I0818974

art, annotated

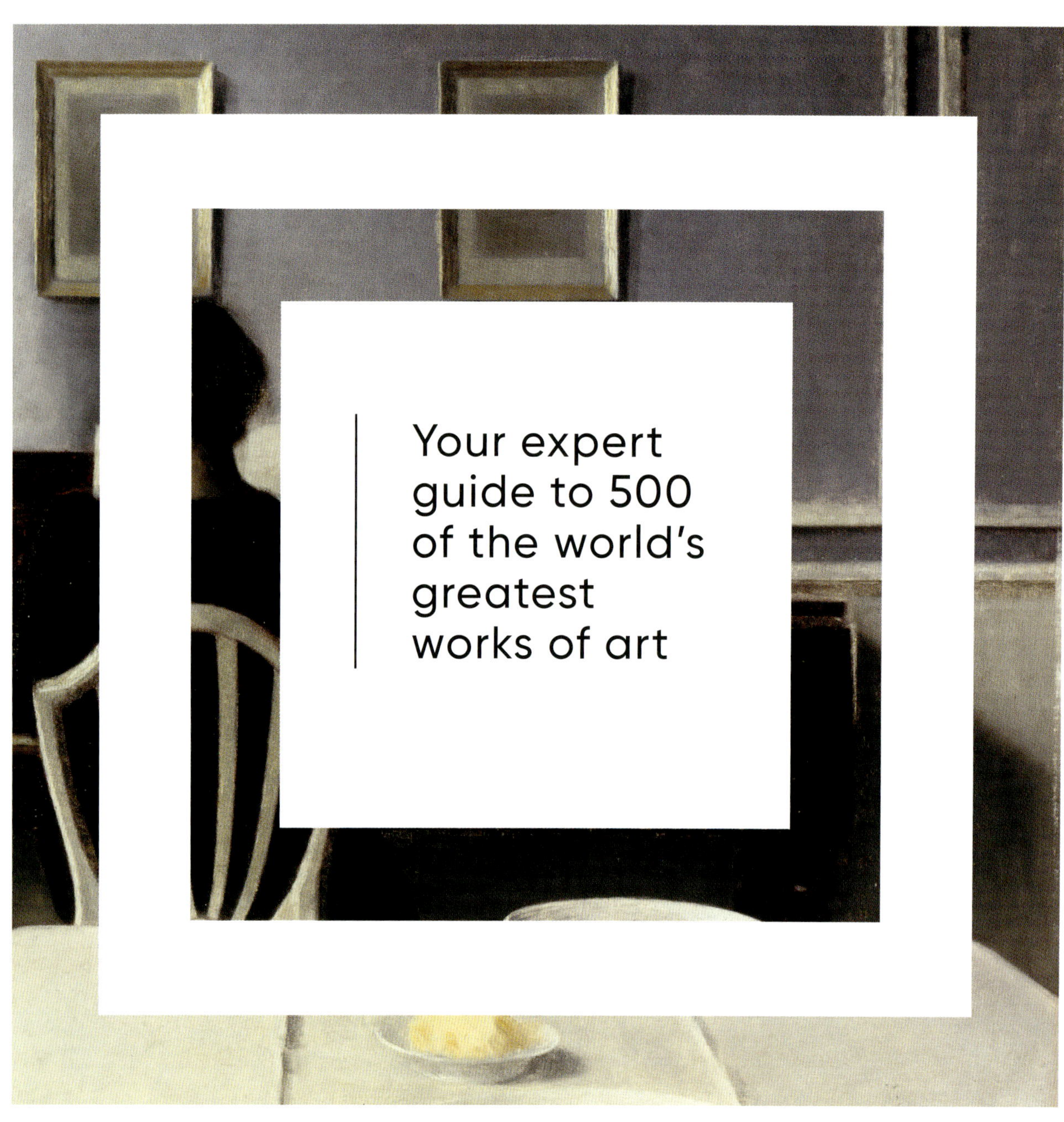

Your expert guide to 500 of the world's greatest works of art

art, annotated

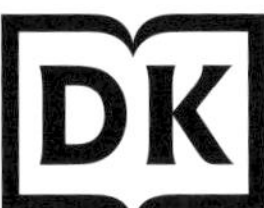

CONSULTANTS

Aliki Braine
Dr Diana Greenwald
Dr Nigel Spivey

CONTRIBUTORS

Joanne Bourne
Dr Sonia Coman
Helen Douglas-Cooper
Dr Lynne Ann Ellsworth Larsen
Autumn Green
Yuya Kawata
Michael Kerrigan
Chaeri Lee
Ruixi Li
Dr Kate Lingley
Richard Mead
Dr Sujatha Meegama
Dr Anthony Meyer
Ruby Ming
Dr Jill Mollenhauer
Dr Khristin Montes
Dr Jeanette Nicewinter
Pas Pascal
Mike Robbins
Brian Robinson
Freya Sackville-West
Dr Hannah Sigur
Dr Nigel Spivey
Dr Maya Stanfield-Mazzi
Dr Emma Stein
Geoff Swimer
Shane Talia
Aiken Unni
Dr Gabrielle Vail
Irina Zhambaldorzhieva

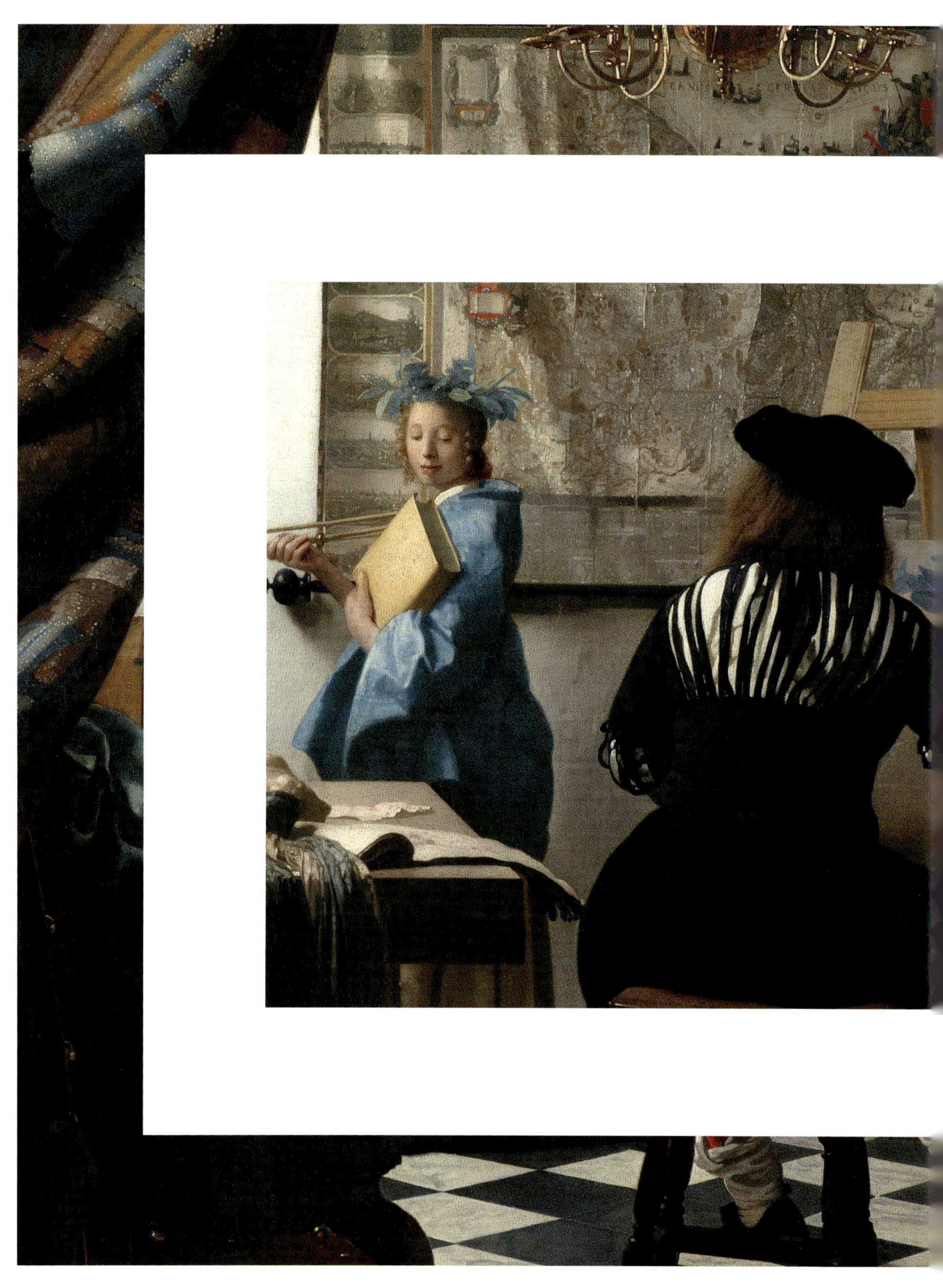

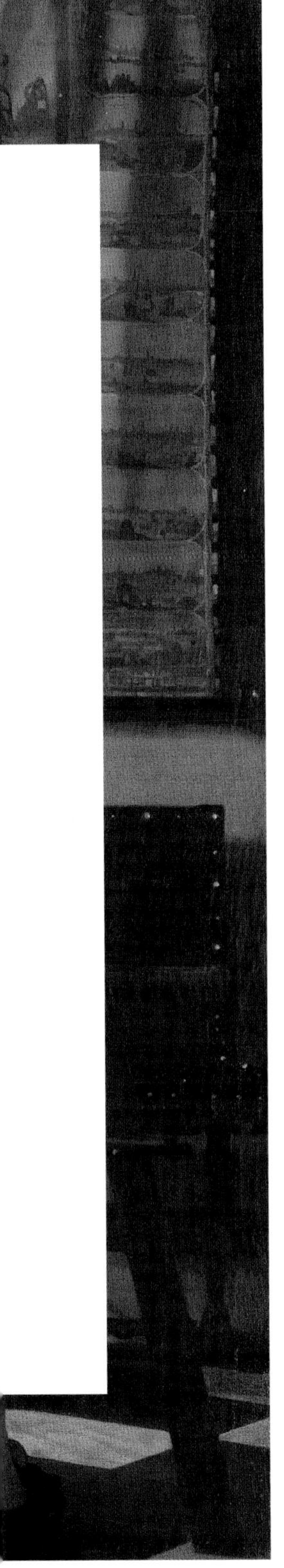

The book provides a sense of how art has changed over time, in different parts of the world, beginning with the 28,000-year-old carving of the *Venus of Willendorf* and continuing with cave paintings from as far apart as France and Central Africa. It moves on to the art of ancient Greece, with its emphasis on an idealized form of naturalism; ceremonial art from Central America; temple sculptures of Hindu deities; early images of the Buddha; and early Christian altarpieces and devotional items. It shows how religion has continued to inspire and influence art right up to the modern day.

Art, annotated also traces the varying landscape traditions of East Asia, Europe, and the US over the centuries, and the changing nature of portraiture in painting and sculpture. It examines the varied ways in which artists have responded to the upheavals and changes of the modern world, such as industrialization and the effects of war. It ends with 21st-century artists, whose themes include race, gender, and sexuality, and environmental and postcolonial issues.

How the book works

The artwork is arranged in chronological order. Each entry is illustrated with a large reproduction, accompanied by information that will help you understand and enjoy the work. An introduction provides a brief overview of the subject matter, the artist's source or inspiration, and the historic or stylistic background, to provide context and other key insights.

The annotations draw attention to key features of each work. These include pointers to what is going on—the story being told, the identities of the people portrayed, or the symbolic meanings of figures and objects. They also highlight examples of style and technique, different ways in which the artist has used their materials, and the characteristics of artistic styles and movements. Pull-out images provide a close look at small details, such as incidents in a distant landscape that are easy to overlook, or draw attention to particular aspects of the work, such as the way an artist uses brushwork, colors, and textures to create form or effect. Each work is also accompanied by illustrated Toolbox features. These include analysis of the work's composition, color palette, use of perspective and other ways of creating spatial depth, or describe specific techniques or influences on the artist's work.

Feature spreads on popular themes such as myths, portraits, landscapes, still lifes, and animals are interspersed throughout the book. These show how different cultures have approached subjects common to all traditions.

▶ ***Fantômas*** (detail), Juan Gris, 1915

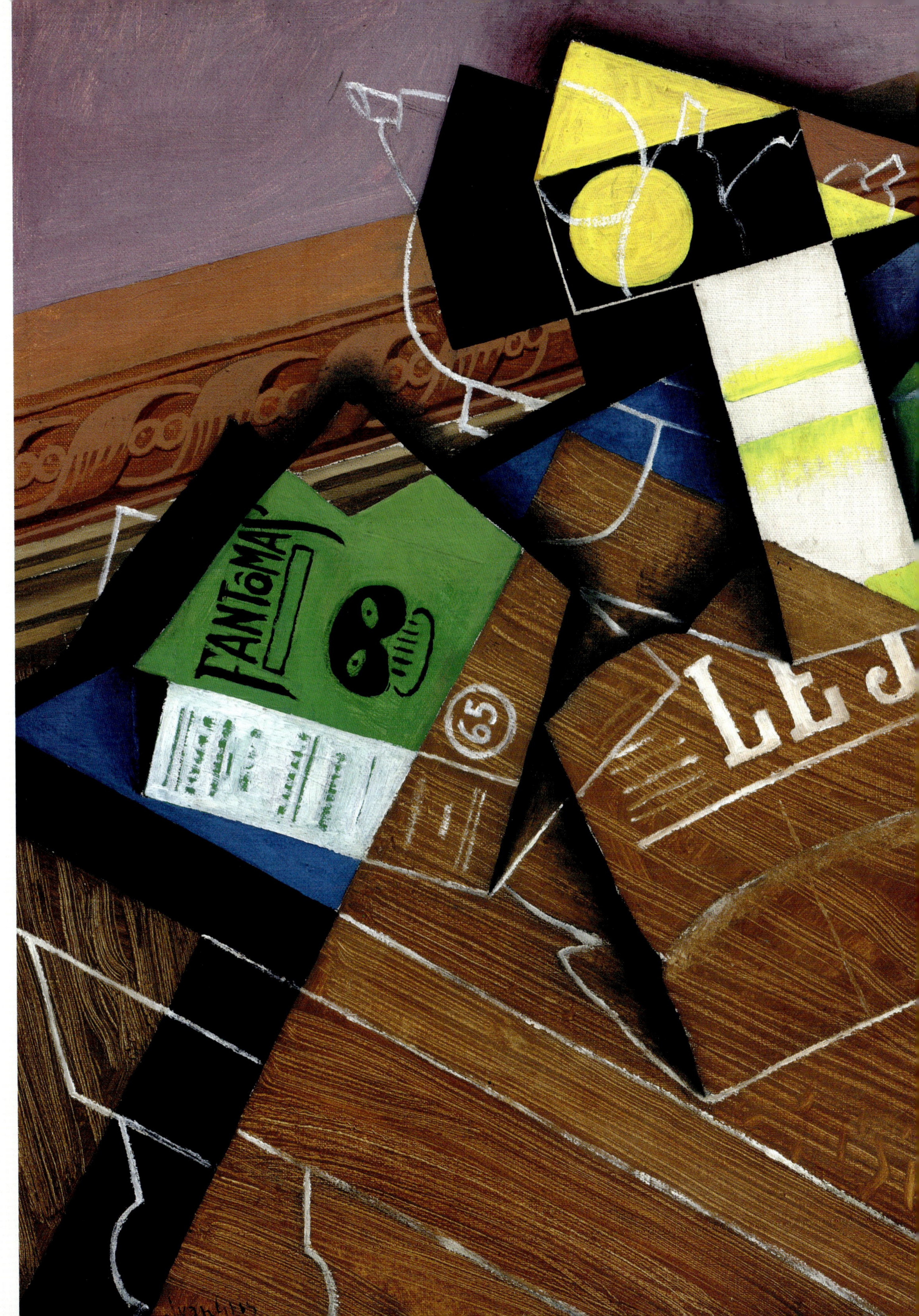
FANTOMAS
65
LE J

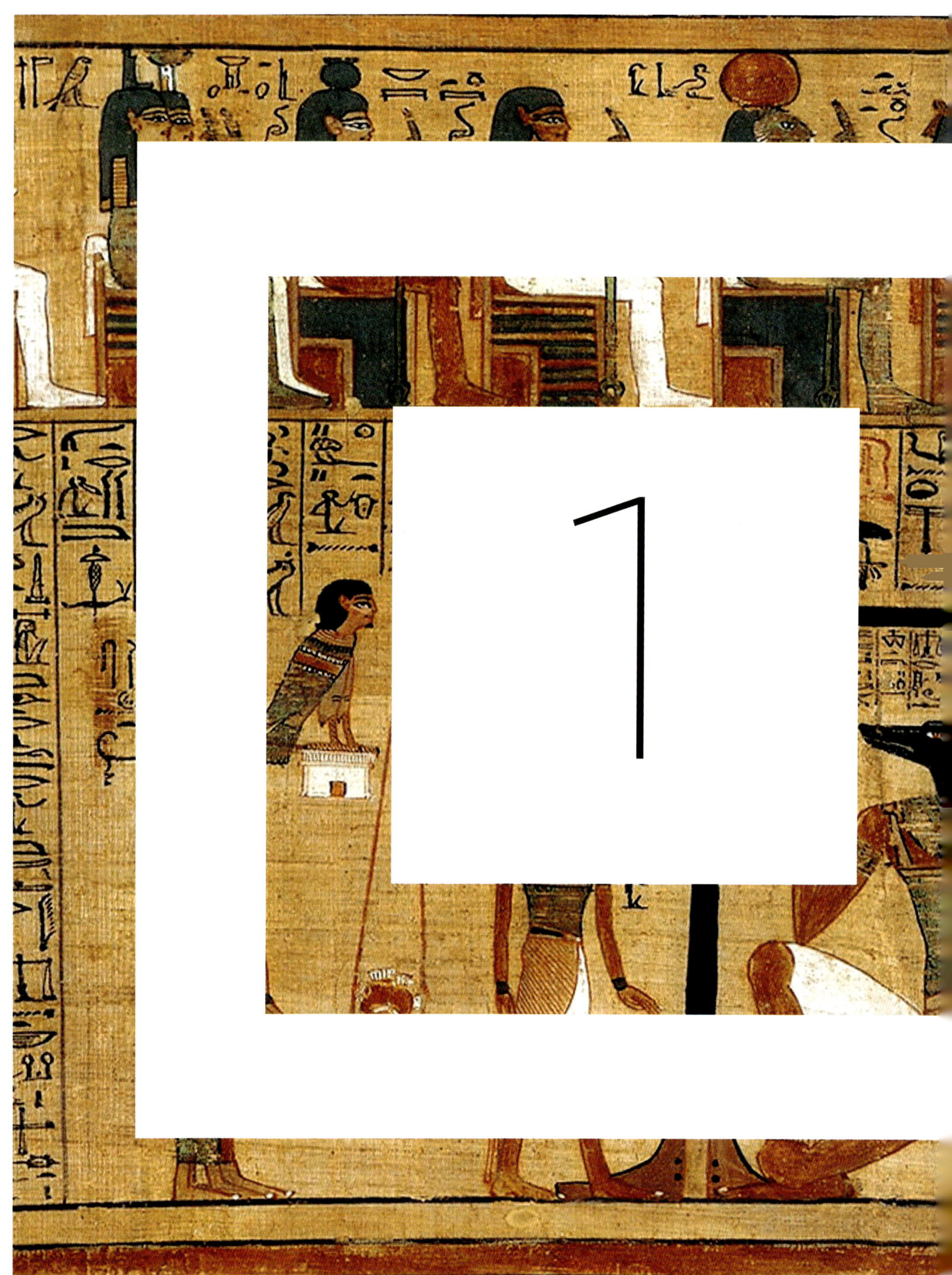

1

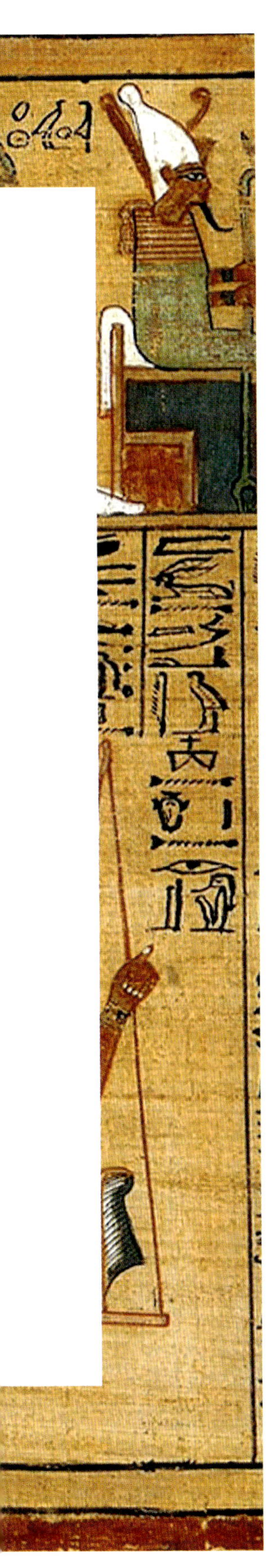

Beginnings

28,000 BCE - 1400 CE

Venus of Willendorf

Artist unknown c. 28,000–25,000 BCE, oolitic limestone, height 4 in (11 cm), Natural History Museum, Vienna, Austria

This Paleolithic statuette of a simple, female form with exaggerated sexual characteristics is one of the oldest examples of three-dimensional art. Worked with a flint tool, it is often interpreted as a fertility goddess, designed to encourage sexual reproduction. Its size made it portable; it is thought to have been carved in what is now Italy, far from where it was found in Austria.

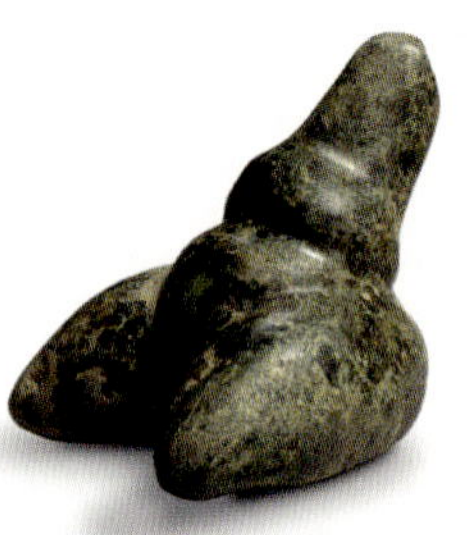

Goddess figures
Prehistoric sculptures of the female form with similarly exaggerated features have been discovered in various parts of the world, including Ukraine, Syria (above), and Malta.

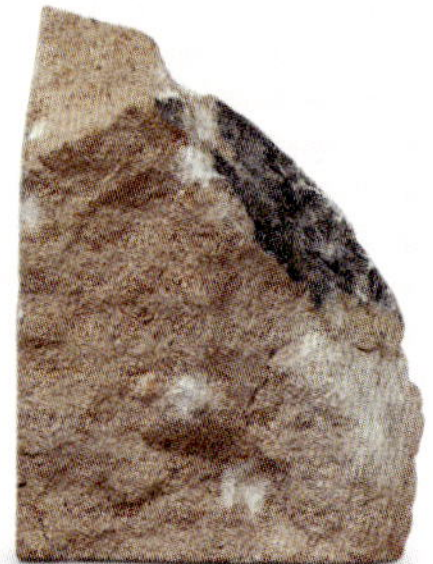

Type of stone
The figure is carved from oolitic limestone, which is not local to Willendorf, Austria, where the statue was unearthed in 1908. Hunter-gatherers of the Gravettian culture of this period traveled large distances to find food as the seasons changed.

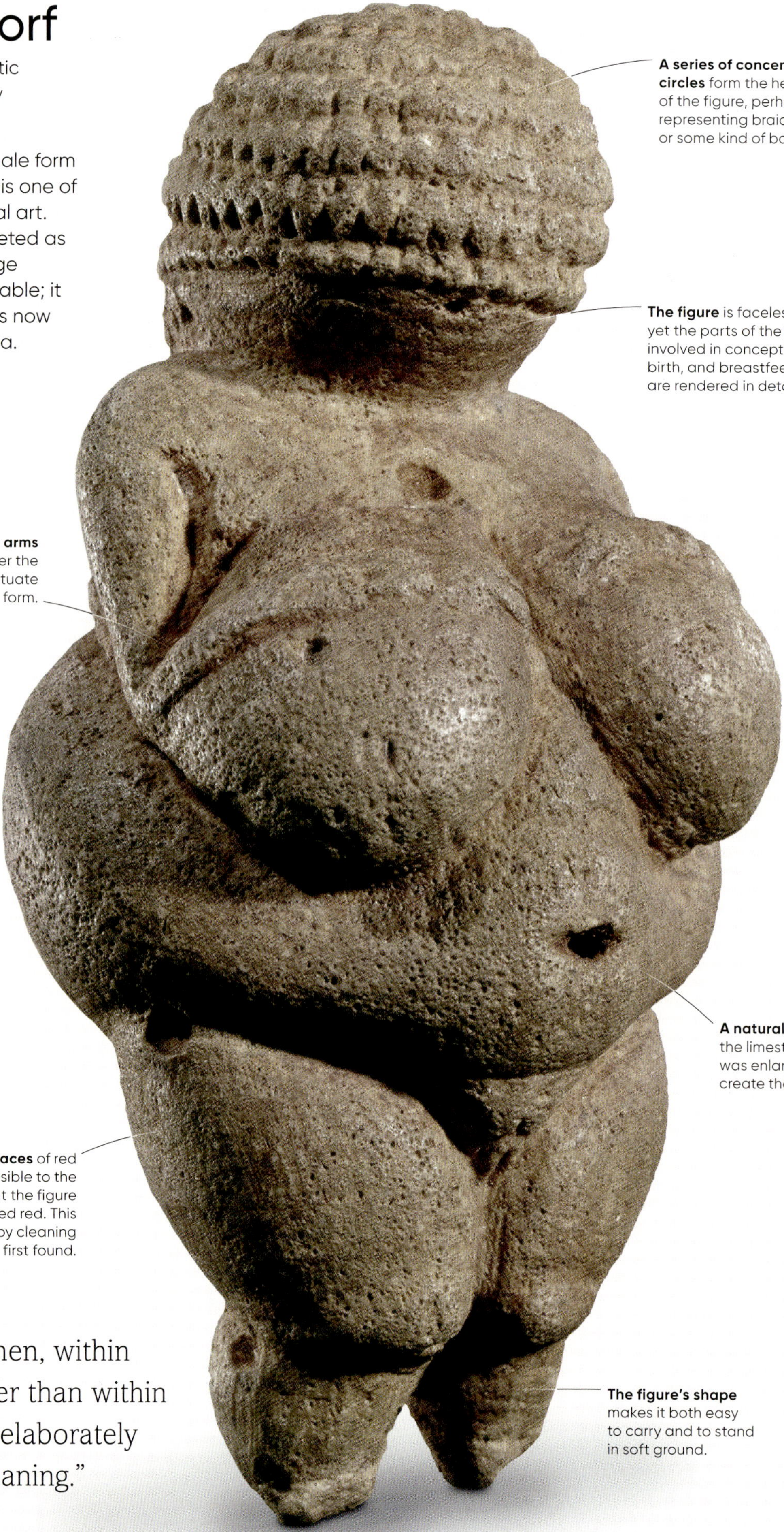

A series of concentric circles form the head of the figure, perhaps representing braided hair or some kind of bonnet.

The figure is faceless, yet the parts of the body involved in conception, birth, and breastfeeding are rendered in detail.

Thin, sticklike arms folded over the breasts accentuate the figure's full form.

A natural hole in the limestone was enlarged to create the navel.

Microscopic traces of red ocher, now invisible to the eye, reveal that the figure was initially painted red. This was removed by cleaning when it was first found.

The figure's shape makes it both easy to carry and to stand in soft ground.

> "The Venus of Willendorf, then, within her culture and period, rather than within ours, was clearly richly and elaborately clothed in inference and meaning."
>
> Alexander Marshack, 1991

Manda Guéli Cave

Unknown 5000 BCE, pigment on sandstone, 138 × 315 in (350 × 800 cm), Ennedi Mountains, Chad

On Chad's vast Ennedi Massif, rocks and cave shelters provide an open-air gallery of animal and human figures painted and incised over millennia. Manda Guéli (sacred stone ax cave), some 13 ft (4 m) above the ground, contains a vibrant, multilayered fresco from a time when the Sahara was lush and green.

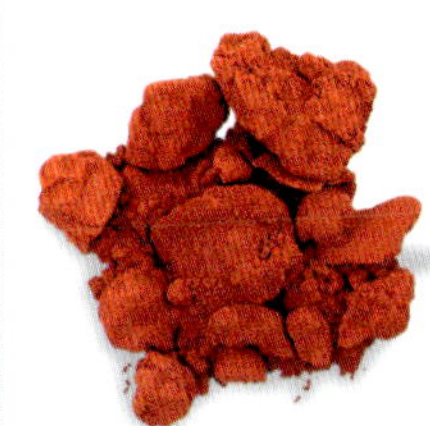

Pigments from the rocks White kaolinite, red-brown hematite, and manganese oxides were pounded with water to make paint. Sheltered from the wind and sun, the figures of the Manda Guéli fresco have retained their original, pristine color.

"Africa's rock art is the common heritage of all Africans, but it is more than that. It is the common heritage of humanity."

Nelson Mandela, 2004

Camels are superimposed over earlier images of livestock, indicating successive groups of people lived in the cave over a long period of time and a shift from a green landscape to more arid conditions.

Crosshatched harnesses show that weaving was a common craft.

Dromedary camels, painted in white, are ridden by red, saddled figures, bearing sticks or spears, and shields. The harnesses are decorated with tassels.

Large "halos" around the heads of some figures suggest styled hair or headdresses.

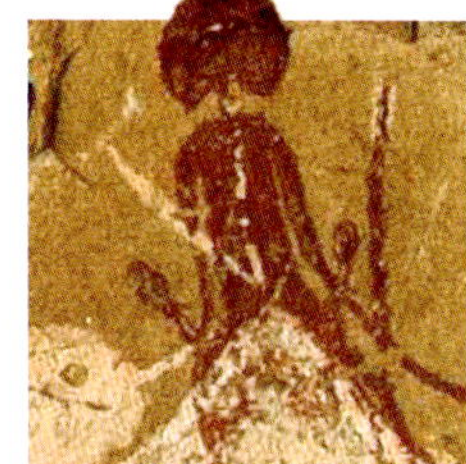

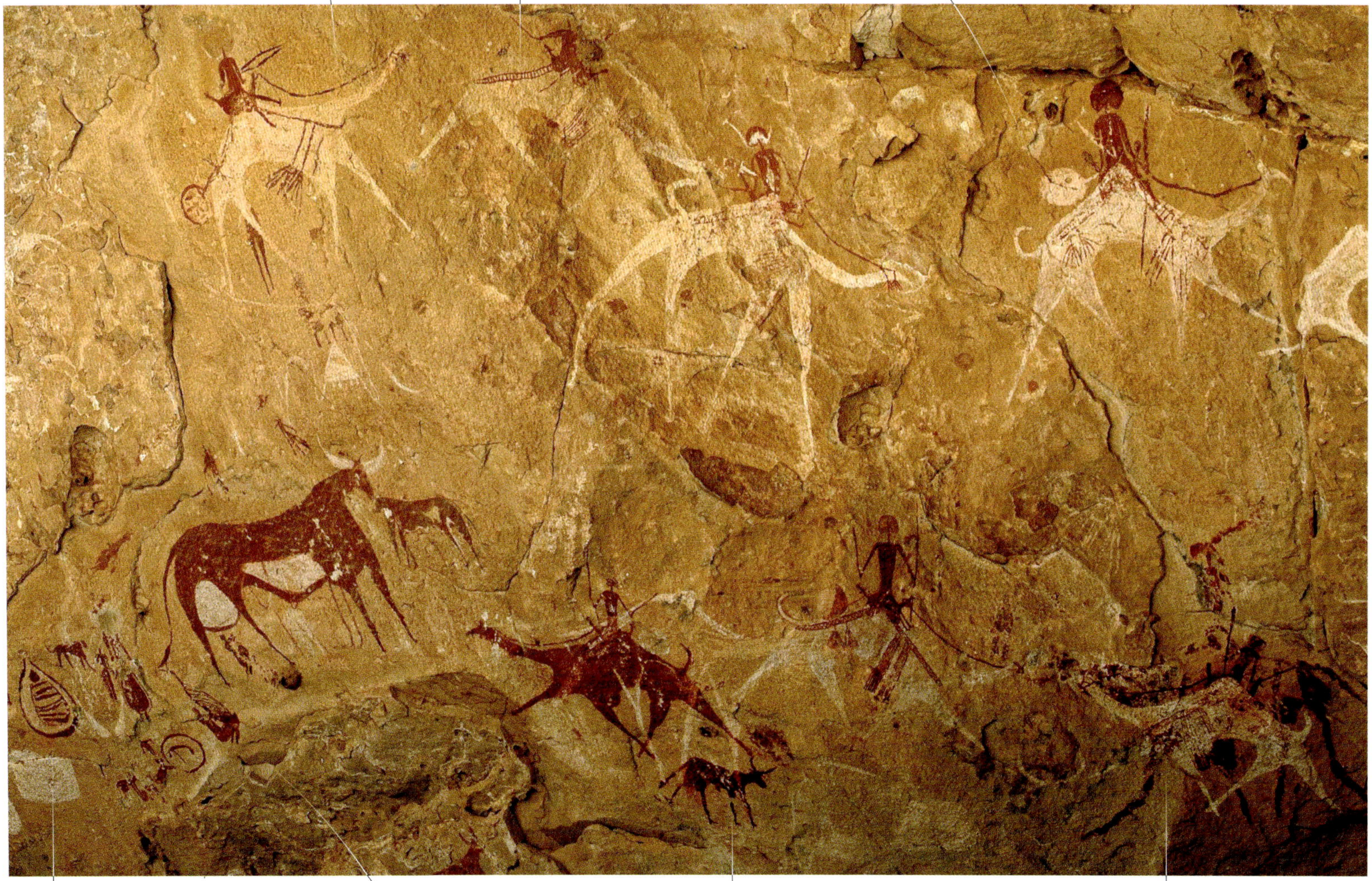

Tear-shaped forms are thought to represent storage baskets of a kind used by herders. These were often hung on trees.

Small human figures are painted in red.

The predominance of cattle, painted in the early phase of the fresco, highlights their value to the herders who painted them.

Some camels are shown walking or running in a flying gallop.

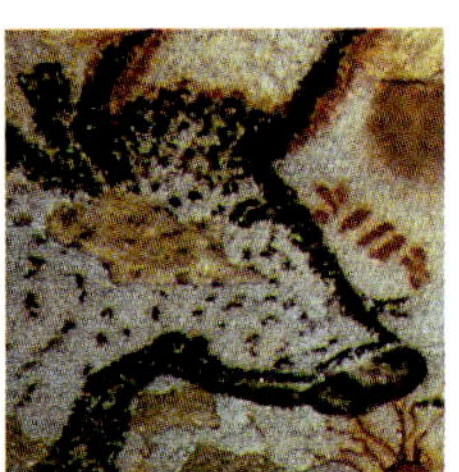

Each animal is individually realized. This auroch has black spots and a tuft of hair between its dual-colored horns.

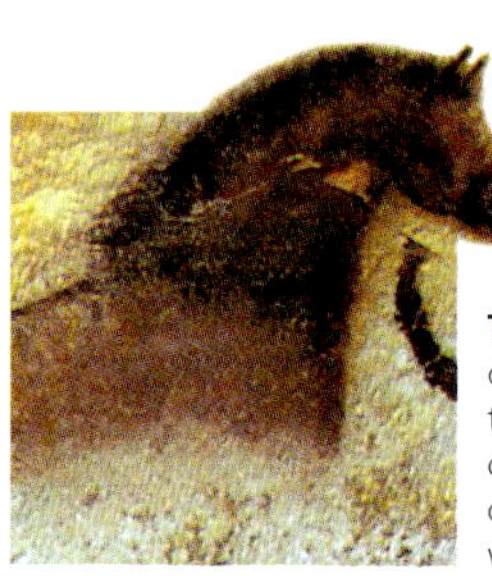

The gradated color of the brown horse suggests that it may have been blown onto the walls using a straw or hollow bone, or applied with pads of fur.

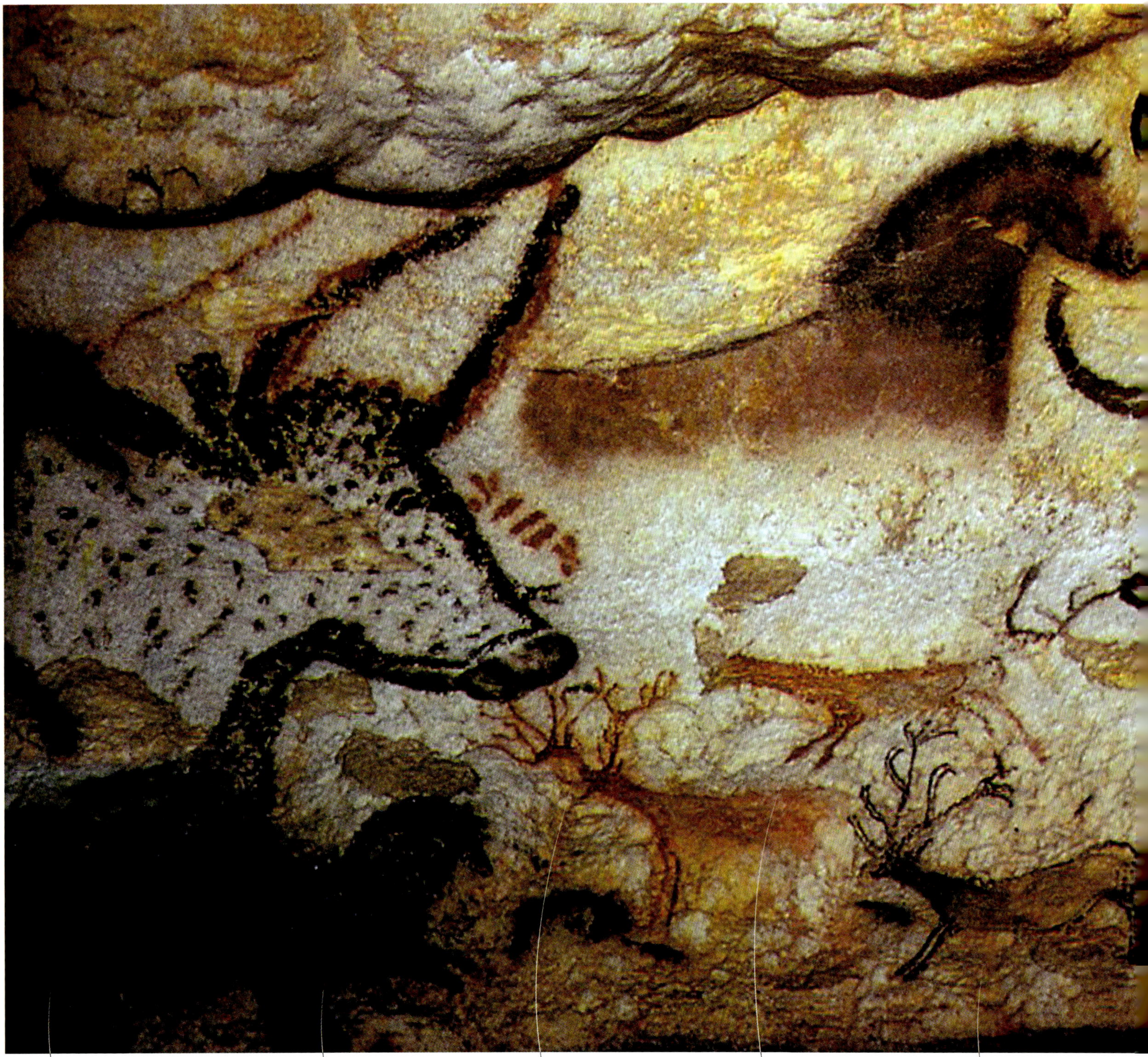

All animals in the panel—and in the wider cave art—are represented in profile.

From the left, a black horse leads a charge of animals toward the center of the panel.

A red stag with a large set of antlers forms part of a distinct group at the base.

The extended neck and legs of the upper stag suggests a creature at full gallop.

The brown stag is drawn from a low perspective.

The Hall of the Bulls (detail)

Artists unknown c. 18,900 BCE, mineral pigments on white calcite, 65½ ft (20 m) in length, Lascaux Cave, Montignac, France

Layered in earth colors on crystalline calcite, the paintings of aurochs, horses, and stags in the Hall of the Bulls is one of many prehistoric artworks in Lascaux Cave, an 820-ft (250-m) cave system in the Dordogne region of France. Working by torchlight and using iron oxide minerals and black manganese ground to a powder and mixed with water, the artists depicted the animals of their world with line, shade, and extraordinary perspective, probably over many years and even generations. Visitors today can see replicas of the paintings in an expertly modeled copy of the cavern, created to protect the original from moisture.

The whole panel was created on the upper wall of the cave's vast rotunda. It curves from left to right and from wall to ceiling, a sweeping but uneven expanse that lends depth to the scene.

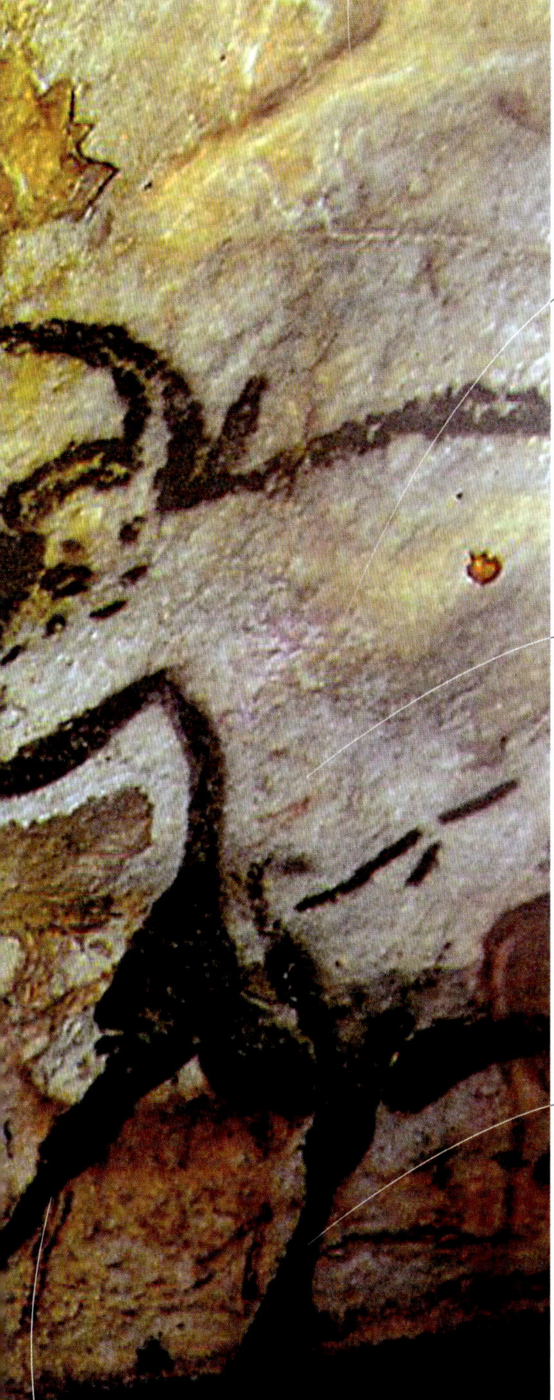

The animals are drawn using "twisted perspective"—their bodies are in profile and their horns turn slightly to the front.

Depictions of horned aurochs, the extinct wild ancestor of modern cattle, dominate the panel. Some are 9 ft (3 m) long.

The aurochs' legs are shaded in black to lend a sense of perspective to the figures.

The figures are layered one on top of the other, as if the other figures were not there.

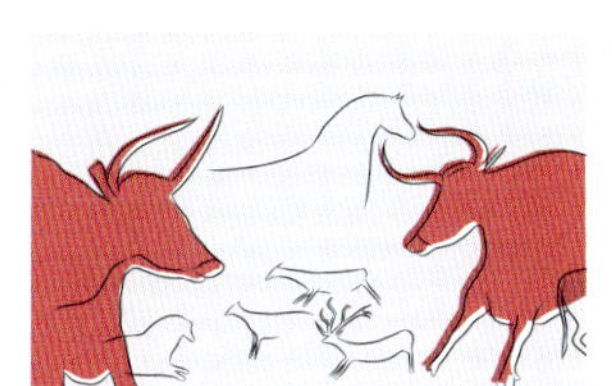

Dramatic impression
The layered ensemble creates an intense feeling of movement, with cantering animals charging away from a face off between two mighty aurochs.

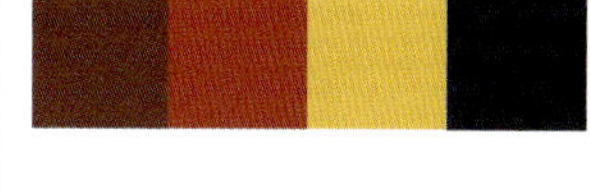

Earth pigments
Brown, red, and yellow pigments derived from the local rocks give form to the animals, filling the black outlines of the larger creatures, and defining the silhouettes of smaller ones.

> "Gazing at these pictures, we sense that something is stirring, something is moving. That something touches us."
>
> George Bataille, 1955

The Standard of Ur—War

Unknown 2500 BCE, shell, red limestone, lapis lazuli, and bitumen, 9 × 20 × 5 in (21.7 × 50.4 × 11.6 cm), British Museum, London, UK

In a lively representation of the Sumerian army, inlaid shells and stone depict rows of soldiers and animals going into battle. The scenes are arranged in three tiers: a wagon charge takes place at the bottom, the infantry marches in the middle, and prisoners are presented to the king at the top. This was found in 1928 in a grave at the Royal Cemetery of Ur in modern-day Iraq, along with a similar peacetime panel. Originally mounted on a hollow wooden box, the Standard is an early example of using inlay to tell a story.

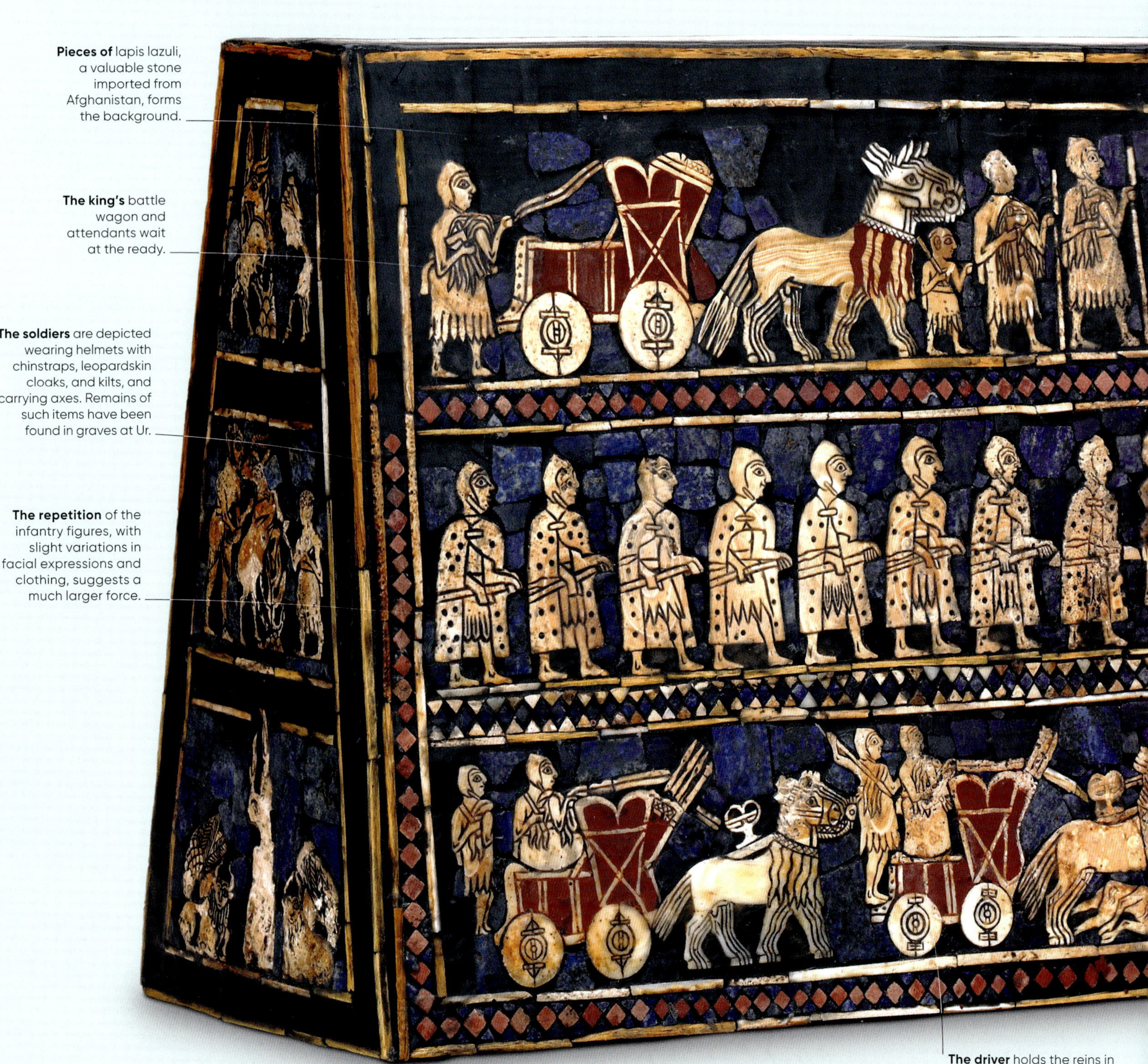

Pieces of lapis lazuli, a valuable stone imported from Afghanistan, forms the background.

The king's battle wagon and attendants wait at the ready.

The soldiers are depicted wearing helmets with chinstraps, leopardskin cloaks, and kilts, and carrying axes. Remains of such items have been found in graves at Ur.

The repetition of the infantry figures, with slight variations in facial expressions and clothing, suggests a much larger force.

The driver holds the reins in one hand and a weapon in the other. The warrior at the rear wields a spear.

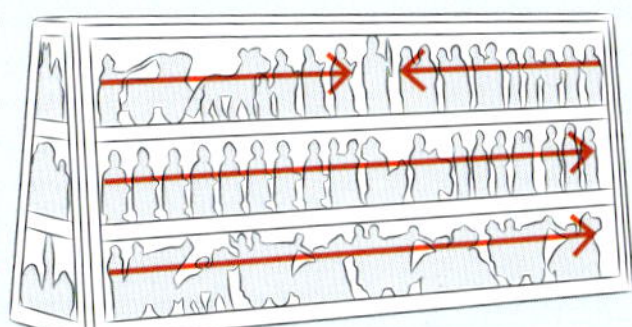

Continuity and space
Each tier of figures is arranged along a ground line across the panel, creating a sense of space. The figures form a continuous procession that has no beginning or end.

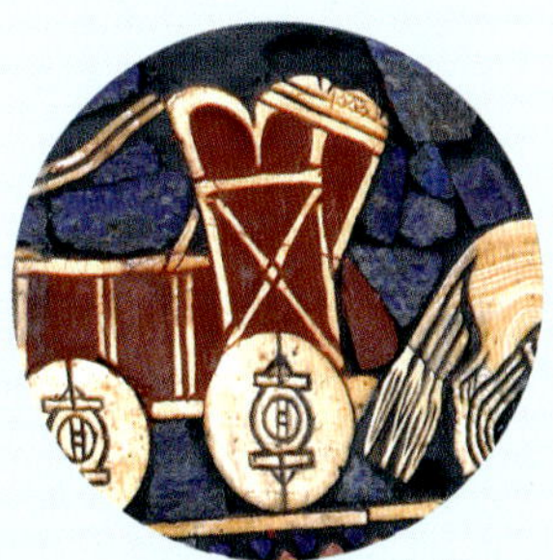

Inlay technique
The pieces of stone and shell are cut with slanting sides so they fit together closely. This allows the artist to achieve a remarkable level of detail.

"Suddenly a loose bit of shell inlay turned up, and the next minute the foreman's hand, carefully brushing away the earth, laid bare the corner of a mosaic in lapis lazuli and shell."

Sir Leonard Woolley, 1954

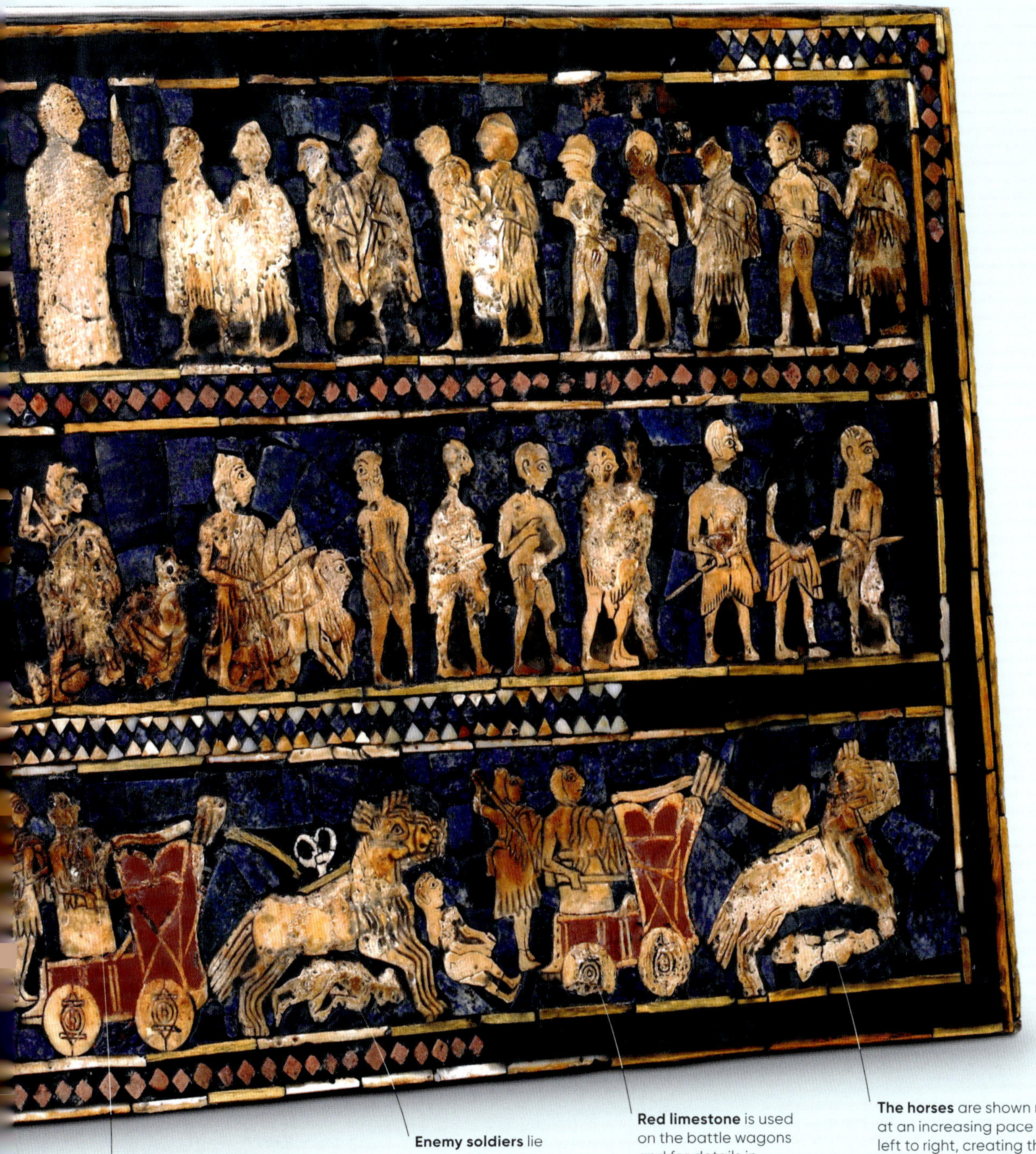

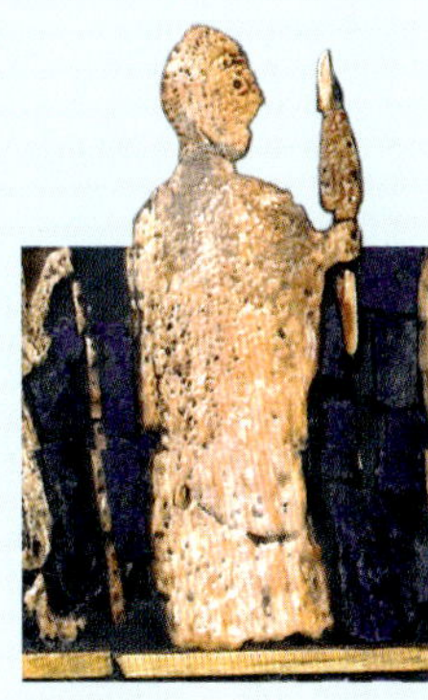

The king is placed in the center of the top tier. His larger size emphasizes his importance.

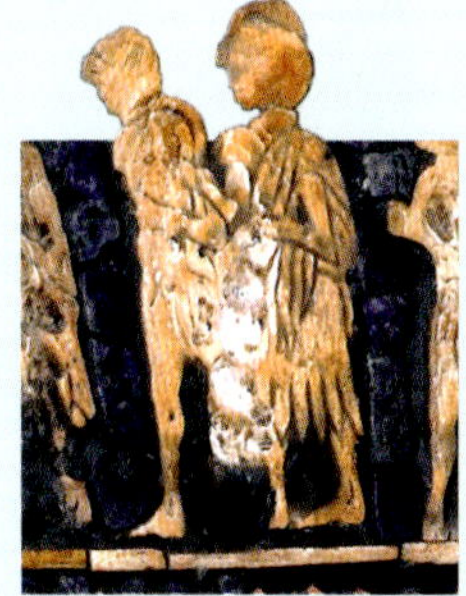

Naked prisoners, some shown bleeding from their wounds, wait for the king to decide their fate.

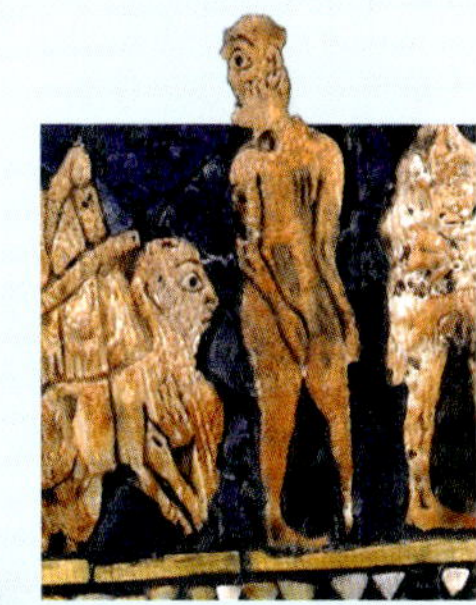

The figures are depicted with a high degree of individuality, as seen in the exchange of looks between this soldier and captive.

Hand-to-hand fighting takes place in the center of the panel while prisoners are led away from the battlefield.

Enemy soldiers lie crushed beneath the battle wagons.

Red limestone is used on the battle wagons and for details in other areas.

The horses are shown moving at an increasing pace from left to right, creating the impression of a charge.

Narmer Palette

Artist unknown c. 3100–3000 BCE, slate, 25 × 17 in (64 × 42 cm), Egyptian Museum, Cairo, Egypt

This palette, found in the Temple of Horus at Nekhen, has been interpreted as a symbolic representation of the unification of Egypt in around 3150 BCE. Carved in bas-relief, one side depicts the Pharaoh Narmer wearing the white crown of Upper Egypt while the other shows him wearing the red crown of Lower Egypt.

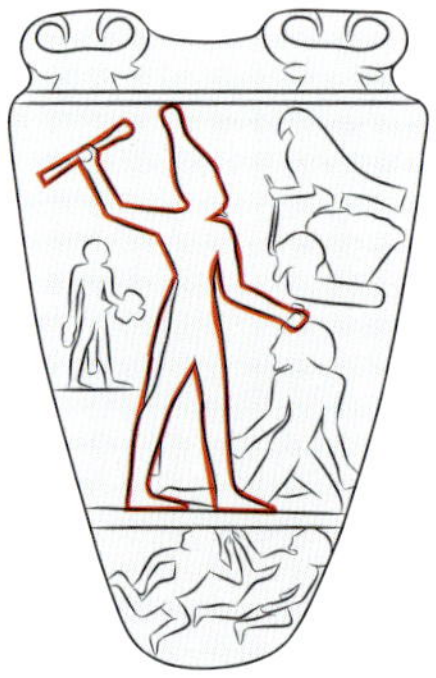

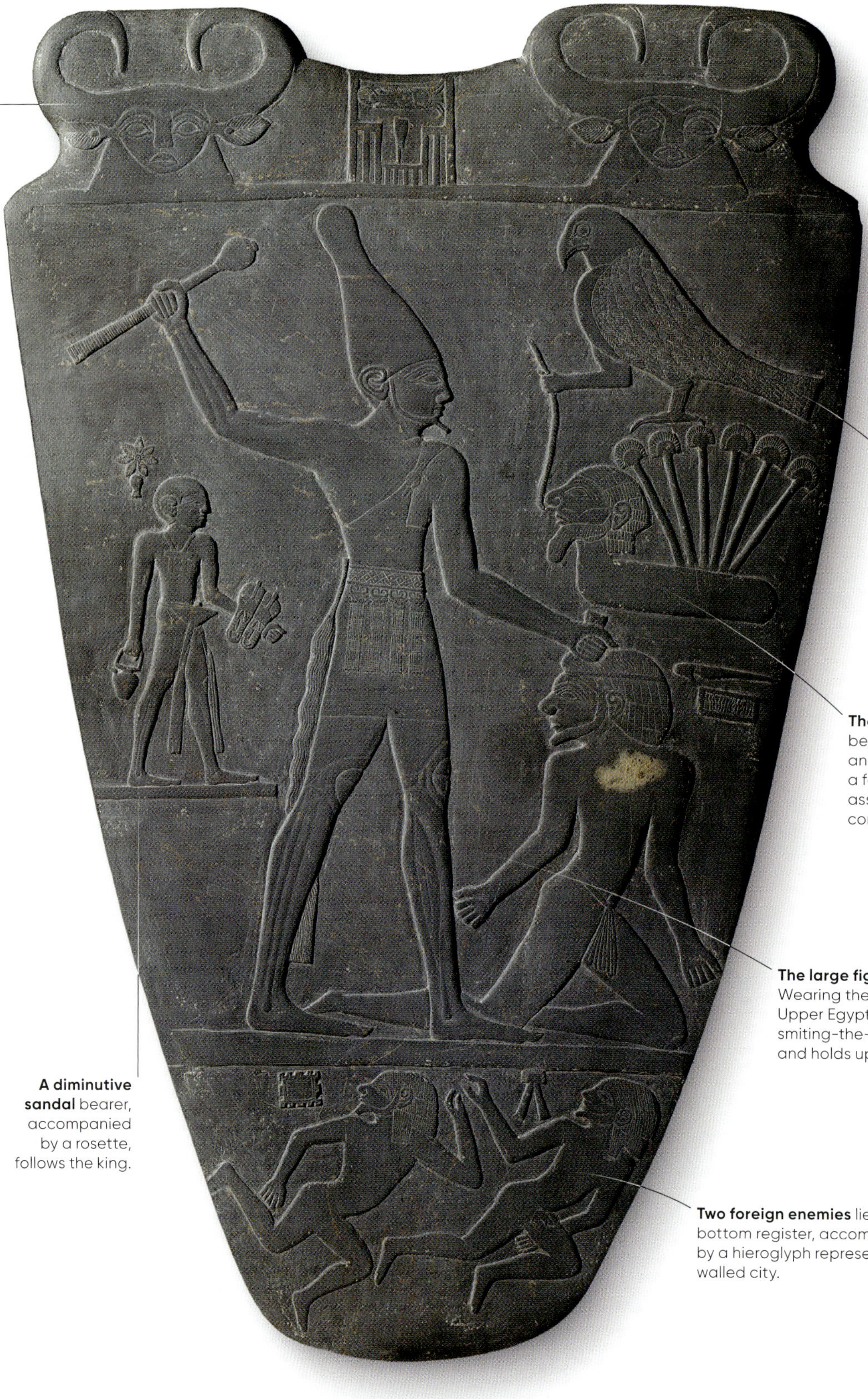

Two cows in the top register represent the sky goddess, Bat.

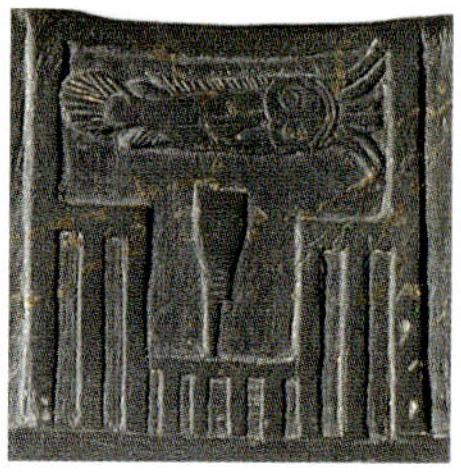

A *serekh*, or royal insignia, identifies the king, Narmer, by the catfish and chisel, the phonetic representation of his name.

The falcon with human arms represents the god Horus. It perches above papyrus flowers symbolizing Lower Egypt.

There are visual parallels between Narmer's restraint of an enemy and Horus controlling a foe. This symbolizes the god's assistance to the king in controlling Lower Egypt.

The large figure is Narmer. Wearing the white crown of Upper Egypt, he adopts the smiting-the-enemy pose and holds up a royal mace.

A diminutive sandal bearer, accompanied by a rosette, follows the king.

Two foreign enemies lie in the bottom register, accompanied by a hieroglyph representing a walled city.

Hierarchy
On both sides of the palette, Narmer is shown larger than the other figures to highlight his authority as pharaoh.

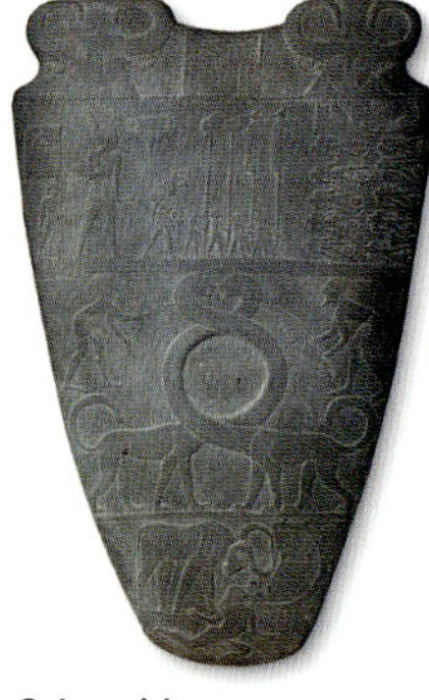

Other side
The palette's other side features horizontal registers depicting Narmer's procession toward the enemy. Mythical creatures encircle a space for mixing cosmetics—the purpose of the palette.

Dancing Girl

Artist unknown c. 2300–1700 BCE, bronze, 4 × 2 × 1 in (10.8 × 5 × 2.5 cm), National Museum, New Delhi, India

This prehistoric bronze sculpture of a young girl from the Indus Valley civilization was cast using the lost-wax method by an artist from the city of Mohenjo-daro (in modern-day Pakistan). It was one of two excavated from a domestic dwelling in 1926 and was described on discovery as a dancer because of her lively, naturalistic pose. The girl is nude, adorned only with a necklace and bangles.

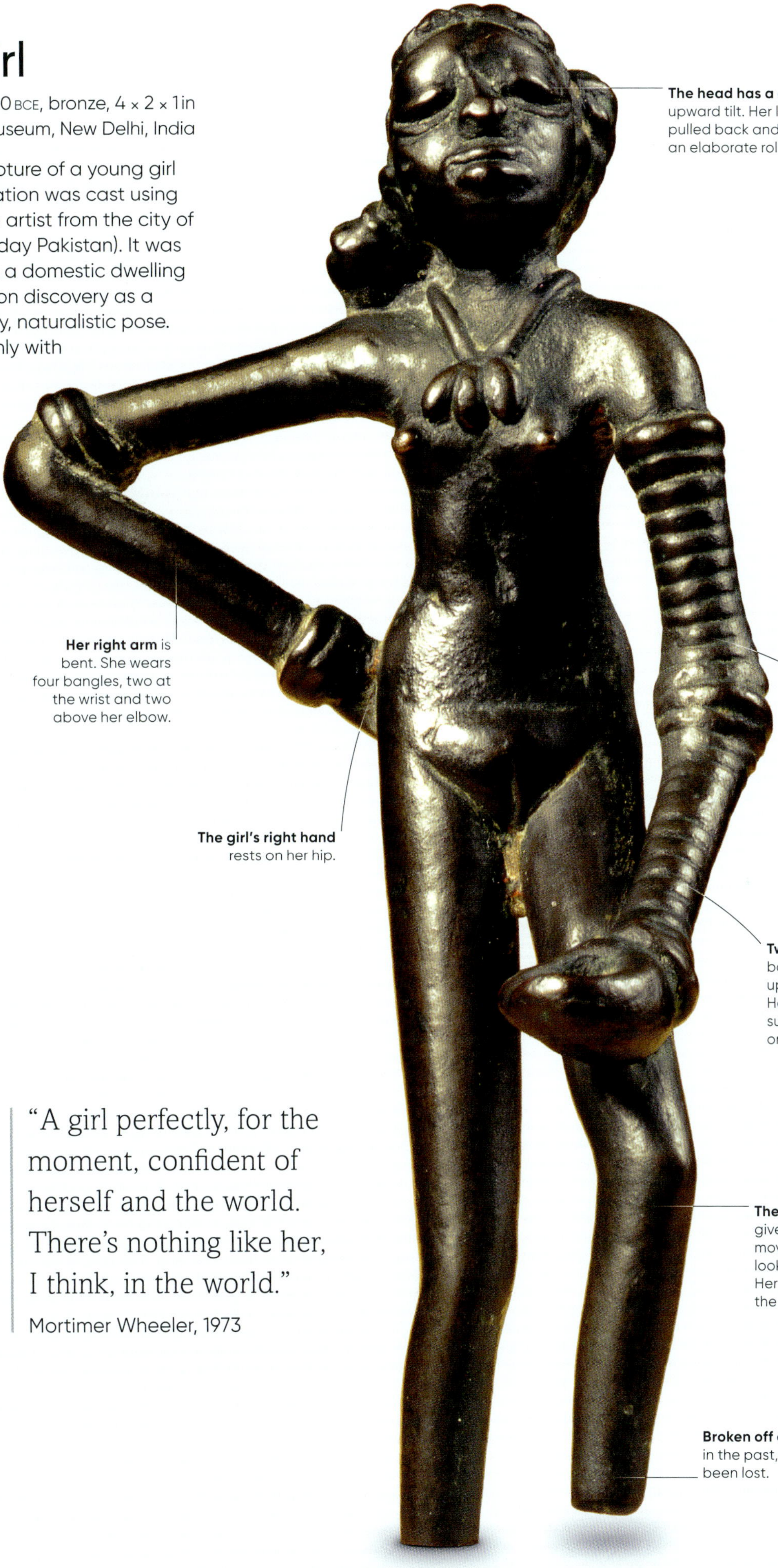

The head has a confident upward tilt. Her long hair is pulled back and braided into an elaborate roll.

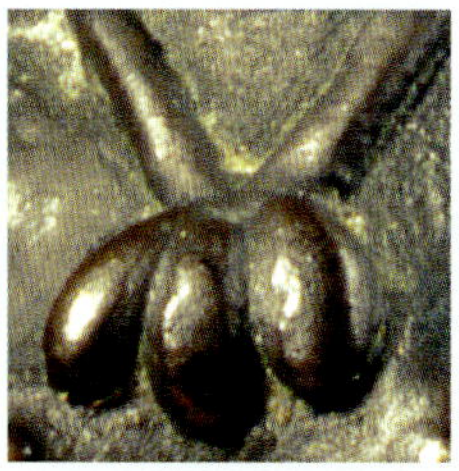

The girl's large necklace is hung with three tear-shaped pendants. Jewelery excavated in Mohenjo-daro was made from gold, blue faience, ivory, jadeite, carnelian, and other colored stones.

Her right arm is bent. She wears four bangles, two at the wrist and two above her elbow.

The limbs are unnaturally long, a common feature of figurines of the time.

The girl's right hand rests on her hip.

Twenty-five large bangles are stacked up on her left arm. Her fist is hollow, suggesting that she once held an object.

The slightly bent leg gives the figure an air of movement and makes her look startlingly modern. Her weight is placed on the other leg.

Broken off at some point in the past, the feet have been lost.

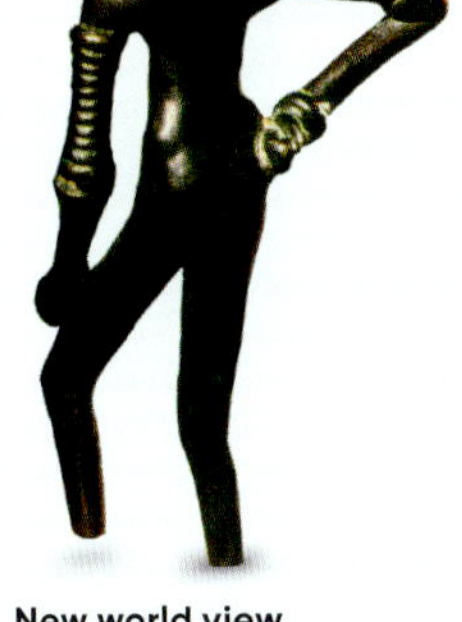

New world view
Exquisitely modeled in the round, the solid bronze stylized girl was one of the artifacts that changed the world view of the ancient Indus Valley civilization.

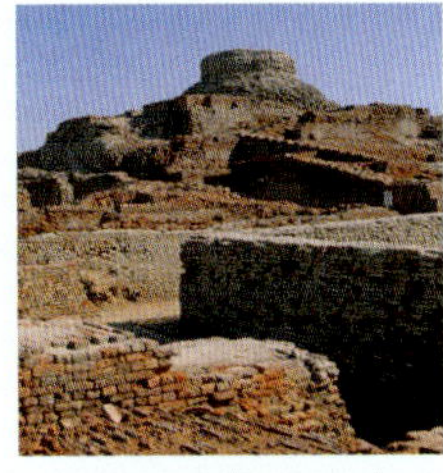

Sophisticated city
The statuette was excavated from one of the world's first urban developments, with houses made of brick, streets laid out on a grid plan, a public bath house, and systematic sanitation.

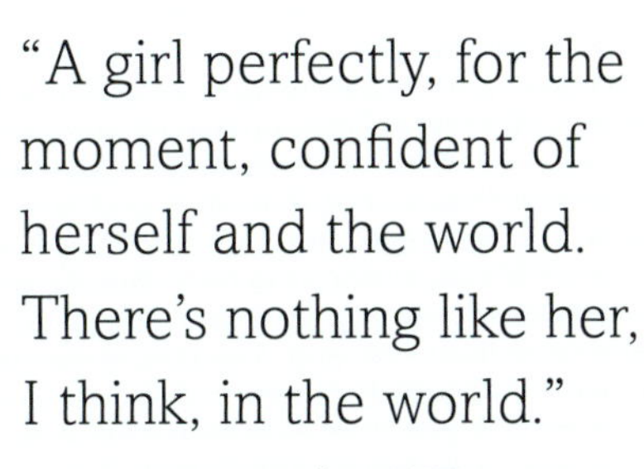

"A girl perfectly, for the moment, confident of herself and the world. There's nothing like her, I think, in the world."

Mortimer Wheeler, 1973

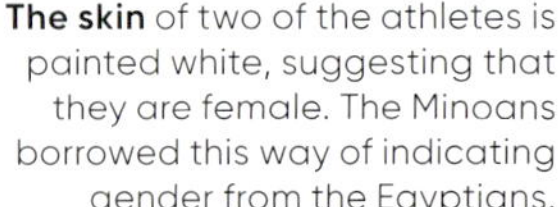

The skin of two of the athletes is painted white, suggesting that they are female. The Minoans borrowed this way of indicating gender from the Egyptians.

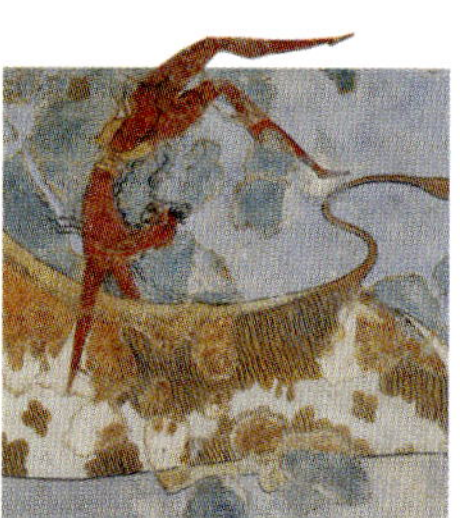

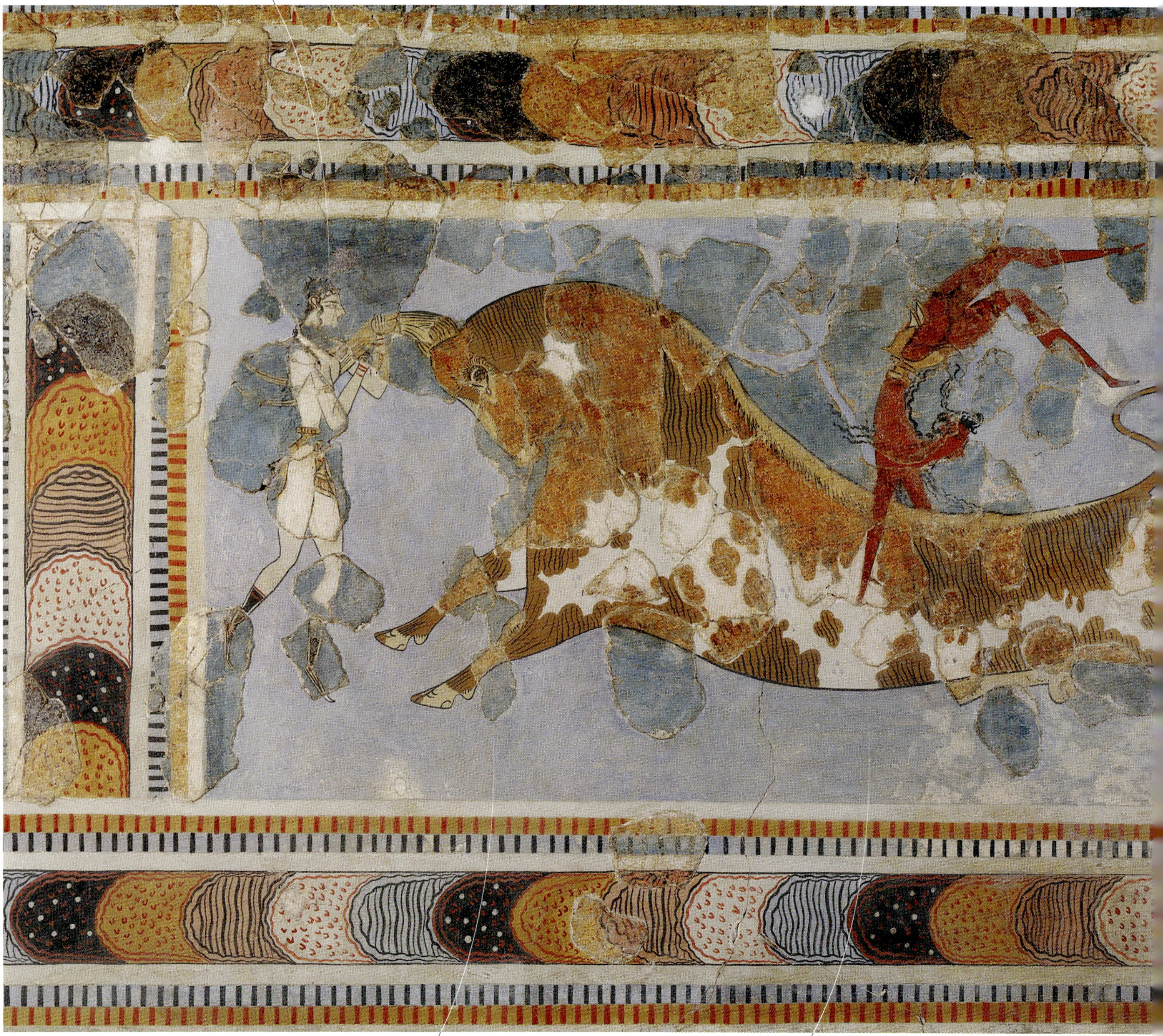

The bull's torso is stretched out to convey that he is charging along at full speed.

Out of proportion with its stubby legs, the bull's broad neck and shoulders convey menace and force.

Earthy-red paint suggests this is a male athlete.

Bull-Leaping Fresco, Knossos

Artist unknown, c. 1450 BCE, stucco panel with scene in relief, 41 × 31 in (104.5 × 78.2 cm), Heraklion Archaeological Museum, Crete, Greece

Depicting the athletic skill and bravery involved in the sport of bull-leaping, the Toreador Fresco once adorned the palace of Knossos on the island of Crete, the center of the Minoan civilization (11,000–3000 BCE). In Minoan art and culture, bulls were a prized symbol of fertility and strength, reflecting a deep spiritual connection to nature. Places where bull-leaping contests were held may have had the status of ceremonial centers. This work is a 20th-century reconstruction, based on rubble fragments from seven different panels discovered by British archaeologist Sir Arthur Evans in 1901. Evans commissioned archaeological restorer Émile Gilliéron to produce a composite scene that some scholars consider highly speculative.

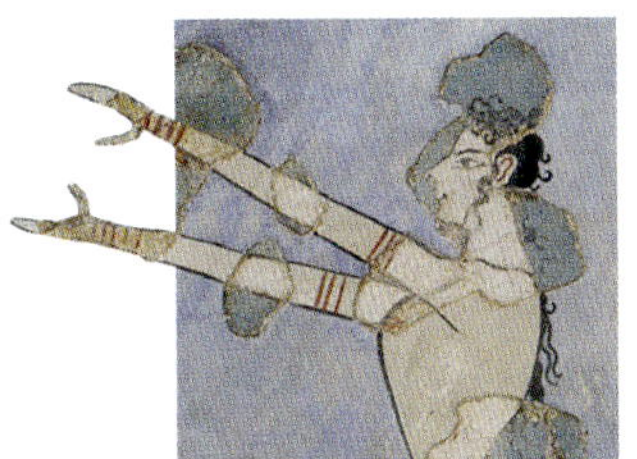

This athlete is waving her arms, possibly to distract or confuse the bull.

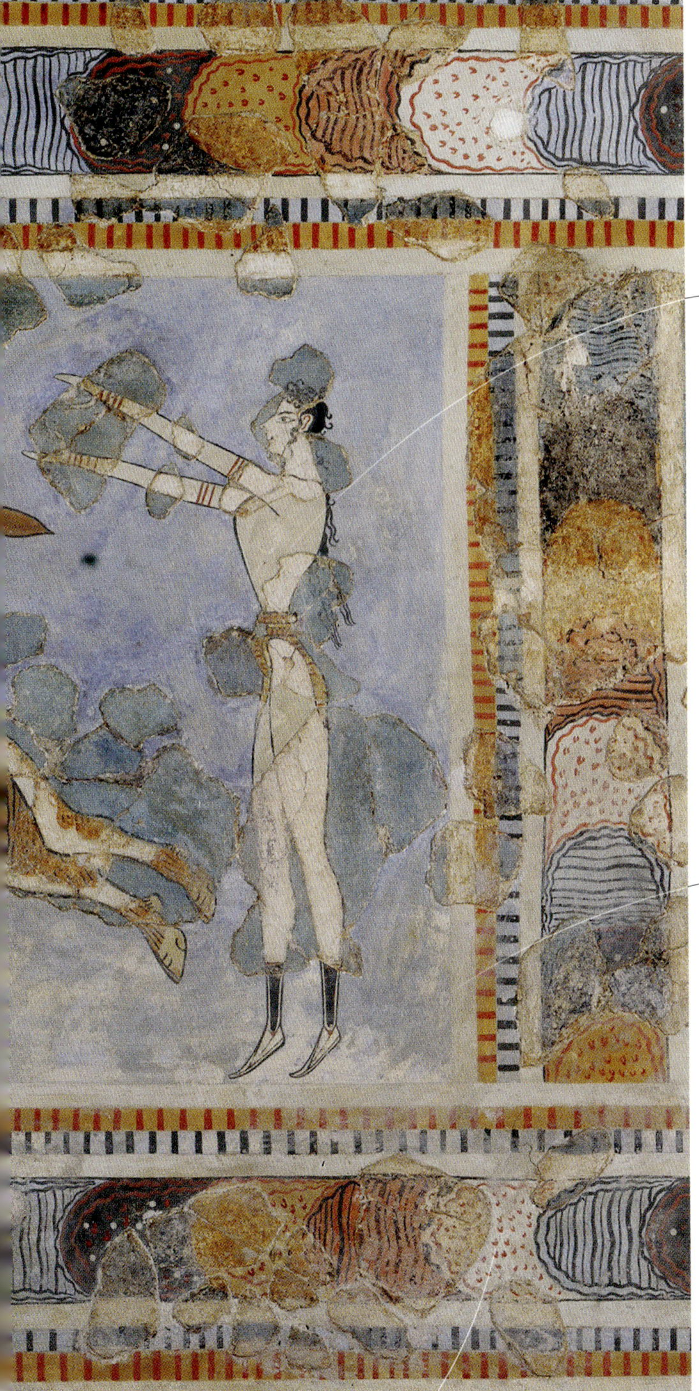

The elaborate hairstyles, jewelery, and footwear of the female athletes show that they are of high social ranking.

The absence of background detail focuses attention on the ritualized displays of athletic action in the foreground.

The original fresco was produced by applying pigments mixed with water to damp plaster.

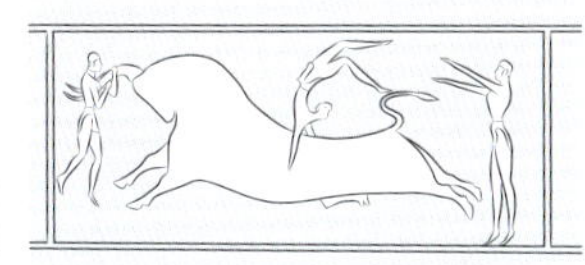

Leaps and vaults
The aim is to convey dynamism and action in one plane rather than consider perspective and depth, as is typical in later Western art.

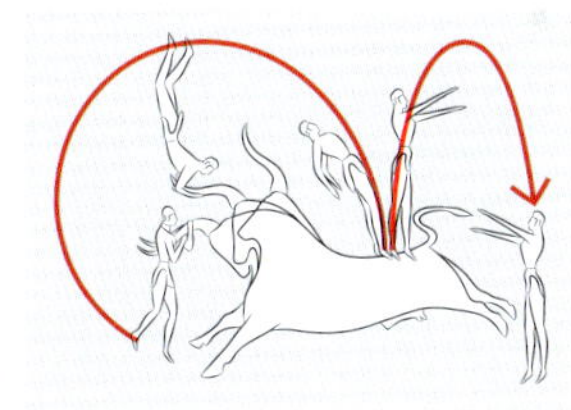

Freeze frame
The fresco may illustrate the different stages of an action sequence rather than a performance by three people.

> "The performance … seems to be of a kind pronounced impossible by modern champions of the sport."
>
> Sir Arthur Evans, 1921

Nebamun Hunting in the Marshes

Artist unknown c. 1350 BCE, fresco, 3 × 4 ft (0.98 × 1.15 m) British Museum, London, UK

An important "scribe and counter of grain" for the Pharaoh Amenhotep III, Nebamun commissioned this fresco to decorate his own tomb on the west bank of the Nile River. According to the hieroglyphic caption, it shows Nebamun "enjoying himself and seeing beauty" in the afterlife. It was designed to encourage his family and friends to visit the tomb and talk about him, guaranteeing him a good afterlife.

The birds appear to erupt out of the ground, representing the vitality—and abundance—of nature. However, they are also evil spirits that Nebamun puts to flight.

Divine symbols in the background suggest that the gods are taking care of Nebamun's soul.

The snake-shaped throw-stick in Nebamun's hand was a weapon often used in hunting.

Nebamun's wife Hatshepsut is wearing fine clothes and jewelery, in contrast to her husband and daughter.

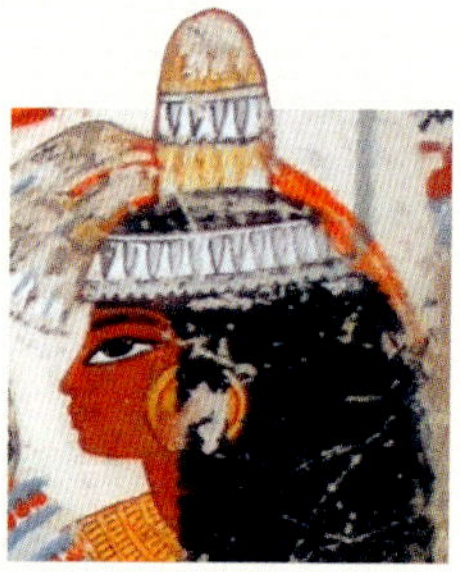

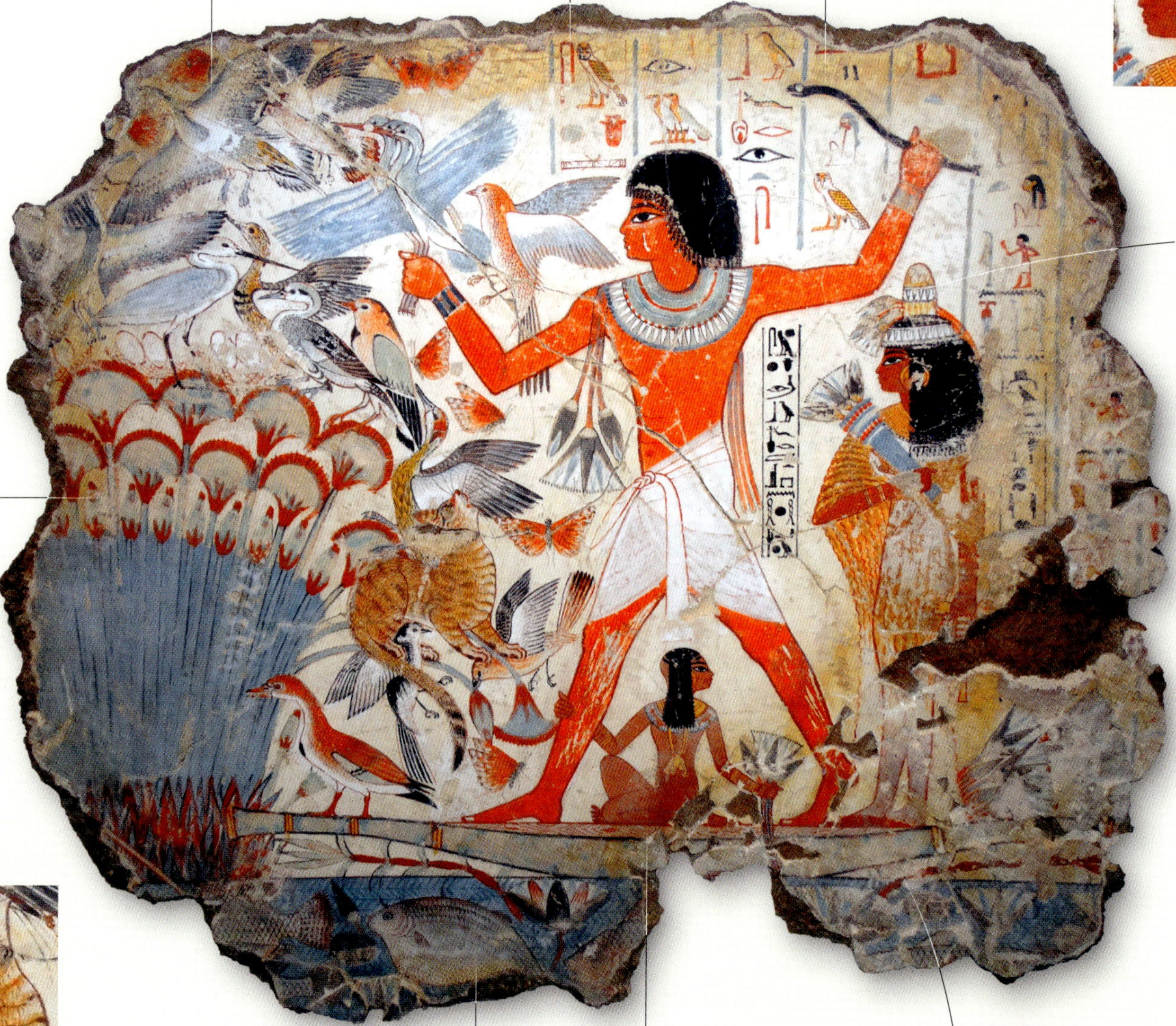

A hieroglyphic caption explains the painting to the viewer.

The papyrus thicket, birds, butterfly, and cat are all realistically represented.

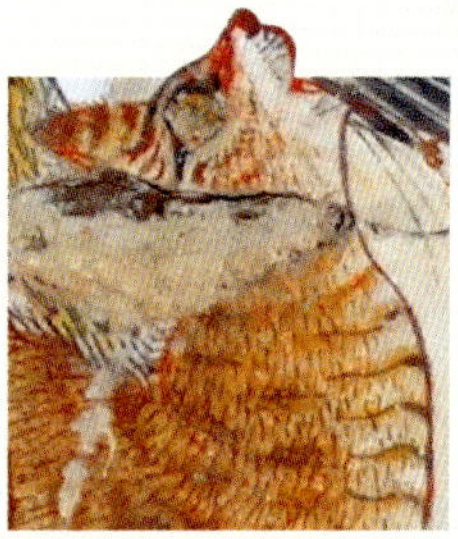

Cats were an emblem of Hathor, the goddess of life and fertility, who was also important as a guardian of the dead. Gold leaf was used to color the cat's eyes.

The fish represent fertility and abundance. They were also emblems of immortality.

Nebamun's daughter clutches her father's leg. Her hairstyle denotes her youth.

The boat is typical of those used in this marshland setting, but it also recalls the vessel that carries the soul to the afterlife.

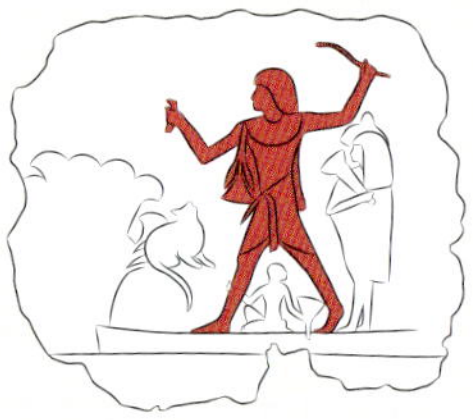

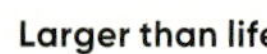

Larger than life
The outsize Nebamun dominates this vivid painting. His resolute stance displays strength, power, and dynamism.

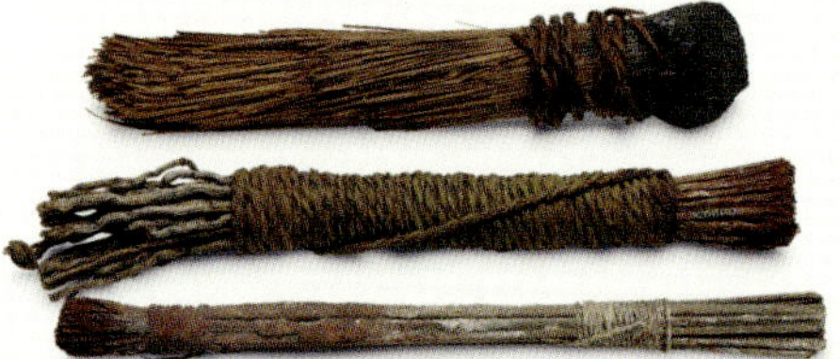

Fresco technique
The outline of the scene would have been sketched onto a layer of fine plaster covering a layer of mud and straw. A team of artists would have added color and details using brushes made from reeds and pigments derived from rocks and mixed with a binder such as gum Arabic.

Bust of Nefertiti

Thutmose c. 1345 BCE, limestone and stucco, 19 in (48 cm) high, Neues Museum, Berlin, Germany

The "great royal wife" of Akhenaten, a pharaoh of Egypt's 18th Dynasty, Nefertiti appears in scenes on the walls of several Theban tombs. This bust, excavated from a studio belonging to the court sculptor Thutmose, gives her a strikingly modern look. Nefertiti's beauty may be lifelike but it is also symbolic, its regularity suggesting the rank she represents.

A Uraeus (stylized cobra) above Nefertiti's brow is an emblem of regal power and wisdom. Only a stump remains where its head once was.

The flat-topped crown resembles that of Tefnut, goddess of life-giving moisture. It broadens as it rises and, with the Uraeus, emphasizes the symmetry of her face.

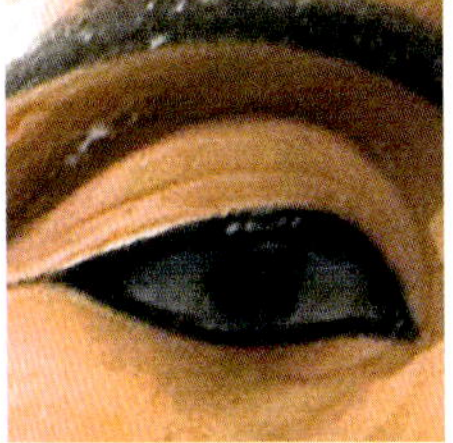

A quartz fragment that has been painted black forms the iris of her right eye. (The one from the left eye is missing.)

Nefertiti is largely unadorned and there is no inscription. The queen's authority speaks for itself.

Iron oxide pigment has been used to give the queen's skin its richness and warmth.

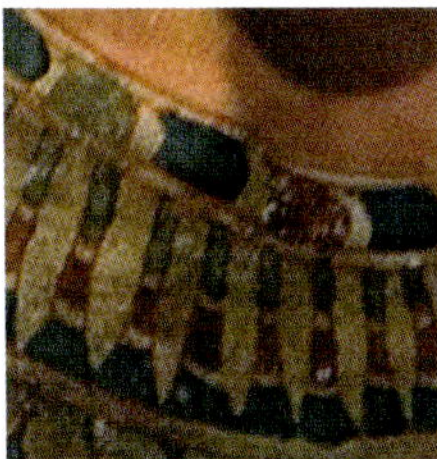

The neckline of Nefertiti's gown mirrors the arc of her eyelashes, eyebrows, and ears.

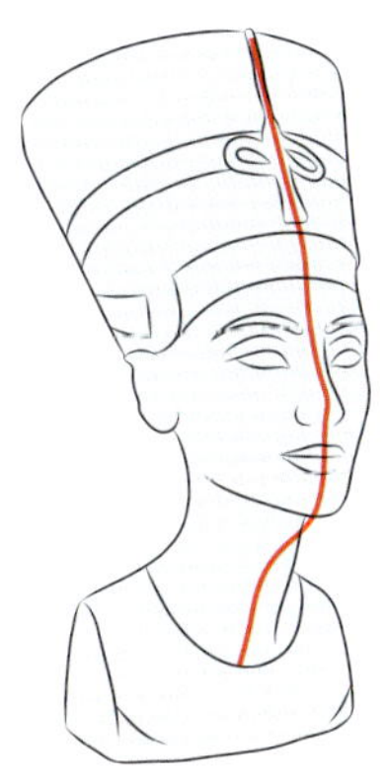

Perfection
The line formed by Nefertiti's elongated neck, her nose, and the Uraeus above them, crosses the band that runs around the crown, reinforcing the sense of symmetrical perfection.

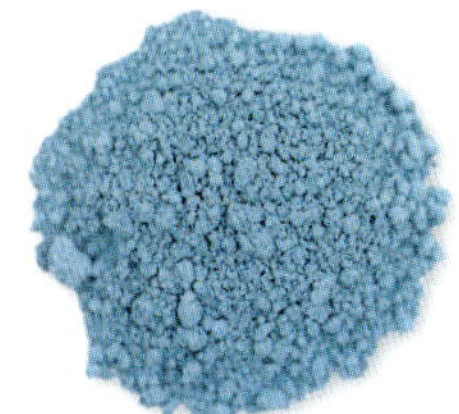

Crowning glory
The blue-green color of Nefertiti's crown is known as Egyptian blue. It was made from copper acetate, which forms a deposit on copper dipped in vinegar.

> "Great in the palace, fair of face … The King's Great Wife whom he loves."
>
> Akhenaten's panegyric, inscription c. 1350 BCE

Colossal Head 1

Artist unknown c. 1200-900 BCE, basalt, 9 × 7 ft (2.85 × 2.11 m), The Museo de Antropología de Xalapa, Veracruz, Mexico

Perhaps the finest of the 17 colossal stone heads attributed to the Olmec culture of southeastern Mexico, Head 1 probably represents a ruler or lord. This portrait is one of the earliest expressions of political authority in ancient Mesoamerica. Lacking metal tools for sculpting, artists carved the head by hammering stone on stone, then polished it with abrasives to create the smoothed surfaces.

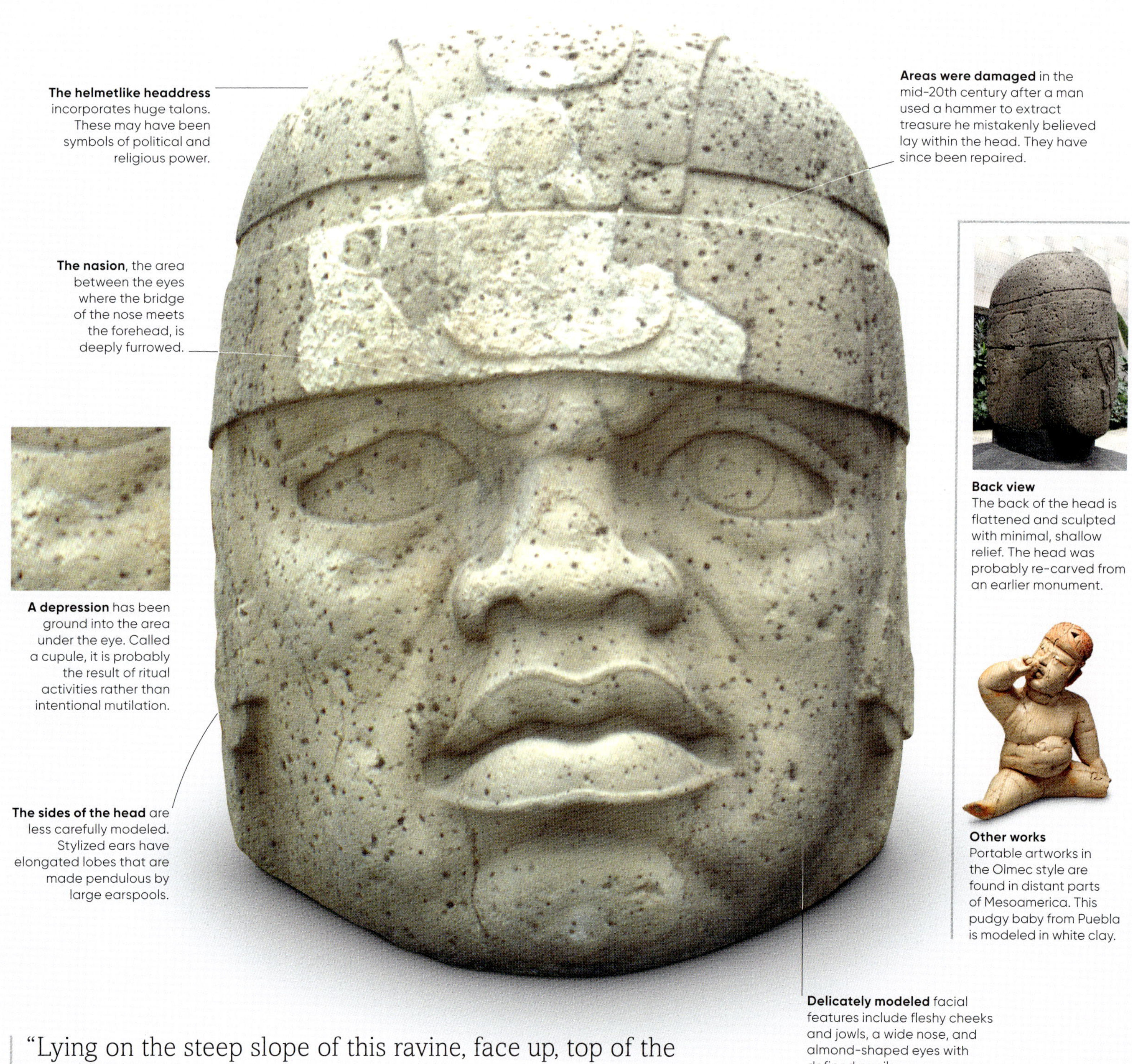

The helmetlike headdress incorporates huge talons. These may have been symbols of political and religious power.

The nasion, the area between the eyes where the bridge of the nose meets the forehead, is deeply furrowed.

A depression has been ground into the area under the eye. Called a cupule, it is probably the result of ritual activities rather than intentional mutilation.

The sides of the head are less carefully modeled. Stylized ears have elongated lobes that are made pendulous by large earspools.

Areas were damaged in the mid-20th century after a man used a hammer to extract treasure he mistakenly believed lay within the head. They have since been repaired.

Back view
The back of the head is flattened and sculpted with minimal, shallow relief. The head was probably re-carved from an earlier monument.

Other works
Portable artworks in the Olmec style are found in distant parts of Mesoamerica. This pudgy baby from Puebla is modeled in white clay.

Delicately modeled facial features include fleshy cheeks and jowls, a wide nose, and almond-shaped eyes with defined pupils.

> "Lying on the steep slope of this ravine, face up, top of the head down, was the colossal head to end all colossal heads."
>
> Matthew Sterling, 1947

Assyrian Lion Hunt

Anonymous c. 640 BCE, alabaster (gypsum) relief sculpture, British Museum, London, UK

The "Lion Hunt" panels from the North Palace at Nineveh (in present-day Iraq) show Ashurbanipal, last of the great kings of Assyria, killing lions with a sword, spear, bow and arrow, and even a mace. Lion hunts such as this were staged as a demonstration of the king's divinely ordained power. The series of panels begins with the release of a lion, probably bred in captivity, from a cage.

It was a king's duty to protect his subjects from lions, and scenes such as these decorated royal reception rooms as testament to his power.

An arrow projecting from the lion's head signifies that it is sufficiently weakened for the king to deal a final blow with his sword.

The lion is sculpted with remarkable attention to detail. The artist must have studied lions, including wounded and dying animals, closely.

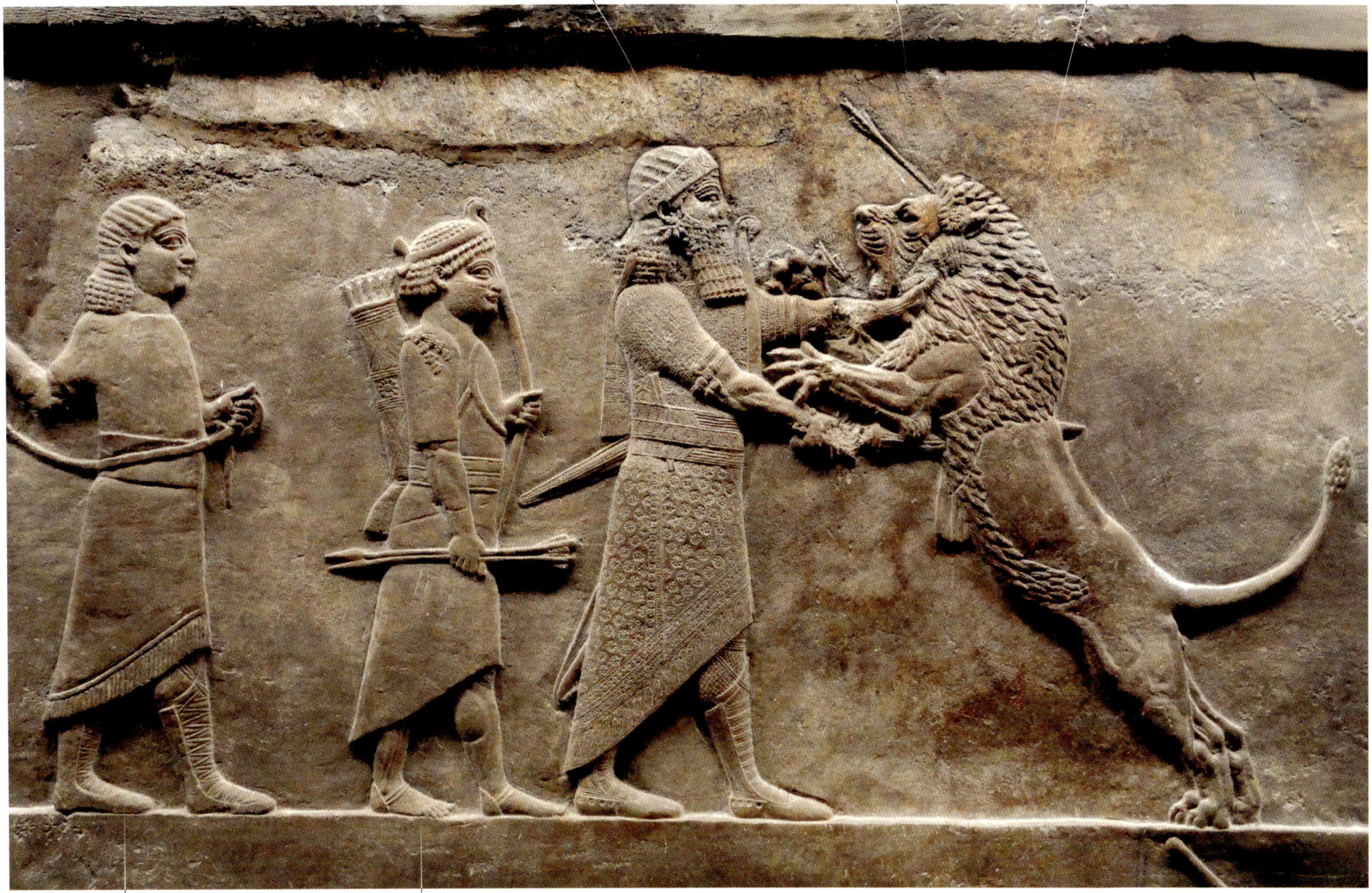

A groom, who holds the king's horse, relates to the previous scene in the series of narrative panels.

An archer stands behind the king, ready to supply fresh arrows. Assistants are always on hand to ensure the king's safety.

> "He hunted the lions, which harried the shepherds all the nights, and he caught the jackals. He, having mastered the lions, let the shepherds sleep soundly."
>
> *Epic of Gilgamesh*, c. 2100–1200 BCE

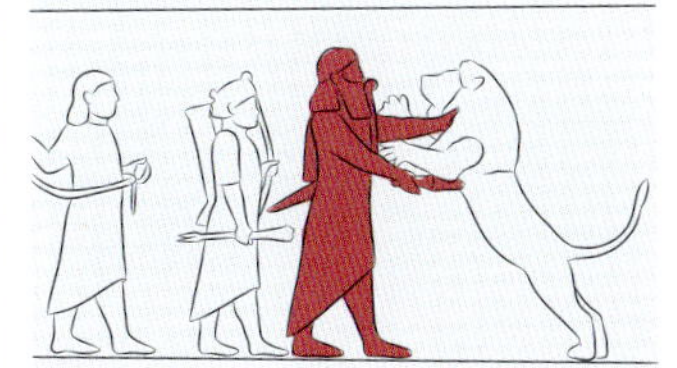

Composition
The king is shown on a larger scale than his courtiers. As usual with Near Eastern and Egyptian art, all figures, including animals, are in profile, and the composition is divided into horizontal bands.

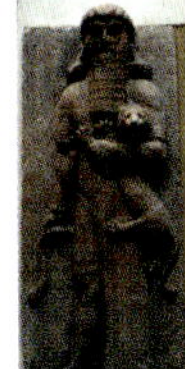

Gilgamesh
The motif of the king holding or killing a lion recalls the exploits of the world's first hero in the poem *Epic of Gilgamesh*, which was retrieved from Ashurbanipal's library at Nineveh.

Attic Black-Figure Amphora

Exekias c. 540–530 BCE, painted ceramic, height 24 in (61.1 cm), Vatican Museums, Vatican City

This wine jar is signed by the Athenian potter and painter Exekias. Painted inscriptions identify the figures as two prominent heroes of the Trojan War: Ajax and Achilles. Both warriors hold spears, suggesting that they have become absorbed by their board game while on guard duty.

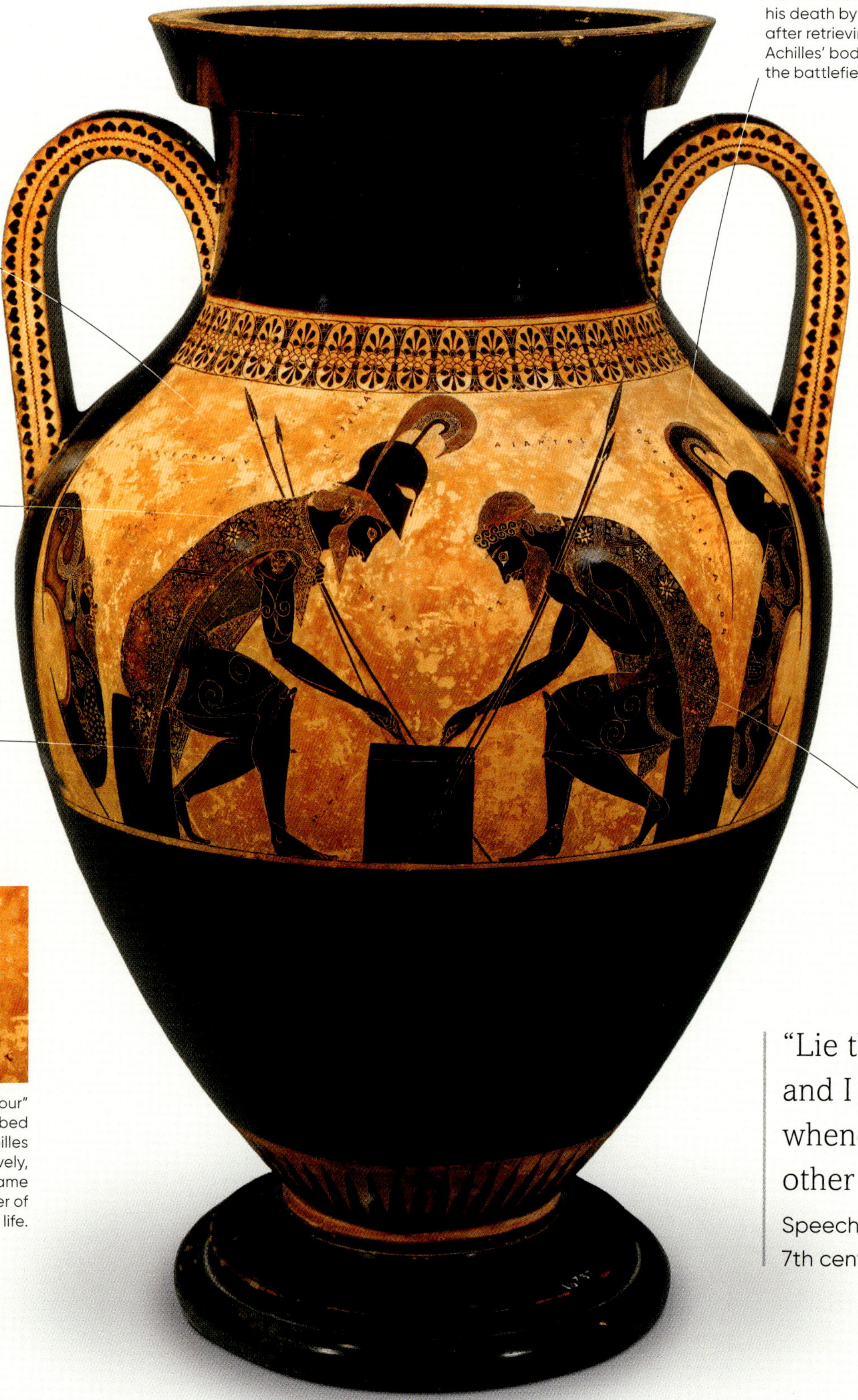

The removal of Ajax's helmet foreshadows his death by suicide after retrieving Achilles' body from the battlefield at Troy.

The strong diagonal lines of the spears reinforce the heroes' focus on the game.

The warriors' eyes have been rendered as if frontal even though the figures are shown in profile.

Fleet-footed Achilles wears leg protectors (greaves) that do not cover the one vulnerable part of his body—his heel.

Ajax's and Achilles' bent postures accentuate the curves of the vase.

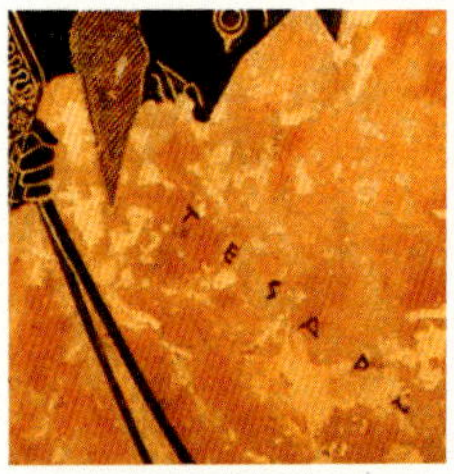

The Greek words for "four" and "three" are inscribed by the mouths of Achilles and Ajax respectively, implying that the game involved dice—a matter of chance and fate, like life.

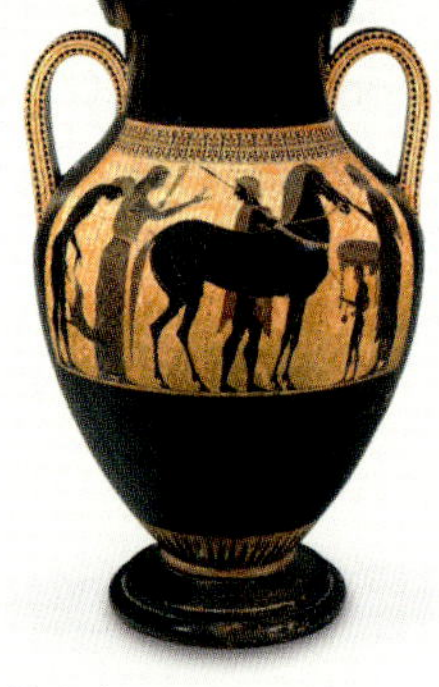

Twin image
The artwork on the other side of the vase depicts the homecoming of the twin half-brothers Castor and Pollux from the hunt. Elaborately decorated vases such as this one often feature mythical scenes.

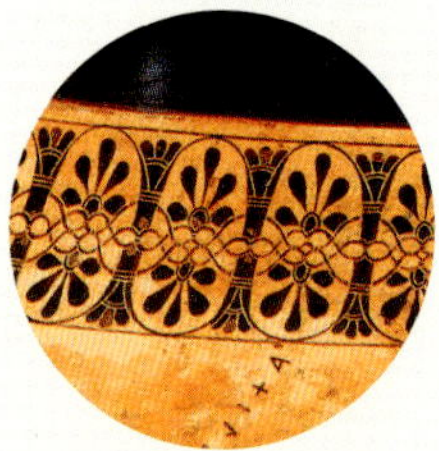

Adding detail
Black-figure motifs were painted in silhouette in black glaze. Details were added by scratching through to the fired clay beneath or by using paint applied with a fine brush.

> "Lie there then in death, and I will face my own, whenever Zeus and the other deathless gods decide."
>
> Speech by Achilles, Homer's *Iliad,* 7th century BCE

Persepolis Relief (detail)

Anonymous c. 500 BCE, limestone relief sculpture, eastern stairway of the Apadana audience hall, Persepolis, Iran

This section of the bas-relief panels that adorn the Apadana palace shows the Persian New Year, or *Nowruz* festival, when the "king of kings" received the homage of subservient delegations from all over his empire. The visitors came with a tribute of products typical of their homeland, such as animals, textiles, or timber. The Apadana reliefs reinforce the power of the Persian king and the breadth of his dominion.

The distinctive dress of these ambassadors identifies them as Syrian or Lydian.

These two bracelets would have been brightly colored, making the material—possibly gold—immediately evident.

A pair of vases offered by a third ambassador probably contained precious oils or wine.

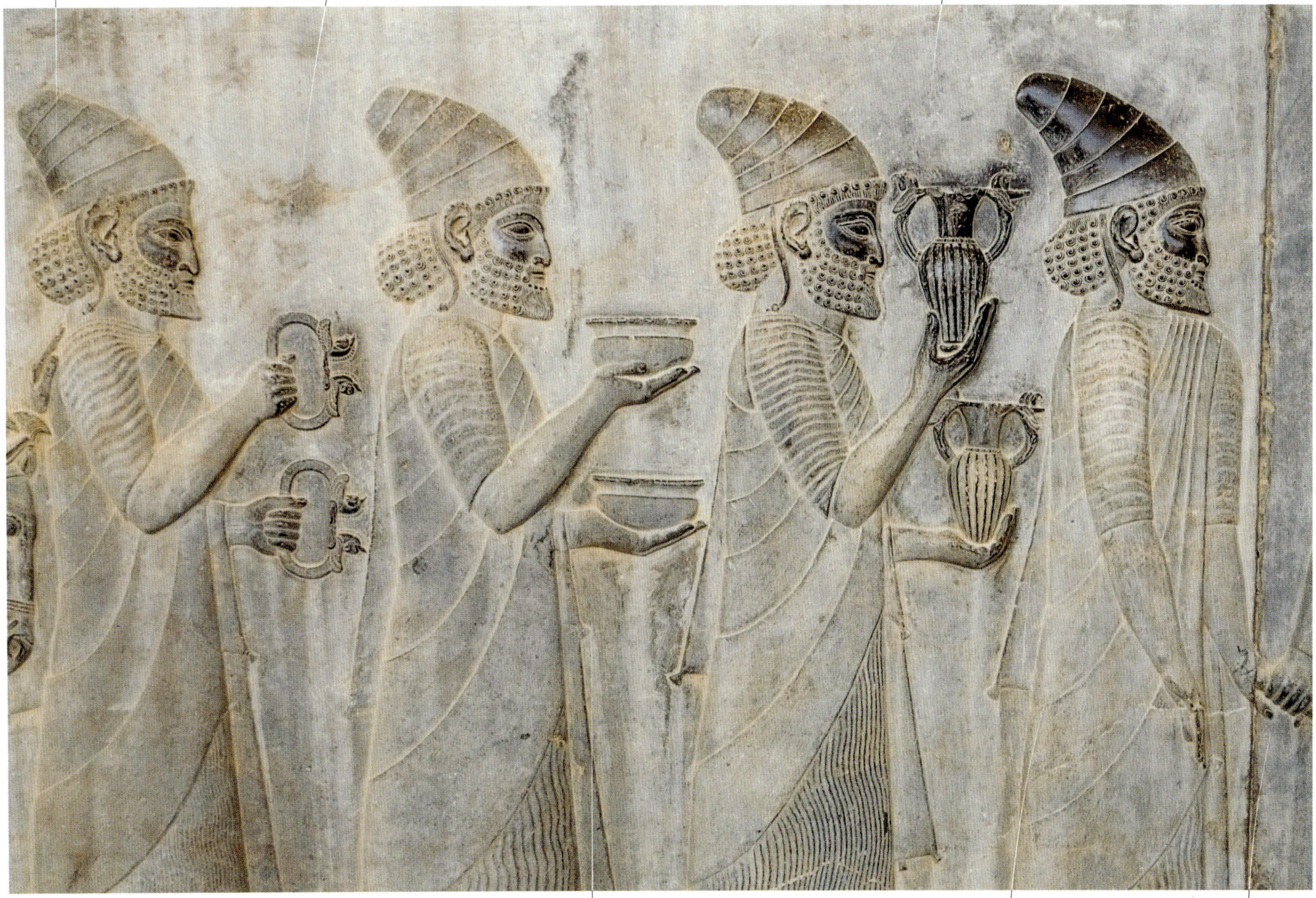

Two bowls may contain precious aromatic liquids, such as frankincense and myrrh.

All the figures file in a procession that leads in one direction only: to the king. The overall effect relies upon the power of repetition.

A royal usher, whose hand is just visible, leads the ambassadors into the audience hall.

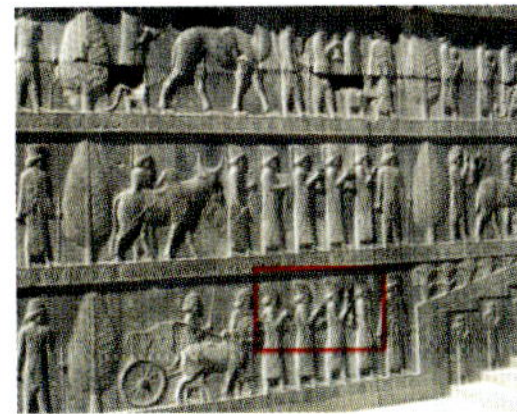

Frieze reliefs
The wall of the Apadana was covered with row on row of people bearing tribute to the king. Representatives of 23 different subject states have been identified in these reliefs.

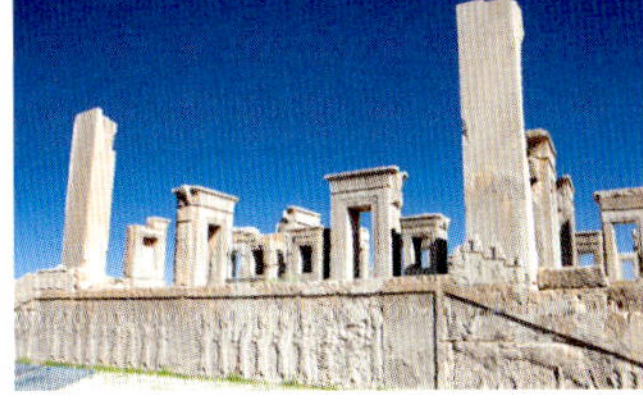

Persepolis
The ceremonial center of the Persian empire, Persepolis was not a regular royal residence. The Apadana was begun by the Achaemenid king Darius I and completed by his son Xerxes. The enormous building could hold some 10,000 people.

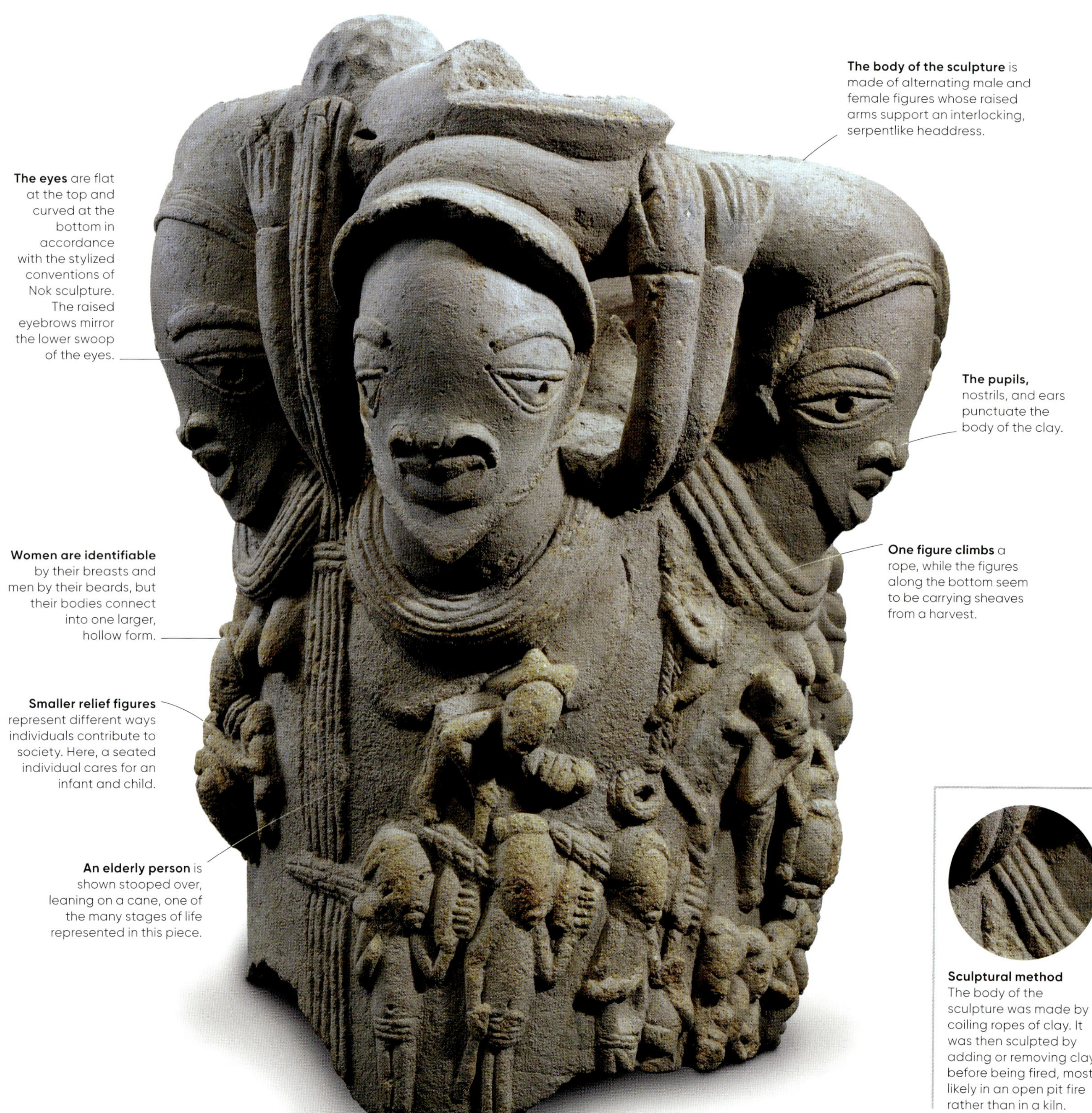

Nok Terra-Cotta Bas-Relief Sculpture

Artist unknown 500 BCE–500 CE, terra-cotta, 21 × 20 × 20 in (54 × 50 × 50 cm), Musée du quai Branly, Paris, France

The Nok culture is famous for its stylized, figurative terra-cotta sculptures and iron smelting. It is one of the earliest known civilizations in West Africa. This piece combines sculpture in the round and relief sculpture to portray ideas about society and to explore the tension between the group and the individual in everyday life. Most Nok sculptures have been found during tin mining operations, rather than by archaeologists, making it difficult to identify what they were originally used for.

Boxer at Rest

Artist unknown 330–50 BCE, bronze, 47 in (120 cm) high, Palazzo Massimo, Rome, Italy

This lifelike and nearly life-size, hollow-cast Greek figure represents a veteran athlete immediately after a contest. He turns his head toward the right as if to acknowledge plaudits from spectators. He must have won to earn an honorific statue, but the cost of victory is shown by his hunched posture and open lesions on his face. He may be seated because he is exhausted or concussed and unable to stand.

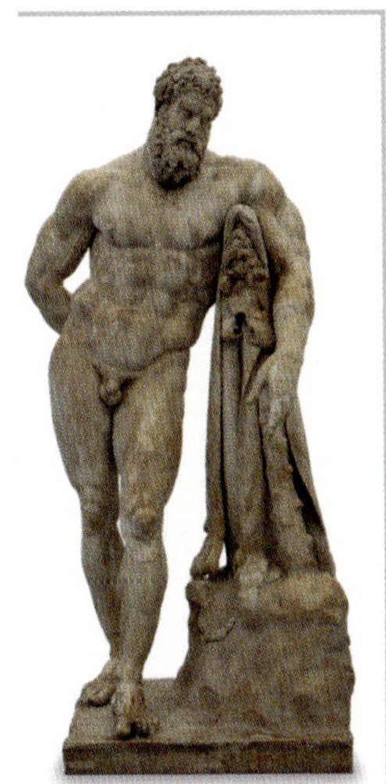

Heroic model Physically and emotionally, the figure evokes the *Weary Herakles*. Created in the late 4th century BCE, this type of sculpture shows a hero who is exhausted yet undefeated by his labors—a model of stoicism.

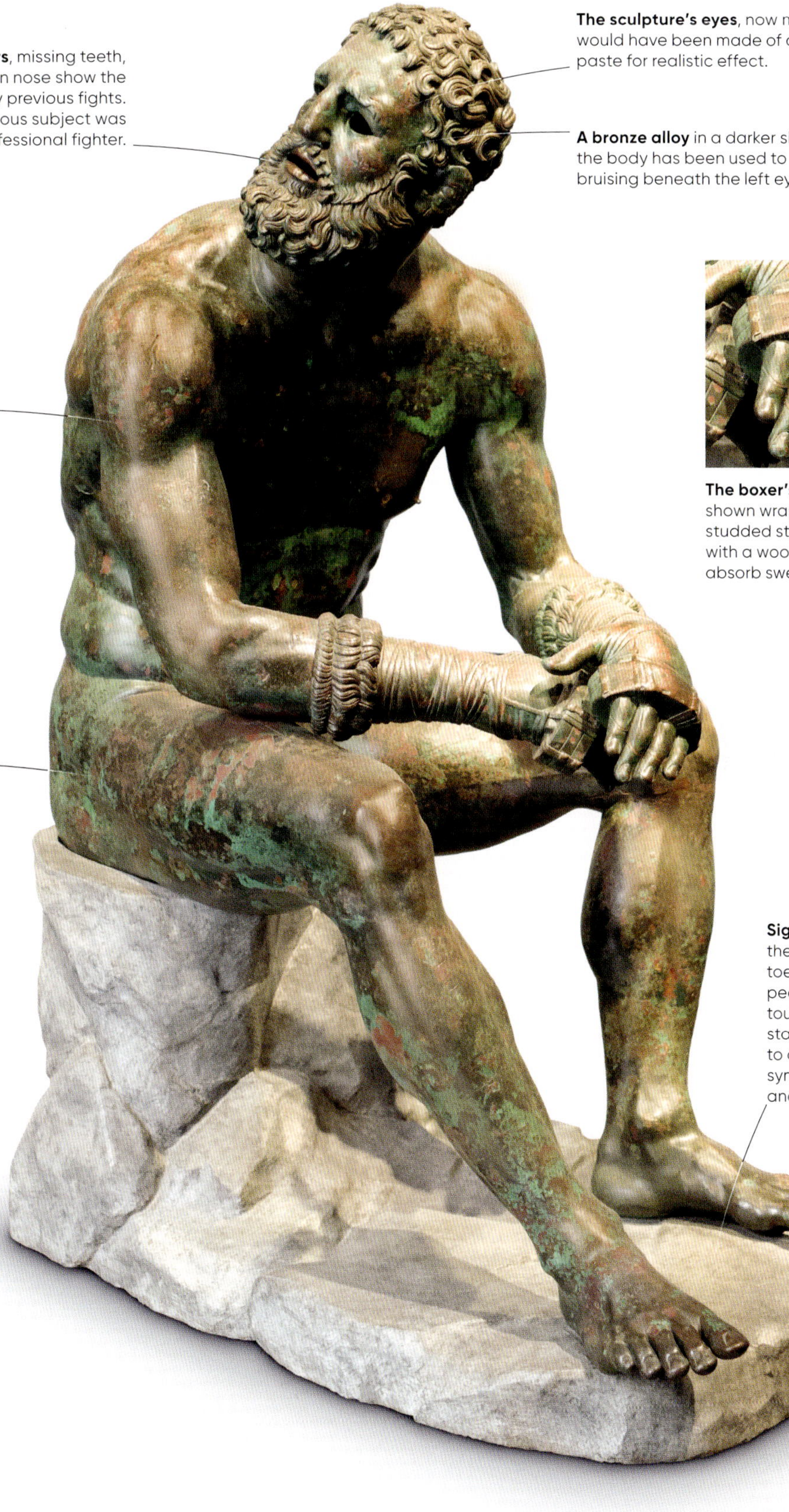

Battered ears, missing teeth, and a broken nose show the damage done by previous fights. The anonymous subject was probably a professional fighter.

The sculpture's eyes, now missing, would have been made of a vitreous paste for realistic effect.

A bronze alloy in a darker shade than the body has been used to show bruising beneath the left eye.

Athletes at the ancient Greek Olympics competed without clothes. The figure's nudity gives it a timeless and heroic character.

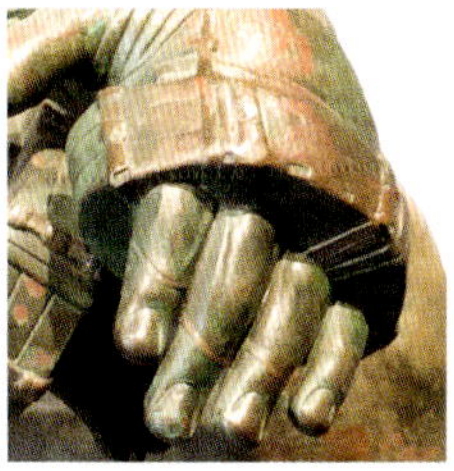

The boxer's hands are shown wrapped in studded strips of oxhide, with a woolen cuff to absorb sweat and blood.

Copper inlays on the right arm and thigh evoke flesh wounds and drops of blood.

Signs of wear to the fingers and toes suggest that people frequently touched the statue, as if to absorb its symbolic strength and resilience.

> "I have never felt such an extraordinary impression as the one created by the sight of this magnificent specimen of a semi-barbaric athlete, coming slowly out of the ground."
>
> Rodolfo Lanciani, 1888

The Terra-Cotta Army

Anonymous c. 210 BCE, terra-cotta, 69–79 in (175–200 cm) high, Mausoleum of the First Qin Emperor, Xi'an, China

Ying Zheng (258–210 BCE) made himself Qin Shi Huangdi (First Divine Emperor) in 221 BCE. He built himself an appropriately imposing tomb and commissioned 8,000 life-size ceramic figures to accompany him to the afterlife, including civilian officials, entertainers, and a formidable army complete with archers, chariots, and horses. The soldiers may have originally carried real weapons, which were looted by robbers in later times.

Soldiers are identified by different types of armor.

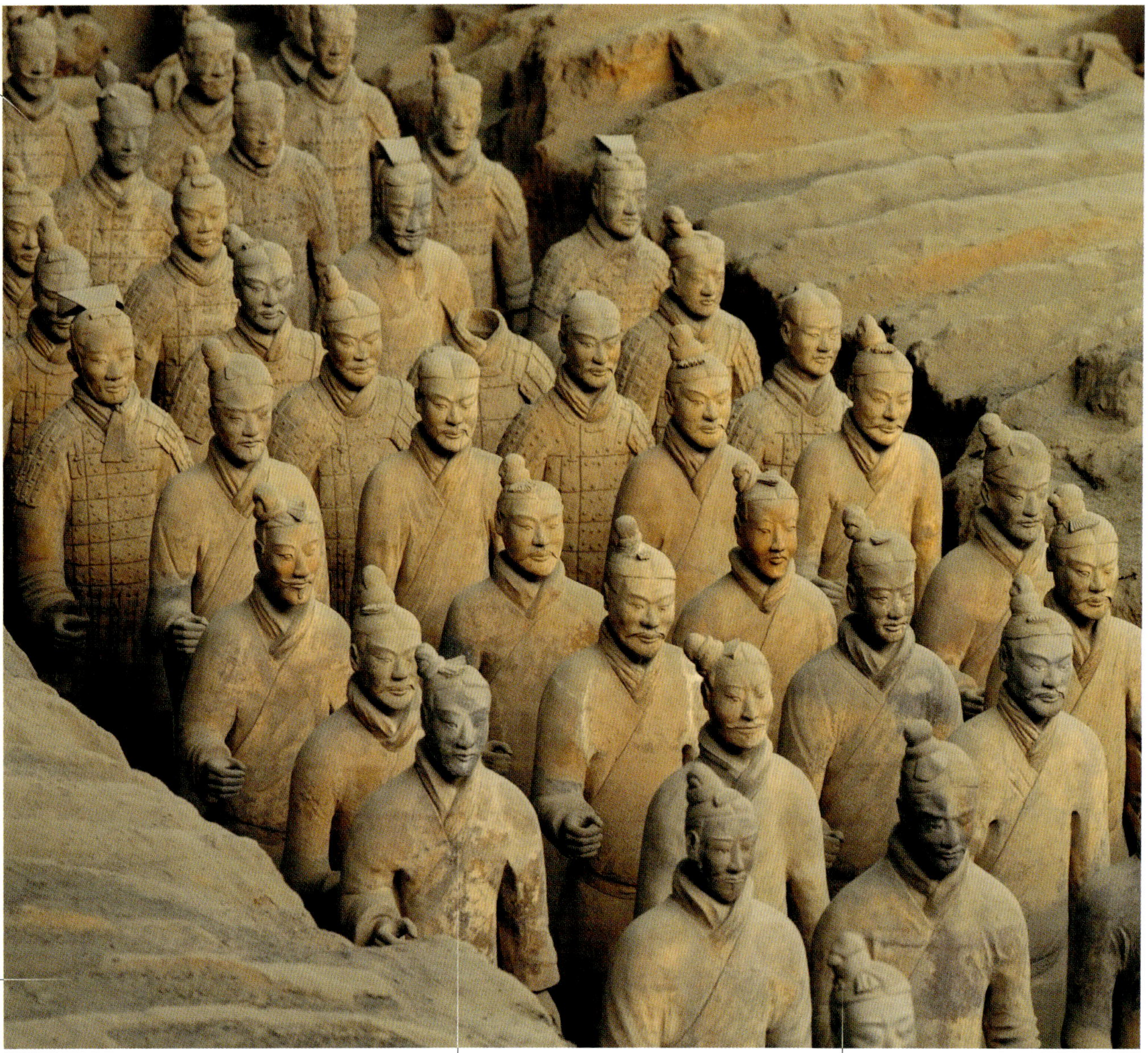

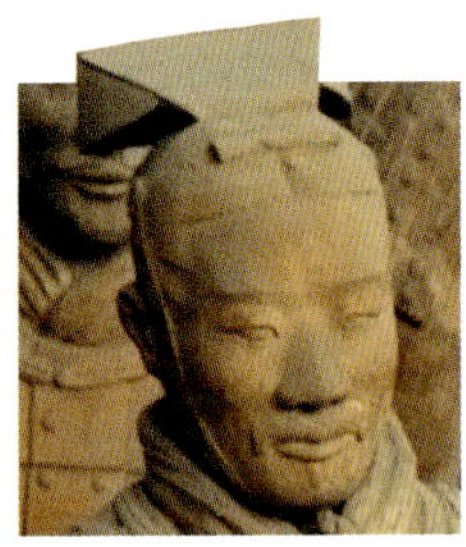

Flattened headdresses identify officers. Status was also communicated by size: generals are taller than the rank-and-file.

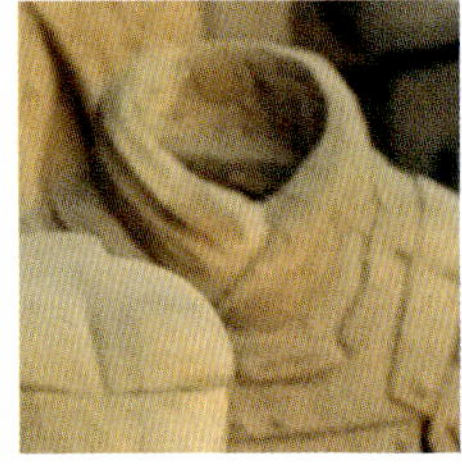

The head of this figure is missing. Heads, torsos, arms, and legs were sculpted and fired separately before being assembled in situ.

The tomb was discovered in 1974, after villagers digging a well came across remnants of clay figures.

Faces were first cast in molds, of which ten basic forms have been identified. Clay was then sculpted onto these templates to give each statue individualized features.

The hairstyles are differentiated as carefully as the faces.

> "The universe entire is our Emperor's realm."
>
> Sima Qian, 104–87 BCE

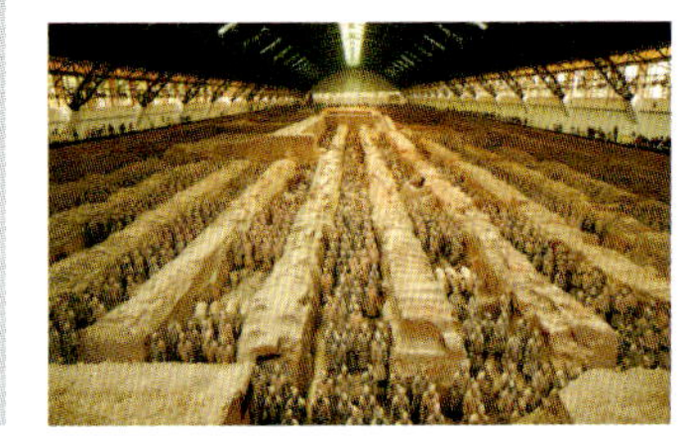

Arrangement
Pit 1 is the largest of the four pits. The figures, all facing east, are arranged in 11 columns, with three rows of infantry at the front of the formation.

Chinese purple
The clay figures were painted with a range of pigments, including the rare synthetic barium copper silicate ("Chinese purple"), but these colors did not survive exposure to the air after the tomb was opened.

Venus de Milo

Alexandros of Antioch c. 150 BCE, marble, 80 in (204 cm) high, Louvre, Paris, France

This classical sculpture, discovered on the Greek island of Milos, shows the goddess of love, known to the Greeks as Aphrodite and to the Romans as Venus, half-naked, as if caught unawares. A further fragment of the statue, however, suggests that her left hand was extended to display an apple—her prize as winner of the mythical divine beauty contest known as "the Judgment of Paris."

The missing ear lobes were probably knocked off during the theft of precious earrings—the statue was once embellished with gold or gilded bronze jewelery.

The goddess's right arm would have reached down in an attempt to gather her falling robes.

The left hand once held an apple, possibly a pun on the name of the island where it was found—Milos sounds like "apple" in ancient Greek.

Marble from the island of Paros was prized for its luminous, fine-grained quality.

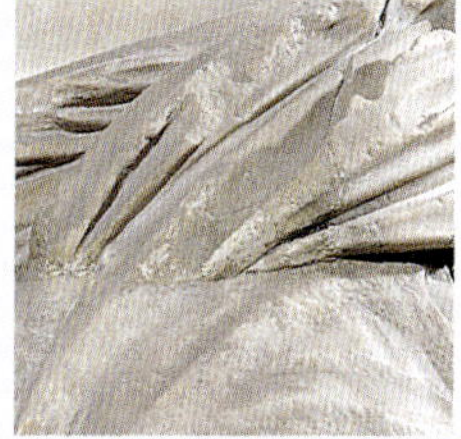

The statue is carved from two pieces of marble, joined diagonally beneath the upper line of drapery.

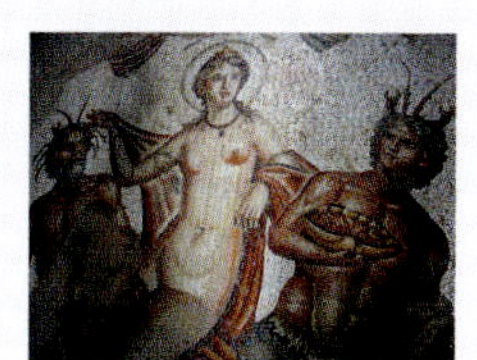

Iconography
According to myth, Venus rose from the ocean. She is often shown attended by sea creatures, as in this Roman mosaic.

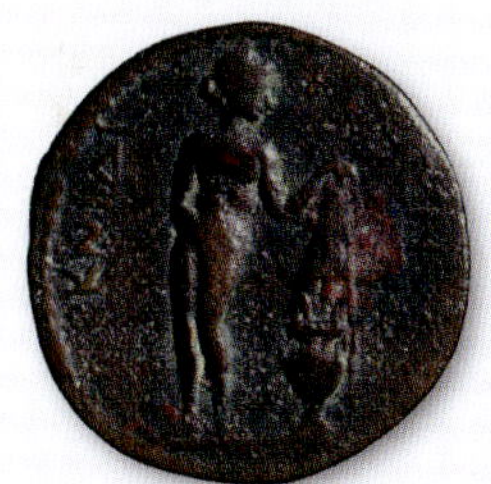

Classical tradition
The first image of a nude Aphrodite is attributed to the Greek sculptor Praxiteles, around 360 BCE. It was displayed at a temple in the port city of Knidos. The original is lost but various copies survive.

> "So great was the power of the craftsman's art that the hard unyielding marble did justice to every limb."
>
> Lucian on Praxiteles' Venus, c. 150 CE

Deep folds of drapery, carved with a running drill, convey a sense of movement and accentuate the shape of the body beneath.

Laocoön and His Sons

Agesander, Athenodoros, and Polydorus c. 1st century BCE–1st century CE, marble, height 95 in (242 cm), Vatican Museums, Vatican City

Horror is etched on the face of Laocoön, the priest who prophesied that the gift of a huge wooden horse would bring doom to the city of Troy. He is assailed, together with his sons, by a pair of giant sea serpents, which entwine themselves around their limbs. Their fate was seen as a sign of divine anger. Ancient Romans admired the statue as epitomizing both the end of Troy and the rise of Rome.

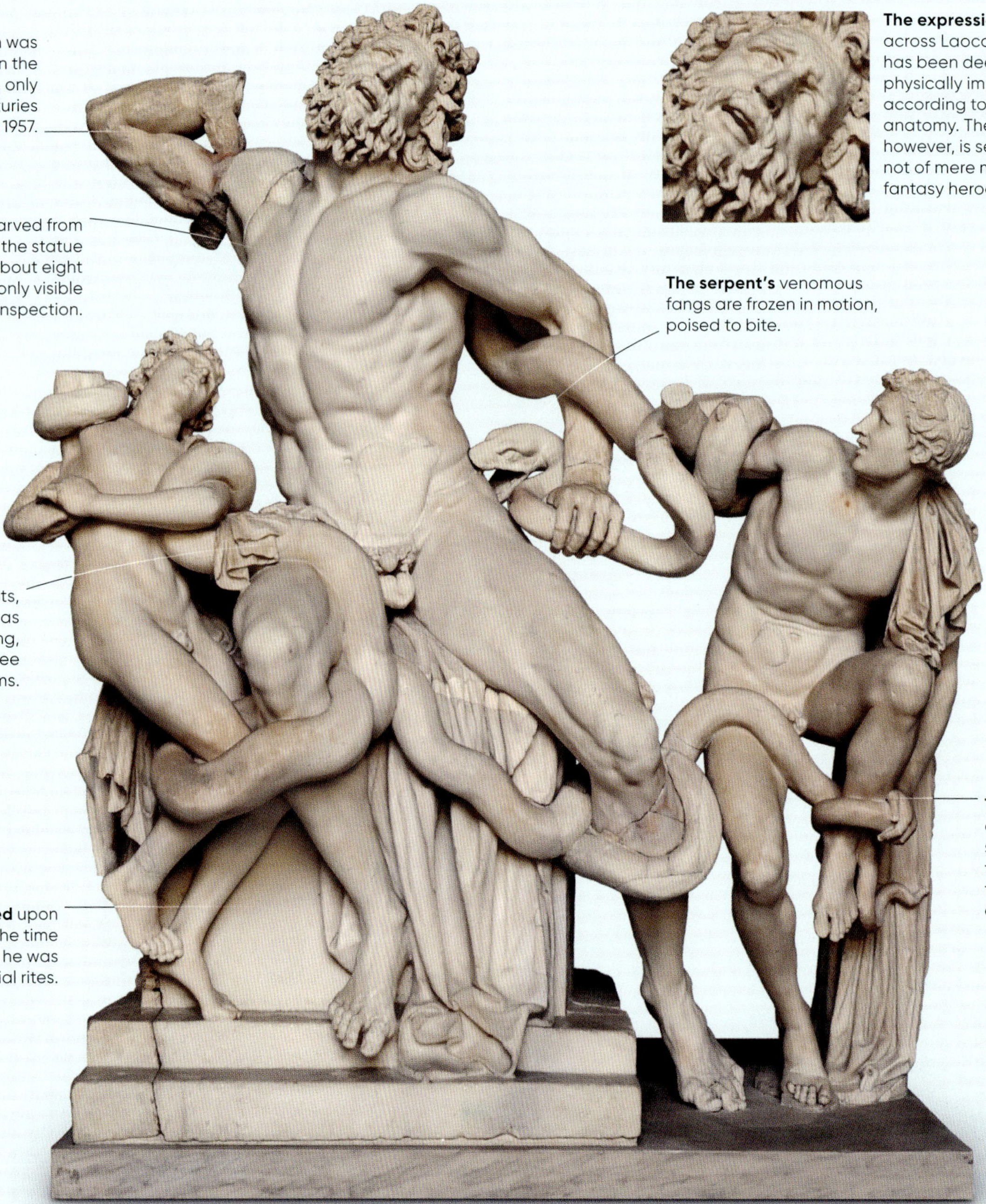

Laocoön's right arm was missing in 1506 when the statue was excavated, only to be recovered centuries later and reattached in 1957.

Reputed to have been carved from a single block of marble, the statue is in fact composed of about eight sections. The joints are only visible on very close inspection.

The coils of the serpents, regarded by some critics as unnatural and unconvincing, serve to unite the three flailing victims.

Laocoön is seated upon the altar where, at the time of the attack, he was conducting sacrificial rites.

The expression carved across Laocoön's forehead has been deemed physically impossible according to human anatomy. The Trojan saga, however, is set in the realm not of mere mortals but of fantasy heroes.

The serpent's venomous fangs are frozen in motion, poised to bite.

The entangled sons are proportionally smaller than their tormented father so that Laocoön stands out as the focus.

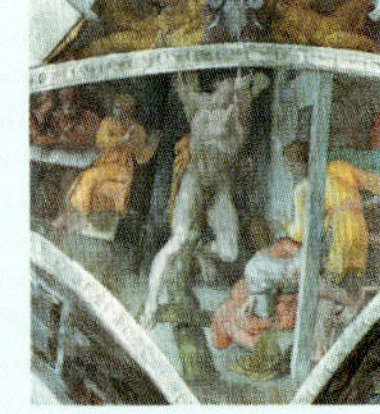

Renaissance echoes
The statue's influence can be seen in the poses of certain figures painted by Michelangelo in the frescoes of the Sistine Chapel. Michelangelo was reportedly present at the excavation of the statue.

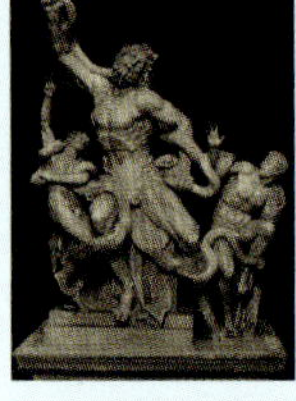

Restoration
Before the original was recovered and reattached, Laocoön's missing right arm was replaced with an arm that reached vertically and emphasized the group's pyramidal structure.

"In the history of Western art, one antique sculpture furnishes us with the prototypical icon of human agony."
Nigel Spivey, 2001

Portrait of Terentius Neo and Wife

Anonymous mid-1st century CE, fresco, 24 × 28 in (60 × 70 cm), National Archaeological Museum of Naples, Italy

Two well-to-do, even literary, citizens look out from this double-portrait painted directly onto the plaster walls of a house in Pompeii. Electioneering graffiti in the house suggests that Terentius Neo, a bakery owner, aspired to political office. The portrait would have been seen by the bakery's customers.

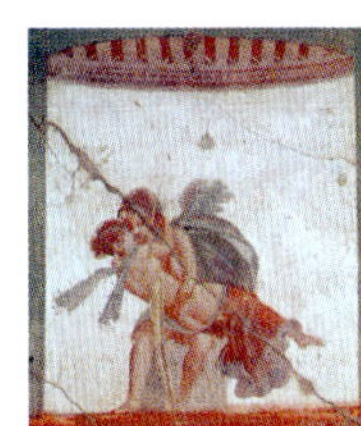

Companion piece
An image of Cupid and Psyche once sat above the couple, as if to confirm their love. After Pompeii was excavated, the two images were separated and sent to the National Archaeological Museum of Naples.

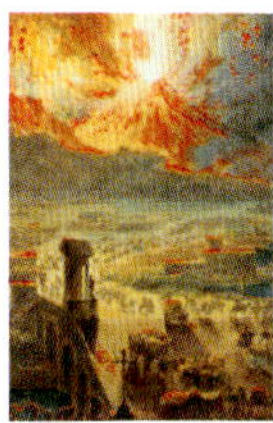

A window into the past
Houses at Pompeii were decorated throughout with frescoes of still lifes, landscapes, and scenes from classical mythology, many of which survived the eruption of Vesuvius.

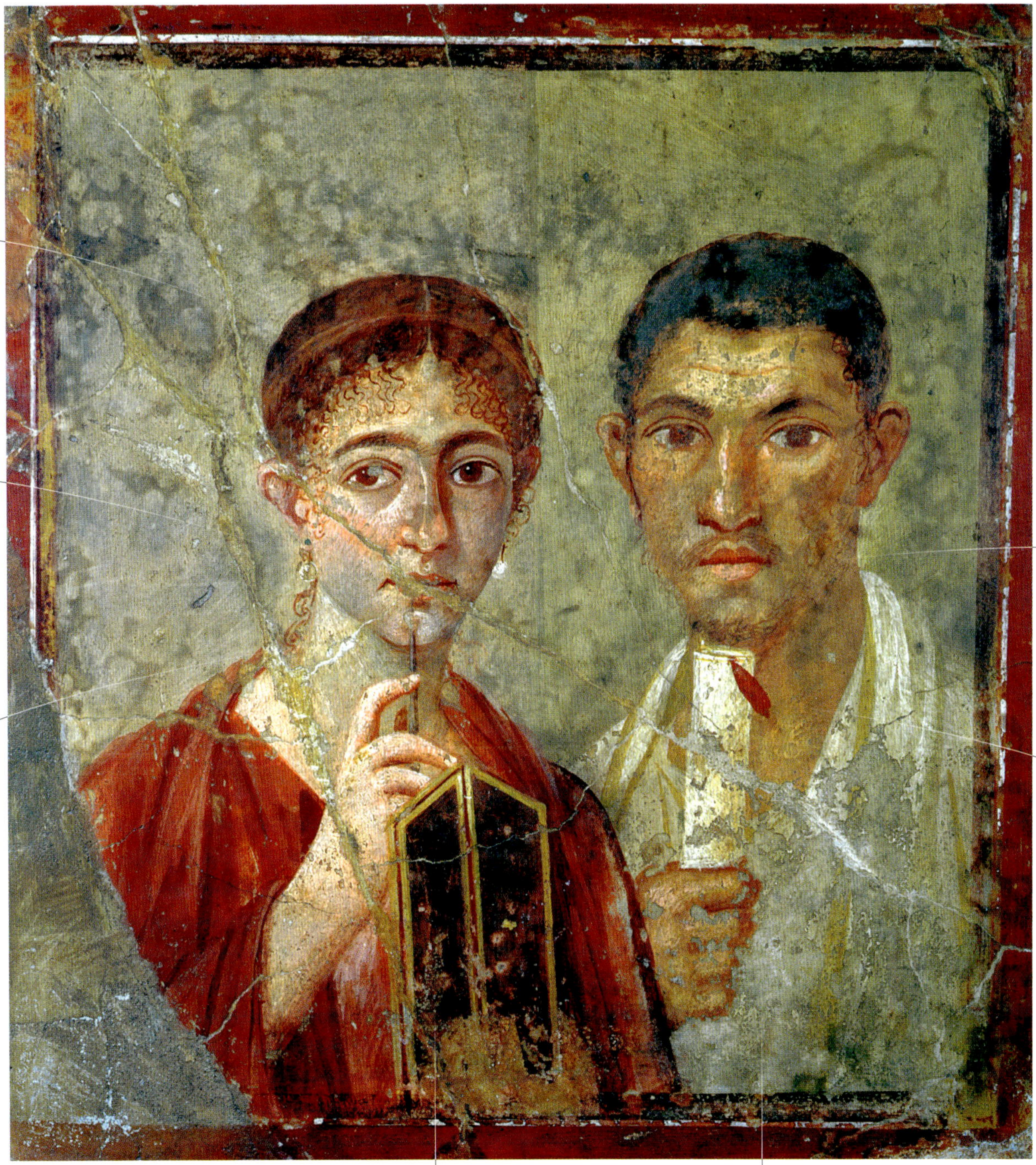

The woman's hair is parted in the center and arranged in fashionable ringlets under a red headband.

Her complexion is markedly lighter than her husband's, perhaps because she spent more of her time indoors.

The woman raises the stylus, used to write on wax tablets, to her lips. This may suggest she is writing poetry.

Terentius Neo's beard is painted with quick brushwork and light touches, indicating a portrait done from life.

He holds a papyrus scroll sealed with red wax.

Wax tablets were used for business accounts, and for letters and poetry.

His white toga (*toga candida*) suggests that he is a political candidate and confirms his status as a Roman citizen.

The nude

A universal motif in art, the nude transcends culture and time, capturing our beauty, sensuality, and vulnerability as humans. Ancient Greek statues of nude heroes and goddesses set a benchmark for physical beauty that was rediscovered and celebrated during the European Renaissance. Countless artists have since harnessed the power of the nude, often in non-idealized forms, to convey personal narratives, challenge social norms, and explore sexual politics.

3

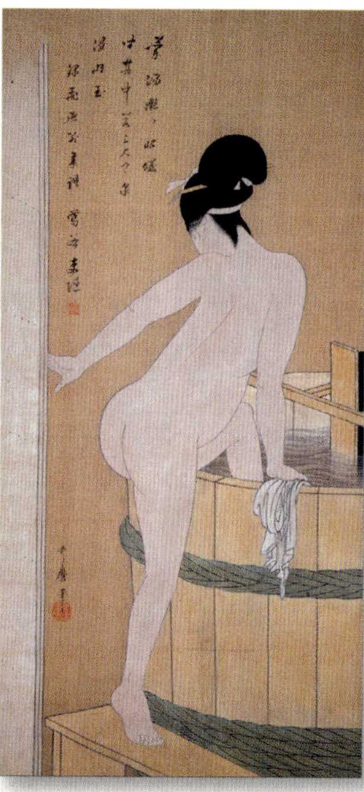

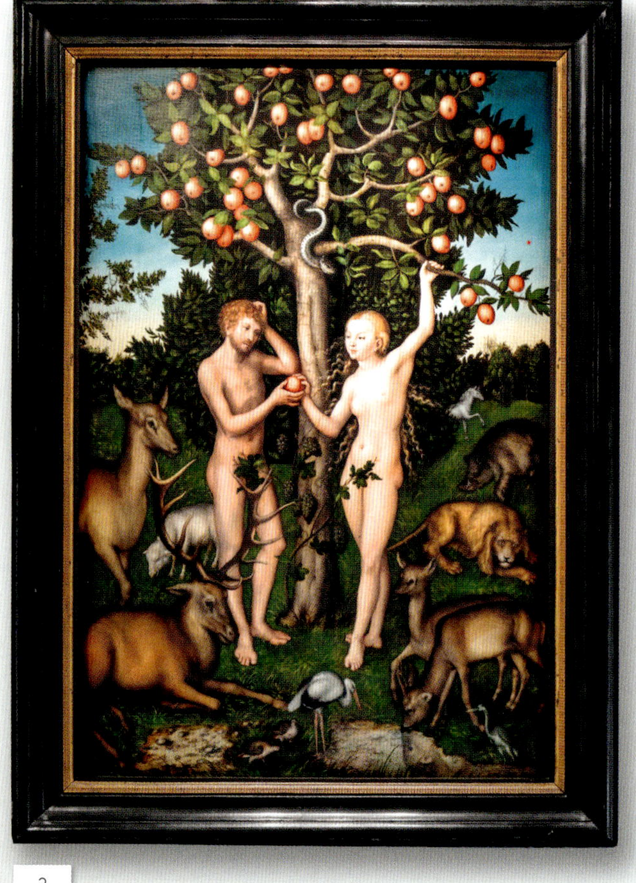

2

1

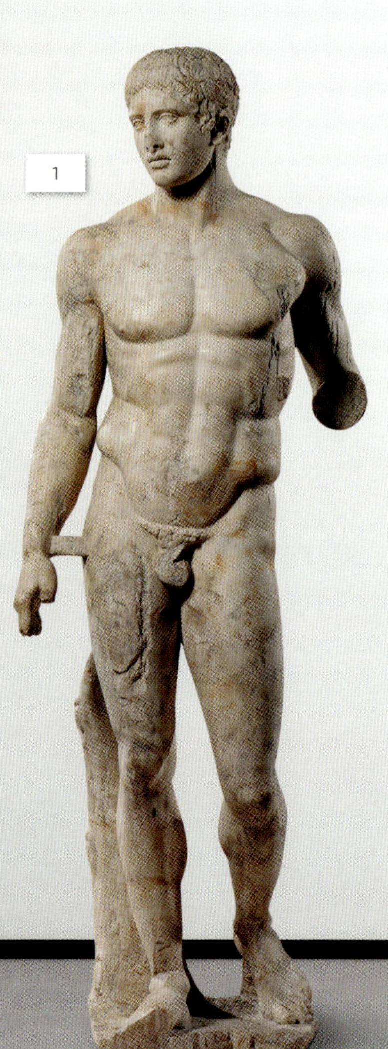

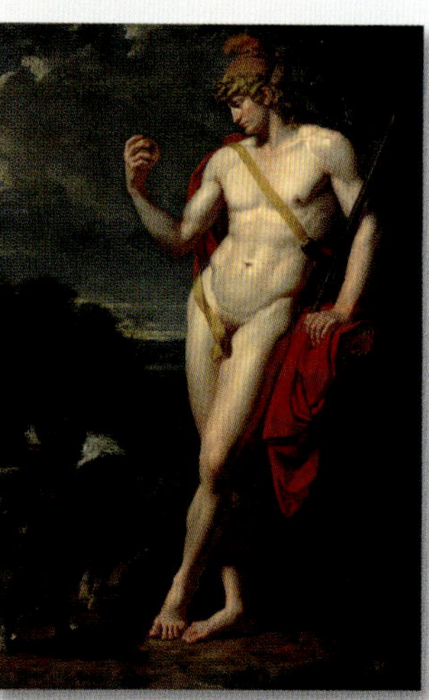

4

1. ***Doryphoros*** **(Spear Carrier), Polykleitos, c. 440 BCE.** This statue (originally made of bronze but now known only through a Roman copy in marble) set a standard for proportion and balance in the male torso. Its *contrapposto* posture idealized male nudity by enhancing muscular tension.

2. ***Adam and Eve,*** **Lucas Cranach, 1526.** Cranach's depiction of the Bible's first couple reveals a clever twist. The fig leaves hiding Adam and Eve's modesty are, on closer inspection, grapes, symbolizing the wine and blood of Christ through whom original sin will be redeemed.

3. ***Bathing in Cold Water,*** **Kitagawa Utamaro, 1770.** In this delicate depiction of the female body during Edo-period Japan, *ukiyo-e* artist Utamaro emphasizes the sensuous softness of this lady-in-waiting's skin and the graceful contours of her back and nape.

4. ***The Shepherd Paris,*** **Jean-Baptiste Frédéric Desmarais, 1787.** Desmarais demonstrated expert command of anatomy in this nude portrayal of Paris of Troy. This Neoclassical painting emphasizes an idealized male nude in a serene pastoral setting.

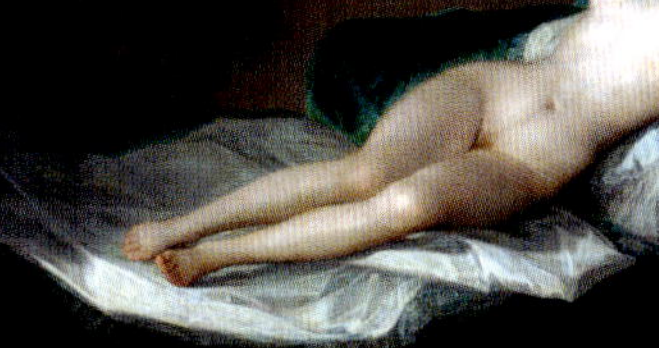

5

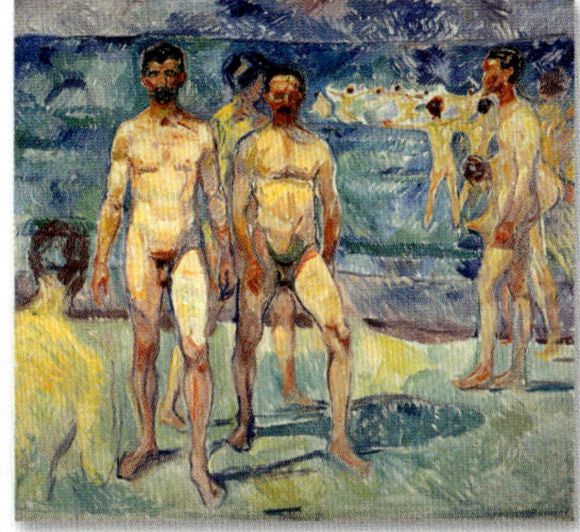

7

6

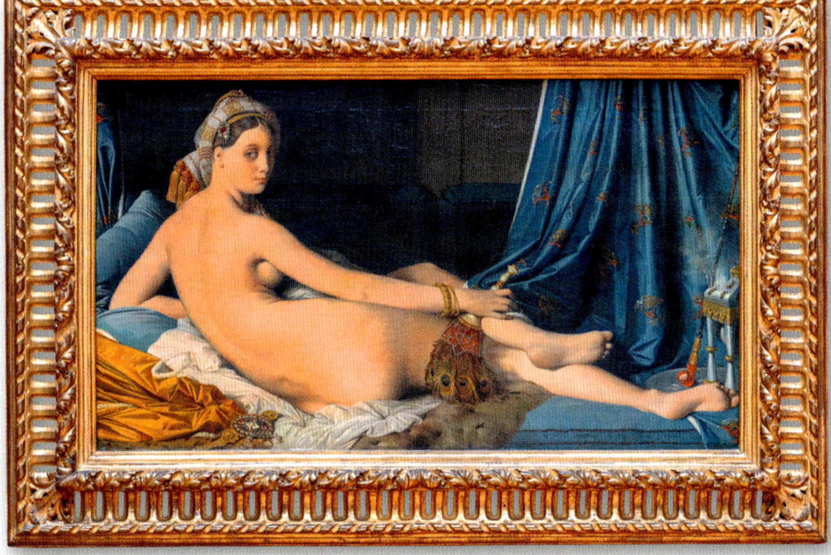

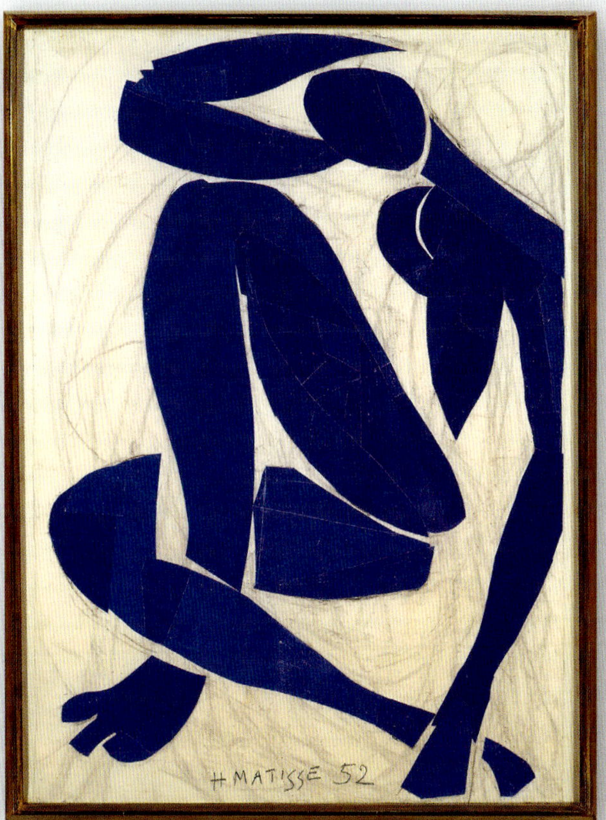

8

The fig leaf

In the 1500s, the Catholic Church issued a decree demanding that "figures shall not be painted with a beauty ... exciting lust." This launched a campaign to conceal genitals in artwork across Italy and beyond with loincloths, foliage, and fig leaves—a movement famously termed the Fig Leaf Campaign.

5. ***The Naked Maja*, Francisco Goya, 1797.** Goya created paired paintings of a clothed and nude Maja, known as "pendant" pieces. In this naked version, the Maja meets the viewer with a direct, steady gaze. Her eyes evoke empowerment and she makes no apologies for being naked.

6. ***The Grande Odalisque*, Jean-Auguste-Dominique Ingres, 1814.** Critics initially derided Ingres's harem concubine for anatomical inaccuracy. Yet her small head and elongated body are now viewed as symbolizing her sensuality, mirroring the folds of sheets and drapery.

7. ***Bathers*, Edvard Munch, 1907.** Exploring the male nude in the context of an everyday activity, Munch transforms the nude into a bold experiment in Expressionist color and form. He uses vigorous brushwork to convey a sense of vitality and masculinity.

8. ***Blue Nude IV*, Matisse, 1952.** In Matisse's striking cut-out, completed late in his career, when he could no longer paint due to ill health, the female nude is abstracted into essential lines and shapes in cobalt blue hues. The composition has a sense of playfulness and movement.

Trajan's Column (detail)

Artists unknown early 2nd century CE, marble, 1500 in (3800 cm) high (including pedestal), Fori Imperiali, Rome, Italy

This monument shows the Roman emperor Trajan's campaigns against the Dacians in present-day Romania. Its sculpted narrative spirals upward—a length of some 656 ft (200 m)—reaching its finale with the pursuit and death by suicide of Decebalus, the Dacian king. The visual composition anticipates modern cinematic techniques, such as montage, cut-aways, and multiple perspectives.

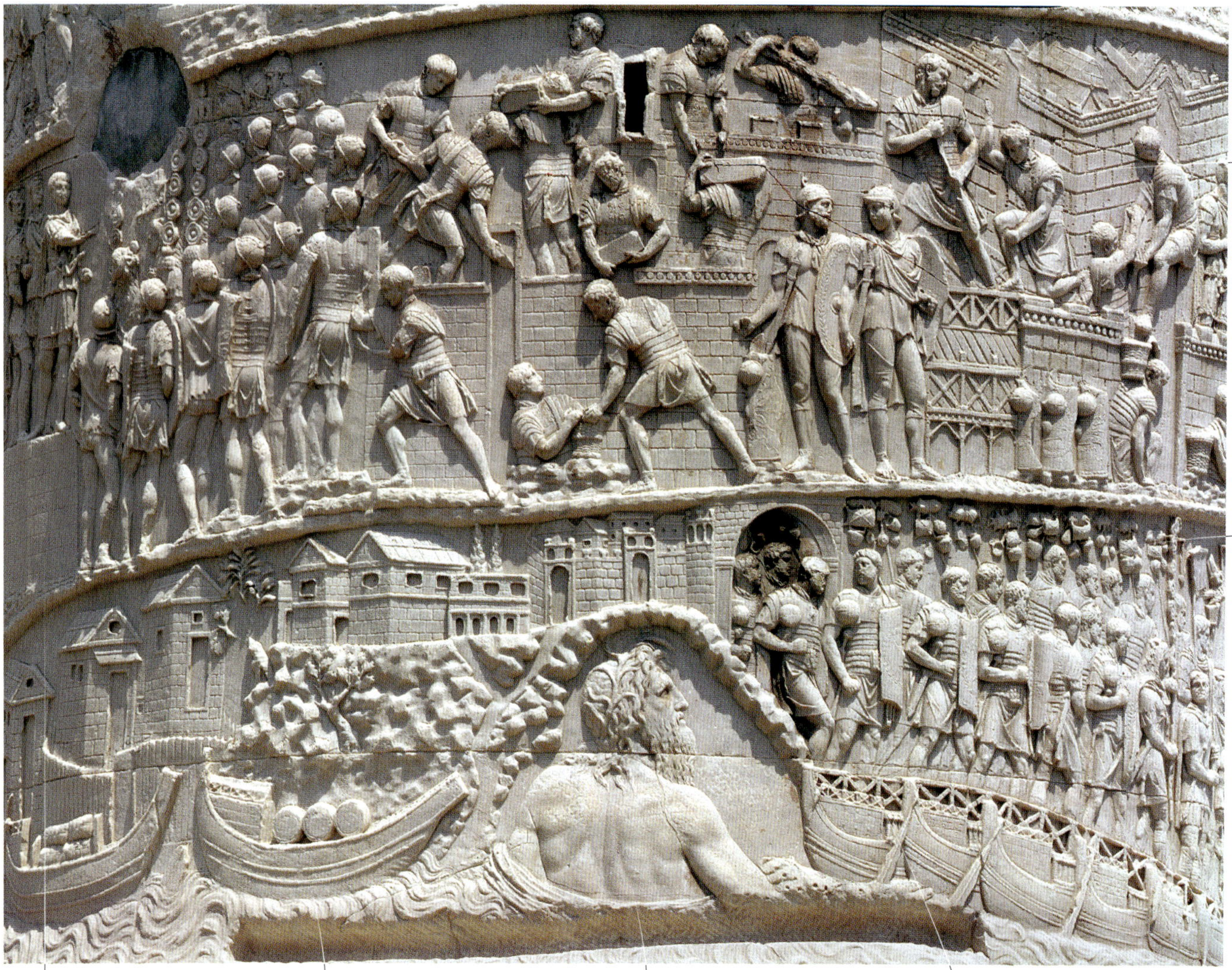

Roman soldiers prepare for military action, clearing woodland, digging trenches, and here constructing a fort.

Led by standard bearers, legionnaires carry their personal items attached to long spears. Such details may have been recorded by artists traveling with the Roman army.

Troops gather to listen to an address from Trajan, their commander (imperator), who is raised above them to signal his importance.

Roman ships are loaded with supplies; the sculptors paid careful attention to routine military logistics as well as the ceremonial aspects of Roman imperialism.

A large, bearded figure personifies the Danube River. He steadies the boats with his right hand.

Legionnaires march through an arch onto pontoon bridges. This detail, at the first level of the column, shows troops crossing the Danube.

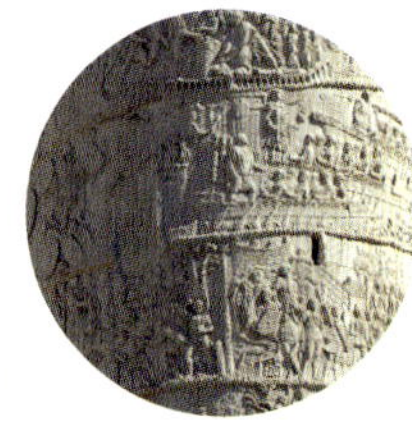

Carrara marble
To construct the column, 17 blocks of marble were brought by boat from the town of Carrara in northern Italy, renowned for the quality of its stone.

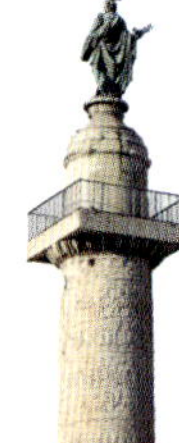

The column
Teams of sculptors worked on a scaffold to carve the marble. The relief-ribbon winds around 23 times, with no breaks, the scenes blending into one another. Trajan once stood atop the column but his statue was replaced by one of St. Peter in 1587.

> "And he set up in the Forum an enormous column, to serve at once as a monument to himself and as a memorial of his work in the Forum."
>
> Cassius Dio, 211–233 CE

Seated Buddha with Two Attendants

Artist unknown India, 131 CE, red sandstone, 37 × 34 × 6 in (93 × 85.4 × 16 cm), Kimbell Art Museum, Fort Worth, Texas, US

This sculpture is one of the earliest extant images of the Buddha in human form. (He had previously been represented by symbols such as footprints.) He is seated cross-legged on a throne, smiling and dressed in a monk's robe. Flanking the Buddha are two royal attendants, each with similarly soft smiles. They are depicted at a smaller scale to visually indicate the hierarchy.

The raised right hand represents *abhaya-mudra* (protection).

This depression once held an *ushnisha* (cranial bump). This, along with the *urna* (spiral dot) on the forehead, identifies the subject as the Buddha.

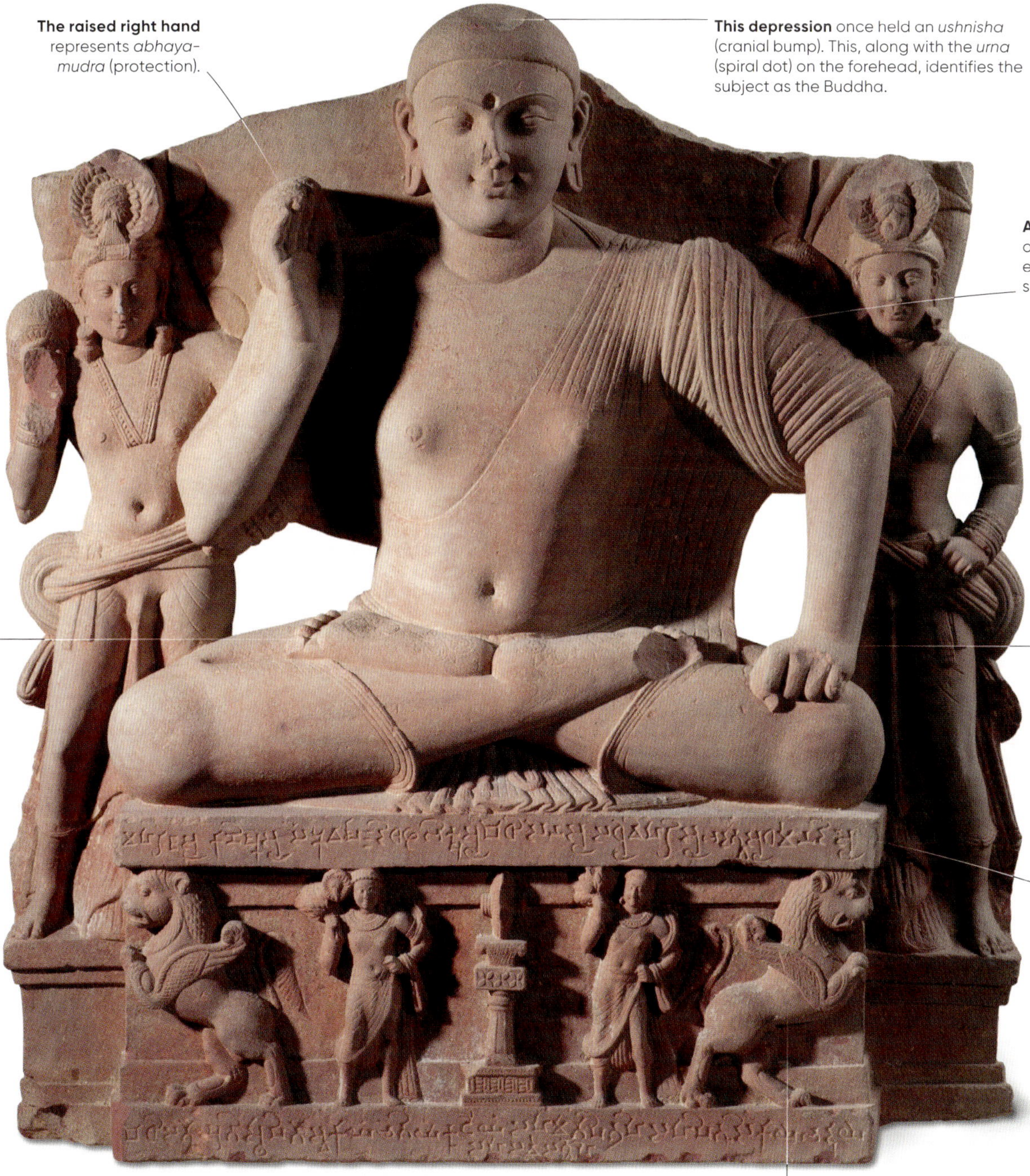

A monk's robe draped over one shoulder exposes a soft, gently sculpted body.

Symbols inscribed on the soles of the Buddha's feet and palms—the lotus and wheel—represent his divine teachings.

Forming a fist, the left hand rests on the knee, signifying the Buddha's power.

An inscription in hybrid Sanskrit records that a monk established this sculpture in the fourth year of King Kanishka's reign in the Kushan Empire.

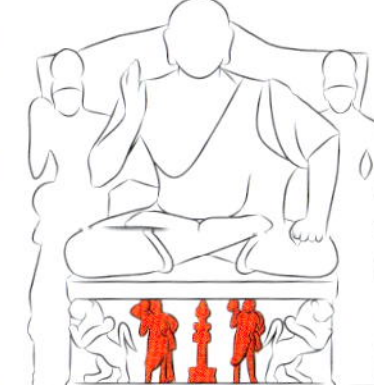

Mirror image
The relief panel on the Buddha's throne repeats the triad scene above: a pillar crowned with a wheel, symbolizing the Buddha and his sermon, is similarly flanked by the two attendants.

Traditional medium
Mathura, a city in northern India, was a significant art production hub for the Kushan Empire (c. 1st century BCE–3rd century CE). Mathura's art is built on Indigenous Indian traditions. It often used the local mottled-red sandstone.

Winged lions on the panel indicate the sharing of cultural and artistic ideas between West Asia and India during the early centuries BCE.

Vishnu Rescues Bhudevi

Artist unknown c. 400 CE, sandstone, 79 in (200 cm) high, Cave 5, Udayagiri Caves, Madhya Pradesh, India

A story in the *Bhagavata Purana*, an ancient Hindu text, tells how a demon captured Bhudevi, "the goddess who is the Earth," and confined her in the depths of a cosmic ocean. This temple relief sculpture shows the god Vishnu setting out to rescue her, thus restoring the natural order.

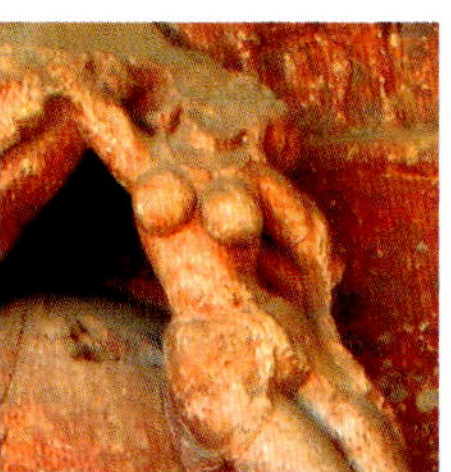

An admiring assembly of deities, spirits, and wise men (brahmins) watch the heroic rescue from a series of upper registers.

Vishnu appears as Varaha, one of his many incarnations, who has the head of a boar. The colossal scale and vigorous stance of Varaha's body signify the infinite capacity of Hindu deities.

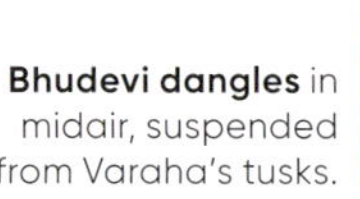

Bhudevi dangles in midair, suspended from Varaha's tusks.

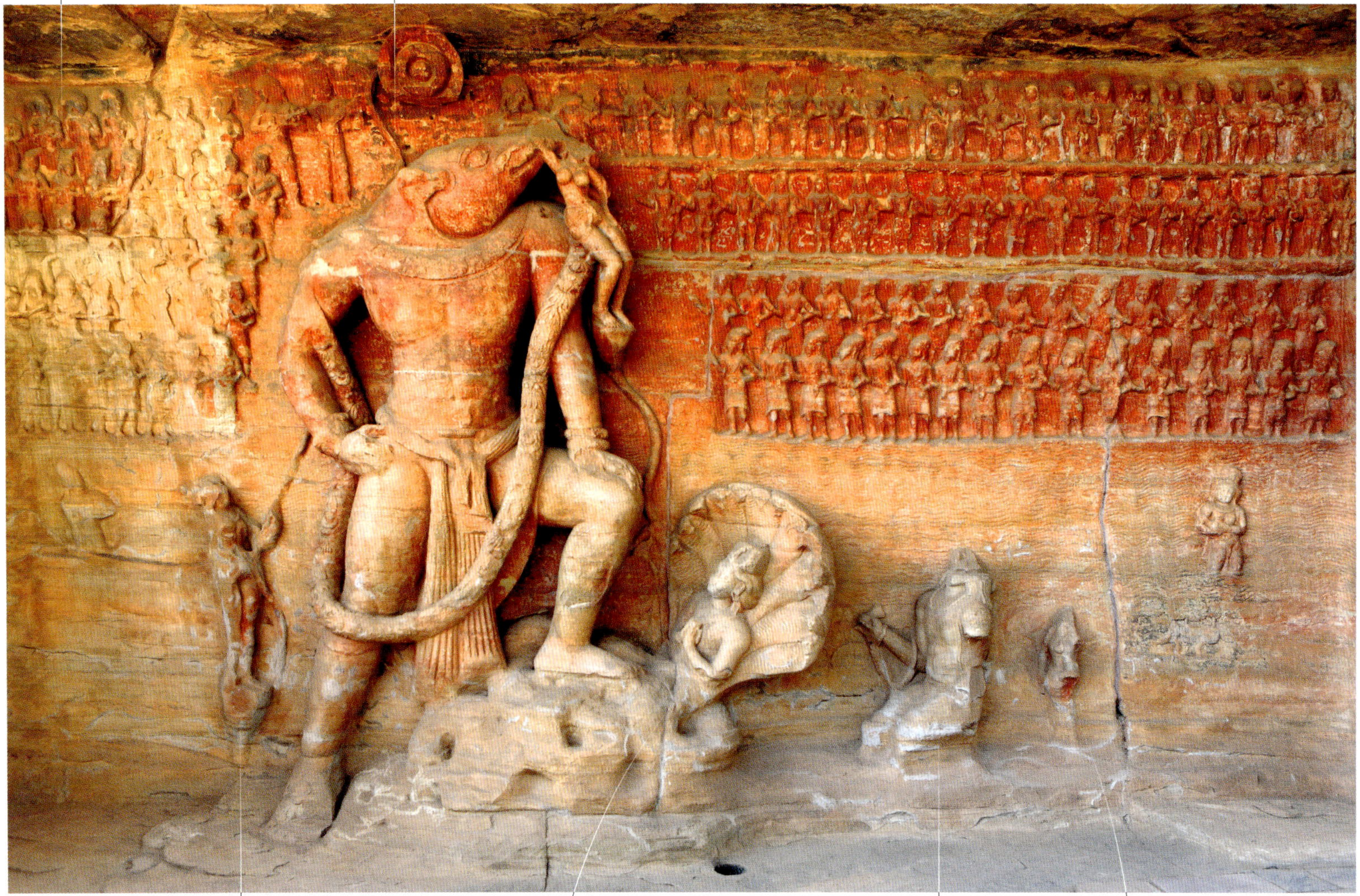

The goddess Lakshmi, attached by a cord to the god's right wrist, is Vishnu's consort.

A female Naga, a snakelike creature of the underworld with coiling body and cobra hoods, acclaims Varaha's victory.

King Chandra Gupta II, who commissioned this sculpture, is represented on a larger scale than the onlookers above, though the figure is now fractured.

The king's most important minister is shown at his side, but on a much smaller scale.

> "He [Vishnu] appeared extremely resplendent when he rose up, pulling out by his tusks the submerged Earth from the *rasātala* [Hell]."
>
> Vyasa, *Bhagavata Purana*

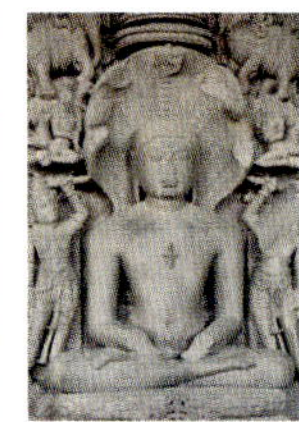

Sacred caves
The sanctuary precincts in the caves of Udayagiri (literally "Sunrise Mountain") are sacred to Buddhism, Jainism, and Hinduism. Cave 20 contains this relief sculpture of the Jain savior, Parshvanatha, sitting under a serpent hood.

A vast empire
The Gupta empire extended across a large swathe of the Indian subcontinent during the 4th to 7th centuries CE. Gupta dynasties were Hindu, but their patronage was also generous to the art and literature of other faiths.

Nose Ornament with Decapitator

Artist unknown 200–900 CE, gilded copper, silver, green stone and brown stone inlays, 3 × 4 in (7 × 10 cm), Metropolitan Museum of Art, New York, US

In the Moche culture, ritual specialists conducted ceremonies, including human sacrifice, atop large adobe pyramids. Metallic nose ornaments, glinting in the desert sun, were worn by these elite men and women. The Moche culture, located on the north coast of what is now Peru, flourished from 200 to 900 CE.

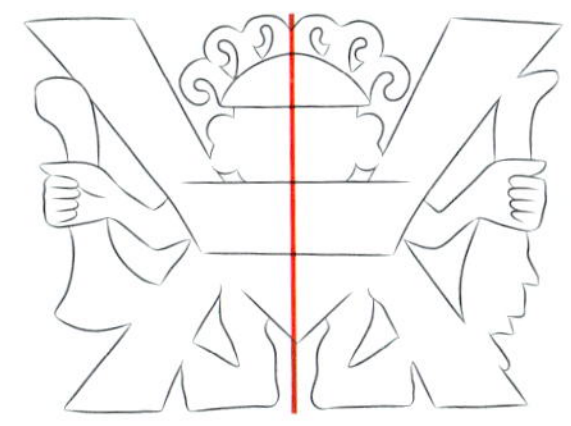

Symmetrical composition The nose ornament uses low relief hammered metal to depict a male figure in a frontal position with diagonal lines radiating out from the center.

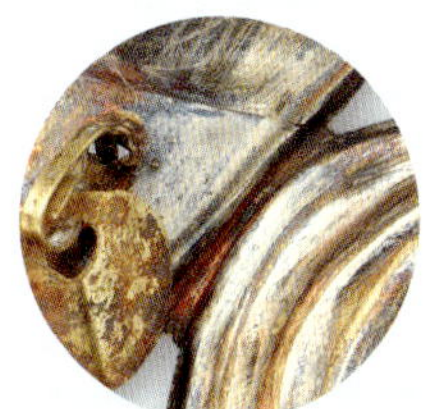

Depletion gilding The Northern Moche used a process called depletion gilding. Silver and copper were dissolved from the surface of a gold alloy by placing it in a salt bath and heating it. A thin layer of gold was then left behind.

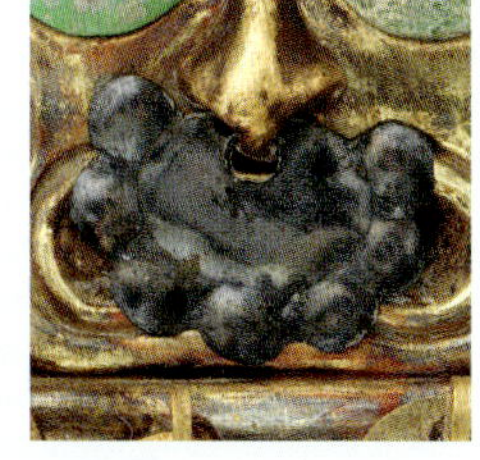

The nose ornament on the decapitator figure shows how the piece would have been worn.

The metal *tumi* knife has a semicircular blade and long handle with a rope attached at the top.

Ear flares were an indicator of elite status.

Fronds on the headdress either refer to an octopus or to the waves of the Pacific Ocean.

Gold attachments create movement and sound; they tinkled and glinted as the wearer moved.

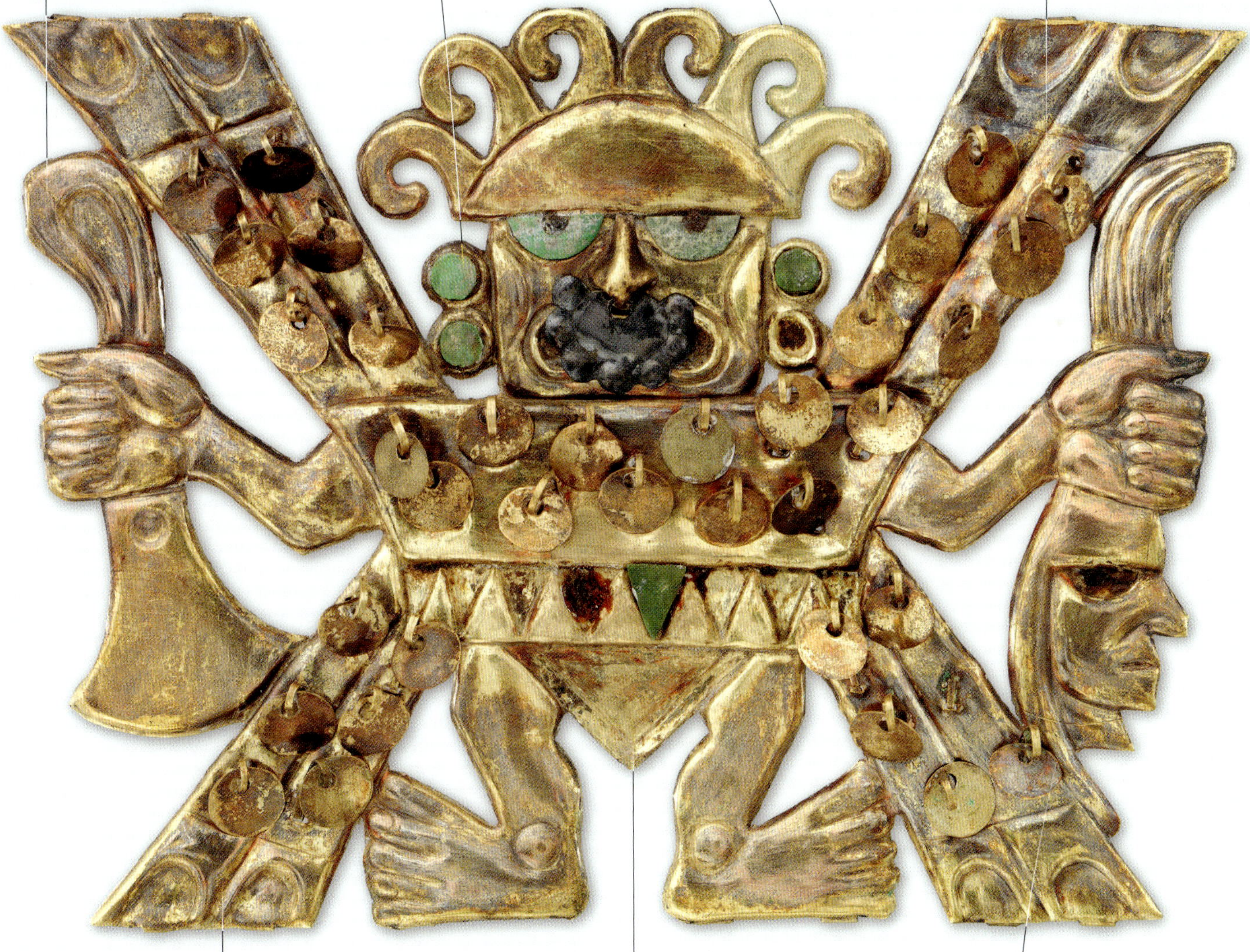

Four pairs of appendages refer to the eight legs of a spider, which is often associated with the decapitator.

The tunic and loincloth were both common men's attire among the Moche.

The decapitator holds a human head, which he presumably removed using the *tumi* knife.

Hunting Scene

Anonymous 400–450 CE, ink, pigments, and lime plaster on stone walls, north wall of the main chamber, Muyongchong Tomb, Ji'an City, China

The artist captured the dynamic motion of a chase in this scene of men on horses pursuing a tiger and two deer. Painted on a tomb wall, probably for a noble family, it illustrates an aspect of life in the great Koguryo kingdom of ancient Korea (now northeast China and North Korea).

The cloud motif is an auspicious symbol in East Asian culture. It represents notions of good fortune and longevity.

The archer twists around to shoot the deer behind him in a display of athleticism.

A white preparation layer was applied to the wet plaster to enhance the brilliance of the pigments.

Vivid oranges and red contrast with the deep black and brown hues, adding vibrancy to the mural.

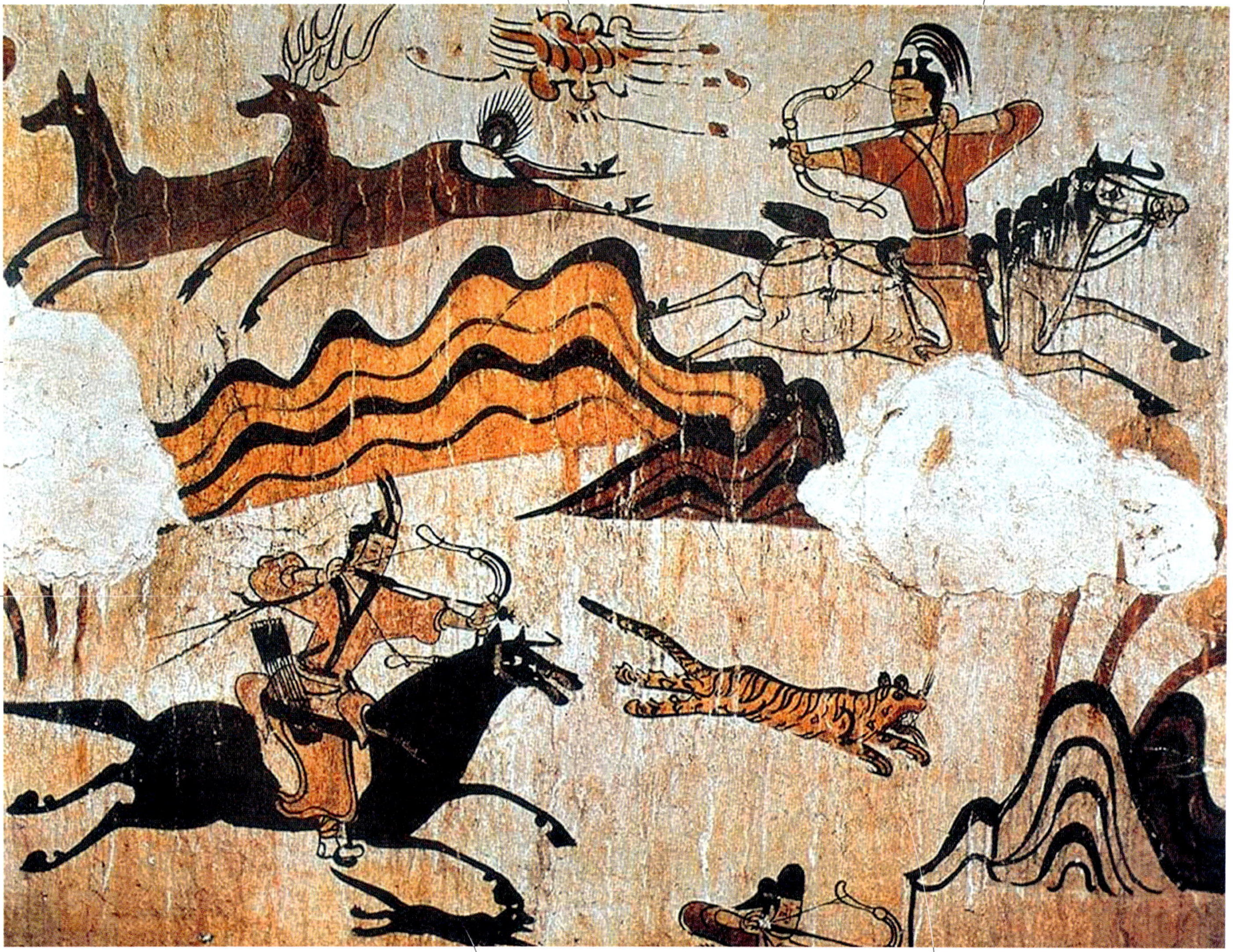

Korean Jindo dogs were renowned for their hunting skills.

The fleeing tiger is appropriately tinted orange with thin, black lines of patterning.

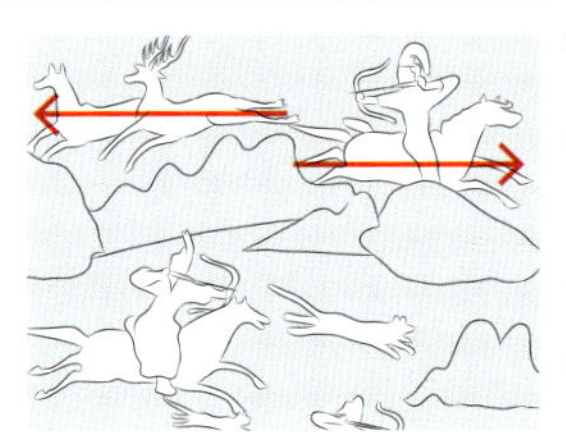

Tension and pace
Drawn bows, the twisting archer, galloping horses, and racing prey portray the thrill and speed of the hunt and also its confusion, as the horsemen ride in one direction and the deer flee in the other.

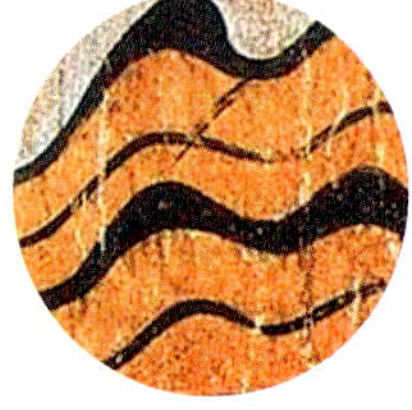

Stylized mountains
Scale creates a sense of depth. The mountains are represented by undulating lines of varying thickness in bright earth colors that recede into the background, suggesting rather than depicting the setting for the hunt.

Vyala with Rider

Artist unknown, 5th century CE, sandstone, 35 × 23 in (90 × 58 cm), Archaeology Museum, Sarnath, northeast India

Two armed nature spirits (*yakshas*) attack a lionlike beast (*vyala*) in this sandstone relief, one of a pair. *Vyalas*, composite animal figures, are depicted in many South Asian temples and on the thrones of seated Buddha figures carved at Sarnath, site of the Buddha's first sermon and an important pilgrimage destination.

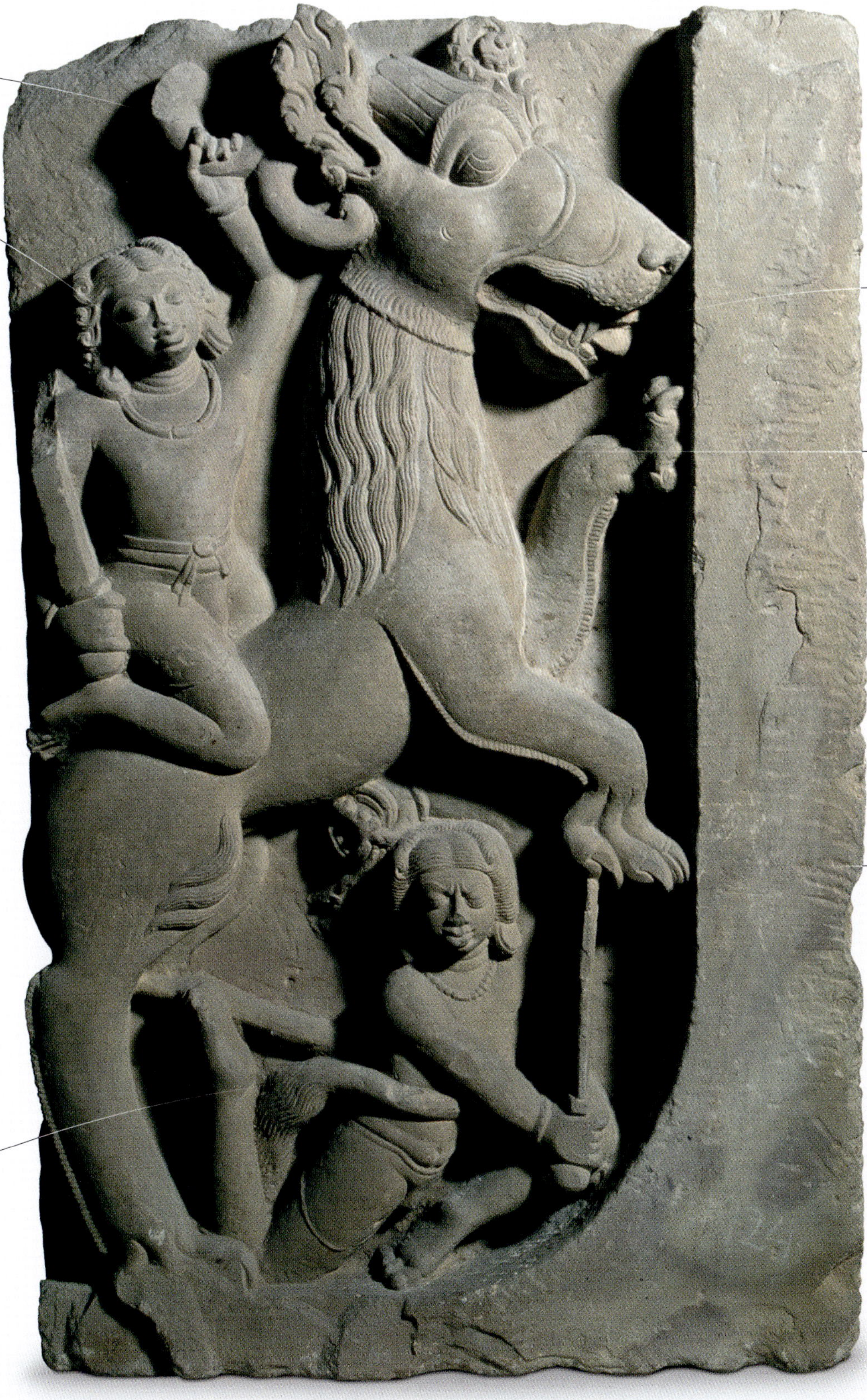

The rider grabs the *vyala*'s horn while smiling nonchalantly.

The figure wears ornaments including necklaces, belts, and two types of earring—one plug disk and one ring.

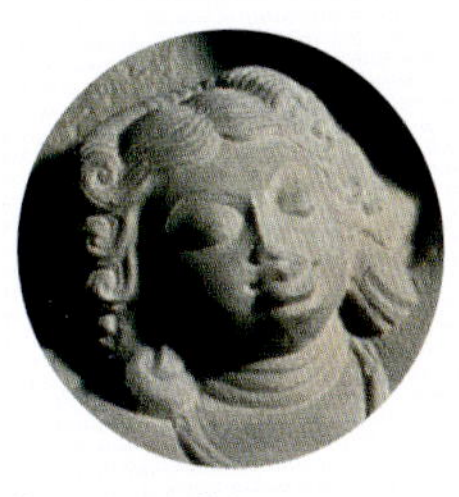

Iconography
Bulging eyes, arched brows, and plump lips suggest the rider is a *yaksha*—a nature spirit who could be benign or malevolent.

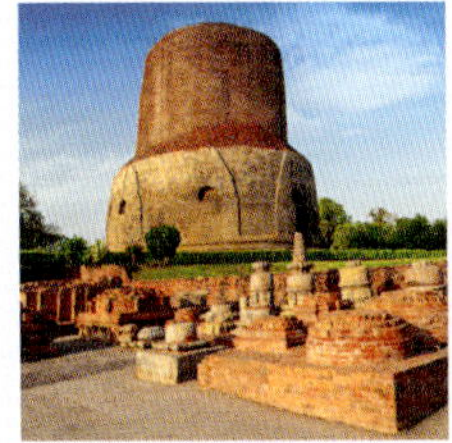

Setting the style
Artists across the Buddhist world were inspired by the artistic style developed at Sarnath monastery during the Gupta Empire (c. 320–550 CE).

The *vyala's* tail loops around the second *yaksha*, whose bent legs suggest that he is leaping through the air to prick the beast's foot with his sword.

Protruding between its teeth, the *vyala*'s extended tongue indicates that the beast is agitated and angry.

The thick locks of the *vyala*'s lionlike mane stream down its neck.

The sculpture's friable edges reveal the layered structure of its sandstone composition.

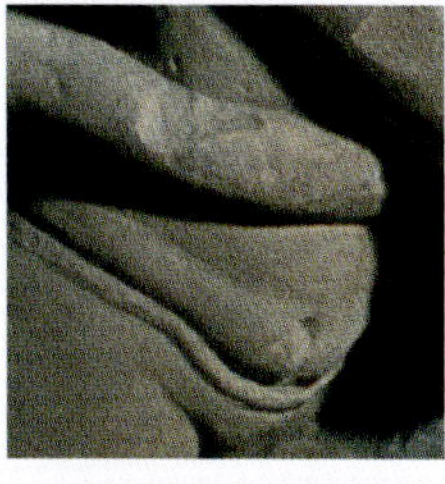

A subtle fold of belly flesh is a hallmark of Gupta-period style.

A man draws back the curtain, as though leading the procession into the church.

The chalice is decorated with precious stones and presents the empress as a generous patron.

Architectural motifs such as columns, arches, and doorways reinforce the connection between the mosaic and the architectural setting.

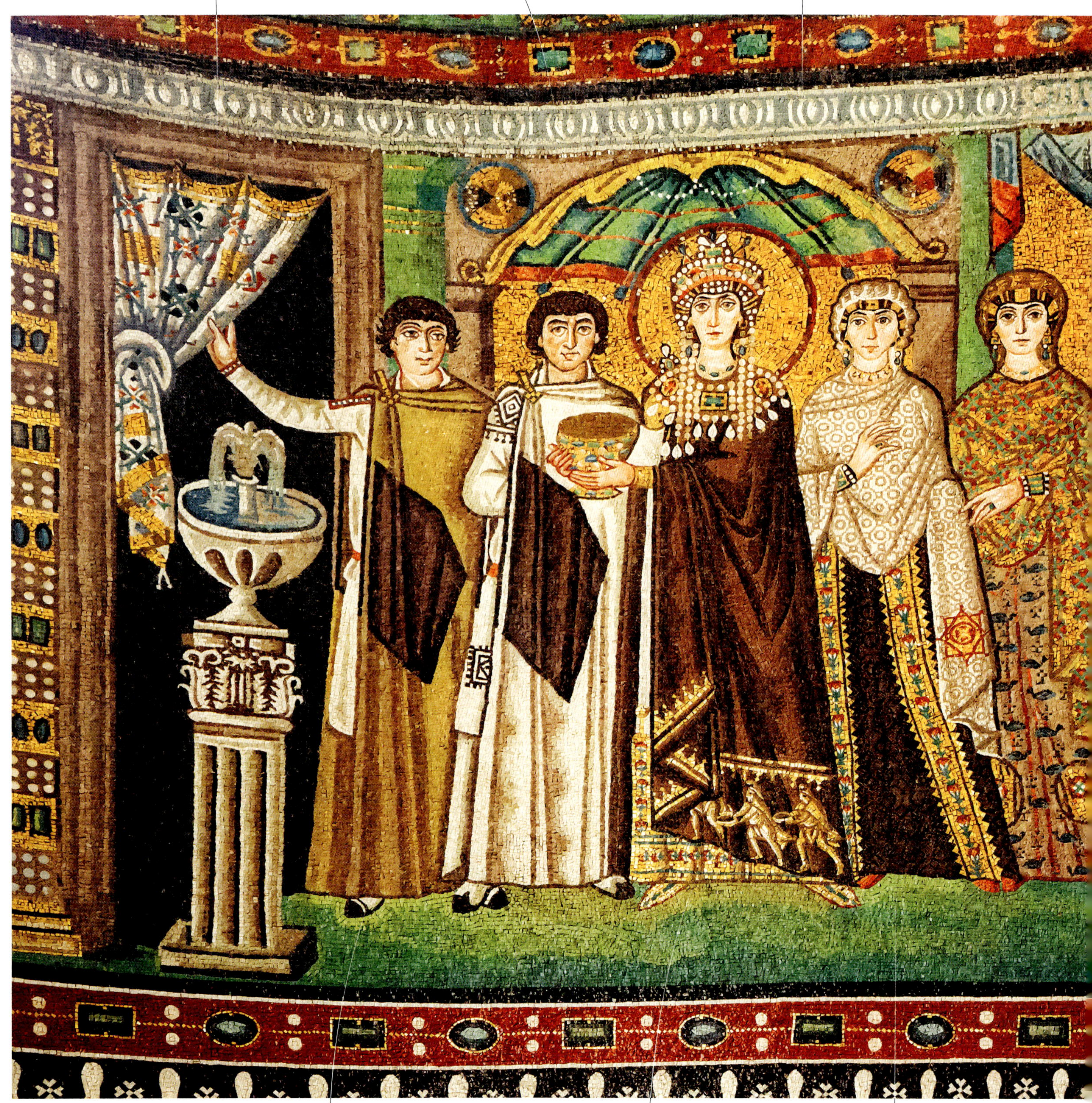

Two clergymen lead the procession toward the church.

The brocade at the bottom of Theodora's robe depicts the three Magi offering gifts.

Antonina, wife of Belisarius, who led the Byzantine reconquest of Italy, is one of Theodora's attendants.

Theodora's Procession

Artists unknown c. 547 CE, mosaic, Basilica of San Vitale, Ravenna, Italy

This mosaic from a church in Ravenna depicts the powerful and influential Byzantine Empress Theodora participating in a religious ceremony. It faces a similar mosaic of her husband, Emperor Justinian I, flanked by soldiers and priests. Built during the reign of Justinian and Theodora after Ravenna became the capital of Byzantine Italy, the basilica was an expression of religious and imperial power. The mosaics, including this one, reflect the merging of Roman and Byzantine iconography, as well as local Italian artistic influences. Dressed in fine clothes and jewels, the empress is shown bearing the chalice for the Eucharist as she prepares to enter the church.

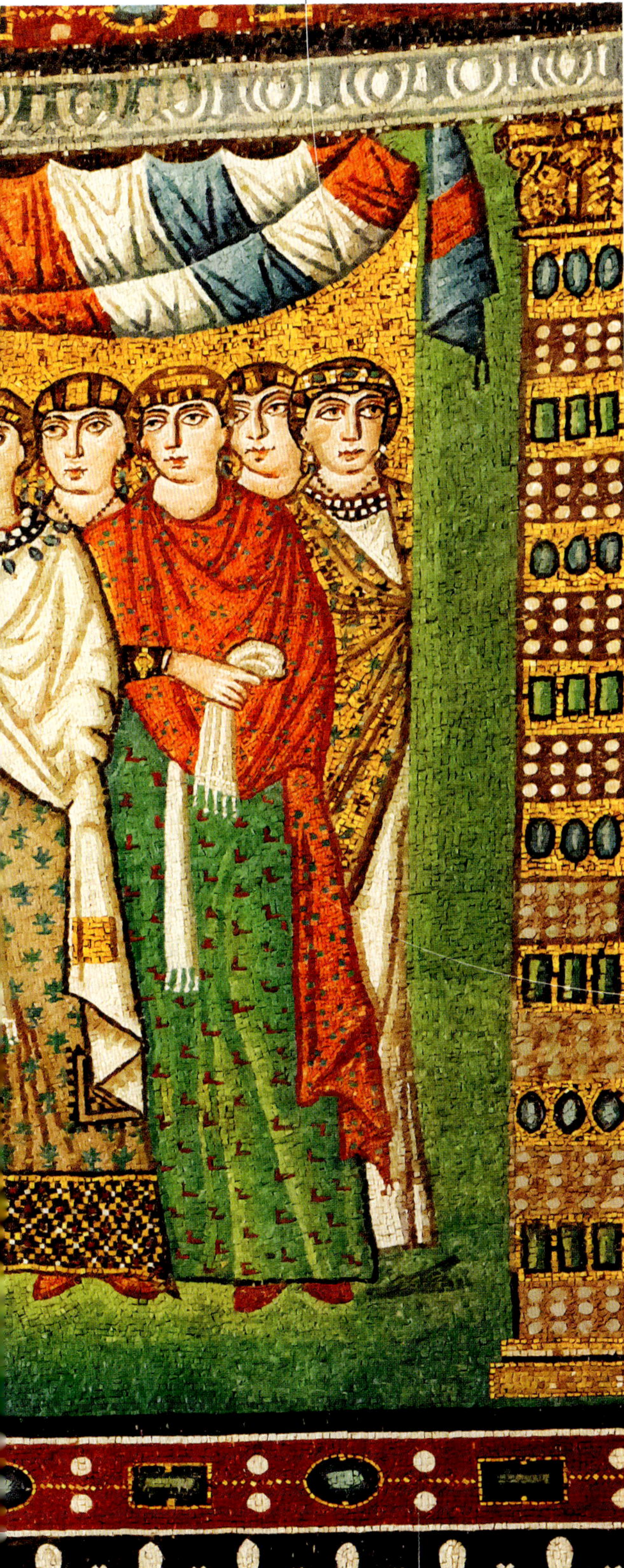

Gold represents the divine light of God and gives the mosaic a celestial quality.

Theodora's female attendants follow the empress in descending order of importance. Their status is indicated by their clothing and their size.

Decorative borders feature a row of medallions and leaves and a second row of pearls and blue and green gems.

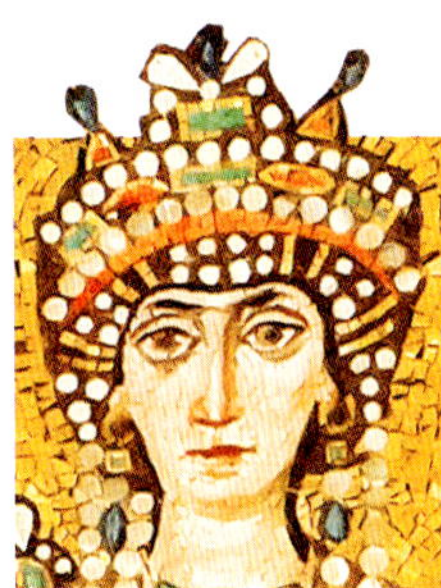

Empress Theodora wears a purple robe and a crown with a halo, signifying her political and religious status.

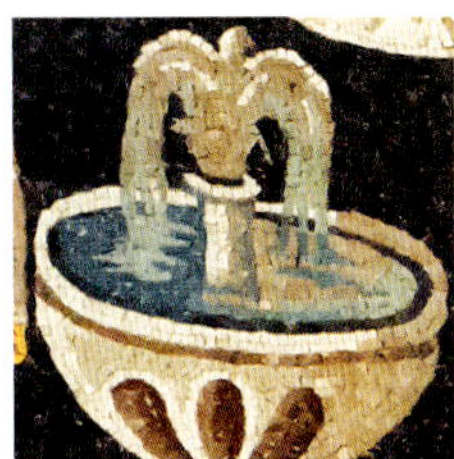

Holy water for cleansing the body is depicted just in front of the curtain.

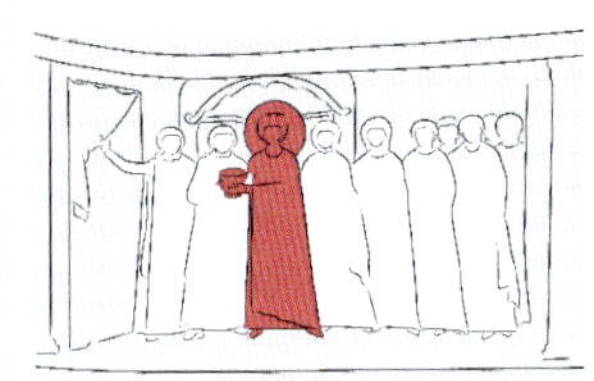

Center stage
The hierarchical arrangement places the empress at the center under an arch. She is shown as slightly taller than her attendants.

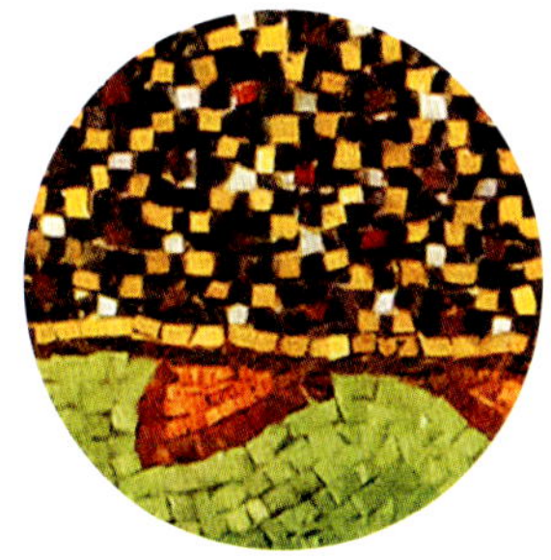

Tesserae
Mosaics were constructed using tesserae—small blocks of stone, tile, glass, or other material. They were often used in Byzantine art because they could incorporate intricate details and vibrant colors to create a sense of opulence.

> "Grand figures in gleaming mosaics stalking in solemn progression along the walls, or looking down from domes & apses—perfect as if executed yesterday."
>
> Lady Eastlake, 1860

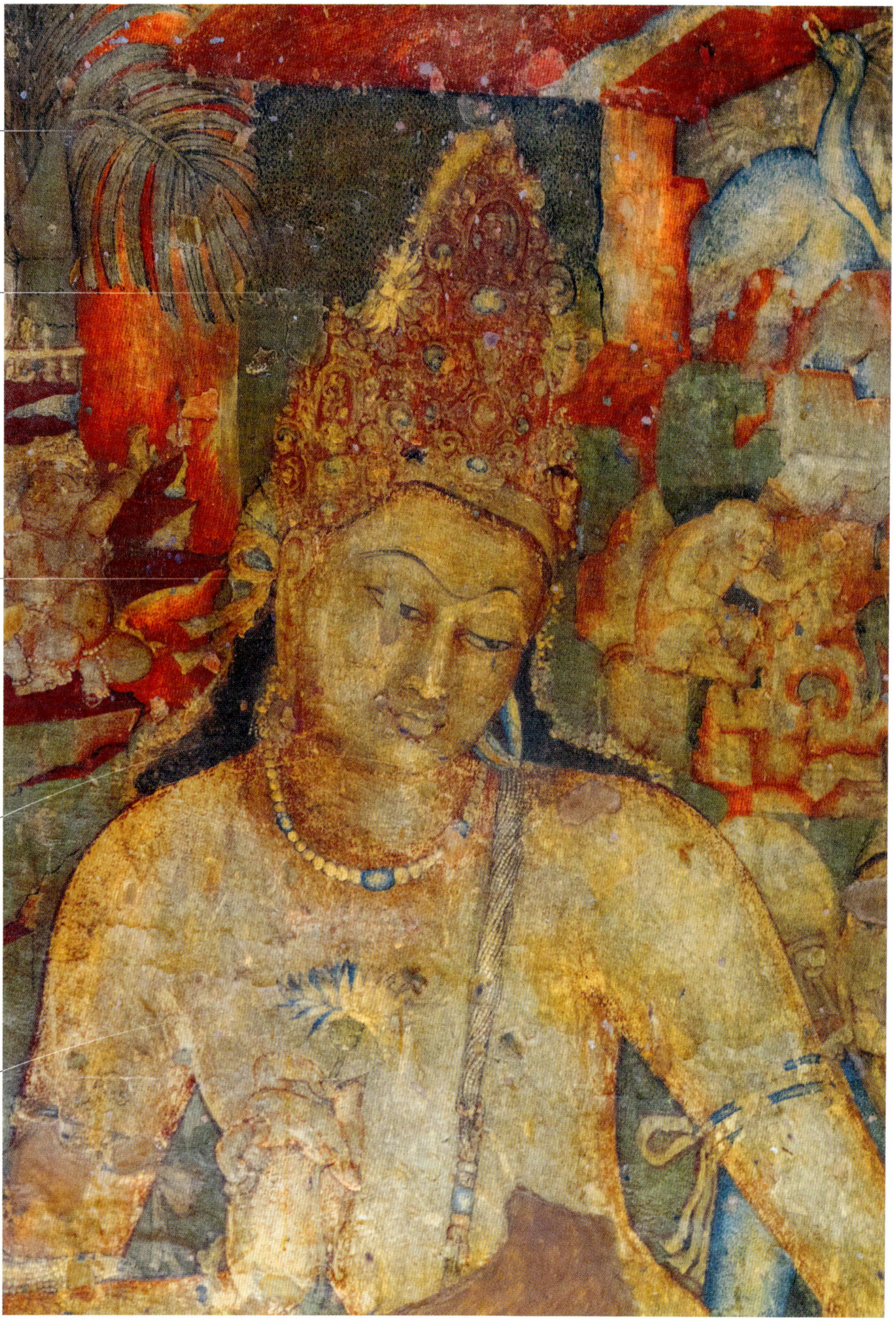

The leaves of the areca palm are remarkably realistic.

A magnificent crown, exquisite jewelery, and twisted strings of pearls emphasize high worldly and divine status.

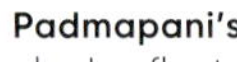

Padmapani's look reflects unlimited compassion and the burden of remaining in *samsara* (cyclic existence) for the benefit of all sentient beings.

Mismatched earrings may indicate how they were worn by Indian kings of the past.

The lotus flower is a symbol of purity and an attribute of the *bodhisattva* of compassion.

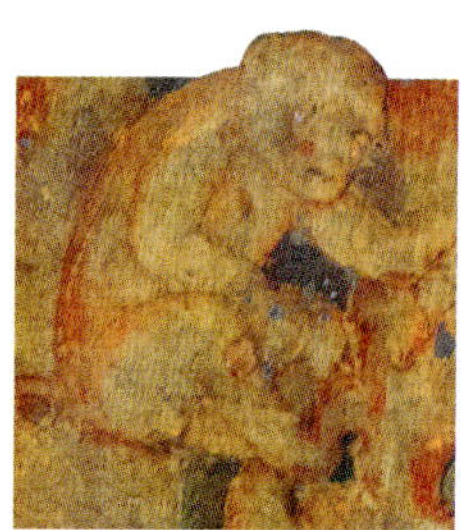

The monkey, a metaphor for the restless and distracted mind, contrasts with the peaceful inner state of the *bodhisattva*.

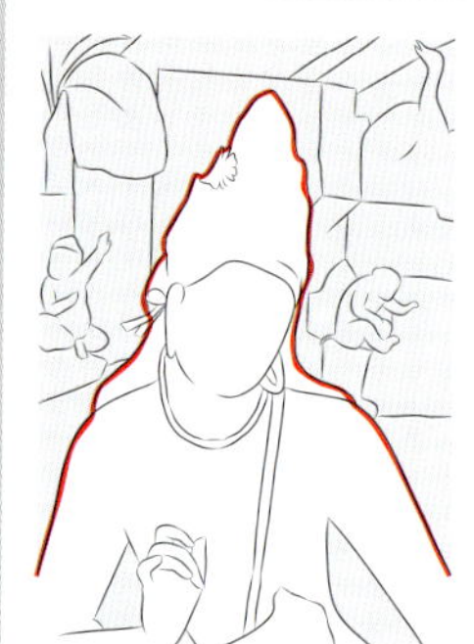

Two worlds
The deep inner world of the main figure contrasts with the lively outer world: vibrant trees, a peacock, a monkey playing, and a cheerful dwarf. The whole mural has many more figures including devoted attendants and loving couples.

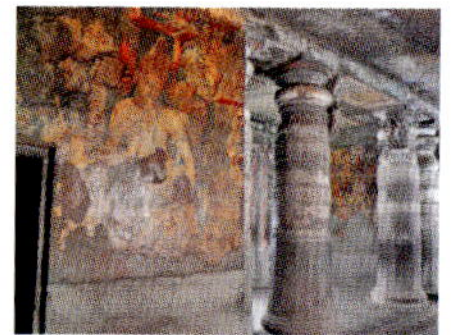

Context
The *Bodhisattva Padmapani* adorns the wall of this pillared hall in the Buddhist monastic complex at Ajanta, which consists of 30 rock-cut caves. Cave 1 was created under the lavish patronage of the Vakataka emperor Harishena who ruled from about 460 to 477 CE.

Bodhisattva Padmapani

Artist unknown late 5th century CE, mural, tempera on wall, 70 × 30 in (177 × 75 cm), Ajanta Caves, Aurangabad, India

In this mural, a *bodhisattva* (one seeking awakening to liberate all beings) named Padmapani (Lotus Bearer), along with a companion painting of Vajrapani (Thunderbolt Bearer), flank a statue of the Buddha at the entrance to Cave 1. Noble and compassionate, he stands in contemplation amid a world teeming with life. Padmapani and Vajrapani are not yet Buddhas (enlightened ones) but are his close attendants.

Buddha

Artist unknown c. 550 CE, agalmatolite, 5 in (13.5 cm) high, National Museum of Korea, Seoul, Korea

This small Buddha figure, which is shown here slightly larger than actual size, sits in a state of tranquil meditation. Created during the Baekje Kingdom, which ruled the southwestern part of the Korean peninsula from 18 BCE to 660 CE, it was unearthed from a temple site, Gunsu-ri, in the capital, Sabi (now known as Buyeo) in 1936.

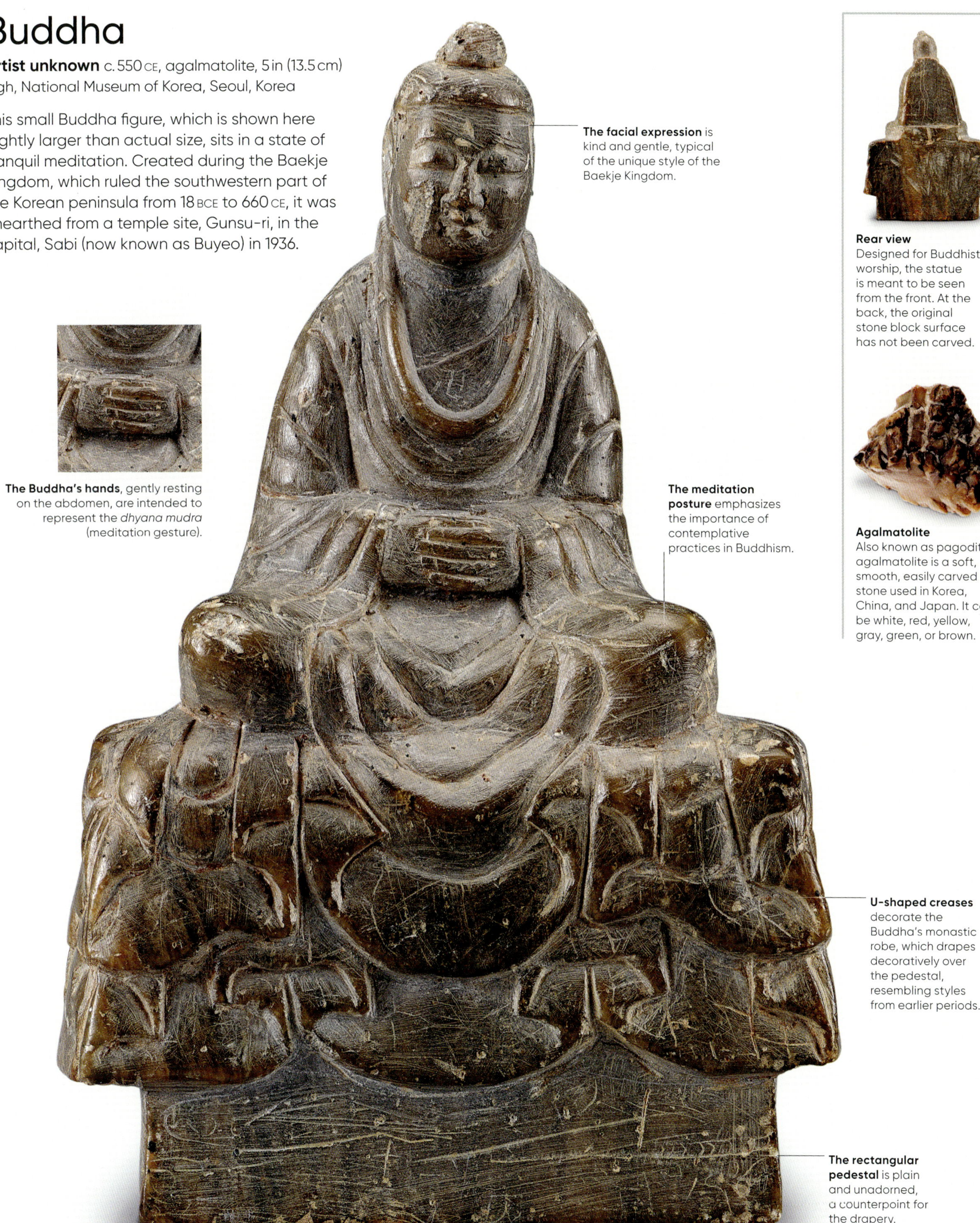

The facial expression is kind and gentle, typical of the unique style of the Baekje Kingdom.

Rear view
Designed for Buddhist worship, the statue is meant to be seen from the front. At the back, the original stone block surface has not been carved.

The Buddha's hands, gently resting on the abdomen, are intended to represent the *dhyana mudra* (meditation gesture).

The meditation posture emphasizes the importance of contemplative practices in Buddhism.

Agalmatolite
Also known as pagodite, agalmatolite is a soft, smooth, easily carved stone used in Korea, China, and Japan. It can be white, red, yellow, gray, green, or brown.

U-shaped creases decorate the Buddha's monastic robe, which drapes decoratively over the pedestal, resembling styles from earlier periods.

The rectangular pedestal is plain and unadorned, a counterpoint for the drapery.

Emperor Wu

Attributed to Yan Liben late 7th century, ink and color on silk, 20 × 209 in (51.3 × 531 cm), Museum of Fine Arts, Boston, US

Emperor Wu Di (r. 560–578) of the Northern Zhou was famous for uniting northern China in 577 and for banning Buddhism and Daoism from 574. In this detail from a hand scroll celebrating 13 emperors from five dynasties, Emperor Wu appears larger than the others. His stature and solid presence emphasize his righteous authority.

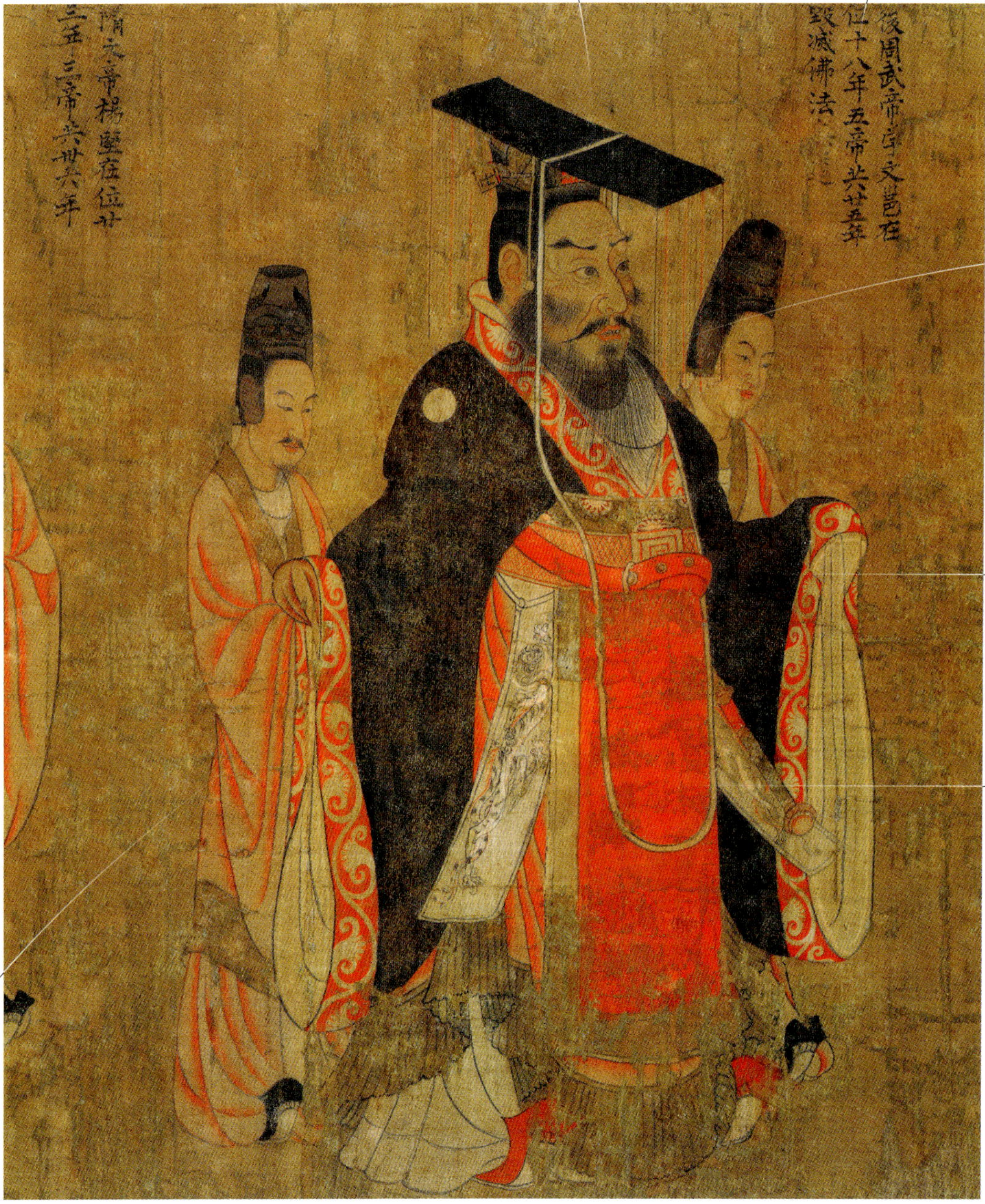

A flat-topped headpiece sits above the emperor's head, with 12 beaded strings hanging from both the front and back.

Inscriptions identify the emperors. This one notes that Wu Di "occupied the throne for 18 years ... and destroyed the Buddha's Law."

Wu Di appears as a mature ruler. He was celebrated for his full facial hair.

Like seven of the 13 emperors in the scroll, Wu Di wears a black robe and red skirt decorated with auspicious emblems, such as a tiger and dragon.

Although the scroll depicts emperors from multiple dynasties (from 171 BCE to 617 CE), they are all shown in Tang-period imperial dress.

The attendants are disproportionately smaller than the emperor, indicating their inferior status.

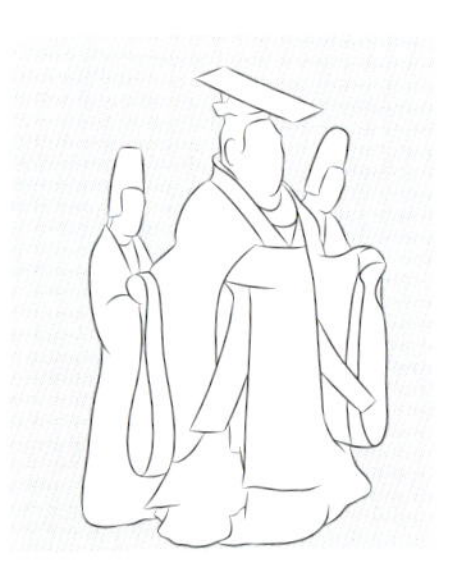

Imperial portrait
The Emperor's power is projected through his solid bearing, upright stance, and regalia decorated with symbols reserved only for the Son of Heaven.

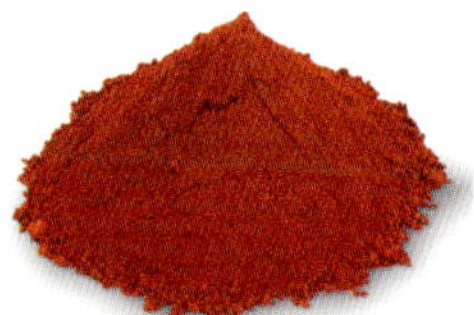

Pigments
Colors were made from plants or minerals, such as malachite for green, cinnabar for red, and calcite for white, mixed with animal glue and water. They were applied to paper or silk with a brush.

> "To 'read' a Chinese painting is to enter into a dialogue with the past ... An intimate experience ... shared and repeated over the centuries."
>
> Maxwell K. Hearn, 2008

Funerary Mask of K'inich Janaab' Pakal

Artist unknown c. 683, jade with obsidian inlay, 10 in (25.6 cm) high, National Museum of Anthropology, Mexico City, Mexico

This jade death mask was made for the great king K'inich Janaab' Pakal, who ruled over the Maya city of Palenque for 68 years after ascending the throne at the age of just 12. Jade was valued by the ancient Maya for its blue-green color, symbolizing water and newly grown corn—key to survival in the jungles of Mesoamerica. Wearing the stone ensured that after his death, Pakal would move through a cycle of rebirth.

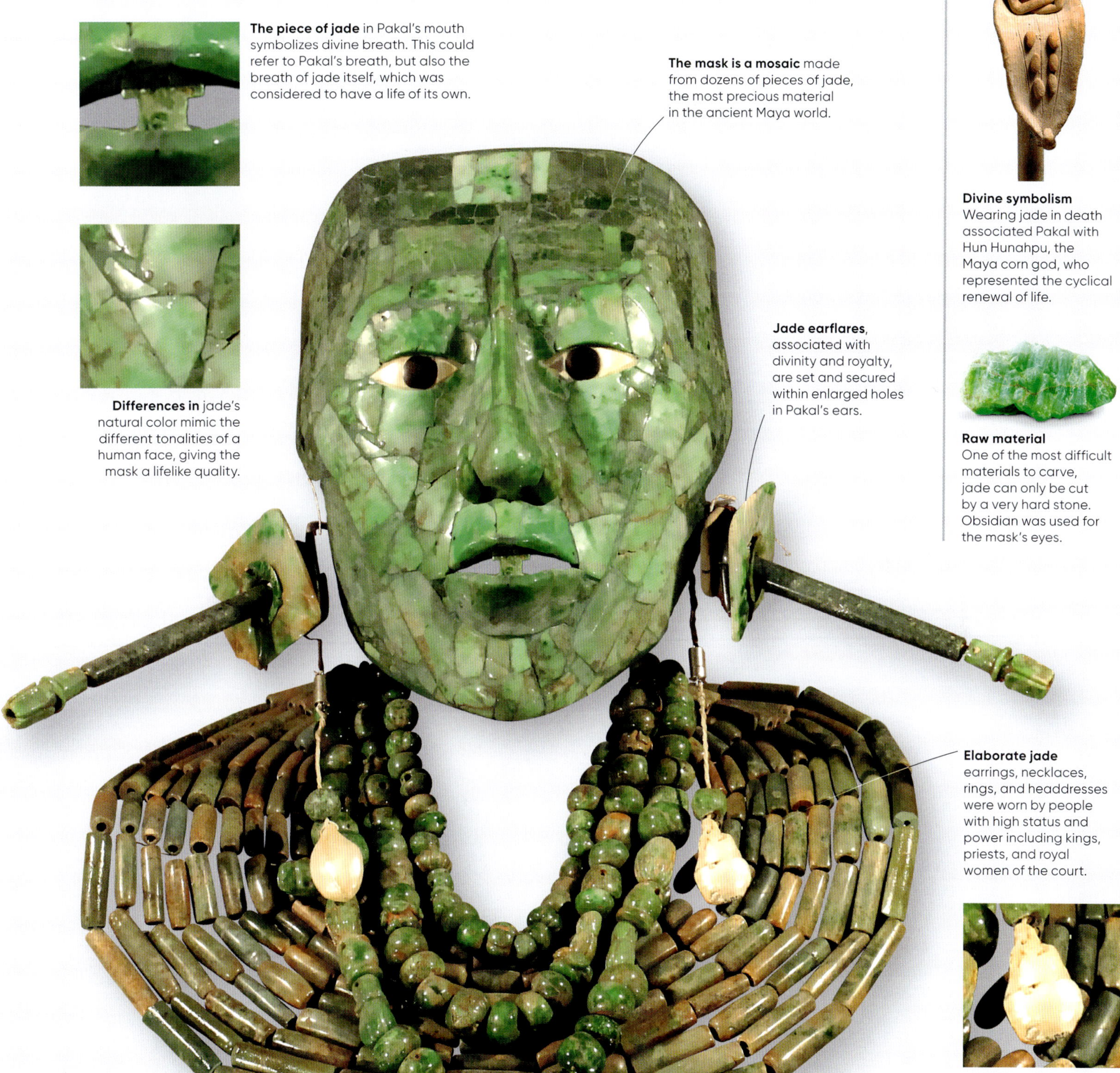

The piece of jade in Pakal's mouth symbolizes divine breath. This could refer to Pakal's breath, but also the breath of jade itself, which was considered to have a life of its own.

Differences in jade's natural color mimic the different tonalities of a human face, giving the mask a lifelike quality.

The mask is a mosaic made from dozens of pieces of jade, the most precious material in the ancient Maya world.

Jade earflares, associated with divinity and royalty, are set and secured within enlarged holes in Pakal's ears.

Divine symbolism
Wearing jade in death associated Pakal with Hun Hunahpu, the Maya corn god, who represented the cyclical renewal of life.

Raw material
One of the most difficult materials to carve, jade can only be cut by a very hard stone. Obsidian was used for the mask's eyes.

Elaborate jade earrings, necklaces, rings, and headdresses were worn by people with high status and power including kings, priests, and royal women of the court.

Pearl and shell are incorporated in the mask's ornamentation, matching the jewelery that Pakal would have worn in life.

Lindisfarne Gospels, St. Matthew the Evangelist

Eadfrith c. 700 CE, folio 25v, 11 × 9 in (28.2 × 22.8 cm), British Library, London, UK

St. Matthew sits, hard at work, illuminating the book this folio is part of—the Lindisfarne Gospels—the ultimate endorsement of its value. The monk who produced this sacred script on the island of Lindisfarne, off Northumberland in northeast Britain, must have felt a sense of kinship with the apostle.

The script above the winged figure, St. Matthew's emblem, says *Imago hominis* (the image of a man).

Golden halos—stylized representations of a blaze of light—indicate that these are saintly, sacred figures.

Greek and Latin, the two languages of medieval scripture, both feature: *Hagios* means "saint" in Greek, *Mattheus* "Matthew" in Latin.

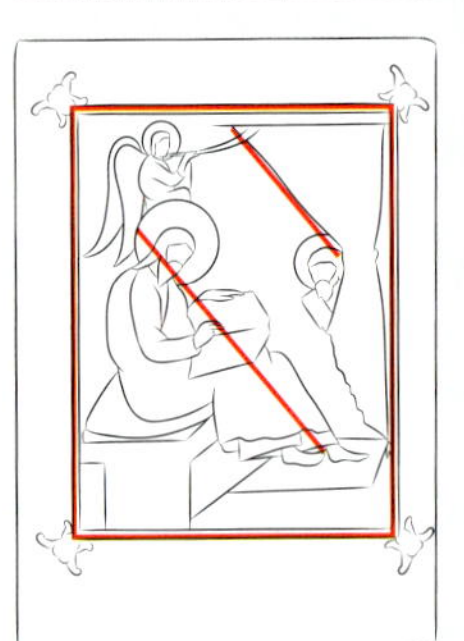

Composition
The simple scene is beautifully balanced, with the line of the curtain mirroring the figure of St. Matthew and Matthew's cell serving as an ornate frame. A series of squares convey the mystic associations of the number four, such as the four Gospels, seasons, and corners of the Earth.

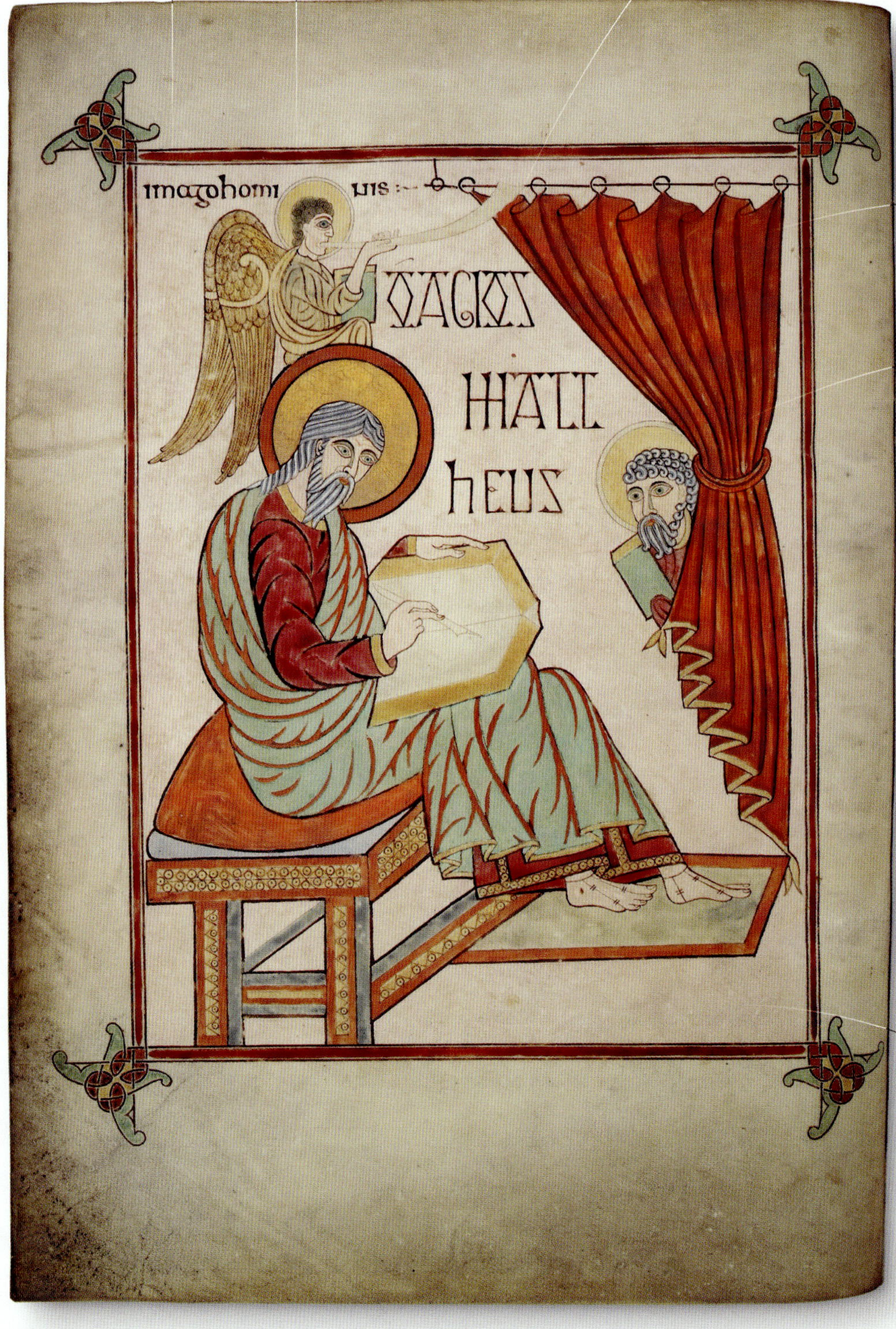

The curtain may represent the everyday reality that scripture pulls aside to reveal the divine truth within.

The man behind the curtain may be St. Luke, whose Gospel was influenced by Matthew's.

> "It is one of the world's masterpieces of book painting."
> Bishop of Durham, 1998

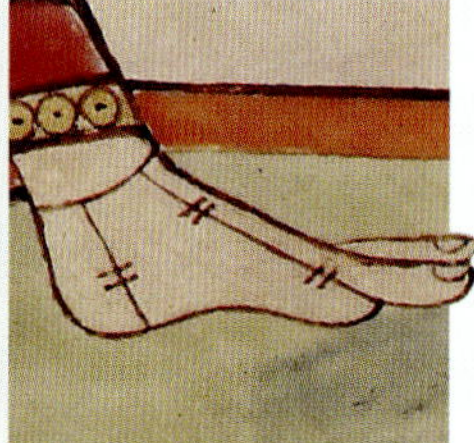

Matthew's feet are bare, a reference to the humility of the former tax collector.

The empty room suggests the purity of Matthew's inspiration: he simply recorded what he had seen as one of Christ's apostles.

Court Officials and Emissaries

Artist unknown 706–711, mineral pigments on white-painted wall, 79 × 118 in (200 × 300 cm), tomb of Li Xian, Prince Zhanghuai, Qianling Mausoleum, Xi'an, China

This scene from the tomb of Tang-dynasty crown prince Zhanghuai depicts imperial court officials receiving emissaries from distant lands, as far apart as modern Uzbekistan, South Korea, and the Russian Far East. The artist uses body language, gaze, gesture, and facial expressions to convey dramatic tension between the foreigners who have come to petition the court and the prince's staff.

The court officials face inward, reinforcing the sense of a closed group as they consult among themselves.

This man's deep-set eyes and large nose reflect Tang stereotypes about Iranian peoples. His partially shaven head is a Central Asian nomadic style.

The second emissary's small cap and full-sleeved white garments indicate a Korean origin, probably from the state of Silla.

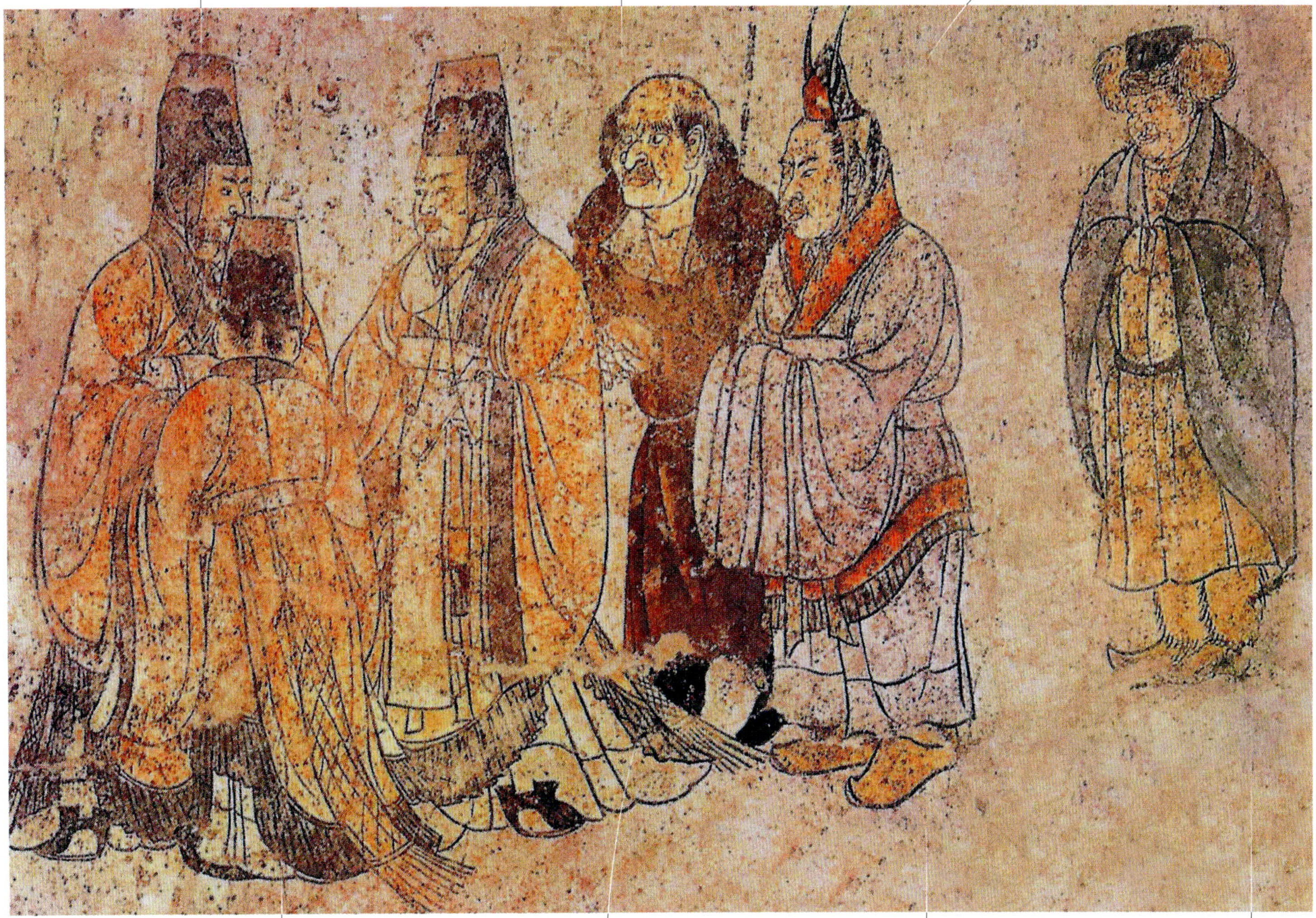

The Tang officials wear official court attire, including distinctive tall caps.

This emissary wears a Central Asian tunic over trousers and boots, a style also adopted by many men of Tang.

All three emissaries look on apprehensively as the officials confer. One wrings his hands while he awaits a decision.

The third emissary wears a fur cap and trousers, probably indicating an Eastern Siberian people from the Yalu River region.

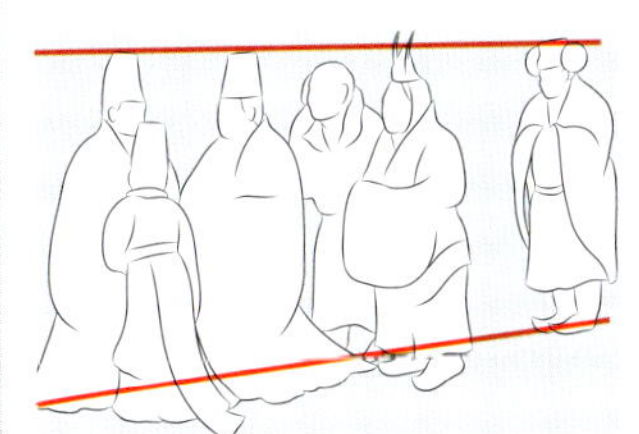

Movement
The implied ground plane slopes because the mural is on the wall of a descending passage. However, the slope also suggests a recession in space between the figures.

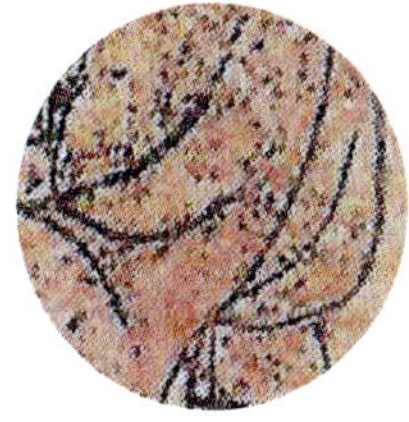

Technique
The figures are drawn with a black outline of even weight, then known as an "iron-wire line." The artist began by sketching an underdrawing in red ocher, then drew the final outline in a black ink made from soot.

Lady K'ab'al Xook Undertaking a Bloodletting Ritual

Artist unknown c. 723–726, limestone, 43 × 31 in (109 × 78 cm), British Museum, London, UK

This carved relief from the site of Yaxchilan, Mexico, shows a sacred ritual. Lady K'ab'al Xook kneels before King Itzamnaaj B'ahlam III, and threads a spiny cord through her tongue. Drops of her divine blood spill onto bark-paper strips as an offering to the gods, ensuring the security of the realm.

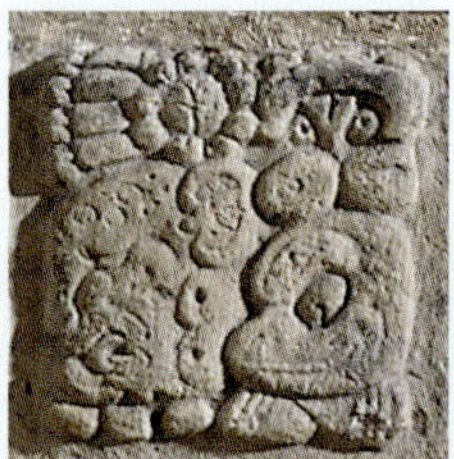

Maya glyphs inscribed above and to the side of the king describe the ritual and provide the names of the participants.

The king's hair is decorated with quetzal feathers and a deity mask, associating him with divine power.

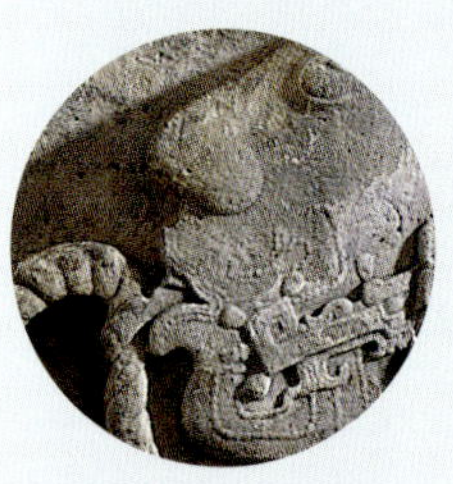

Ritual representation
Bloodletting from the royal body was believed to ensure that the world and sacred cycles of time would continue.

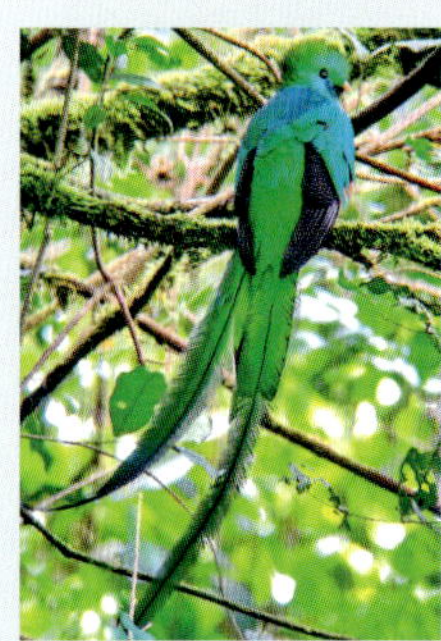

Animal symbolism
The quetzal feathers in King Itzamnaaj B'ahlam III's hair link him to this tropical bird, whose resplendent blue-green feathers were associated with royalty and divinity.

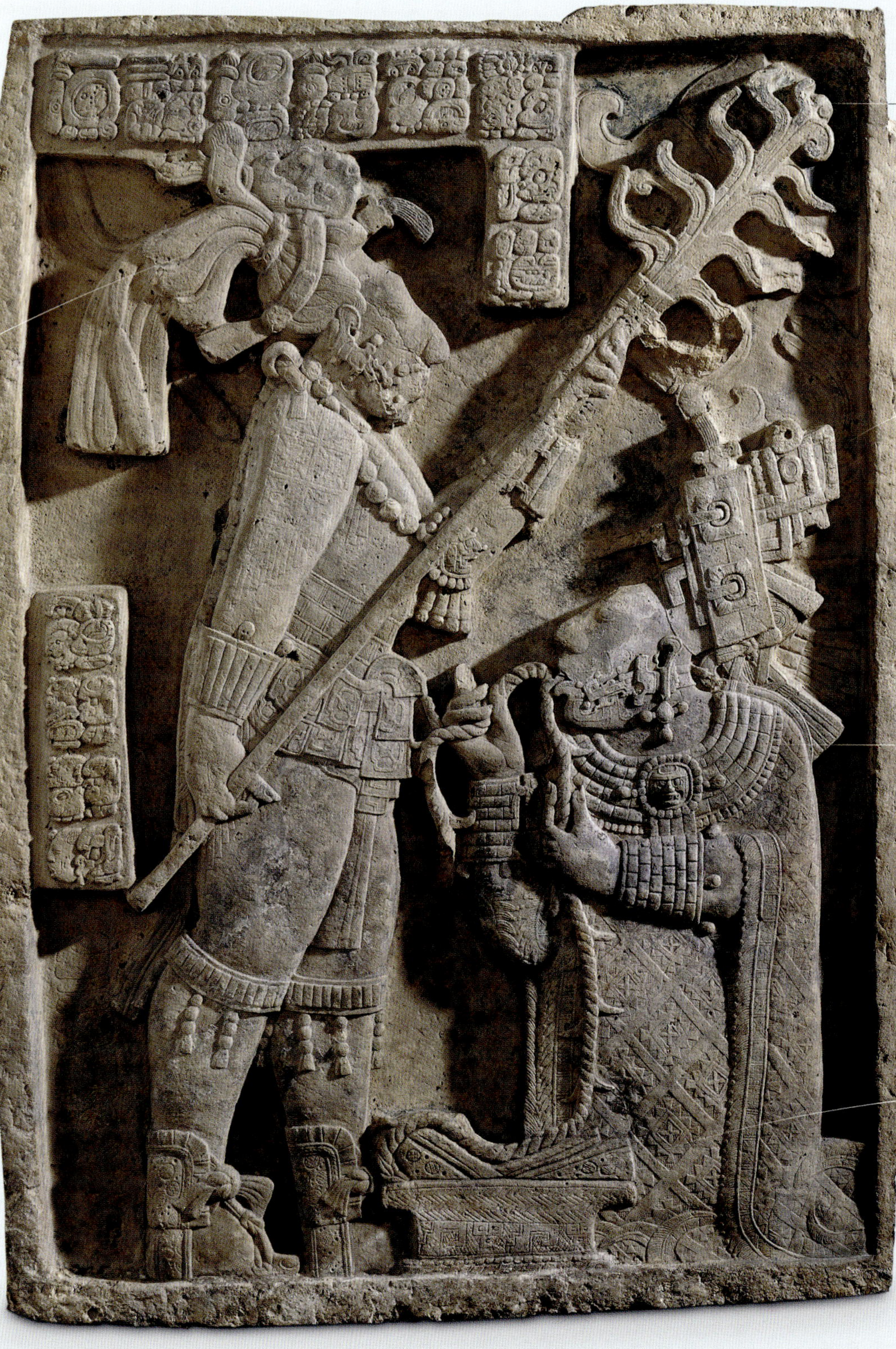

The sacred flaming torch that the king holds over Lady Xook signifies the tremendous importance of the ritual.

Deep relief carving gives the impression that the figures are nearly three-dimensional, making them appear more lifelike.

Lady K'ab'al Xook's fine woven *huipil* (dress), jade jewelery, and elaborate headdress signify her high status.

The sacred blood falls onto bark-paper strips nestled within a vessel.

Ratnacuda Shows Sudhana His Palace

Artist unknown 9th century, carved basalt, approx. 79 × 39 in (200 × 100 cm), Borobudur Temple, Magelang Regency, Central Java, Indonesia

This carved panel depicts the story of Sudhana, a Buddhist pilgrim on a journey to spiritual awakening. He meets Ratnacuda, a wealthy merchant and Buddhist patron, who shows him a magnificent palace. Each floor of the palace displays the perfections that one develops on the bodhisattva's path to awakening. The narrative takes place in South India at the time of the Buddha, about 6th–5th century BCE.

On the lower stories, Sudhana is shown acts of charity such as distributing food and riches. The higher he progresses, the more subtle are the perfections of his personality.

The parasols above both Ratnacuda and Sudhana emphasize their secular wealth and equal spiritual status.

Local flora and fauna are often used to create familiar settings that would help devotees connect with the stories.

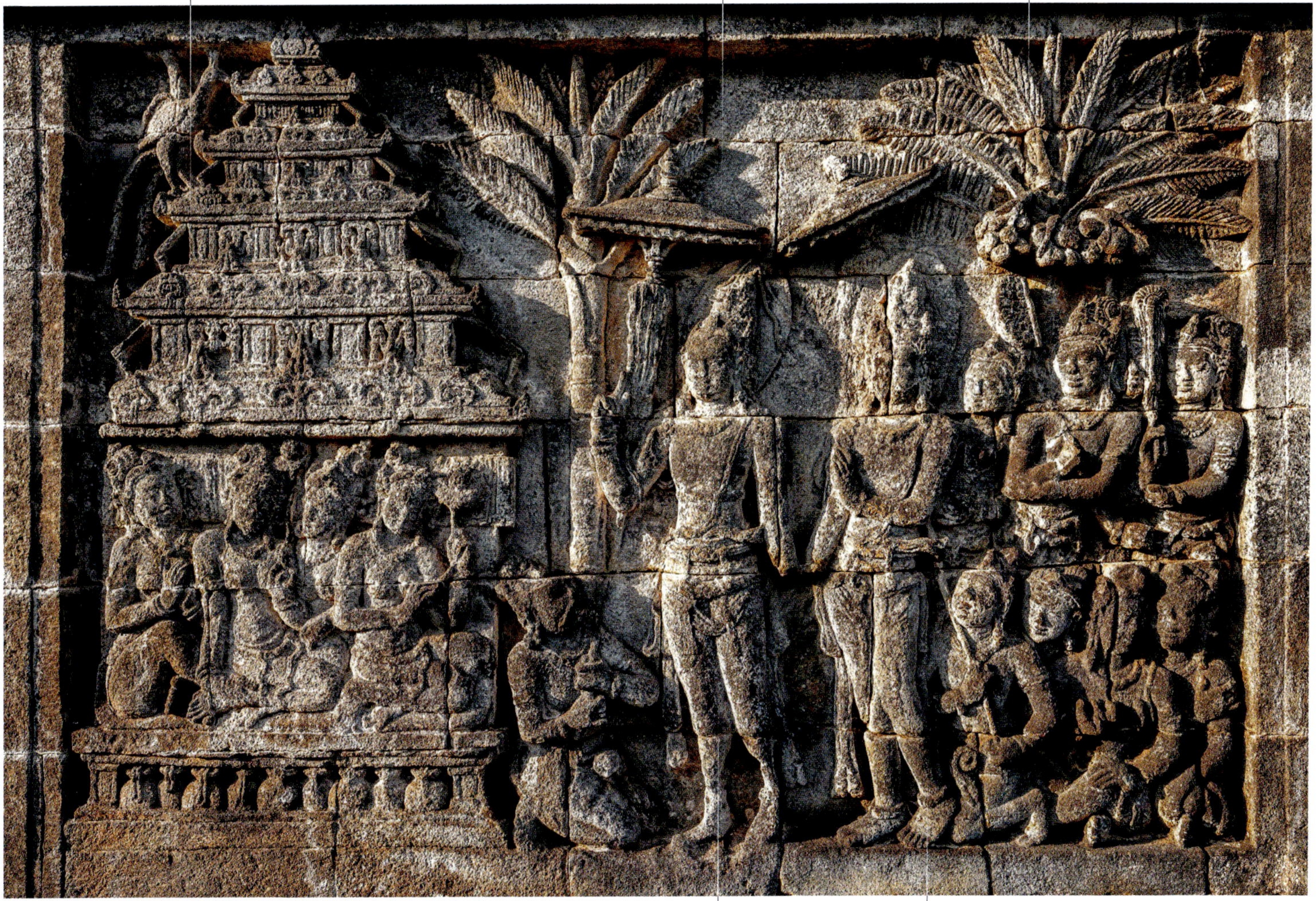

Ratnacuda shows Sudhana his 10-story palace, which allegorically demonstrates the 10 bodhisattva levels leading to the Buddha's state of awakening.

The crown, jewelery, and attire of the figures are inspired by both local Javanese styles and South Indian aesthetics.

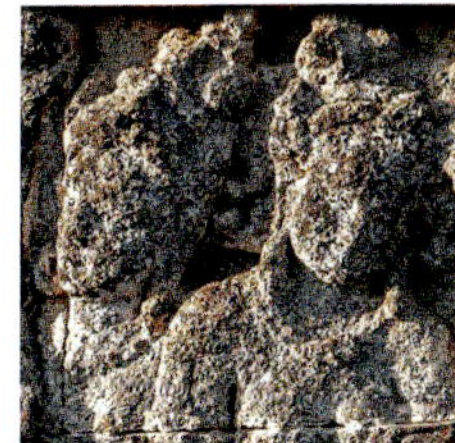

Consorts and attendants add to the impression of wealth and status.

Meru structures
Multistory structures such as Ratnacuda's palace may not have existed in Java, but multitiered roof structures known as "Meru" were common in palatial and temple architecture all over Southeast Asia.

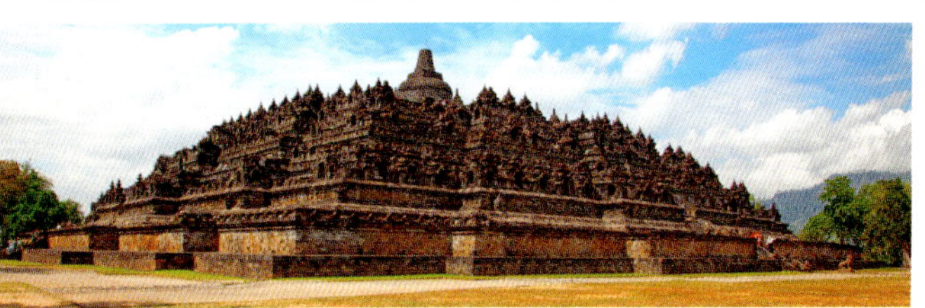

Borobudur Temple
The temple complex, containing 504 Buddha statues and 2,672 carved panels, was built in the Kedu Valley, Java, during the Shailendra dynasty, which flourished from about 750 to 850.

The Chi Rho Page (Folio 34r)

Artist unknown c. 800 CE, ink, gold, and silver on vellum, 13 × 10 in (33 × 25 cm), Trinity College Dublin, Dublin, Ireland

Chi (X) and *rho* (P) are the first characters in the Greek spelling of "Christ," and the *Chi Rho* symbol became a monogram for Christ. This page is taken from the *Book of Kells*, a set of the four gospels of the New Testament, thought to have been compiled by Celtic monks in the Columban monastery on the Scottish island of Iona. This page marks the first mention of Christ in St. Matthew's Gospel. The monk who illuminated this manuscript wished to evoke wonder at the importance of its words.

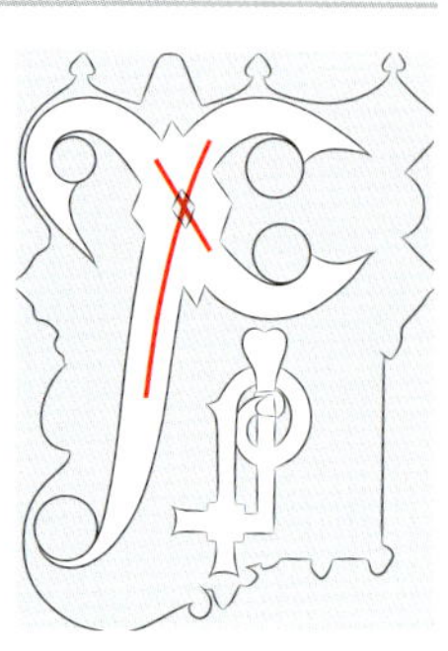

Focal point
The "X" made by the arms of the letter *chi* as they cross over are emblematic of the cross on which Christ would die and are given special emphasis.

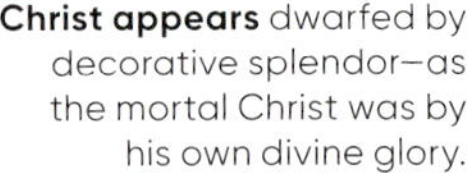

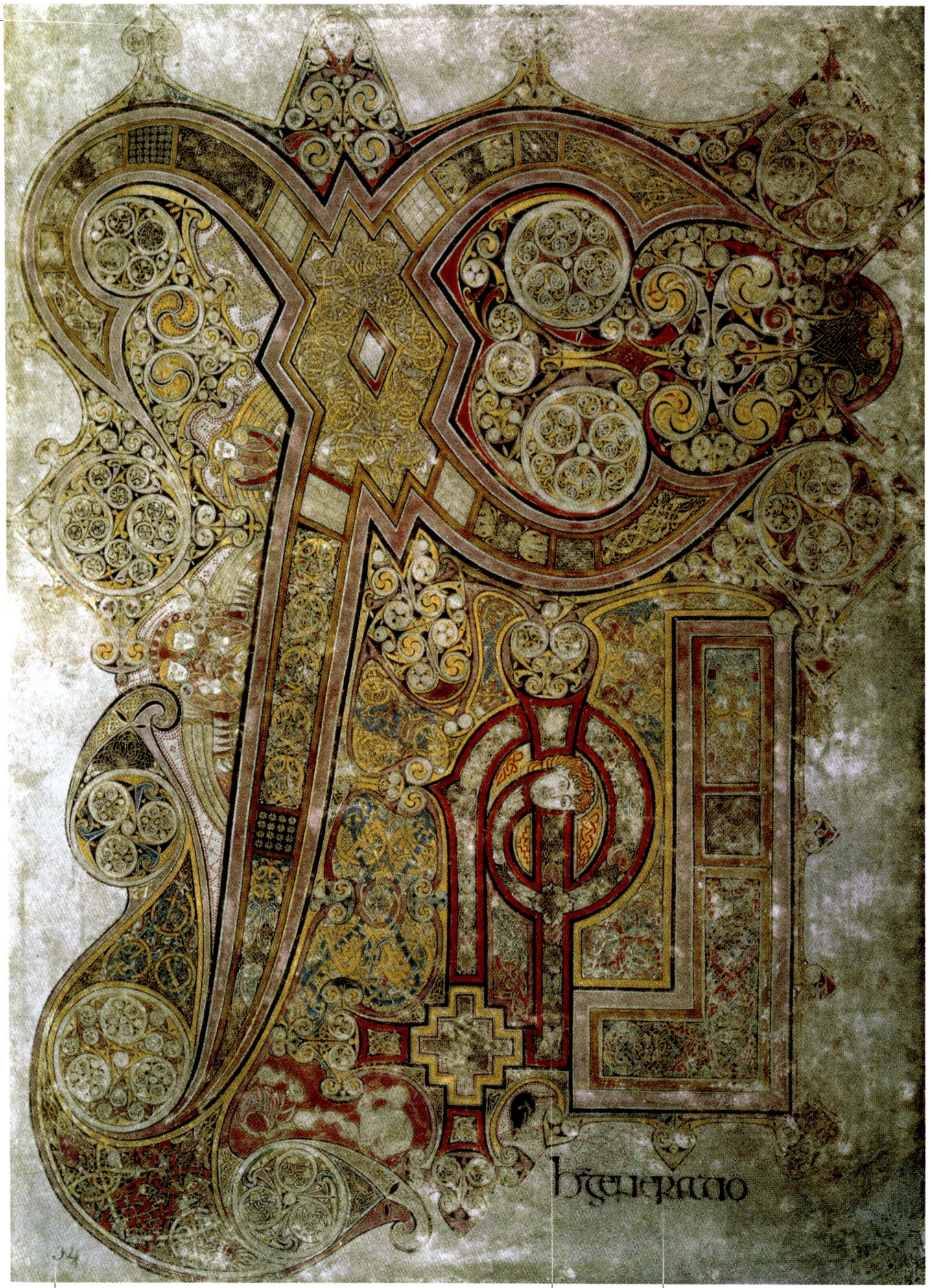

Christ appears dwarfed by decorative splendor—as the mortal Christ was by his own divine glory.

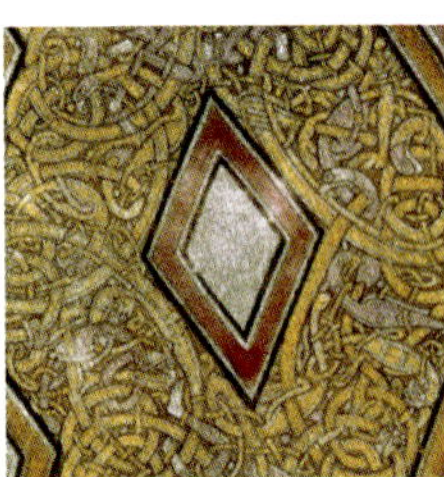

Interlacing patterns recall the filigree metalwork of 9th-century Ireland.

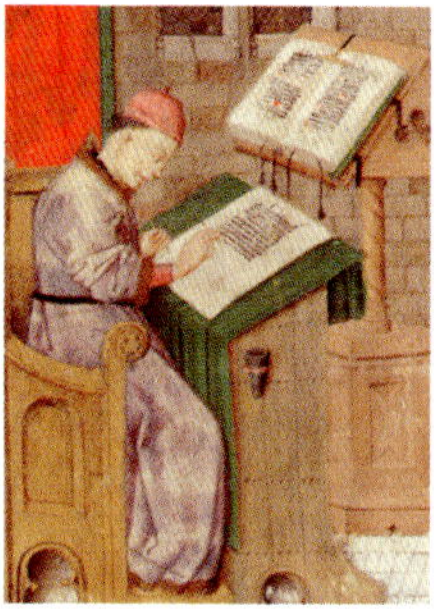

Scribes and illuminators
Illuminated manuscripts were produced by monks in a room called a scriptorium. Normally, scribes would copy texts onto vellum using ink and a quill pen and then an illuminator would add embellishments using gold leaf and natural pigments.

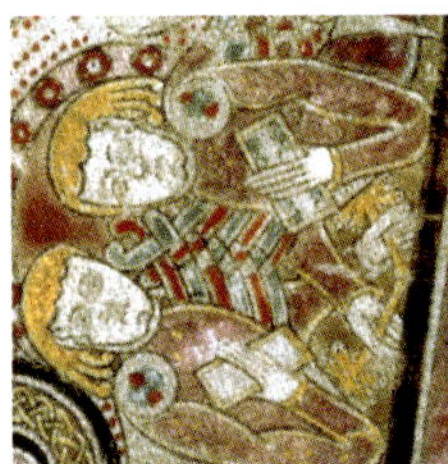

Angels are reminders of the heavenly origins of the Gospel's words.

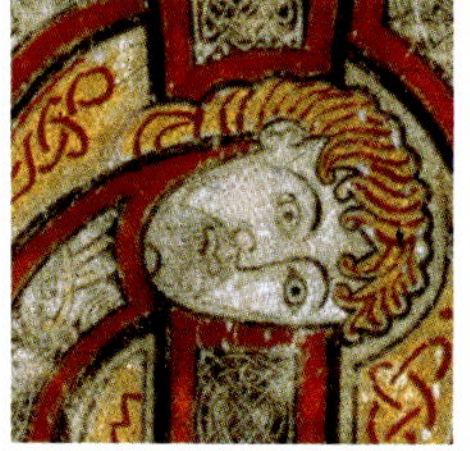

The human head that forms the end of *rho* (P) also dots the *iota* (I).

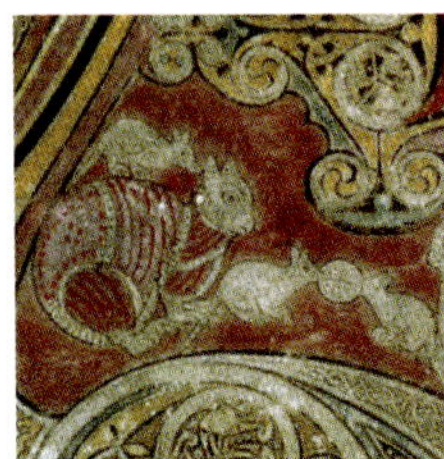

Cats catch mice stealing a communion host, an engaging detail and a reminder of the need for spiritual vigilance.

The pages of the *Book of Kells* are made from vellum (calfskin).

***Iota* (I)**, the third letter in Christ's Greek name, is tucked in beneath the curling *rho* (P).

The script completes the phrase begun by the illuminated letters: *XPI autem generatio*, "Now, the birth of Christ."

A saint holds out a compassionate hand to help a soul into Heaven.

Gold light suffuses Heaven. The color has faded but still contrasts starkly with the darkness of Hell below.

Stars shine in their respective spheres, in a stylized representation of the medieval theory of the universe.

Horseshoe arches interlock in one of this illumination's most obviously Islamic touches.

Demons treat the sinful with brutal violence, dragging them down to their damnation.

Snakes guard Satan's captives. They reference the serpent that tempted Eve with forbidden fruit in the Garden of Eden (Genesis 3:1-24).

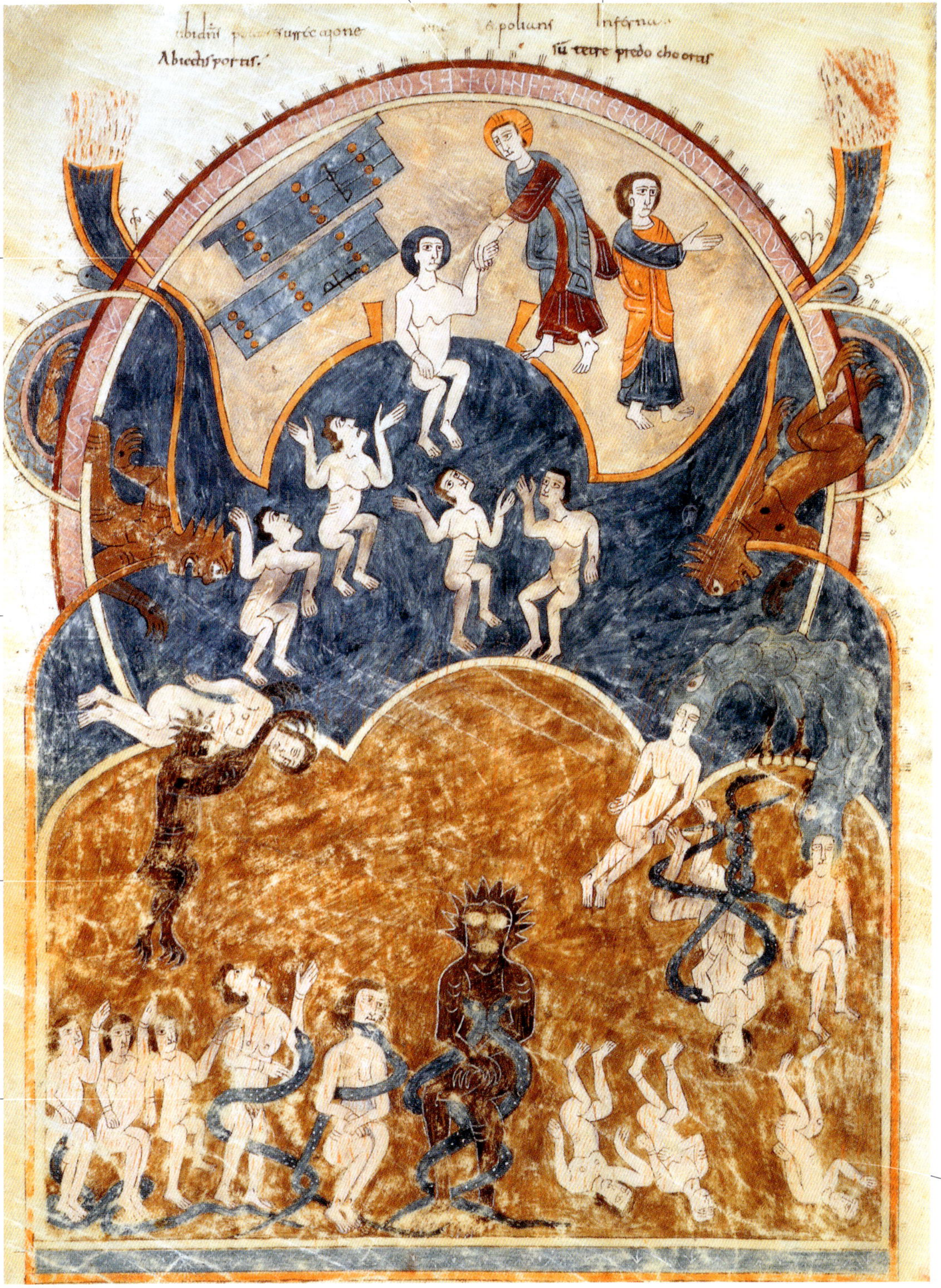

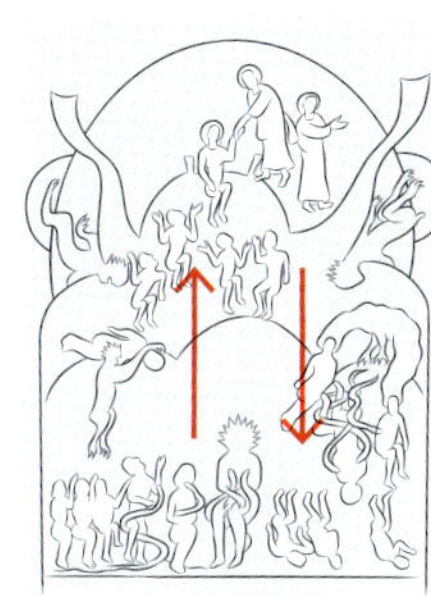

Creating tension
Tension between the saints who are laboring upward, and the sinners who are moving downward, creates energy and coherence.

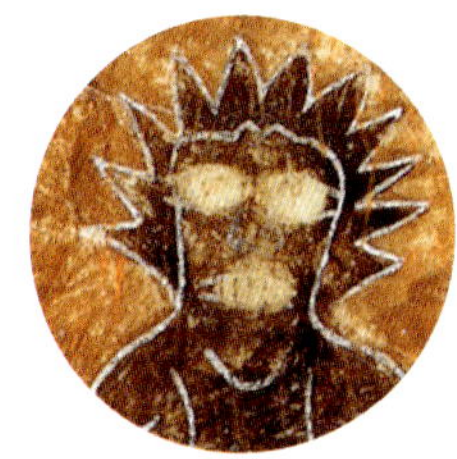

Expression
The blankness of Satan's face contrasts with the warm kindness in the faces of the saints, just as his spiky crest appears to parody their halos.

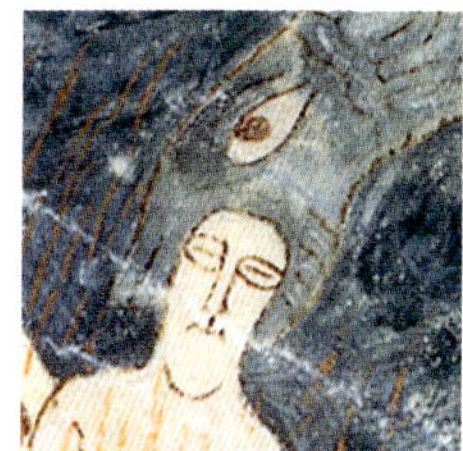

A monstrous serpent swallows up a soul that seemed set to escape from Hell.

The downward direction of these lost souls is a reminder that they damned themselves with their sinful lifestyles.

Last Judgment

Ende c. 975 CE, ink, gold, and silver, illuminated manuscript, 14 × 10 in (36 × 26 cm), Girona Cathedral, Girona, Catalonia, Spain

This page of the illuminated manuscript *Gerona Beatus* was produced by a Catholic nun in Catalonia, not long after it had been recaptured from Muslim forces. Mozarabic in style, its vibrant colors and geometric forms are typical of a Spanish Christian culture in which Islamic aesthetic attitudes had become embedded. Gold and silver decorate the pages, a mark of the value its makers attached to the divine Word.

Standing Parvati

Artist unknown c. 900–925, bronze, 27 in (69.5 cm) high, Metropolitan Museum of Art, New York, US

This magnificent representation of Uma (as the Hindu goddess Parvati is called in Tamil Nadu, where this sculpture was made) embodies ideal beauty and femininity. Regal, maternal, and alluring, the abundantly adorned deity shifts her weight sideways, her left arm elegantly following the contour of her hip.

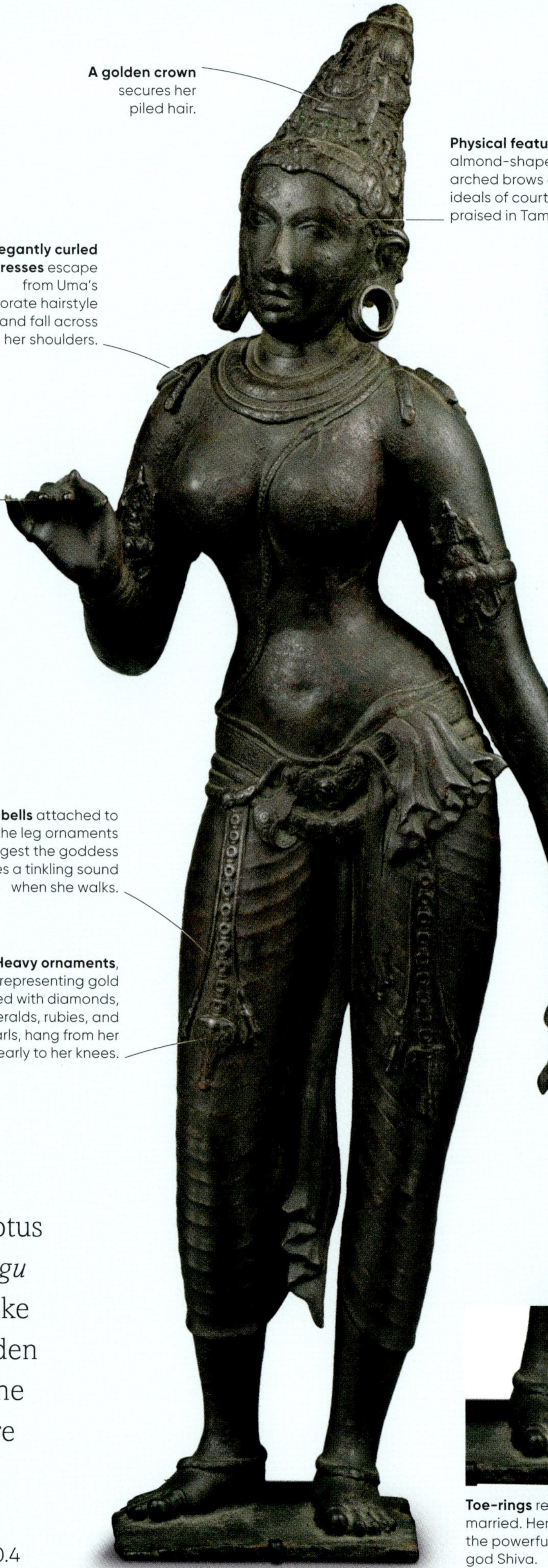

A golden crown secures her piled hair.

Physical features including almond-shaped eyes and arched brows conform to ideals of courtly beauty praised in Tamil poetry.

Elegantly curled tresses escape from Uma's elaborate hairstyle and fall across her shoulders.

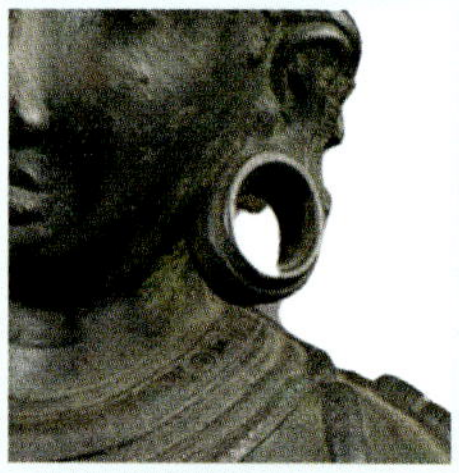

Her earlobes stretch around large plug-disk rings which were worn by royalty.

Her right hand is raised as if she is about to pluck a flower—an attribute of the goddess.

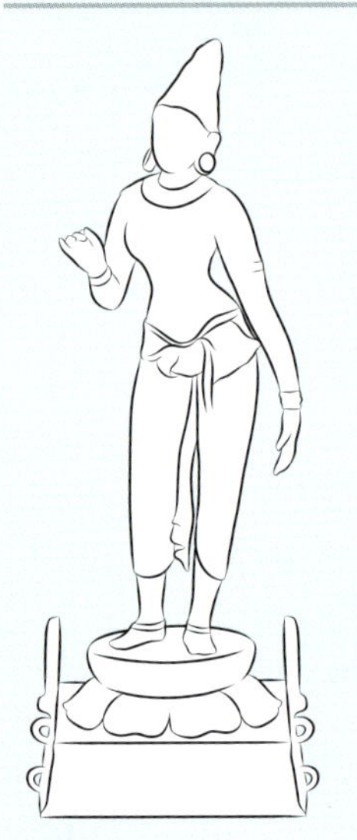

Display
The square base was set into a lotus-shaped pedestal—a sign of divinity—which would have been mounted onto a palanquin during processions.

Tiny bells attached to the leg ornaments suggest the goddess makes a tinkling sound when she walks.

Heavy ornaments, representing gold studded with diamonds, emeralds, rubies, and pearls, hang from her waist nearly to her knees.

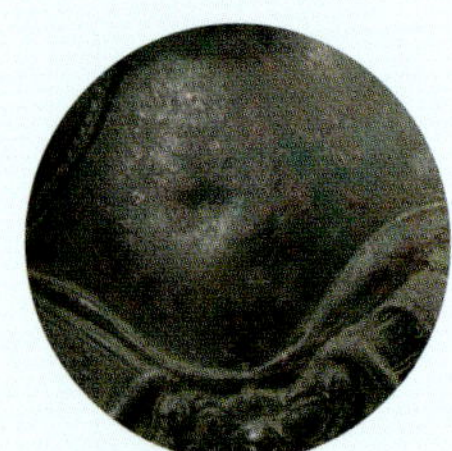

Survival
Surface corrosion reveals that the sculpture was buried for centuries. South Indian bronzes were often buried for safekeeping in times of instability.

"Fresh as newborn lotus buds, lustrous as *kongu* blossoms, honeyed like young coconuts, golden [vessels] filled with the nectar of the gods are the breasts of the resplendent Uma."

Saint Sambandar, hymn 260.4

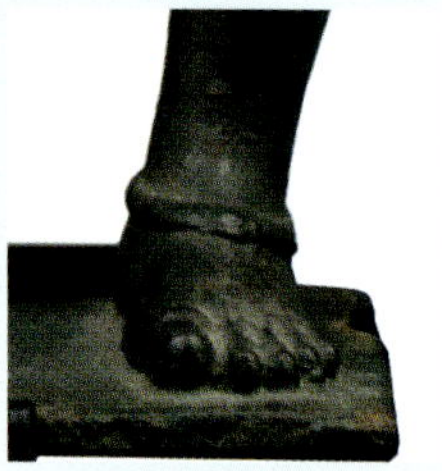

Toe-rings reveal she is married. Her husband is the powerful Hindu god Shiva.

Norse Dragon-Prowed Ship

Artist unknown 10th century, Anglo-Saxon manuscript, 11 × 9 in (27.6 × 23.2 cm), British Museum, London, UK

The Northumbrian monk who illuminated this manuscript would have feared the Norsemen, naval raiders from Scandinavia who terrorized the coastal communities of Britain and Europe between the 8th and 12th centuries. Here, however, his artistic enthusiasm shines through in this representation of a Viking longship, which is full of colorful (and eccentric) detail.

There was no single accepted convention for depicting dragons—this one resembles a horse.

Both sides of the dragon's mane are shown, suggesting that the artist was more interested in decorative detail than in realism.

The cabin resembles a multistory house; again, artistic exuberance prevails over accuracy.

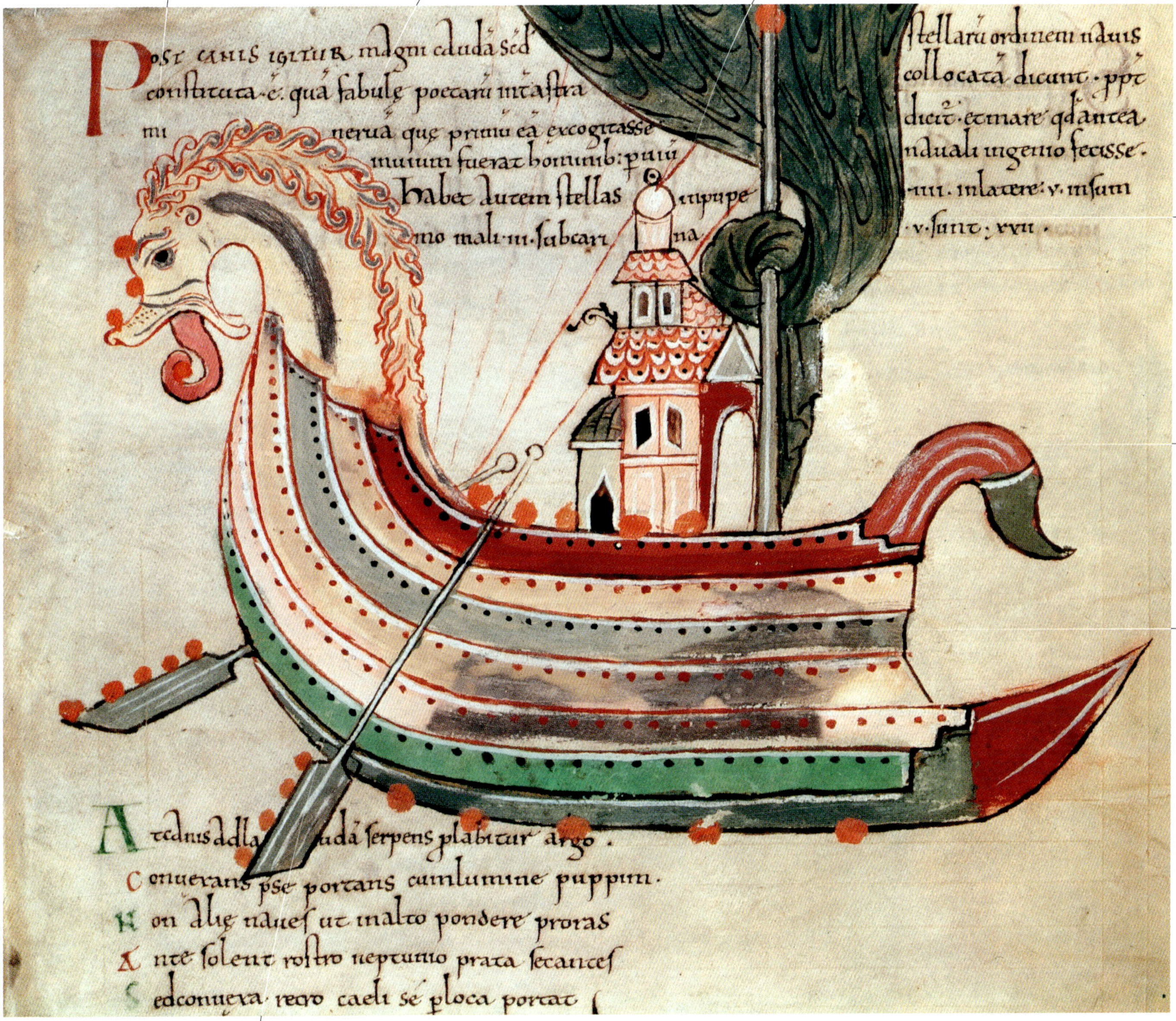

The fluid line of the sail furled around the ship's mast echoes the curve of the dragon's arching neck.

The tail of the dragon dips downward, mirroring the curve of the rising prow.

Owing to the focus on the decorative bow and stern, the artist has shortened the boat considerably.

The overlapping planks of the boat, typical of Norse ship construction, are realistically shown, apart from their bright colors.

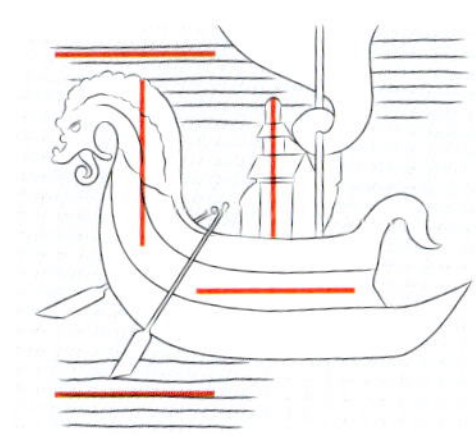

Composition
The vertical lines of the dragon's "neck" and the vessel's central cabin, mast, and sail balance out the horizontal planks of the hull and the lines of text.

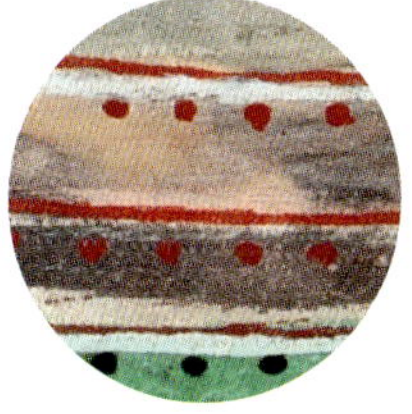

Visual interest
The red dots that punctuate the outline of the ship serve no obvious representational purpose. Like the manuscript's brightly colored capitals, they have likely been included to add a greater sense of vibrancy overall.

Myths

Created by cultures around the world, myths have long been a source of subjects for painters and sculptors. During the European Renaissance and Baroque periods, artists looked back to Greek and Roman myths for inspiration. Later, during the political upheavals of the 19th century, legends often provided a vehicle for celebrating national identity. In the late 19th century, some artists reimagined ancient myths to explore radical new ideas such as psychoanalysis.

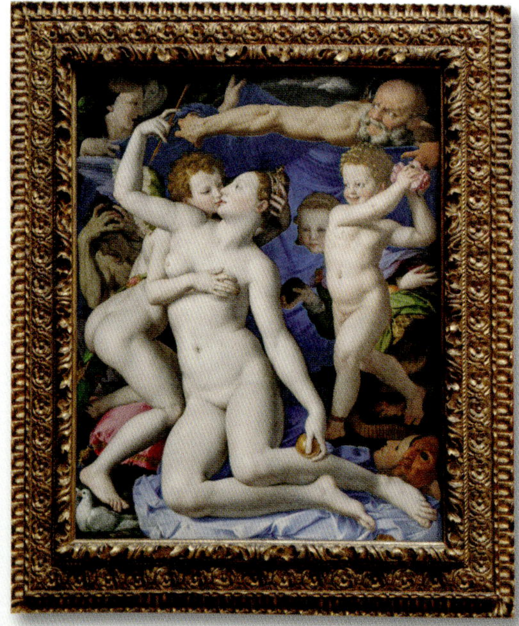

2

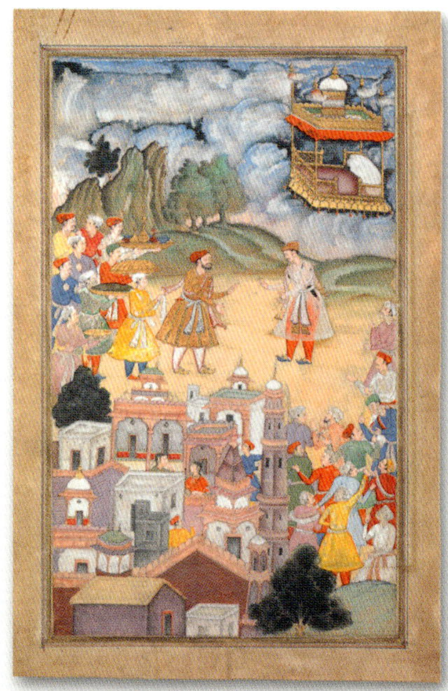

3

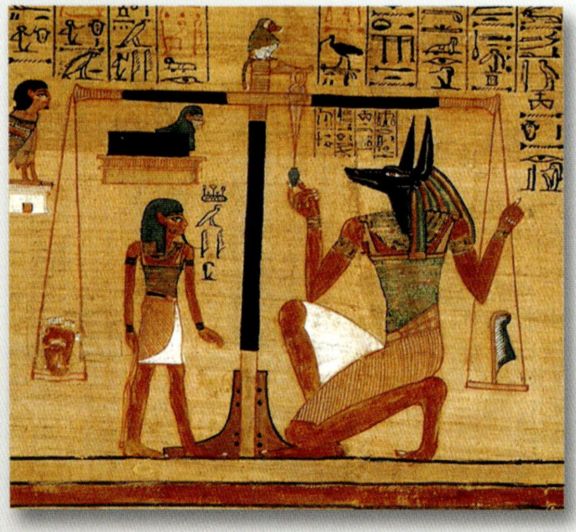

1

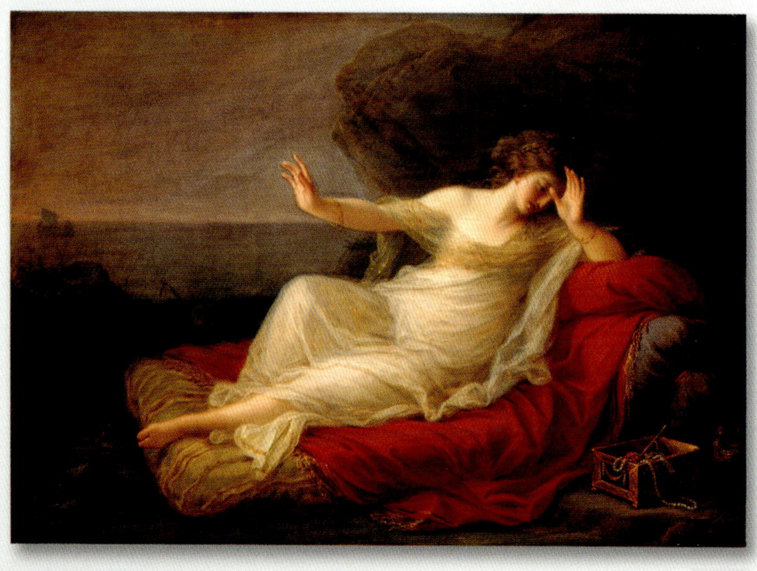

4

1. ***Weighing of the Heart Against the Feather of Truth*, c. 1275 BCE.** The ancient Egyptian Book of the Dead was designed to guide the deceased through the afterlife. The episode on the weighing of the heart against the feather of truth would decide if the dead went to paradise.

2. ***Allegory with Venus and Cupid*, Agnolo Bronzino, c. 1540–1550.** The Roman deities of love embrace each other, surrounded by personifications of Pleasure, Deceit, Jealousy, and Oblivion. Unraveling the meaning of the painting would have provided entertainment for courtiers.

3. ***King Salya Visits Kala Yavana*, unknown artist, c. 1590–1595.** The *Harivamsa* (*The Legend of Hare Krishna*) describes the youth of the Hindu god Krishna. Here King Salya, his traveling throne floating overhead, meets Kala Yavana, who had led an army against Krishna.

4. ***Ariadne Abandoned by Theseus*, Angelica Kauffman, 1774.** The story of Ariadne, taken from classical mythology, was a popular subject among Renaissance and Baroque artists. Kauffman has chosen the moment when Ariadne realizes that her lover, Theseus, has betrayed her.

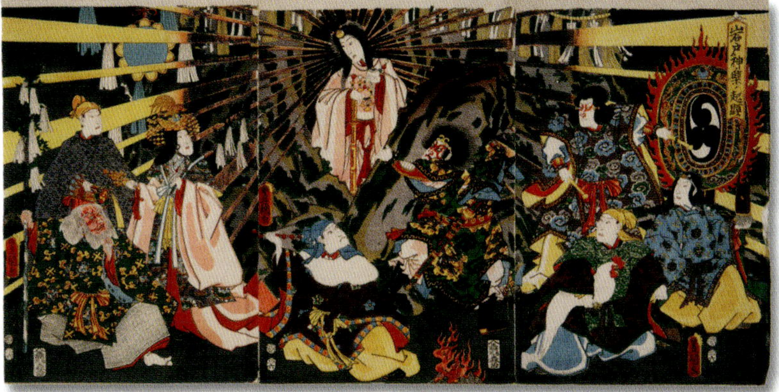

5

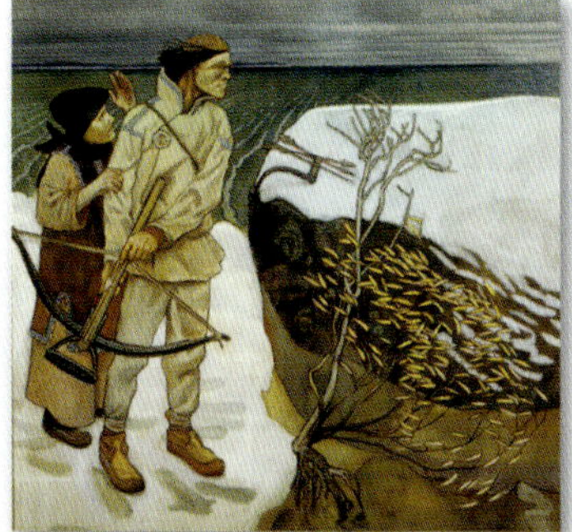

7

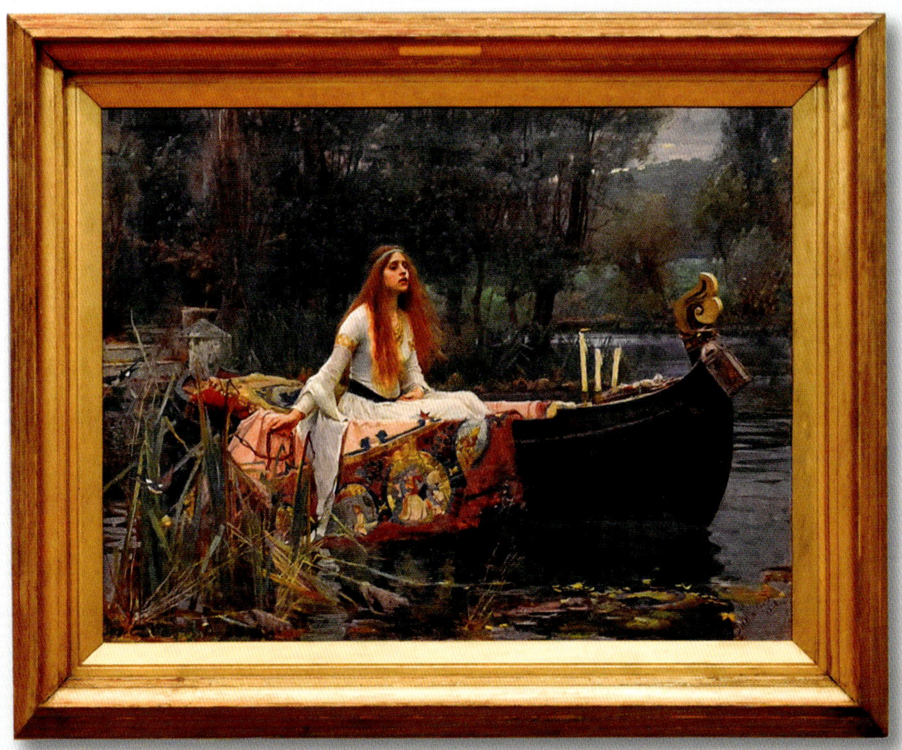

6

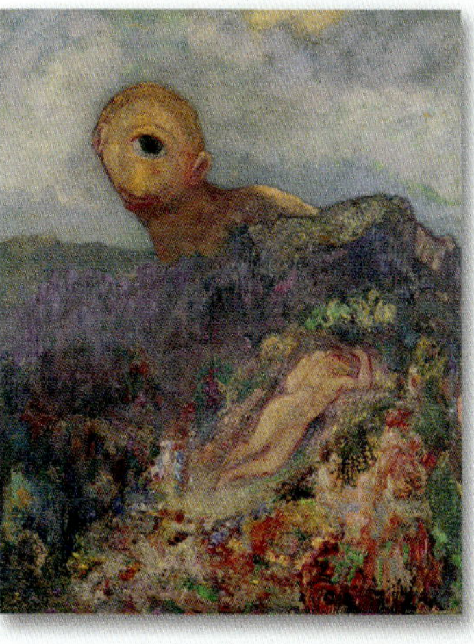

8

The hero quest

Many myths, from those of ancient Greece to the Arthurian quest for the Holy Grail, are based on a journey made by a male hero figure. Along the way, he meets allies and enemies and completes trials. Eventually, after overcoming a final challenge, he returns to his people a changed person.

5. ***Goddess Amaterasu Emerges from a Cave*, Utagawa Kunisada, c. 1860.** In Japanese mythology, stories of the gods explain natural phenomena. In one, the sun goddess Amaterasu retreats into a cave, turning the world dark. When the other gods lure her out, light returns.

6. ***The Lady of Shalott*, John William Waterhouse, 1888.** Pre-Raphaelite painters such as Waterhouse turned to Arthurian legends for subject matter, seeing the romance and chivalry of the medieval world as an antidote to the harsh industrialized world in which they lived.

7. ***Joukahainen's Revenge*, Akseli Gallen-Kallela, 1897.** Joukahainen's attempt to exact revenge on the hero Väinämöinen by killing him with a crossbow is an event in the *Kalevala*, a collection of ancient origin myths and folk tales that make up Finland's national epic.

8. ***Cyclops*, Odilon Redon, c. 1914.** A Symbolist painter, Redon used Greek myth in this evocation of a world drawn from the subconscious. *Cyclops* is based on a story in Ovid's *Metamorphoses* about the one-eyed giant Polyphemus's unrequited love for the nymph Galatea.

Luohan

Artist unknown 907–1125, stoneware with sancai glaze, 41 in (103 cm) high, British Museum, London, UK

This life-size figure from China's Yizhou Caves depicts a Buddhist *luohan* (or *arhat*)—one who has come to understand the true nature of existence and is therefore freed from the cycle of *samsara* (life, death, and rebirth). It is one of a set numbering at least eight figures, which were probably installed in a temple. The *luohan*'s serene expression and delicate features reflect his role as a teacher and protector of Buddhism.

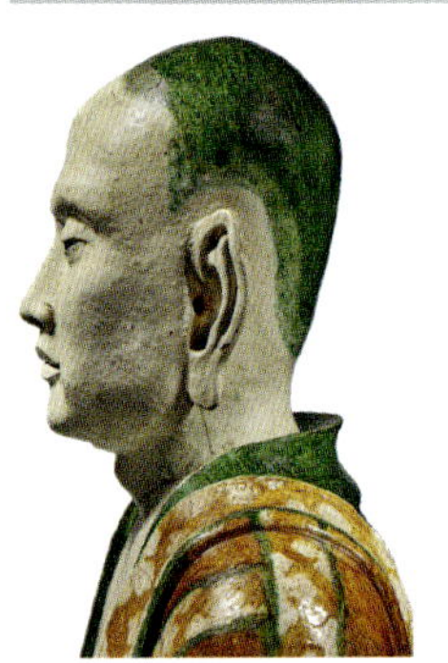

Firing technique
This clay figure was built in multiple stages and fired twice, initially at a high temperature to solidify the body, then at a lower temperature to fuse the glazes. The figure is hollow, with openings in the base and the ears to allow air to circulate during firing.

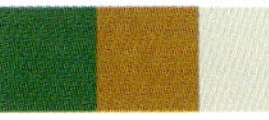

"Three-color" glaze
Sancai—green, amber, and cream—glaze is primarily silica, fluxed with lead oxide. Copper oxides produce the green, and iron produces the amber color.

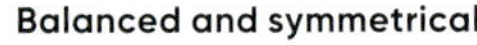

The shaved head and robes indicate his status as a monk.

The monk's face is youthful and unlined, in contrast to some other figures from the same set, which depict older men.

Elongated earlobes, stretched by heavy earrings, imply a past life of luxury that the monk has renounced.

The mantle, made of patches of discarded fabric, was intended to recall his vows of poverty.

These patches are decorated with a pattern suggesting scraps of fine silk brocade given by a wealthy donor.

Folded hands form a version of *dhyana mudra*, a symbolic gesture indicating a meditative state.

Balanced and symmetrical, the figure is seated with legs crossed in the lotus position. His downward, even inward, gaze contributes to the sense of stillness and repose.

The rustic base is meant to suggest a wilderness or mountain setting.

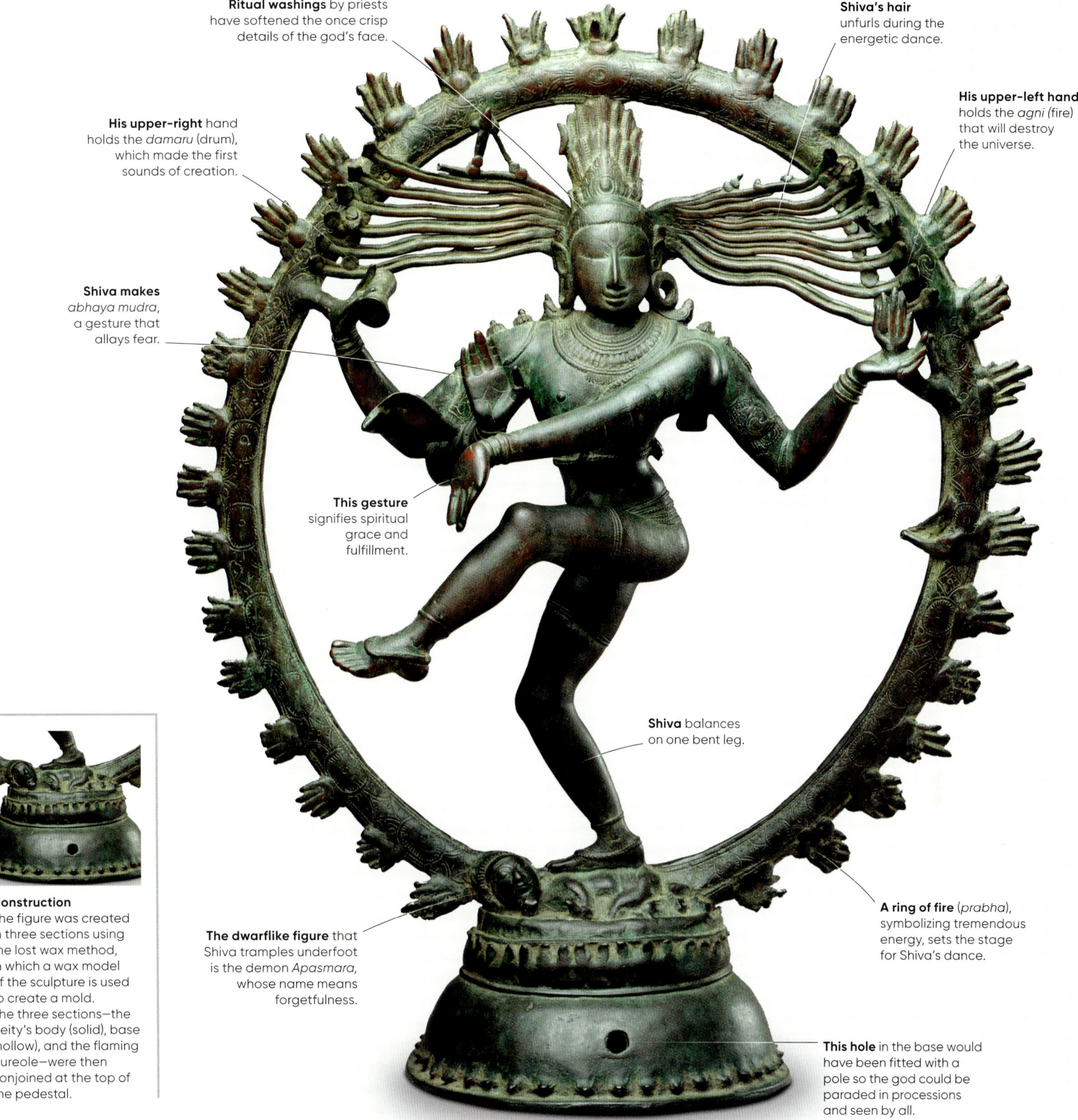

Construction
The figure was created in three sections using the lost wax method, in which a wax model of the sculpture is used to create a mold. The three sections—the deity's body (solid), base (hollow), and the flaming aureole—were then conjoined at the top of the pedestal.

Shiva as Lord of the Dance (Nataraja)

Artist unknown 11th century, bronze, 27 in (68.3 cm) high, Metropolitan Museum of Art, New York, US

In this iconic image from Tamil Nadu in south India, the Hindu god Shiva appears as Nataraja, or Lord of the Dance, who dances the universe into destruction so it can be born anew. The sculpture was regularly carried through the streets in resplendent processions. On those occasions, it would have been bathed in sacred substances, dressed in fine textiles, bejeweled, and adorned with fragrant flowers and other offerings.

Rain God Vessel

Artist unknown c. 1100–1400, polychrome ceramic, 10 × 8 × 11 in (24.7 × 21 × 28.5 cm), Kimbell Art Museum, Fort Worth, Texas, US

This elaborately decorated spouted vessel merges the roles of warrior and rain god within the same figure. The iconography is that of the Mixtec god of rain, Tlaloc, who was crucial for a bountiful harvest. The shield and the crouching position, however, identify the figure as a warrior.

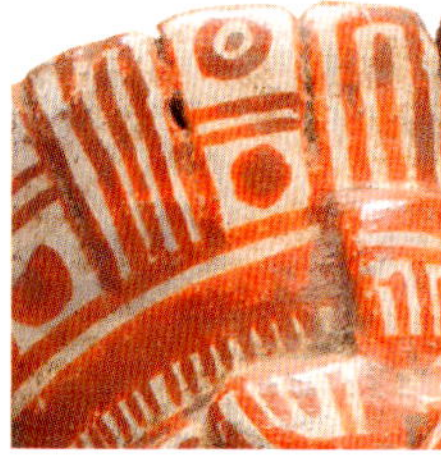

Geometric feather patterns occur across the figure, notably on the headdress, identifying the deity.

The mask emerges from the open mouth of a coyote-head helmet, a reference to the ferocity of warriors.

This object may be either a club or corn. If corn, it alludes to Tlaloc's role in the cultivation of this vital crop.

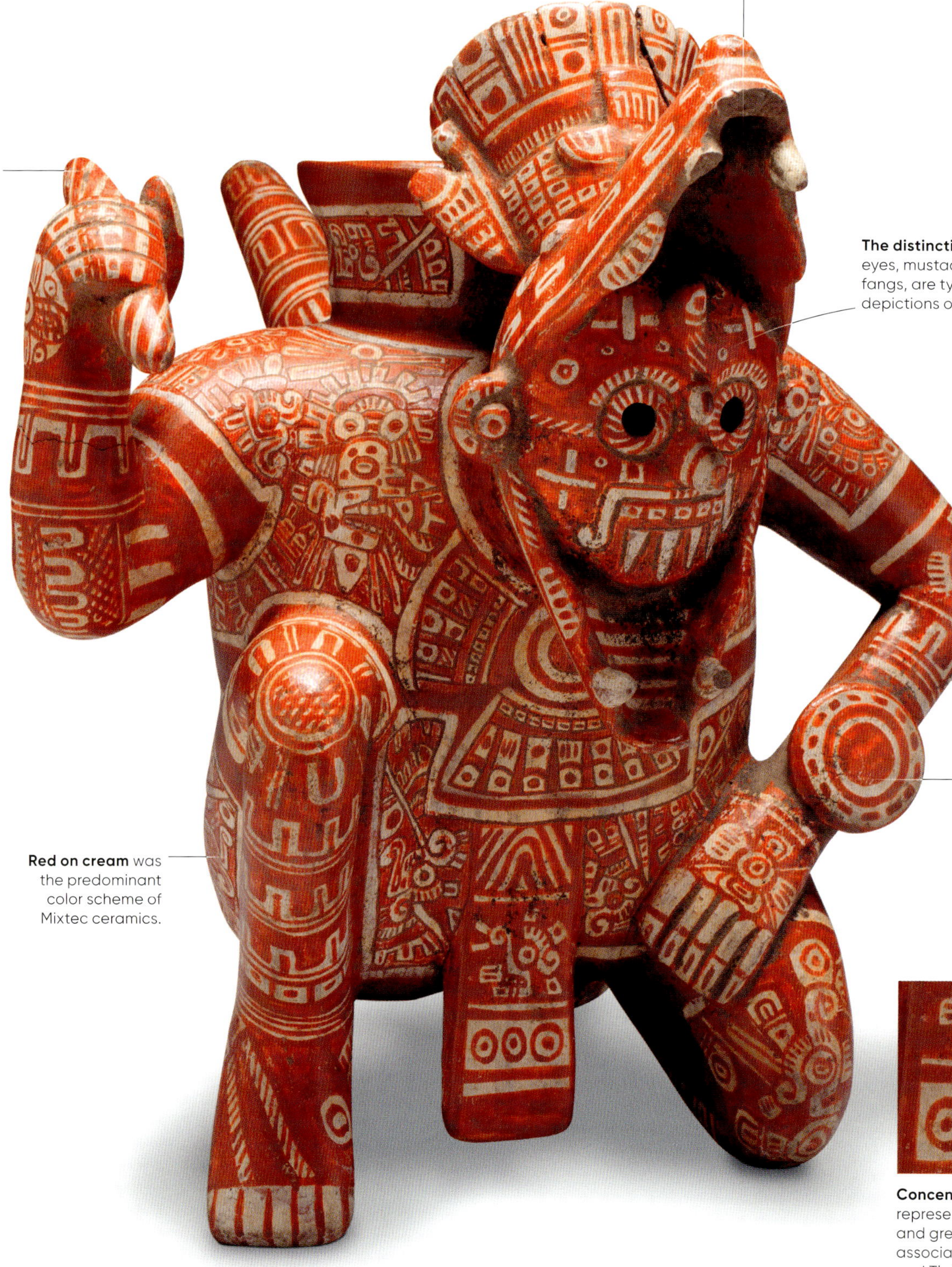

The distinctive circular eyes, mustache, and fangs, are typical of Mixtec depictions of the rain god.

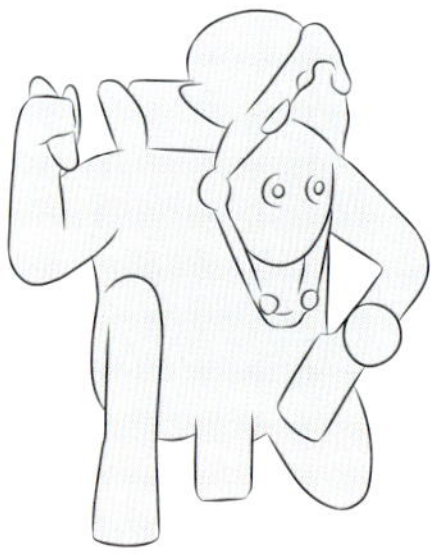

Composition
The figure adopts a crouching stance, with its left knee on the ground and right arm raised, evoking a sense of balance and stability.

This small shield tied around the god's wrist is a symbolic allusion to the warrior archetype.

Red on cream was the predominant color scheme of Mixtec ceramics.

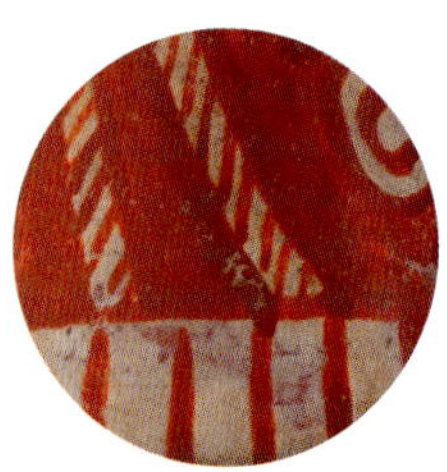

Technique
After an initial firing, the clay vessel was burnished to a high sheen. A white slip was then applied, onto which red pigments were added before undergoing a second firing.

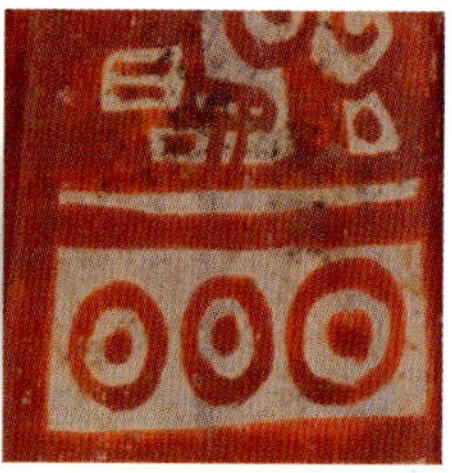

Concentric circles represent precious jade and greenstone, both associated with water and Tlaloc.

Shiva Embracing His Consort, Uma (Alinganamurti)

Artist unknown late 11th century, bronze, 15 × 8 in (38.1 × 20.3 cm), Metropolitan Museum of Art, New York, US

Lord of destruction and family man to Hindus in the Indian state of Tamil Nadu, where this sculpture was made, the god Shiva curls his arm around his beloved wife, Uma (Parvati), and raises his lower-right hand in a gesture of reassurance (*abhaya-mudra*). Medieval poet-saints extolled the divine couple's beauty, here expertly cast in bronze.

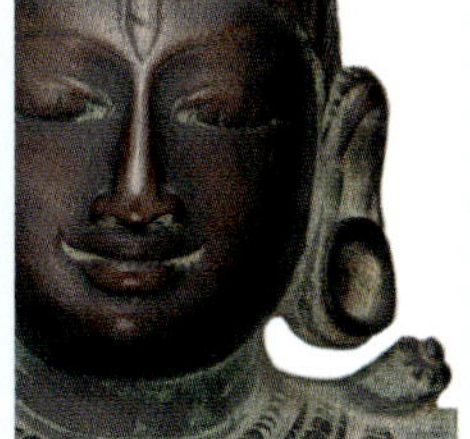

The couple wear large, plug-disk and makara-shaped earrings, which were reserved for royalty.

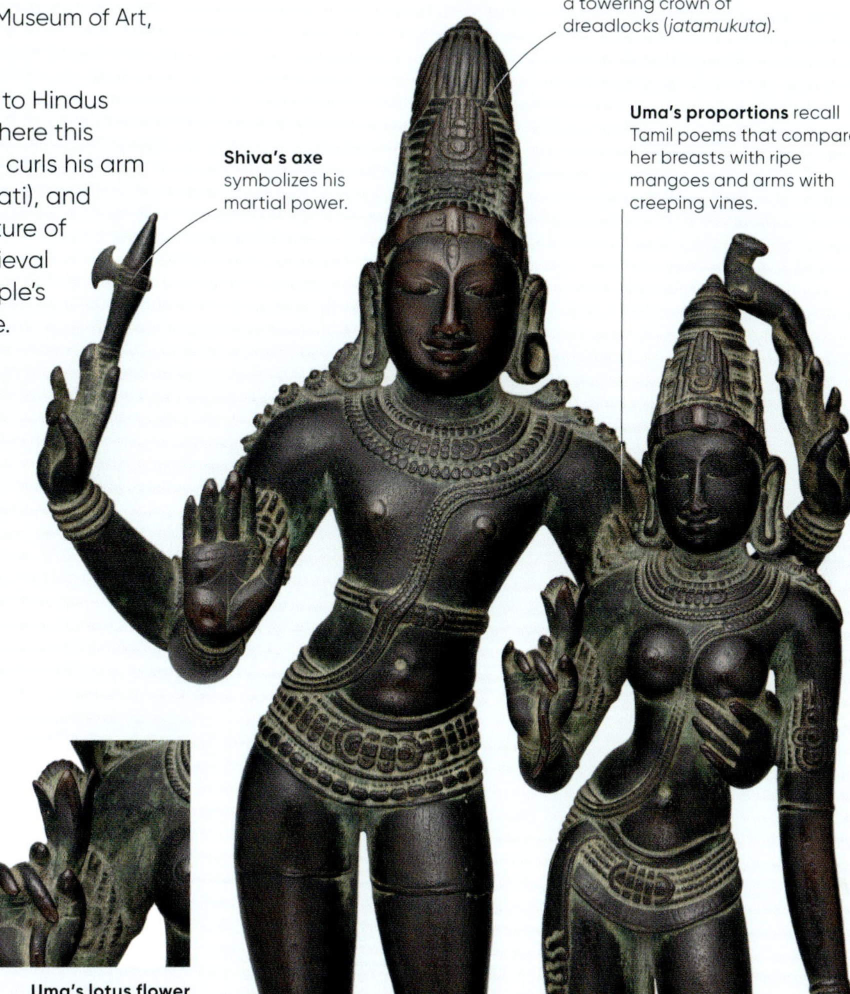

Shiva's hair is arranged in a towering crown of dreadlocks (*jatamukuta*).

Shiva's axe symbolizes his martial power.

Uma's proportions recall Tamil poems that compare her breasts with ripe mangoes and arms with creeping vines.

Uma's lotus flower symbolizes her gentle disposition.

Bracelets, belts, necklaces, and anklets were cast directly on the bronze. The sculptures were also ritually adorned with gold jewelery.

A ring of flames (*prabha*) symbolizing cosmic energy would have been attached to the upturned prongs rising from the pedestal.

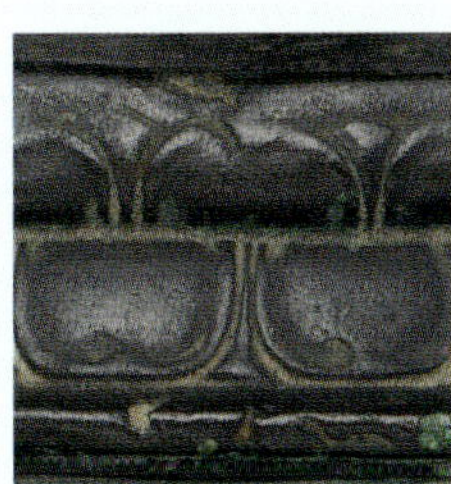

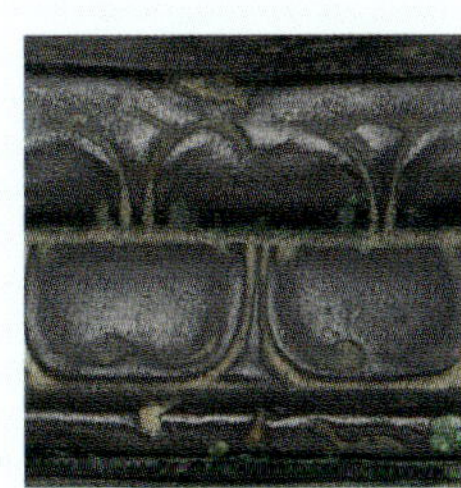

The lotus-flower pedestal indicates the couple's divine status.

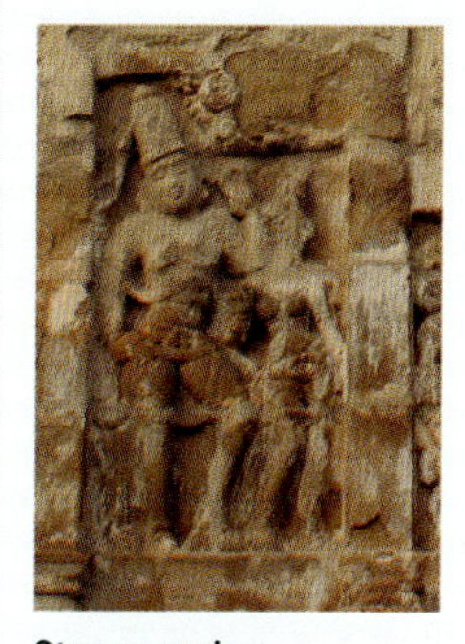

Stone carving
The earliest surviving *Shiva Embracing Uma* is an 8th-century relief carving at the Muktesvara Temple, Kanchipuram, India.

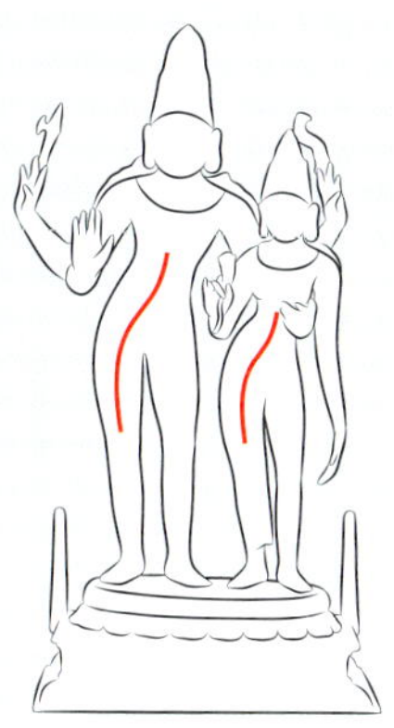

Posture
The god and goddess shift their weight onto their right hip, in the *tribhanga* (three-bend) stance typical of classical Indian art.

Boat styles and rigging methods of 1,000 years ago are drawn in such detail that historians refer to them.

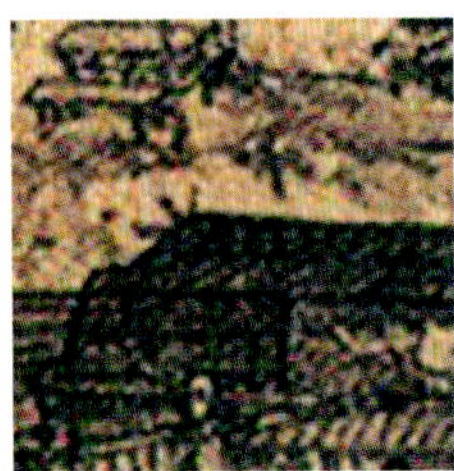

The silk has aged to a deep, golden yellow, while the ink has retained its rich black hue.

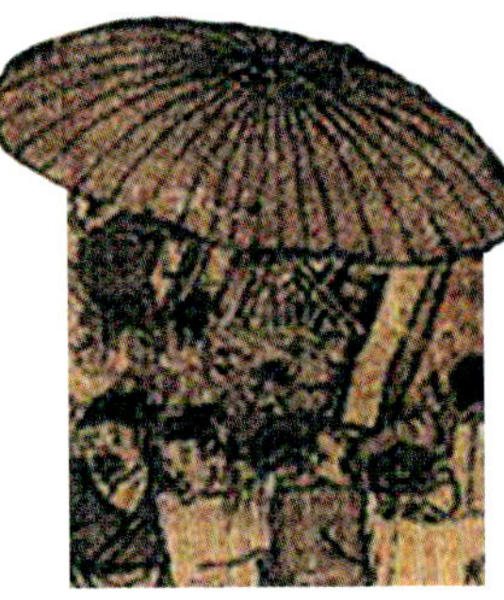

Large bamboo umbrellas shield customers as well as sellers and their wares.

A bustling marketplace lining the bridge and nearby streets offers food and goods sourced locally and from the Silk Road.

Oxen pulling carts, as well as horses and camels moving goods, are among the 80 animals shown.

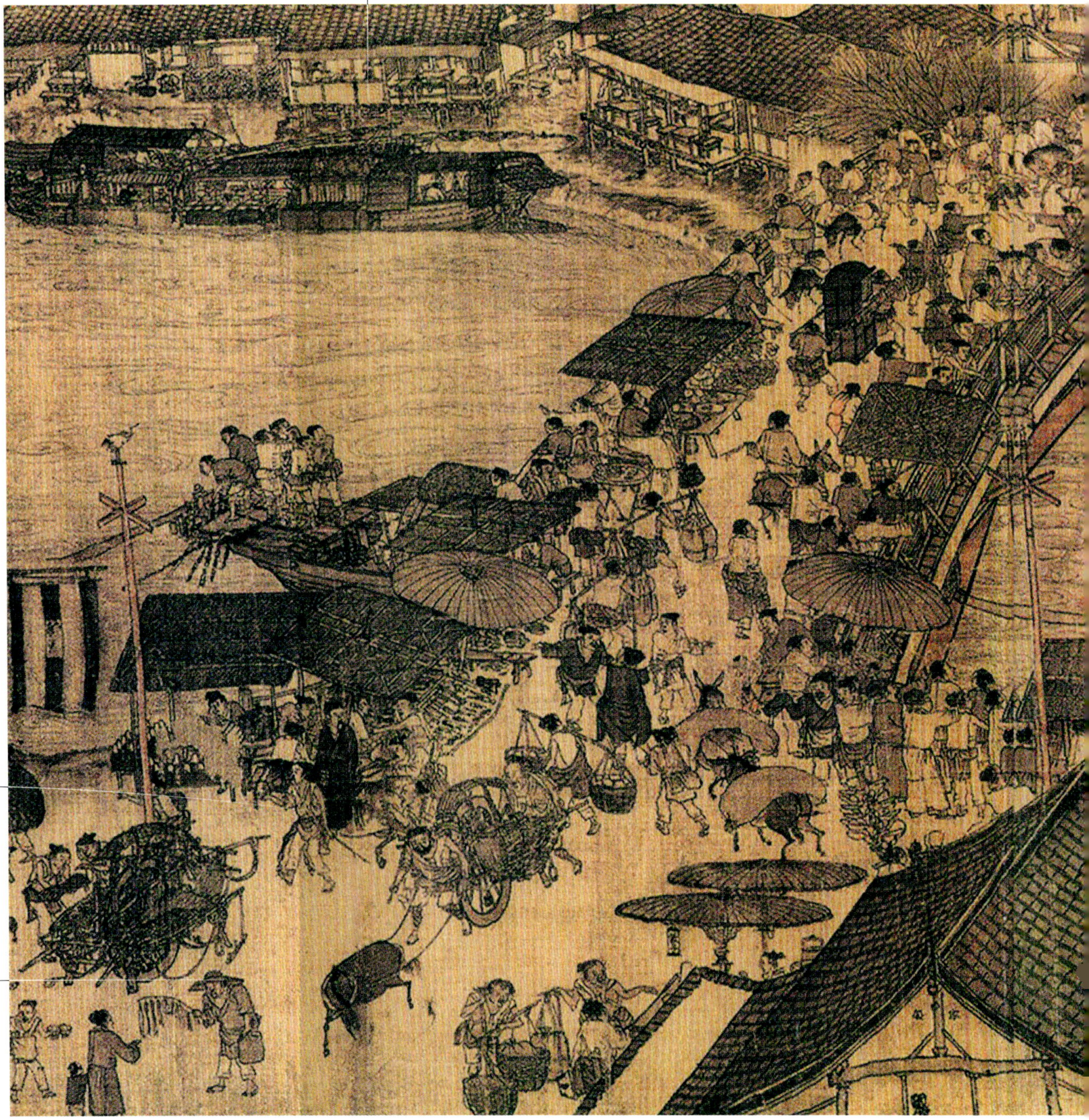

Along the River During the Qingming Festival

Attributed to Zhang Zeduan 12th century, ink and color on silk, 10 × 208 in (24.8 × 528 cm), Palace Museum, Beijing, China

Painted in minute detail, this monochromatic handscroll provides a panoramic view of 12th-century life in a prosperous city during the Northern Song Dynasty (960–1127). Hundreds of people of all classes, almost all male, run errands and carry out chores; only about 20 women are represented and they are mostly depicted indoors. Despite the remarkable wealth of detail provided by this bird's-eye view, questions remain. Which city does it depict? And why does the title refer to the ancestor-honoring Qingming Festival, but show no activities, such as tomb sweeping and prayers, associated with it?

Onlookers hang over the bridge to get a better view.

The boat's crew seems to be in danger of losing control and crashing into the bridge.

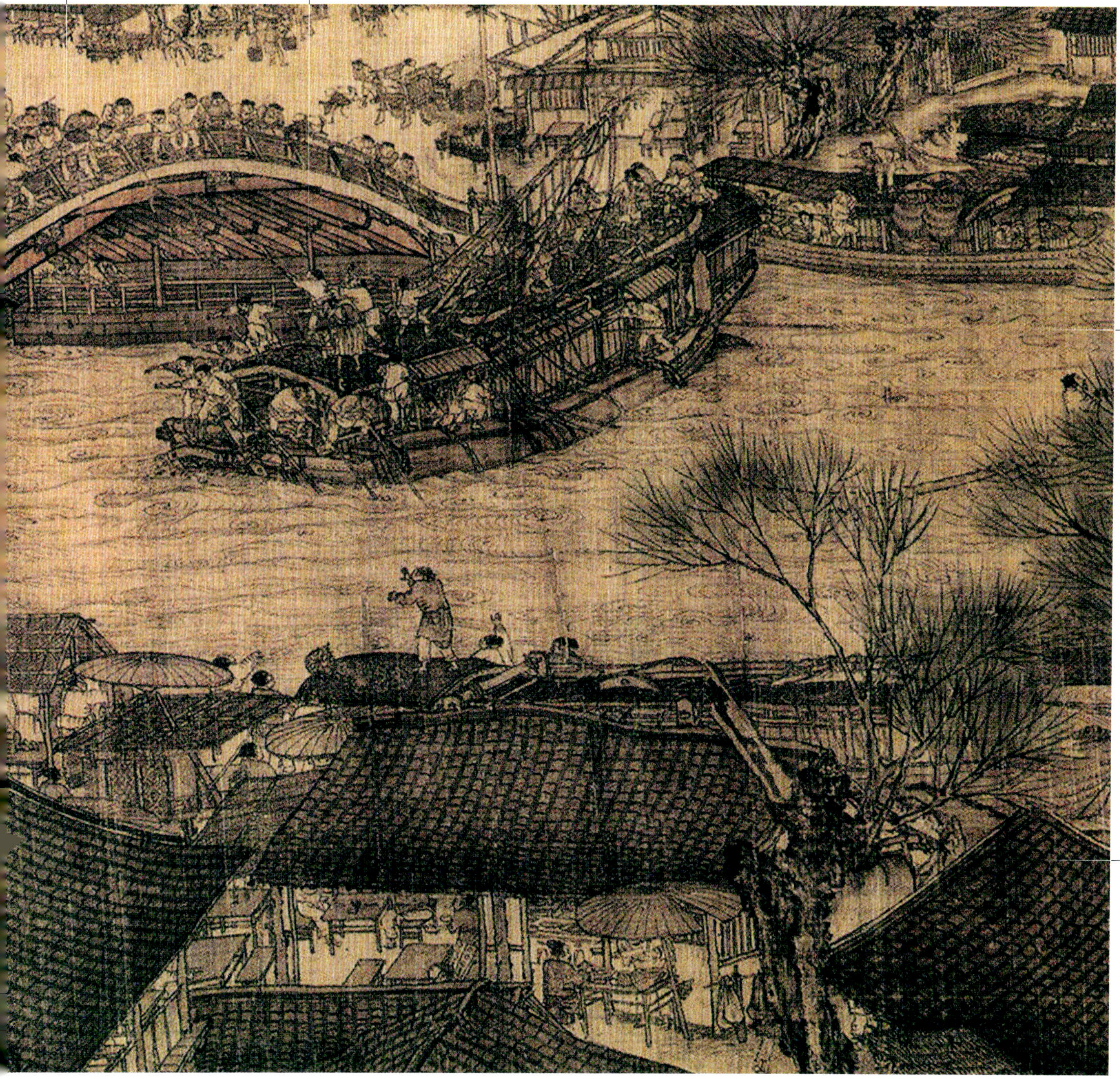

The river depicted here may be the Bian River flowing through the Northern Song capital (present-day Kaifeng).

Architectural details are clearly depicted, with curving ceramic roof tiles and wooden support beams.

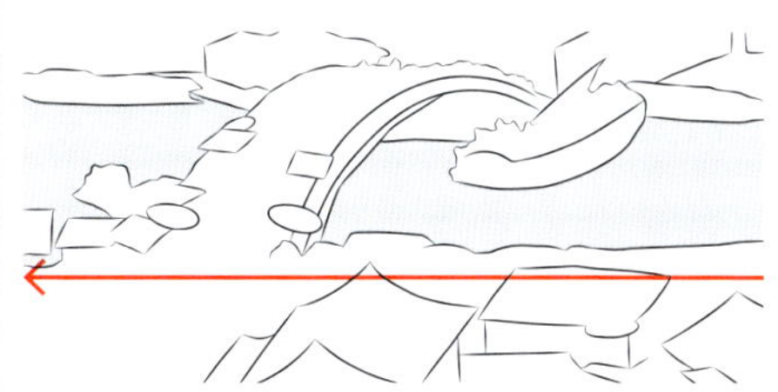

A journey into the city
Handscrolls should be viewed by unfurling from right to left, revealing the scenes one section at a time, as if traveling along a path. Here, the viewer walks along the river, from the country to the city.

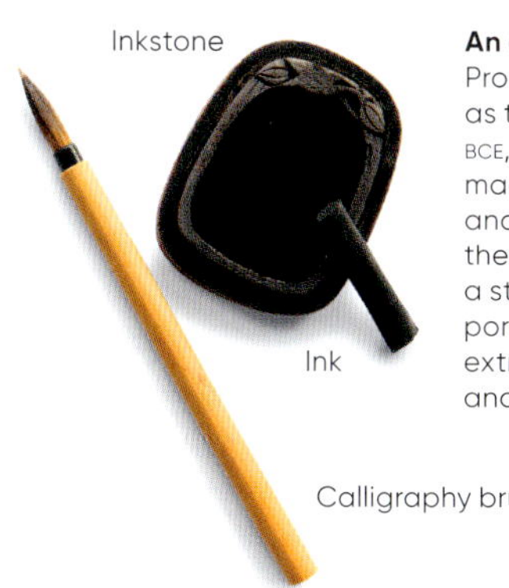

An ancient recipe
Produced as early as the 3rd century BCE, Chinese ink is made from soot and animal glue, then formed into a stick, for portability. It is extremely stable and does not fade.

"[Its] spellbinding artistry, coupled with the lack of documentation about its maker and subject, guarantee that future generations will find the scroll as tantalizing—and rewarding—as their predecessors."

Valerie Hansen, 1996

Pisa Griffin

Artist unknown c. 950–1150, bronze, 42 × 35 × 18 in (107 × 90 × 46 cm), Museo dell'Opera del Duomo, Pisa, Italy

The magnificent bronze figure of a griffin, a mythical winged creature—part eagle, part lion—decorated with Islamic patterning, may originally have been a noise-producing instrument. Probably made in Spain to grace an Islamic palace, the griffin was later taken to Pisa as war booty and installed on top of the cathedral.

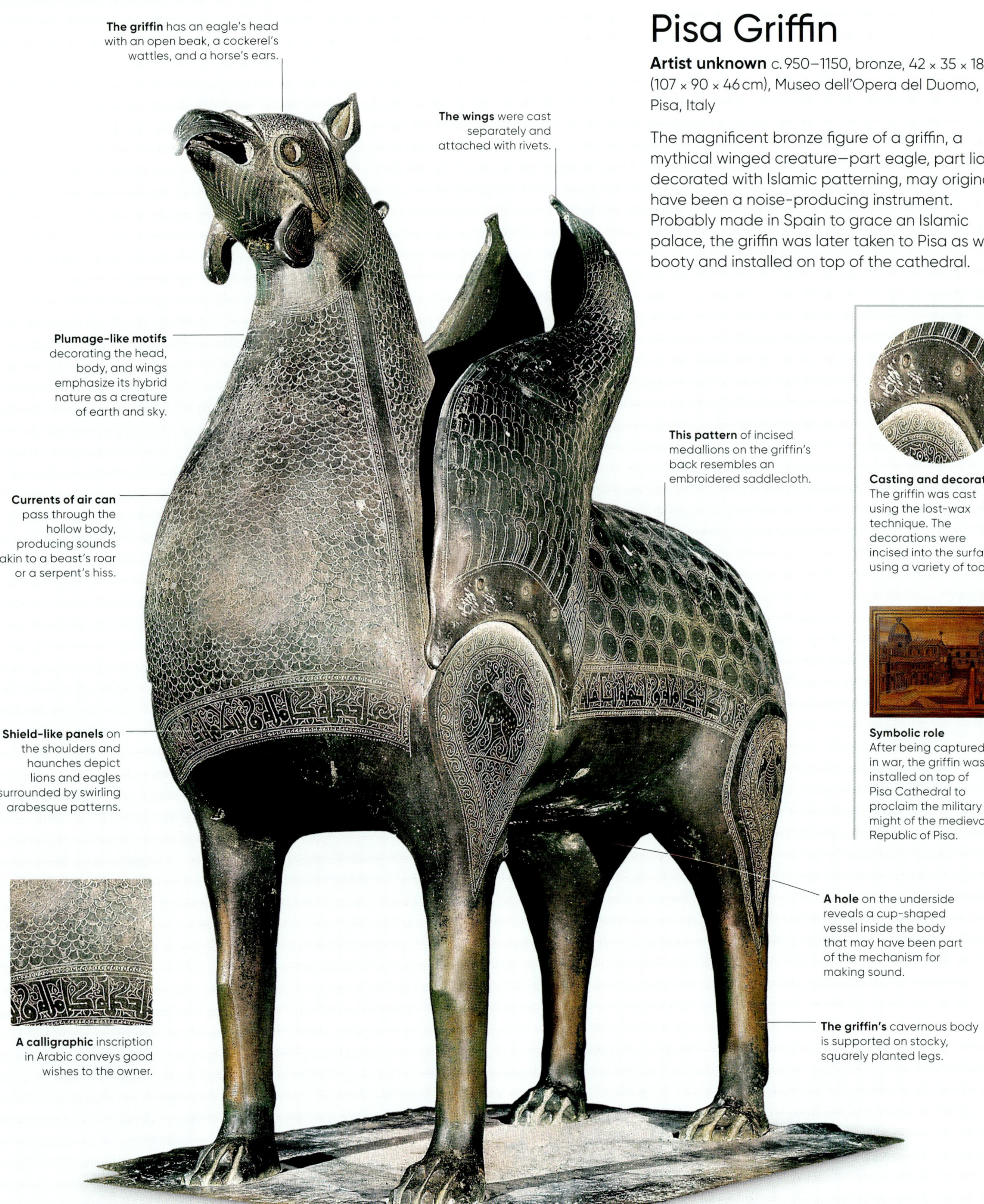

The griffin has an eagle's head with an open beak, a cockerel's wattles, and a horse's ears.

The wings were cast separately and attached with rivets.

Plumage-like motifs decorating the head, body, and wings emphasize its hybrid nature as a creature of earth and sky.

This pattern of incised medallions on the griffin's back resembles an embroidered saddlecloth.

Currents of air can pass through the hollow body, producing sounds akin to a beast's roar or a serpent's hiss.

Shield-like panels on the shoulders and haunches depict lions and eagles surrounded by swirling arabesque patterns.

A hole on the underside reveals a cup-shaped vessel inside the body that may have been part of the mechanism for making sound.

A calligraphic inscription in Arabic conveys good wishes to the owner.

The griffin's cavernous body is supported on stocky, squarely planted legs.

Casting and decoration
The griffin was cast using the lost-wax technique. The decorations were incised into the surface using a variety of tools.

Symbolic role
After being captured in war, the griffin was installed on top of Pisa Cathedral to proclaim the military might of the medieval Republic of Pisa.

Homilies on the Virgin

James of Kokkinobaphos 12th-century, manuscript, 13 x 9 in (33.8 x 23.3 cm), Vatican Library, Vatican City

The *Kokkinobaphos Homilies* are a set of six sermons, written in Greek in Constantinople in the 12th century. The sermons draw moral and spiritual lessons from the life of the Virgin Mary. In this vibrant image focusing on Christ's Ascension, Mary watches her son reclaim his divine status after redeeming humankind.

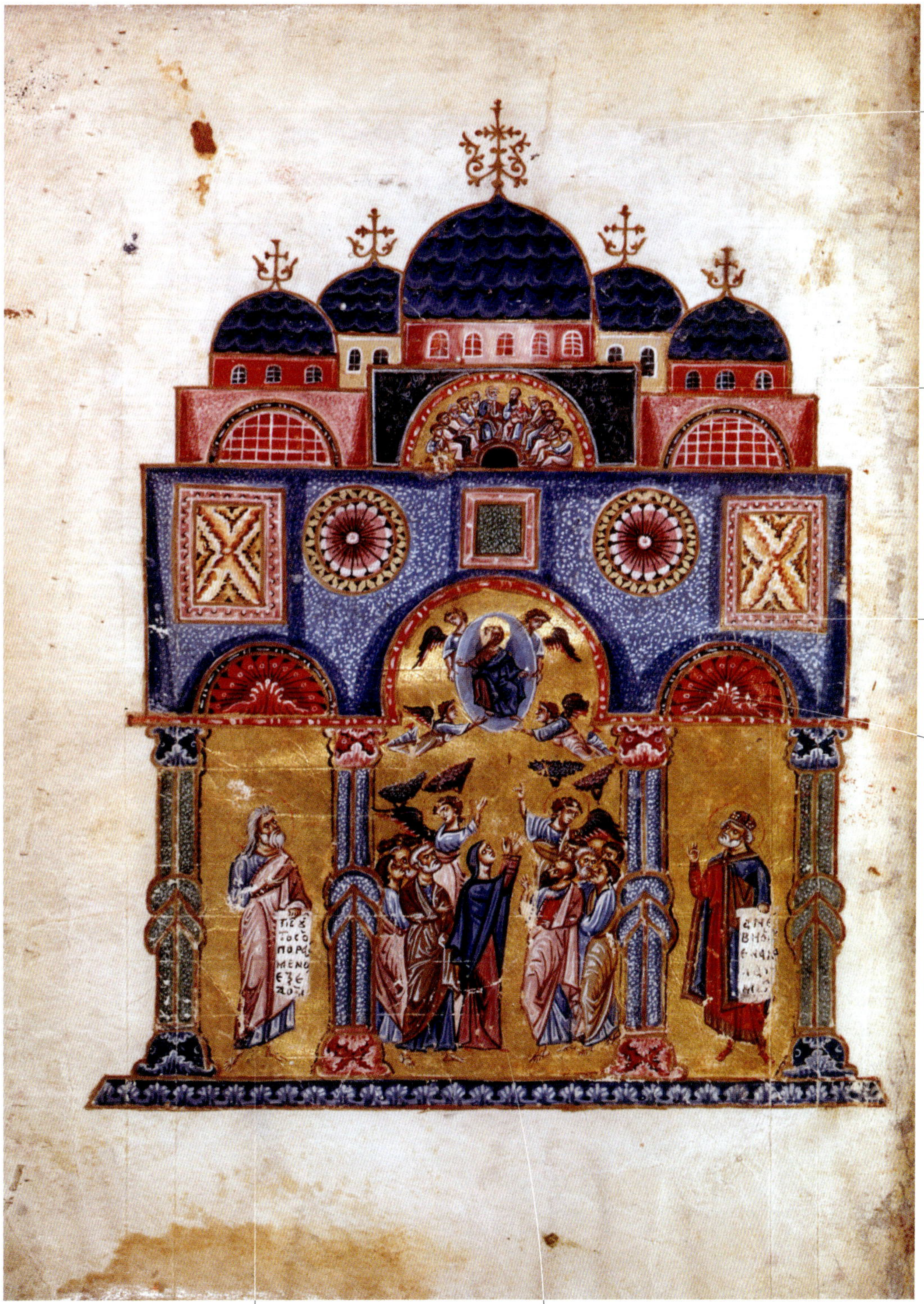

Gold leaf has been used lavishly.

Christ and his Apostles line up beneath the church's dome, recalling the sacred ministry of the Church.

Heaven seems to be indoors. The scale and opulence of the building is a reminder that salvation can only be achieved through the institution of the Church.

Christ's Ascension is depicted as a mosaic or painting inside the church.

The prophet Isaiah, who had predicted the Virgin birth and Christ's purpose, is present to see his prophecy fulfilled.

Mary stands among the disciples. She reaches upward as her son ascends.

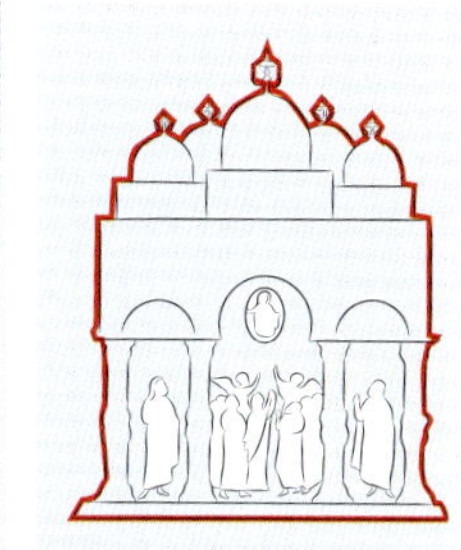

Byzantine church
The church has symbolic importance as the means by which Christ's mission will be fulfilled, but it also acts as a frame for the protagonists. Its Byzantine structure incorporates multiple domes, columns, gold embellishments, and sumptuous mosaic tiling.

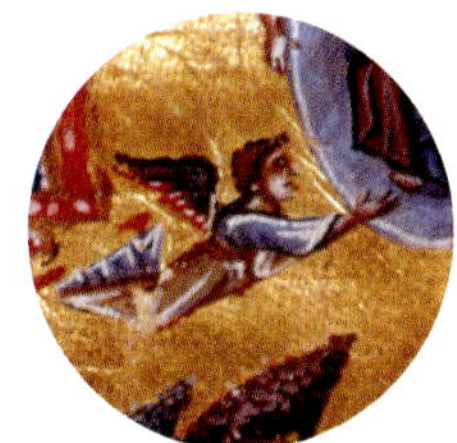

Individuals
As stylized as this image first appears, the human figures (and the angels) are all unique and clearly differentiated. Mary's portrayal shows emotion as well as reverence.

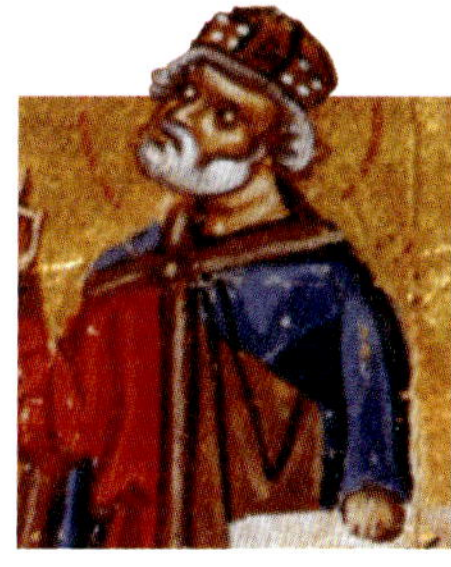

King David is identified by his crown. According to the Gospels, Mary and Christ were descended from the line of David.

Ife Head

Artist unknown c. 1250–1450, brass, 14 × 5 in (35 × 12.5 cm), British Museum, London, UK

Celebrated for its naturalism and craftsmanship, this near life-size head was one of 13 heads discovered behind the royal palace of Ife, Nigeria, in 1938. The Yoruba people, who make up more than a fifth of Nigeria's population, consider the city to be the origin of creation and the center of their culture. While its exact purpose is debated, the head undoubtedly represents someone of noble status, possibly a king (*ooni*).

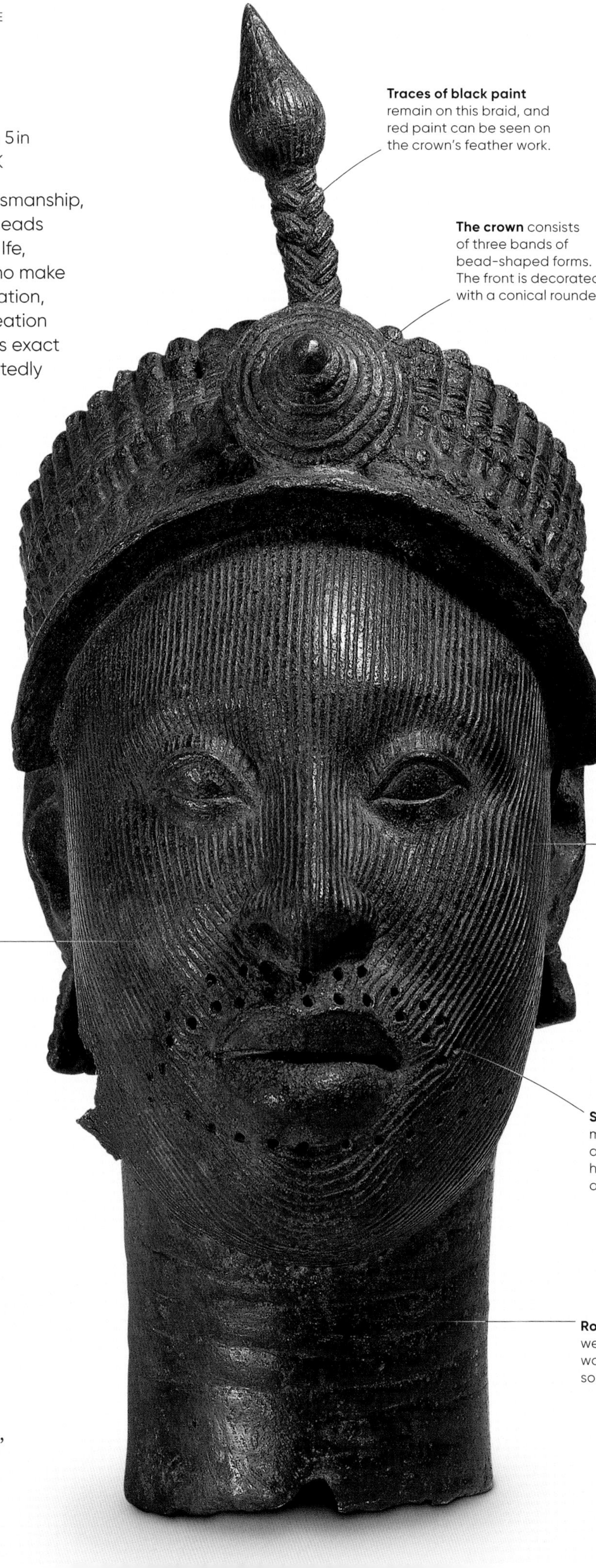

Traces of black paint remain on this braid, and red paint can be seen on the crown's feather work.

The crown consists of three bands of bead-shaped forms. The front is decorated with a conical roundel.

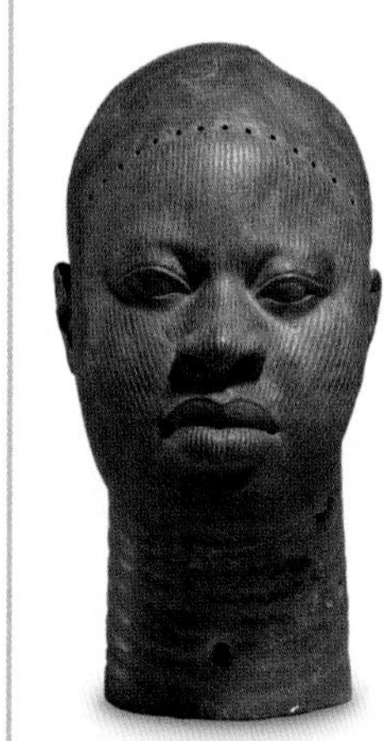

Processional figure Some Ife heads, as shown in this cast, have large punctured holes around the base of the neck. Originally, they may have been attached to dressed wooden mannequins for processions.

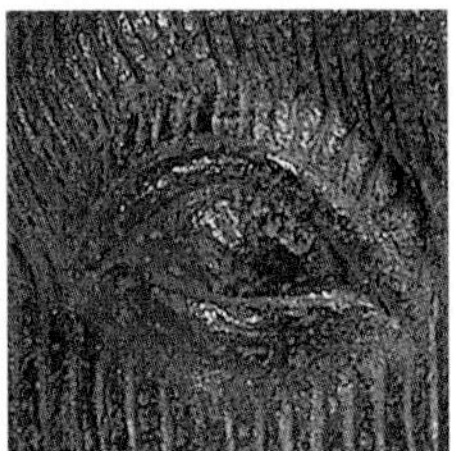

The eyes of Ife heads are small, slanted, and blank, though pigment traces elsewhere indicate that they may have originally been painted.

The striations cover the face except the lips and lower eyelids. They could represent a beaded veil, scarifications, or face paintings, or could have been added to accentuate the contours of the face.

The composed and contemplative expression is typical and prized in Yoruba art.

Strings of black beads may once have been attached to these holes. They acted as facial hair.

Rolls on the neck indicate wealth and beauty—they would be attributes of someone who is well fed.

> "Because of the overwhelming political influence, advanced technology, and highly developed religious traditions of the city of Ifè, it was regarded as a civilization above all others in Yoruba thought."
>
> Rowland Abiodun, 2014

Virgin and Child

Artist unknown 1260, ivory, 16 in (41 cm) high, Louvre,Paris, France

The Virgin Mary bends her body at the hip to bear the weight of the infant Christ, a pose that emphasizes her slender figure. Sculpted in the round by an anonymous artist, the statue was carved out of a single tusk of ivory. For many years, it was kept in Paris's Sainte-Chapelle.

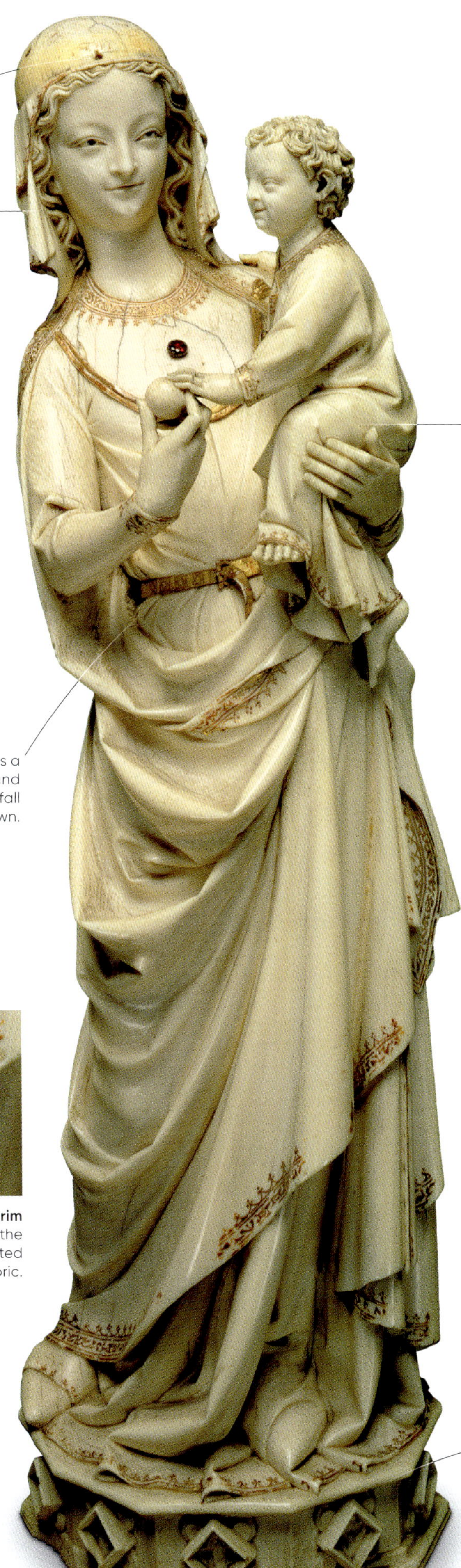

A golden crown was once attached by these holes.

Mary's headdress, like her gown, follows the aristocratic fashion of the 13th century.

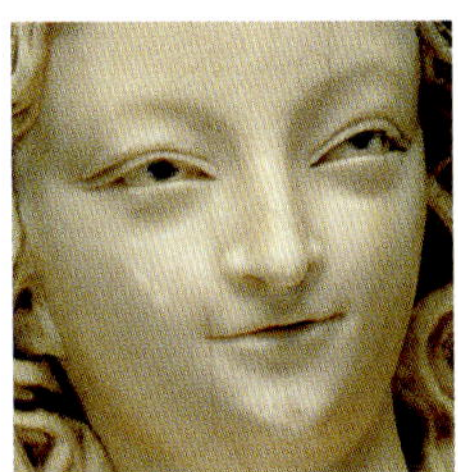

Mary's expression is cheerful, even humorous, rather than solemn or spiritual.

The belt provides a color contrast and adds interest to the fall of the gown.

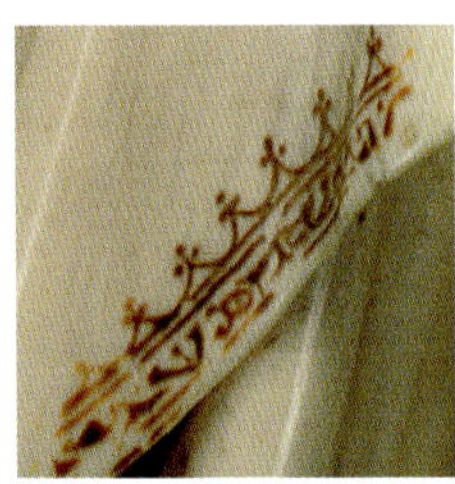

The ornate trim draws the eye to the sumptuously sculpted folds in the fabric.

In order to convey wisdom, the Christ Child is often portrayed as an older, miniature child in medieval art. Here, his body balances his mother's stance.

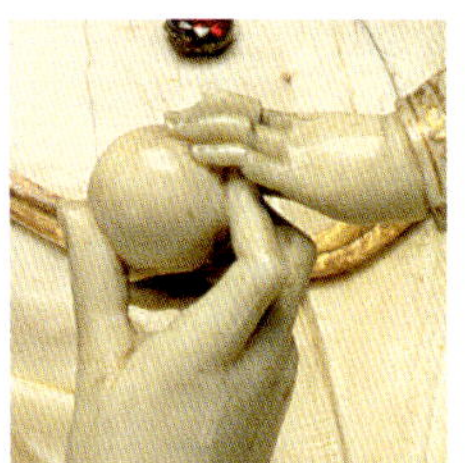

The apple recalls the fruit taken by Eve in the Garden of Eden. According to Church doctrine, Mary reversed that "original sin" by giving birth to Christ.

> "that most beautiful of chapels, the chapel of the king …"
>
> Jean de Jandun, 1323

The Virgin stands on a pedestal, increasing the impression of height.

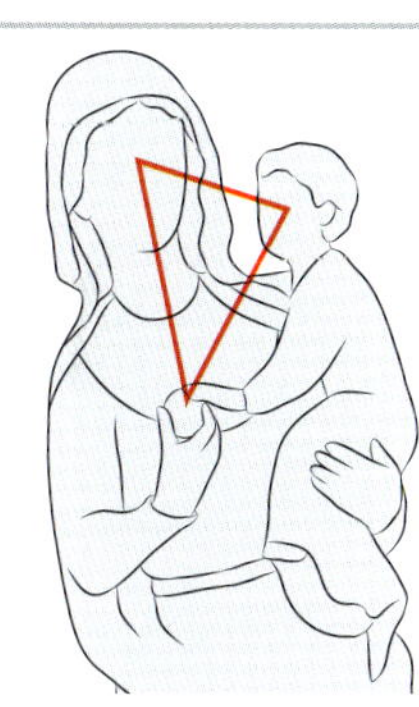

Sacred triangle
The child reaching out for the apple adds a touch of realism. The apple also forms a triangle with the faces of Christ and the Virgin, suggesting Christ's wish to redeem humanity by assuming responsibility for its sins.

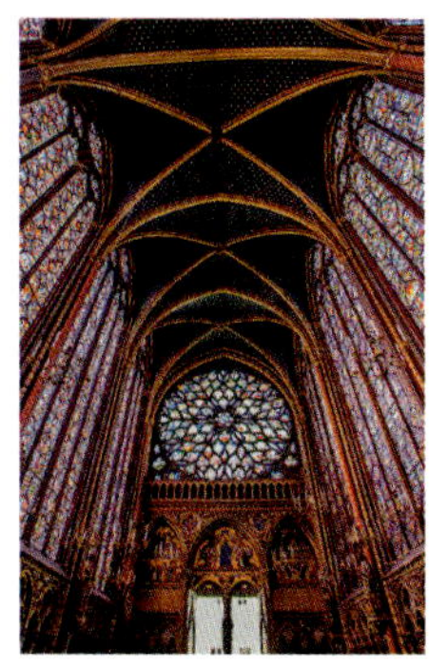

Gothic setting
The Virgin's slender proportions conform to 13th-century standards of feminine beauty, but also with the Gothic aesthetic. Paris's Sainte-Chapelle, where the statue was once kept, exemplifies the Gothic style with its soaring windows and arches.

Annunciation and Nativity

Nicola Pisano 1260, marble relief, 33 × 44 in (85 × 113 cm), Baptistry of Pisa Cathedral, Pisa, Italy

This panel is one of six that together form a hexagonal pulpit. It features significant events in the early life of Jesus: the Annunciation of the Incarnation; a Nativity scene; and the bathing of the infant Christ. The style of the sculpted reliefs was a powerful, unprecedented blend of ancient classicism and French Gothic.

Mary draws back with disbelief as the Archangel Gabriel announces that she will bear the Son of God.

Emanating serenity, a reclining Mary dominates the panel's center. Her form is classical, her emotion typical of Gothic art.

Angels and shepherds attend the Nativity. Christ's crib beside them resembles a coffin—an allusion to his later Crucifixion.

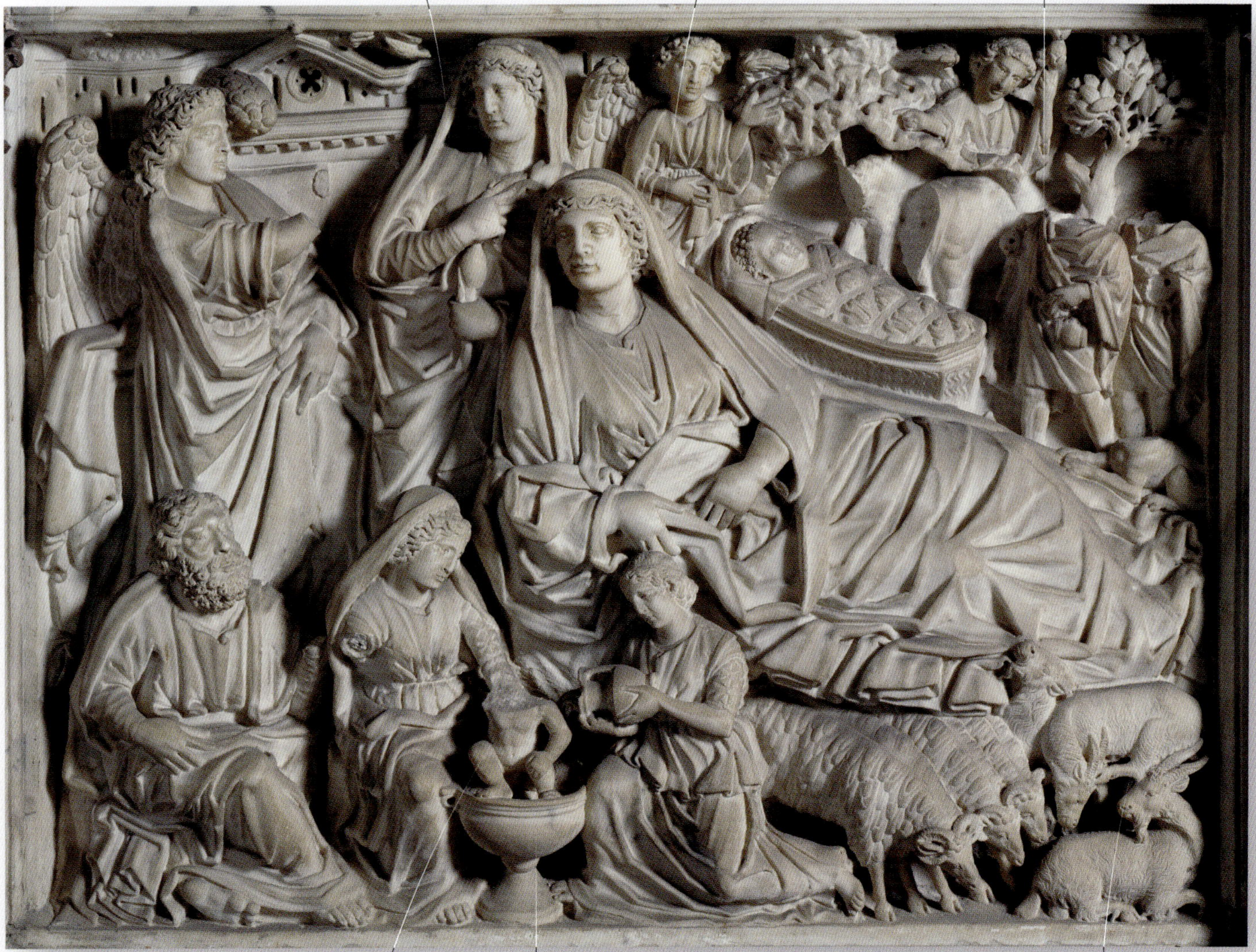

The Christ Child's upright pose as he is bathed (the head and right arm now lost) anticipates his death and Resurrection.

Christ's bathing vessel is a reminder that the pulpit is within a baptistry. Its form also references the Communion chalice.

Precisely observed animals, particularly the ear-scratching goat, demonstrate Pisano's love of natural details.

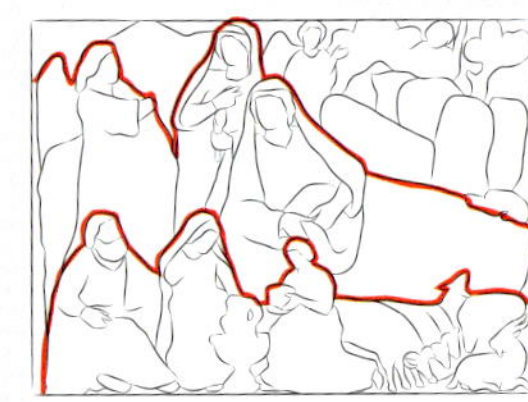

Composition
Pisano forsakes the single plane traditionally used in Gothic sculpture in favor of a lively, overlapping set of three scenes that proceed with their own spatial logic.

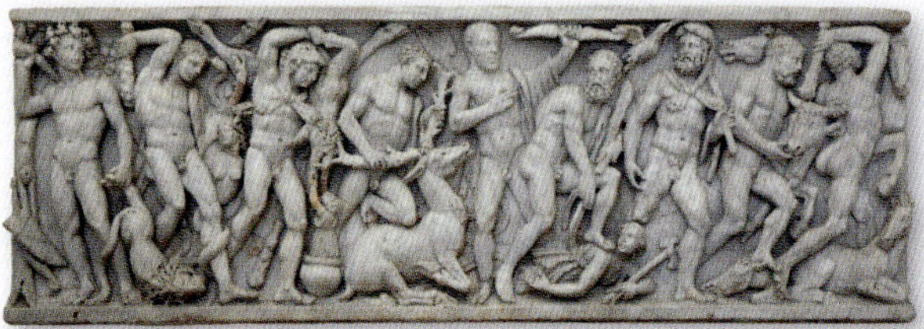

Classical influence
Pisano's figures have a convincing sense of movement in the space they inhabit, recalling figures on ancient Roman sarcophagi.

Night Attack on the Sanjô Palace

Artist unknown 13th century, ink and color on paper, detail from handscroll, 16 × 276 in (41.3 × 700.3 cm), Museum of Fine Arts, Boston, US

Depicting an episode from a notorious 12th-century Japanese insurrection, this work effectively conveys the terror and chaos of the surprise attack that destroyed the Sanjô Palace in Japan's then capital, Kyoto. The individualized figures and the dynamic composition create a gripping narrative as the violence escalates. It is a fine example of "otoko-e", a masculine style that often depicted fighting.

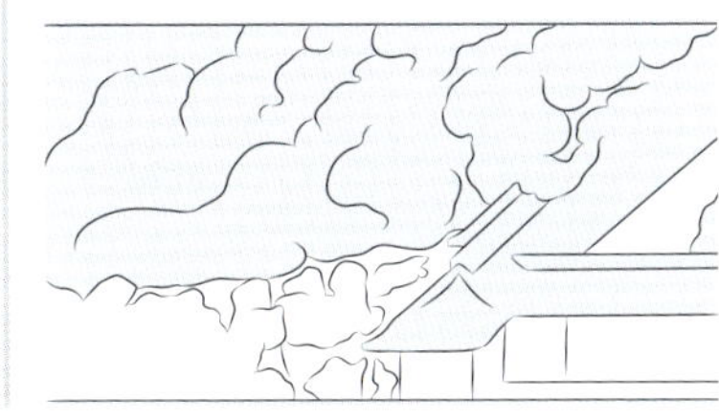

Composition The handscroll (*emaki*) format, often used for narrative paintings, typically presents a bird's-eye view from above and at an angle.

Fire swirls, smolders, and wavers, creating one of the most powerful images of a burning building in art.

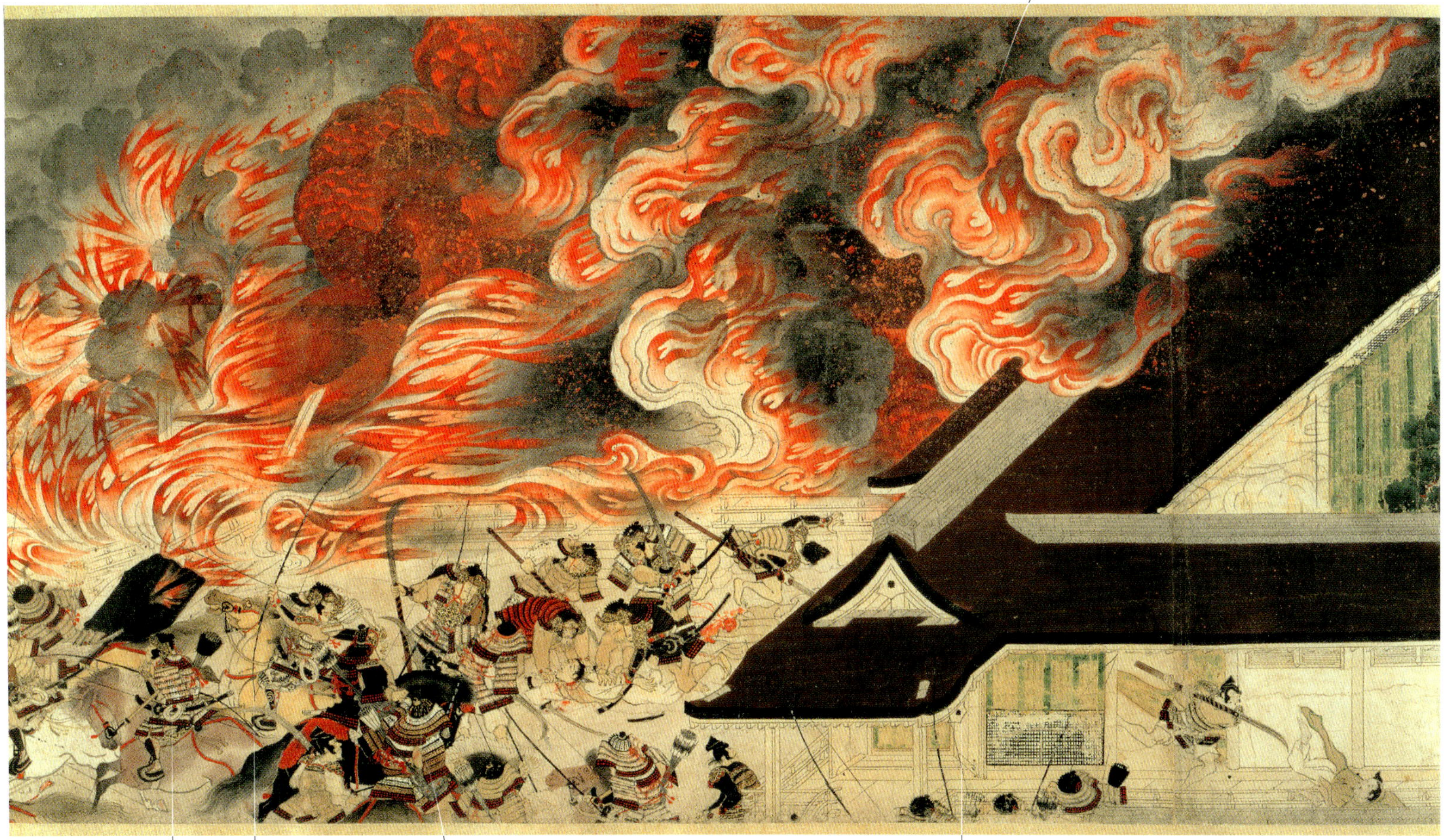

The cavalry heads toward the palace, leading the viewer's eye on to the next scene.

Bows were more commonly used than swords in medieval Japan.

This high-ranking soldier wears *ō-yoroi* (great armor) designed for cavalry officers and accurately depicted here.

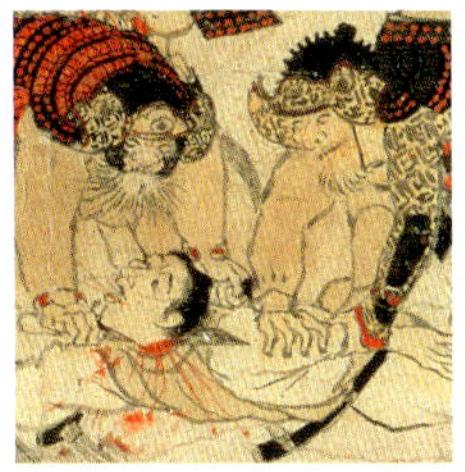

A man escapes from the burning palace only to be captured by the soldiers and decapitated.

The palace, depicted in fine architectural detail, was the home of retired emperor Go-Shirakawa, who was abducted by the insurgents during the attack.

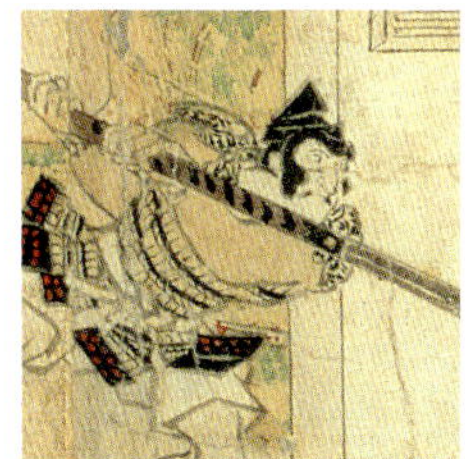

The animallike faces of the soldiers suggest the brutality of their acts.

The Virgin and Child Enthroned, with Narrative Scenes

Margarito d'Arezzo c. 1263–1264, tempera on wood, 36 × 72 in (92.1 × 183.1 cm), National Gallery, London, UK

Characteristic of the Italo-Byzantine style, Margarito d'Arezzo's painting uses Byzantine motifs, iconography, and hierarchy while also incorporating novel elements such as an increased naturalism and narrative scenes. Renaissance critics such as Giorgio Vasari and 19th-century art historians tended to dismiss such early Italian paintings and only referred to them in order to show the evolution of the Italian Renaissance. Nevertheless, the fine craftsmanship and artistic self-awareness exemplify the artist's mastery.

The two scenes top left show the Nativity (left) and St. John the Evangelist being tortured in a cauldron of boiling oil.

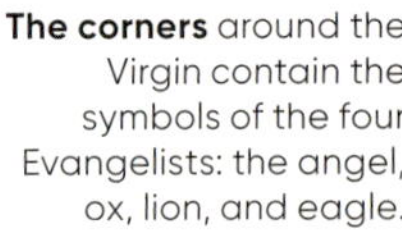

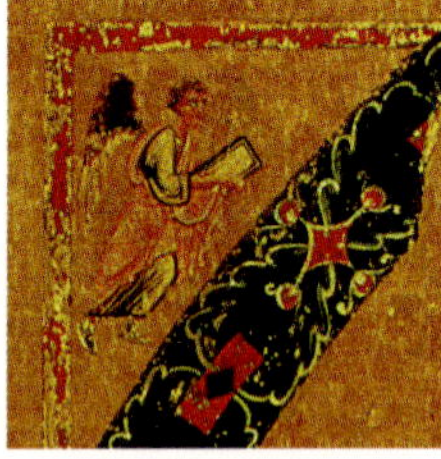

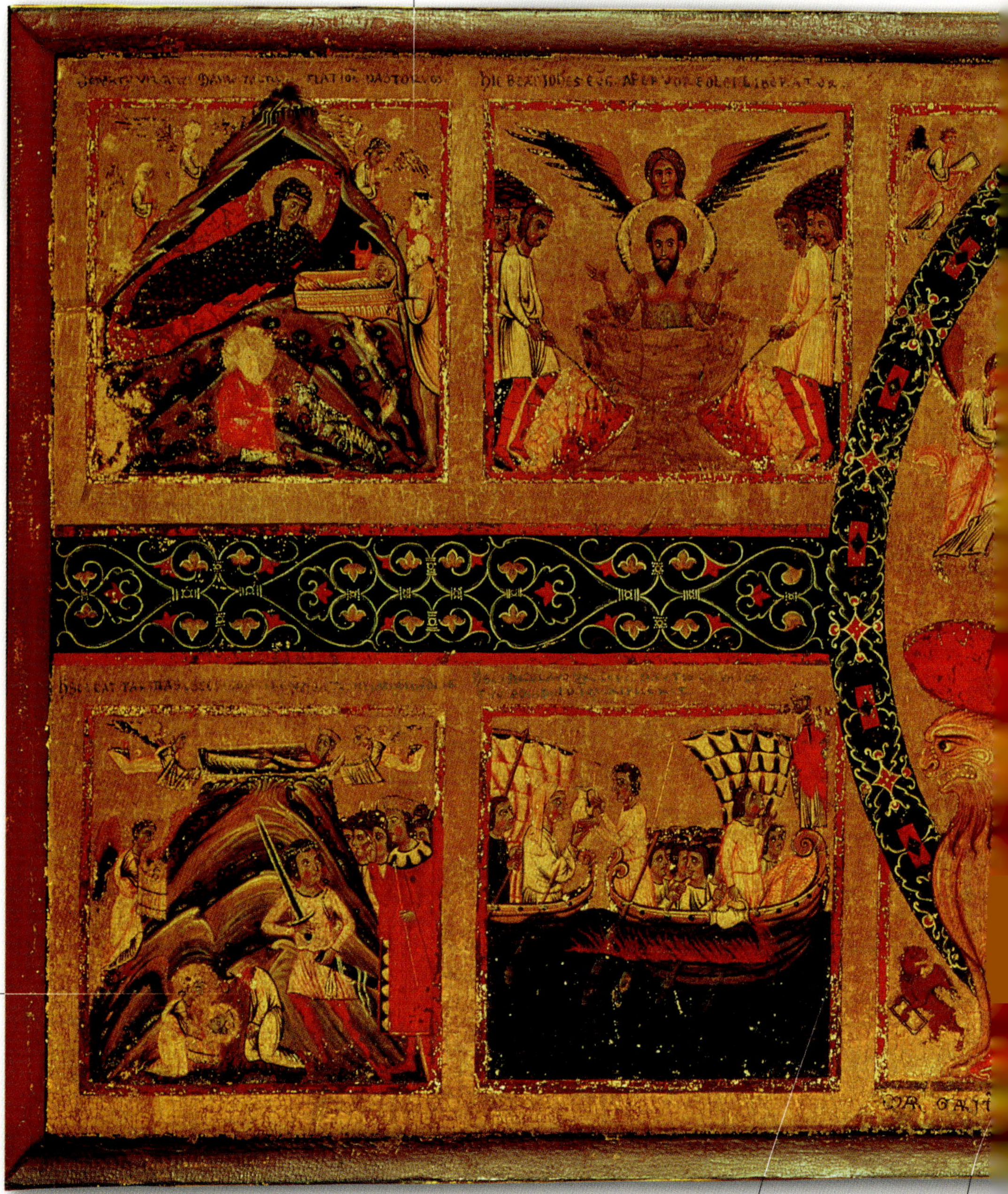

The corners around the Virgin contain the symbols of the four Evangelists: the angel, ox, lion, and eagle.

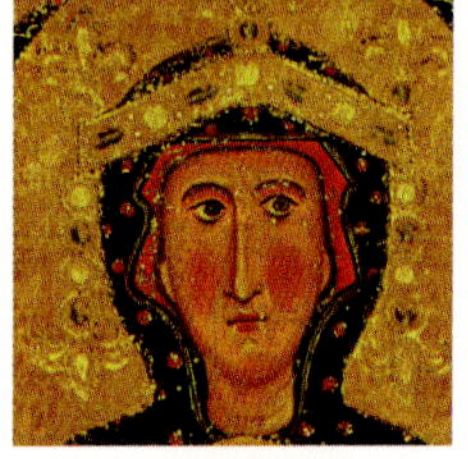

Similar to those worn by Byzantine empresses, the Virgin's headdress emphasizes her divinity while grounding her in contemporary styles.

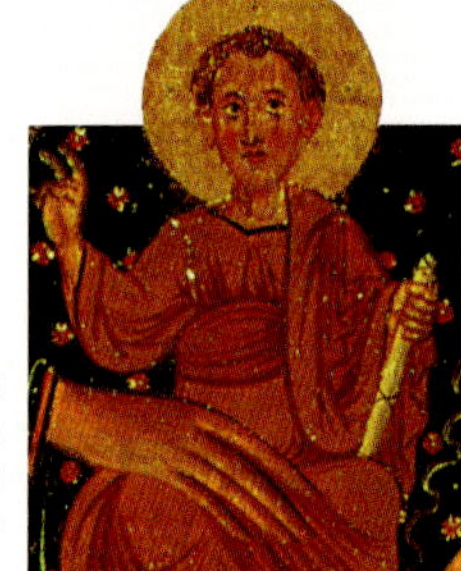

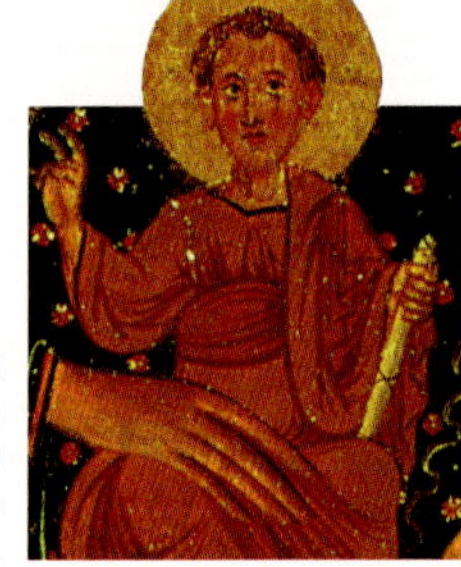

Christ is depicted as a small man, rather than a child, and holds a scroll symbolizing the Word of God.

Two panels bottom left show the beheading of St. Catherine of Alexandria (left) and St. Nicholas saving a ship from the devil, who is disguised as a nun (right).

The throne on which the Virgin sits is carved with lions, alluding to King Solomon's throne in the Old Testament (1 Kings 10:20).

Margarito d'Arezzo signed his name on this panel.

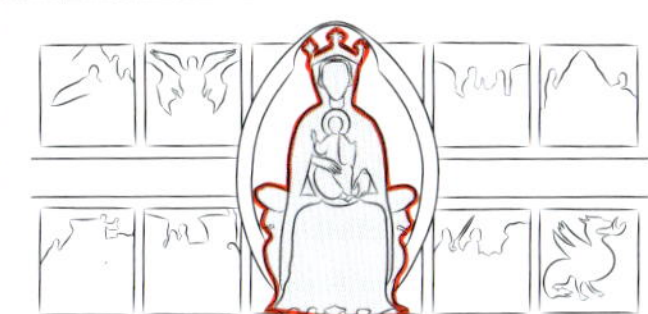

Strict hierarchy
The central and devotional focus of the composition are the Virgin and Child. They are emphasized by their size and proportion; the smaller narrative scenes illustrate the lives of saints.

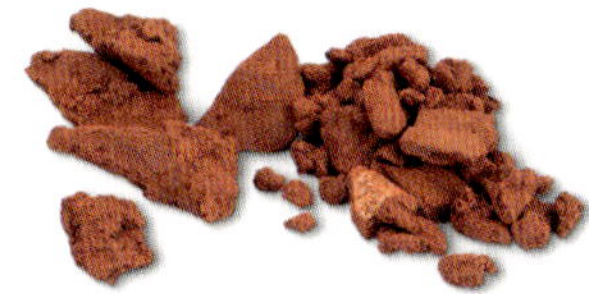

Lustrous effect
Margarito d'Arezzo applied bole, a red clay, on top of the gesso (primer) and under the gold leaf to intensify the luster of the gilding.

"He was the inventor of the method of applying Armenian bole, and of spreading gold-leaf thereon and burnishing it. All these things, never seen before, are seen in many of his works ..."

Giorgio Vasari, 1568

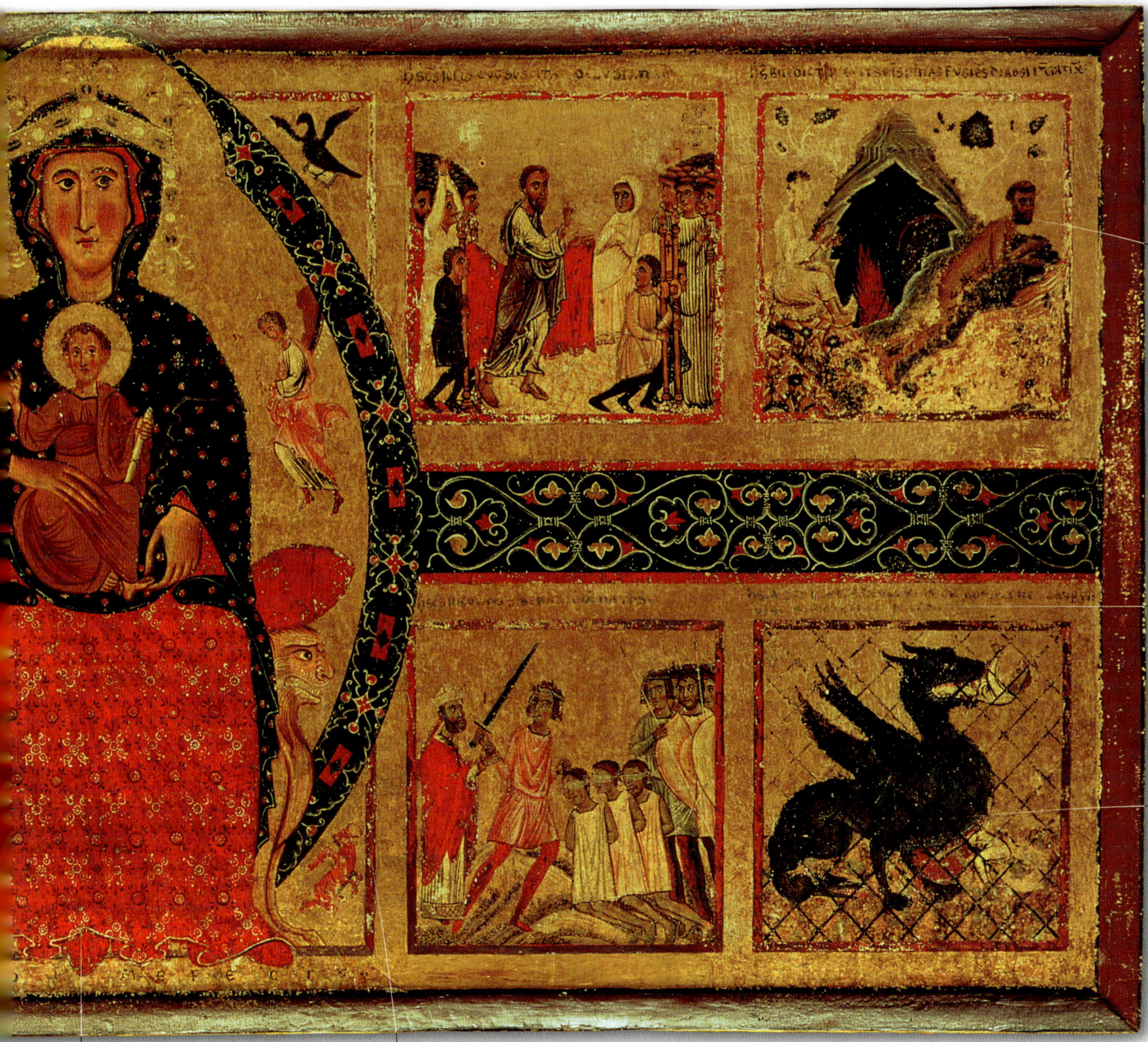

Two scenes top right show St. John the Evangelist raising Drusiana, a Christian woman, from the dead (left) and the temptations of St. Benedict (right).

Inscriptions above each narrative scene identify the protagonist and describe what is taking place.

Two scenes bottom right show St. Nicholas saving three men from being beheaded (left) and Margaret, the patron saint of childbirth, being eaten by a dragon (right).

The Virgin's frontal pose was known as Theotokos, or "Mother of God," in Byzantine art. It is found in both paintings and sculpture.

A mandorla (almond shape) frames the Virgin. This device was used in Byzantine painting to express the divinity and majesty of icons.

Madonna and Child Enthroned with Six Angels

Cimabue c. 1280, tempera and gold on wood panel, 167 × 109 in (424 × 276 cm), Louvre, Paris, France

Against a gold background, the blue-robed Virgin, flanked by angels, sits on an elaborate throne and holds the Christ Child, who holds his hand out in a blessing. This huge work, originally made as an altarpiece for the church of San Francesco in Pisa, is suffused with an air of melancholy at Christ's suffering to come.

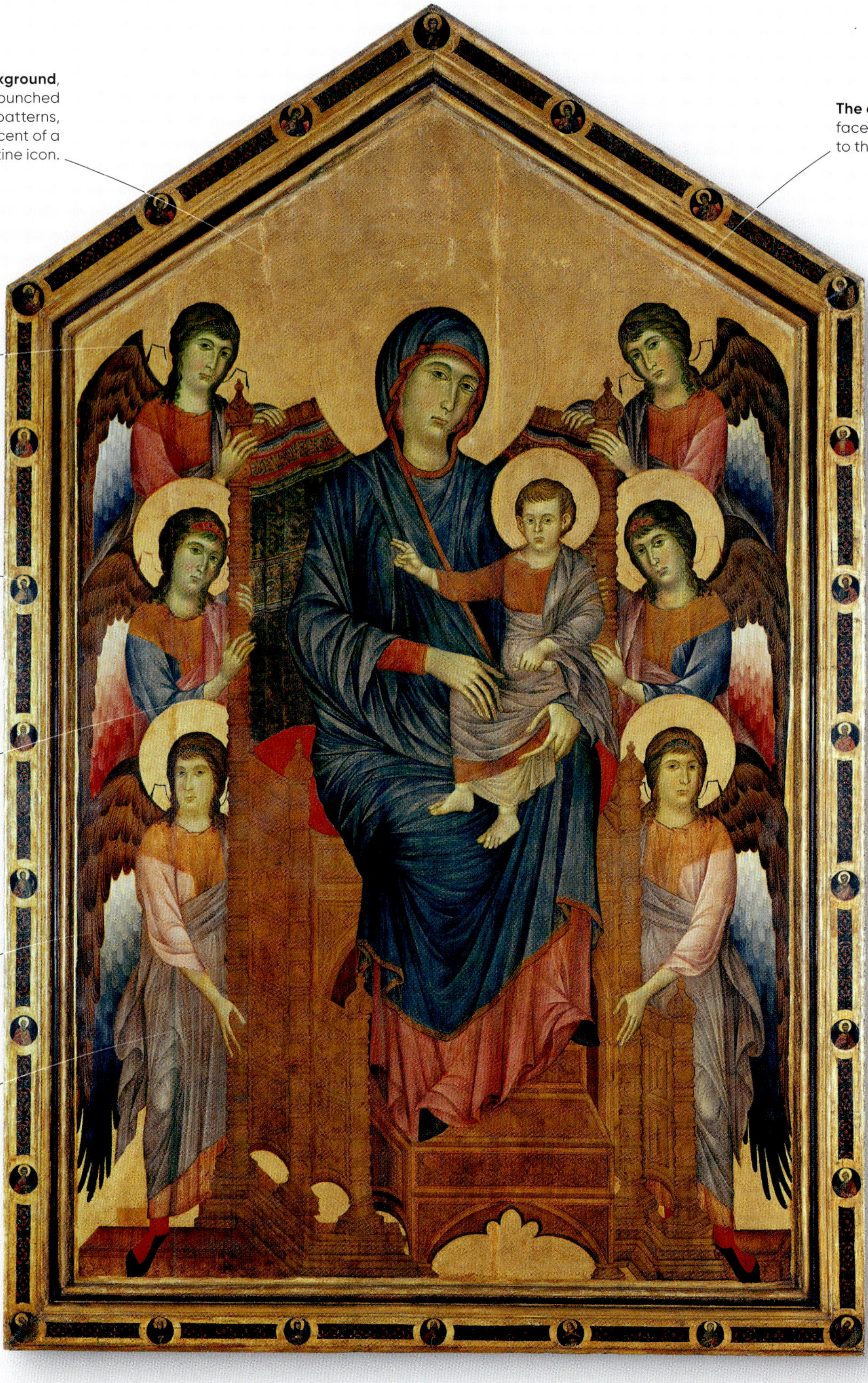

The gold background, covered with punched gold-leaf patterns, is reminiscent of a Byzantine icon.

The angels' unsmiling faces have a stillness to them.

All eyes are looking directly at the viewer, adding to the intensity of the picture.

The frame contains 26 miniature portraits of saints, including the Evangelists on each of the four corners and the Apostles on the sides.

Mary sits on an oversized throne of complex construction. The fabric on the back includes inscriptions resembling Arabic script.

The angels' wings are beautifully colored in shades of brown, white, red, and blue.

The hands are gently elongated to suggest purity and holiness.

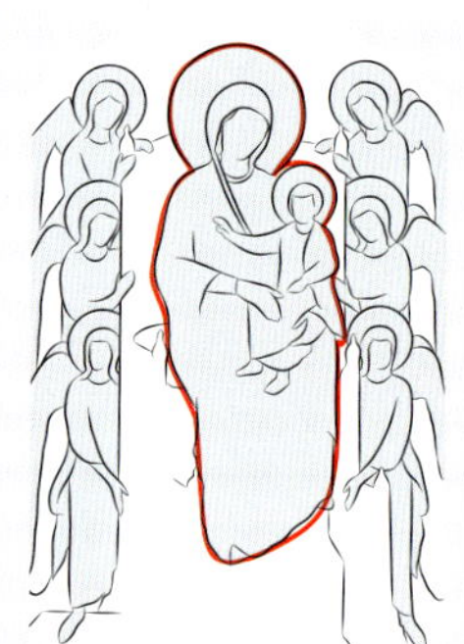

Mirror images
The poses of the six angels to the right and left of the Virgin and Child mirror each other, framing Mary and directing the viewer's focus to her and the Christ Child.

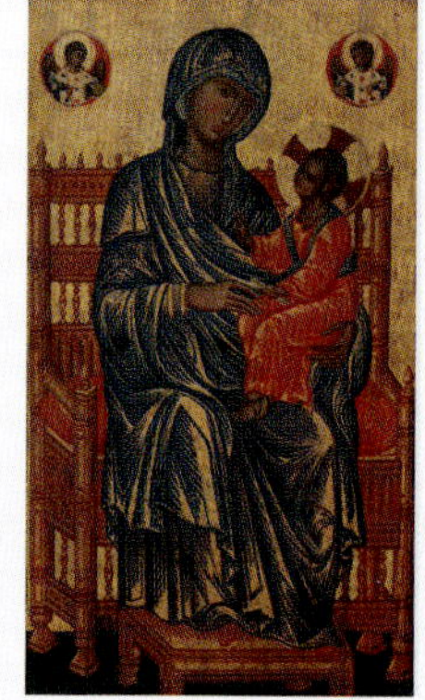

Inspiration
The image of the Virgin and Christ Child sitting on an elaborately carved throne was a common subject of Byzantine icons. Brought to Italy after the Fourth Crusade in 1204, such icons had an enormous influence on Italian art in the 13th century.

Grooms and Horses (detail)

Zhao Mengfu 1296, ink and color on paper, hand scroll, 12 × 70 in (30.2 × 178.1 cm), Metropolitan Museum of Art, New York, US

In the early Yuan period, when ruling Mongols curtailed the employment of Chinese scholar-officials, the groom and horse symbolized a plea for the proper use of scholarly talent. The groom was associated with the legendary figure Bole, whose ability to judge horses was a metaphor for recruiting able government officials. Zhao painted his portion of the hand scroll for an official who may have been a government recruiter.

> "At his leisure he delighted himself with brush and ink. The refinement of his calligraphy and painting and the magic of his brushwork, therefore, were among the best under heaven."
>
> Shen Danian, 1403

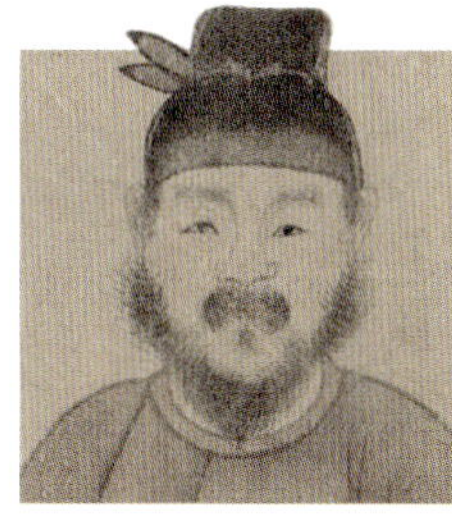

Gazing out at the viewer, the groom stands tall in a symmetrical pose, transmitting an air of quiet confidence. This may be a self-portrait of the artist.

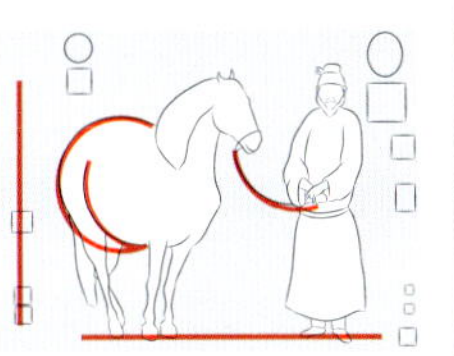

Circles and squares
The arcs in the figures, vertical inscription, and alignment of the horse and groom along the bottom of the image imply the use of a compass and square.

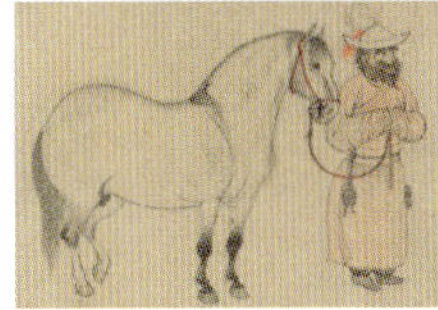

Artistic dynasty
Zhao's wife was the famous poet and painter Guan Daosheng. In 1359, their son Zhao Yong and grandson Zhao Lin were asked to add their own "groom and horse" to this hand scroll.

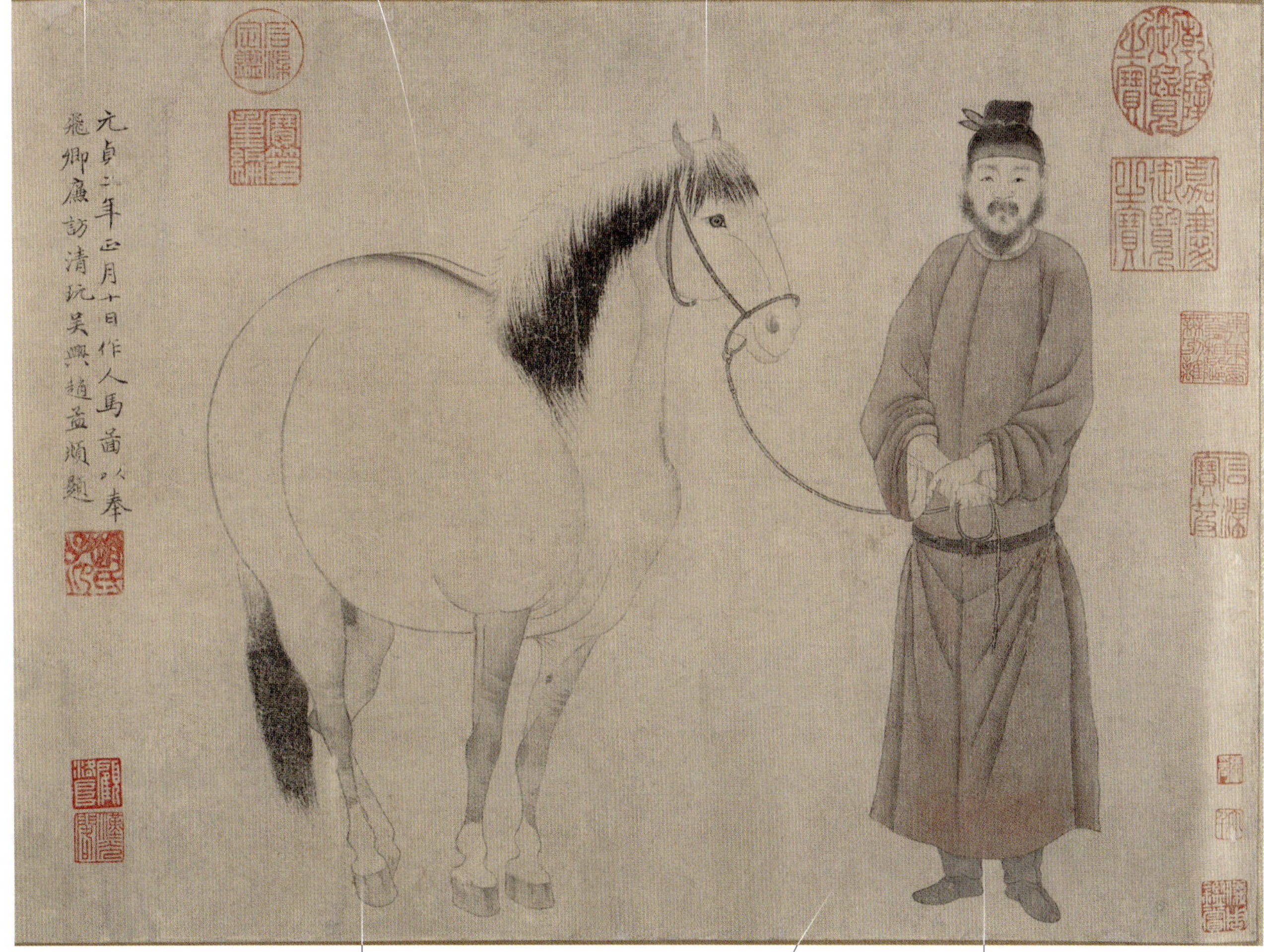

This inscription includes the date and the name of the Surveillance Commissioner Feiqing, for whom the painting was created.

The horse, despite being mostly unpainted, seems muscular and solid, in a relaxed pose.

With a neatly combed mane and tail, and pricked-up ears that face forward, the horse appears interested and alert.

Although simply depicted, the horse represents strength, competence, and readiness to serve—ideal traits in a government official.

Neither a floor nor a background have been depicted, yet the figures seem to stand firmly on the ground.

The groom's calm poise was recognized by an early commentator as reflecting the qualities of the Confucian gentleman, or *junzi*.

Dresden 74

Artist unknown c. 1250–1521, pigment on paper, 8 × 4 in (20.5 × 9 cm) per page, Saxon State and University Library, Dresden, Germany

This page from the *Dresden Codex* shows Itzam Kab' Ayin, the earth crocodile in Maya creation myth, rising into the sky in the context of an eclipse and torrential downpour, likely referencing the destruction of a previous world era. By conflating events from mythic and historical time, the painter emphasizes the dire prophecies arising from Venus's first appearance as the evening star coinciding with an eclipse prediction occurring during a 65-day period before the planting and rainy season.

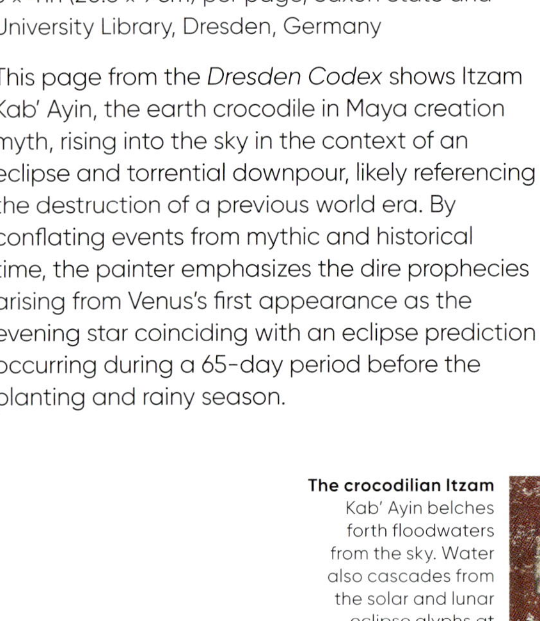

References to "black sky, black earth" describe conditions occurring during solar eclipses, which foretold the end of a world age.

The four glyphs forming the sky band describe Venus as being in the sky and the sun as darkened.

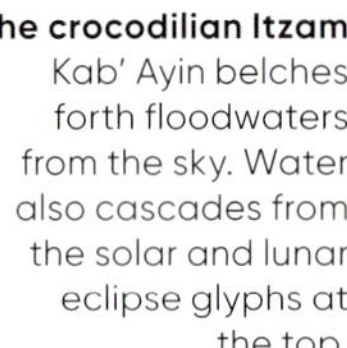

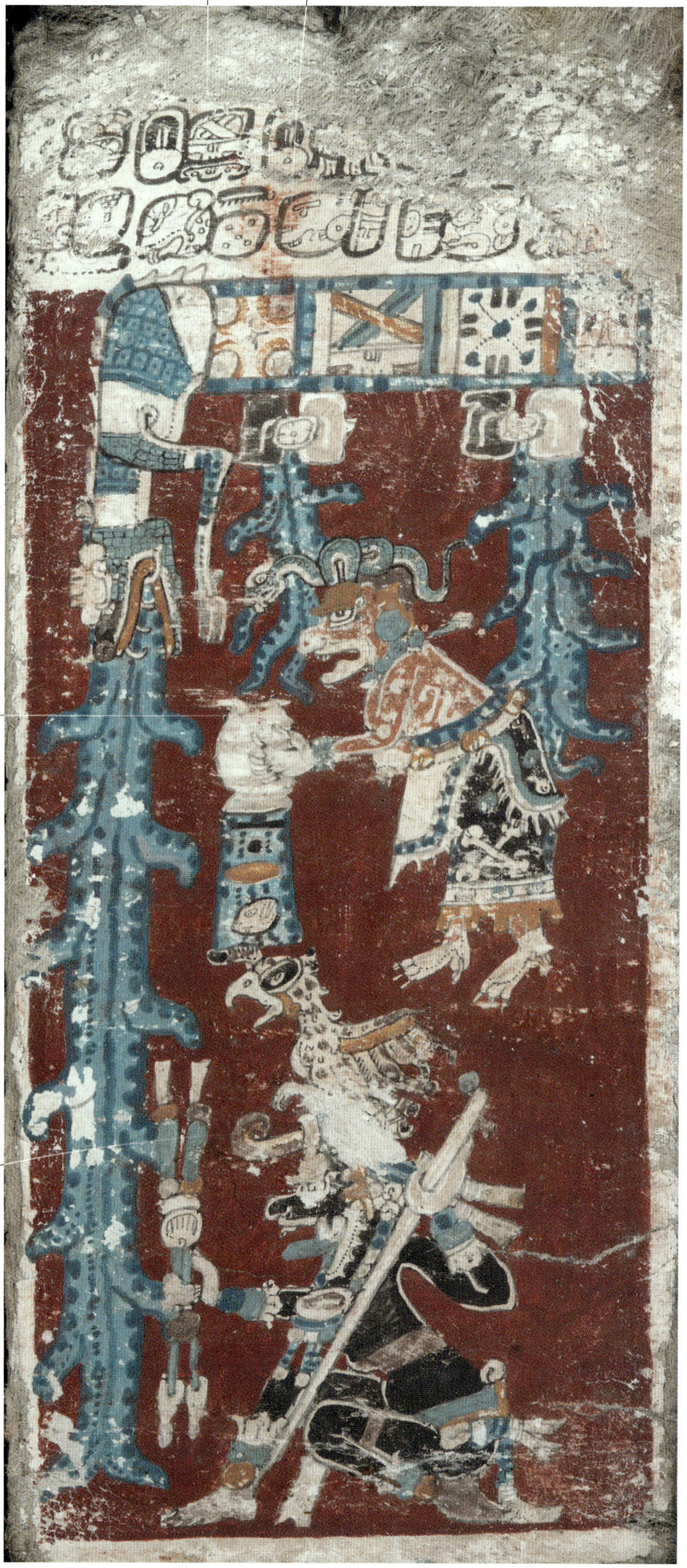

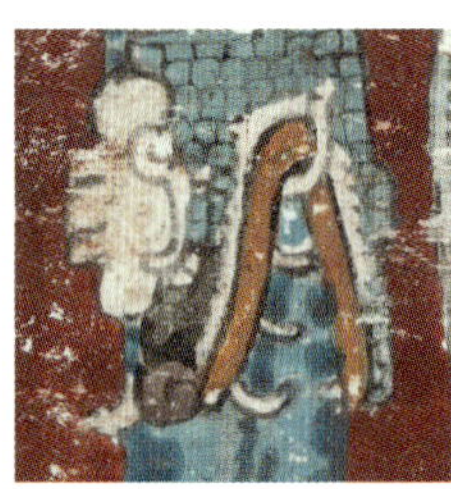

The crocodilian Itzam Kab' Ayin belches forth floodwaters from the sky. Water also cascades from the solar and lunar eclipse glyphs at the top.

Overturning her water jar to announce the prophecies for the rainy season, Chak Chel assumes her jaguar aspect, linking her to the underworld, a region associated with regeneration as well as death.

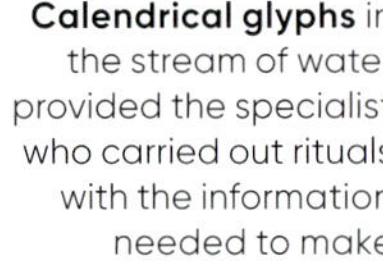

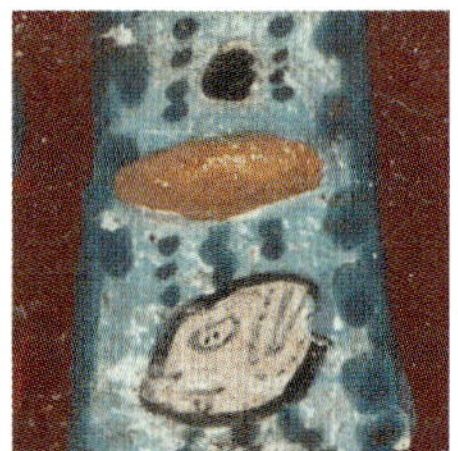

Calendrical glyphs in the stream of water provided the specialist who carried out rituals with the information needed to make predictions.

Damage sustained during the fire-bombing of Dresden in 1945 can be seen in this region.

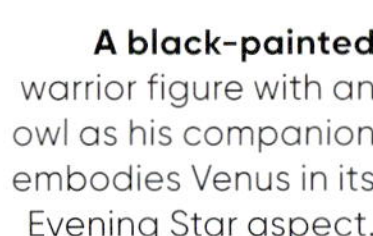

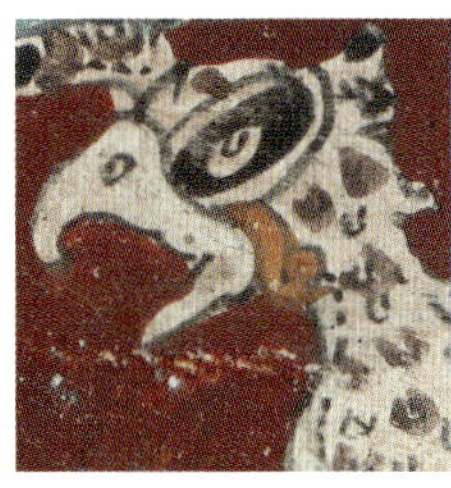

A black-painted warrior figure with an owl as his companion embodies Venus in its Evening Star aspect.

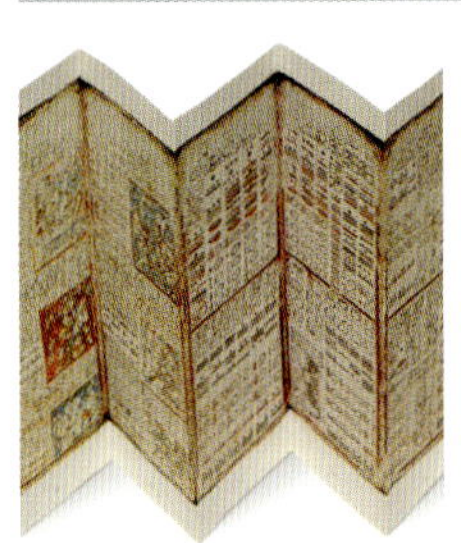

Screenfold book
The *Dresden Codex* has 78 pages and a total length of 11 ft 7 in (3.56 m). The screenfold format can only be seen in facsimiles; the codex itself is encased in glass and cannot be removed without damaging it.

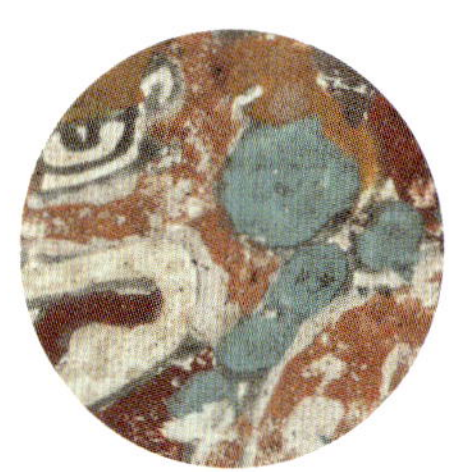

Maya blue
Formed of indigo mixed with palygorskite (found in only a handful of clay sources in the Yucatán Peninsula), blue pigments were used sparingly. Here they signify the jade jewelery worn by Chak Chel.

Walking Buddha

Artist unknown c. 14th century, cast bronze, 11 in (28 cm) high, British Museum, London, UK

The most recognizable silhouette in Thai Buddhist sculpture is the Walking Buddha. Unique to Southeast Asia, it first appeared in the Sukhothai period (c. 1238–1438 CE). Small-scale images are used for private devotion or as votive offerings in temples.

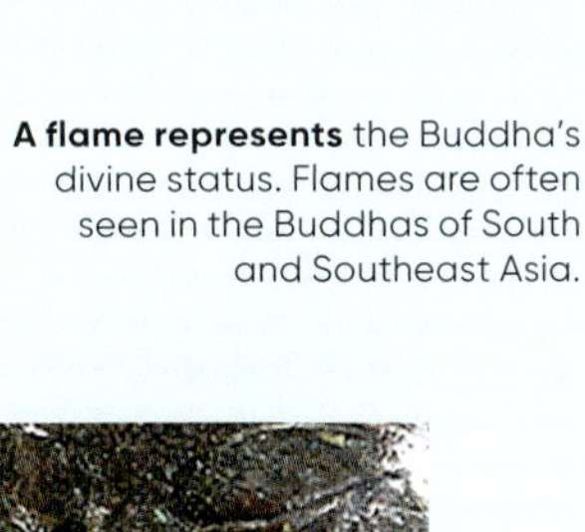

A flame represents the Buddha's divine status. Flames are often seen in the Buddhas of South and Southeast Asia.

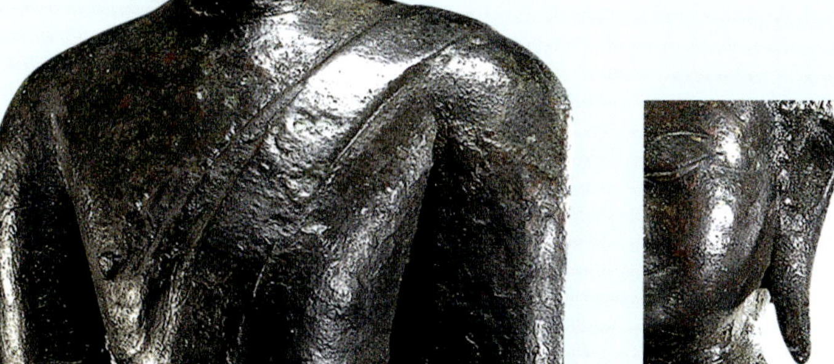

The facial expression is sweet and gentle.

Elongated earlobes are due to the heavy jewelery the Buddha wore as a prince, before his renunciation.

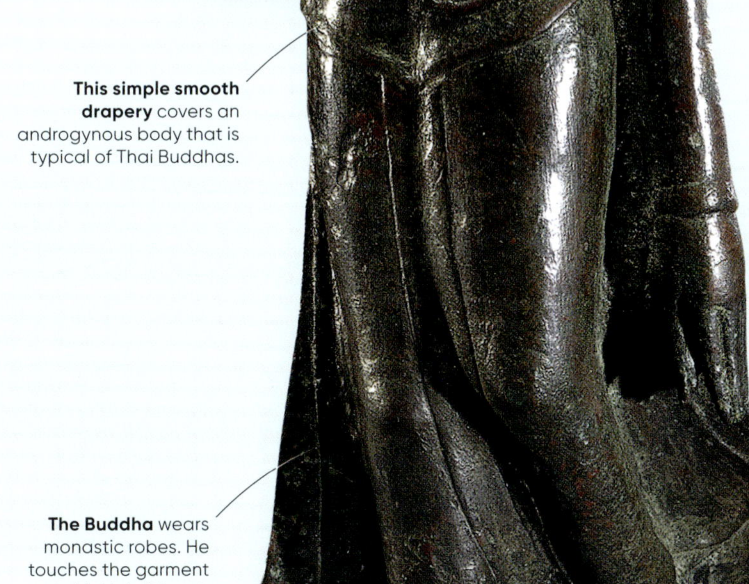

The Buddha raises his hand in *abhaya mudra*, the gesture of protection.

This simple smooth drapery covers an androgynous body that is typical of Thai Buddhas.

The Buddha wears monastic robes. He touches the garment with his left hand.

One foot is lifted, the leg poised in a walking motion. Walking images of the Buddha are still made in Thailand to this day.

> "He by that noble insight gave discourse on the Abhidhamma to the spirits who came, led by his mother, from the myriad worlds."
>
> Buddhaghosa, c. 370–450 CE

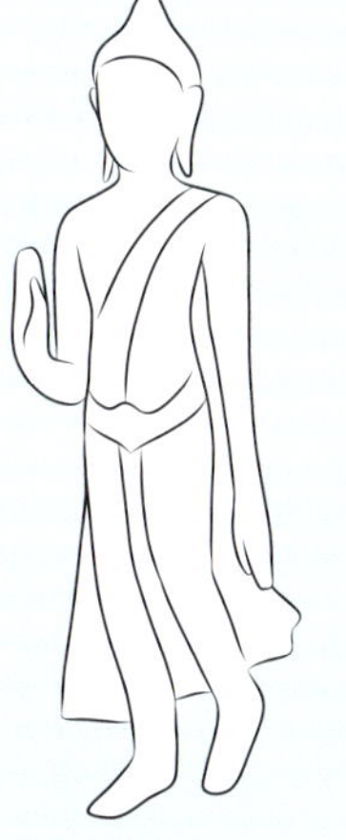

Finely balanced
This bronze work illustrates the mastery of weight distribution calculations to balance the sculpture.

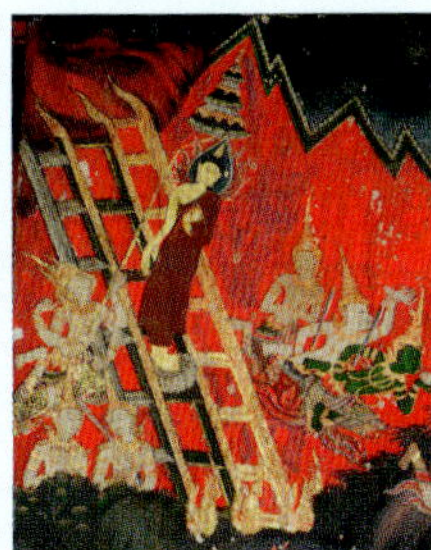

Descent From Heaven
In this mural, located in Buddhaisawan Chapel, Bangkok National Museum, the Buddha is shown descending from heaven and returning to Earth, having preached to his deceased mother.

The Lamentation of Christ

Giotto c. 1305, fresco, 79 × 73 in (200 × 185 cm), Scrovegni Chapel, Padua, Italy

In this pre-Renaissance masterpiece, one in a cycle of frescoes depicting the life of Christ, Giotto shows the dead Christ surrounded by his grieving family and friends while a host of distraught angels fly above.

Using a more natural and expressive style than his predecessors and incorporating perspective, Giotto tells the story of Christ's death and entombment with a new emotional depth.

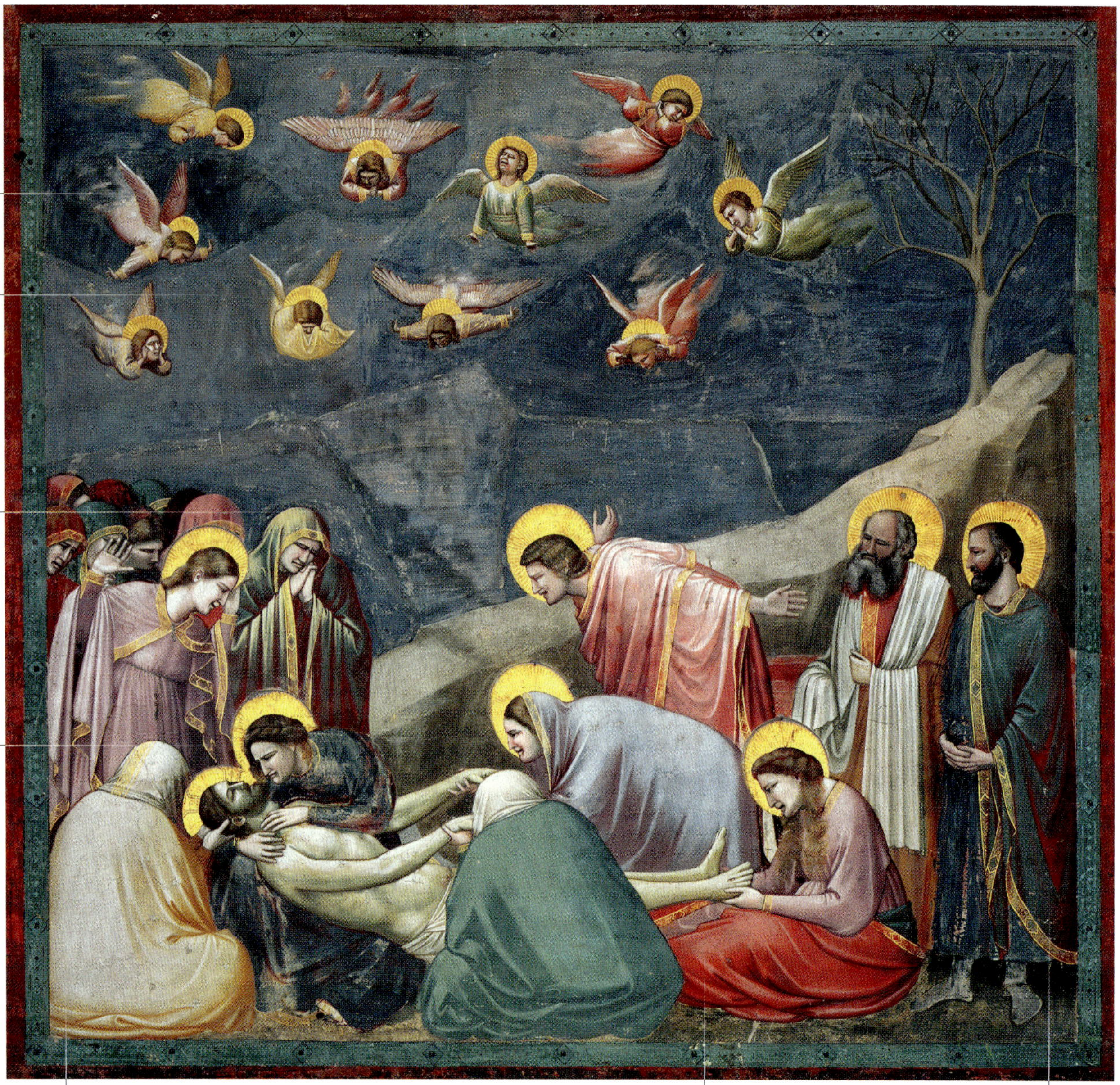

The pink wings and robes of the angels give a delicate lightness to the dark and brooding background.

The angels learn of Christ's death at the same time as the humans. They react just as powerfully.

The most expressive figure is St. John the Baptist. He occupies a central position, his arms outstretched in grief and reminiscent of a crucifix.

The composition focuses on Mary, who is heartbroken. She cradles her dead son as she did when he was a baby.

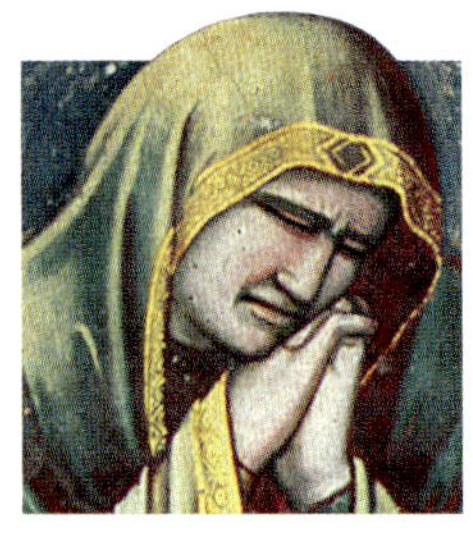

Grief is potently expressed. The mourners' gestures, the way their eyes stare in disbelief, and their contorted mouths evince deep emotion.

Two figures with their backs to the viewer watch what is happening and help draw attention to Christ and Mary.

Mary Magdalene washes Christ's feet, an act she previously performed when he was alive.

To the far right, two saints—probably Joseph of Arimathea and Nicodemus—appear the most restrained in their grief.

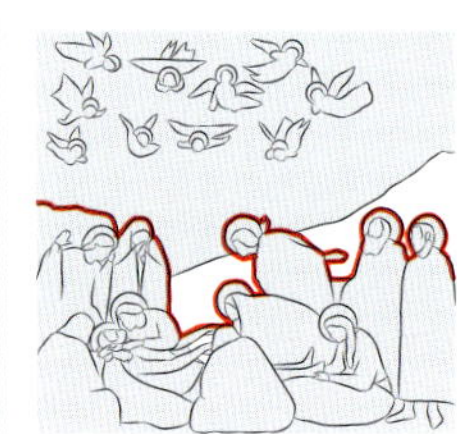

Line of vision
The rocky outcrop behind the figures separates the heavenly and the worldly arenas. It also helps focus attention on Christ and the mourners.

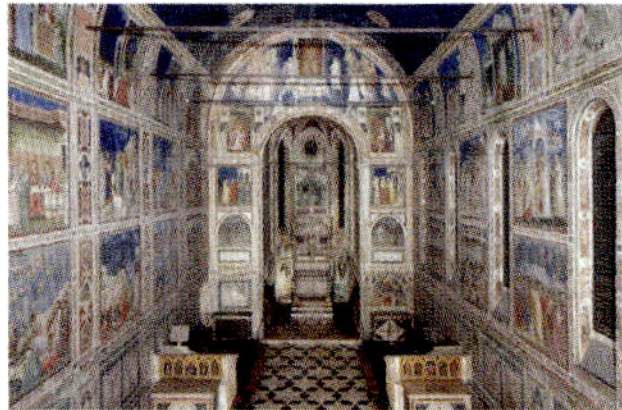

Scrovegni Chapel
The Scrovegni Chapel, also known as the Arena Chapel, was connected to the palace of the Scrovegni, a wealthy banking family. The walls are covered in frescoes and the ceiling is painted with a star-studded sky dotted with images of the saints.

Bamboo Groves in Mist and Rain (detail)

Guan Daosheng 1308, ink on paper, 9 × 45 in (23.1 × 113.7 cm), National Palace Museum, Taipei, Taiwan

One of the few publicly acclaimed female artists of her time, Guan Daosheng was a painter, calligrapher, and poet. While she was adept at painting diverse subjects, her singular style of depicting groves of young bamboo along misty waterways after the rain inspired generations of artists.

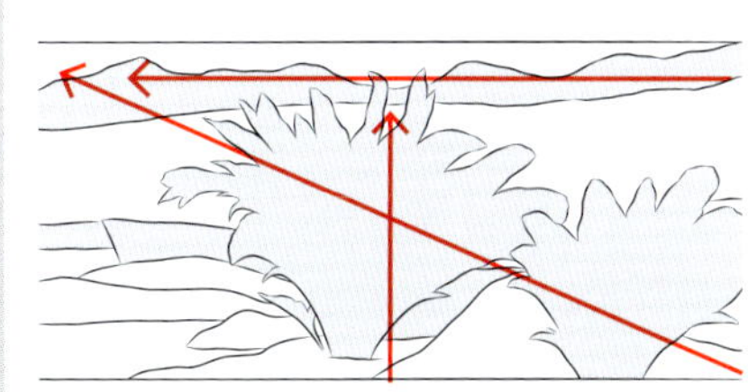

Composition
Transitions from dark to light and large to small create a diagonal path from lower right to upper left, and from foreground to background. In the top half, the mist creates a strong horizontal that leads the eye from right to left as the viewer unrolls the handscroll.

Imperial inscription
To the left of the detail shown here, the Qianlong Emperor (1711–1799) added a poetic inscription: "The long smoke blows down the green ripples." He added his own inscription and seal to many artworks that were held in the imperial collection.

Bamboo, which bends in the wind and stays green in winter, represents strength, flexibility, and perseverance—considered ideal masculine virtues.

Painting bamboo as isolated branches was typical until Guan reintroduced the integration of whole bamboo plants into landscape settings.

This unpainted area represents the mist, floating between the bamboo in the foreground and the stalks behind.

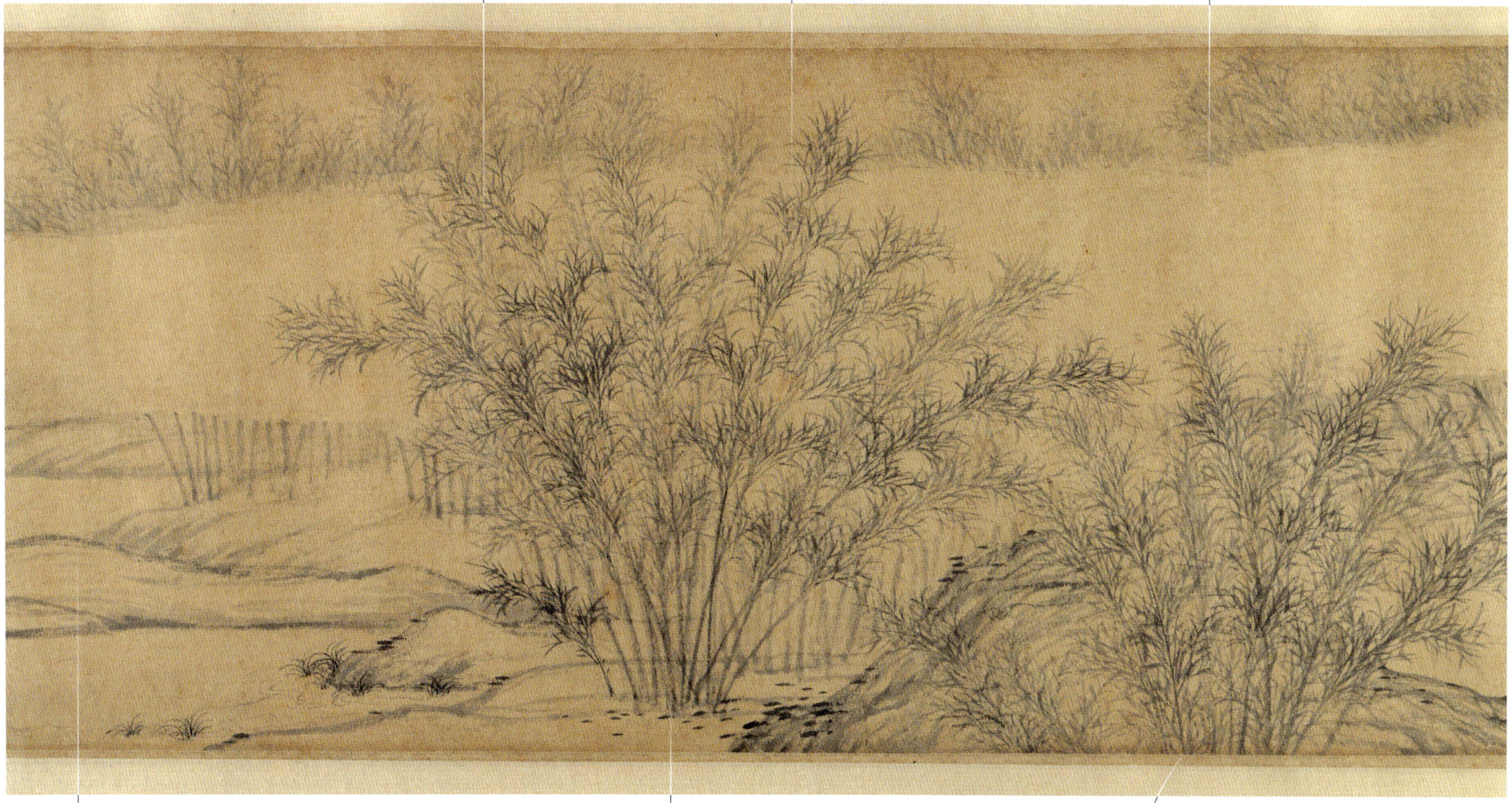

The waterway, with its small inlets, meanders alongside the bamboo.

Clumps of young bamboo spread fanlike along the waterway.

By cropping the bamboo in the foreground, Guan suggests immediacy and naturalness.

> "To play with brush and ink is a masculine sort of thing to do, yet I made this painting. Wouldn't someone say that I transgressed [propriety]? How despicable, how despicable."
>
> Guan Daosheng, 1310

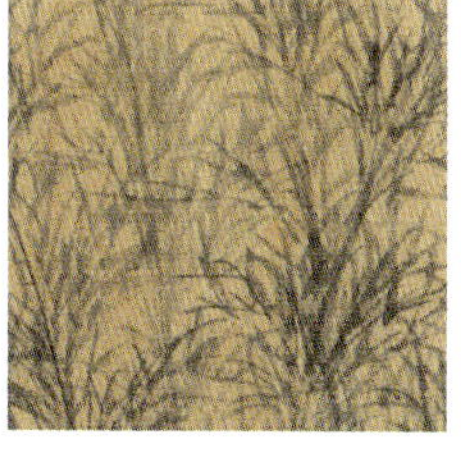

The dark and light tones of the leaves create livellness and a sense of movement, as well as depth.

Maestà

Duccio di Buoninsegna 1308–1311, tempera and gold on wood, 84 × 162 in (214 × 412 cm), Museo dell'Opera Metropolitana del Duomo, Siena, Italy

The central panel of a double-sided altarpiece commissioned for the cathedral of Siena, *Maestà* (The Virgin Mary in Majesty) depicts the Virgin and Child while also celebrating the city's wealth and power. Duccio was one of the leading artists of the Sienese school, which marked the shift from the flat Byzantine style of painting to the more humanistic approach adopted in the early Italian Renaissance. The tender gestures and emotional expressions between the Virgin and Child convey maternal love and affection.

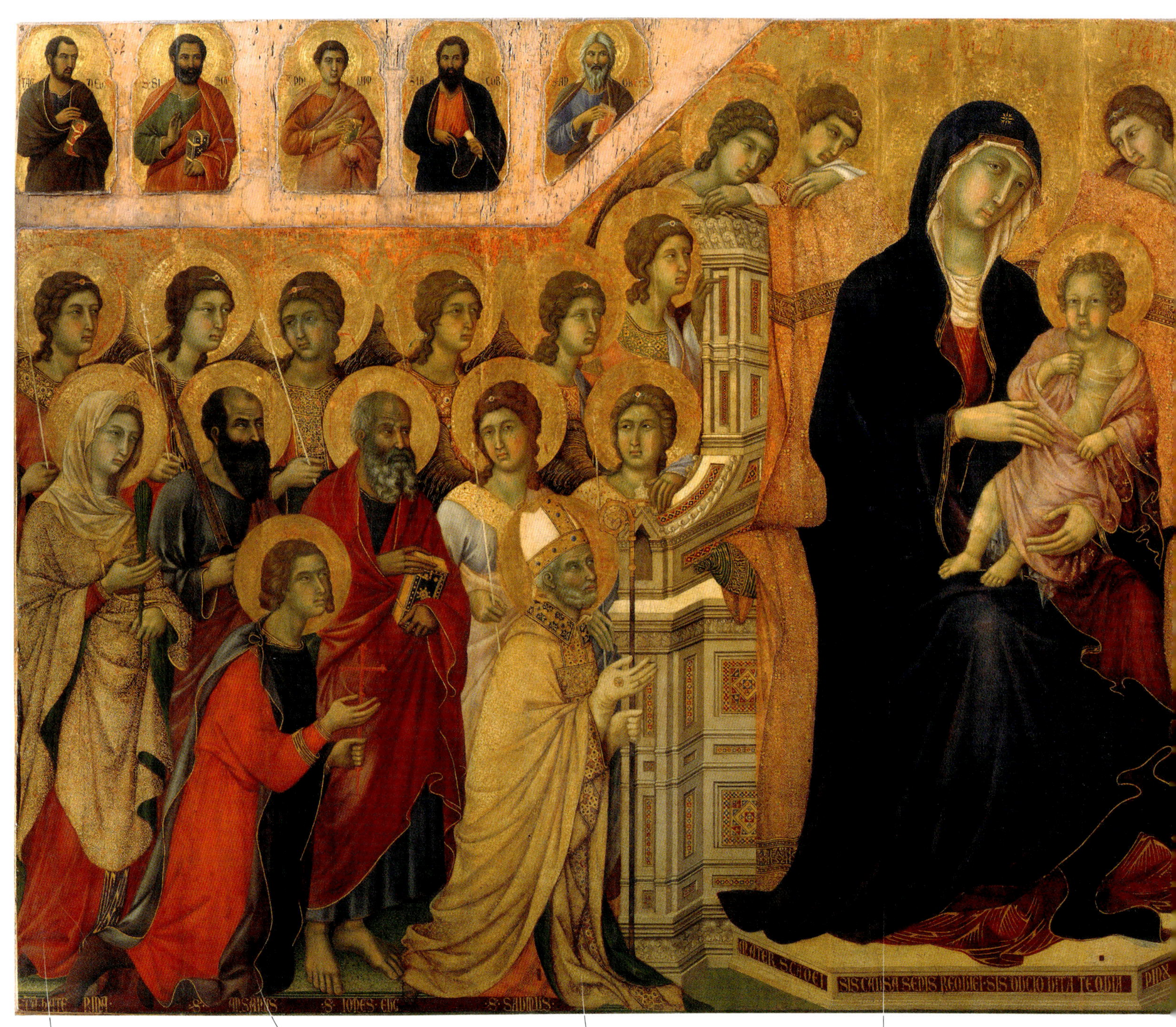

St. Catherine of Alexandria holds a palm branch, a symbol of her martyrdom.

Asano, one of Siena's four patron saints (here all shown kneeling), baptized the first Christians in the city.

Savino, another patron saint, was a Roman soldier. He is usually depicted as a bishop.

The expensive ultramarine pigment used for the Virgin's robe reflects her divinity.

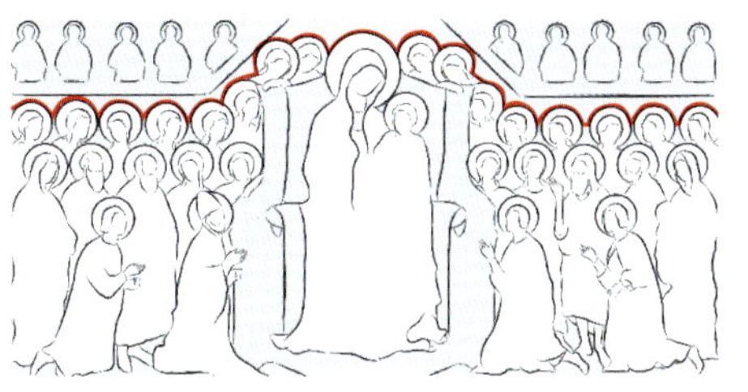
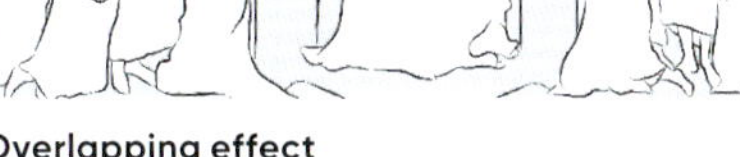

Overlapping effect
The figures overlap to achieve the illusion of depth. Distant figures, such as those of the apostles, are significantly smaller.

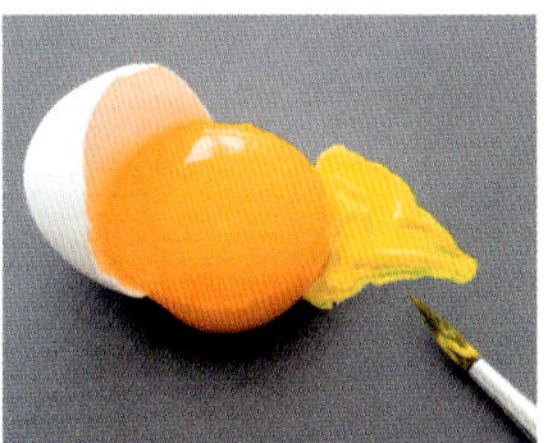

Using tempera
To achieve a luminous depth, tempera—pigment mixed with egg to bind it—was applied in many thin layers using fine brushes. Duccio was one of the first artists to use tempera successfully.

> "Duccio may in fact be called the most gifted manipulator of the Italo-Byzantine style of his time."
>
> Charles Rufus Morey

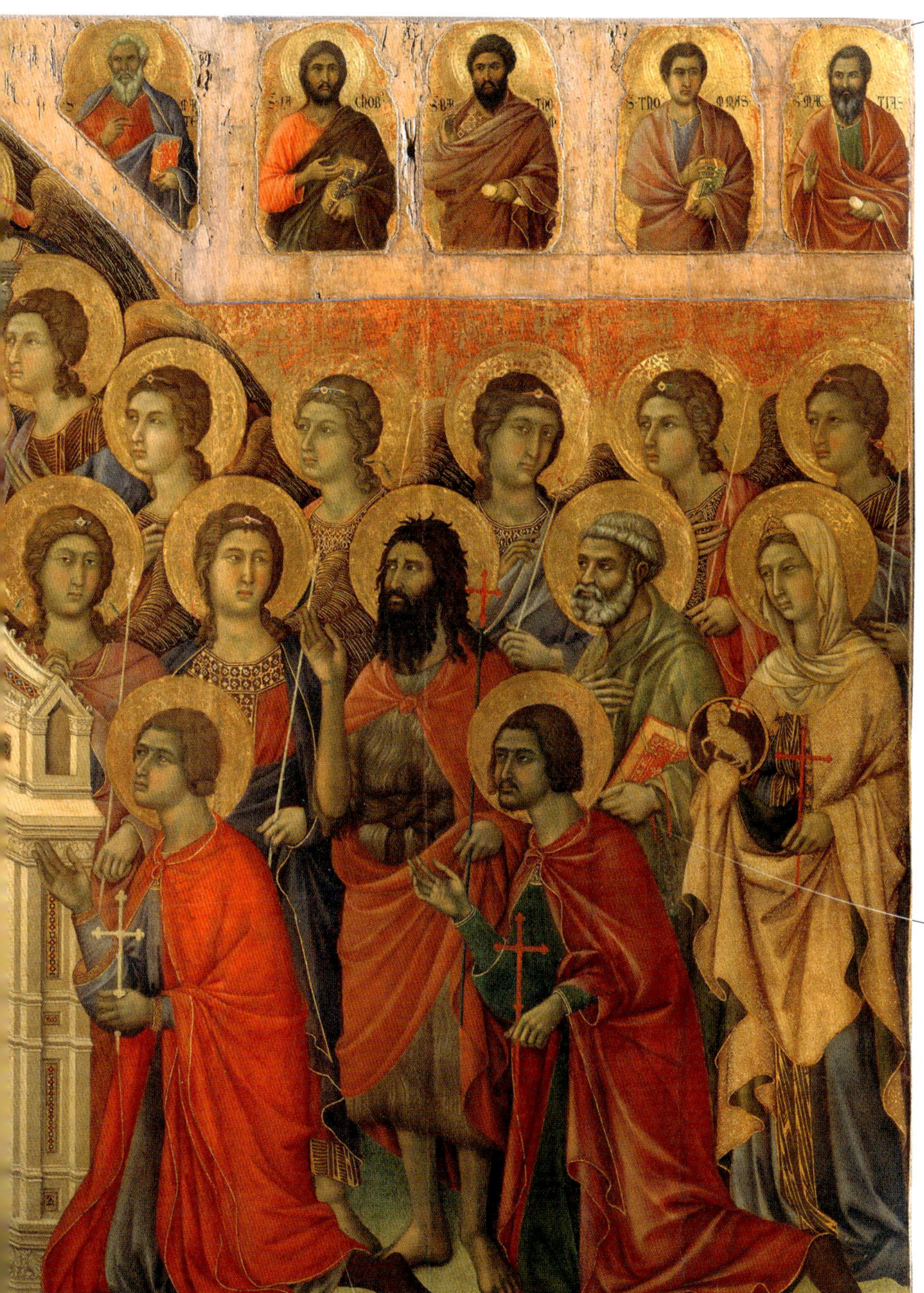

Ten apostles, identified by abbreviated inscriptions and the attributes they carry, are ranged across the top of the painting.

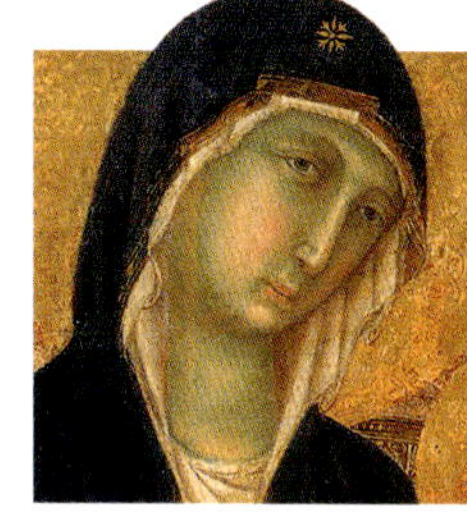

The exaggerated size of the Virgin and Child, and the symmetrical arrangement of the saints and angels on either side of them, reflect their divinity.

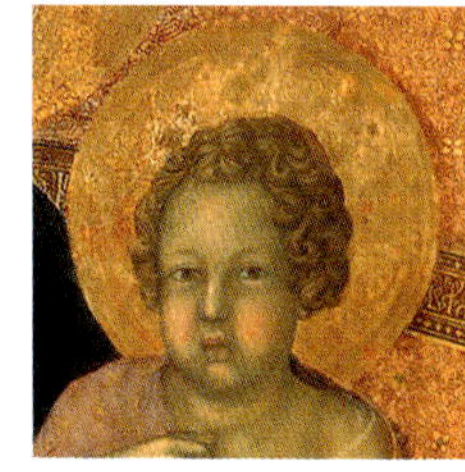

Gold leaf has been used extensively, to reflect light onto the central figures but also to indicate Siena's great wealth.

Light and shadow give the faces three-dimensional and lifelike qualities.

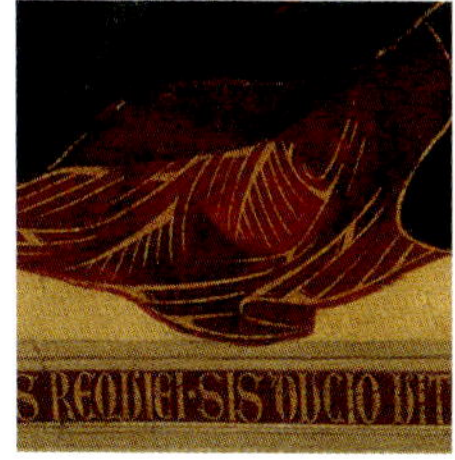

An inscription in Latin entreats the "Holy Mother of God" to "grant peace to Siena and life to Duccio who has painted you thus."

The saints kneeling before the Virgin and Child are identified at the base of the painting.

Crescenzio was a child martyr. His remains were taken to Siena's cathedral in 1058.

Vittore, the fourth patron saint, was a Christian soldier born in Syria.

Belleville Breviary

Jean Pucelle 1323–1326, grisaille and tempera on vellum, 9 × 7 in (24 × 17 cm), Bibliothèque Nationale, Paris, France

A "breviary" was a book that brought together the appointed prayers and readings for the Christian year. This is a page from one made for Jeanne de Belleville, a devout noblewoman. It was a deeply personal item and a symbol of her wealth and education. Cautionary scenes from the Bible and images of animals and mythical beasts decorate the margins, while stylized renderings of plants curl around the columns of text.

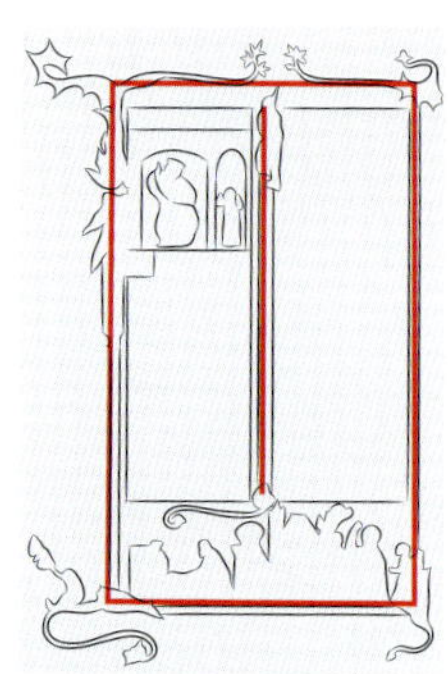

Imposing order
The rigid division and containment of the text contrasts with the extravagant decoration, just as the breviary imposes devotional order on the vagaries of everyday life.

Flowers and foliage lend vibrancy. They also imply that religious truth is integral to the natural order.

Illustrating the theme of jealousy, King Saul is shown throwing a spear at the young David, whom he sees as a threat (1 Samuel 18:11).

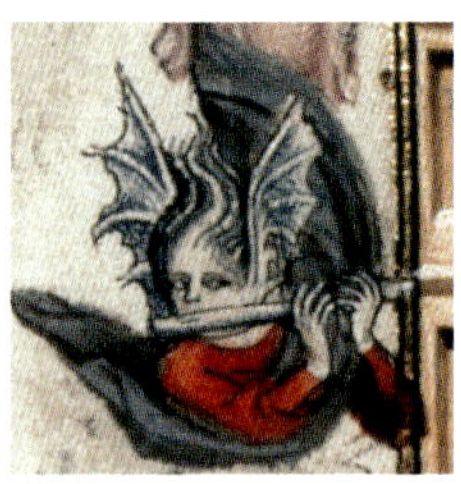

Demonic figures provide a colorful reminder of what is at stake if religious observations are ignored.

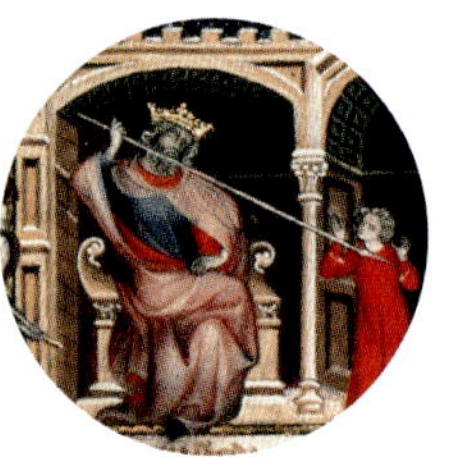

Structural echoes
The figures of David and Saul are contained within a stylized palace. The lines of the building and furniture echo their poses and the fall of their clothing.

A dragonfly, a bird (below), a moth (bottom left), and what may be a monkey (also bottom left) underline the variety of God's creation.

"A very beautiful breviary, very perfect, well written, very nobly illuminated and very richly written."

Inventory, 1380

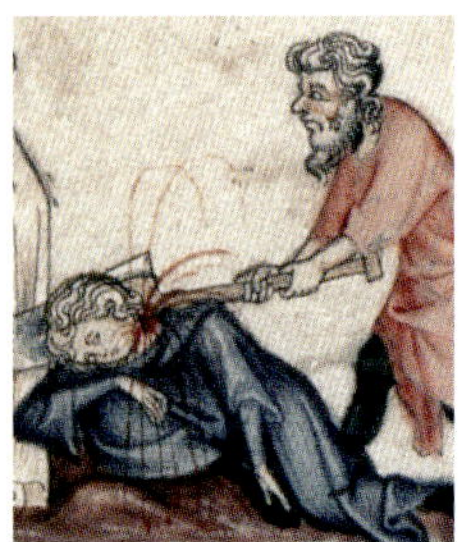

Cain, a farmer, signified by a wheat sheaf, kills Abel, his shepherd brother (Genesis 4).

A saint (unknown) is blessed for her acts of charity. Religious piety was nothing without good works.

The Annunciation With Two Saints and Four Prophets

Simone Martini 1333, tempera and gold leaf on wood, 72 × 66 in (184 × 168 cm), Gallerie degli Uffizi, Florence, Italy

The Archangel Gabriel announces to Mary that she will conceive and bear the son of God through a virgin birth. The triptych (three-part altarpiece), designed for a chapel in Siena Cathedral, is an exquisite rendition of this episode in the Christian story, infused with emotional drama. The elongated figures, rich colors, and detailed patterns are typical of the Sienese Gothic style.

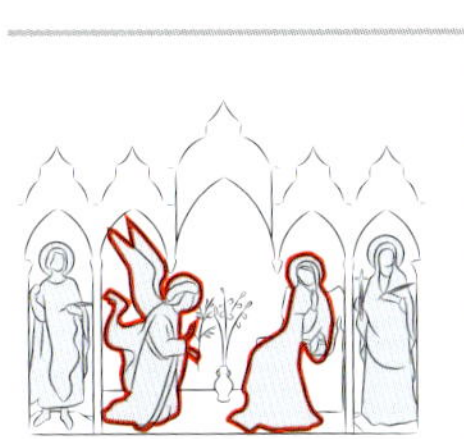

Composition
The figures are arranged across the painting in the manner of a frieze. Gabriel and Mary, the most important figures, occupy most of the space.

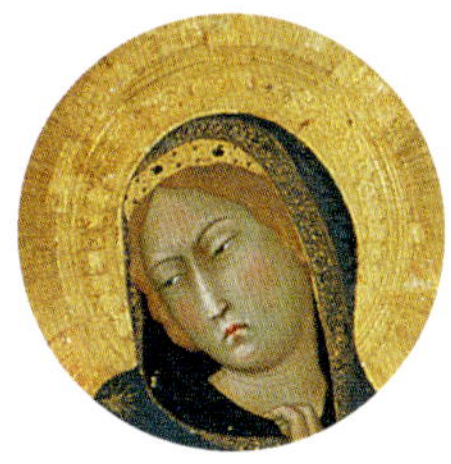

Gold-leaf tooling
The halos have been depicted by creating patterns in gold leaf. Tools known as punches were used to engrave or stamp out the pattern.

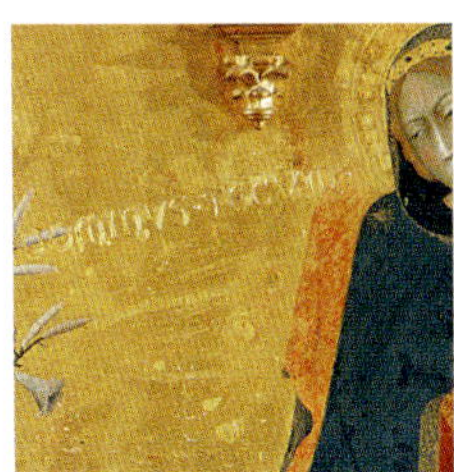

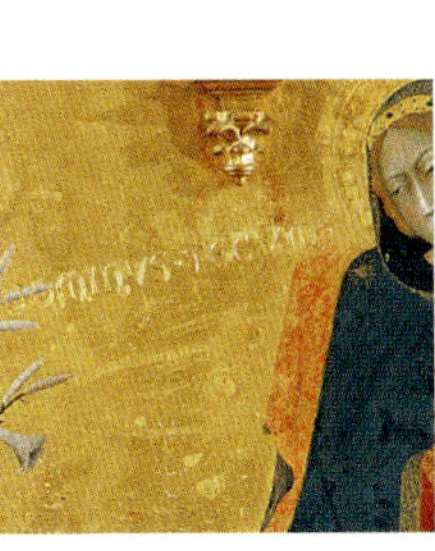

Gabriel's message is inscribed across the background: "Ave Gratia Plena Dominus Tecum" (Hail, full of grace, the Lord is with thee).

In the four roundels, the prophets Jeremiah, Ezekiel, Isaiah, and Daniel hold scrolls with Bible quotes.

The Holy Spirit in the form of a dove emerges from a cluster of eight angels to descend upon the Virgin.

The Gothic-style frame is a 19th-century construction.

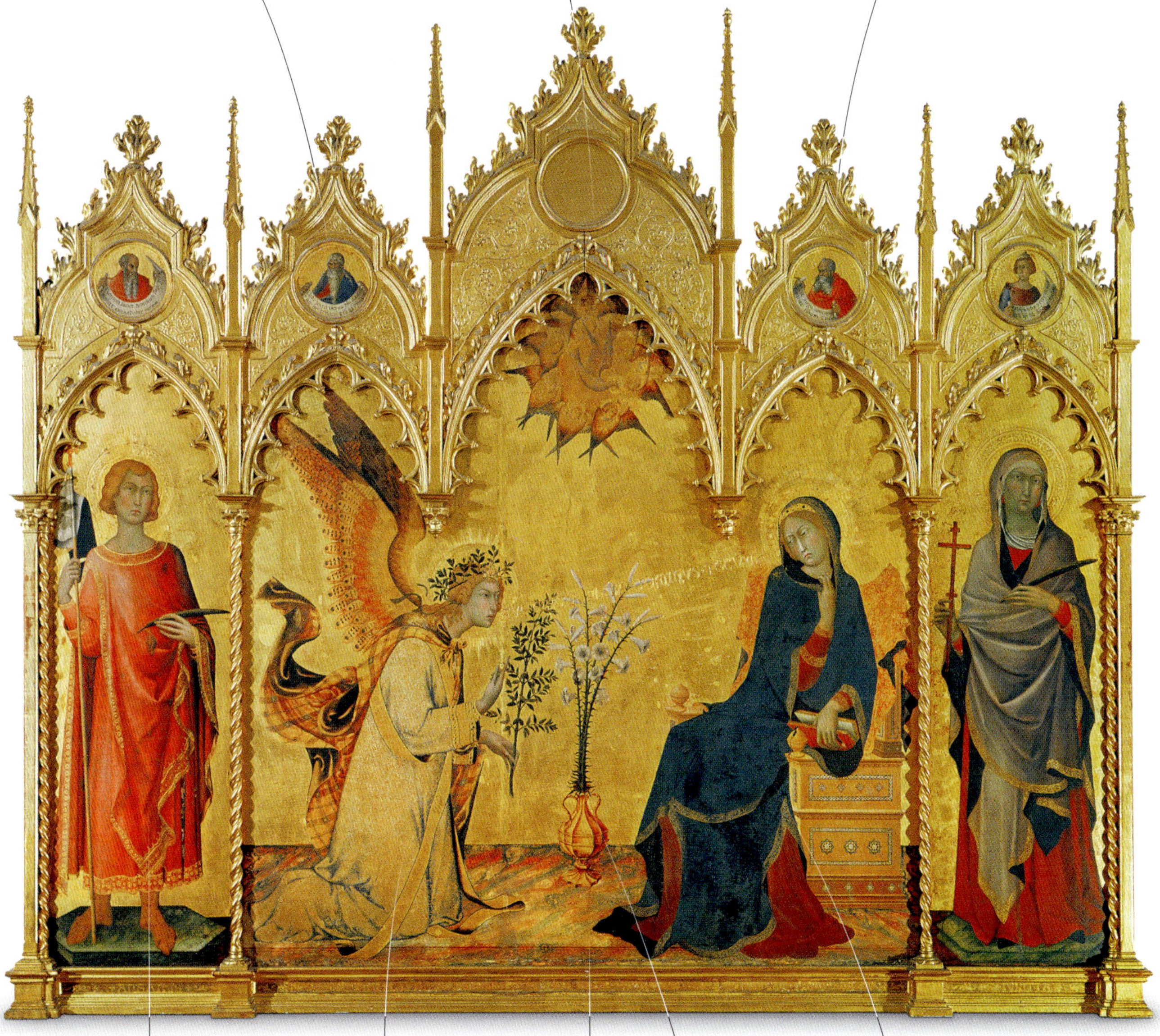

The patron saints of Siena Cathedral, St. Ansanus (left) and St. Margaret (right), flank the central figures.

The Archangel Gabriel's outspread wings and billowing robe indicate that he has just arrived. He leans forward to deliver his message.

Perspective lines in the marble flooring create a sense of depth against the golden backdrop.

Gabriel's olive branch symbolizes peace; the potted lily is a symbol of the Virgin's purity.

Mary, interrupted while reading, recoils at the angel's news. Later in the story, she will submit to God's will.

The Effects of Good Government in the City

Ambrogio Lorenzetti 1338–1339, fresco, 25 × 47 ft (7.7 × 14.4 m), Fondazione Musei Senesi, Siena, Italy

This fresco depicts a bustling and prosperous city. Its inhabitants buy and sell goods in the market, celebrate a wedding, and come and go freely through the city gates. It is a picture of harmonious living. Belonging to *The Allegory of Good and Bad Government*, a cycle of three frescoes in Siena's Palazzo Pubblico, it depicts the positive effects of good government, such as stability, prosperity, and the rule of law, considered essential in 14th-century city states. The secular and civic nature of these frescoes, as statements of political ideology, deviates from the dominance of religious subject matter at the time.

The distinctive dome and bell tower of the city's cathedral can be seen in the background.

Red- and brown-brick buildings with crenellations are characteristic of Sienese architecture.

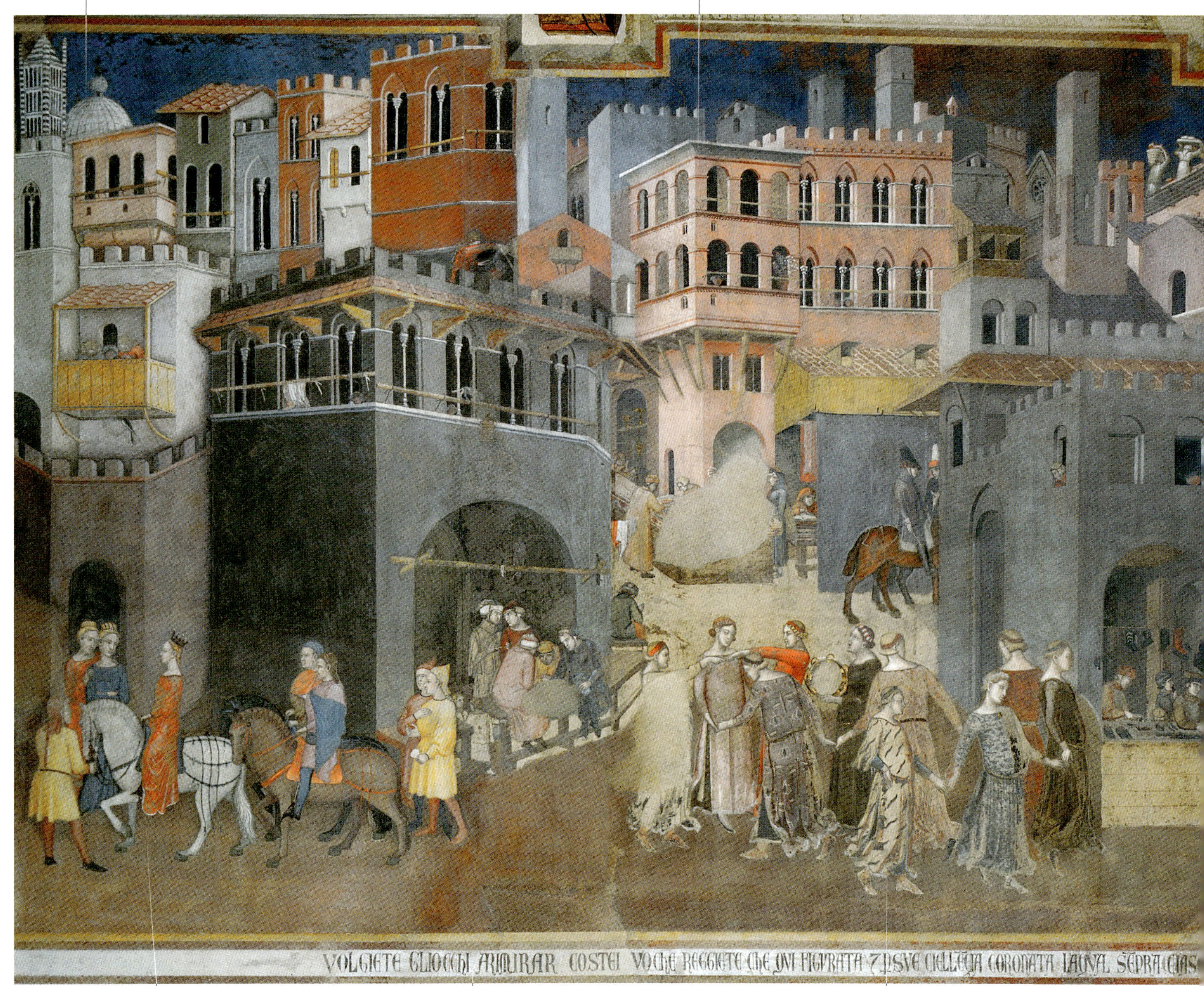

A wedding procession is led by a bride riding a horse. The spectacle is watched by two women.

This inscription reminds the city's rulers to be fair as Justice (shown in another panel) "always renders to everyone his due."

Nine female dancers are an allegory for cultural wealth and social harmony in an ideal civic society.

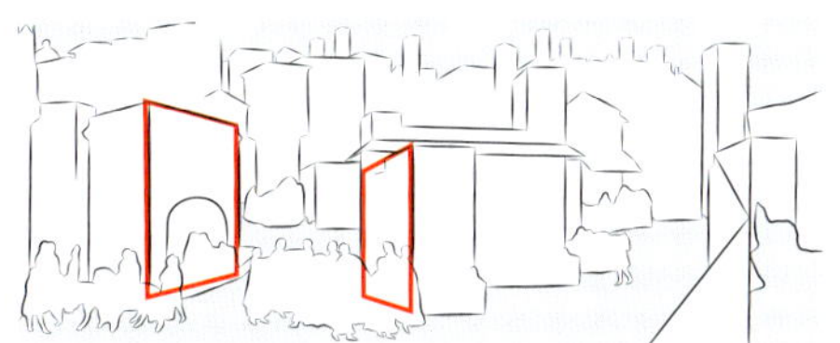

New sense of perspective
Most of the buildings are shown at the same three-quarters angle, an attempt by Lorenzetti to create a sense of depth. Within just a few years, the concept of single-point perspective would revolutionize art.

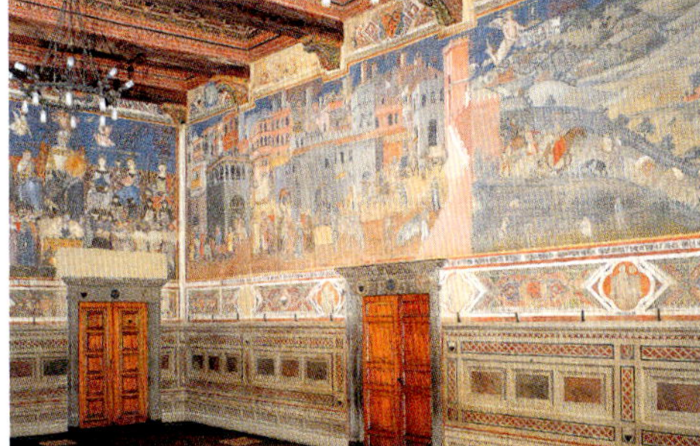

Wall art
Frescoes are made by painting pigments mixed with water onto a wet plaster surface; they bind together as they dry. The artist must work quickly and cannot correct mistakes without applying fresh plaster.

Porta Romana, one of the city's medieval gates, identifies the scene as Siena.

The winged figure of Security flies over the city.

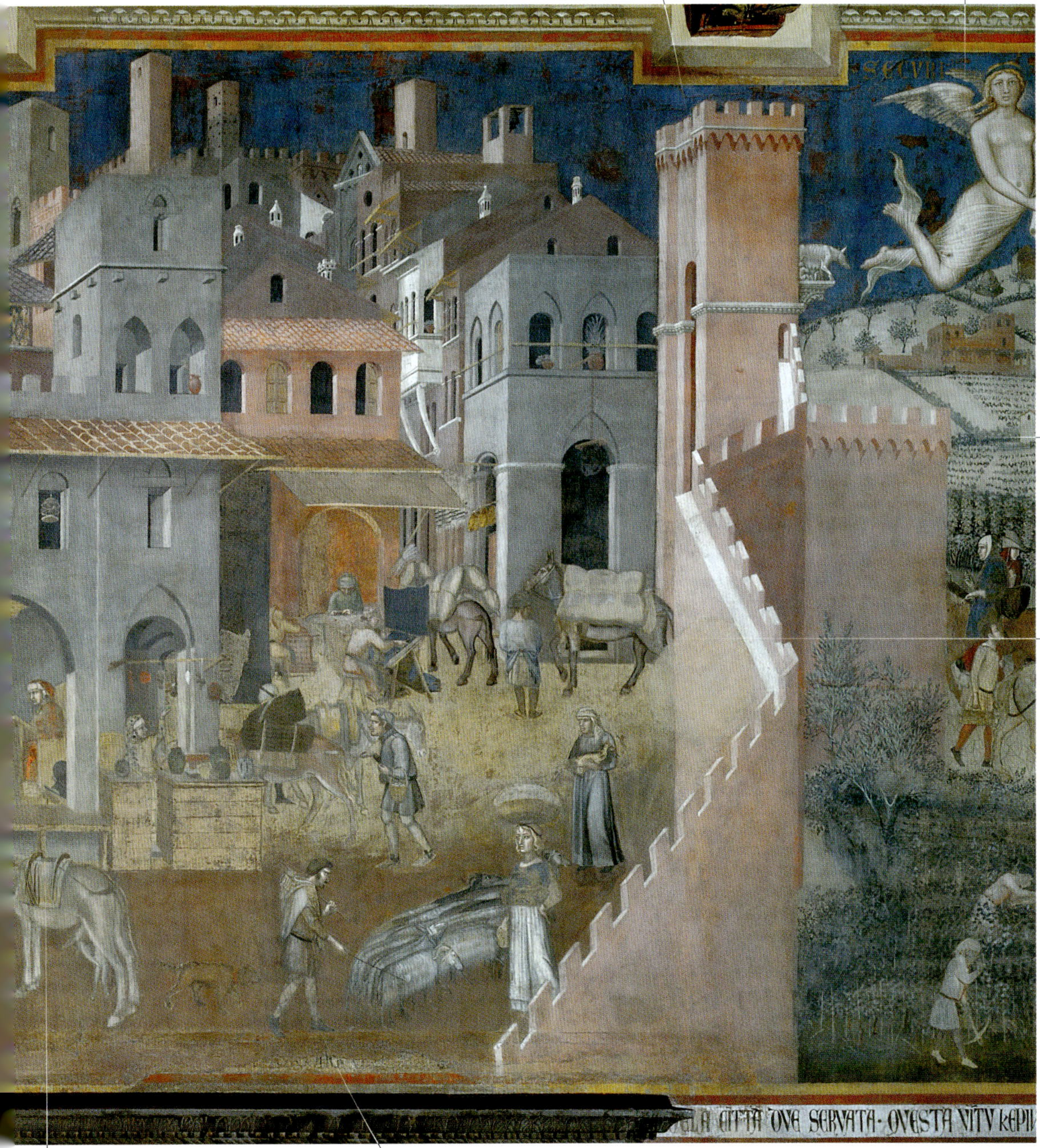

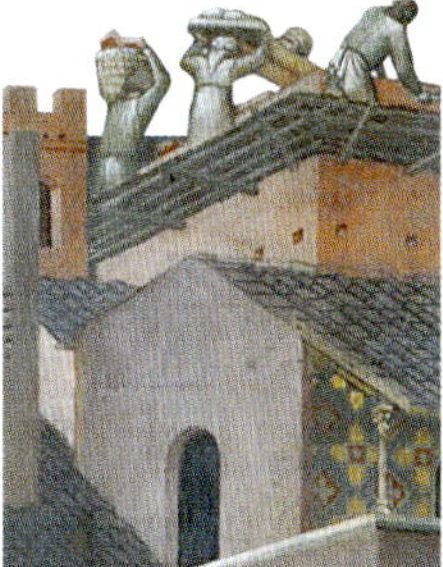

Masons are erecting new buildings, highlighting the prosperity of a well-run city.

An extension to the scene shows the effects of good government in the countryside.

Donkeys are laden with grain, suggesting a plentiful harvest, providing food for all.

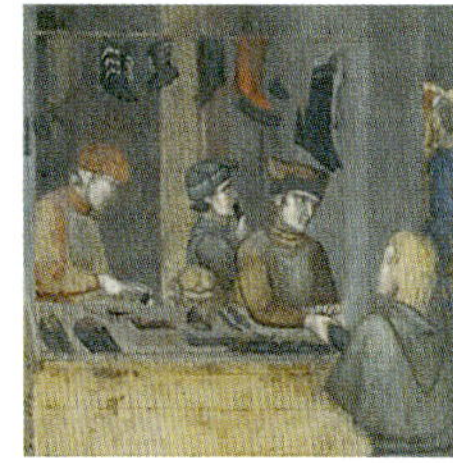

Scenes set inside this cobbler's workshop and a shop selling wine and meat indicate the thriving economy of the ideal city.

Education is important to the city. A teacher lectures to a class of attentive students.

A shepherd takes his sheep to graze in the Tuscan countryside beyond the Porta Romana.

Quetzalcoatl

Artist unknown c. 1325–1521, jade, 13 × 9 × 6 in (33.1 × 24 x 15.3 cm), British Museum, London, UK

The god Quetzalcoatl was believed by the Aztecs to be the creator of humankind. His name in Nahuatl, the language spoken by the Mexica, means "feathered serpent." This carved stone bust adorned with a feather headdress represents Quetzalcoatl's dual nature, signifying that he can both fly in the sky like a bird and slither on the ground like a snake, alongside humans and animals.

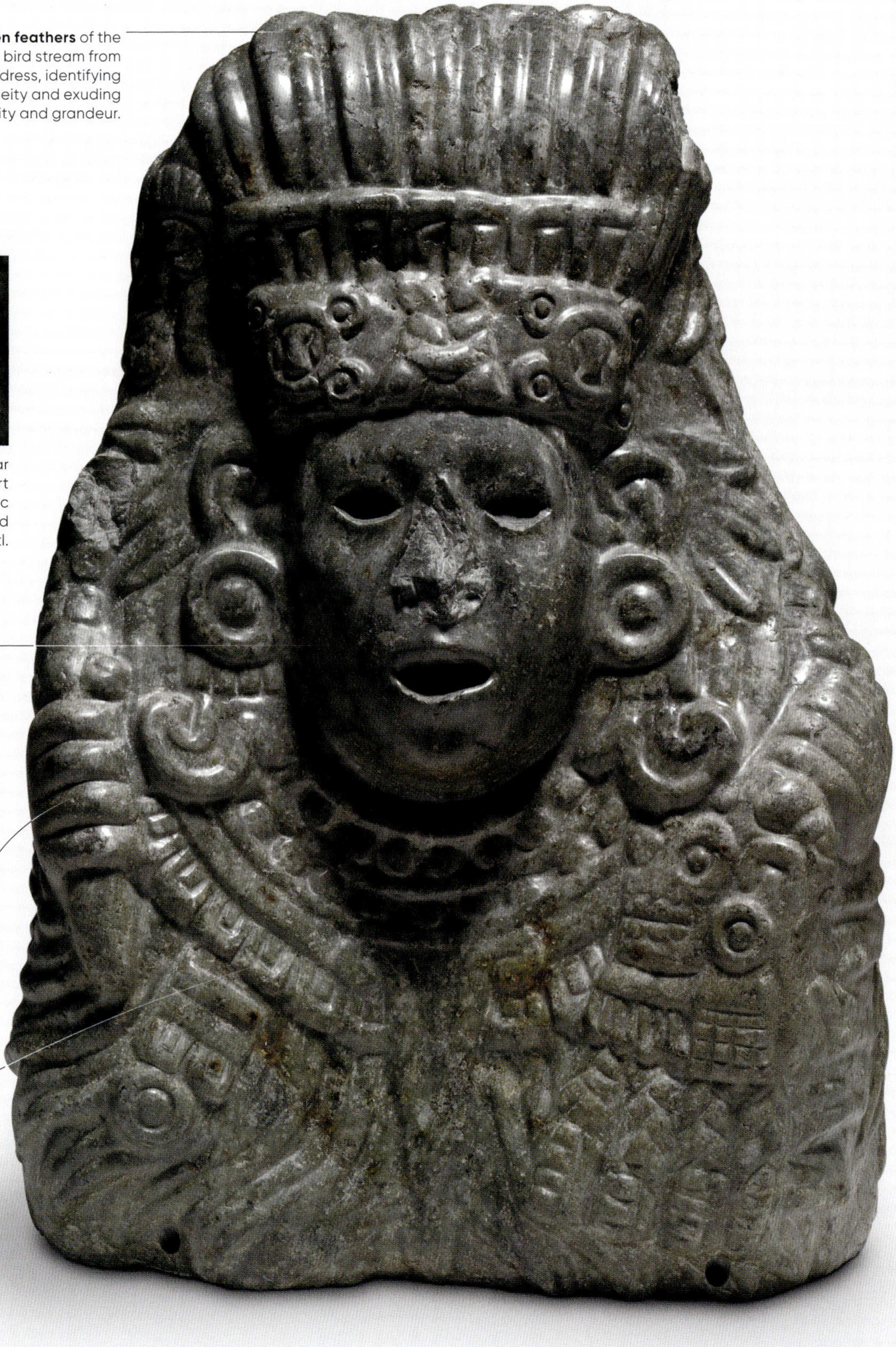

Long, green feathers of the quetzal bird stream from the headdress, identifying the deity and exuding authority and grandeur.

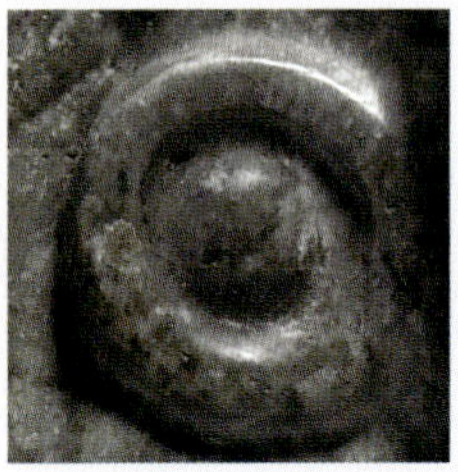

Curved, conch-like ear ornaments, are part of the iconographic symbols associated with Quetzalcoatl.

A human mask personifies the deity. The hollow mouth and eyes add a sense of depth to its expression.

The god's right hand holds a short club, possibly a cob of corn.

This necklace depicts part of an Aztec solar disk. It alludes to Quetzalcoatl's celestial role.

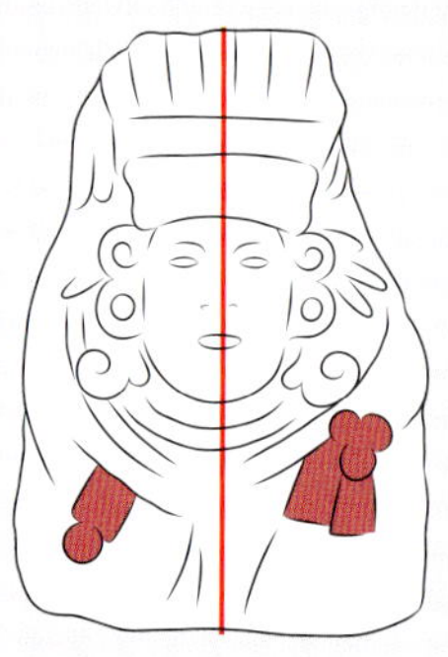

Symmetry disrupted
The bust is presented front-facing, creating a compositional symmetry that is subtly disrupted by the carved decorations, which differ slightly on either side.

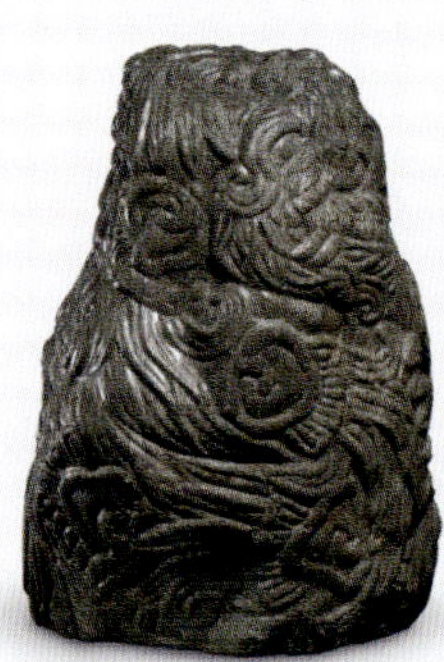

Feathered serpent
Coiling motifs on the reverse of the bust are also adorned with feathers, alluding to the duality of the deity.

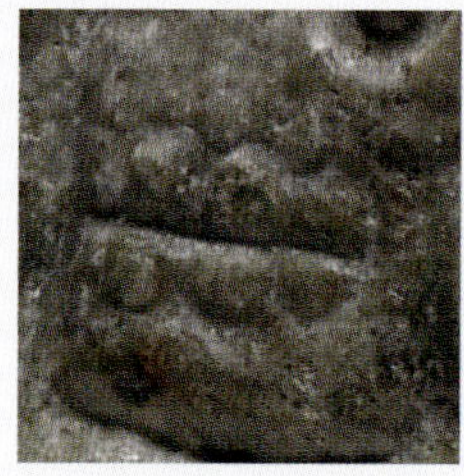

A serpent's jaw, surrounded by feather motifs, is visible on the bust's left shoulder.

Wind Among the Trees on the Riverbank

Ni Zan 1363, ink on paper, 23 x 12 in (59.1 x 31.1 cm), Metropolitan Museum of Art, New York, US

Artist Ni Zan lived during China's turbulent transition from the Yuan to Ming dynasties. To escape the political upheaval, he left behind his wealth and lived a simple, itinerant life, painting only for friends. He developed an expressive, relaxed style that embodies the essence and mood of a landscape.

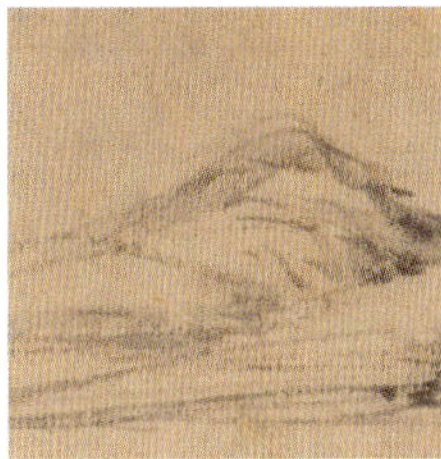

A dry-brush technique creates a sketchy, spontaneous effect that is impressionistic rather than rigidly representational.

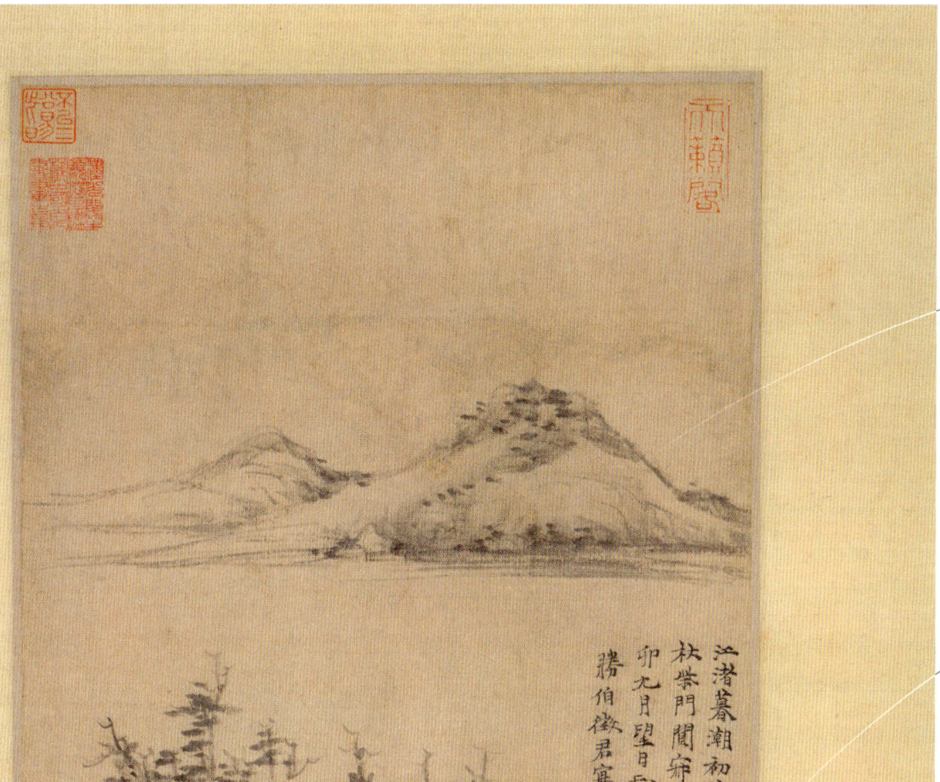

The viewer looks at the mountains in the distance while simultaneously taking in the foreground.

A poem about the landscape at dusk may reference Ni's late wife: "I think of my friend—the glow is nearly gone from the hills."

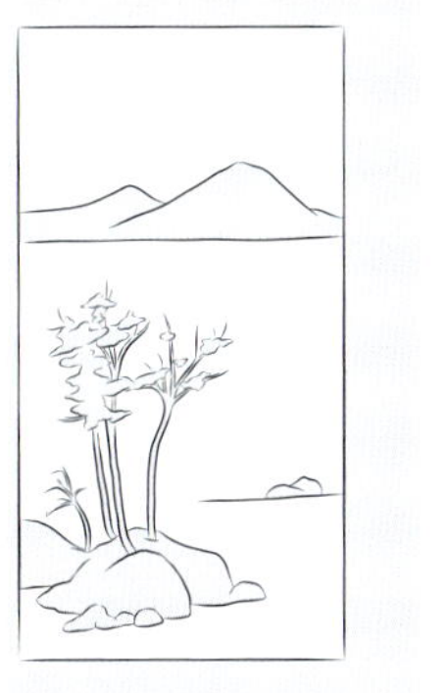

Negative space
Unpainted areas are common in Chinese paintings and may represent water, sky, or a surface such as a leaf or tree trunk.

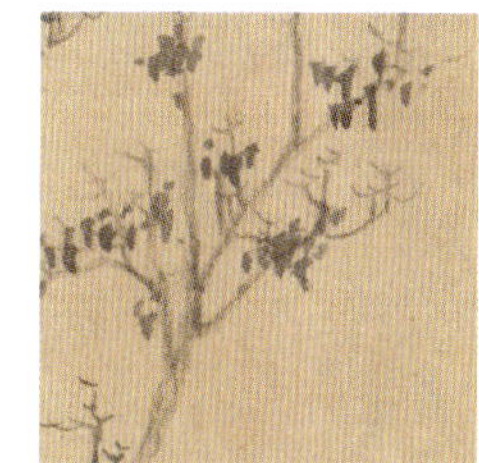

"Frost-covered leaves" mentioned in the inscription indicate that it is late fall.

This blank space represents a body of water.

Red seals
Chinese artwork often includes red seals that belong to the collector, not the artist. Later admirers may add inscriptions and their own seals.

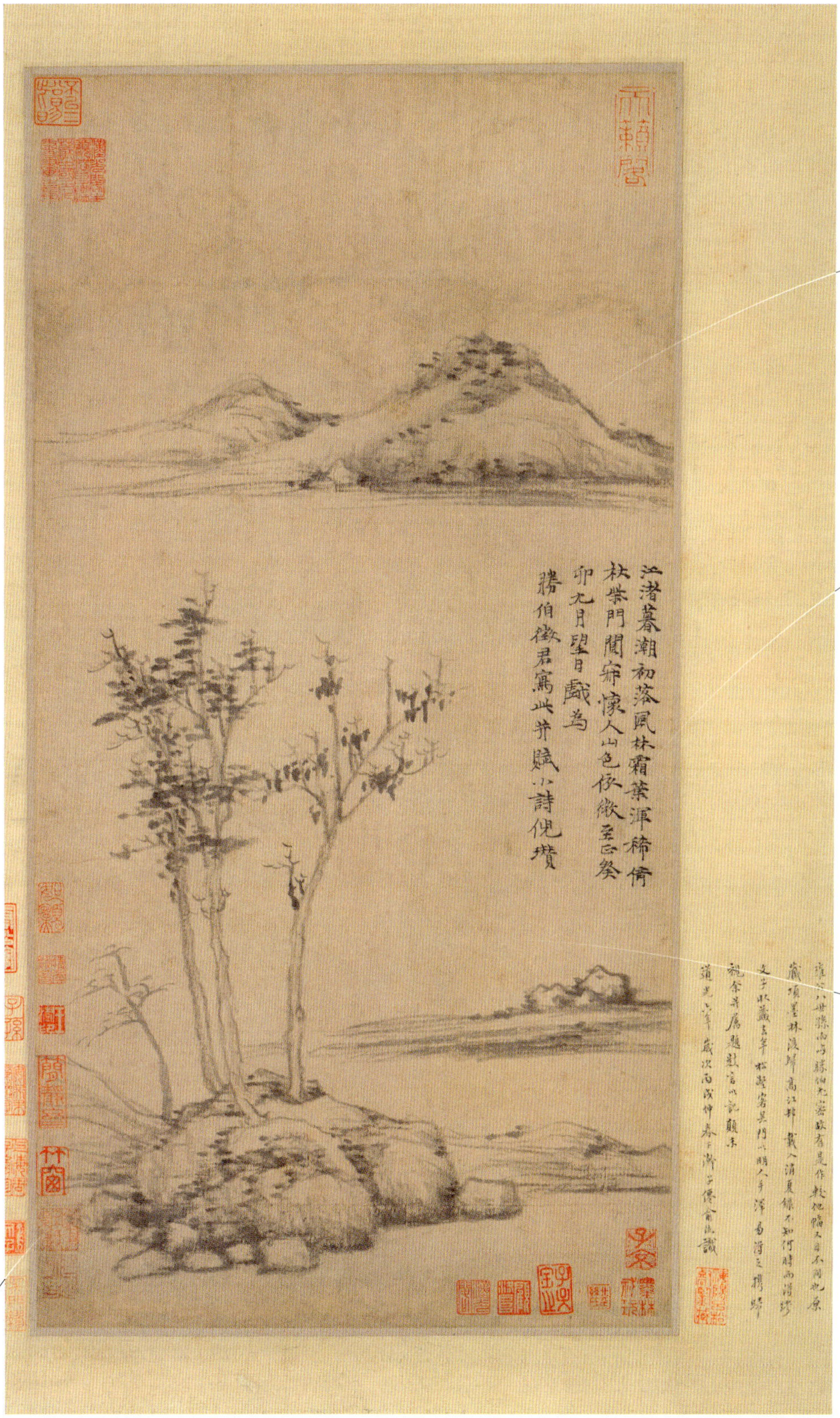

The red seals were stamped by more than two dozen collectors of this artwork over its 660-year history.

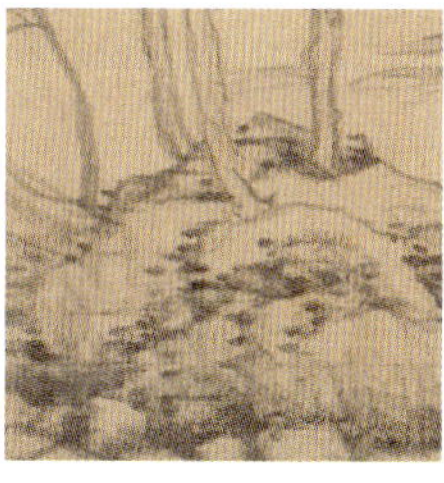

The few trees growing from rocks might allude to resilience and perseverance in the face of adversity.

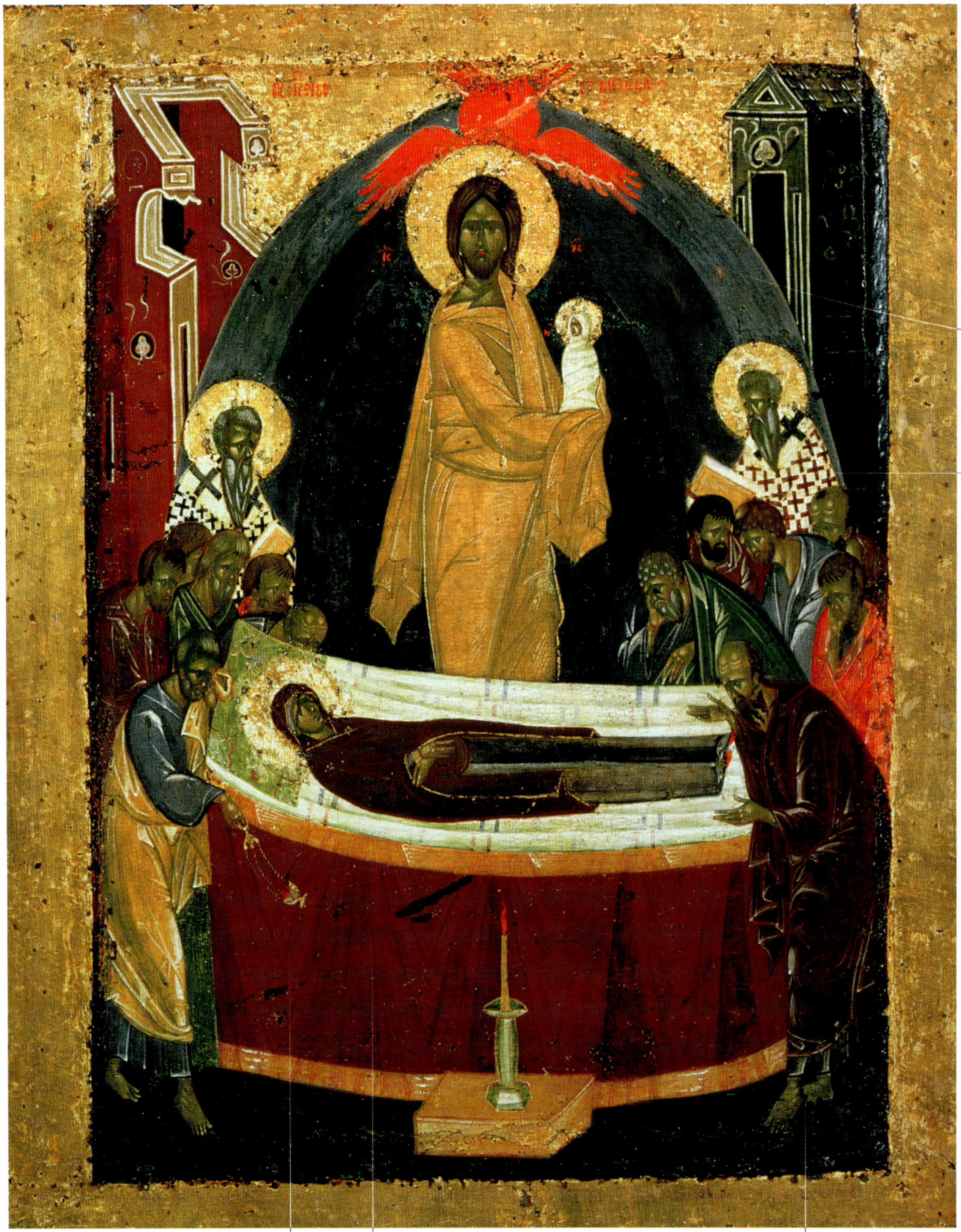

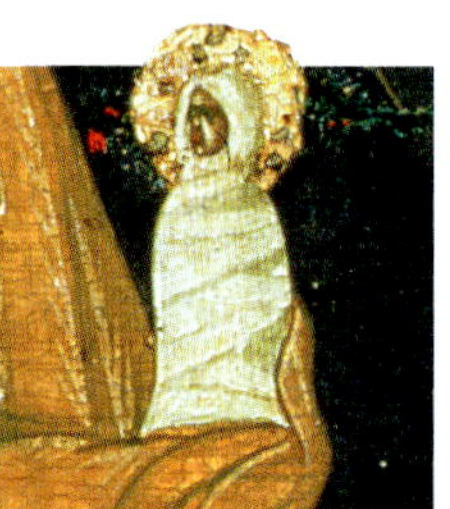

Christ holds the Virgin's soul, in the form of a swaddled baby.

A red-winged angel crosses its wings over Christ's head.

Two Church fathers wearing contemporary robes with bishop's stoles join the mourners.

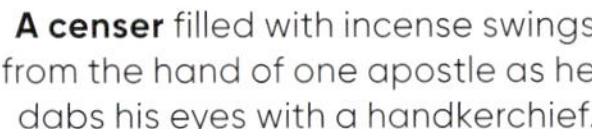

A censer filled with incense swings from the hand of one apostle as he dabs his eyes with a handkerchief.

The Virgin lies on a bier, in preparation for being entombed.

Six apostles stand on each side, mourning the Virgin's death.

The Dormition of the Virgin Mary

Theophanes the Greek 1392, tempera on wood, 34 × 27 in (86 × 68 cm), State Tretyakov Gallery, Moscow, Russia

The Orthodox church teaches that Mary, as the Mother of God and untainted by original sin, did not die but only slept before being taken body and soul into Heaven by Christ. In an apocryphal tale, depicted here, the apostles arrived on a cloud to be by Mary's side for three days before her repose (dormition).

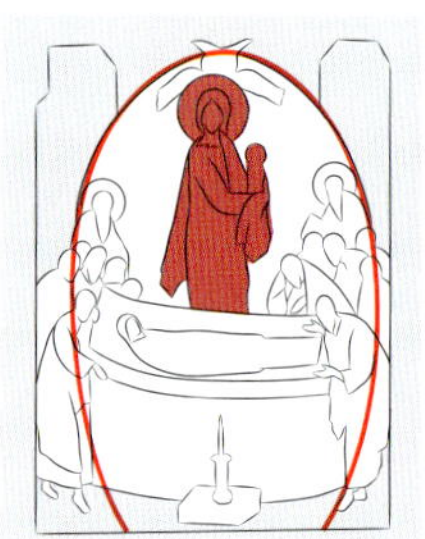

Mandorla
Christ appears within a *mandorla*, an almond shape, which includes Mary and the saints. The apostles outside the form bend their bodies toward it.

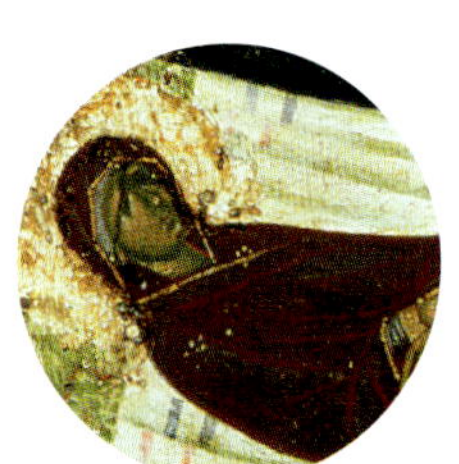

By candlelight
The work was designed to be viewed in dark, candlelit spaces, so Theophanes painted Christ with a paler color to make him easier to see. The Virgin stands out against the white cloth.

The Wilton Diptych

Unknown c. 1395–1399, tempera on oak, 21 × 15 in (53 × 37 cm), National Gallery, London, UK

Created for the English king Richard II, the diptych, a religious painting in two parts, is a portable altarpiece, primarily used for private devotion. On it, Richard is shown kneeling before the infant Christ, who is held by his mother and surrounded by angels. Beside Richard stand the English saints St. Edmund and St. Edward the Confessor, who with John the Baptist are Richard's intercessors with the divine.

The gold-leaf background is delicately patterned and here represents the sky. The rocky ground below contrasts with the flowers of Heaven in the second panel.

St. Edward the Confessor was an English king and saint in the 11th century.

St. John the Baptist was Richard's patron saint.

The infant Christ reaches out to Richard and the banner of St. George (England's patron saint), reinforcing the idea of the king's divine right to rule. Medieval artists also used the flag to symbolize Christ's victory over death.

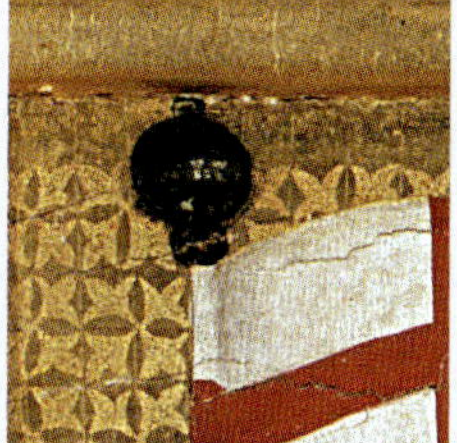

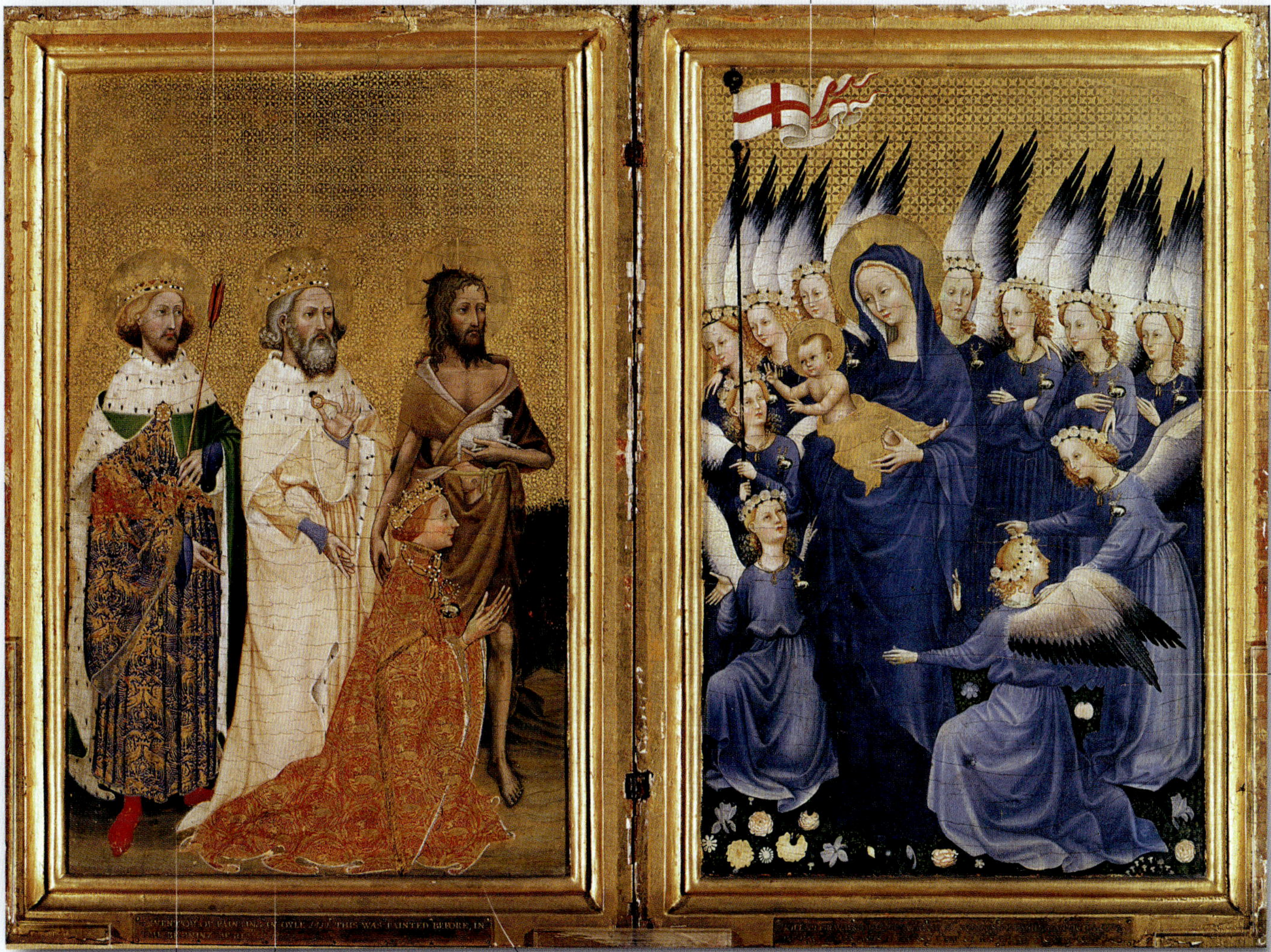

The orb is decorated with an island on which stands a castle.

Angels wear Richard's stag emblem. They are crowned with roses.

Christ, Mary, and the angels occupy a heavenly garden representing paradise. They are painted in the elegant international Gothic style.

St. Edmund, a 9th-century king of East Anglia and a martyr, holds his attribute, an arrow.

Richard's personal emblem, a white stag, can be seen on his clothes and on a chain of pearls around his neck.

Although the diptych was commissioned when Richard was an adult, he is depicted as a youth at his coronation.

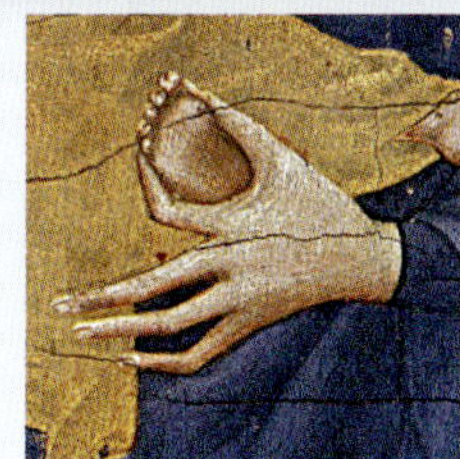

Mary holds out Christ's foot to show where the nails will go, while his halo is decorated with the crown of thorns he will wear at his crucifixion. These symbolize the possibility of salvation through Christ's death.

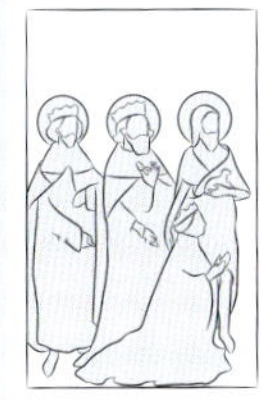

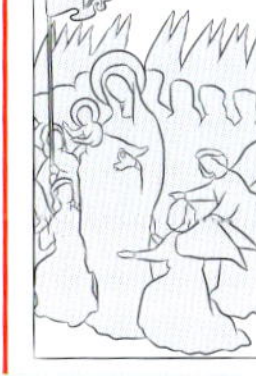

Moving situation

The still figures on the left-hand panel contrast with those on the right-hand panel, where movement is conveyed by their gestures and the wind in the flag.

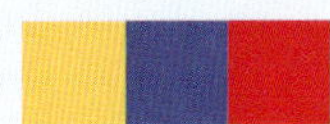

Regal colors

Costly sheet gold and ultramarine (ground lapis lazuli) contrast with splashes of red vermilion.

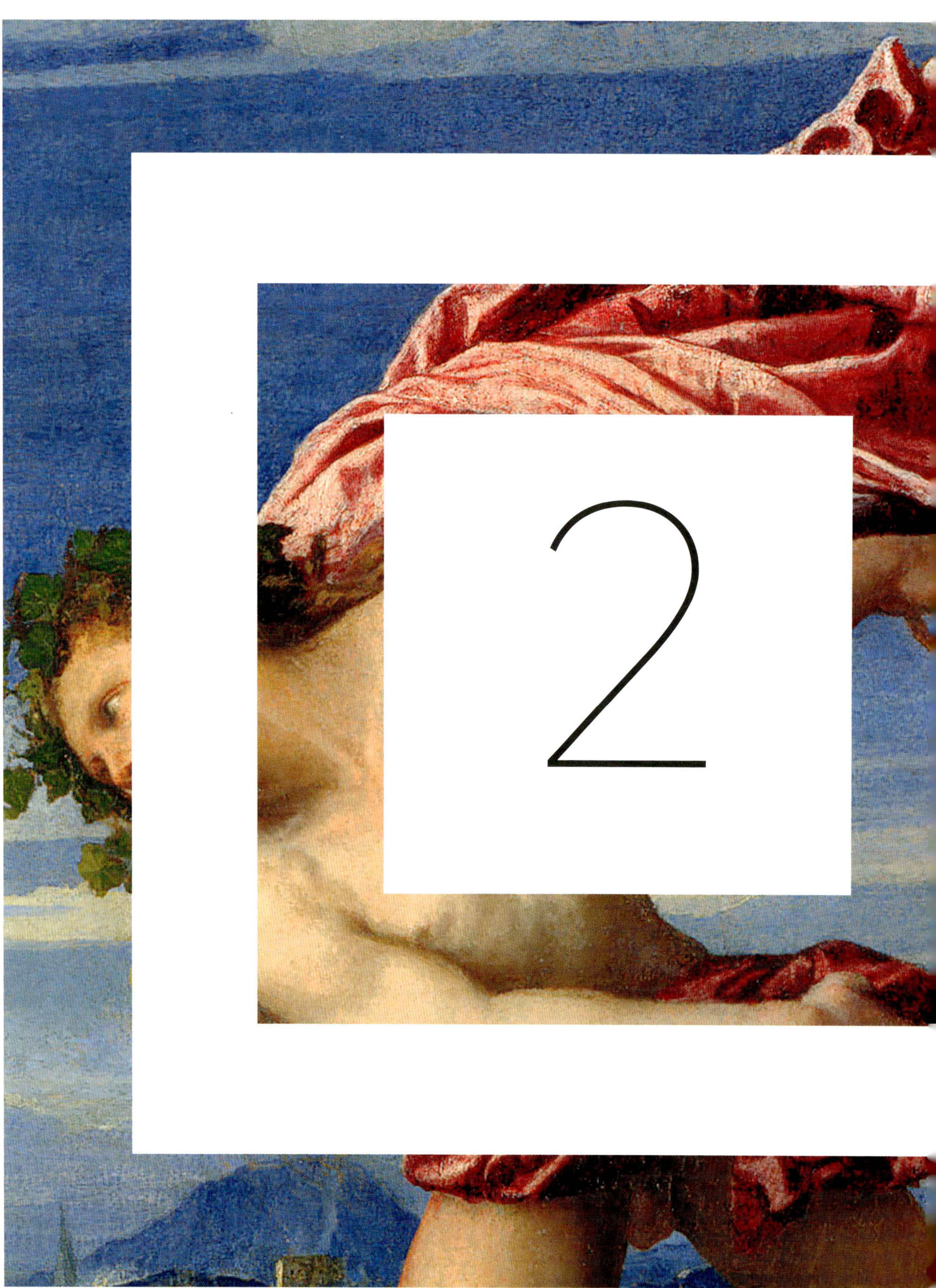

2

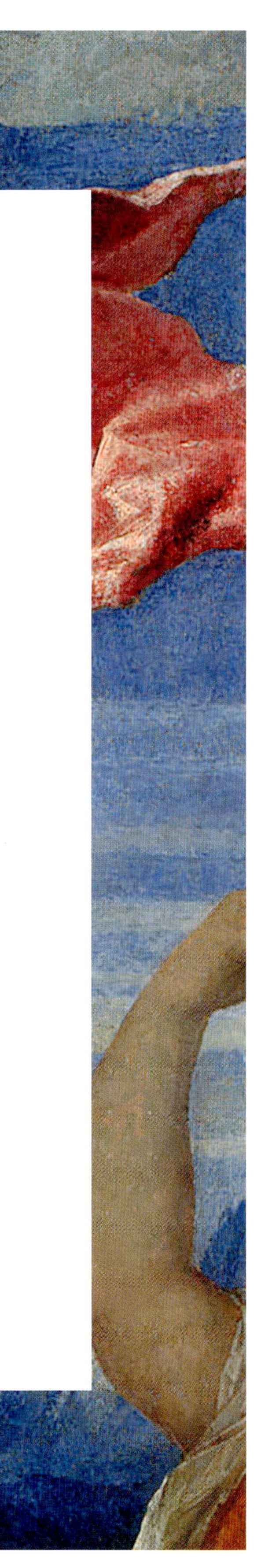

Illusion and observation

1400 - 1600

The Sacrifice of Isaac

Lorenzo Ghiberti 1401–1402, bronze and gilding, 21 × 17 in (53.3 × 43.2 cm), Museo Nazionale del Bargello, Florence, Italy

Ghiberti portrays the moment in the Old Testament when Abraham is about to sacrifice his son Isaac, a test of faith set by God (Genesis 22:1-19). The scene in bronze, one of 28 relief panels created for the north doors of Florence's Baptistry, particularly demonstrates Ghiberti's skill at depicting human anatomy.

The angel points to the ram as he orders Abraham to sacrifice the animal instead of his son.

Foreshortening projects the angel from the background and shows Ghiberti's skill as a goldsmith and his ability to work in high-relief sculpture.

The rocky landscape, a detail from the Bible story, unifies the composition, which is set in a quatrefoil frame.

Abraham's left arm holds Isaac's shoulders, while his right hand grips a dagger close to his son's neck as if he is still considering whether to carry out the sacrifice.

The flowing robes of the two servants on a donkey who accompanied Abraham and Isaac up the mountain show Ghiberti's ability as a sculptor.

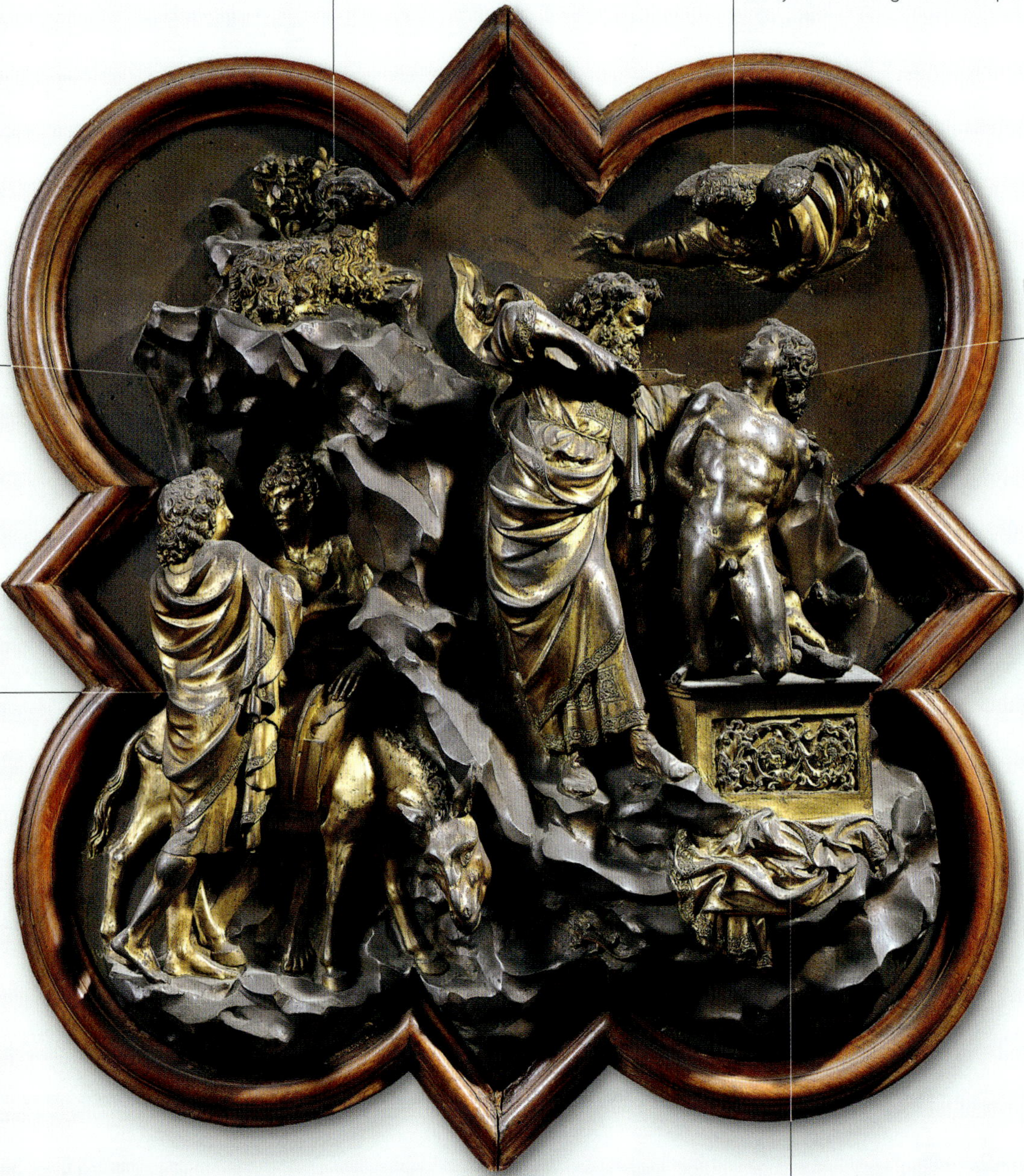

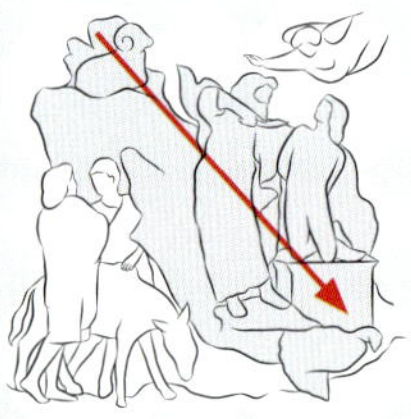

Narrative sequence The rocky mountain directs the composition from the ram at the top left to the altar—the focal point—at the bottom right.

The altar on which Isaac kneels has an intricate decorative pattern based on the friezes on Roman temples.

> "The whole was finished with so great diligence, that it appeared not made by casting and polished with tools of iron, but blown with the breath."
>
> Giorgio Vasari, 1568

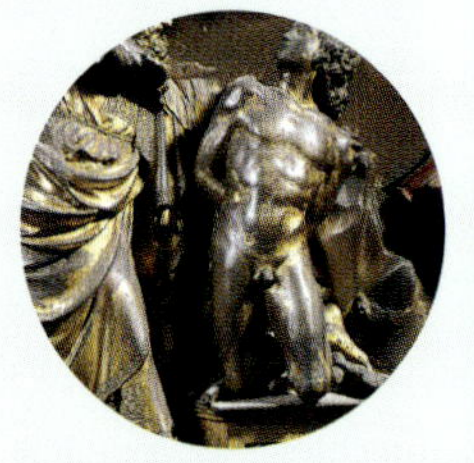

Isaac's pose, with his weight on one leg, is reminiscent of classical sculpture and echoes his father's body as he pulls back the knife.

Tomb of Philip the Bold, Duke of Burgundy

Claus Sluter 1410, Italian and Dinant black marble, gilded alabaster, and polychrome, 8 × 8 × 12 ft (2.43 × 2.54 × 3.6 m), Musée des Beaux Arts, Dijon, France

This monumental tomb marks the transition from the Gothic to the Northern Renaissance style. Unlike earlier tombs, where the subject was depicted like a statue, here the body looks naturalistic, and the mourners are highly expressive. Philip the Bold commissioned the tomb for his own burial.

The size of the tomb means that the viewer can hardly see the effigy of the Duke. Both he and the mourners are raised on slabs of black marble.

The lion at the Duke's feet symbolizes power and strength.

Only the Duke's hands and the lion at his feet are original. The effigy was damaged during the French Revolution and was re-created using 18th-century drawings.

Two angels hold the Duke's helmet above his head.

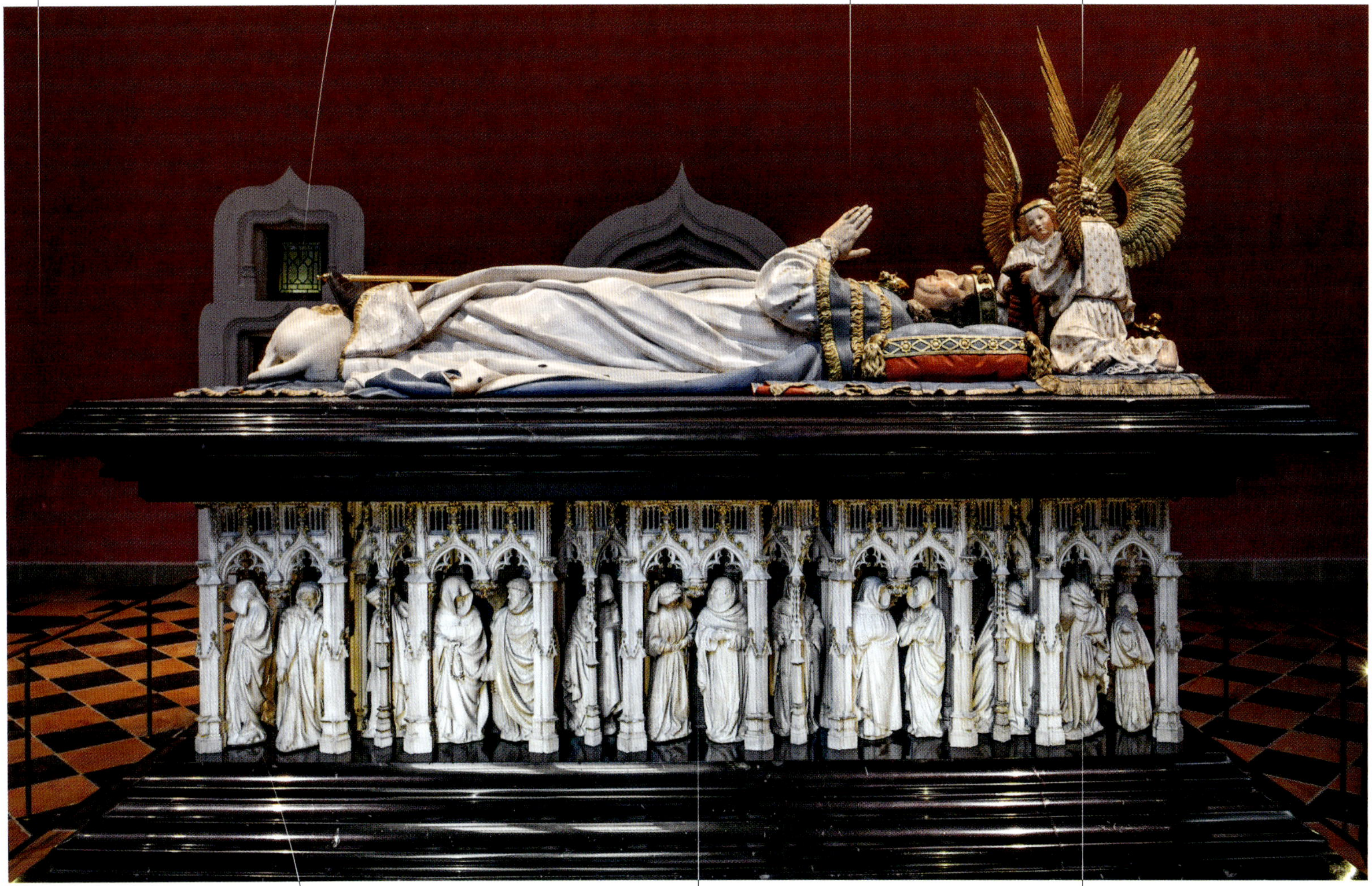

Hooded mourners in the frieze express their grief through their posture and the way they wrap their mourning cloaks around their bodies.

Alternate double arches and triangular recesses along the procession create a sense of architectural depth and highlight the sculptor's technical skills.

The mourners are set in a cloister with pointed trefoil cusped arches, which are characteristic of French Gothic architecture.

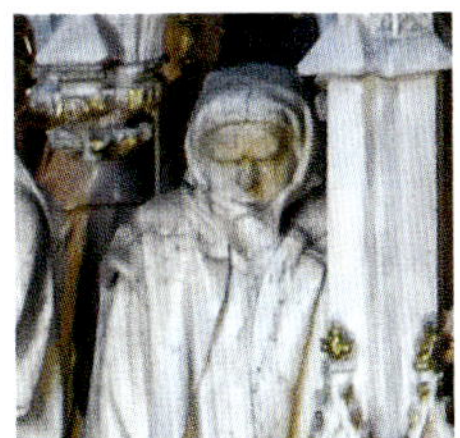

The faces of the mourners are highly expressive, a characteristic of the transition to the Renaissance style.

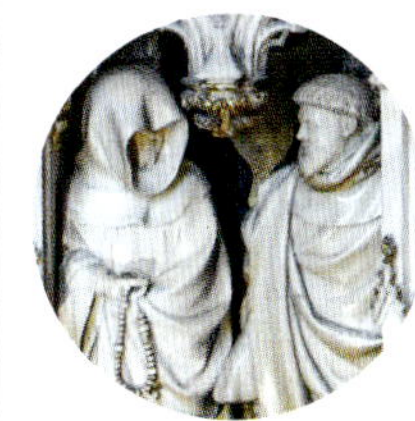

Alabaster
The mourners are carved from alabaster, a soft stone that can be carved into precise and elaborate shapes.

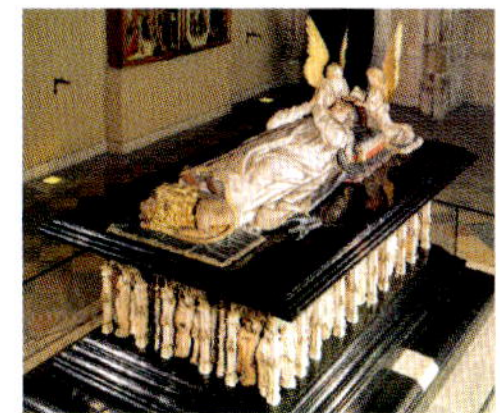

Context
The tomb was made for the monastery of Chartreuse de Champmol, which Philip founded. It was incomplete when he died, and still unfinished when Sluter died. It was finished by Claus de Werve, Sluter's nephew.

Holy Trinity

Andrei Rublev c. 1411–1425, tempera on wood, 56 x 45 in (142 x 114 cm), Tretyakov Gallery, Moscow, Russia

This icon is based on the Old Testament story of Abraham's hospitality to three angels (Genesis 18:1-15), but rather than simply depicting the narrative, it uses it to convey the Christian doctrine of God the Trinity, replacing the angels with God the Father, God the Son, and God the Holy Spirit.

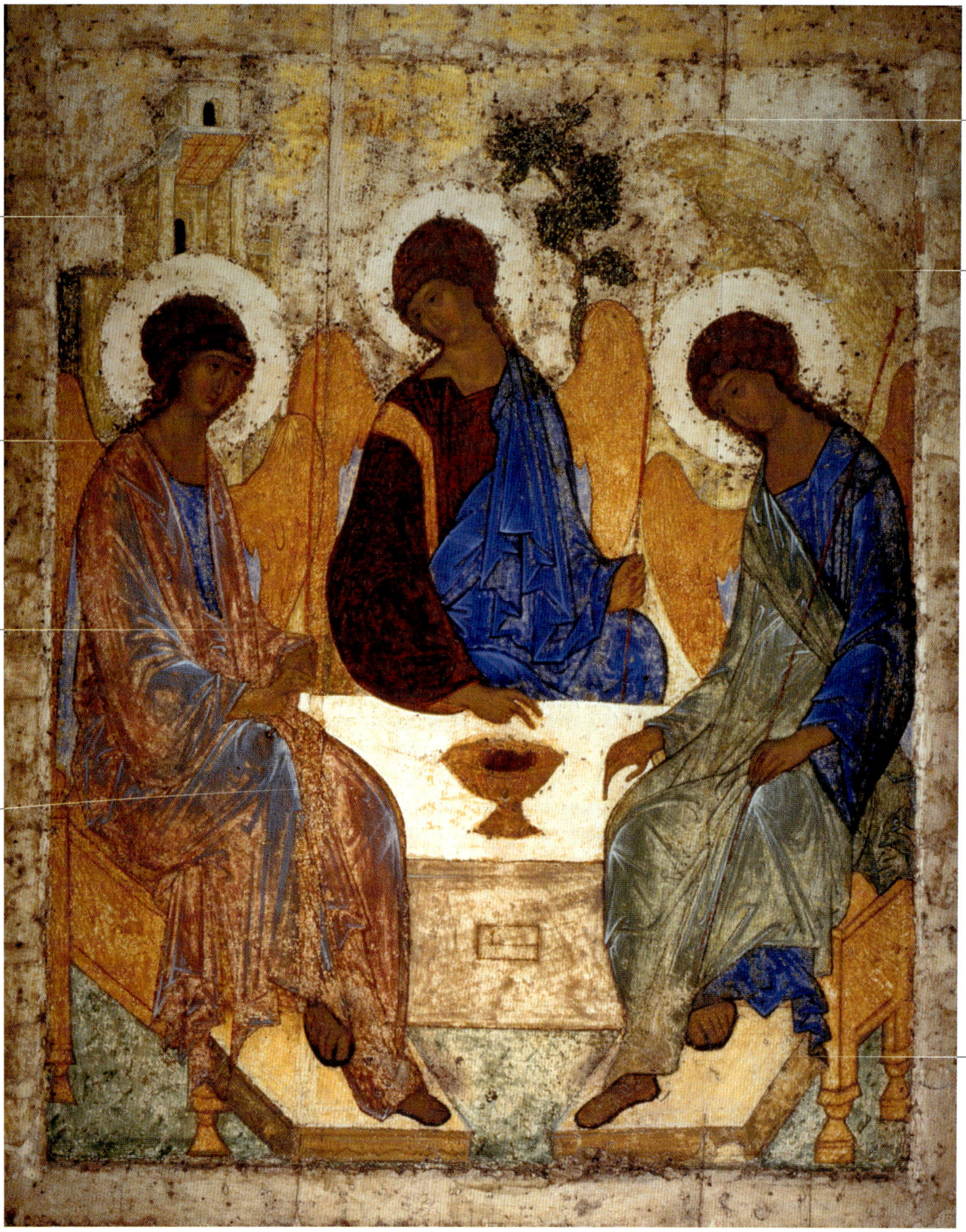

The house of Abraham in the background refers to the Bible story.

God the Father holds out his hands in blessing toward the chalice.

God the Son (center) and the Holy Spirit (right) look toward God the Father (left) with their heads bowed.

The chalice is the focal point of the work and refers to the Christian sacrament of the Eucharist.

The tree is the Oak of Mamre, where Abraham is said to have met the three figures.

The mountain gives compositional symmetry to the house. It also refers to the spiritual ascent toward God.

The flat colors, sharp contours, and gold decoration show the influence of Byzantine icons.

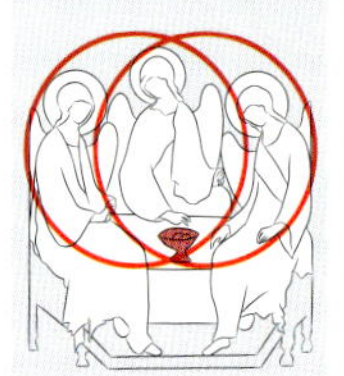

Circular form
The figures' faces, halos, and wings, and the way they are arranged, create circular patterns that meet at the chalice in the center of the work.

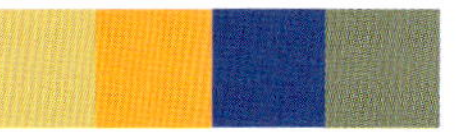

Symbolic colors
The gold and yellows of the background bathe the scene in a spiritual light. The blue used in the figures' robes indicates their divinity, while green represents new life.

"[Rublev is] Russia's answer to the Italian Renaissance."

The Guardian, 2008

Très Riches Heures du Duc de Berry

Limbourg Brothers c. 1412–1416, tempera and gold leaf on vellum, 12 × 8 in (30 × 21.5 cm), Musée Condé, Chantilly, France

May's calendar page from a book of hours made for the Duke of Berry shows an aristocratic outing to celebrate the beginning of spring. The elaborate decoration, naturalistic details, and rich colors used by the Limbourg brothers are characteristic of the courtly International Gothic style.

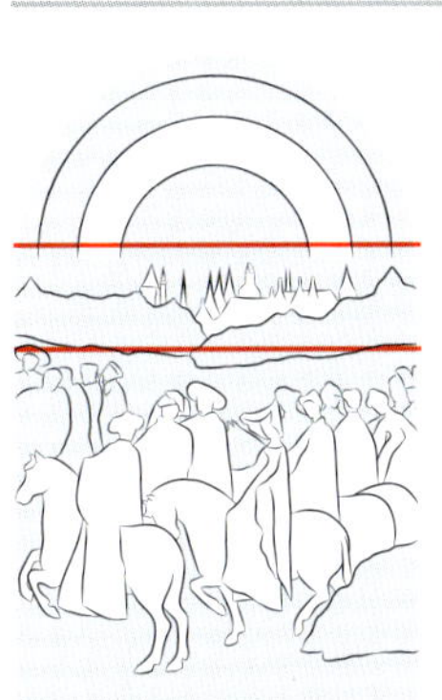

Three levels
The composition divides into three. The lunette represents the heavenly realm; the palace, the political administration; and the procession, the royal court

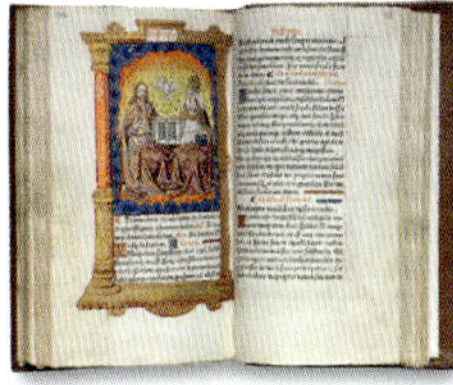

Books of hours
Intended for personal use, books of hours are Christian prayer books containing psalms, prayers, and other devotional texts for reading at set times during the day. In the Middle Ages, they were often highly illustrated.

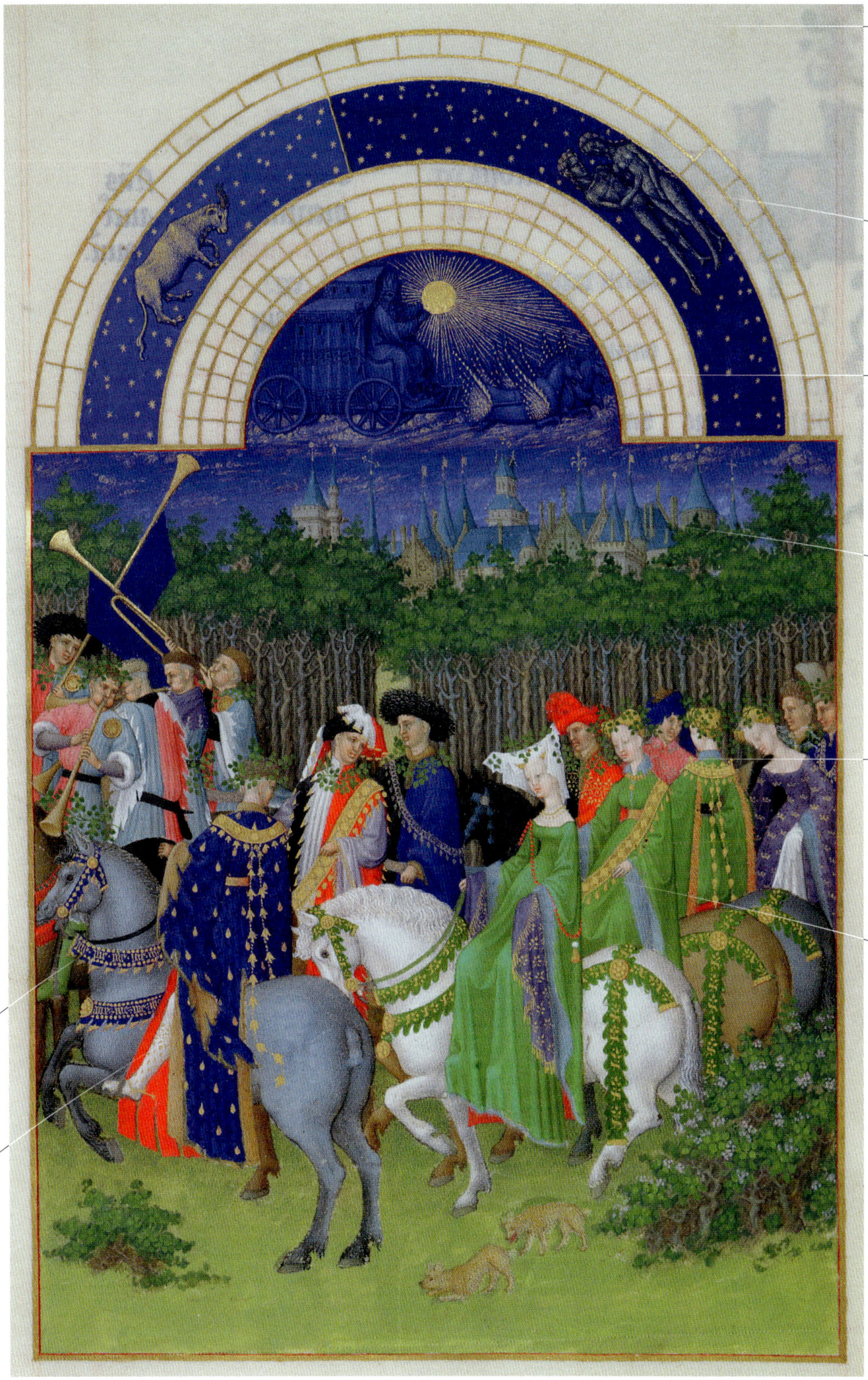

The book of hours is made up of 206 leaves of fine quality parchment. Each month offers a view of medieval life in France from the viewpoint of the book's aristocratic patron.

The lunette depicts May's zodiac signs, the bull (Taurus) and twins (Gemini).

A figure rides a chariot pulling the sun. This was based on a medal owned by the Duke that depicted Heraclius returning the Cross to Jerusalem.

The palace on the Île de la Cité, the center of government in 15th-century Paris, is visible in the distance.

The illustration is typical of the Limbourg brothers' elegant work, combining naturalism and attention to detail with a highly decorative finish.

In the center, Marie de Berry, the daughter of the Duke, rides her white horse. Marie and her attendants wear crowns of leaves and green dresses—symbolizing spring and renewal.

Gilding has been used to add the word *vie*, or "life," to the harness of John de Bourbon's horse.

John de Bourbon, who married Marie, wears a blue cloak decorated with gold details. He looks back toward his wife.

The Tribute Money

Masaccio c. 1426, fresco, 8 × 19½ ft (2.47 × 5.97 m), Brancacci Chapel, church of Santa Maria del Carmine, Florence, Italy

When a temple tax collector demands payment from Peter, one of Christ's disciples, Christ sends Peter to catch a fish, which has a coin in its mouth. Masaccio's rendering of this Bible story uses continuous representation to tell the different episodes in the story simultaneously, so Peter is shown being told to go and catch the fish in the center of the painting while also landing the fish on the left of the painting. The work departs from flat Gothic forms and embraces three-dimensional representation, achieved through the new techniques of the Italian Renaissance, such as foreshortening, one-point perspective, chiaroscuro (light and shade), and aerial perspective.

The white hair and beard, as well as the blue and orange robes, identify this figure as Peter.

Hazy outlines and colors help create a sense of distance, a technique known as aerial perspective.

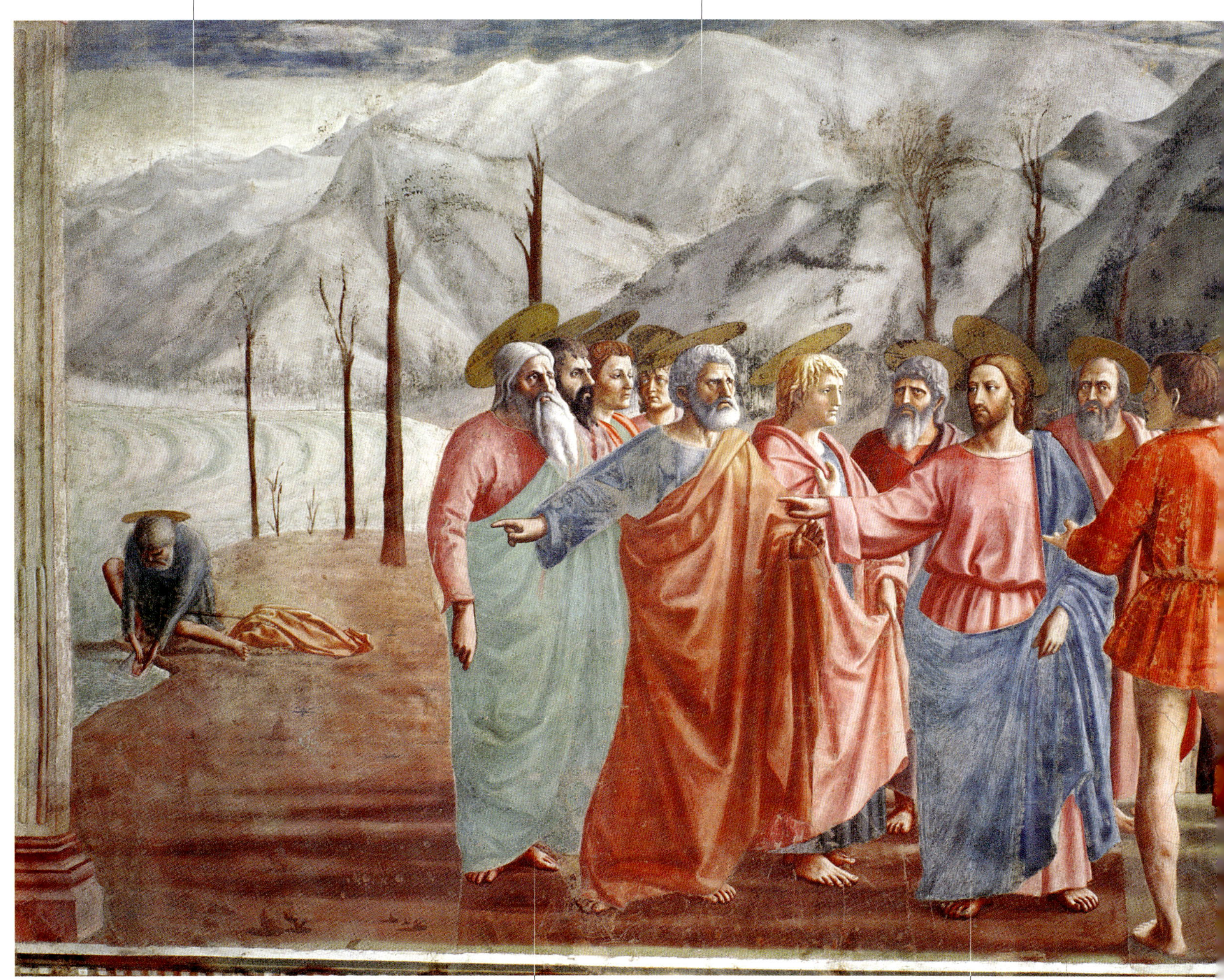

Masaccio gives each apostle weight and form, with a large space around Christ. Groups were previously depicted as heads clustered together.

The central scene is colored blue, pink, and green, in contrast to the muted background. Christ's robe was originally bright azure blue.

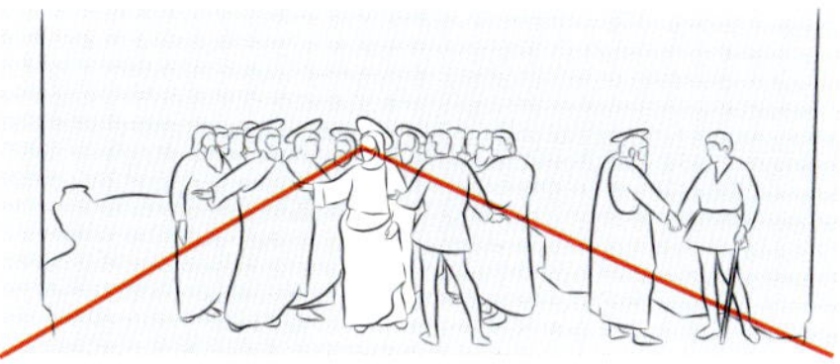

Focused on Christ
One-point perspective leads the eye to Christ, who directs the action of the scene from the center of the painting.

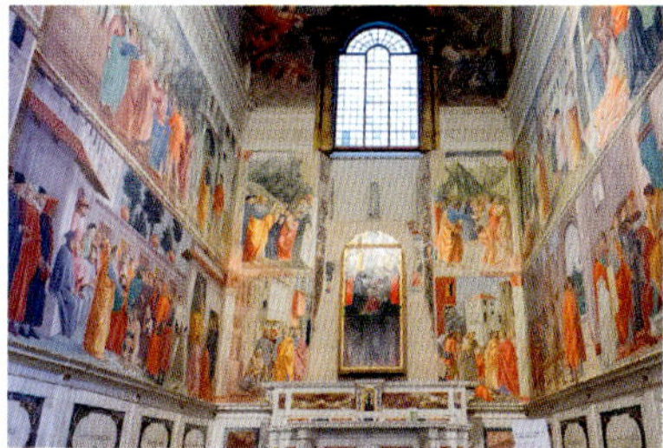

Adorning the Brancacci Chapel
The Tribute Money is just one in a series of frescoes depicting scenes from the life of St. Peter. The Brancacci family commissioned Masaccio and Masolino da Panicale to paint the frescoes between 1425 and 1427.

"To tell the truth, the works created before Masaccio can be described merely as paintings, while his creations, compared to those executed by others are lifelike, true, and natural."

Giorgio Vasari, 1568

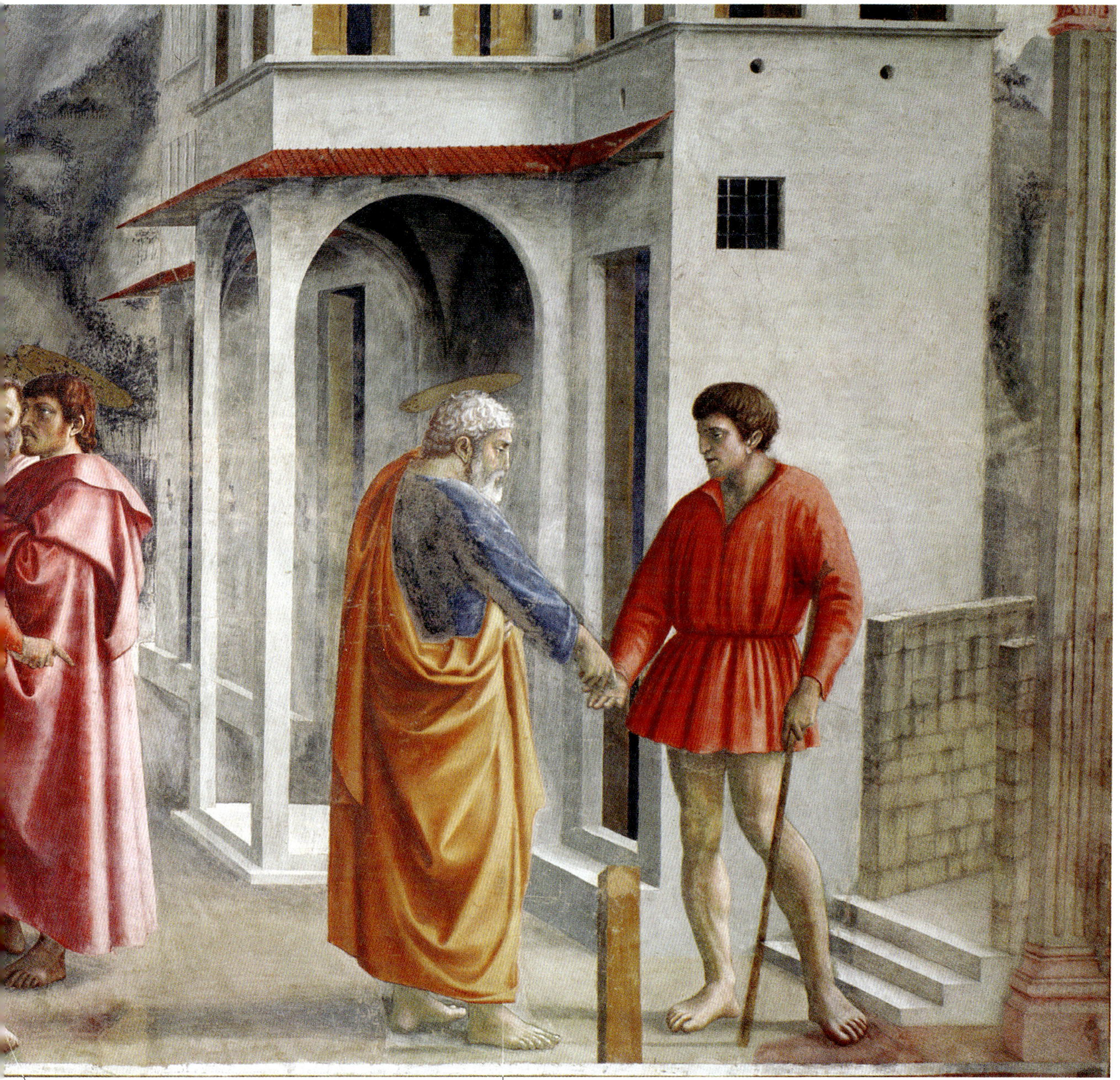

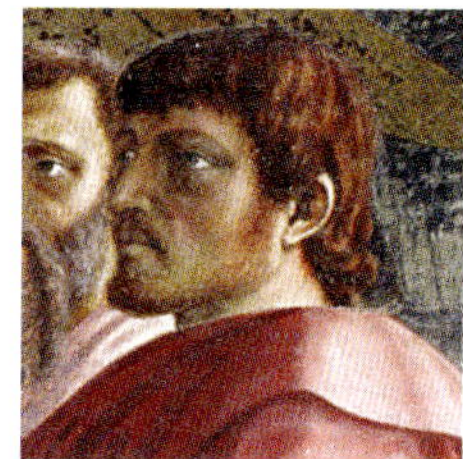

The cloaked man may be a self-portrait of the artist, a theory promoted by one of the first art historians, Giorgio Vasari.

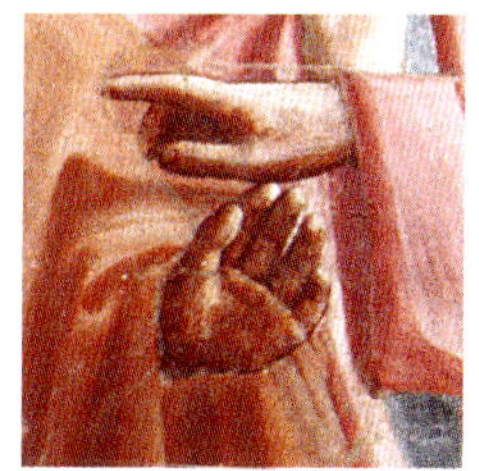

Peter's hand is an example of extreme foreshortening. This technique makes the body more lifelike.

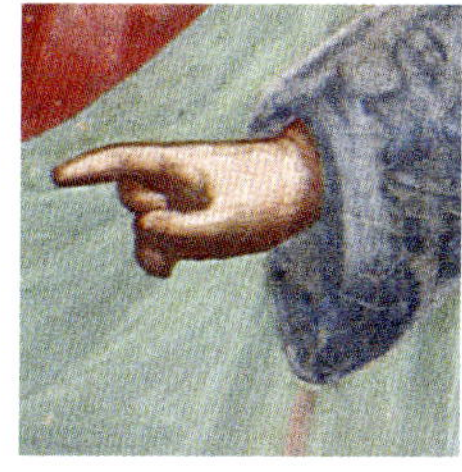

Christ and Peter point to the next part of the narrative, in which Peter catches the fish with the coin in its mouth.

Excluded from the holy group, the tax collector has his back to the viewer and wears a different form of clothing.

Here the story concludes, with Peter paying tribute. The building separates it from the earlier part of the story.

Adoration of the Mystic Lamb

Hubert and Jan van Eyck 1432, oil on wood, 138 x 181 in (350 x 460 cm) (open), St. Bavo's Cathedral, Ghent, Belgium

As a hinged altarpiece, *The Adoration of the Mystic Lamb*, also known as the Ghent Altarpiece, was closed for most of the year, but on holy days, this masterpiece of the Northern Renaissance was opened, putting the 12 exquisitely detailed interior panels on show. In the center at the top, God the Father wears a papal crown and is flanked by the Virgin Mary and John the Baptist. Below them, a bleeding lamb, representing Christ, stands on an altar, receiving the adoration of angels, saints, and popes. The altarpiece was probably designed by Hubert van Eyck, who died in 1426, but primarily painted by his brother Jan. During services, it would have seemed to the congregation that they were being blessed by God himself.

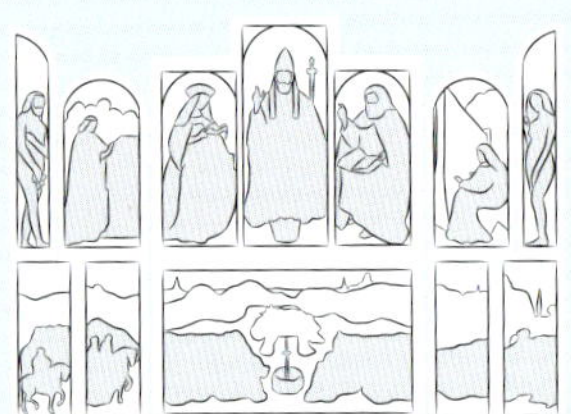

Corresponding motifs The figures lean toward the center of the altarpiece, where the Trinity (God as Father, Son, and Holy Spirit) are aligned with a fountain of Holy Water.

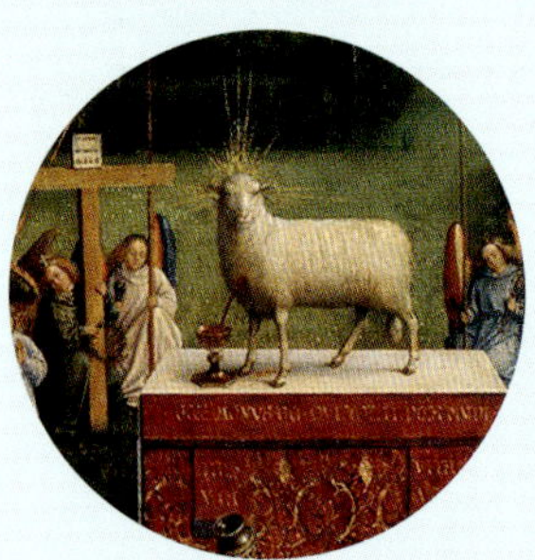

Symbol of Christ In 1550, the humanoid eyes and pursed lips of the Mystic Lamb (bottom panel, center), representing Christ, were painted over. They were revealed during an eight-year restoration of the altarpiece, completed in 2020.

> "The painter Hubert van Eyck, a greater man than whom cannot be found, began this work. Jan, his brother, second in art, completed this weighty task."
>
> Inscribed in Latin on the painting

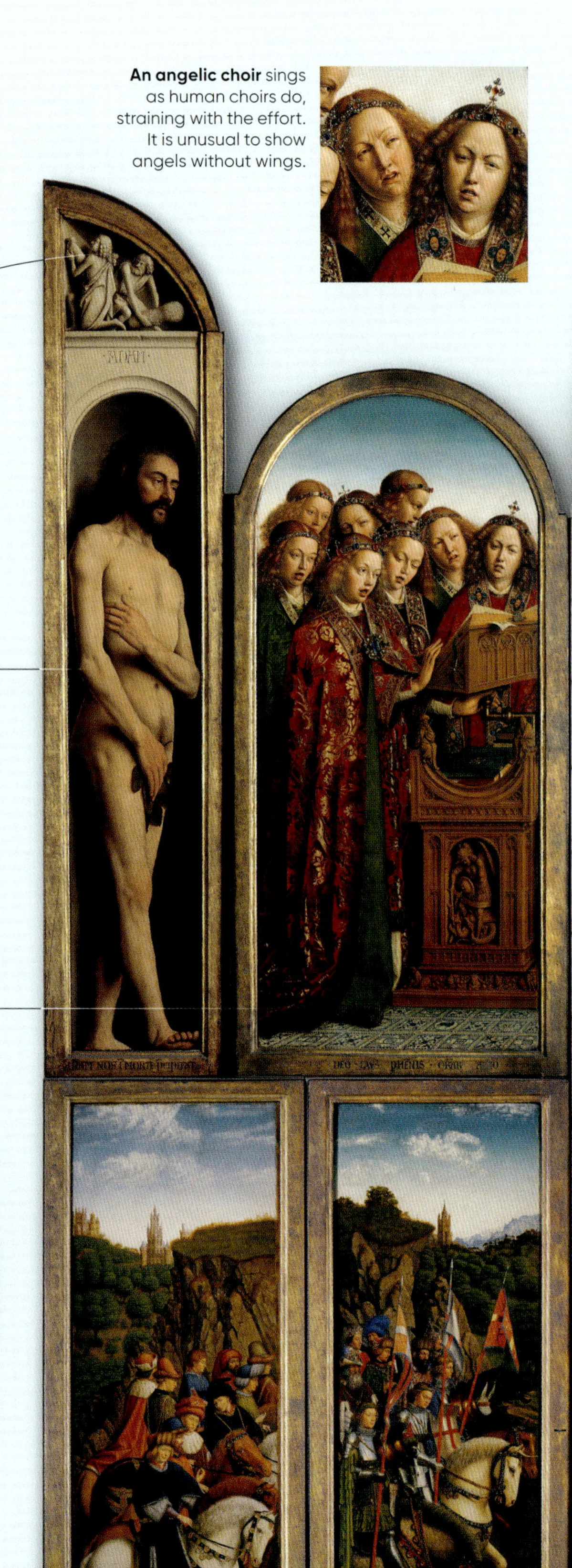

An angelic choir sings as human choirs do, straining with the effort. It is unusual to show angels without wings.

Grisaille (shades of gray) is used to produce a trompe-l'œil effect of statues in a niche.

Adam and Eve are portrayed with natural realism. In more prudish times, their panels were removed from view.

Layers of oil paint and glaze highlight the silk fringe on this angel's cloak.

An idealized city is shown in the background. Aerial perspective—in this case, the use of cool blues and green—is used to create the illusion of distance.

The Just Judges panel is a reproduction. The original panel was stolen in 1934 and has not been recovered.

The Virgin Mary is shown reading to indicate that she conceived Christ according to the Word of God.

Tin relief imitates brocade, giving a solid texture.

Northern Renaissance artists inherited the Gothic method of depicting crowds; a tight group of heads is used to indicate multitudes.

Eve's forbidden fruit is a citron—an ancestor of lemons and limes. Van Eyck probably saw one when traveling in Portugal.

The detail on the organist's ermine-trimmed robe shows Van Eyck's technical skill. The organist may be St. Cecilia, the patron saint of music and musicians.

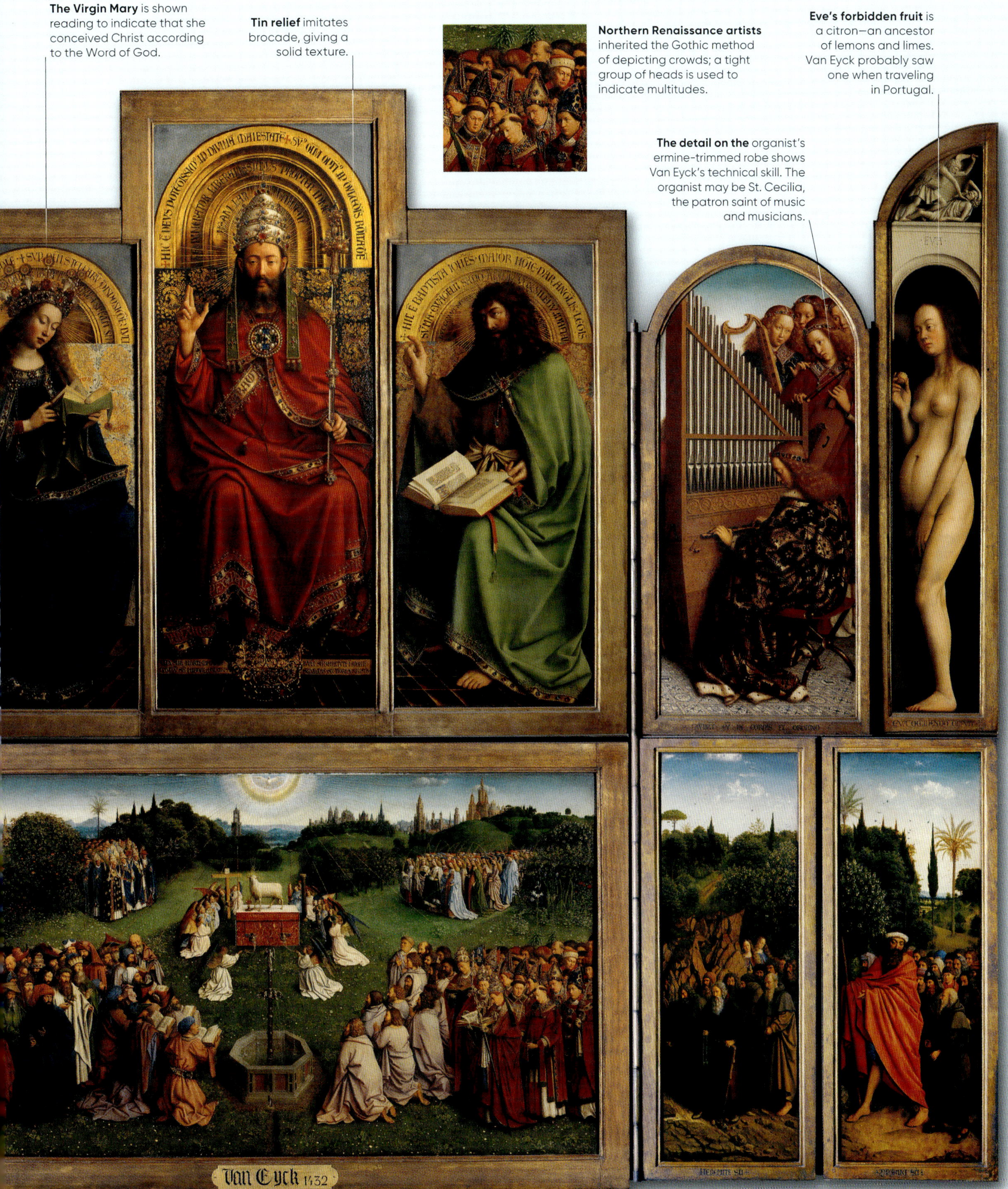

Descent from the Cross

Rogier van der Weyden c. 1435, oil on panel, 81 × 103 in (204.5 × 261.5 cm), Museo del Prado, Madrid, Spain

Depicting the moment when Christ's body is removed from the cross, this painting focuses on the grief and pain of the mourners, all but three of whom are weeping. The dynamic composition, the use of light to accentuate Christ, and the palpable sense of shared grief create a work of emotional intensity.

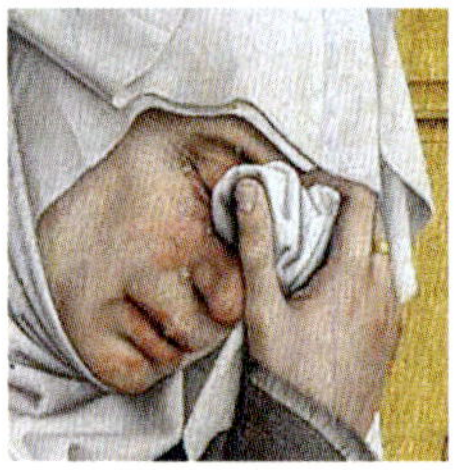

Glistening teardrops intensify the sorrow and passion of the scene.

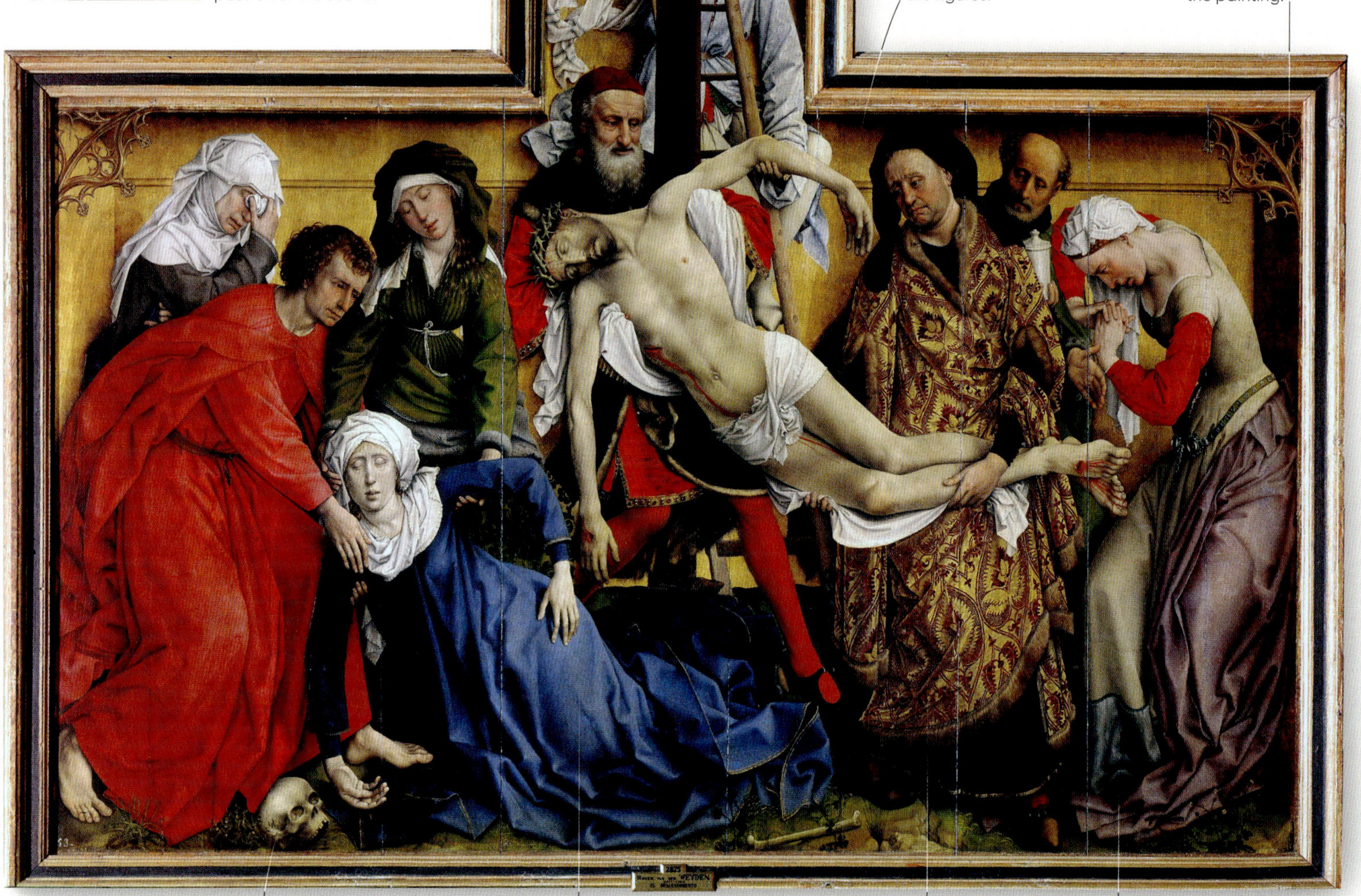

The scene is set within a gilded box, which is similar to an altar shrine. The gold reflects the light, highlighting the figures.

Tracery at the corners of the work forms the shape of crossbows. Leuven's Great Crossbowmen's Guild commissioned the painting.

A skull symbolizes Golgotha (meaning "skull" in Aramaic), the place where Christ was crucified.

The Virgin Mary collapses in grief. Her body echoes the shape of Christ as he is lowered from the cross.

The silk, fur, and embroidery in Joseph of Arimathea's gown show the artist's ability to paint texture and detail.

Mary Magdalene's posture echoes that of John the Evangelist (far left), who is traditionally shown in red at the Crucifixion.

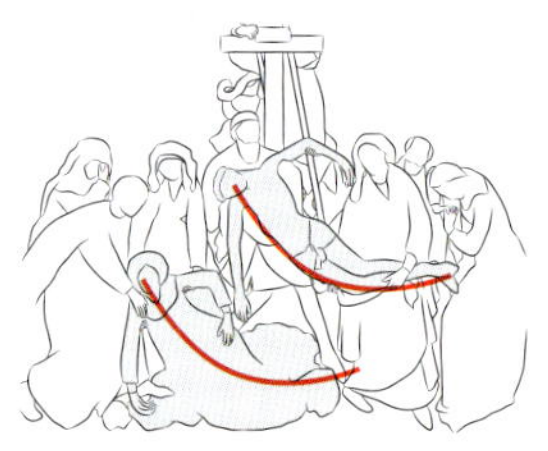

Directing the viewer Lines from the bodies of Christ and Mary point the narrative from Christ's descent from the cross to his entombment, which Joseph of Arimathea will organize.

> "The painted tear, a shining pearl born of the strongest emotion, epitomizes that which Italians most admired in Early Flemish painting: pictorial brilliance and sentiment."
>
> Erwin Panofsky, 1953

The Baptism of Christ

Piero della Francesca 1437–1445, tempera on poplar, 66 × 46 in (167 × 116 cm), National Gallery, London, UK

Author of the first treatise on the art of perspective, Piero captures a moment in the life of Christ. Standing in a stream, he is anointed by John the Baptist as three angels look on and the Holy Spirit, in the form of a dove, hovers overhead. A sense of calm and lightness suffuse the scene.

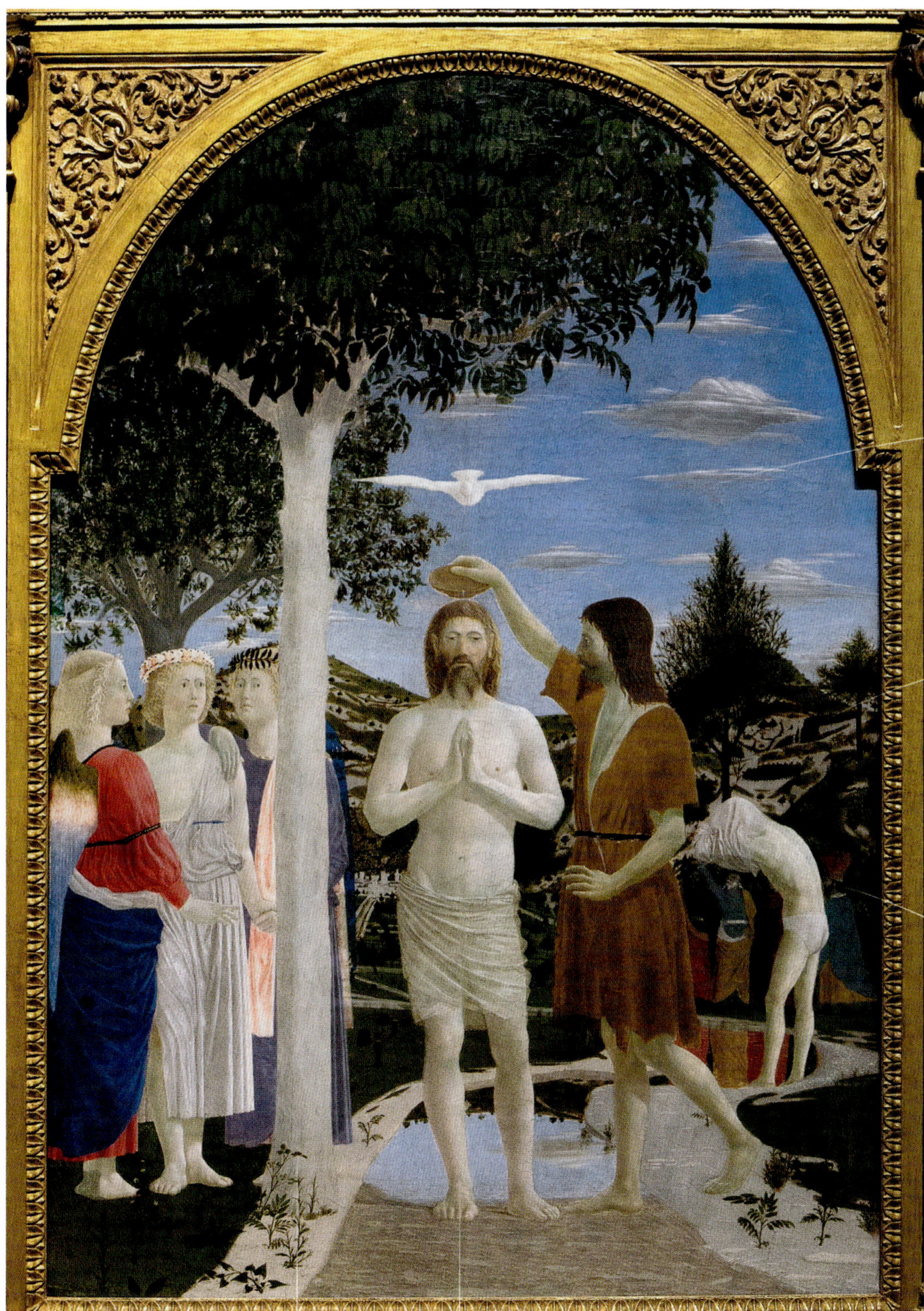

A soft dawn light reflects the mystical transformation that is taking place.

The background resembles the landscape around Sansepolcro, Piero's hometown in Tuscany. The various plants and trees are all from the area.

Unlike the angels, who wear heavy clothing, the figure removing his shirt to expose his flesh symbolizes Christ's new life.

The tree is a reminder of Christ's eventual Crucifixion on a cross of wood.

Each figure is distinctly three-dimensional, in contrast to the conventions of the late Gothic style.

Secret geometry
Christ is aligned with the dove, the water, and his own hands, creating a vertical line that intersects in a cross formation with the line of the horizon.

Muted colors
Piero's limited palette and soft tones unite the figures with the paradisiacal landscape in the background.

> "Piero differs from almost all the great colorists in European painting in that his color is pale and cool … without degenerating into mere coldness."
>
> Kenneth Clark, 1951

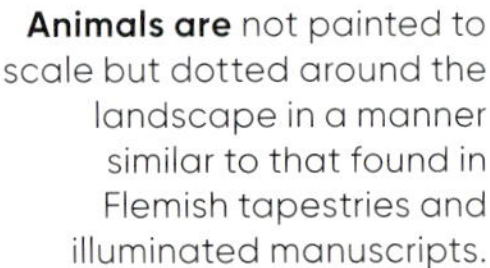

Animals are not painted to scale but dotted around the landscape in a manner similar to that found in Flemish tapestries and illuminated manuscripts.

Believed to pierce its own breast with its beak to feed its young with blood, the pelican was a symbol of Christ.

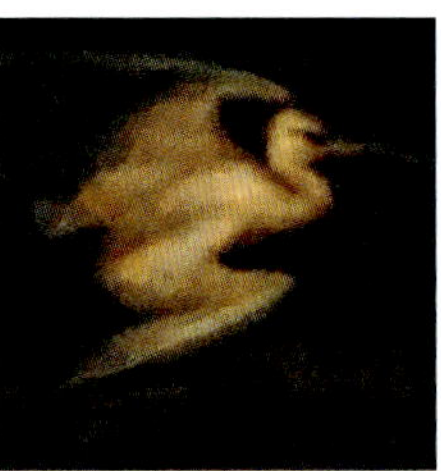

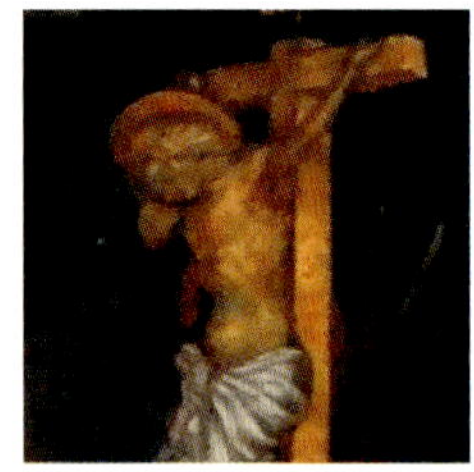

The painting combines the ideals of Christian chivalry and the excitement of the hunt, making it appealing to patrons.

Eustace is dressed as a prince in contemporary court fashion, with a blue headdress, gold jacket, and gilded spurs.

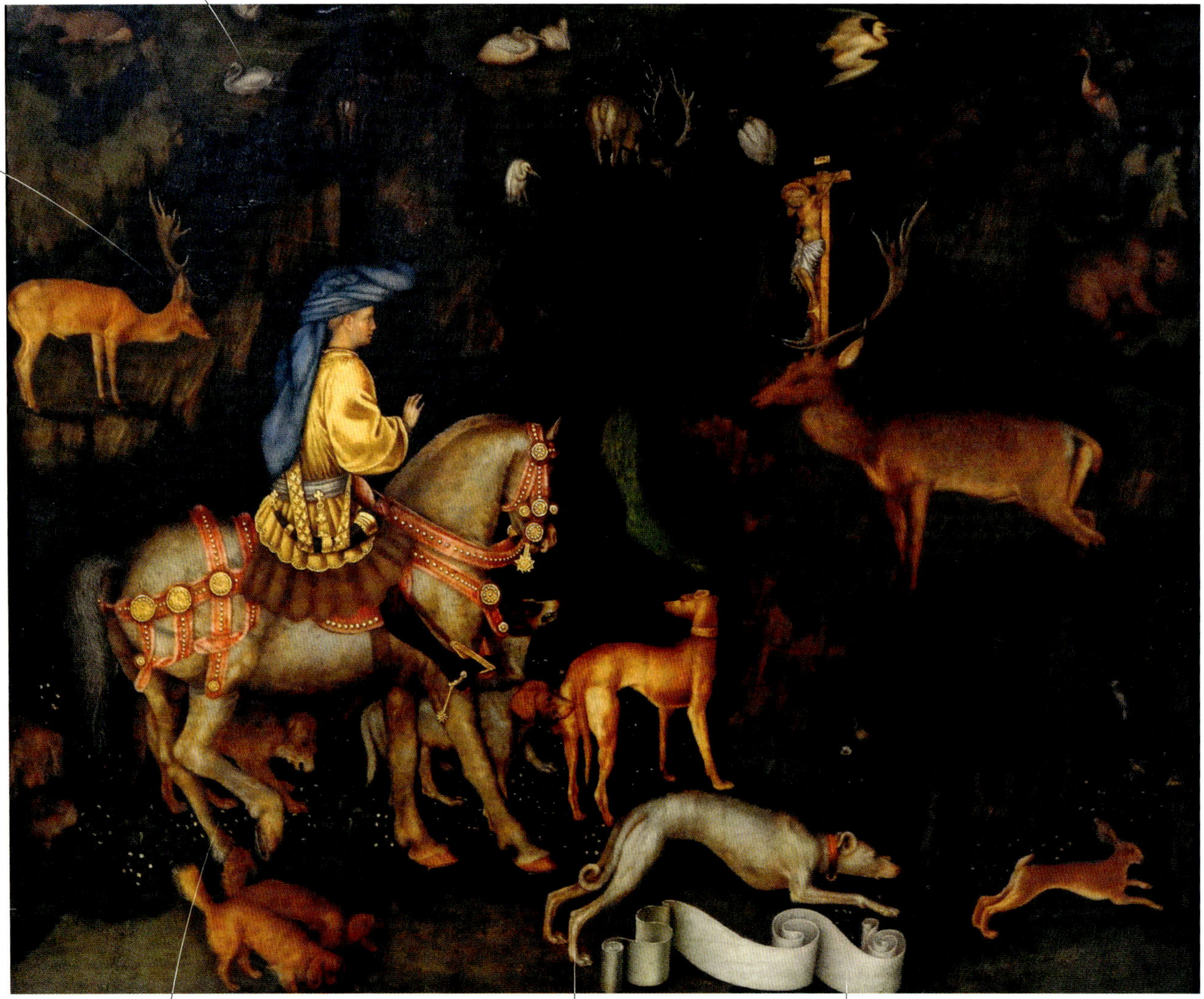

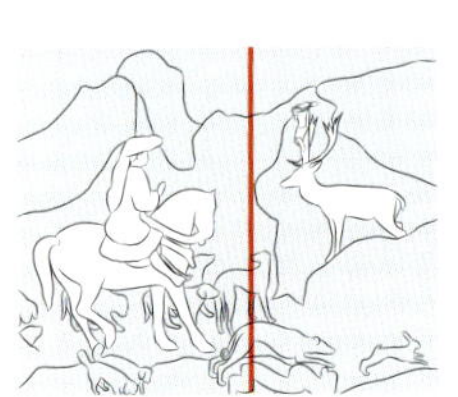

Two halves
The painting divides into two. The sumptuously clad hunter is balanced by the vision of the crucifix and stag.

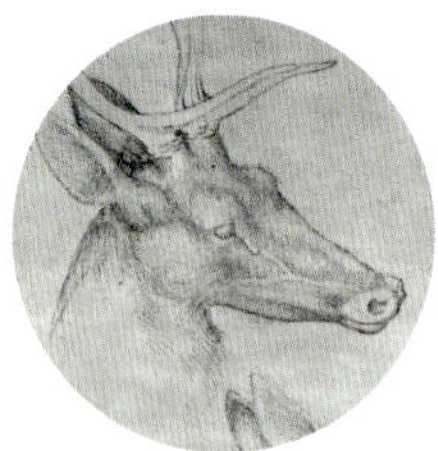

Natural world
Pisanello's skill in depicting different animals was celebrated. Like other early 15th-century artists, he often included animals in his work and made many preparatory sketches.

The bent hind leg of the horse conveys its arrested motion.

Certain breeds of dog were used to hunt specific quarry. This greyhound would have coursed hares, and the spaniels (bottom left) would have been used to flush out birds.

A small scroll is left blank. No one knows why it is there, but a similar scroll can be seen in a work by one of Pisanello's pupils.

The Vision of Saint Eustace

Pisanello c. 1438-1442, tempera on poplar, 22 × 26 in (54.8 × 65.5 cm), National Gallery, London, UK

Out hunting in the forest, Eustace, a Roman soldier, has a vision of a stag with a crucifix between its antlers. This dramatic moment, witnessed by an array of birds and animals, leads to his conversion to Christianity. Pisanello's exquisite painting on a small wooden panel was intended for personal religious devotions at home.

The Annunciation

Fra Angelico 1442–1443, fresco, 91 × 126 in (230 × 321 cm), Museo Nazionale di San Marco, Florence, Italy

Portraying the moment when the angel Gabriel tells Mary that she will conceive a child by the Holy Spirit, this fresco was commissioned for a stairway in the convent of San Marco. The monks passed the scene daily, entering into its quiet spirituality before dispersing to their dormitories. Fra Angelico exaggerated the size of the central characters in the scene to heighten the drama.

The only decorative element is the angel's wings, designed by God rather than Man.

The angel looks directly into Mary's eyes, creating a moment of intimacy that the viewer witnesses.

Mary and Gabriel are presented with plain halos. In Fra Angelico's earlier *Annunciation* of 1426, the halos are more elaborate.

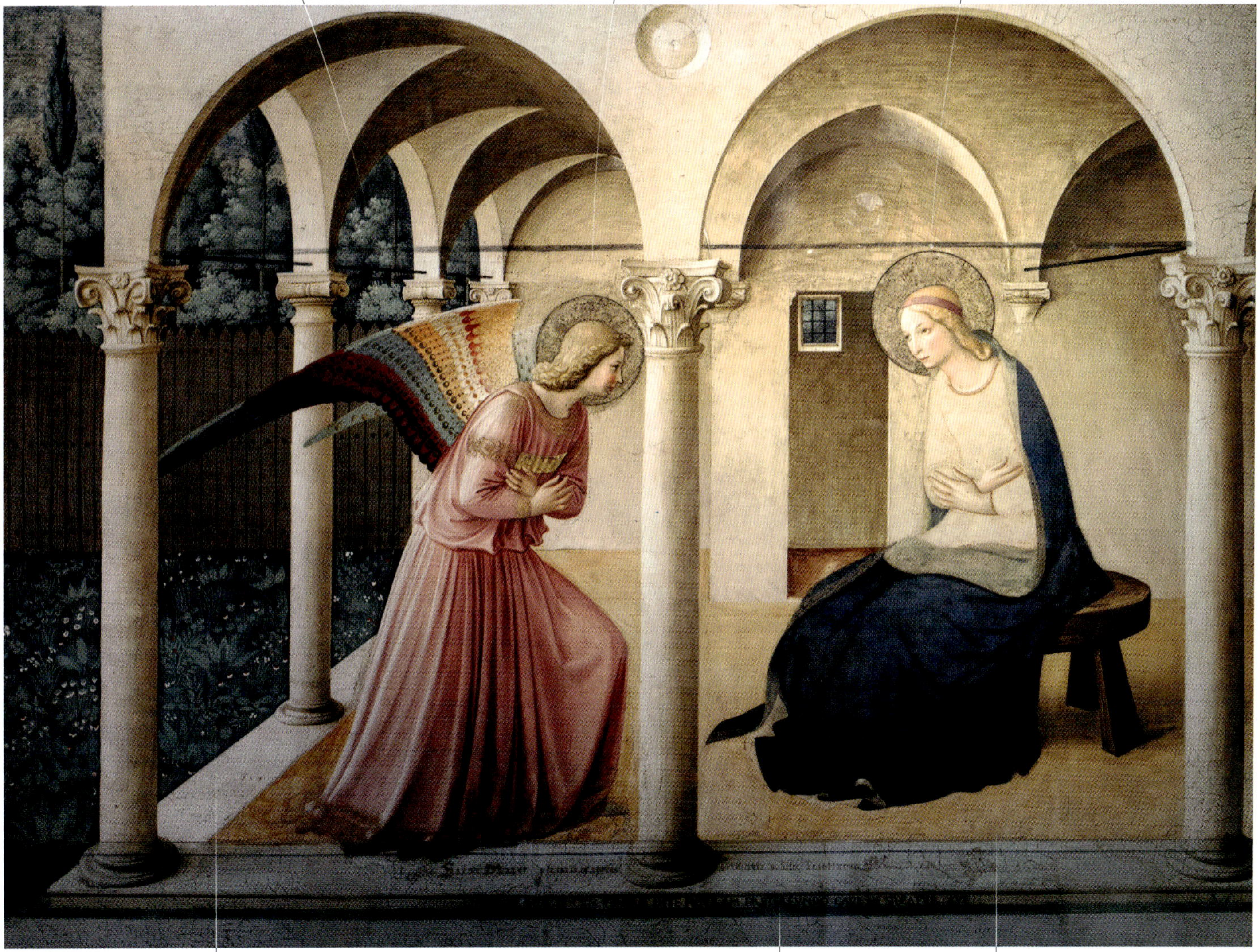

A garden, representing the Garden of Eden, lies behind a high fence, reminding visitors of the Fall and the salvation promised by Christ.

The Latin inscription translates as "Hail Mother of Piety and noble couch of the Trinity." It comes from a hymn written for the feast of the Nativity of the Blessed Virgin.

The plain loggia is similar to the cloisters of the convent of San Marco.

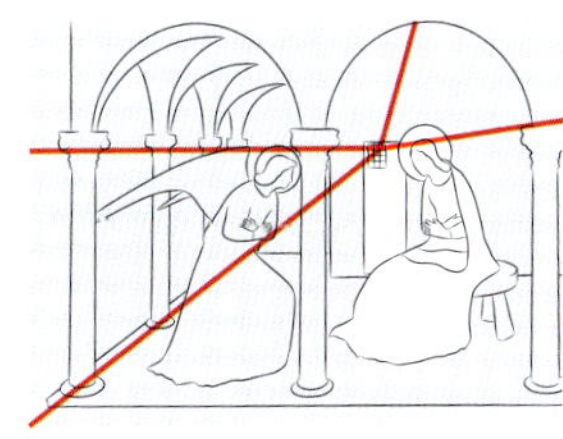

Symbolic window
The vanishing point for this Annunciation occurs in the barred window in the room beyond the Virgin Mary, a symbol of her chastity.

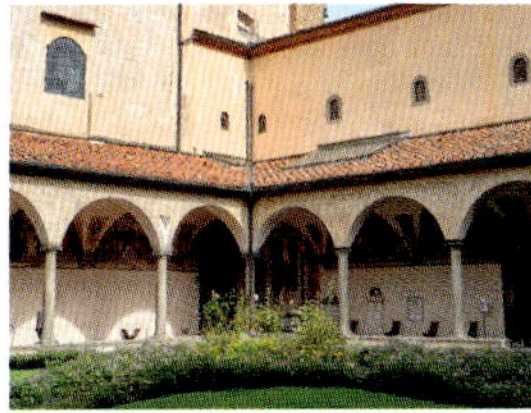

Convent decoration
Fra Angelico was commissioned to paint 50 frescoes to decorate the walls of the convent of San Marco when it was rebuilt by Cosimo de'Medici in 1437.

> "… as you pass by, take care that you do not fail to say Ave!"
>
> Inscription, Convent of San Marco

The Florentine army's massed ranks follow the commander into battle.

A forest of lances pierces the sky; the two at the front point toward the vanishing point.

The serenity of the farmland in the background contrasts with the chaos of the battlefield.

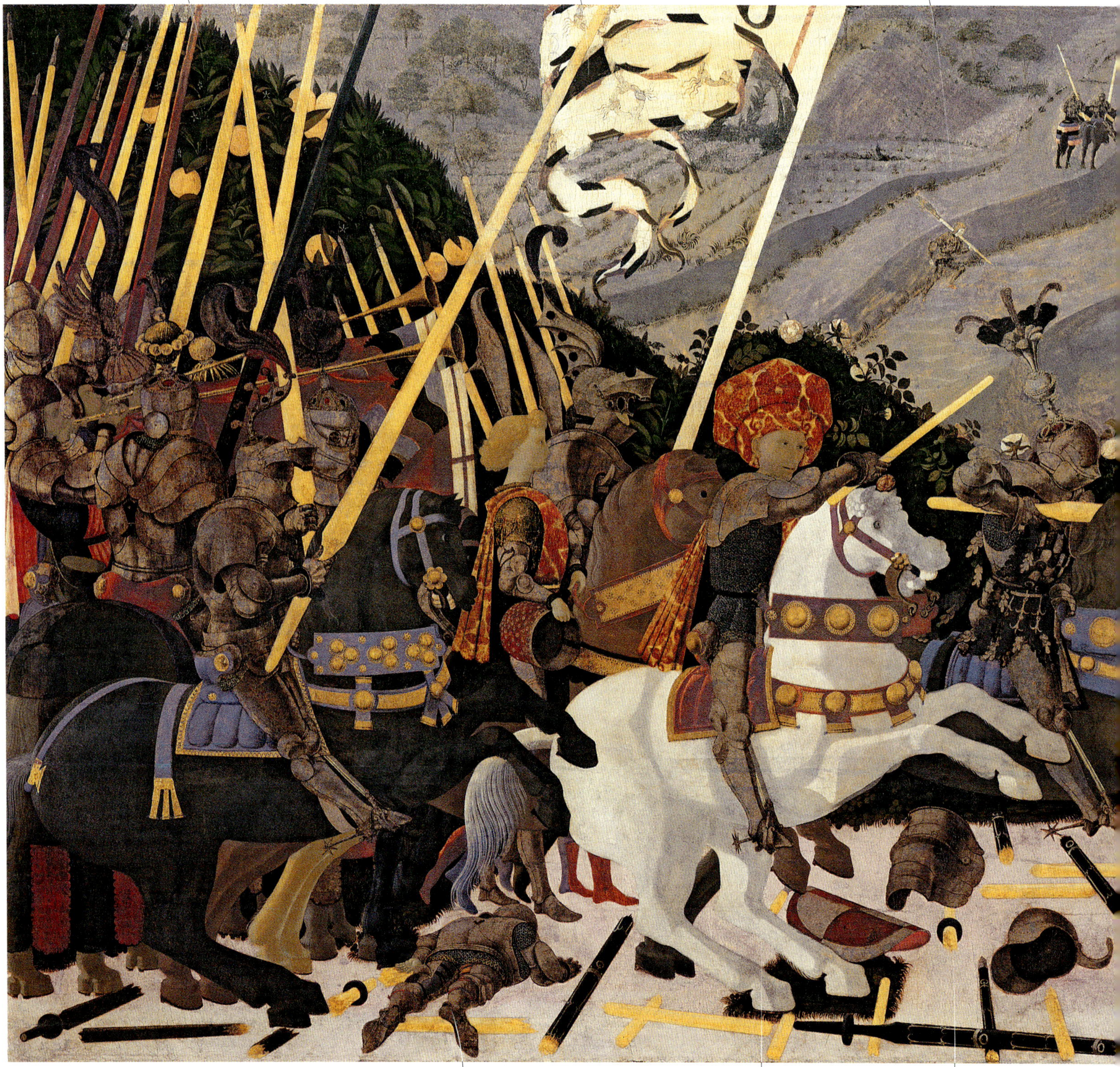

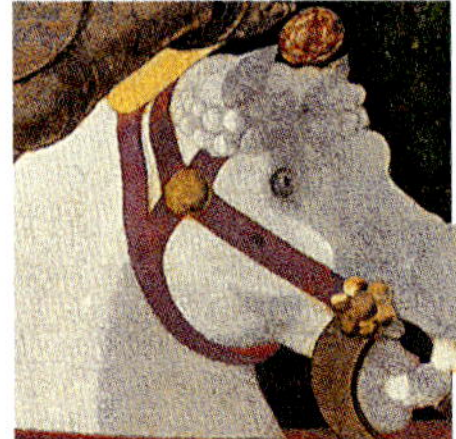

Bulging eyes and flared nostrils convey the white horse's terror.

The fallen soldier is an attempt at foreshortening in a single figure. An artist creates perspective by mimicking the distortion seen by the human eye.

The colorful turban and distinctive white horse of the Florentine commander are the focus of attention.

Fallen armor lying at various angles shows Uccello's mastery of foreshortening.

A soldier loads a crossbow while other background figures run in panic.

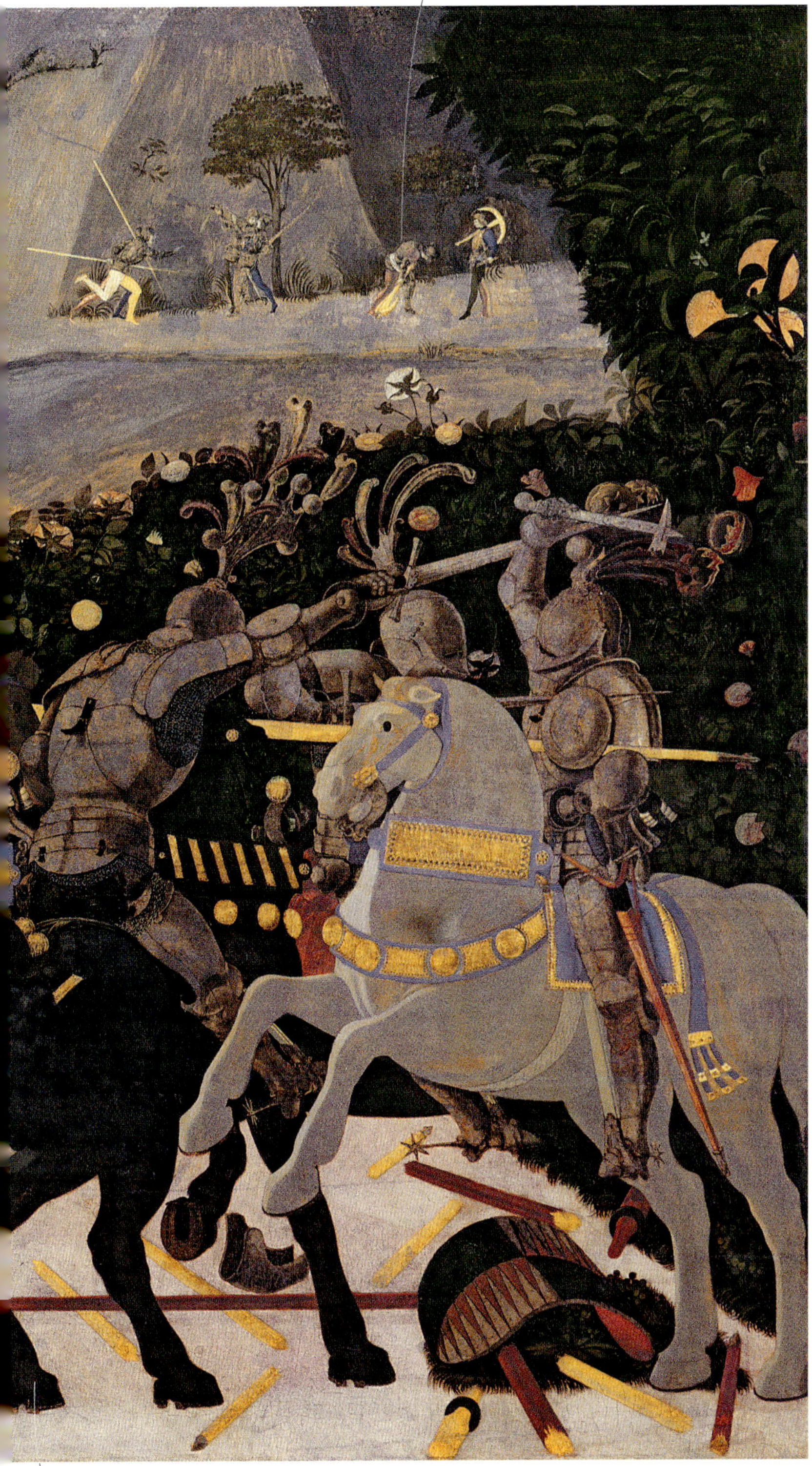

Horses generally wore armor in battle, but Uccello portrays them without it to display their beauty.

The knight on the gray horse is the lone representative of the opposing army.

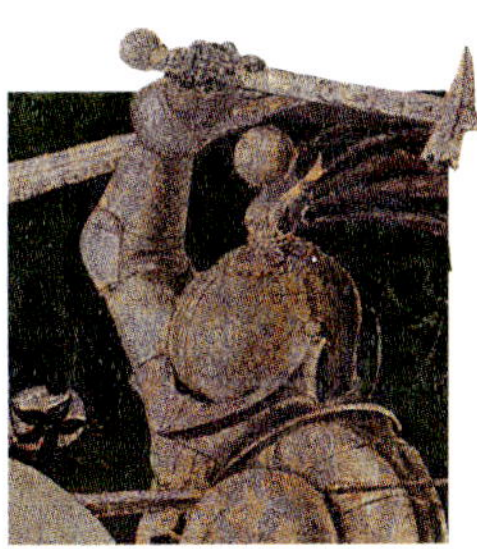

The Battle of San Romano

Paolo Uccello 1456, egg tempera with walnut oil and flaxseed oil on poplar, 72 × 126 in (182 × 320 cm). National Gallery, London, UK

In 1432, Florence vanquished the cities of Lucca, Siena, and Milan in battle. Twenty-four years later, the victory was immortalized by Uccello in a set of three panels, including this one centering on Niccolò Mauruzi da Tolentino, the Florentine commander. Uccello's use of perspective was groundbreaking. The vegetation and people seem to recede into the distance, and the angles of the lances create a sense of depth. The knights on their rocking-horse chargers are far from the reality of war, yet the broken armor and fallen knight are reminders of its cost.

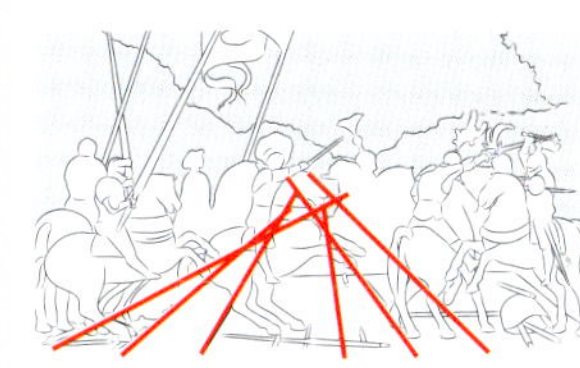

New perspective
Broken lances point to a cluster of vanishing points above the head of the white horse, creating a sense of depth.

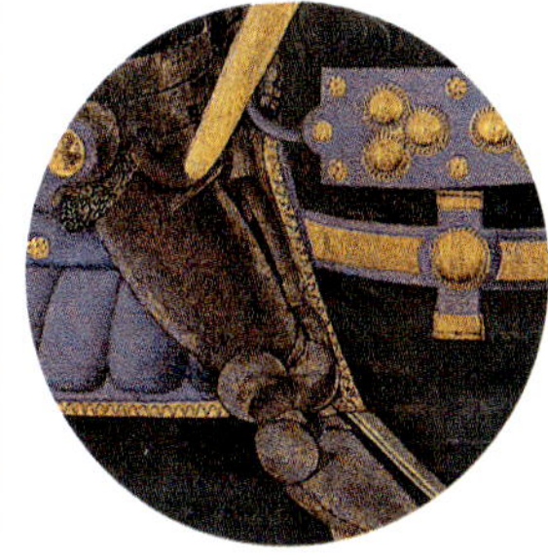

Embellishments
The bright blue of the horses' saddles and barding stand out against the mellow browns of the background. Uccello used real silver and gold for the metallic embellishments.

> "Ah, Paolo, this perspective of yours makes you abandon the substance for the shadow."
>
> Donatello

The Virgin in the Rose Bower

Stefan Lochner c. 1440–1442, oil on oak, 20 × 16 in (50.5 × 40 cm), Wallraf-Richartz-Museum, Cologne, Germany

Lochner's Virgin Mary sits in a *hortus conclusus* (enclosed garden), a symbolic representation of her untouched womb. Her humble blush and the childlike bodies and soft curly hair of the angels and the Christ Child imbue the work with innocence and sweetness. It is likely that this panel was originally part of a diptych, with a kneeling donor presented by a patron saint in the second panel.

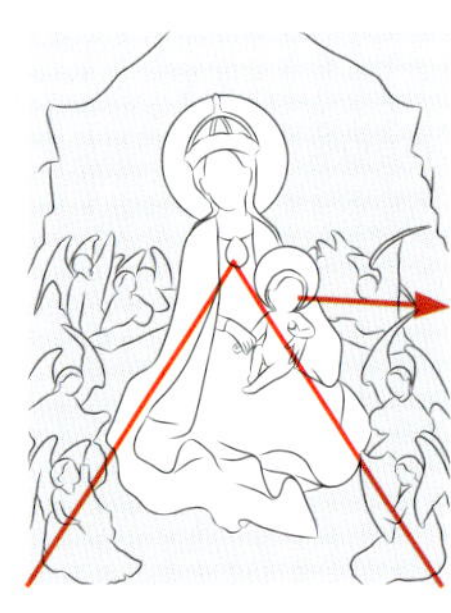

Lines of focus
Christ regards the donor on his left, while the vanishing point centers on the Virgin's brooch, another representation of her purity.

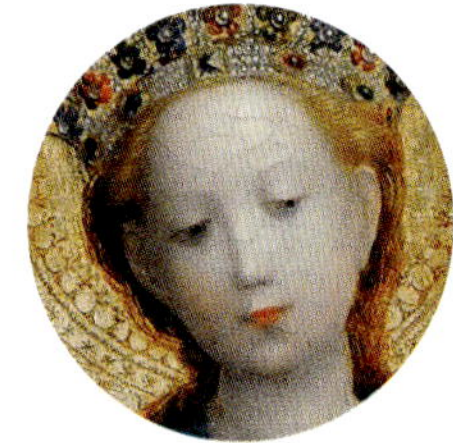

Enhanced effect
Lochner used red to outline the features of his figures, increasing the translucent porcelain quality of their skin.

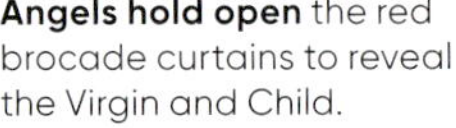

Angels hold open the red brocade curtains to reveal the Virgin and Child.

God the Father and God the Holy Ghost peer down on God the Son, together representing the Trinity.

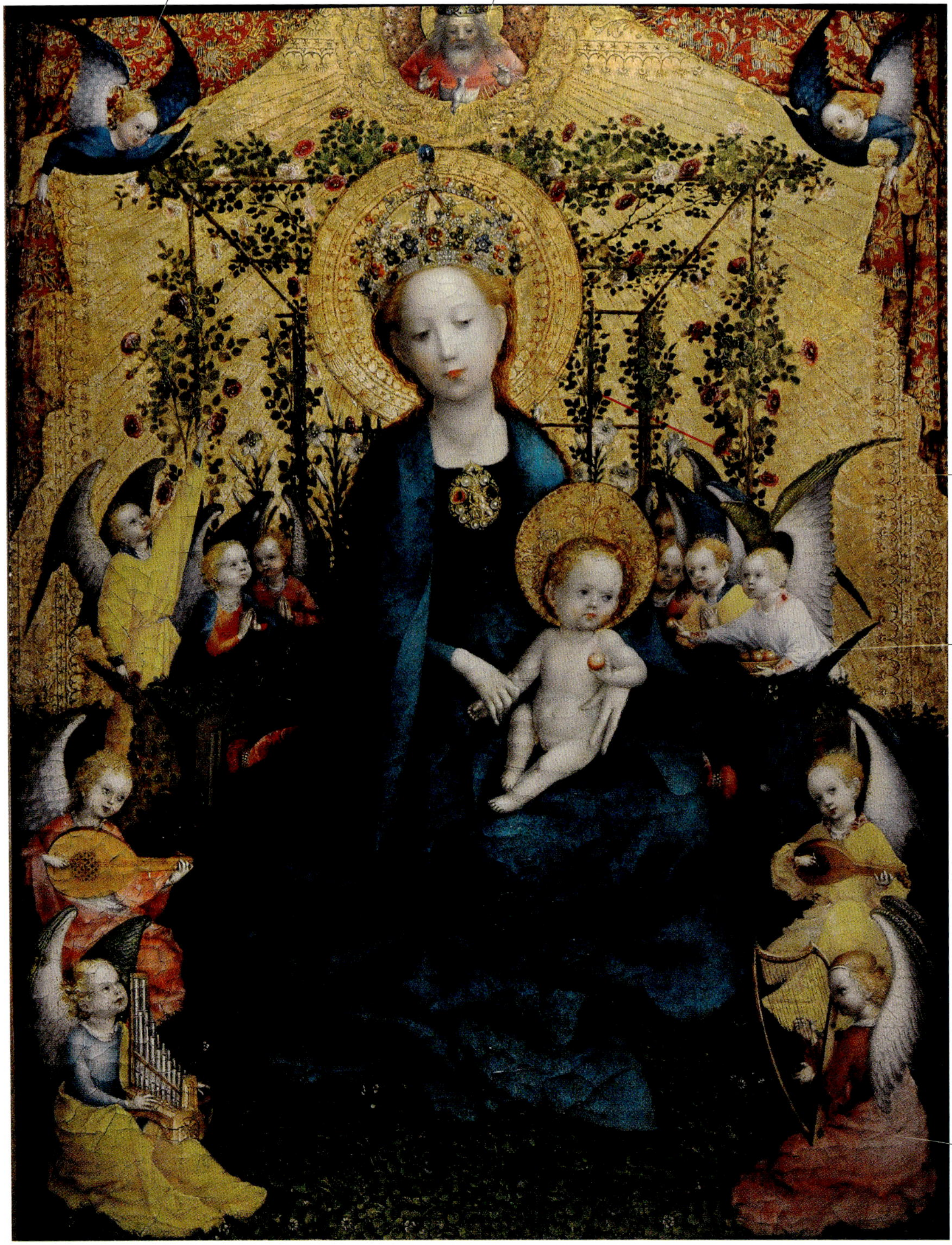

Lochner created gilding by building up layers of chalk ground that were carved and then covered with gold leaf.

As the "new Adam," Christ holds an apple, signifying salvation from the fall of humankind in the Garden of Eden.

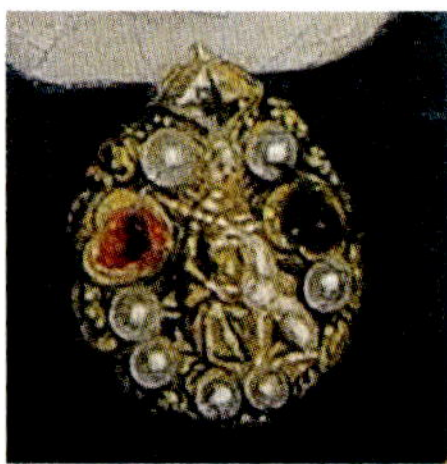

A bejeweled brooch on Mary's chest shows a young girl holding a unicorn, in the same way that Mary holds Christ.

The Virgin and Child appear in an earthly paradise, with roses, strawberries, and lilies blooming while an angelic band plays.

David Victorious

Donatello c. 1440s, partly gilded bronze, 62 in (158 cm), Museo Nazionale del Bargello, Florence, Italy

The Biblical hero David contemplates his victory over the tyrannical giant Goliath. Donatello's statue was probably commissioned by the wealthy Medici family to inspire 15th-century Florentines to defend their city against its enemies at home and abroad. It was the first large, freestanding, bronze male nude in a thousand years of Western art, and inspired Michelangelo's statue of the same name.

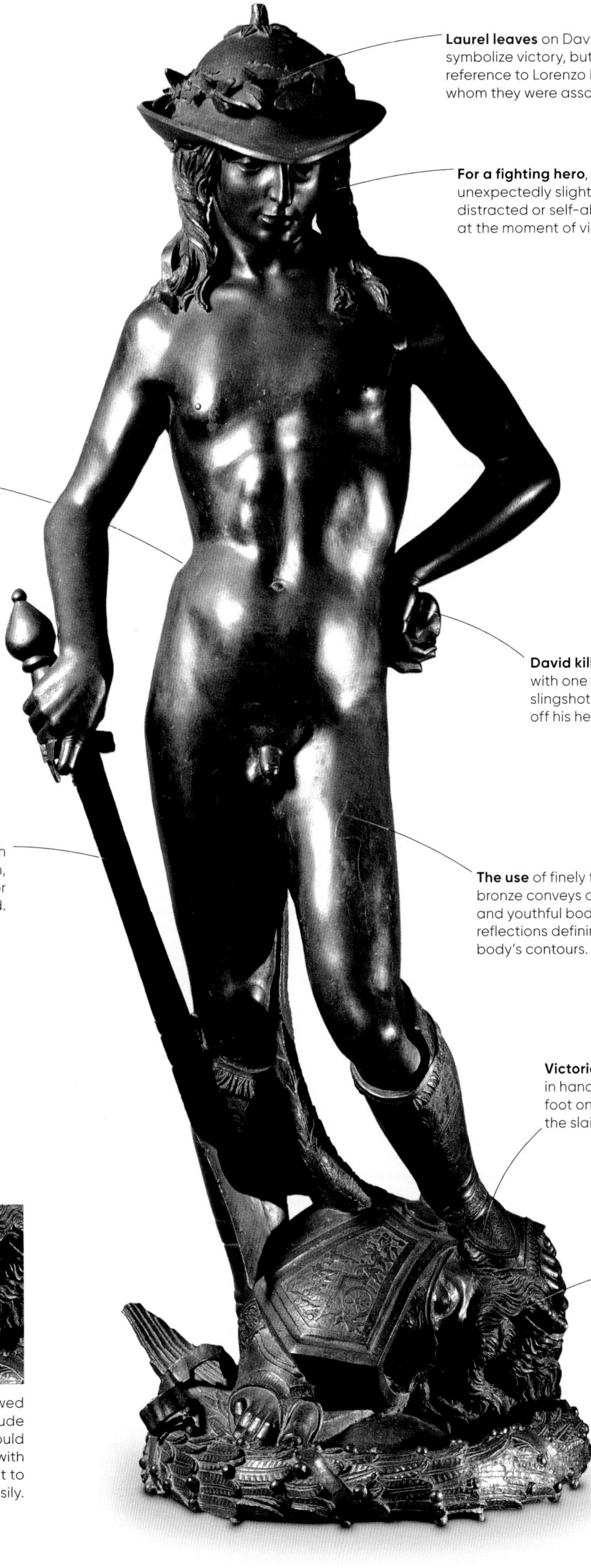

Laurel leaves on David's hat symbolize victory, but could be a reference to Lorenzo Medici, with whom they were associated.

For a fighting hero, David is unexpectedly slight. He is also distracted or self-absorbed at the moment of victory.

With his pelvis pushed forward and his weight on one leg, David's body is contrapposto, a sculptural stance favored by the ancient Greeks.

David killed Goliath with one stone from his slingshot. He then cut off his head.

Goliath's sword, which may be a falchion, looks too large for David to wield.

The use of finely finished bronze conveys a smooth and youthful body, its reflections defining the body's contours.

Victorious with sword in hand, David rests his foot on the head of the slain Goliath.

Goliath's gruesome head contrasts with the sensuality of David's body.

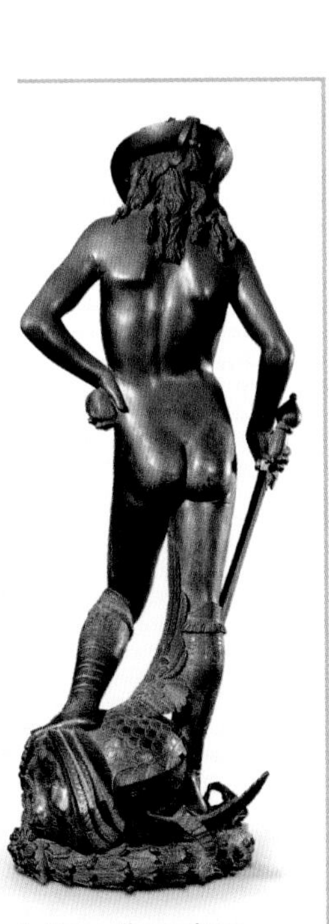

In three dimensions
Originally placed on a pedestal in the Medici palace courtyard, the statue was designed to be viewed in the round.

Reviving an ancient art
Donatello used the lost wax method to cast *David*, an old technique that Renaissance artists revived. The artist first carves the work from wax, then encases it in clay and fires it in a kiln. The mold that is left behind is then filled with molten bronze.

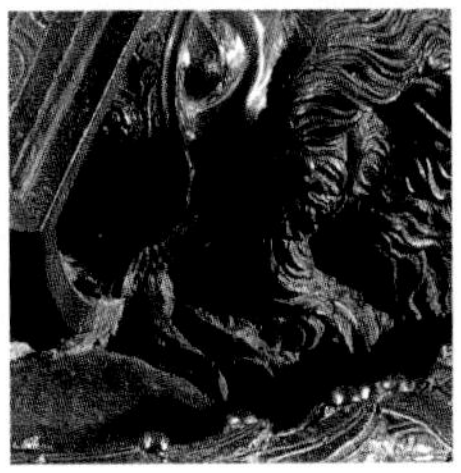

Using casting allowed Donatello to include intricate details. This would not have been possible with marble, which is difficult to work and fractures easily.

The Miraculous Draft of Fishes

Konrad Witz 1444, oil on panel, 53 × 60 in (134.6 × 153.2 cm), Musée d'Art et d'Histoire, Geneva, Switzerland

Christ stands by the shore while his disciples struggle to pull a net of fishes into their boat. The scene reflects two Biblical passages when Christ—alive and later resurrected—helps his disciples secure a huge catch. It is the first known work to depict a recognizable landscape; Lake Geneva represents the Sea of Galilee.

The view looking southwest from Lake Geneva would have been familiar to those seeing the painting. The work was originally part of an altarpiece at St. Peter's Cathedral in Geneva.

Witz placed Christ in the shallows by the lake's edge, leading some to suggest that the scene also reflects Christ walking on water.

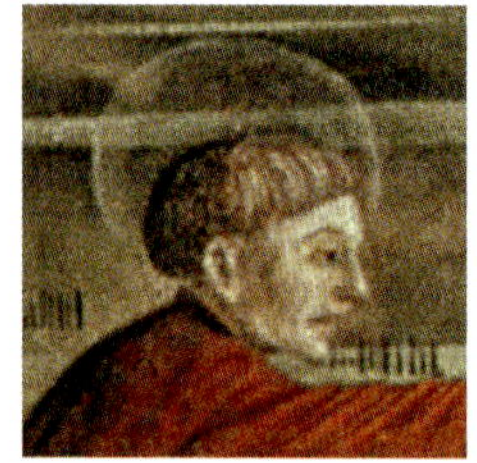

The disciples' halos are almost imperceptible. There are no distracting elements to prevent the viewer from focusing on the story.

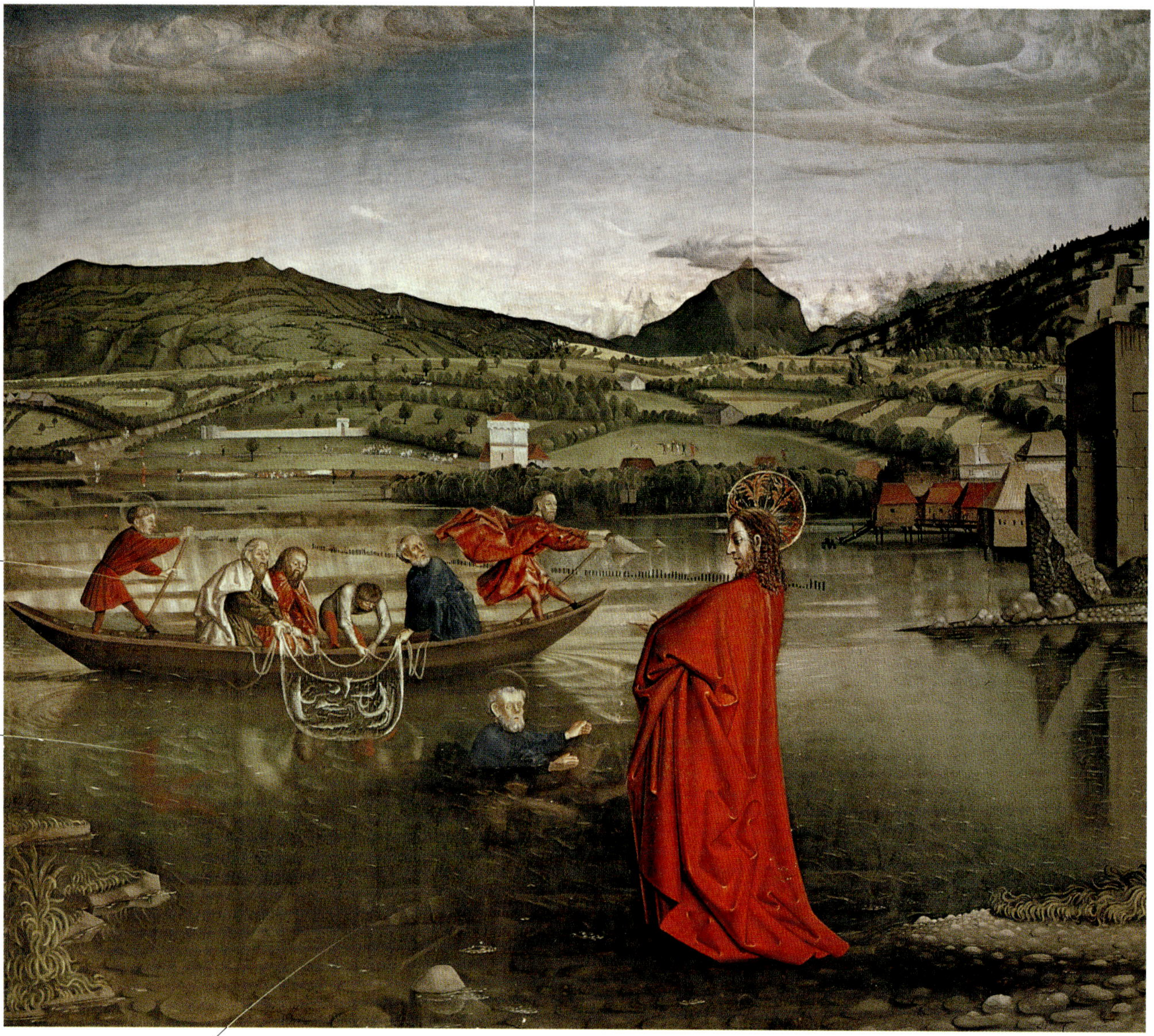

In St. John's Gospel (21:1–7), the resurrected Christ tells the disciples to cast their nets on the right side of the boat. They do so, and their catch is huge.

Reflections of the boat and the disciples, including St. Peter who has jumped out to thank Christ, are perfectly rendered.

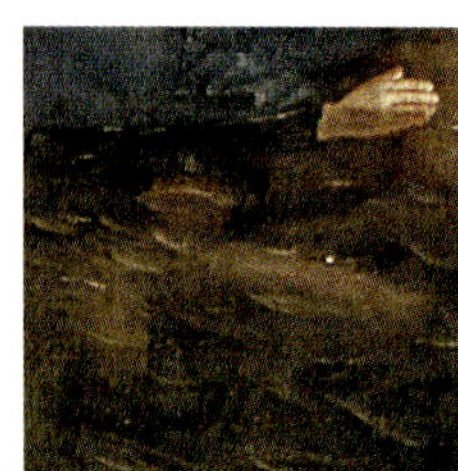

St. Peter's legs are distorted by the water. This is the first time that refraction had been shown in painting.

Light reflected off the surface of the water and off the stones in the shallow area of the lake is painted in a naturalistic manner.

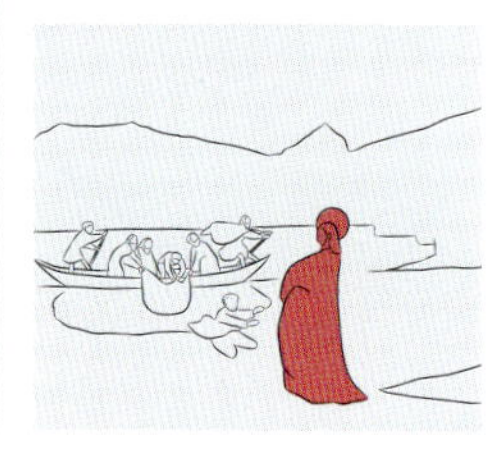

Supernatural focus
The tall, dominating figure of Christ in a flowing red cloak seems to float on the water. Unlike the figures of the disciples, it has no reflection.

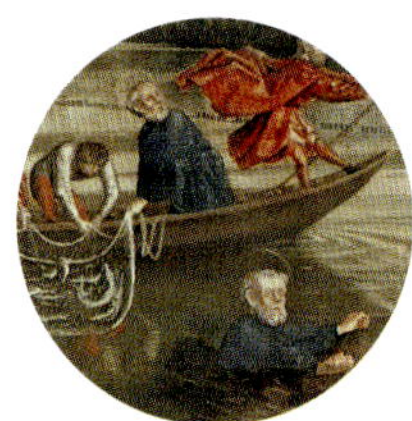

Time shift
The painting shows two scenes at once. One shows St. Peter (in blue and with a beard) pulling the net with the other disciples and turning to recognize Christ. The other shows Peter swimming toward Christ.

St. Catherine's skin is pale, almost like porcelain. Lochner was known for his ability to render flesh tones.

Although she was tortured on a wheel, St. Catherine was later killed by a sword.

St. John the Evangelist drank poison and survived. He holds a chalice with a serpent representing the poison.

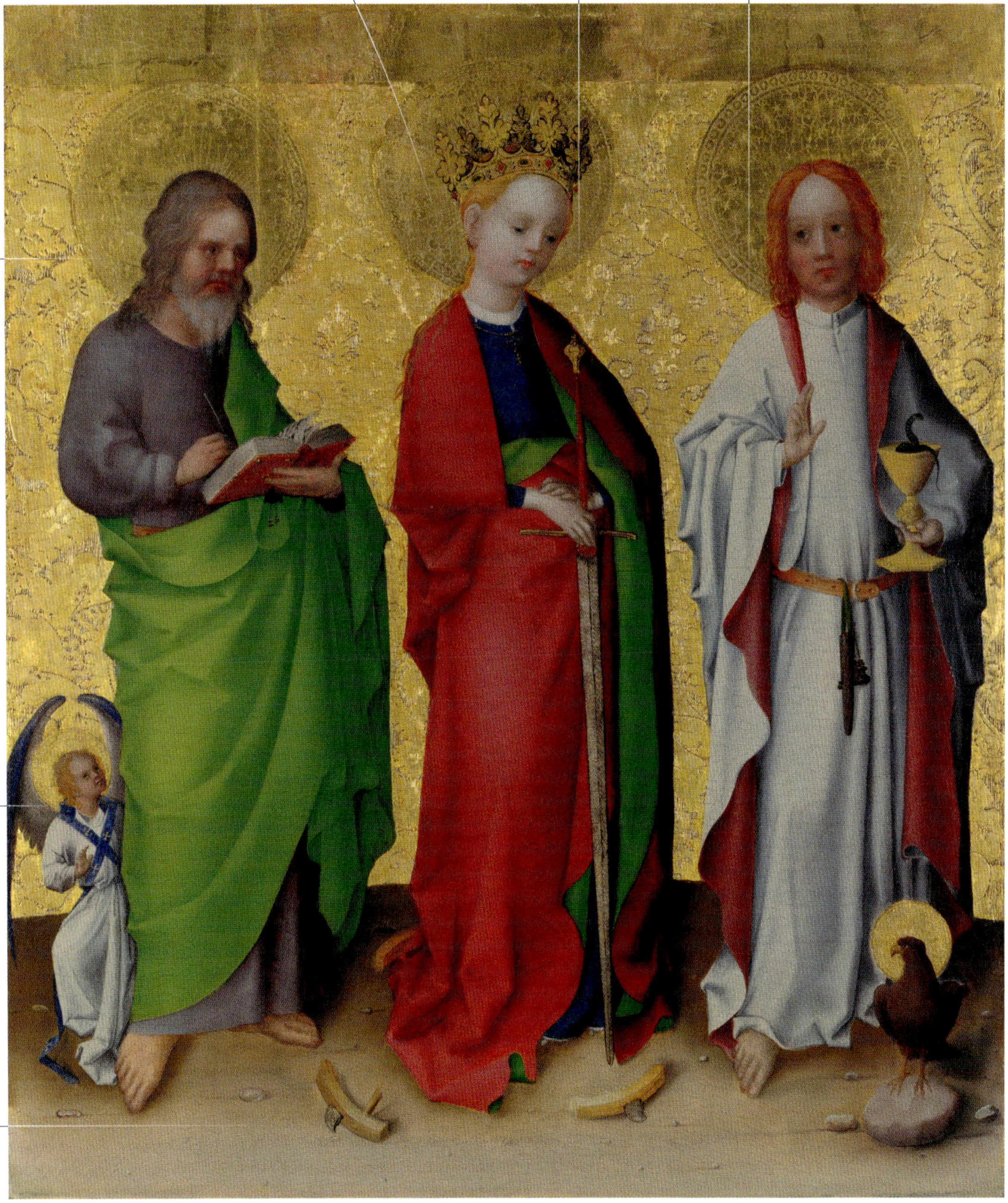

St. Matthew, in the act of writing his gospel, holds a pen.

An angel, another symbol of St. Matthew, peeks out from behind his robes.

Pieces of the wheel on which Catherine was tortured lie on the floor. Catherine was saved when the wheel miraculously shattered.

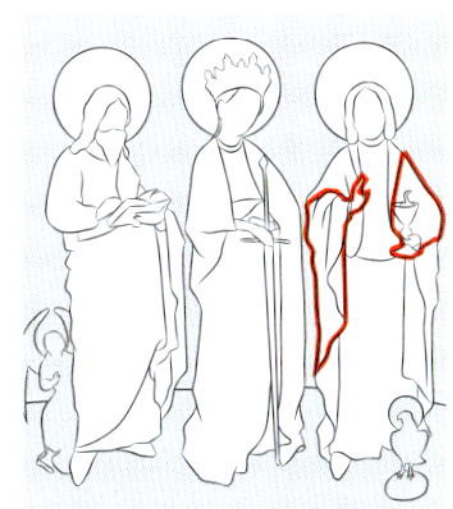

Three-dimensionality
Lochner gives his figures a real, three-dimensional quality. For instance, he uses receding folds in the sleeves of St. John's right arm to create the hand's blessing motion and foreshortens the left arm to hold the chalice.

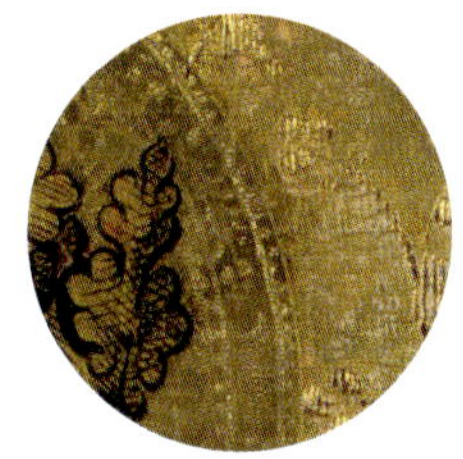

Mystical effect
In a church setting, candlelight would have reflected off the uneven gold surface of the background. Crosshatching on the trees of the crown gives the effect of shadow.

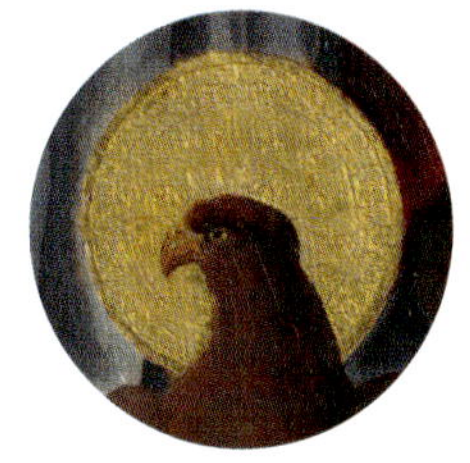

Iconography
The eagle at St. John the Evangelist's feet is his attribute (symbol). In paintings, saints were often depicted with their personal attributes, so ordinary people in 15th-century Europe would recognize them.

Saints Matthew, Catherine of Alexandria and John the Evangelist (The Three Saints)

Stefan Lochner c. 1445–1450, oil on oak panel, 27 × 23 in (68.6 × 58.1 cm), National Gallery, London, UK

This painting formed the left-hand shutter of an altarpiece in Cologne. It is an outstanding example of International Gothic, a style characterized by rich color, gold backgrounds, and elongated figures. By the 1440s, Renaissance ideas of naturalism were replacing this style, but Lochner made innovative advances in techniques by making the figures seem three-dimensional. He may have trained with Netherlandish artists such as Robert Campin and Jan van Eyck, as well as metalworkers and goldsmiths.

Pale skin signified status in premodern Europe. It also suggested spiritual purity.

The perfect roundness of Mary's face and breasts (outlined with compasses) makes her the embodiment of universal order.

Mary's magnificent crown and throne show her as the Queen of Heaven while highlighting her pared-back beauty.

Angels in monochrome red and blue create a stark contrast with the pale foreground.

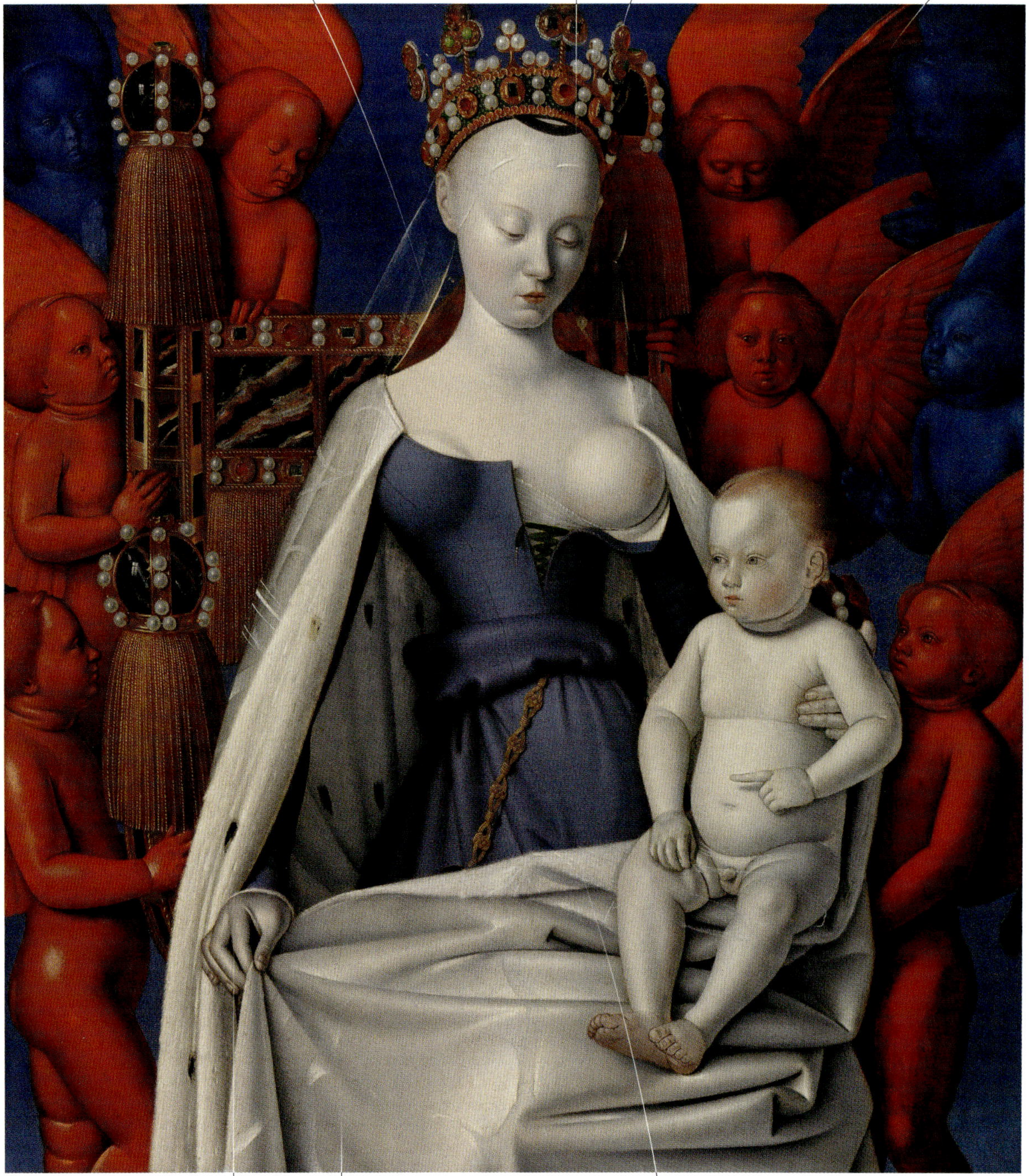

The ermine cloak creates a sense of intimacy, even as she is exposed.

The child's swaddling suggests the shroud that will one day enfold him in the tomb.

This ultramarine pigment was so closely associated with the Virgin that it is still known as "Marian blue."

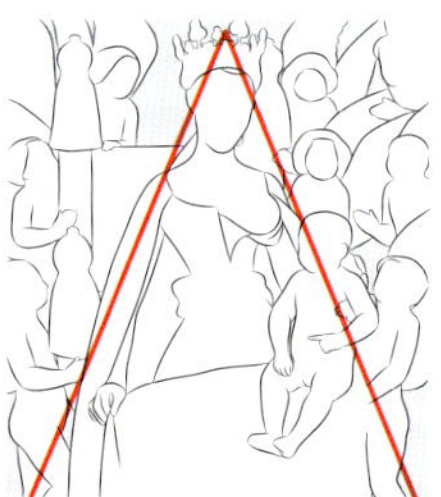

Framing device
The pyramidal shape of Mary and the Christ Child is accentuated by the frame of red and blue angels.

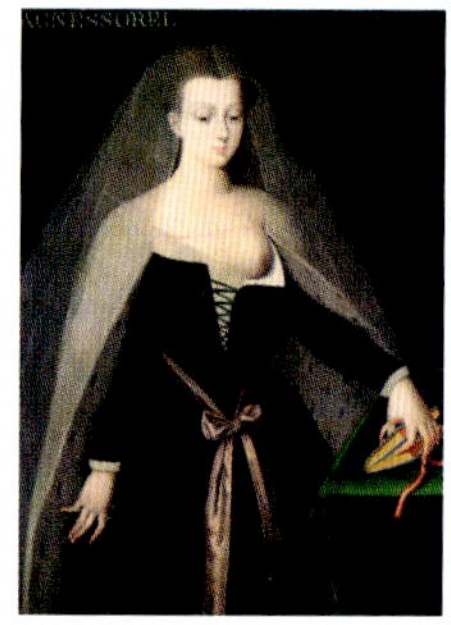

Model for Mary
Fouquet's choice to portray the Virgin's naked breasts was controversial—not least because the model was rumored to have been King Charles VII's mistress, Agnès Sorel.

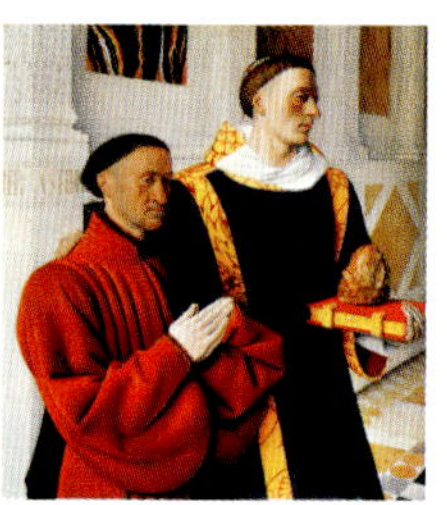

Patronage
Virgin and Child forms one side of a diptych, a two-panel painting. Christ's pointing finger once indicated the man depicted in the other panel of the diptych: Étienne Chevalier, Charles VII's treasurer. He is shown kneeling in prayer beside the figure of St. Stephen.

Virgin and Child

Jean Fouquet c.1452, oil on wood, 44 × 41 in (113 × 104 cm), Koninklijk Royal Museum of Fine Arts, Antwerp, Belgium

The figure of the *virgo lactans* (breastfeeding virgin), which formed the right-hand panel of the Melun Diptych, was popular in medieval religious art. The mother's milk lovingly bestowed upon the Christ Child foreshadows the sacrificed Savior's blood. Fouquet's Virgin is striking for her milk-white pallor and partially unclothed state, which scandalized contemporary viewers and unsettles modern viewers.

The Agony in the Garden

Andrea Mantegna c. 1455–1456, egg tempera on wood, 25 × 31 in (62.9 × 80 cm), National Gallery, London, UK

In this painting, Mantegna arranged different elements of Christ's betrayal by the disciple Judas in a single landscape. Christ is shown kneeling before a group of cherubs as Judas leads a band of soldiers to arrest him, while the disciples Peter, James, and John sleep. The approaching soldiers, emerging from darkness on the right, create a sense of drama and foreboding in a scene that prefaces Christ's trial and Crucifixion.

Five muscular cherubs present objects of Christ's imminent torture and death: the Crucifixion cross, the column, the sponge, and the lance.

An otherworldly Jerusalem—its architecture a composite of Roman and Renaissance architectural styles—rises amid a barren, mountainous landscape.

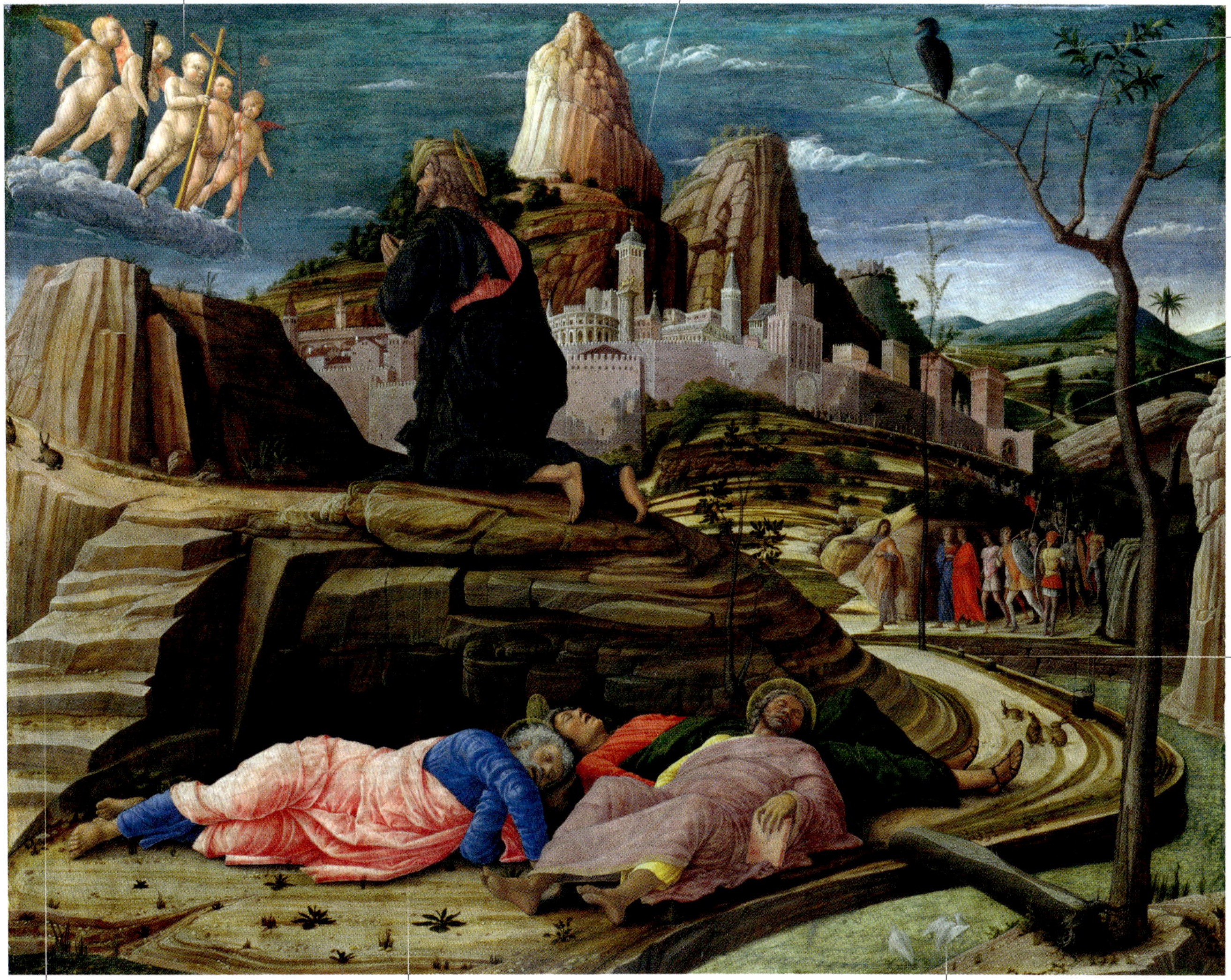

A vulture waits ominously, perched on the dead branch of a tree.

Judas leads the soldiers from Jerusalem to the Garden of Gethsemane, where they will arrest Christ. Their march implies the passage of time.

A young fig tree grows from a crevice in the rock. According to folklore, Judas hung himself from a fig tree after betraying Christ.

Rabbits may symbolize future followers who will put their faith in Christ's message.

Falling asleep, though told by Christ to keep watch, the disciples resemble toppled Roman statues, their robes folded like togas.

Egrets in the stream represent the purification that follows baptism.

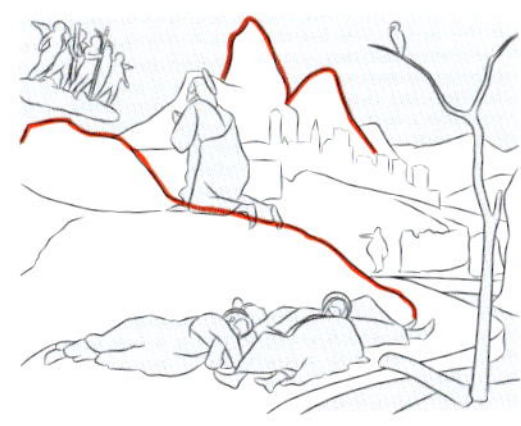

Conic composition
Mantegna devised a series of cone shapes in the landscape to create three-dimensionality and lead the eye to different scenes.

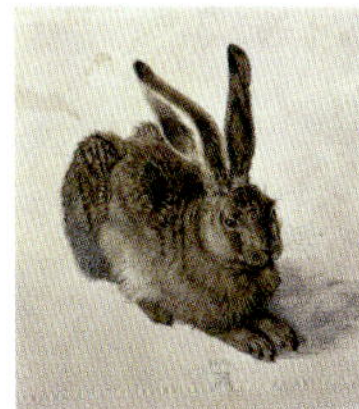

Animal depiction
Mantegna had a profound influence on German artist Albrecht Dürer, whose realistic images of animals include this hare.

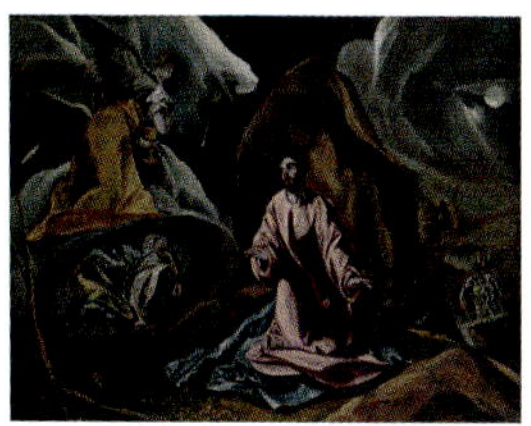

El Greco's version
Some 150 years later, El Greco painted his own *Agony in the Garden of Gethsemane*, but showed Christ facing the viewer. While El Greco's composition and colors link the work to Mantegna's version, El Greco emphasized the dreamlike qualities of the story.

The Procession of the Magi

Benozzo Gozzoli 1459, fresco with tempera and oil, 159 × 203 in (405 × 516 cm), chapel of the Palazzo Medici Riccardi, Florence, Italy

One of three frescoes in which Gozzoli used the Christmas story of the Magi to honor the Medici family, this is devoted to Caspar, the youngest magus. The painting is packed with sumptuous detail, much of which alludes to the Medicis' great wealth and status. Caspar is portrayed as the young Lorenzo de' Medici, later known as "Il Magnifico," leading his retinue through a Tuscan landscape.

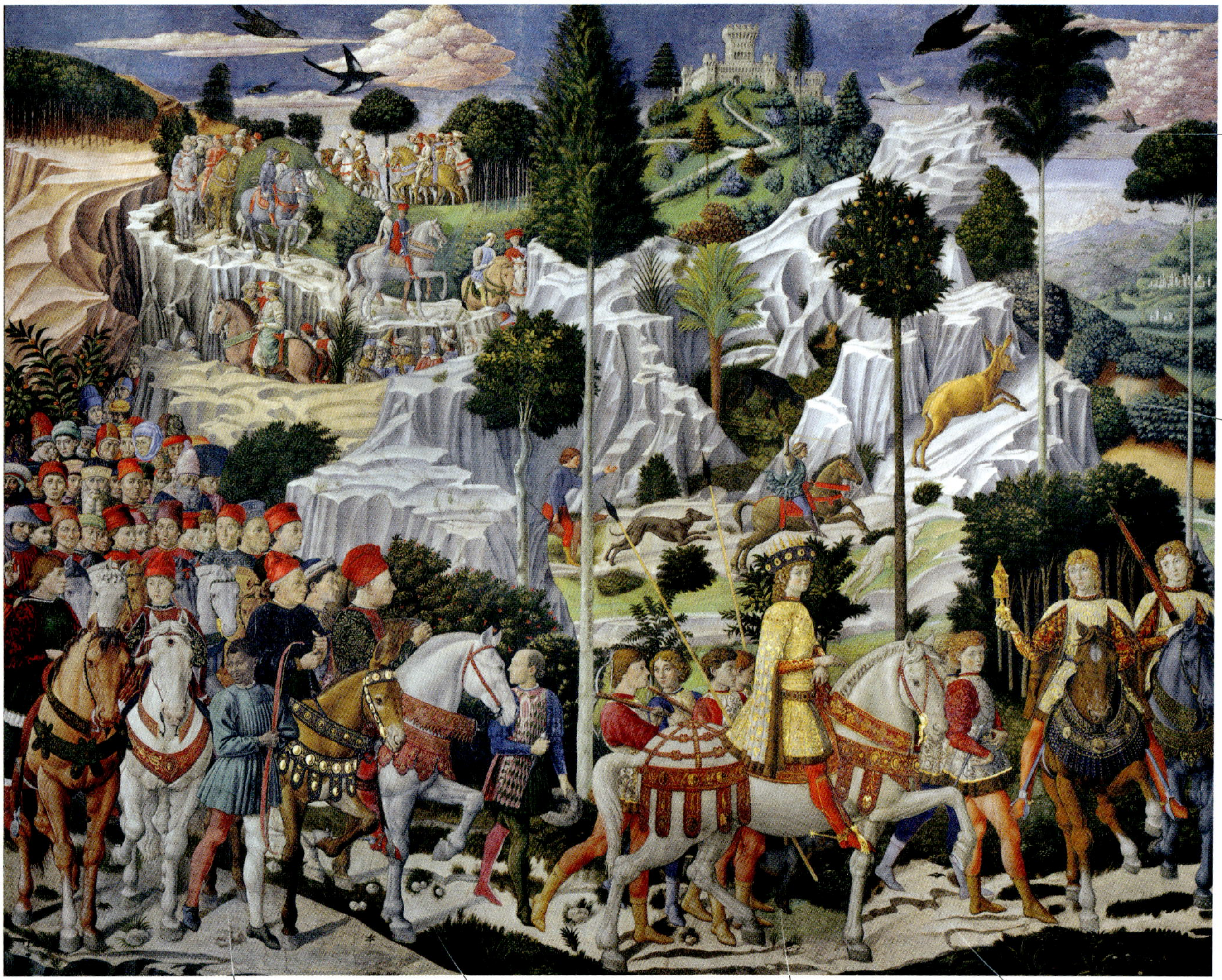

Details in the landscape present a stark contrast between rocky outcrops and lush vegetation.

A deer hunt is underway in the background, reflecting the Medicis' love of a noble sport.

A single Black man, possibly a member of the Medici household, is depicted as a bowman.

Behind Lorenzo, the cavalcade parades, led by his close relatives and associates. Piero di Cosimo de' Medici is in front, and Cosimo (his father) rides the donkey.

Lorenzo was 10 years old when the painting was produced, but Gozzoli depicted him as an adolescent.

The family coat of arms appears in the oval medals on the bridle worn by Lorenzo's horse.

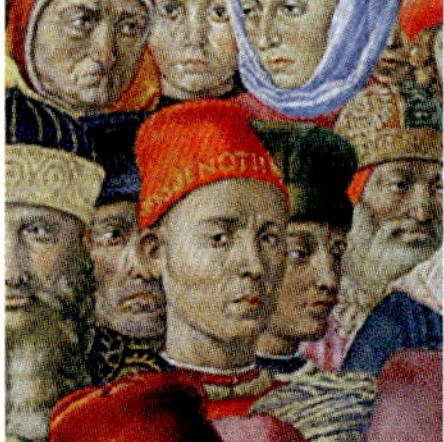

In a self-portrait, Gozzoli depicts himself as a member of the Florentine elite. On his hat, the words "Opus Benotii," a play on his name, trumpet his artistic achievement.

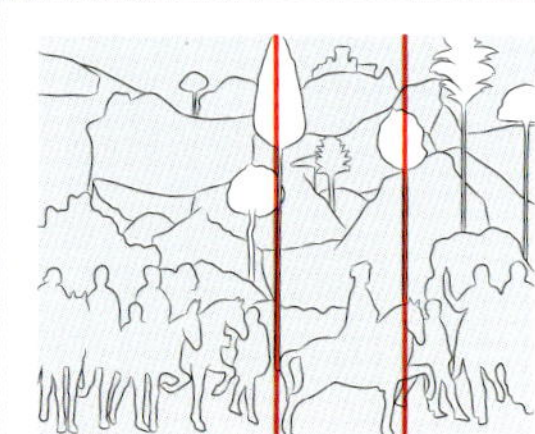

Bringing order
The slender stylized trees divide the image into separate sections in a style reminiscent of contemporary Flemish tapestry.

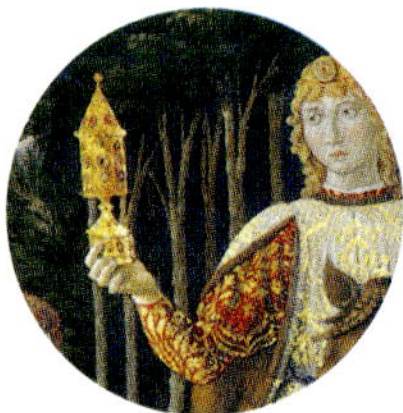

Master of jewels
A former goldsmith, Gozzoli paid great attention to the clothing and jewels of the retinue.

The Virgin of the Dry Tree

Petrus Christus c. 1465, oil on oak panel, 6 × 5 in (14.7 × 12.4 cm), Museo Nacional Thyssen-Bornemisza, Madrid, Spain

This devotional work references the Book of Ezekiel in the Bible, in which God promises to bring life to the dead tree. It was painted by Christus after he and his wife became members of the Confraternity of Our Lady of the Dry Tree in Bruges in 1462. Its small size indicates that it was intended for personal, spiritual use.

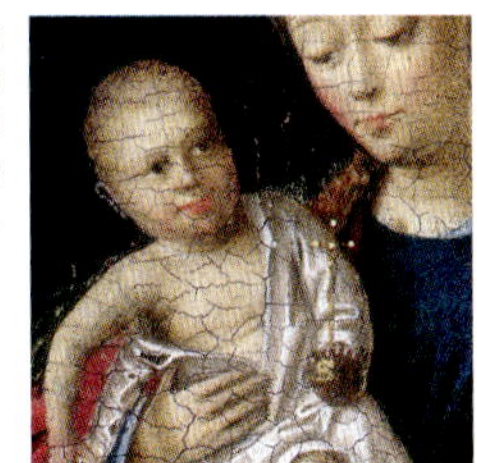

Christ holds a golden globe crowned with a cross. This is a symbol of his mission to redeem the world.

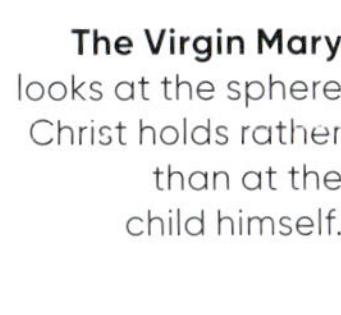

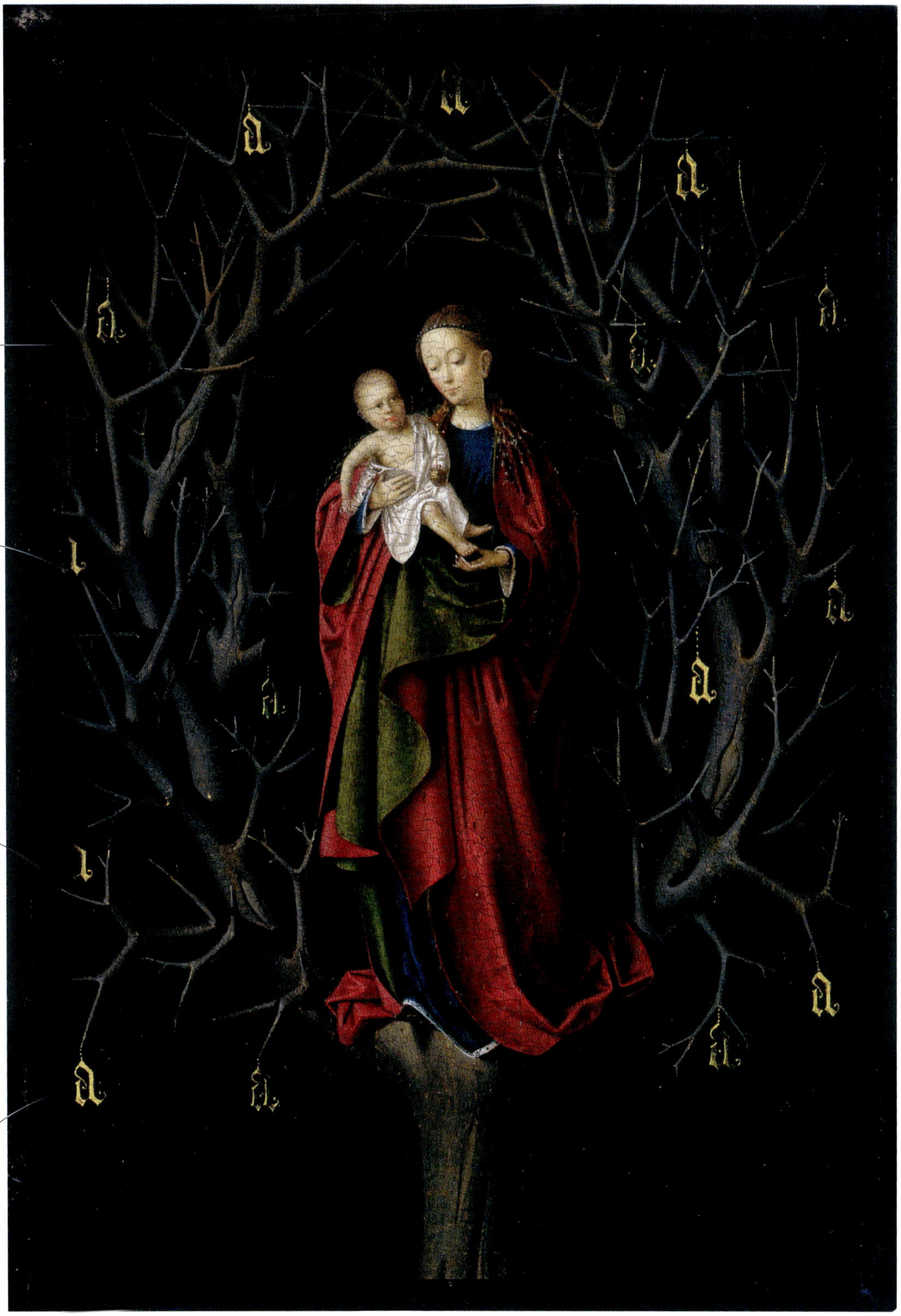

The Virgin Mary looks at the sphere Christ holds rather than at the child himself.

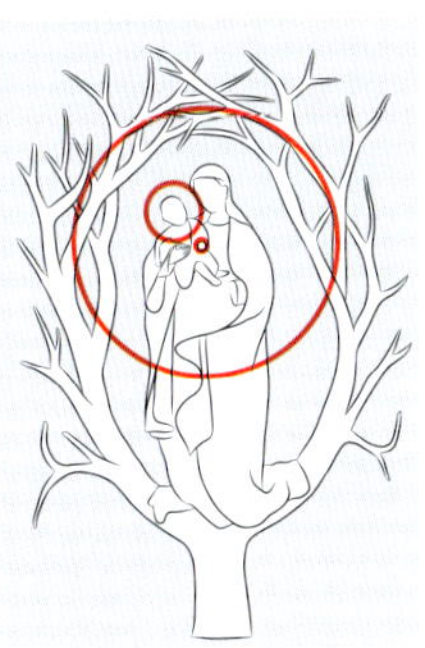

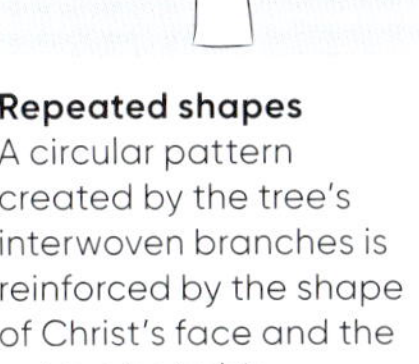

Repeated shapes A circular pattern created by the tree's interwoven branches is reinforced by the shape of Christ's face and the sphere he holds.

The dry tree represents the Tree of Knowledge in the Garden of Eden and the Christian belief that salvation can only be found through Christ.

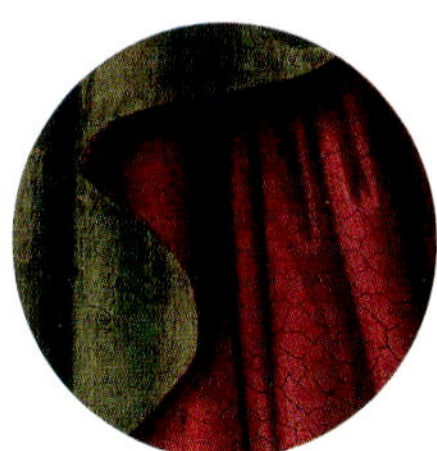

Swathes of fabric The use of light and shade to convey the sheen and heavy folds of the Virgin's dress and cloak show Christus's skill as a painter.

Spiky branches and the tree's oval shape suggest the crown of thorns that Christ wore at his Crucifixion.

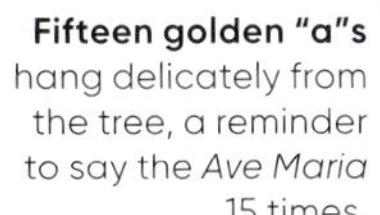

Fifteen golden "a"s hang delicately from the tree, a reminder to say the *Ave Maria* 15 times.

Religion

Art is closely linked to many religions. The purpose of Hindu art is to connect the spiritual and human worlds. In Buddhism, monks and lay artists have used it to recount the life of the Buddha and to provide a focus for meditation since the 1st century CE. In the Christian faith, art has been used to tell stories from the scriptures and to aid spiritual contemplation. The representation of God is forbidden in Islam on the grounds of idolatry, so most Islamic art focuses on intricate patterns and exquisite calligraphy.

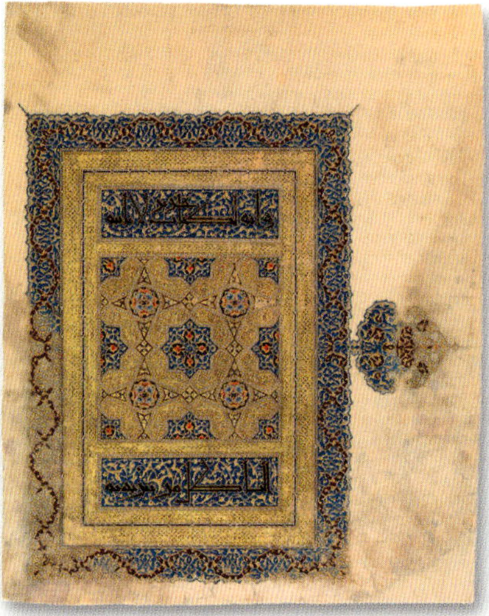

3

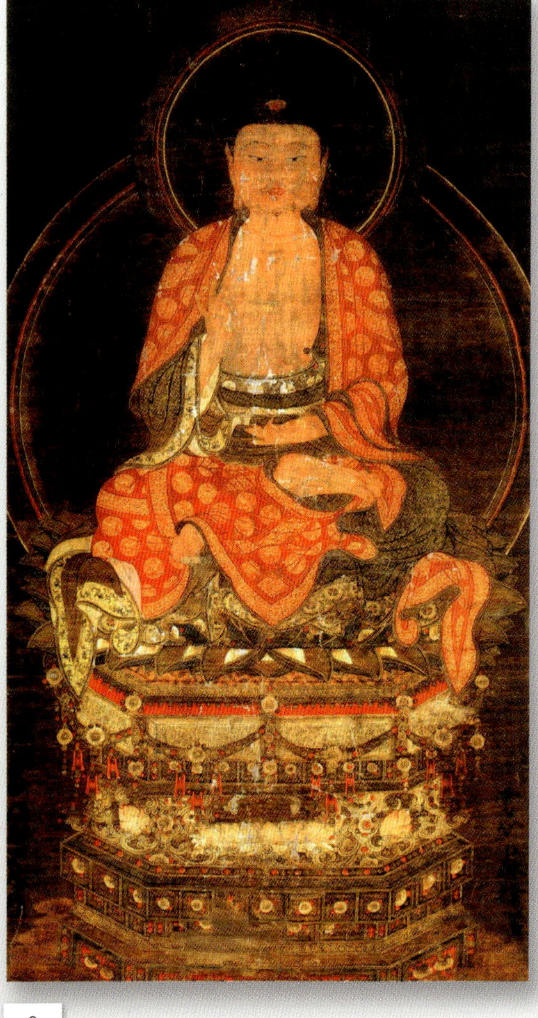

2

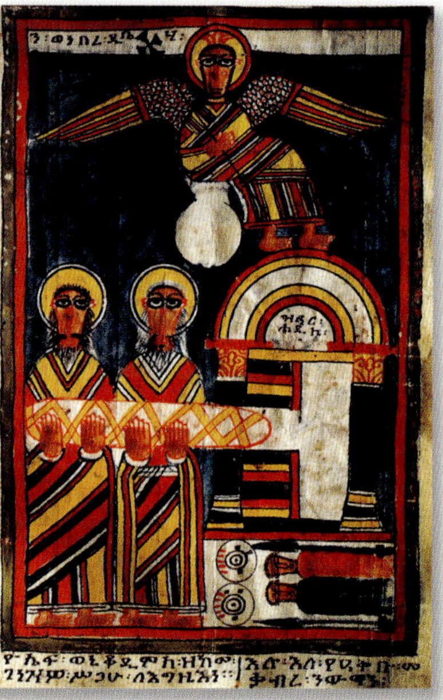

4

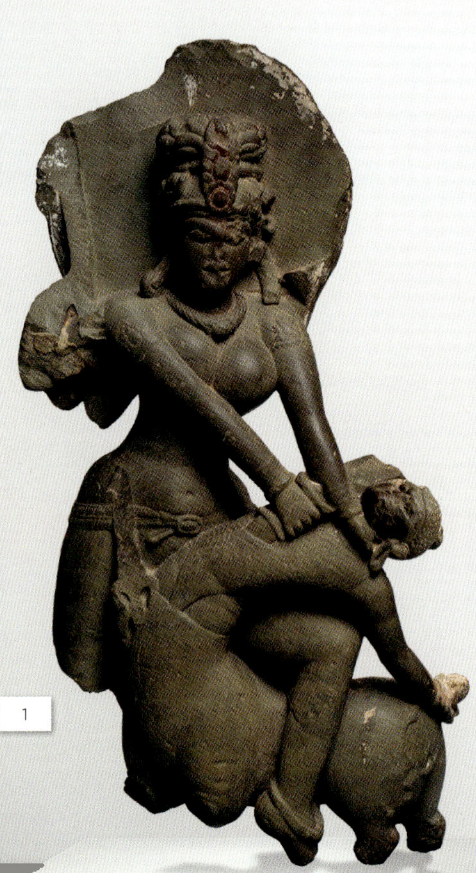

1

1. ***Durga Destroying the Buffalo Demon*, unknown artist, c. 800 BCE.** The Hindu goddess Durga slays Mahishasura, the Buffalo Demon, who has been ravaging the universe. Hindus believe that the beauty of a sculpture of a god attracts the god to inhabit its own image.

2. ***Amitabha Buddha*, unknown artist, c. 14th century.** During the Korean Goryeo dynasty, wealthy families commissioned paintings of Amitabha Buddha, which they placed beside the dying. The style is characterized by rich, subtle color and patterns outlined in gold.

3. ***Anonymous Baghdad Qur'an*, Muhammad ibn Aibak ibn' Abdallah, c. 1306–1307.** Qur'ans illustrated with intricate designs and calligraphy express the beauty of the word of God. This one is the combined work of Ibn' Abdallah and the calligrapher Ahmad ibn al-Suhrawardi al-Bakri.

4. ***Jesus and the Thieves*, Ethiopian School, c. 1300.** In Ethiopia, illuminated manuscripts of the Gospels were illustrated in a highly stylized fashion with front-facing figures and geometric patterning. They were commissioned by wealthy individuals as gifts for churches.

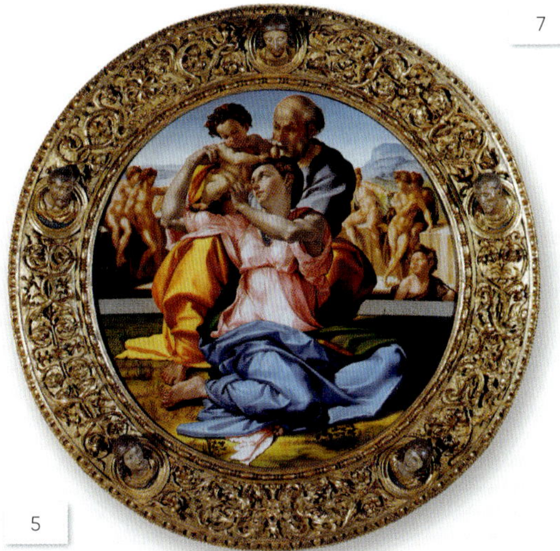

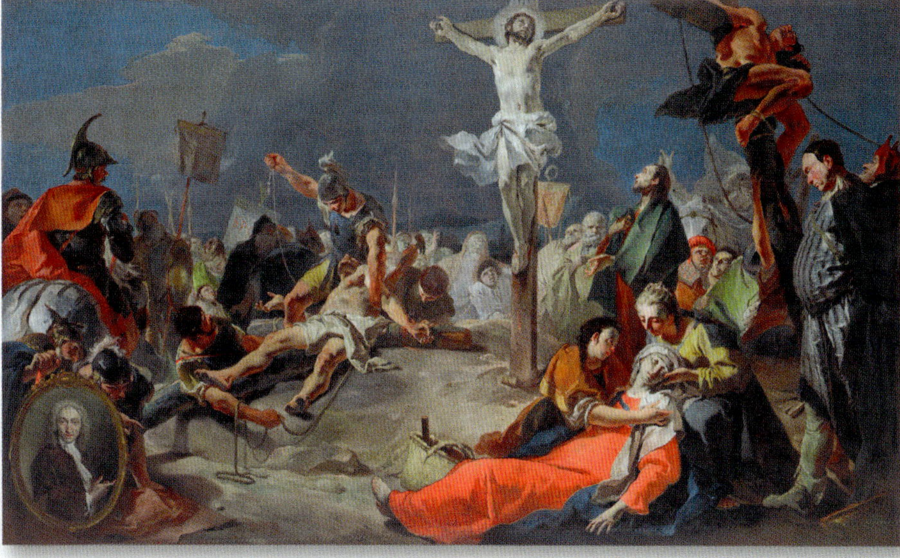

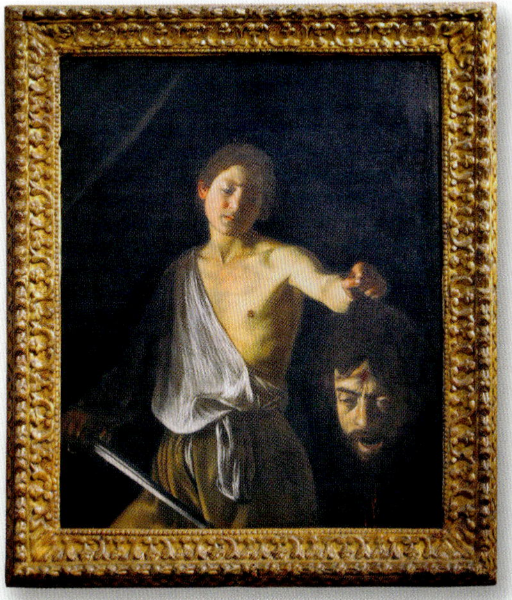

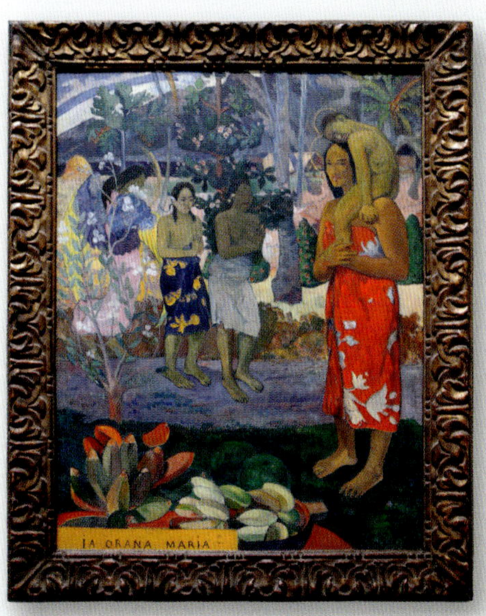

7

5

6

8

Representing God in Christianity

According to the Old Testament's Book of Genesis, God created man in his own image, and depictions of God first appeared in Christian art during the early medieval period. At first, he was represented simply by a hand, then by a face, and finally as a figure. The representation of God as a patriarchal figure with white skin and long flowing hair and beard developed during the early Renaissance.

5. ***Doni Tondo*, Michelangelo Buonarroti, c. 1504–1506.** The theme of the Holy Family—Mary, Joseph, and Jesus—was popular as a celebration of family life. This example was commissioned by the Doni family, probably to mark a marriage or christening.

6. ***David with the Head of Goliath*, Caravaggio, c. 1607.** Stories about the battle of good and evil from the Old Testament, such as that of David and Goliath, were perennially popular subjects. Caravaggio added a personal dimension by making Goliath a self-portrait.

7. ***The Crucifixion*, Giambattista Tiepolo, c. 1724-1725.** Tiepolo portrays the crucified Christ flooded with light, surrounded by his grieving followers. Painted for a church, the scene was designed to engage the congregation's emotions as they contemplated Christ's sacrifice.

8. ***La Orana Maria* (*Hail Mary*), Paul Gauguin, 1891.** Two Tahitian women and an angel greet Mary and Jesus, who are also portrayed as Tahitian. Seeking alternatives to Christianity in the spiritual traditions of Polynesia, Gauguin combined Christian scenes with depictions of Indigenous culture.

The Last Judgment

Hans Memling 1467–1471, tempera and oil on oak panel, 87 × 63 in (220.9 × 160.7 cm) central panel, 88 × 29 in (223.5 × 72.5 cm) each wing, Muzeum Narodowe, Gdańsk, Poland

In this monumental altarpiece, Hans Memling portrays the central theme of the New Testament's Book of Revelation—the end of days and the destiny of souls. The central panel of the triptych depicts the Last Judgment, the left panel shows the saved being led into paradise, and the right panel imagines the damned falling into the pits of hell.

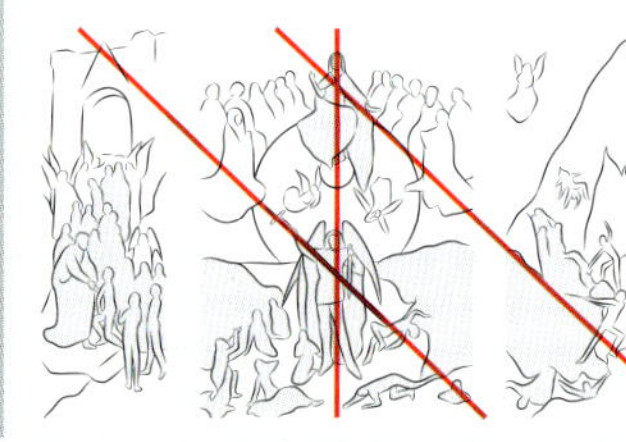

Triptych focus
The triptych balances around a central axis formed by Christ and St. Michael the Archangel, introducing a diagonal movement toward paradise and hell on each wing.

Tempera painting
The opacity of tempera provided Memling with a solid underpainting. He then added more transparent layers of oil paint to achieve a rich interplay of luminosity, depth, and texture.

St. Peter guides the saved as they climb the stairs, through the doors, and into paradise. He is identified by the key he is holding.

A sword and a lily branch on either side of Christ's head symbolize judgment and purity respectively.

Two angels hold the instruments of the Passion (Christ's suffering before the Crucifixion), including the crown of thorns and a hammer and nails, reminders of Christ's sacrifice.

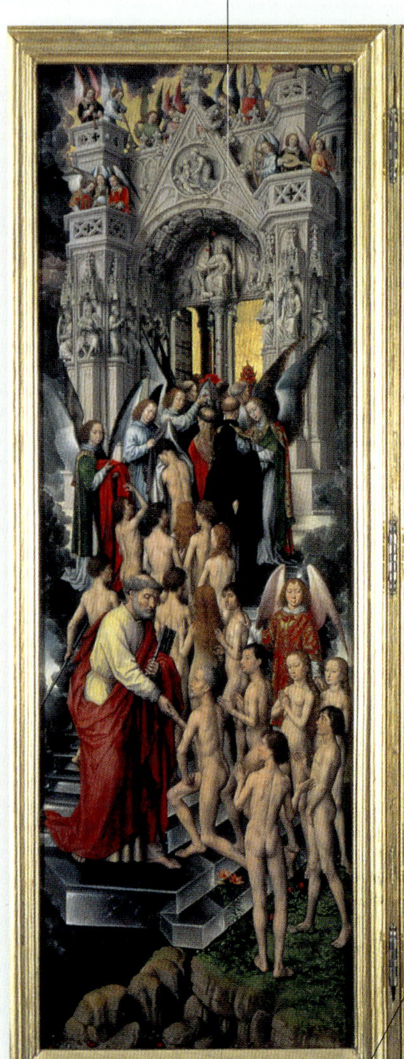

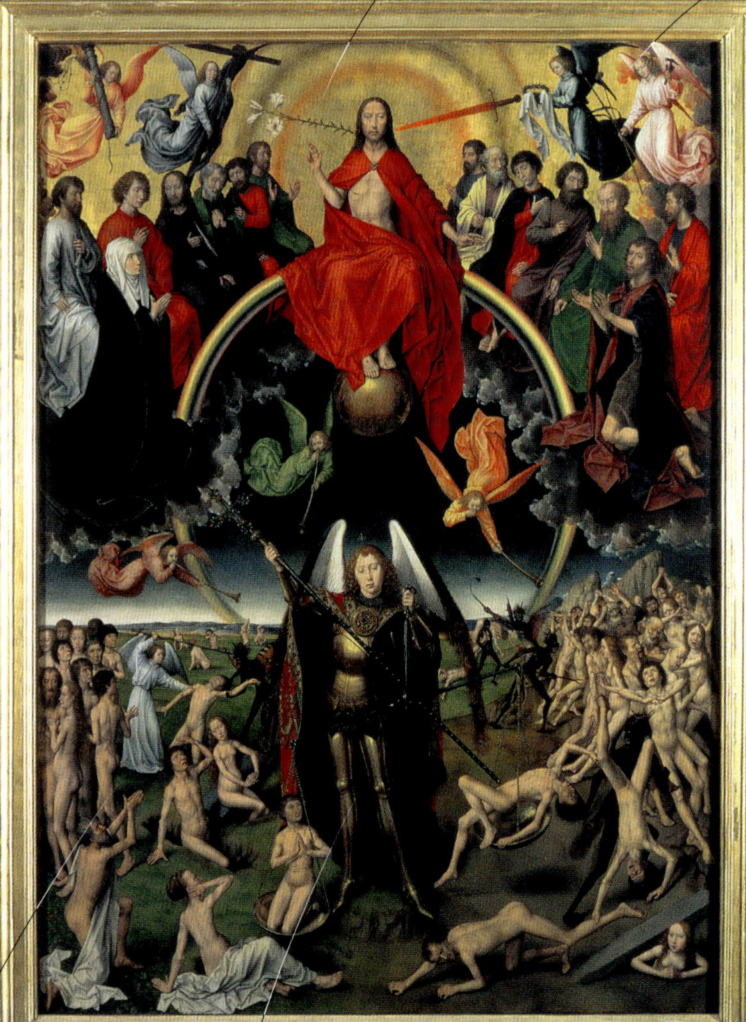

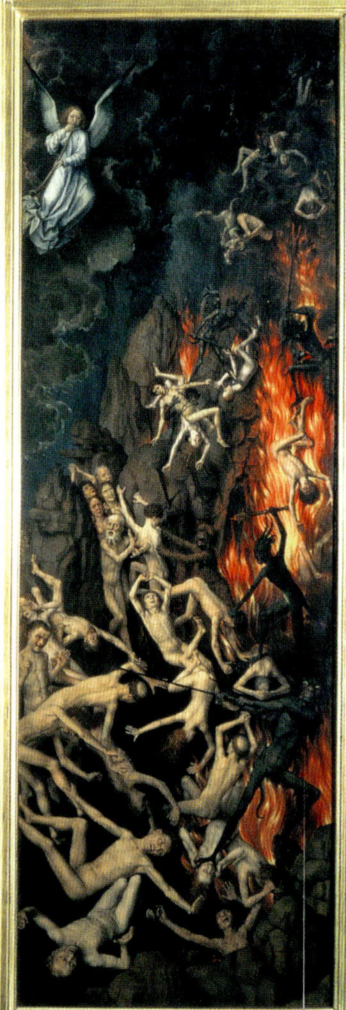

A struggle unfolds between an angel and a devil with butterfly wings, symbolizing the conflict over the human soul.

Archangel Michael holds a scale, weighing the souls of those being judged.

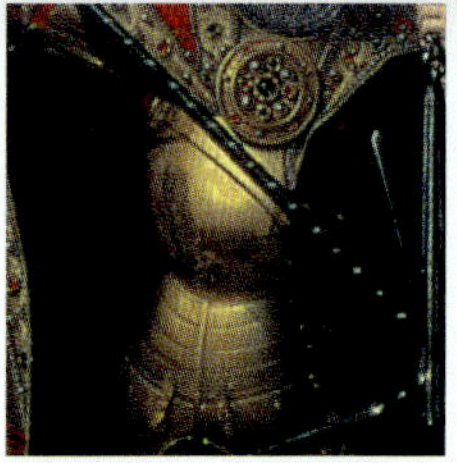

St. Michael's body armor acts like a convex mirror to reflect the space behind the viewer, outside the pictorial frame.

Devilish creatures grasp the bodies of sinners, dragging them into the fires of hell.

Apollo and Daphne

Piero del Pollaiuolo c. 1470–1480, oil on wood, 12 × 8 in (29.5 × 20 cm), National Gallery, London, UK

Set against a Florentine landscape, this painting depicts a scene from Ovid's *Metamorphoses*, in which Apollo's unwanted pursuit of the nymph Daphne leads her to appeal to her river god father, who turns her into a laurel tree. It is both a startling warning against the dangers of desire and an exquisite rendering of nature.

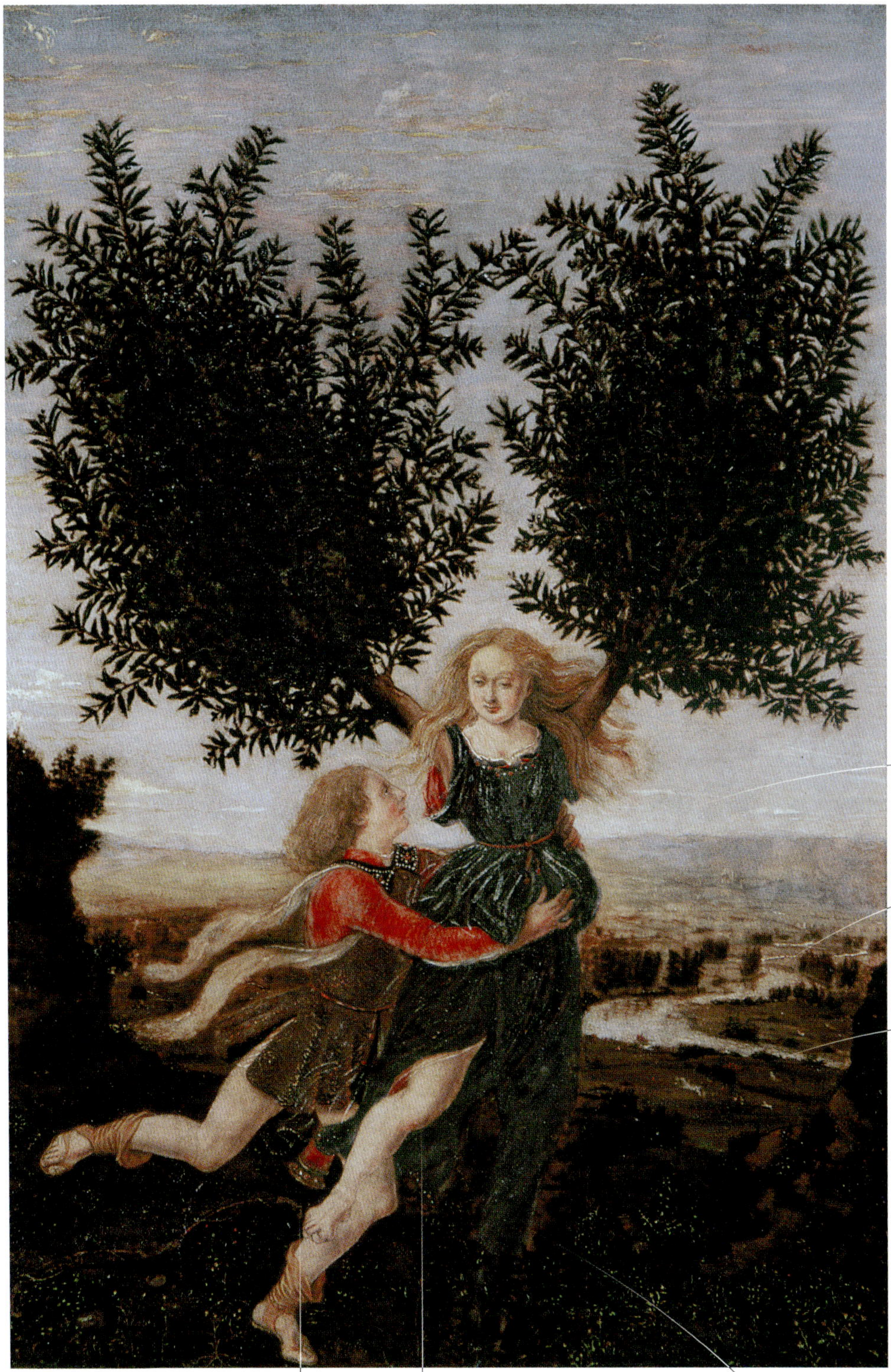

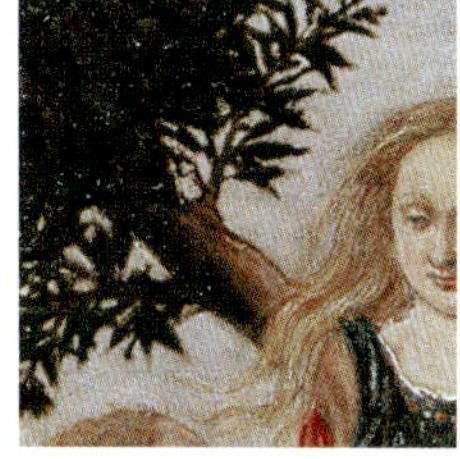

Daphne's arms, raised in an appeal for help, have been transformed into laurel branches. After her demise, Apollo gifted laurel leaf crowns in Daphne's memory.

Dressed in blue with golden hair, Daphne represents the pinnacle of Renaissance beauty.

The winding Arno River and the distant cityscape set the tale in 15th-century Florence.

A hunting scene unfolds in the background, echoing Apollo's pursuit of Daphne.

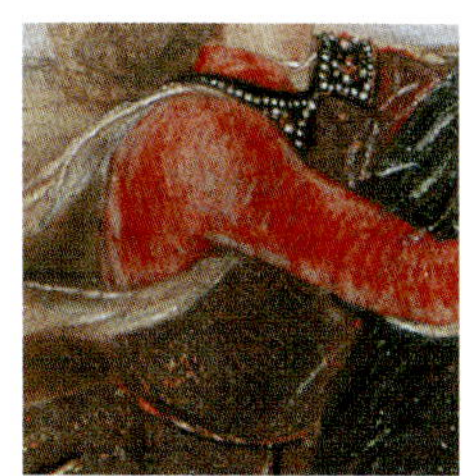

Apollo is dressed in a fine hunting outfit, reflecting the courtly Florentine style.

The bottom of Apollo's quiver is just visible, a reminder of his divine role as god of archery.

Daphne's bare leg is provocatively revealed through a slit in her skirt, adding an alluring sensuality to the composition.

As Daphne's transformation takes hold, her left leg becomes rooted in the ground.

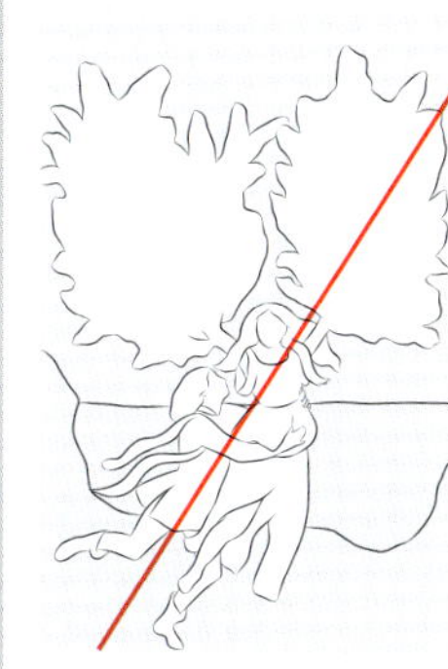

Line of action
The balanced composition unfolds dynamically, with a diagonal line from Apollo's lunge on the left, through their entangled bodies, to the laurel branch sprouting from Daphne's left arm.

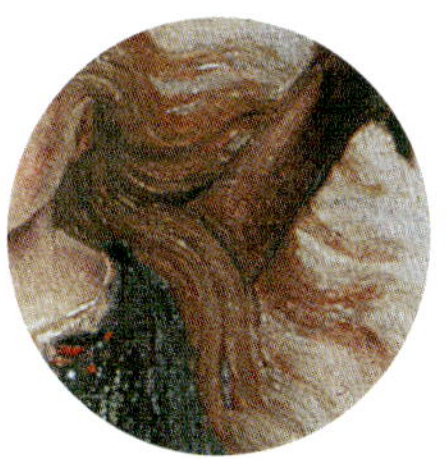

Attention to detail
This tiny painting is full of detail, exemplified by the meticulous rendering of each strand of Daphne's hair and the reflection of trees in the waters of the Arno River.

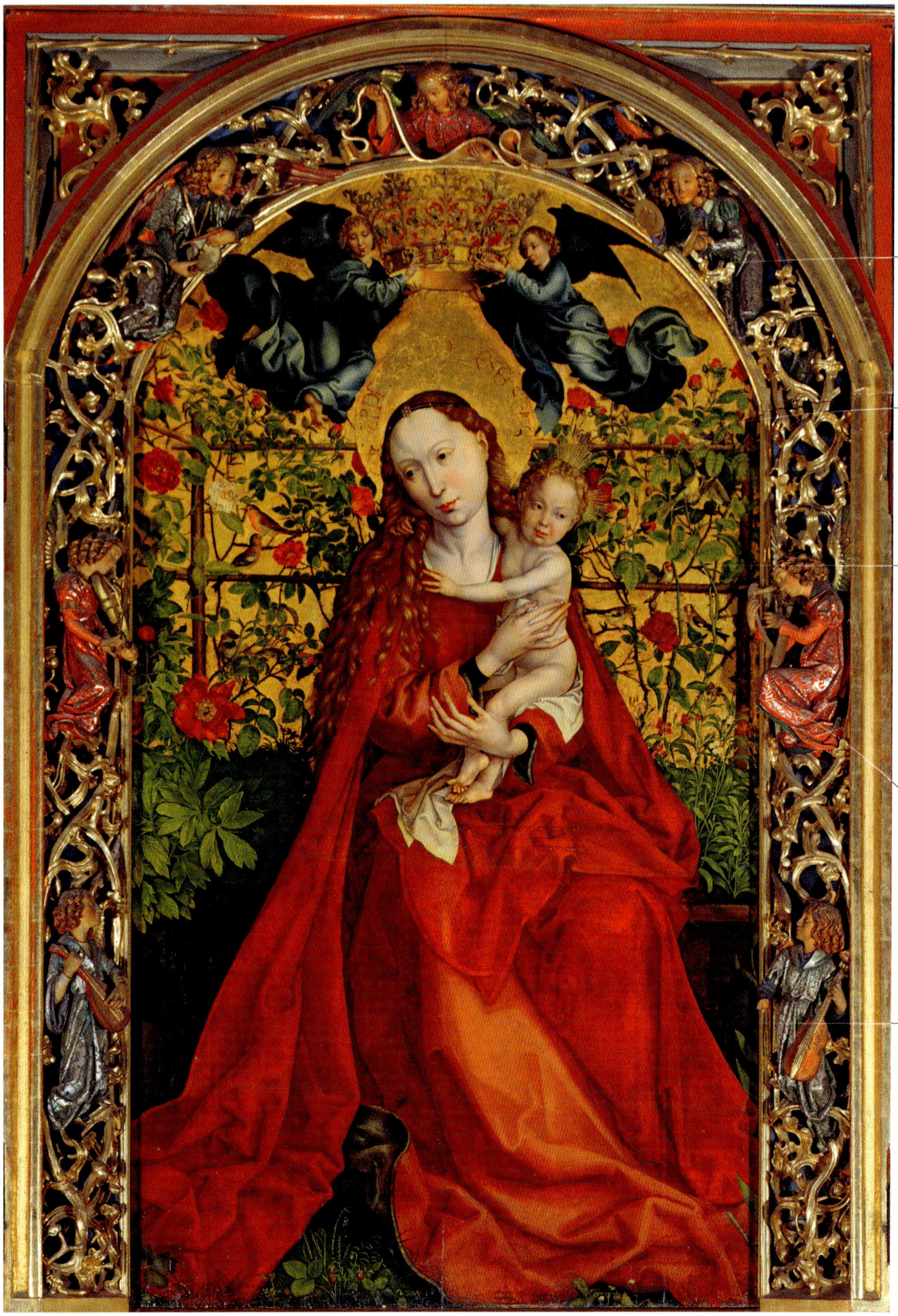

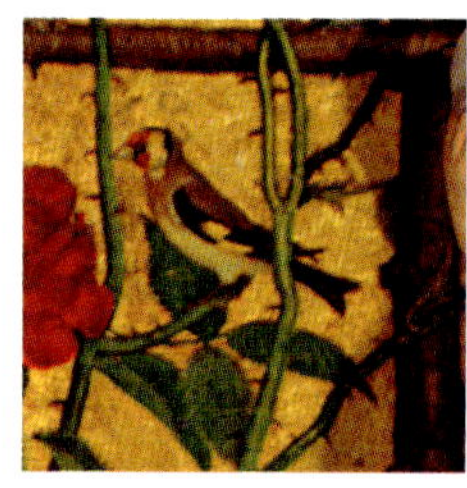

The goldfinches symbolize Christ's Passion. According to legend, a drop of blood fell on a goldfinch from the crown of thorns worn by Christ to his Crucifixion.

Angels are lowering the crown, signaling that Mary is the Queen of Heaven.

Roses are the main feature of the garden, but there are also tree peonies and strawberries.

While the Virgin and Child are close—Christ's arms encircle Mary's neck—they gaze in opposite directions, prefiguring their future sorrow and separation.

The gold background emphasizes that they are in a heavenly space, rather than a garden on earth.

An early copy of the painting shows that these leaves belong to a lily, a flower that represents purity and royalty.

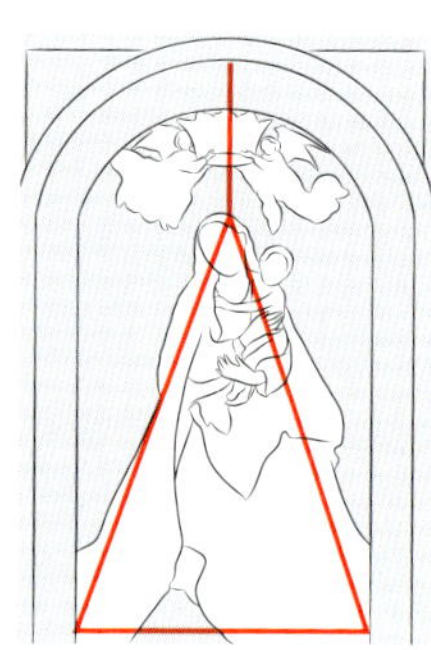

Unifying device
Originally, God the Father and God the Holy Spirit formed a direct line above the seated figures, who form a triangle.

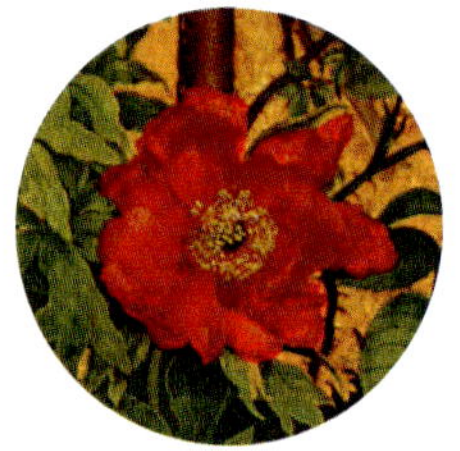

Blood of Christ
Traditionally blue, Mary's orange-red dress and deeper red cloak symbolize Christ's blood. Red roses also represent the blood shed by Jesus on the cross.

Madonna of the Rose Bower

Martin Schongauer 1473, oil on wood panel, 79 × 45 in (200 × 114 cm), Dominican church of Saint Martin, Colmar, France

Martin Schongauer has made the subject of the *hortus conclusus* (enclosed garden) his own with the pained expressions of the Virgin and Child in this monumental panel painting. The work is still in its original home, but was cut down on all sides sometime before the 20th century.

Portraits of the Duke and Duchess of Urbino

Piero della Francesca 1475, oil on wood, 19 × 13 in (47 × 33 cm) each, Uffizi, Florence, Italy

This celebrated portrait of the Italian Renaissance was originally a diptych (two joined paintings) of Federico da Montefeltro, Duke of Urbino, and his wife, Battista Sforza. The duke was the commander of a band of mercenary soldiers. His young wife died soon after childbirth, before the painting was finished.

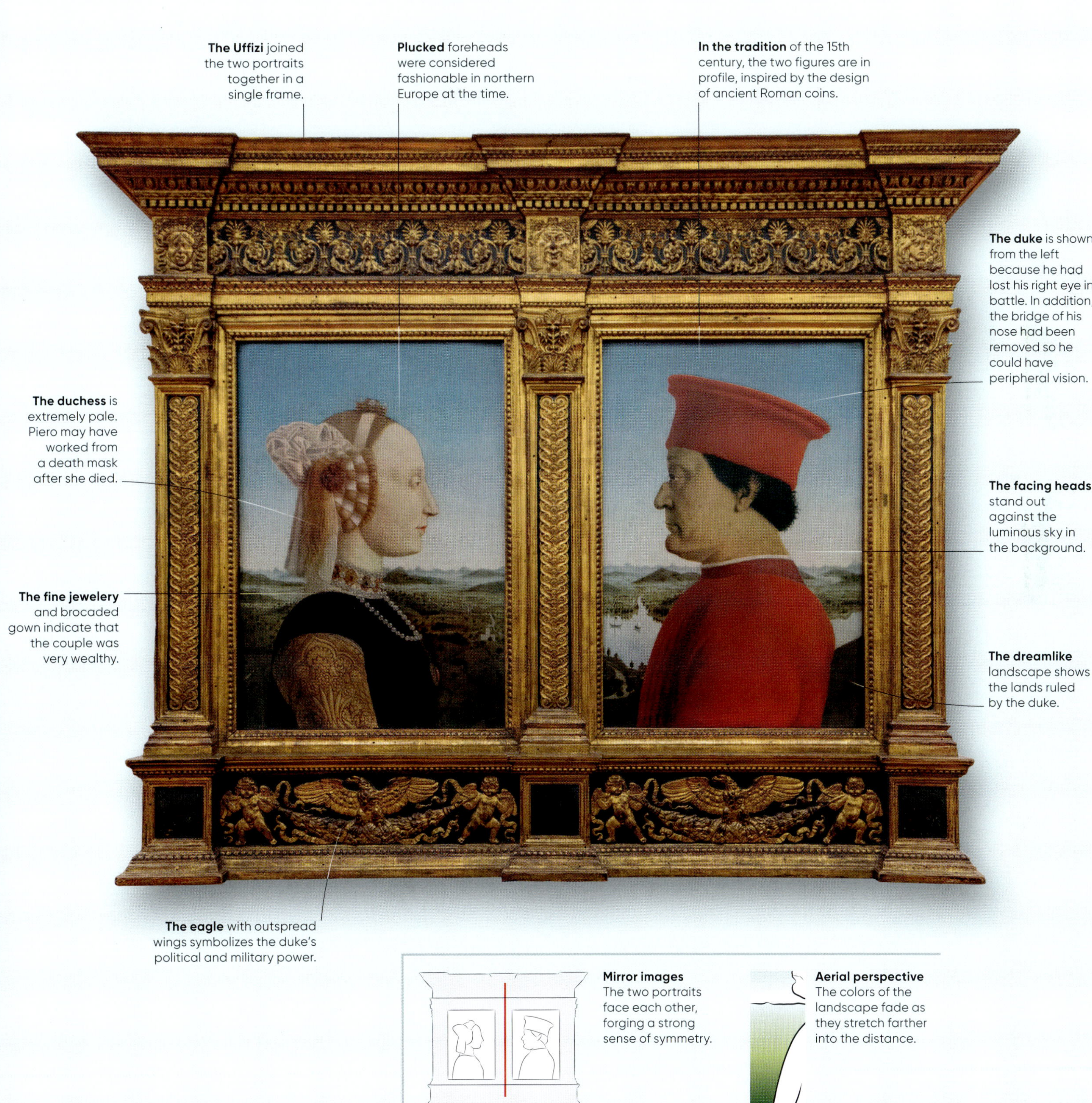

The Uffizi joined the two portraits together in a single frame.

Plucked foreheads were considered fashionable in northern Europe at the time.

In the tradition of the 15th century, the two figures are in profile, inspired by the design of ancient Roman coins.

The duke is shown from the left because he had lost his right eye in battle. In addition, the bridge of his nose had been removed so he could have peripheral vision.

The duchess is extremely pale. Piero may have worked from a death mask after she died.

The facing heads stand out against the luminous sky in the background.

The fine jewelery and brocaded gown indicate that the couple was very wealthy.

The dreamlike landscape shows the lands ruled by the duke.

The eagle with outspread wings symbolizes the duke's political and military power.

Mirror images
The two portraits face each other, forging a strong sense of symmetry.

Aerial perspective
The colors of the landscape fade as they stretch farther into the distance.

St. Dominic of Silos Enthroned as a Bishop

Bartolomé Bermejo 1474–1477, oil on panel, 95 × 51 in (242 × 130 cm), Prado, Madrid, Spain

Intended as the central panel of a high altarpiece, this painting shows Bermejo's skill at depicting minute detail and monumental scale. St. Dominic, an 11th-century monk, looks up from his book, a powerful figure seemingly unaware of the magnificent throne on which he is seated. Executed in the Hispano-Flemish style, the work marks the transition between the Spanish Gothic and Spanish Renaissance periods.

Fleshy hues, a characteristic of Bermejo's work, create a vivid and lifelike portrait that underscores the saint's mortality.

Charity sits above the throne. Niches around the throne are occupied by the other Virtues.

The golden backdrop symbolizes St. Dominic's transcendence beyond the earthly realm as he ascends to divinity.

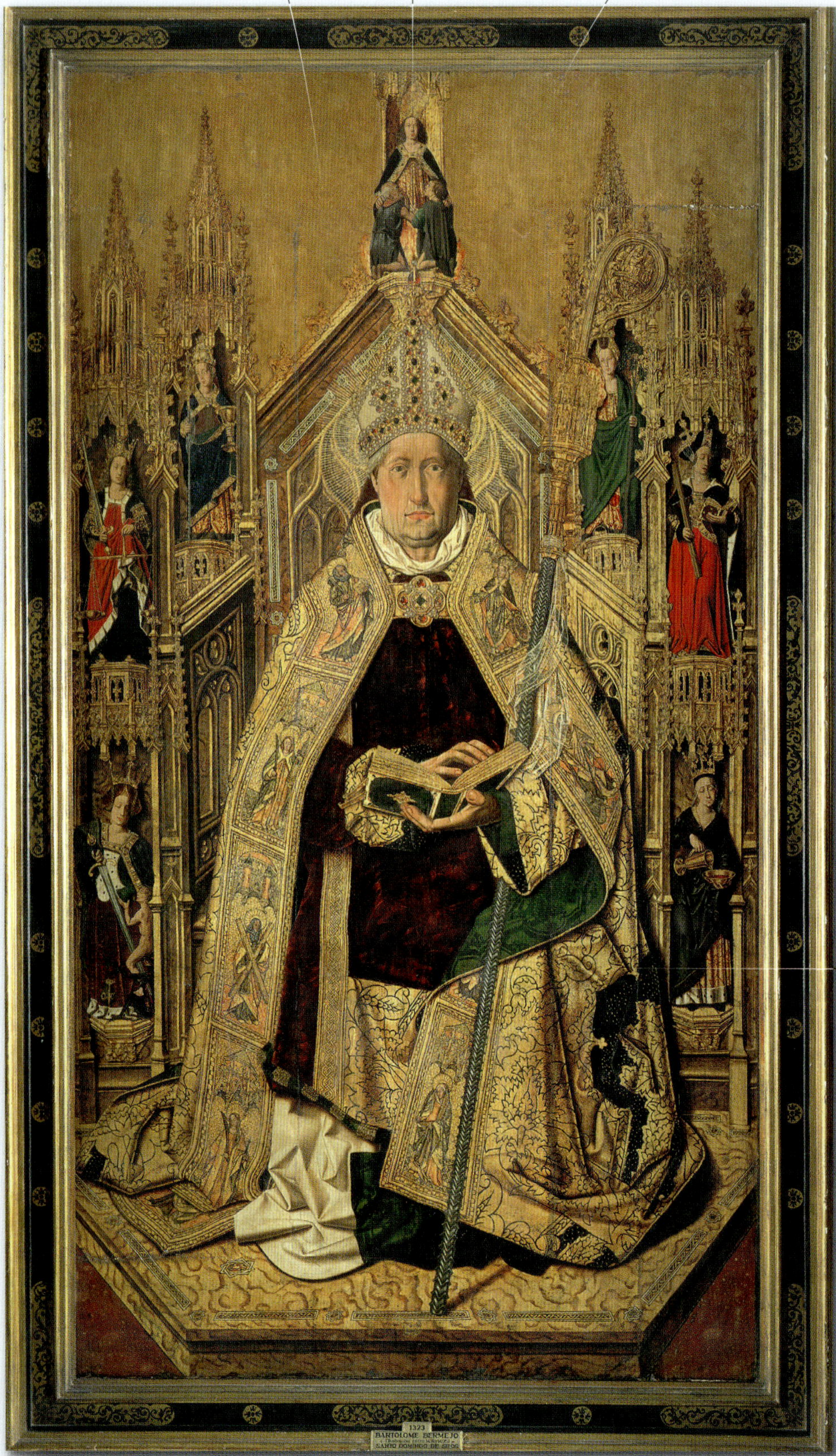

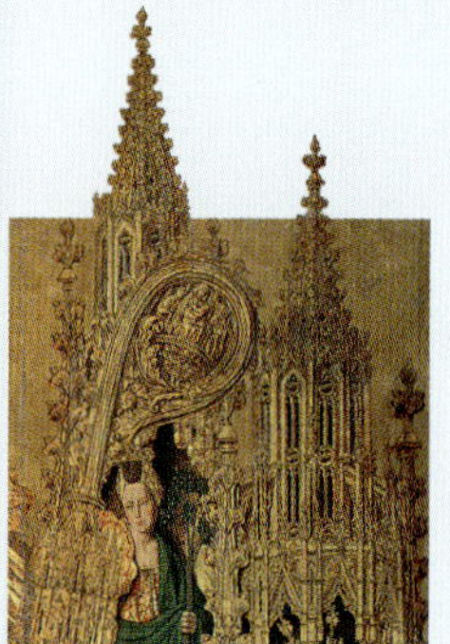

Gothic architecture, characterized by vertical proportions, pointed arches, and ornate decoration, symbolizes the glorification of God.

The angular folds and varied textures of St. Dominic's clothing suggest the influence of Flemish paintings.

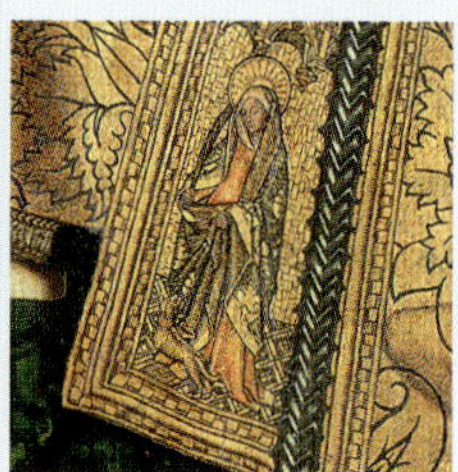

Various saints are intricately depicted on St. Dominic's cope.

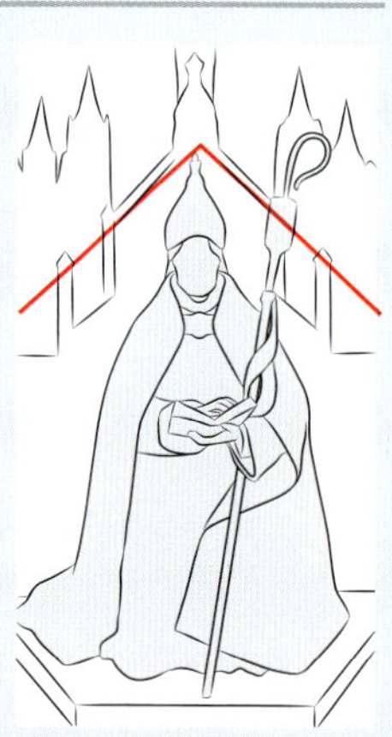

Focal figure
The balanced composition focuses on St. Dominic, who forms the apex of a triangle outlined by the architectural lines of his throne.

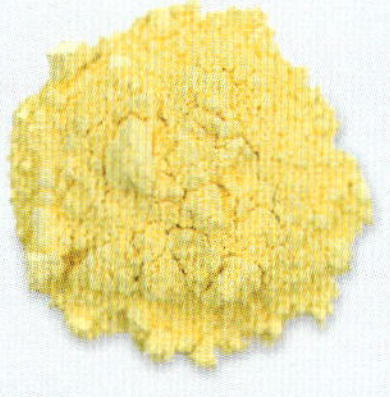

Gilding
Thin lead-tin yellow and dark red-brown oil glaze were applied over gold leaf to replicate the interplay of light on the garments and architectural details.

St. Francis in the Desert

Giovanni Bellini 1475–1480, oil on panel, 49 × 56 in (124.6 × 142 cm), Frick Collection, New York, US

After stepping out of his secluded cave, St. Francis receives the stigmata—wounds corresponding to the nail marks of the crucified Christ. Abandoning the 15th-century archetypes employed by artists, Bellini created a naturalistic scene in a Tuscan landscape infused with a mystical and spiritual aura.

St. Francis receives the stigmata from a golden light in the top left corner.

A donkey, heron, and sheep in the background allude to St. Francis's solitary life, surrounded by nature.

The Tuscan town on the hill in the background suggests the New Jerusalem—Heaven on Earth.

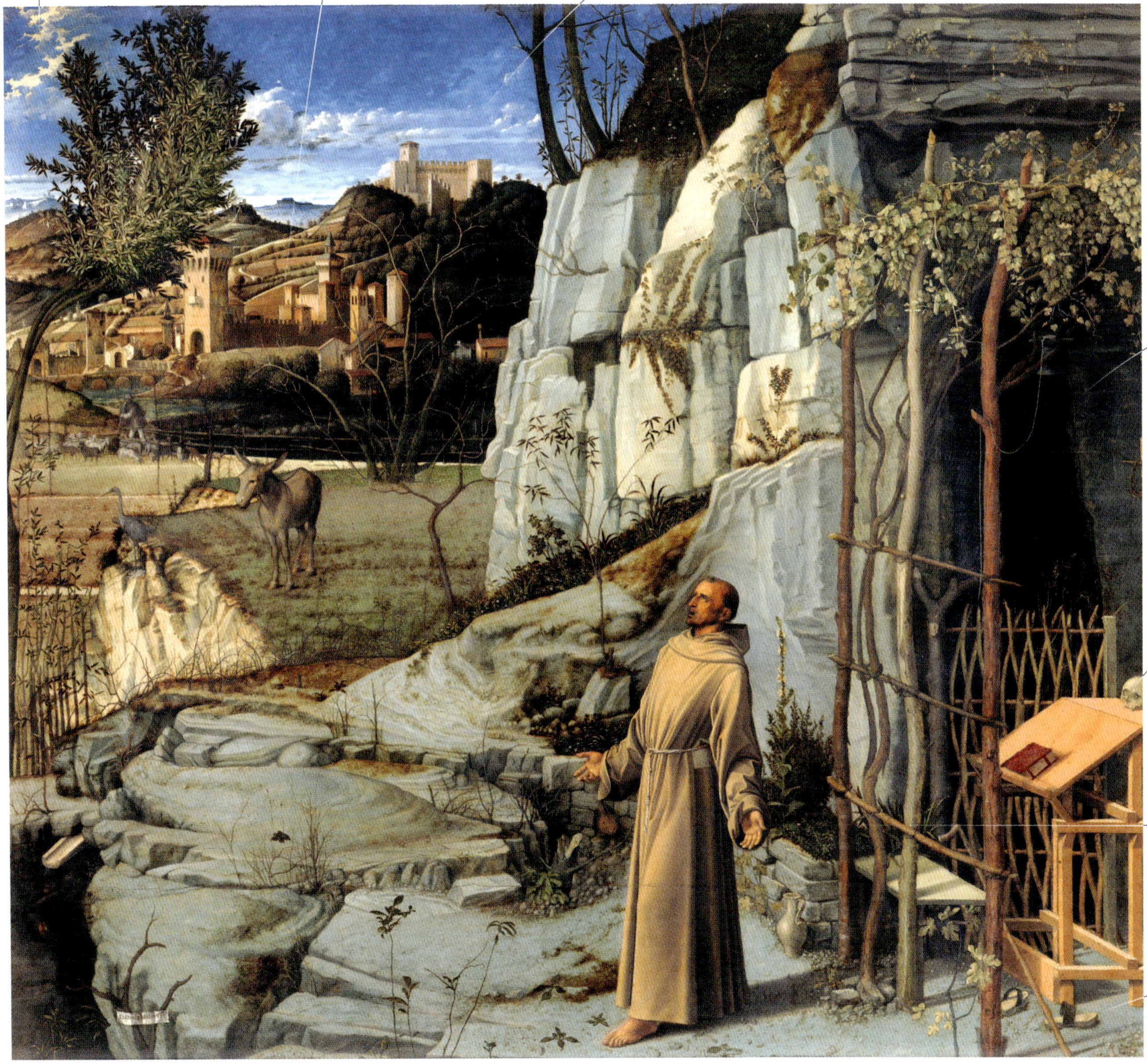

The dark cave where St. Francis lives creates a striking contrast to the radiant light bathing the rest of the scene.

The skull resting on St. Francis's desk is a reminder of mortality.

Stigmata, evidence of St. Francis's deep identification with Christ, are visible on St. Francis's palms.

The saint has left his sandals behind, suggesting that he has been interrupted.

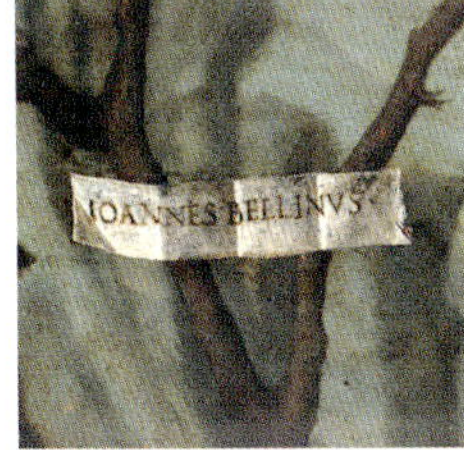

Bellini signed his name on a *cartellino*, a piece of paper incorporated into the painting.

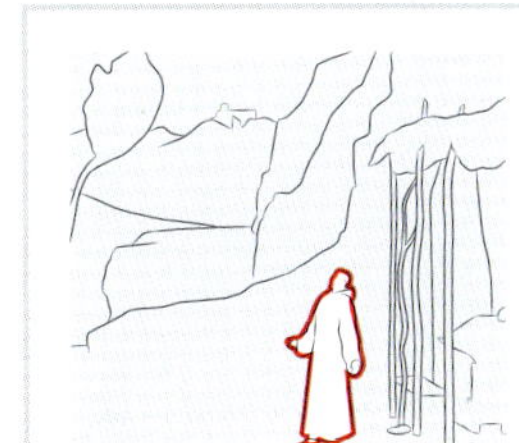

New light
The figure of St. Francis is illuminated. As he opens his body to receive the stigmata, he gazes in ecstasy toward the source of the radiant light.

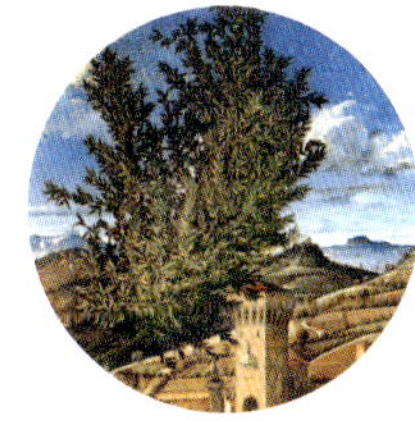

Divine detail
The natural world is painted in fine detail, reinforcing the sense of divine agency within nature.

Portinari Altarpiece

Hugo van der Goes 1475–1476, oil on panel, 100 × 120 in (253 × 304 cm), Uffizi, Florence, Italy

Theatrically composed and packed with symbolic details, the Portinari Altarpiece depicts the story of the shepherds' visit to see the newborn Christ, told in St. Luke's Gospel (2:8–20). The central panel of the altarpiece immerses viewers in the wonder of the shepherds as they pay homage to the Christ Child.

Joseph has removed his sandal, out of respect for the holy ground beneath him. His red gown is a reference to Christ's blood.

At the center of the composition, the Virgin looks lovingly at her son.

The moment when the angels announce the birth of Christ to the shepherds is depicted in the background.

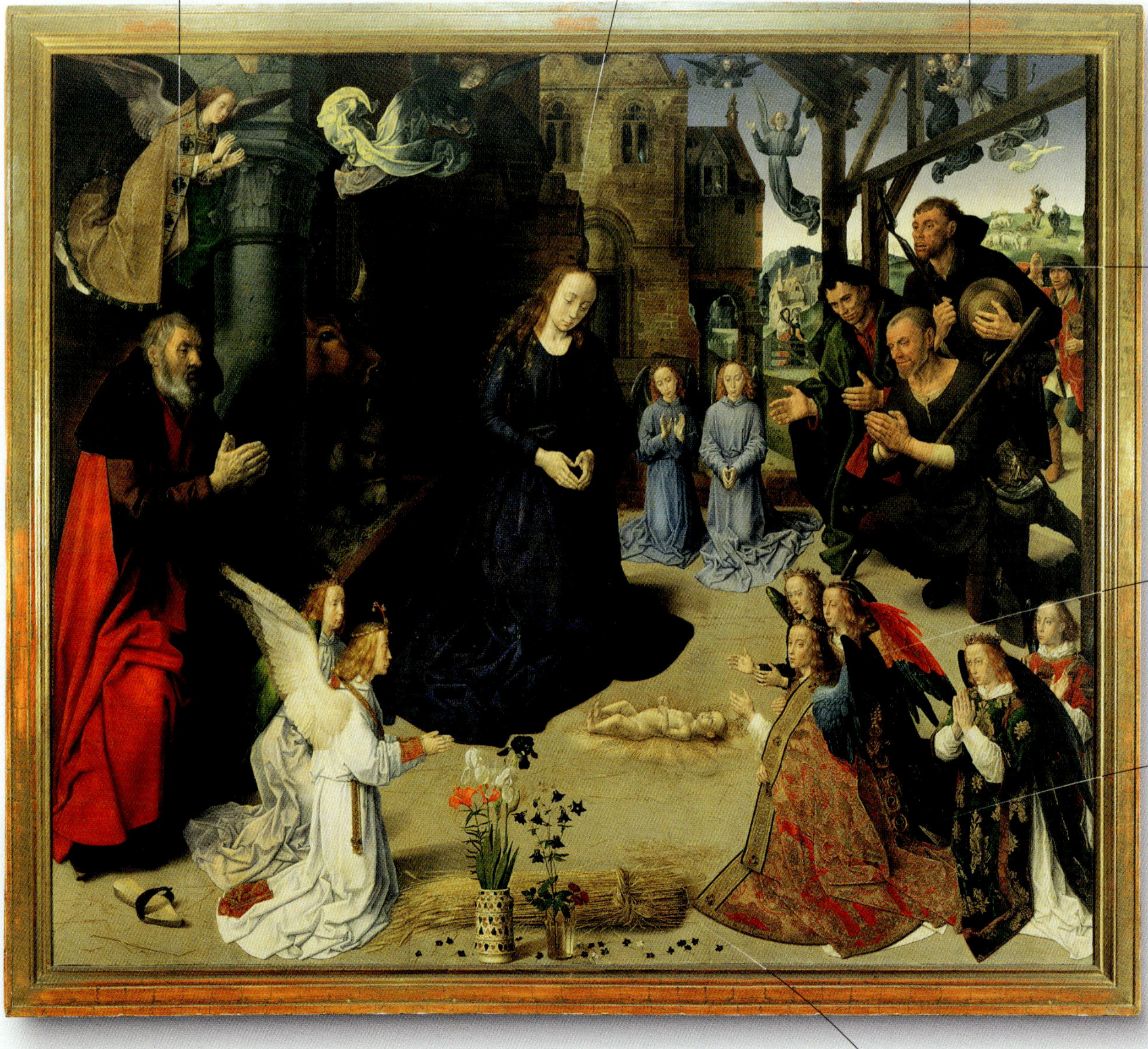

The three shepherds arrive to admire the baby. Their faces are weathered by labor and form a stark contrast to the tranquil demeanor of the angels.

The Infant Jesus lies on a bed of wheat, a symbol of the bread of the Eucharist.

All the angels wear liturgical garments with decorative brocades. The word SANCTUS (holy), is embroidered on the trim of this angel's cloak.

A sheaf of wheat alludes to the bread of the Eucharist.

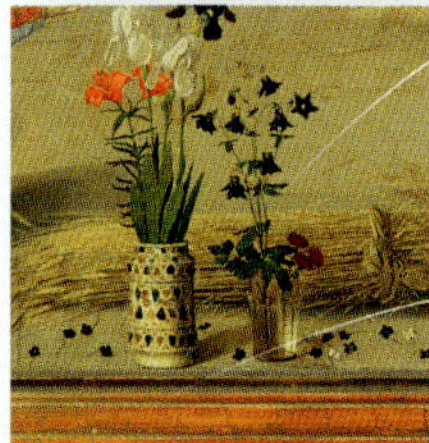

Three carnations in a glass jar refer to the Holy Trinity—the belief that God is the Father, Son, and Holy Spirit.

An earthenware vase holds white and blue irises, symbolizing Mary's purity, and red lilies, foreshadowing Christ's arrest, trial, and death.

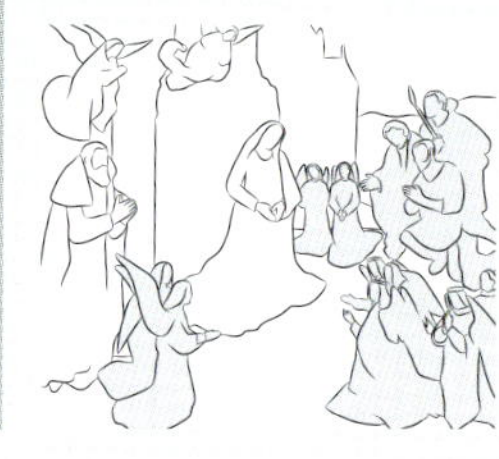

Multilayered
Van der Goes created a sense of depth in the painting by layering the groups of angels and shepherds.

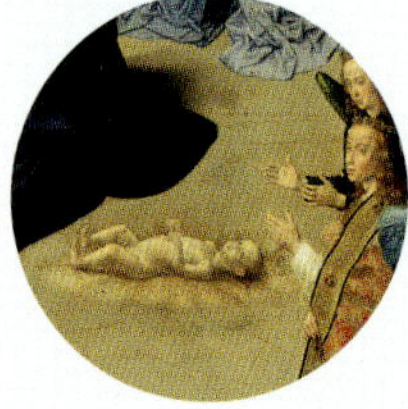

All eyes
The newborn Christ, bathed in golden light at the center of the composition, captivates the onlookers. With bowed heads and hands in prayer, they tenderly fix their gaze on him.

Saint Sebastian

Andrea Mantegna 1480, tempera on canvas, 100 × 55 in (255 × 140 cm), Louvre, Paris, France

Depicted in a crumbling classical ruin, St. Sebastian, a Roman soldier has been shot with arrows for refusing to deny his Christian faith. This painting—the second of three depictions of the saint by Mantegna—is a comment on the triumph of faith over the pagan world. It reveals Mantegna's love of antique ruins and his careful study of the human body.

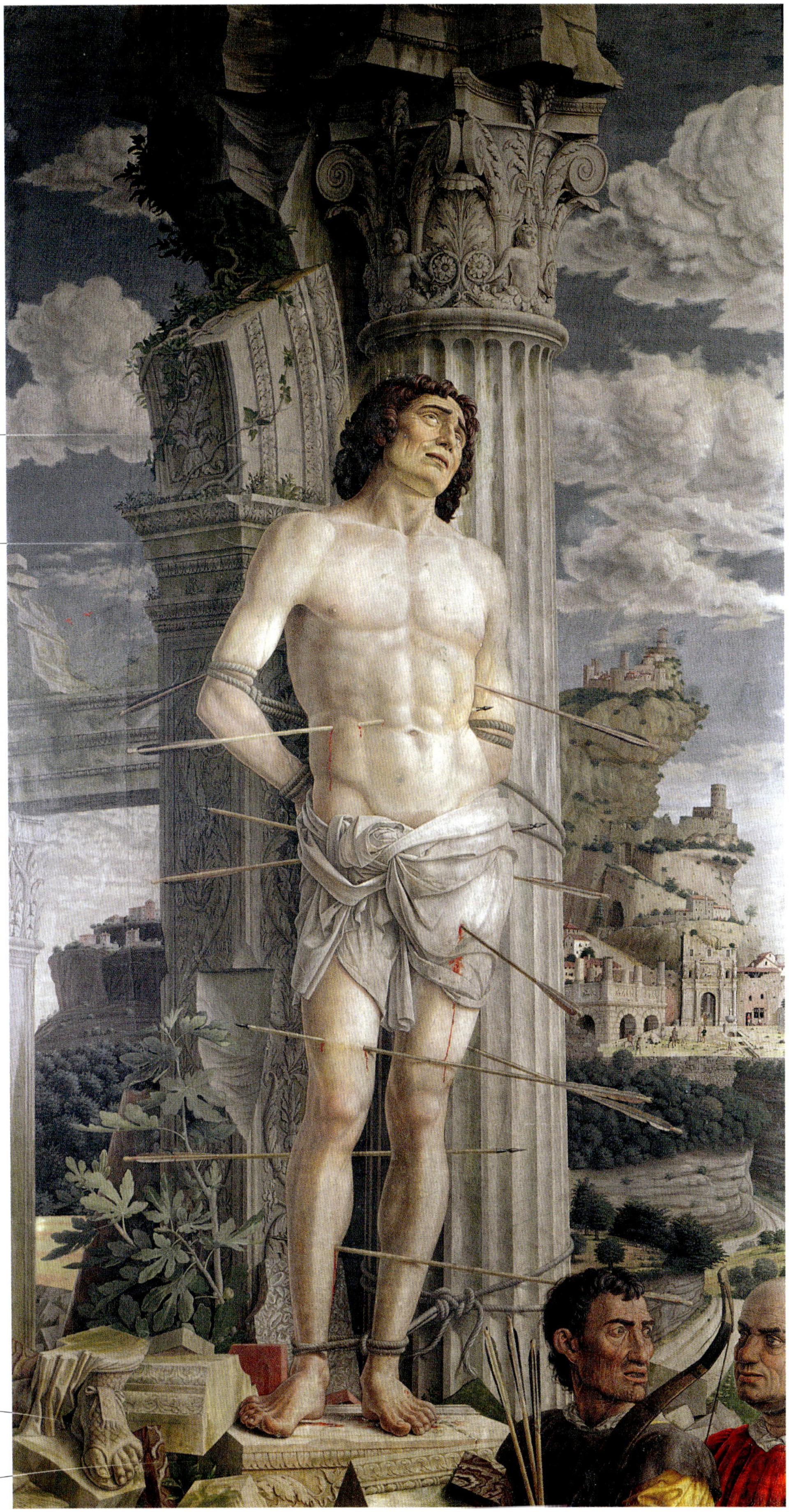

St. Sebastian looks up to heaven, resolved to bear his martyrdom.

A realistic arch resembles authentic Roman remains surviving in northern Italy.

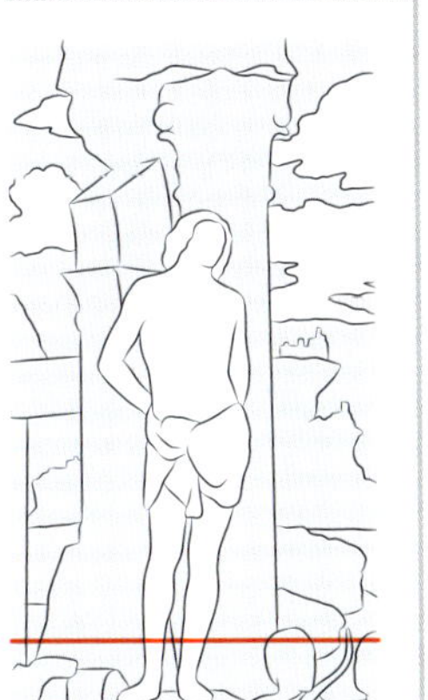

Low viewpoint
The saint is observed from an unusually low viewpoint, enhancing the impression of solidity and the dominance of his figure. The archers' heads are at the same level as the viewer.

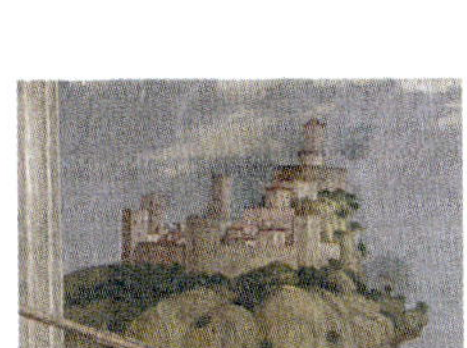

The rocky path, gravel, and caves allude to the difficulties of reaching celestial Jerusalem, the fortified city on top of the mountain.

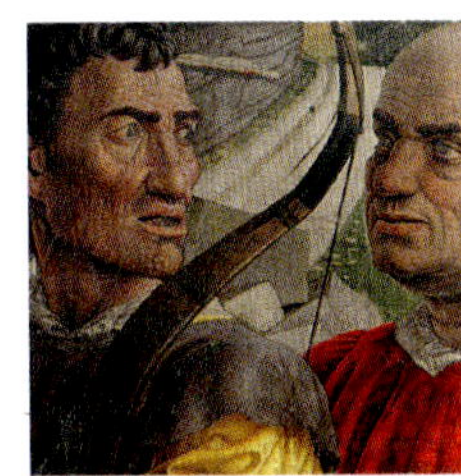

Brightly colored archers create a contrast between the man of transcendent faith and those who are only attracted by profane pleasures.

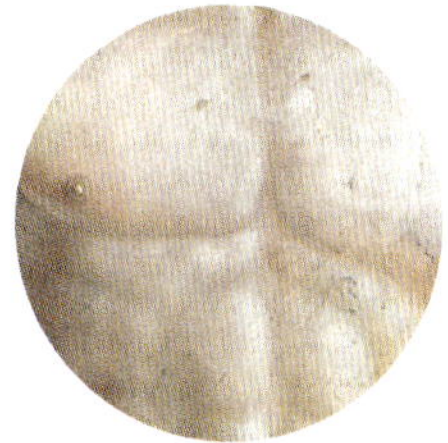

Sculptural effect
The modeling of the body, achieved through light and shade, has a sculptural feel, as though carved from stone.

A sculpted foot in a Roman sandal symbolizes the triumph of Christianity over paganism through sacrifice. Mantegna is also comparing his painting to classical sculpture.

A fragment of building, acts as a pedestal.

The Greek god Zephyrus, the personification of the west wind, blows Venus to the shore.

This figure is probably the nymph Chloris, who was abducted by Zephyrus and became Flora, the goddess of flowers.

Venus's small head, long neck, sloping shoulders, and rounded stomach match the 15th-century Italian ideal of female beauty.

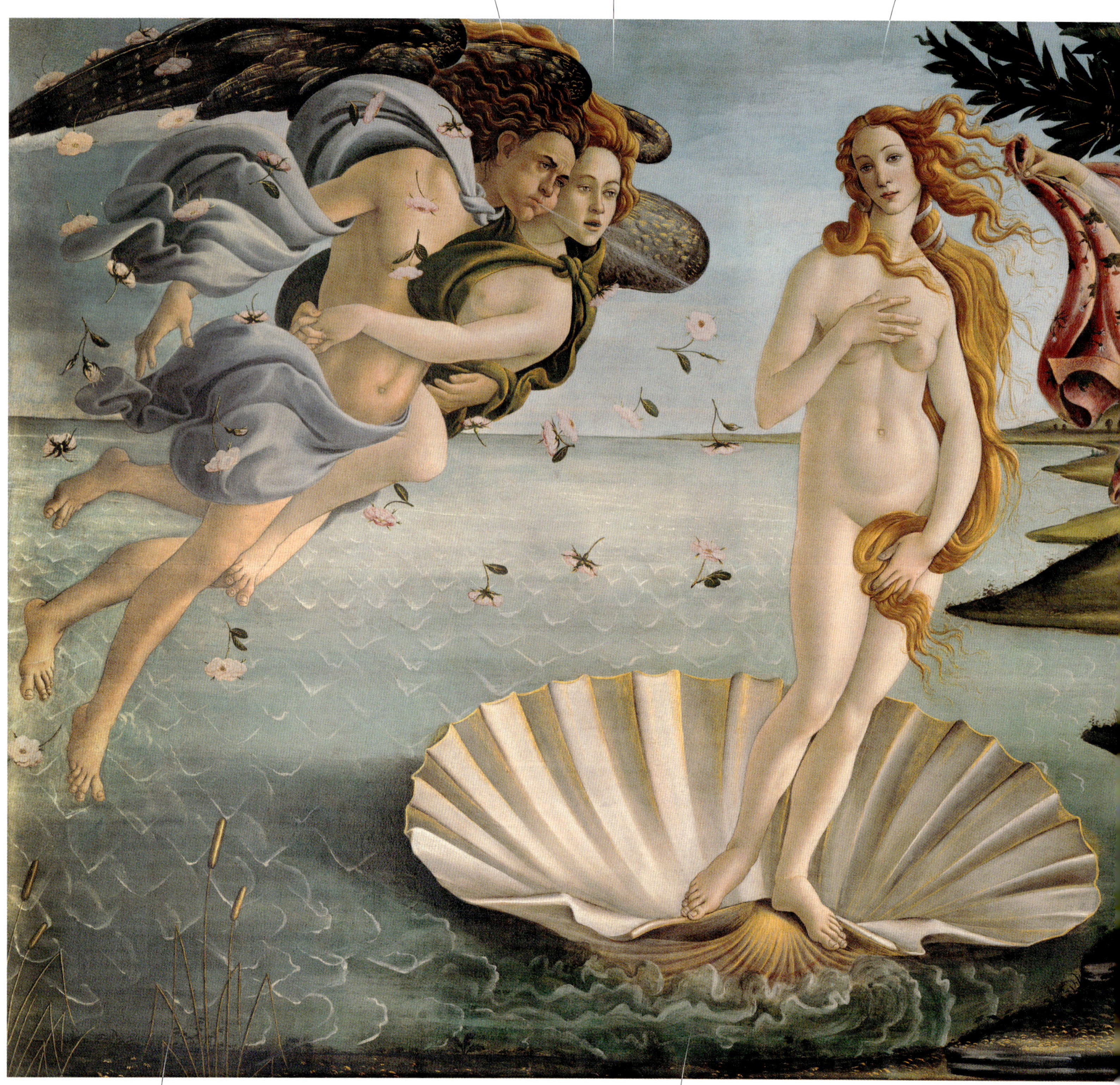

A pattern of V shapes on the surface of the water represents waves.

Venus appears fully grown on a scallop shell boat—her story in the original myth has more violent origins.

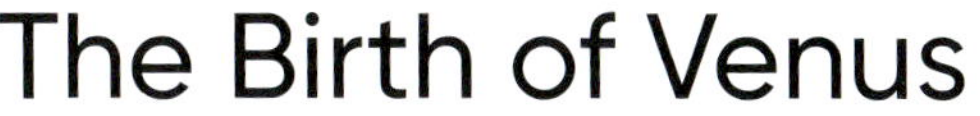

The Birth of Venus

Sandro Botticelli c. 1485, tempera on canvas, 68 × 110 in (172.5 × 278.5 cm), Uffizi, Florence, Italy

The Birth of Venus depicts Venus, the Roman goddess of love and beauty, arriving on the shores of a Greek island standing on a scallop shell. It was the first large-scale Renaissance artwork on canvas to feature a mythological subject and was probably commissioned by a member of the Medici family. In 15th-century Italy, artists tended to portray mythological scenes on a much smaller scale than Botticelli's Venus, often to decorate furniture. Bigger paintings were more likely to have a religious subject. Although *The Birth of Venus* is a pagan image, it is a celebration of spiritual beauty.

A nymph representing Spring wears a myrtle leaf necklace and a sash of roses. She holds out a cloak to cover Venus.

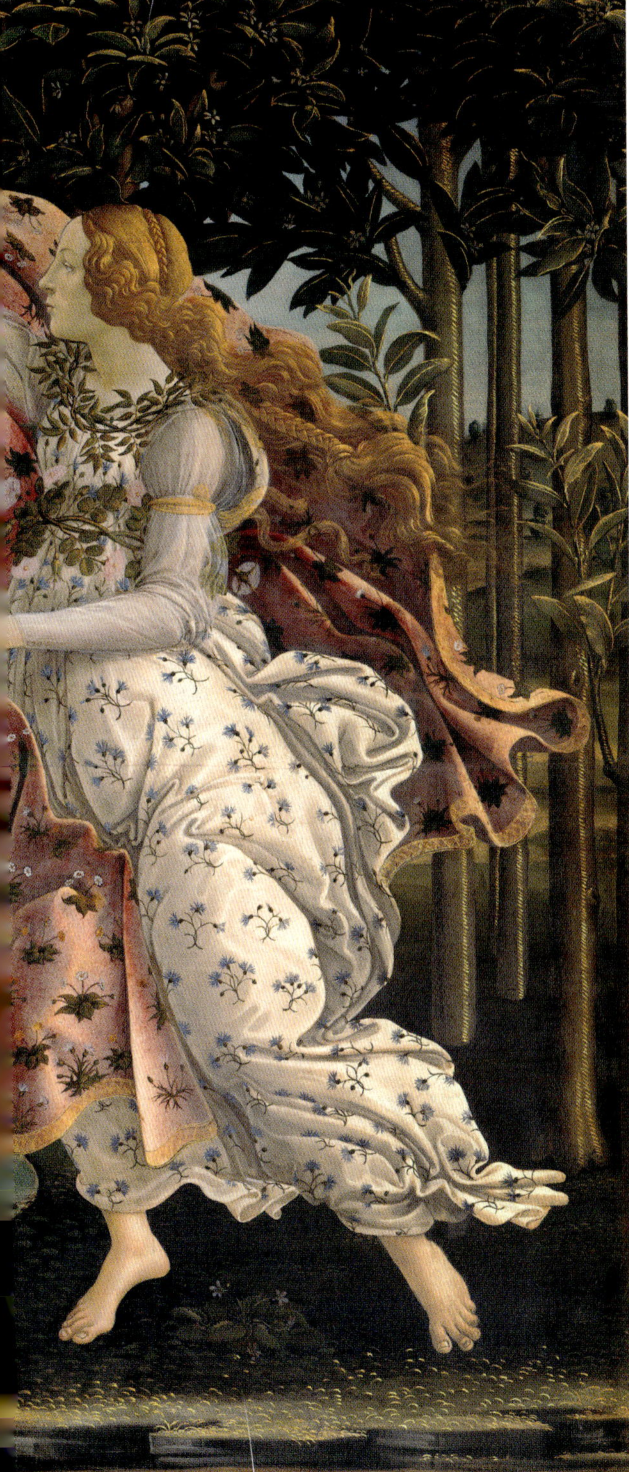

A lone blue anemone at the nymph's feet further associates the scene with Spring's arrival.

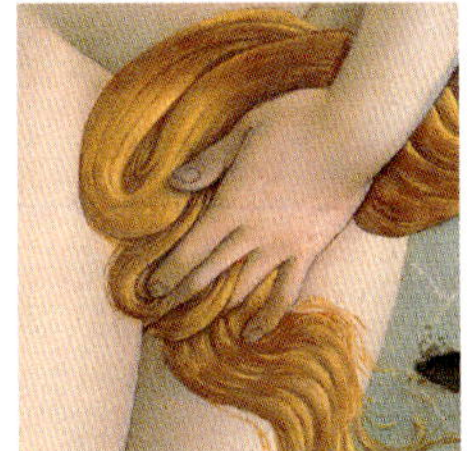

Botticelli's goddess is known as a "modest Venus" because her breast and pubic region are covered up.

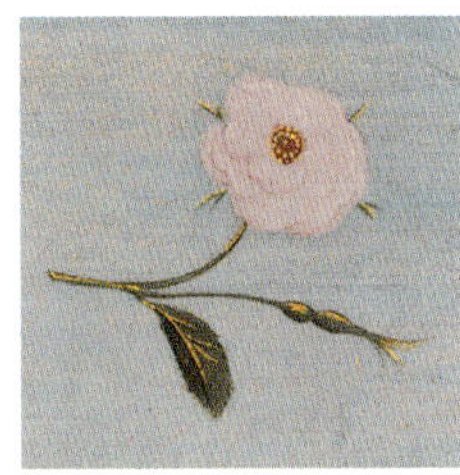

Roses are a symbol of love, and are known as the flowers of Venus.

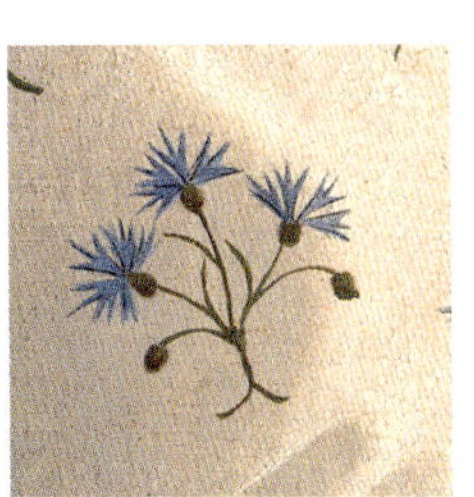

Ultramarine, an expensive blue pigment derived from lapis lazuli stones, indicates that Botticelli was well funded.

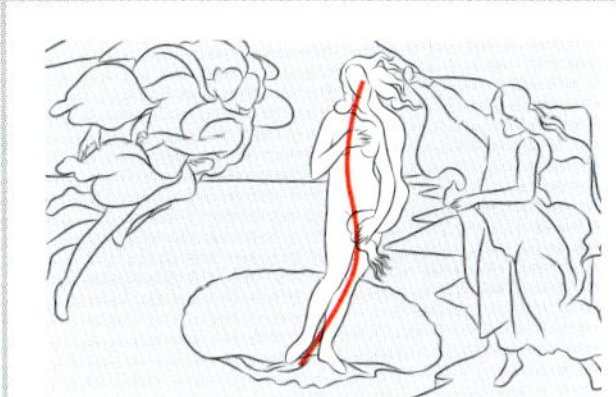

Floating figure
Venus has an ethereal quality, created by the delicate S-shaped curve of her pose and the lack of shadows.

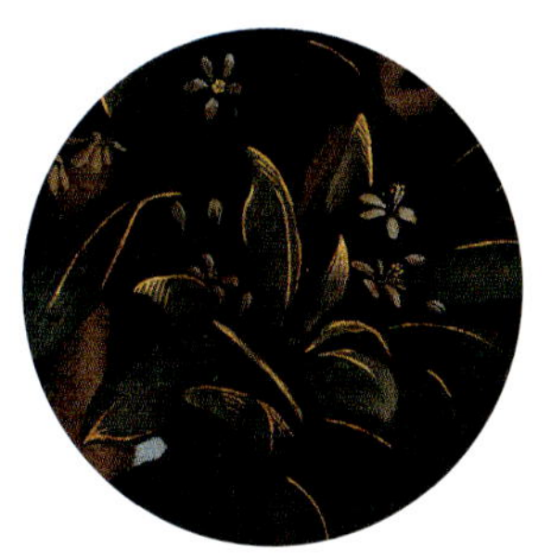

Gilded goddess
Gold highlights would have made the painting shimmer when viewed by candlelight.

> "Botticelli is the painter of Florence; he has given his soul to the city."
>
> Giorgio Vasari, 1568

Madonna and Child with Cherubim

Andrea della Robbia c. 1485, glazed terra-cotta with polychrome and gilt wood frame, 38 x 35 x 6 in (95.25 x 88.27 x 14.61 cm), National Gallery of Art, Washington, D.C., US

This intimate portrait of the infant Jesus and his mother Mary is in tondo, or circular form. Sculptor Andrea della Robbia continued the production of glazed terra-cotta reliefs developed by his uncle Luca in the 1440s. They were used as objects of devotion in churches and homes, and mounted on the walls of outdoor shrines.

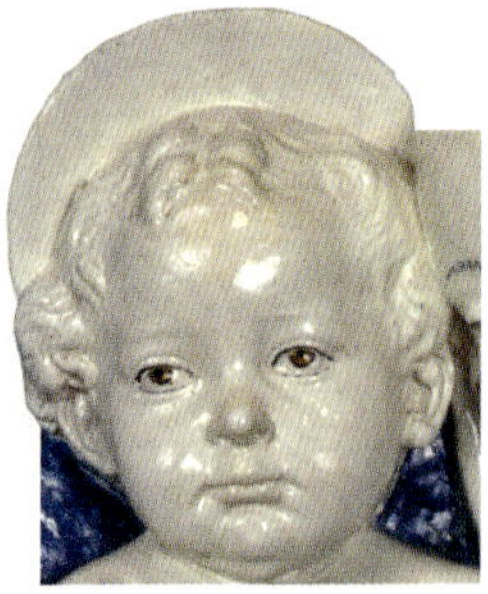

The child turns his face toward the world, but his eyes suggest quiet contemplation.

Angelic spirits known as putti hover over the Virgin and Child, their wings crossed.

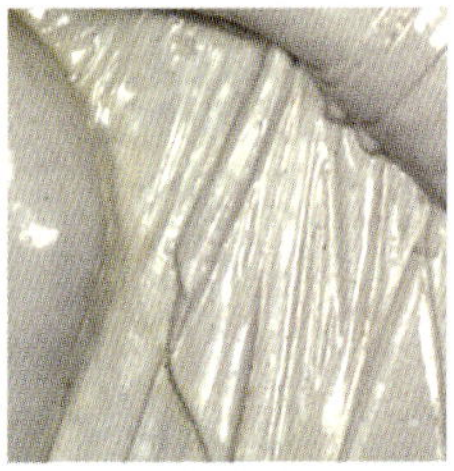

The detailing of the folds of Mary's robe, and the scale, suggest a work intended to be viewed close-up for private devotion.

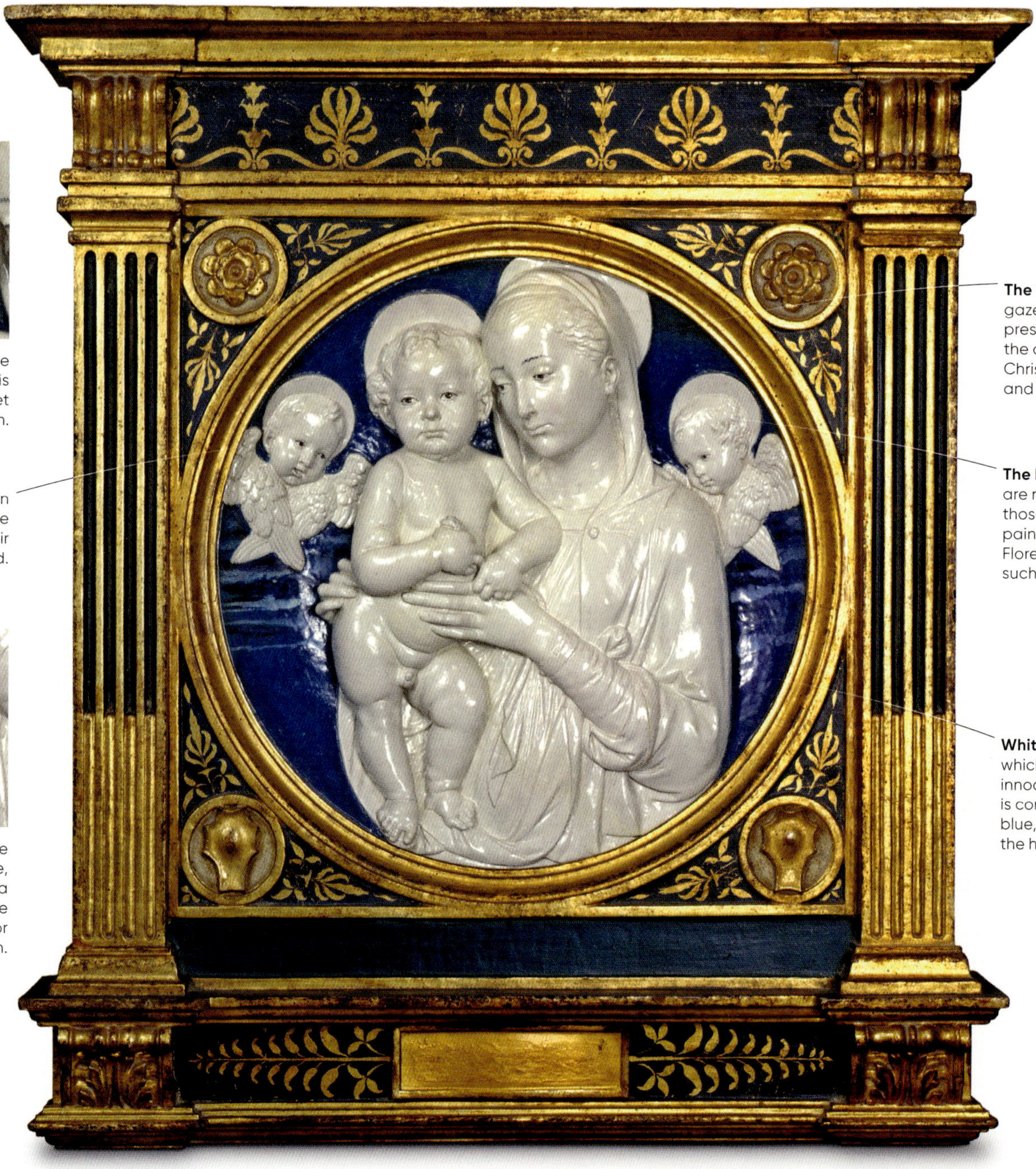

The Virgin's downcast gaze suggests a presentiment of the child's fate: Christ's Passion and Crucifixion.

The beautiful faces are reminiscent of those depicted by painters of the Florentine school, such as Botticelli.

White glaze, which symbolized innocence and purity, is complemented by blue, representing the heavens.

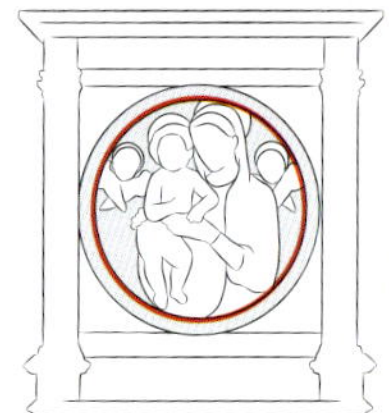

Intimate relationship
The circular form and close crop enclose the Virgin and child in an intimate embrace, made more so by the flanking putti.

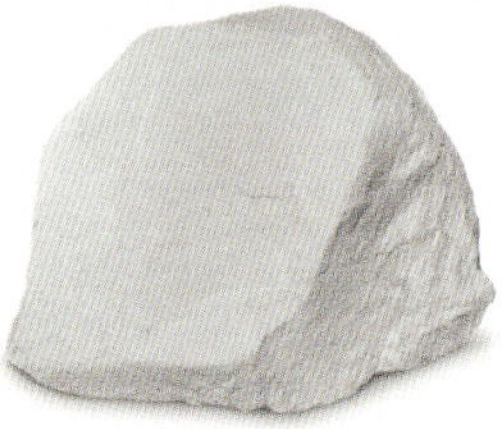

Method
The Della Robbia workshop collected fine-quality white clay from the riverbank then pressed it into molds and fired it in a kiln. The glazed coating was applied with a brush; it gave the colors a much greater durability than that of painted sculpture.

The Annunciation, with St. Emidius

Carlo Crivelli 1486, egg and oil on canvas, 81 × 58 in (207 × 146.7 cm), National Gallery, London, UK

The Archangel Gabriel has come to tell Mary she is to be the mother of God. Beside him kneels Emidius, patron saint of Ascoli Piceno, the "city of 100 towers." Crivelli's work, which interweaves Christian imagery with symbols of Ascoli Piceno's wealth, is as much a civic celebration as a religious one.

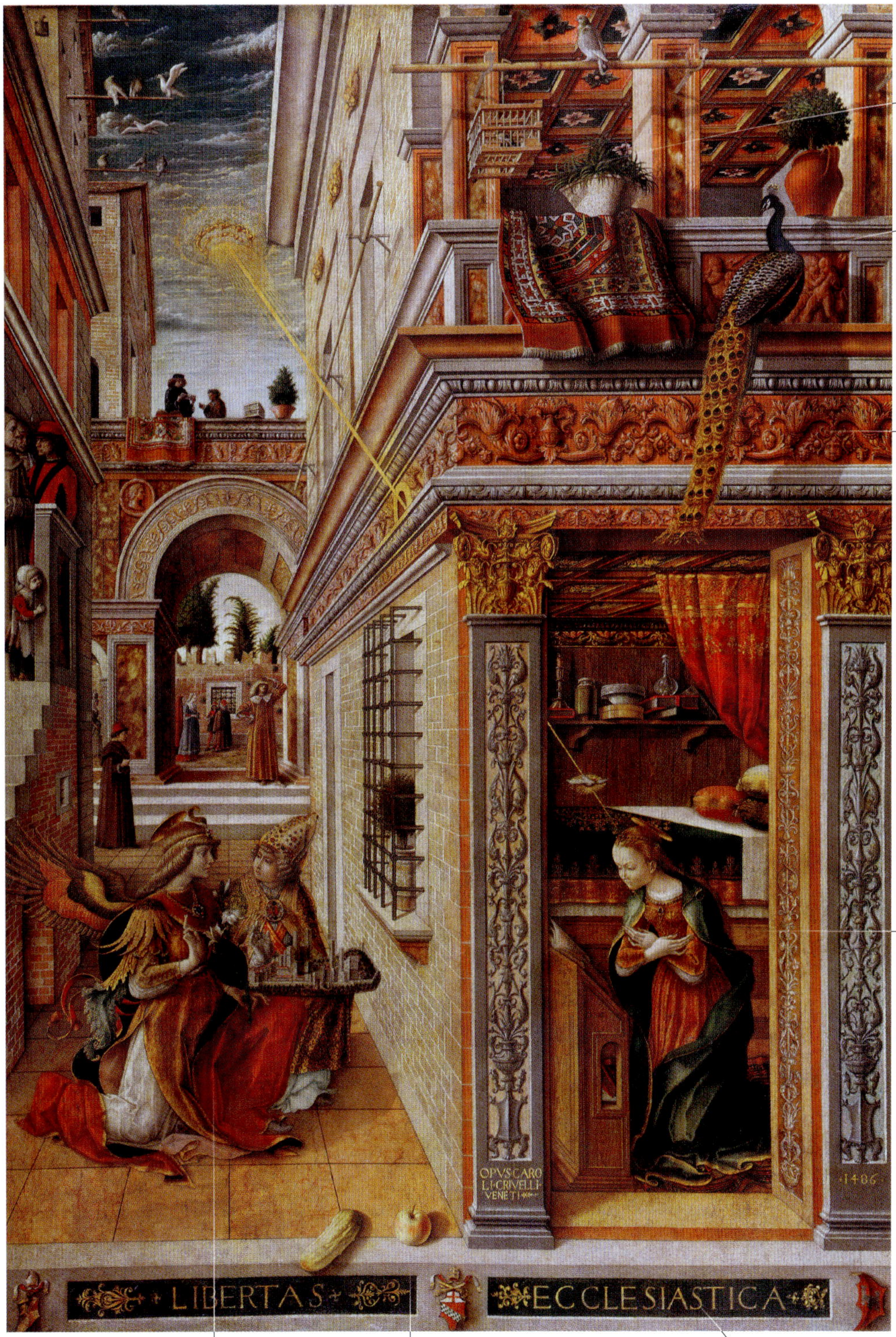

A beam of light from Heaven causes Mary to conceive. The dove is the emblem of God's Holy Spirit.

The peacock was widely recognized as a symbol of immortality because the ancient Greeks believed its flesh never decayed.

Elaborately carved stonework and costly furnishings reflect Ascoli Piceno's prosperity.

Mary's outfit gives her the look of a wealthy merchant's daughter. She prays, crossing her hands in submission to her destiny.

The angel Gabriel brings Mary lilies in recognition of her purity.

In Christianity, the apple conventionally represents the Fall of humankind, while the cucumber is an emblem of redemption.

The inscription at the base—*Libertas Ecclesiastica* (Church Freedom)—honors the autonomy recently granted to Ascoli Piceno by Pope Sixtus IV.

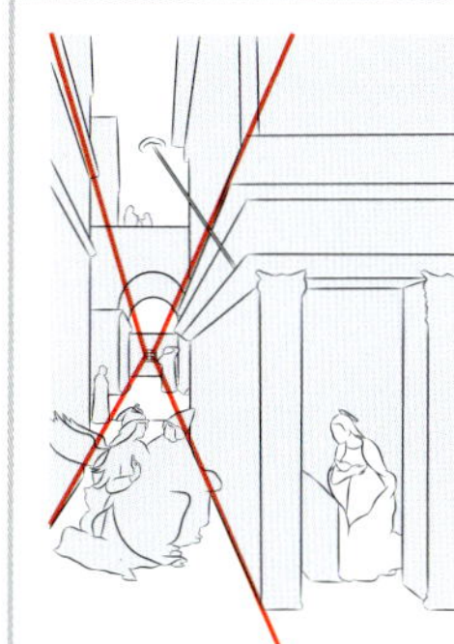

Linear perspective
The vanishing point leads the eye along the lane on the left-hand side of the picture to a dead end, sealed off with an iron grille. This is said to represent Mary's virginity.

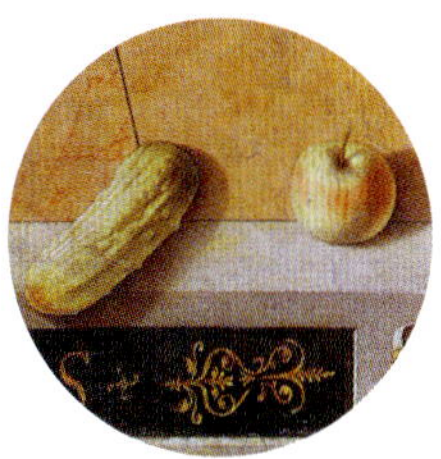

Trompe l'oeil effect
Crivelli deploys the technique of geometric perspective by which the apple and cucumber seem to emerge from the frame.

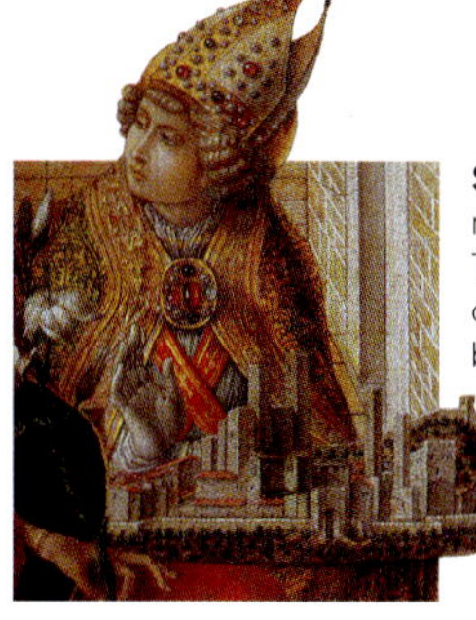

St. Emidius carries a model of Ascoli Piceno. The German-born bishop of the town was martyred by the Romans.

Bosch probably copied these exotic animals from illustrated travelogues. They would have been unfamiliar to most European viewers in the 15th century.

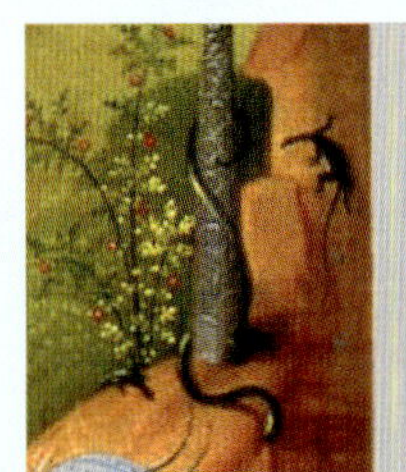

Coiled around a palm tree, the serpent symbolizes the temptation to commit sin.

Bizarre, fleshlike structures symbolize the fleeting nature of the delights being enjoyed by the people in the garden.

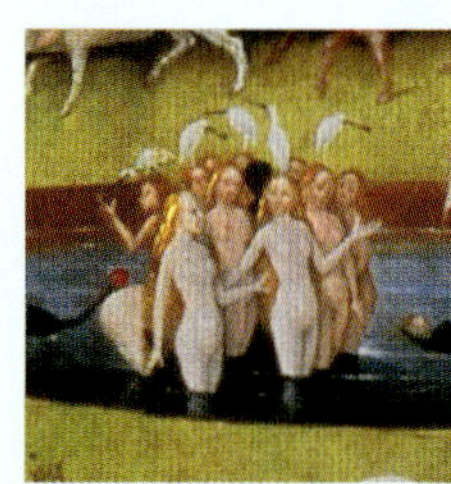

Naked women bathe in a pool at the center of the triptych, encircled by male hunters.

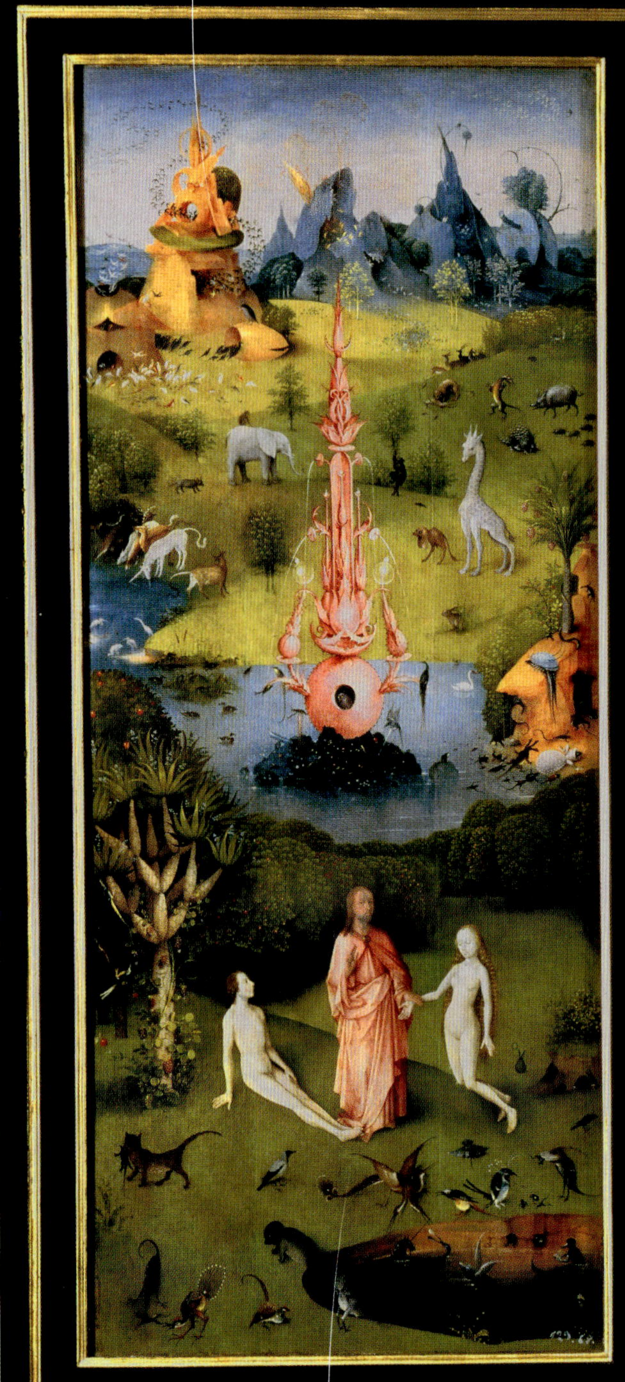

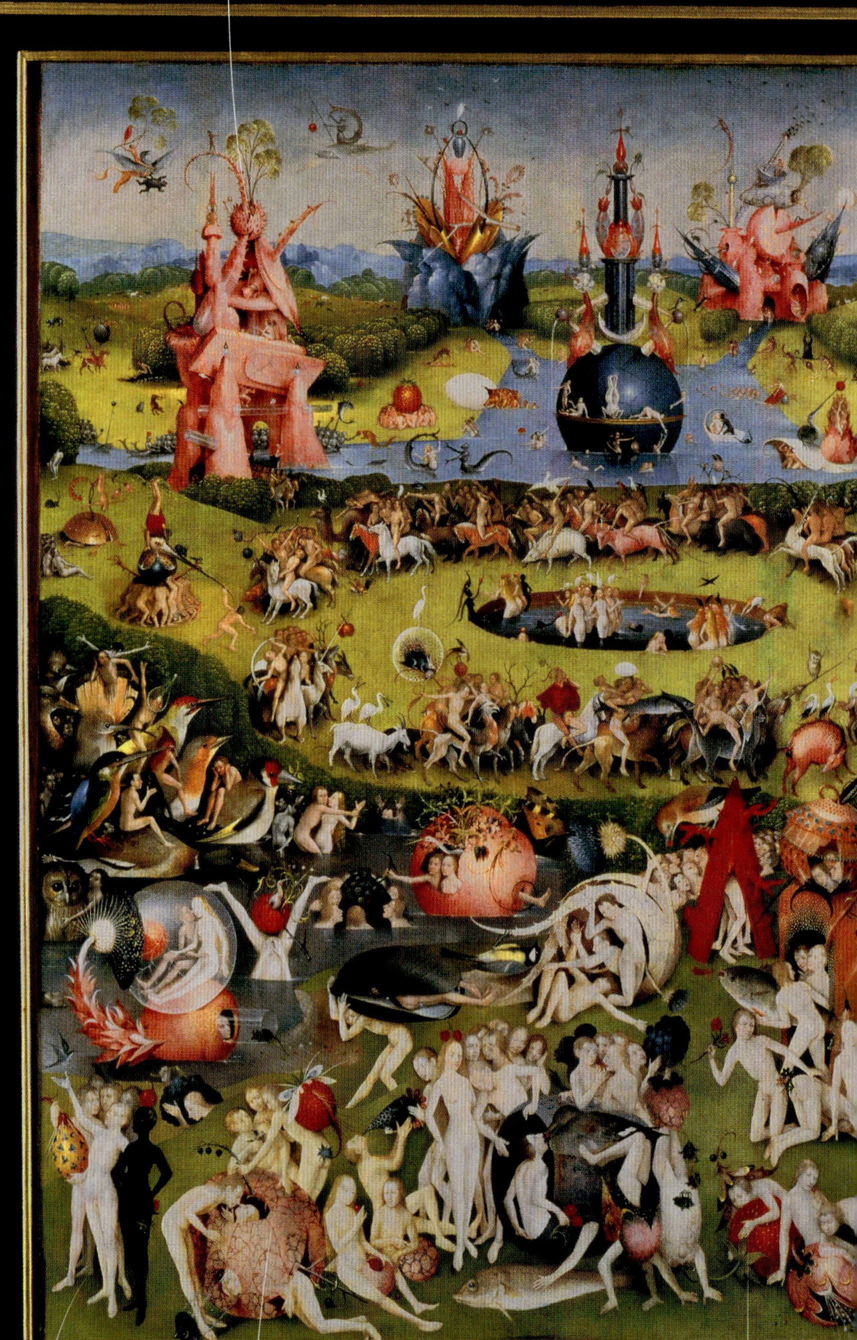

God presents Eve to Adam in the Garden of Eden.

Naked men and women, a state usually restricted to the figures of Adam and Eve in art, populate this section.

Scenes of sexual intimacy and lust fill the central panel.

Figures gorging on red fruit mirror Adam and Eve eating the forbidden apple, the act of transgression that caused their expulsion from Eden.

The Garden of Earthly Delights

Hieronymus Bosch 1490–1500, oil on oak panel, 73× 128 in (185.8 × 325.5 cm), Prado, Madrid, Spain

Made for a private home, this triptych reflects the moral and philosophical preoccupations of society during the Northern Renaissance, yet it is also an astonishing departure from the art being produced at the time. Rich in fantastical symbolism and allegory, it explores the themes of paradise, temptation, and the consequences of sin described in the Bible. The left panel shows Adam and Eve in Eden; the central panel depicts a false paradise in which sin and lust prevail; and the right panel illustrates hell, where grotesque creatures exact or endure punishment.

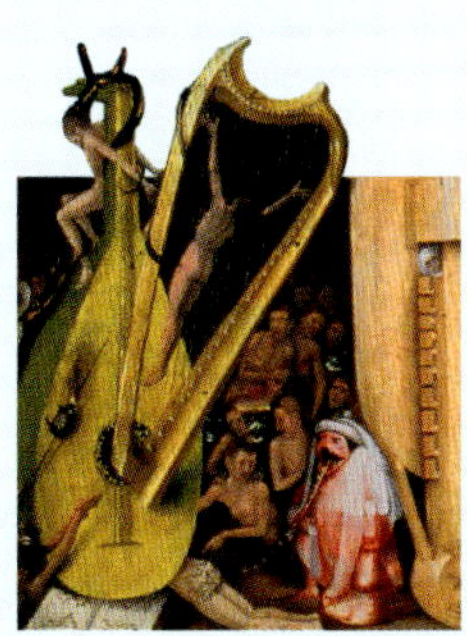

Musical instruments, formerly objects of pleasure, become tools for torture.

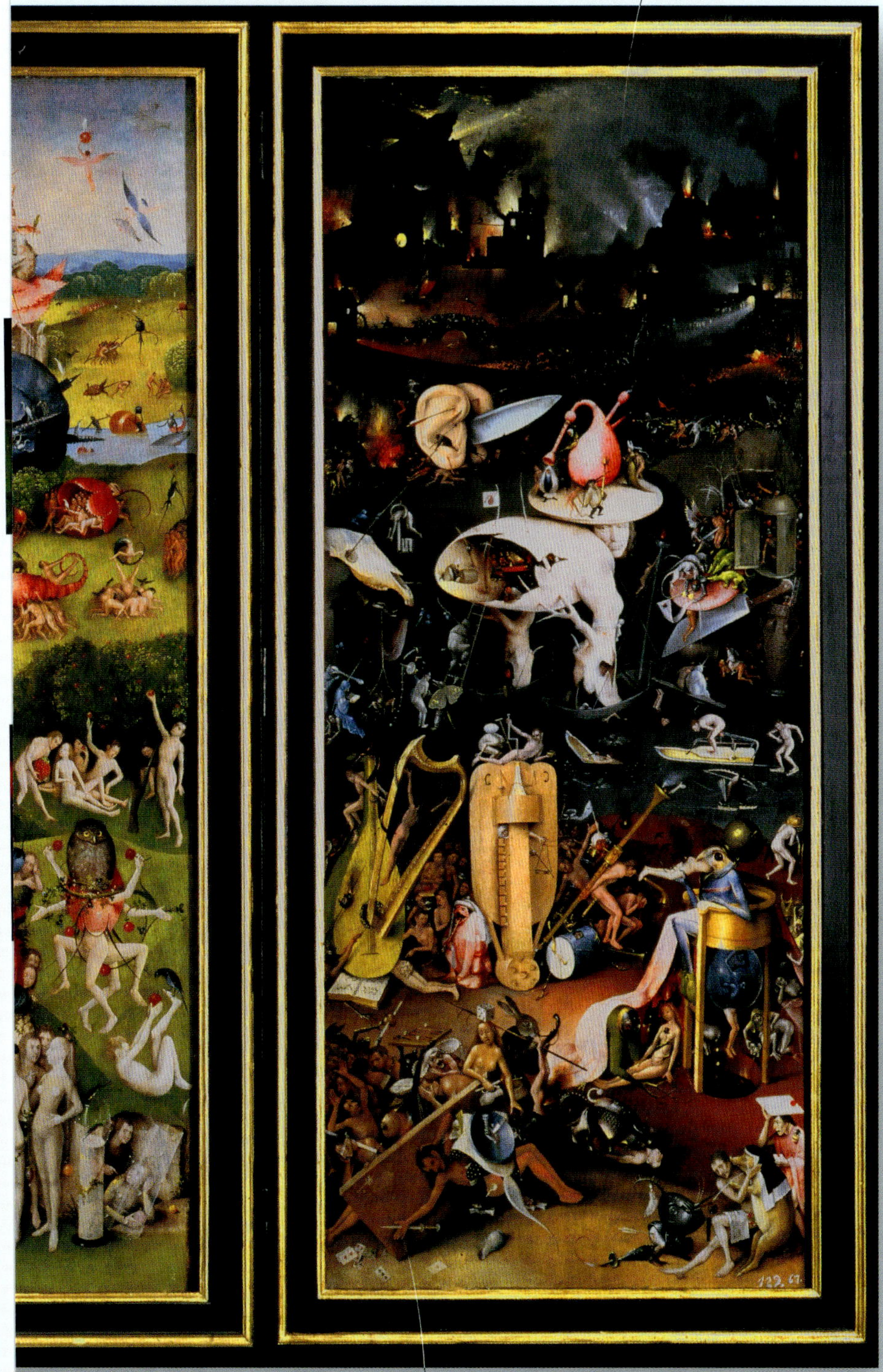

Burning buildings set the scene in the fiery depths of hell.

Christ's blessing hand is punctured by a knife. Nearby are dice, playing cards, and a board game, all symbols of gambling.

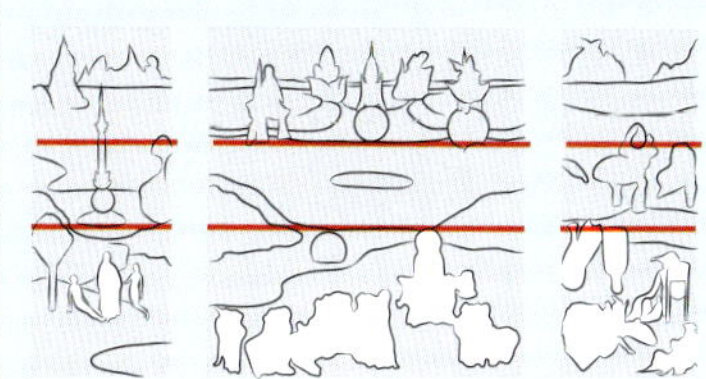

Method in the mayhem Despite its apparent chaos, each panel contains a background, middle ground, and foreground, with most of the details reserved for the latter.

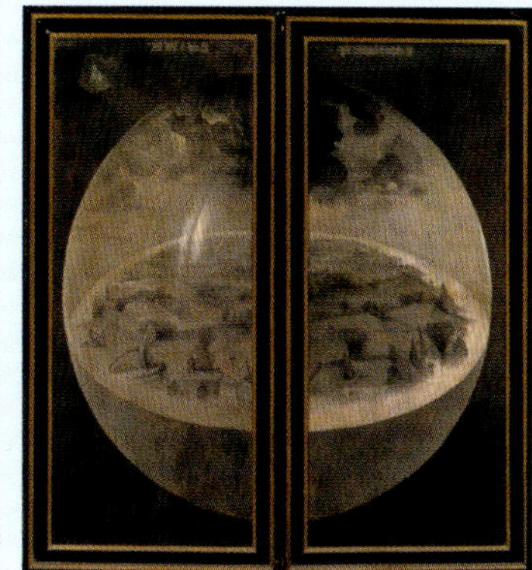

Monochrome image The closed panels of the triptych depict the Third Day of Creation in grisaille (shades of gray). According to the Bible's Book of Genesis, this was when God separated the waters from the earth and created vegetation. God is shown sitting in the top left corner, with a Bible in his lap.

> "For the first and perhaps for the only time, an artist had succeeded in giving concrete and tangible shape to the fears that had haunted the minds of man in the Middle Ages."
>
> E. H. Gombrich, 1950

The Last Supper

Leonardo da Vinci 1495, mural, 15 × 29 ft (4.6 × 8.8 m), church and convent of Santa Maria delle Grazie, Milan, Italy

One of the masterpieces of the European Renaissance, *The Last Supper* captures the moment when Jesus Christ, celebrating a Passover feast with his apostles, reveals he will be betrayed by someone at the table. The poses of the apostles convey their horror and confusion.

The mural took four years to complete; when the prior of the church where the work was painted complained about the delay, Leonardo threatened to use him as the model for Judas, Christ's betrayer. The work deteriorated badly over time, and has been extensively restored.

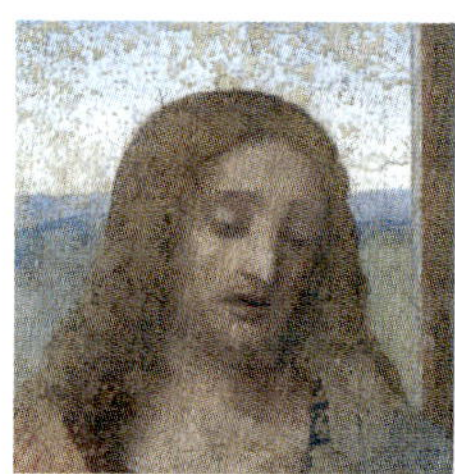

Leonardo used a small nail and string to create the one-point perspective. The hole for the nail is still visible to the right side of Christ's temple.

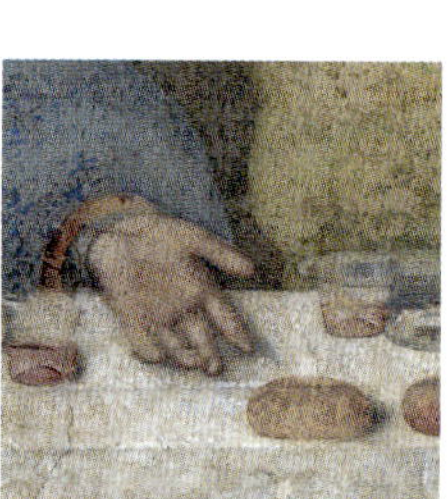

Christ points toward the bread and wine, instructing his disciples in the ritual of the Eucharist, in which Christians consume bread and wine in remembrance of Christ.

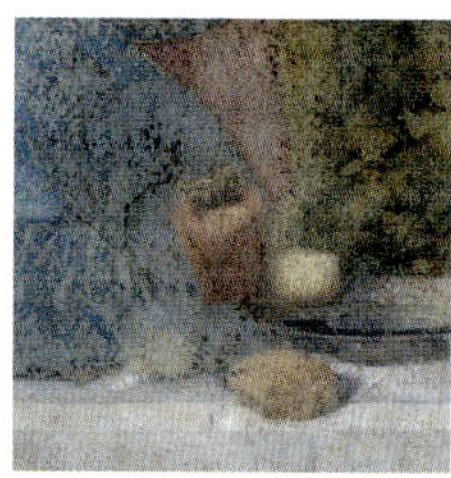

Judas holds a purse, symbolizing the 30 pieces of silver that he received for betraying Christ.

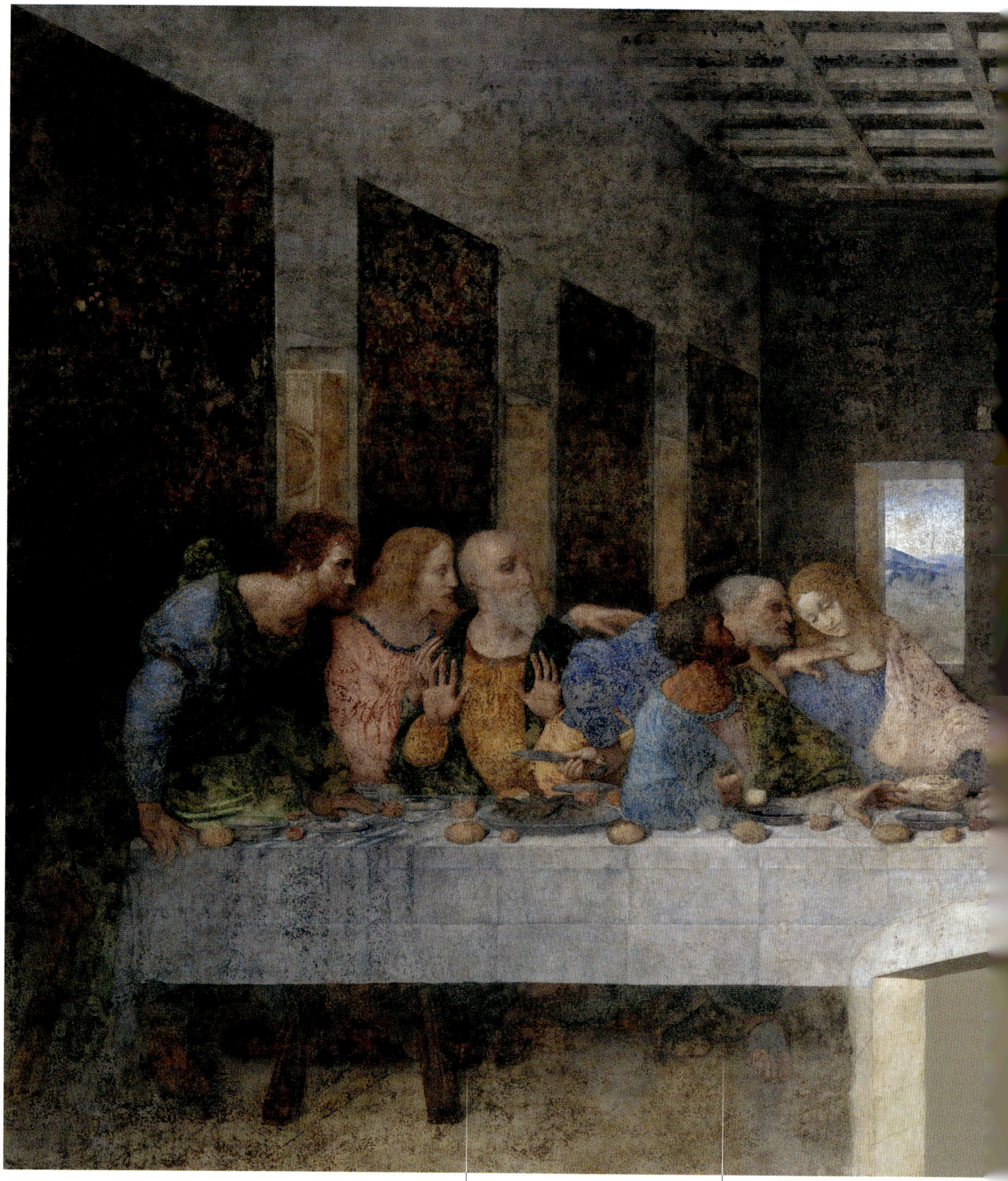

From left to right: Bartholomew, James son of Alphaeus, Andrew, Judas Iscariot, Peter, John, Christ, Thomas, James the Greater, Philip, Matthew, Jude Thaddeus, and Simon the Zealot.

Judas is depicted in shadow and lower than the other disciples.

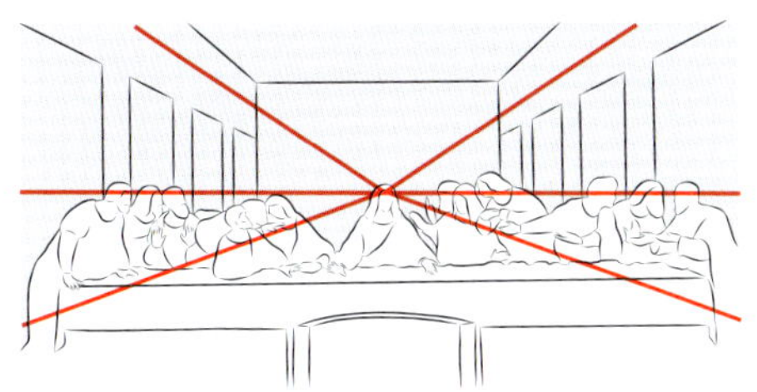

Creating depth
One-point perspective leads the eye to Christ. This point also creates the horizon line, dividing the work in two.

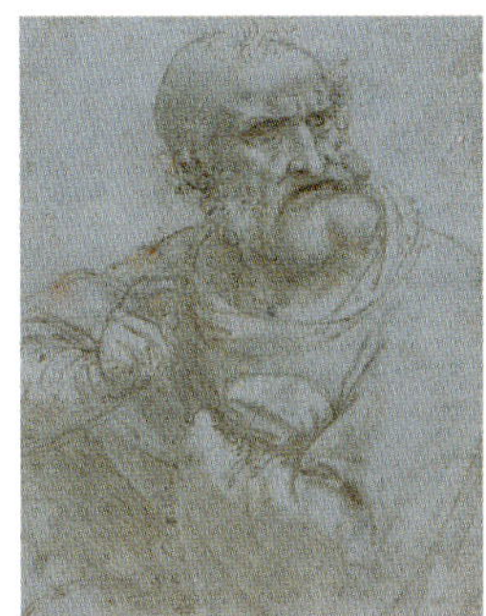

Physiognomies
Leonardo made many preparatory drawings of the disciples. He aimed to capture their particular characteristics through their gestures, features, and expressions.

> "Perspective is the guide and entrance, without which nothing can be well done."
> Leonardo da Vinci

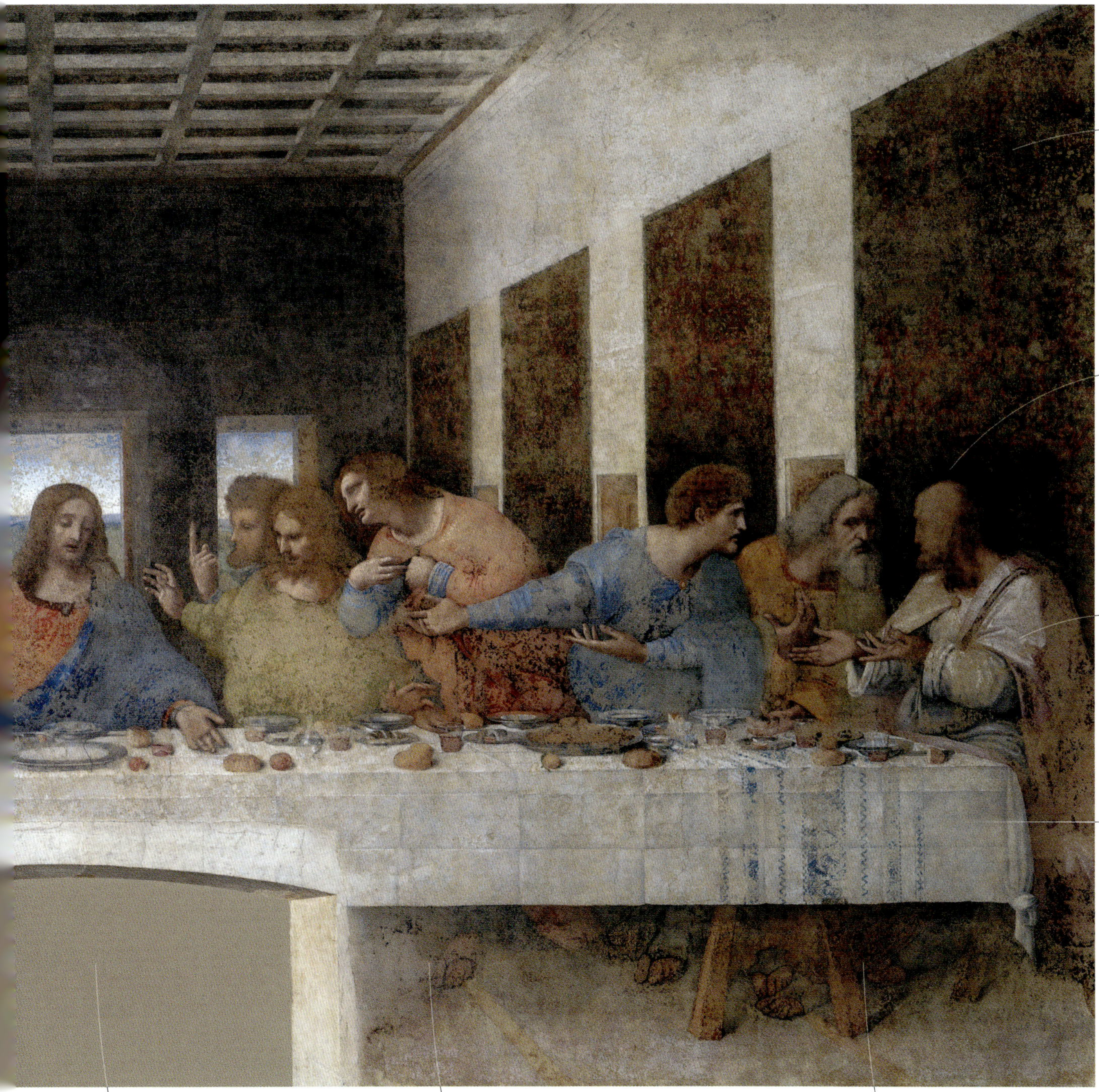

The dark squares on the walls behind the diners were once filled with depictions of tapestries, but these deteriorated beyond repair.

Leonardo's experimental attempt to paint on dry plaster rather than wet, as was traditional, meant that the painting began to deteriorate almost immediately.

After numerous attempts at restoration, only 20 percent of the paint is original.

Blue embroidery decorates the white tablecloth.

Christ's feet were removed when monks cut a door through the wall in 1652.

Leonardo chose to show Christ and the apostles as human rather than holy, so he did not give them their customary halos.

The apostles are placed in four groups of three.

Miracle of the Relic of the Holy Cross at the Rialto Bridge

Vittore Carpaccio c.1494–1496, oil on canvas, 146 × 154 in (371 × 392 cm), Gallerie dell'Accademia, Venice, Italy

Carpaccio contributed this painting to a cycle of nine, commissioned from various artists for the premises of the Confraternity of St. John the Evangelist, a Venetian charity. It shows a possessed man being healed by exorcism through the power of the relic of the Holy Cross—a fragment of wood—owned by the group. The painting presents a vibrant picture of the city as a hub on the east–west trade route.

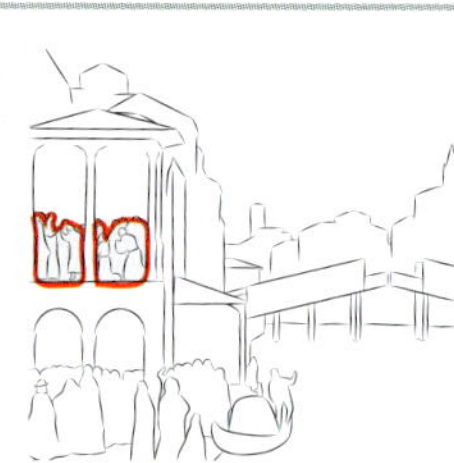

Composition
By placing the subject of the painting on the far left of the canvas, Carpaccio fulfills his main aim—to present an overview of life in the heart of Venice. He excelled at capturing open-air spectacles.

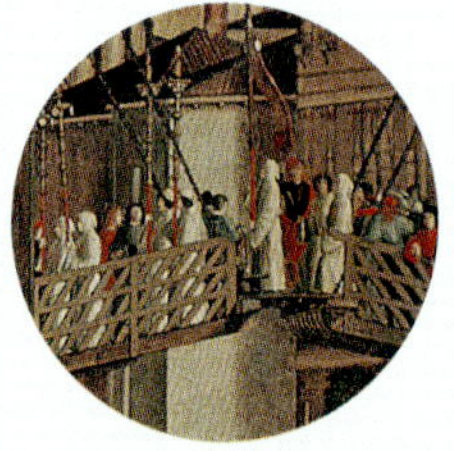

Continuous narrative
Carpaccio employs the device of continuous narrative—depicting sequential events simultaneously. The Relic of the Holy Cross is shown being carried across the Rialto Bridge and as the instrument of the exorcism in the loggia (enclosed balcony).

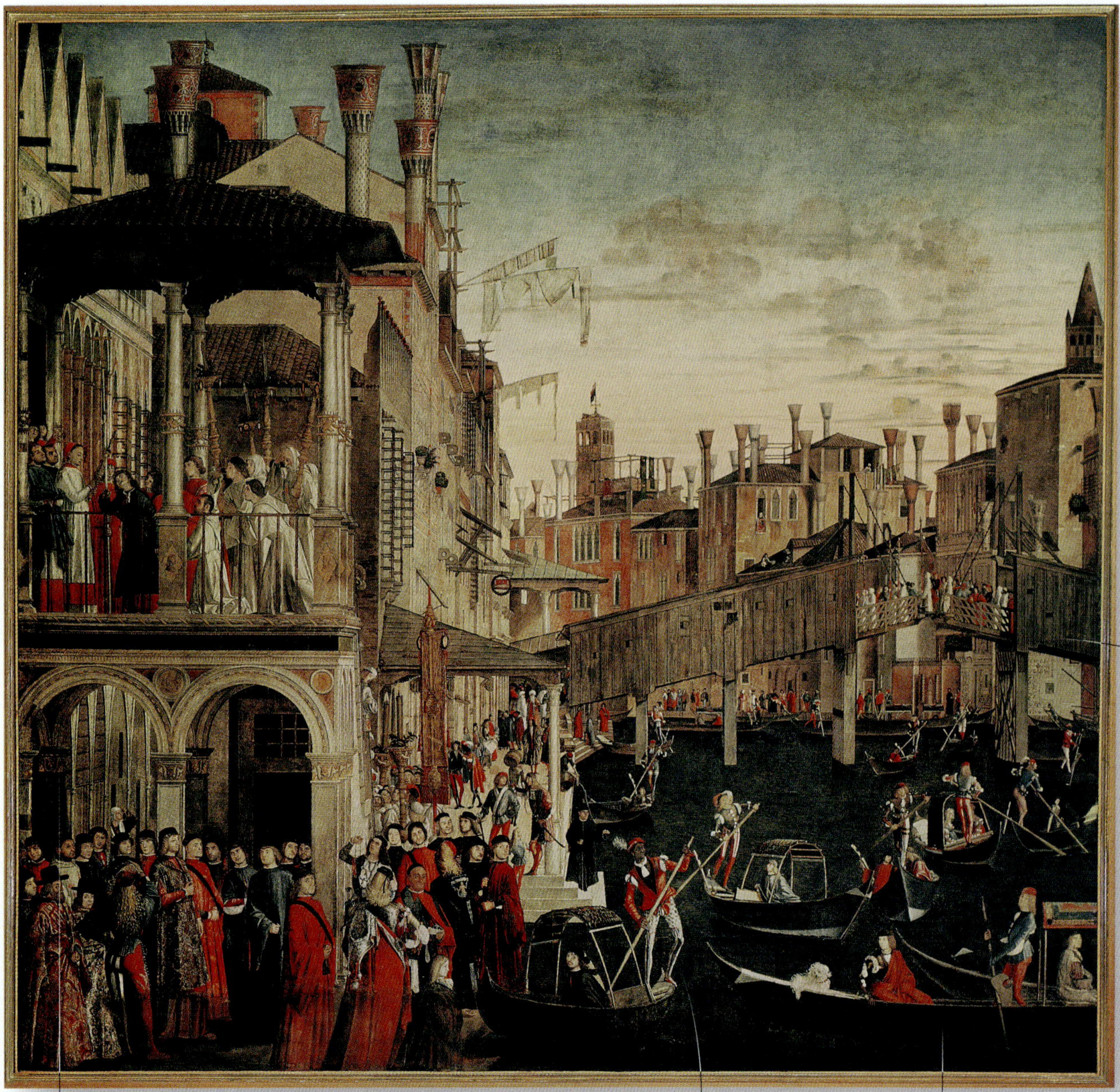

The Rialto Bridge shown in the painting is the original wooden structure that collapsed in 1524. It was replaced in 1588–1591 by a stone bridge, which still stands today.

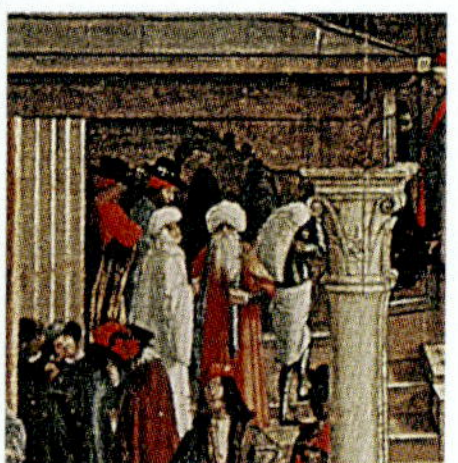

Some figures wear turbans, evidence that Venice was a European gateway to the East.

Exorcism takes place in the loggia of the palace of the Patriarch, Francesco Querini, overlooking the Grand Canal.

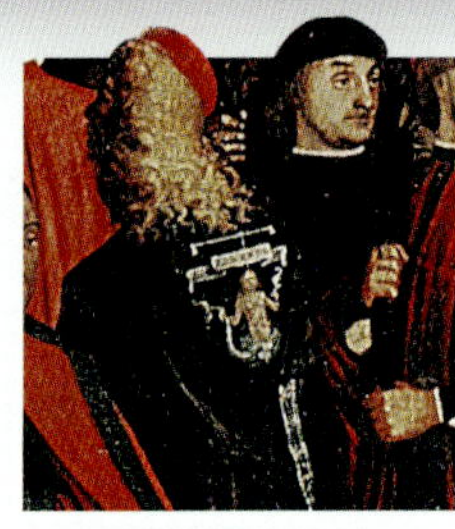

A man wears a cloak bearing a mermaid motif. The badge shows that he belongs to the Compagnia della Calza, an elite group that staged theatrical spectacles.

Black gondoliers were a common sight in 15th-century Venice. There is evidence that men who had formerly been enslaved obtained work on gondolas.

Gondolas transport many kinds of passengers, including wealthy merchants. The Grand Canal around the Rialto Bridge was a busy hub for the city's trade.

Haboku sansui

Sesshū Toyō c. 1495–1498, ink on paper, 59 × 13 in (148.6 × 32.7 cm) (full scroll), Tokyo National Museum, Tokyo, Japan

The best-known work of Zen Buddhist monk-painter Sesshū Toyō, *Haboku sansui* (*Broken Ink Landscape*) is unprecedented in its use of abstracted forms and loose brushwork to create a visually appealing rendition of a mountainous, waterside landscape. The image suggests that it was painted swiftly and evokes an intuitive approach to representation. This style was emulated by Japanese painters in later centuries.

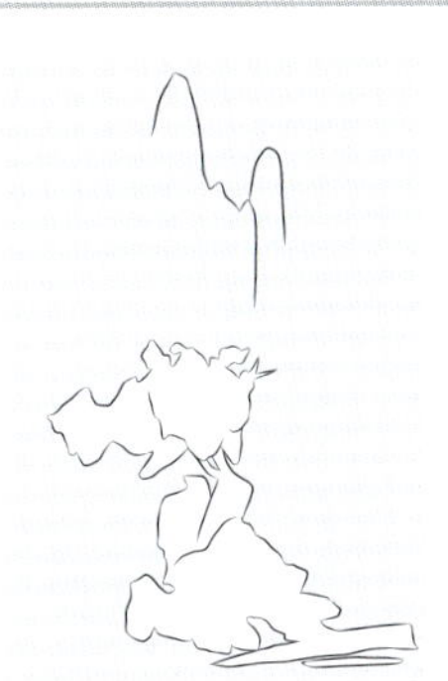

Linked zones
The landscape is organized vertically. The darkest areas of ink wash in the center connect the rocky shores in the foreground with the mountains in the background.

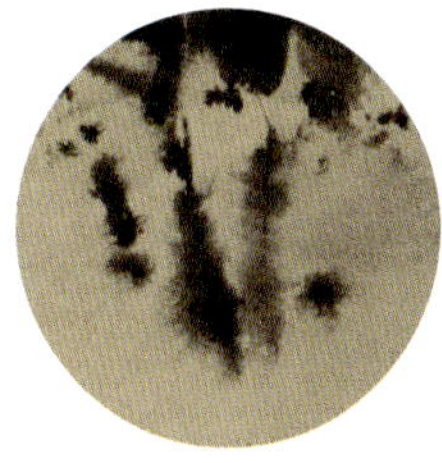

***Haboku* brushwork**
The *haboku* technique is known as "broken ink," or "spilled ink," because the artist creates the image without using any outlines, only layers of splashed ink wash.

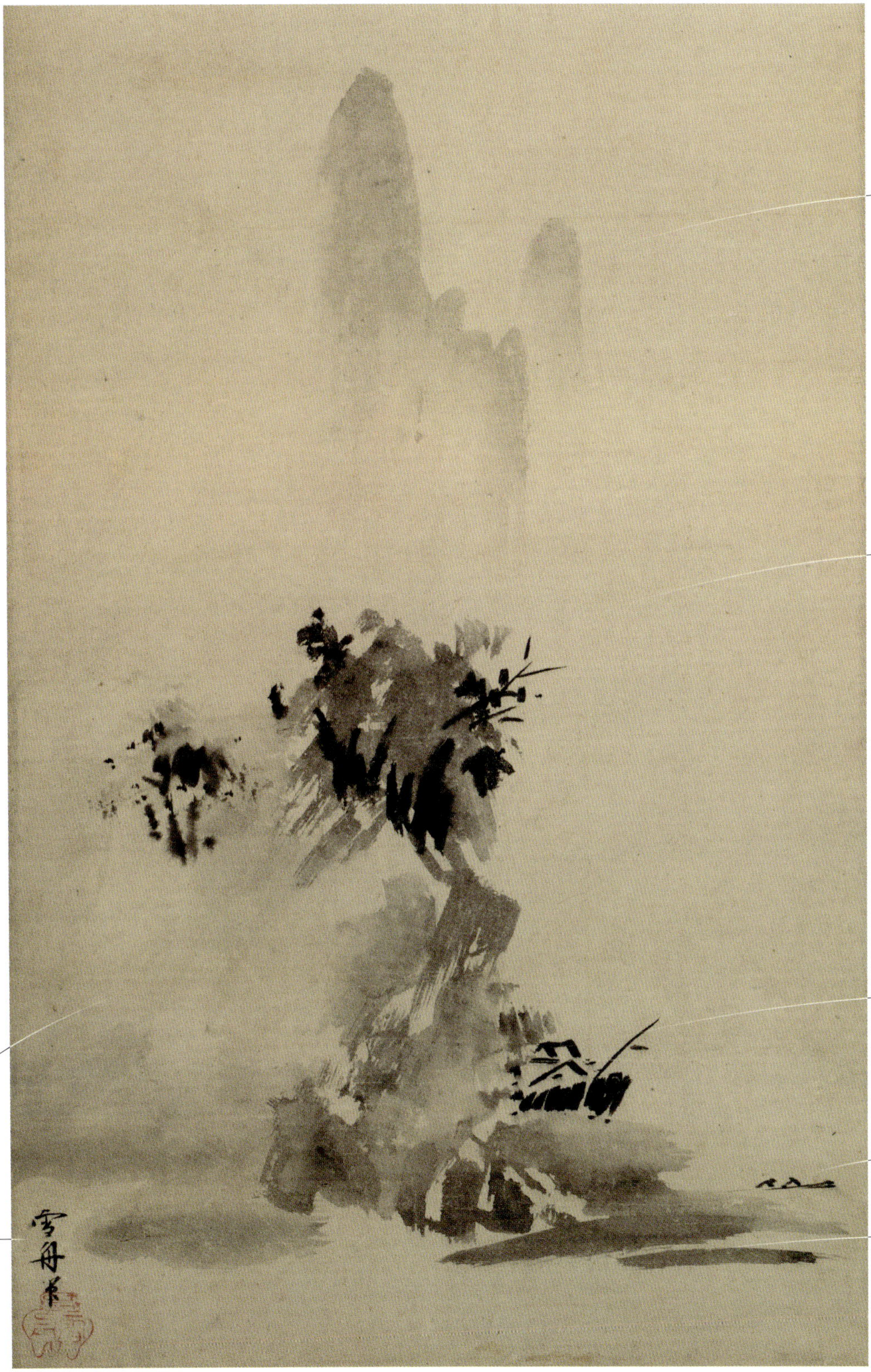

Distant mountains convey a sense of depth and illustrate the painting's debt to the East Asian ink-painting tradition.

This dense center, built up with hair-thin strokes and dark splashes, unites the bottom and top halves of the painting.

Using quick brushstrokes, the artist creates an abbreviated impression of rooftops behind a fence.

Almost untouched by ink, this blank space creates a powerful contrast to the adjacent areas, making their otherwise minimal treatment appear more detailed.

Thinner lines are minimally deployed to represent figures in a boat.

The signature says *Sesshu hitsu* (by Sesshū) but the inscription accompanying the painting was multi-authored, indicating the role of ink painting in Zen monastic culture.

Quasi-horizontal strokes suggest waves, inviting the viewer to imagine an expanse of water.

Pietà

Michelangelo Buonarroti 1499, marble, 69 × 77 in (174 × 195 cm), St. Peter's Basilica, Vatican City

Michelangelo's masterpiece of Renaissance sculpture depicts the dead Christ in his mother's arms after the Crucifixion. Carved from a single block of marble by the artist when he was 24 years old, it shows all the naturalism, idealized beauty, and anatomical accuracy that are characteristic of his work.

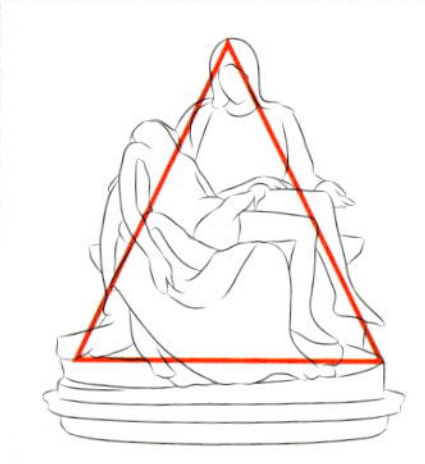

Naturalistic
The pyramidal form captures the sensitivity of a mother cradling her adult son. A series of downward curves emphasize the weight of his body.

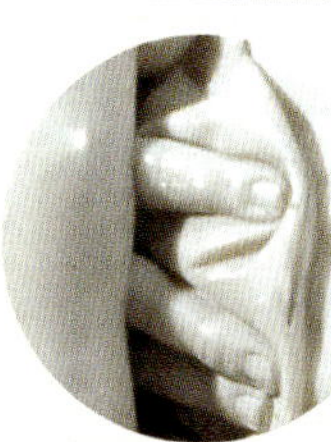

Taking hold
Mary's fingers are tense and dig into Christ's side, indicating the strength needed to hold on to his body with just one hand.

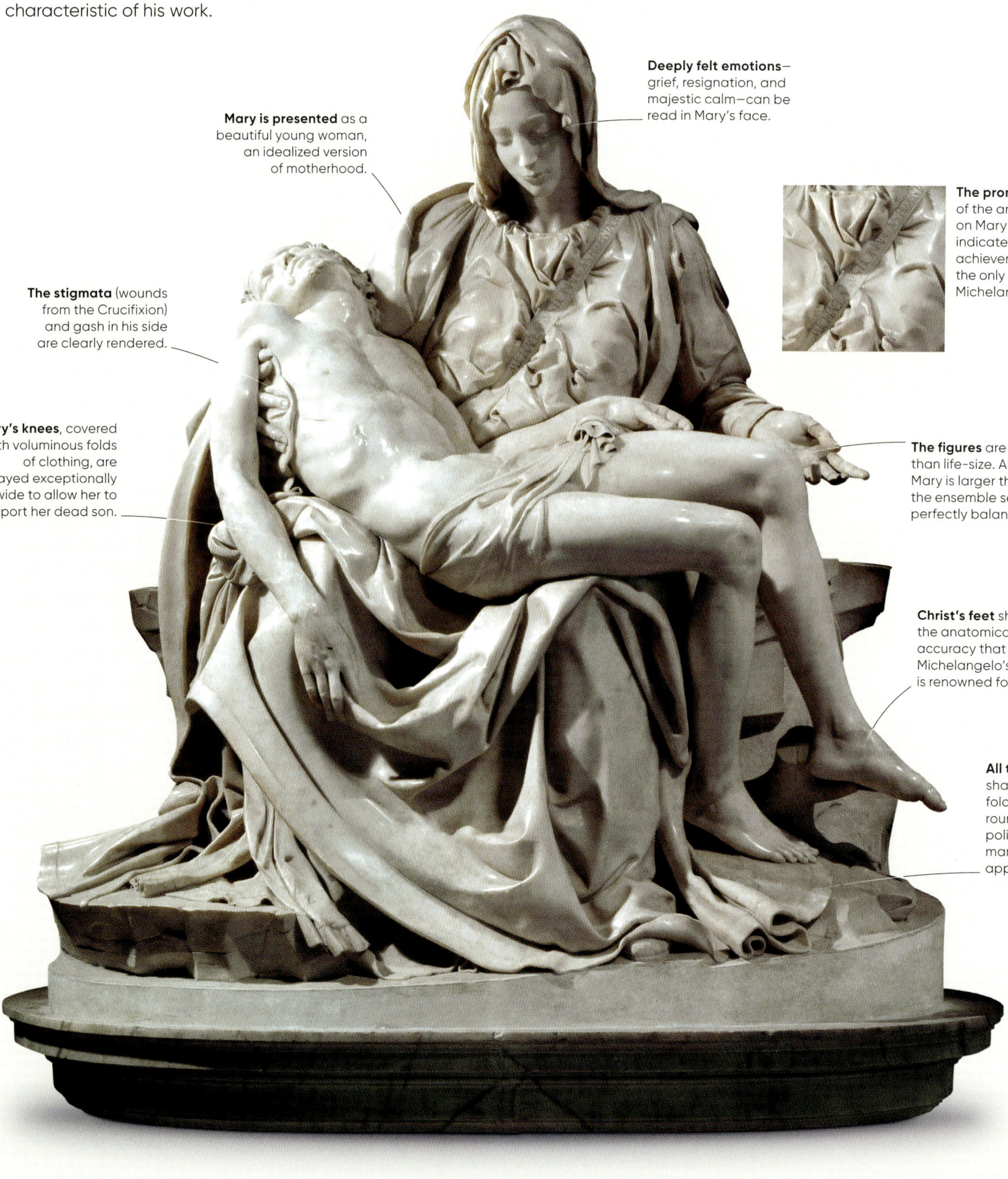

Deeply felt emotions—grief, resignation, and majestic calm—can be read in Mary's face.

Mary is presented as a beautiful young woman, an idealized version of motherhood.

The prominent position of the artist's signature on Mary's sash may indicate pride in his achievement. This is the only work that Michelangelo signed.

The stigmata (wounds from the Crucifixion) and gash in his side are clearly rendered.

Mary's knees, covered with voluminous folds of clothing, are splayed exceptionally wide to allow her to support her dead son.

The figures are larger than life-size. Although Mary is larger than Christ, the ensemble seems perfectly balanced.

Christ's feet show the anatomical accuracy that Michelangelo's work is renowned for.

All the forms, including sharp edges along the folds of cloth, are rounded off and highly polished, giving the marble a soft, ivory-like appearance.

Standing against an impenetrable black background, the figure's coat merges into the darkness, giving a somber, melancholy impression that may reflect his state of mind.

The self-portrait is asymmetric: the face is off-center, the hair does not part exactly in the middle, and the eyes look slightly to the left.

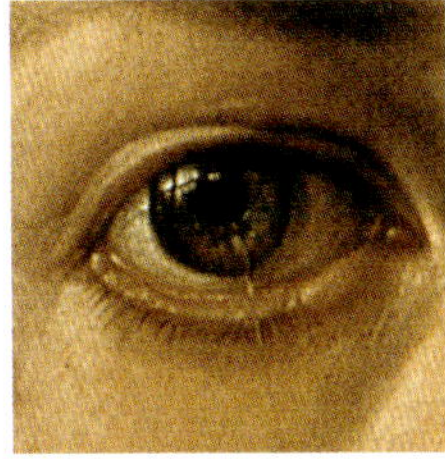

His right eye reflects the window frame, which is the light source for the portrait. Dürer's detailed brushwork is particularly apparent here.

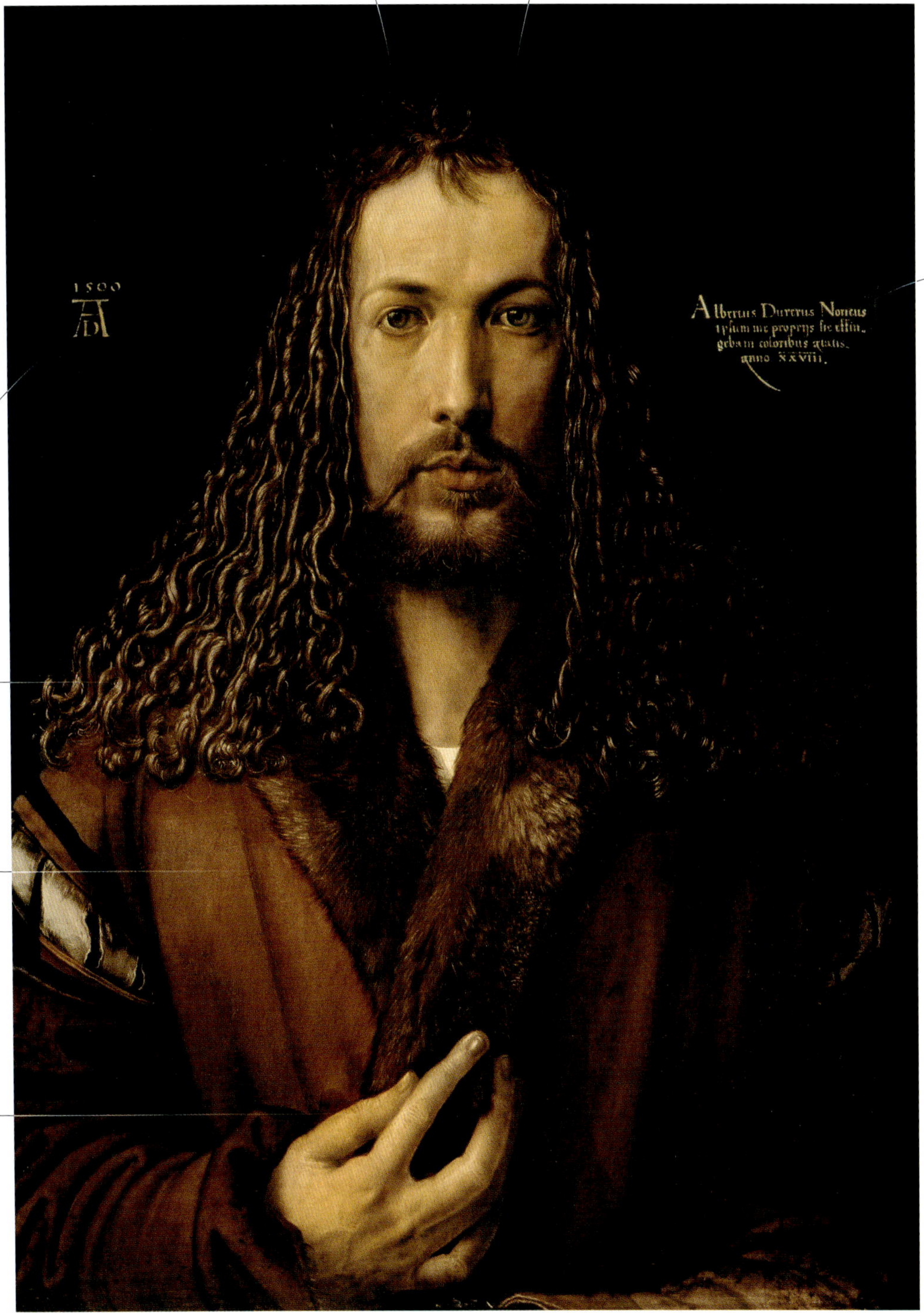

Latin text in gold translates as, "I, Albrecht Dürer of Nuremberg, painted myself thus, with indelible (or everlasting) colors at the age of twenty-eight years." This was considered the year of transition from youth to maturity.

Dürer designed his own monogram: the initials AD with the date above (AD standing for both *Anno Domini* and Albrecht Dürer).

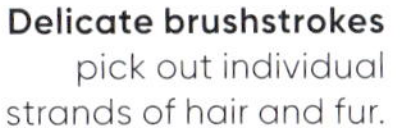

Delicate brushstrokes pick out individual strands of hair and fur.

Only people of high status wore fur. Dürer included it to show that he was a successful artist, confident of his abilities.

The artist holds the marten fur on his lapel in the way that fingertips grip a paintbrush. At the time, marten fur was used to make paintbrushes.

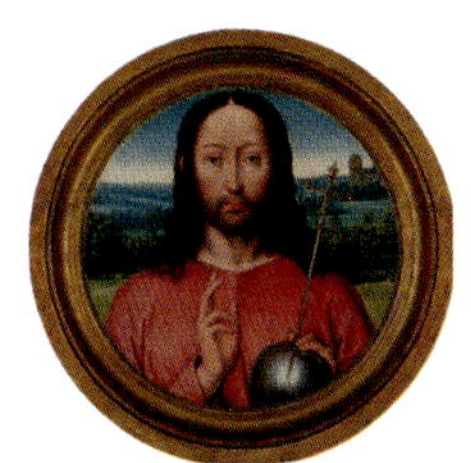

Divine inspiration
The image of Christ as the savior of the world, or *Salvator Mundi*, was first used by Byzantine artists. Portraits copying this pose, in imitation of Christ, were a feature of the northern European humanist movement.

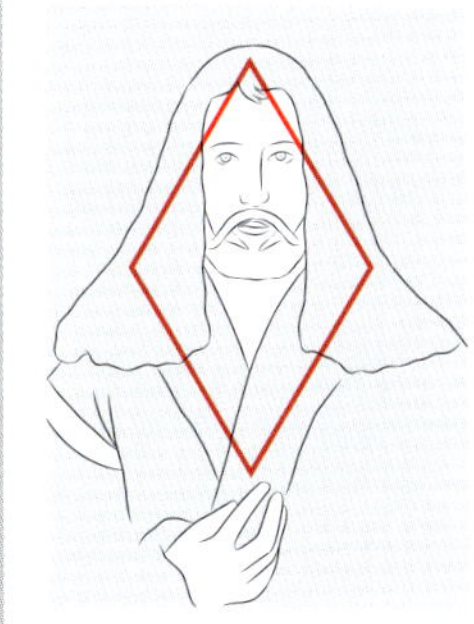

Diamond shape
Dürer's hair and neckline form two triangles that combine to createa a diamond shape, framing his face. The white slash on his right sleeve points to the hand at the base of the diamond, while his index finger follows the line of his collar to create a circular path for the eye.

Self-Portrait in a Fur Coat

Albrecht Dürer 1500, oil on wood, 26 × 19 in (67.1 × 48.9 cm), Alte Pinakothek, Munich, Germany

In this unusual self-portrait, Dürer depicts himself facing the viewer in the style of paintings of Christ the Savior, with his hand almost raised in a blessing. Rather than being blasphemous, the gesture conveys Dürer's view that his skills as an artist were given to him by God and his skill of creation is derived from the divine.

Mandarin Ducks and Cotton Rose Hibiscus

Lü Ji late 15th century, ink and color on silk, 68 × 39 in (172.7 × 99.1 cm), Metropolitan Museum of Art, New York, US

Symbolism is prevalent in Chinese art, often appearing as rebuses, or visual puns, based on homophones, words that sound the same but have different meanings. In this work by Lü Ji, the most esteemed bird-and-flower painter of his day, the symbolism refers to marital bliss, appropriate for celebrating a wedding.

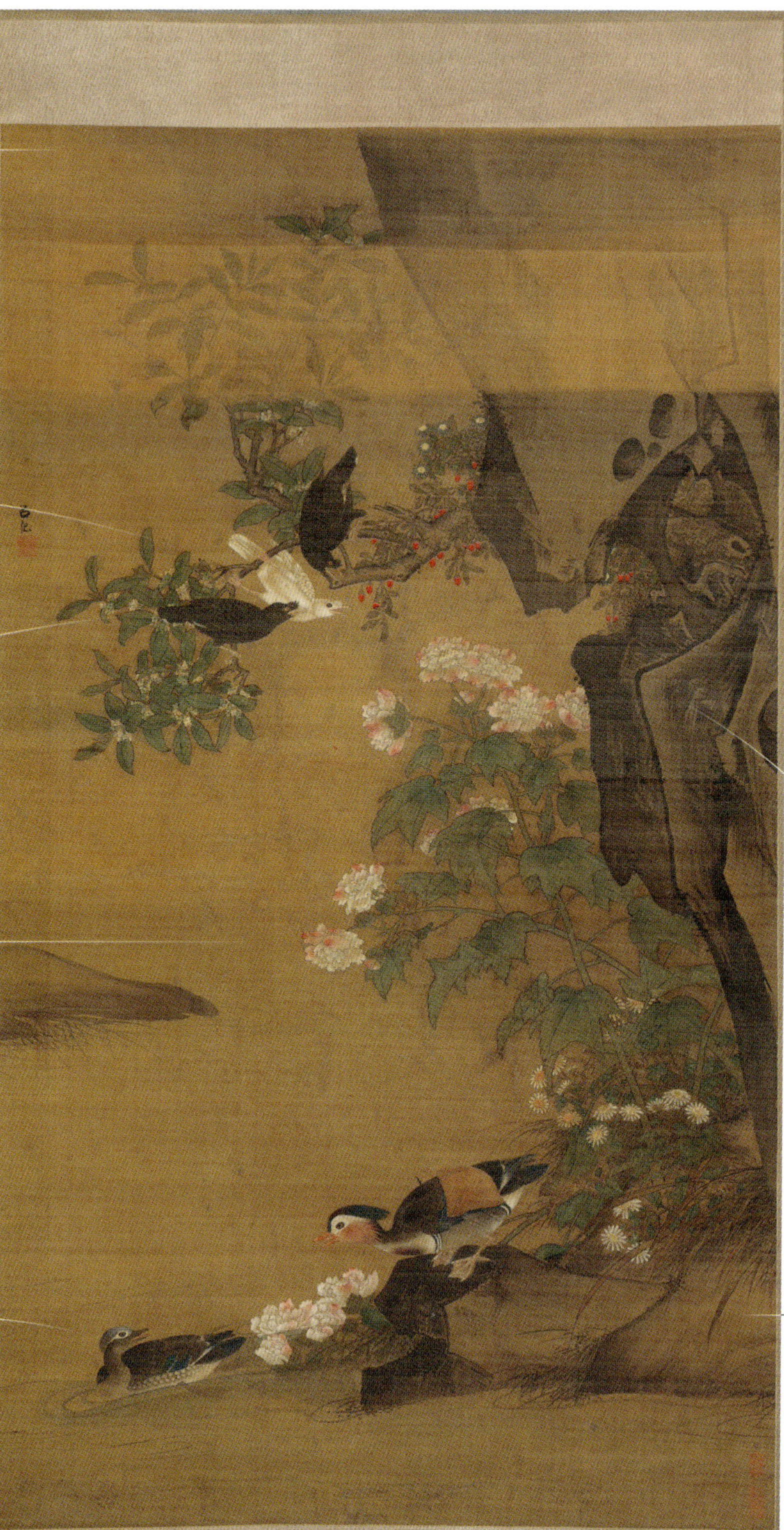

Now a golden hue, the silk was once much paler, providing a brighter background for the colorful scene.

The words for "white mynah" create a rebus meaning "hundreds of them," referring to a wish for many sons.

A pair of mynah birds indicates a longing for conjugal bliss and many sons.

The words for this flower, hibiscus, and cassia (where the mynah birds perch) together sound like those for "prosperous groom, honorable bride."

Mandarin ducks, believed to mate for life and die if separated, are apt symbols of marital bliss and fidelity.

Sculptural rocks are an important feature of Chinese gardens. Top-heavy, deeply textured stones with cavities are highly prized.

Unpainted silk depicts both the water and the sky. It is also used as a color, as in the rock's surface.

> "In recent times the paintings of Lü Ji are the best."
>
> Hang Huai

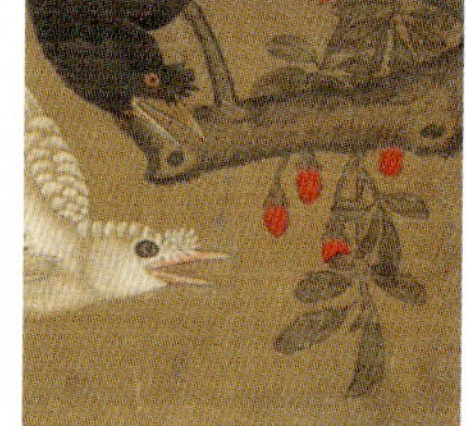

The birds are attracted by jujube fruit. This usually symbolizes fertility in Chinese art. Here it conveys a wish to have a baby soon.

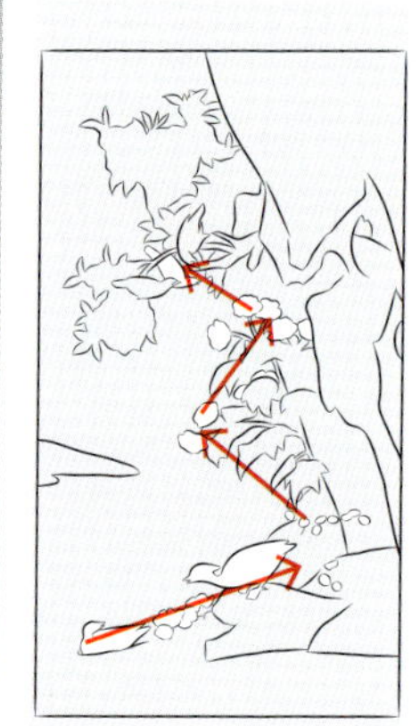

Meandering path
The bright white of the flowers and ducks leads the viewer's eye along a zigzagging path through the painting.

Hanging scrolls
Unlike hand scrolls, which are meant to be viewed scene by scene, hanging scrolls are hung vertically and display the entire painting at once

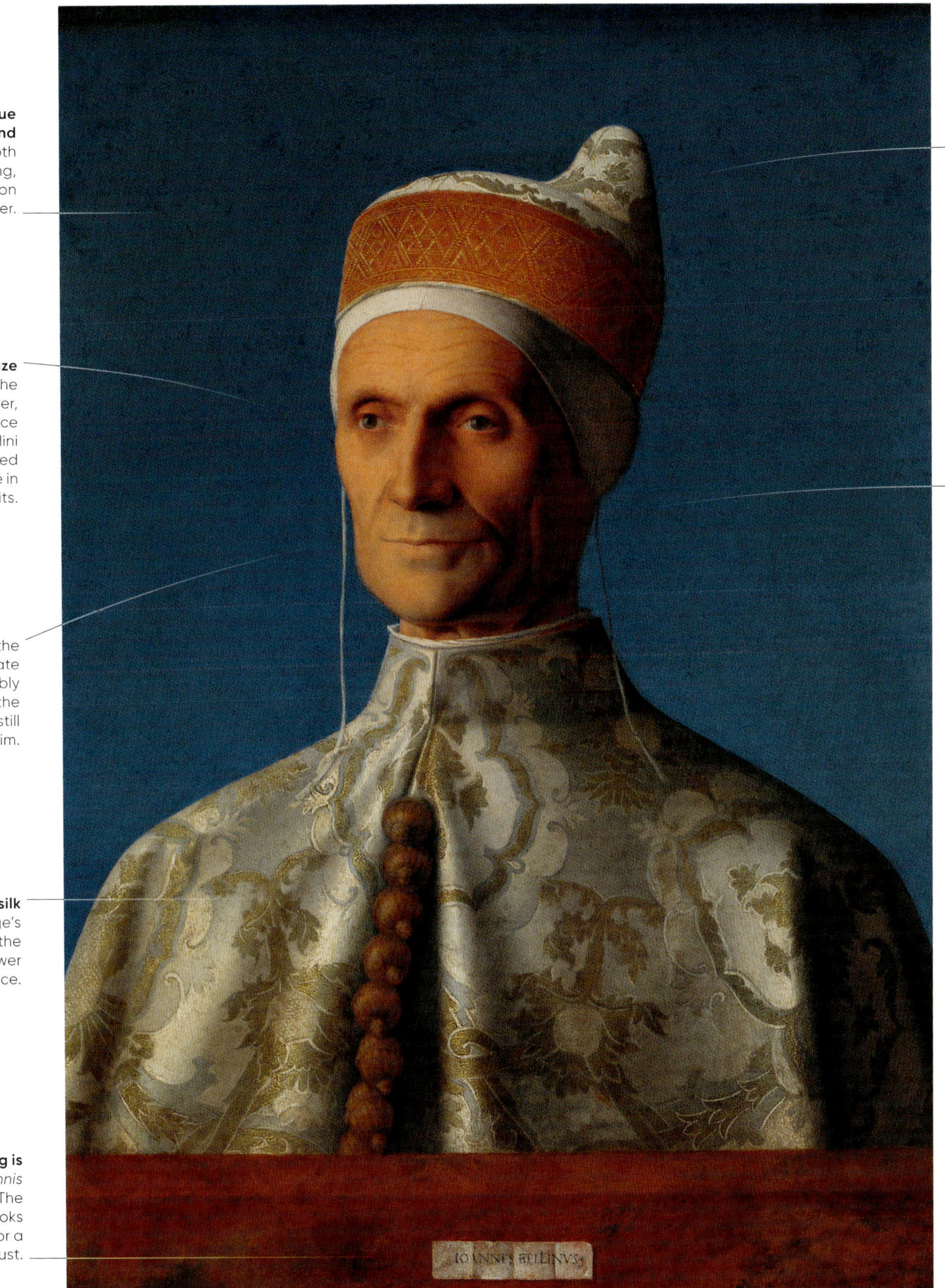

A flat blue background eliminates depth in the painting, focusing attention on the sitter.

The subject's gaze is fixed to the left of the viewer, toward the source of light. Bellini often employed this technique in his portraits.

The quality of the light suggests late afternoon, possibly implying that the elderly doge still has life in him.

Made of gold silk damask, the doge's cape reflects the wealth and power of Venice.

The painting is signed *Ioannis Bellinus*. The parapet looks like a plinth for a monumental bust.

This ceremonial headdress was known as a *corno*.

The doge has lifelike facial features, including wrinkles and stubble. His faint smile suggests a confident self possession befitting high office.

Pose
Official portraits often showed their subjects in profile, but this is a frontal view referencing an imperial Roman bust.

Achieving realism
Lifelike details were achieved by using transparent layers of paint on the face, in contrast to the thick layers used on the clothing. Bellini was one of the first Italian artists to fully master the potential of oil paint, using methods developed by Flemish artists.

Portrait of Doge Leonardo Loredan

Giovanni Bellini 1501–1502, oil on panel, 24 × 18 in (61.4 × 44.5 cm), National Gallery, London, UK

This work depicting the elected ruler of the Venetian Republic is considered Bellini's greatest achievement in portrait painting. Doge Leonardo Loredan ruled Venice from 1501 to 1521, when the city-state was a powerful and wealthy political force. Loredan's subtle expression seems lifelike and immediate as well as distant and imposing. The portrait is more about the office of the doge than it is about the man.

The Sun Stone

Artist unknown c. 1502–1520, stone, 141 in (358 cm) across, 39 in (98 cm) deep, Museo Nacional de Antropología, Mexico City, Mexico

Moteuczoma II, Aztec emperor from 1502 to 1520, commissioned this carved stone disk. Arranged in concentric rings and rich in iconography, it represents Aztec cosmology and mythology, drawing on the belief in the cyclical nature of time and the existence of previous eras of creation and destruction. The circular shape and radiating motifs emulate the sun.

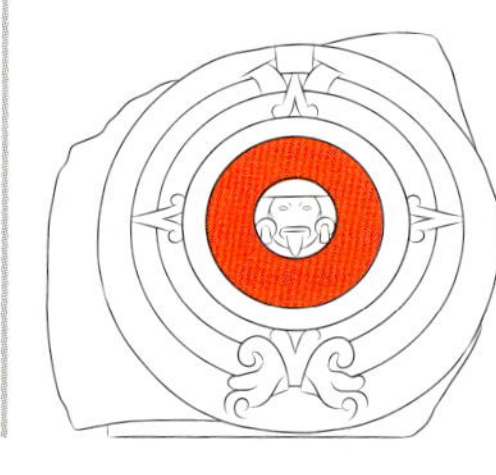

End of an era
The Aztec symbol *Ollin* around the central figure represents the era when it was made, "Four Movement" (*Nahui Ollin*).

Medium
The stone disk was originally painted with red and ocher pigments and there are possibly traces of blue, black, and white pigments.

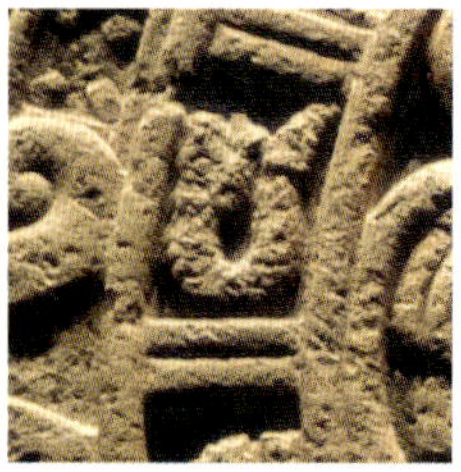

The inner ring comprises 20 glyphs representing the Aztec days. The fifth day is represented by *coatl*, meaning serpent.

Curved spirals decorate the four large arrows that point to the cardinal directions.

The royal insignia of Moteuczoma II dates this work to his reign.

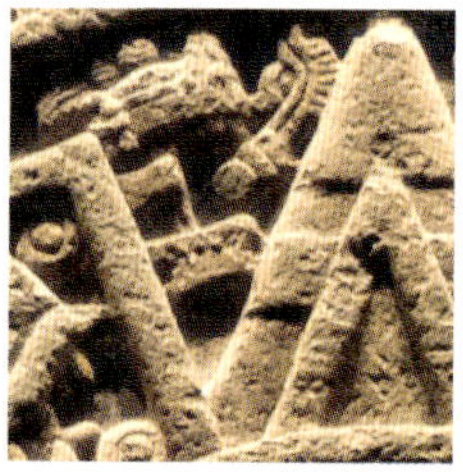

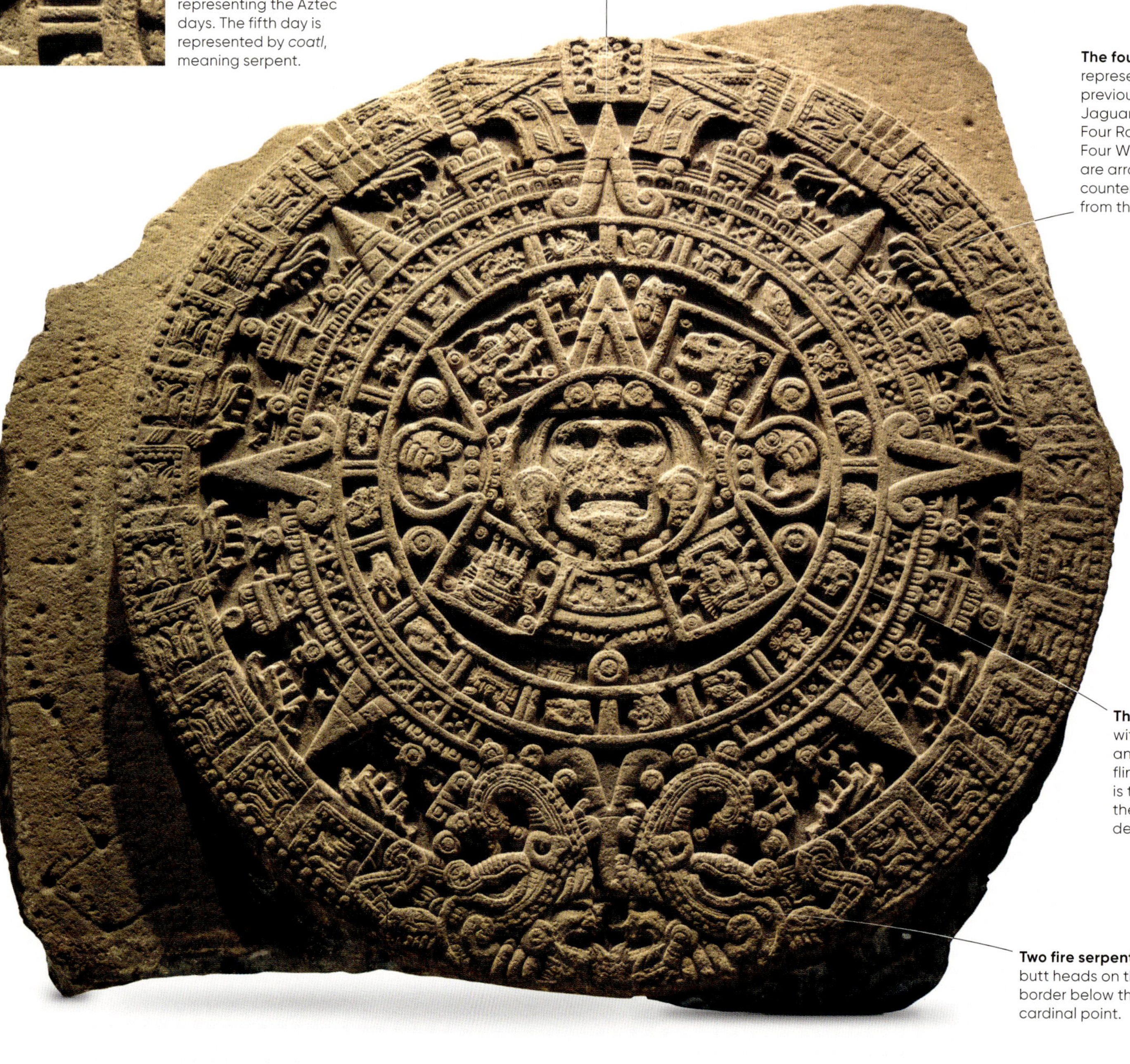

The four squares represent the four previous eras: Four Jaguar, Four Wind, Four Rain, and Four Water. They are arranged counterclockwise from the top right.

The central face with its wide mouth and protruding flint-knife tongue is thought to be the Aztec sun deity, Tonatiuh.

Two fire serpents (*xiuhcoatl*) butt heads on the outer border below the south cardinal point.

The Great Piece of Turf

Albrecht Dürer 1503, watercolor, pen, ink, and gouache on paper, 16 × 12 in (40.3 × 31.1 cm), Albertina, Vienna, Austria

Using an intricate and systematic approach, Dürer reveals a seemingly unassuming patch of meadow to be an astonishing microcosm of grasses, leaves, and dandelions. The minutely observed details, low viewpoint, and elegant shaping honor the richness and beauty found in nature.

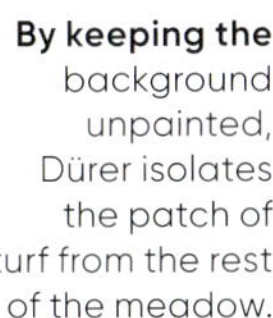

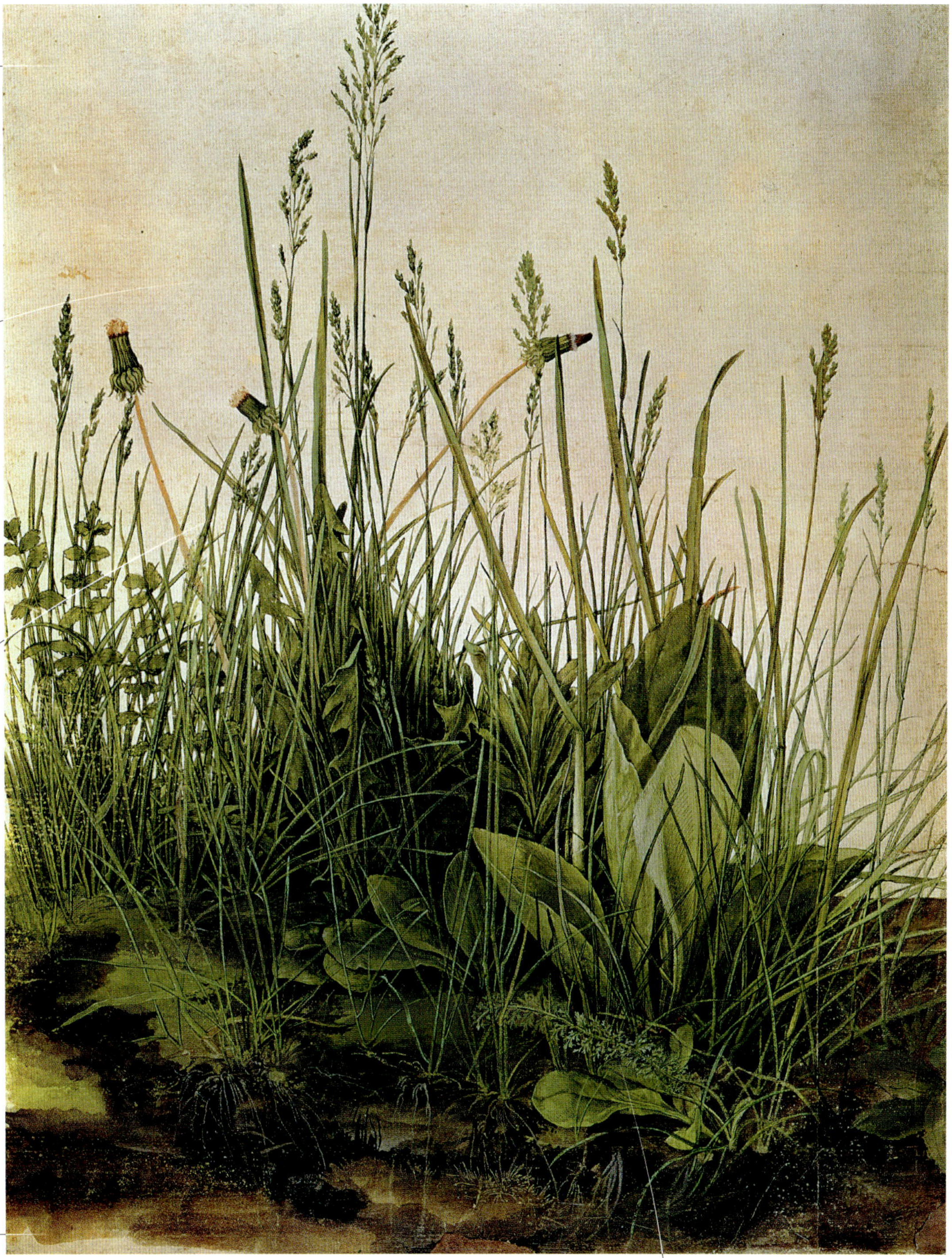

By keeping the background unpainted, Dürer isolates the patch of turf from the rest of the meadow.

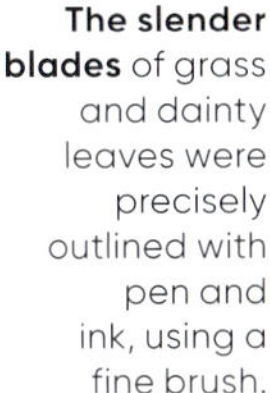

The slender blades of grass and dainty leaves were precisely outlined with pen and ink, using a fine brush.

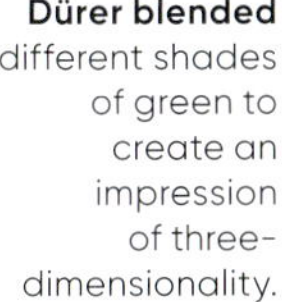

Dürer blended different shades of green to create an impression of three-dimensionality.

The watercolor does not fill the bottom-left corner. This suggests that it may have served as a preliminary work or as a study for a larger, possibly religious, composition.

Bulky leaves in the mid-ground add weight to the center of the composition.

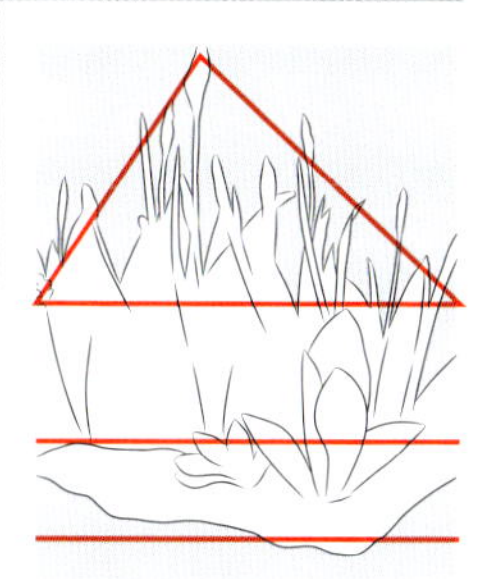

Composition
The tall and wispy grasses gracefully form a balanced triangle in the upper half of the composition, while the lower portion is divided into denser foliage, soil, and roots.

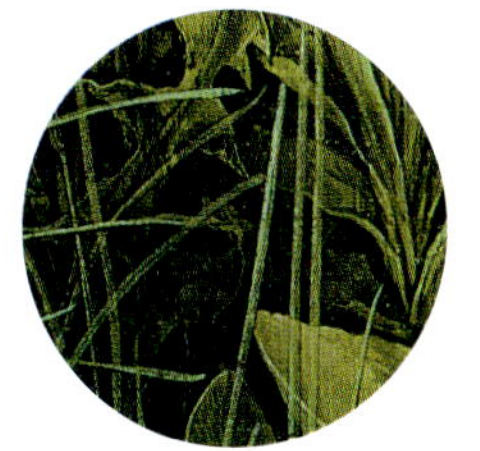

Color
Hues of green dominate the composition. Darker shades cluster toward the center and lighter greens accentuate the distinctive features and individuality of each plant.

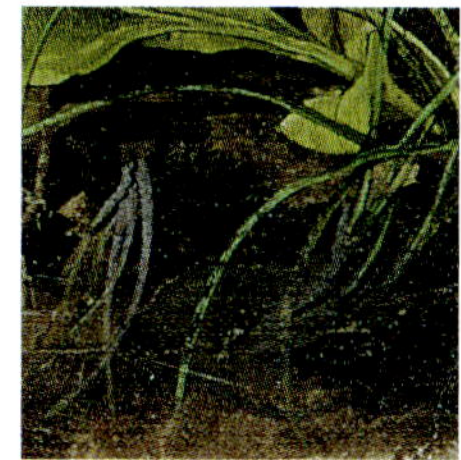

The sprawling roots under the soil show scientific precision.

> "Geometry is the right foundation of all painting."
>
> Albrecht Dürer, 1528

Coronation Stone of Moteuczoma II

Artist unknown 1503, stone (basalt), 22 × 26 × 9 in (55.9 × 66 × 22.9 cm), Art Institute of Chicago, US

This carved stone block commemorates the reign of Moteuczoma II, ruler of the Aztec Empire, and was originally located in its capital, Tenochtitlan (present-day Mexico City). It depicts the iconography associated with Aztec cosmology, illustrating the five suns that symbolize the five eras of creation.

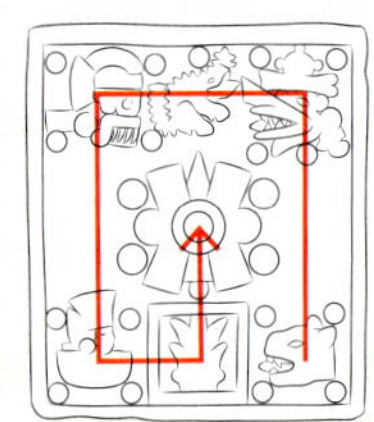

Composition
The eras begin with the *ocelotl*, representing the first era, in the bottom right corner, and follow counterclockwise. The sequence ends with the present era in the center.

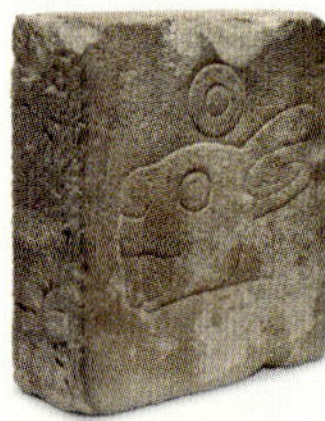

Creation symbol
The underside of the stone depicts a rabbit and one circle, representing the creation of the cosmos by the Aztec gods.

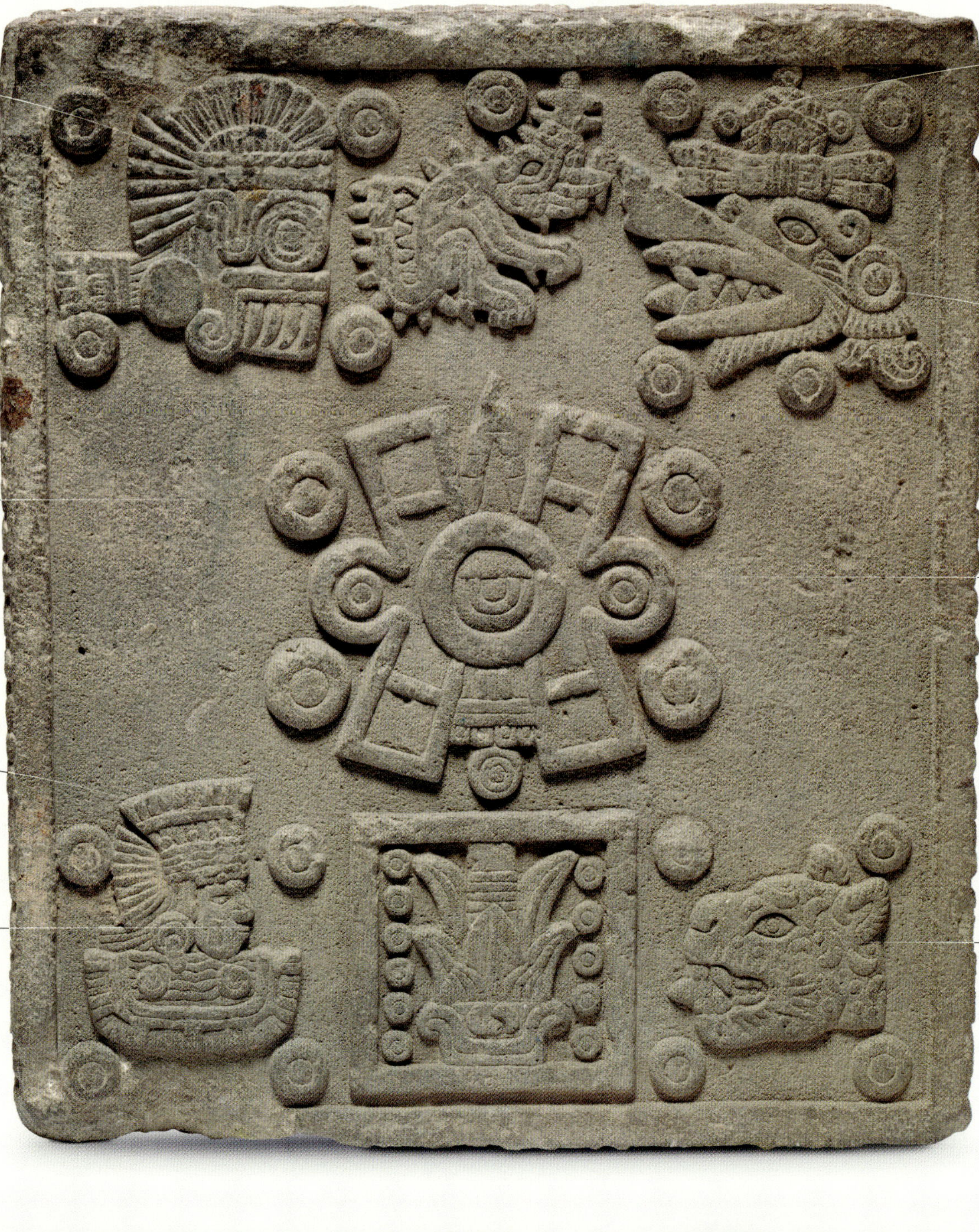

An icon representing Four Rain refers to the third sun. It depicts the god Tlaloc who presided over this era.

Circled dots correspond to numbers associated with the icons around which they occur.

Chalchiuhtlicue, the goddess of water, represents the fourth era, Four Water, in which inhabitants perished in floods.

Eleven circled dots and a reed motif refer to the hieroglyphic year, "11 Reed"–1503, in the Gregorian calendar.

A crocodile icon with one circled dot corresponds to July 15, possibly marking the date of the coronation of Moteuczoma II.

The glyph for *ehecatl* (wind) symbolizes the second sun, Four Wind, ruled by the god Quetzalcoatl, in which the inhabitants were killed by a hurricane.

The *ollin* (movement) glyph at the center represents the present sun, Four Movement, situating Emperor Moteuczoma II as ruler of the current era.

The *ocelotl* (jaguar) symbol represents the first sun, Four Jaguar, which ended when the Aztec god Tezcatlipoca instructed his jaguars to devour the people.

Mona Lisa (La Gioconda)

Leonardo da Vinci c. 1503–1519, oil on poplar, 30 × 21 in (77 × 53 cm), Louvre Museum, Paris, France

This haunting portrait of Italian noblewoman Lisa Gherardini, wife of Francesco del Giocondo, a Florentine textile merchant, is possibly the most famous painting in the world. This is partly because of the sitter's enigmatic smile, but it is Leonardo's innovative technical skills that make the painting exceptional.

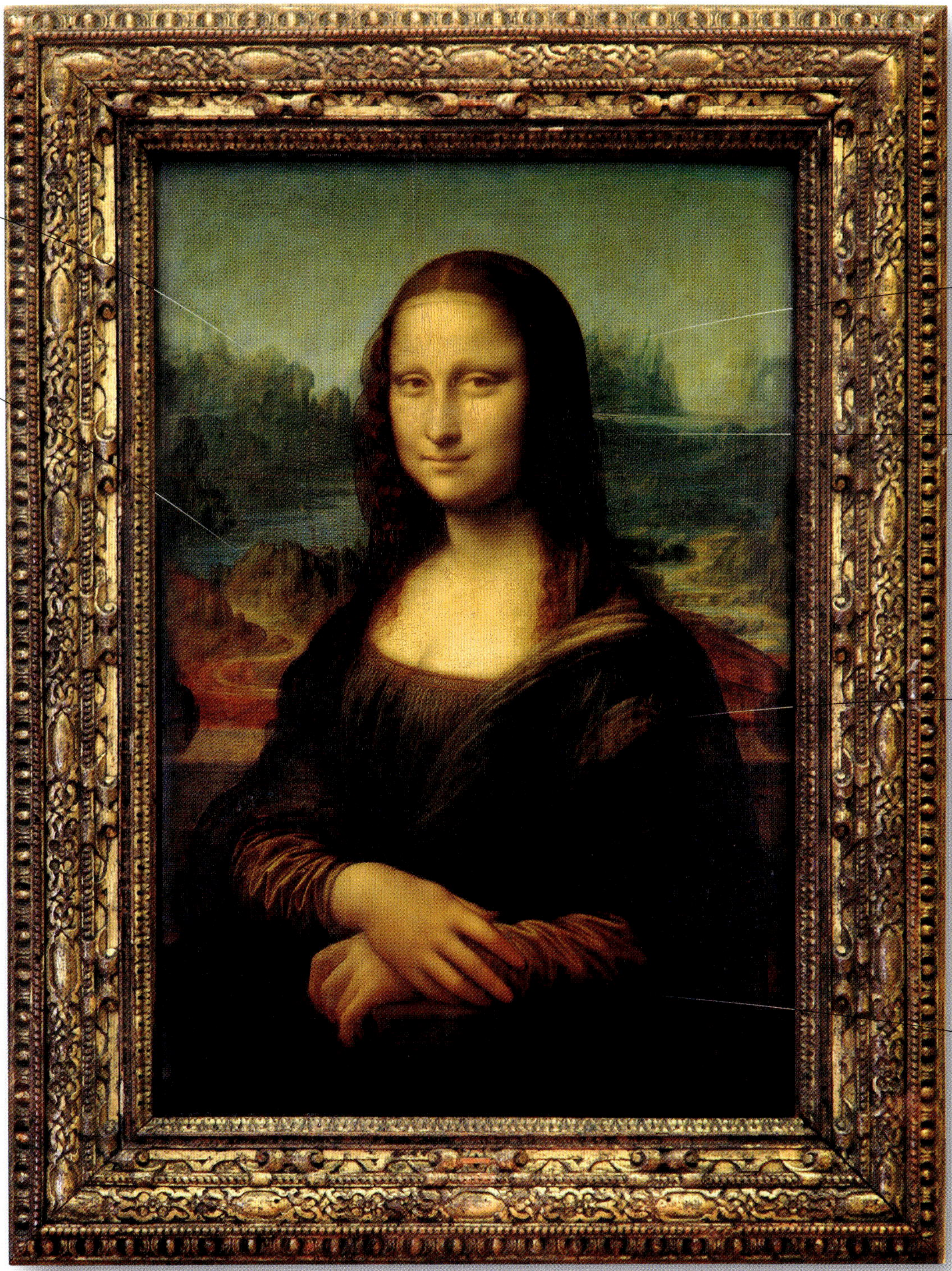

The horizon is at her eye level, linking the figure with the landscape and adding an air of mystery.

The distant landscape and the parapet frame her figure. The view was influenced by northern European portrait artists such as Memling.

Her eyes look directly at the viewer. The wrinkles at the corners are particularly lifelike.

The subtle blending of tones in the face creates a sculptural quality.

Unlike in other contemporary portraits, the sitter is not wearing furs, highly embroidered fabrics, or jewelery. The simplicity of her clothing maintains the focus on her face.

The way the woman's hands rest on each other symbolizes fidelity, although she wears no wedding ring.

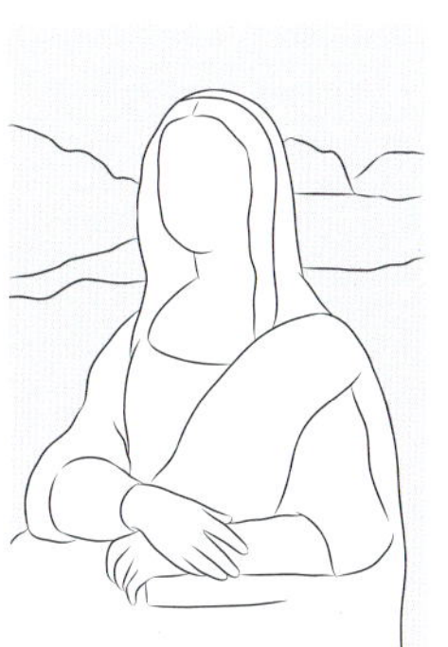

New techniques
Several aspects of the painting were innovative, including the pose (face and shoulders turned toward the viewer), the inclusion of the hands, and the three-dimensional depiction of the body.

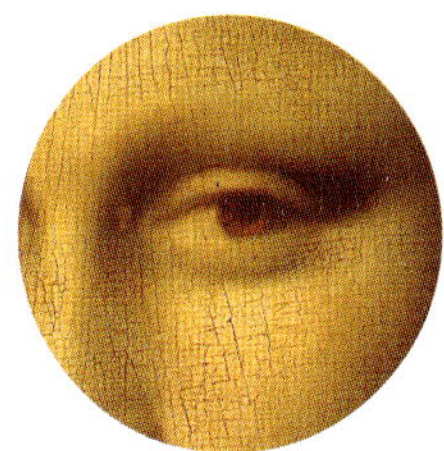

Sfumato technique
Leonardo perfected the technique of *sfumato*—the hazy blending of tones to create an imperceptible, lifelike gradation.

> "La Gioconda is, in the truest sense, Leonardo's masterpiece … Perhaps of all ancient pictures time has chilled it least."
>
> Walter Pater, 1922

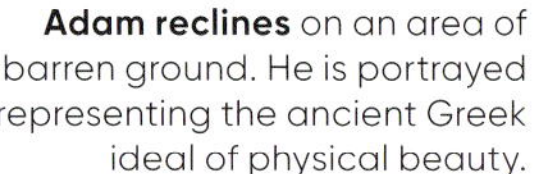

Adam reclines on an area of barren ground. He is portrayed representing the ancient Greek ideal of physical beauty.

Adam's raised arm mirrors God's outstretched arm to illustrate the belief that God made man in his own image.

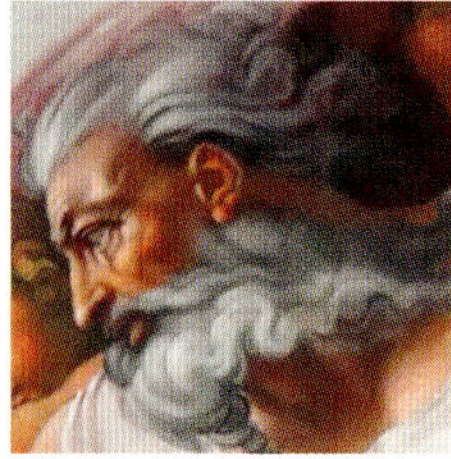

A sense of movement is created by God's flowing hair and beard and the trailing ends of his cloak.

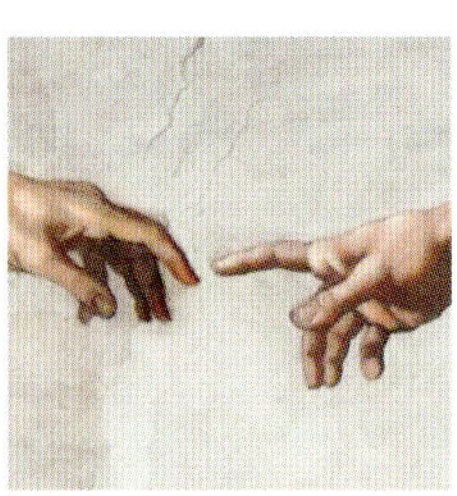

The hands provide the focal point. The fingers are a split-second away from touching each other, and the small gap creates tension.

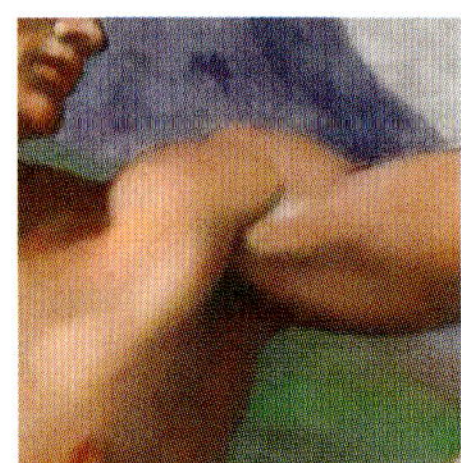

Tonal modeling of the musculature gives the figure a sculpted, three-dimensional look.

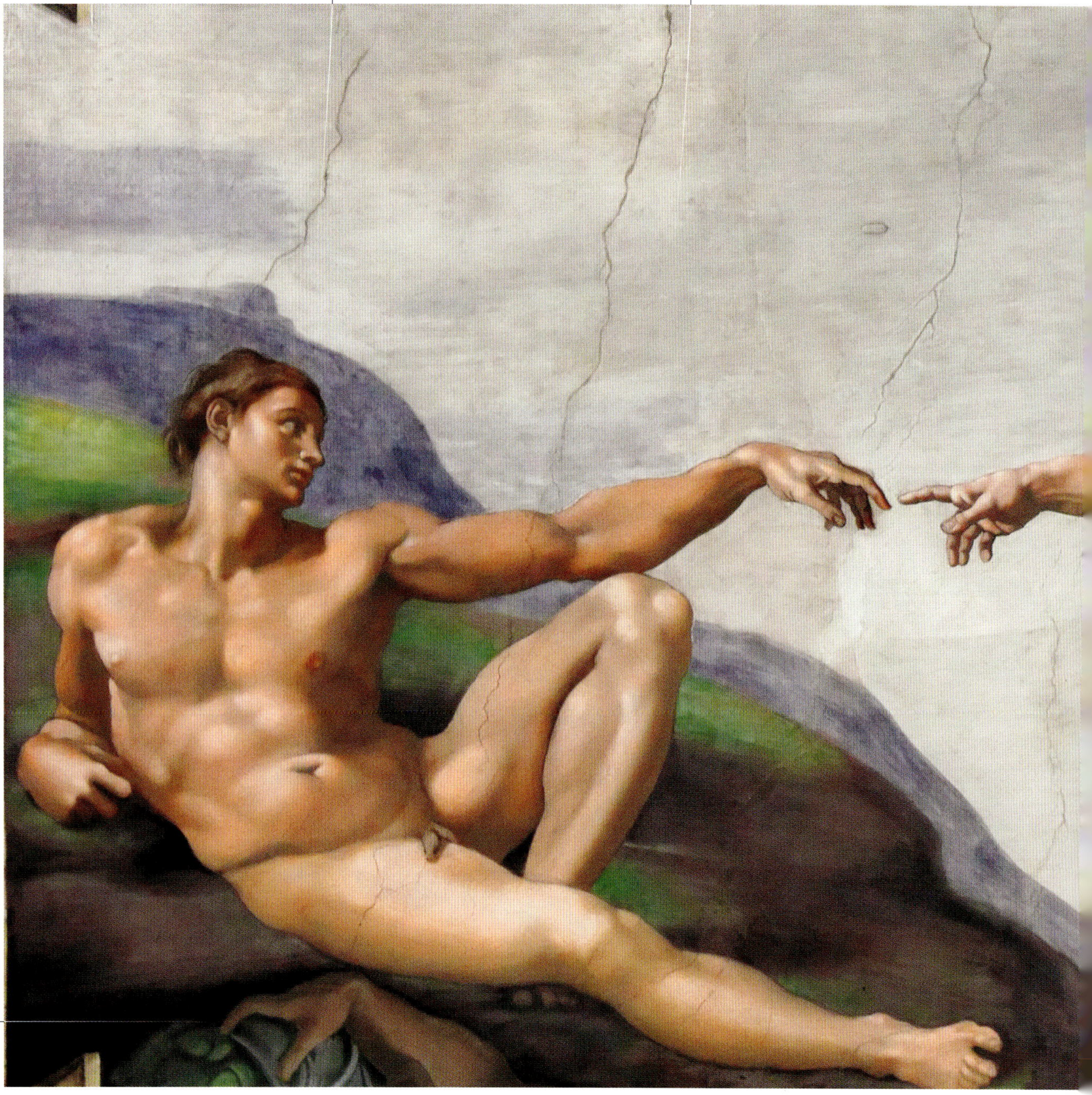

A figure from an adjacent space on the ceiling encroaches into the scene.

The Creation of Adam

Michelangelo 1508–1512, 110 × 224 in (280 × 570 cm), fresco, Sistine Chapel, Vatican Museums, Vatican City

This famous fresco captures the instant when God creates Adam, the first human, a moment of electrifying energy representing the imparting of the divine breath of life. It is one of the Creation stories from the Old Testament Book of Genesis that Michelangelo illustrated on the ceiling of the Sistine Chapel in the Vatican. Seen from the chapel floor below, the two figures, monumental in scale, appear to be reaching out across the width of the chapel. Michelangelo took 16 days to complete the panel using the fresco technique of painting directly onto wet plaster.

Small details on the figures were painted over the fresco after it had dried.

The identity of the female figure is disputed. She could represent Eve or the Virgin Mary, or be a personification of the human soul or of wisdom.

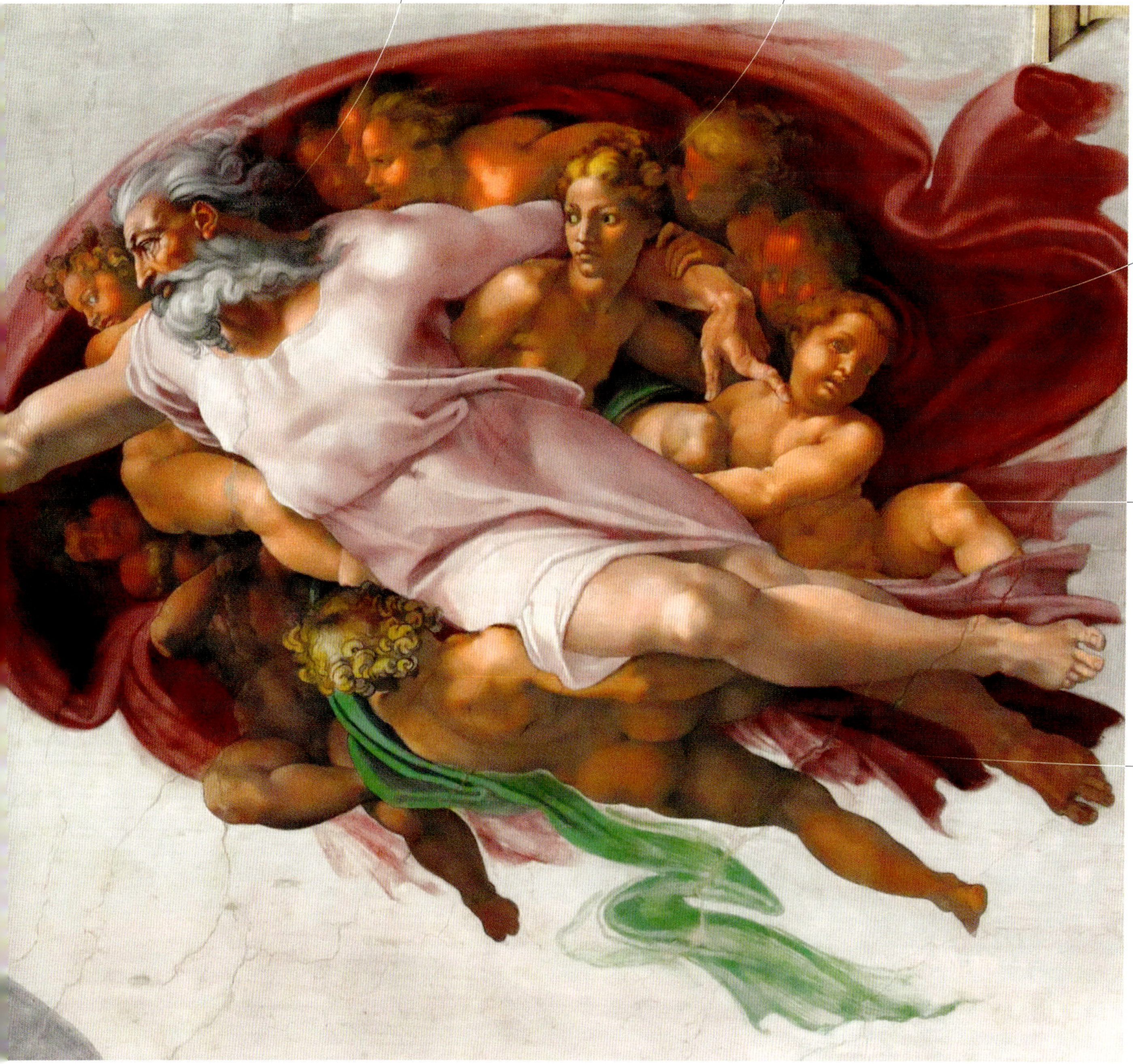

The child could be Christ if the female figure represents the Virgin Mary.

God is portrayed as an elderly yet muscular father figure. He wears a simple robe, making him look human and accessible.

Angels support God as he travels through the air, and the group is bounded by a billowing cloak.

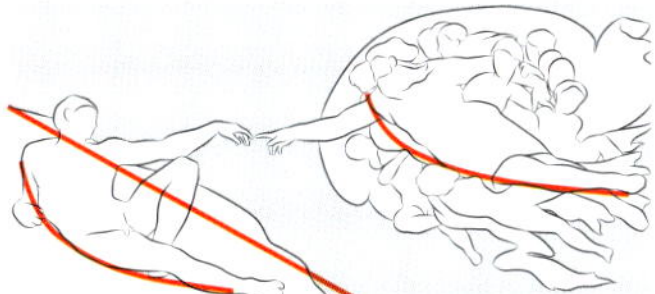

Separation of heaven and earth
A diagonal line along the edge of the green area divides the painting into an earthly and a heavenly realm. A series of curving lines link the figures horizontally.

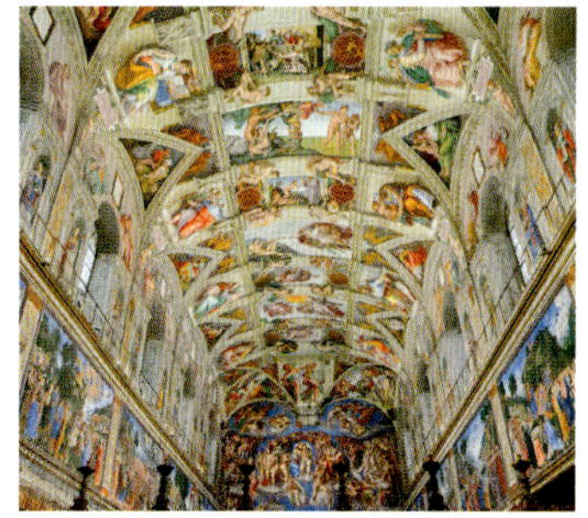

The Sistine Chapel
Located in the Apostolic Palace, the Pope's official residence in Vatican City, the Sistine Chapel takes its name from Pope Sixtus IV, who had it built in 1473–1481. Conclaves, baptisms, and other official events are held inside. The walls are decorated with works of art commissioned by the popes over the centuries.

> "So God created man in his own image, in the image of God created he him."
>
> Genesis 1:27 (King James Version)

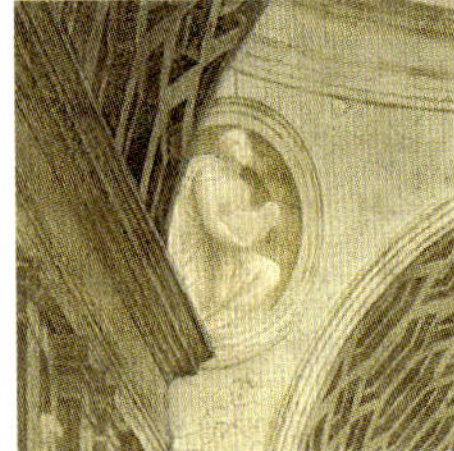

The building in the painting is inspired by classical Greek architecture.

Apollo, the Greek sun god, represents philosophical enlightenment. Raphael based the figure on a sculpture by Michelangelo.

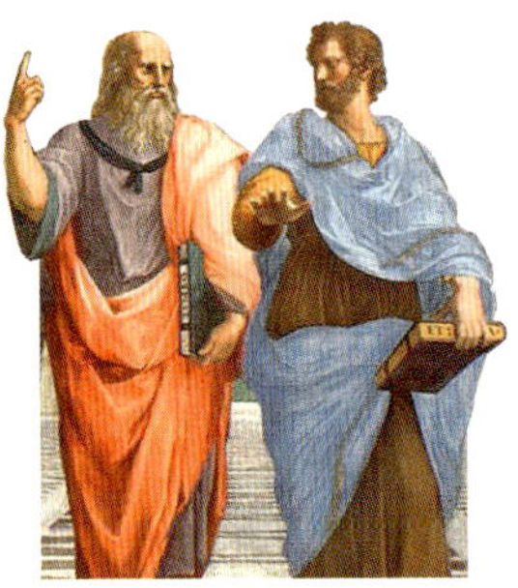

Plato, representing theoretical philosophy, points to the heavens, while Aristotle, who favored empirical philosophy, gestures toward the ground.

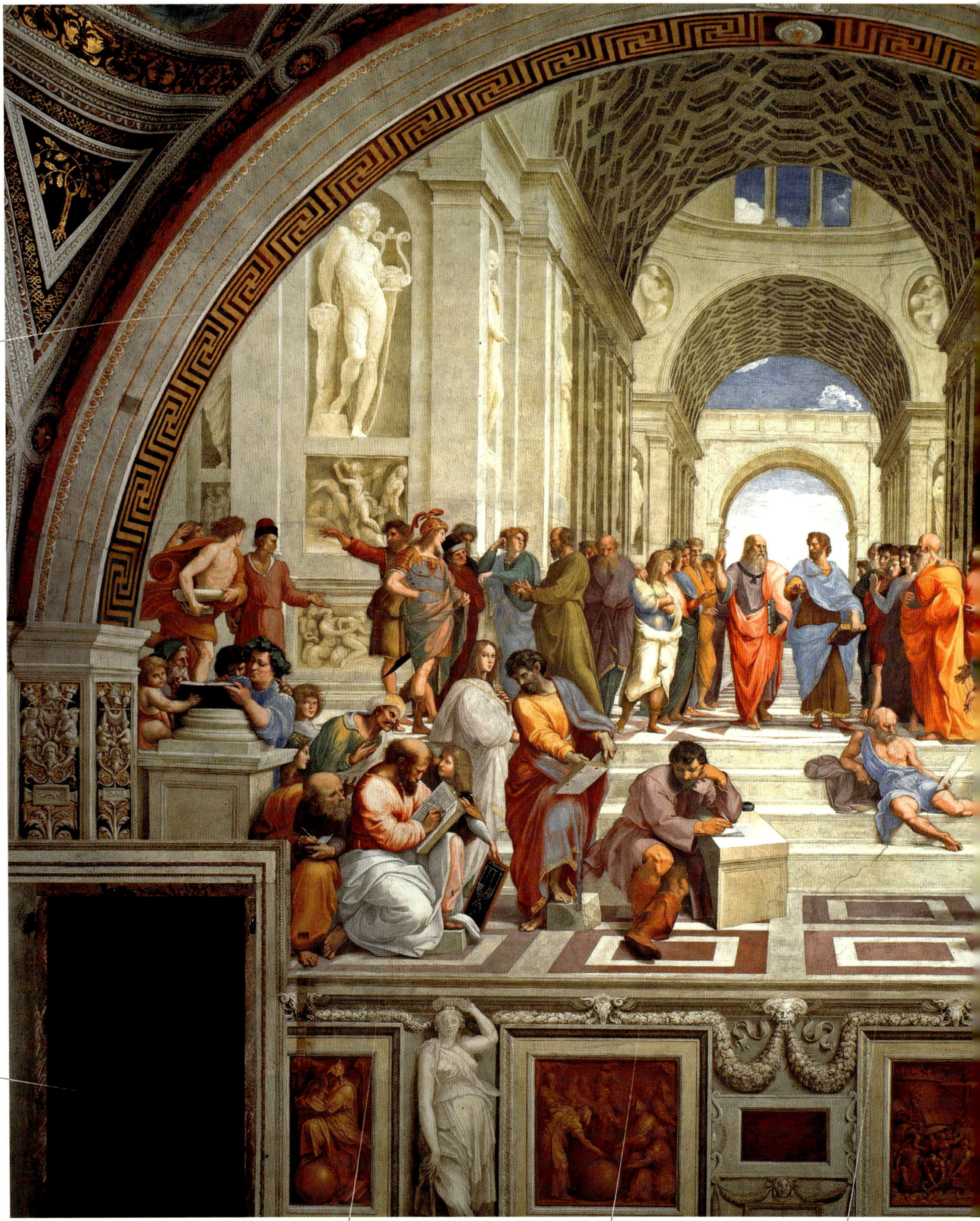

This black rectangle is a doorway to another part of the Vatican.

Greek mathematician and philosopher Pythagoras sits surrounded by enthusiastic listeners, including Archimedes, who holds a slate.

Added after the artist's preliminary drawings, this representation of the pessimist Heraclitus is actually a likeness of Michelangelo.

This partially clothed figure is the Cynic Diogenes, who disliked possessions and society, and chose to live in a large ceramic jar.

The School of Athens

Raphael 1509–1511, fresco, 197 × 303 in (500 × 770 cm), Vatican Museums, Vatican City

Raphael was 25 and relatively unknown when Pope Julius II commissioned him to decorate his private chambers at the Vatican Palace. In one room, the Stanza della Segnatura, his frescoes illustrate what were considered the greatest human endeavors: theology, poetry, and law. Representing philosophy, *The School of Athens* depicts some of the most illustrious scholars of ancient times explaining, arguing, and demonstrating their theories. It is filled with expressive activity, yet this is carefully controlled and contained by the classical architectural setting. Plato and Aristotle, with their contrasting schools of thought, are depicted in the center. Raphael did not confirm the identities of the other figures that he included, but historians tend to agree on the names assigned here.

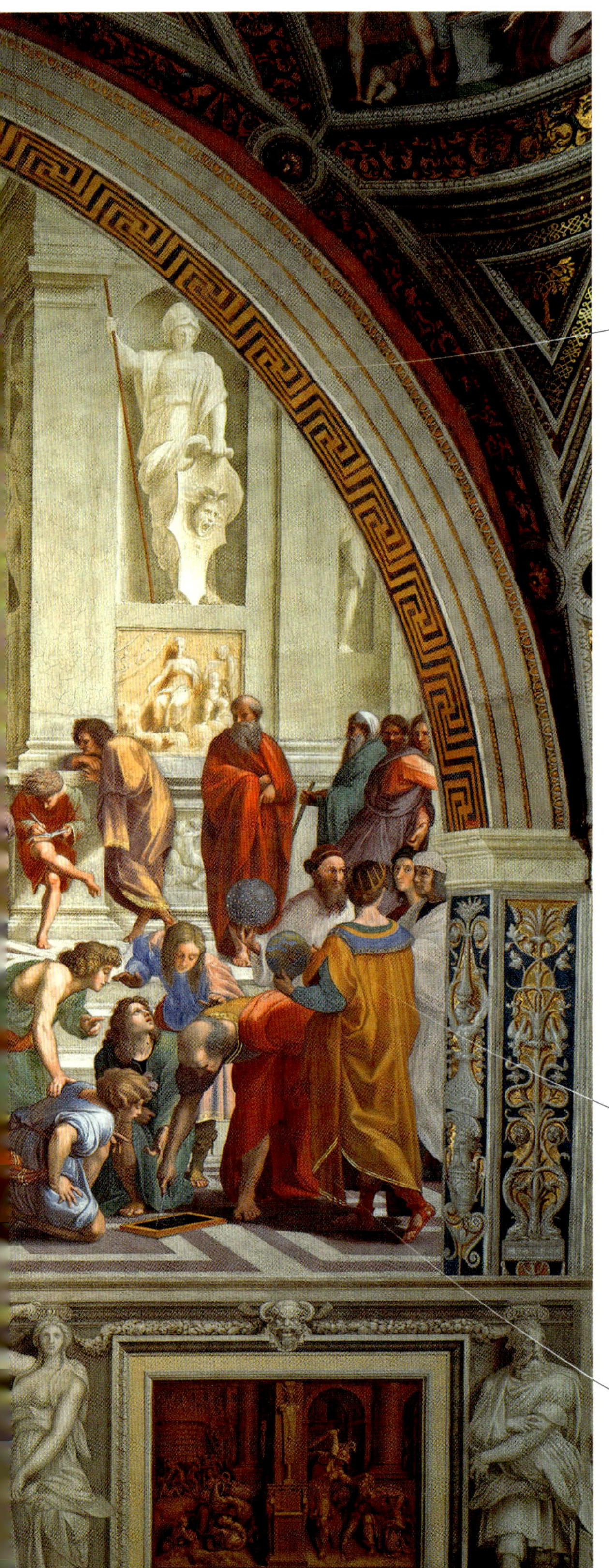

The goddess Athena, who embodies wisdom and justice, is also the sponsor of the arts and the pursuit of knowledge.

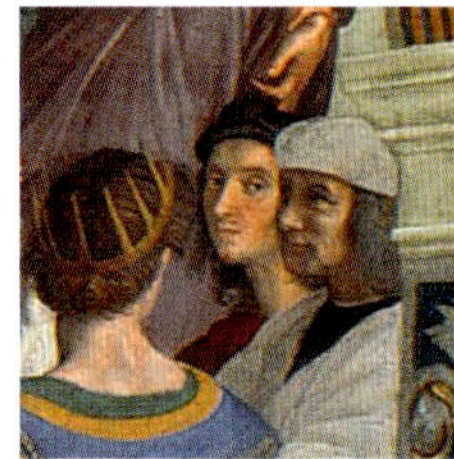

Raphael included himself in the painting, wearing a cap that was associated with poets.

Ptolemy, balancing a terrestrial globe, converses with Zoroaster, who holds a celestial one, despite the fact that the pair lived centuries apart.

Euclid, the "Father of Geometry," demonstrates a mathematical concept.

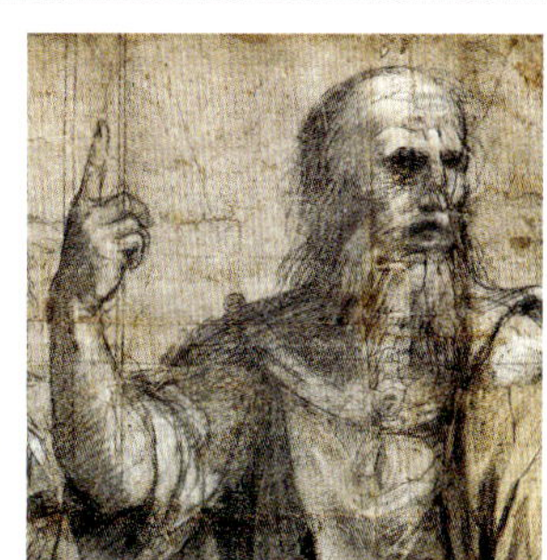

Cartoon method
To transfer his composition to the walls of the Stanza della Segnatura, Raphael used what is known as pouncing. A preparatory sketch—called a cartoon—was drawn onto paper and pasted to the wall. The artist then pricked holes in the outlines of the cartoon and dabbed them with charcoal to transfer the outlines to the walls.

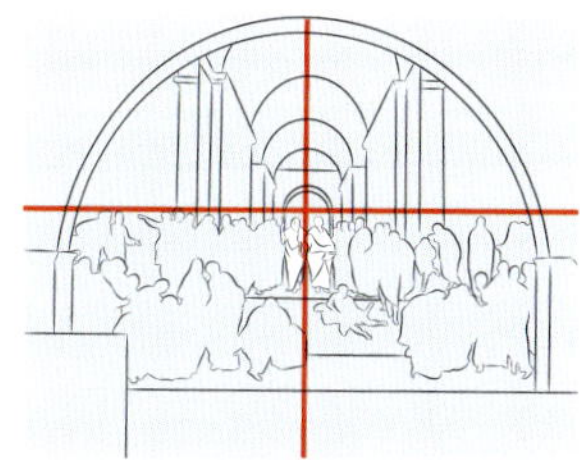

Center of attention
Plato and Aristotle stand where the horizon line meets the central vertical. The decreasing size of the arches create depth.

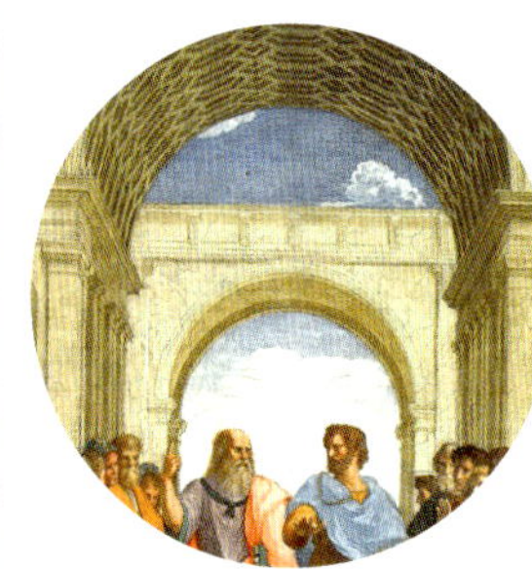

Graduating shades
The blue of the sky becomes lighter as the eye scans down the artwork. In this way, Raphael created a sense of aerial perspective.

> "The medieval principles led up to Raphael and the modern principles lead down from him."
>
> John Ruskin, 1853

The Tempest

Giorgione 1505-1508, oil on canvas, 32 × 29 in (82 × 73 cm), Gallerie dell'Accademia, Venice, Italy

This mysterious painting, one of the first paintings in Western art to be described as a "landscape," captures the moment when a storm breaks. The work has baffled viewers for centuries—what do the lightning flash, cluster of buildings, and the two enigmatic figures on either side of a riverbank mean?

The winged lion of St. Mark on the tower is a symbol of the city of Venice; Padua was part of the Venetian Republic.

A lightning flash illuminates the scene. It has been interpreted as God, or merely Giorgione's attempt to depict the unpaintable—thunder.

The city is probably Padua: the emblem above the arch depicts a four-wheeled cart, the coat of arms of the Carrara family.

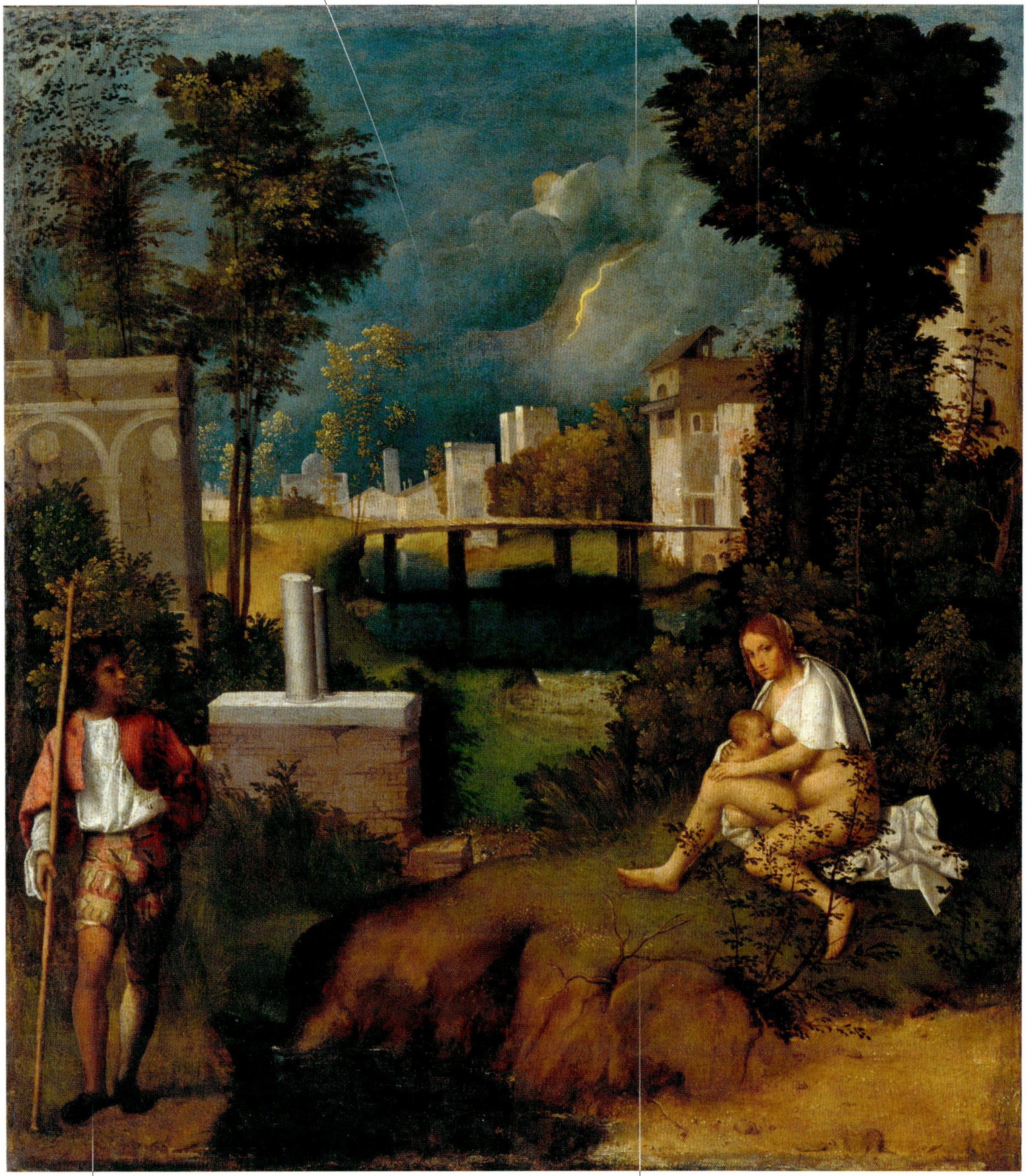

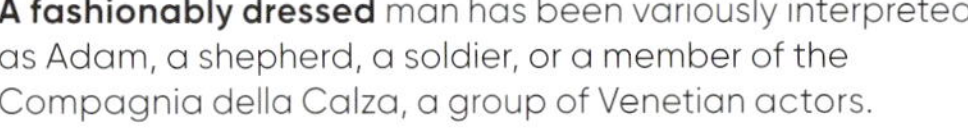

A fashionably dressed man has been variously interpreted as Adam, a shepherd, a soldier, or a member of the Compagnia della Calza, a group of Venetian actors.

The female figure may represent Eve or Charity. Her direct gaze and the fact that she is breastfeeding while naked unsettle the viewer.

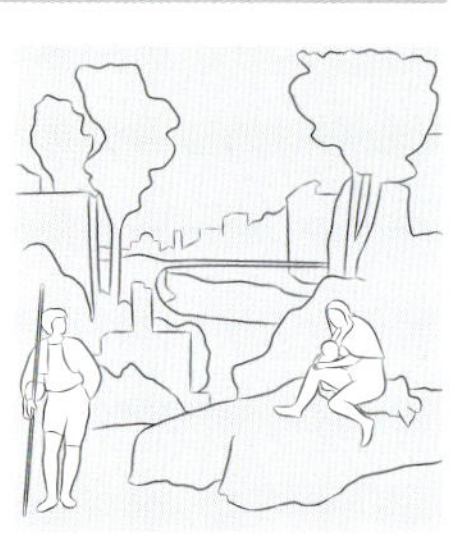

New emphasis
Traditionally, figures in a painting were given prominence over the background. In this painting, the setting is as important as the two protagonists.

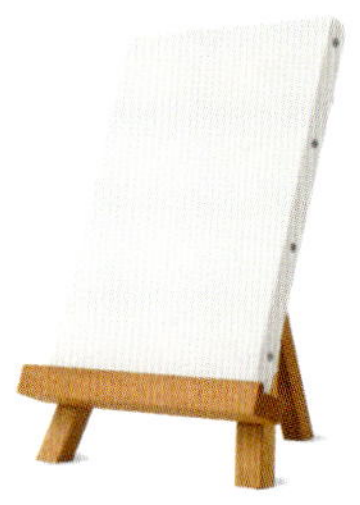

New materials
Giorgione was innovative in using oil paint on canvas. Previously, paintings were typically made on wood panels.

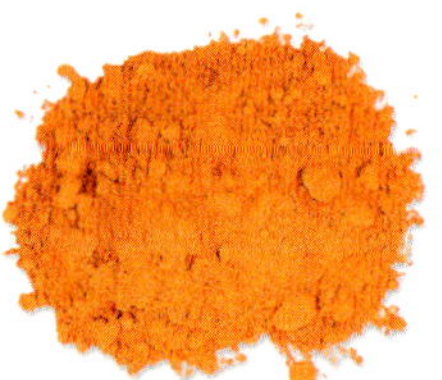

Yellow and orange
The strangely atmospheric lighting is enhanced by the use of yellow orpiment and orange realgar, two pigments derived from arsenic sulfide.

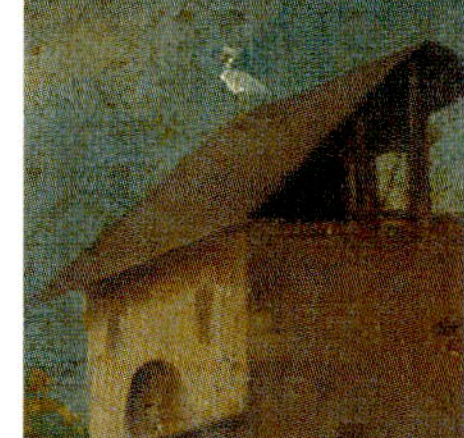

The stork on the roof might symbolize the birth of the child.

The Adoration of the Kings

Jan Gossaert (Mabuse) 1510–1515, oil on oak, 71 × 64 in (180 × 163 cm), National Gallery, London, UK

A Netherlandish painter, Gossaert spent two years in Italy, where he was influenced by the art of Raphael and Michelangelo. Painted after his return to the Netherlands, *The Adoration of the Kings* altarpiece reflects the tension between Roman classicism in the modeling of the bodies and Northern Gothic influences in the density of detail. Gossaert's teeming scene captures the excitement at Christ's birth.

An angel holds a scroll proclaiming "Gloria in Excelsis Deo," a declaration made by the shepherds.

The star appears directly above the Holy Spirit (shown as a dove) and the Christ Child.

Classical arches and capitals are crumbling. The Roman world is giving way to a Christian dawn.

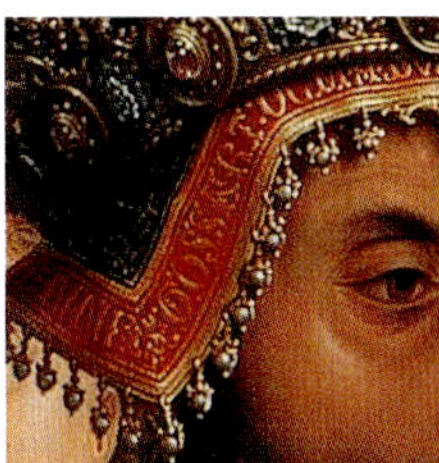

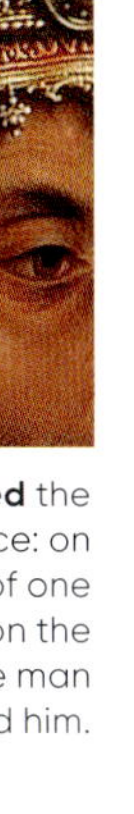

Gossaert signed the painting twice: on the headdress of one of the kings and on the collar of the man standing behind him.

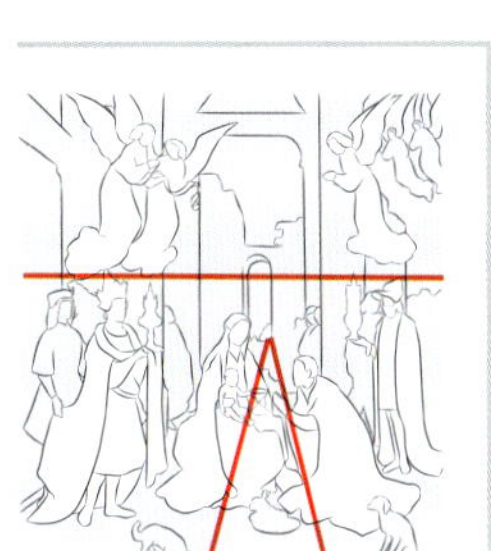

Composition
The heavenly and earthly realms are divided by a horizontal split. The shepherds appear at the painting's vanishing point.

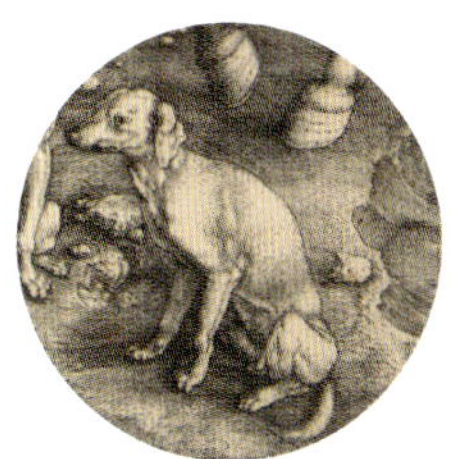

Dürer's influence
The dog in the bottom right corner was copied from an engraving (c. 1501) by German painter and printmaker Albrecht Dürer.

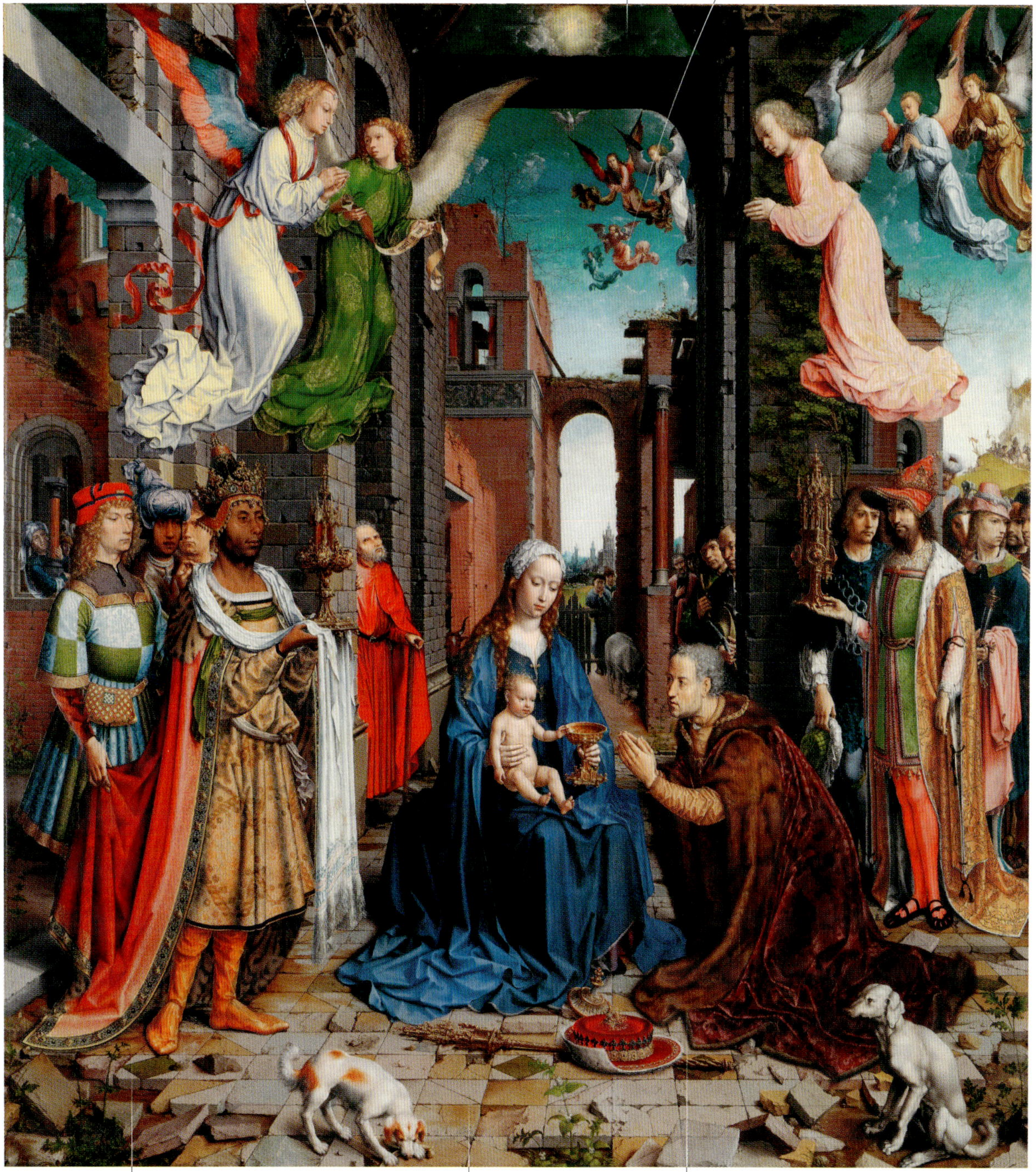

The Adoration of the Kings occurs in the foreground, while the humble shepherds look on in the background.

The diagonal patterns in the tiles lead the eye to the center of the painting.

The kneeling king is probably modeled on Daniel van Boechout, the wealthy nobleman who commissioned the work.

The Sistine Madonna

Raphael c. 1512–1513, oil on canvas, 111 × 168 in (281 × 426 cm), Gemäldegalerie Alte Meister, Dresden, Germany

One of the last Madonnas completed by Raphael before his death at age 37, *The Sistine Madonna* was painted for Pope Julius II to hang above the altar in the church of San Sisto, Piacenza, Italy. The Madonna stares out from a carpet of clouds, flanked by St. Sixtus and St. Barbara as she cradles the Christ Child protectively.

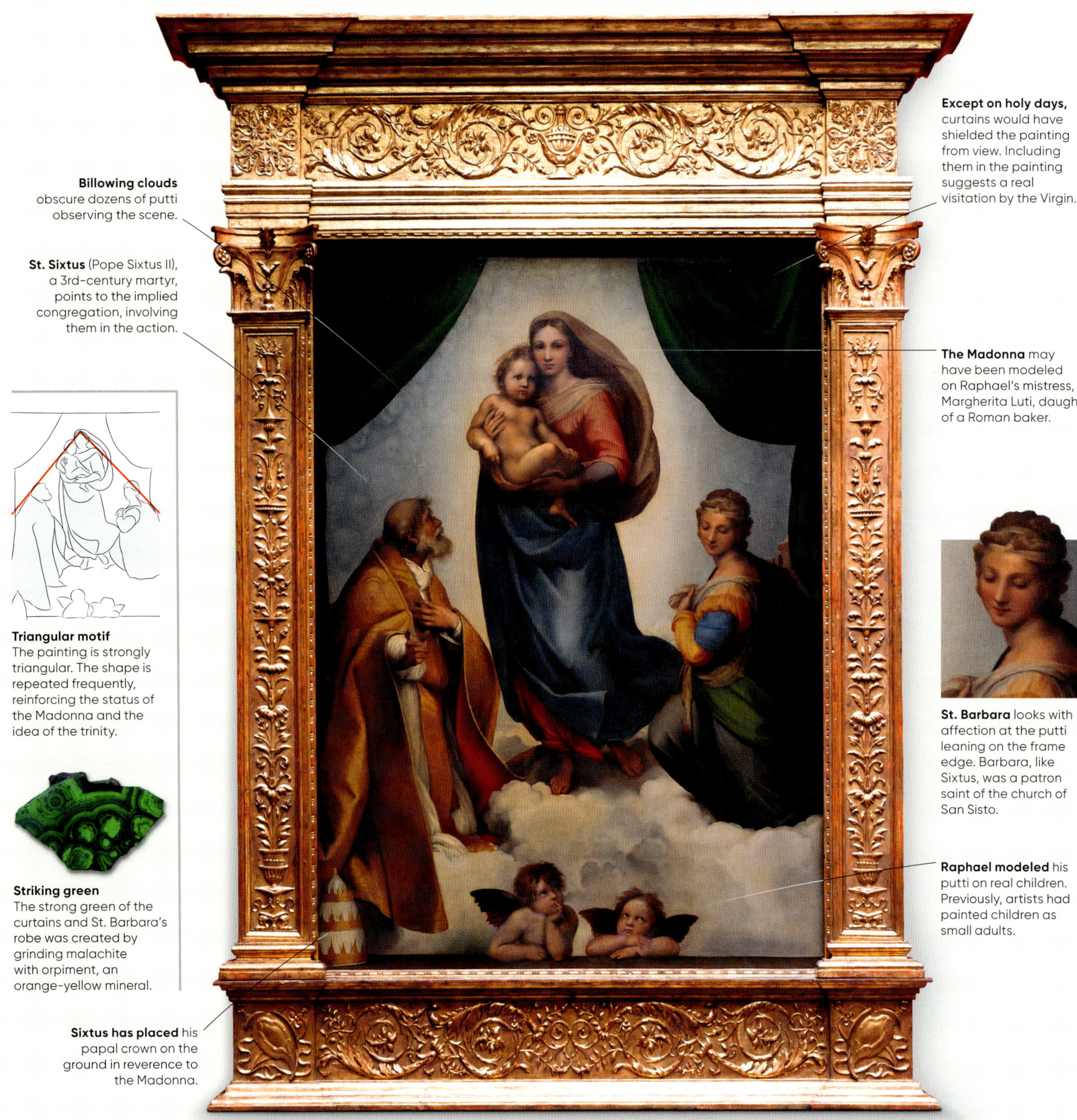

Billowing clouds obscure dozens of putti observing the scene.

St. Sixtus (Pope Sixtus II), a 3rd-century martyr, points to the implied congregation, involving them in the action.

Triangular motif
The painting is strongly triangular. The shape is repeated frequently, reinforcing the status of the Madonna and the idea of the trinity.

Striking green
The strong green of the curtains and St. Barbara's robe was created by grinding malachite with orpiment, an orange-yellow mineral.

Sixtus has placed his papal crown on the ground in reverence to the Madonna.

Except on holy days, curtains would have shielded the painting from view. Including them in the painting suggests a real visitation by the Virgin.

The Madonna may have been modeled on Raphael's mistress, Margherita Luti, daughter of a Roman baker.

St. Barbara looks with affection at the putti leaning on the frame edge. Barbara, like Sixtus, was a patron saint of the church of San Sisto.

Raphael modeled his putti on real children. Previously, artists had painted children as small adults.

Isenheim Altarpiece Crucifixion

Mathis Neithart Grünewald 1512–1516, oil and tempera on wood panel, 148 × 210 in (376 × 534 cm), Musée Unterlinden, Colmar, France

Mathis Grünewald's *Crucifixion* forms the central panel of an altarpiece in a monastery dedicated to sufferers of ergotism, caused by eating poisoned rye. Christ's body has been tortured, with the marks of flagellation on his skin similar to those of ergotism patients. This moving image is a study of physical and mental pain.

> "This tortured man hanging there. It's a wonderful picture. It is comforting simply because it is beautiful."
>
> Gerhard Richter, 2016

Christ's hands and feet are brutally misshapen, emphasizing his agony.

Christ's body is covered with wounds and abrasions. His blue lips signify the approach of death.

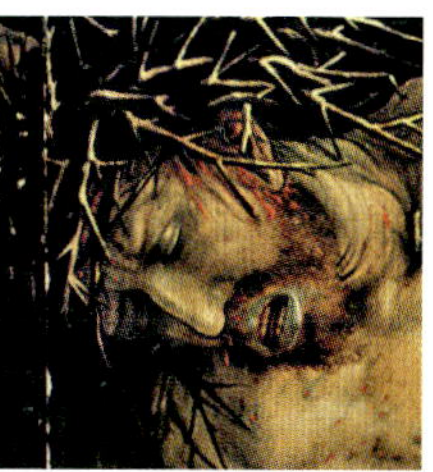

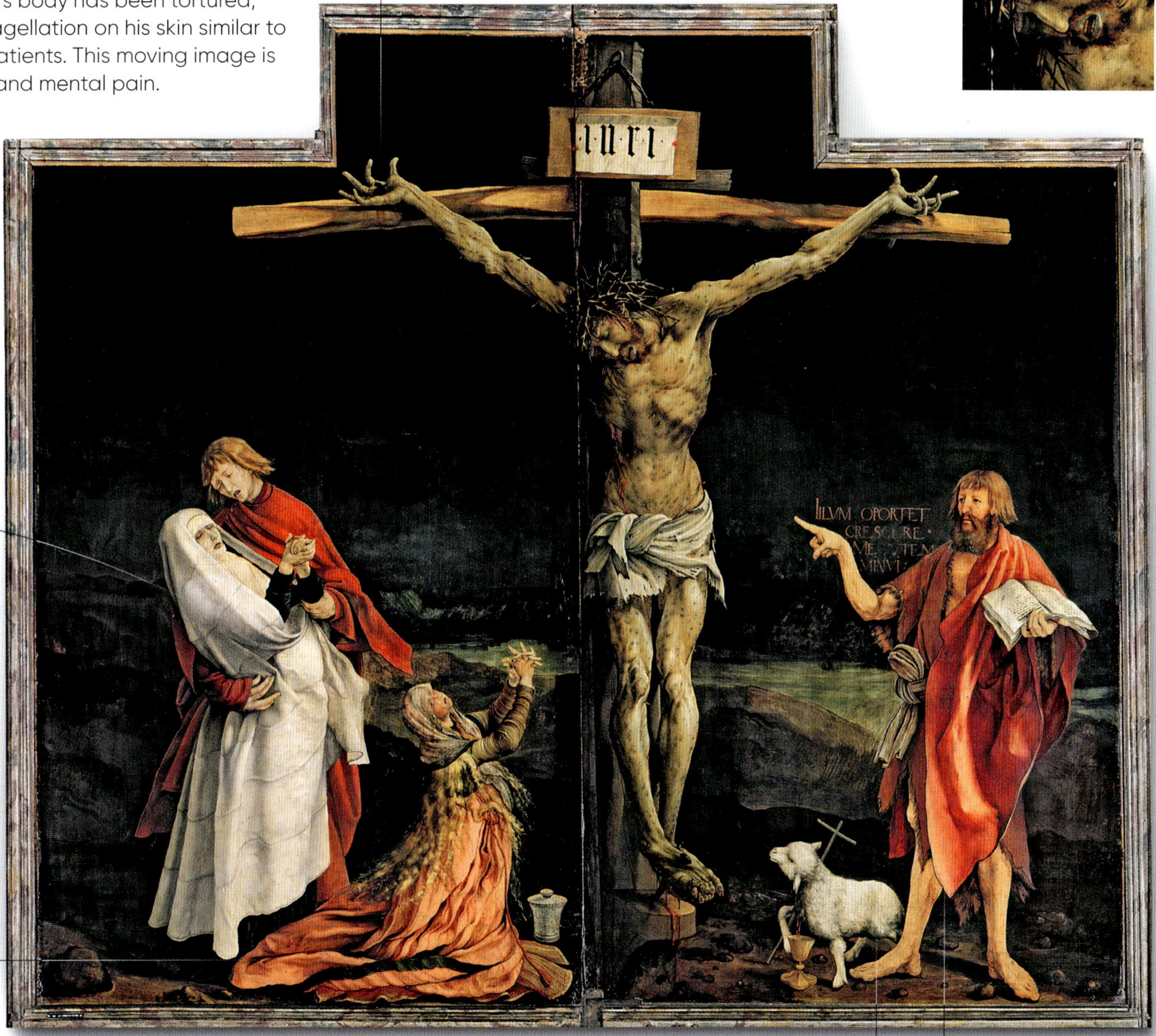

The Virgin Mary swoons in the arms of St. John.

Mary Magdalene can be identified by her position at Christ's feet and the jar of ointment, used for anointing them.

The lamb carries a cross and bleeds into the golden chalice, a symbol of the Christian Eucharist in which wine is said to become the blood of Christ.

John the Baptist calmly points to Jesus Christ, the lamb of God bleeding at his feet. Behind him is the Jordan River, where he baptized Christ.

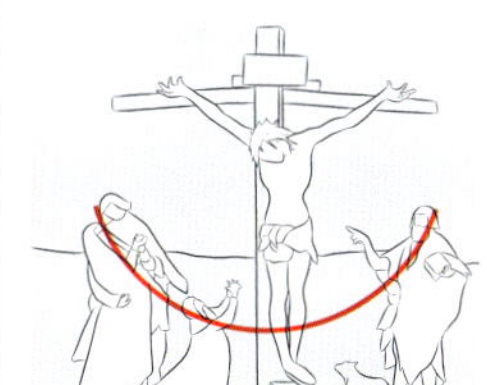

Focus on Christ
The figures form a loose semicircle around Christ, whose body has been amplified to twice the size of the others.

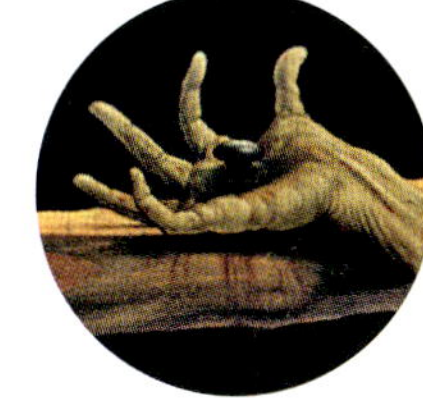

Distortions
The right arm of St. John has been artificially elongated to support Mary's body, while Christ's feet and hands are contorted. Grünewald used such distortions to intensify the emotional impact.

The Feast of the Gods

Giovanni Bellini and Titian 1514/1529, oil on canvas, 67 × 74 in (170.2 × 188 cm), National Gallery of Art, Washington, D.C., US

In the shade of trees, drunken deities attended by nymphs and satyrs enjoy an orgiastic party organized by Bacchus, the god of wine. The subject matter was a departure for the elderly Bellini, who was best known for his religious and historical scenes or portraits. The painting was commissioned by Duke Alfonso d'Este, who later employed Titian to repaint elements of the scene and to produce other works on mythological themes.

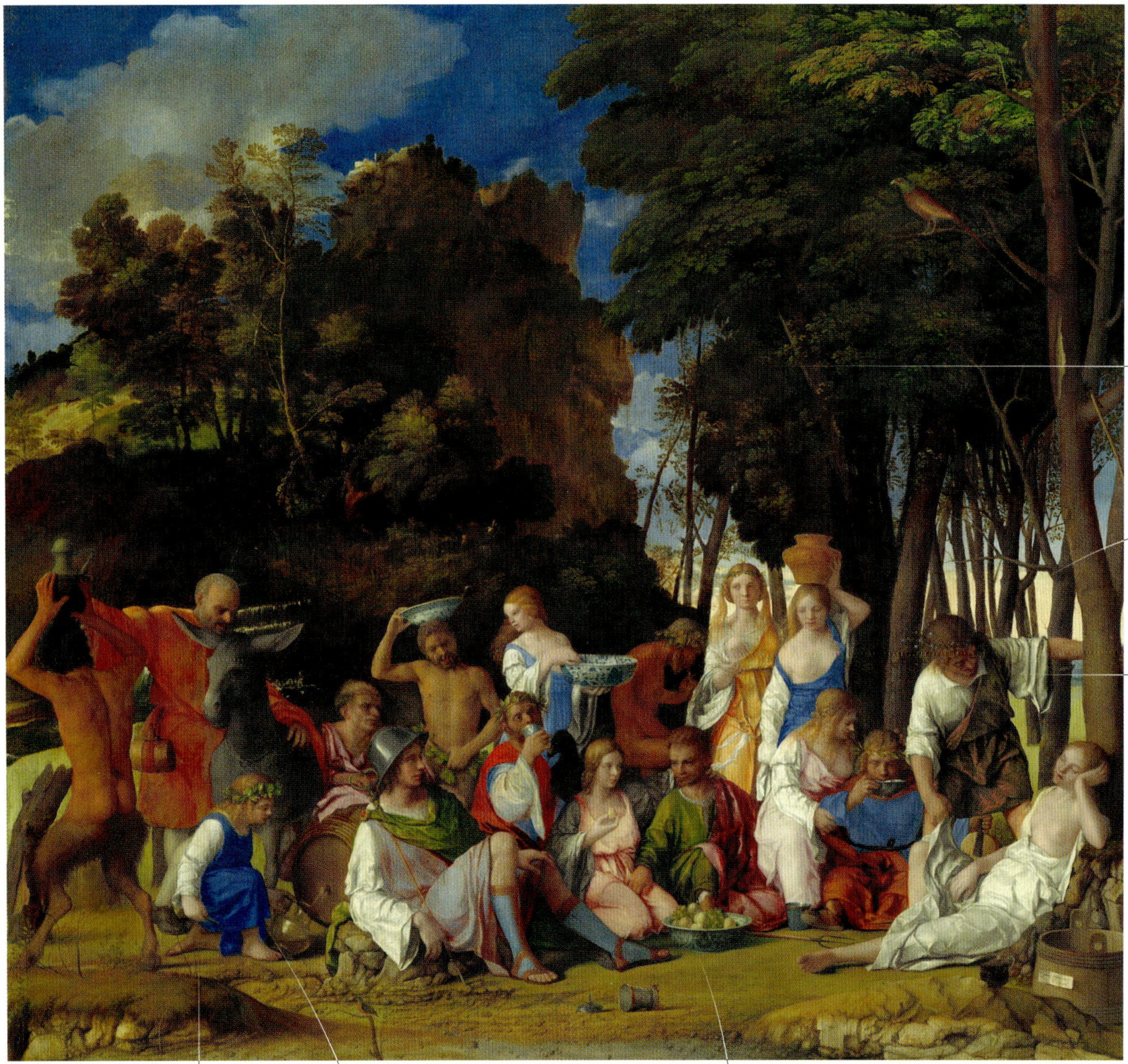

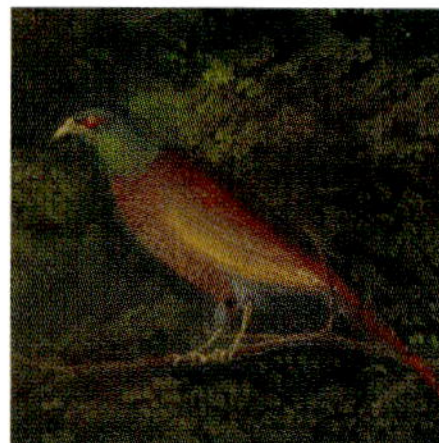

The pheasant was added by Dosso Dossi, Duke Alfonso's court artist, and left in place by Titian.

Titian's alterations include the wooded hillside. He also replaced what had been a simple line of trees with sky.

There are two sources of light: one from between the trees in the background, and one that bathes the revelers.

Priapus, the god of fertility, lifts the dress of the sleeping nymph Lotis. According to the story, he is caught in the act when Silenus's donkey brays and wakes her up.

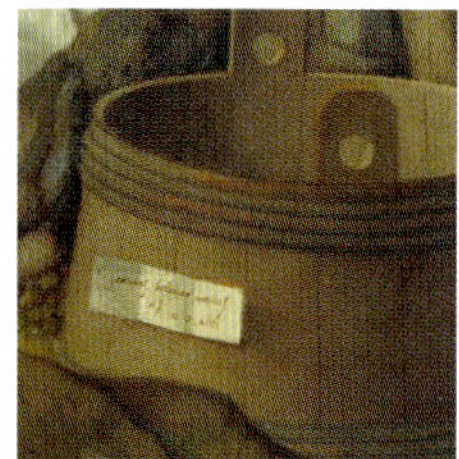

A scroll on the wooden tub says "joannes bellinus venetus/p MDXIIII"—Bellini's signature and the date.

Bacchus, who is depicted as a young boy, pours wine into a crystal jug.

Bellini balanced the intensity of ultramarine in the clothing by using pink, mauve, and green undercoats. Bacchus's robe is the deepest blue.

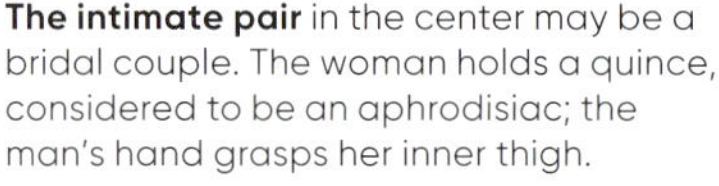

The intimate pair in the center may be a bridal couple. The woman holds a quince, considered to be an aphrodisiac; the man's hand grasps her inner thigh.

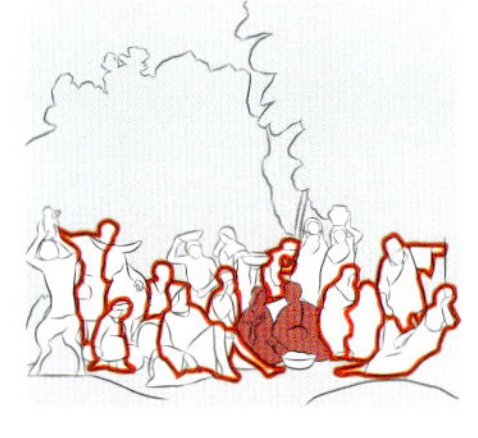

Featured cast
The main characters pictured are, from left to right, Silenus, Bacchus, Silvanus, Mercury, Jupiter, Pan, Ceres, Apollo, Priapus, and Lotis. The couple at the center have sometimes been identified as Neptune and Amphitrite, or Persephone and Hades.

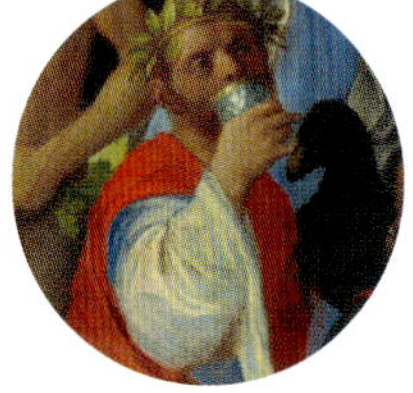

Ancient and modern
The composition resembles a classical frieze, although the gods are wearing the brightly colored clothing of 16th-century Venetians rather than the robes of ancient Greece and Rome.

Portrait of Pope Leo X with Two Cardinals

Raphael 1518, oil on wood, 61 × 47 in (154 × 119 cm), Uffizi, Florence, Italy

The last picture Raphael painted for Pope Leo X was one of his finest. Leo was born Giovanni de' Medici, son of Lorenzo the Magnificent, and became pope in 1513. He is shown here with his two nephews, the cardinals Giulio de' Medici and Luigi de' Rossi, together representing the power of the Medici family.

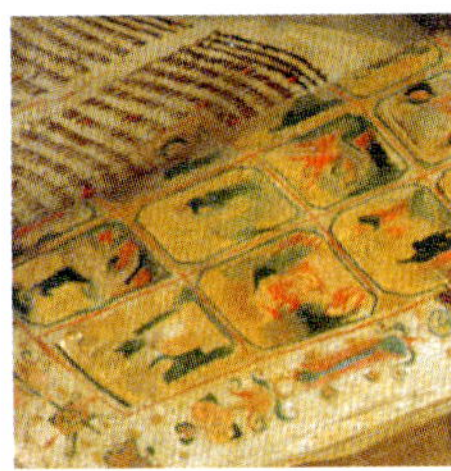

The illuminated Bible is so accurately painted that it is has been identified as the Hamilton Bible, now in the Berlin State Museum, Germany.

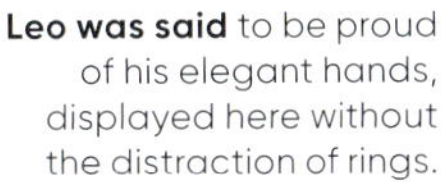

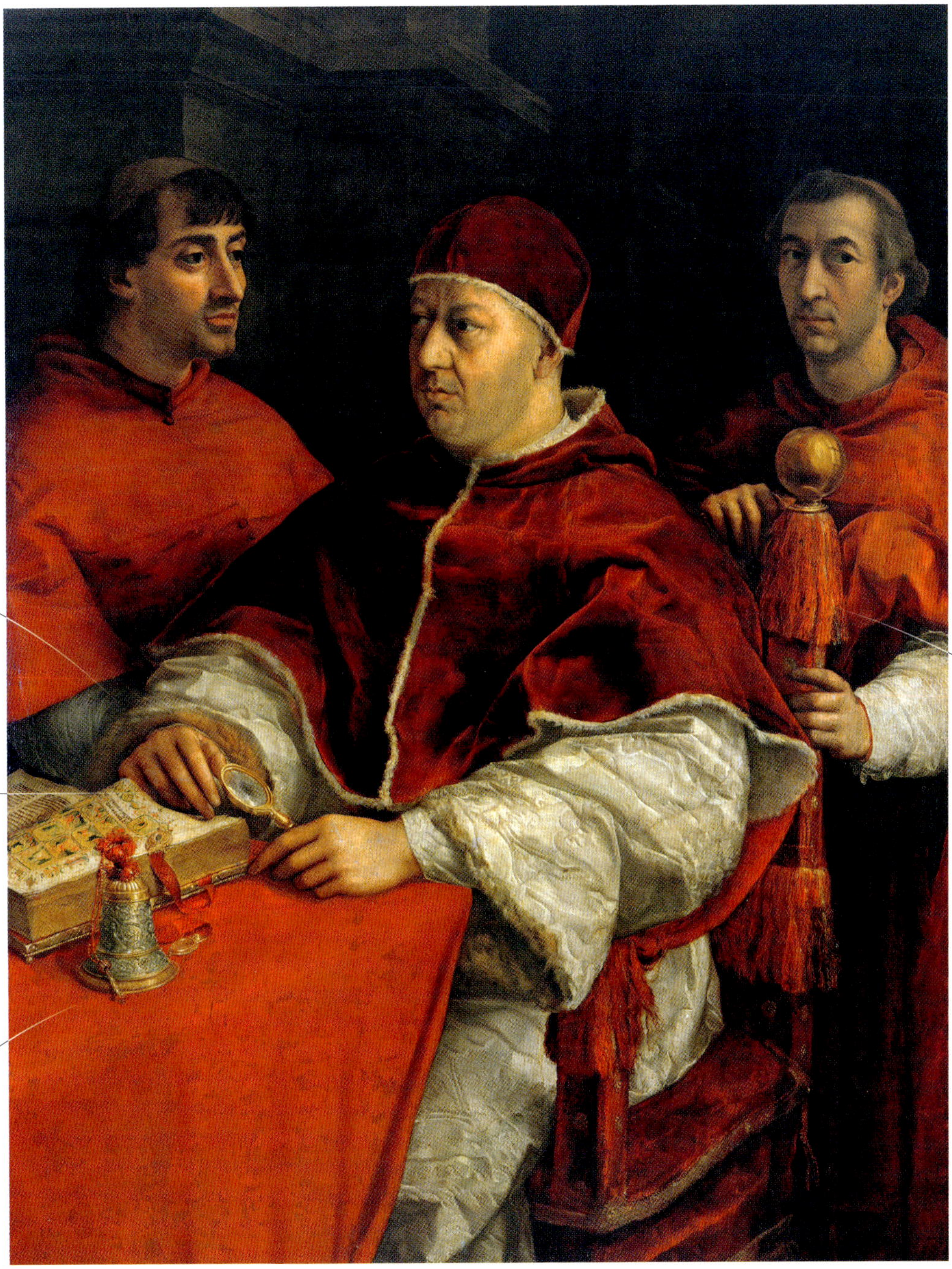

Leo was said to be proud of his elegant hands, displayed here without the distraction of rings.

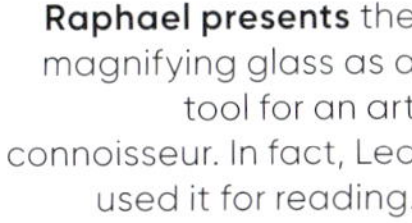

Raphael presents the magnifying glass as a tool for an art connoisseur. In fact, Leo used it for reading.

A delicately wrought gold and silver bell with a red silk tassel signals that the pope was a man of culture, who collected fine objects.

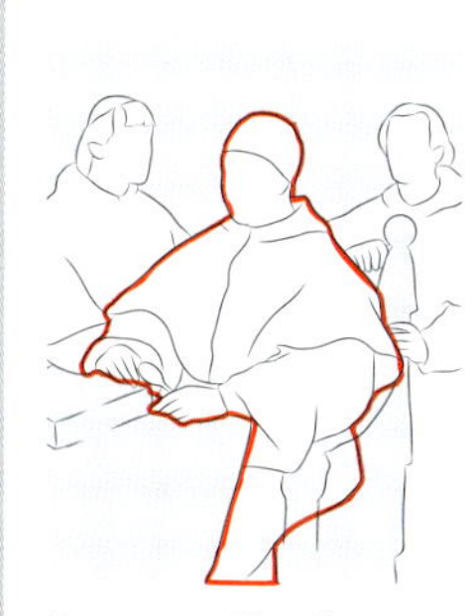

Foregrounding the subject
The two cardinals are placed slightly behind the pope. This provides depth—reinforced by the receding architecture—and emphasizes Leo as the main subject of the portrait.

The elaborate chair indicates Leo's high status as well as demonstrating Raphael's skill: the reflection of a window in its golden finial is reminiscent of the work of Flemish artists.

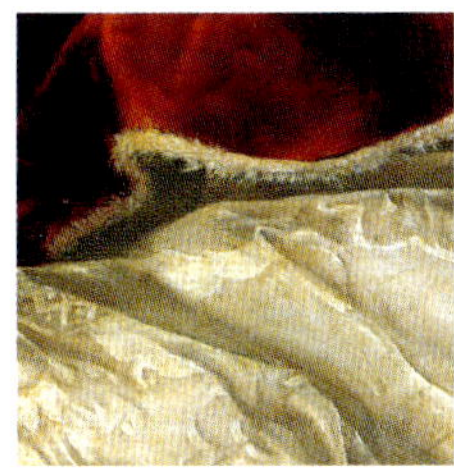

A lover of luxury, Leo wears a silk brocade robe with fur-lined sleeves, not the traditional papal shirt.

> "It may be surely said that those who are the possessors of such rare and numerous gifts as were seen in Raffaello da Urbino are not merely men, but, if it be not a sin to say it, mortal gods."
>
> Giorgio Vasari, 1568

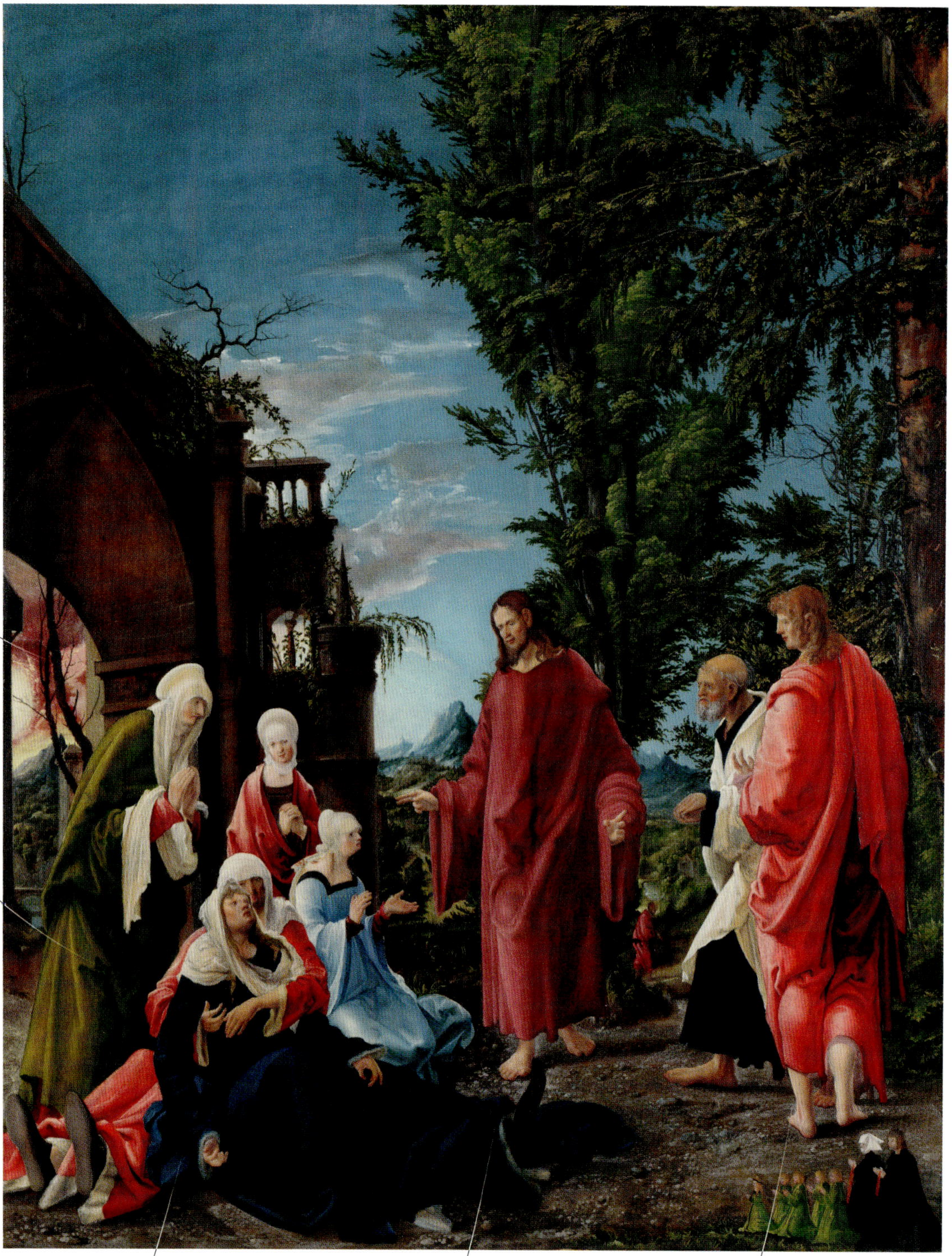

Framed by an arch, the withered tree and crimson colored clouds allude to the blood of the Crucifixion.

Altdorfer used pose and gestures to convey emotion, deliberately elongating the figures and enlarging their hands and feet.

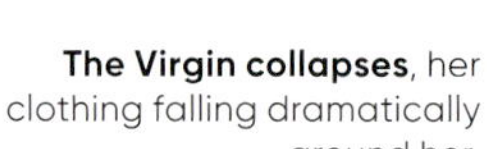

The Virgin collapses, her clothing falling dramatically around her.

Christ bestows his blessing on his mother.

St. John the Evangelist (in red) and St. Peter witness the scene. Their expressions are calm and reassuring.

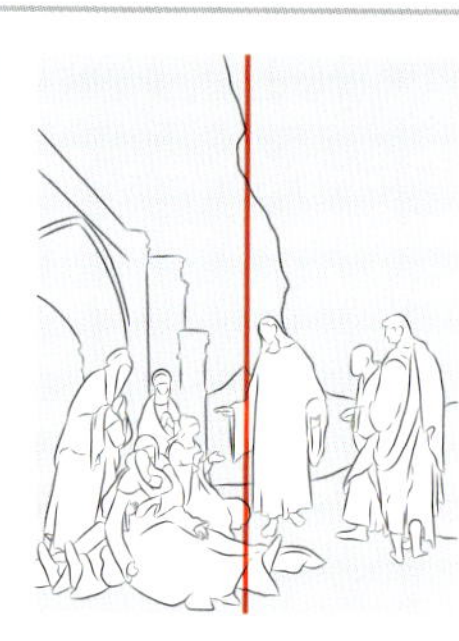

Two sides
The composition divides vertically, with the barren landscape and grief-stricken women on the left, juxtaposed with the lush foliage and calmer apostles on the right of the painting.

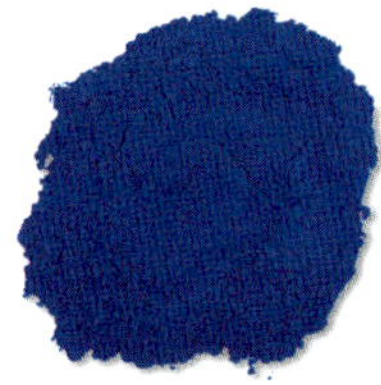

Azurite
The pigment azurite was widely used during the Renaissance as a cheaper alternative to ultramarine. In this painting, it was used for the blue gowns and mixed with lead white for the sky.

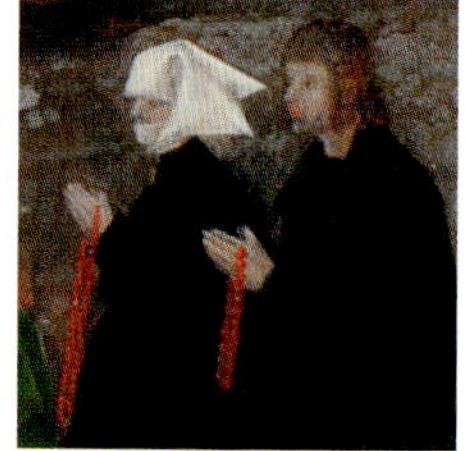

The miniature figures in the bottom right-hand corner are "donor portraits," referencing the family who commissioned the painting.

Christ Taking Leave of His Mother

Albrecht Altdorfer c.1520, oil on lime, 56 × 44 in (141 × 111 cm), National Gallery, London, UK

In a scene drawn from devotional texts rather than the Bible, Altdorfer has imagined Jesus calmly blessing his shocked mother after telling her that he is traveling to Jerusalem to face his impending death. The landscape encompasses both suffering and hope; its wealth of natural detail, such as the large tree and other background foliage, marked the rise of landscape painting as an independent genre.

Bacchus and Ariadne

Titian 1520–1523, oil on canvas, 69 × 75 in (176.5 × 191 cm), National Gallery, London, UK

This painting shows the moment when Bacchus, the Roman god of wine, first sees Ariadne, who has been abandoned on the island of Naxos by her lover, Theseus. It illustrates Titian's skill in translating a classical mythological text into dramatic visual imagery. He uses composition, color arrangement, and allegorical details to tell the story, drawing the viewer's eye along the story arc from left to right.

The stars show the constellation that Ariadne will become.

Ultramarine, an expensive pigment made from lapis lazuli, is used for the sky.

Silenus, Bacchus's tutor and friend, and chief of the satyrs, is in a drunken stupor.

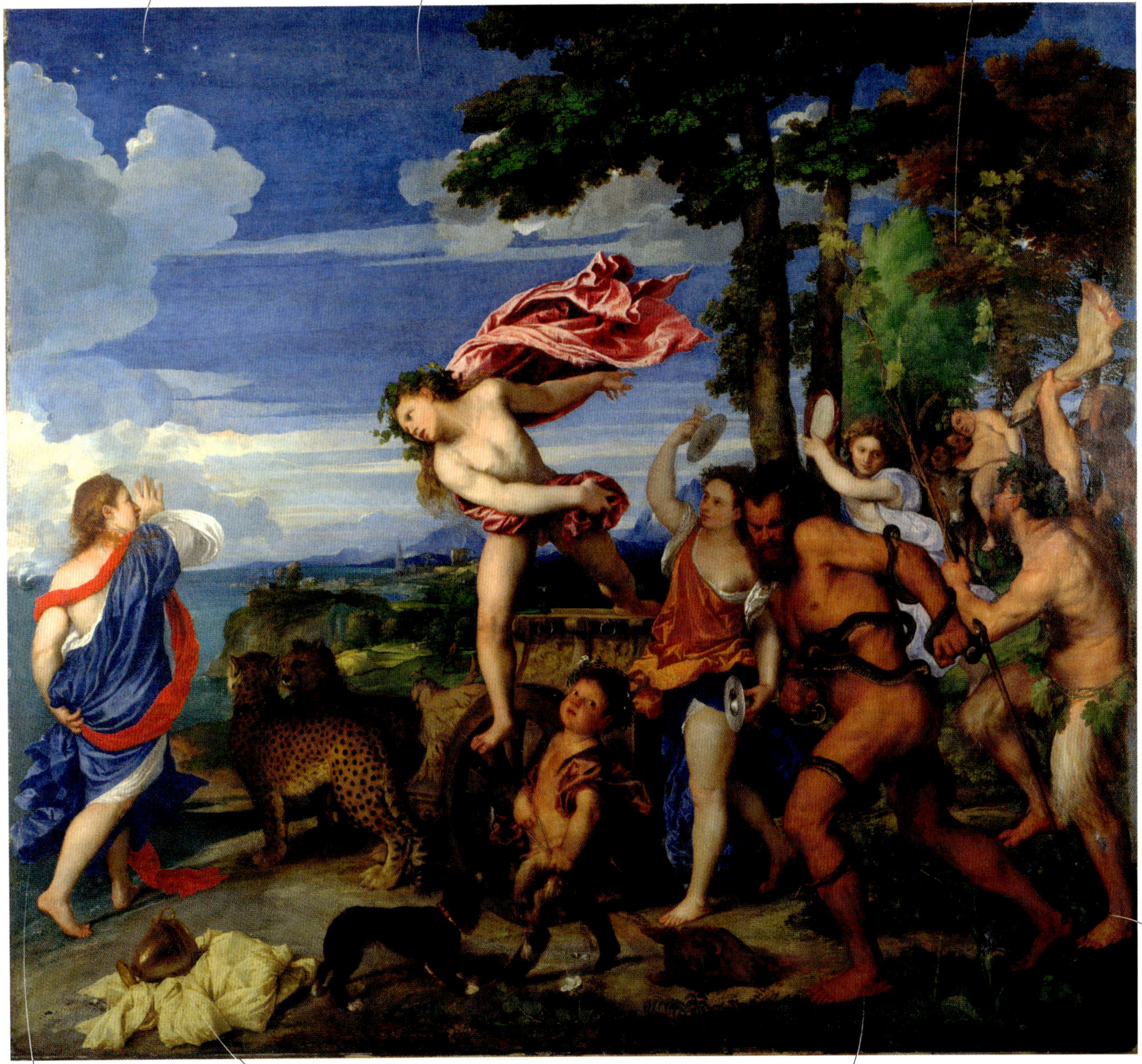

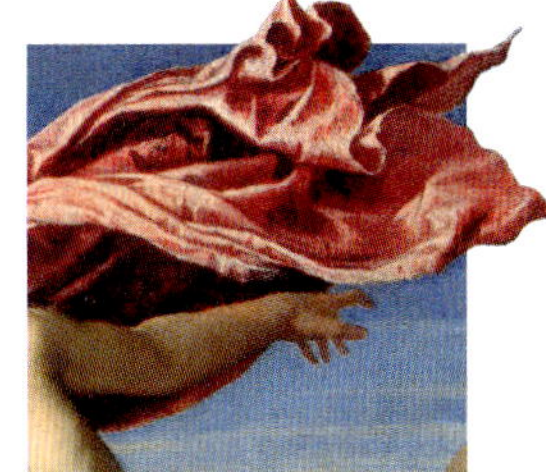

Poised in midair, Bacchus links the realm of the gods and the earthly domain. His cloak looks like a crumpled set of wings. As he turns toward Ariadne, he seems to trap her where she stands.

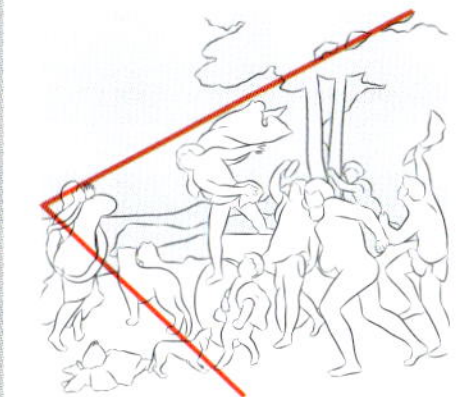

Composition
The painting is divided in two diagonally, the left side dominated by blue and the right by warm, earthy reds and oranges, splitting the world of the painting into a distant, ethereal sphere and the worldly terrain of the revelers.

Bacchus is attended by a rowdy band of satyrs and female followers.

A strong contrast between Ariadne's blue dress and red sash attracts the eye. Her clothing creates a swirl of movement as she turns to see Bacchus.

Titian's signature can be seen on the urn. It stands out against a pale yellow cloth, which draws attention to it.

The man wreathed in snakes is based on *Laocoön*, a famous classical sculpture that had been rediscovered in Rome in 1506. The statue was often used as a model by Renaissance painters.

> "It is not bright colors but good drawing that makes figures beautiful."
>
> Titian

Faces peek through every multicolored nook and cranny, adding lively detail.

Blossoming trees and billowing clouds are motifs from the Chinese artistic tradition that Persian artists incorporated into their work.

The angel Surush warns Kayumars of an evil plot to murder his beloved son, Siyamak, who sits opposite on rocks on the right.

The landscape is painted with rich pigments such as ultramarine, created from ground lapis lazuli.

Multiethnic courtiers, clothed in leopardskin robes, gather around the idyllic garden.

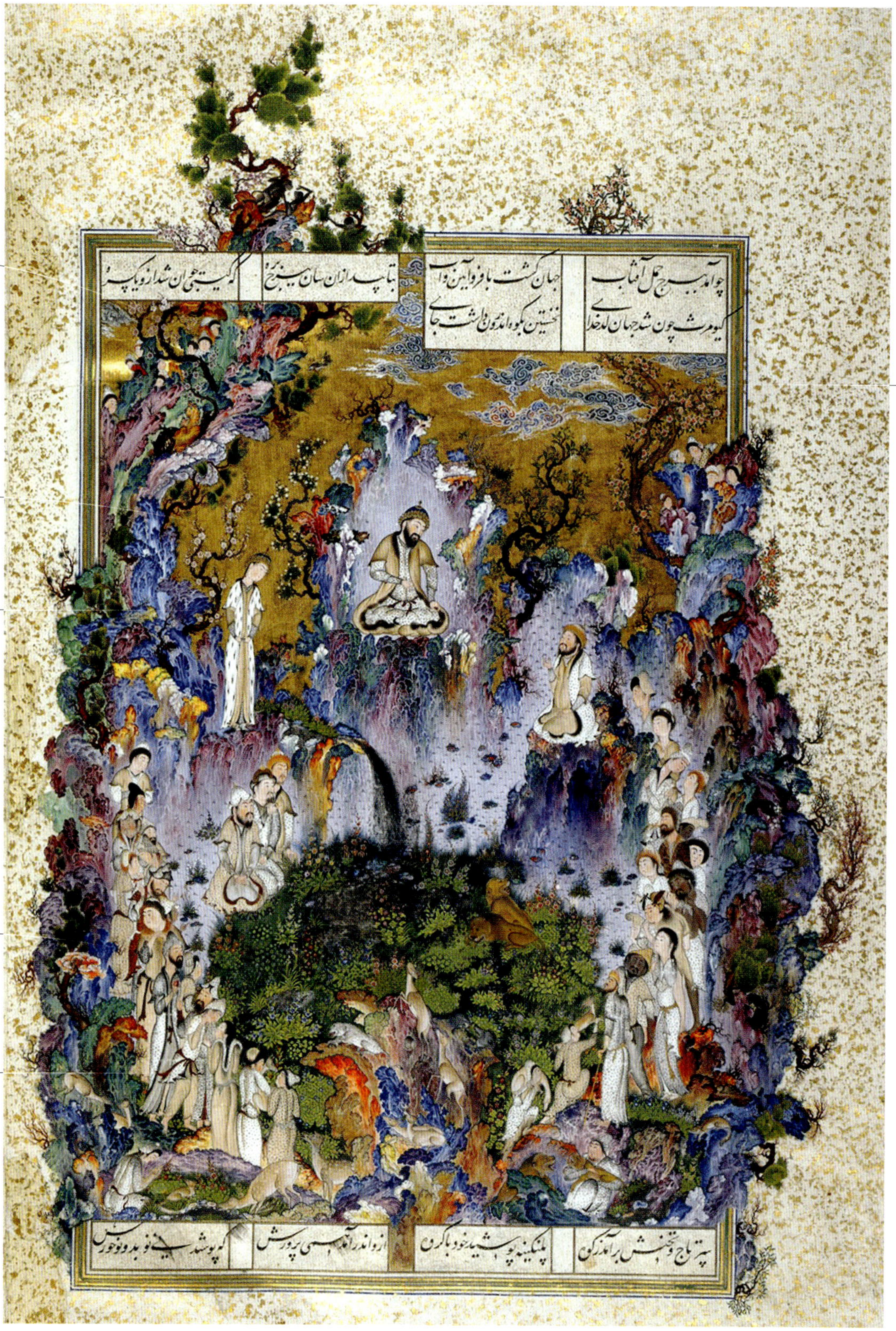

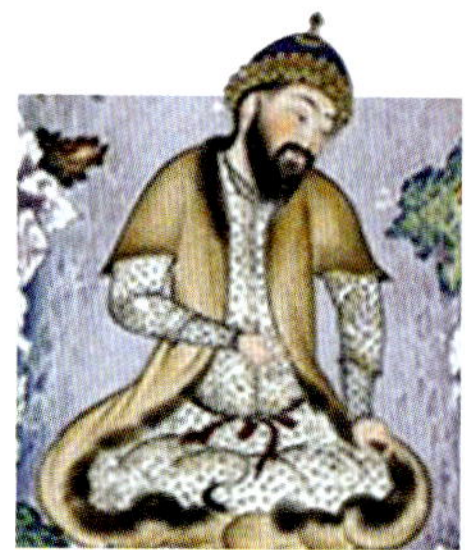

Kayumars, the mythical first king of Iran, sits cross-legged on a throne of jewellike boulders.

Monkeys play among branches that burst out into the rich, gold-speckled border.

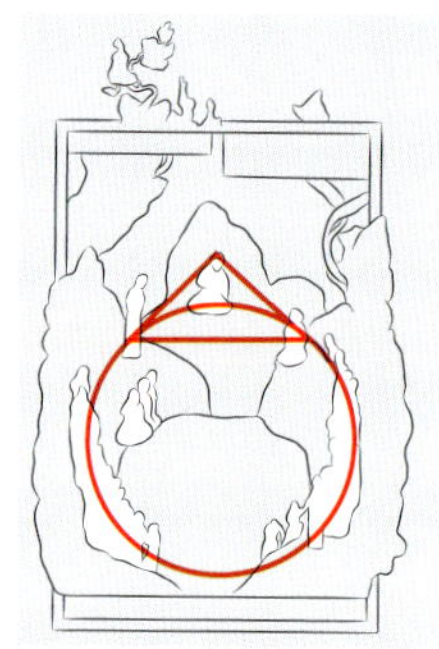

Composition
The circular formation of courtiers grounds the painting at its base and heightens the ethereal quality of the triangle of angel, king, and prince floating above.

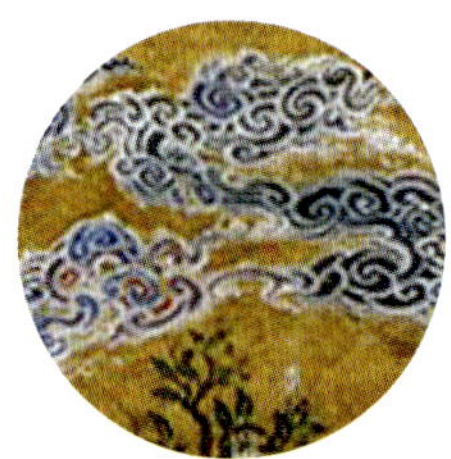

Everlasting sun
Gold signifies daylight in the Persian painting tradition, suggesting that an everlasting sun shines on the court of King Kayumars.

The Court of Kayumars

Sultan Muhammad c. 1524–1525, opaque watercolor, ink, and gold on paper, 18 × 12 in (45 × 30 cm), Aga Khan Museum, Toronto, Canada

Humans and beasts exist in perfect harmony under the rule of King Kayumars in this illuminated folio from the *Shahnameh* (Book of Kings) of Shah Tahmasp. The poetic work, chronicling the history of pre-Islamic kingship in Iran up to the Arab conquest of 642 CE, is a masterpiece of Persian art.

The Deposition from the Cross

Jacopo Pontormo 1525–1528, tempera on wood, 123 × 76 in (313 × 192 cm), Capponi Chapel, Florence, Italy

Pontormo's altarpiece is a fine example of Mannerism, a self-consciously artificial style developed in opposition to naturalism. The work features two angel-like youths carrying the body of Christ, while a group of sympathetic women support the Virgin Mary. The complex composition of overlapping individuals highlights Mary's swirl of bitter emotions as she is separated from the body of her dead son.

While the figures are lit from the right, a single cloud is illuminated from above—from heaven.

A burial cloth is held by the woman at the top of the painting, possibly an allusion to the Turin Shroud, a revered relic.

A woman carries a cloth, a reference to the Veil of Veronica, said to have been imprinted with the image of Christ's face after St. Veronica used it to wipe his face.

Pontormo modeled the figure of Christ on Michelangelo's *Pietà*, a marble sculpture of Mary cradling her dead son.

Elongated, distorted torsos reject the naturalism of the Renaissance.

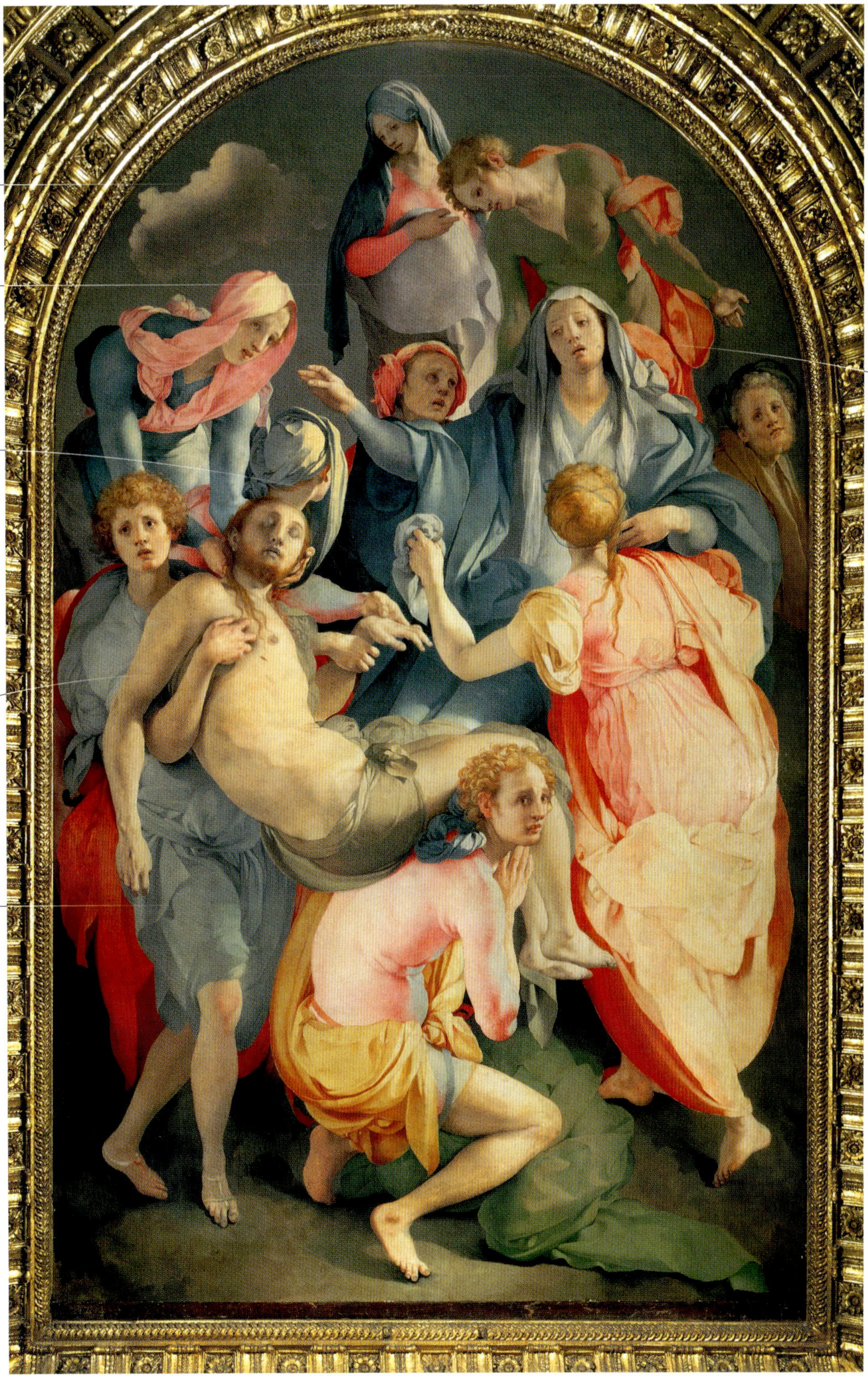

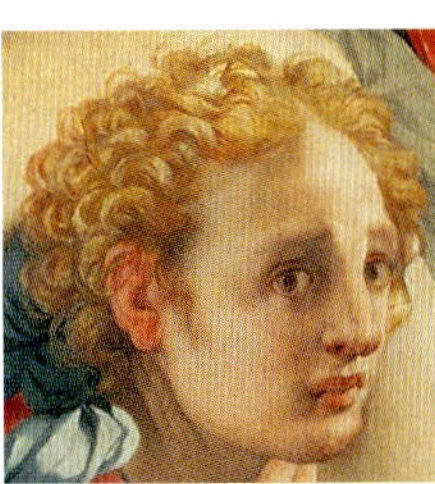

The melancholy angel-like figure, straining under the weight of Christ, looks out at the viewer as if appealing for help.

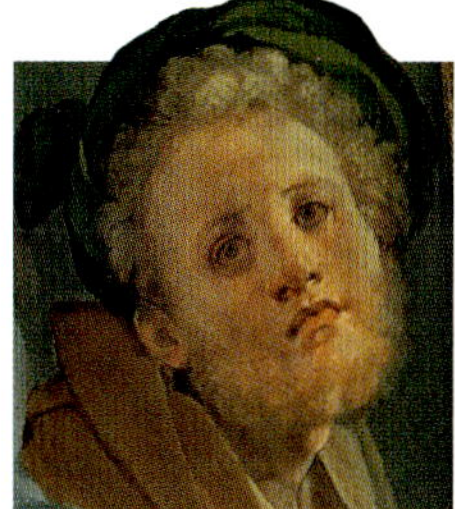

Pontormo may have included a self-portrait in this figure, possibly representing Joseph of Arimathea, who buried the body of Christ.

The oversize Virgin, with her voluminous blue robe, dominates the painting.

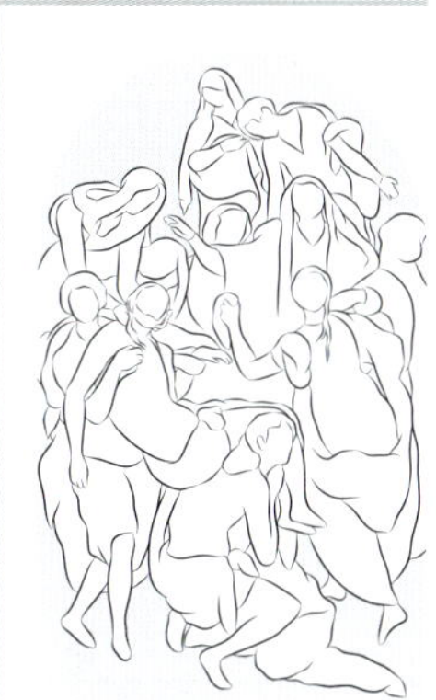

Illuminating effect
Extensive use of white lead underpainting gives the work a luminous, ethereal quality which befits its subject matter.

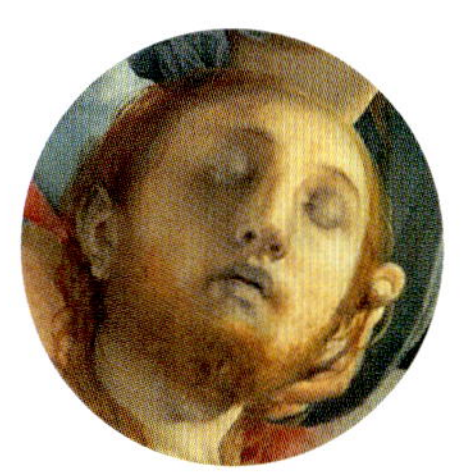

Sfumato
Pontormo paints Christ's face with soft *sfumato* shading in the manner of Leonardo da Vinci. The gentle gradation of the color conveys a sense of great calmness and beauty.

The dark foliage of the forest contrasts with Venus's pale skin.

Venus wears a feather-trimmed hat and a gold choker and chain. Cranach was court painter to the Saxon kings, and such accessories would have been fashionable in court circles.

The Latin inscription is based on a poem, "The Honeycomb Stealer," by the 3rd-century Greek poet Theocritus.

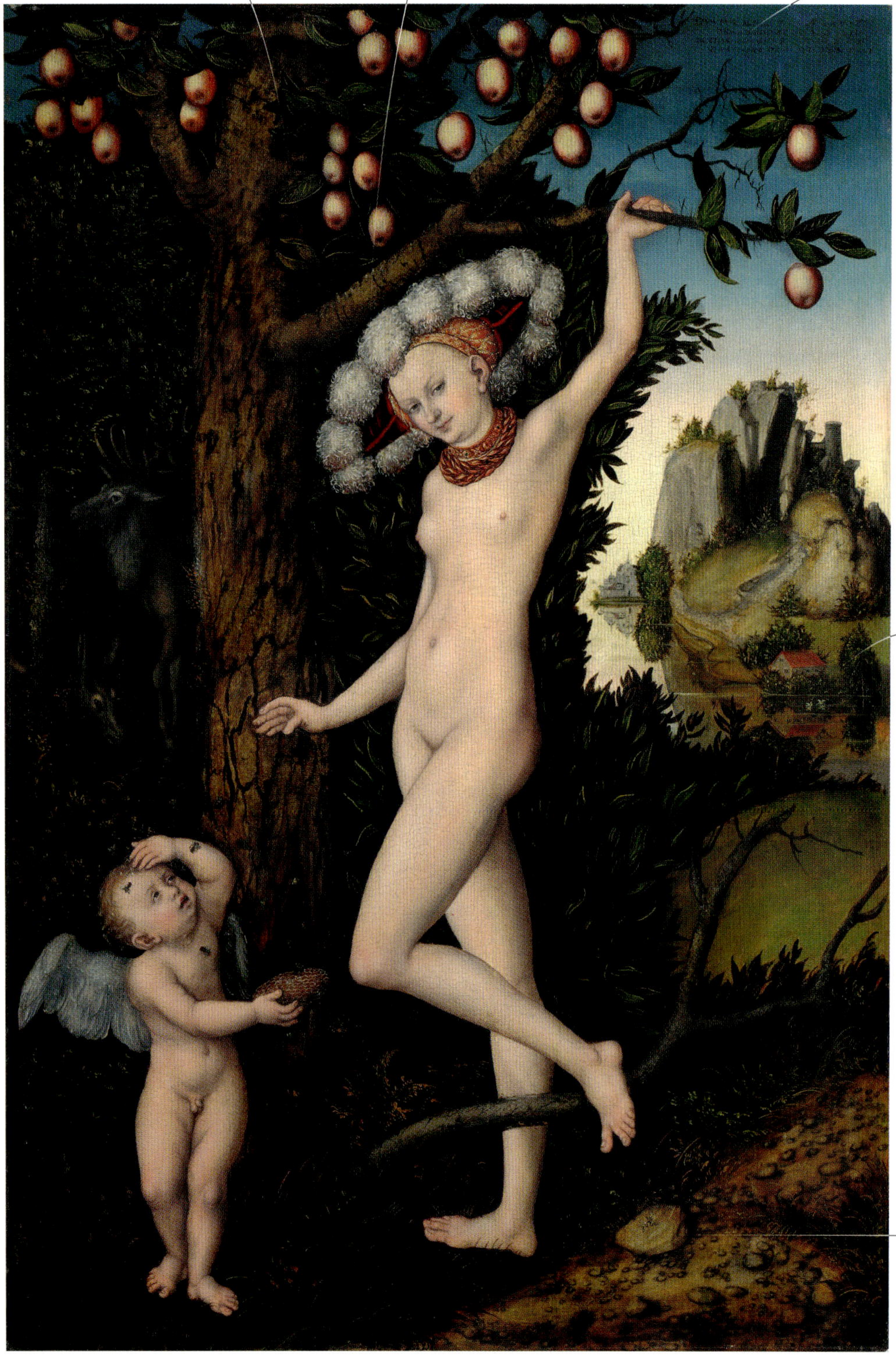

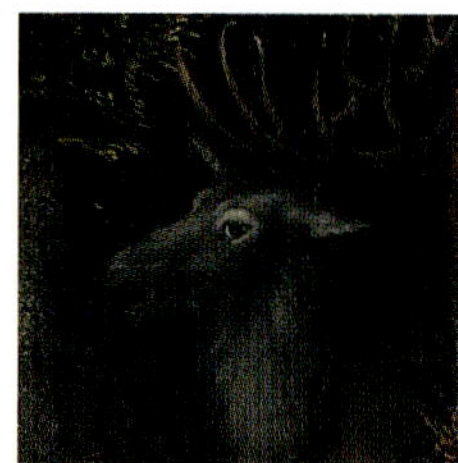

The stag and the doe were attractive to viewers who enjoyed hunting them. The stag also represented the resurrected Christ, while roe deer were known for their virtue and loyalty to one mate.

A rustic cottage and detailed trees are perfectly reflected in the still water.

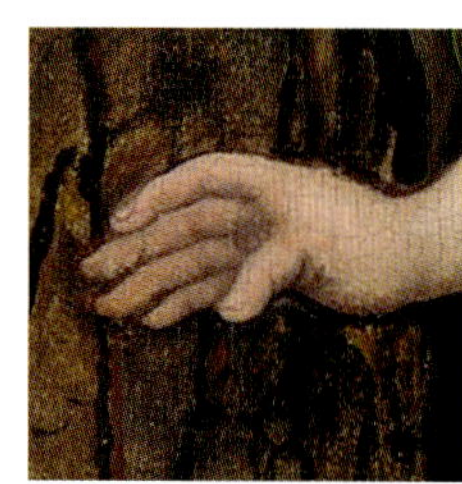

Venus raises her right arm. Her gesture tells Cupid that his arrows cause pain like the bee sting and pleasure like the sweet honey.

Cranach put his signature, or emblem, on this stone. He used the motif of a winged serpent with a crown on its head after Elector of Saxony Friedrich the Wise granted him a coat of arms in 1508.

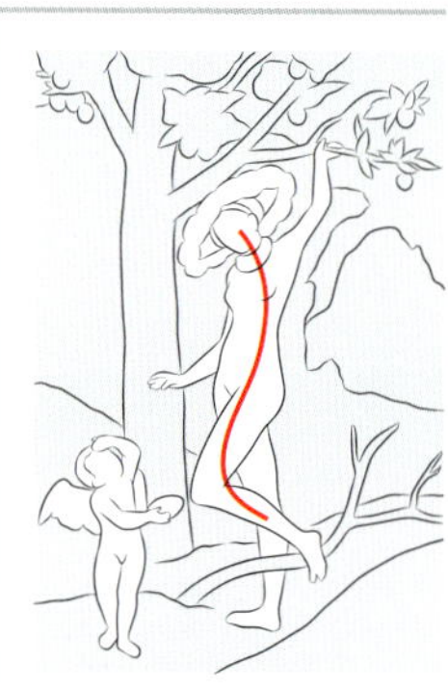

In Eve's shadow
Venus's sinuous S shape suggests her seductive powers. Her pose is almost the same as that of Eve in Cranach's *Adam and Eve*, which he painted shortly before this painting.

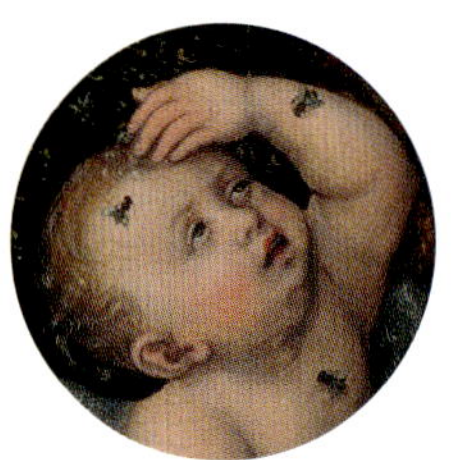

Exquisite detail
Cranach's skills are especially evident in the expression of anguish on Cupid's face and the rendering of his hair.

Cupid Complaining to Venus

Lucas Cranach the Elder 1526–1527, oil on wood, 32 × 21 in (81.3 × 54.6 cm), National Gallery, London, UK

In a moral message that short-lived pleasures derived from temptation can result in suffering, Cupid holds a honeycomb that he has taken from a bees' nest, the bees buzzing angrily around him. He complains of pain to his mother Venus, but she is uninterested; instead, she looks at the viewer, her arm raised seductively.

Queen Mother Pendant Mask: Iyoba

Artist unknown 16th century, ivory, 9 × 5 × 3 in (23.8 × 12.7 × 6.4 cm), Metropolitan Museum of Art, New York, US

This mask would have been worn over the hip or chest of the king, or *oba*, on ceremonial occasions. It is one of four ivory works representing Idia, the Queen Mother of Oba Esigie (reigned 1504–1550). It is an idealized portrait of a woman who was instrumental in helping her son retain the throne of the Benin Kingdom.

Her corona is composed of alternating representations of mudfish and Portuguese traders, both of whom come from the water and have liminal associations.

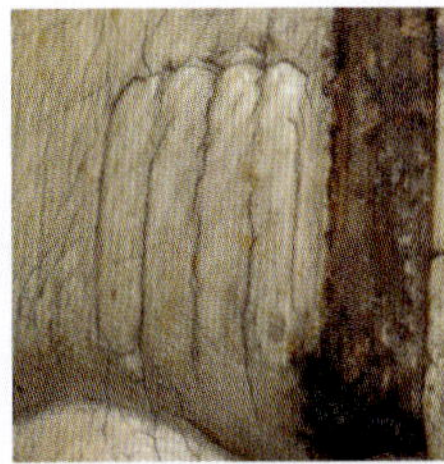

The four short vertical marks and larger, iron-inlaid bars over each eye indicate scarification—a source of power and prestige.

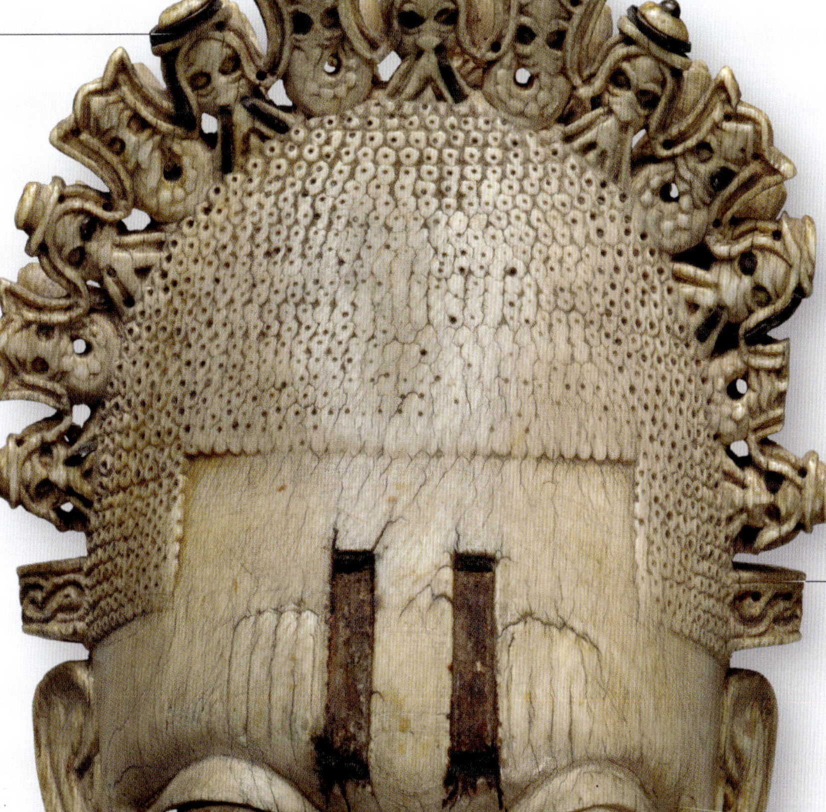

Mudfish survive the dry season by burrowing into the mud. They represent the supernatural aspects of Benin royalty.

Decorated loops were used to attach the pendant mask to the waistband of the wearer.

Metal was inlaid in the eyes. It was also added to the mudfish and Portuguese faces that frame the mask.

Bearded Portuguese sailors echo the upper corona while also alluding to economic prosperity gained by trade.

Only the open mouth and nostrils are pierced through to the back of the mask.

Beads represent the costly red coral beads worn by the Benin court and associated with Olokun, god of the sea.

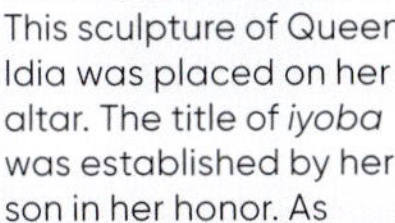

Commemorative head
This sculpture of Queen Idia was placed on her altar. The title of *iyoba* was established by her son in her honor. As with the hip mask, the eyes and vertical bars on this brass head were inlaid with iron that has since oxidized.

Stolen goods
The treasury of the Kingdom of Benin (now southern Nigeria) was looted during the British Punitive Expedition of 1897. Some museums and institutions are working to repatriate these objects.

Five angels create visual interest in the upper part of the painting, a space usually left blank on altarpieces.

The column in the background reflects the tradition of locating Christ's birth in a classical setting.

Joseph is relegated to the background as he struggles with the donkey that brought them to Bethlehem and will carry Mary and the baby on their flight to Egypt.

The midwife is physically affected by the brilliance of the Christ child.

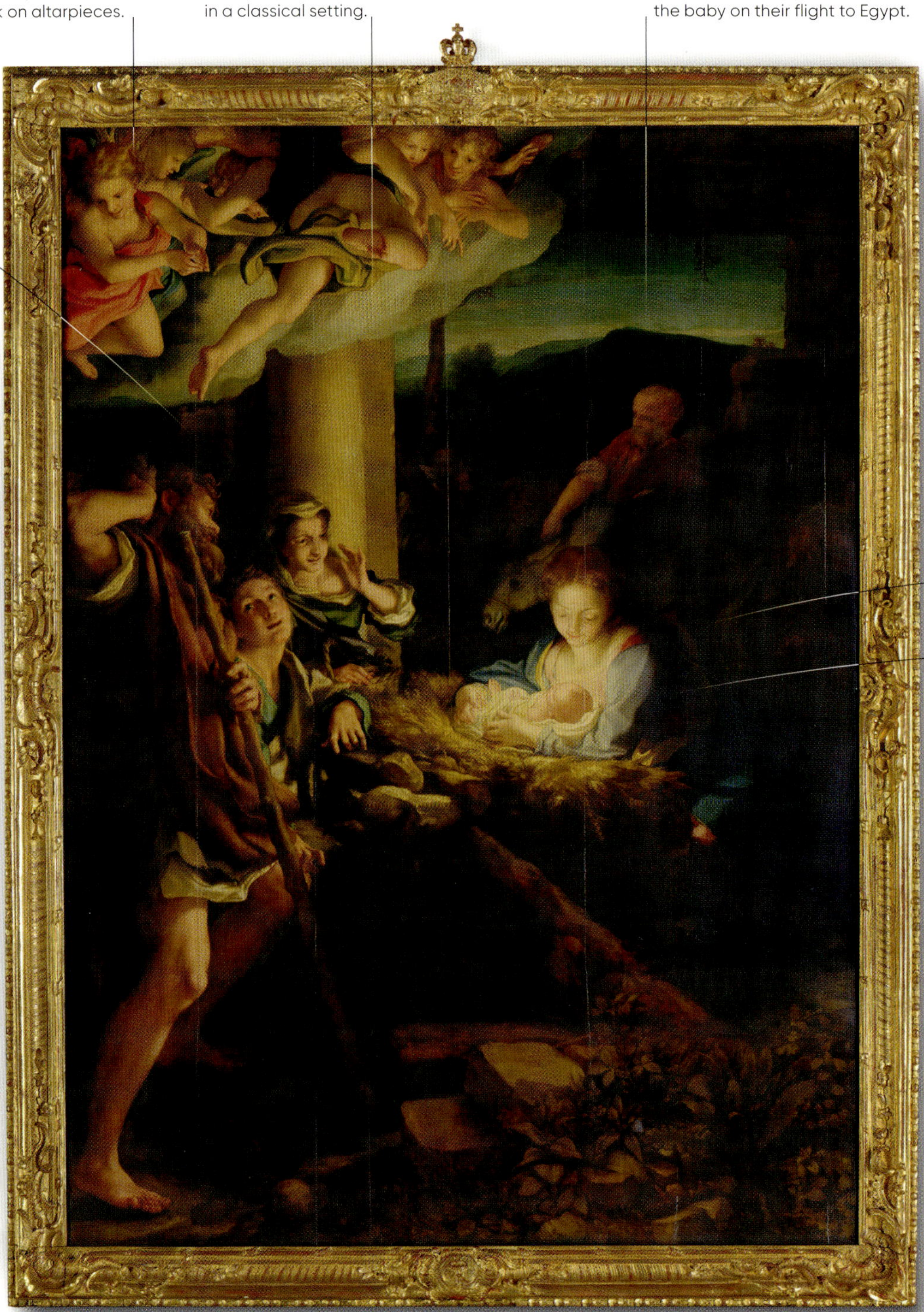

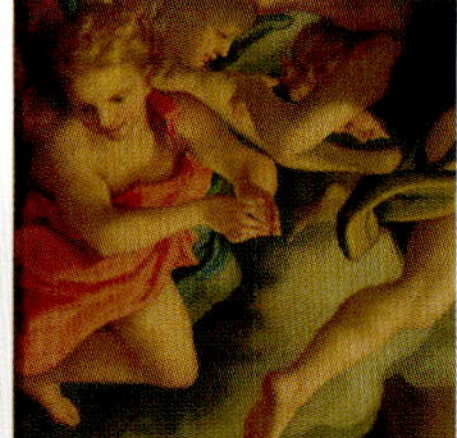

Foreshortening Transported on a cloud, the angels are shown in foreshortened perspective, adding to the illusion of depth.

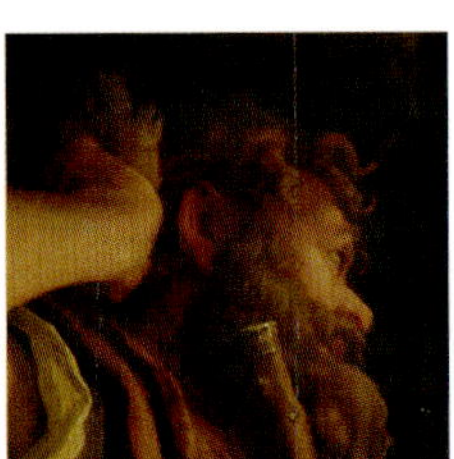

Rapture and perplexity are conveyed by the stance of the bearded shepherd as he takes off his hat in a gesture of respect.

Oblivious to the activity around her, Mary remains focused on her child. Her subtle smile was influenced by the work of Leonardo da Vinci.

Light emanates from the baby. It symbolizes his divinity and the miracle of his birth.

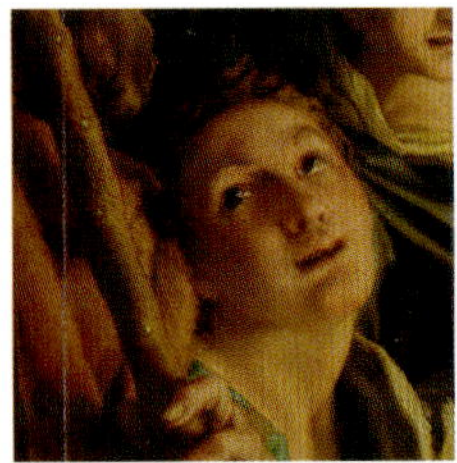

The face of the younger shepherd expresses pure joy. The ability to capture spiritual ecstasy helped establish Correggio's popularity.

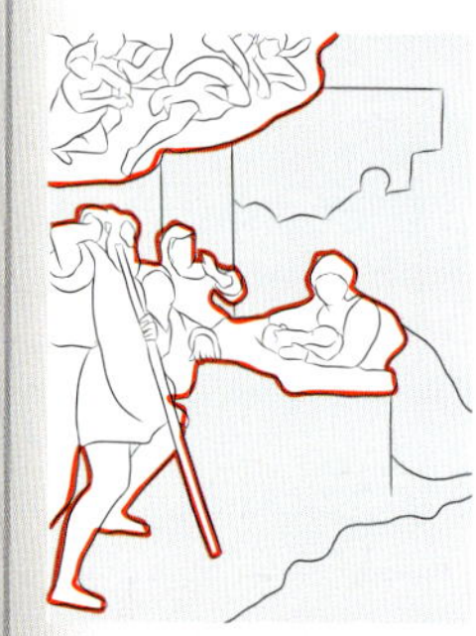

Highlights and lowlights Pockets of light draw attention to the action in the painting, forcing the eye to move around in search of component parts in shadow.

The Holy Night

Antonio Correggio c. 1528–1530, oil on panel, 101 × 74 in (256.5 × 188 cm), Gemäldegalerie Alte Meister, Dresden, Germany

Correggio captures the joy of the Holy Family, shepherds, and angels following Christ's birth. The arresting play of light and shadow conveys the sense of wonder among the protagonists and was intended to inspire a similar response in viewers of the work, which was created as an altarpiece.

Portrait of a Young Man

Bronzino 1530s, oil on panel, 38 × 29 in (95.6 × 74.9 cm), Metropolitan Museum of Art, New York, US

A handsome, fashionably dressed young man stares through the viewer with an enigmatic look that could be aristocratic aloofness or youthful arrogance.

Bronzino, who became court painter to the Medici family, was renowned for his striking Mannerist portraits of the Florentine elite.

His eyes look in two directions, a feature of Bronzino's portraits. It suggests his subjects may have secret inner lives.

An austere, windowless background rendered in tones of blue-gray does not distract from the subject of the painting.

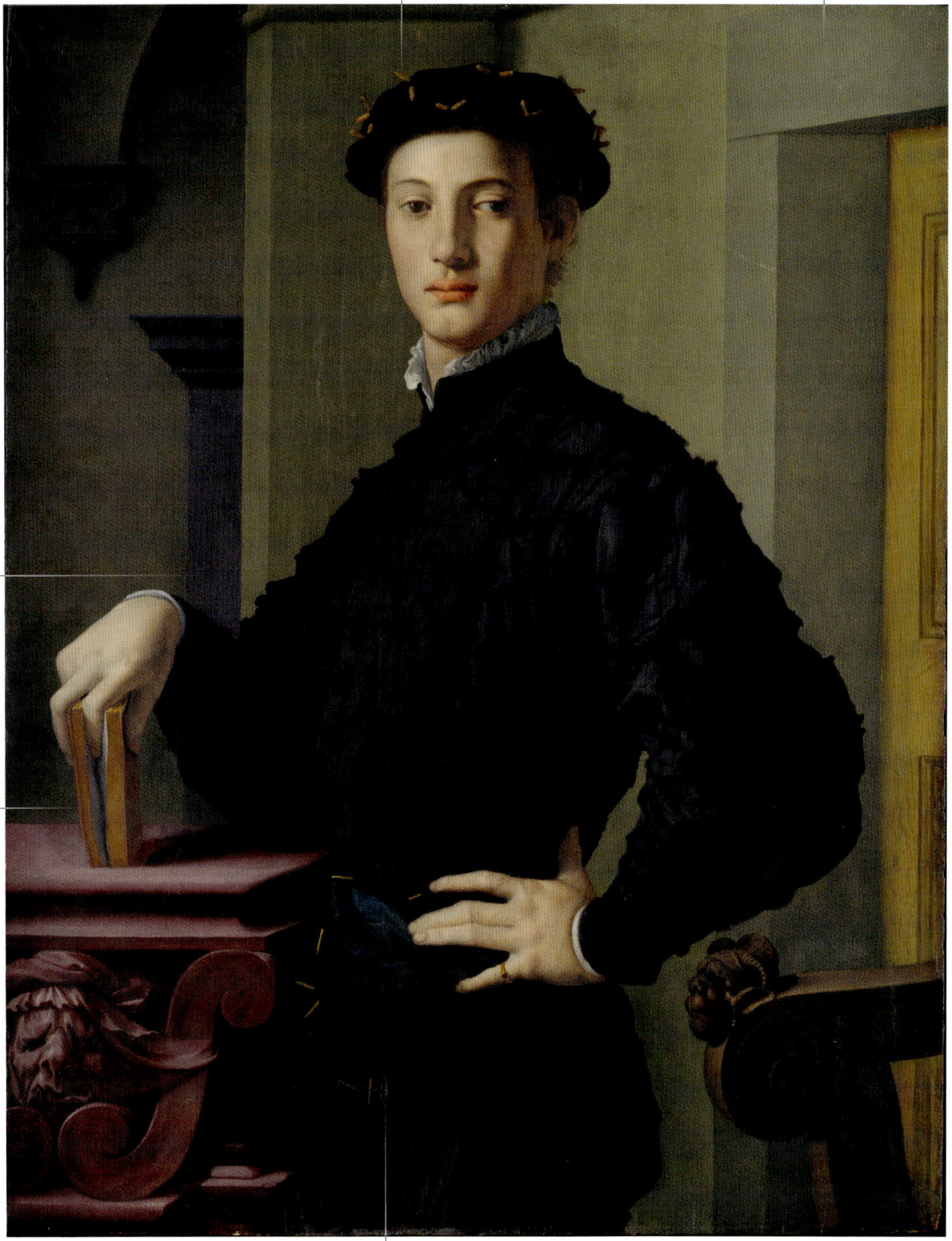

The man's elegant doublet is slashed to reveal a silk lining, in a style popular at this time.

This may be a volume of poetry. Bronzino was a poet and part of a sophisticated literary circle.

In a witty conceit, the young man's breeches create another mask.

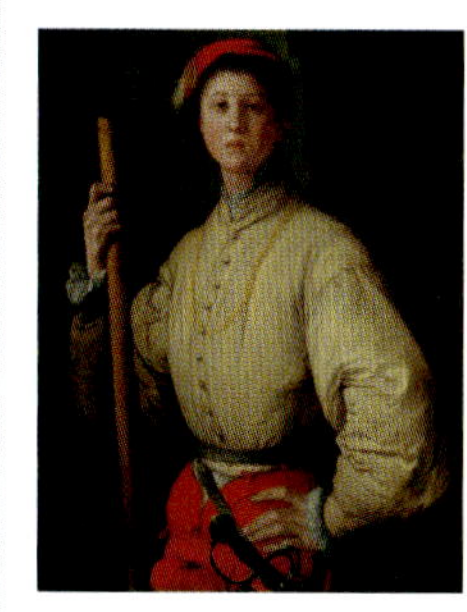

Pontormo's influence *Portrait of a Halberdier* (c. 1530), a work by Jacopo Pontormo, Bronzino's teacher, probably inspired the distinctive hand-on-hip pose.

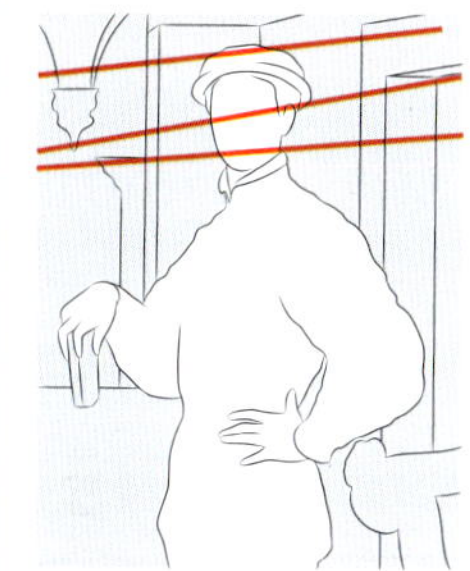

Breaking the rules Bronzino departed from the usual laws of perspective—the door panels, lintel, and molding on the wall above the door do not seem to have a common vanishing point.

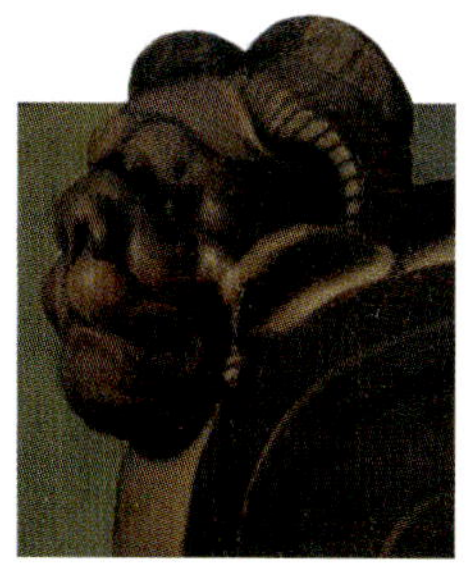

The masks may suggest that the young man's appearance is another form of mask.

Hawk on a Pine

Kanō Yukinobu mid-16th century, ink on paper, 33 × 16 in (83.5 × 41.7 cm), Metropolitan Museum of Art, New York, US

This striking image of a hawk perching on a pine branch is emblematic of the popular Kanō painting school in 16th-century Japan. Kanō artists such as Yukinobu adapted Chinese ink-painting techniques and styles to satisfy the aesthetic taste and symbolic preferences of their patrons among the Buddhist clergy and regional warlords. The style remained popular for around 300 years.

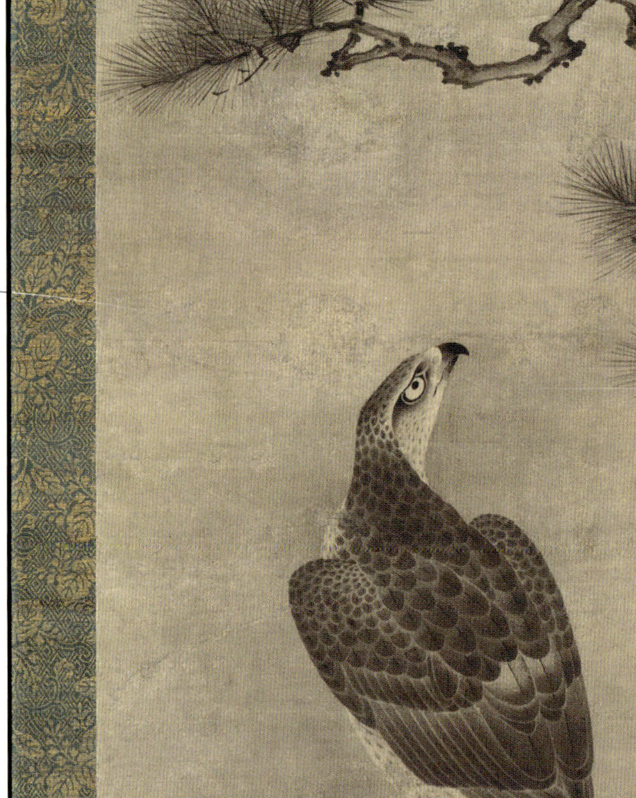

Pine needles are rendered with fine, overlapping lines of ink wash, in contrast to the thicker and darker brushwork of the branches.

This mainly empty space emphasizes the fragmentary nature of the painting. Parts of the pine tree emerge along the borders and at the corners, inviting the viewer to imagine the rest of the setting.

The precisely delineated eye of the hawk suggests sharp eyesight and a keen gaze, indicative of the strength that birds of prey symbolized.

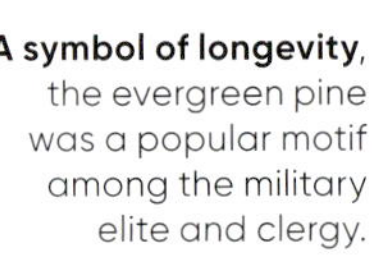

A symbol of longevity, the evergreen pine was a popular motif among the military elite and clergy.

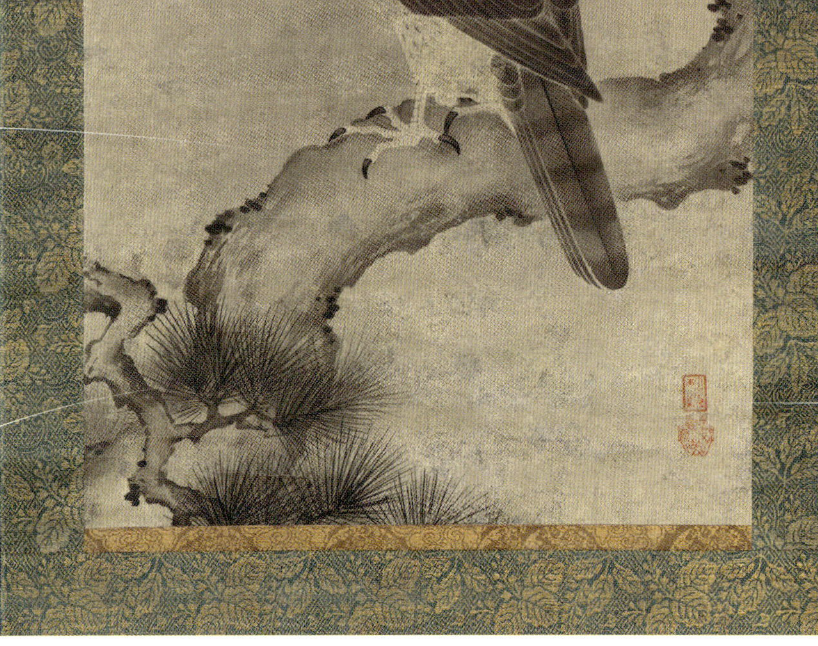

Pine needles have been painted on top of the tree trunk, creating a sense of shallow depth.

The two seals, which read *Moin*, are identified with the artist Kanō Yukinobu.

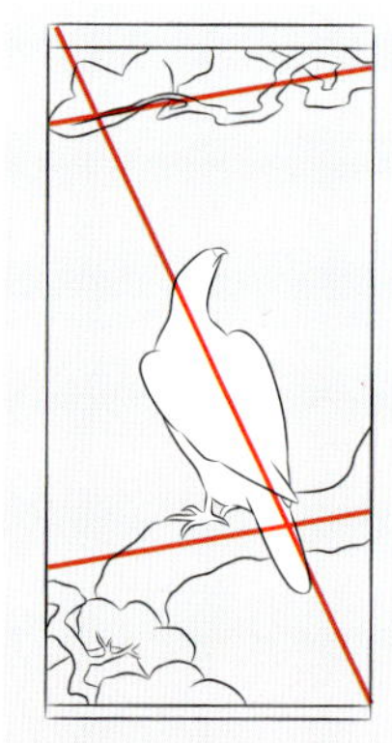

Composition
Centrally placed, the diagonal orientation of the hawk disrupts the parallel rhythm of the two pine branches that frame it. This creates visual tension.

Ink-painting
Yukinobu's refined technique recalls that of the founder of the Kanō school, Motonobu, who adopted the Chinese style to respond to demand from influential Zen temples.

The fine lines and controlled washes used for the bird's plumage convey a velvety texture.

Jean de Dinteville and Georges de Selve or The Ambassadors

Hans Holbein the Younger 1533, oil on oak panel, 81 × 82 in (207 × 209.5 cm), National Gallery, London, UK

This lavish double portrait shows off the affluence of the French ambassador and his friend, the Bishop of Lavaur. Holbein demonstrates his skillful rendering of textures in the sumptuous fabrics and furnishings, the visual richness of which is disrupted by the strangely distorted skull in the foreground.

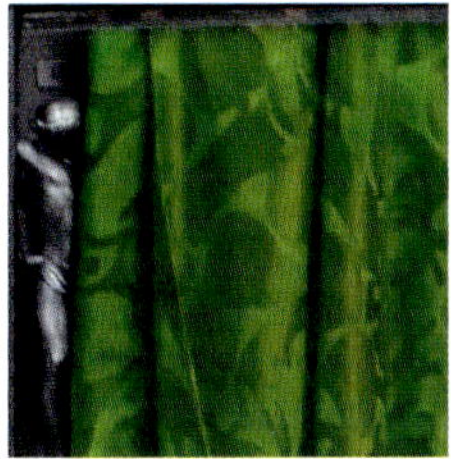

A crucifix is unveiled behind the sumptuous green damask curtain. It serves as a reminder of mortality and also introduces the concept of salvation.

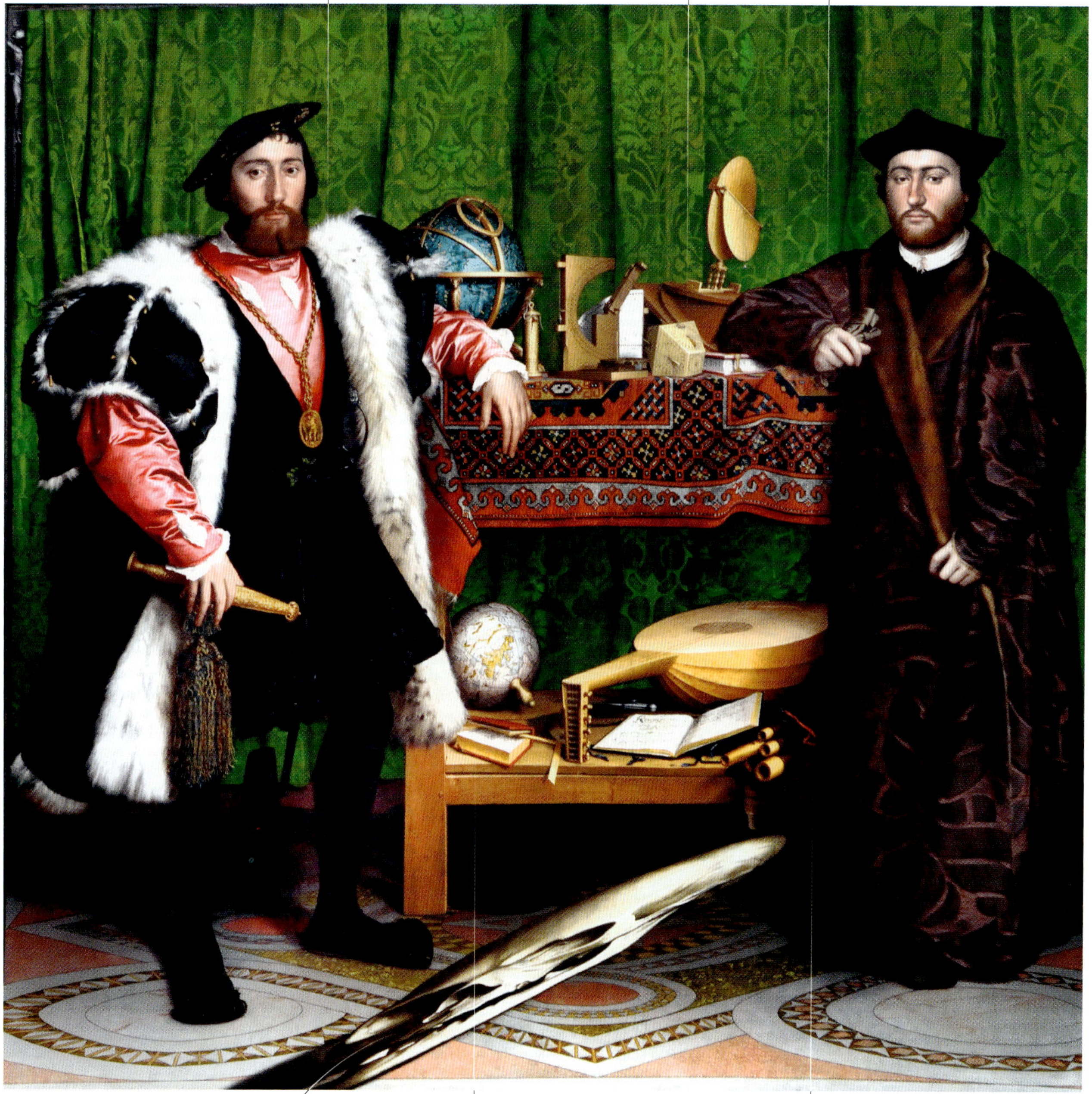

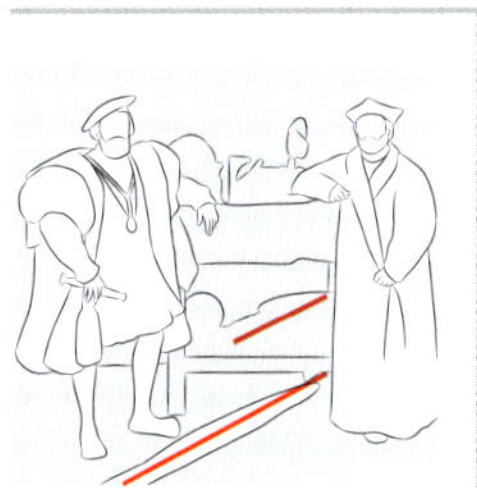

Creating illusions The foreshortening of the skull and the lute in parallel directions conveys the idea that perspective is a form of illusionism.

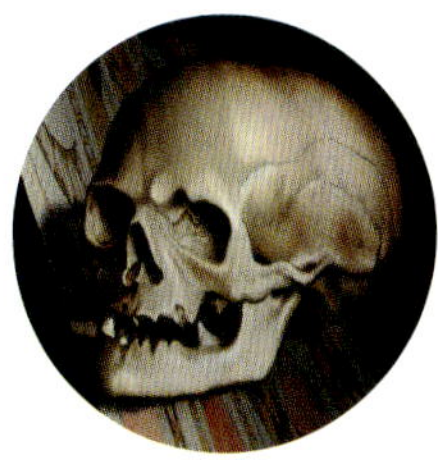

Distorted projection The skull is painted to create an effect called anamorphosis, in which the viewer must stand at a particular vantage point to see the non-distorted image

French ambassador Jean de Dinteville is shown dressed in pink satin, draped in a fur-lined cape, and clutching a gilded dagger.

Astronomical instruments and time-measuring tools lie on the table, highlighting the men's knowledge.

Bishop Georges de Selve's coat is meticulously painted, with fine brushstrokes representing individual strands of fur.

The skull functions as a memento mori, a poignant reminder of death in this otherwise celebratory portrayal of earthly pleasures.

A terrestrial globe on the lower shelf mirrors the celestial globe above, establishing a visual dialogue between the earthly and the divine.

The lute has a broken string, alluding to Henry VIII's split from the Roman Catholic Church in the year the work was painted.

Venus of Urbino

Titian 1538, oil on canvas, 47 × 65 in (119 × 165 cm), Uffizi, Florence, Italy

A beautiful nude woman calmly meets the viewer's gaze—is she a depiction of Venus, the goddess of love, as the title suggests, or a courtesan? Historians now believe she is a bride, preparing for *il toccamano*, a ceremony in which the woman wears formal clothing and consents to marriage by touching the hand of her betrothed, an interpretation supported by the symbolism in the painting. In the homes of the wealthy, nude images often decorated the bedroom, where they were thought to encourage maritally sanctioned fertility.

Figural pose
The classical pose is adapted from Roman statues commonly called *Venus pudica* (modest Venus) because a hand always hides the genitals. The painting influenced the work of other artists and began a revival of female nudity in art.

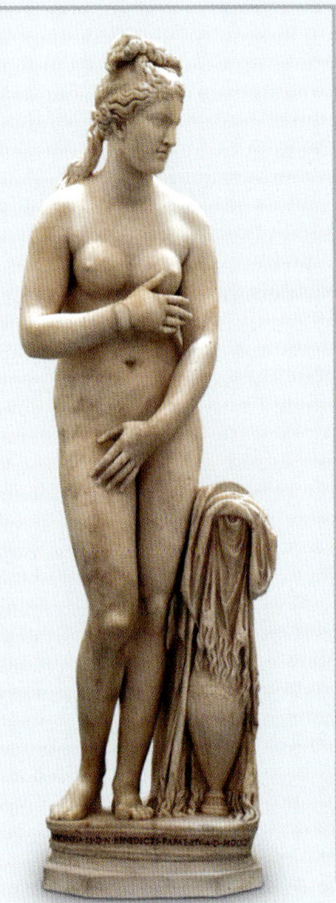

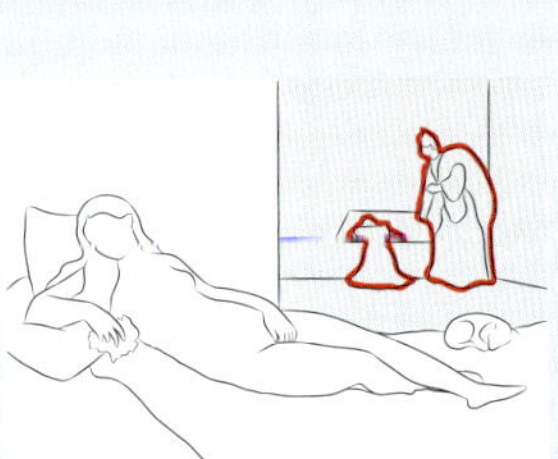

Perspective points
An L-shaped foreground places the viewer directly in front of the figure, perhaps kneeling. The maids' diminutive size indicates their distance.

> "So long as Nature lives Titian will also live. He was the very mirror of nature, only that the mirror reflects whilst Titian creates."
>
> Marco Boschini, 1664

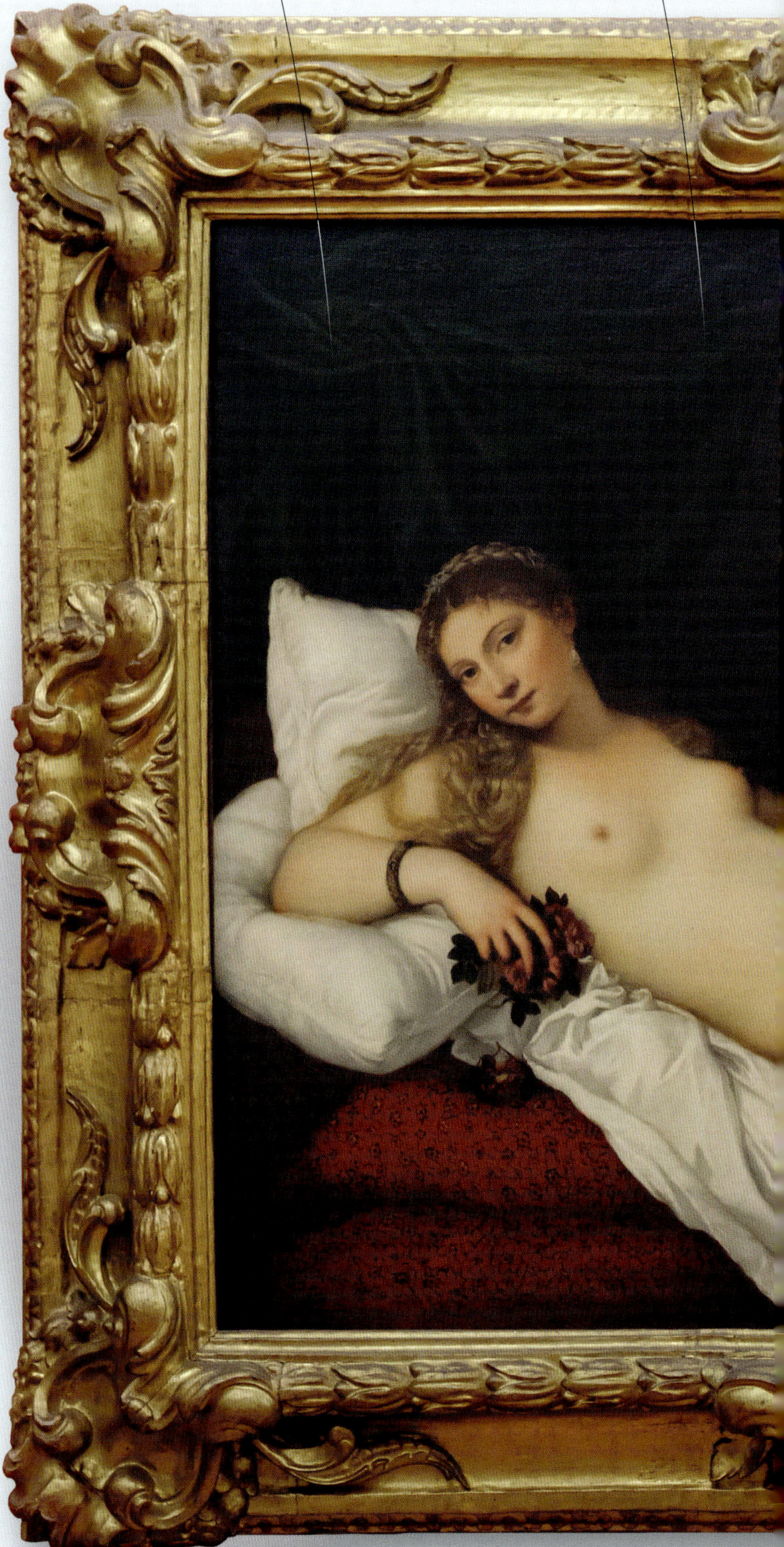

A red posy draws out the blush in the woman's skin.

The soft rendering of the velvet curtain and smooth sheen of the sheets show Titian's gift for painting texture.

Two maids are working at the *cassone*, a wedding chest designed to hold the bride's trousseau.

The maid holds a blue and gold dress over her shoulder, an expensive gown with ruffled details.

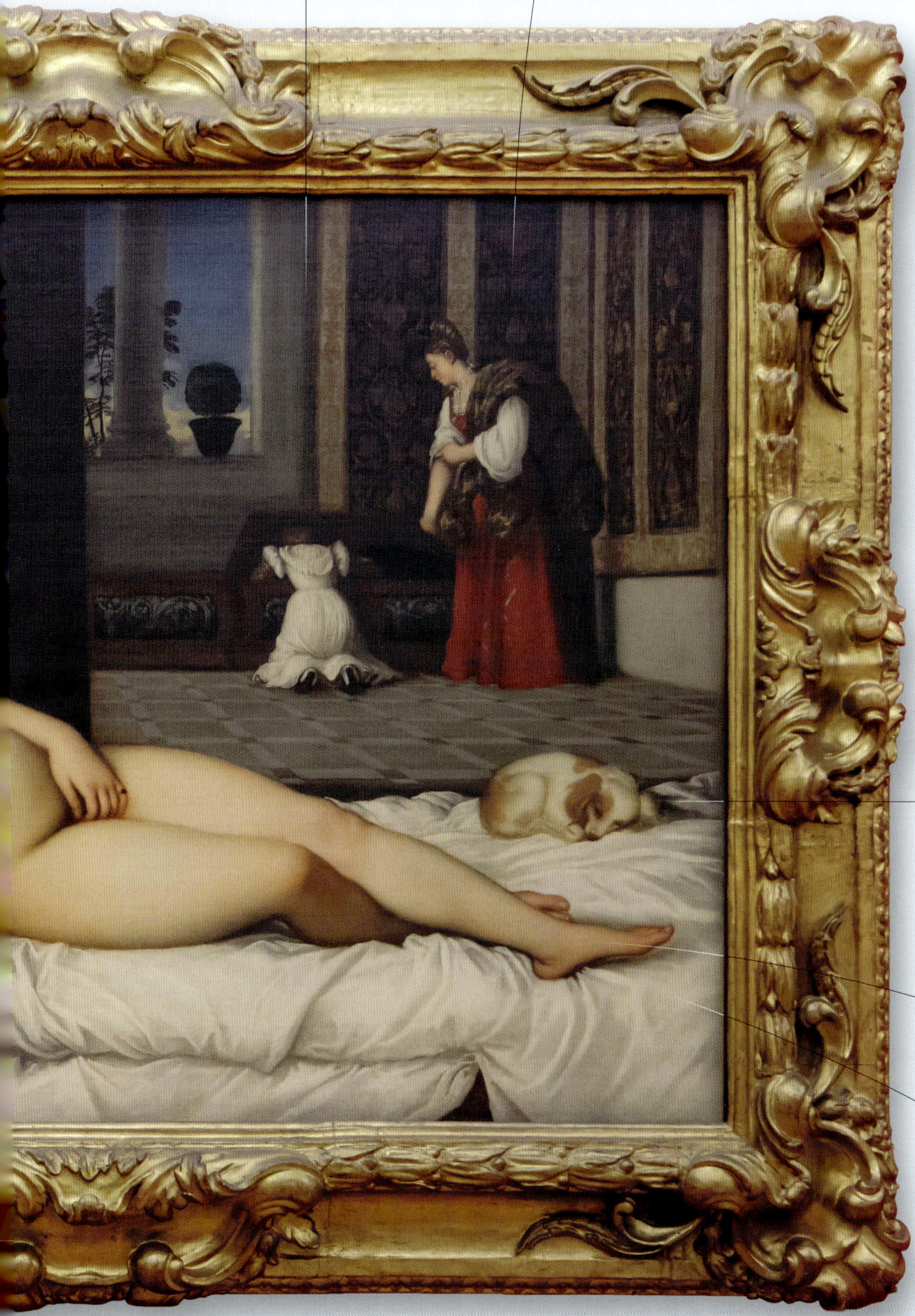

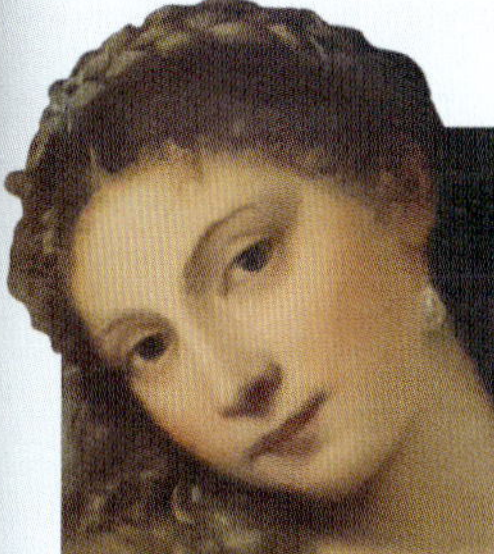

Young Italian women only wore their hair down when single. This woman also wears pearls, which symbolize sexual purity.

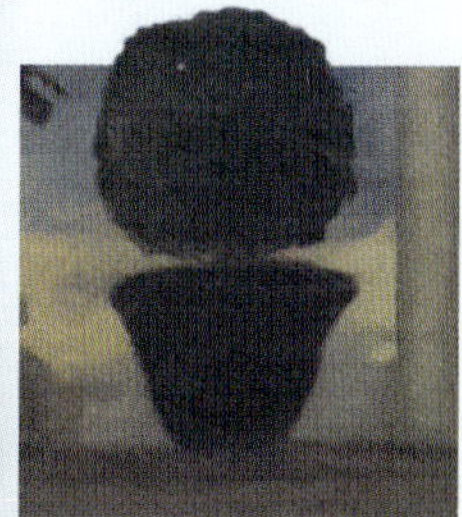

Myrtle can be seen in the window. Sacred to Venus, the plant is associated with love and desire.

Dogs represent fidelity. This puppy appears in another Titian painting, *Portrait of Eleonora Gonzaga, Duchess of Urbino* (1537).

The modeling of the flesh creates an impression of sensuality.

Titian used the same model in his painting *Girl in a Fur* (c. 1535).

Madonna with the Long Neck

Parmigianino 1534–1540, oil on panel, 85 × 52 in (216.5 × 132.5 cm), Uffizi, Florence, Italy

A fine example of Mannerist elegance and harmony, Parmigianino's *Madonna* has fascinated art historians for its eccentricity. Instead of conforming to Renaissance ideals of naturalism and classical proportions, Parmigianino distorted his figures, because he believed artists should create rather than copy.

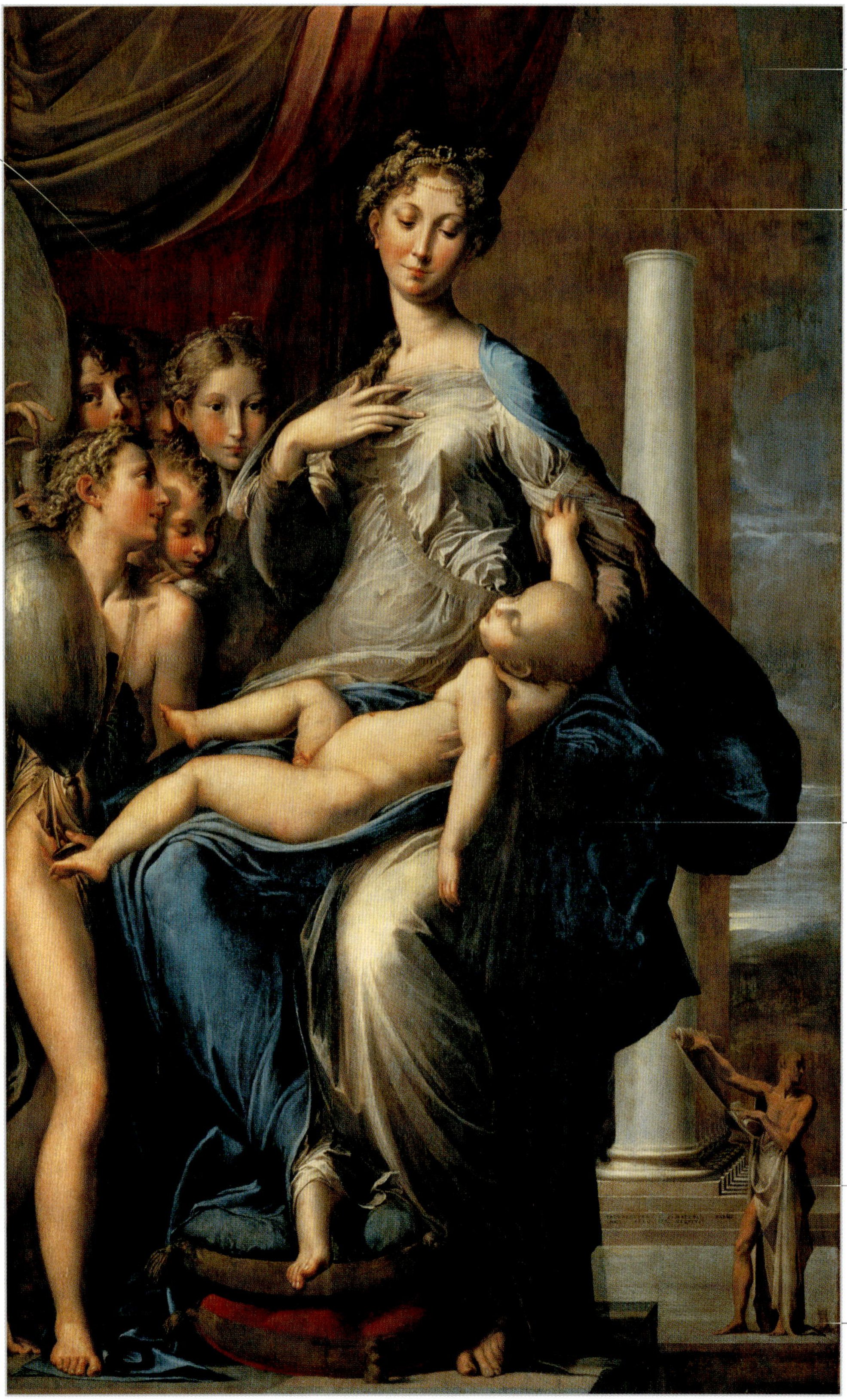

Parmigianino conveyed the scene as a revelation, the curtains theatrically drawn back to reveal the Virgin and Child with six angels.

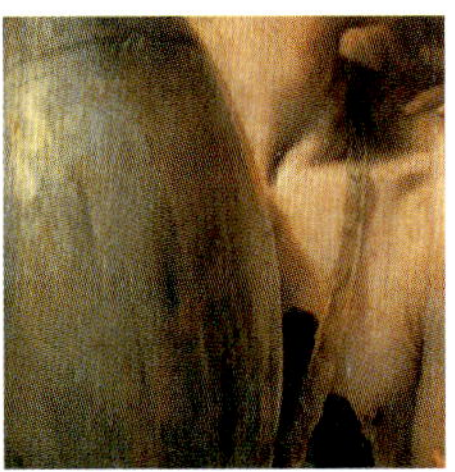

An angel holds an amphora on which appears an image of the cross—an allusion to Christ's Crucifixion.

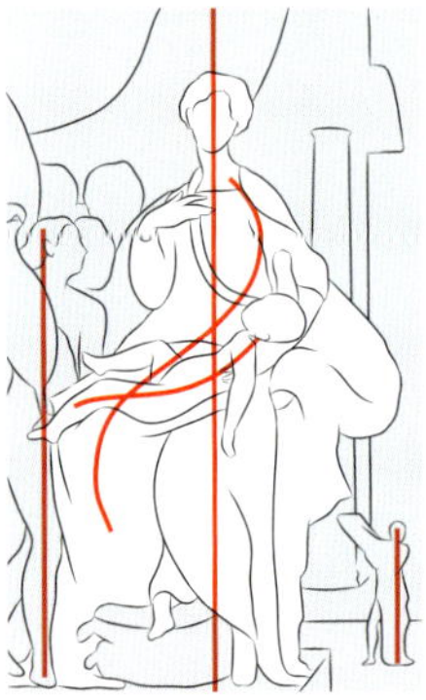

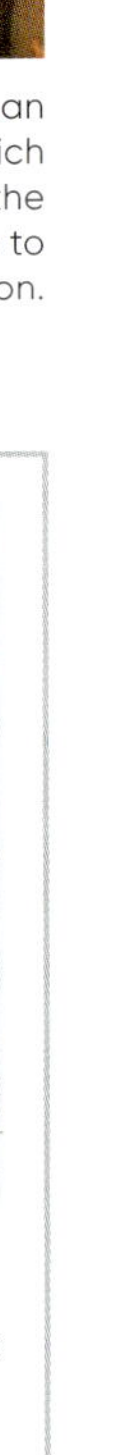

Echoing lines
A serpentine line down the Virgin's body weaves either side of the central axis. Curving lines through Christ's body echo the vertical line, as do the lines through the angel and St. Jerome.

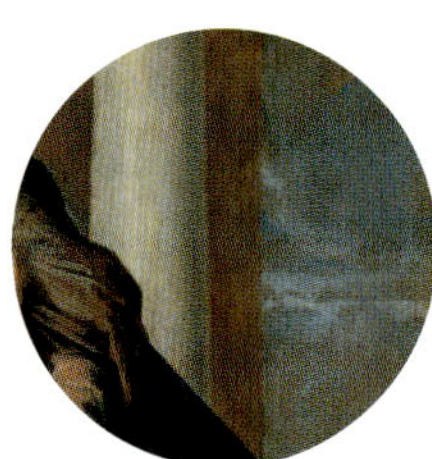

Colored ground
The unfinished area shows how the painting was built up in thin layers of paint over a colored ground.

The painting is unfinished. More of the temple was planned for the top right section of the canvas.

Mary's exaggerated beauty and elongated but graceful form are typical features of Mannerism.

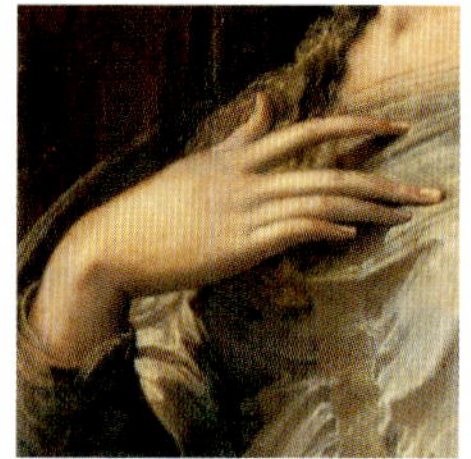

The hand on Mary's breast suggests the *Virgo Lactans* (nursing Madonna), a common subject among Renaissance artists.

This pose, with the Christ Child's left arm dangling lifelessly is similar to a pietà—an image of Mary holding her dead son.

In a strange change of scale, the small figure reading a scroll is St. Jerome, champion of Mary's Immaculate Conception.

The foot suggests that another figure was due to be added.

Lidded salt cellar

Artist unknown 15th–16th century, ivory, 12 × 4 in (29.8 × 10.8 cm), Metropolitan Museum of Art, New York, US

Exquisitely detailed and elegantly proportioned, this vessel was created by the Sapi peoples in what is today Sierra Leone to sell to European customers. Meant to hold salt, a precious commodity in the 16th century, it would have been a prestigious and interesting addition to a dining table. The object exemplifies the carver's skill and ability to blend European and African styles and motifs.

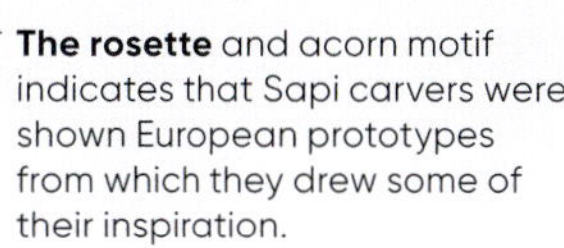

The rosette and acorn motif indicates that Sapi carvers were shown European prototypes from which they drew some of their inspiration.

This openwork carving is in visual conversation with the snakes and ridge-back dogs below, and emphasizes the piece's verticality.

The zigzag seam marks the divide between the lid and bowl of the salt cellar.

Serpents slither down the central section to confront the dogs face to face.

Two male warriors, holding swords and shields, and two women, finely dressed and wearing necklaces and skirts, adorn the base.

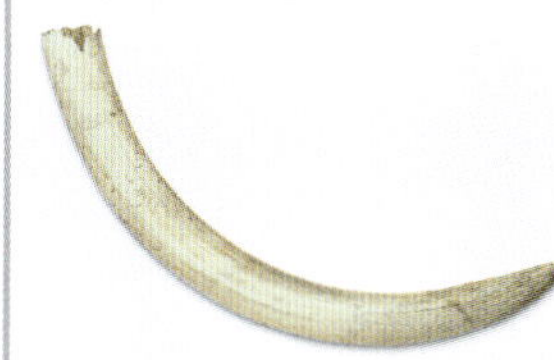

Ivory
Early European traders referred to elephant tusk ivory as "white gold." It is conducive to capturing and retaining detail and can be polished to a beautiful luster.

The Sapi people
Now dispersed, the Sapi people once lived along the western Guinea coast. Their descendants include the Baga, Bullom, and Landuma peoples who now live in Guinea and Sierra Leone.

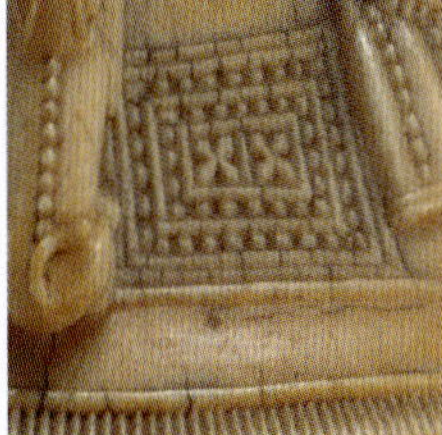

The textile-like, precisely carved sections at the base add visual variety and texture.

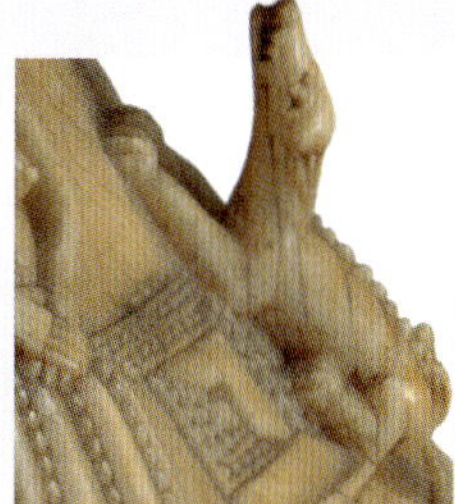

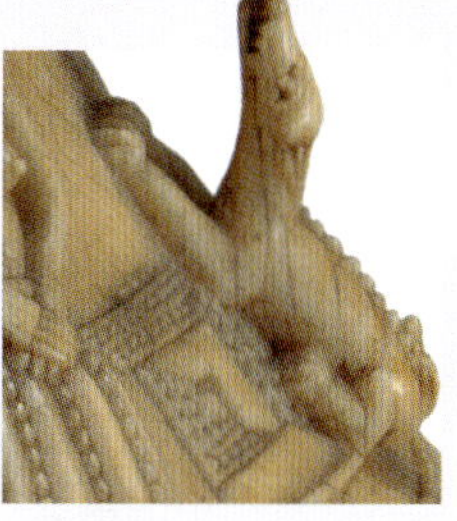

The dogs, considered spiritually intelligent by the Sapi people, add tension. Their teeth are bared, their ears are laid back, and the hair bristles along their backs.

Perseus with the Head of Medusa

Benvenuto Cellini c. 1545–1554, bronze, 120 in (306 cm), plinth: 84 in (213 cm), Loggia dei Lanzi, Piazza della Signoria, Florence, Italy

In Greek mythology, Perseus kills Medusa, one of the three Gorgons who turned people to stone if they looked at them. In Cellini's sculpture, commissioned by Cosimo de' Medici and placed outside Florence's town hall, Perseus holds Medusa's head up while his foot rests on her lifeless body.

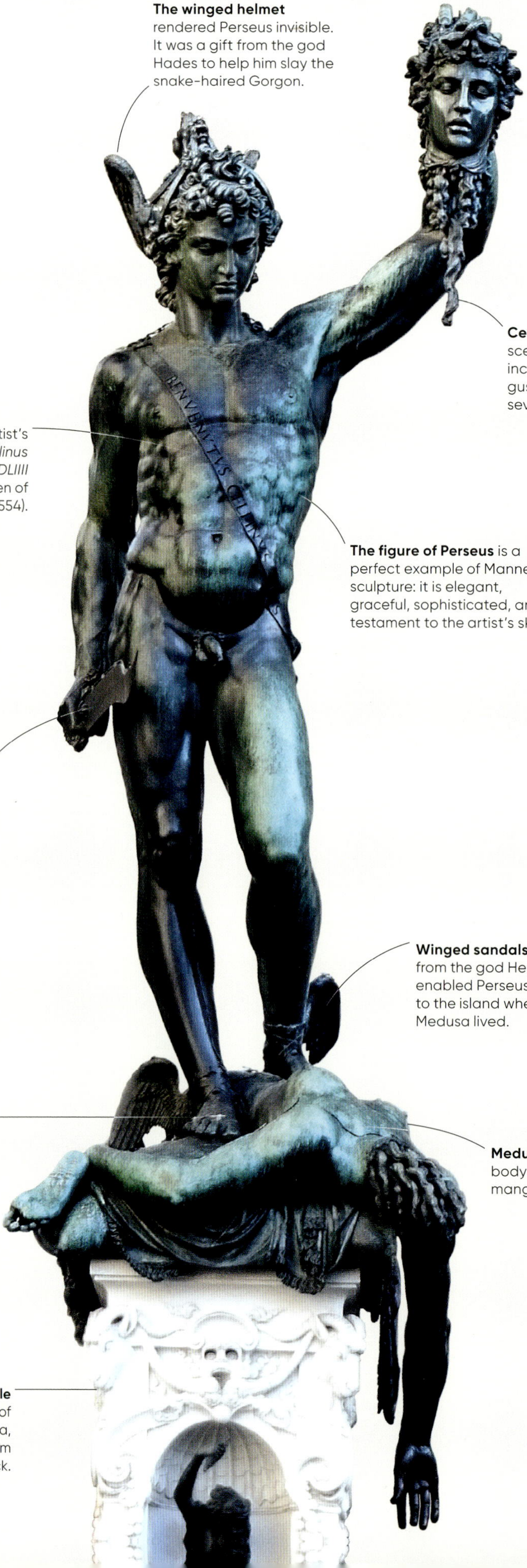

The winged helmet rendered Perseus invisible. It was a gift from the god Hades to help him slay the snake-haired Gorgon.

Cellini presents the scene in all its goriness, including the blood gushing from Medusa's severed head and neck.

This strap carries the artist's signature: *Benvenutus Cellinus Civis Flor Faciebat MDLIIII* (Benvenuto Cellini, citizen of Florence, made in 1554).

The figure of Perseus is a perfect example of Mannerist sculpture: it is elegant, graceful, sophisticated, and a testament to the artist's skill.

According to Greek mythology, Zeus gave Perseus the sword. Cellini's sword was replaced by a copy in 1945 due to deterioration.

Winged sandals, a gift from the god Hermes, enabled Perseus to fly to the island where Medusa lived.

Perseus stands triumphantly on the lifeless body of Medusa.

Medusa's decapitated body is reduced to a mangled heap.

Panels on the marble base depict the story of Perseus and Andromeda, a beautiful princess whom he rescues from a rock.

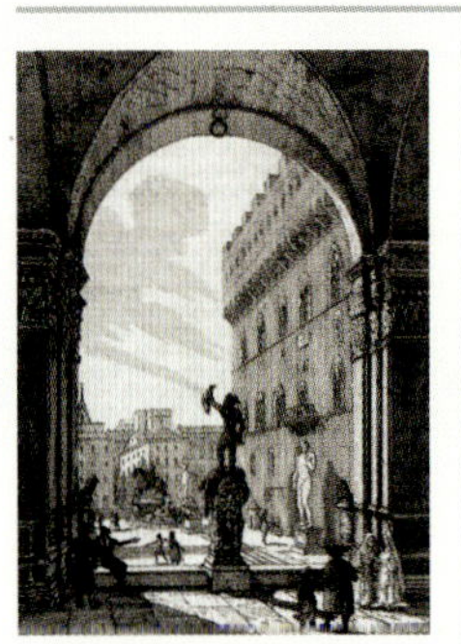

Political point
Florence's Piazza della Signoria also contained Michelangelo's *David* and Bandinelli's *Hercules*, both symbols of the Republic of Florence. By placing *Perseus with the Head of Medusa* opposite these statues, Cosimo de' Medici was asserting his power over the city-state.

Sculptural success
Casting such a large sculpture from bronze was technically difficult as the metal was likely to become too cool to flow into all the spaces in the mold. Managing to do so was a great achievement.

Spring Dawn in the Han Palace (detail)

Qiu Ying c. 1545–1552, handscroll, ink and colors on silk, 12 × 226 in (30.6 × 574.1 cm), National Palace Museum, Taipei, Taiwan

This section of a long handscroll painting is a fantasy glimpse into the amusements of palace ladies, shut away in luxurious quarters from which most men were banned. The artist, who painted during the Ming Dynasty (1368–1644), set it in the distant past of the Han Dynasty (202 BCE–220 CE) to avoid charges of voyeurism. Many of the figures are modeled on women in older palace-lady paintings.

This group of women sewing together at an embroidery frame is a quotation from a painting of court ladies attributed to the Tang painter Zhou Fang (c. 730–800).

A court lady tends to two small children.

A female official of the women's quarters is dressed in a man's robe and headgear to indicate her position.

The palace's green-painted beams and carved white marble plinth do not resemble actual Han Dynasty architecture, but are a Ming fantasy of imperial decor.

A table laden with books, scrolls, and antiques alludes to the refined pleasures of the collector.

The ornamental garden rocks in the palace courtyard are painted bright blue, enhancing the scene's unreality.

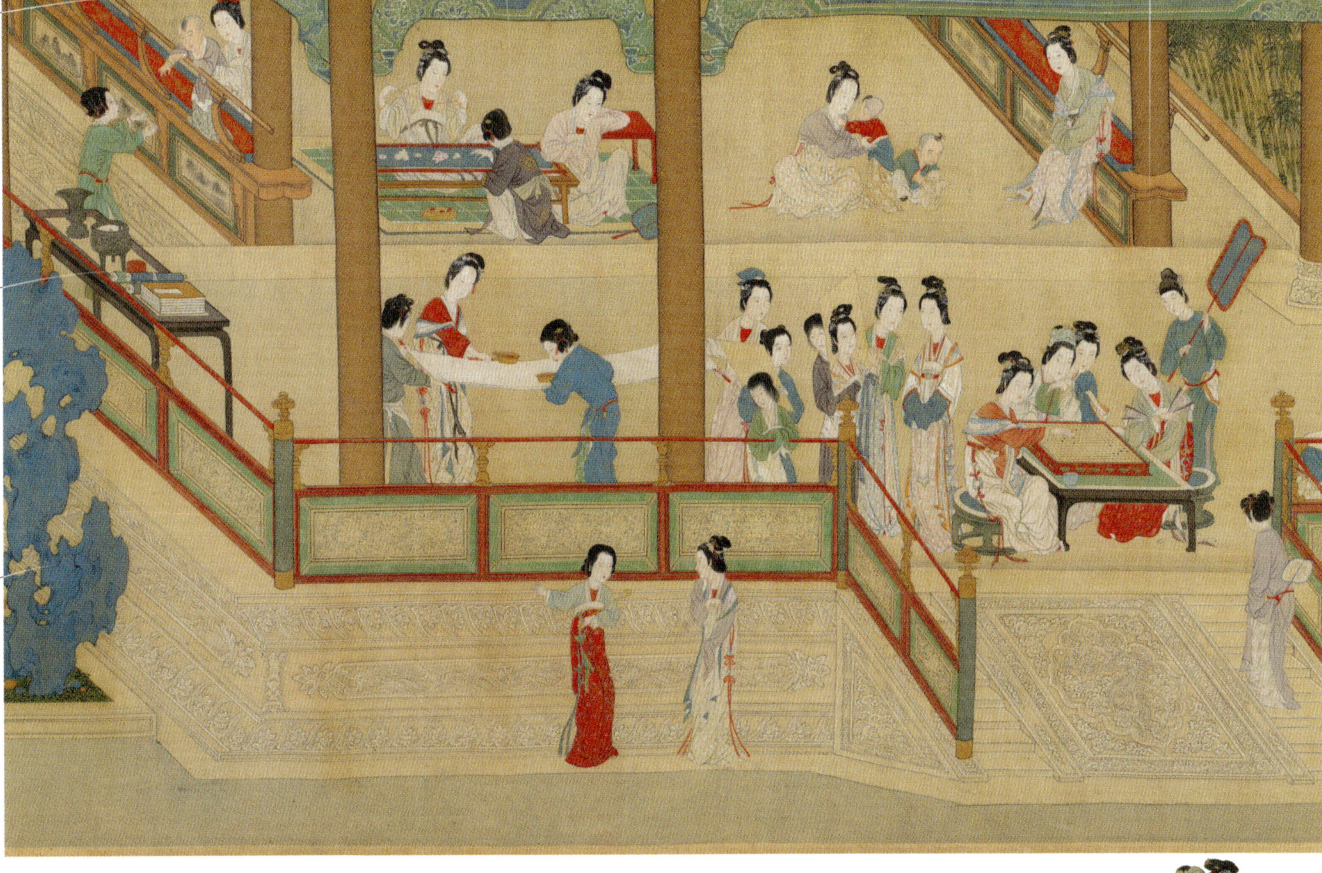

These women, ironing a length of silk, are taken from a painting of court ladies preparing silk, after the Tang painter Zhang Xuan (713–755).

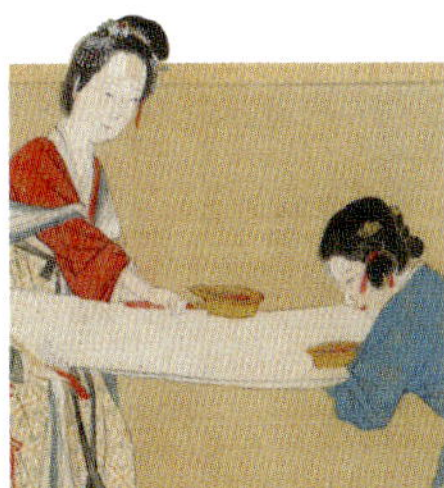

Various courtly activities are included, such as looking in the mirror, dancing, singing, and dressing up.

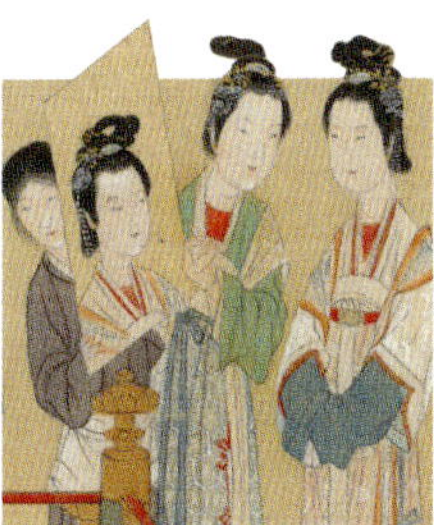

Weiqi, a game also known by its Japanese name, "Go," was a genteel pastime in the Ming era.

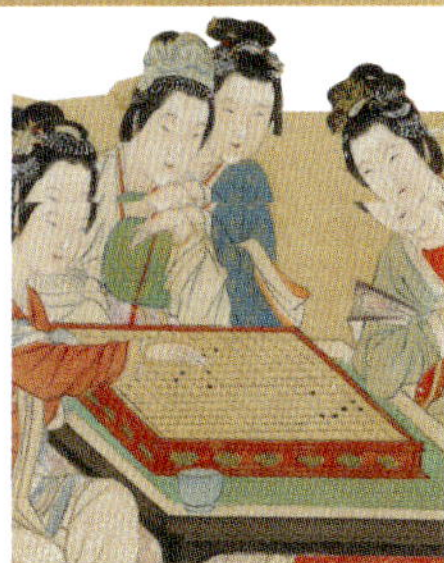

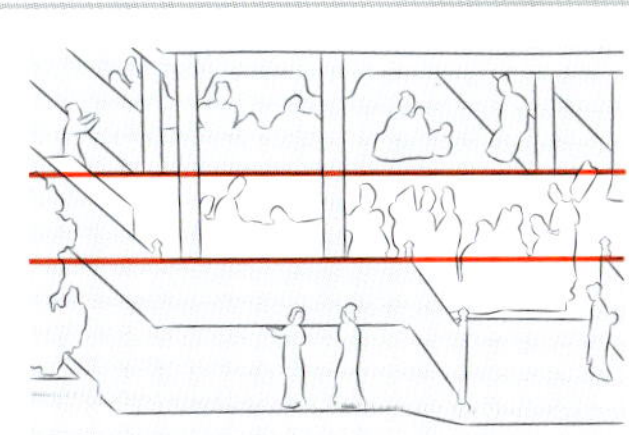

Private view
An elevated viewpoint enables the viewer to see inside the palace. The scene is divided horizontally into three private spaces: the courtyard in the foreground, the columned porch in the mid-ground, and the palace interior in the background.

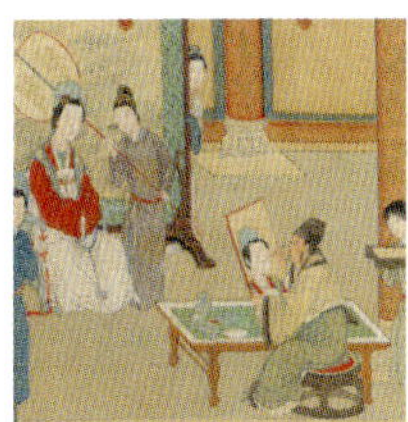

Reference to a legend
In one scene, an artist is shown painting the court ladies. According to legend, Wang Zhaojun, the most beautiful, is the only one who does not bribe the artist, so he makes her ugly. When the emperor later realizes his error in giving her away on the basis of the portrait, he has the artist executed.

Self-portraits

Artists in antiquity are known to have painted self-portraits, but it was in Renaissance Europe that they gained popularity among artists and their clients. During this time artists became public figures. Wanting painting to be recognized as a profession rather than a craft, many artists presented themselves surrounded by signs of learning and worldly success. Others treated self-portraiture as an exploration of identity, painting themselves repeatedly through their lives, recording their ups and downs in fortune and their evolving painting style. The subject of a self-portrait was always a willing model who did not expect to be paid.

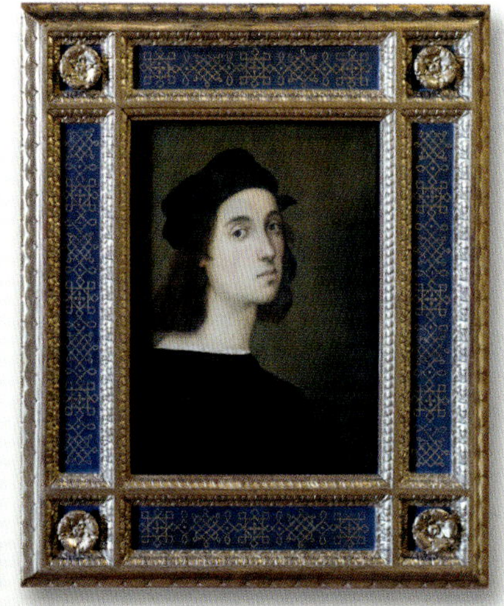

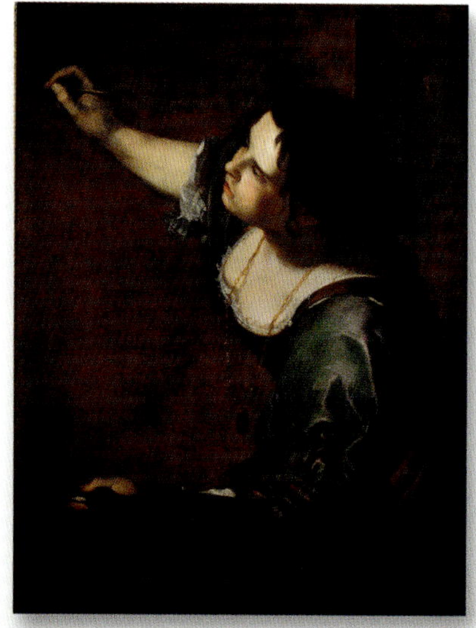

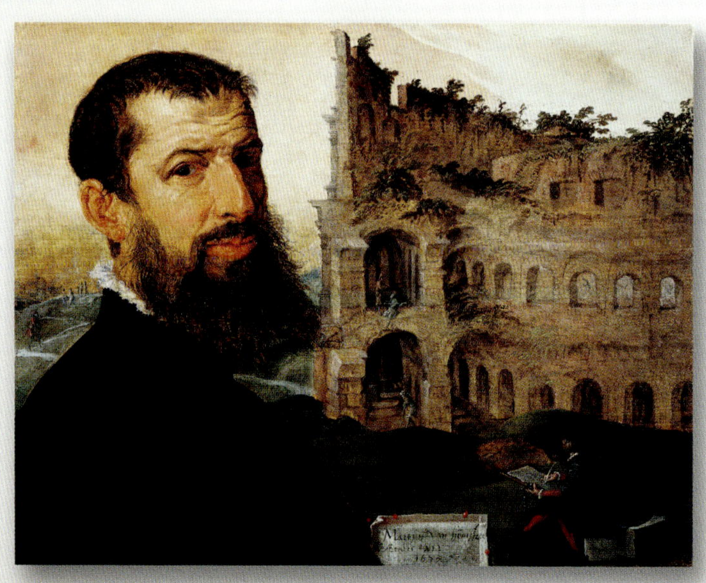

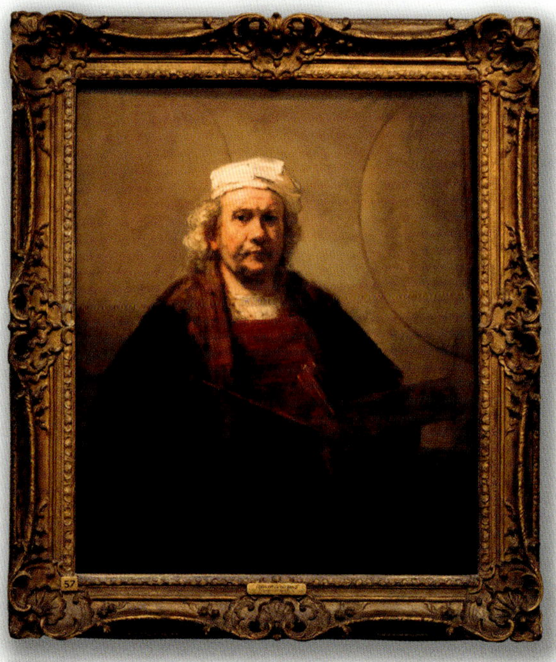

1. ***Self-Portrait*, Raphael, 1506.** In this small panel painting, executed when he was in his early twenties, Raphael represents himself as a thoughtful and elegant young man. With its careful modeling, it shows the technical brilliance and restraint for which he was already famous.

2. ***Self-Portrait, with the Colosseum, Rome*, Maarten van Heemskerck, 1553.** The artist presents himself as a learned individual. He has included the figure of an artist drawing, creating a double self-portrait: of himself at work and as the creator of the painting.

3. ***Self-Portrait as the Allegory of Painting (La Pittura)*, Artemisia Gentileschi, 1638.** Gentileschi combines a self-portrait with a personification of Painting as a woman. The way in which she is depicted shows her extreme self-confidence.

4. ***Self-Portrait with Two Circles*, Rembrandt, 1665.** In one of his last self-portraits, started when he was 59, Rembrandt paints himself in the studio. Rembrandt was a prolific self-portraitist and painted his own image at least 85 times. These works show how his style developed.

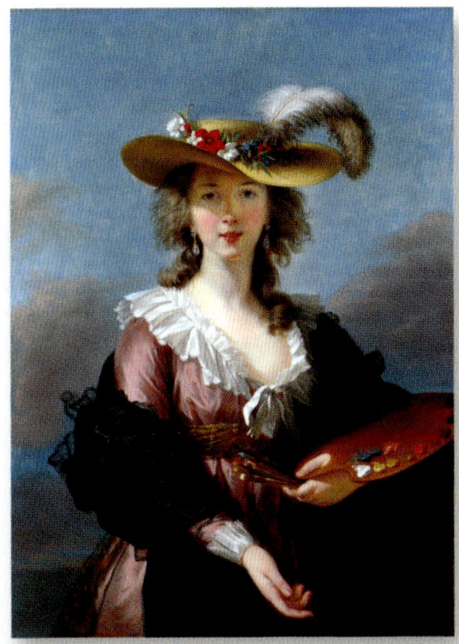

5

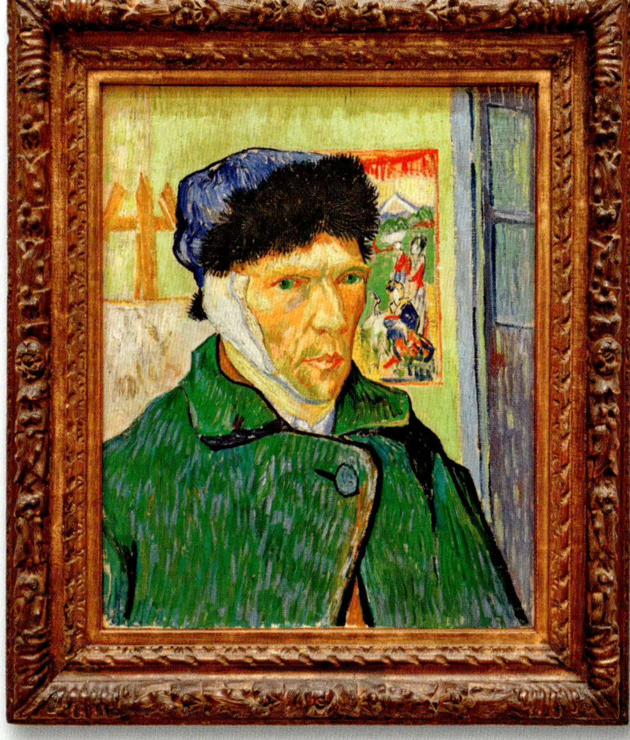

7

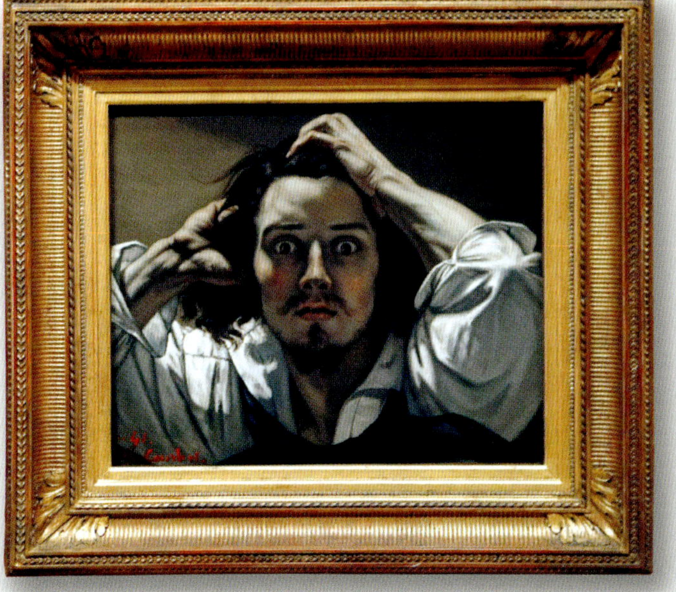

6

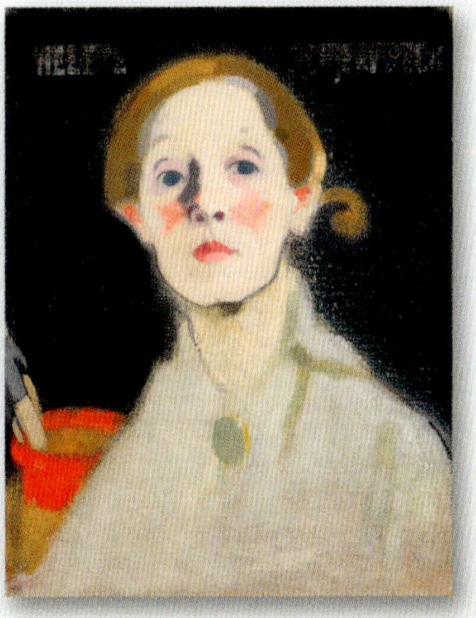

8

Artist at work

When painting themselves, artists had to decide on how they wanted to be perceived. Some presented themselves as successful members of society. Others showed the realities of life in the studio. A few artists, such as Velázquez and Goya, found ways to include themselves working at an easel in paintings of their patrons.

5. ***Self-Portrait in a Straw Hat*, Elisabeth Vigée Le Brun, 1782.** Le Brun has presented herself as a fashionable member of society, confident, informally dressed, and engaging directly with the viewer. The painting was intended to appeal to her aristocratic clients.

6. ***The Desperate Man*, Gustave Courbet, 1843.** Courbet painted this dramatic self-portrait at the age of 24. Drawing on the Romantic idea of the tortured genius, and conscious of his status as a social outsider, he conveys all the anxiety of a young artist trying to build a career.

7. ***Self-Portrait with Bandaged Ear*, Vincent van Gogh, 1889.** A prolific painter of self-portraits, van Gogh produced this one after a stay in a mental hospital, having cut off his own ear. The canvas behind him indicates his determination to keep painting.

8. ***Self-Portrait, Black Background*, Helene Schjerfbeck, 1915.** Schjerfbeck painted self-portraits throughout her life, recording changes in her painting style as well as the process of aging. This one, painted when she was 52, presents a masklike face and distant look.

Self-portrait at the Easel

Catharina van Hemessen 1548, oil on oak panel, 32.2 × 25.2 cm, Kunstmuseum Basel, Switzerland

Van Hemessen paints herself painting a portrait of herself with an expression full of seriousness and concentration. It is a confident expression of her skill and one of the earliest self-portraits in European art showing an artist at work at the easel. The simple, dark background creates an atmosphere of quiet intimacy.

The inscription reads "I Catharina van Hemessen painted myself in 1548. Aged 20". It echoes the inscription on Albrecht Dürer's self-portrait of 1500.

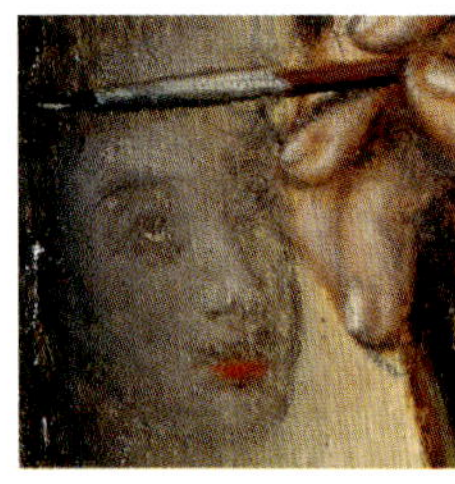

The face she is painting appears on the left of the panel – perhaps because the artist is looking at herself and her work in a mirror.

The artist rests her hand on a mahlstick so that it does not come into contact with the paint surface.

Details such as the brushes and peg-holes in the easel are meticulously painted.

The colours shown on the palette – white, ochres, and earth colours – are those she is using in the painting.

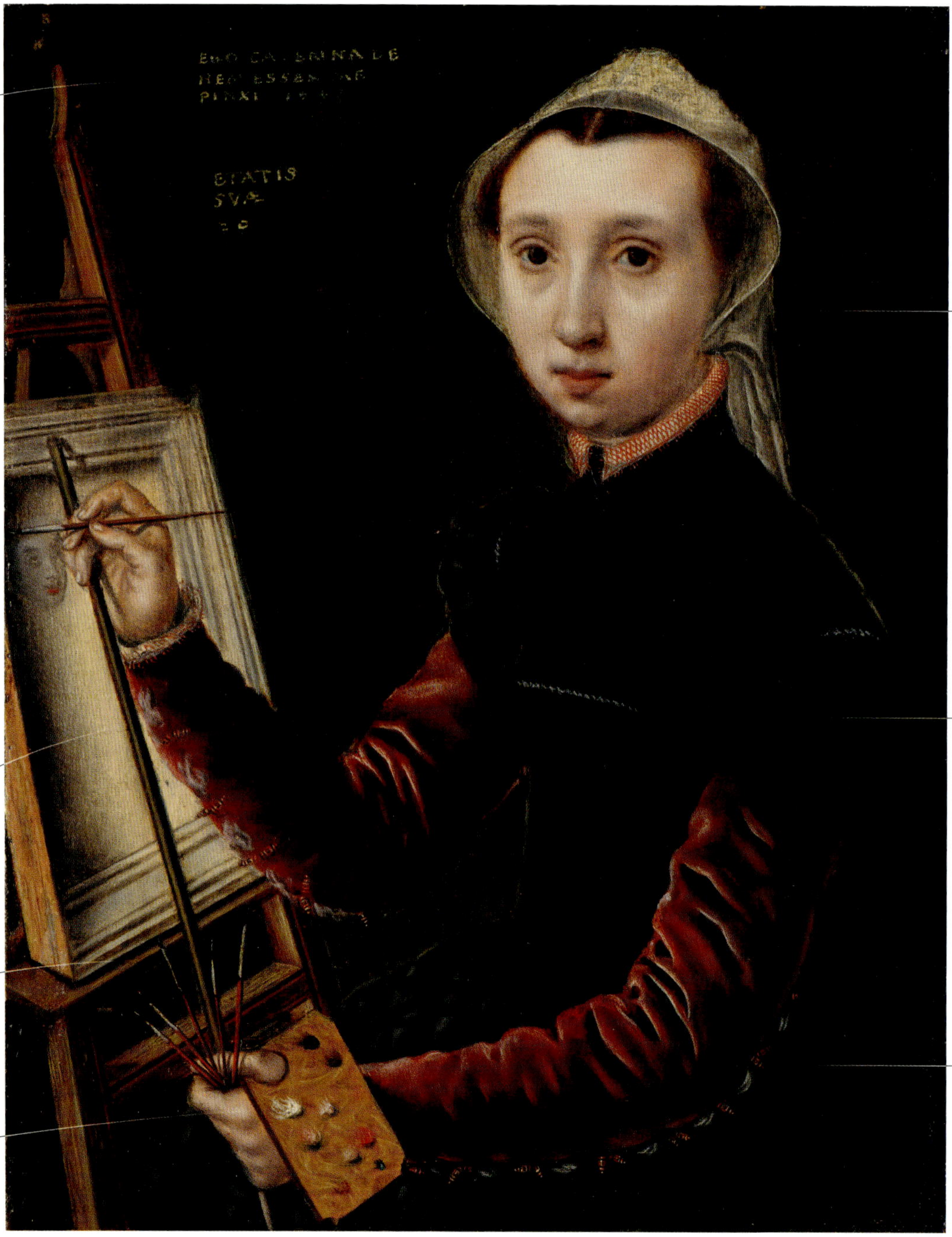

Gentle contrasts of light and dark model the features of the face.

The velvet dress and lace cap indicate her social rank as a talented painter and daughter of notable Renaissance artist, Jan van Hemessen.

White highlights drawn in with thick paint outline the shoulders and sleeves of the dress and the folds in the fabric.

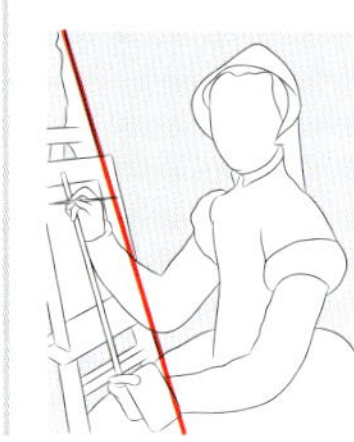

Two worlds
The canvas is divided between the world of the painting and the world of the artist.

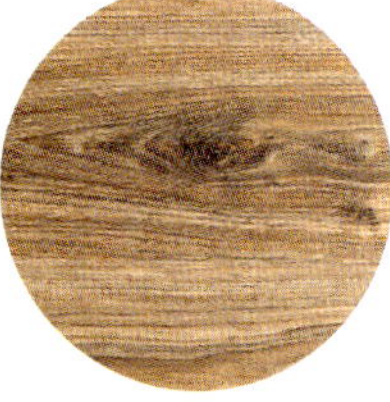

Wood panels
The oak panel on which she painted was prepared by sanding it smooth and applying layers of gesso, a mixture of white chalk and animal glue. The panel was then sanded again and burnished.

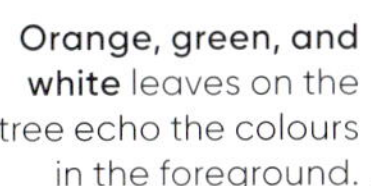

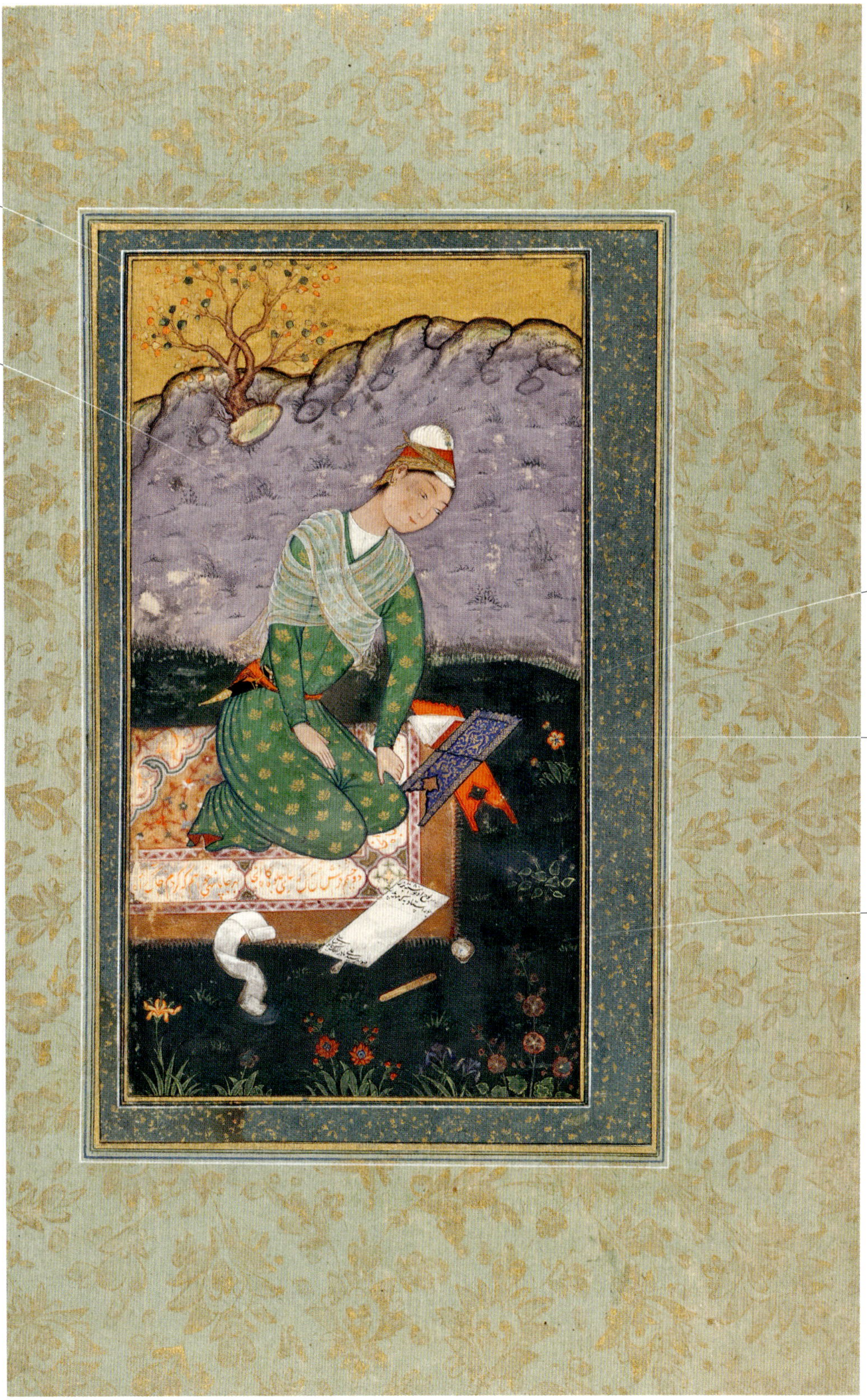

Orange, green, and white leaves on the tree echo the colours in the foreground.

A gauzelike shawl is depicted with delicate precision.

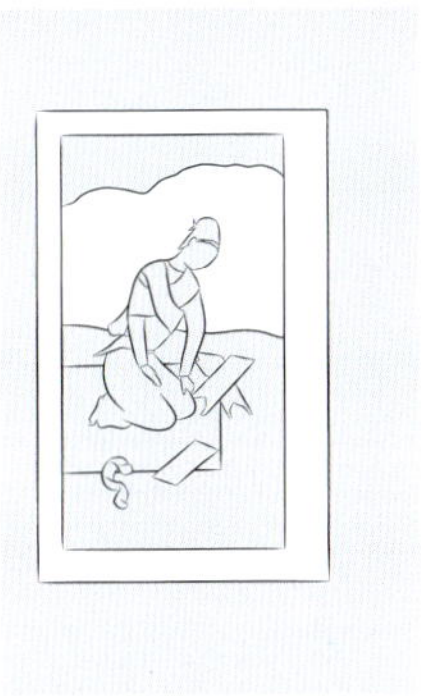

Three colour registers
The painting has three receding registers distinguished by colour: green foreground, pale-violet background, and golden sky.

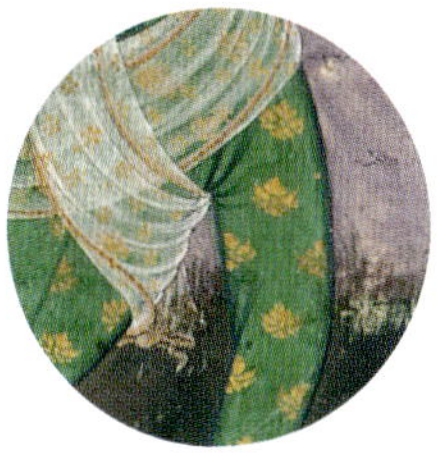

Colour wash
Opaque washes of colour create an overall sense of flatness against which motifs such as the gold pattern on the green robes stand out.

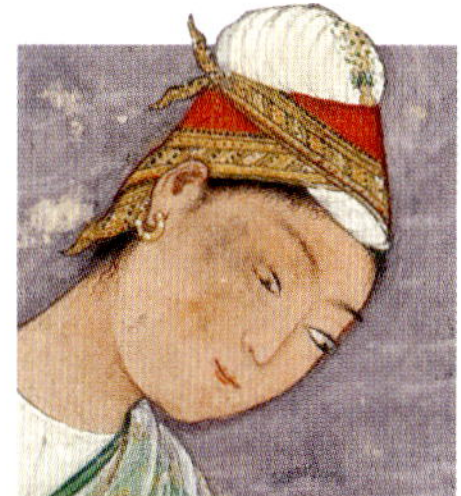

Mir Sayyid Ali appears content and serene, his delicate features carefully delineated with single ink brushstrokes.

The youth pores over a book that is propped open on a lavishly decorated bookstand.

Various species of flowering plants frame the figure.

An inkwell and a bronze pen box are strewn near a paper scroll and writing tablet.

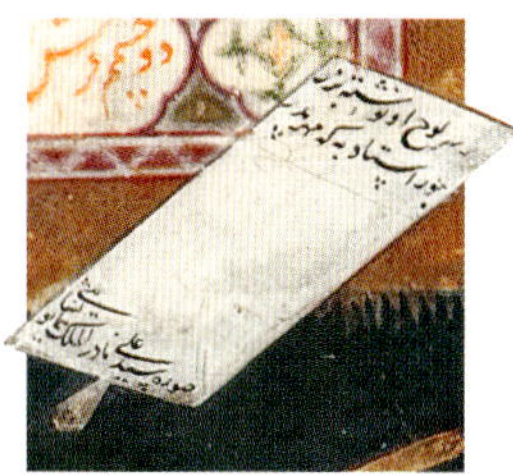

The name of the artist and his patron, Humayun Shah, the Mughal ruler, are inscribed on the paper.

Self-Portrait of Mir Sayyid Ali

Mir Sayyid Ali c. 1550, ink, opaque, and gold on paper, 31.6 × 20 cm, Los Angeles County Museum of Art, Los Angeles, US

In this idealized self-portrait, an elegant young courtier – Mir Sayyid Ali – leans forward to read a book while kneeling on a carpet in an outdoor setting. The mastery of expressive line and harmonious colour combinations paved the way for this Persian émigré artist's success at the Mughal court in India.

Eight Songs of the Xiao and Xiang Rivers

After Wen Zhengming 16th–17th century, ink on paper, each leaf 8 × 8 in (21 × 19.7 cm), Metropolitan Museum of Art, US

In the album Eight Songs, each of the Eight Scenic Views of the Xiao and Xiang Rivers (in what is now China's Hunan province) is paired with a poem by the artist. Such scenes became a popular subject for artists in China from the 10th century, and the style was later adopted by painters in Korea and Japan. The leaf shown here depicts the scene "Misty temple, evening bell."

A distant mountain peak is rendered in ink wash, without an outline, to create the effect of aerial perspective.

Parts of the buildings disappear behind banks of mist indicated by stretches of unpainted paper.

The temple, probably Qingliang Temple in Hengyang, and its pagoda are drawn with a controlled line, using only the very tip of the brush.

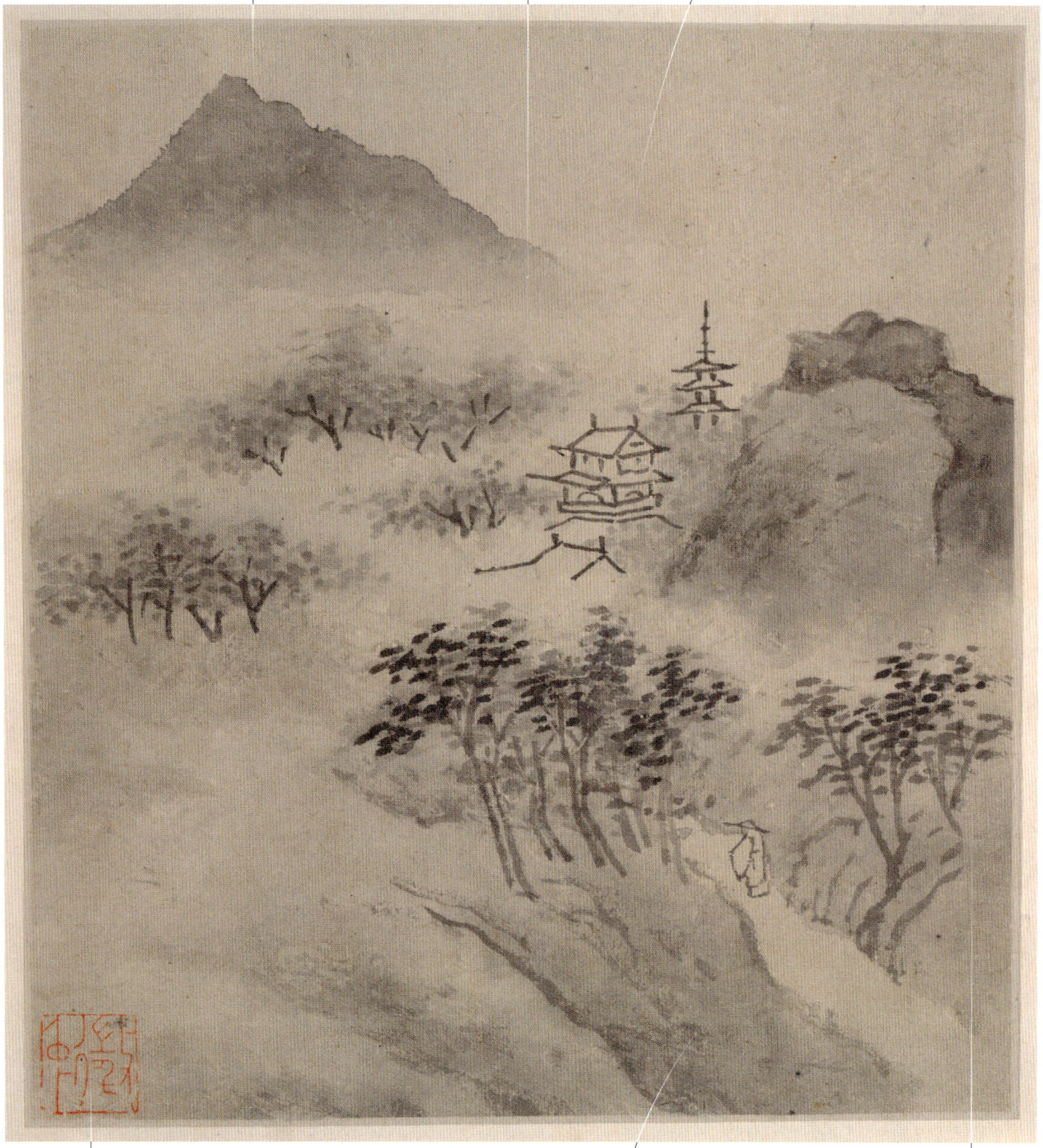

Though the red seal is that of Wen Zhengming, this painting was likely created after his death.

Hills and banks in the foreground have a loose outline. Texture strokes have been used to create volume.

All the trees are painted using the same stroke, but the artist varies the saturation of the ink to indicate misty effects.

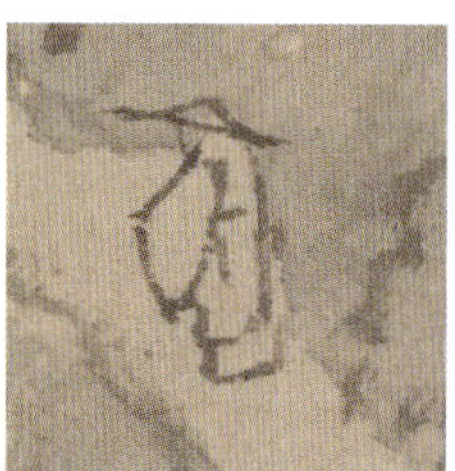

A white-robed monk wearing a straw hat makes his way up the trail leading to the temple.

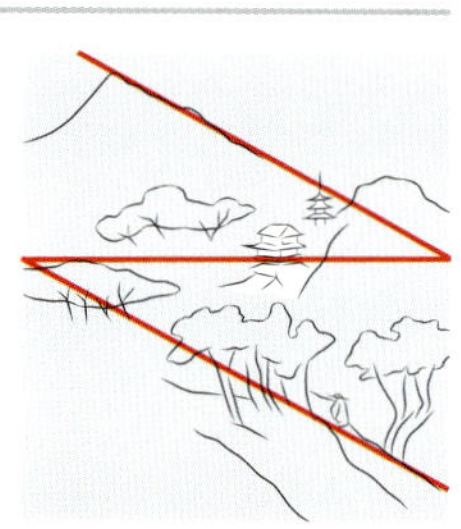

Blurred lines
The composition is defined by two strong diagonals sloping down from left to right to frame the temple, and one running horizontally from right to left to anchor its location.

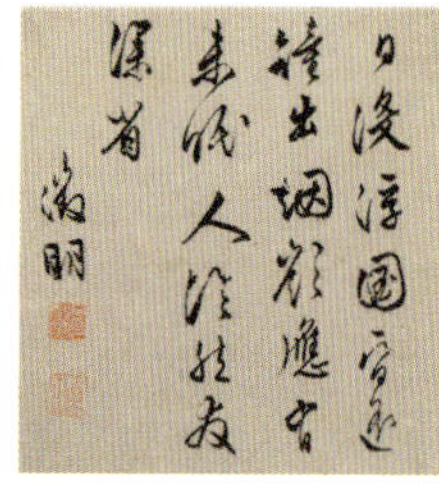

Companion piece
The painting is incomplete without the poem. It has four lines of five characters each, but the artist does not insert line breaks or punctuation in his calligraphic rendition.

Chinese ink
Traditional Chinese painters such as Wen Zhengming ground their own ink, adding water to create a more saturated or more dilute black. The same brush was used for writing and painting, which explains the connection between painting and calligraphy.

The Chess Game

Sofonisba Anguissola 1555, oil on canvas, 28 × 38 in (70 × 97 cm), Narodowe Museum, Posnán, Poland

This joyful portrait of the artist's sisters playing chess, while a servant looks on, was painted quickly and with great verve. Anguissola paid great attention to the exquisite detail of her sisters' elaborate dresses.

> "It was done with such diligence and quickness that they all seemed truly alive and only lacking in speech."
>
> Giorgio Vasari, 1568

Soft blues and grays give the background a *sfumato* (smoky) effect, common in paintings of the Italian Renaissance.

By depicting her sisters in different poses, Anguissola was able to show her considerable abilities as a painter.

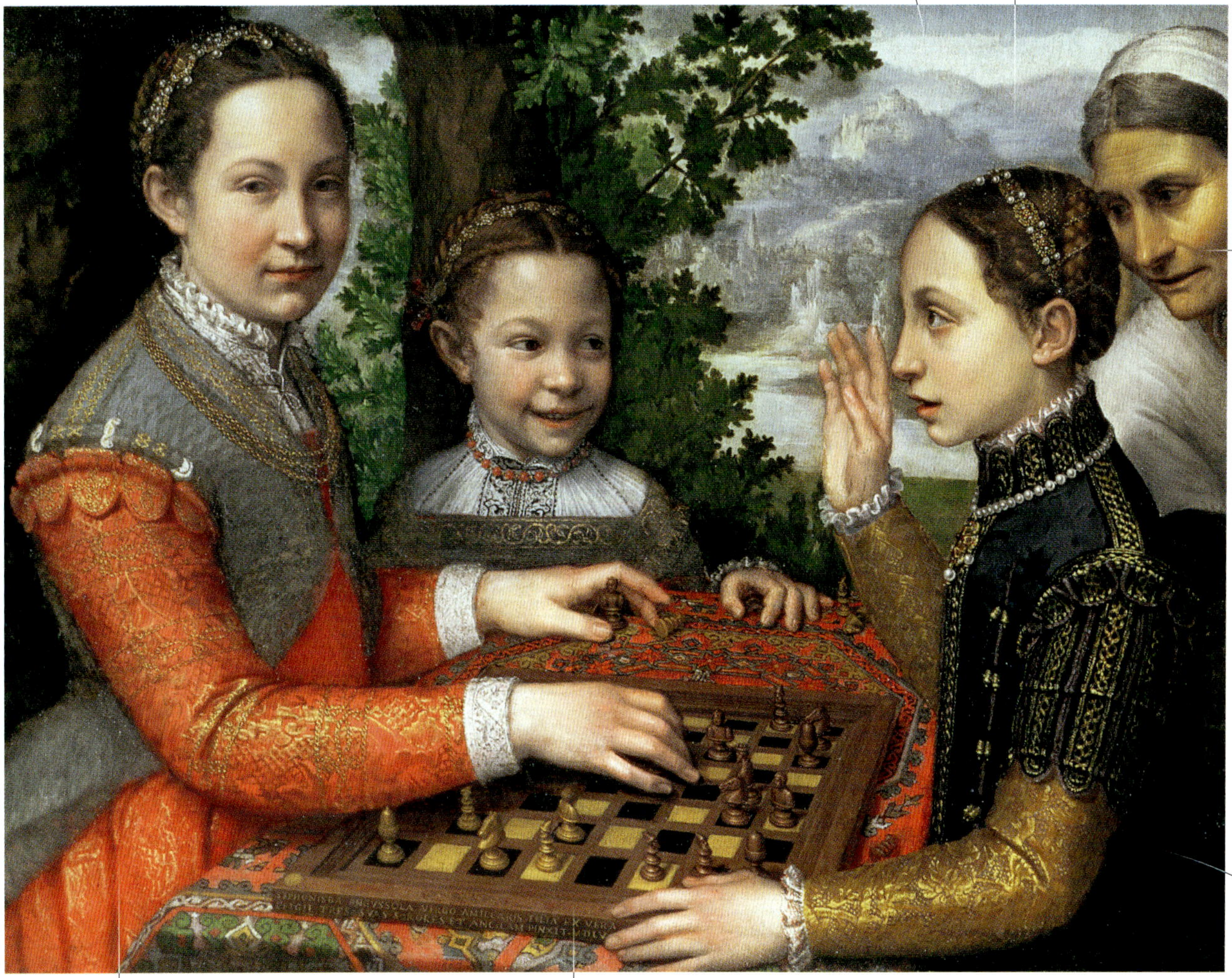

A servant looks on. Servants rarely featured in portraiture at this time, suggesting that the sisters may have been fond of this woman.

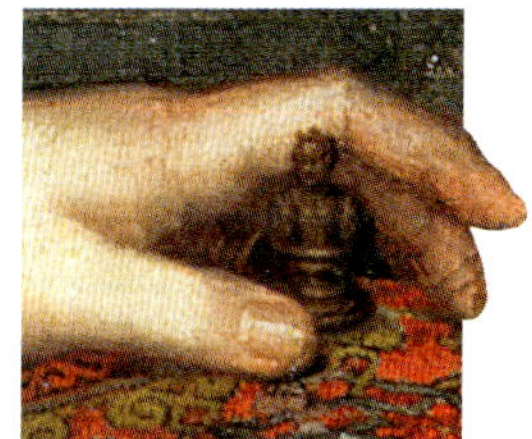

The square U-shape formed by Lucia's left hand is a signature of the artist seen in many of her paintings.

Silks and velvets trimmed with jewels and gold thread are immaculately rendered.

Lucia also became a professional artist but she died in her late twenties, and her talent was never fully realized.

A Latin inscription on the board means: "Sophonisba Anguissola, maiden daughter of Amilcare, painted this true likeness of her three sisters and a servant in 1555."

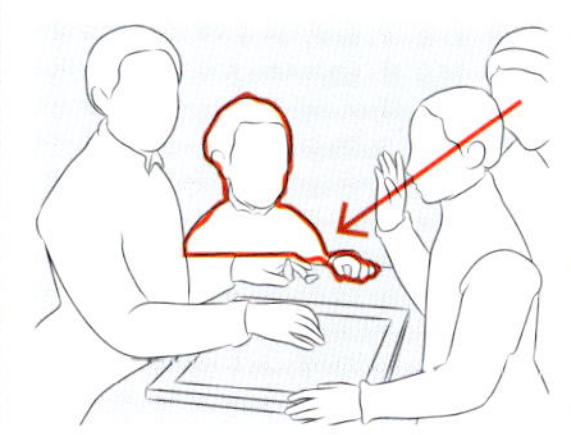

Close relationship
There is a playful interaction as Minerva (right) reacts to the move made by Lucia (left) making young Europa (center) smile. The viewer is also drawn into the painting by Lucia's gaze.

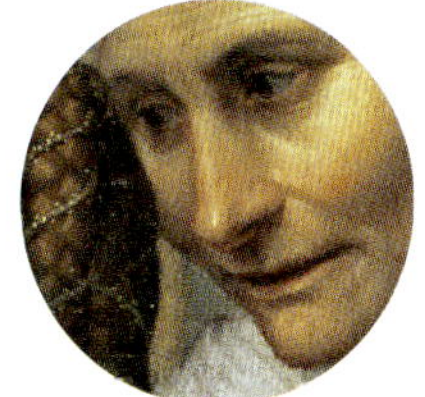

Michelangelo's influence
The delicately rendered features of the old woman's face reflect the influence of Michelangelo. Anguissola had met Michelangelo and possibly studied with him.

The Wedding Feast at Cana

Paolo Veronese c. 1562–1563, oil on canvas, 267 × 391 in (677 × 994 cm), Louvre, Paris, France

Commissioned for the refectory of a Benedictine monastery, *The Wedding Feast at Cana* depicts the Biblical story of Christ changing water into wine at the request of his mother, Mary. Yet the great banquet is held in a Palladian loggia in typical Venetian splendor, the tables laden with food and the guests richly dressed. Veronese uses color to depict a scene of ideal beauty, signaling the Mannerist period with which he is associated. Rather than depicting the miracle—he expects viewers to know the story—he focuses on the guests, servants, and fine details of Venetian life.

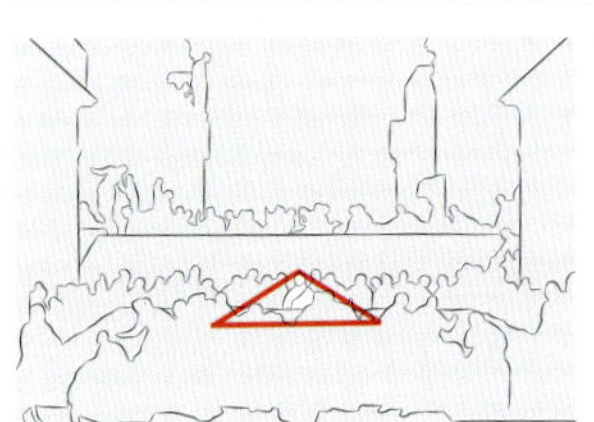

Triangular form
Christ forms the top of a triangle with the wine taster on the right and wine server on the left.

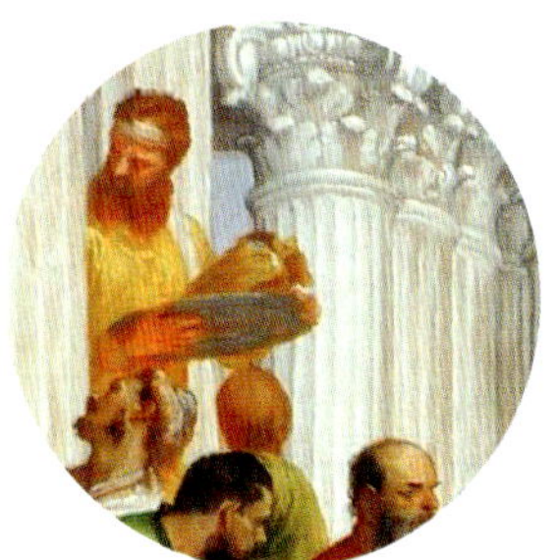

Lighting the scene
Strong light emanates from the right, illuminating the left side and leaving much of the right in shadow.

“Never was a painter more nobly joyous, never did an artist take a greater delight in life, seeing it all as a kind of breezy festival and feeling it through the medium of perpetual success … He was the happiest of painters.”

Henry James, 1909

Greco-Roman architecture provides the backdrop to the scene. The new tower right of center echoes the much admired buildings of 16th-century architect Andrea Palladio.

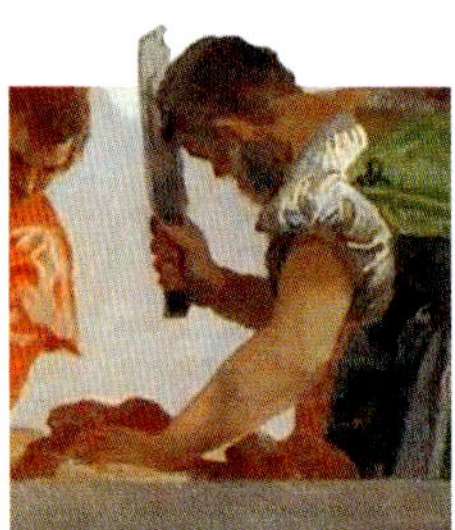

A butcher carves meat for the serving platter directly above Christ, a reference to Christ's role as the sacrificial lamb.

Historical figures such as Cardinal Pole (in red) and Suleiman the Great (in gold) appear alongside Venetian notables.

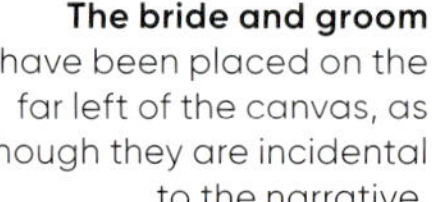

The bride and groom have been placed on the far left of the canvas, as though they are incidental to the narrative.

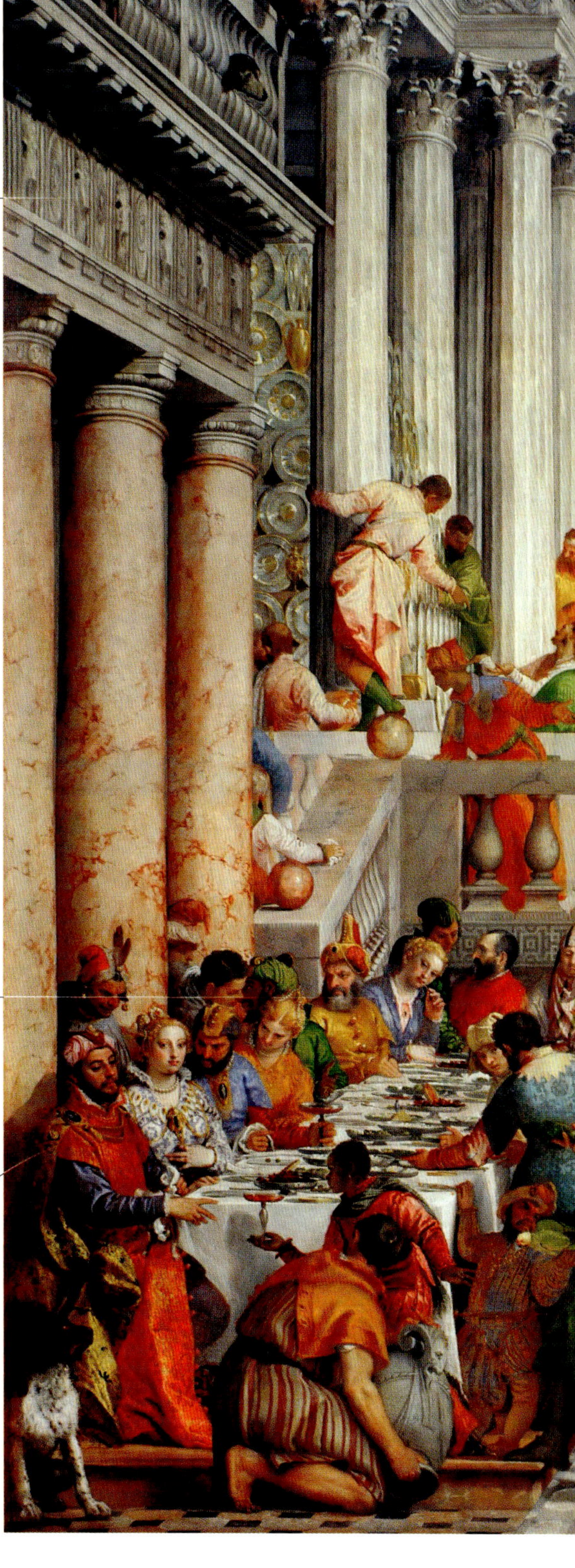

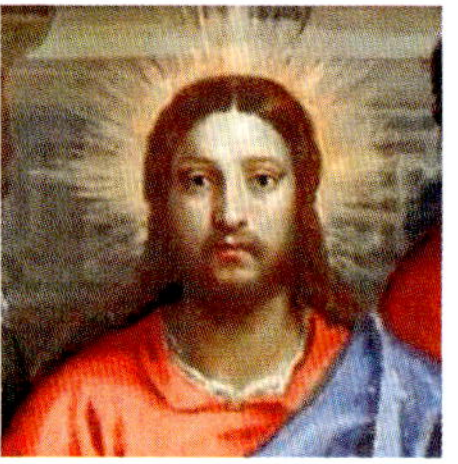

Christ sits at the table as the guest of honor and is illuminated by a halo. Mary, who sits next to him, also has a halo but it is not as bright.

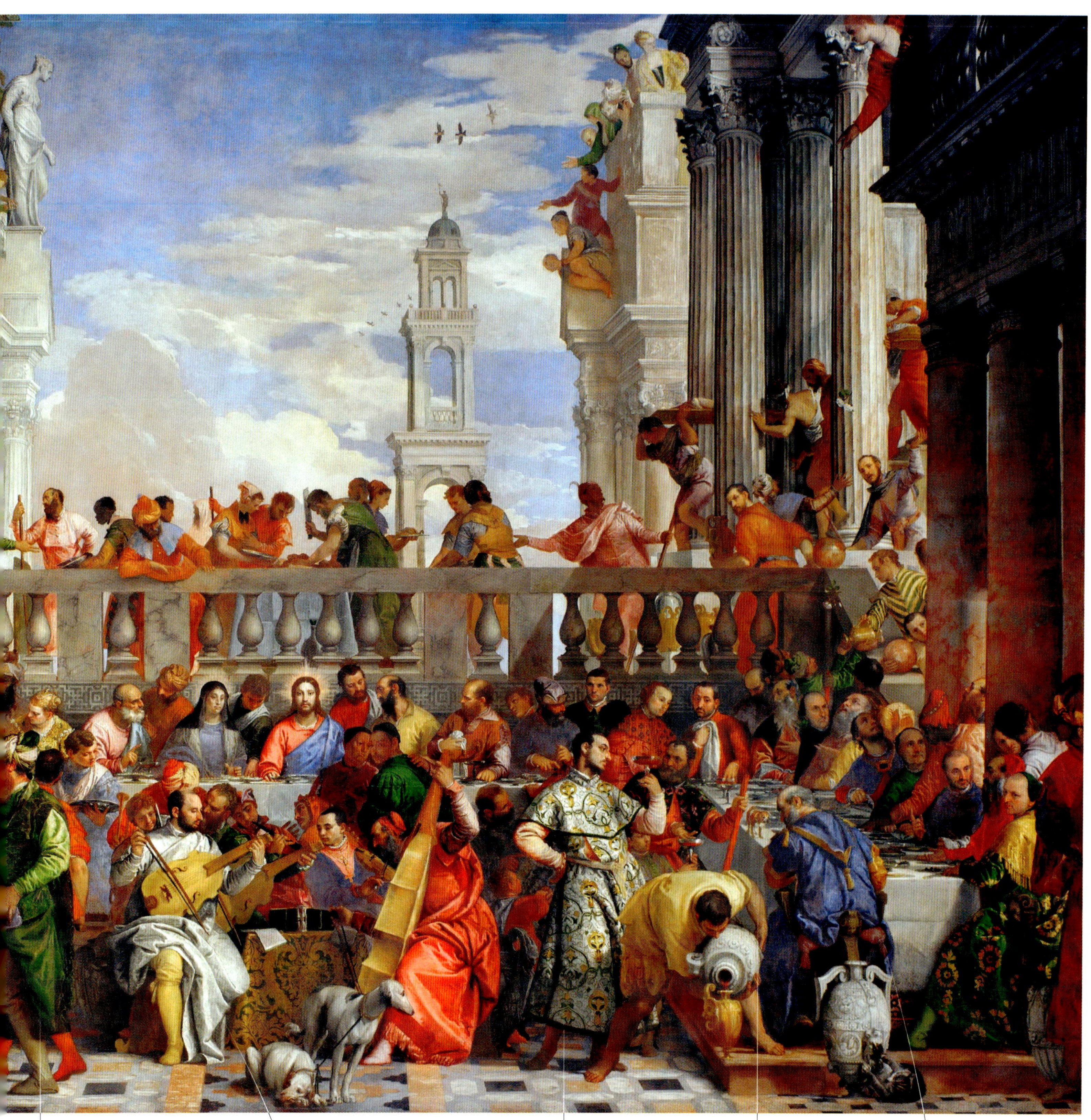

Before extensive restoration in the 1980s, the steward's coat was red. An association of artists protested about the color change, insisting that Veronese himself had changed it from green to red.

The group of musicians depicts Venetian artists popular at the time, including Veronese himself (in white).

A wine taster inspects the water that has been turned into wine.

Venetian weddings were opportunities to show off. Guests are nobly dressed and the table is set with silver, glasses, and exotic foods.

The Benedictine monks who commissioned the painting specified that Veronese must use ultramarine, an expensive blue pigment derived from lapis lazuli.

Hunters in the Snow (Winter)

Pieter Bruegel 1565, oil on canvas, 46 × 64 in (117 × 162 cm), Kunsthistorisches Museum, Vienna, Austria

In the depths of winter, a group of hunters returns from an expedition almost empty-handed, while villagers carry on with life in the valley below. With skeletal trees, dark skies, and snow-covered ground, Bruegel creates a scene of unremitting coldness, while details hint at the privations and the possibility of starvation to come.

Warm colors in the buildings heighten the overall coldness of the scene.

An inn sign hanging precariously from one corner depicts St. Hubert, patron saint of hunters, with a stag.

The trees are depicted with quick strokes of thin paint.

The blue-gray color in the leaden sky is echoed in the frozen ponds and river.

Subtle changes in tone model the trees and distant crags against the snow.

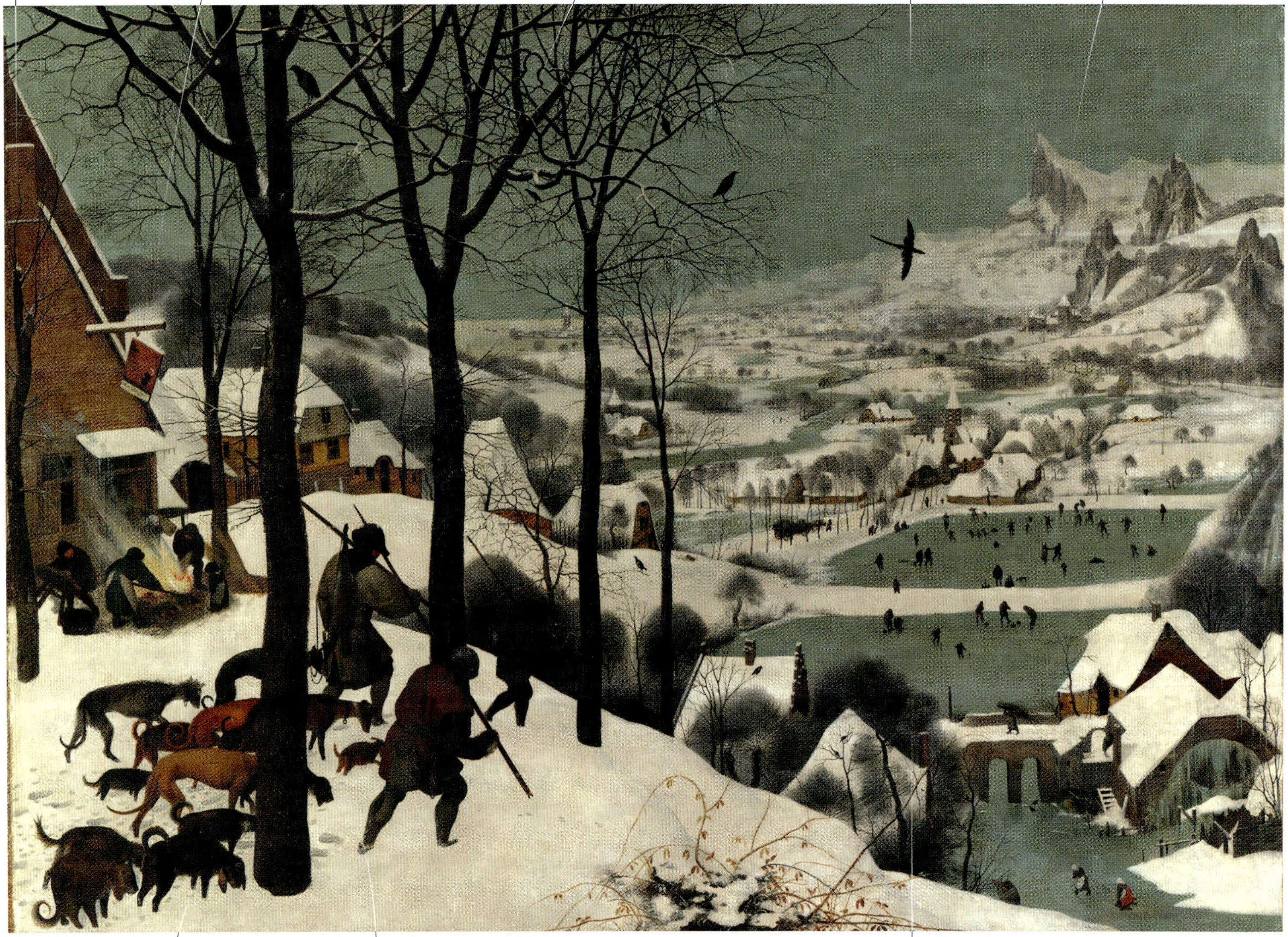

One dog looks out of the painting, catching the viewer's eye.

This hunting group forms a stark contrast with the white snow. Deep footprints show the depth of the snow.

The villagers' activities on the ice include ice hockey and curling.

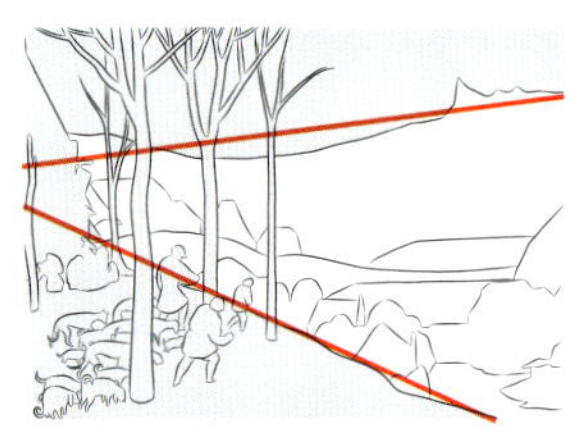

Three areas of focus
Diagonals divide the painting into three main areas: the foreground containing the hunters, the valley, and the sky.

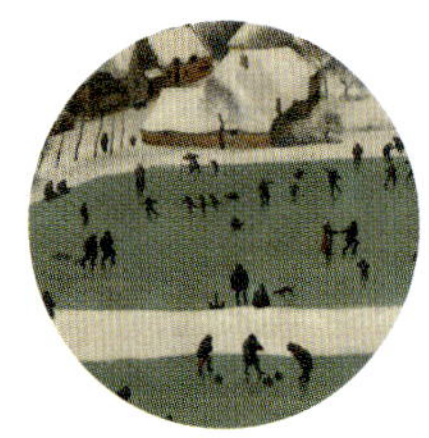

Recession
Figures and trees reduce quickly in size between the foreground and the valley, creating a sense of an endless icy landscape sweeping into the distance.

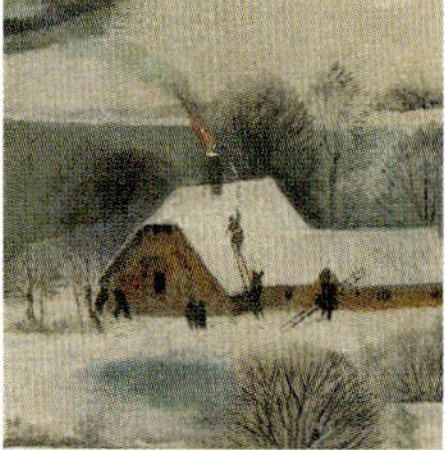

A chimney on fire, a constant hazard in cold weather, is one of many incidental details shown.

> “Moroni is one of the most subtle portrait artists of all time, and deserves to be much more famous than he is.”
>
> Jonathan Jones, 2014

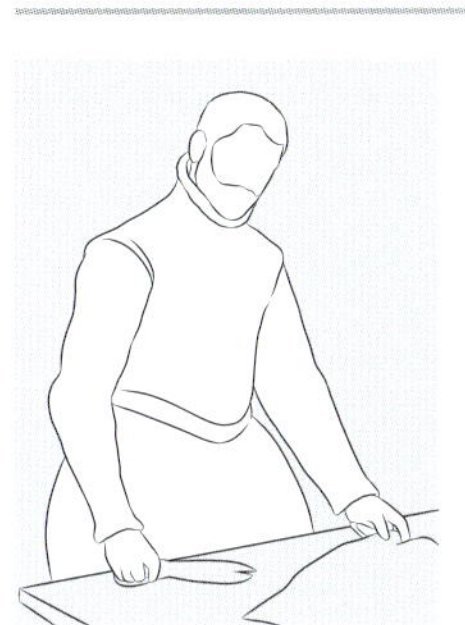

Brought to life
The figure is slightly off-center and set at an angle to the picture plane. In contrast, the turn of the head toward the viewer creates a sense of movement.

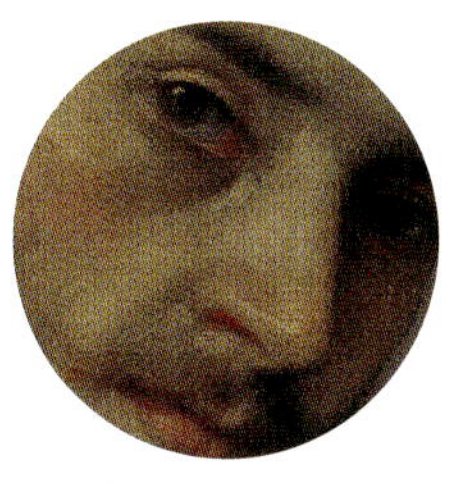

Modeling
The features have been modeled with restrained contrasts of light and shadow and subtle changes in color.

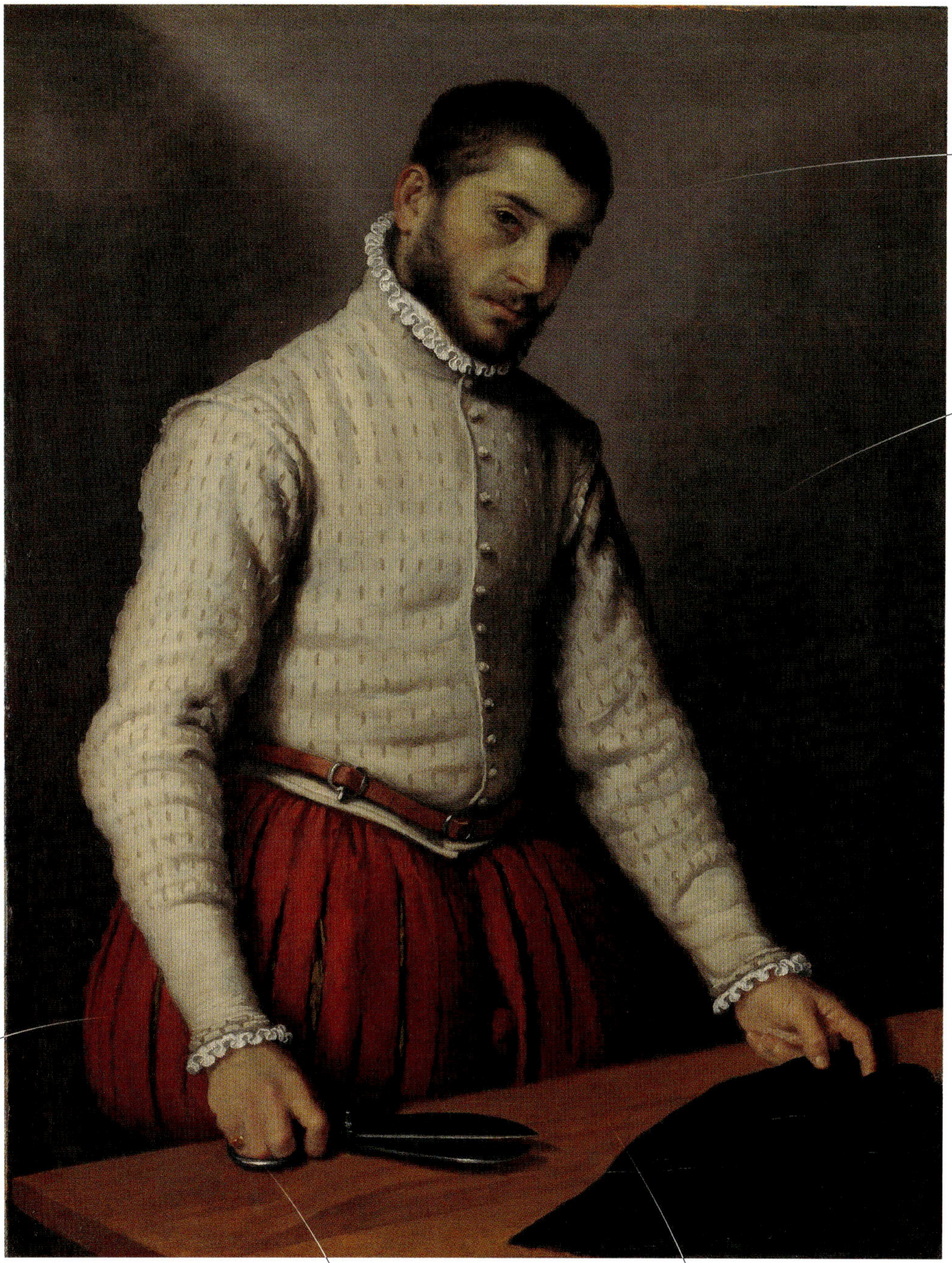

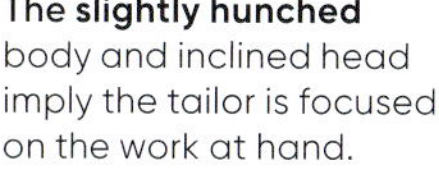

The slightly hunched body and inclined head imply the tailor is focused on the work at hand.

This doublet would have been made of wool, because silk was reserved for the nobility. Nevertheless, the tailor exhibits signs of wealth.

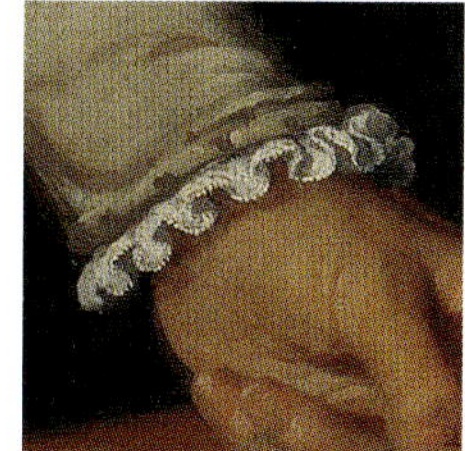

Very thin paint is used throughout, except for the lace trim, which is rendered with thick dots to suggest the texture of lace.

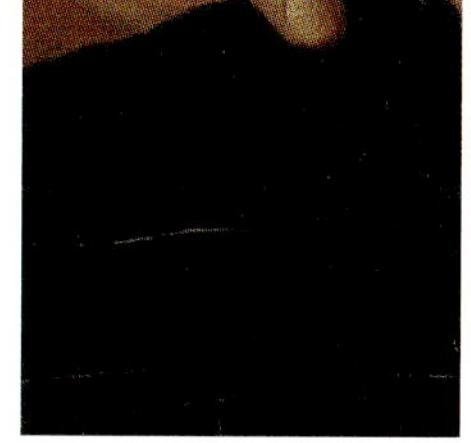

Chalk lines have been drawn on the black cloth in preparation for cutting, a technique still used by tailors today.

Fashionable clothing—an ivory-colored doublet and full, rust-colored breeches with codpiece—is vividly depicted. The sword belt denotes high status—a master craftsman perhaps or a cloth merchant.

His right hand grasps the tailor’s scissors; an elegant ring with a red stone indicates sophistication.

The gentle angle of the table draws the viewer into the space.

The Tailor

Giovanni Battista Moroni c. 1570, oil on canvas, 39 × 30 in (99.5 × 77 cm), National Gallery, London, UK

Moroni specialized in portraits, and this picture of a craftsman in his workshop preparing to cut cloth is innovative in showing someone at work and dramatic in its approach. The tailor looks straight out at the viewer, as if he has been interrupted. Moroni painted directly from life without preliminary drawings, which gives the portrait an air of vitality, spontaneity, and psychological realism as it captures a fleeting moment.

Benin Plaque of Warrior and Attendants

Artist unknown 16th–17th centuries, brass, 19 x 15 x 4 in (47.6 x 38.1 x 10.8 cm), Metropolitan Museum Art, New York, US

Originally displayed among other such plaques in the royal palace of the Benin Kingdom (now Nigeria), this piece portrays a high-ranking warrior flanked by two other soldiers coming to meet the *oba*, or king. Remarkably preserved, it exemplifies the style and craftsmanship of Edo artists in the Benin Kingdom.

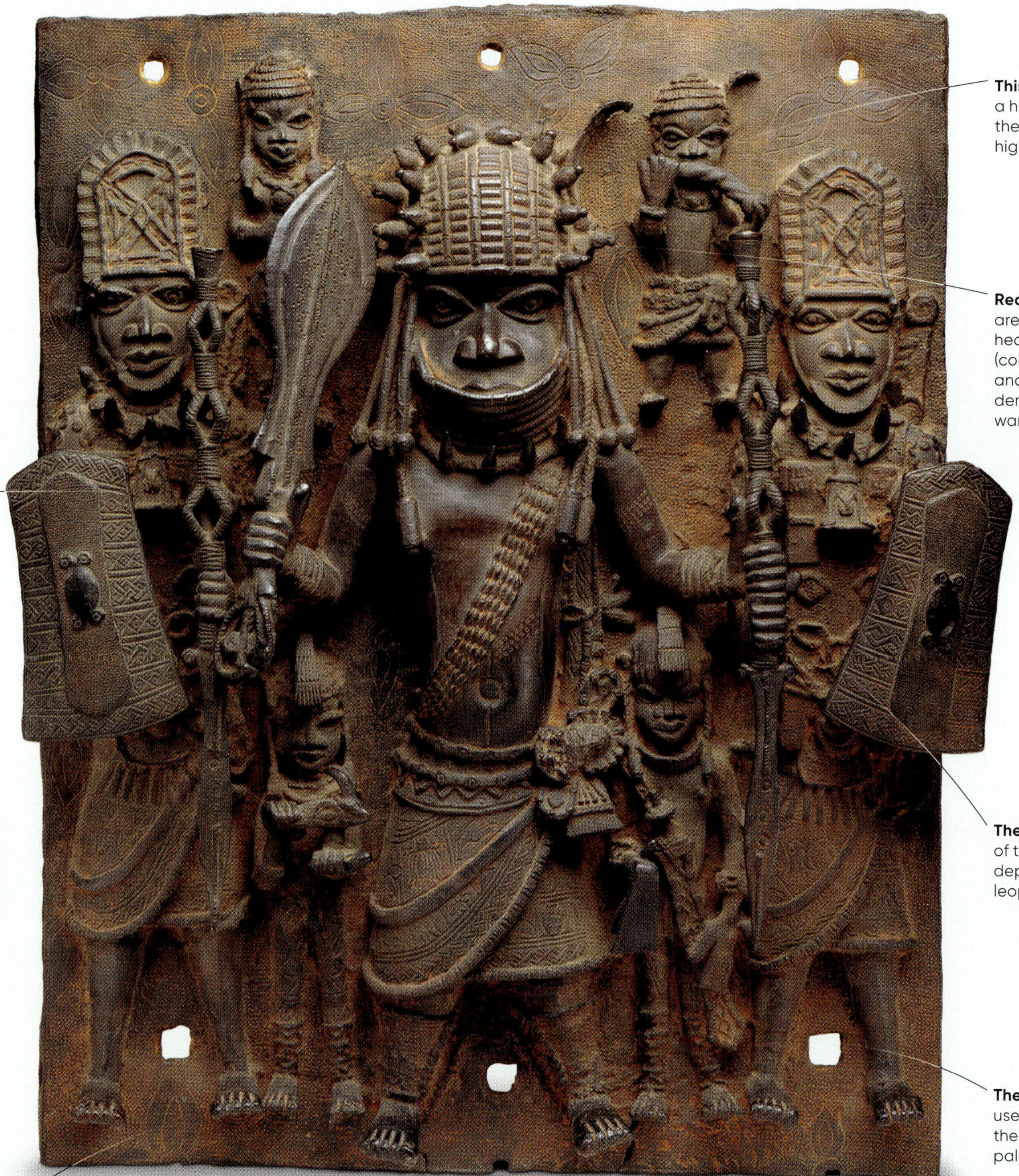

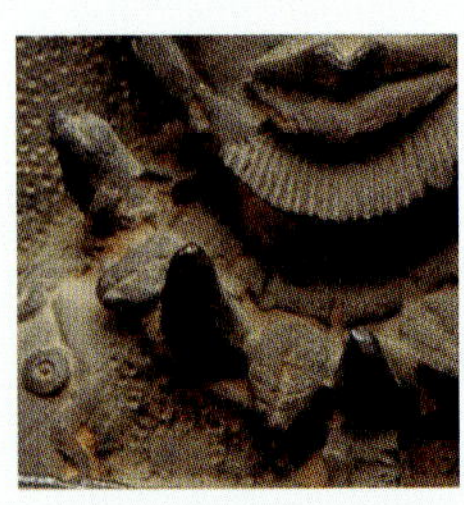

Leopard-tooth necklaces adorn the warriors. On the side figures, the leopard teeth are interspersed with cowrie shells, a precolonial currency.

Warriors wore four-sided, flat-topped bells to incite panic in battle and provide spiritual protection. A larger version of this type of bell was placed on palace altars.

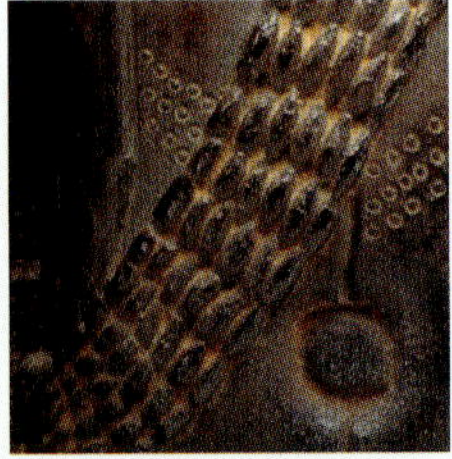

The spotted scarification, called *iwu*, alludes to the leopard—an animal associated with ferocity as well as with Benin kingship.

Aquatic leaves allude to *Olokun*, god of the sea. It is thought that the patterned background and rectangular format were influenced by illuminated books brought by the Portuguese.

This attendant blows a horn to announce the arrival of the high-ranking warrior.

Red coral beads are depicted on the headdress, *odigba* (collar), sash, and lower legs to demonstrate this warrior's elite status.

The breastplates of these warriors depict stylized leopard faces.

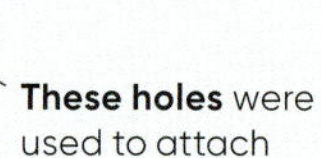

These holes were used to attach the plaque to a palace post.

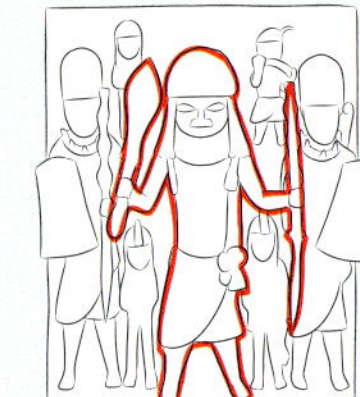

Hierarchical scale
The artist employs hierarchical scale by making the high-ranking warrior the largest, those of lesser ranks slightly smaller, and the attendants the smallest.

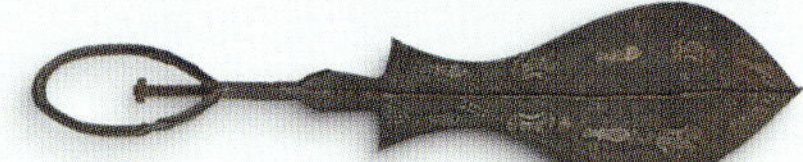

Ceremonial sword
The central warrior carries an *eben* (a ceremonial sword with a circular handle and openwork blade). Such swords are spun and danced with in celebration of the *oba* to the present day.

St. Luke Painting the Virgin

Giorgio Vasari 1565–1570, fresco, 126 × 115 in (320 × 293 cm), St. Luke's Chapel, Santissima Annunziata, Florence, Italy

Vasari is known for his monumental *Lives of the Artists*, dedicated to the artists of the Renaissance and said to be the first art historical text. He was also an artist in his own right, and it is fitting that he painted this fresco of St. Luke, the patron saint of artists and painter of the first religious devotional image, for an artists' chapel.

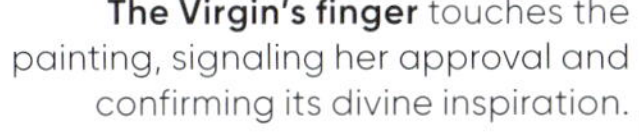

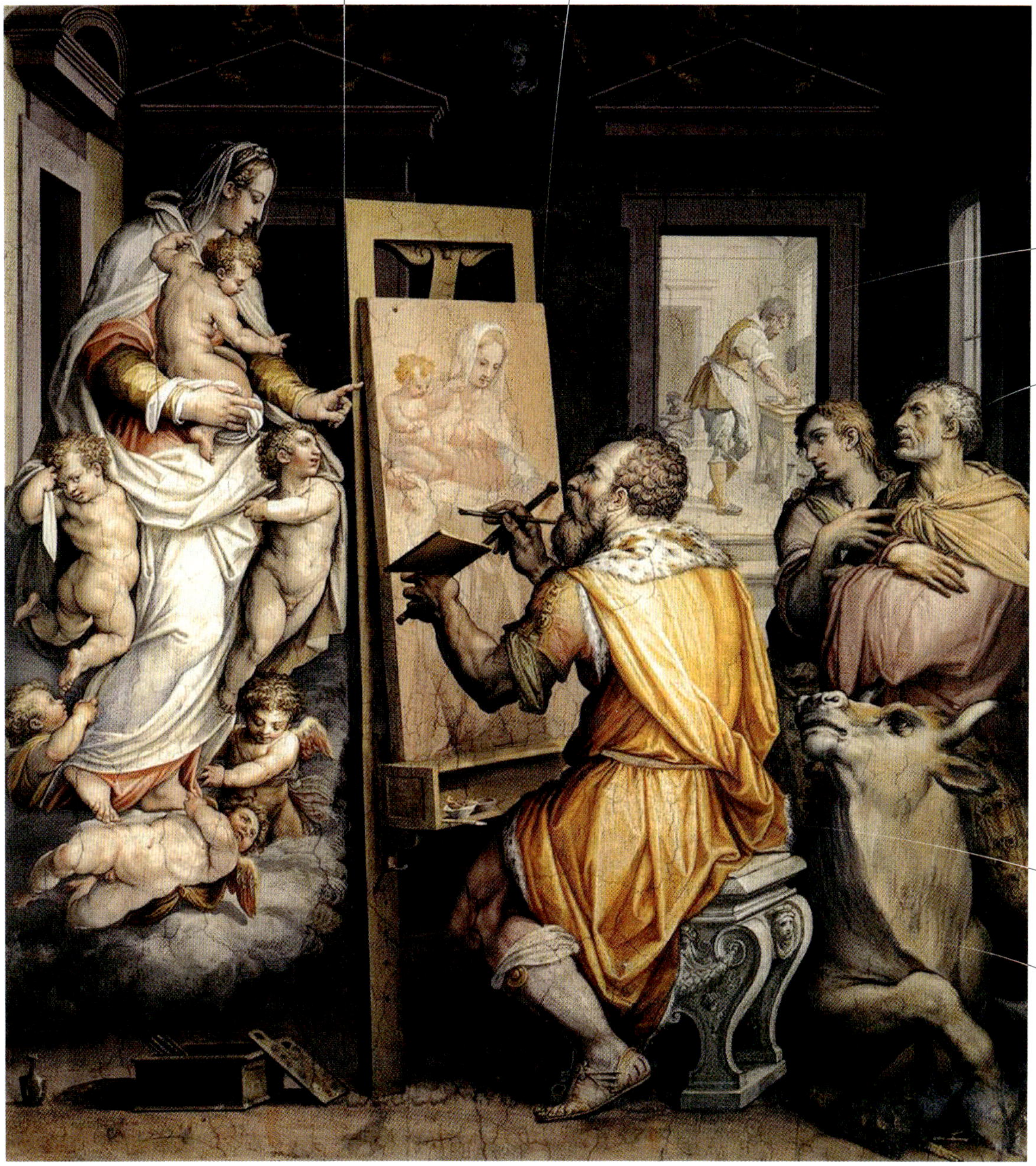

The Virgin's finger touches the painting, signaling her approval and confirming its divine inspiration.

St. Luke's maulstick, a tool to steady the artist's hand, seems to be guided by the Mary in the painting.

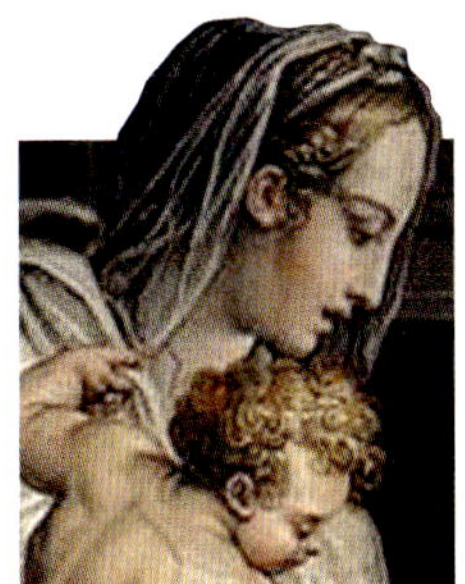

Surrounded by angels and borne on a cloud, the Virgin is a vision rather than a real presence.

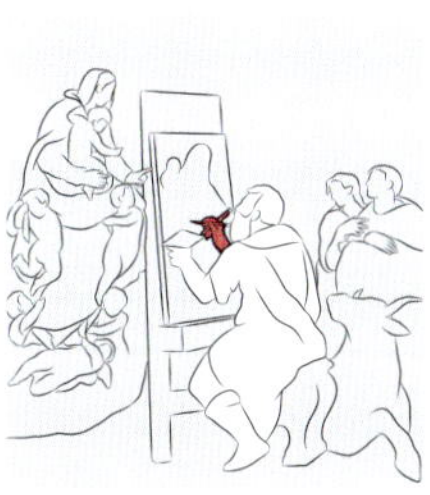

Through the doorway, a man prepares pigment, using a muller to grind the powder and combine it with oil.

These two figures are thought to be the sculptors Giovanni Angelo Montorsoli (right) and his student, Martino Montanini (left).

Hand of the artist
St. Luke's painting hand is in the very center of the fresco, a deliberate placement to emphasize the significance of artistic creativity.

Vasari used a limited palette of pale yellows, browns, and reds.

The ox, a sacrificial animal and a reminder of Christ's sacrifice on the cross, is the traditional symbol of St. Luke.

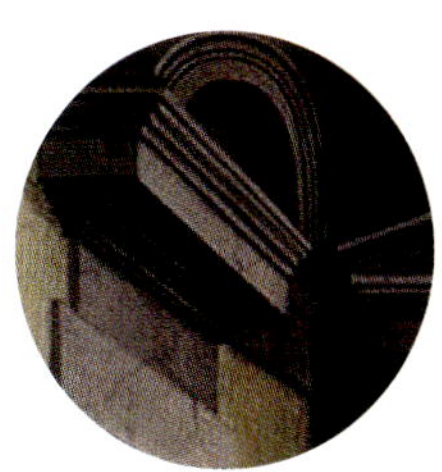

Architectural motifs
As well as being a painter and historian, Vasari was an architect. Signs of this can be seen in how he painted architectural elements in the painting.

> "The greatest geniuses sometimes accomplish more when they work less, since they are searching for inventions in their minds, and forming those perfect ideas which their hands then express."
>
> Giorgio Vasari, 1568

Queen Elizabeth I

Nicholas Hilliard 1572, watercolor on vellum, 2 × 1¾ in (51 × 48 mm), National Portrait Gallery, London, UK

In this portrait—the earliest-known miniature of Elizabeth I, painted when she was 38 years old—the artist combines technical precision with intricate details, creating rich textural depth despite the small size and developing a recognizable iconography of the queen that became pervasive during her reign. Portable, novel, and easily hidden, miniature portraits were hugely popular during the Elizabethan period.

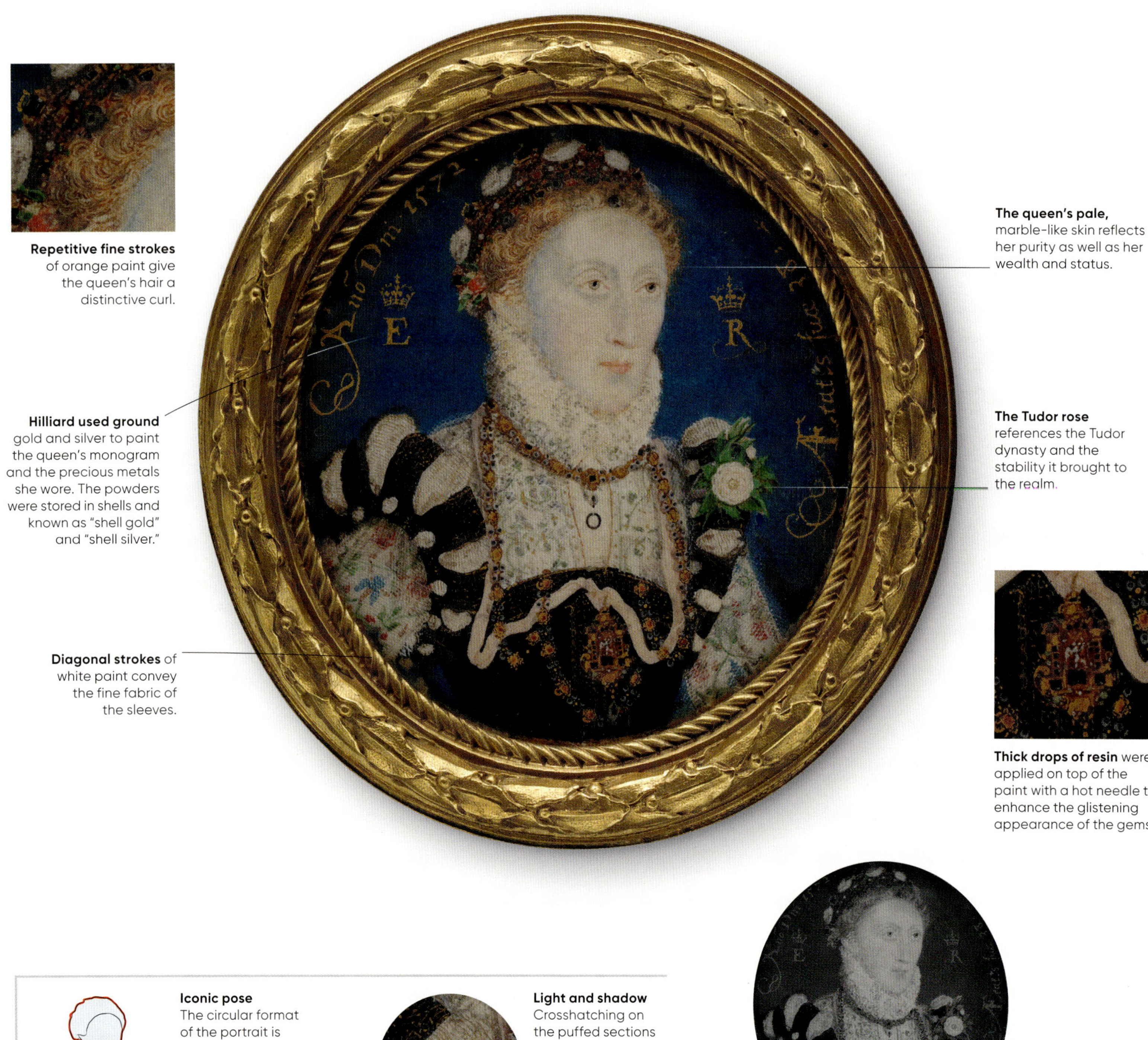

Repetitive fine strokes of orange paint give the queen's hair a distinctive curl.

Hilliard used ground gold and silver to paint the queen's monogram and the precious metals she wore. The powders were stored in shells and known as "shell gold" and "shell silver."

Diagonal strokes of white paint convey the fine fabric of the sleeves.

The queen's pale, marble-like skin reflects her purity as well as her wealth and status.

The Tudor rose references the Tudor dynasty and the stability it brought to the realm.

Thick drops of resin were applied on top of the paint with a hot needle to enhance the glistening appearance of the gems.

Iconic pose
The circular format of the portrait is characteristic of Hilliard's early miniatures. Elizabeth I's frontal pose, with her head turned, became the standard way of depicting her.

Light and shadow
Crosshatching on the puffed sections of the sleeves adds depth to the composition.

Actual size

Spring

Giuseppe Arcimboldo 1573, oil on canvas, 30 × 25 in (76 × 64 cm), Louvre, Paris, France

Flowers, buds, and leaves associated with spring form the portrait of a young woman in profile, a symbol of the changing of the seasons and the beauty of nature. The painting, by Giuseppe Arcimboldo, artist at the Court of Rudolf II in Prague, is designed to look like a portrait from afar, but close up, it reveals a wide range of painstakingly painted plants. At the time, it was considered an amusement as much as a work of art.

A peony represents the ear. The earring is a white columbine flower.

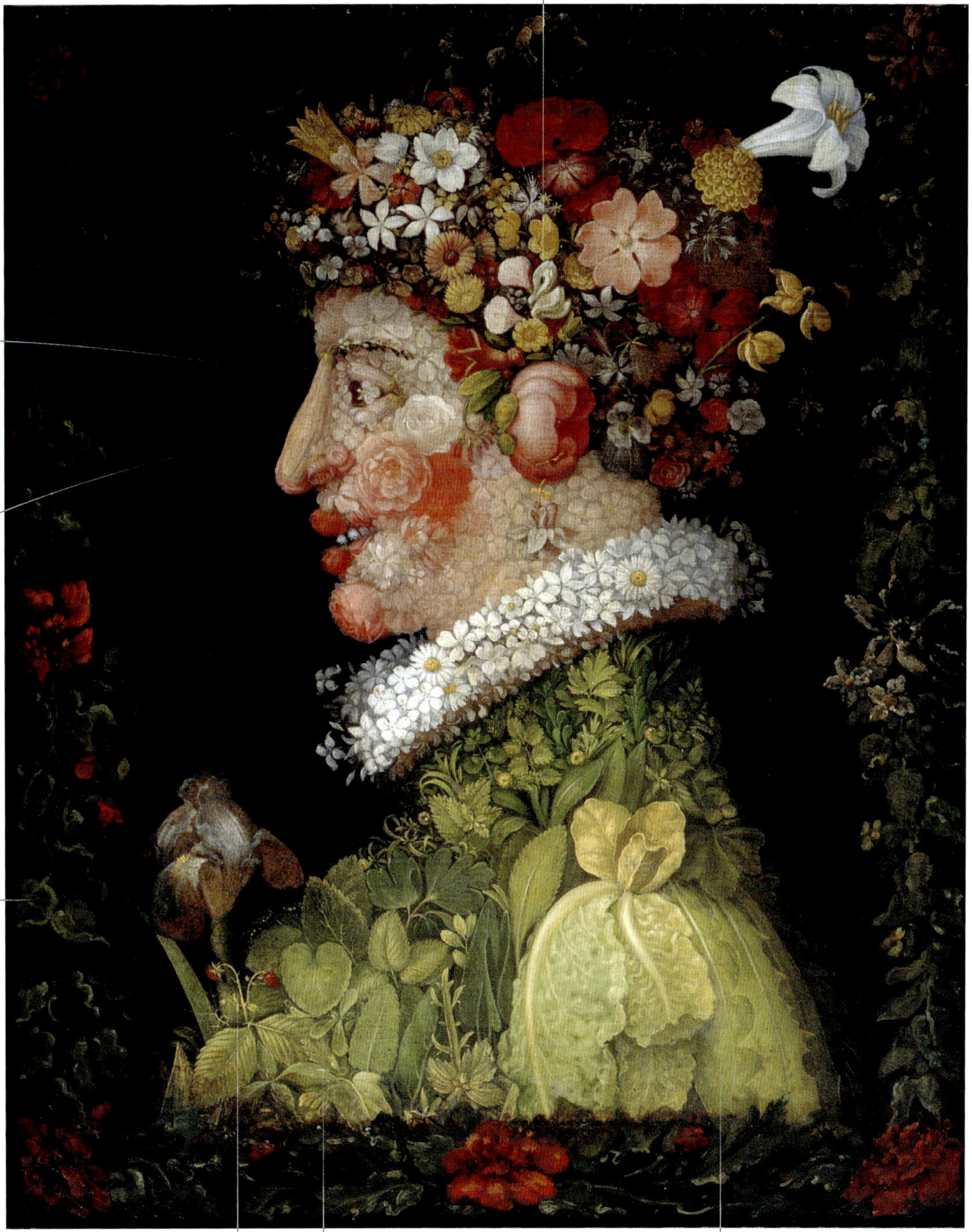

The woman looks out of the painting toward *Air*, which would have hung next to it. Arcimboldo's Elements series complemented his paintings of the Seasons.

A lily bud forms the bridge of the nose. There are 80 distinct plant species in *Spring*.

The border was probably added after Arcimboldo's death—it is not on Arcimboldo's other versions of *Spring* and lacks his usual precision.

The ***Iris germanica*** forms a jewel on the woman's bust. It was probably chosen to honor the Hapsburg's Austro-Germanic empire.

The bust confirms that this figure is female.

Curved lettuce leaves form the shoulder. Lettuce was one of the few food plants that grew well in the cool Italian spring.

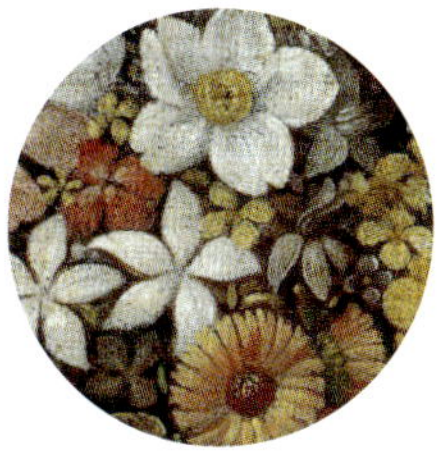

Natural world
The flowers and vegetables are painted with great attention to detail, reflecting the tremendous interest in the natural sciences during the Renaissance.

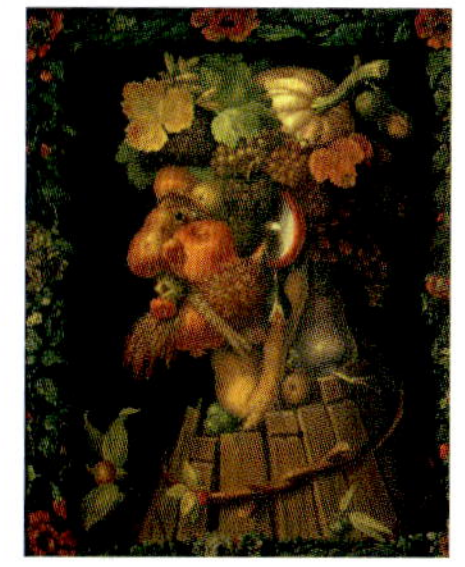

Other seasons
Arcimboldo created "composite heads" for the other seasons. Autumn depicts a man with grape hair, apple cheeks, and a beard of wheat.

The Nativity

Jacopo Tintoretto c. 1570s, oil on canvas, 61 × 141 in (155.6 × 358.1 cm), Museum of Fine Arts, Boston, US

This atmospheric depiction of the Nativity, painted in the late 1550s and reworked in the 1570s, shows the Holy Family in an outdoor stable. Its monumental scale offers an impressive vision of larger-than-life figures—including a woman who is probably Mary's mother, St. Anne, and a shepherd—and a range of animals. The varied painting styles and unusual composition have puzzled critics.

The Magi, on their journey to find the Christ Child, are believed to have been added by Tintoretto's workshop.

The Christ Child and background figures lack the bold brushwork of Tintoretto's signature style.

St. Anne appears to be looking at the lamb, a symbol of Christ, her arms open wide in a gesture of surprise.

The scene on the right depicts the Annunciation to the shepherds. It was also added by studio assistants.

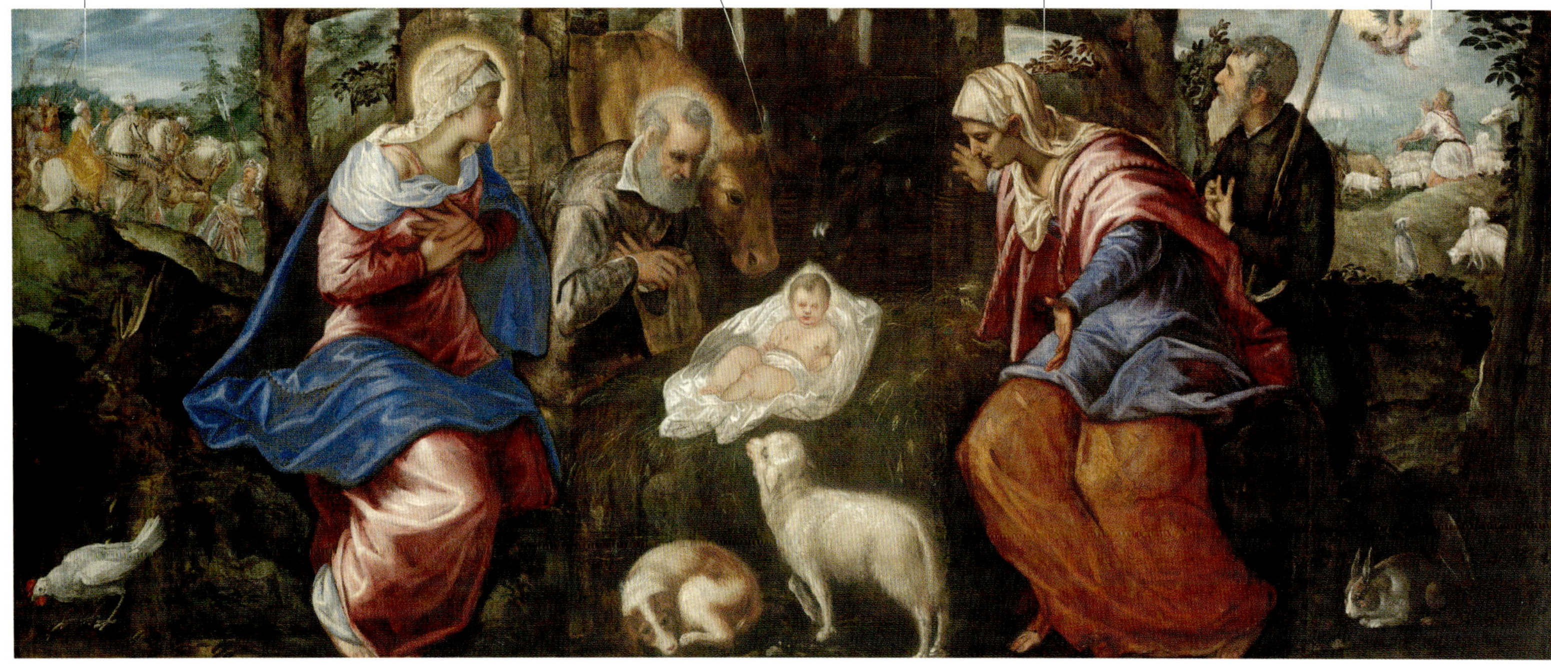

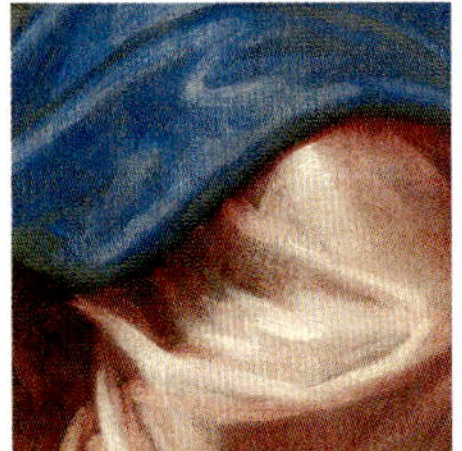

Tintoretto specialized in dramatic lighting. There is no single source of illumination in the work, and there are striking highlights on the clothing.

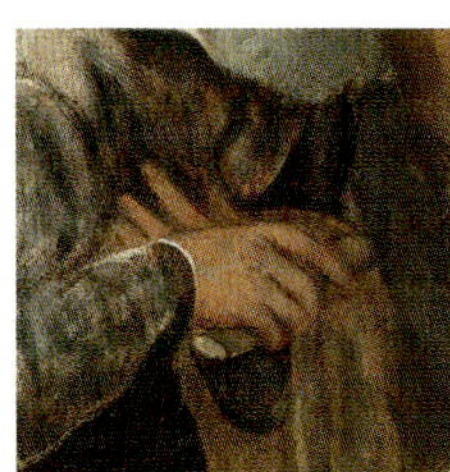

Joseph holds his hands together as though in prayer. Mary and the shepherd do the same.

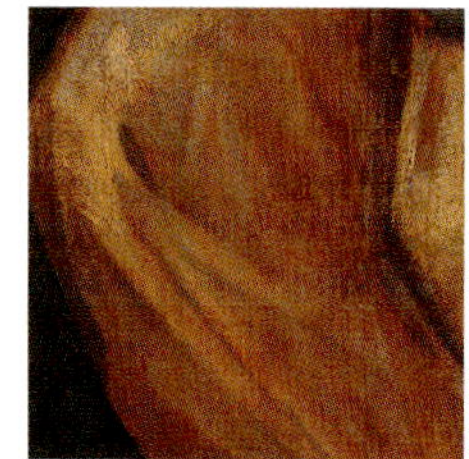

Tintoretto's technique of using long, loose brushstrokes was criticized in his lifetime, although it became fashionable later.

> "Tintoretto […] wanted to explore new ways of representing the legends and myths of the past."
>
> E. H. Gombrich, 1950

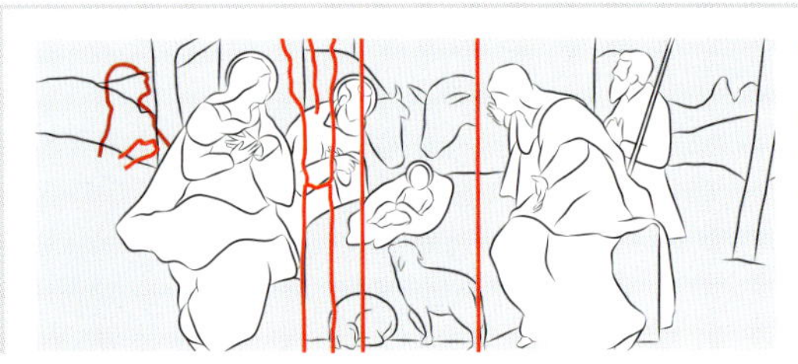

Repurposed
X-rays of this painting have revealed other figures and joins in the canvas, indicating that another work has been repurposed.

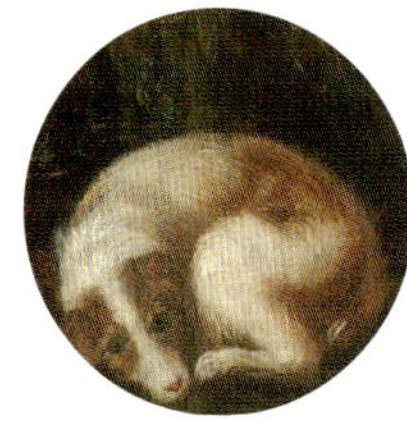

Iconography
Animals are significant in Christian iconography: the cockerel represents redemption; the dog, fidelity; the lamb, Christ; and the rabbit, resurrection.

Lady in a Fur Wrap

Alonso Sánchez Coello 1580–1588, oil on canvas, 31 × 26 in (79.8 × 65.7 cm), Pollock House, Glasgow, UK

An anonymous noblewoman draped in an elegant fur-lined robe emerges from the darkness, gazing out at the viewer. The intimacy of this half-length portrait, accentuated by her soft lips and the gleam in her eyes, was unusual for 16th-century depictions of women. Until recently, the work was attributed to El Greco.

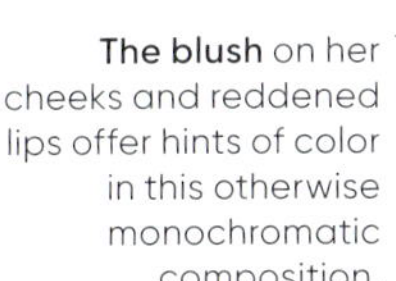

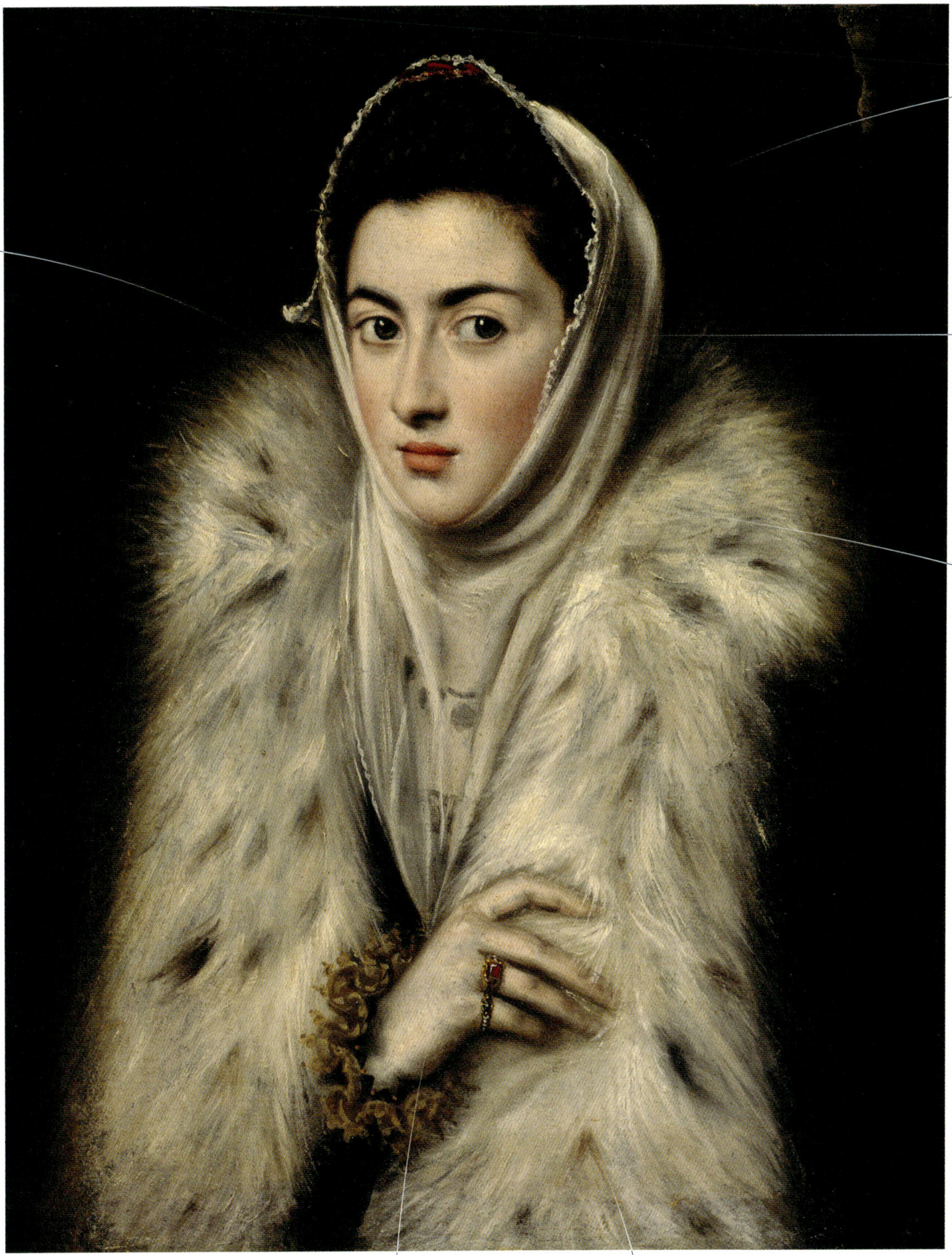

The blush on her cheeks and reddened lips offer hints of color in this otherwise monochromatic composition.

Analysis of the work found its base layer to be light gray, rather than brownish-red as used by El Greco. Early lines on the canvas were also in Coello's style.

A delicate veil with a scalloped trim is wrapped around her head. A thin layer of oil paint was used to show its transparency.

The woman's veil softly frames her oval chin, accentuating the contours of her jawline.

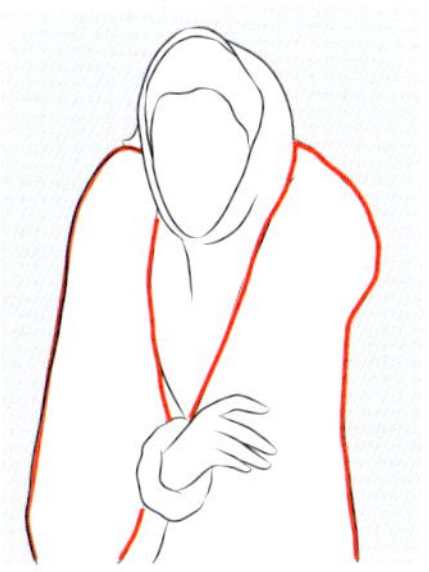

Natural frame
The composition achieves harmony through the parallel fur lapels that frame the sitter. Her turned head and hand reinforce the sense of balance and visual cohesion.

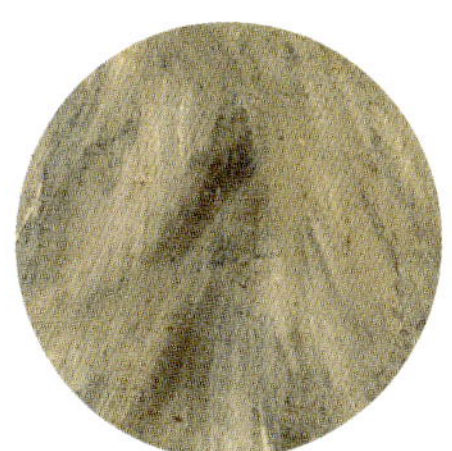

Fur texture
Coello used dense but fine brushstrokes to create the rich and tactile texture of the sumptuous fur.

Her hand gracefully reaches for one side of her robe, introducing a sense of movement that highlights her jewelery and lace cuff.

The fur may have been ermine or lynx. The robe falls into darkness behind this dramatic lining.

Gold leaf drew attention to a patron's wealth, while the reflective surface brought light into the dim palace interiors.

Masking a view of distant crags, Eitoku transformed the delicate mists of Chinese paintings into opaque, scalloped-edged clouds of gold leaf.

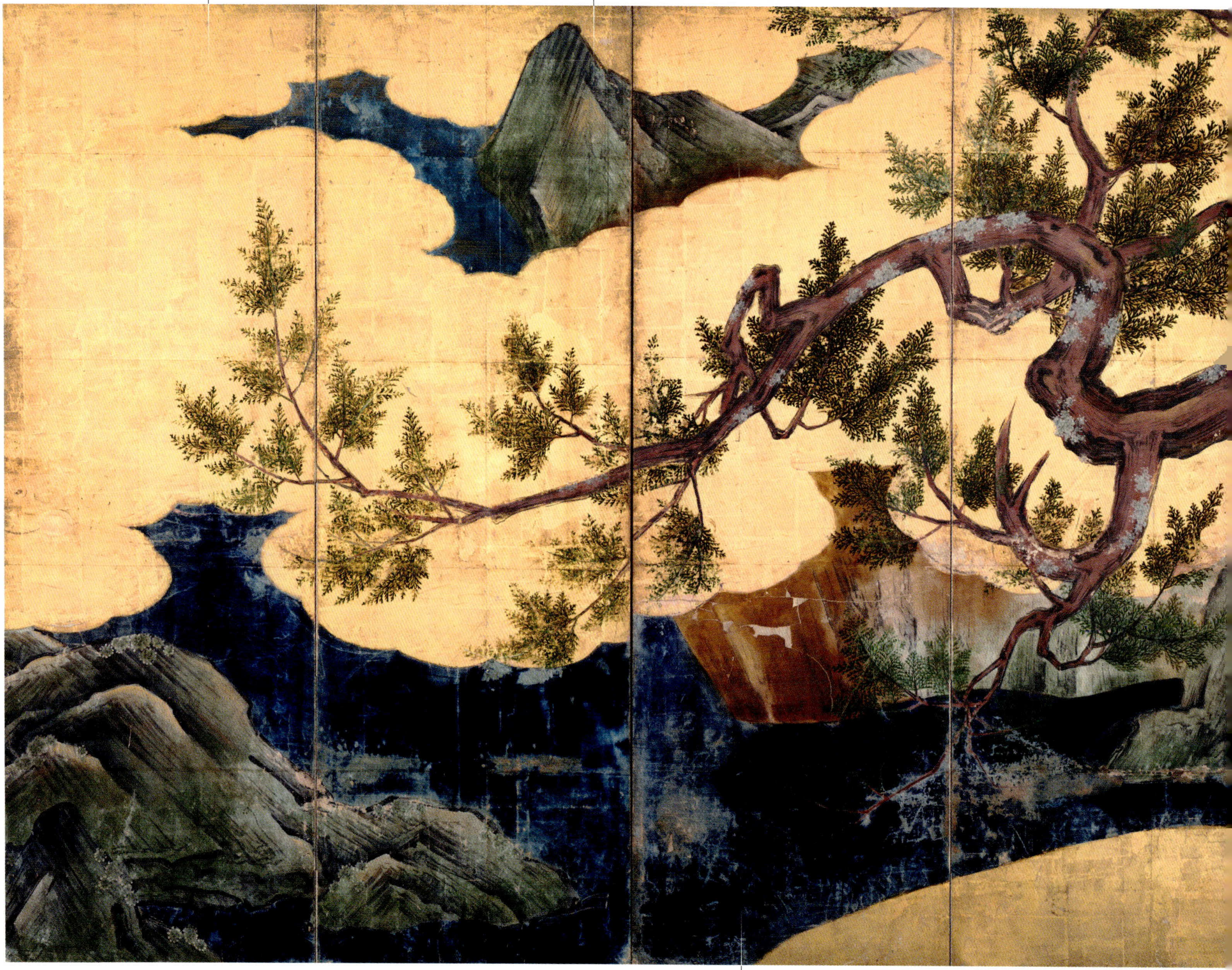

Ground azurite, a copper carbonate, is used for the dark-blue water.

Cypress Trees

Attributed to Kanō Eitoku c. 1573–1615, 170.3 × 460.5 cm, colour and gold leaf on paper, Tokyo National Museum, Tokyo, Japan

A cypress tree clings to the gilded banks of a rocky stream in this folding screen attributed to Kanō Eitoku, the greatest artist of 16th-century Japan. The scene once filled one wall of sliding panels in the palace of a Japanese prince but was later remounted. The theme is inspired by images of aged evergreen trees in mountainous settings depicted on scrolls, fans, and album leaves taken to Japanese Buddhist monasteries by Chinese monks.

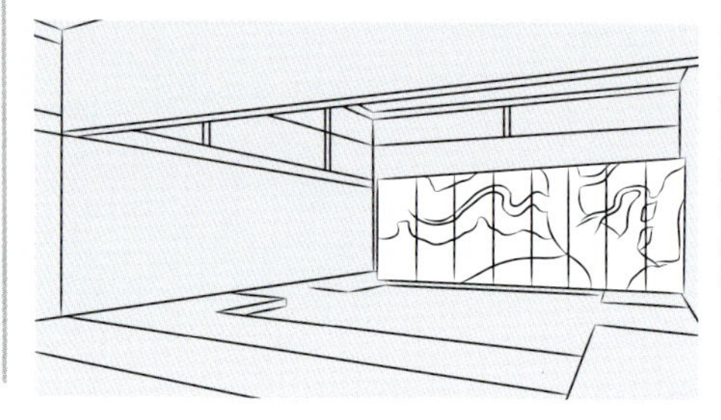

Immersive wall panels It seems likely that Eitoku conceived the work as sliding wall panels. Anyone standing in a room whose walls were decorated with closely packed trees would have felt as if they were in a forest.

The forms of rocks and tree trunks are boldly outlined or accented in textural strokes in black ink.

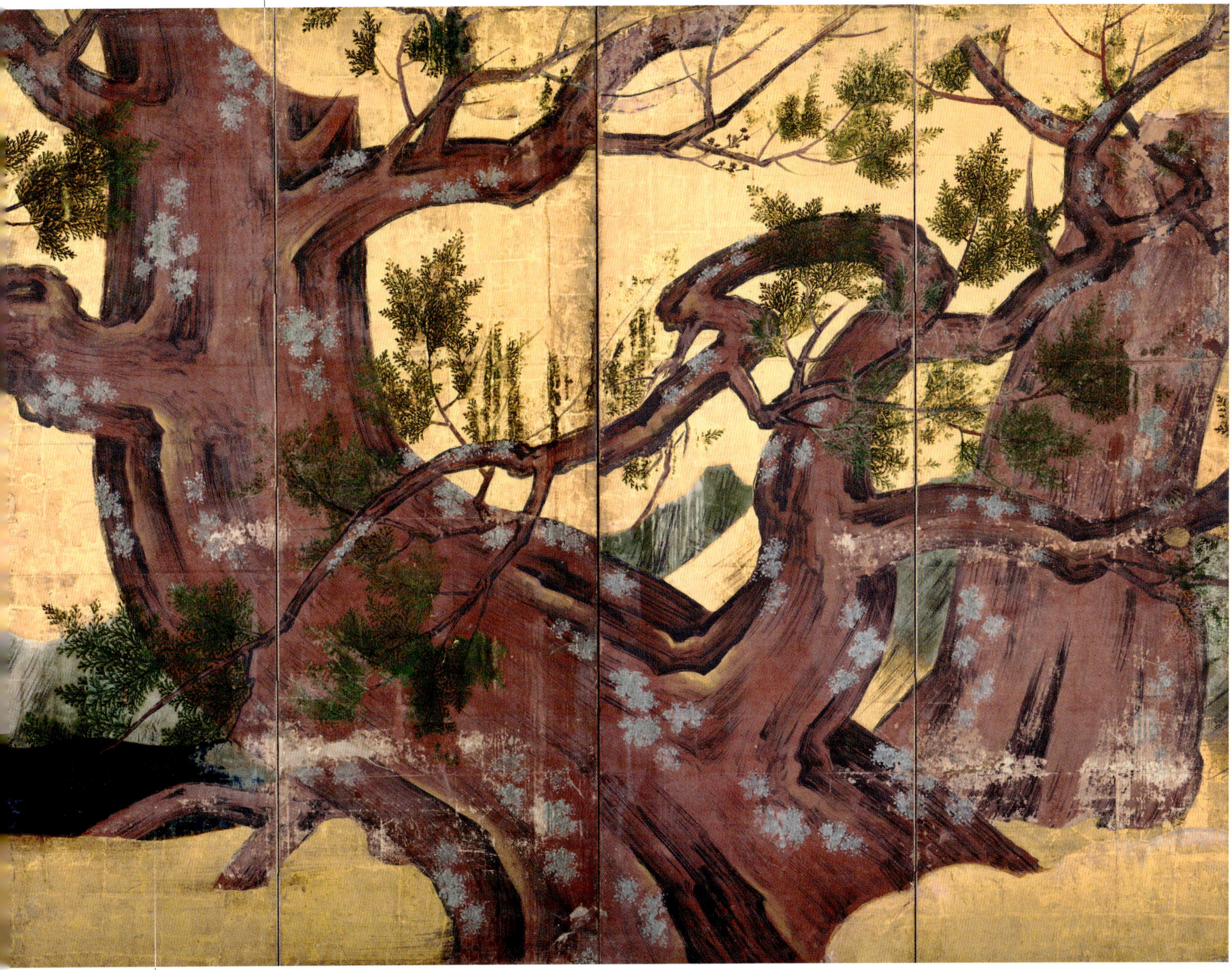

The great age of the cypress is revealed by fingerlike roots grasping the bank and the massive, gnarled, lichen-covered trunk and branches.

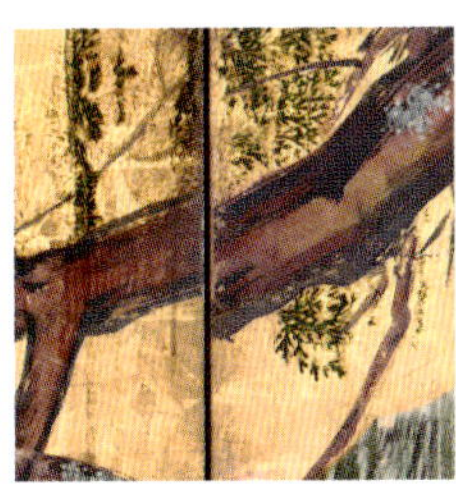

The tree's spreading branches often do not match as they extend, indicating that the work has been reduced in size.

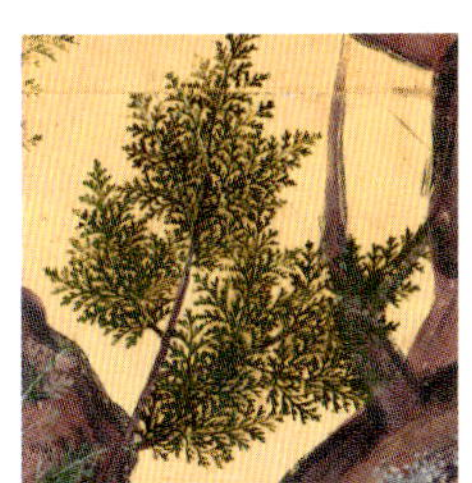

Ground malachite, a semiprecious stone, is used for the green leaves.

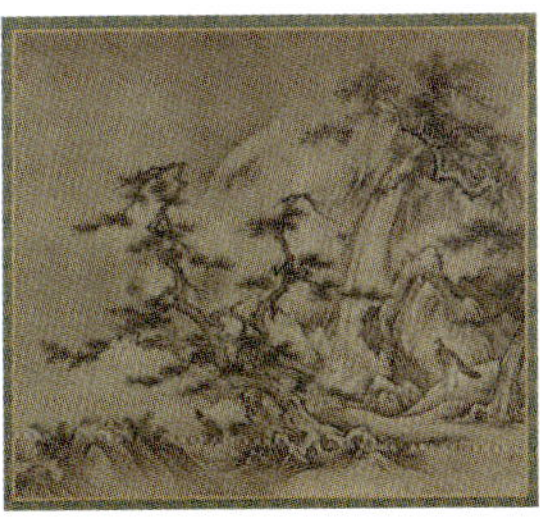

Ancient inspiration
Ancient Chinese concepts anthropomorphized certain wild plants. An aged, gnarled evergreen tree gripping a rocky bank, for example, embodied a person of loyalty, fortitude, and wisdom. Water, mist, and distant peaks represented spiritual solitude from the corrupt outer world.

> "It's only in winter that the pine and cypress are known to be evergreens."
>
> Confucius

Marriage Portrait of a Bolognese Noblewoman

Lavinia Fontana c. 1580, oil on canvas, 45 × 35 in (115 × 89.5 cm), National Museum of Women in the Arts, Washington, D.C., US

An unidentified bride shows off her family's wealth in a portrait that was probably painted to celebrate her marriage. The fine silks and velvets, as well as the jewels she wears, indicate her family's wealth. Fontana was one of Bologna's leading portraitists. Her paintings are notable for their luminous coloring.

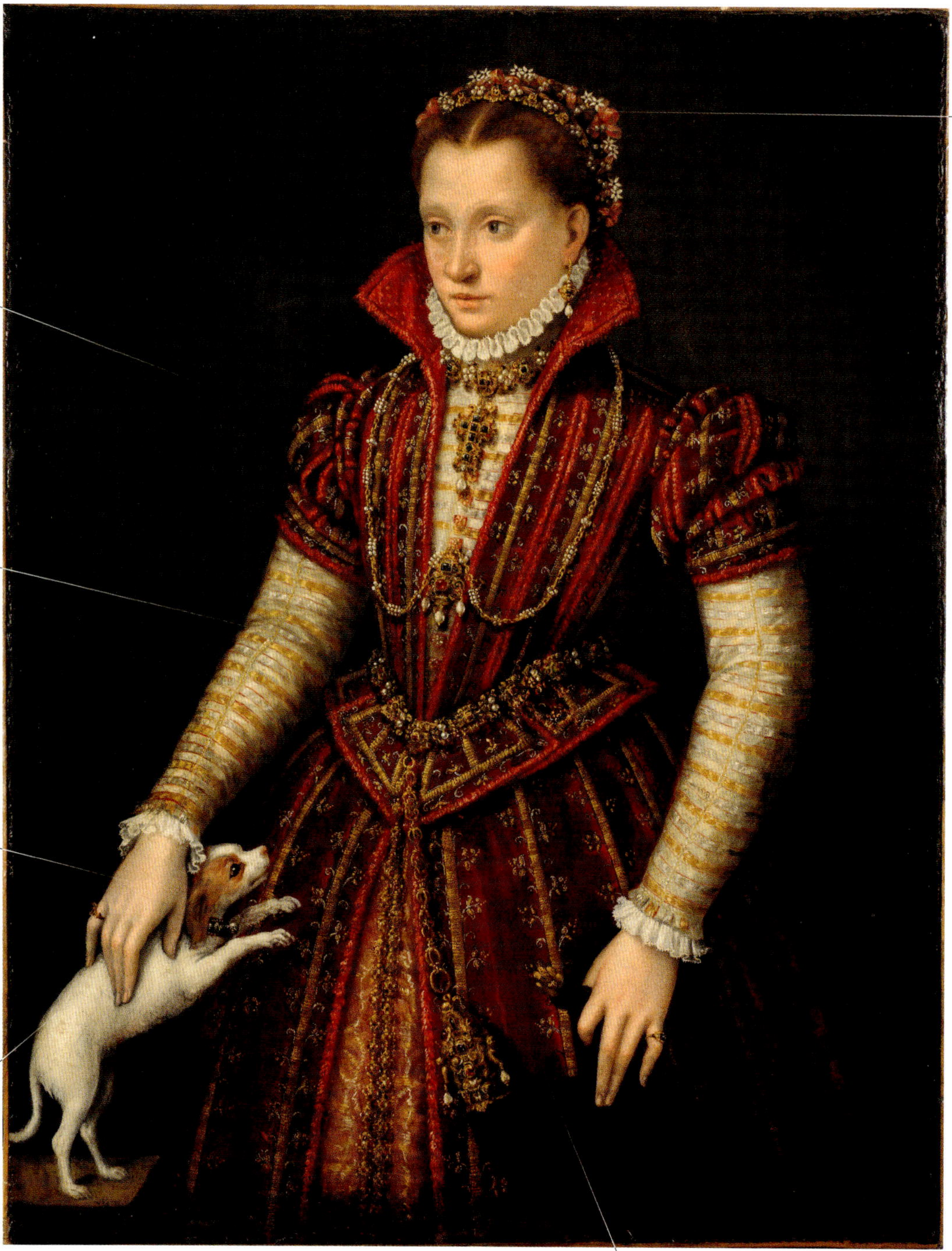

A crown of jewels and flowers confirms that the woman is a bride.

Bolognese brides traditionally wore red dresses at this time.

A fine velvet, worn over a striped silk doublet with a gold lamé underskirt, was a popular fashion.

The elongated, curved fingers are typical of the cultivated elegance and sophistication of Mannerism.

The dog, a symbol of marital fidelity, offers a contrast to the stiff pose of the woman and humanizes the painting's formality.

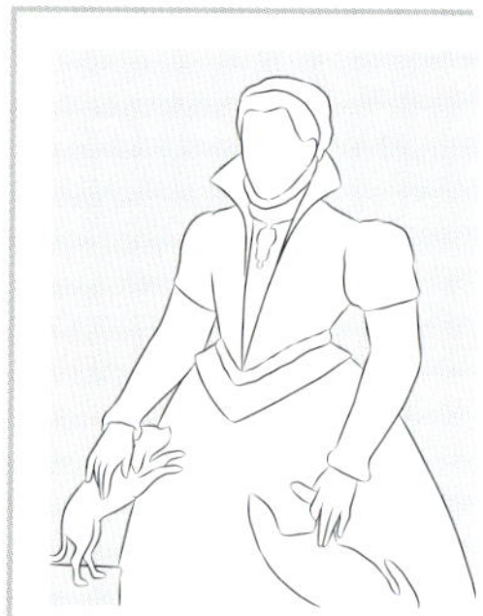

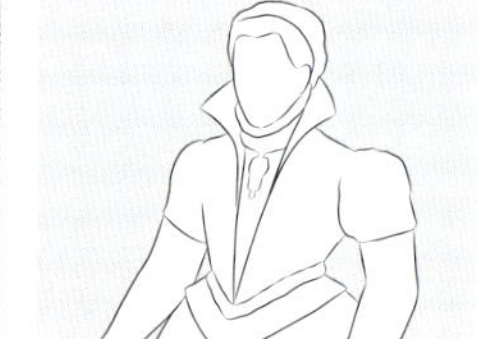

Contrasting styles
The sitter, depicted using a limited palette of red, white, and gold, is the focus of the painting. The dark background offers no distractions.

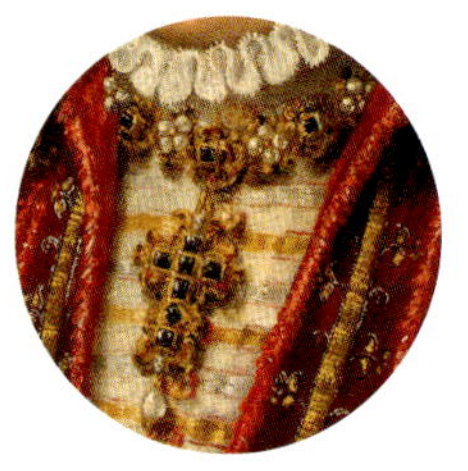

High fashion
Fashion historians believe that Fontana's depiction of fabrics and jewels are authentic records of Italian fashions of the time. The fine detail in the jewelery suggests it was painted in the studio without the presence of the sitter.

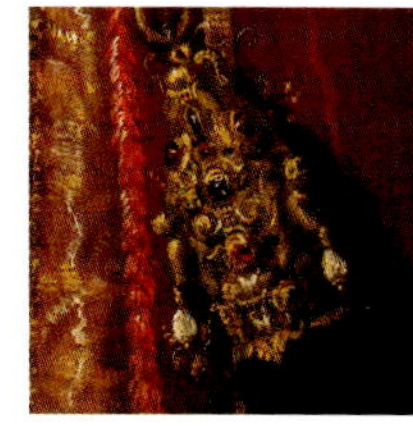

Suspended from the woman's belt is a fertility talisman known as zibellino. It is the pelt of a marten with gem-studded head and paws.

The sumptuous fabrics and jewels are rendered in intricate detail.

The Burial of the Count of Orgaz

El Greco c.1586, oil on canvas, 189 × 142 in (480 × 360 cm), Iglesia de Santo Tomé, Toledo, Spain

This altarpiece, reminiscent of scenes of Christ's entombment, depicts the Count of Orgaz being lowered into his tomb by saints Stephen and Augustine. The earthly funeral procession is imbued with a sense of the divine, as Jesus and Mary emerge from the swirling, celestial clouds above.

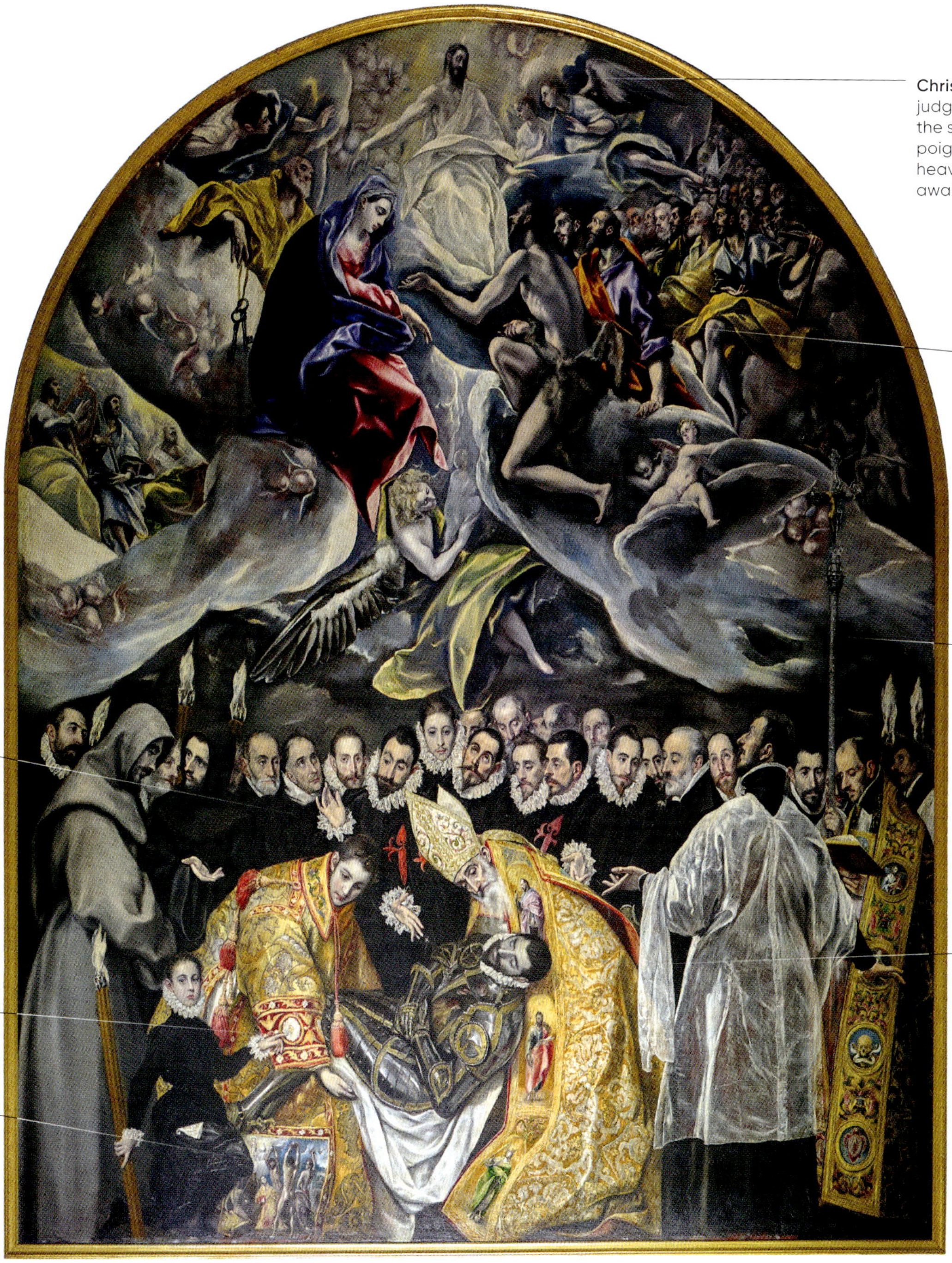

Christ's presence as judge, presiding over the scene, serves as a poignant reminder that heavenly judgment awaits after death.

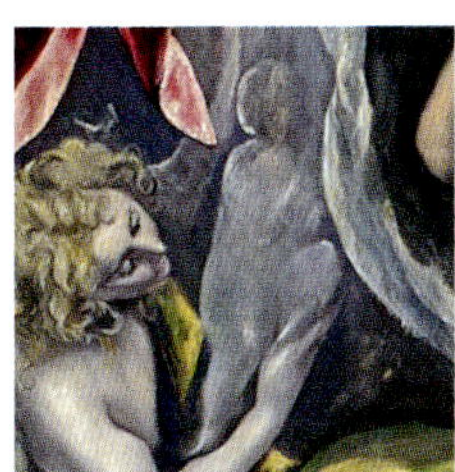

An angel guides the count's soul, which is represented as a baby, to meet its maker.

Use of cool blue tones in the flesh heightens the expressive qualities of the work and reflects the somber atmosphere of the painting.

El Greco's elongation of the figures amplifies their expressive gestures. This is particularly notable in hands, one pointing to the count and the other toward heaven.

The painting divides into two—the mortal world and the heavenly sphere. They are united by the upward gaze of some of the mourners as well as the crucifix.

In the center of the composition, the Count of Orgaz is carried by the two saints. He wears military dress to emphasize his courtly status.

Amid the dark hues, hints of yellow in the saints' vestments, draped fabric, and the hazy light behind Christ reinforce the upward movement of the composition.

Stephen's intricate vestment features a miniature scene of his martyrdom, adding another narrative while showcasing the artist's technical brilliance.

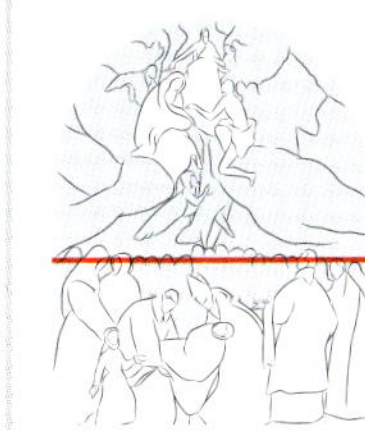

Contrasting styles
The static, friezelike funeral procession in the lower half of the painting contrasts with the dynamic movement above, where the clouds arch upward toward Christ at the apex.

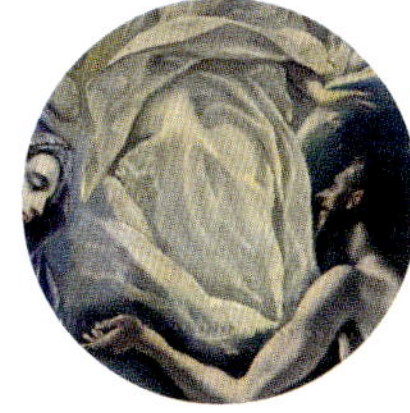

Two realms
El Greco's intricate brushwork on the ruffs and the saints' vestments contrasts sharply with the broader strokes in the upper composition, enhancing the visual distinction between earthly and sacred realms.

> "The spirit of creation is an excruciating, intricate exploration from within the soul."
>
> El Greco

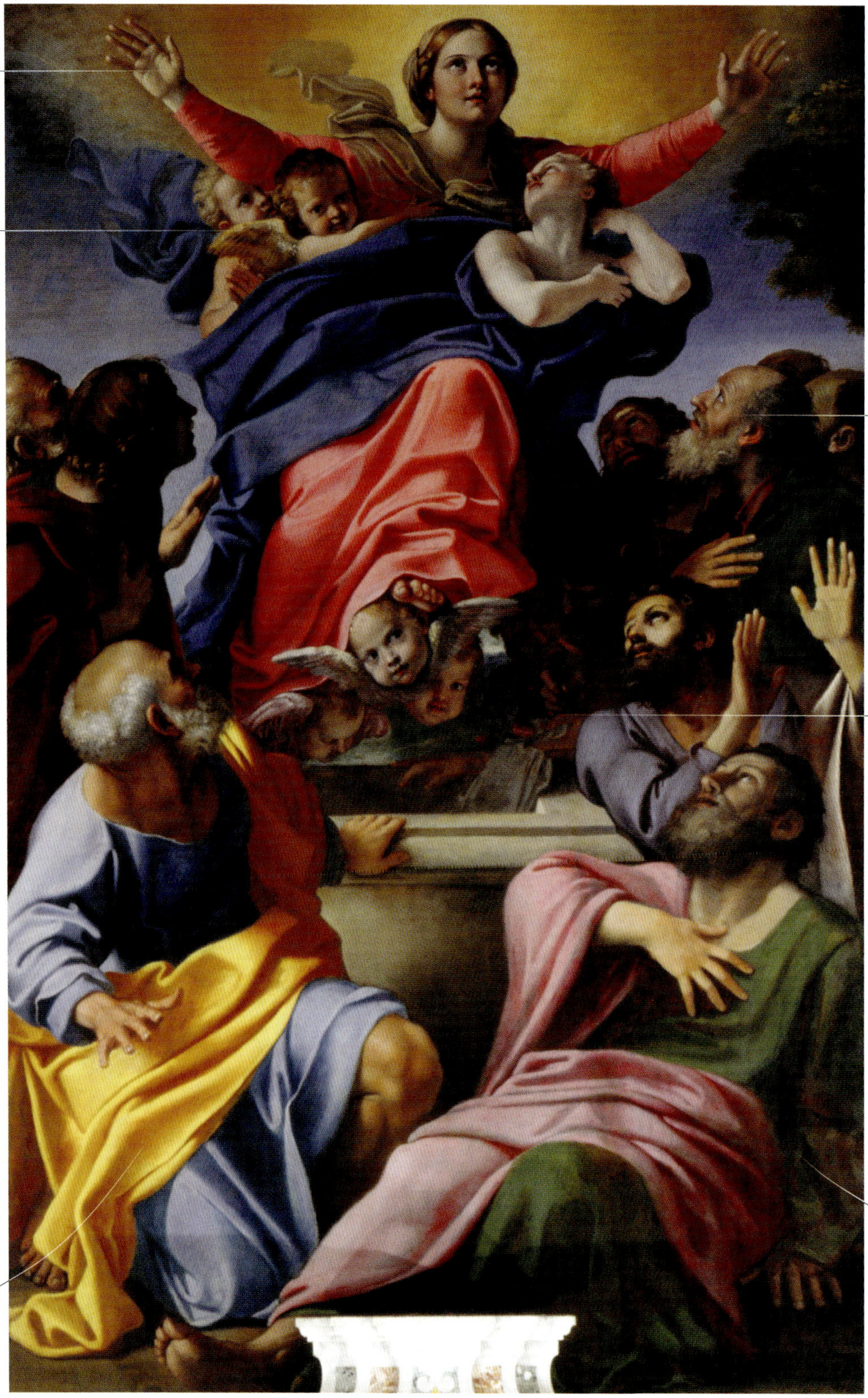

The Virgin's outstretched arms and awkward position make her seem off-balance, evoking movement.

A group of putti raises the Virgin to heaven.

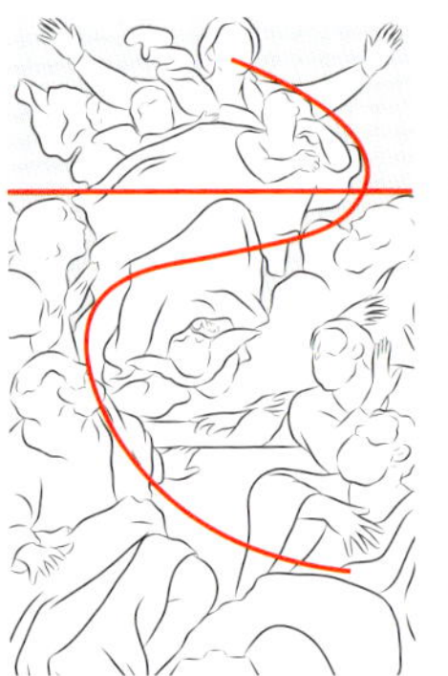

Upward thrust
The eye follows a serpentine movement up the canvas through the figures of St. Paul, St. Peter, and the Virgin.

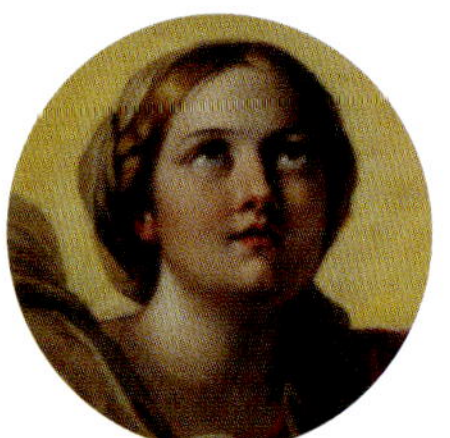

Golden cast
The heavenly glow radiating from the Virgin is reflected in the faces around her.

St. Peter was one of the founders of the Christian Church.

An implied horizontal line at the level of the apostles' heads separates the realms of heaven and earth.

Roses and strips of linen symbolize the Virgin's empty tomb. The Virgin leaves no mortal remains.

St. Paul spread Christ's teaching through the Mediterranean and laid down the doctrines of the Church.

Assumption of the Virgin

Annibale Carracci 1600–1601, oil on panel, 96 x 61 in (245 x 155 cm), church of Santa Maria del Popolo, Rome, Italy

According to the Roman Catholic Church, the Virgin Mary was taken up to heaven (assumed) body and soul on her death. The crowded composition, sense of movement, and emotional drama in Carracci's version of the Assumption are key elements of Baroque painting. All eyes are on the Virgin as she ascends.

The Supper at Emmaus

Caravaggio 1600–1601, oil on canvas, 56 x 77 in (141 x 196 cm), National Gallery, London, UK

In this expressive painting, Caravaggio captures the surprise of two followers of Christ when they realize he is with them after the Resurrection. He uses theatrical gestures, realistic details, and dramatic contrasts to bring the protagonists alive. The lack of a distracting background reinforces the sense of intimacy.

The innkeeper is still. He has not realized he is in the presence of the risen Christ.

Christ blesses the bread and wine, which symbolize the Christian sacrament of the Eucharist.

This man's hand appears to break through the picture plane and draw in the viewer.

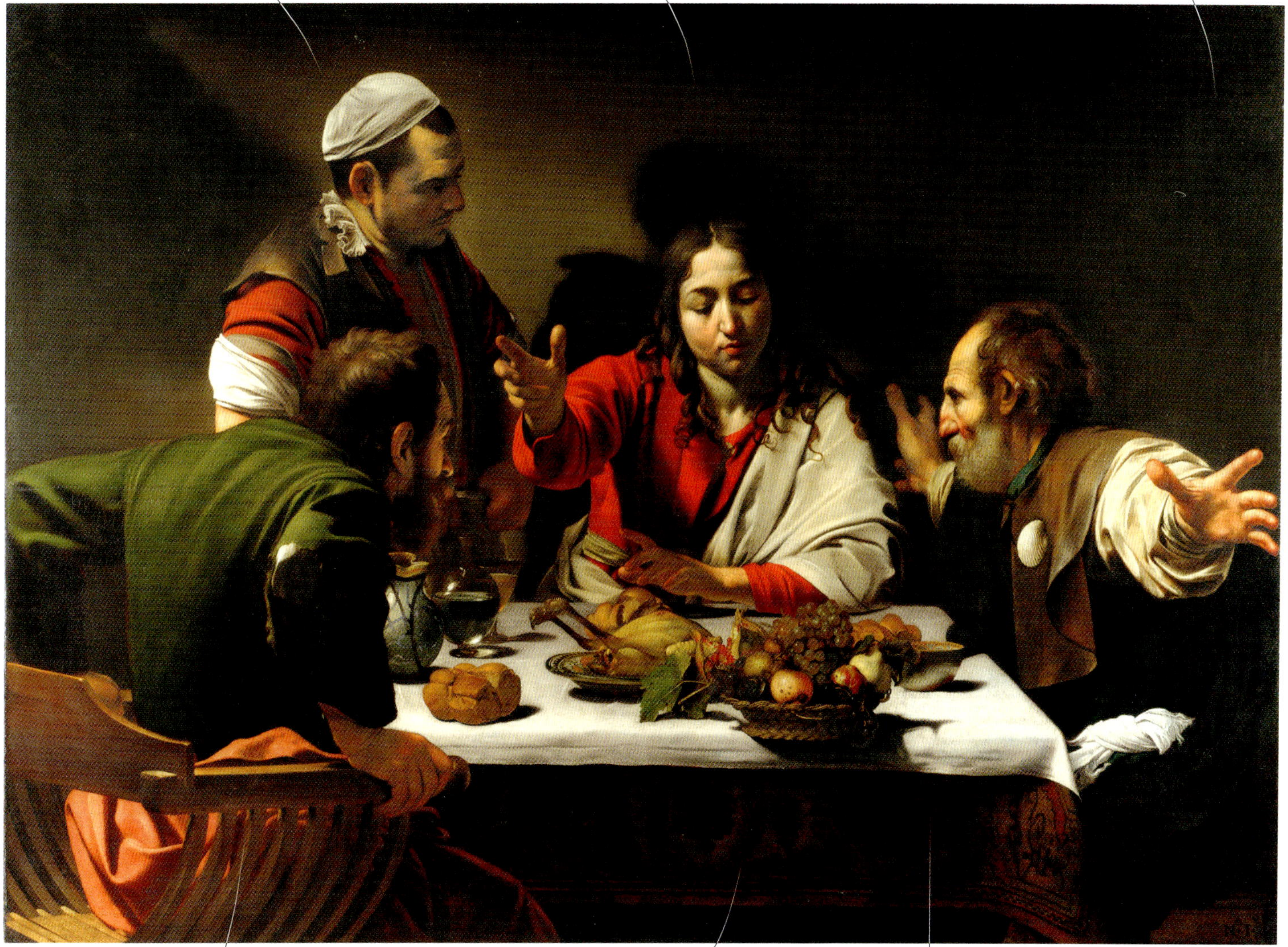

The figures fill the canvas, bringing the scene close to the viewer.

Blemished fruit represents the Christian doctrine of original sin.

The fruit basket casts a shadow in the shape of a fish—a secret symbol used by early Christians.

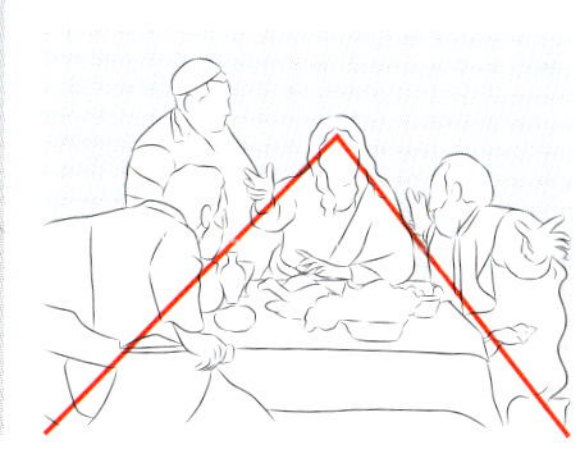

Top and center
Christ's face, more youthful than those of his followers, is at the apex of a triangle rising from the bottom corners of the painting.

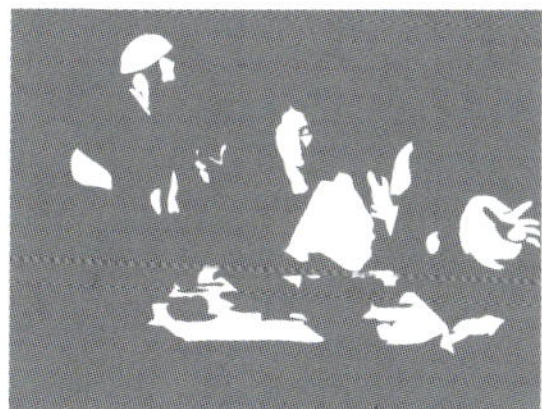

Light and dark
Caravaggio used chiaroscuro—strong contrasts of light and shadow—to create drama, a style known as tenebrism that was emulated by his contemporaries.

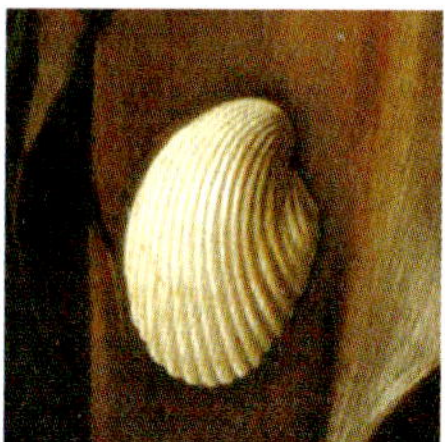

A scallop shell on the jacket of the figure on the right associates him with the apostle James the Great. It is also a symbol of pilgrimage.

Still Life with Quince, Cabbage, Melon, and Cucumber

Juan Sánchez Cotán c. 1602, oil on canvas, 27 × 33 in (68.9 × 84.5 cm), San Diego Museum of Art, US

A quince and a cabbage dangle into the frame while a cut melon and a cucumber rest on a stone surface in an austere yet luminous *bodegón*, a Spanish still-life showcasing simple foods. This style of painting contrasts with the opulence found in Dutch still life paintings of the time.

An intense light source from the top left creates a dramatic chiaroscuro effect, infusing the simple composition with dynamic contrasts.

Vegetables were suspended in cellars to prevent decay. Some critics think Cotán's quince and cabbage represent planets, reflecting a celestial harmony.

A stone window frame and dark backdrop showcase the fruit in its unadorned splendor.

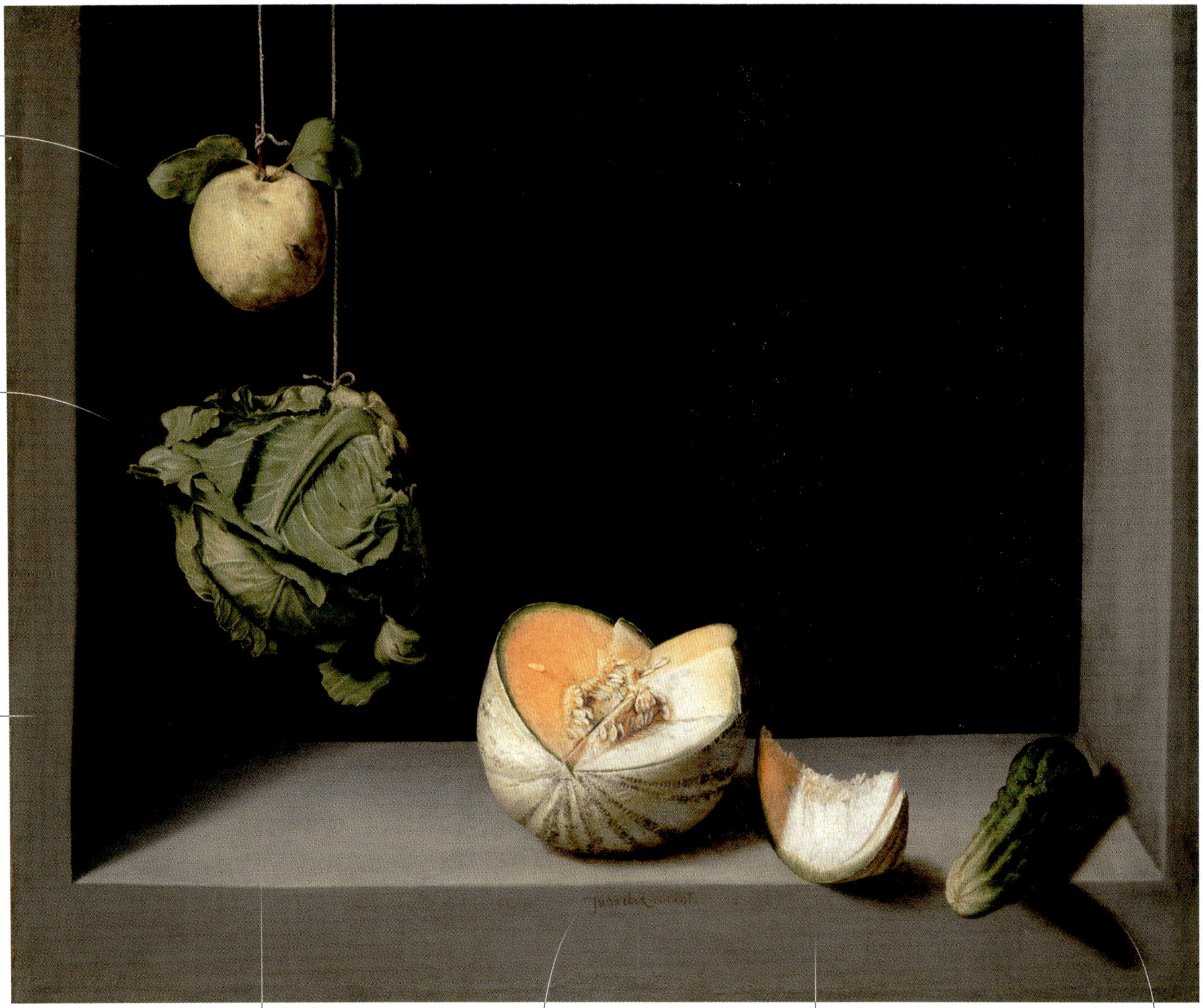

Painted in an uncomplicated, naturalistic style, this depiction of fruit and vegetables could simply be in praise of God's most basic creations.

Cotán signed this work at the center of the shelf, just below the melon.

A slice of melon has been cut off, subtly suggesting a human presence.

Foreshortening the cucumber allows it to protrude beyond the confines of the stone frame, inviting the viewer into the space.

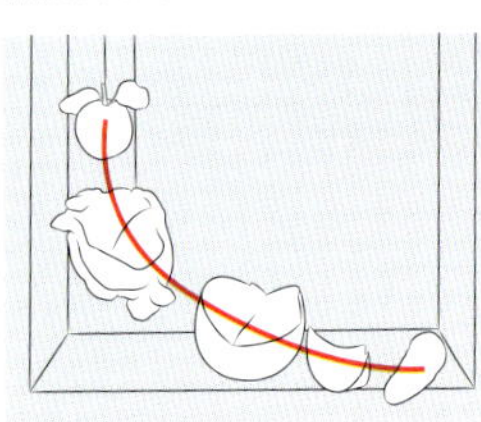

Compositional asymmetry
The fruits form a dynamic arch, starting with the quince in the top left and descending toward the cucumber in the bottom right.

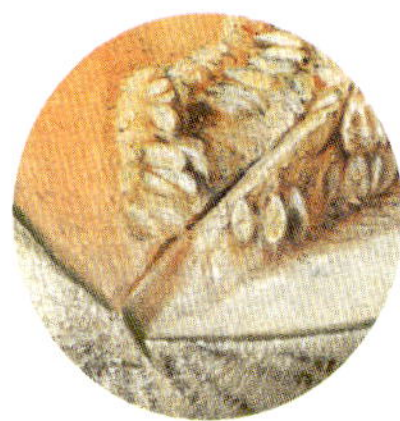

Lifelike textures
Cotán used fine yet discernible brushstrokes to show a variety of textures, from the smooth but uneven surface of the quince to the succulent flesh and seeds of the melon.

Flight Into Egypt

Adam Elsheimer 1609, oil on copper, 12 × 16 in (31 × 41 cm), Alte Pinakothek, Munich, Germany

In the oldest-known nocturnal landscape in European painting, German artist Elsheimer shows the Holy Family fleeing from Herod, a story that was usually set in daylight. The painting is divided into three scenes—the shepherds around a fire, the escaping family, and a moonlit landscape—linked by a vast, overarching sky.

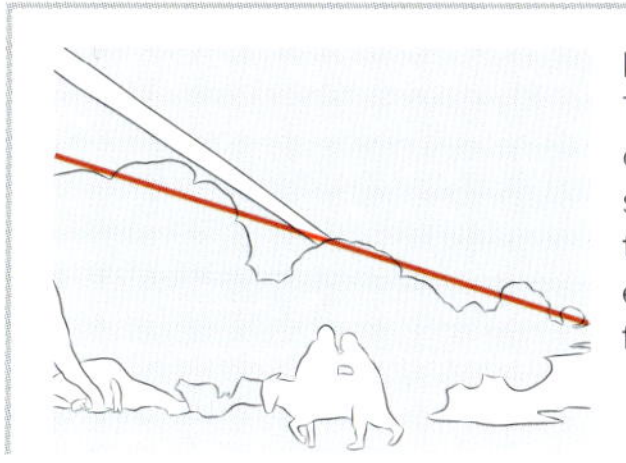

Linking line The three scenes are linked by a strong diagonal that leads the eye into the far distance.

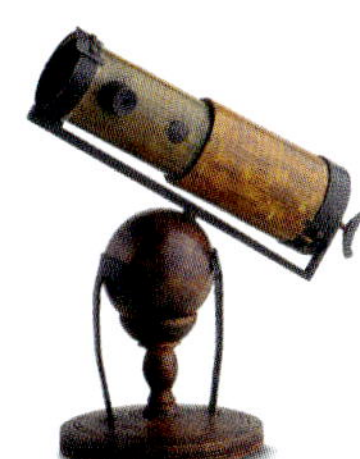

Detailed stars The constellations are depicted accurately. Elsheimer had used a telescope, a recent invention, to study the night sky on a visit to Rome.

The Milky Way, which symbolizes the path to heaven, is portrayed as a mass of individual stars.

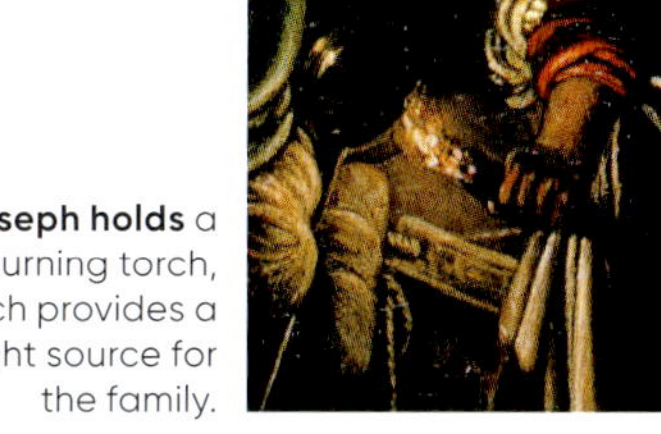

Joseph holds a burning torch, which provides a light source for the family.

The constellation Leo, the lion, associated with kingship, is shown above the Holy Family.

The reflective surface of the copper support intensifies the luminosity of oil paint, especially in lighter areas.

The moon illuminates the landscape. Its surface is shown pitted with craters.

Reminiscent of the shepherds in the Nativity story, these figures are set back in space and lit by a fire.

The Holy Family is positioned close to the front of the picture. Essential details are highlighted against the dark background, a style known as chiaroscuro.

Landscape with Tobias Laying Hold of the Fish

Domenichino c. 1610–1613, oil on copper, 18 × 13 in (45.1 × 33.9 cm), National Gallery, London, UK

A classical landscape serves as a setting for a scene from the *Book of Tobit*, an apocryphal work (outside the accepted Biblical canon) about a devout man who has been blinded. Instructed by an angel, Tobias, Tobit's son, kneels on the bank of the Tigris River and catches an enormous fish, which goes on to play a part in restoring Tobit's sight. Domenichino's carefully constructed landscape reveals a growing interest in an idealizing style that came to define landscape painting in 17th-century Italy.

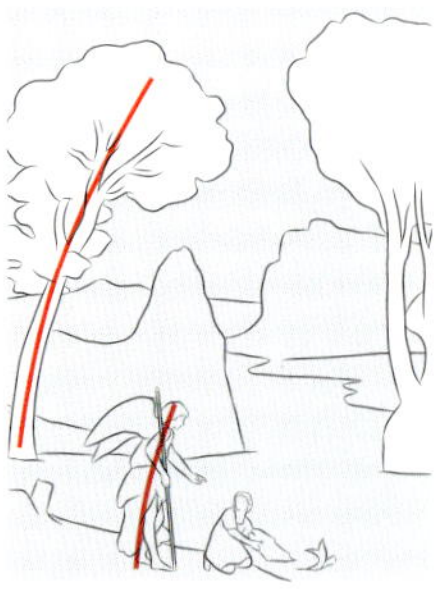

A building on a mound in the distance adds depth to the composition.

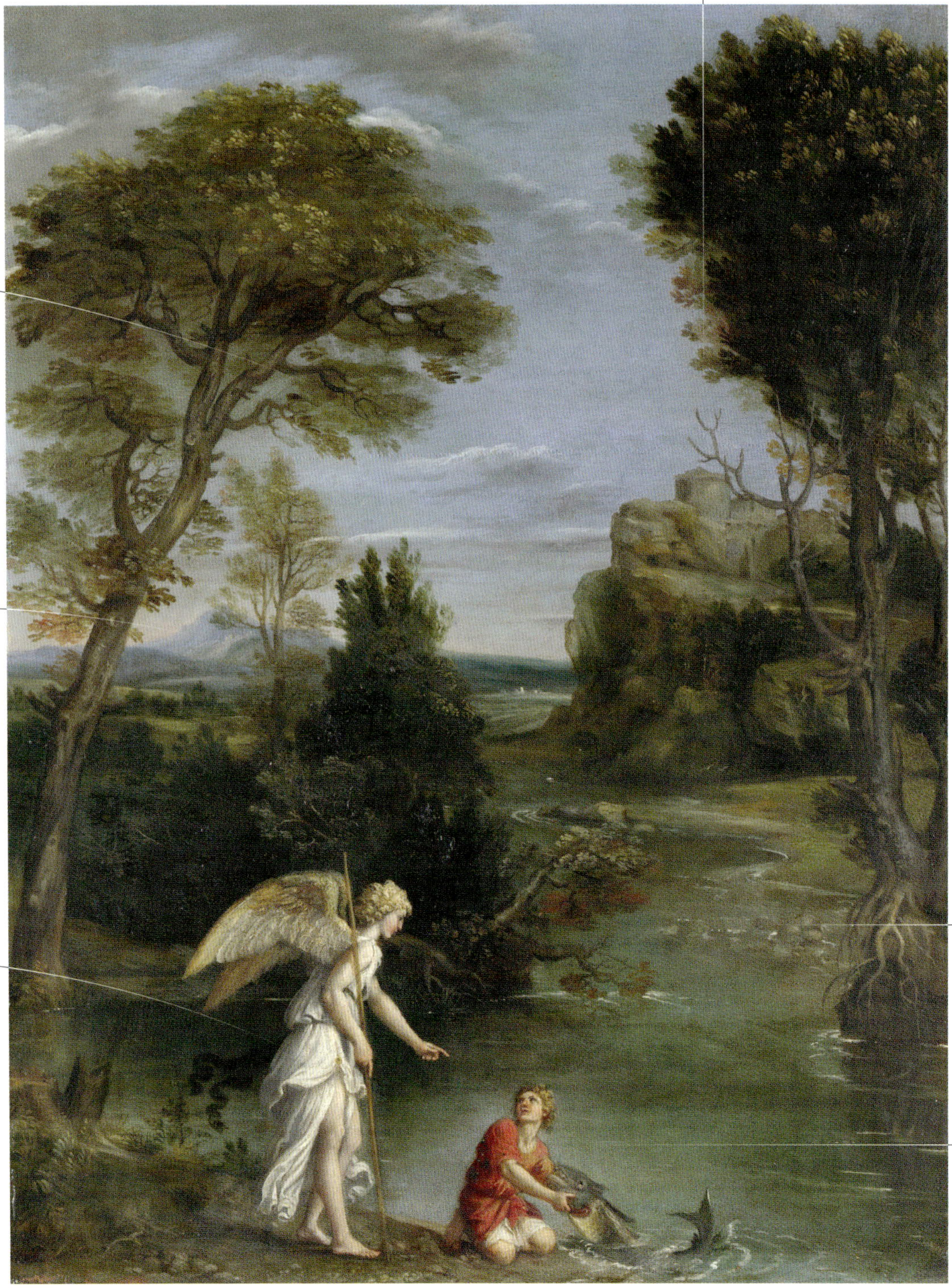

Depicted with transparent layers of paint, the leaves look as though they are moving in the wind.

The artist's main interest seems to be the landscape. The narrative occupies a relatively small portion of the composition.

The angel is bathed in light, accentuating its white drapery and celestial status.

Painting with oil on copper produces a smooth, almost slippery surface that complements the fluidity and reflectivity of the water.

Tobias's red tunic stands out against the muted blues and greens.

Two trees
The composition is balanced by two trees (one of which follows a parallel diagonal axis to that of the angel), creating a visual tension that gives the scene dynamism.

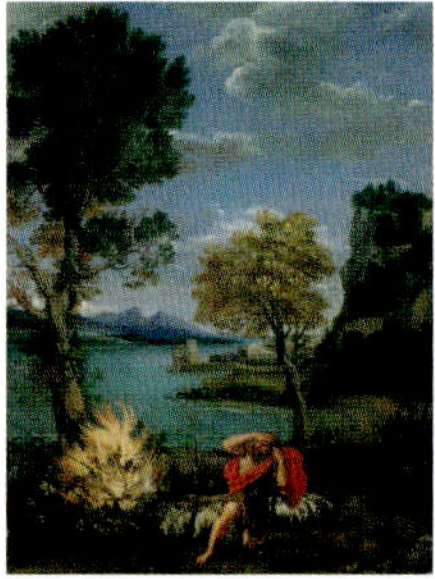

Shared elements
Domenichino's *Landscape with Moses and the Burning Bush* (1610–1616) is very similar to his Tobias painting. Produced around the same time, it depicts a similarly receding landscape, framing trees, and a burst of red color in the clothes of the main protagonist.

Peaches in a Pierced White Faience Basket

Fede Galizia c. 1610, oil on panel, 12 × 16 in (30 × 41.5 cm), private collection

Six plump peaches are carefully arranged in a white tin-glazed, earthenware basket, illuminated against a dark backdrop. Two pairs of plums on the shallow tabletop balance the composition. The fruit, at the peak of ripeness, is both a celebration of nature's bounty and a subtle reminder of the passage of time.

A theatrical light shines from the top left, spotlighting the fruit in the front of the basket and casting shadows over those on the far right.

Warm red and bright yellow tones make the peaches glow vibrantly against the dark background.

The hard basket contrasts with the soft fruit. Galizia used this basket in several paintings.

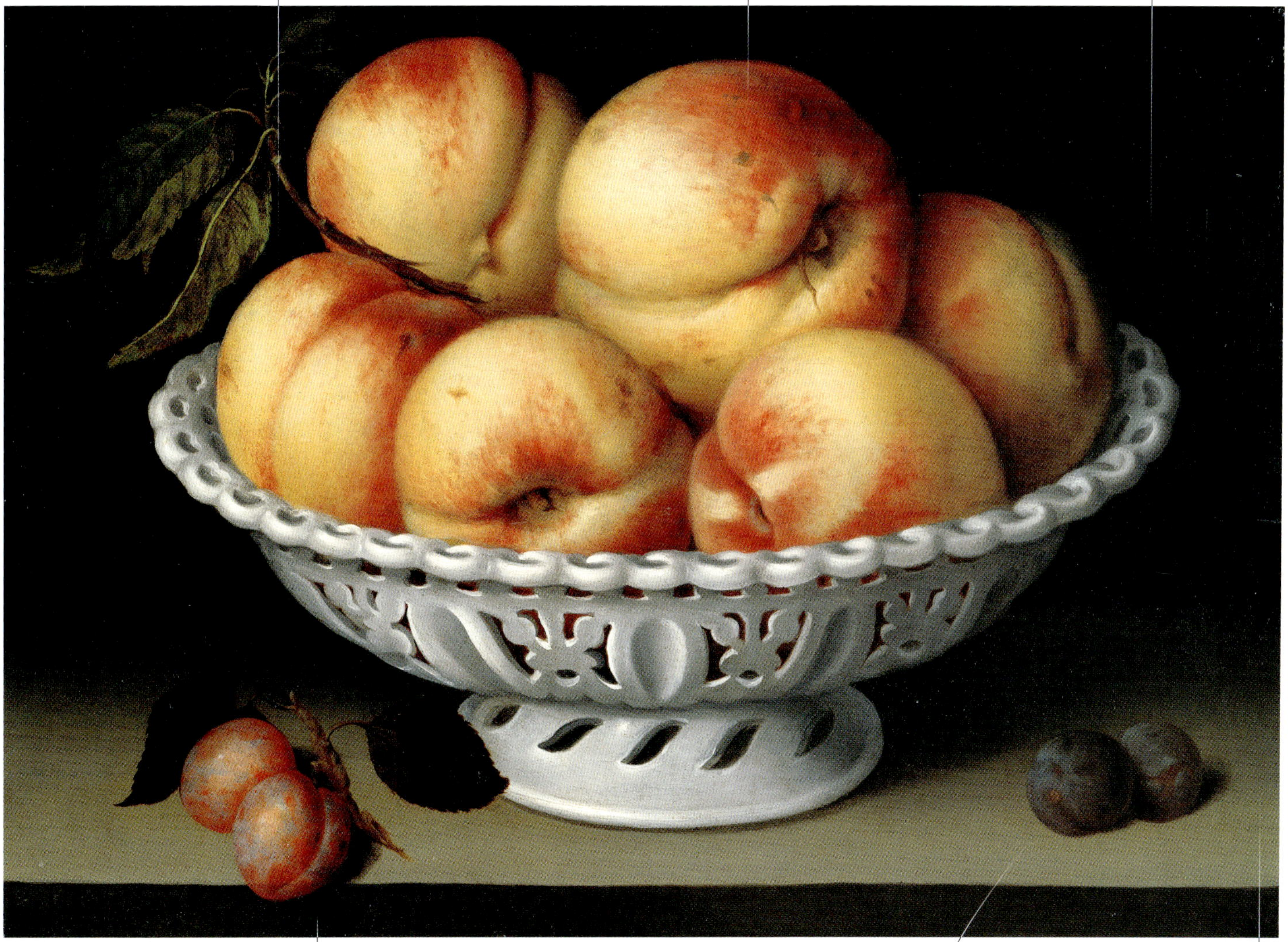

One of the plums hangs over the edge of the table, adding a hint of precariousness and bridging the gap between the viewer's world and the world of the painting.

The darker plums recede into the darkness. Unlike the plums on the left of the basket, they are past their best.

Dramatic chiaroscuro is most pronounced on the receding tabletop, where the light abruptly gives way to the darkness behind.

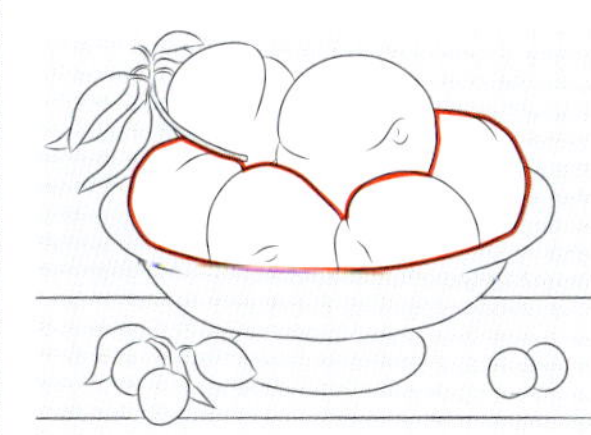

Cropping the subject
The four peaches sitting in the bowl elevate the two larger central peaches. The composition is tightly framed around the basket, deliberately excluding any background distractions.

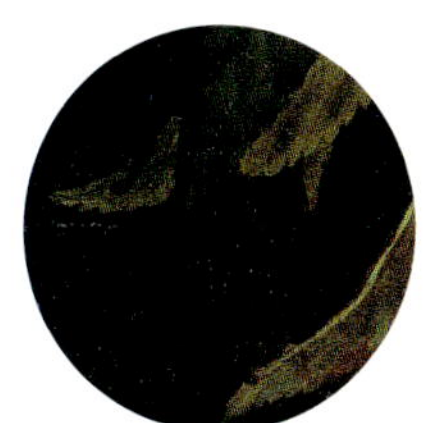

Movement in the stillness
The green leaves on the left-hand side give the otherwise still composition a sense of movement, as do the plums overhanging the edge of the table.

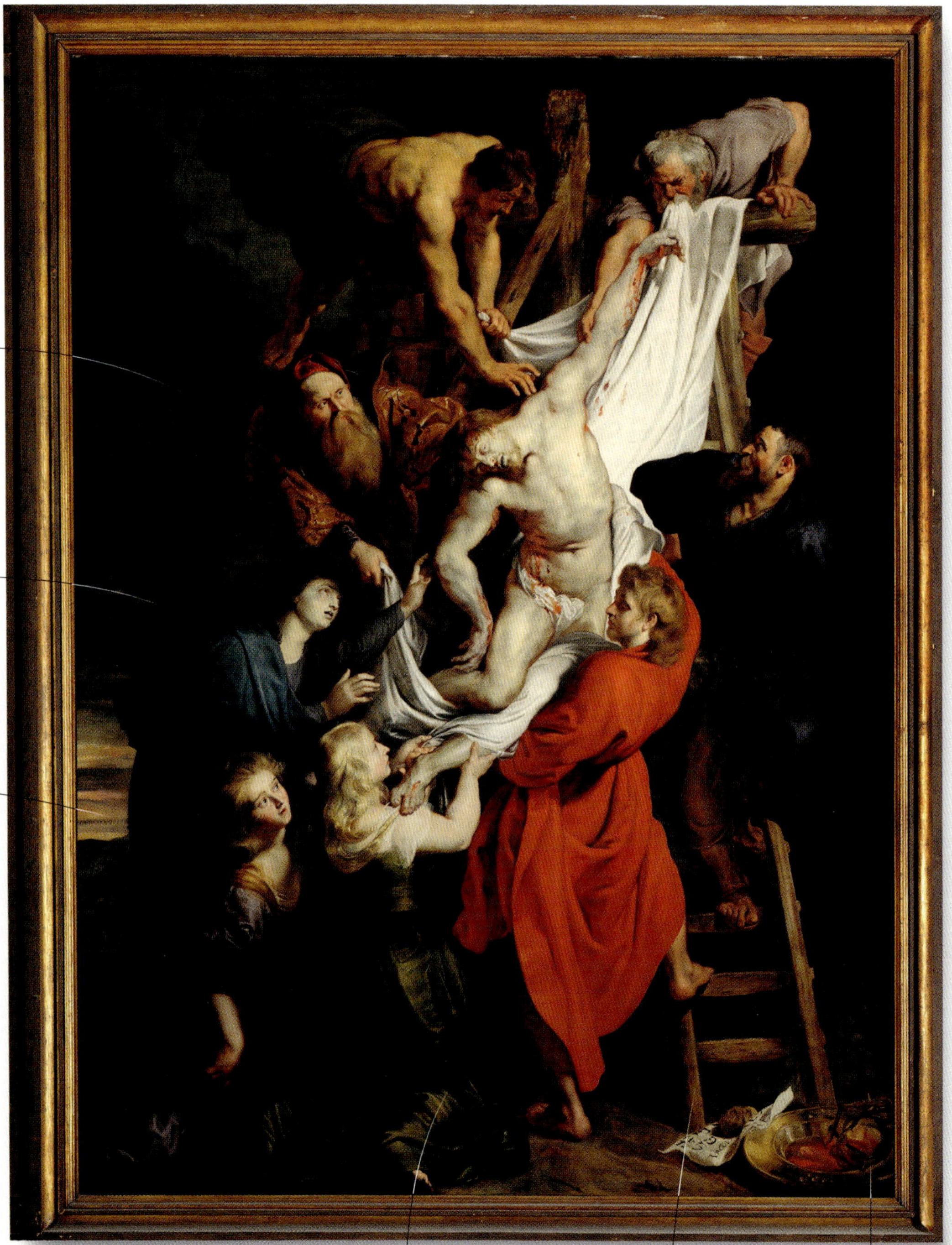

The richly dressed figure is Nicodemus. According to the Gospel of St. John, he helped Joseph of Arimathea prepare the body for burial.

The Virgin's sorrow is reflected in her pale complexion.

The evening light glows in the distance, extending depth beyond the immediate scene.

St. John wears a bright-red cape, accentuating the symbolic connection to the blood from Christ's wounds.

Joseph of Arimathea is said by the Gospels to have provided his own tomb for Christ's burial.

The crown of thorns lies in a copper basin filled with blood.

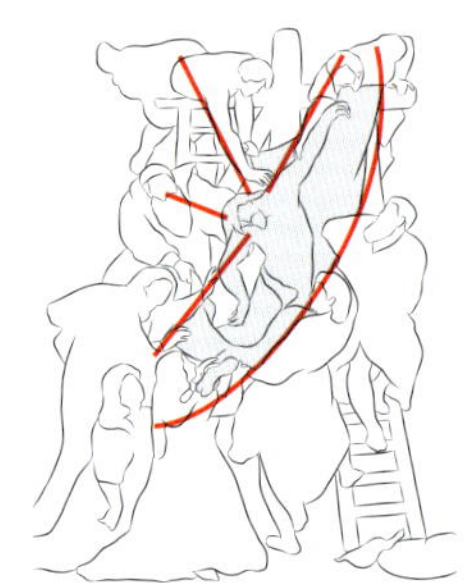

Reading the scene
The white shroud emphasizes the sweeping motion of Christ's descent from the cross. His followers' focused gazes and outstretched arms converge on his face.

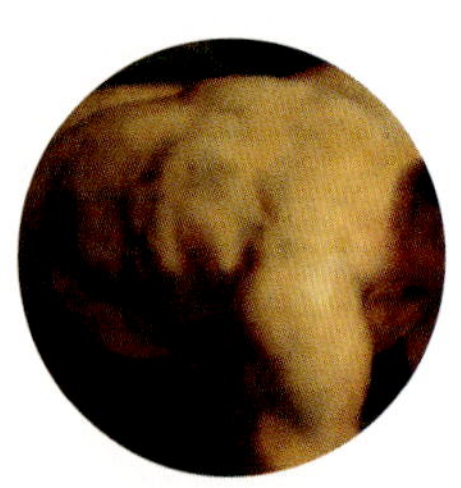

Body and mind
Rubens used color and light to emphasize the sculptural quality of the naked bodies. His use of chiaroscuro conveys emotional drama.

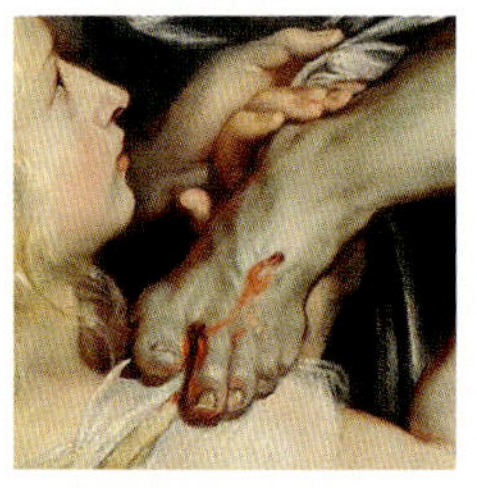

Christ's foot rests on Mary Magdalene's shoulder. This alludes to the story of a woman, sometimes identified as Mary Magdalene, who washed Christ's feet with her tears and dried them with her hair (Luke 7:37–38).

The Descent from the Cross

Peter Paul Rubens 1612–1614, oil on panel, 166 × 126 in (420.5 × 320 cm), Cathedral of Our Lady, Antwerp, Belgium

Draped in a white shroud and lit by a radiant light, Christ's broken body is gently lowered from the cross by an inner circle of followers. Forming the central panel of a triptych, the image is flanked by two other New Testament scenes in which Christ is carried by others—the Visitation and the Presentation.

Still Life with Cheeses, Almonds, and Pretzels

Clara Peeters 1615, oil on panel, 14 × 19 in (34.5 × 49.5 cm), Mauritshuis, The Hague, the Netherlands

In this *banketjes*, or banquet piece, Peeters captures the texture of ripe cheese, softening butter, and dried figs. The foods and costly goods reflect the wealth and economic production of the new Dutch Republic. The artist included a portrait of herself in the composition, to remind the viewer of her skills.

Golden light from the top left bathes the food, while the jug and glass recede into the shadow, enhancing the sense of depth.

The red, brown, and golden hues envelop the scene in a warm glow, making it seem intimate.

Gilded Venetian glass gleams in the light, suggesting opulence.

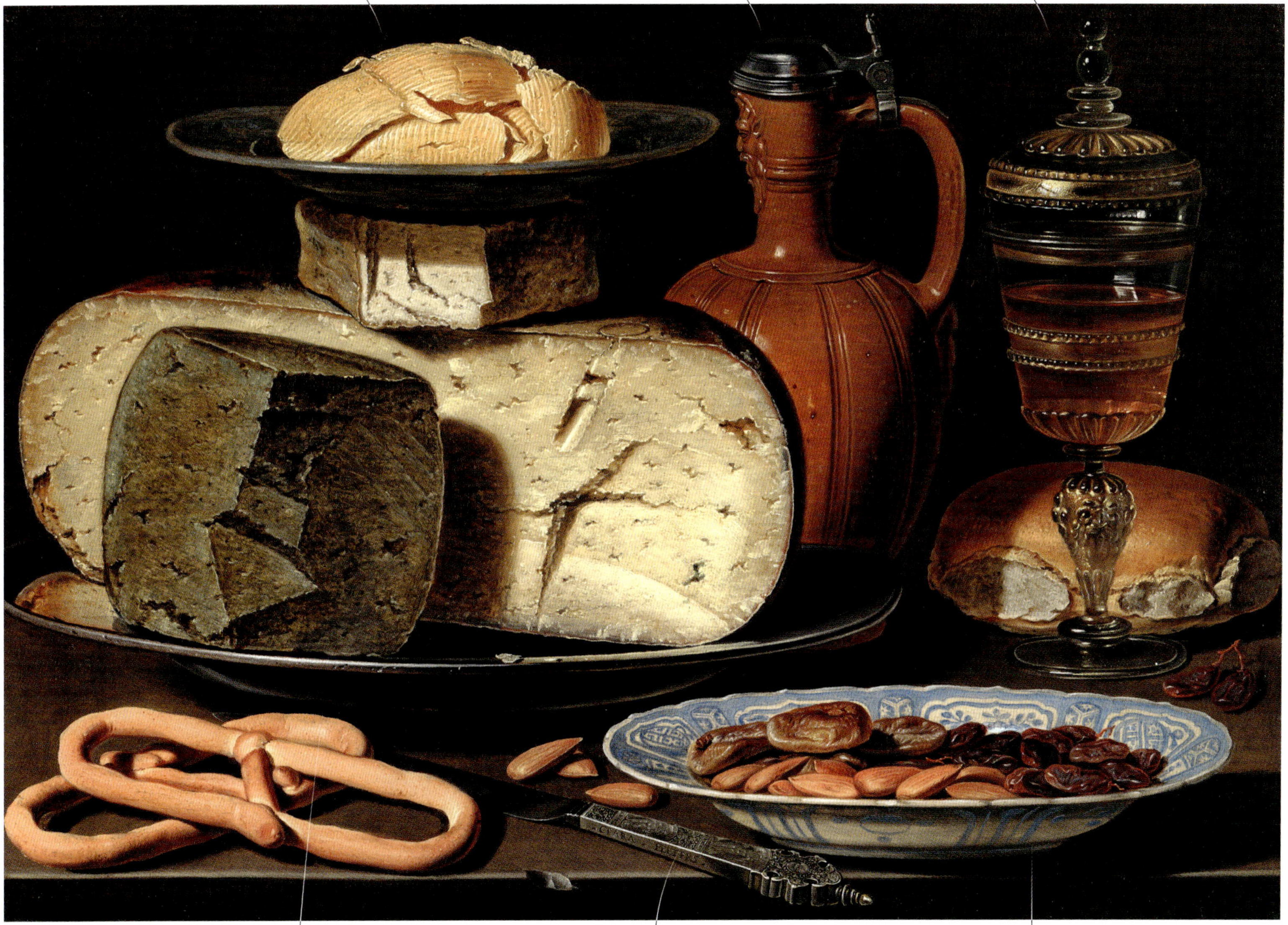

The cheese and butter stand as symbols of Dutch pride, yet their abundance could also serve as a cautionary reminder about the dangers of excess.

Decorative figures on the handle of the knife allude to love. The side of the knife is engraved with the artist's name.

The blue-and-white porcelain dish not only adds color to the composition but also refers to the popularity of imported Chinese porcelain in the Netherlands.

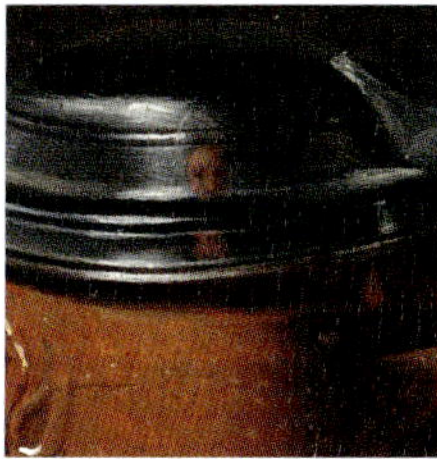

A self-portrait of Peeters is visible in the reflection on the pewter lid of a jug.

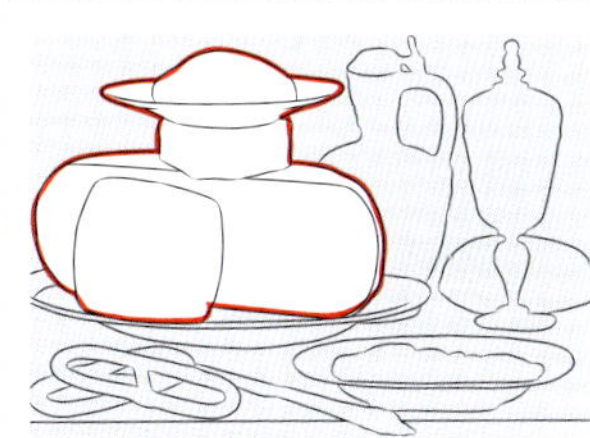

Cheese centerpiece
The pyramid of cheese, crowned by the soft butter, is the focal point of the painting. Its off center placement heightens the sense of depth in the composition.

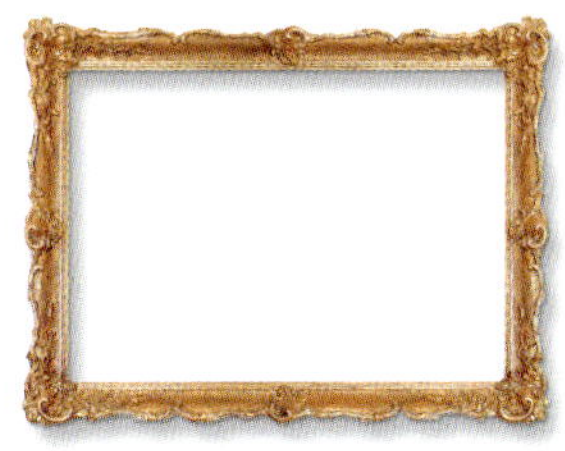

Tight crop
The tight framing of the painting, low vantage point, and dark background create a sense of intimacy.

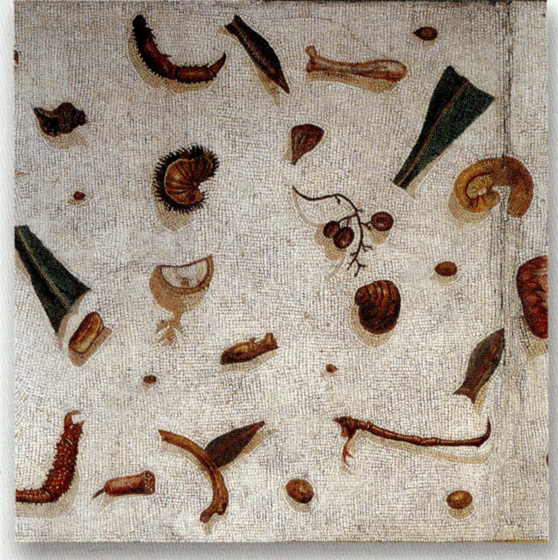

1

Still life

Still life, which refers to paintings of groups of natural and human-made objects, emerged as an independent genre in 17th-century Holland and Flanders. Illusions of reality were much admired, and artists could show off their skill at re-creating every type of surface and texture. In the 19th century, artists concentrated on the aesthetic qualities of objects. Still life remained popular with modern artists, as a means for self-expression and experimentation.

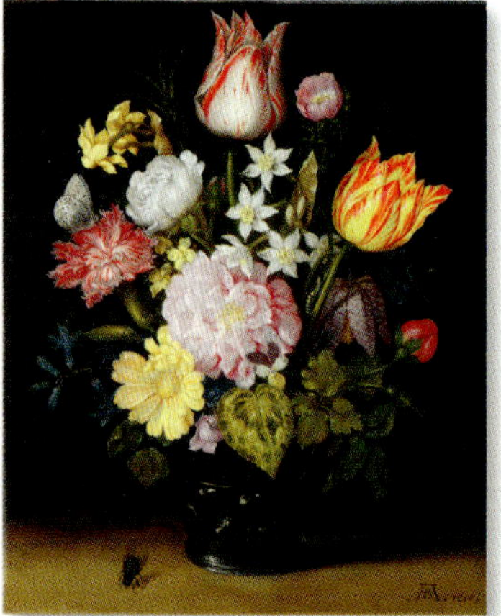

2

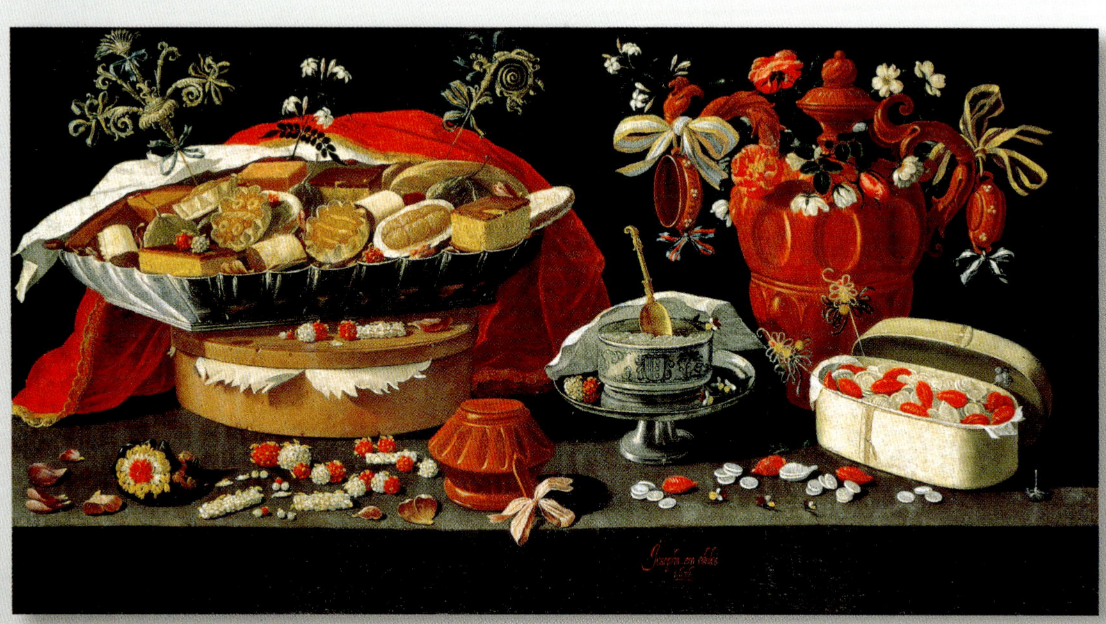

3

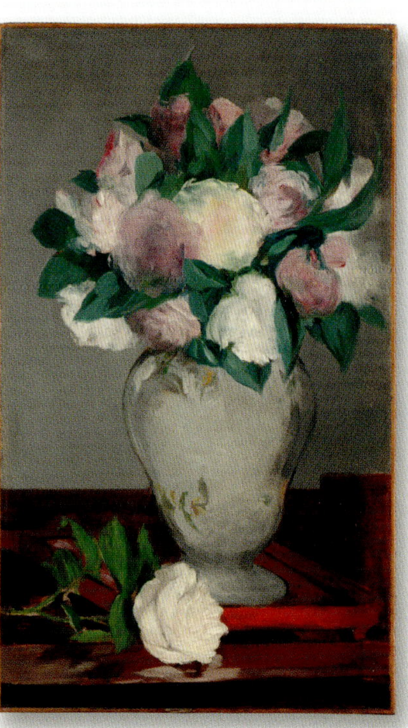

4

1. ***Unswept Room*, Heraclitus, 2nd century CE.** The idea of illusion was highly prized in ancient Greece and Rome. In this mosaic, which runs around the edge of a dining room, the objects are painted to make them look like the remains of a banquet scattered on the floor.

2. ***Flowers in a Glass Vase*, Ambrosius Bosschaert the Elder, 1614.** Bosschaert specialized in flower painting. His precise renditions were a reminder that beauty is fleeting. They were assembled from studies of flowers that bloom at different times and so can only exist in art.

3. ***Still Life with Sweets*, Josefa de Óbidos, 1679.** The Spanish type of still life, called a *bódegon*, usually celebrated simple items of food laid out on a plain stone slab. Óbidos has used the form to depict luxurious delicacies together with an elegant china pot and silver sugar bowl.

4. ***Peonies*, Édouard Manet, 1864–1865.** Manet's approach departed from the tradition that flower paintings had to be botanically accurate. Instead, he used simplified flower forms and sensuous brushwork to explore the relationship between light and color.

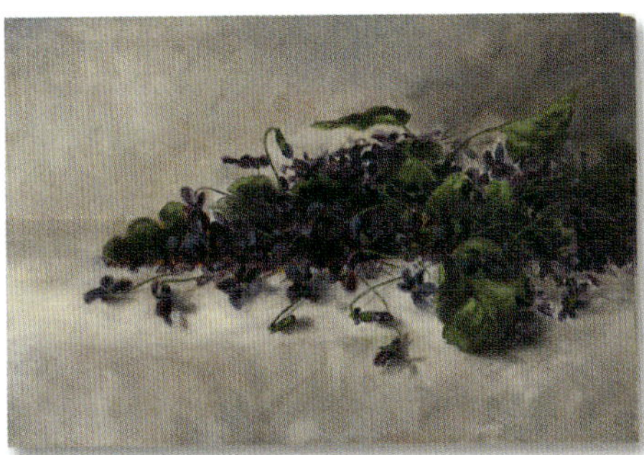

5

Symbolism

Still life has always been a vehicle for symbolism. Religious meanings attach to some objects: white lilies, for example, represent the Virgin Mary. In the 17th century, there was a fashion for vanitas paintings, which depicted candles, flowers, and hourglasses—references to the transience of life and worldly wealth.

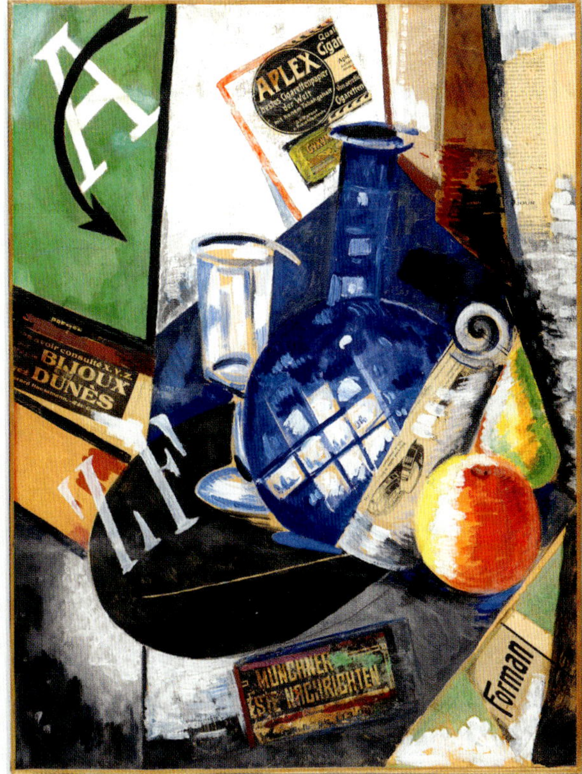

7

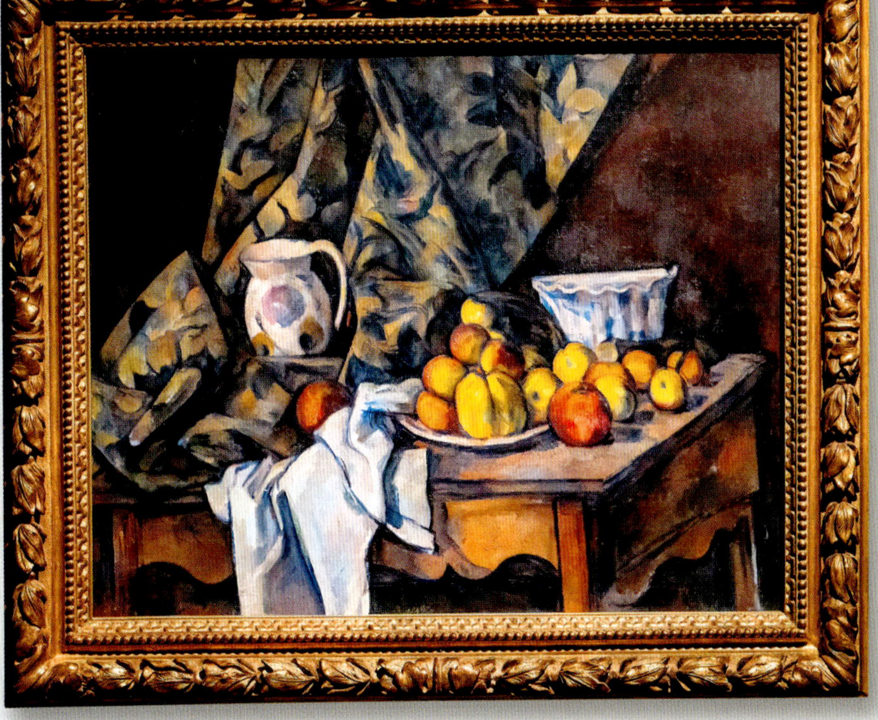

6

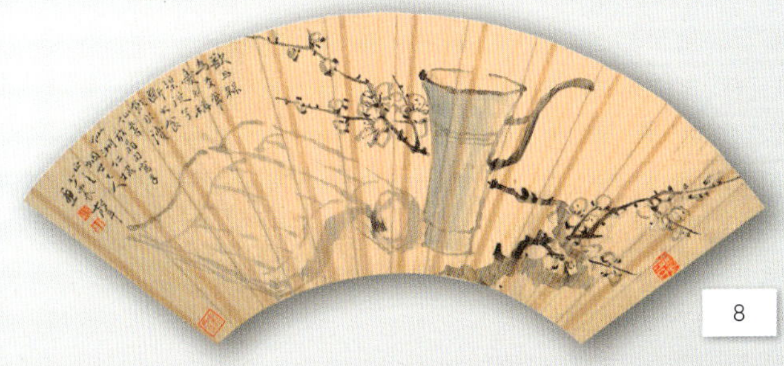

8

5. ***Violets*, Pauline Powell Burns, c. 1890.** Burns was a skilled flower and still-life painter. In 19th-century Europe, people ascribed meanings to flowers, and would express their feelings by sending particular blooms to others. Violets were given as a symbol of faithfulness and love.

6. ***Still Life with Apples and Peaches*, Paul Cézanne, c. 1905.** Cézanne painted the same few objects repeatedly. In an innovative and influential approach, he combined subtle variations in viewpoint and used contrasts in color to convey solidity and depth.

7. ***Still Life*, Alexandra Exter, 1913.** Influenced by Cubism, Exter has combined actual objects—cuttings from newspapers—and painted depictions of objects, showing them from different viewpoints. Also, the flat letters on the picture plane contrast with the modeled objects.

8. ***Still Life with Plum*, Wang Zhensheng, early 20th century.** Originally produced as a fan, this delicate ink drawing in the style of traditional Chinese art combines sprigs of plum blossom (representing blessings and noble virtue) with a loosely drawn cup and scroll.

The Garden of Eden with the Fall of Man

Jan Brueghel the Elder and Peter Paul Rubens 1615, oil on panel, 29 × 45 in (74.3 × 114.7 cm), Mauritshuis, The Hague, the Netherlands

This collaborative painting of the expulsion of Adam and Eve from the Garden of Eden combines Brueghel's meticulous and encyclopedic depiction of the natural world with Rubens's dramatic narrative. Packed with Christian symbols, it captures an enchanting paradise moments before the Fall.

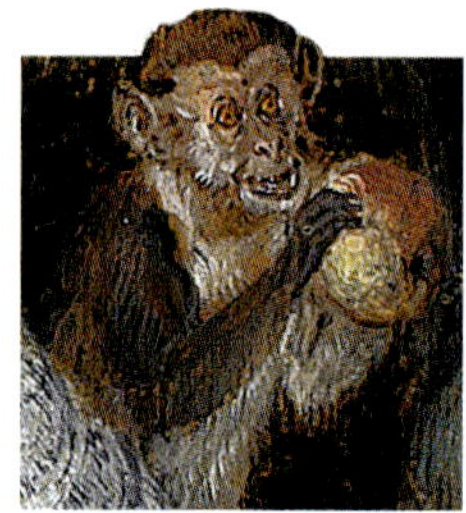

A monkey takes a bite of an apple, foreshadowing the actions that led to the Fall of Man.

Bunches of grapes emerge from the dark foliage above Adam's head, referring to the Eucharist and Christ's redemption of our sins.

As a court painter to Archduke Albert of Austria, Brueghel was able to study exotic birds and animals in the archduke's menagerie.

The lush vegetation is infused with a soft blue light that recedes into the background.

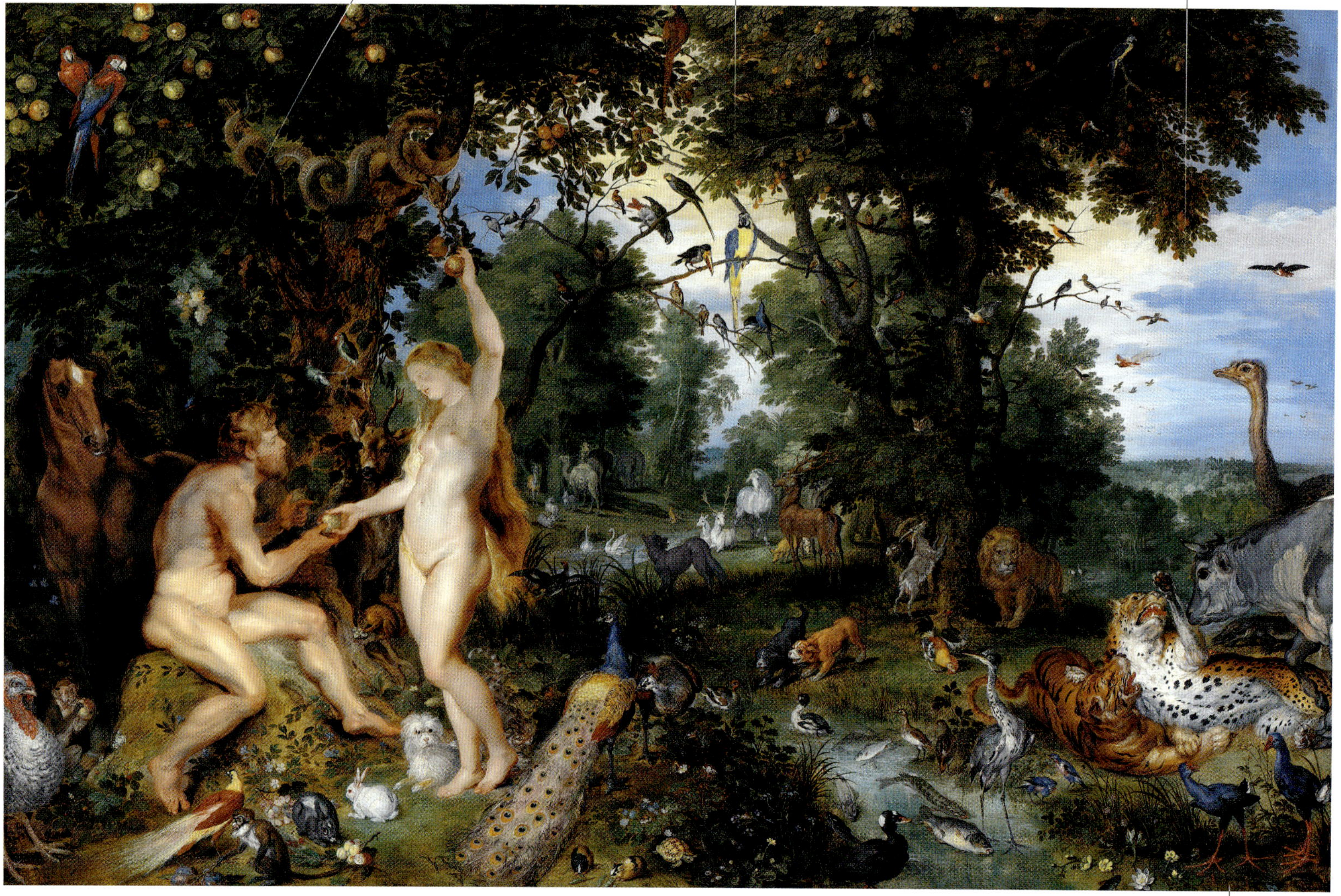

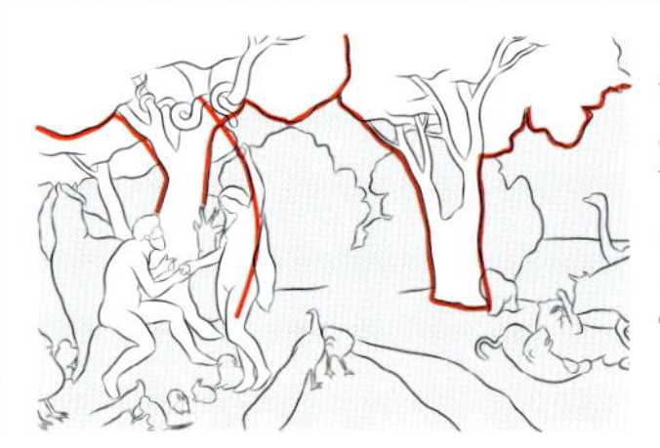

Balanced composition
The narrative unfolds along an arc from the serpent to Eve. Two trees add compositional balance: one (left) provides a backdrop while the other (right) adds depth to the landscape.

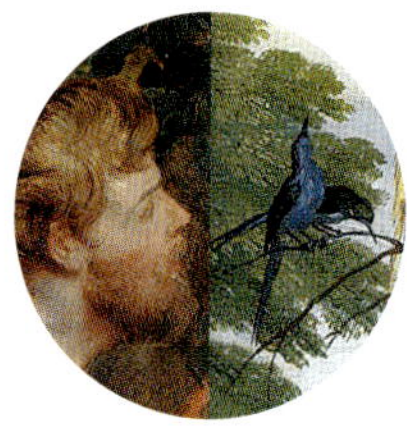

Characteristic techniques
Rubens used broad, fluid brushstrokes to depict Adam, Eve, the horse, the tree, and the serpent. Brueghel, who relied on underdrawings, used fine brushstrokes.

Brueghel signed the bottom right while Rubens signed the bottom left—below the portion of the painting that each artist completed.

Shah Jahan

Abu'l Hasan c. 1616, ink, opaque watercolor, and gold on paper, 15 × 10 in (38.7 × 26.6 cm), Victoria and Albert Museum, London, UK

Abu'l Hasan's single-page painting of Shah Jahan exemplifies the mastery of naturalistic portraiture and passion for the natural world at the Mughal court in northern India. The ruler's halo emanates a soft glow that permeates the painting's subtle shading and warm color palette.

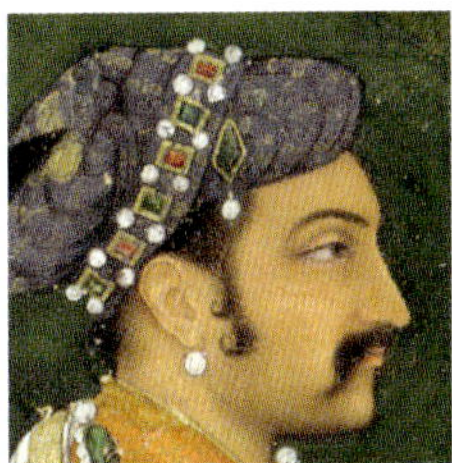

Shah Jahan's right profile is shown in an extremely detailed and naturalistic manner, down to the folds of his ear.

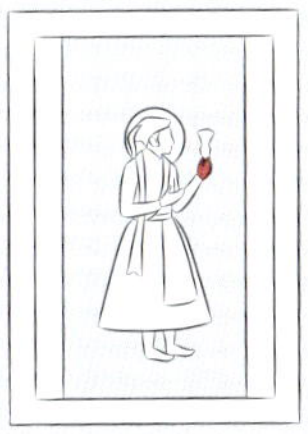

Elongated composition
The painting's narrow width and vertically oriented borders elongate Shah Jahan's figure. The strong diagonal gesture focuses attention on his left hand.

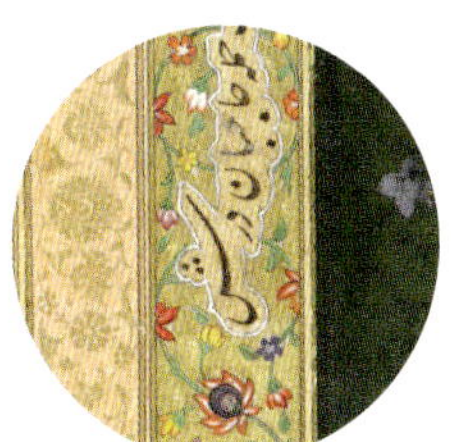

Gold inscriptions
The golden inscriptions identify Abu'l Hasan as "the leading artist of the era" and praise Shah Jahan as the "master of mankind."

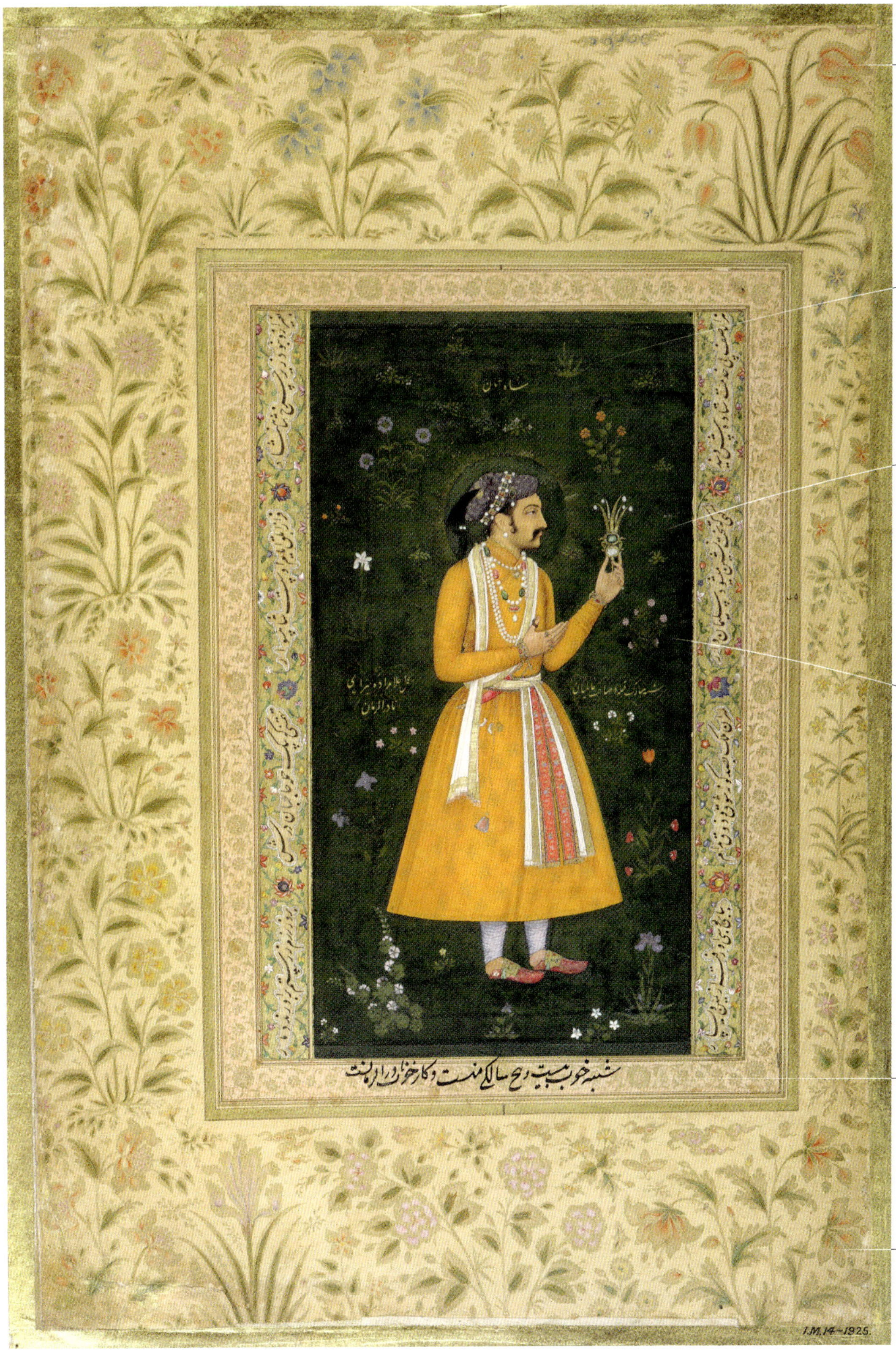

Mughal artists were inspired by flowers found in European engravings of Christian religious imagery as well as botanical studies.

A Persian inscription in *Nasta'liq* gold script identifies the young prince as Shah Jahan, meaning "King of the World."

Shah Jahan emphasizes his imperial stature by holding up a plumed, gem-studded turban ornament. This was worn only by the emperor.

Shah Jahan's vibrant orange *jama* sets off a spectacular array of precious stones and pearls.

Sometime after its completion, Shah Jahan added an inscription describing the portrait as "a good likeness" of himself at the age of 25.

The outer borders, now very faded, are filled with flowering plants, painted in gold and various colors.

Abra, the maid, is rendered here as a young woman and participant. Other artists painted her as an older woman and onlooker.

Sumptuous fabrics add a decorative element that seems incongruous in the circumstances.

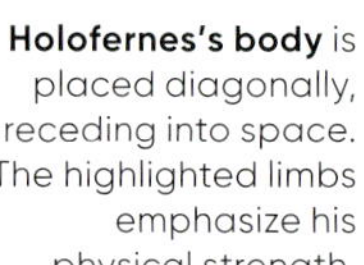

Holofernes's body is placed diagonally, receding into space. The highlighted limbs emphasize his physical strength.

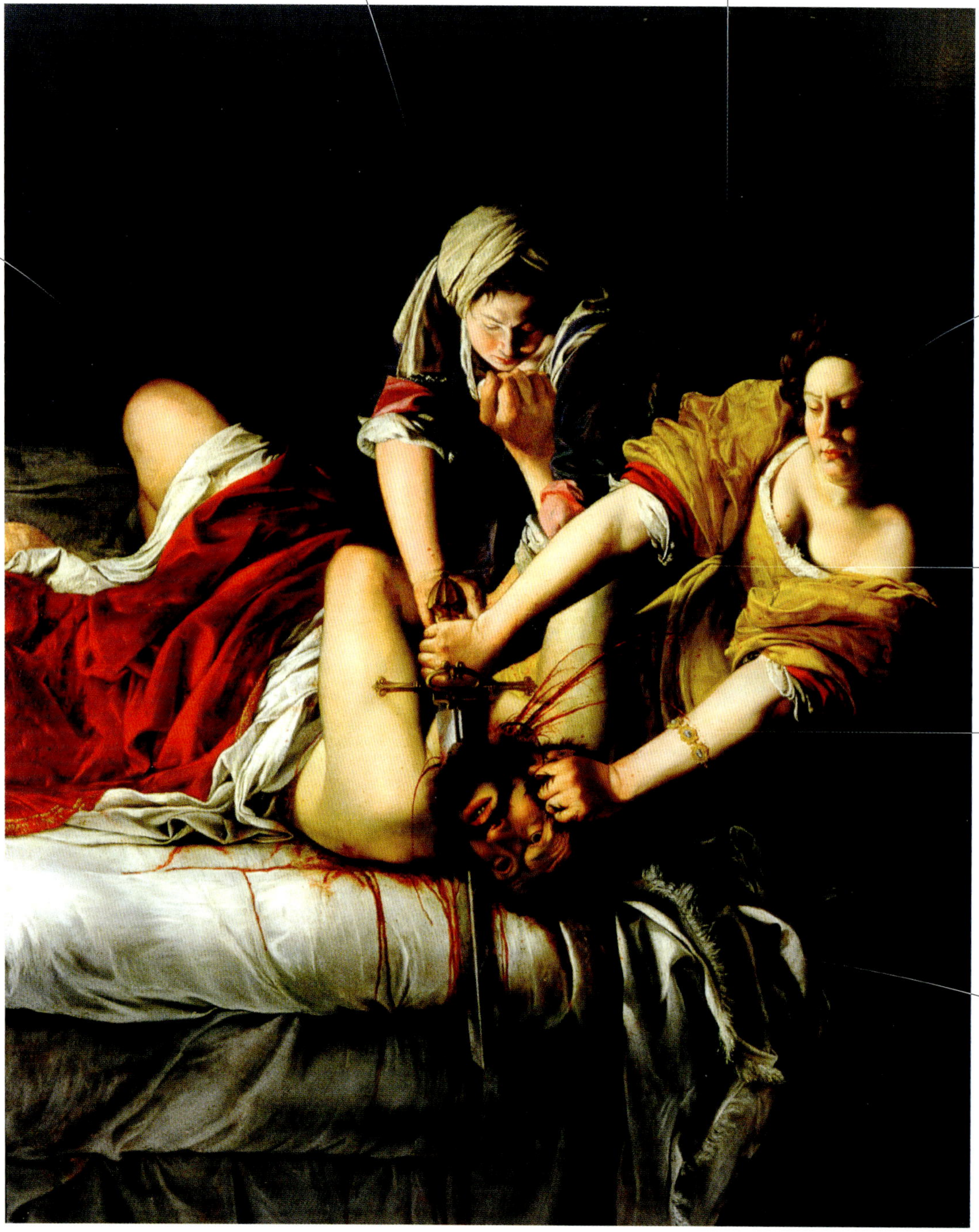

The features of Judith's face are picked out in strong light–dark contrasts.

The emphasis is on Judith's powerful arms. Her head is set back in space and positioned close to the dark edge of the painting.

The spurting blood is painted in realistic detail. Spatters of blood appear on the women and their clothing.

Holofernes's head is placed at the front of the picture space. It is turned toward the viewer, increasing the sense of horror.

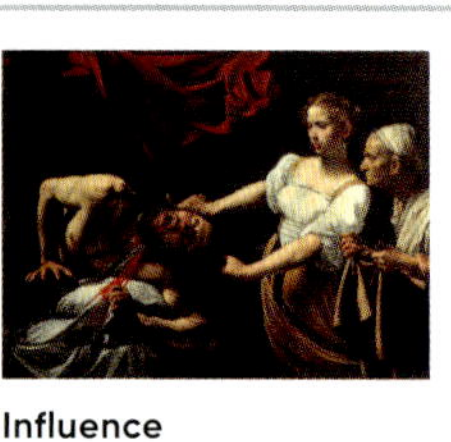

Influence
Caravaggio's use of light–dark modeling and foreshortening in his own *Judith Beheading Holofernes* (1598–1599) influenced Gentileschi. Many art critics think that Gentileschi's painting achieves greater realism and drama.

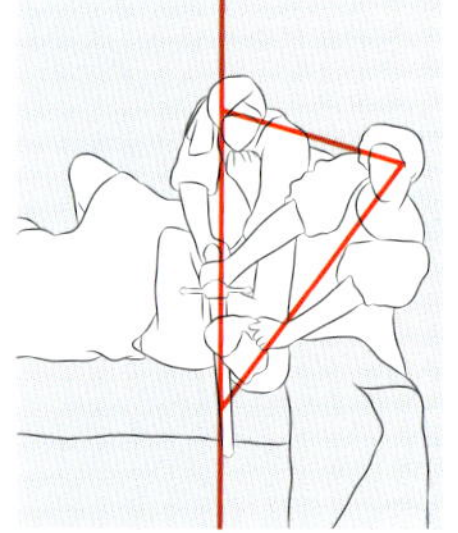

Composition
A strong vertical line divides the painting in half, with the drama concentrated in the right side. The action is contained and therefore amplified within a tight triangle.

Judith Beheading Holofernes

Artemisia Gentileschi c.1620, oil on canvas, 58 × 43 in (146.5 × 108 cm), Uffizi, Florence, Italy

Two women pin a man down, while one of them draws a sword through his neck. Judith is a Biblical character who seduces and then beheads an enemy general, Holofernes, to save her people. A tangle of criss-crossing limbs brings a sense of power and movement to a disturbing scene. Some art historians believe Gentileschi may have drawn upon her own experience of being raped by the artist Agostino Tassi at the age of 17.

Susannah and the Elders

Guido Reni c. 1622–1623, oil on canvas, 46 × 59 in (116.6 × 150.5 cm), National Gallery, London, UK

Enveloped in a soft glow, Susannah recoils from the advances of two lewd men, who threaten to accuse her of adultery if she does not give in to their advances. This moralizing scene from the Old Testament captures Susannah's vulnerability and discomfort and the men's predatory intent and power.

One man silences Susannah by pressing his finger to his mouth, threatening to falsely accuse her of adultery if she resists their lust.

The central man holds his hand up toward Susannah, ready to touch her breast.

The background foliage alludes to the Biblical narrative in which the two men spy on Susannah as she bathes in her garden.

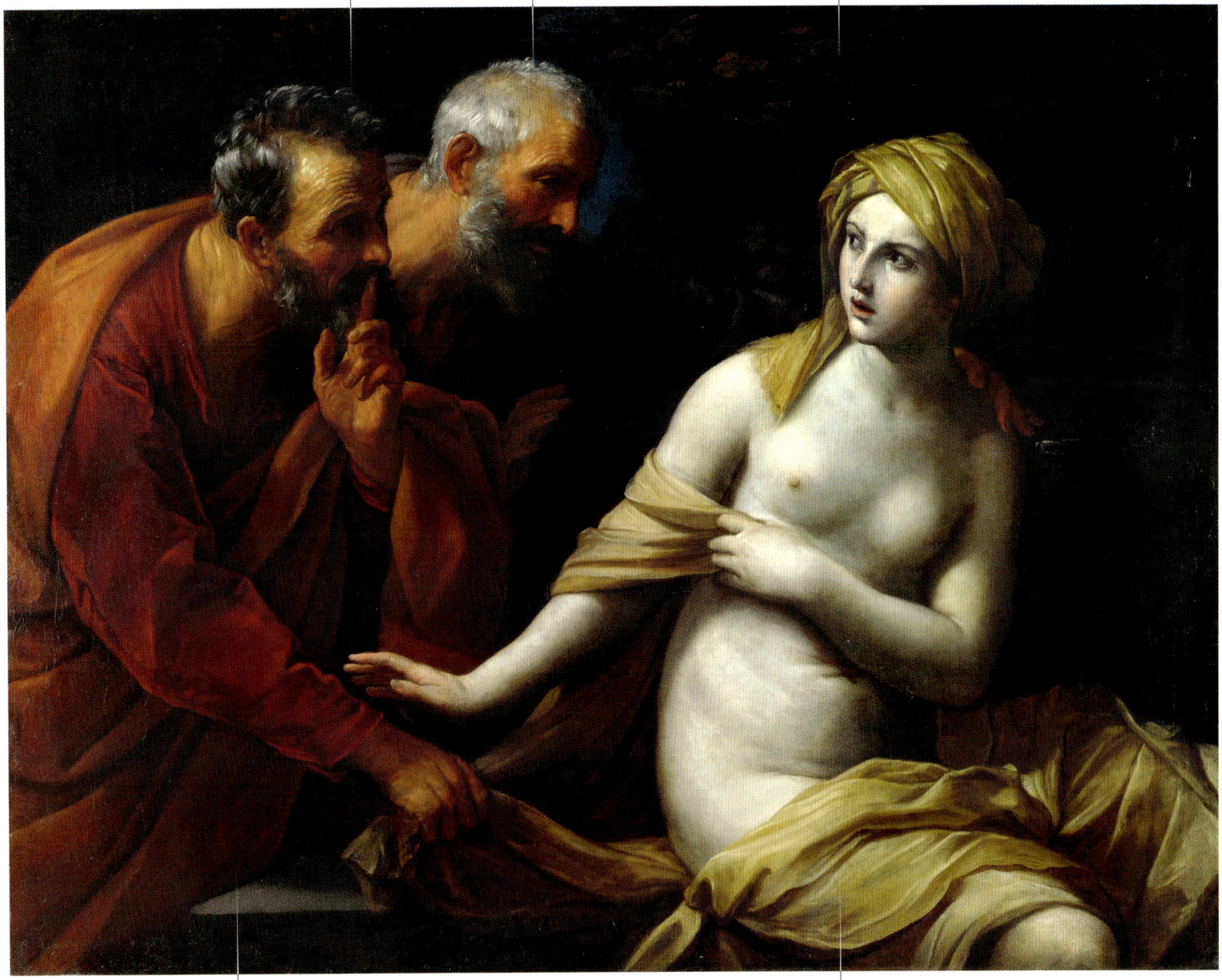

The rich red-orange tones of the men's clothing and flesh establish a tonal division between the men and Susannah, heightening the dramatic impact.

Susannah's naked figure is statuesque, painted with cool, pale tones, emphasizing her vulnerability.

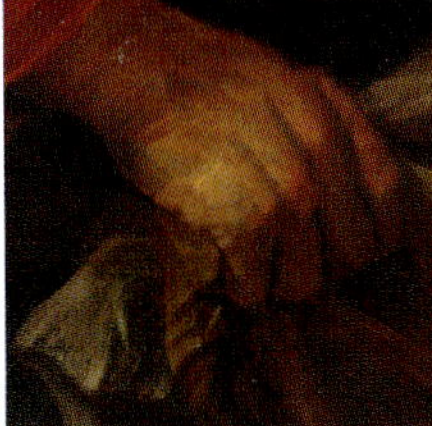

The man tugs at Susannah's robe, prompting her to cover herself, intensifying the visual drama.

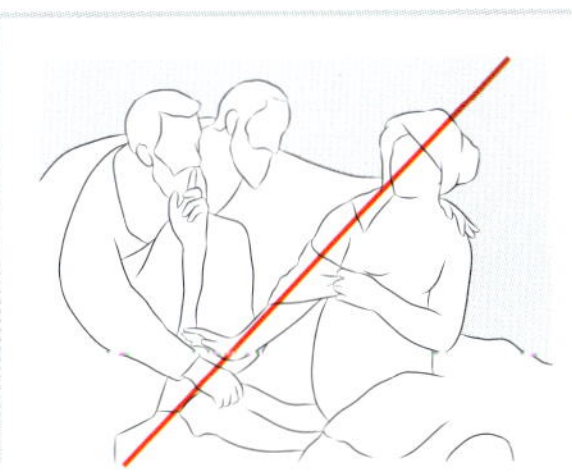

Diagonal division
Compositional movement unfolds along a diagonal axis, traced by Susannah's outstretched arm. The two men incline toward the center while Susannah retreats, creating a balanced visual tension.

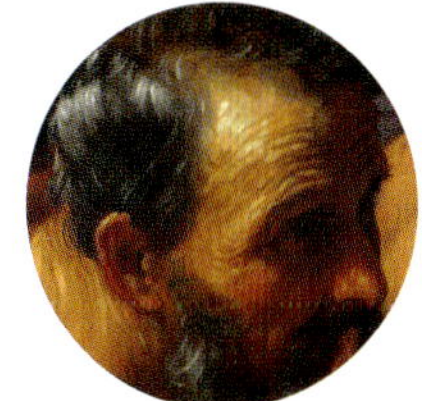

Creating texture
Reni used loose and expressive brushstrokes. White daubs capture the textural richness and interplay of light, especially evident in the men's hair and wrinkled foreheads.

Apollo and Daphne

Gian Lorenzo Bernini 1622–1625, marble, 96 in (243 cm) high, Borghese Gallery, Rome, Italy

Bernini, a leading Baroque sculptor, was in his mid-twenties when he made this highly expressive, dynamic, and disturbing life-size representation of the story of Apollo and Daphne in Ovid's narrative poem *Metamorphoses*. The god Apollo is in love with the nymph Daphne, who is sworn to virginity. When she asks the gods to help her escape his advances, she is transformed into a laurel tree.

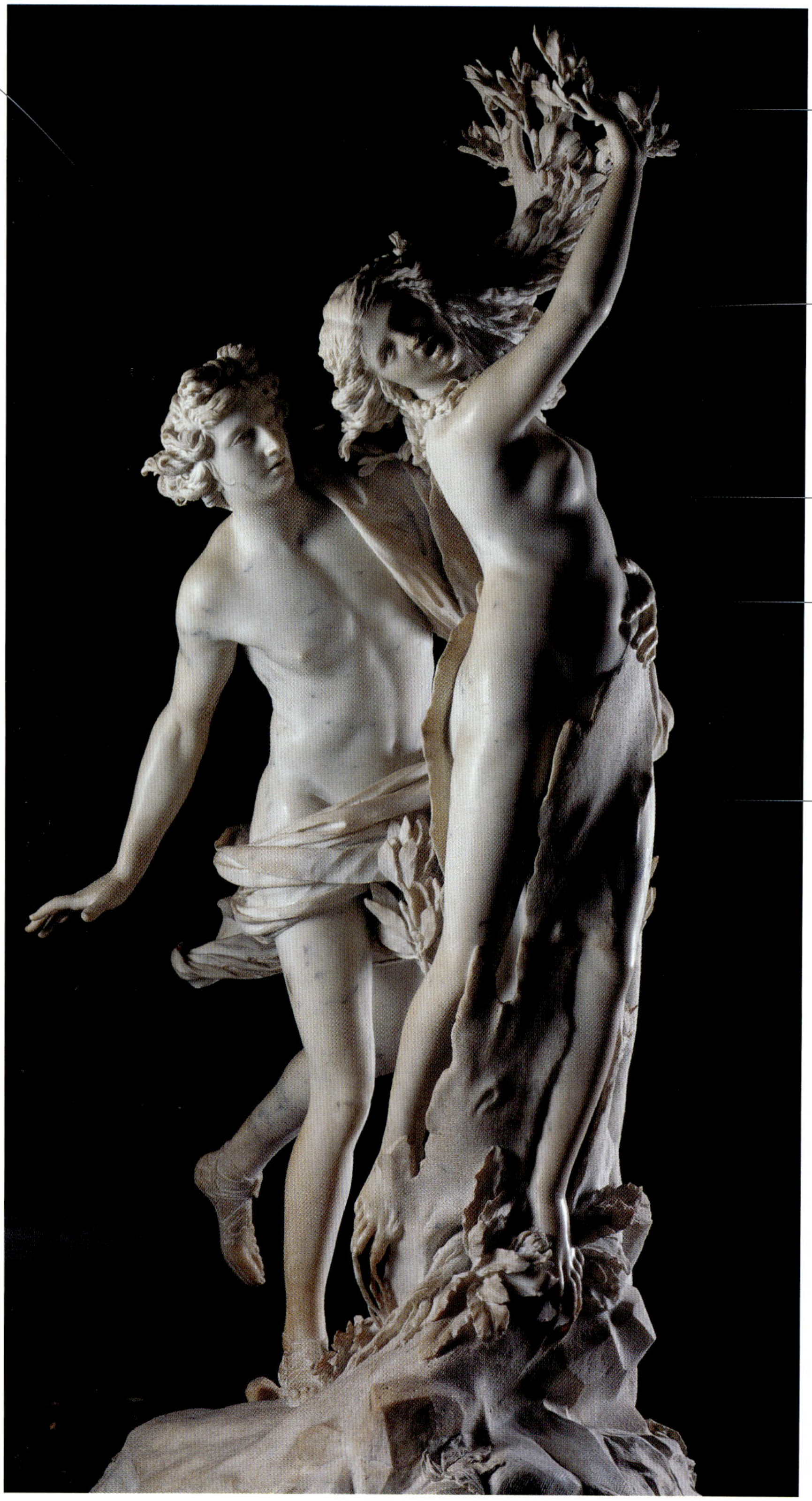

Apollo seems unaware of what is happening to Daphne.

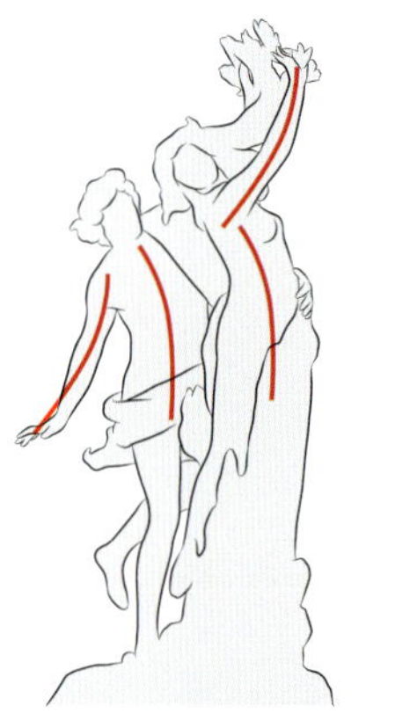

Close connection
The two figures move as if dancing together. A series of curving lines echo each other, reinforcing their connection.

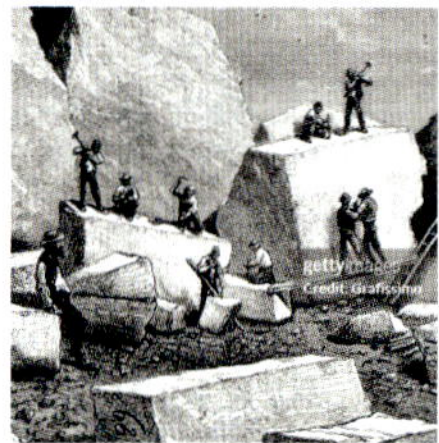

Carrara marble
This fine-grained white or blue-gray marble has been quarried from around the city of Carrara, in modern-day Tuscany, since ancient times. The Romans called it Luna marble.

Daphne's fingers sprout leaves and her hair turns into twigs.

Her face fills with fear as she becomes rooted to the spot.

Carrara marble is a soft ivory color. It has been highly polished to bring out its innate warmth.

Apollo grasps Daphne as bark covers part of her body and she twists upward, slowly turning into a tree.

Running full tilt in pursuit, Apollo's flowing robes slip from his body.

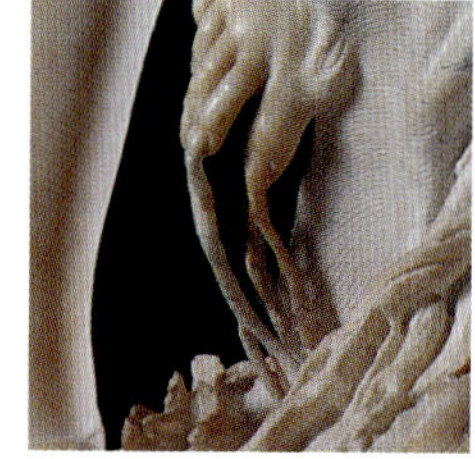

The level of detail creates a strong sense of realism. Daphne's toes extend into very fine roots, connecting her to the ground.

> "Immediately when it was … finished there arose such a cry that all Rome concurred in seeing it as a miracle."
>
> Filippo Baldinucci

The feathered hat is part of the musician's costume, hinting at the theatricality of the scene.

Rosy cheeks and a red nose suggest a lively character and allude to the impact of the wine.

Depicted using delicate yet fluid brushstrokes, the feathers and facial hair animate the scene, amplifying the violinist's expressive gesture.

The glass of wine alludes to the tavern setting, but also refers to the theme of the drunken fool, common in Dutch theater at the time.

An undefined, flat background makes the figure of the musician stand out.

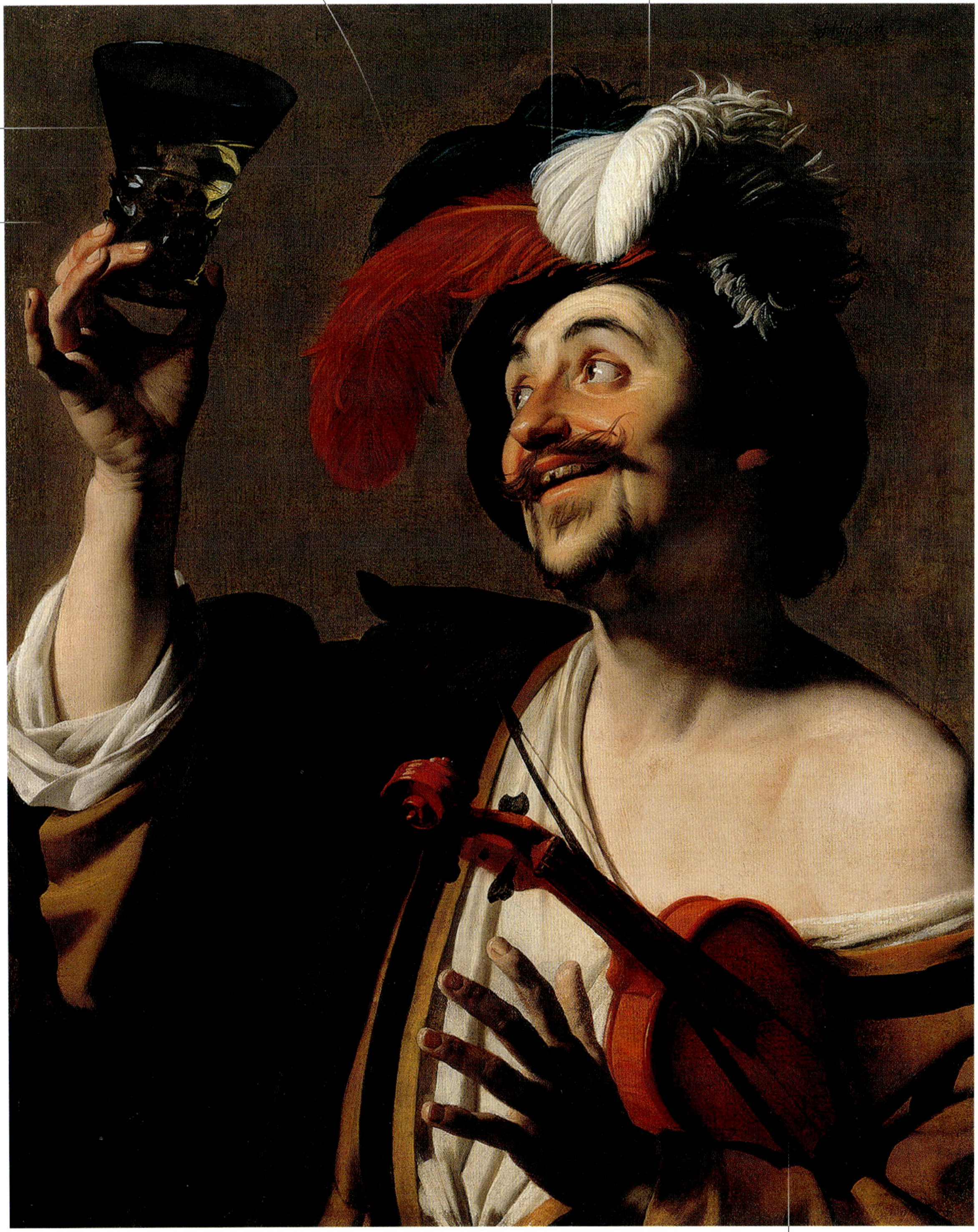

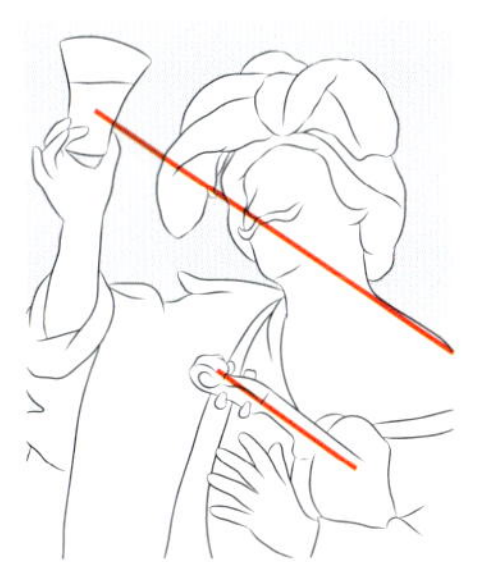

Follow his glance
A dynamic diagonal axis extends from the violinist's shoulder and through his gaze toward the wine glass. This narrative movement is echoed by the neck of the violin.

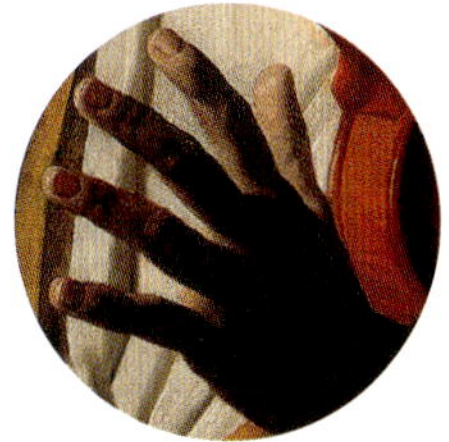

Light and dark
Soft illumination from the left envelops the wine glass, the violinist's face, and his shoulder in a unified glow. Meanwhile, his left hand and neck are in deep shadow.

The violin rests under his arm, indicating that a performance has just taken place.

The Happy Violinist

Gerrit van Honthorst c. 1624, oil on canvas, 33 × 27 in (83 × 68 cm), Museo Nacional Thyssen-Bornemisza, Madrid, Spain

An exuberant musician raises his glass of wine in a theatrical gesture, his mood conveyed by his radiant gaze, which attracts the viewer's attention. Inspired by Caravaggio, Honthorst captures an intimate and joyful moment, using dramatic lighting to infuse the scene with vitality and anticipation.

The Lomellini Family

Anthony van Dyck c. 1625–1627, oil on canvas, 106 × 100 in (269 × 254 cm), Scottish National Gallery, Edinburgh, UK

This portrait reflects nobility and prestige. The father, Giacomo, was head of the government in Genoa. His portrait could not be painted while he was in office in case it was used to augment his power. Instead, his eldest sons assume a commanding presence over Giacomo's second wife and two younger children.

Everyone is looking in a different direction, giving this formal portrait an informal air.

The Doge's wife sits at the center of the composition, her pale complexion framed by her lace ruff.

The arch and columns in the background frame Nicolò, one of the Doge's sons, subtly signaling his elevated status within the painting.

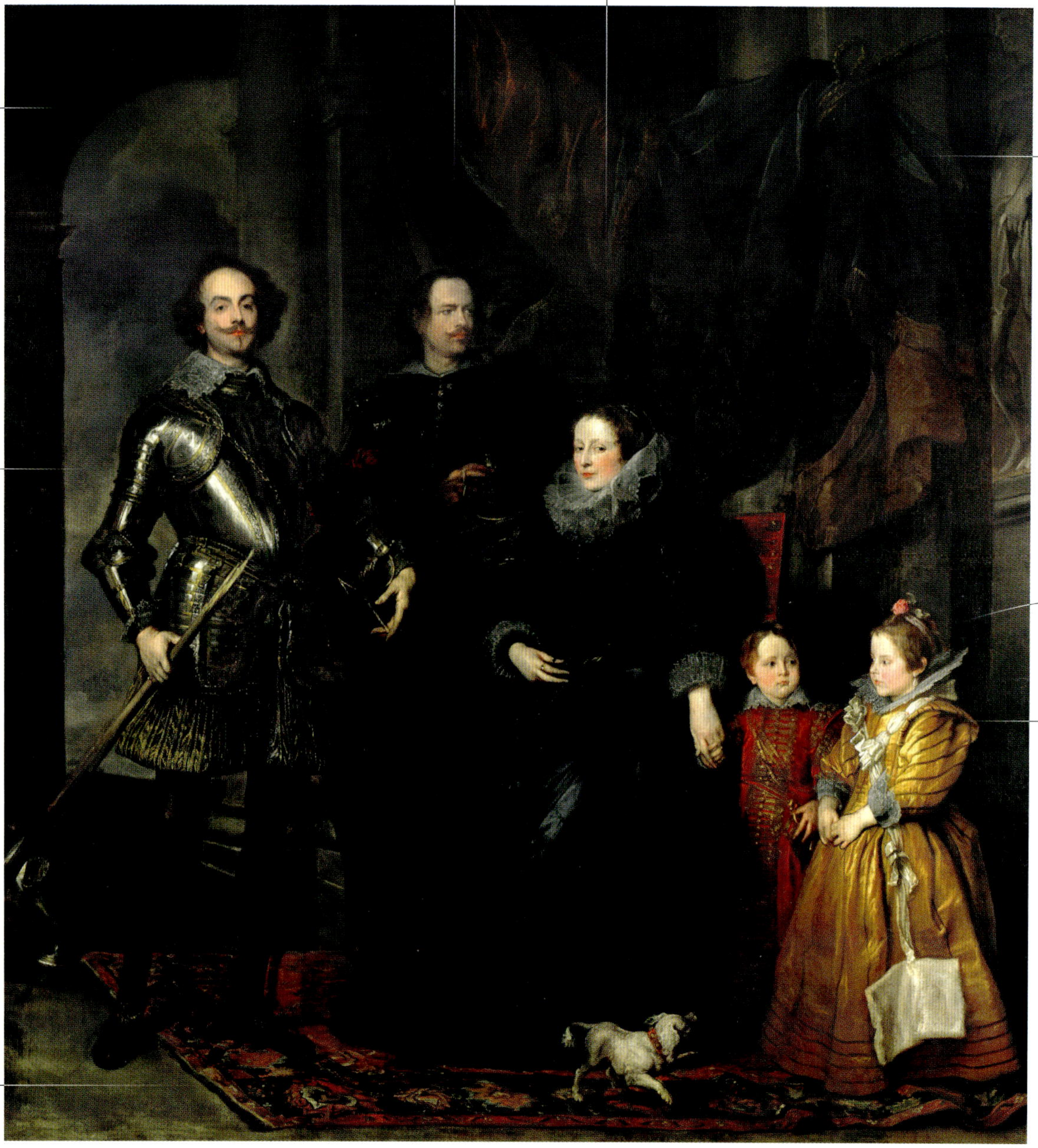

Velvet drapery provides interest in the top-right corner.

Nicolò is dressed in armor. It glimmers in the light and reflects his nobility.

Van Dyck captured the character of each family member. Agostino looks bored, while his sister Vittoria is amused by something happening beyond the frame.

The young children wear bright clothing, adding a vibrant touch to the predominantly dark composition.

An intricately patterned carpet hints at material wealth.

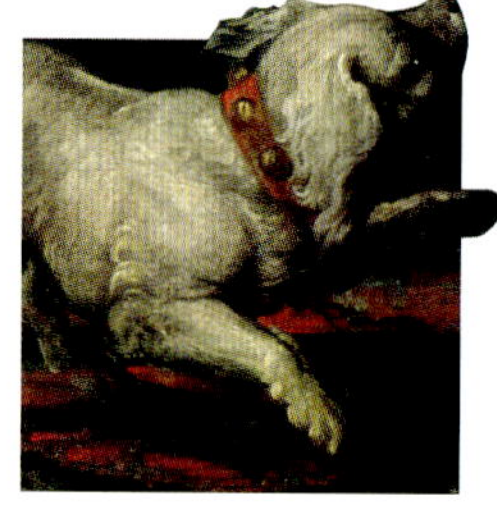

The inclusion of the family's dog—a symbol of loyalty—at the children's feet adds a playful intimacy to an otherwise formal composition.

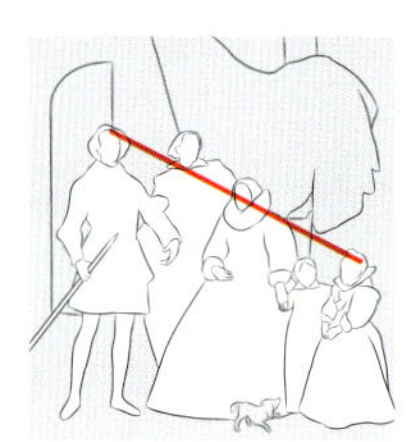

Family order
The hierarchical arrangement of the family according to gender and age creates a diagonal movement, with the eldest sons at the top.

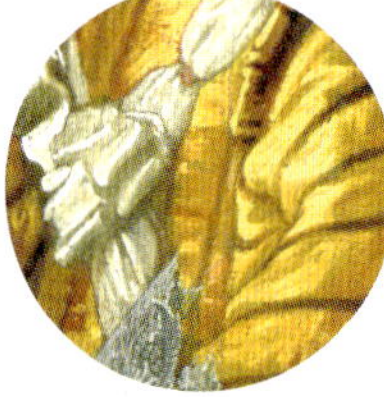

Fine fabrics
The brushwork on the children's clothes ranges from fine white dots on the lacework to broad strokes that emulate the texture of the silk.

Young Man Holding a Skull (Vanitas)

Frans Hals 1626–1628, oil on canvas, 36 × 32 in (92.2 × 80.8 cm), National Gallery, London, UK

A boy with rosy cheeks and softly parted lips holds a skull with one hand, while his other hand reaches out toward the viewer. This intimate allegorical painting focuses on the themes of fleeting youth, the transience of life, and mortality. Hals's technique of painting freely and quickly set him apart from other artists of the time.

The boy appears distracted, his gaze directed to his left, beyond the frame, giving the composition a sense of intrigue.

A muted, earthy palette is punctured by hints of red, infusing the scene with vibrancy and life.

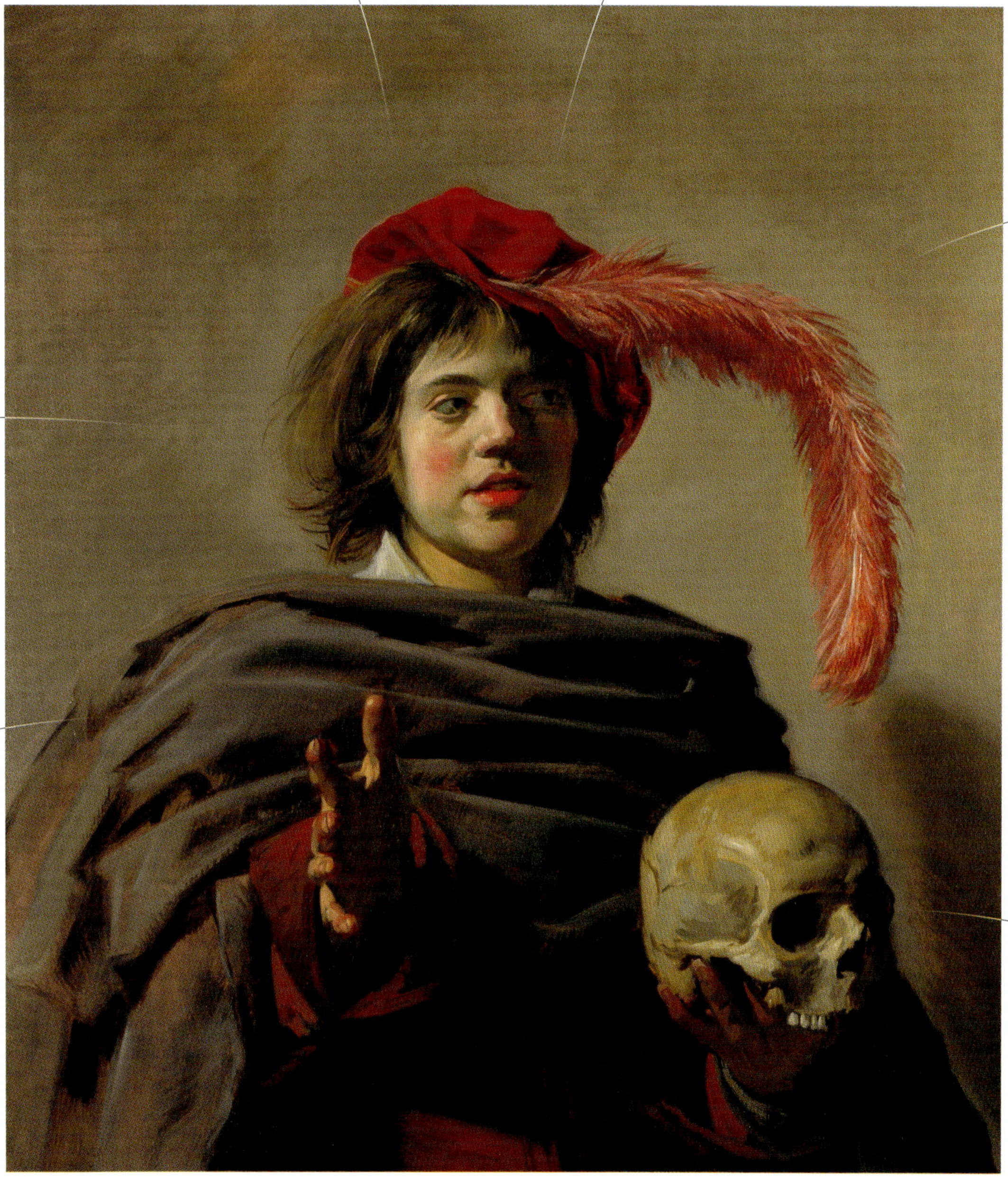

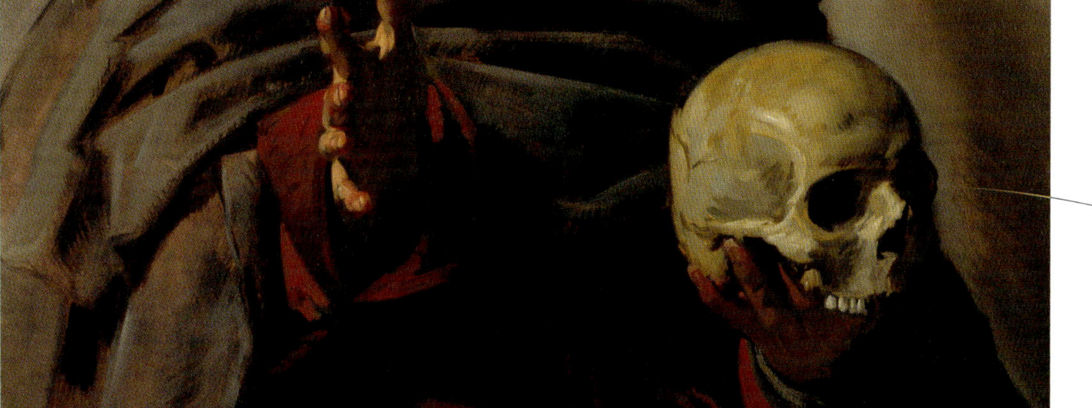

The red ostrich feather alludes to the theatrical and allegorical nature of this painting.

Hals used cross-hatching—applying paint wet-on-wet to blend colors—to create tonal depth in the boy's face and on the skull.

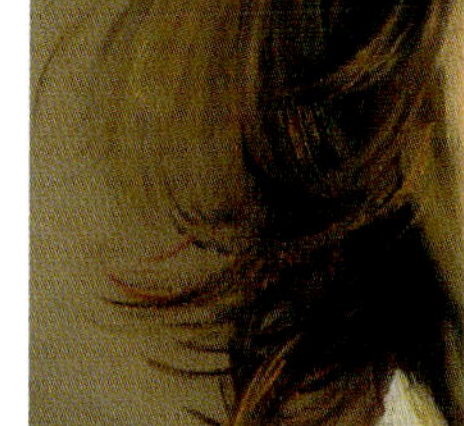

Fine, wispy brushstrokes, which vary in tone, define the boy's hair and the feather.

Fabric around his shoulders was applied using a thin layer of paint, revealing the reddish-brown ground layer beneath it.

The skull symbolizes *vanitas* (vanity). It was used to encourage the viewer to contemplate the transient nature of earthly pleasures. It is also known as *memento mori*, a reminder of life's fragility.

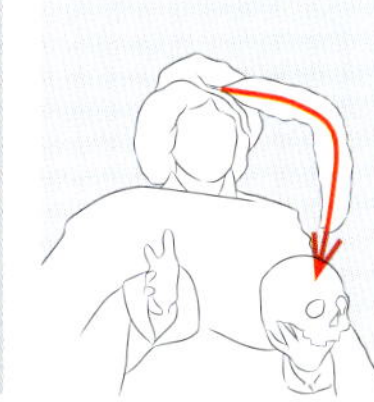

Follow the feather
The ostrich feather directs the viewer's eye from the boy's face to the skull, crafting a symbolic narrative of life and death.

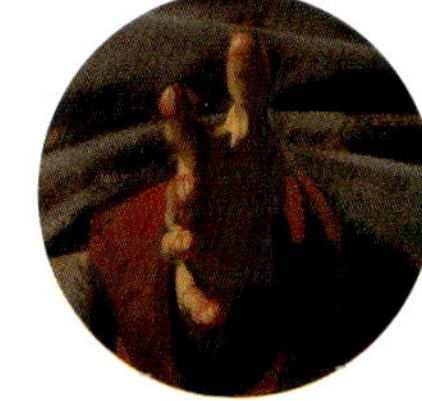

Sense of movement
The boy's fingers are dramatically foreshortened, reaching out toward the viewer. This adds a dynamic forward motion while also creating the illusion of depth.

> "It is worth as much as Dante's *Paradise* and the Michelangelo's and Raphael's and even the Greeks."
>
> Vincent van Gogh, 1888

Man Offering Money to a Young Woman

Judith Leyster 1631, oil on panel, 12 × 10 in (30.9 × 24.2 cm), Mauritshuis, The Hague, the Netherlands

A woman concentrates on her needlework, ignoring the advances of a man who is offering her money while studying her response. Also known as *The Proposition*, this is a genre painting (scene from everyday life), in which Leyster specialized. Dutch genre scenes frequently had a clear moral message, but this one is ambiguous. Is it an unwanted proposition or the beginning of a courtship?

The man is painted in dark tones, giving him a threatening quality.

The woman's expression is a study in concentration, and her clothing is simple and modest.

The domestic setting is plain and simple, like other depictions of virtue in Dutch genre scenes.

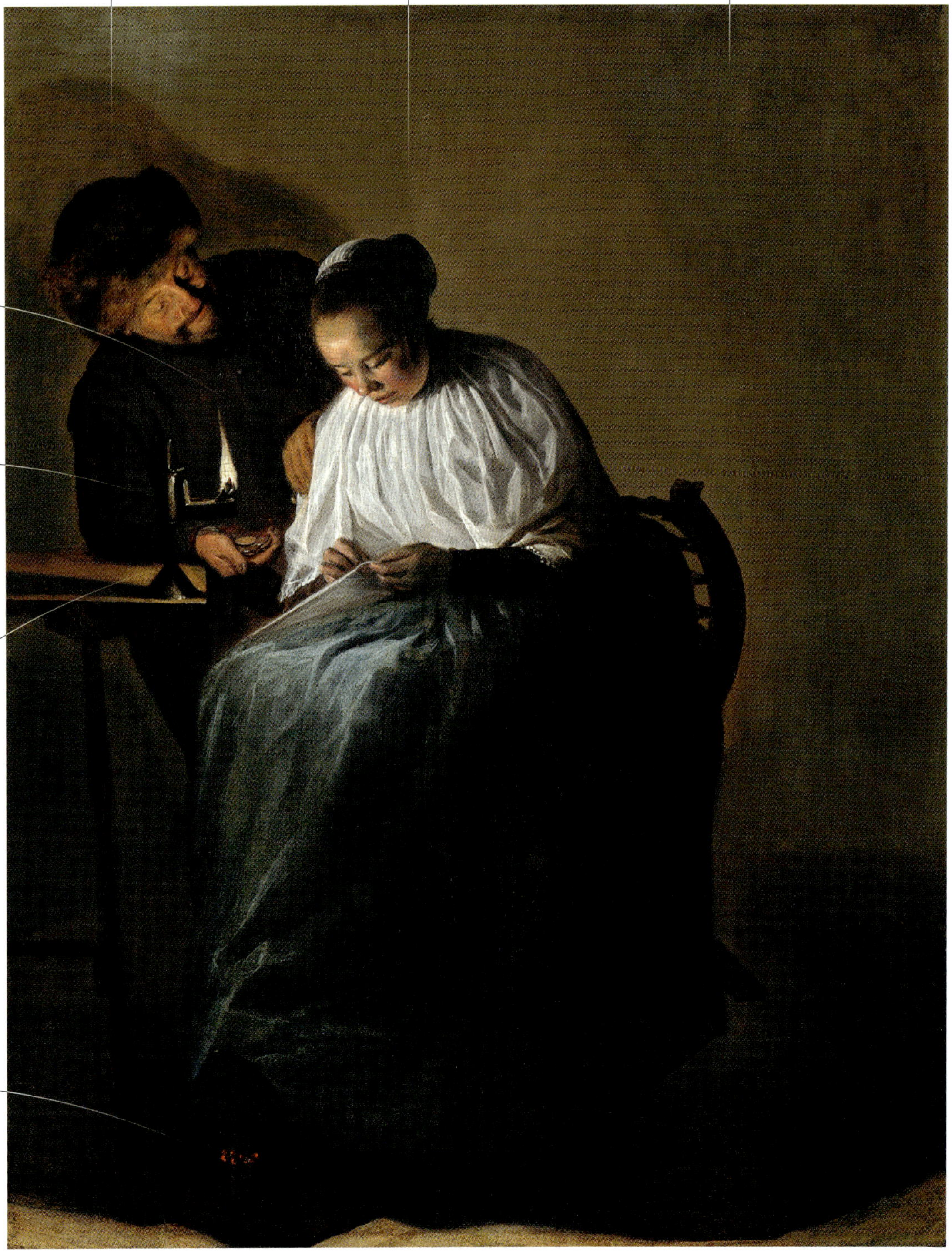

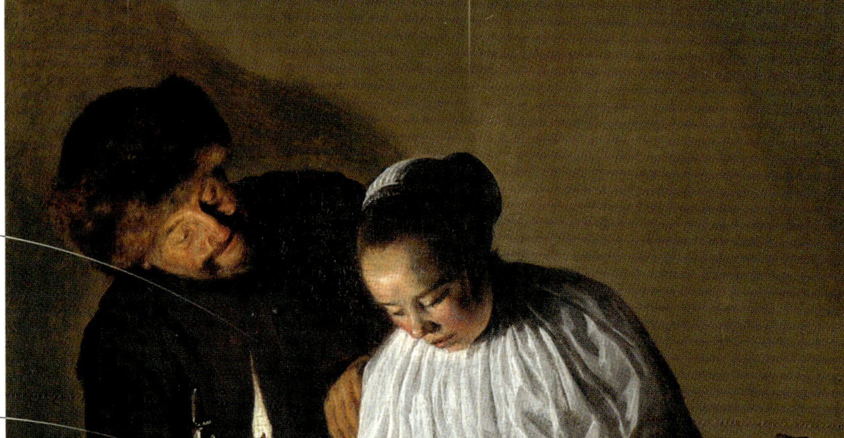

The man's hand is on the woman's shoulder to try to distract her.

An oil lamp, the only light source in the painting, focuses attention on the faces, hands, and needlework.

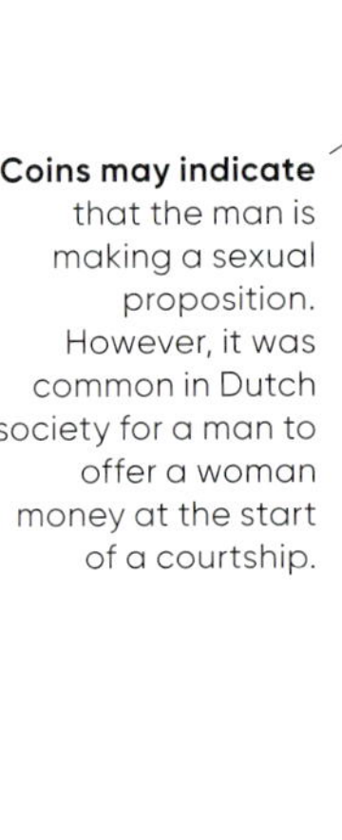

Coins may indicate that the man is making a sexual proposition. However, it was common in Dutch society for a man to offer a woman money at the start of a courtship.

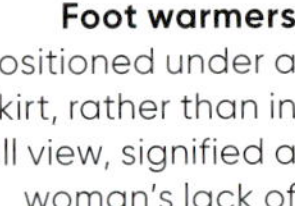

Foot warmers positioned under a skirt, rather than in full view, signified a woman's lack of interest in a man.

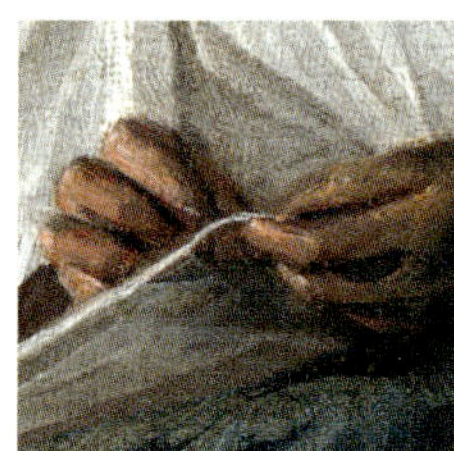

Needlework was considered a respectable occupation for a woman.

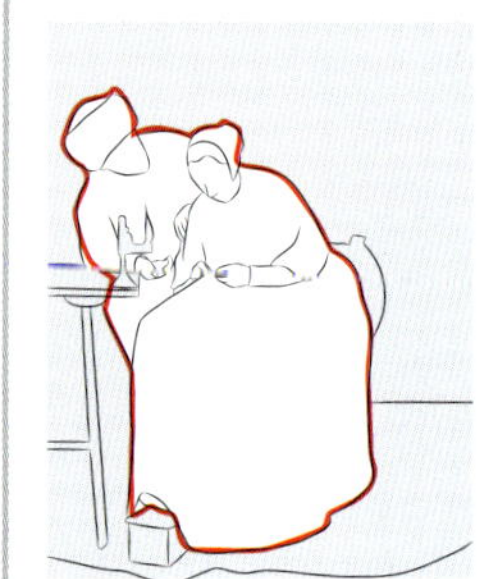

Composition
The couple are off-center. However, damage to the wooden panel on the left side of the painting indicates that part of the work is missing. The figures were probably originally positioned nearer the center of the space.

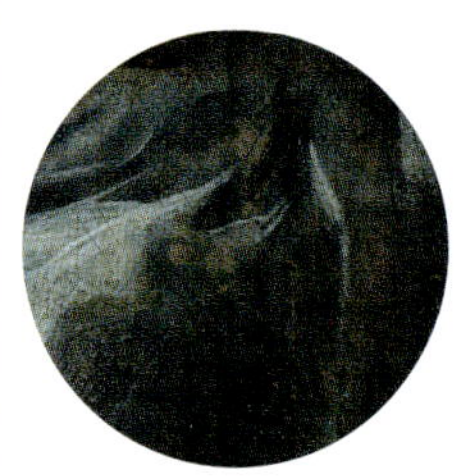

Brushwork
The brushwork is spontaneous but restrained. The highlights on the skirt were added with strong blue brushstrokes over a dark ground.

The Martyrdom of St. Bartholomew

Jusepe de Ribera 1634, oil on canvas, 41 × 44 in (104 × 113 cm), National Gallery of Art, Washington, D.C., US

A popular subject for paintings in Counter-Reformation Italy and Spain, St. Bartholomew is said to have been flayed alive and beheaded after jealous priests complained about his success in converting people to Christianity. Portraying the apostle's final moments, this tightly cropped, emotionally charged painting imagines Bartholomew with the soldier who arrested him, the priest who accused him, and the man who will kill him.

Strong light beams down from the far left. Both the saint and the cloaked priest look upward.

The executioner's features are partially in shadow, a dramatic effect called tenebrism.

The knife is sharpened against a honing rod, symbolically placed to look like a cross.

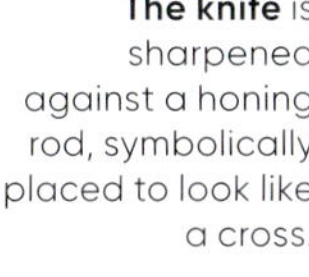

St. Bartholomew's hand gestures both to the heavens and the instrument of his torture.

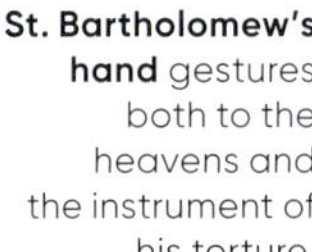

Emotional intensity is increased by the tight crop and plain background.

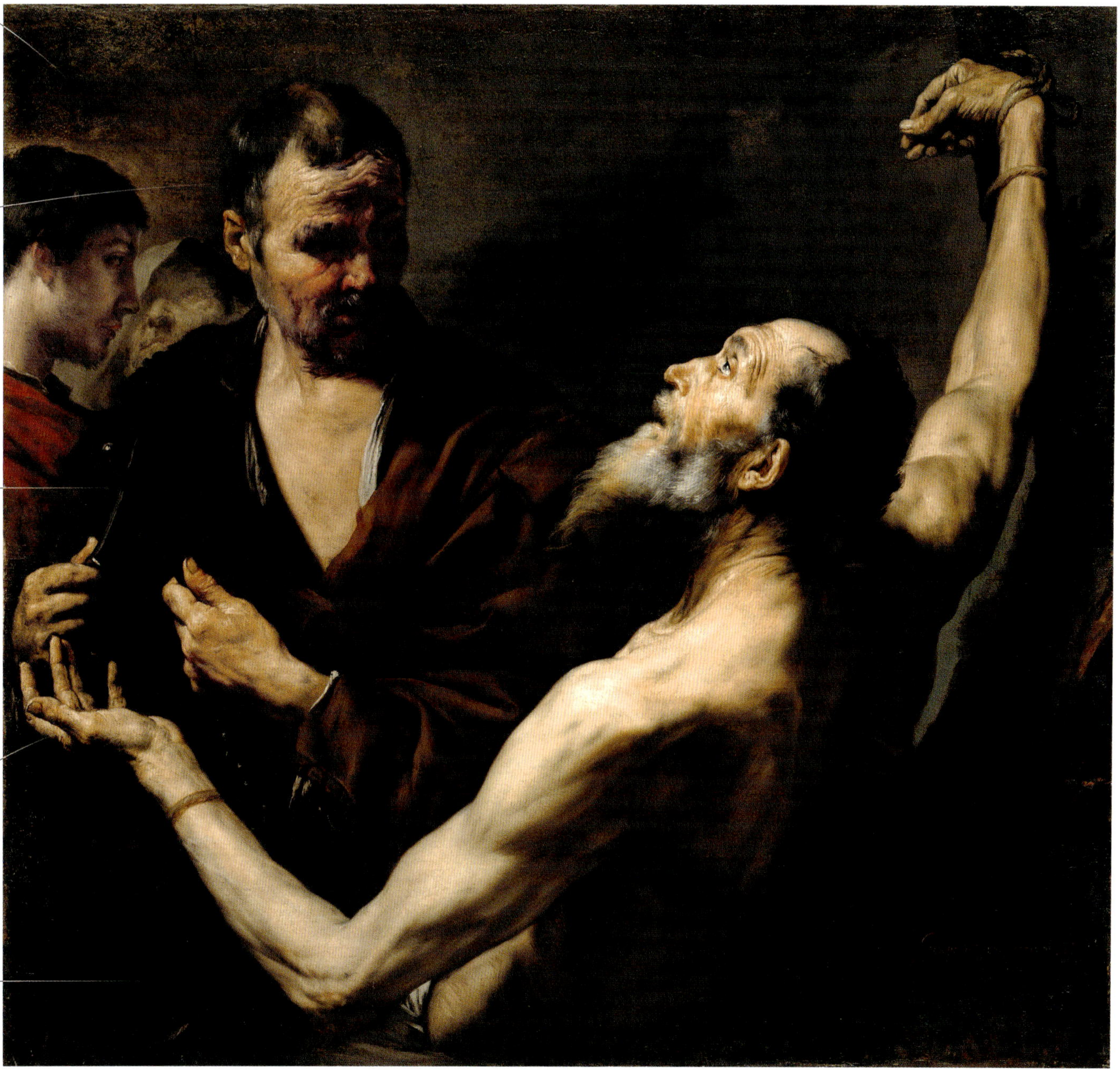

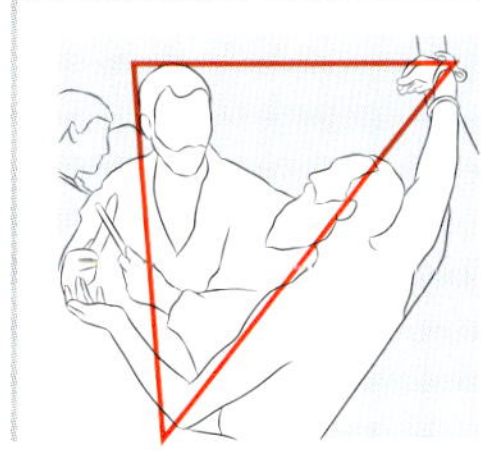

Triangular form The strongly triangular shape of the work frames the executioner's head and points to the heavenly vision experienced by St. Bartholomew just before his death.

St. Bartholomew's face is brightly illuminated and wholly in profile, with an expression of wonder rather than fear.

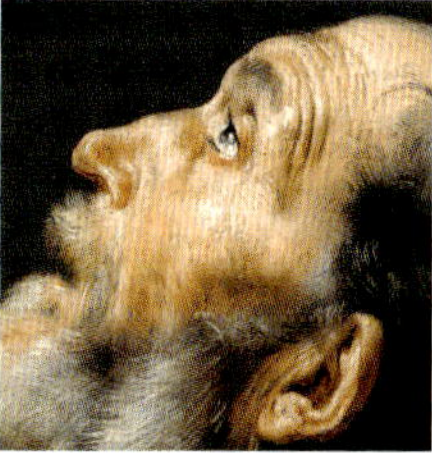

"Jusepe de Ribera was a miraculous painter of the male body."

Charlotte Higgins, 2018

Still Life with Lemons, Oranges, and a Rose

Francisco de Zurbarán 1633, 24 × 42 in (60 × 107 cm), oil on canvas, Norton Simon Museum of Art, Pasadena, California, US

Using simple everyday objects—fruit, a basket, a plain cup—arranged in three groups, equidistant from each other on a polished tabletop, Zurbarán produced an image of intense serenity. He was often known as "the Spanish Caravaggio" for his mastery of chiaroscuro, or modeling with light and dark. He mainly painted religious subjects and the three groups here are seen by some commentators as a reference to the Holy Trinity of the Father, Son, and Holy Spirit. The painting is also a study in the play of light on contrasting textures and surfaces.

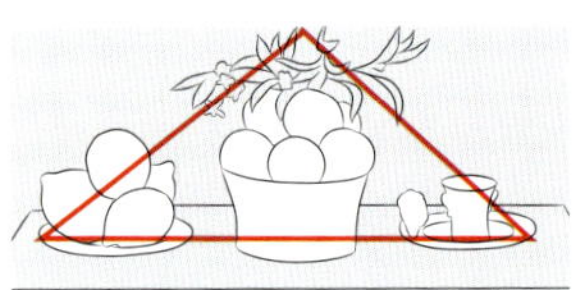

Pyramidal organization The basket of oranges and flowers in the center flanked by smaller groups on either side creates a centralized composition based on a triangle.

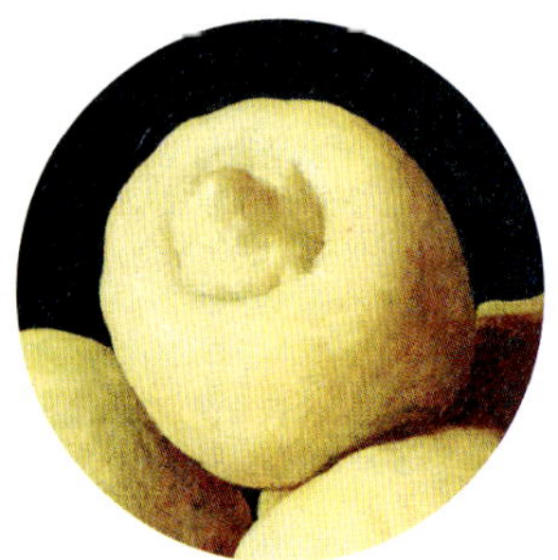

Tenebrism The brightly lit objects are set against a dark background, creating a shallow picture space that evokes a timeless, mystical intensity.

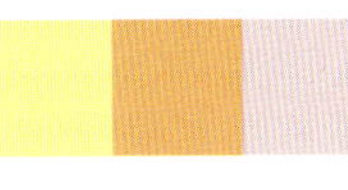

Delicate colors The light tones of yellow, orange, and pink in the fruit and flowers are carefully harmonized.

> "The drama in a still life is the drama found in a juxtaposition, a placing, an encounter, within a protected space."
>
> John Berger, 2000

Tiny brushes were used to paint the pitted texture of the rough-skinned fruit.

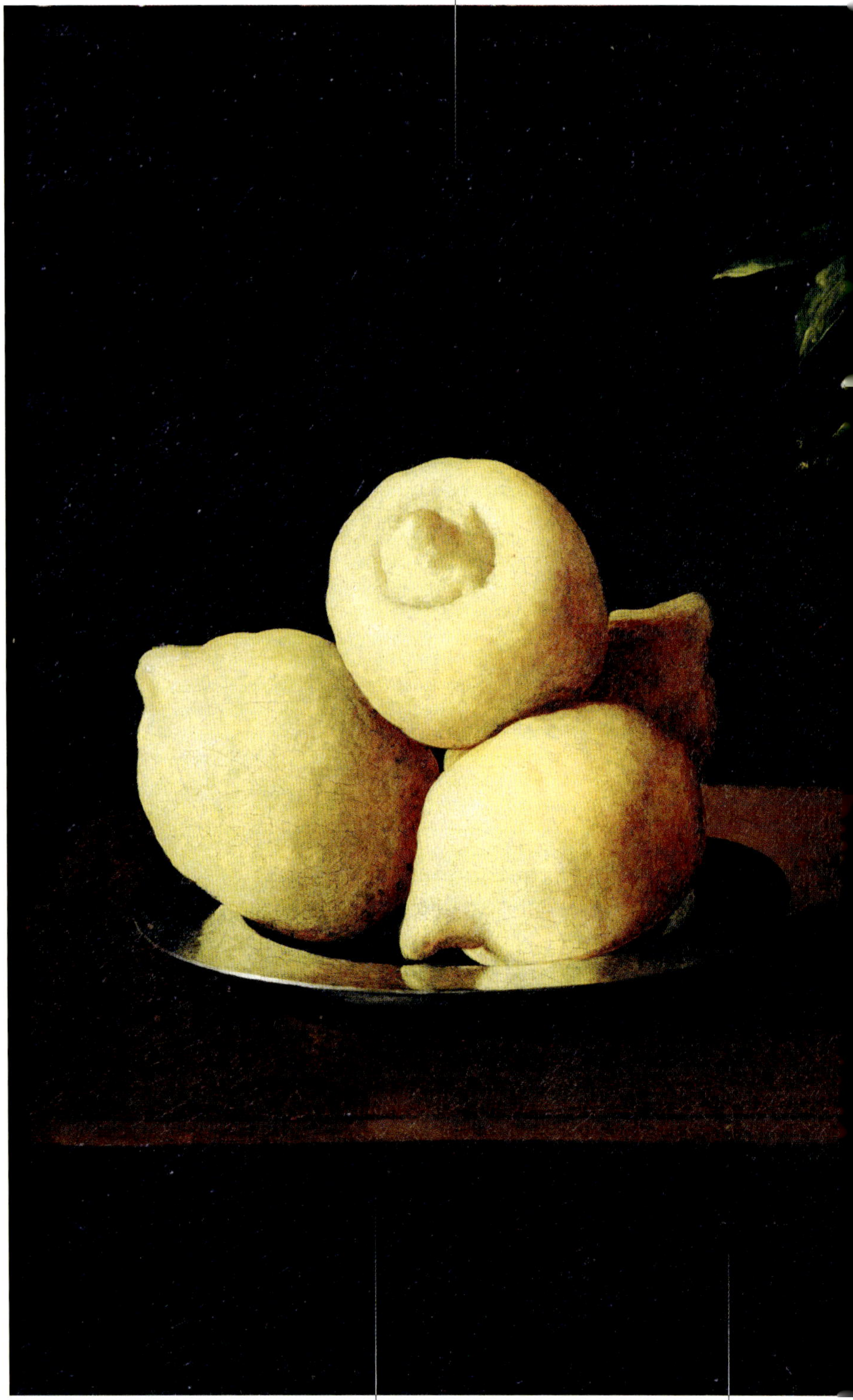

The citrons are modeled using contrasts of light and dark. Adding hints of green and russet suggests the fruit's protuberances and weight.

The polished surface of the table reflects little light and is very close in tone to the background.

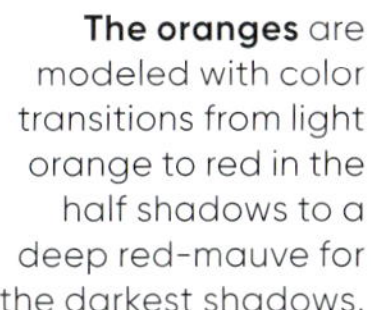

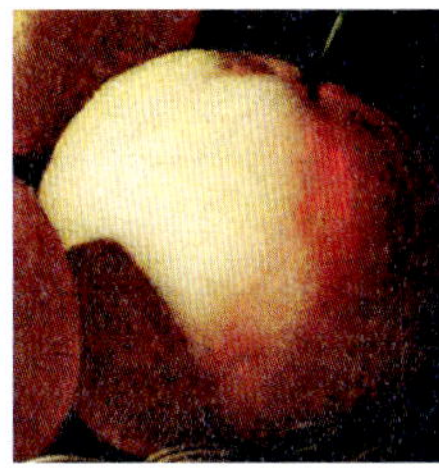

The oranges are modeled with color transitions from light orange to red in the half shadows to a deep red-mauve for the darkest shadows.

Orange blossom symbolizes fertility. It could also refer to the Virgin Mary, the mother of Christ.

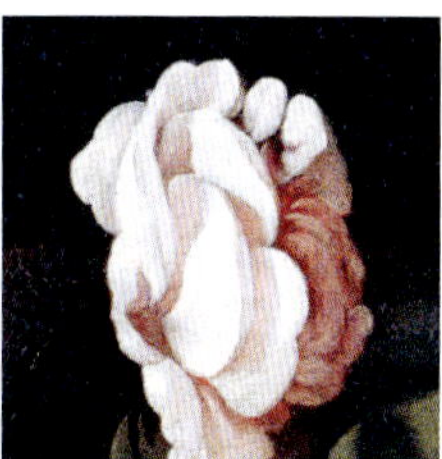

A pink rose represents the Virgin Mary, who is often called "the rose without thorns," a reference to the Immaculate Conception of Christ. It also symbolizes love.

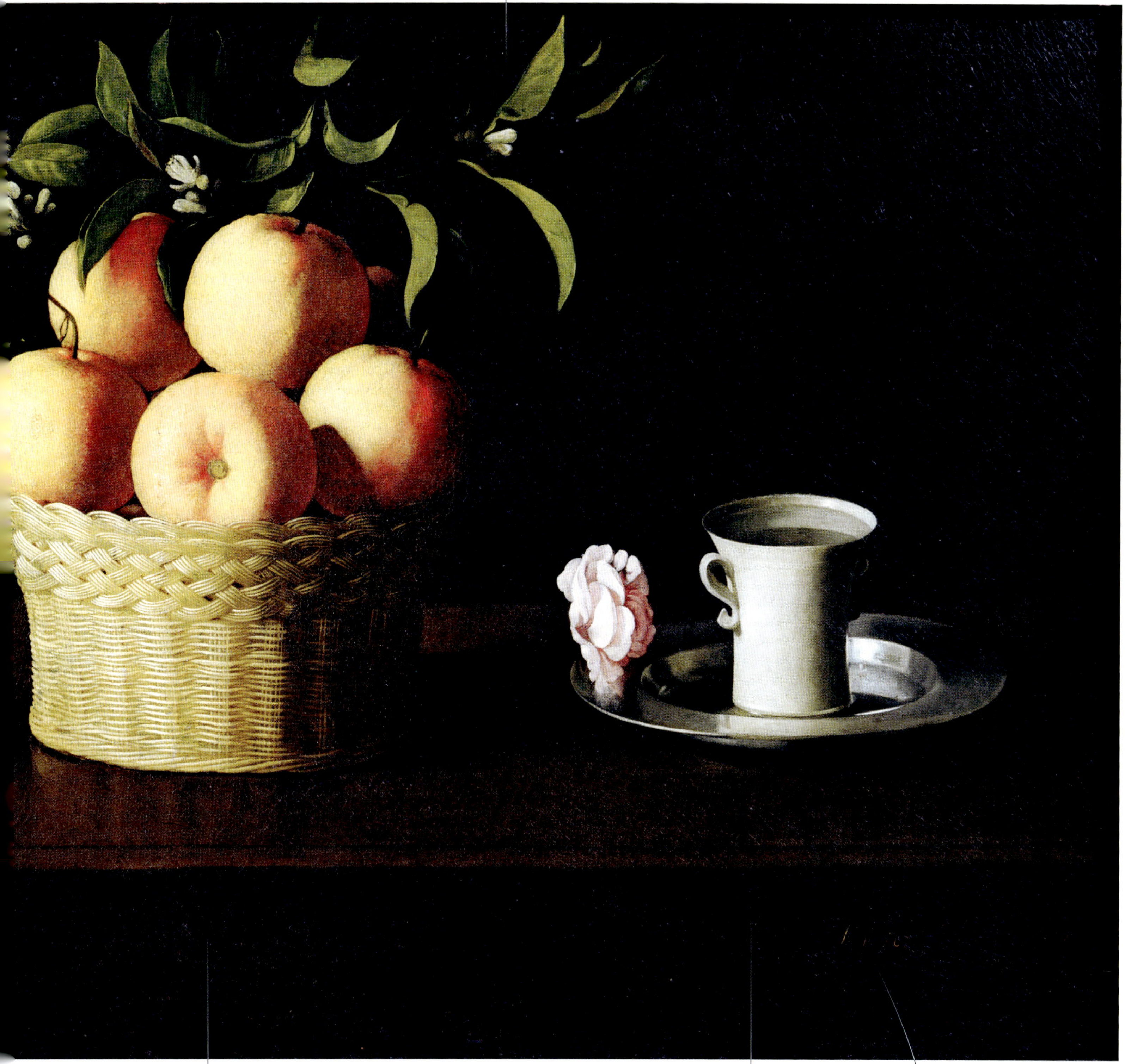

A slanting light falling from the left brings out the textures of the objects.

The cup of water symbolizes the purity of the Virgin.

This is the only still life that Zurbarán signed and dated, suggesting he was pleased with the result.

Et in Arcadia Ego

Nicolas Poussin 1637–1638, oil on canvas, 33 x 48 in (85 x 121 cm), Louvre, Paris, France

This pastoral scene is set in a landscape known as Arcadia, a paradisal land in Greek mythology where people follow a simple life. A group of shepherds have discovered a massive tomb in the middle of the beautiful countryside. There is an air of curiosity and melancholy as they study the inscription on the stone, which reads *Et in Arcadia Ego* (Even in Arcadia, there am I). An allegory of death, the painting is a reminder that the end comes to everyone, even in Arcadia.

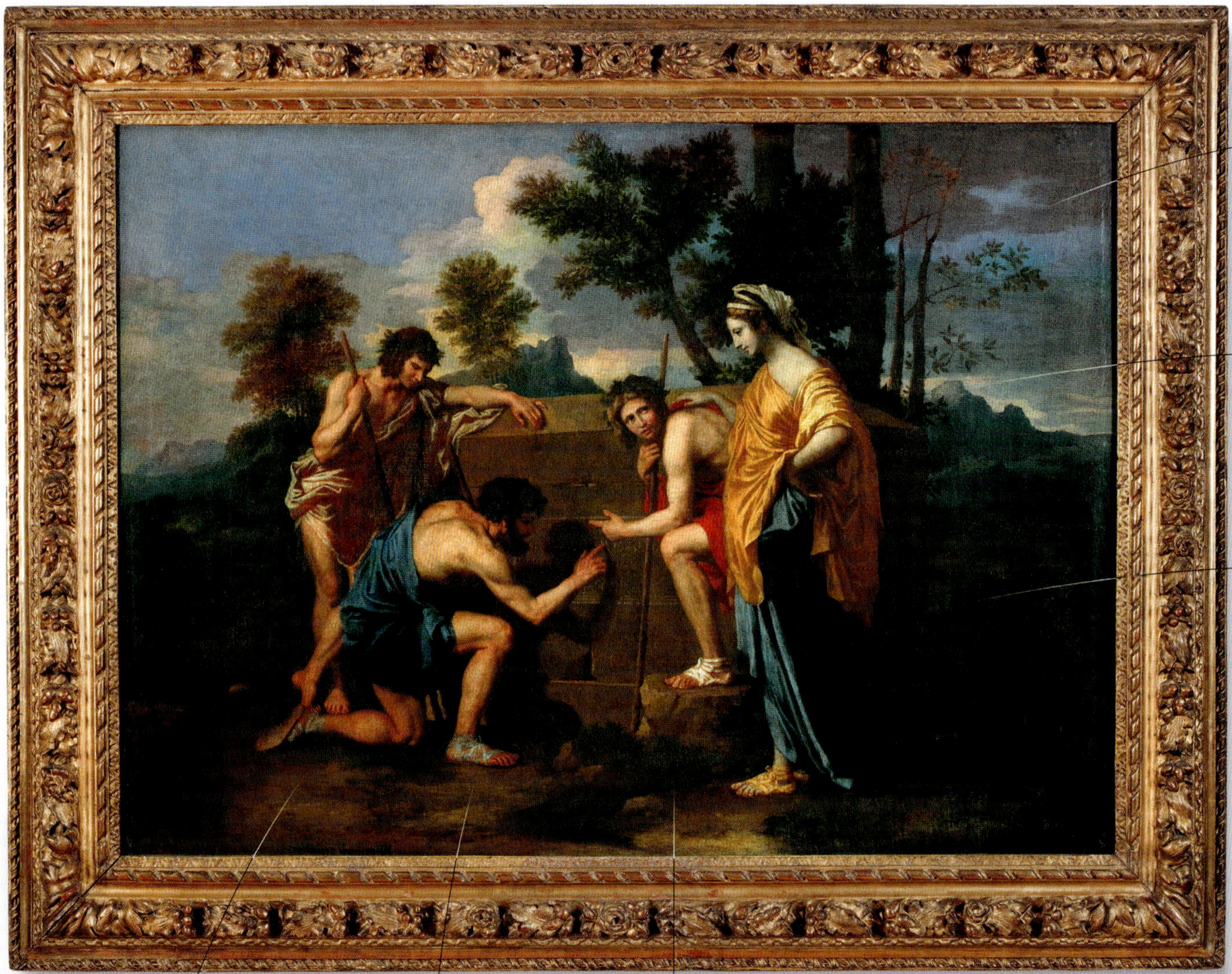

Dark clouds gather in the skies of Arcadia.

The static, clearly outlined poses of the figures are based on studies of classical art.

The female figure may represent the personification of Reason.

The shepherds represent innocence, as was the convention in 16th-century art and literature.

The angles formed by the shepherds' arms and legs introduce an element of discord.

Linked looks and gestures draw the eye to the inscription.

The circular shadow echoes circular motifs found on ancient Roman funerary monuments, symbolizing the cycle of life and death.

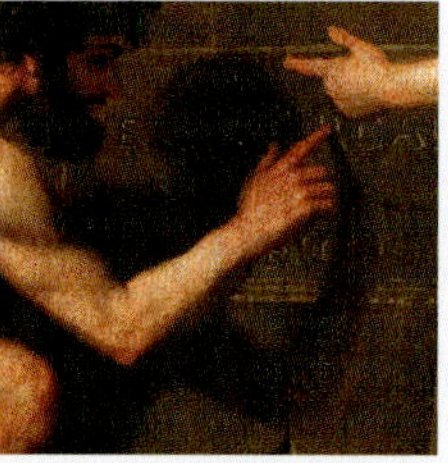

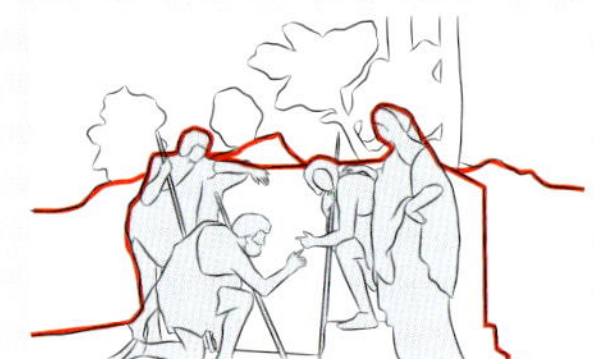

Recession
Successive planes are placed parallel to the picture plane. The elements reduce in size toward the distance, creating spatial recession.

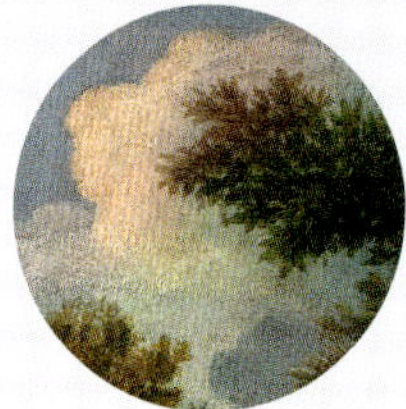

Minimal texture
A smooth finish has been achieved by eliminating all visible signs of brushwork, making the scene appear hard, cold, and static.

> "Even in complete happiness death is ever present."
>
> Anthony Blunt, 1958

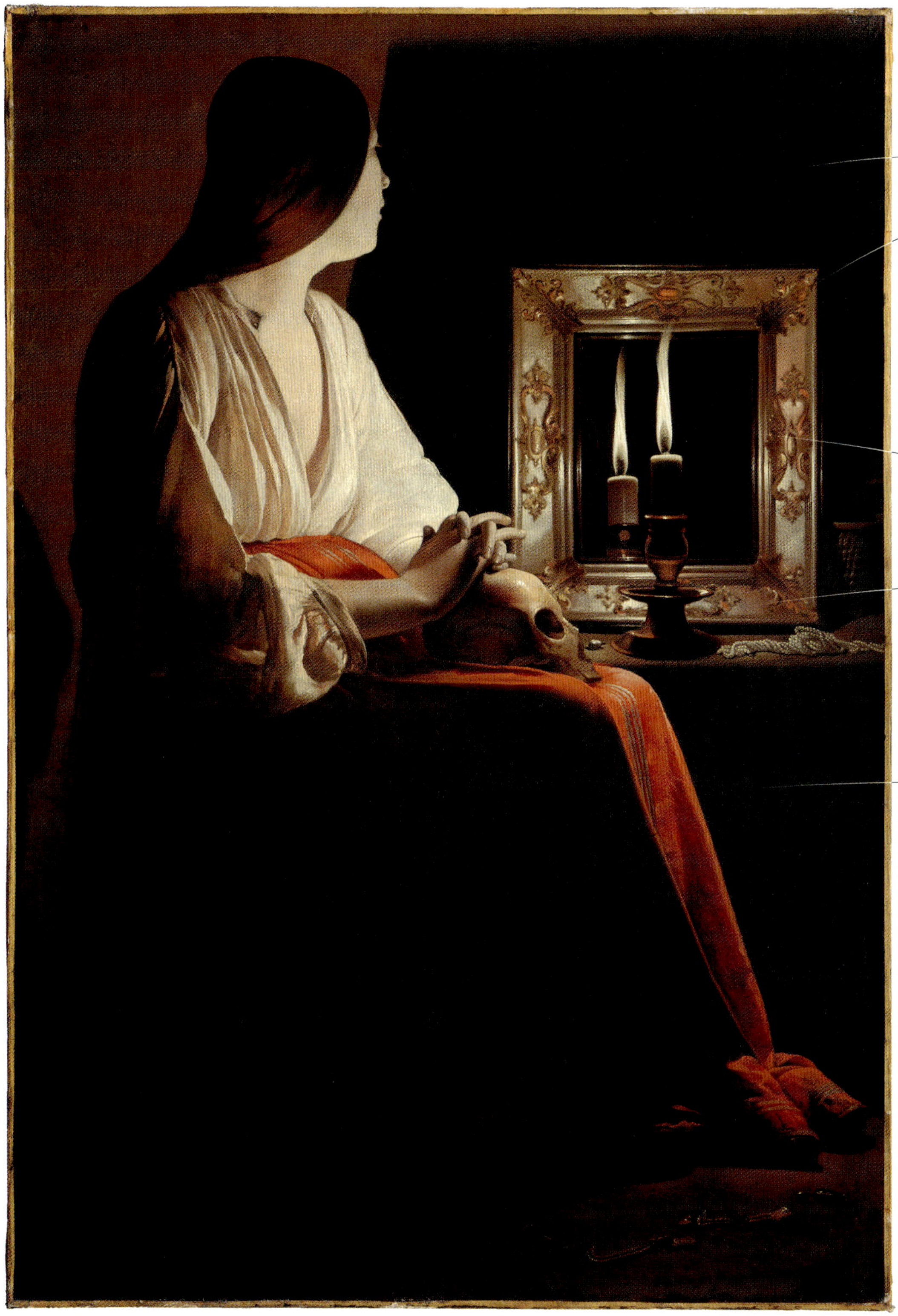

Mary's pale profile is bathed in the glow of the candlelight. This is accentuated by the intense shadow behind her and the cascade of her brown hair.

A gilded mirror, a symbol of vanity, glints in the candlelight. Dabs of yellow, orange, and red paint bring out details in the molding.

A flickering candle serves as a poignant reminder of the ephemeral nature of life.

The illuminated forehead of a skull suggests the inevitability of death.

The warm tones of the painting are enriched by the red skirt.

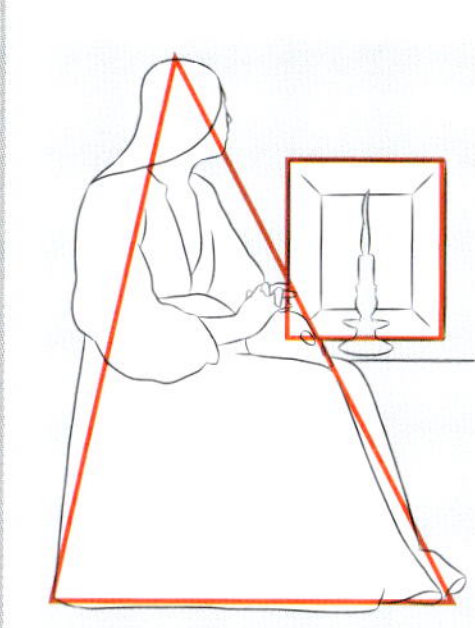

Painted geometry
The contemplative tone of the painting is enhanced by its harmonious stillness. This is achieved through the geometric composition—Mary's body forms a triangle that is complemented by the square mirror.

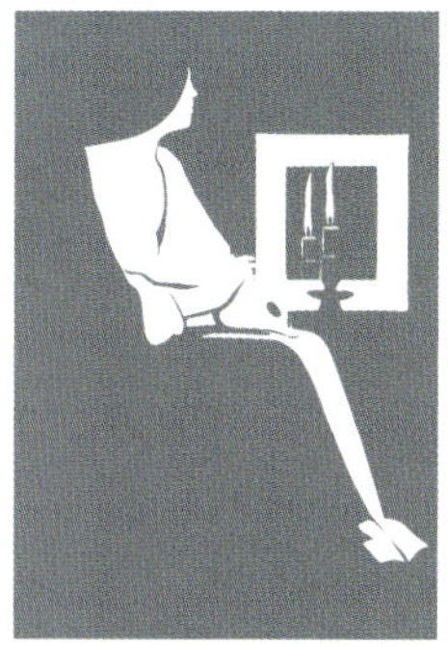

Intense chiaroscuro
A single candle and its reflection in the mirror illuminate Mary while plunging the rest of the scene into darkness.

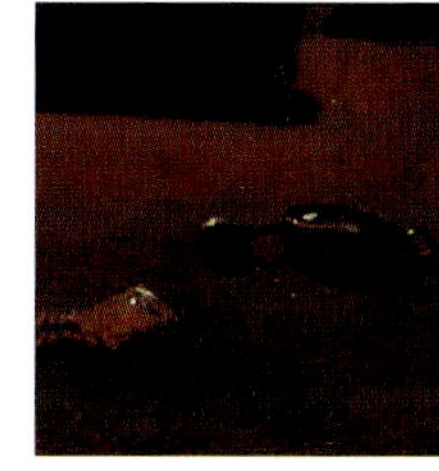

Jewelery and a pocket watch lie discarded on the floor. They allude to Mary's renouncement of her previous life filled with worldly pleasures.

The Penitent Magdalen

Georges de La Tour c. 1640, oil on canvas, 53 × 40 in (133.4 × 102.2 cm), Metropolitan Museum of Art, New York, US

This emotionally charged painting uses a dramatic contrast between light and dark to capture Mary Magdalene's introspection. It is one of four paintings by La Tour depicting Mary's spiritual repentance as she turns to Christ, all including allusions to *vanitas*—still-life reminders of the transience of life.

Triple Portrait of Cardinal de Richelieu

Philippe de Champaigne and studio c. 1642, oil on canvas, 23 × 29 in (58.7 × 72.8 cm), National Gallery, London, UK

Cardinal Richelieu, a French statesman as well as a religious figure, wears the traditional red robes and attributes of his sacred office. Depicting him from three perspectives, Champaigne's portrait is a meticulous examination of the man as much as the role and served as a reference for Francesco Mochi, an Italian sculptor tasked with creating a bust of the cardinal.

The left-hand portrait was probably painted by someone in Champaigne's studio. It is less accomplished than the other two, known to have been painted by the artist himself.

The warm tones of the cardinal's skull cap and robes are accentuated by the redness of his lips.

Delicate brushstrokes use subtle tonal variations of gray and white to depict light reflecting off individual hairs.

The scarlet skull cap identifies the sitter's role as a cardinal.

The sumptuous red cape and broad white collar stand out against the dark background, enhancing the cardinal's authoritative pose.

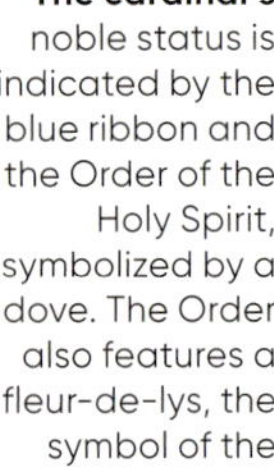

The cardinal's noble status is indicated by the blue ribbon and the Order of the Holy Spirit, symbolized by a dove. The Order also features a fleur-de-lys, the symbol of the French king.

Dabs of white paint mimic the texture of the tassels that dangle from the collar.

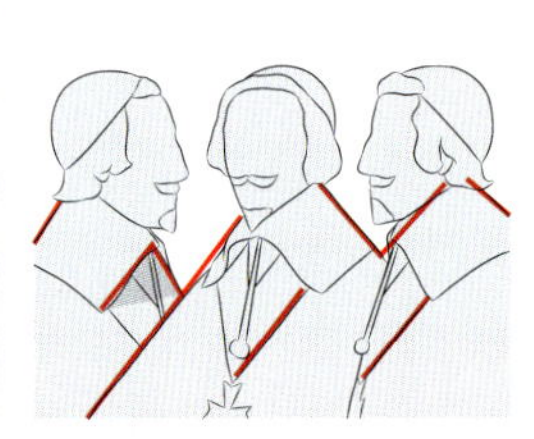

Sense of balance Sharp, angular lines create triangles that contribute to the balance of the composition.

> "Secrecy is the first essential in affairs of state."
>
> Cardinal de Richelieu, 1641

The Triumph of Bacchus

Michaelina Wautier c. 1634–1659, oil on canvas, 116 × 149 in (295 × 378 cm), Kunsthistorisches Museum, Vienna, Austria

Bacchus, the Roman god of wine, is surrounded by his followers as one of them squeezes grape juice into his open mouth. This lively composition, featuring semi-naked male bodies, is unusual in being by a woman at a time when women were not allowed to attend life drawing classes unless they were the model.

Bacchus drunkenly reclines on a wooden wheelbarrow at the center of the composition.

A man squeezes grape juice into the mouth of Bacchus—a reminder that Bacchus is the god of wine.

A satyr—half-man, half-goat—is a Greek symbol of excess and male lust, contributing to the sexual undertones of the painting.

An older man lusts after the artist, touching her face and hair.

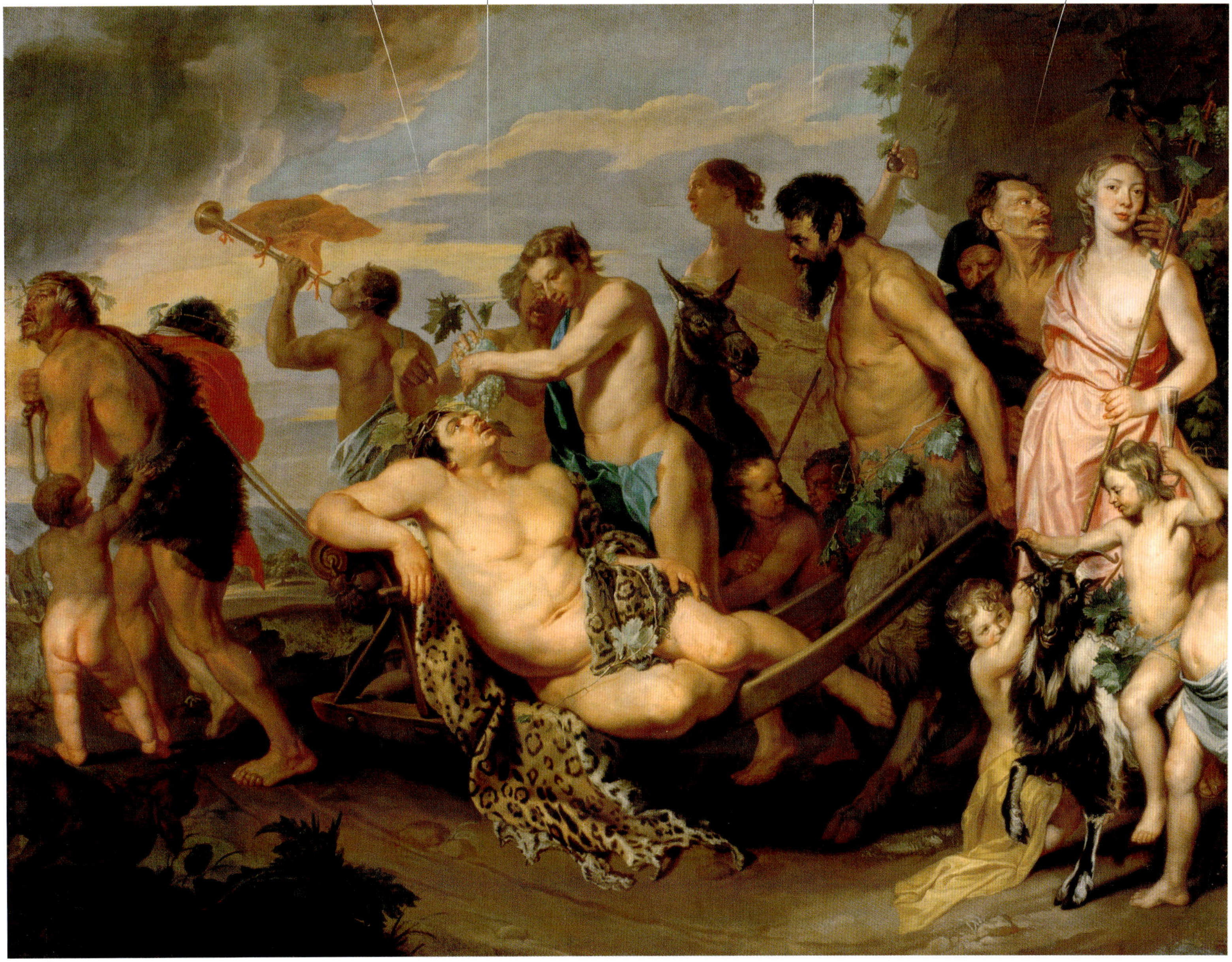

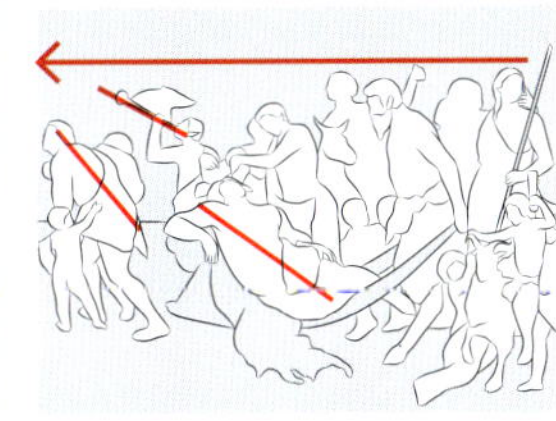

Sense of movement
The joyful procession moves across the composition toward the left; the movement is accentuated by the leaning bodies and the raised trumpet.

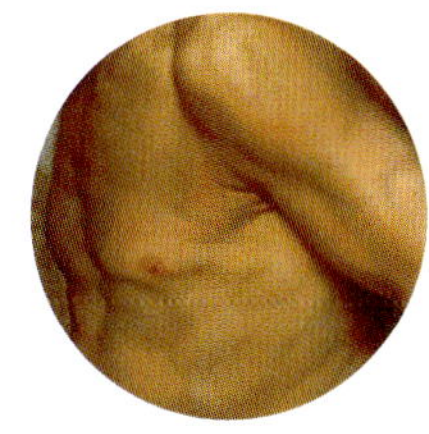

Flesh and muscles
The sculptural rendering of the naked bodies is achieved by employing light and shadow to enhance their three-dimensionality. Wautier may have had access to life drawing at her brother's studio.

A self-portrait of the artist, disguised as one of Bacchus's female followers, is the only figure who gazes out toward the viewer.

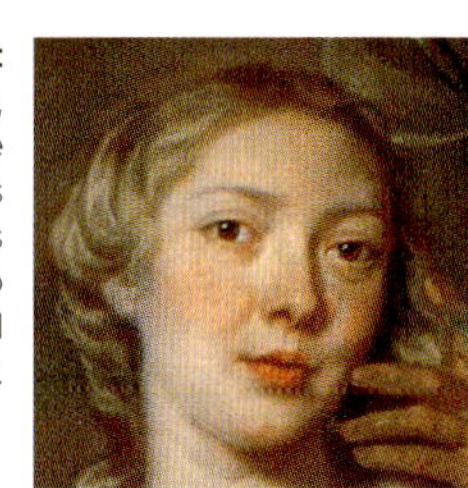

The painting was trimmed in order to fit the space allotted to it in Amsterdam's town hall. The left-hand side alone was reduced by more than 2ft (half a meter).

A white and blue flag depicts the colors of the civic guard.

Gold on the clothes and armor highlights the wealth and status of the guardsmen.

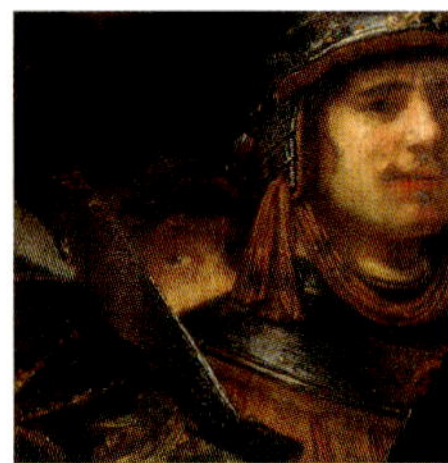

This person peeping over the shoulders of one of the guardsmen is believed to be a self-portrait.

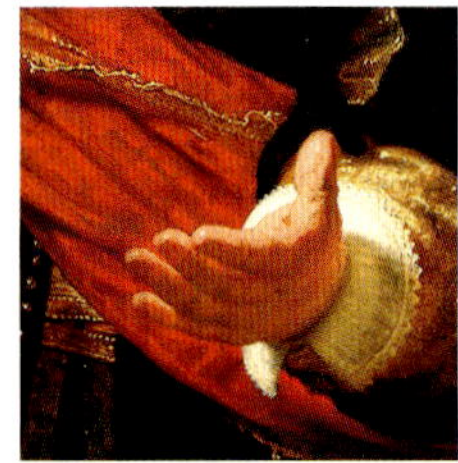

Captain Banninck Cocq gives an order to Lieutenant van Ruytenburch with a hand gesture. His red sash designates him as group leader, underlining his authority.

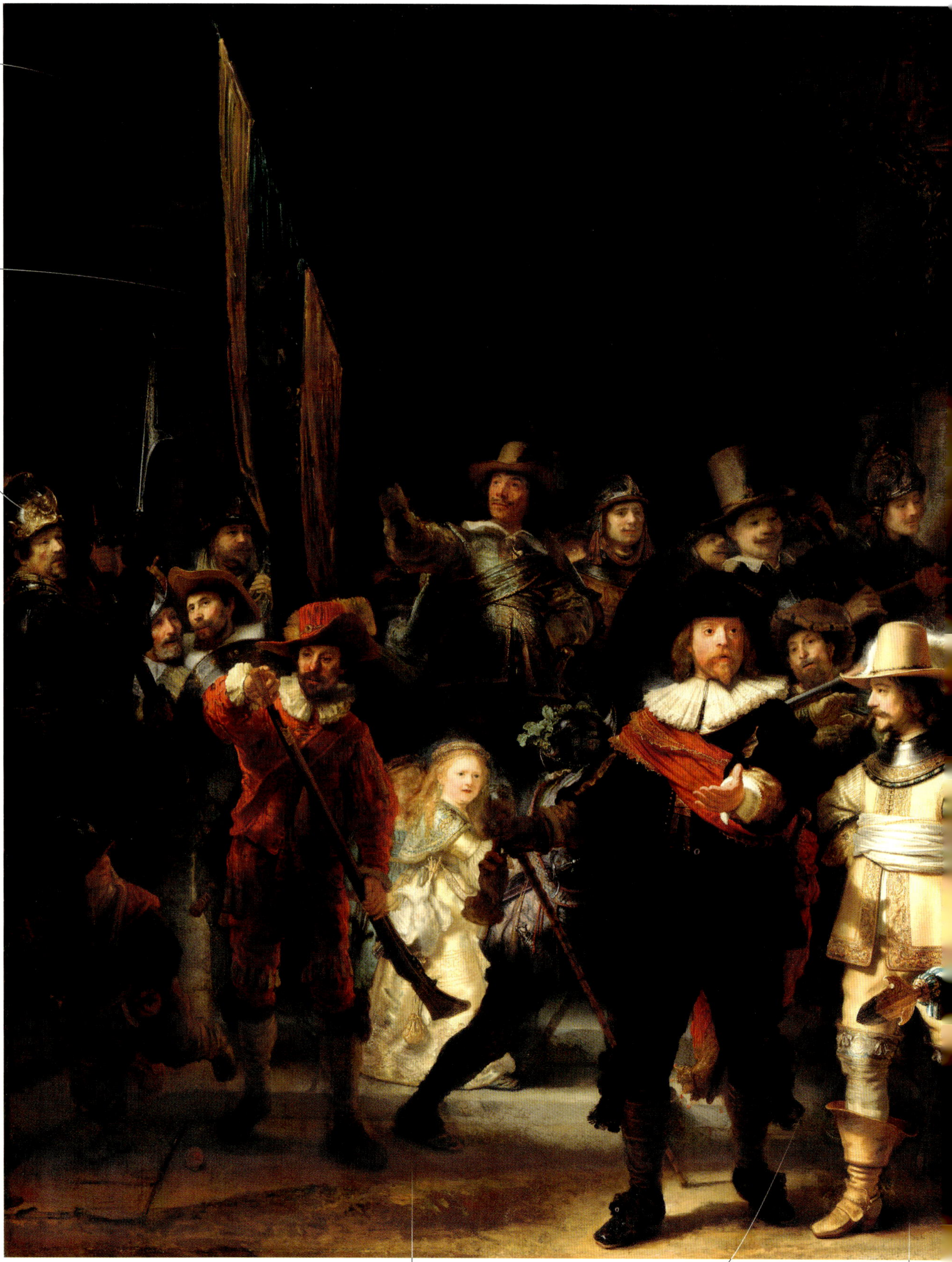

The young girl is the guardsmen's mascot. The chicken and pistol tucked into her waistband are symbols of the Kloveniers company.

The shadow of the captain's hand points to the city's coat of arms woven into the brocade on the lieutenant's coat.

Van Ruytenburch holds a ceremonial pike and wears a steel gorget around his neck to indicate his military status.

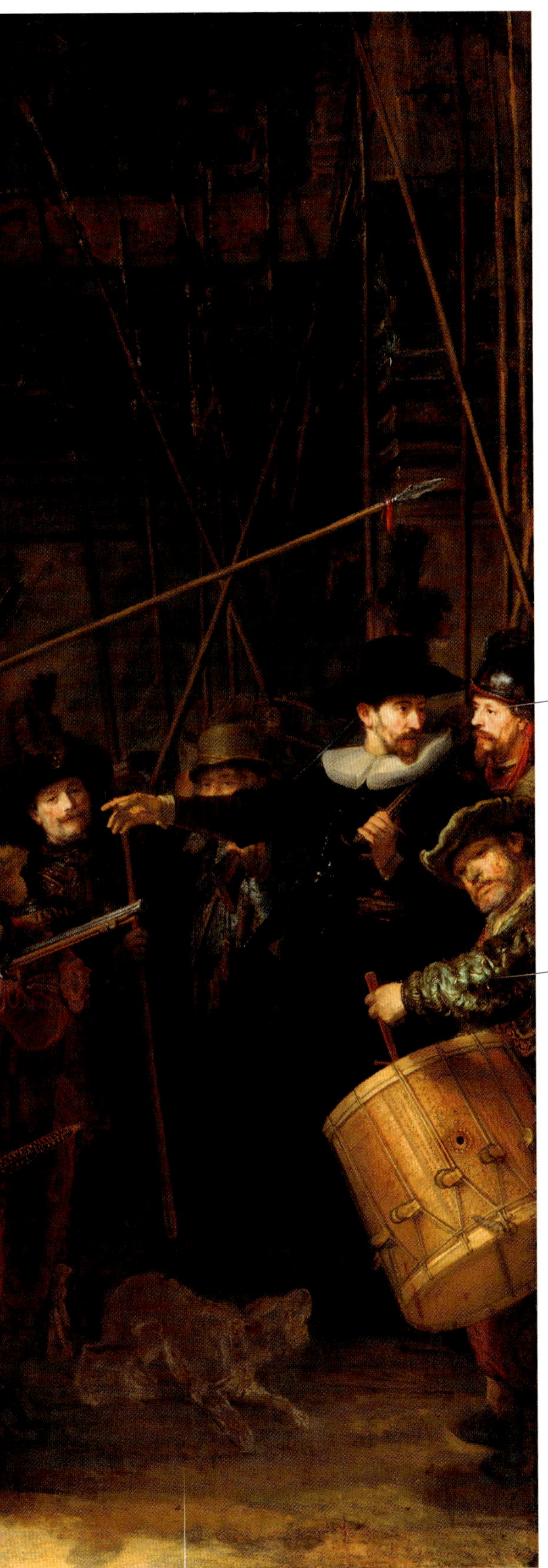

A shield records for posterity the names of the guardsmen depicted in the painting.

Chiaroscuro is used to indicate the status of the various figures. The most important guardsmen are bathed in light.

A drummer—an unusual addition to civic guard portraits—adds to the sense of occasion and underlines the Kloveniers' military role.

The paint on the dog has worn away slightly, exposing Rembrandt's preparatory underdrawing.

The Night Watch

Rembrandt van Rijn 1642, oil on canvas, 149 × 179 in (379.5 × 453.5 cm), Rijksmuseum, Amsterdam, Netherlands

Rembrandt was commissioned to paint this group portrait by Amsterdam's Kloveniers, a company of civic guardsmen, each of whom would have contributed to the cost. The painting departed from the convention of depicting the members of such companies in a static row. Rather, it shows the guards in action, as they receive orders to march out to defend the city. The striking contrast between light and dark creates a sense of drama and movement. Rembrandt illuminates the captain and lieutenant, making them the focal point.

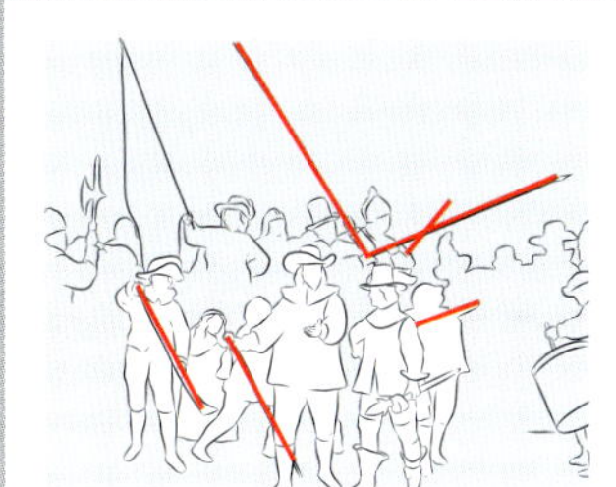

Steering the eye
The figures look and move in all directions, but the firearms and pikes point toward the captain and lieutenant at the center of the painting.

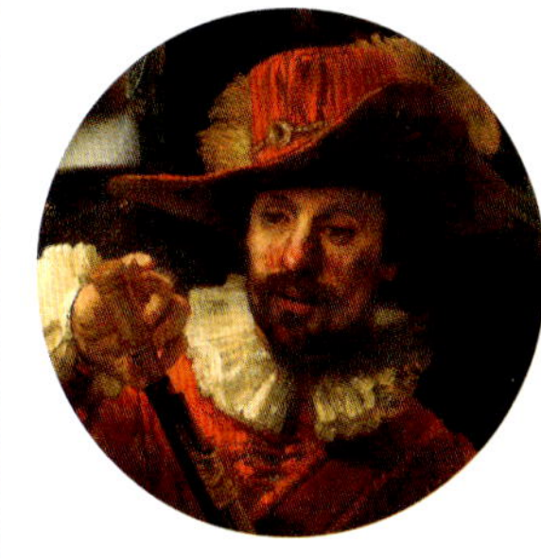

Color as code
Saturated reds, yellows, blues, and bright white details are used in the outfits of important figures, who stand out against a darker background.

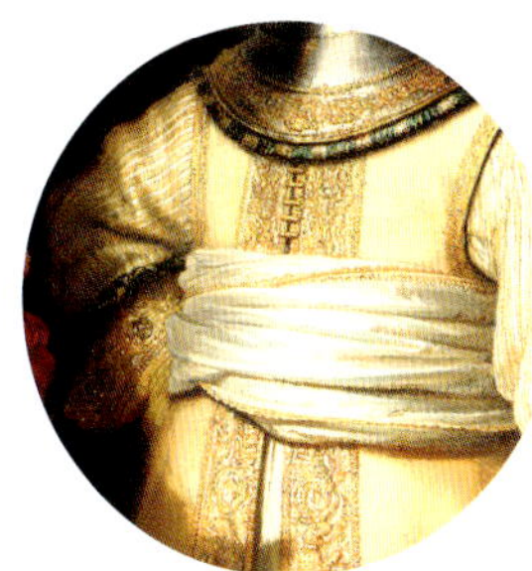

Lavish paintwork
Rembrandt uses impasto—areas of thick paint—to create a textured surface, particularly on decorative areas of clothing such as the brocade on the lieutenant's coat.

> "In this masterpiece of masterpieces, Rembrandt eclipsed all pontifical ostentation, the coronations of princes, noble tournaments, and the apotheosis of the ideal."
>
> Pierre-Joseph Proudhon, 1865

The Interior of the Buurkerk at Utrecht

Pieter Saenredam 1644, oil on oak, 24 × 20 in (60.1 × 50.1 cm), National Gallery, London, UK

The Dutch artist Pieter Saenredam specialized in architecturally complex, carefully observed church interiors of great beauty in which light pours in through tall windows and plays across the surfaces of stone walls and columns. He based his paintings on meticulously accurate drawings that he made, but also introduced small distortions to increase the impression of scale and luminosity.

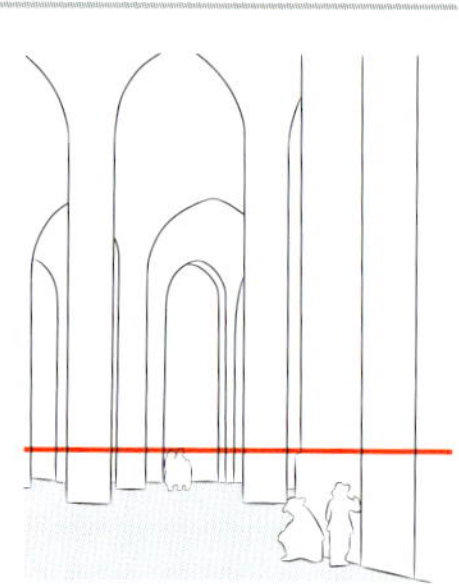

Composition Receding diagonals meet at the level of the distant figures' heads. The low eyeline creates a sense of height in the building.

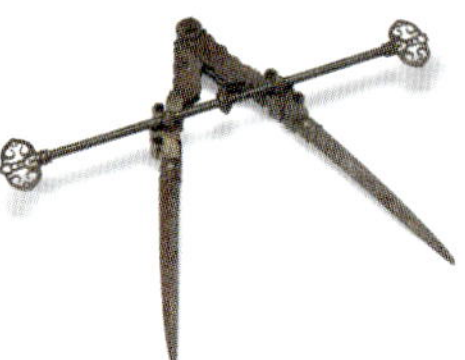

Working method Saenredam combined a freehand drawing done on the spot with carefully measured perspective drawings to arrive at the final image. The painting was produced in the studio several years later.

Saenredam has exaggerated the height of the columns and windows and increased the space beneath the arches.

A sword and shield are mounted high on the wall.

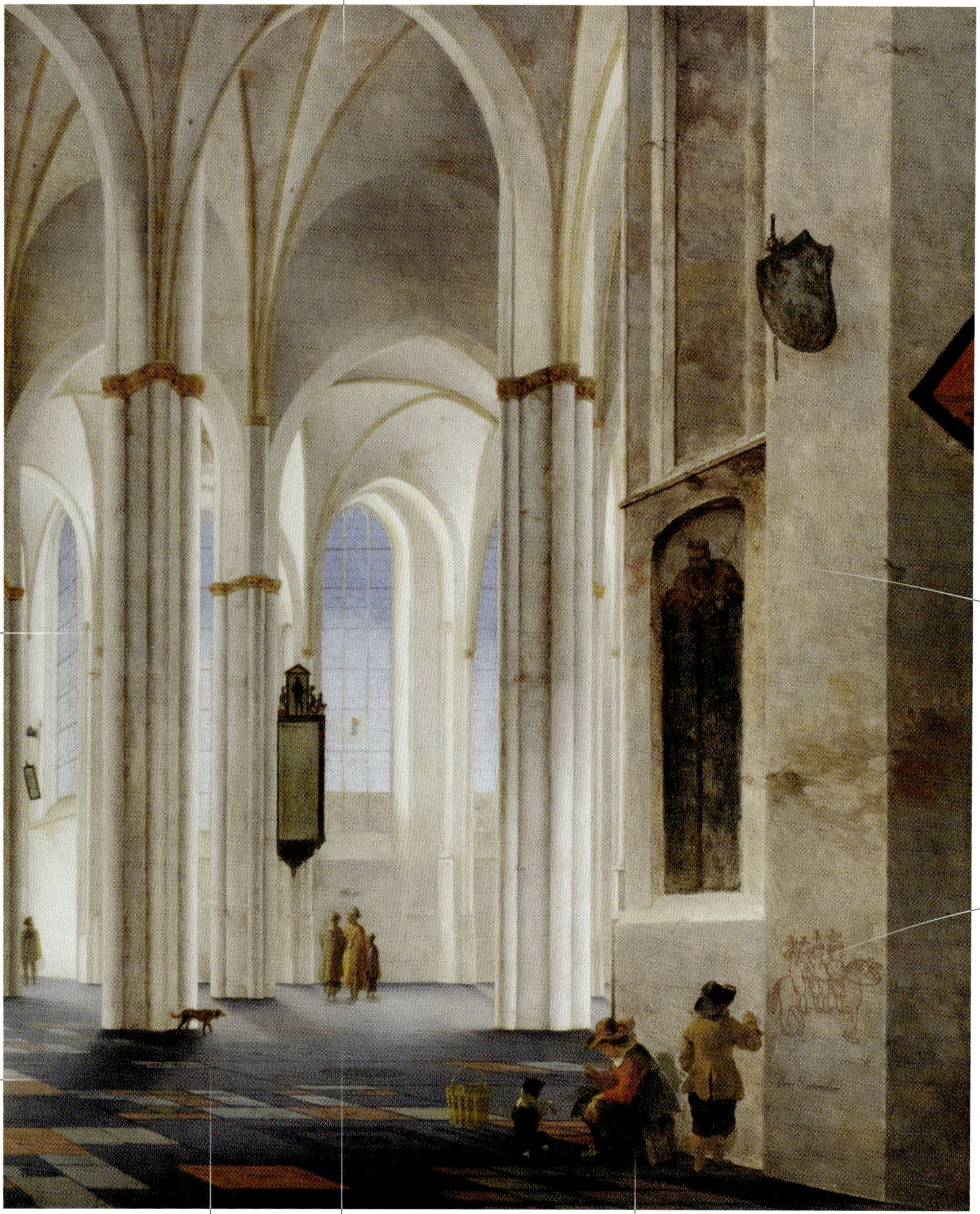

The interior of this medieval church has been stripped of its Catholic paintings and statues in line with Protestant beliefs after the Reformation.

A bust of Moses tops a list of the Ten Commandments, the laws for living a moral life that the Bible claims God gave to Moses on Mount Sinai (Exodus 20:1–26).

The younger boy drawing on the wall introduces an element of rebellion into the well-ordered interior.

The tiled floor and slanting shadows combined with the small figures in the distance create the illusion of receding space.

A dog introduces an air of informality and suggests that the church is a public space.

Small figures add human interest and give the interior a sense of scale.

The older boy is training a dog, an illustration of obedience.

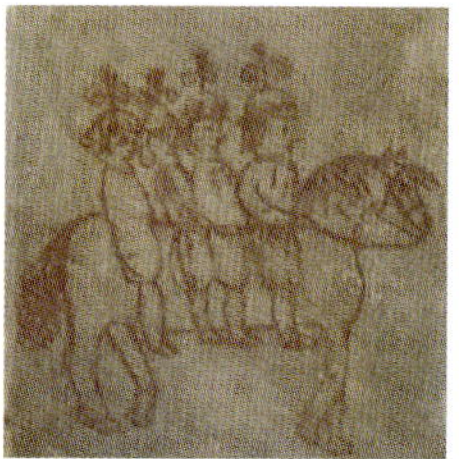

The drawing illustrates a popular medieval French legend about four brothers who travel to the Crusades on a magic horse called Bayard.

Juan de Pareja

Diego Velázquez 1650, oil on canvas, 32 × 28 in (81.3 × 69.9 cm), Metropolitan Museum of Art, New York, US

Pareja, the subject of this portrait, was an artist in his own right who was enslaved in Velázquez's studio for 20 years. Velázquez has painted Pareja in the simple, restrained style popular for informal portraits at the time, but the portrait's likeness to the sitter stunned his contemporaries. Velázquez was known for his fluent and naturalistic style, and this particular work captures the innate spirit of Pareja with exceptional subtlety.

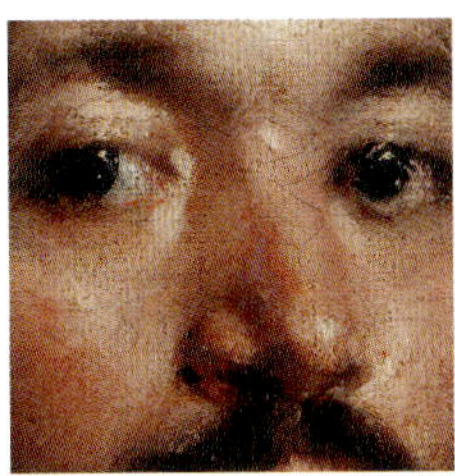

Highlights in the eyes were put in with tiny dabs of white paint.

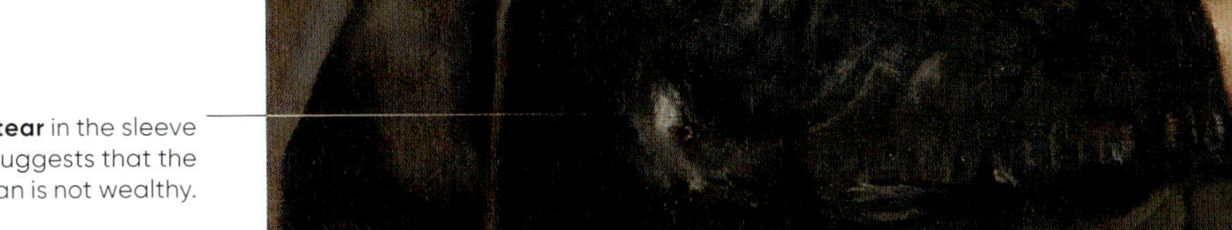

The plain, empty background concentrates attention on the face of the sitter.

The arm is positioned close to the front of the painting, setting the body and face of Pareja farther back in space, creating a sense of distance and reserve.

A tear in the sleeve suggests that the man is not wealthy.

The sitter is shown in a three-quarter view with his face turned toward the viewer. This conveys a dignified demeanor.

Pareja's lace collar has been roughly sketched in over gray without any attempt at detail.

The gray clothing and background provide a foil for the warm tones of the face.

Chiaroscuro is used to model the forms, but the contrasts of light and dark are restrained.

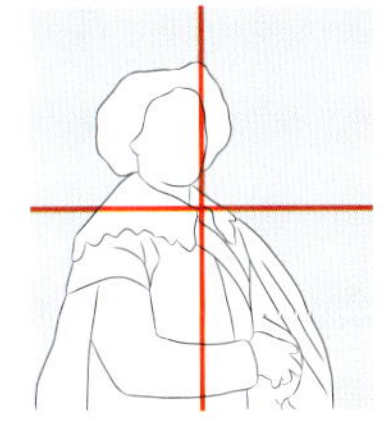

Composition
The head is just off-center in the upper part of the canvas. Folds in the clothing create strong lines that converge on the face.

Technique
Velázquez applied wet paint onto wet paint and blended adjacent areas to produce changes in tone rather than building up the painting in layers.

Plate of Cherries, Pod, and Bumblebee

Giovanna Garzoni c. 1640–1660, tempera on parchment, 10 × 15 in (24.5 × 37.5 cm), Museo della Natura Morta, Poggio a Caiano, Italy

Art and science combine in this intensely detailed still life depicting glistening cherries piled up on a plate lined with leaves, branches, and blossom. This composition stands as a testament to Garzoni's training in botanical illustration and direct observation of the natural world.

The bare parchment background isolates the subject matter, focusing attention on the marvels of nature.

Fine brushstrokes of brilliant reds, with nuanced variations in hue and tone, give a fleshy texture to the cherries at various stages of ripeness.

The departing bumblebee, having savored the ripe fruit, is a reminder of the transient nature of life.

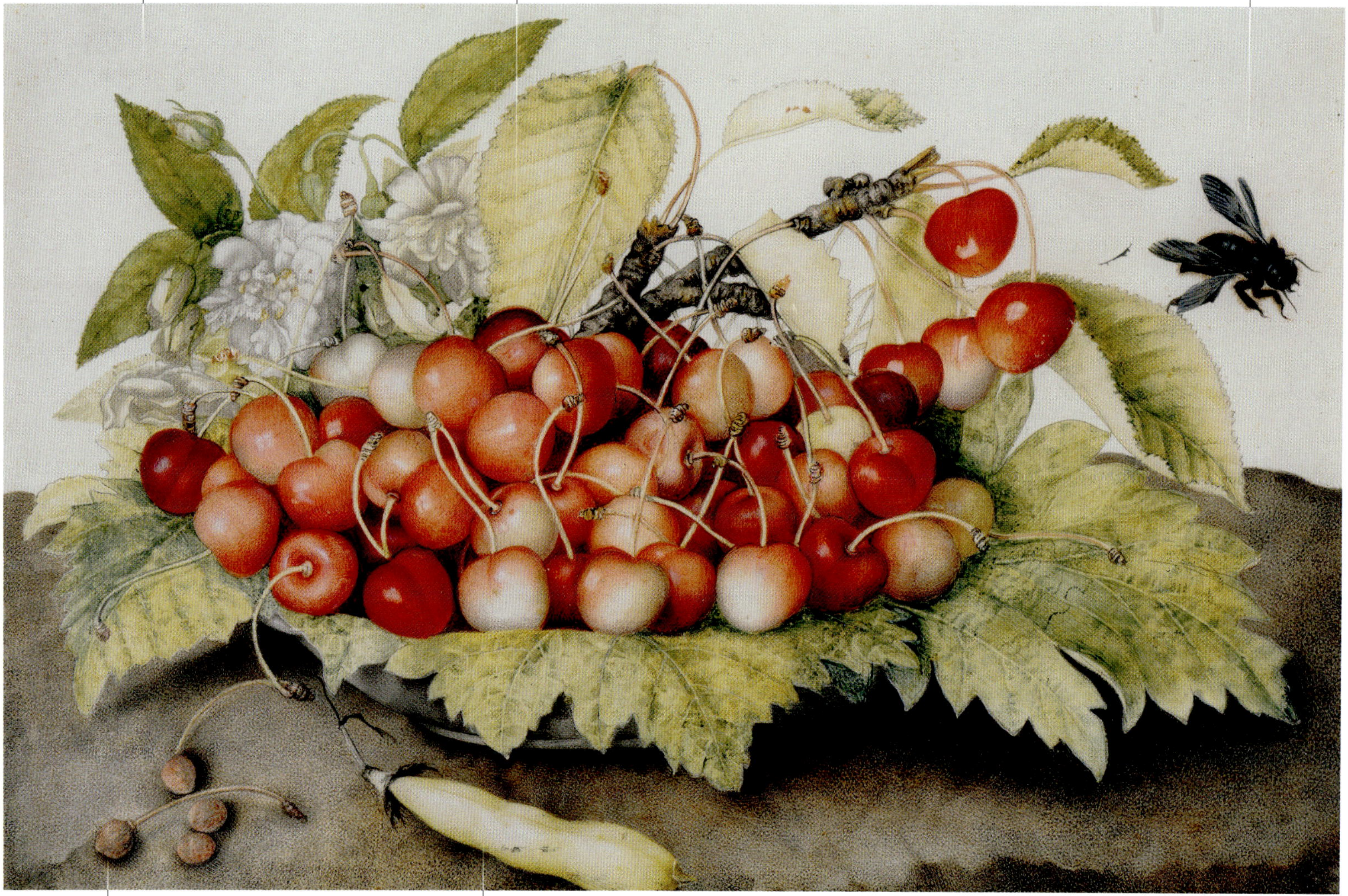

Four cherry stones subtly suggest a human presence, perhaps that of the artist herself, underscoring the deliberate arrangement of the composition.

A lone bean pod seems out of place among the abundance of cherries, giving Garzoni's composition a touch of playfulness.

The reflection of a window is visible on some of the cherries, offering a glimpse of the interior setting in which the artist worked.

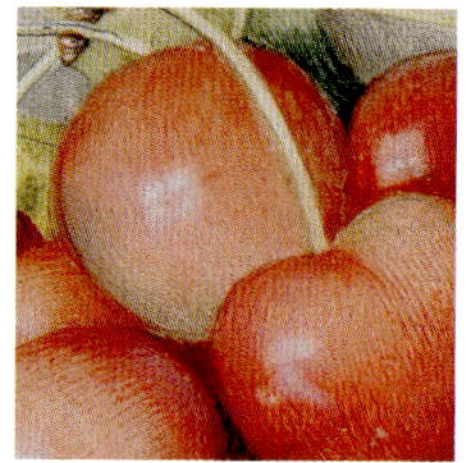

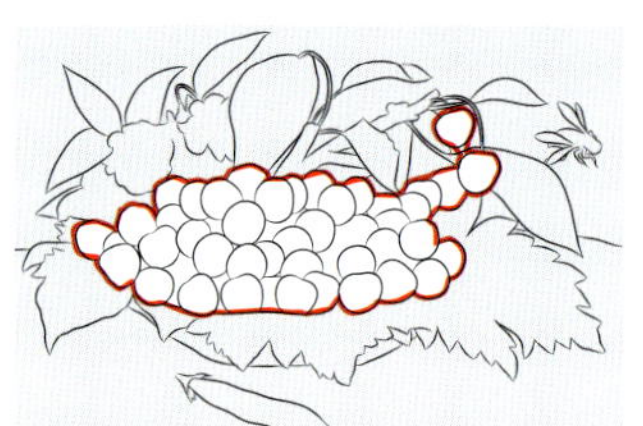

Point of view
A slightly elevated perspective enables the viewer to peer into the bowl, revealing as many cherries as possible.

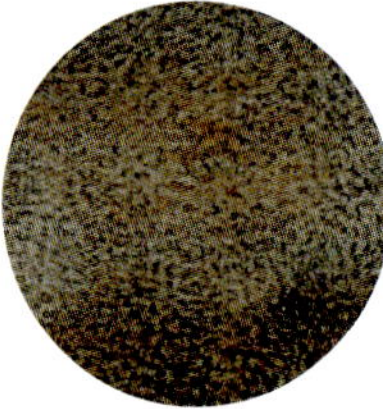

Creating perspective
Garzoni used stippling, a technique that employs dots of color to create shadows and textured surfaces as well as a sense of depth. This is especially evident on the tabletop.

Las Meninas

Diego Velázquez 1656, oil on canvas, 126 × 111 in (320.5 × 281.5 cm), Prado, Madrid, Spain

In this royal portrait, Velázquez plays with perspective and lighting to create a visual mystery. The artist appears to be painting the king and queen while their daughter and servants look on, but he also invites viewers into the composition, so they become both the watcher and the watched. Some have compared the work to a photograph because it presents such a wealth of action.

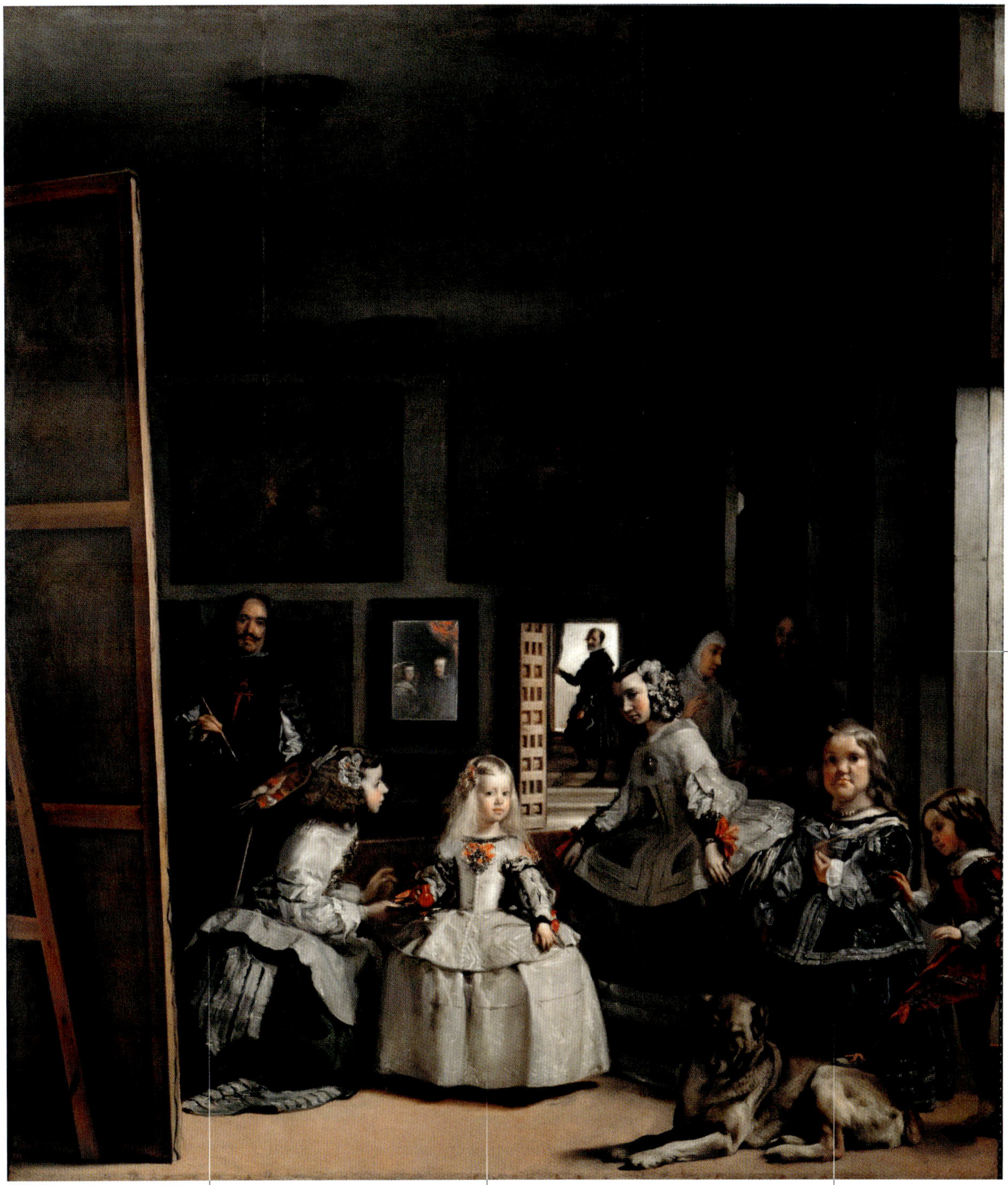

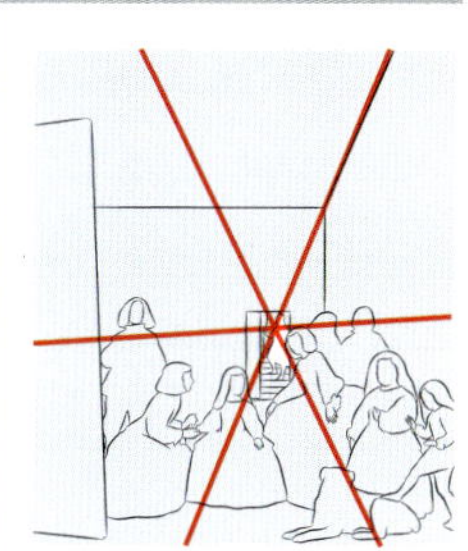

Life outside the room
The queen's chamberlain in the doorway at the far end of the room marks the vanishing point, where the perspectival grid converges. This suggests depth beyond the composition.

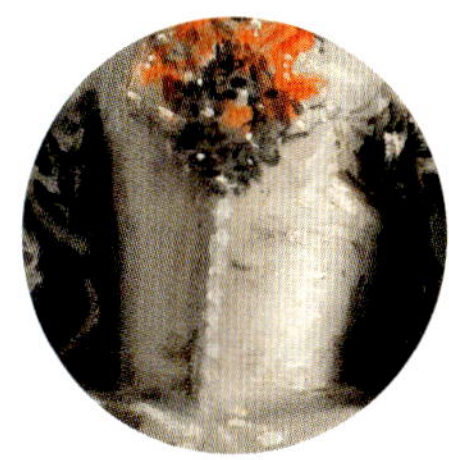

Technique
Velázquez applied thick layers of fresh paint on top of paint that was still wet to build up textural details and colors. This technique gave his work a striking sense of movement.

Light divides the composition into thirds, illuminating the foreground and doorway while casting the mid-ground into darkness, heightening the drama and mystery.

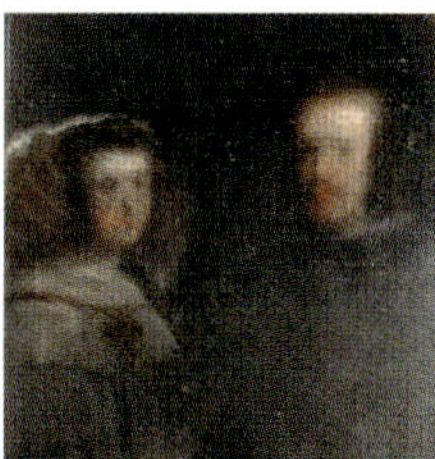

King Philip IV and Queen Mariana of Austria are reflected in a mirror at the back of the room. Are they the subject of the painting or have they merely come to see how Velázquez is getting on?

Velázquez included a self-portrait of himself working on a large canvas; the subject was probably the royal couple.

In the center is the Infanta Margarita. She is attended by two of her mother's ladies-in-waiting (*meninas*).

Dwarves played an important part in daily life at the Spanish court. They were admired as curiosities, yet Velázquez paints them with a tender individuality.

Personification of Music

Elisabetta Sirani c. 1659, oil on canvas, 37 × 29 in (94.6 × 74.3 cm), private collection

A woman sings in a room full of instruments, creating a harmonious fusion of the visual and audible arts. The significance of this painting lies in its layered meanings: it is a self-portrait in the guise of an allegory, in which Italian artist Sirani contemplates her own artistic identity and status as a woman painter.

The woman's upward gaze signifies her musical prowess, echoing Sirani's awareness of her artistic ability.

A collection of musical instruments hangs in the background. It belonged to Sirani's father, who was also an artist, and reflects the family's musical interests.

The three-quarter-length portrait format creates a sense of intimacy, reminiscent of a private musical performance.

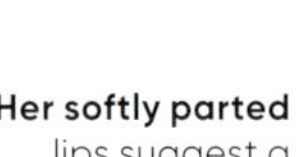

Her softly parted lips suggest a melodic voice.

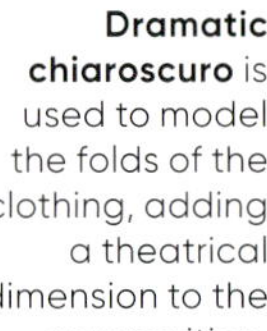

Dramatic chiaroscuro is used to model the folds of the clothing, adding a theatrical dimension to the composition.

Vibrant colors convey a joyful celebration of music as an art form.

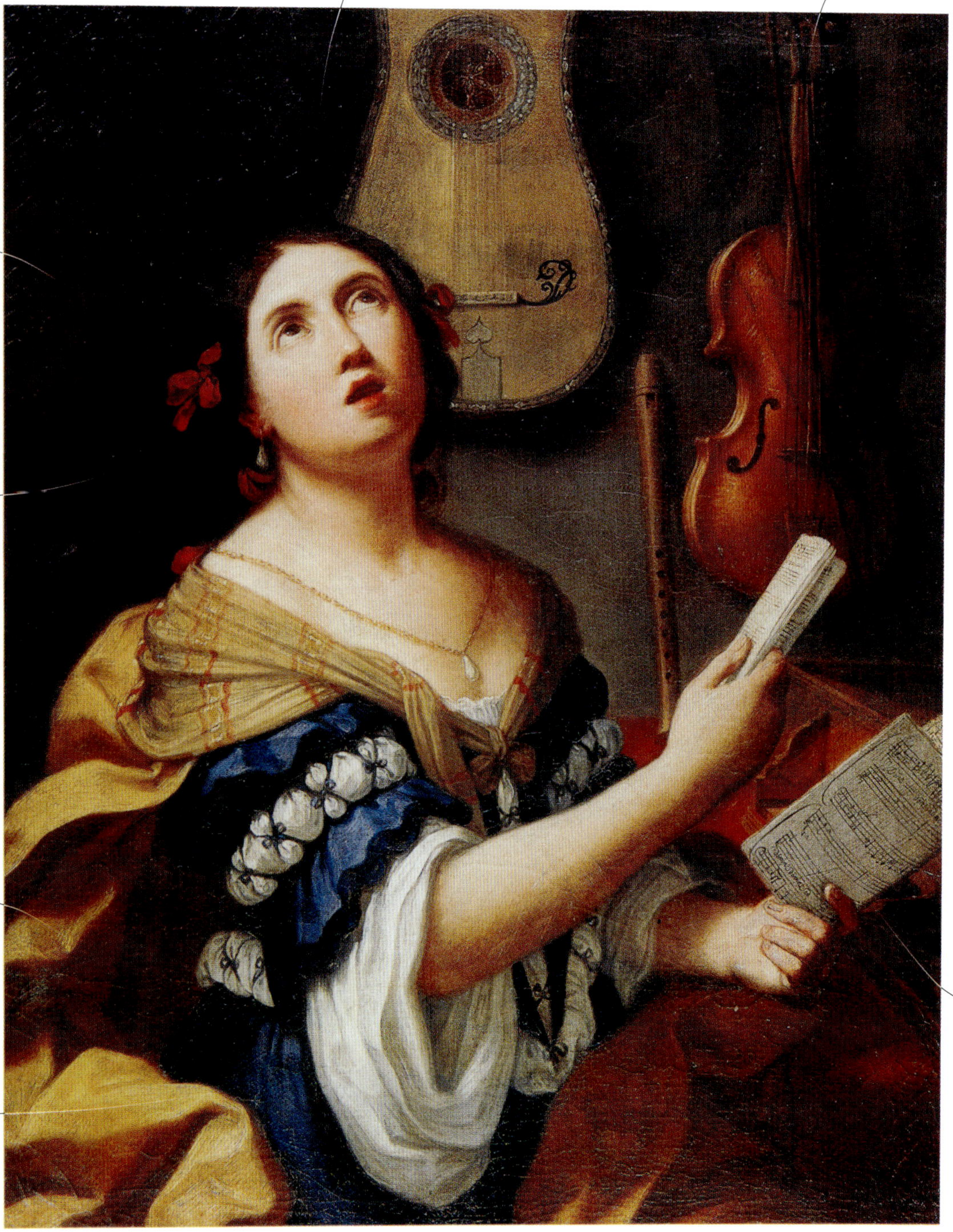

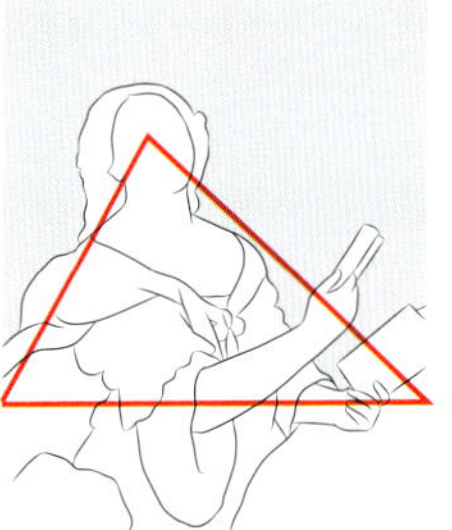

Drawing focus
The woman's cloak and posture create a graceful movement, drawing the viewer's eye to her face positioned at the pinnacle of an off-center pyramidal composition.

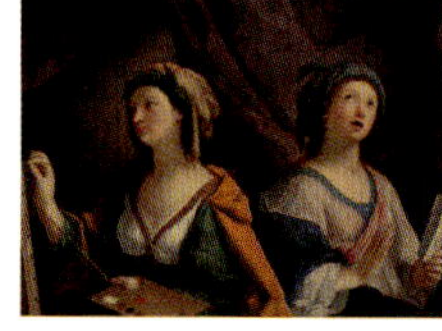

Memorable look
The woman's pose is reminiscent of that used by the artist's father, Giovanni Andrea Sirani, in his painting *Allegory of Painting and Music* depicting two women engaged in the arts.

In the 17th century, sheet music became widely available as music started to become popular in the home.

The Calling of St. Matthew

Juan de Pareja 1661, oil on canvas, 89 × 128 in (224.9 × 325 cm), Prado, Madrid, Spain

This painting depicts a scene from the Gospel of St. Matthew (9:9–13) in which Christ summons Matthew, a tax collector, to be one of his disciples. Pareja, a Black artist formerly enslaved in Velázquez's studio, weaves social commentary, dramatic storytelling, and reflections on his own status into a carefully structured painting. Behind Christ, a doorway leads into an idyllic landscape suggesting divine salvation.

Pareja depicts himself in the painting, just as Velázquez did in *Las Meninas* (1656). The piece of paper in his hand says "Juan de Pareja made this."

A radiant white halo encircles Christ's head.

Bright stars hover above the heads of the three disciples accompanying Christ and also over Matthew.

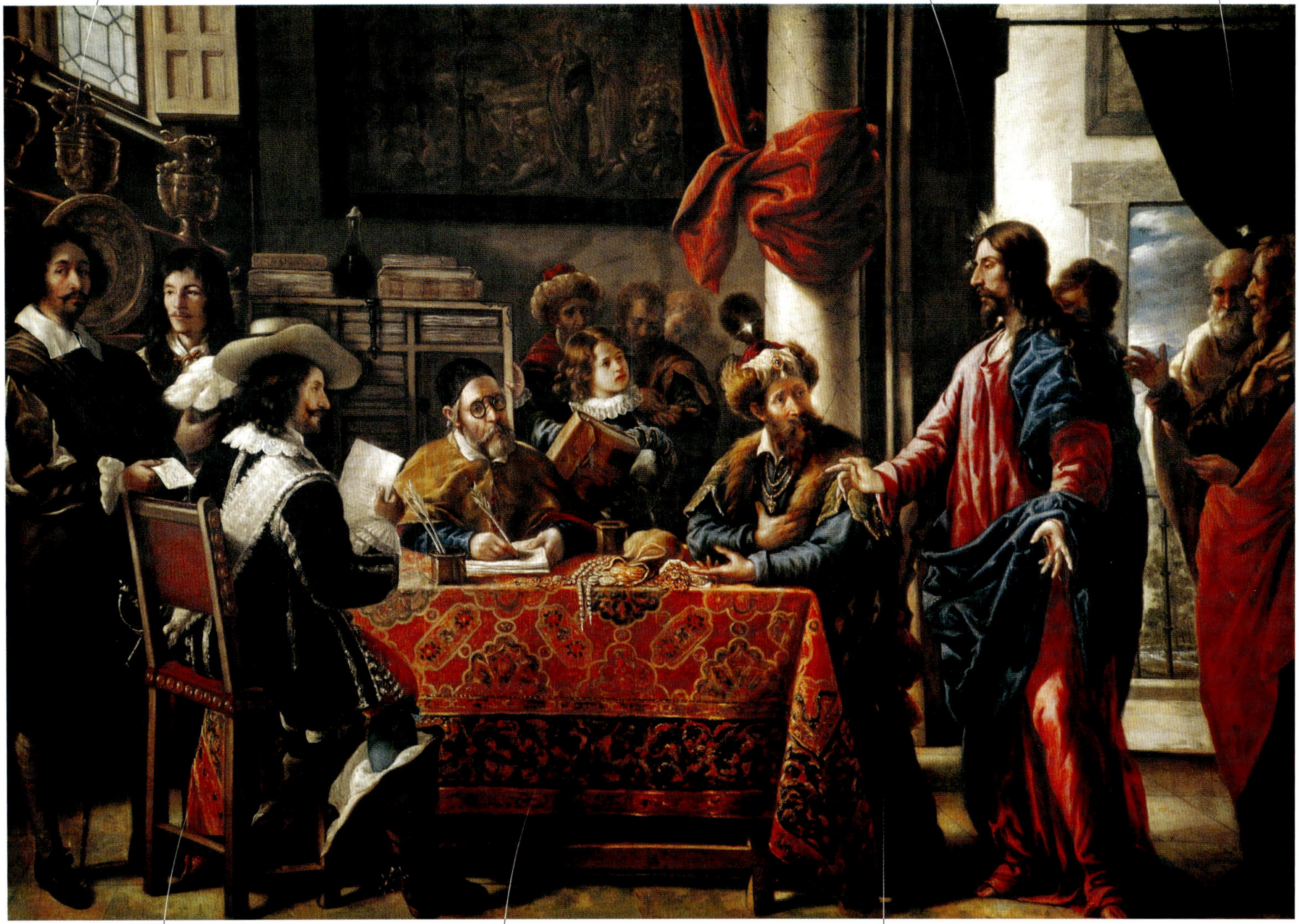

The men are dressed in the courtly fashion of 17th-century Spain.

Money and jewelery cover the richly furnished table, allusions to the earthly pleasures Matthew will abandon.

Matthew, dressed in opulent fur and golden chains, gestures toward himself, surprised at Christ's request.

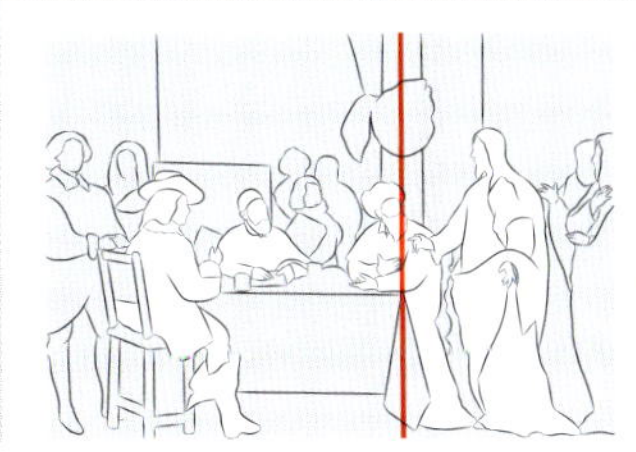

Composition
Architectural elements structure the composition. A column divides the earthly and spiritual realms, with Matthew occupying the liminal space between them.

"Pareja's artistic legacy reverberates across the canons of Western art and the African diaspora into our time."

Vanessa K. Valdés, 2023

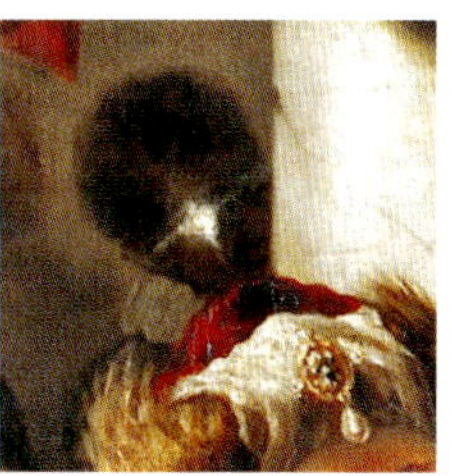

A Black boy references Spain's enslaved African population and the story of Matthew converting an Ethiopian king to Christianity.

View of Delft

Johannes Vermeer c. 1660–1661, oil on canvas, 38 × 46 in (96.5 × 115.7 cm), Mauritshuis, The Hague, Netherlands

This oil painting of Vermeer's hometown was one of the most famous works of the 17th-century Golden Age of Dutch painting, and his only cityscape. Popular in the Netherlands at the time, such scenes celebrated civic pride and prosperous commerce. The subtle interplay between light, shadow, and reflection imbues the scene with tranquility, while the people going about their daily activities in the foreground animate the painting. Composition was important for Vermeer, and he altered architectural details and the position of buildings to achieve balance in the scene.

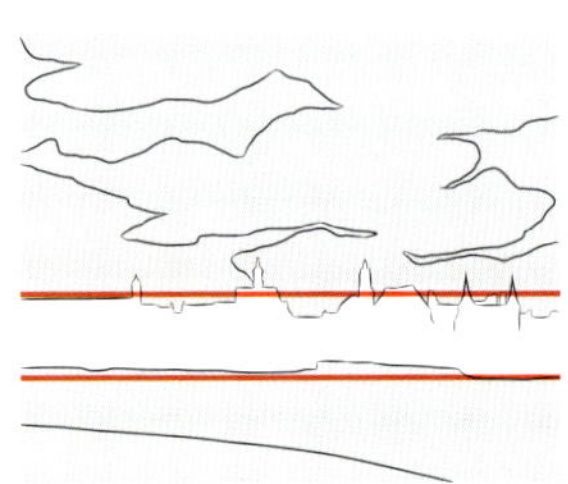

Depth and layering
The composition is divided into three unbalanced, horizontal layers, with the sky taking up the top half of the canvas, the city in the middle, and the water in the foreground. The diminishing size of the clouds creates perspective.

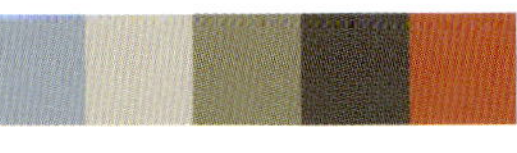

Against the blue
Blues and grays dominate the image. The browns and whites of the boats and the red rooftops stand out against the water and sky.

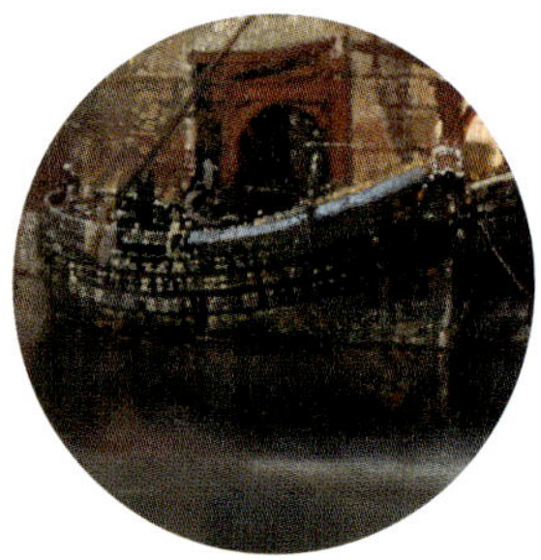

Subtle reflections
Vermeer used thin layers of paint for the reflections of the buildings in the calm river. He used thick spots of white paint on the boats to convey reflections from the water.

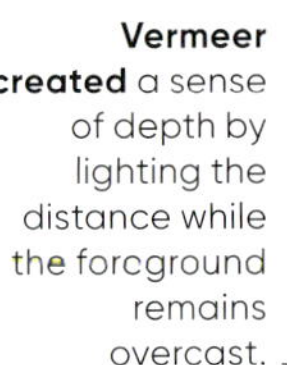

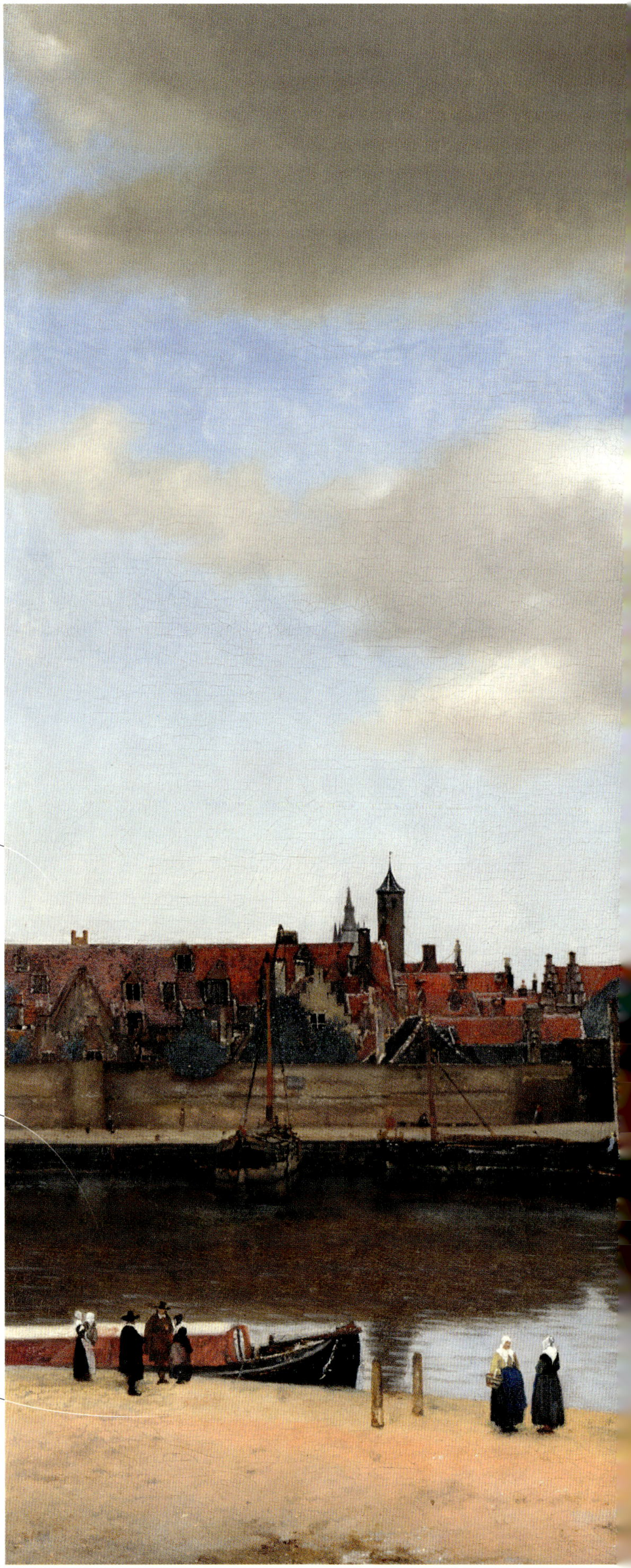

Vermeer created a sense of depth by lighting the distance while the foreground remains overcast.

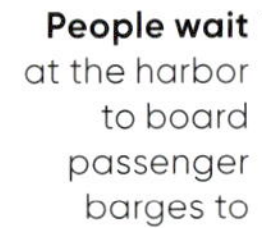

People wait at the harbor to board passenger barges to Rotterdam or Schiedam.

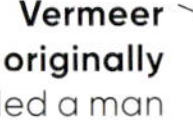

Vermeer originally included a man standing to the right of the two women, but he painted out that detail, possibly to balance the composition.

> "When I saw *A View of Delft* at the Museum in The Hague, I knew that I had seen the most beautiful picture in the world."
>
> Marcel Proust, 1921

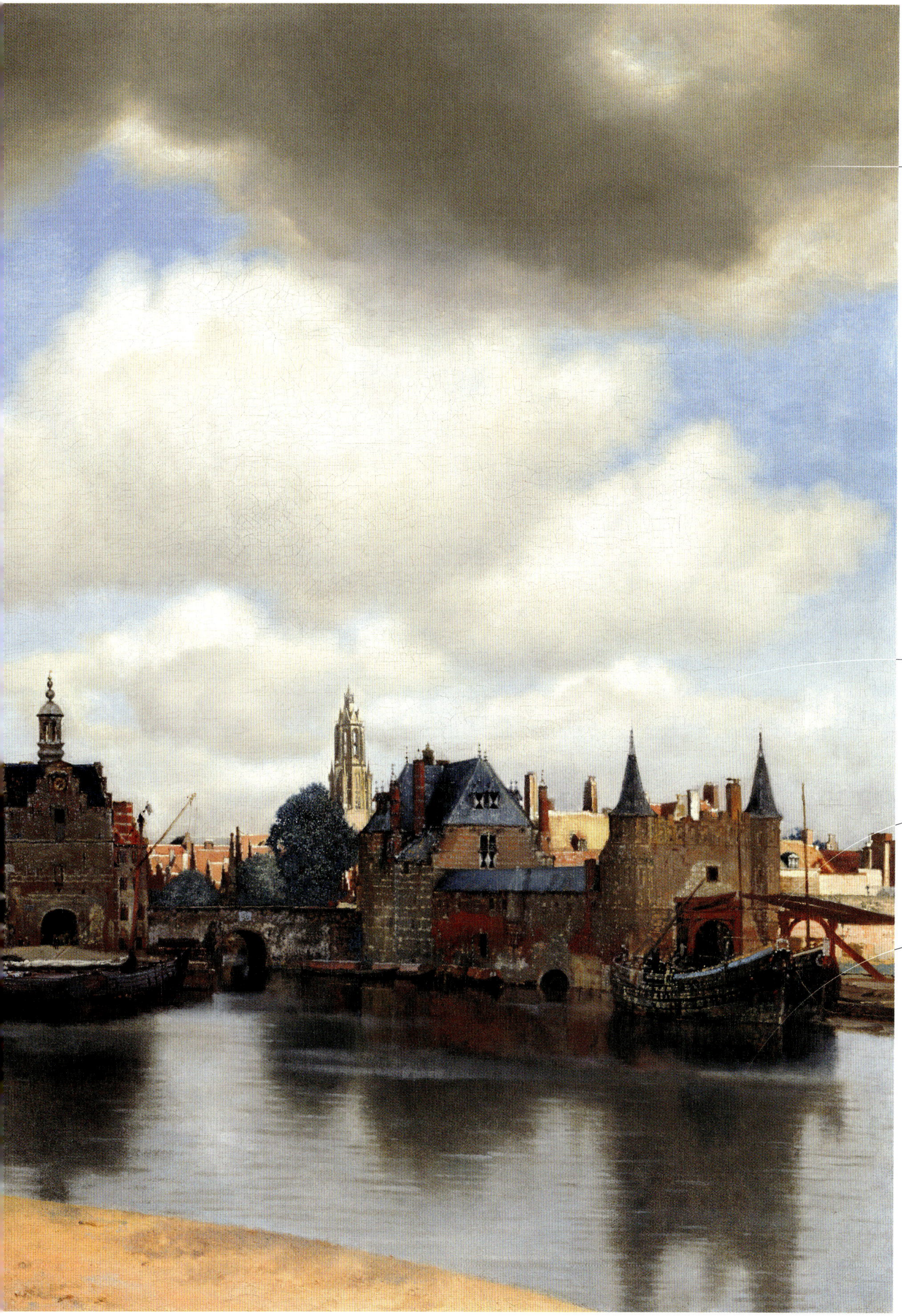

Sky takes up two-thirds of the painting, but an impressive dark cloud pushes the viewer's attention toward the city and quay.

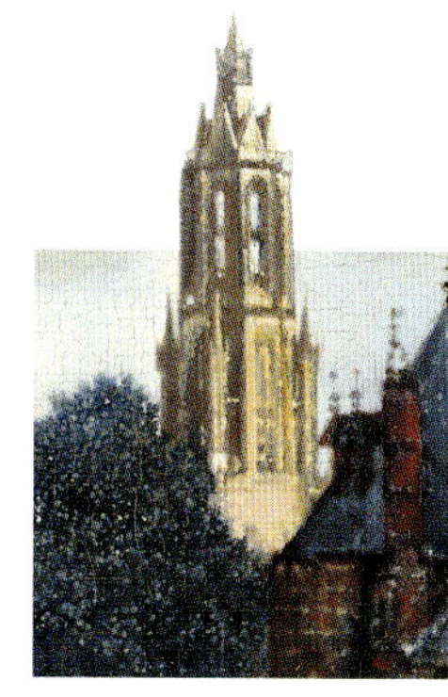

Sunlight illuminates the spire of the Nieuwe Kerk (New Church), where Vermeer was baptized and William of Orange is entombed.

Architectural references to Delft include the two gates at the south of the city: the Rotterdam Gate (right) and the Schiedam Gate (center).

Two herring busses (fishing boats) are moored in the harbor, highlighting a thriving trade.

Vermeer elongated the shadow of the Rotterdam Gate in his attempt to achieve visual balance in the composition.

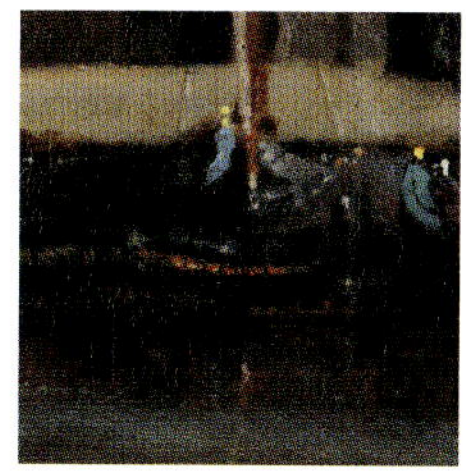

Boats used to carry goods around the canals are moored with their sails lowered.

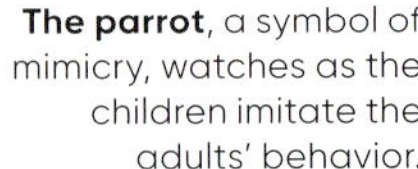

The parrot, a symbol of mimicry, watches as the children imitate the adults' behavior.

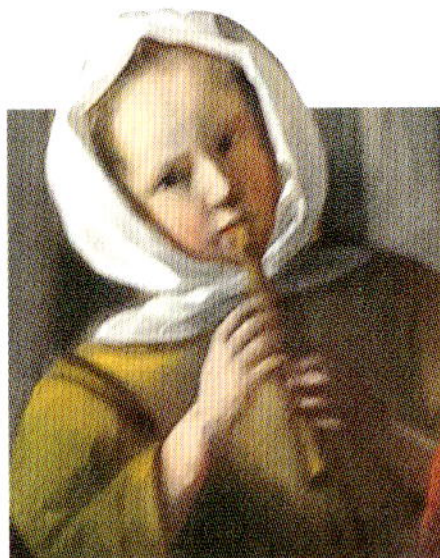

A boy smokes a pipe while a girl plays a pipe, reminding the viewer of the proverb "As the old sing, so the young pipe."

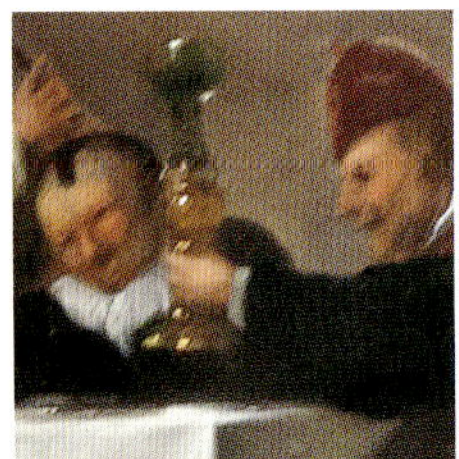

Adults drink excessively in the background, setting a bad example.

The baby sleeps, under the influence of a group of responsible adults in the foreground.

The paper contains the Dutch version of the proverb used in the title of this work.

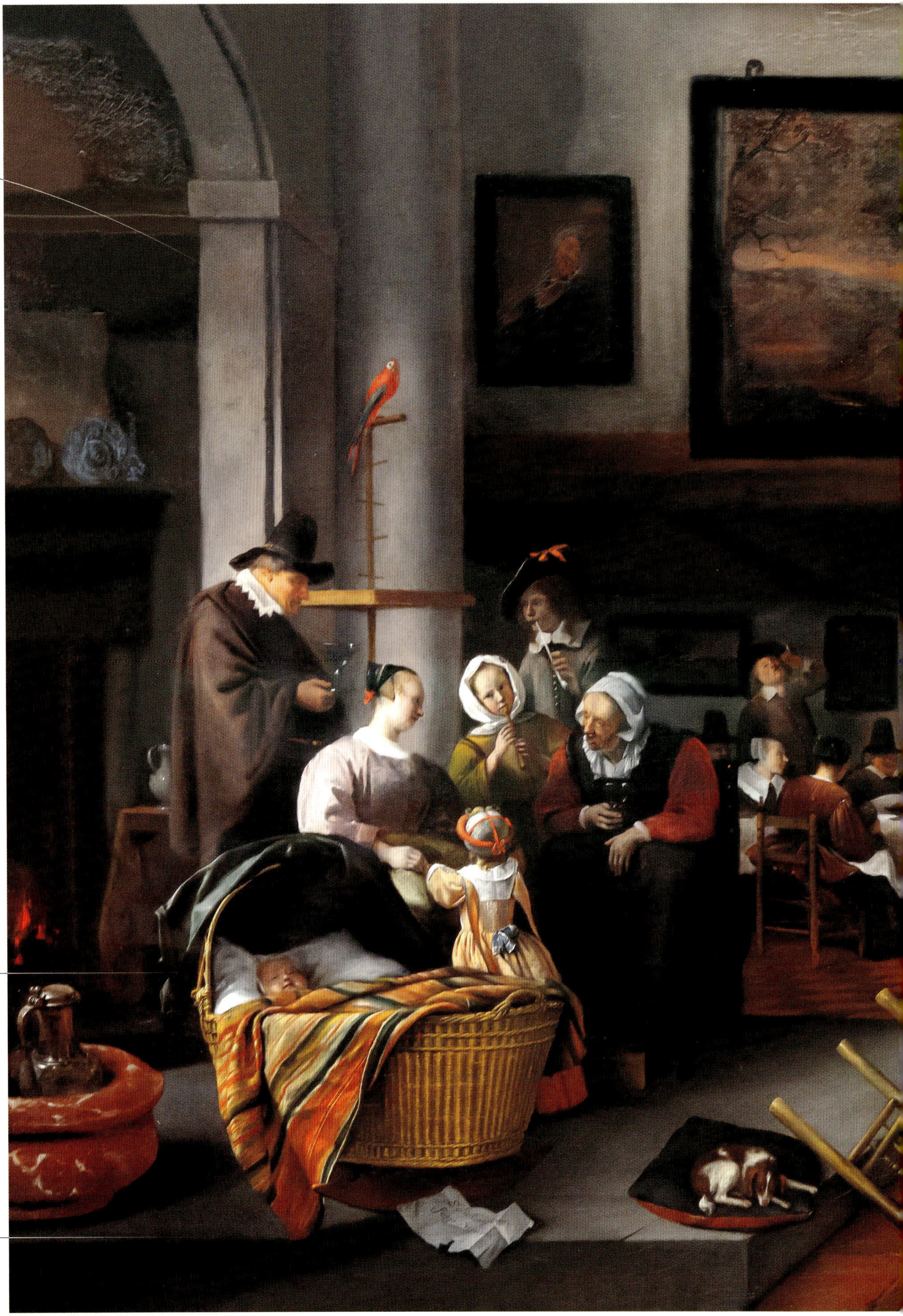

As the Old Sing, So the Young Pipe, or The Christening

Jan Steen 1665–1670, oil on canvas, 34 × 40 in (85.1 × 100.5 cm), Gemäldegalerie, Staatliche Museen, Berlin, Germany

Imbued with satire and visual puns, this glimpse into 17th-century Dutch society has a moralizing message about behavior and vices. Like several other genre paintings by Steen, including others depicting a christening, it references the old Dutch proverb "As the old sing, so the young pipe," warning adults that children will copy their misbehavior. While one group of adults carouse in the background, and another group keep an eye on the baby, the children wreak havoc. Though similarly animated and colorful, Steen's painting departed from other works of this kind by contrasting good and bad behavior rather than simply satirizing the latter.

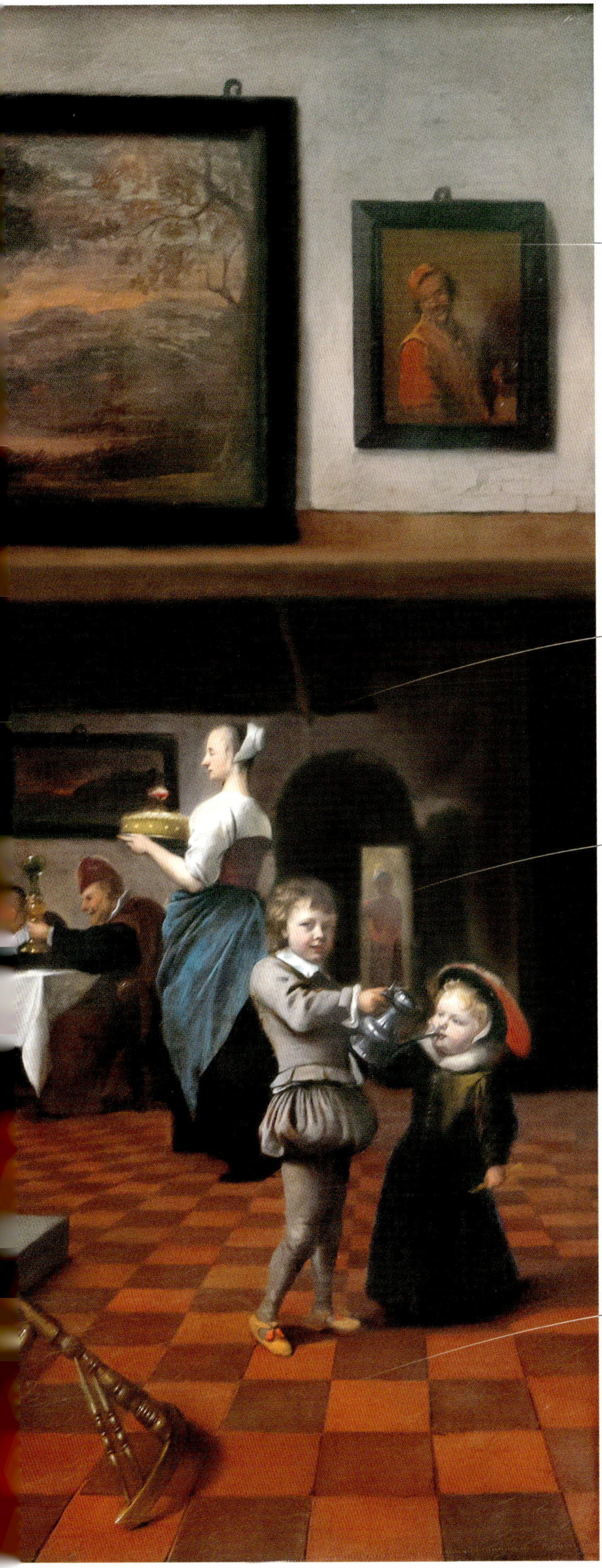

Paintings by Frans Hals depicting stock comic drunkards hang on the wall.

A maid carries a cake with a candle toward the adults at the back of the room, a reminder of the brevity of life.

A young boy gives wine or beer from a jug to an even younger boy.

A chair has tumbled over. Broken objects, a common motif in Steen's painting, indicate frivolity and disorder.

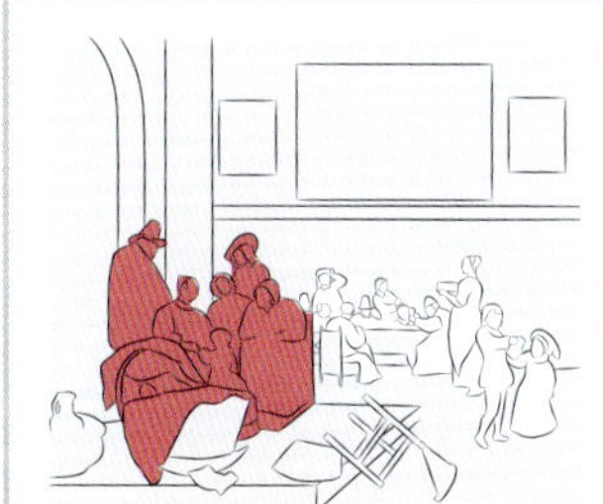

Good versus bad
The top half of the composition confirms the interior setting. The group in the foreground represents responsible behavior; the one in the background, bad behavior.

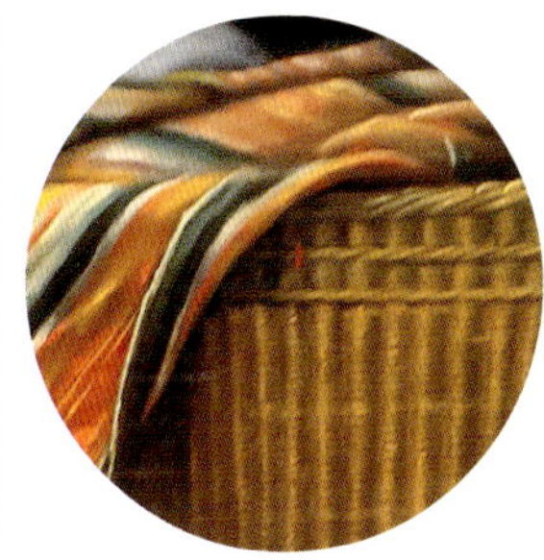

Fine detail
Steen used fine, smooth brushstrokes to suggest contrasting textures, such as the wicker basket and luxurious textiles.

> "Steen produced genre scene after genre scene of domestic uproar."
>
> Simon Schama, 1988

A Landscape with a Ruined Castle and a Church

Jacob van Ruisdael 1665–1670, oil on canvas, 43 × 57 in (109 × 146 cm), National Gallery, London, UK

In an idealized scene based on the Dutch countryside, a landscape extends in every direction beneath a sky filled with darkening clouds. Using religious images for worship had been banned by the Protestant Dutch Republic, but Biblical paintings were still being made. Ruisdael used elements of landscape painting, such as a flash of sunlight and a dramatic sky, to suggest a divine presence and celebrate the new republic.

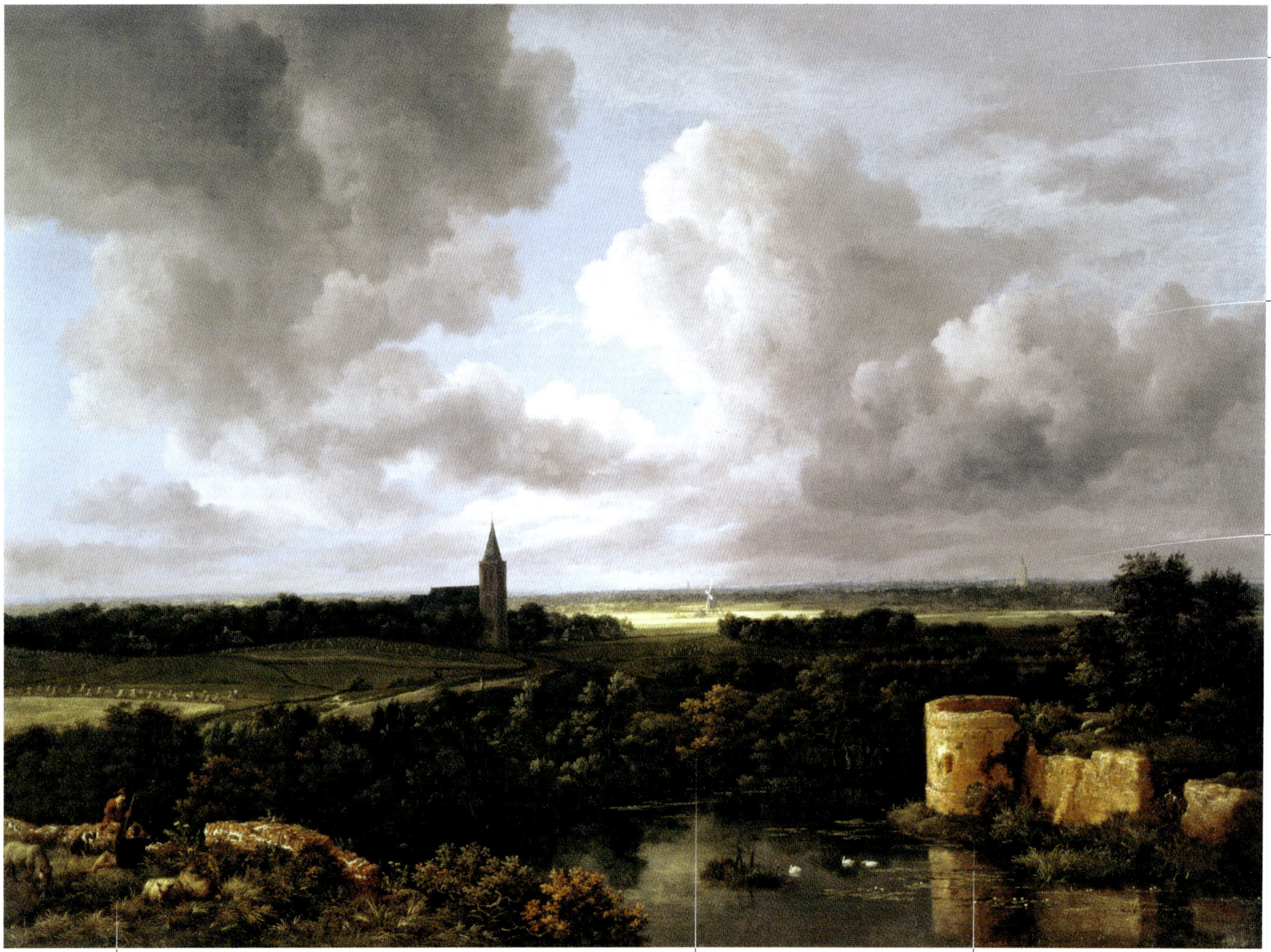

The clouds are shown in perspective: broad at the top of the picture and tapering toward the horizon.

Brushstrokes in the clouds convey the sense that they are moving and changing.

The horizon is low and broken by increasingly small church spires, creating an illusion of receding space.

Shepherds, once a familiar presence in religious paintings, provide an echo of pre-Reformation art.

The harvest and windmill celebrate a productive countryside and are a reminder that this low-lying land had been reclaimed from the sea.

The ruined castle is a reminder of the country's recent struggle against Spanish rule.

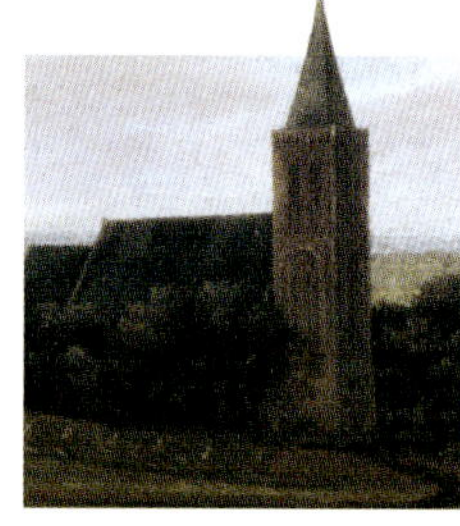

The prominent church silhouetted against the sky suggests the importance of religion in Dutch society.

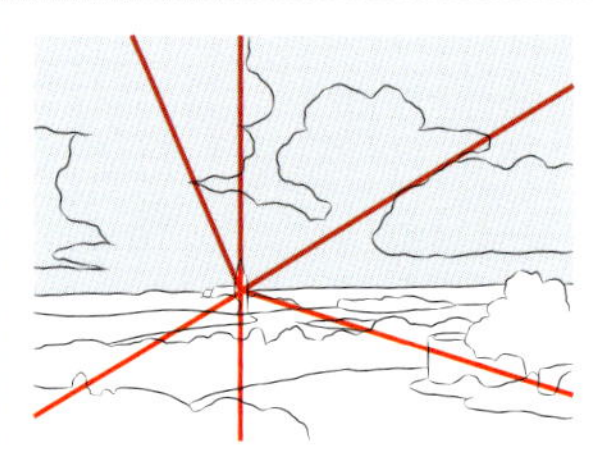

Focal point
The church is placed off-center, and diagonals lead to it from all sides of the canvas.

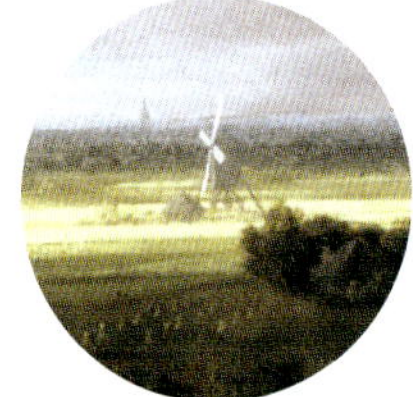

Illuminating detail
Light is used to pick out details at different points on the canvas, creating depth by drawing the eye through the scene and into the distance.

The Art of Painting

Johannes Vermeer 1666–1668, oil on canvas, 47 × 39 in (120 × 100 cm), Kunsthistorisches Museum, Vienna, Austria

A stylishly dressed artist works in a room filled with the trappings of prosperity. The artist is painting Clio, the muse of history in Greek mythology, but Vermeer's real subject is the status of painting and the role of the artist. The map on the wall and the references to honor and fame seem to imply that the artist brings distinction to his city and country—the Dutch Republic—and should be afforded a place in history.

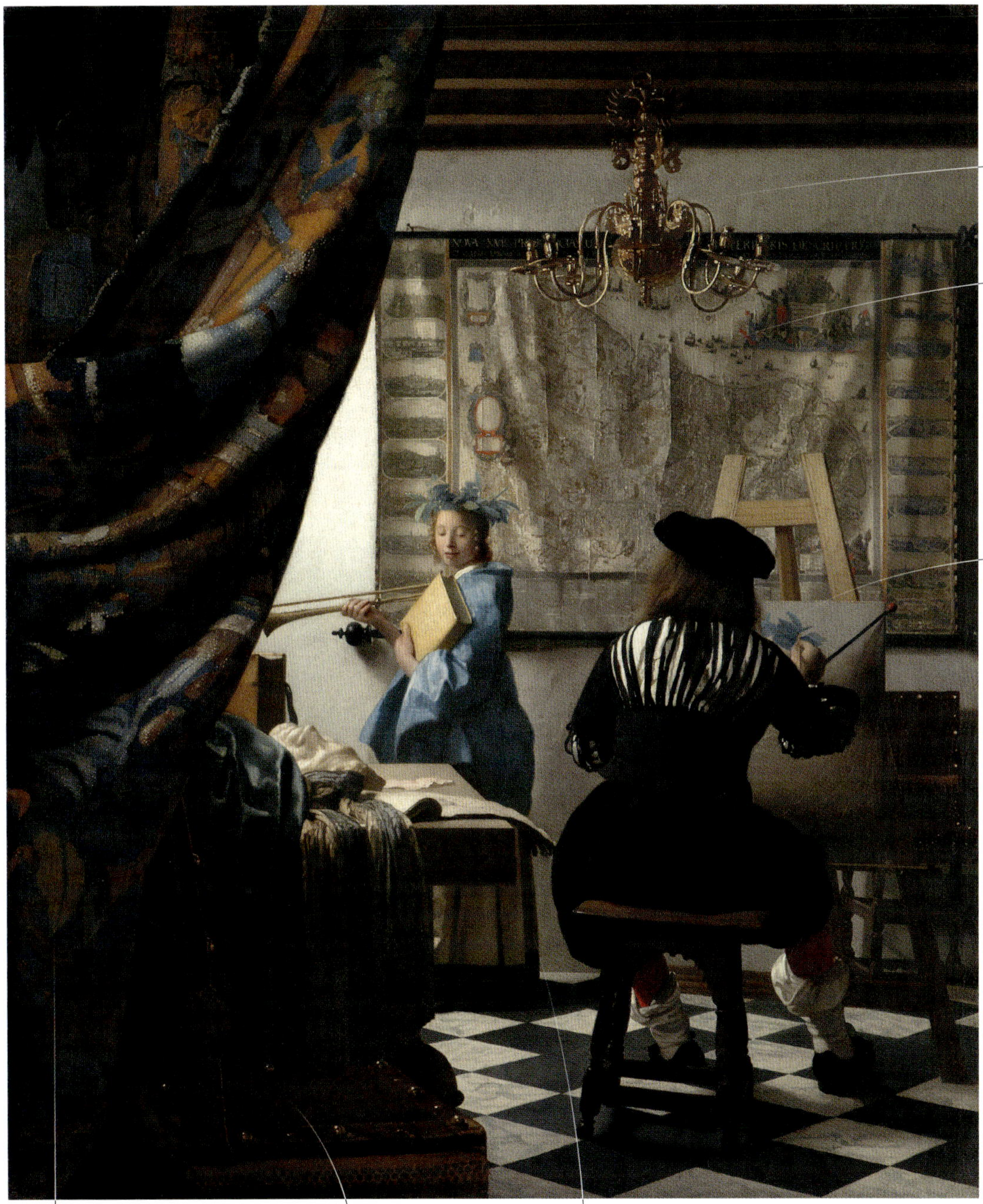

Highlights on the chandelier were put in with thick brushstrokes of lead-tin yellow, a common pigment until the early 18th century.

The map illustrates the Hapsburgs' Seventeen Provinces in the Dutch Republic. The frame features vignettes of their major cities.

The artist wears 15th-century Burgundian clothing, revealing that he is of a high social class.

The curtain is drawn back to reveal a staged scene. This dark area at the front of the painting pushes everything else back into the room.

A chair invites the viewer into the painting to ponder its meaning.

The model is identified as Clio by her laurel wreath, which stands for honor; the trumpet signifies fame; and the book represents the muse of history.

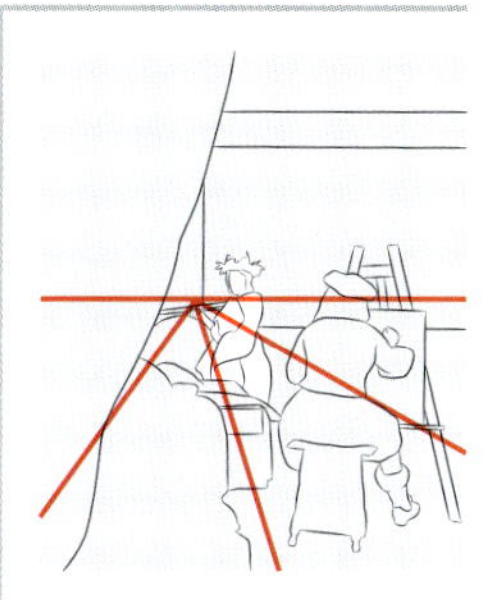

Perspective
The vanishing point is just above the model's hand. Vermeer attached a piece of string covered in chalk to a pin pushed into the canvas and used it to "print" straight lines across the canvas leading to this point.

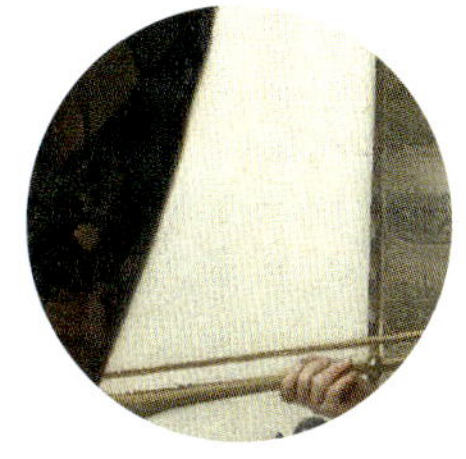

Light source
The light enters from a window hidden behind the curtain and spreads across the room, catching the model, the chandelier, objects on the table, the floor tiles, and the artist's white stockings.

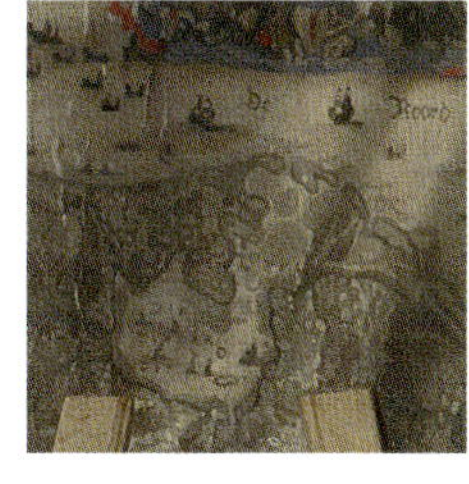

Vermeer conveyed the texture of the map by creating the impression of raking light—the exaggerated illumination of surfaces facing the light.

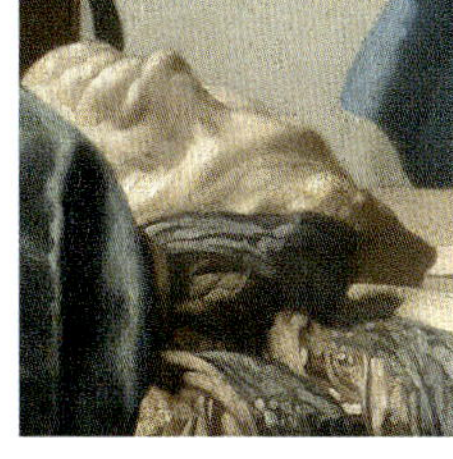

A plaster cast of a classical statue on the table implies that the artist is familiar with the arts and culture of ancient civilization.

> "Such a brilliantly executed work that it is hard for us to remove our eyes."
>
> Alejandro Vergara, 2003

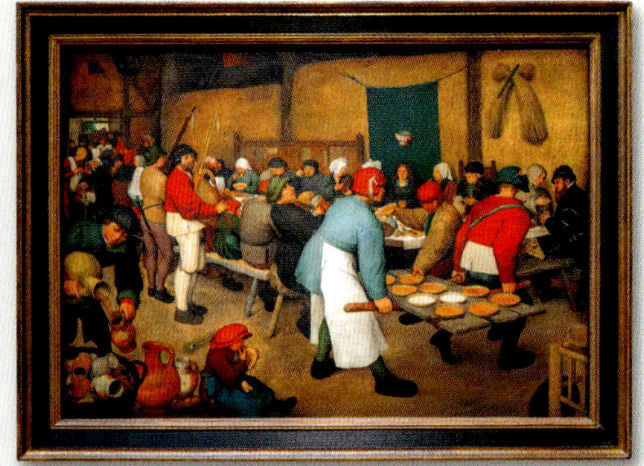

1

Genre painting

Scenes of everyday life were often included in the backgrounds of religious and mythical paintings, but in Northern Europe during the 17th century, they became a subject in their own right. They usually depict ordinary people in contemporary settings and in a naturalistic style. Some contain moral messages, while others were intended to be entertaining. In the 19th century, subjects included the effects of industrialization and life of the rural and urban poor.

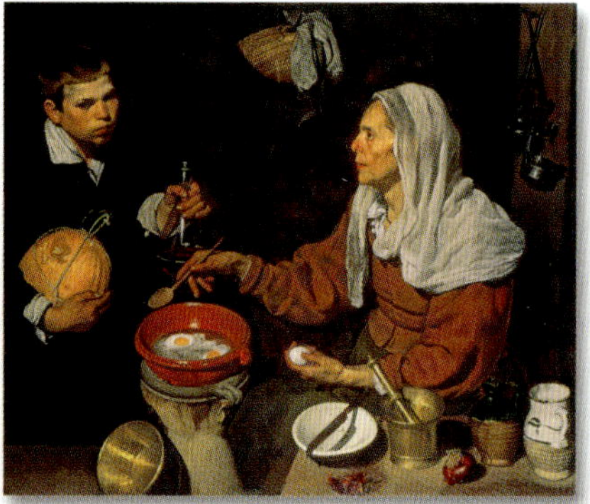

2

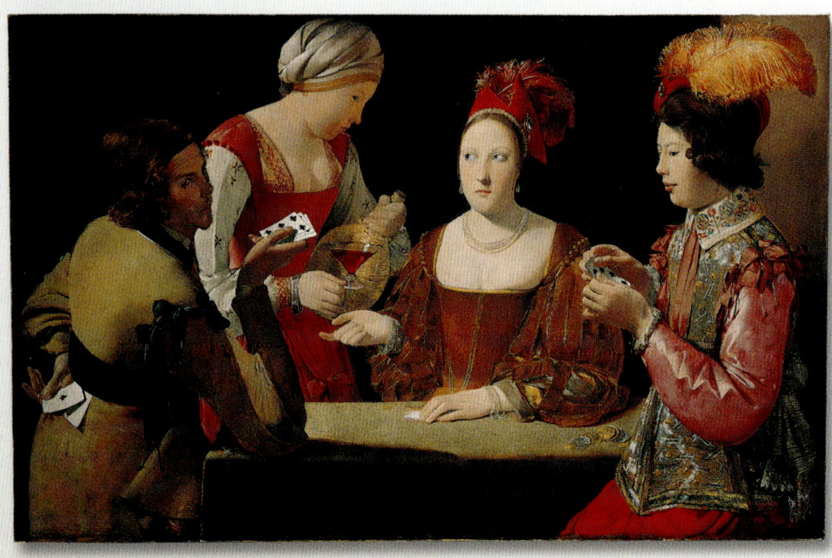

3

4

1. ***Peasant Wedding*, Pieter Bruegel the Elder, 1568.** Bruegel, known for his lively scenes of village life, was one of the first painters to specialize in depicting ordinary people engaged in everyday activities. His paintings contain moral messages.

2. ***Old Woman Frying Eggs*, Diego Velázquez, 1618.** *Bodegónes* were a Spanish kitchen or tavern scene. The contrast between the old woman and the young man represents the transience of life. It also shows his fascination with different textures, such as the eggs in the hot oil.

3. ***The Cheat with the Ace of Clubs*, Georges de la Tour, 1630–1634.** In an entertaining moralizing scene, a cardsharp (left) reveals his plan to cheat the naive young man out of his money, while the two women, the cheat's accomplices, prepare to distract the youth with wine.

4. ***Milkmaid*, Johannes Vermeer, c. 1660.** Although Vermeer has included a foot warmer and an image of Eros on one of the tiles (both symbols of female sexual arousal in Dutch paintings at the time), the painting is mainly a celebration of domestic work.

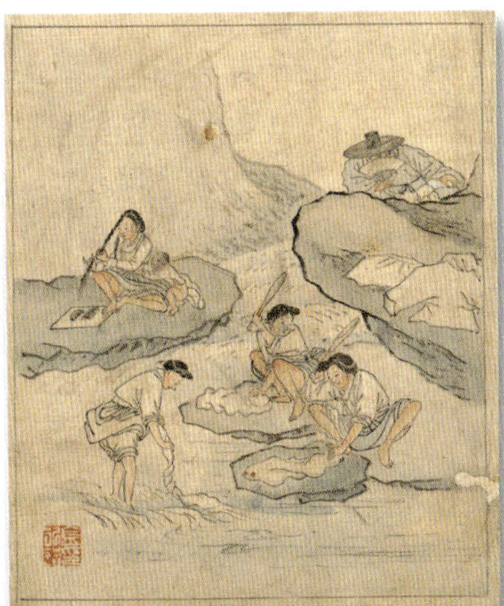

5

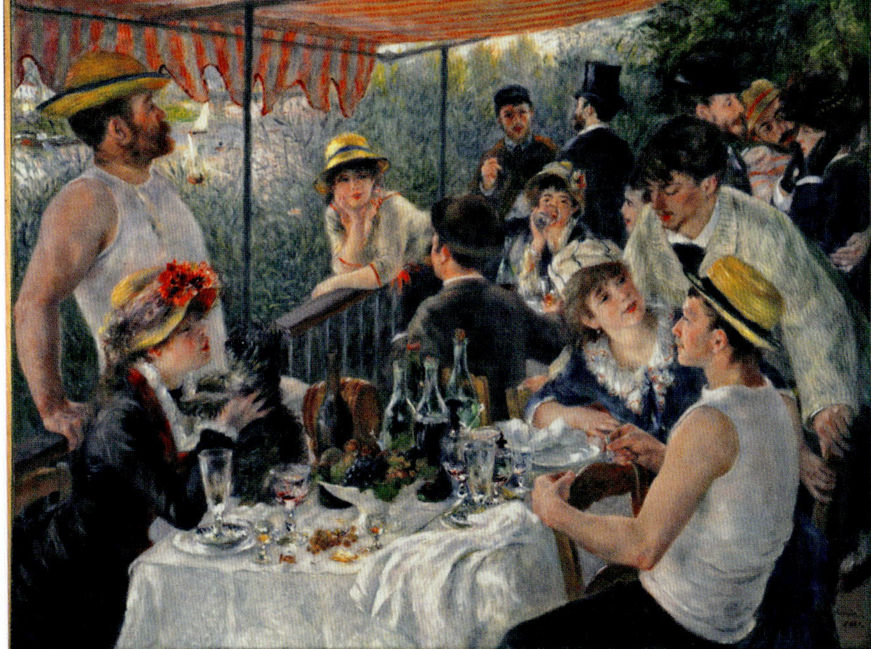

7

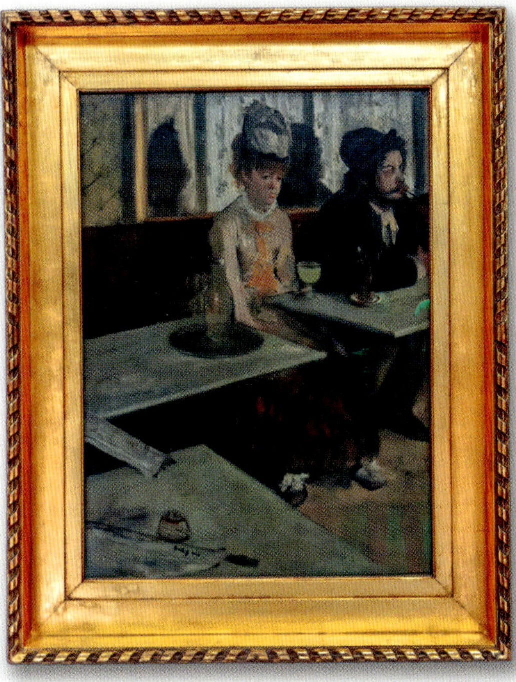

6

Dutch genre painting

Religious paintings were considered idolatrous in the Protestant Dutch Republic of the 17th century. Instead, moralizing genre paintings were produced to celebrate good behavior and warn against vices that could lead to the breakdown of the family and, by extension, society.

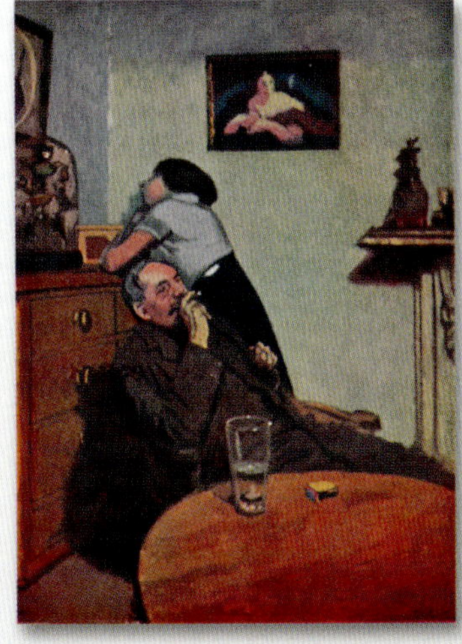

8

5. ***A Wash Place*, Kim Hong-do, 1780.** Hong-do was one of the first Korean artists to depict ordinary people engaged in everyday activities. Minimal detail and restrained color emphasize the interplay between the women, transforming an ordinary activity into a story.

6. ***L'Absinthe*, Edgar Degas, 1875-1876.** In this portrayal of a woman drinking absinthe, known as the "queen of poisons" for its addictiveness, Degas captures the loneliness of the poor in late 19th-century Paris. Even though a man sits next to the woman, a sense of alienation prevails.

7. ***Luncheon of the Boating Party*, Pierre-Auguste Renoir, 1880-1881.** In an animated scene that includes figures, still life, and landscape, Renoir portrays his friends on a trip to the countryside. Rail travel had made this possible for middle- and working-class Parisians.

8. ***Ennui*, Walter Sickert, 1914.** Sickert has portrayed a private moment in a marriage. A couple who seem to have nothing left to say to each other appear trapped in a room and a marriage. This is one of five similar works that Sickert painted on the theme of boredom.

Vanitas Still Life

Maria van Oosterwijck 1668, oil on canvas, 29 × 35 in (73 × 88.5 cm), Kunsthistorisches Museum, Vienna, Austria

A table is piled with objects that speak of beauty, wealth, and human knowledge, but they are interspersed with reminders of passing time, death, and the futility of worldly wealth. Such works, known as *vanitas* paintings, were popular in the 17th century. In this example, Oosterwijck, a leading Dutch flower and still-life painter, shows her skill in rendering light, reflections, and different textures and surfaces.

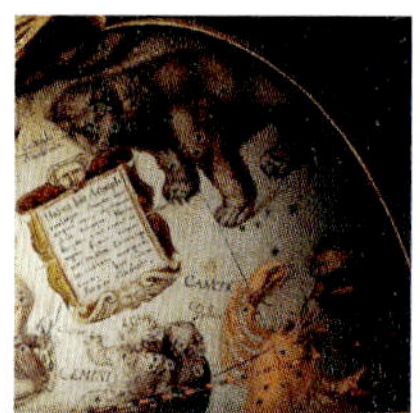

The celestial globe symbolizes heaven. It shows the constellations of Ursa Major and Cancer.

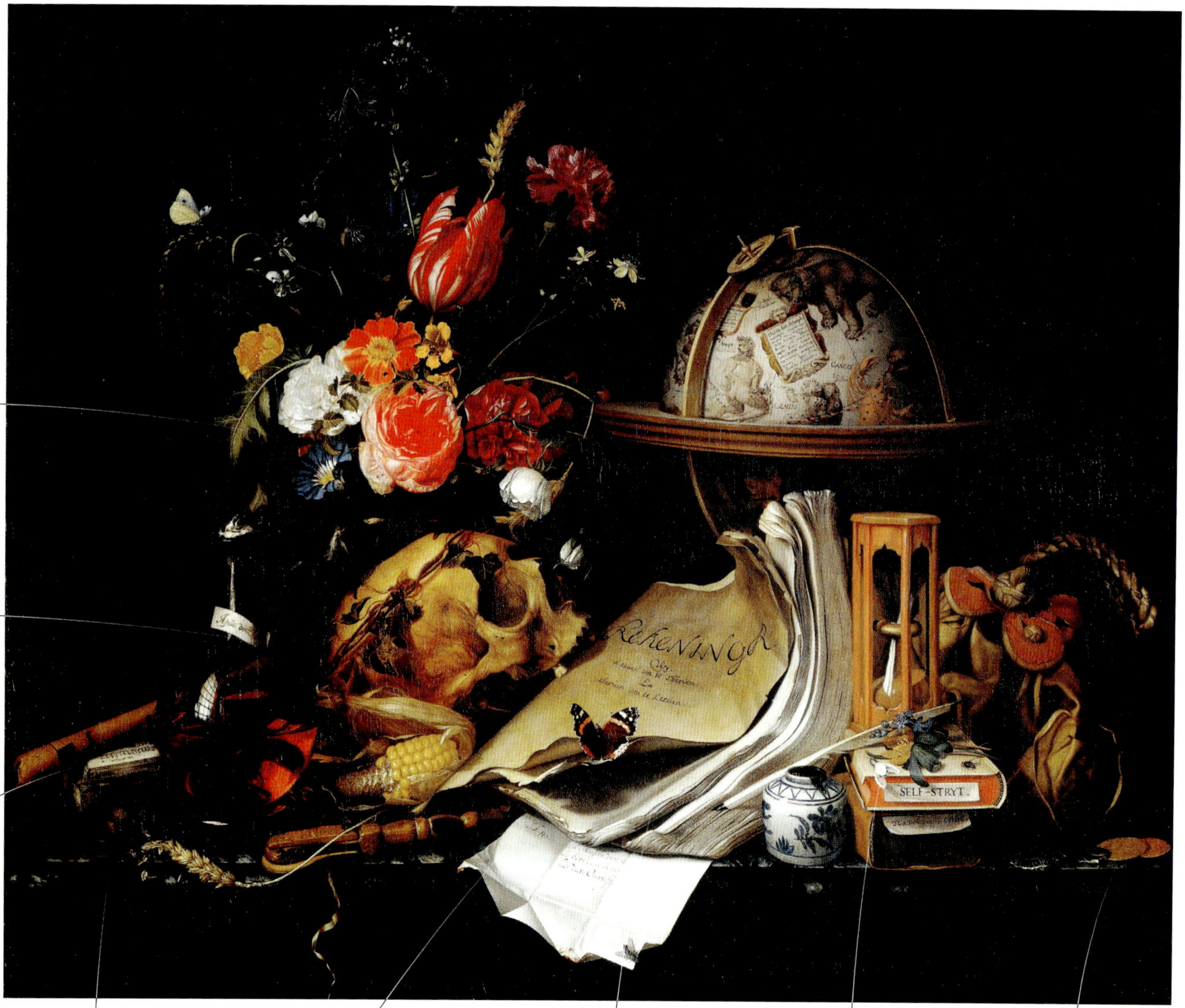

A vase contains 17 types of flowers that bloom in different seasons, representing a whole year. They also symbolize wealth and the fleeting nature of beauty.

The skull is a reminder that death comes to everyone. Its shape is echoed by the globe on the right.

The flute and musical score refer to the nature of musical notes—they resonate briefly and are gone.

A mouse nibbles on an ear of corn, signifying that nothings lasts.

The butterfly is a symbol of ephemerality.

The inscription on the book reads "We live unto death and die unto life," referring to the hope for eternal life.

An hourglass is a classic reference to the passing of time.

Gold and silver coins and a money bag symbolize worldly wealth.

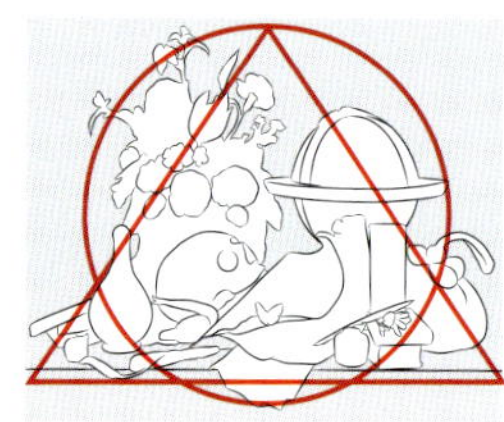

Composition
A triangle provides a solid base for the composition. All the main objects are contained within a circle.

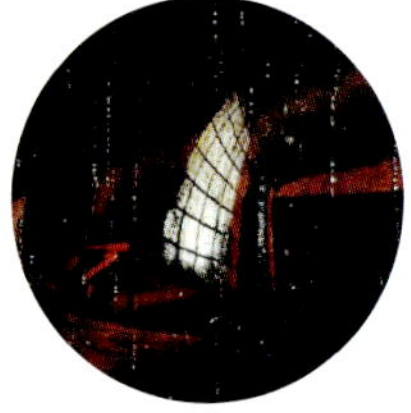

Self-portrait
A reflection on the bottle shows the artist in her studio. All the elements, including the window and its reflection on the opposite wall, follow and draw attention to the bottle's curving surface.

Landscape with Ascanius Shooting the Stag of Sylvia

Claude Lorrain 1681–1682, oil on canvas, 47 × 59 in (120 × 150 cm), Ashmolean Museum, Oxford, UK

Claude was celebrated for painting idyllic, luminous landscapes based on the Italian countryside and endowing them with a sense of timelessness by including features and figures from Italy's classical past.

The story of Ascanius, from Virgil's *Aeneid*, tells of a hunting incident in which a pet stag is killed, leading to war between Ascanius, the son of Trojan hero Aeneas, and the Italian country of Latium.

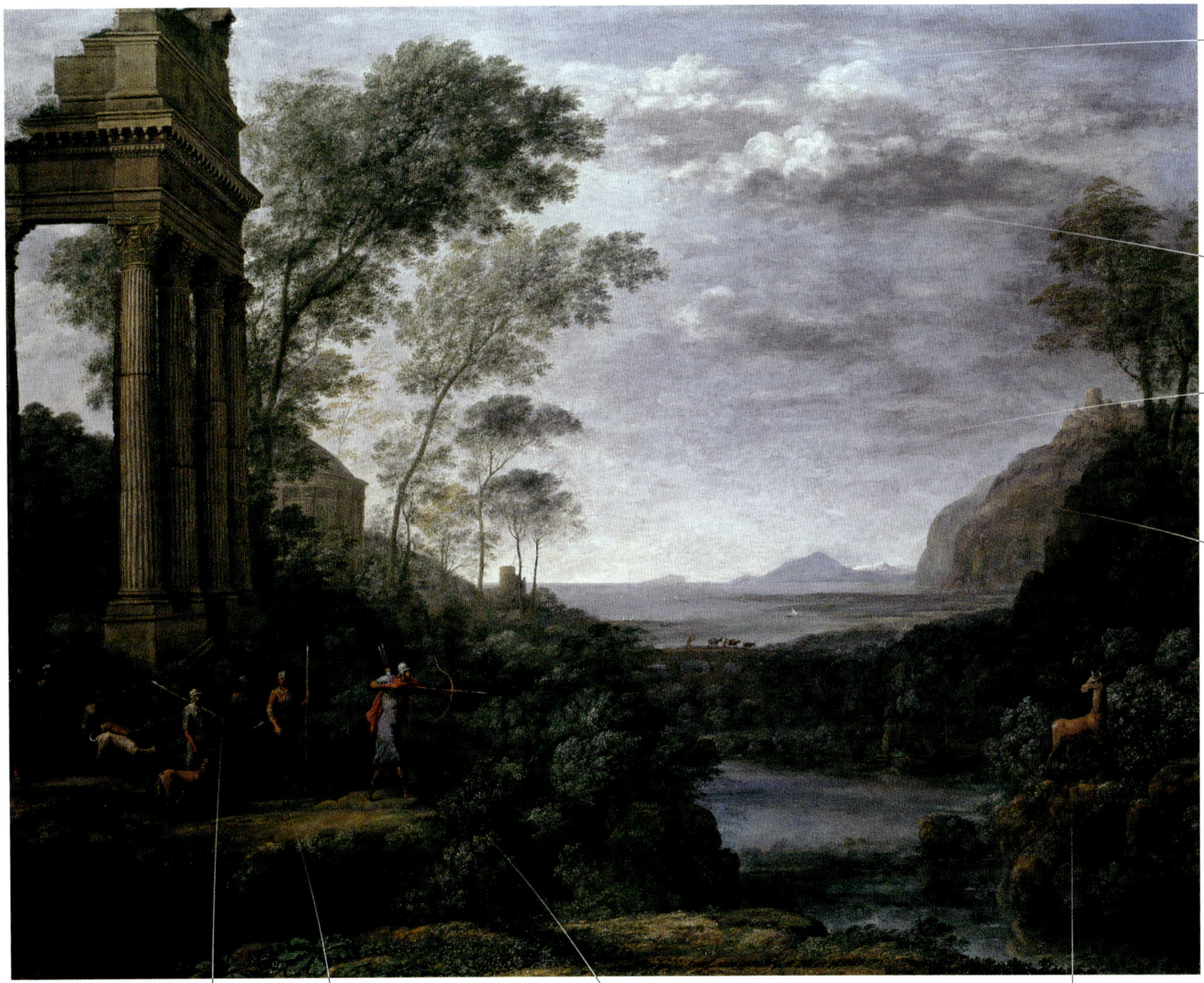

The bending trees represent the Fury Alecto, sent by the Roman goddess Juno to provoke war.

Storm clouds hint at the impending conflict.

A cool, silvery light fills the top half of the painting, suggesting the incident is taking place at dawn.

Features in the landscape are painted in realistic detail.

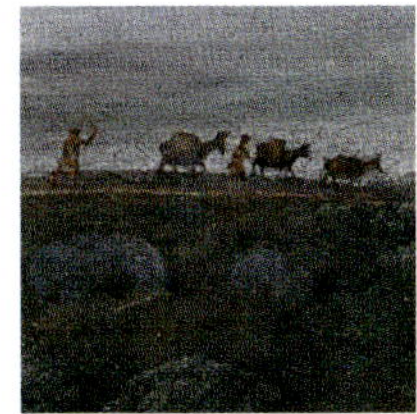

Figures on the bridge draw attention away from the protagonists and into infinity.

The ruins of a Roman temple with Corinthian columns places the story in the ancient world.

The hunting party is dwarfed by the ruined temple and the landscape.

Ascanius takes aim at the stag, which he will mortally wound.

The stag is the pet of Sylvia, daughter of Tyrrheus, a ranger to the king of Latium. It is tame, so does not flee.

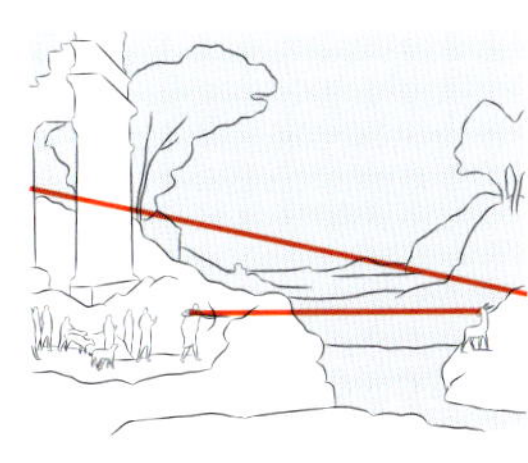

Dividing line
A diagonal divides the painting into foreground and distance. The tension created between Ascanius and the stag creates a strong horizontal movement.

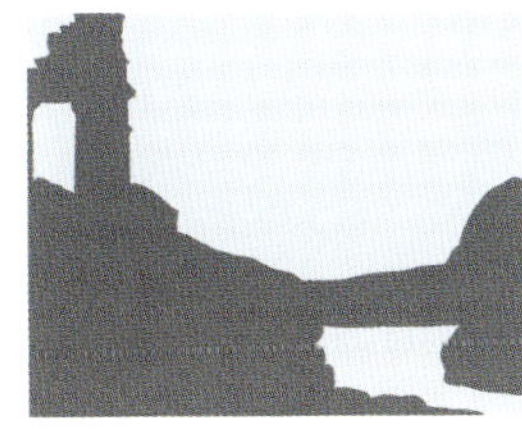

Framing device
The two dark cliff edges, in the center foreground, and on the right-hand side, push lighter areas into the distance, an effect known as *repoussoir*.

> "All is lovely—all amiable—all is amenity and repose; the calm sunshine of the heart."
>
> John Constable

The Kangxi Emperor's Southern Inspection Tour, Scroll Three (detail)

Wang Hui and assistants 1698, hand scroll, ink and colors on silk, 27 × 549 in (67.9 × 1,393.8 cm), Metropolitan Museum of Art, New York, US

This is a section of a long hand scroll painting, one of a set of 12 commissioned by the Kangxi emperor of China to document his grand tour of the regions south of the capital of Beijing. It is based on a diary kept during the journey. This image depicts the emperor's entourage arriving at the foot of the sacred Mount Tai.

The mountain peaks are subtly colored with green and blue mineral pigments, a reference to ancient landscape paintings.

Travelers and pilgrims are shown climbing the path and entering the temple complex at the mountain's peak.

This depiction of Mount Tai, in modern Shandong Province, is based on 17th-century woodcut images that mapped its peaks, trails, and temples.

The rocky surfaces are modeled using layers of "raindrop" texture strokes, while dots are added to indicate greenery.

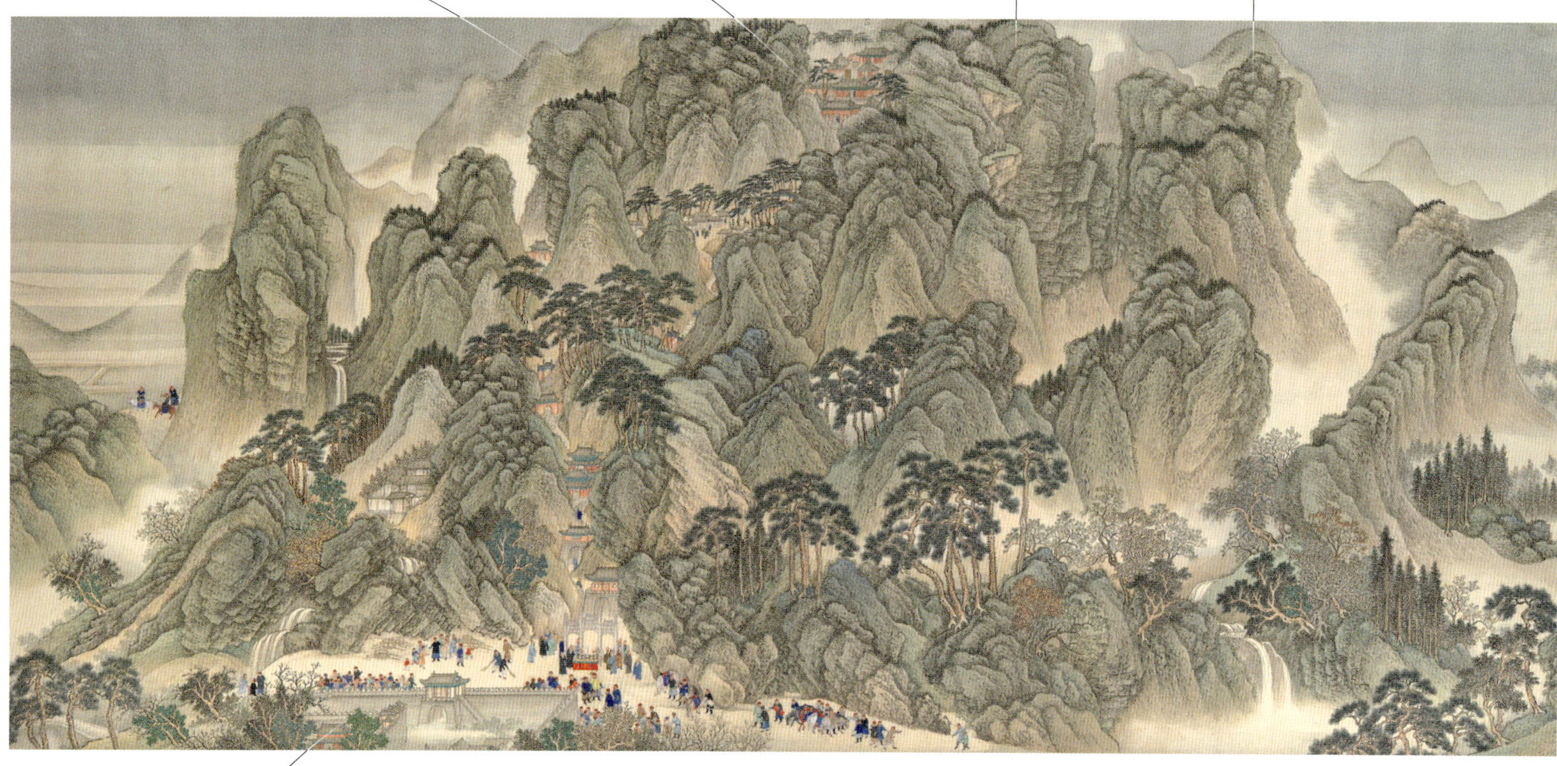

The walled town of Tai'an encloses the Temple to the God of Mount Tai, where the emperor made offerings.

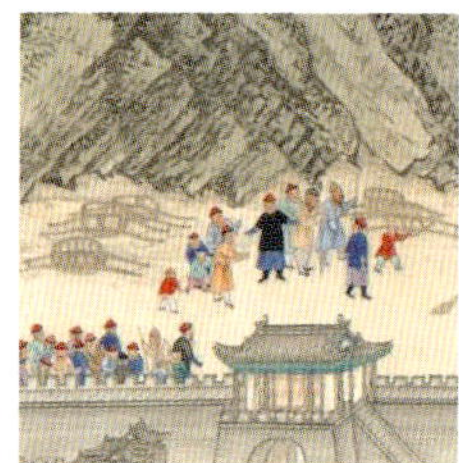

A group of chair-bearers wait to carry the emperor's entourage up the mountain.

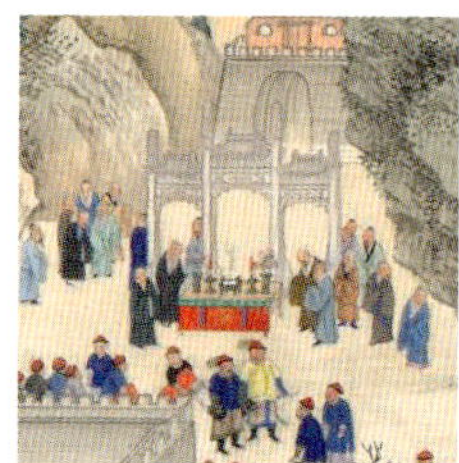

An altar has been set up at the entrance to the mountain, attended by Daoist priests who await the emperor's arrival.

> "Considering the power of brush and ink, real landscape can never equal painting."
>
> Dong Qichang

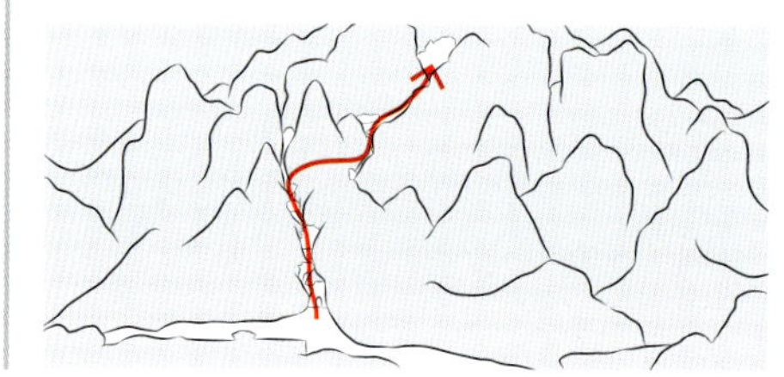

Sinuous passage
The pathway—its steeper sections cut into steps—winds through archways and pavilions, interrupting the mountain's monumental symmetry.

Making scrolls
Wang Hui's assistants produced draft scrolls in light ink on paper for approval. Amendments were made and the approved version was sketched onto silk in charcoal and finished in ink.

Amitabha, the Buddha of the Western Pure Land

Artist unknown c. 1700, distemper with gold on cloth, 56 × 39 in (143 × 100 cm), Metropolitan Museum of Art, New York, US

Amitabha, the Buddha of Infinite Light, is depicted in his Pure Land called Sukhavati, the Land of Delight, in this painting from Tibet. Before attaining awakening, he vowed that virtuous beings who cultivated faith in his teachings would be reborn in Sukhavati, free from suffering and filled with happiness.

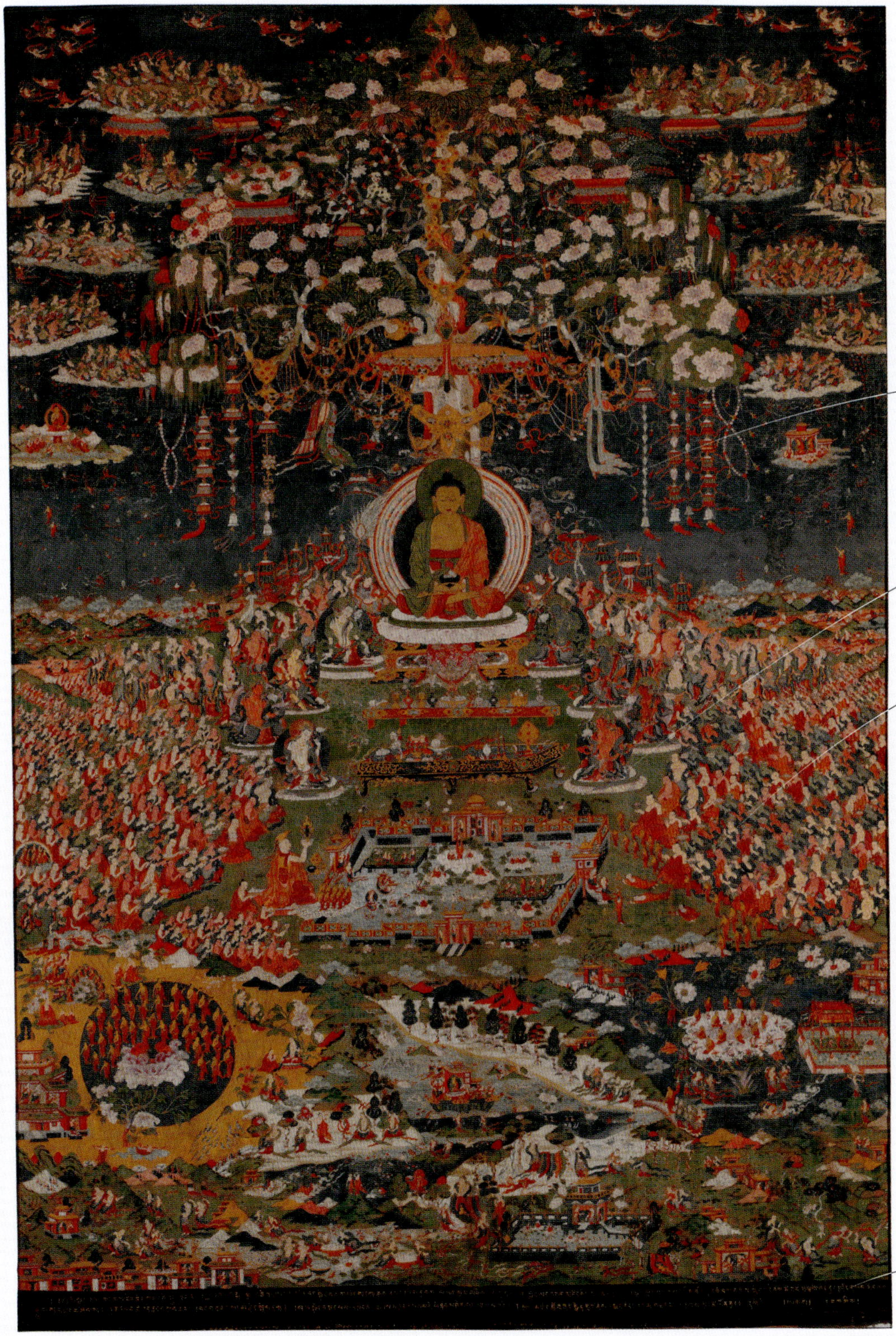

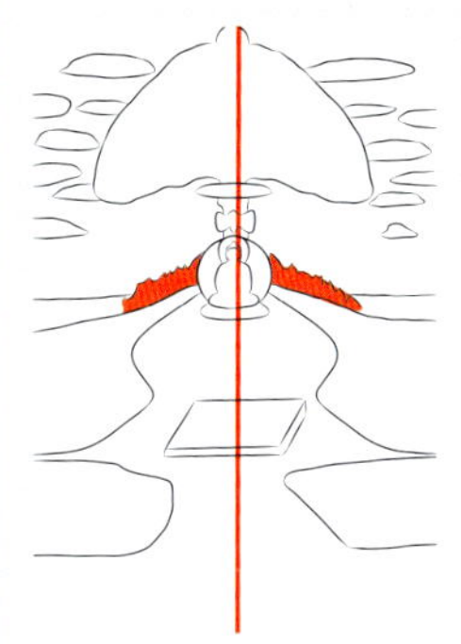

Achieving enlightenment Amitabha is the focus of the symmetrical layout. The victory banners on either side of him may symbolize the path to awakening—the gradual victory over destructive emotions.

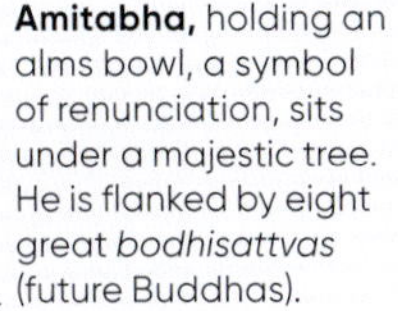

Amitabha, holding an alms bowl, a symbol of renunciation, sits under a majestic tree. He is flanked by eight great *bodhisattvas* (future Buddhas).

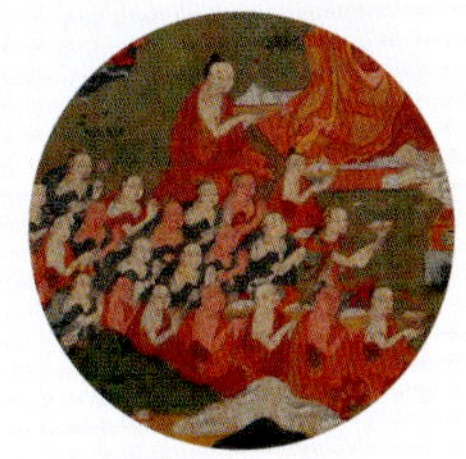

The Pure Land Sukhavati is shown filled with joy, pleasant melodies, and soft light, where all material forms are utterly magnificent, and everyone delights in spiritual activities such as making offerings.

The ponds are covered with large lotus blossoms on which Amitabha's devoted disciples are being reborn in the Pure Land.

Monks prostrate themselves—a practice of devotion and purification.

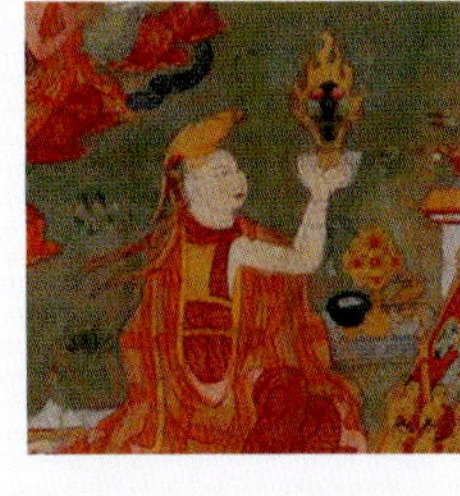

The monk's hat indicates his affiliation with the Gelugpa tradition of Tibetan Buddhism, which was founded by the Tibetan philosopher Tsongkhapa (1357–1419).

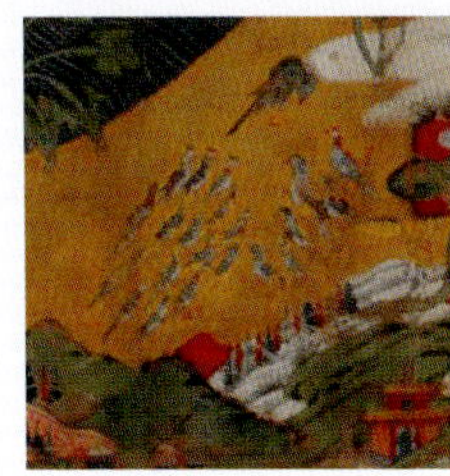

Birds are magically displayed by Amitabha. In Sukhavati, there would be no birds as no being would be reborn as an animal, an unfavorable form of existence in Buddhism.

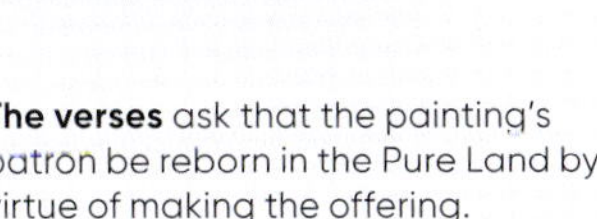

The verses ask that the painting's patron be reborn in the Pure Land by virtue of making the offering.

Seated Couple

Artist unknown 18th–early 19th century, wood and metal, 29 × 9 × 8 in (73 × 21.9 × 20.3 cm), Metropolitan Museum of Art, New York, US

This highly stylized sculpture portrays a couple whose visual parallels communicate the complementary roles of men and women in Dogon society. The man rests a hand on the woman's breast and another on his penis to emphasize their procreative powers. The Dogon live along the Bandiagara Escarpment in Mali.

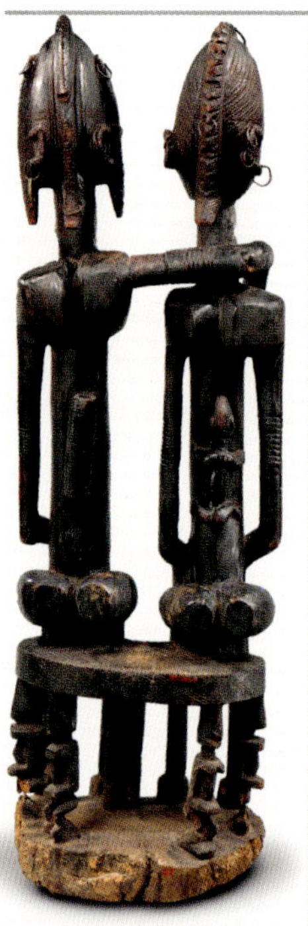

Rear view
The man has a quiver on his back and the woman a baby These indicate their primary roles. The baby has the same ridged hairstyle as its parents.

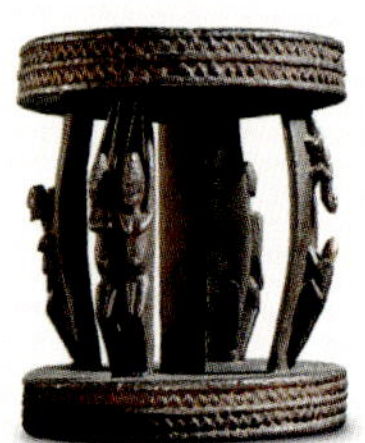

Symbolic meaning
The zigzags around the edge of a Dogon stool have more than one meaning. In some cases, they represent Lébé, the first ancestor to have experienced death by turning into a serpent.

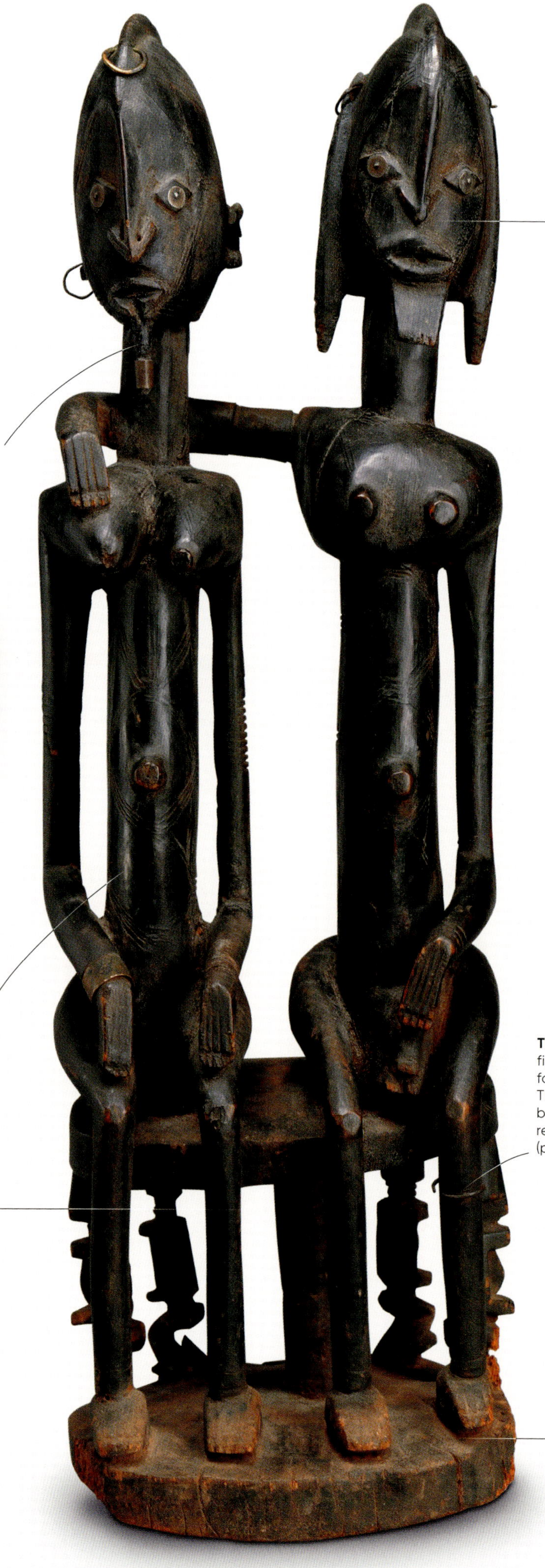

The woman's lip labret echoes the man's goatee. Metal has been added here as well as in the figures' eyes, ears, and hair.

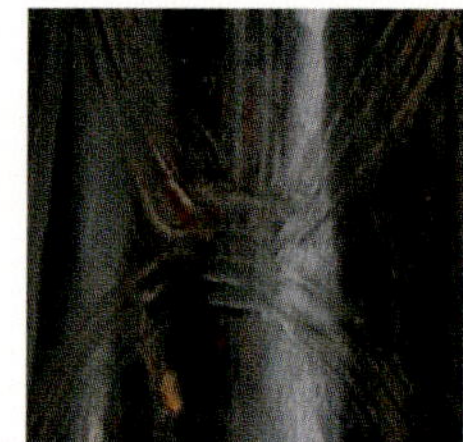

Overlapping circular scarification on the torsos of both figures emphasizes ideas of interconnectedness, harmony, and union.

The long tubular torsos, as well as the arms and necks, add to both the verticality and monumentality of the piece.

The stool is full of symbolism. The two planes connected by a central axis refer to the realms of both the living and their ancestors.

An arrow-shaped nose and C-shaped ears are typical of Dogon sculpture.

The legs of the two figures form the front four legs of the stool. The four legs at the back of the stool represent the *nommo* (primordial ancestors).

Heavy wear at the base indicates use. The statue was probably displayed at the funeral celebrations of prominent men in a Dogon village.

Still Life with Fruit and Insects

Rachel Ruysch 1711, oil on wood, 17 × 24 in (44 × 60 cm), Uffizi, Florence, Italy

An array of fall fruits and vegetables together with insects, a lizard, and a nest containing eggs are presented in scientific detail. This type of still life is known as *sottobosco* (forest floor), and was popular in the Netherlands in the 17th century. Ruysch was one of the most skilled still-life artists working at the time; she wanted her paintings to be enjoyed for their attention to detail and naturalism.

Strong, glowing colors emerge from a dark background, typical of Baroque painting.

The composition is based on studies of each item. These were then combined to create a believable fiction.

A stag beetle is climbing on top of the squash.

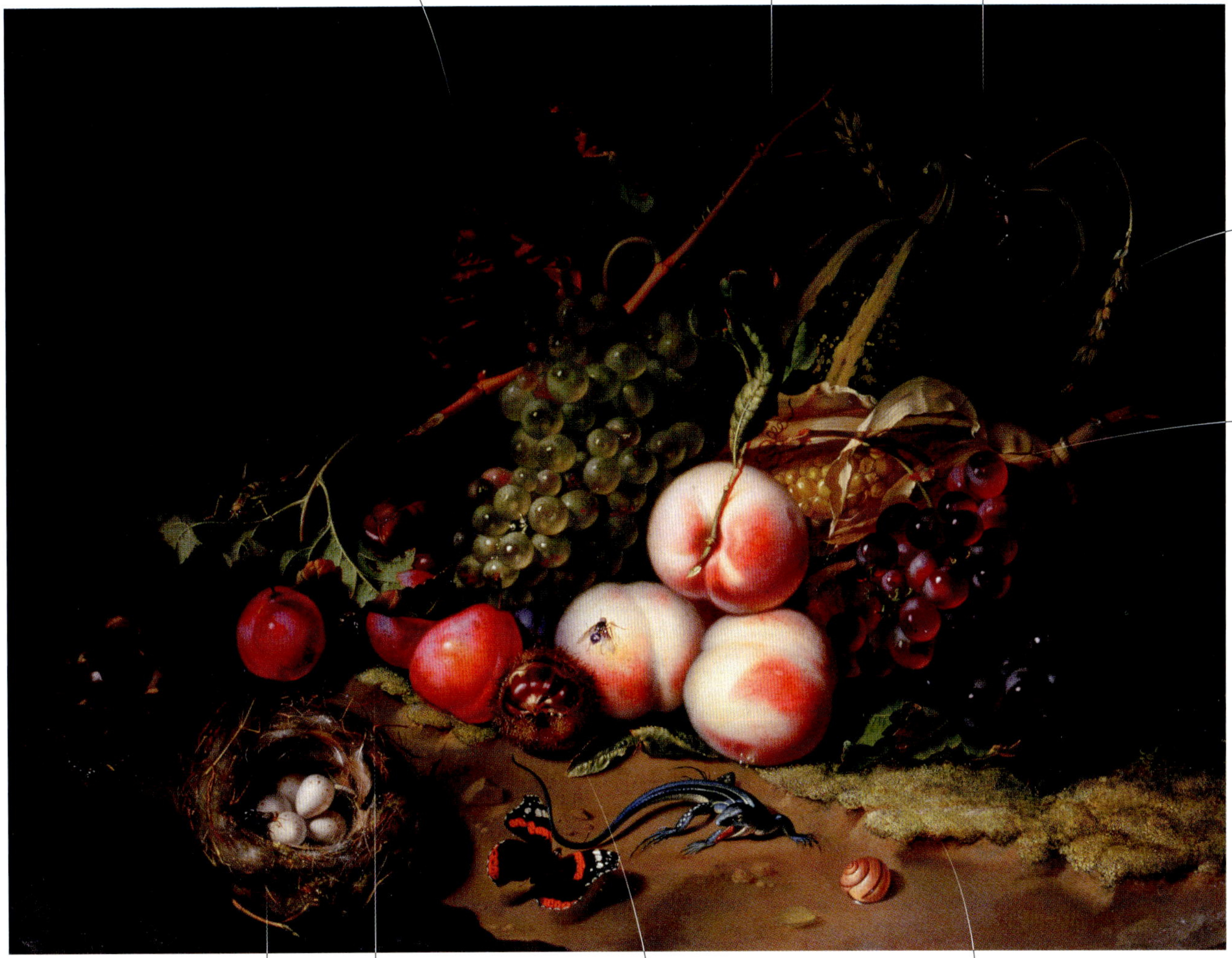

Wheat and grapes may be reminders of the bread and wine used at the Christian sacrament of the Eucharist.

Accurate observation combined with technical skill enabled Ruysch to record the surface details of each piece of fruit.

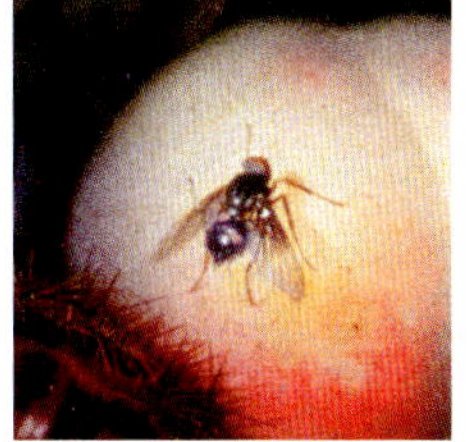

The fly positioned on a peach is a reminder that all things decay and die.

Placing the bird's nest at the front draws in the eye.

Faint touches of light blue create the bloom on the plums.

A chestnut bursting open provides a strong contrast between rough and smooth textures.

Pieces of moss on bare earth simulate the forest floor.

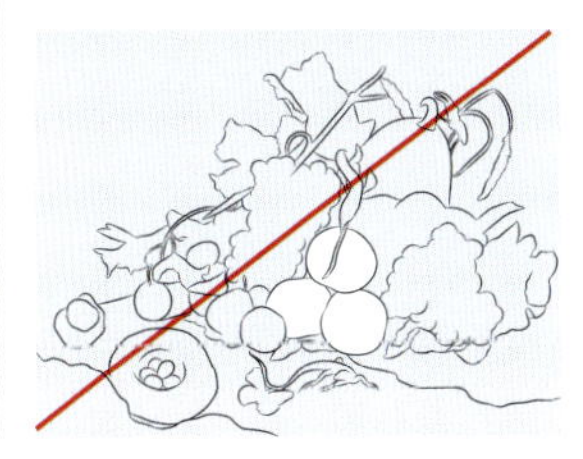

Creating focus
The objects are arranged along a strong diagonal that runs from bottom left to top right. The main focus falls on the three round, light forms at the center.

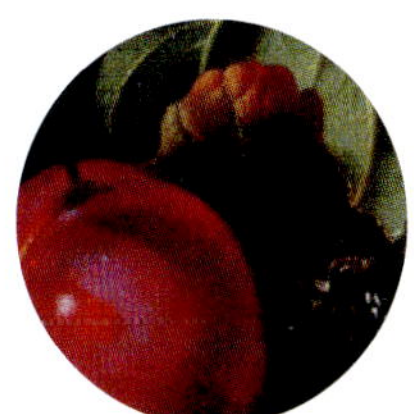

Complementary colors
Contrasts of red and green occur throughout the composition: the red leaves against the green grapes, against the red plums; and the red grapes against the pale green moss.

The sky offers no indication of time. It could be any hour or season, adding to the dreamlike atmosphere.

Delicate brushstrokes create an ethereal feel, the figures merging with air, earth, and water.

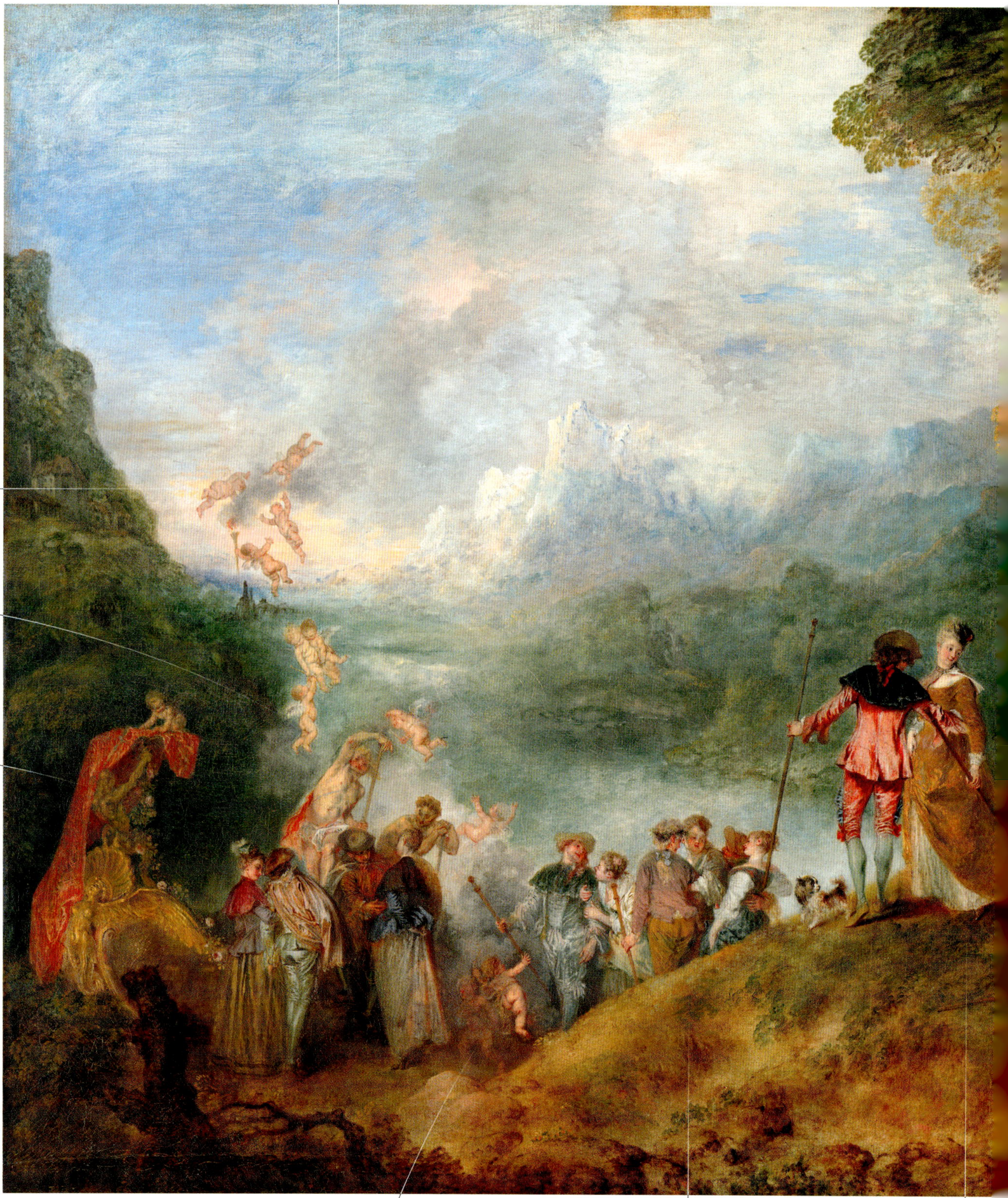

The putti playfully guide the boat as it approaches or departs from the island.

The semi-naked oarsmen embody sensuality and are reminiscent of classical sculpture.

A female nude is carved into the prow of the golden boat that will take the lovers back to their normal lives. It is decorated with a garland of roses, echoing the statue of Aphrodite.

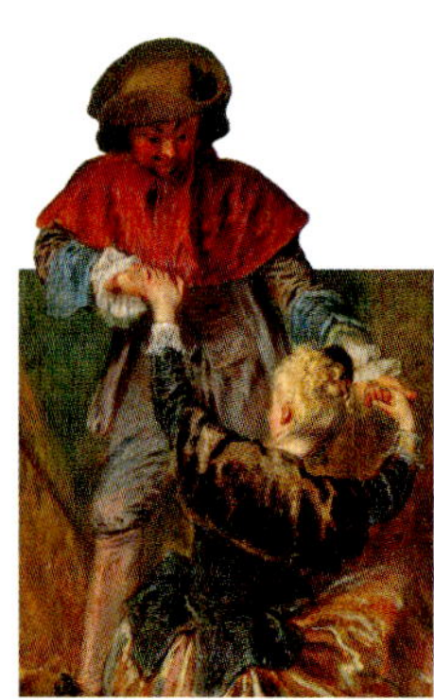

A man pulls his companion from the ground as if they are gracefully dancing. This is characteristic of Watteau's subtle ability to choreograph fluidity and movement.

A putto playfully pulls a couple toward the boat.

The theatrical staging of the scene, reminiscent of the pastoral operas popular in 18th-century France, blurs the lines between reality and performance.

The three couples in the foreground are a humorous comment on the stages of 18th-century courtship: flirtation, surrender, and consummation.

Pilgrimage to the Isle of Cythera

Jean-Antoine Watteau 1717, oil on canvas, 51 × 76 in (129 × 194 cm), Louvre, Paris, France

With this work, Watteau created a *fête galante*, a style depicting a gathering of aristocrats at an amorous—but genteel—gathering set in a pastoral landscape. The genre became a cornerstone of the Rococo period, when art moved away from religious or regal subject matter toward more frivolous themes and the pursuit of pleasure, often using soft colors and curved lines. The title of the painting refers to the Greek island of Kythira, the birthplace of Aphrodite, the goddess of love, adding a classical strand to the narrative.

A statue of Aphrodite wearing a garland of roses watches and blesses the visitors. Roses represent the beauty of love, but their thorns are reminders of the pain it may cause.

The idyllic landscape, with its lush foliage and slender trees, serves as a theatrical yet transitory backdrop.

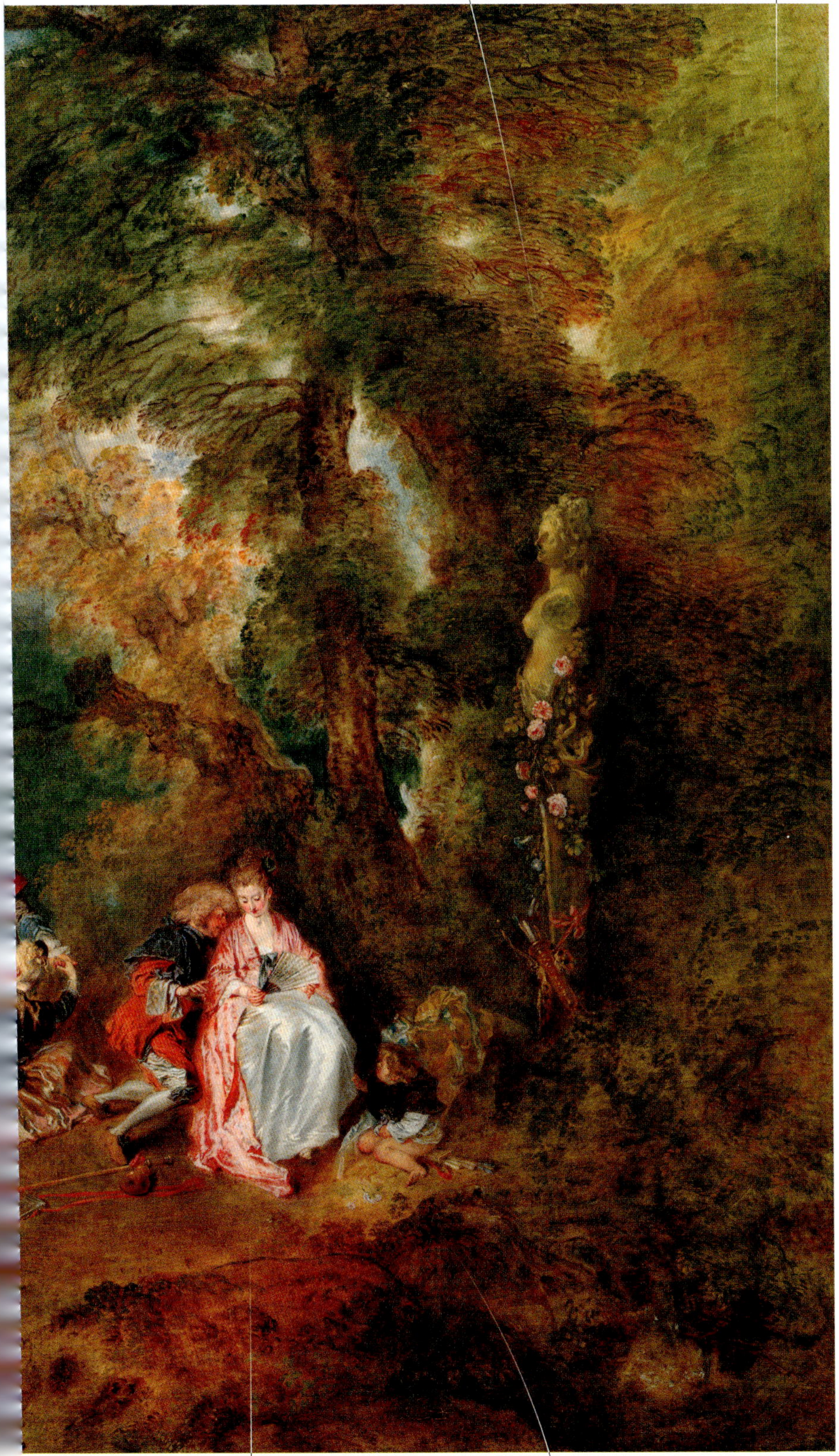

Fashionable clothes in luxurious fabrics with intricate details underscore the aristocrats' wealth and status.

A child, or a half-dressed putto, tugs at a woman's dress, encouraging her to engage in flirtatious conversation.

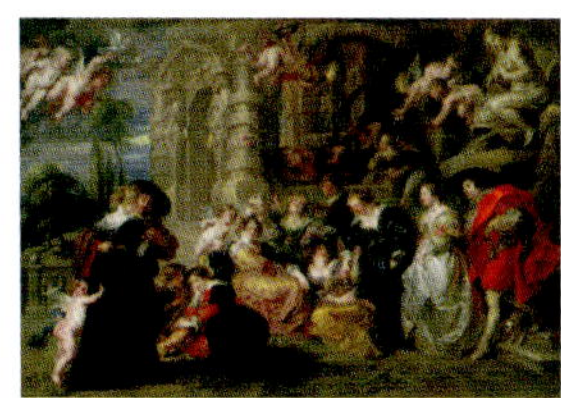

Rubens' influence
Watteau drew inspiration from Peter Paul Rubens, especially in his use of color and theatrical compositions. *Pilgrimage to the Isle of Cythera* bears a striking resemblance to Rubens' *The Garden of Love* (c. 1633).

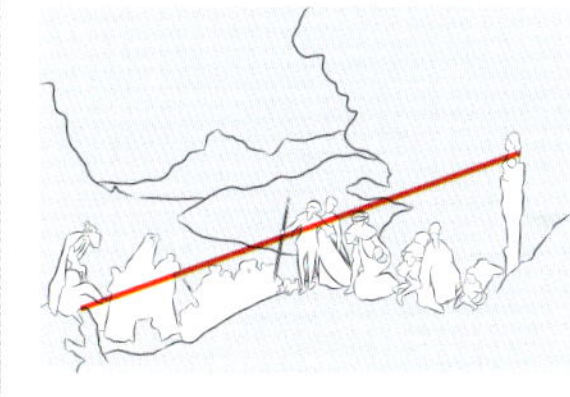

Leading the eye
The composition moves from the sculpture of Aphrodite in the top right, along the procession of lovers, down to the boat in the bottom left.

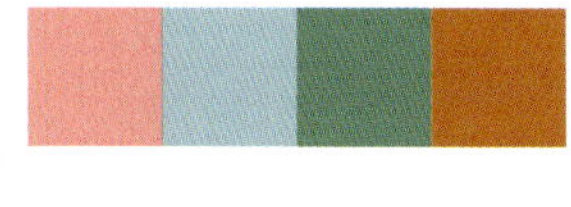

Rococo palette
Watteau uses a traditional Rococo color palette featuring pastel tones, such as gentle pinks and blues for clothing, complemented by greens and warm earthy tones for the landscape.

> "And there lay the enchanted land—there was the island of Cythera, where love was painless and pleasures never pall. Most of [Watteau's] pictures are invitations to that voyage of pure romance."
>
> Roger Fry, 1951

Rama Releases the Demon Spies Shuka and Sarana

Manaku c. 1725, opaque watercolor, ink, and gold on paper, 22 × 31 in (56.5 × 79.4 cm), Metropolitan Museum of Art, New York, US

Within a yellow-green landscape, two events from the *Ramayana* take place. On the right, Vibhishana brings the demon spies Shuka and Sarana to the god Rama, who mercifully sets them free. Returning to Ravana's golden palace, on the left, the demons report the terrifying strength of the bear and monkey armies they must face. This folio, from the Siege of Lanka series, shows the artist's skill in depicting the natural world.

Ravana, demon-king of Lanka, has multiple heads that see in all directions; his dizzying whir of hands hold assorted weapons.

The demons enter the palace gate upon returning from their encounter with Rama.

In a gesture of homage to Rama, the demons join their palms.

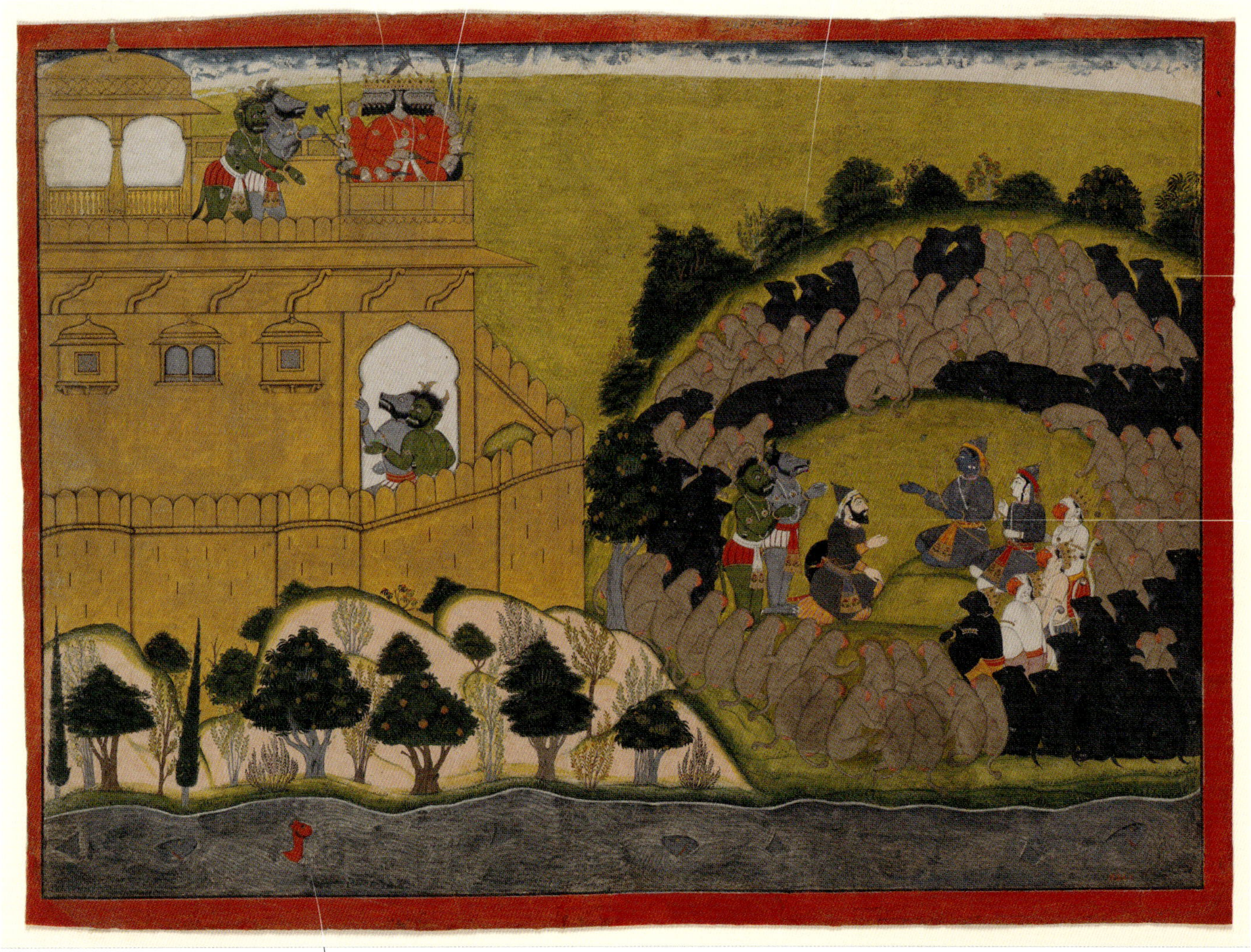

Bears and monkeys encircle Rama in his encampment.

With a pointed hat and beard, Vibhishana (younger brother of demon-king Ravana) kneels humbly before Rama.

Fish and other sea creatures emerge from the water.

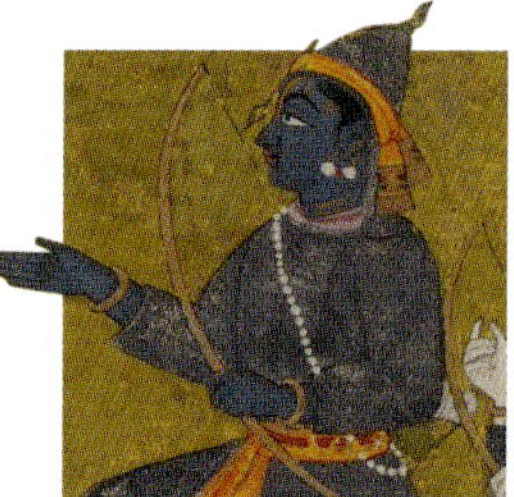

Blue skin, yellow garments, and a bow and arrow identify Rama, a manifestation of the Hindu god Vishnu.

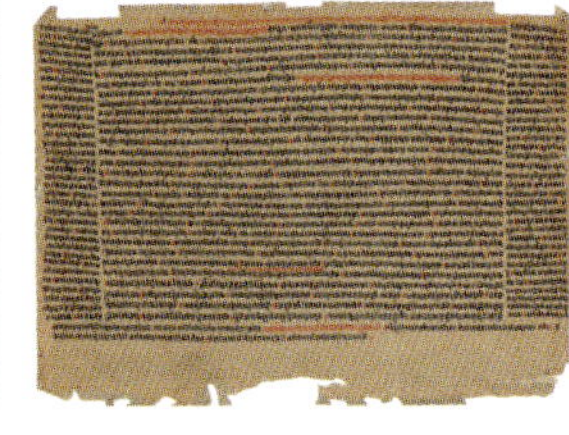

The Ramayana
The painting's verso is completely filled with lines of text from the Sanskrit *Ramayana*, one of India's two great ancient epics. They are elegantly written in black and red Devanagari script.

A family tradition
Painters passed their skills through familial lines in the Pahari hills. Manaku and his brother, Nainsukh learned them from their father and taught their sons.

A Young Lady with a Parrot

Rosalba Carriera c. 1730, pastel on blue laid paper, mounted on laminated paper board, 24 × 20 in (60 × 50 cm), Regenstein Collection, Art Institute of Chicago, US

In this pastel drawing, Carriera skillfully combines allegorical elements with portraiture to focus on the sitter's playful character and seductive beauty. The themes of love and sensual pleasure resonate with the Rococo aesthetic, a testament to Carriera's role in shaping the style.

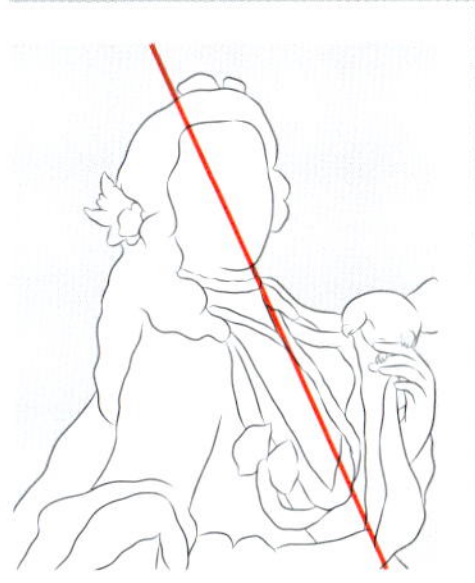

Creating movement
A diagonal axis is created by the woman slightly turning and leaning back, as the bird pulls back her dress to reveal her chest.

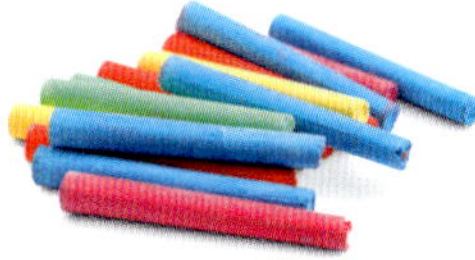

New medium
Carriera transformed the use of pastels, which had traditionally been reserved for preparatory work, into a recognized medium. As a result, pastel portraits became popular among upper-class patrons.

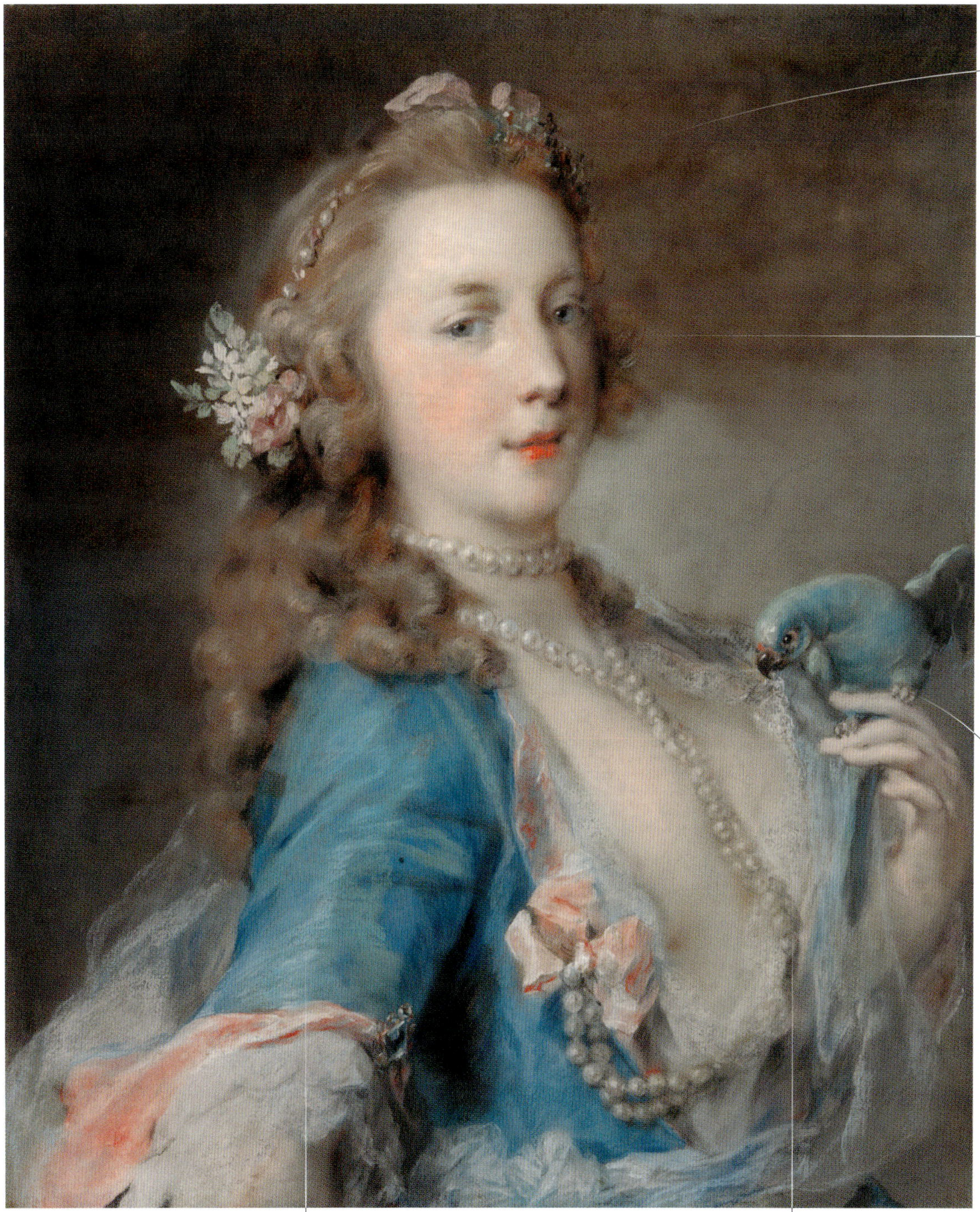

The subject may be one of the daughters of Lord Manchester, the English ambassador in Venice at the time.

Carriera achieved the subtle shading around the sitter's face by blending the pastels with her fingers.

The parrot reveals the woman's breast, displaying a sense of playfulness that the woman appears to share. The parrot also reflects the 18th-century interest in exotic animals.

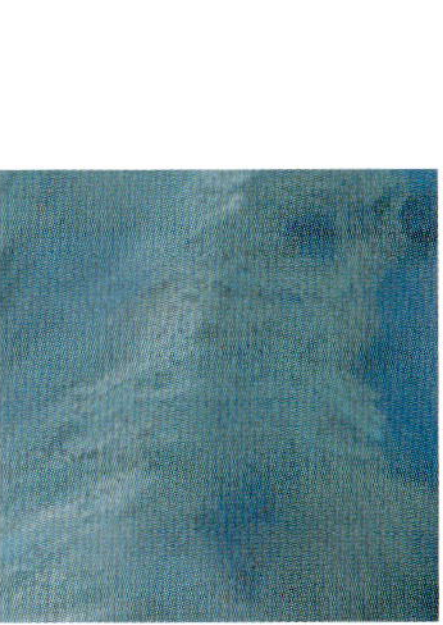

Strokes of dry, lighter blue chalk over the deeper blue dress give it a glossy, satin-like texture.

Matching the parrot's feathers to the color of the dress creates tonal harmony.

Portraits and still lifes were the two genres thought suitable for female painters. The portraits were usually modest, but here the subject stares boldly out of the frame.

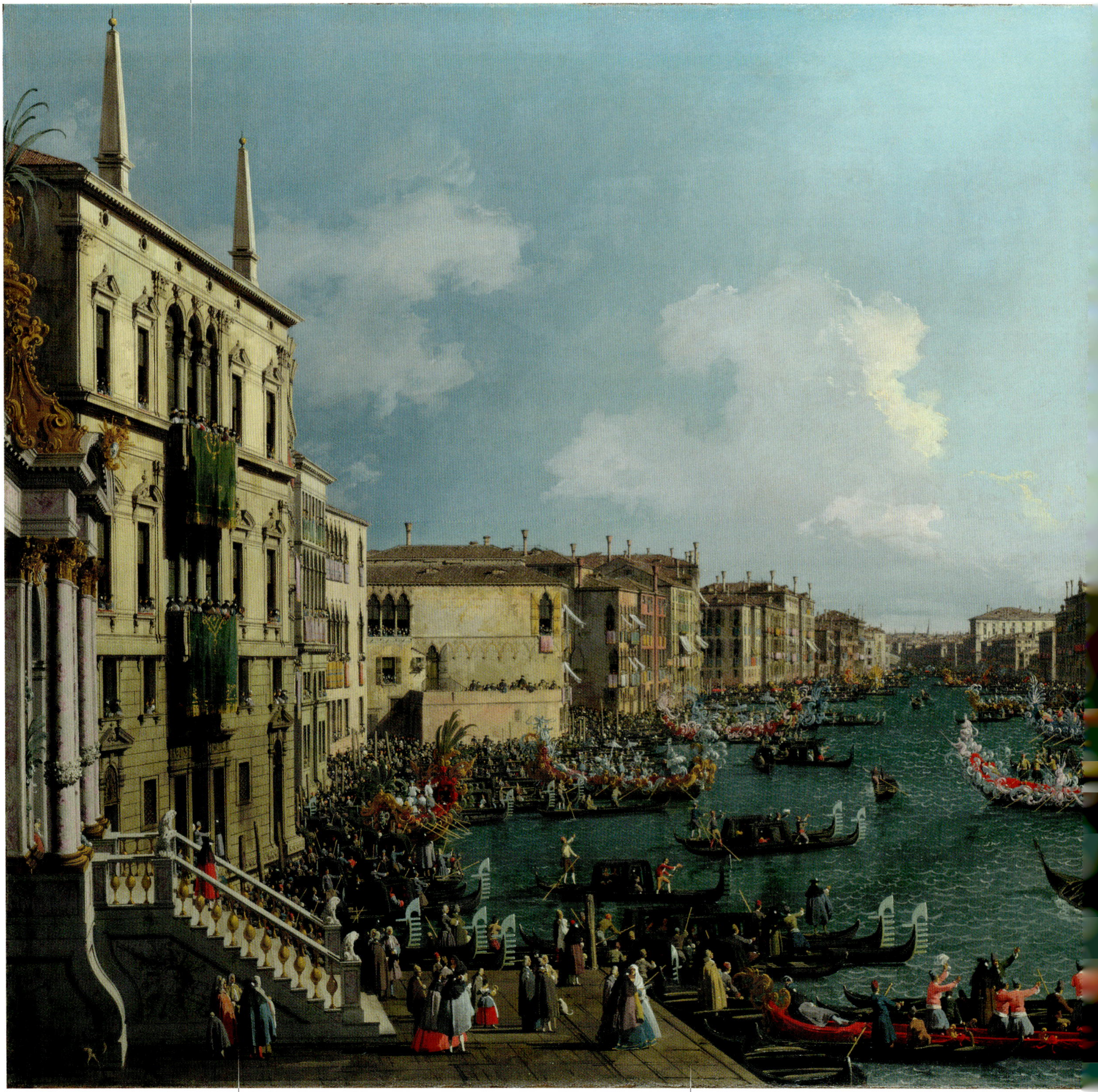

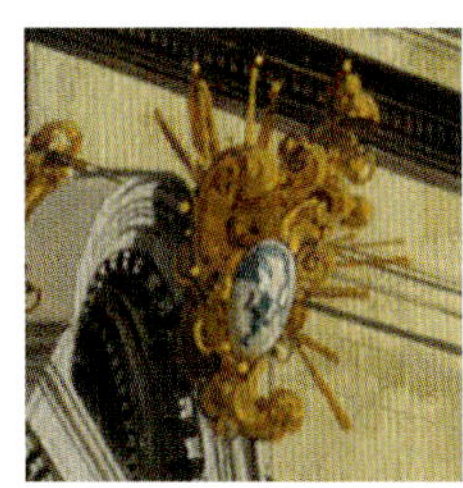

The symbol of the Venetian Republic, the Doge's hat, or *corno*, surmounts the coat of arms.

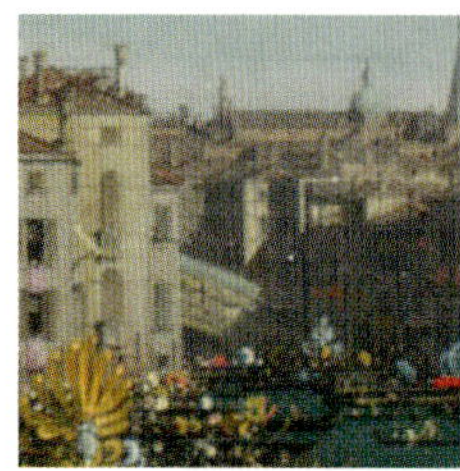

A tiny part of the Rialto Bridge, crossing the narrowest part of the Grand Canal, can be seen in the center.

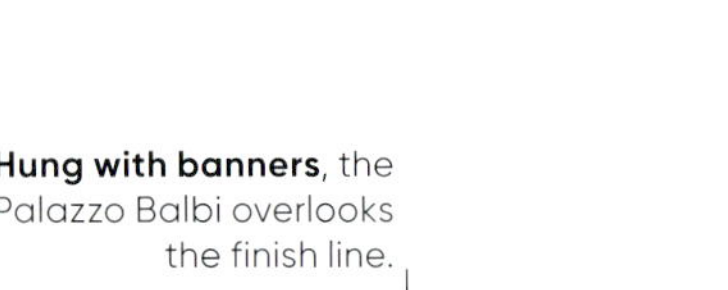

Hung with banners, the Palazzo Balbi overlooks the finish line.

The animated crowd helps create a feeling of excitement. Canaletto painted the spectators at a steep angle to focus the viewer's eye on the race.

The *macchina della regatta*, a temporary floating structure where prizes were awarded, was specially erected for the race.

A Regatta on the Grand Canal

Canaletto 1740, oil on canvas, 48 × 72 in (122.1 × 182.8 cm), National Gallery, London, UK

Canaletto captures the excitement of an annual rowing race on the Grand Canal in Venice. The Venetian tradition of "view paintings," or *vedute*, had begun a generation earlier, and such works were popular with tourists visiting the cultural highlights of Europe on what was known as the Grand Tour. Canaletto made the genre his own and may have used a camera obscura to capture Venice's complex architecture. The energy of a busy and popular city suffuse the painting, conveying a sense of celebration.

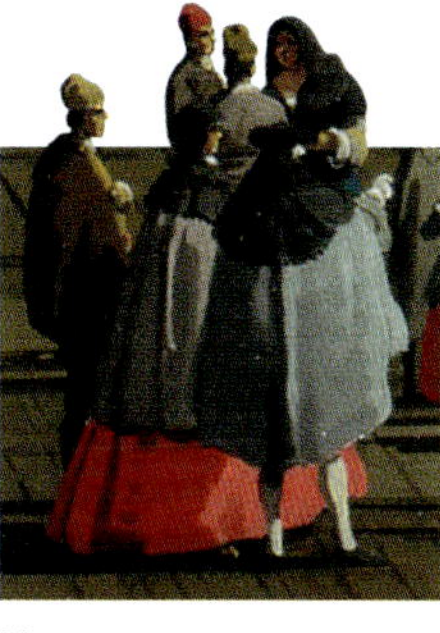

Many spectators are wearing the traditional carnival disguise of tricorn hat, white mask, and cloak. The races were held on February 2, the feast of the Purification of the Virgin.

Every detail of the urban fabric of Venice is captured, from the characteristic chimneys and roof terraces to the particular details of individual palaces

Spectators watch from the canal sides, balcony windows, and gondolas, while the *bissone* (ceremonial gondolas) of the noble families line the canal.

Two gondolas swing around the bend, almost colliding in their attempts to catch up with the leaders.

White ripples fleck the blue-green water, giving it a sense of depth and movement.

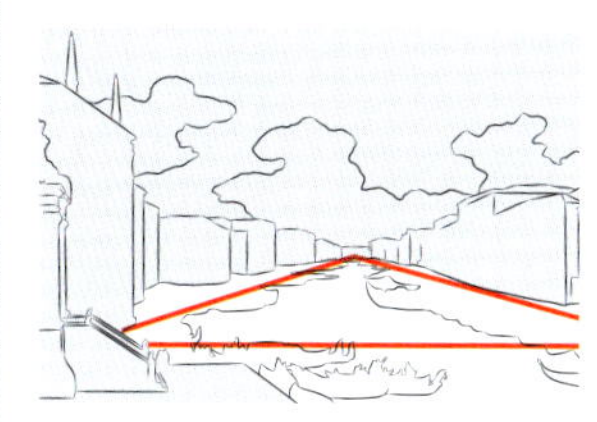

Follow the lines
Although the canal funnels the focus to the vanishing point beside the Rialto Bridge, horizontal lines created by the spectators' gondolas detain the eye, encouraging the viewer to explore other areas of interest.

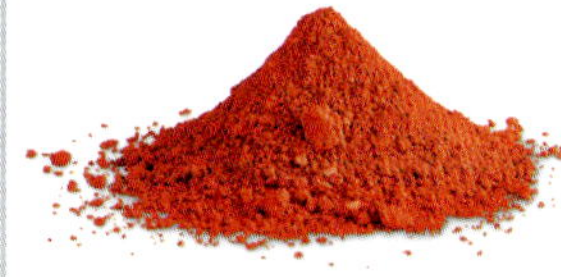

Highlights of red
Canaletto used vermilion and red lake pigments—derived from organic matter—to emphasize key details.

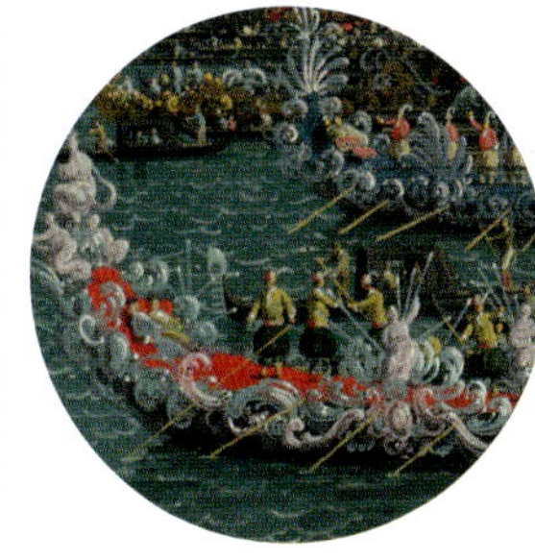

Minimal marks
Character is effectively conveyed with minimal brushstrokes, sometimes just a few dots of paint.

"Great judgment in the choice of views, in the distribution of figures and space, and in the arrangement of light and shade … the effects of a serene personality and happy genius."
Antonio Zanetti

A Rake's Progress II: The Levée

William Hogarth 1734, oil on canvas 25 × 30 in (63 × 75.5 cm), Sir John Soane's Museum, London, UK

A Rake's Progress is a series of eight satirical paintings depicting the fall of the fictional Tom Rakewell. In *The Levée*, the second in the series, Rakewell is shown surrounded by a crowd of hangers-on as he squanders his inheritance on the frivolous interests of the aristocracy. Hogarth intended to deliver a strong message about the importance of morality and the perils of vice.

A crowd of people seeking Rakewell's money spills into an adjoining room.

The man holding quarterstaffs (pole-shaped weapons) is James Figg, a famous prizefighter and self-defense instructor.

This may be landscape designer Charles Bridgeman, who helped popularize informal garden designs in England.

A painting in the background depicts the Judgment of Paris, a Greek myth in which a poor choice causes disaster. Here, it foreshadows Rakewell's fall.

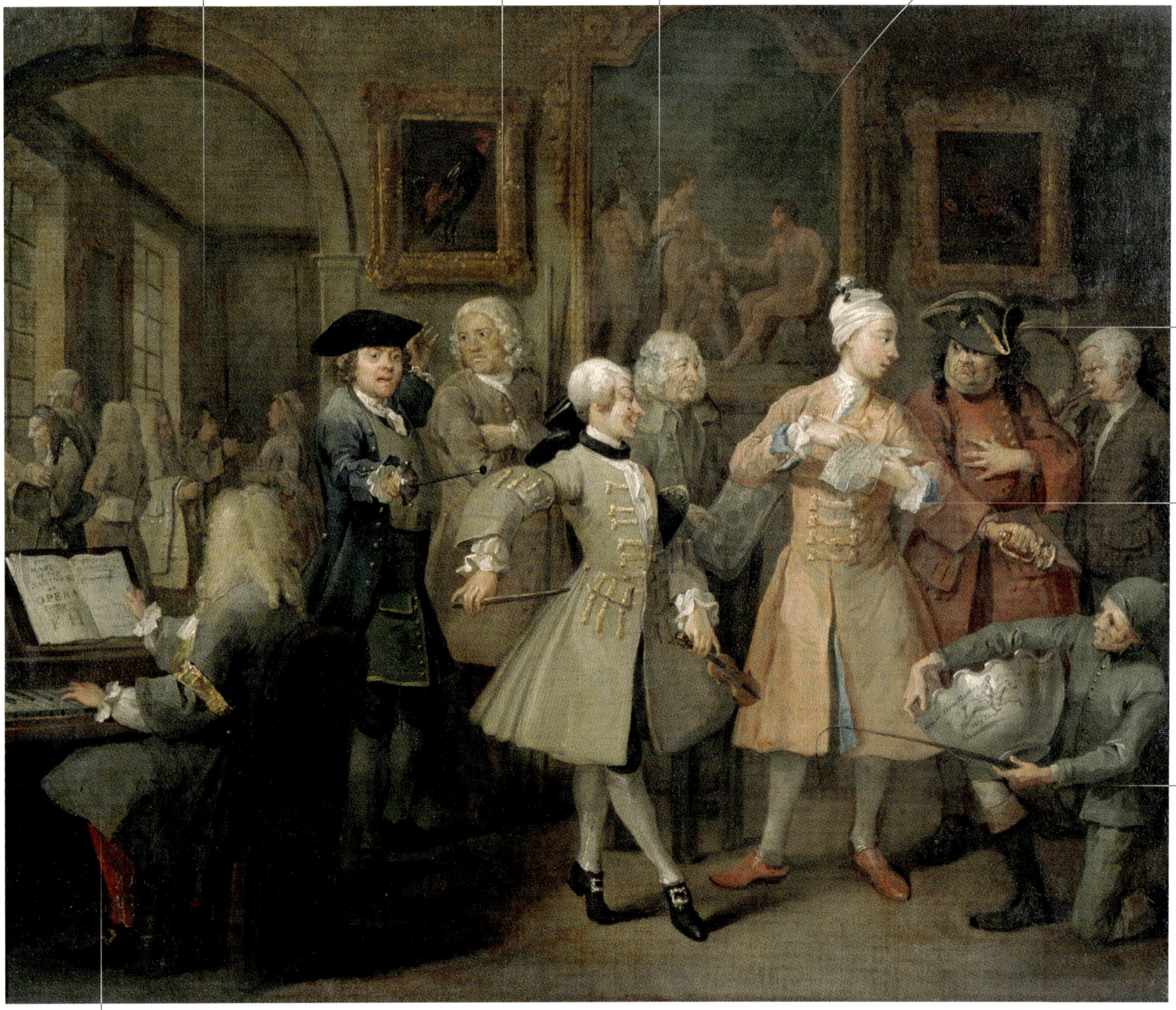

Brutish Captain Hackum, a would-be bodyguard, has handed Rakewell a letter recommending himself as "a man of honor."

Rakewell wears a morning coat and slippers. He receives people seeking his patronage while he is dressing.

A jockey holds a trophy awarded to a horse named "Silly Tom"—a commentary on Rakewell's character.

The harpsichord player might be George Handel or perhaps Nicola Porpora. Hogarth is mocking Rakewell's interest in fashionable foreign opera.

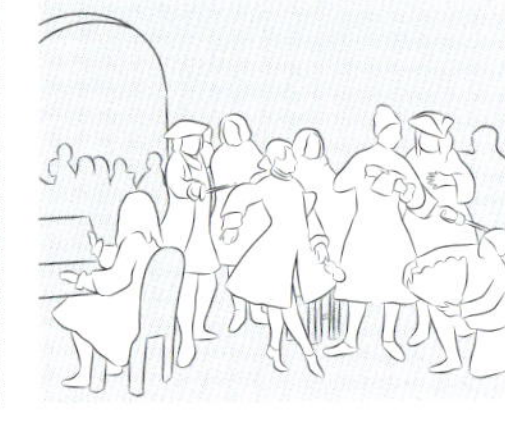

Busy scene
The composition is overcrowded with characters and detail, creating a sense of chaos and cacophony that reflects the tumult of Rakewell's life.

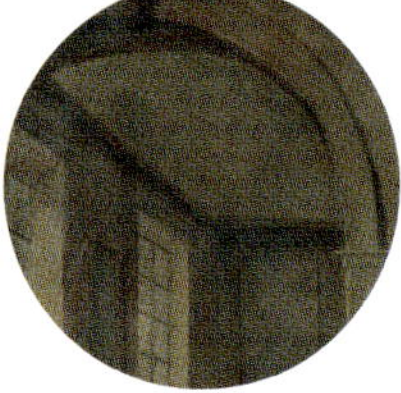

Visual sequence
Doorways and arches appear frequently in the eight *Rake's Progress* paintings, establishing continuation from one image to the next. By creating a series of images that together tell a story, Hogarth helped set the stage for modern comics.

Jeong Seon signed his name alongside the title of the work.

Biro Peak is the highest point in the Diamond Mountains, ascending to the apex of the composition.

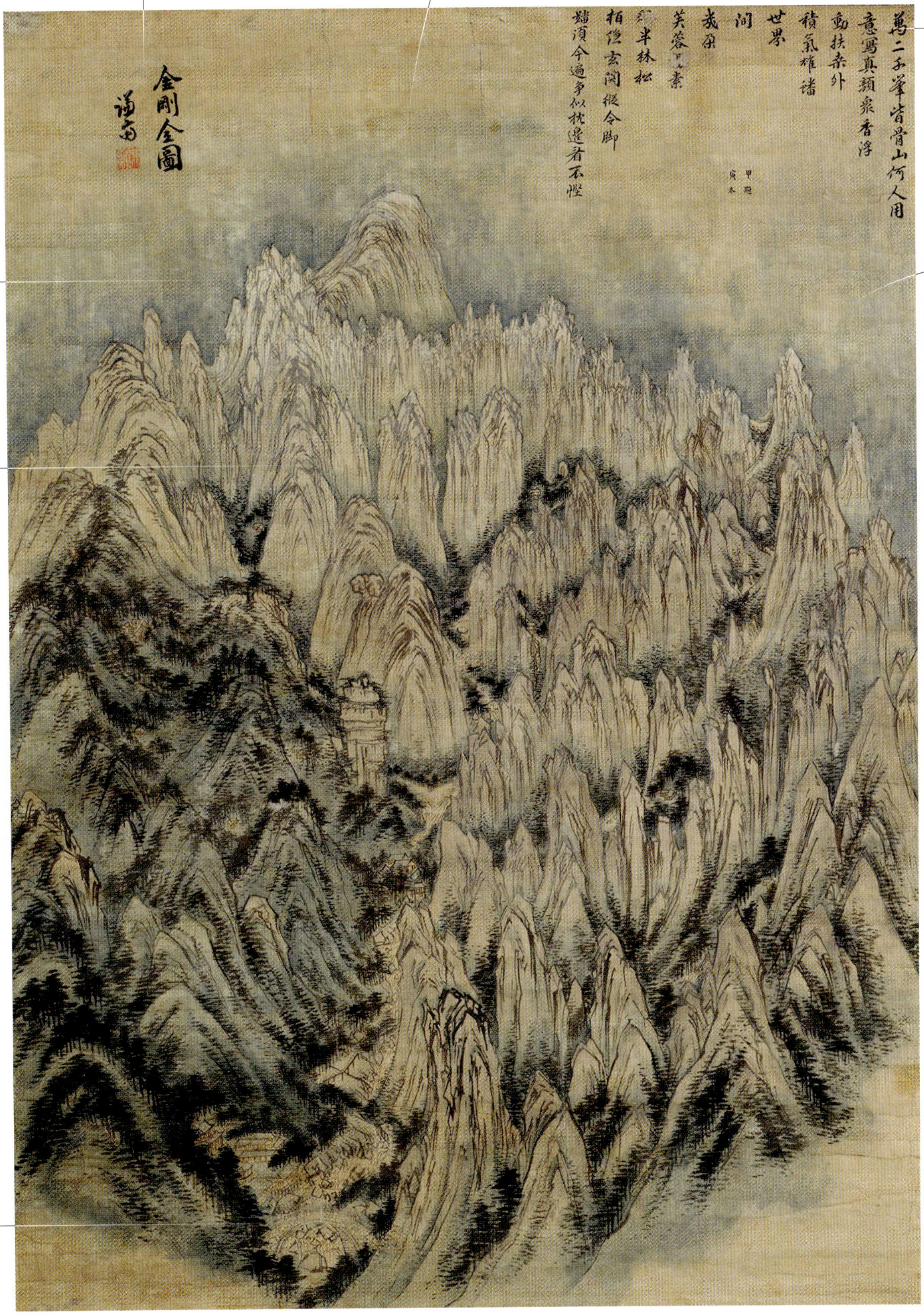

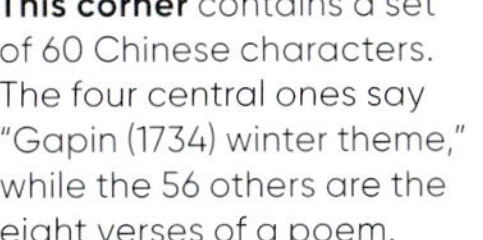

This corner contains a set of 60 Chinese characters. The four central ones say "Gapin (1734) winter theme," while the 56 others are the eight verses of a poem.

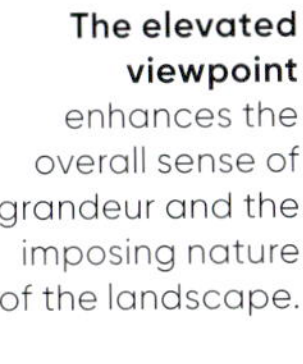

The elevated viewpoint enhances the overall sense of grandeur and the imposing nature of the landscape.

A muted blue wash in the sky and forest areas of the mountains adds color to an otherwise monochromatic composition.

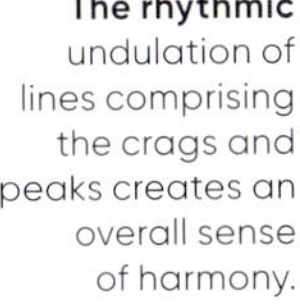

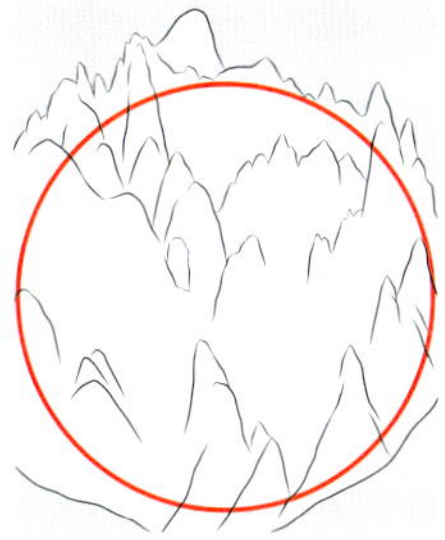

The rhythmic undulation of lines comprising the crags and peaks creates an overall sense of harmony.

Circular arrangement
The mountains are arranged in a circular composition, reminiscent of the *taegeuk*, an icon symbolizing cosmic harmony. This creates an overall balance within the work.

At the base of the peaks, a bridge and temples show the insignificance of human civilization in comparison to nature's grandeur.

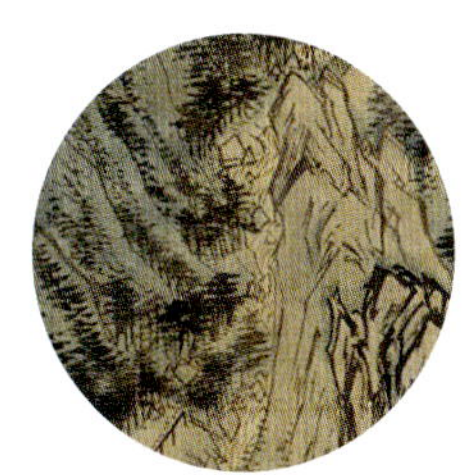

Contrasting sides
Different brushstrokes characterize the two halves of the composition: on the right, sharp, vertical lines mimic the jagged rocks, while the left side showcases stippled strokes depicting trees.

General View of the Diamond Mountains

Jeong Seon 1734, ink on paper, 51 × 37 in (130.7 × 94.1 cm), Ho-Am Art Museum, Yongin, South Korea

This painting depicts the grandeur and magnificence of the Diamond Mountains, a landscape of rugged rocks and dense forest. Jeong Seon relied on his memory to paint this panoramic view of the mountains, conveying his emotional response to the serene atmosphere he encountered there.

Diana Bathing

François Boucher 1742, oil on canvas, 22 × 29 in (57 × 73 cm), Louvre Museum, Paris, France

Diana, the Roman goddess of hunting, and a companion relax beside a pool in a secluded glade. Boucher has given this intimate scene from the Roman poet Ovid's *Metamorphoses* an elegant treatment. The sensuous subject matter and idyllic pastoral setting are typical of Rococo painting.

The lush, blue-green landscape provides a cool tonal contrast to the warm sensuality of the women's bodies.

The close, intimate framing invites the viewer into the scene to observe Diana as she bathes.

Ovid described Diana's secret bathing place as a wide pool with grassy banks.

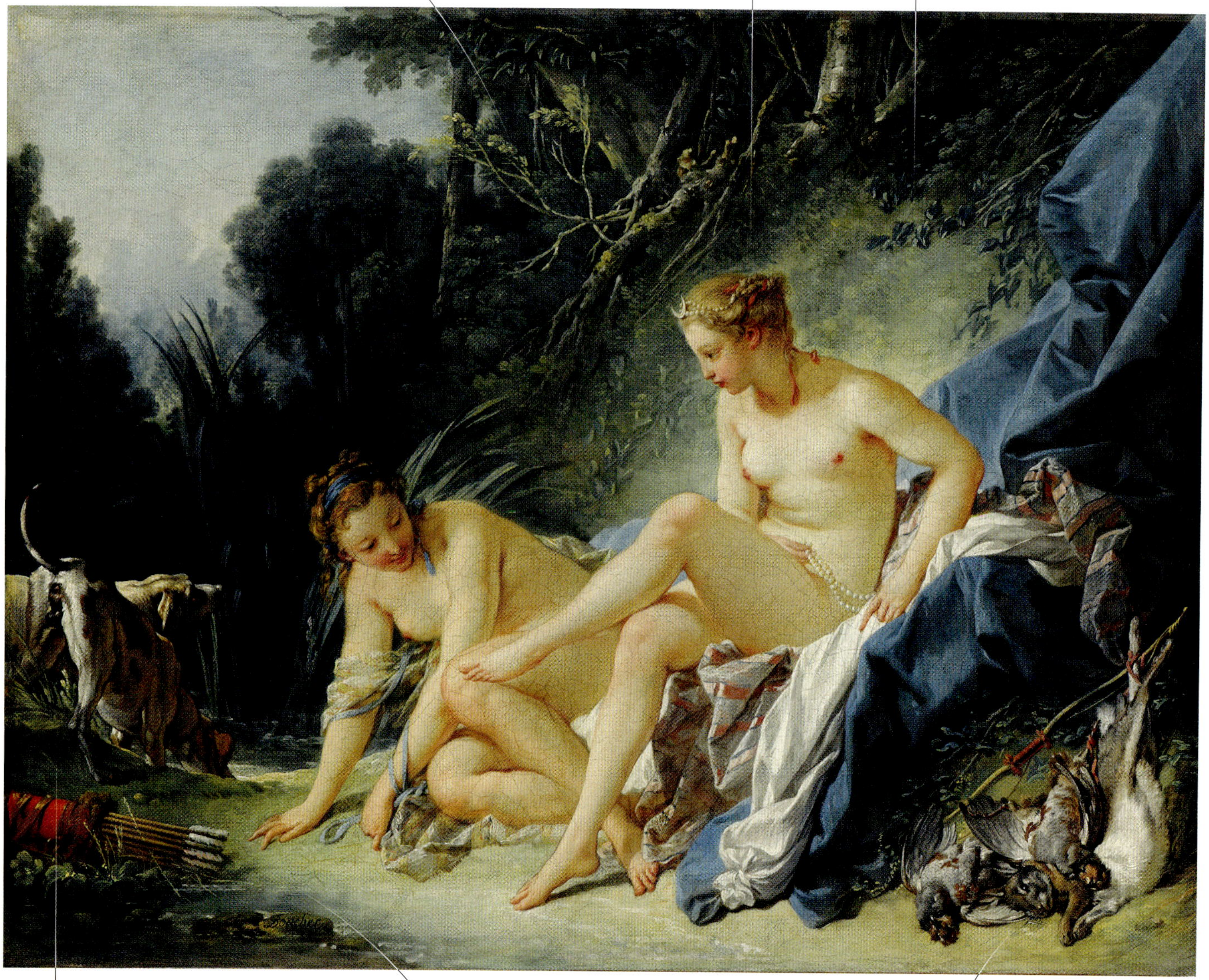

The overt display of the dog's genitals serves as a reminder of male sexuality in this otherwise female scene.

The quiver of arrows and two hunting dogs were often used as symbols to identify Diana.

Dead game beside Diana's bow alludes to the hunt that has just taken place.

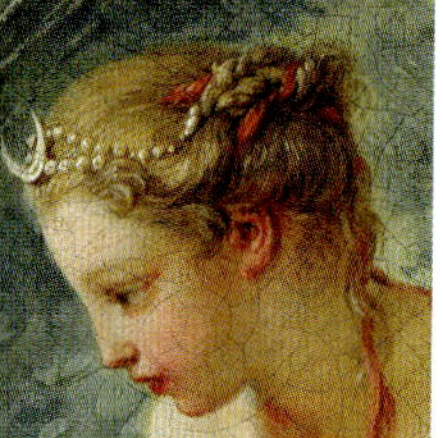

Soft, golden light from the left bathes the women in a warm glow, heightening their allure.

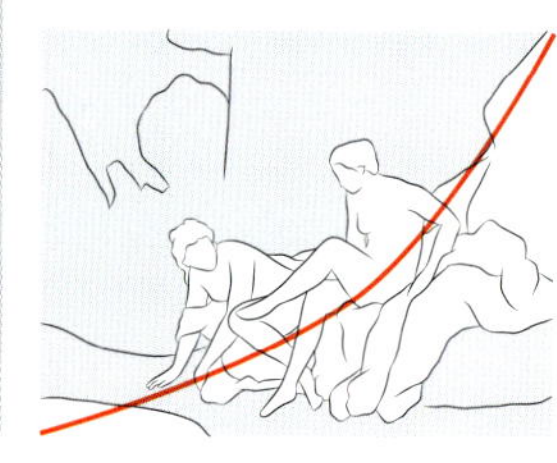

Narrative line
A graceful arc of motion unfolds from the blue drapery at the top right, passing around Diana and her female companion, and ending in the pond.

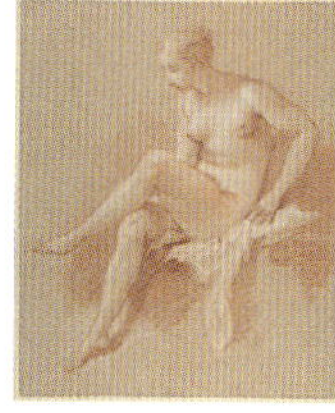

Diana's pose
Boucher was a meticulous draftsman. He used detailed preliminary drawings to plan all aspects of Diana's pose, including the play of light and shadow.

Leaning columns evoke a sense of dread, presaging the imminent downfall of the Ptolemaic Empire.

African servants, modeled after Venetian descendants of enslaved people, emphasize the wealth and decadence of the ruling classes.

The Greco-Egyptian god Serapis bridges the gap between Greek and Egyptian traditions.

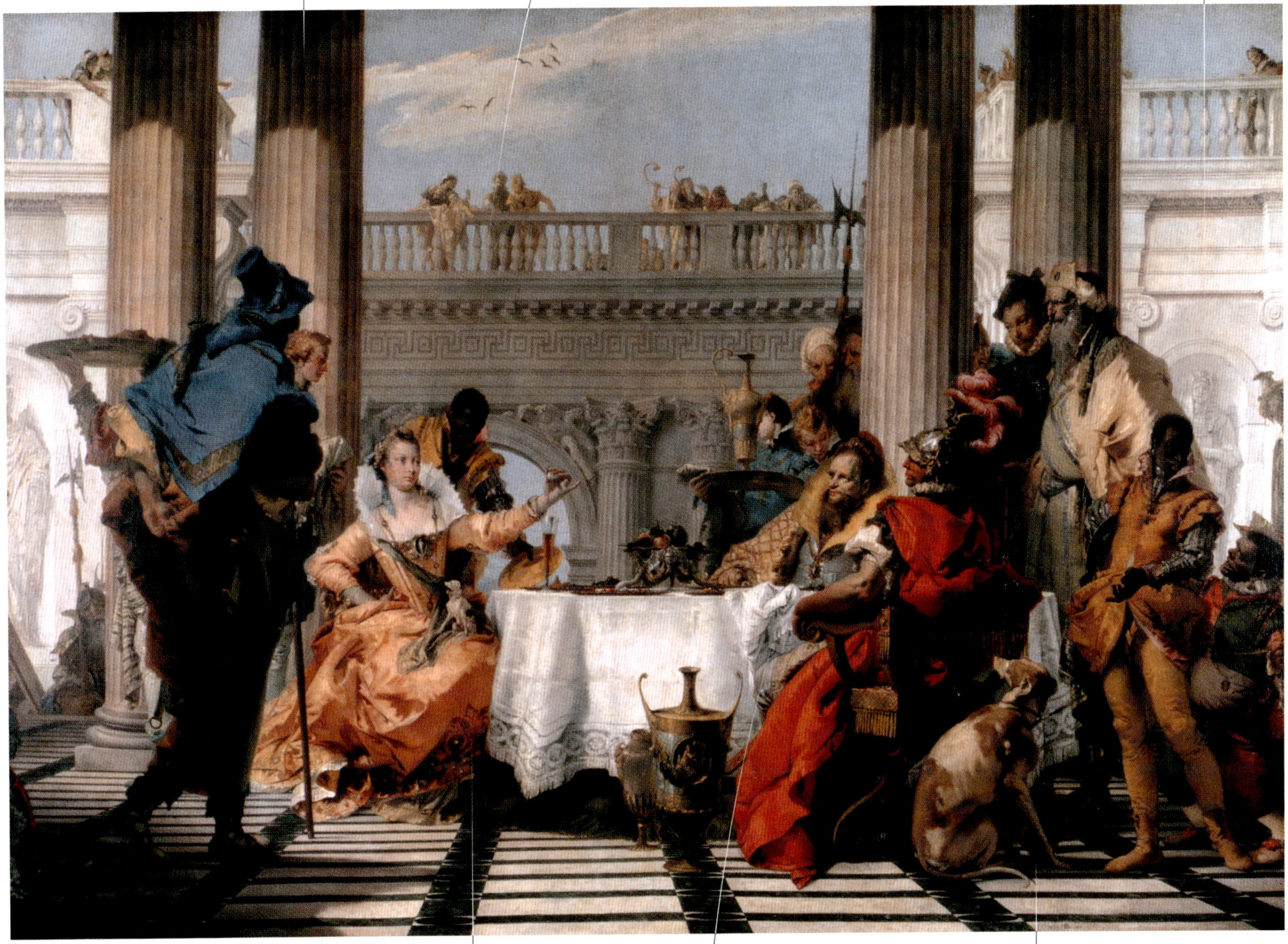

Tiepolo paints Cleopatra in 18th-century attire, juxtaposing the Venetian nobility's extravagance with that of ancient Egyptian rulers.

Roman senator Lucius Plancus, dressed in opulent Eastern attire, adjudicates the wager.

A cowering hound reinforces Mark Antony's authority, in contrast to Cleopatra's lactating lapdog, a symbol of fertility and protection.

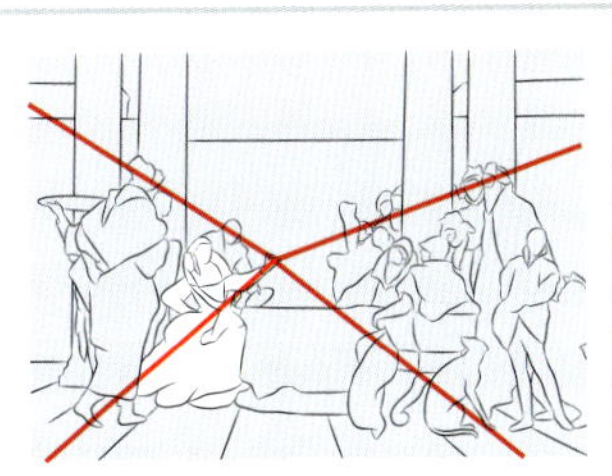

Perspective
Single-point perspective draws attention to Cleopatra's hand and her dangling pearl. The converging lines of stone tiles and onlookers gazing inward guide the vanishing point.

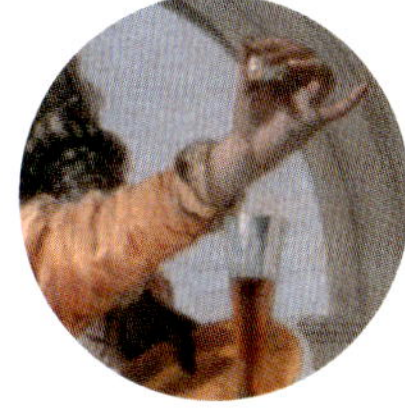

Focus on the left
Left hands dominate in the painting. From Roman times to the Middle Ages, the left side was associated with malevolence and foreboding.

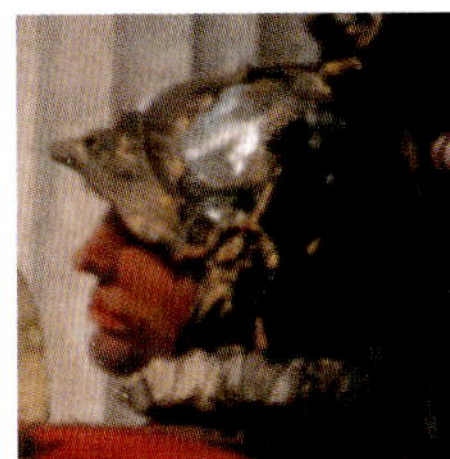

With a scornful gaze, Mark Antony concedes defeat, acknowledging Cleopatra's superior wit and political savvy.

The Banquet of Cleopatra

Giovanni Battista Tiepolo 1744, oil on canvas, 99 × 141 in (250.3 × 357 cm), National Gallery of Victoria, Melbourne, Australia

An ancient tale of rivalry and high theater unfolds in this scene of a banquet. Cleopatra, Queen of Egypt, has boldly wagered that she can stage a more lavish banquet than her Roman lover, Mark Antony. Tiepolo's depiction of the climactic moment when Cleopatra is about to dissolve a priceless pearl in vinegar and then drink it, showcases his mastery in blending Rococo extravagance with tension and intrigue.

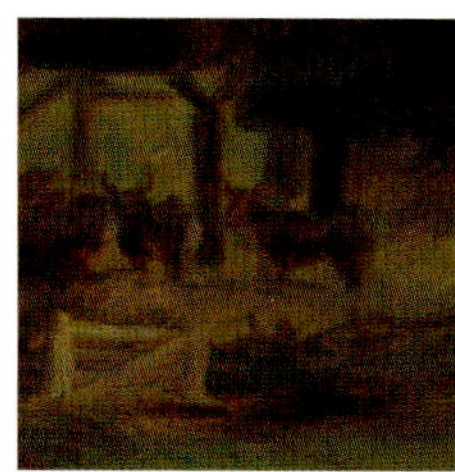

A pair of donkeys under the trees may be intended to represent the Andrewses. If so, it is a deeply unflattering comparison by Gainsborough.

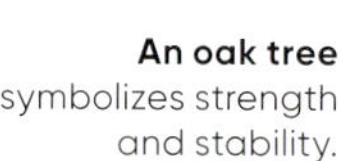

An oak tree symbolizes strength and stability.

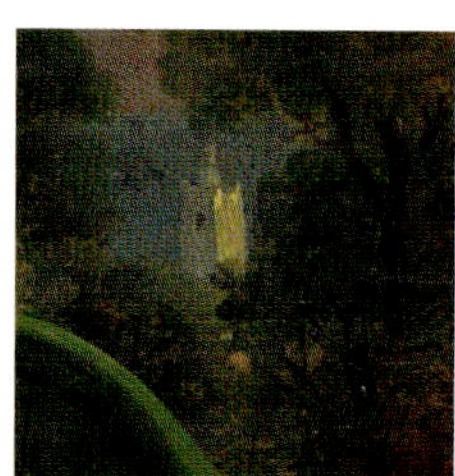

Sudbury's All Saints Church, in the distance, was the venue for the Andrews' wedding, and contains the Gainsborough family mausoleum.

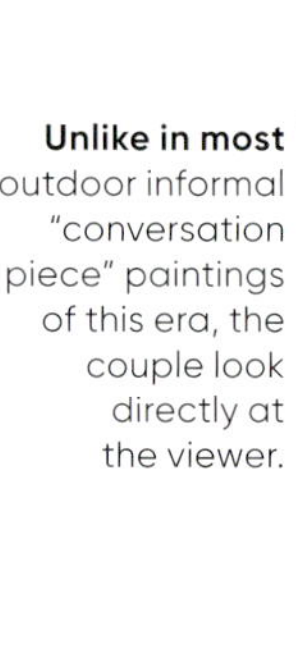

Unlike in most outdoor informal "conversation piece" paintings of this era, the couple look directly at the viewer.

By placing Mr. and Mrs. Andrews off-center, the painting celebrates their land, not just their marriage.

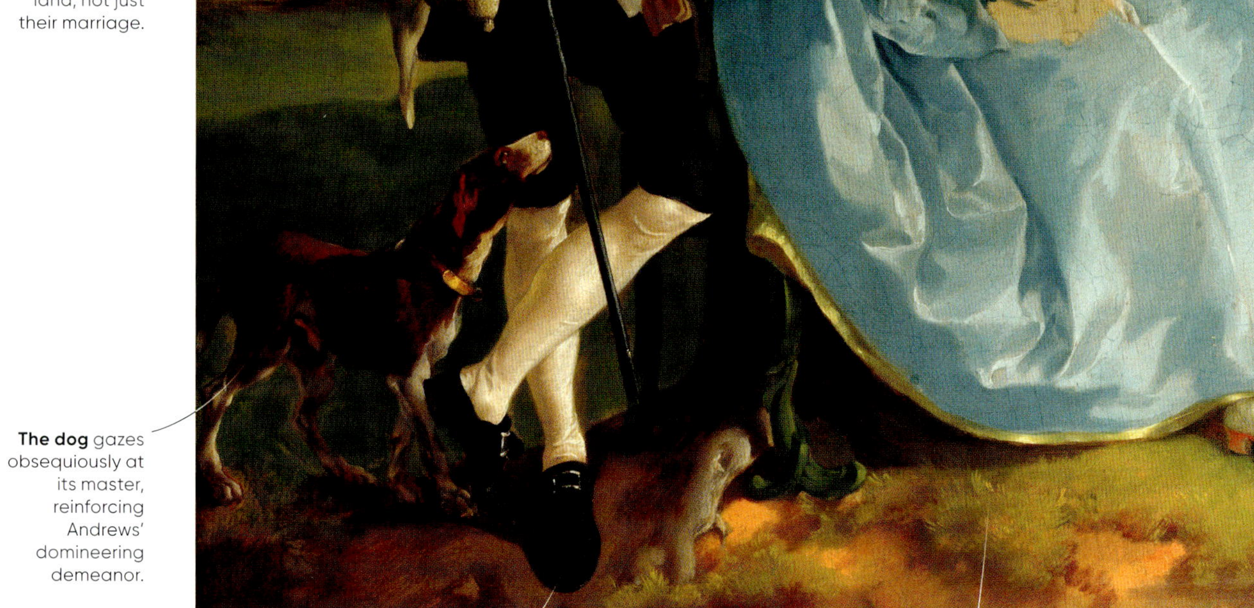

The dog gazes obsequiously at its master, reinforcing Andrews' domineering demeanor.

Robert Andrews has a supercilious air. He and Gainsborough were childhood friends but at some point they fell out, perhaps over this painting.

Experts suggest that the artist might have planned to paint a game bird on Mrs. Andrews' lap, or perhaps a future baby.

In this work, Gainsborough combines his preference for landscape painting with portrait painting, which was more profitable.

Mr. and Mrs. Andrews

Thomas Gainsborough c. 1750, oil on canvas, 27 × 47 in (69.8 × 119.4 cm), National Gallery, London, UK

Both a portrait and a landscape, this early Gainsborough painting depicts newlyweds Robert and Frances Andrews posing in their extensive estate at Sudbury in the English county of Essex. At first glance, it is an idyllic image of a wealthy young couple, but closer inspection hints that Gainsborough might have been satirizing his sitters. Mrs. Andrews wears an unlikeable expression, often interpreted as contempt, and some see symbolic insults hidden in the painting. This may explain why Gainsborough never finished it—a section of Mrs. Andrews' lap remains unpainted.

Cloudy skies may hint that Gainsborough saw trouble ahead for the couple.

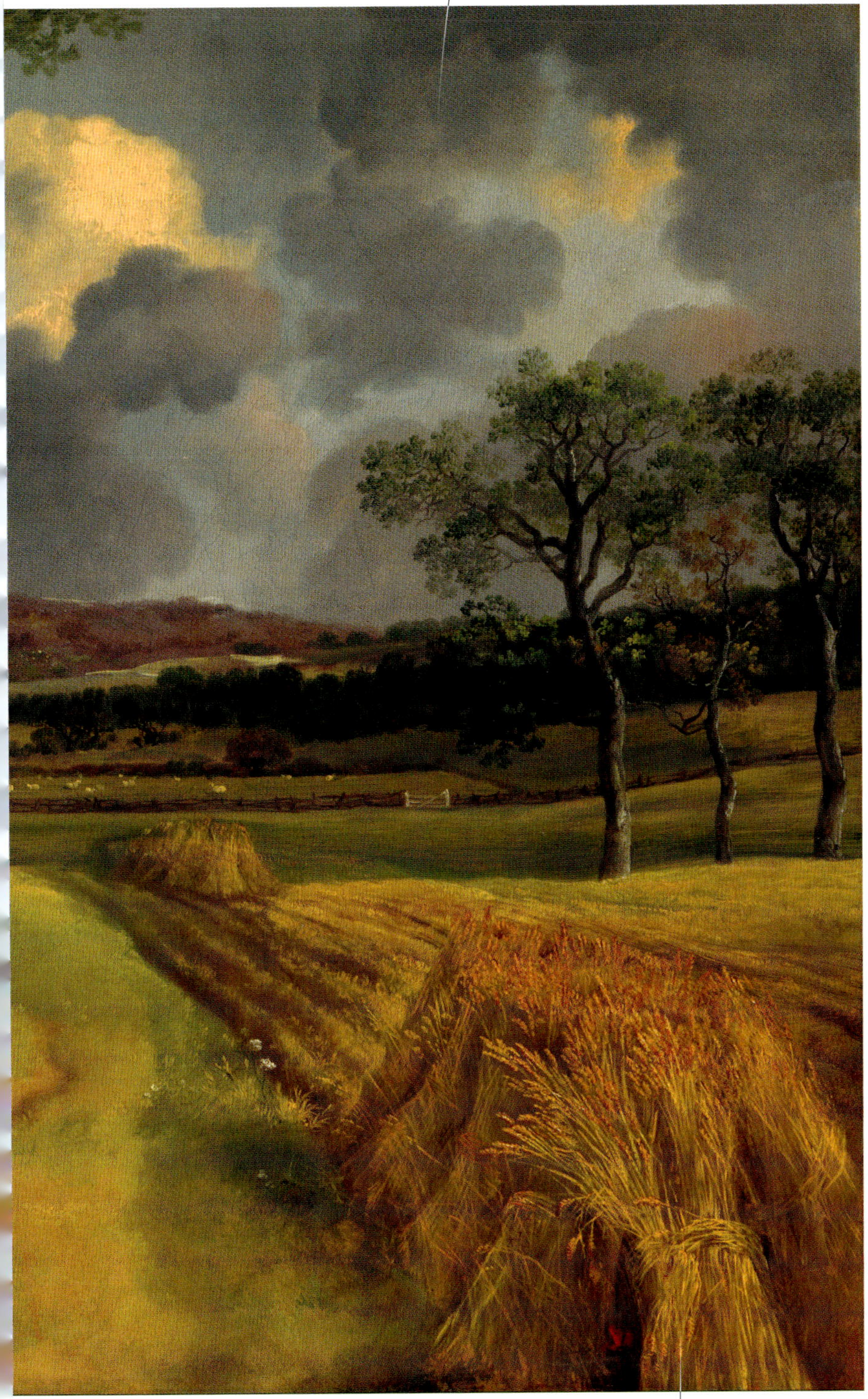

The abundance of wheat and neat furrows suggest that the Andrewses have used the latest methods to get the most from their land.

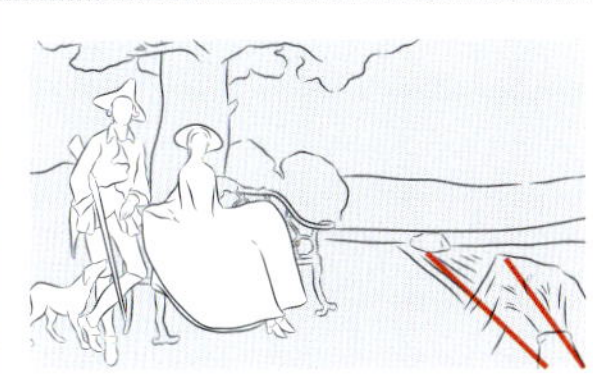

Sense of scale
The vertical lines formed by the rows of cut wheat in the field lead the viewer into the painting, emphasizing the scale of the Andrews' land holdings.

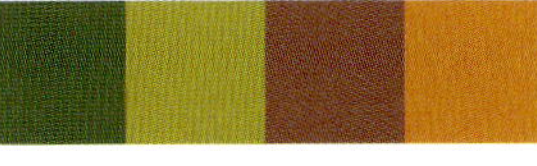

Harvest hues
Warm, natural colors abound. The greens and browns of the trees and the gold of the wheat suggest abundance.

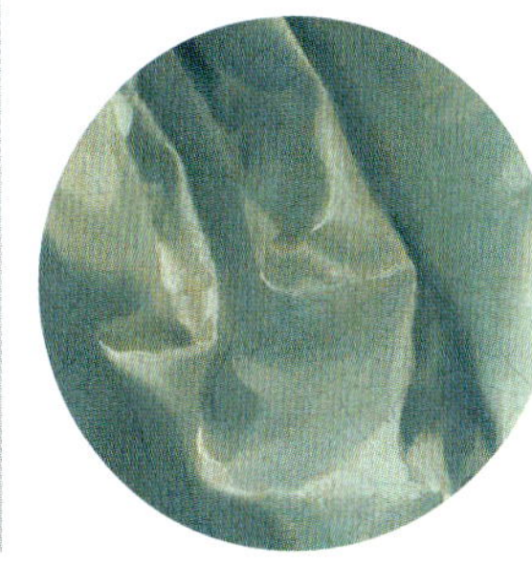

Fine textiles
The eye is drawn to Mrs. Andrews' shimmering blue dress. The son of a luxury cloth trader, Gainsborough excelled at painting silk, satin, and lace, using fine brushstrokes.

> "It has been described as a 'triple portrait'—of Robert Andrews, his wife, and his land."
>
> The National Gallery, UK

Blossoming Plum

Jin Nong 1759, hanging scroll, ink on paper, 49 × 17 in (125.4 × 43.2 cm), Metropolitan Museum of Art, New York, US

The plum tree blooms in midwinter, around the time of the Lunar New Year holiday. Because the blossoms emerge on bare boughs, before the tree grows leaves and often when snow is still on the ground, the tree has come to stand for grace and endurance in adversity. The plum blossom, pine, and bamboo are called the "Three Friends of Winter," with the same symbolic meaning. This very long painting can be hung on a wall for all to see.

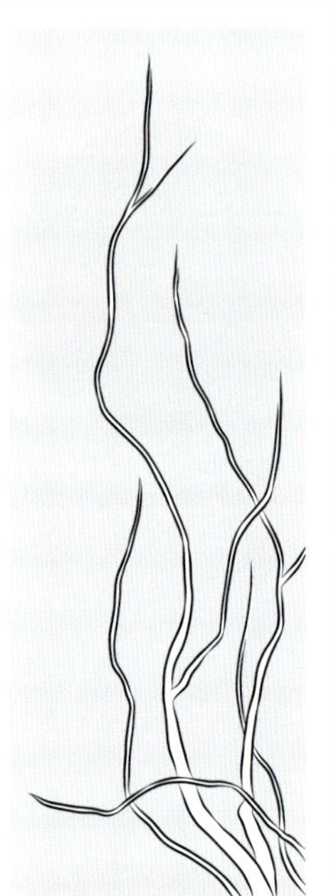

Crossing branches
The plum blossoms are weighted heavily to the lower right corner. The branches reach delicately upward, crossing and recrossing each other, with one narrow horizontal branch reaching across the lower section of the composition.

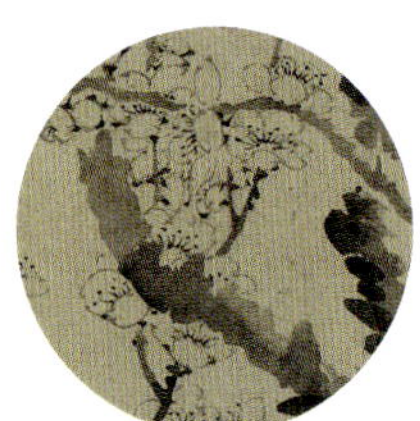

Ink monochrome
Jin did not avoid using colors, as some of his contemporaries did, but here the subject itself—white blossoms against black boughs—is monochromatic.

A later owner of the painting added this inscription in a cursive style in 1804. It describes the painting's history.

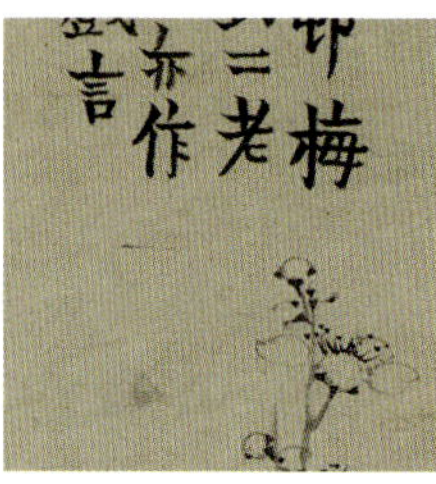

The same brush was used to paint the loose, wet strokes of the branches; the fine, pale outlines of the blossoms; and the angular, black forms of the artist's calligraphy.

The plain background does not reveal the setting or location.

The red seal impressions belong to the artist and three collectors who owned this painting at different times.

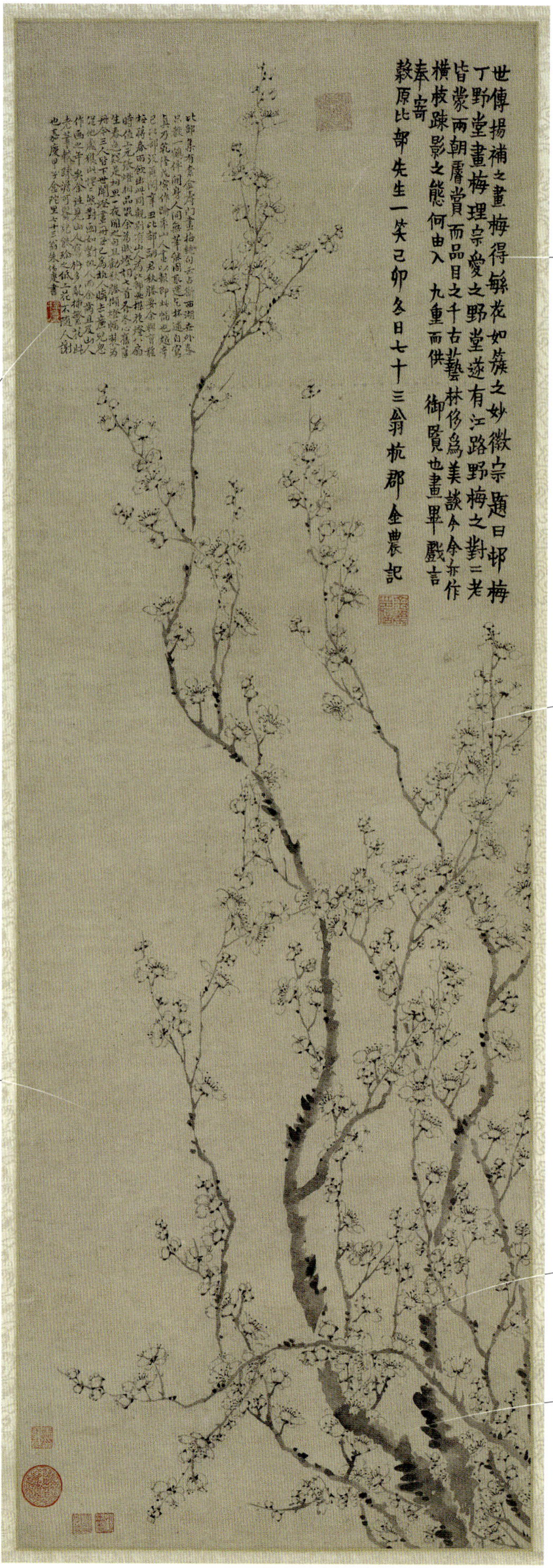

The artist's inscription, in which he compares himself to great plum blossom painters of the past, is written in a vigorous, deliberate style and intensely black ink.

A delicate outline describes the white blossoms, all turning in different directions and depicted at various stages of blooming.

A loose watercolor technique has been used to depict the branches, with darker strokes indicating the knobbly bark.

The contrast between the delicate blossoms and the gnarled branches is the essence of a plum blossom painting.

Basket of Wild Strawberries

Jean-Baptiste-Siméon Chardin 1761, oil on canvas, 15 × 18 in (38 × 46 cm), Louvre, Paris, France

A basket of luscious-looking strawberries is flanked by a glass of water, a pair of white carnations, two cherries, and a peach. From these items, Chardin, a celebrated still-life and genre-scene painter, conjured up an image of compelling stillness. The objects hold no symbolic meaning, but the painting celebrates the beauty of simple things, inviting viewers to retreat from the commotion of the world.

The background is painted with a thin layer of reddish brown, harmonizing with the reds in the fruit.

Green stalks among the strawberries complement the red.

The glass of water provides a contrast in texture with the basket, flowers, and fruit.

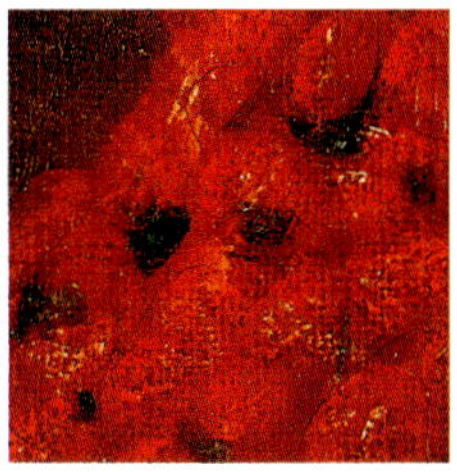

For the strawberries, Chardin used thin layers of different reds, from warm lighter areas to cooler shadows. The weave of the canvas adds texture.

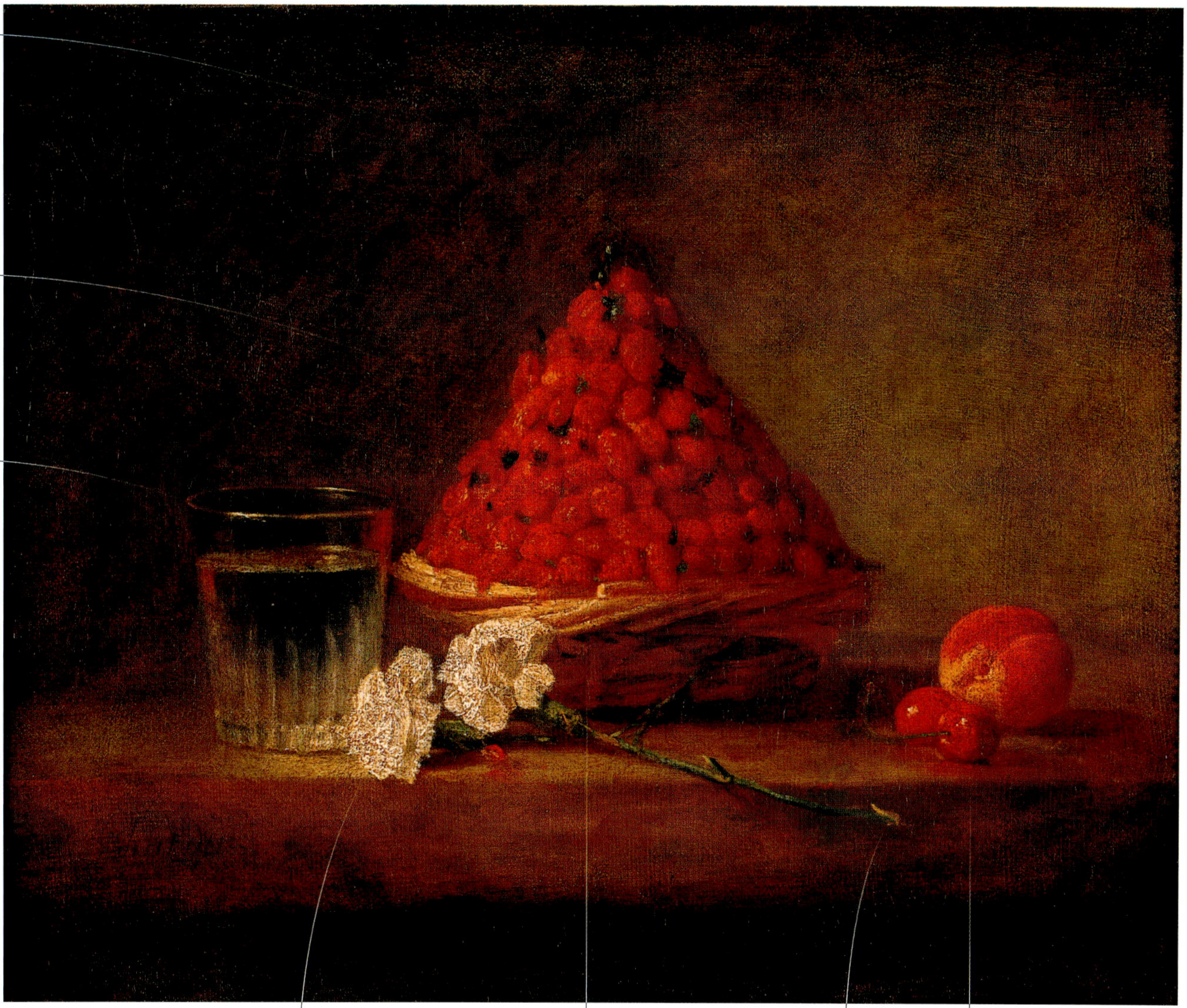

The carnations have been depicted by dragging white paint over darker paint.

Strokes of thick white paint are used for the highlights on the basket.

Stems break the straight line of the table edge and appear to extend in front of the painting.

The red cherries balance the red reflections of the strawberries in the glass.

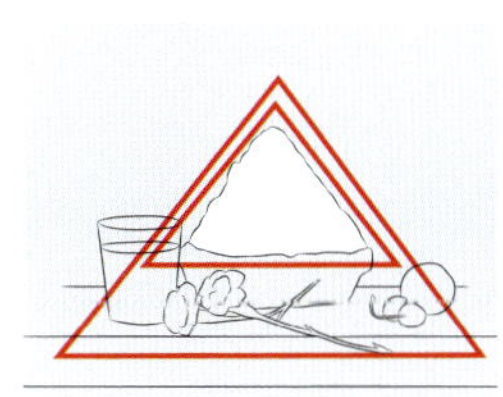

Triangular form
The composition is based on a triangle within a triangle. The shape of the strawberries is echoed by a larger triangle, to produce a balanced image.

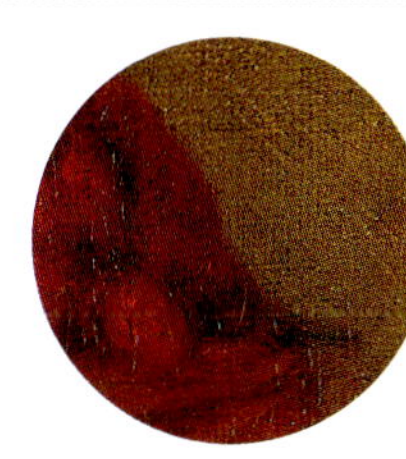

Tonal balance
Light comes from the left. The lit side of the strawberries is set against a darker area of background, the shadow side against a lighter area, creating movement across the canvas.

> "Who said one paints with colors? One employs color, but one paints with feeling."
>
> Jean-Baptiste-Siméon Chardin

The Swing

Jean-Honoré Fragonard c. 1767–1768, oil on canvas, 32 × 25 in (81 × 64.2 cm), Wallace Collection, London, UK

In an overgrown garden filled with statues, a young woman swings through the air between her lover and older husband in one of the most famous (and risqué) French paintings of the 18th century. Commissioned by a "man of the court," the painting would have been considered erotic. Its message suggests that women are inconsistent when they fail to choose between two partners.

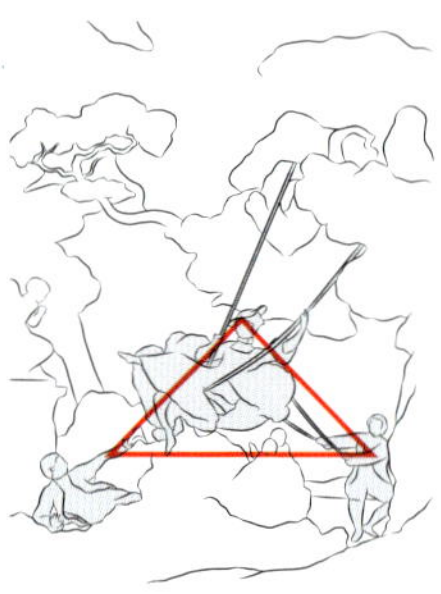

Love triangle
A literal love triangle is reinforced by the ropes held by the older man, the younger man's outstretched arm, and the garden wall. Strong diagonal lines created by the ropes and woman's body also lead the eye toward the lover in the lower left.

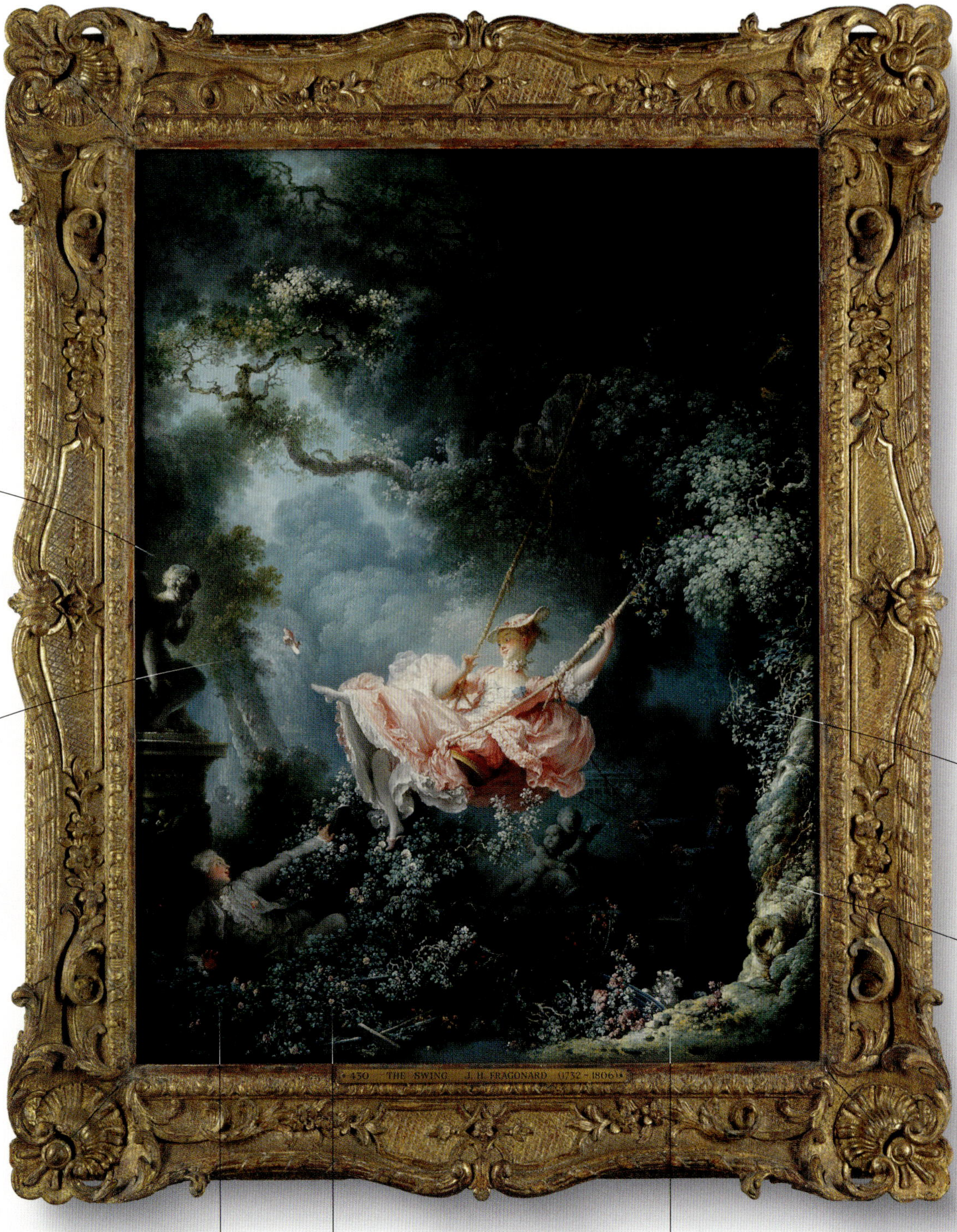

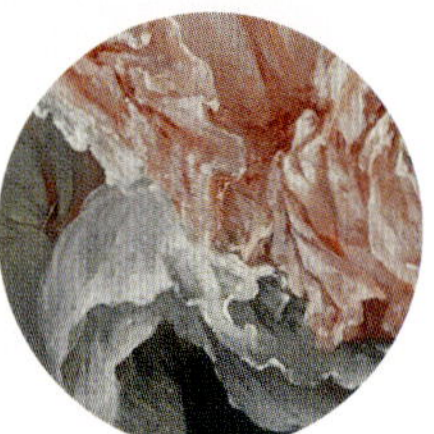

Gestural style
Fragonard's loose brushstrokes capture the exuberance of the moment. The Impressionists, particularly Renoir, were influenced by Fragonard's style.

The statue, *The Menacing Cupid* by French sculptor Étienne-Maurice Falconet, holds its finger to its lips, suggesting that the lovers' relationship must remain secret.

The woman's pink slipper flies in the direction of the statue of Cupid, the Roman god of desire and love.

The fraying rope hints at trouble ahead for the woman. Perhaps her secret lover will soon be revealed.

Holding the ropes that control the swing, the husband believes he is in control of his wife.

The woman's lover is concealed in the bushes, positioned so he can see up her dress.

Phallic imagery has been suggested in the arm aimed toward the woman, while there is a reference to her loins in the triangular hat.

A dog barks and jumps, unlike the docile dogs that symbolize female faithfulness in other portraits of this era.

An Iron Forge

Joseph Wright 1772, oil on canvas, 84 × 52 in (121.3 × 132 cm), Tate Britain, London, UK

The glow of a white-hot iron ingot illuminates a forge master and his family in a scene extolling the transformative power of hard work and, arguably, technology. All three daughters gaze outward, engaging the viewer and encouraging an emotional connection with this working-class family. Wright often painted forges and blacksmith shops, exploring technology with strong contrasts of dark and light.

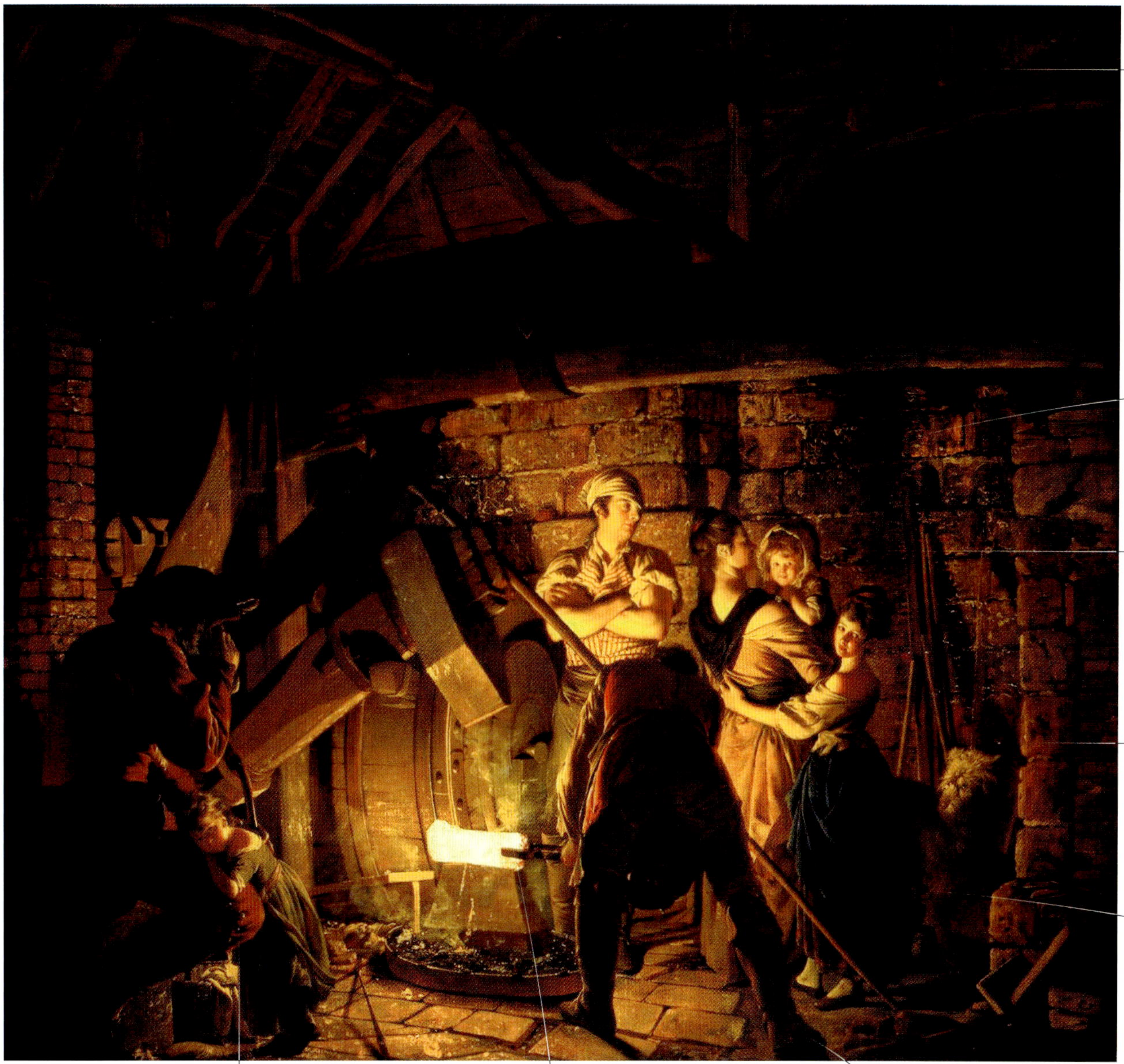

The rafters reach toward the heavens, as do the ladders on the left-hand side.

The powerful, well-dressed forge master gazes proudly at his family. A modern Apollo, he has been called the "new masculine ideal."

Wright has adapted the scale for dramatic effect—a real forge family could not gather quite so close to white-hot iron.

The dog—a pet, not a working dog—is another sign that this family can afford some luxuries.

The girls are well dressed, indicating that this family has achieved a measure of material success.

The old man sits idle. Perhaps the mechanized forge allows him to escape a long life of hard labor.

A tilt hammer is powered by a waterwheel, showing how humans have harnessed nature to do their bidding.

An employee, face unseen, does the hard work.

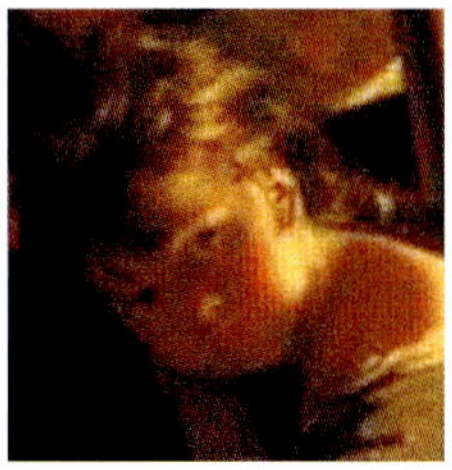

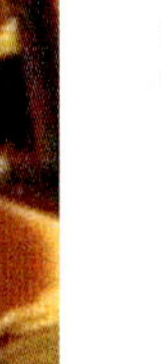

One of the forge owners' children leans against the older man, who is probably a grandparent, not a mere employee.

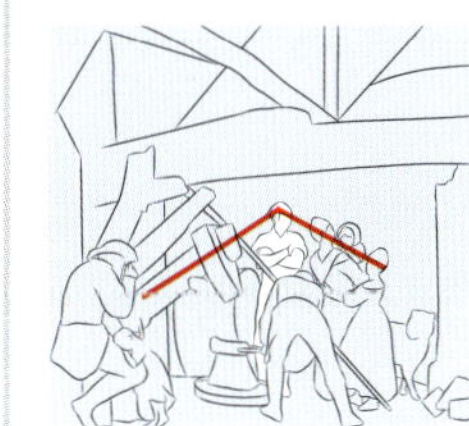

The main man
Diagonal lines formed by the arm of the tilt hammer, the heads of the family, and the roof's support beams direct the viewer's gaze toward the forge master's head. Although he stands at the rear, he is the painting's focal point.

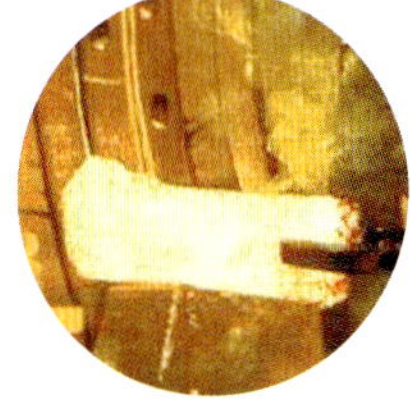

Light source
Wright created glowing iron by attaching gold leaf to the canvas above a white underlayer, then applying yellow paint over it. This is the only light source—its warm upward light imbues the modest forge and forge master with grandeur and drama.

Three Ladies Adorning a Term of Hymen

Sir Joshua Reynolds 1773, oil on canvas, 114 × 133 in (290.2 × 338.2 cm), Tate Britain, London, UK

Commissioned to mark the engagement of Elizabeth, a daughter in the aristocratic Montgomery family, this group portrait shows Elizabeth and her sisters decorating a statue of Hymen, the Greek goddess of marriage and fertility. Sir Joshua Reynolds believed that artists should idealize their subjects, making them more perfect than the original, by drawing on the example of classical and Renaissance art. He called this approach the Grand Style and applied it to portraits as well as history paintings. He depicted the Montgomery sisters as mythical figures in order to ennoble them.

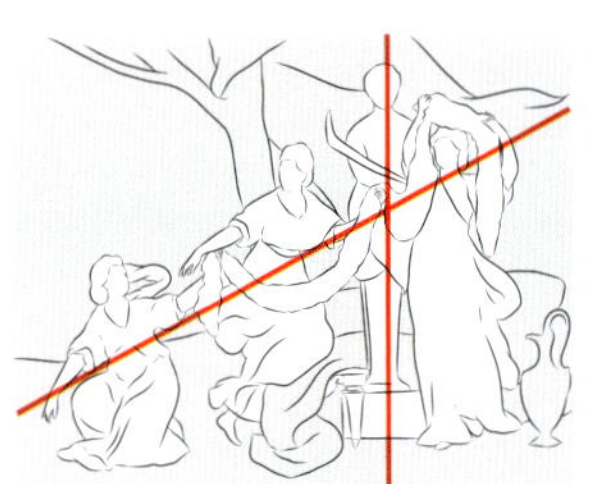

Lines of composition
A strong diagonal from bottom left to top right links the three sisters. A vertical through Hymen stabilizes the composition.

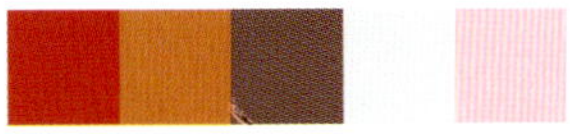

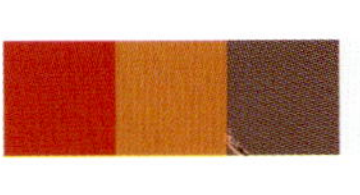

Tonal contrast
Warm reds, oranges, and earth tones in the background and clothing are set off by the pale sky, flesh tones, and white dress.

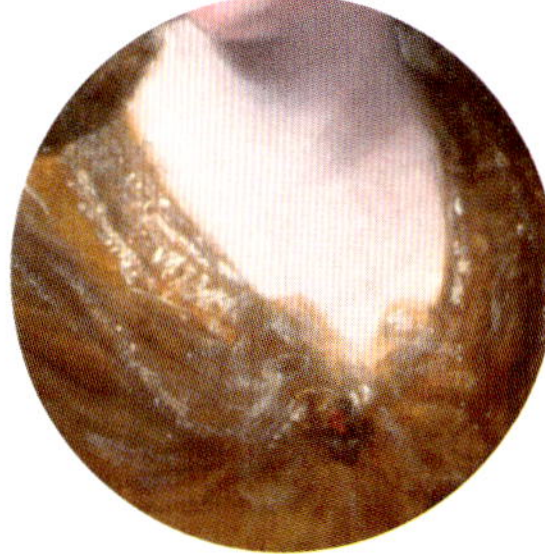

Lace detail
Thick dabs of white paint have been added over a very thin veil of color to suggest the lace collar.

> "It is not the eye, it is the mind, which the painter of genius wishes to address."
>
> Sir Joshua Reynolds, 1770

Barbara, the youngest sister, hands flowers to Elizabeth.

An aristocratic English country estate provides the setting.

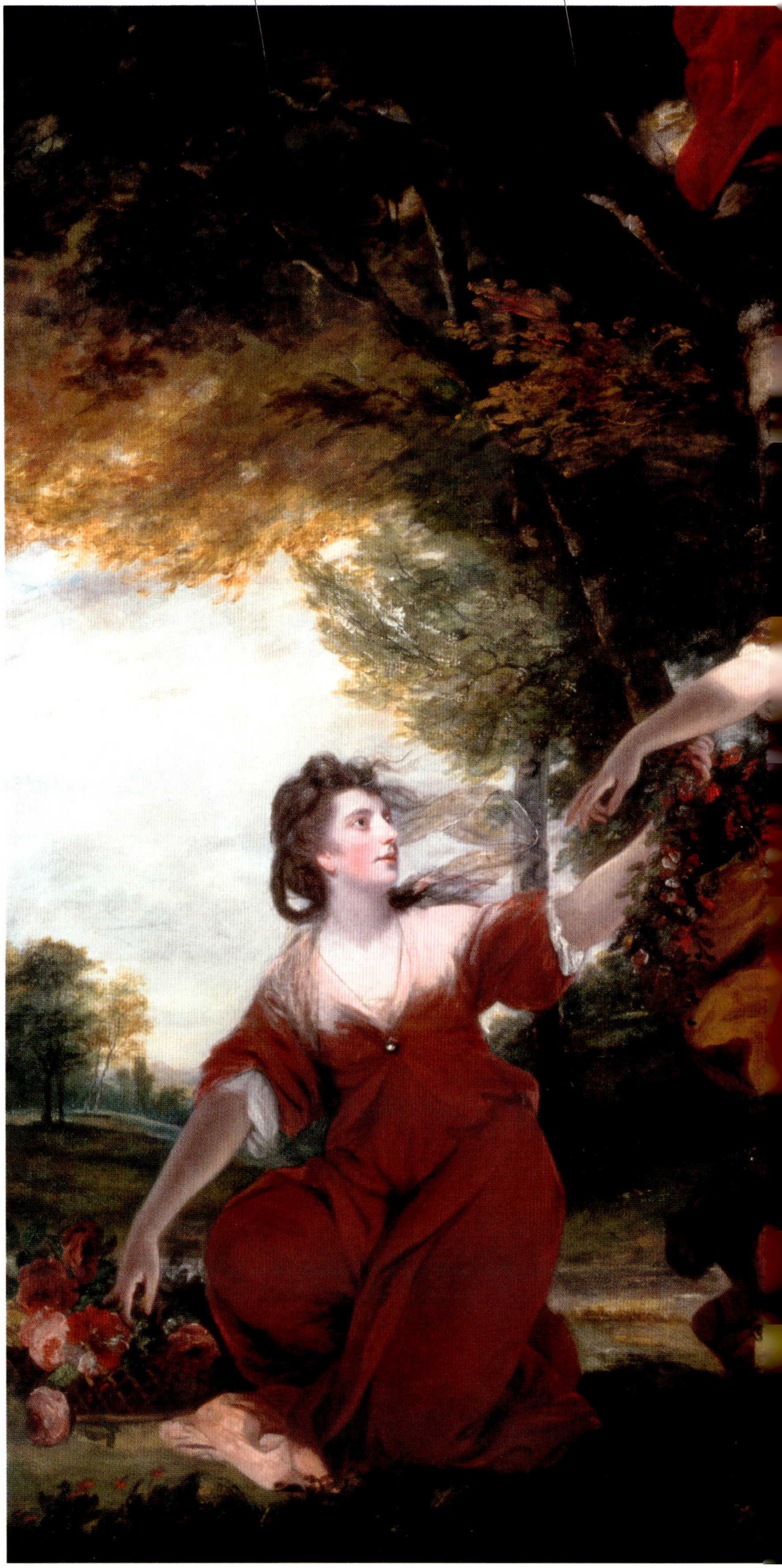

Elizabeth dances in the center.

The oldest sister, Anne, is dressed in white to signify that she is married.

A dark note is struck by the overhanging tree and red drape.

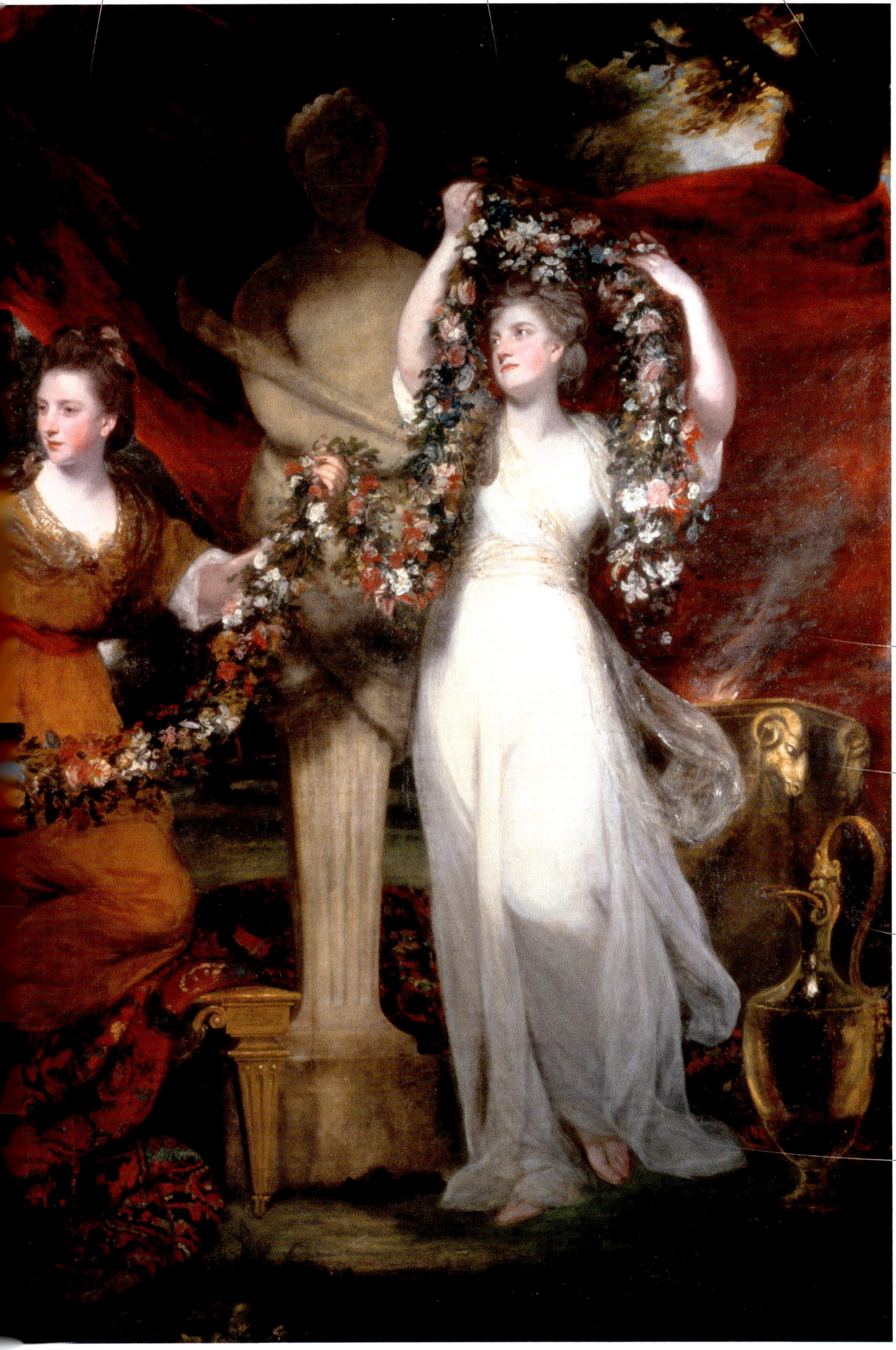

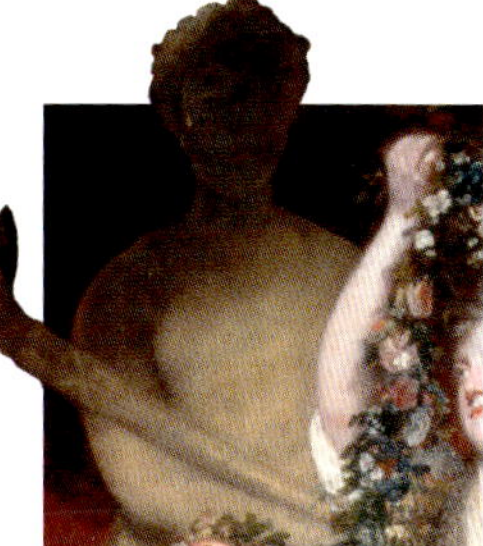

Hymen holds a burning torch, which he carried in wedding processions. A clear flame signified happiness; a smoky flame unhappiness.

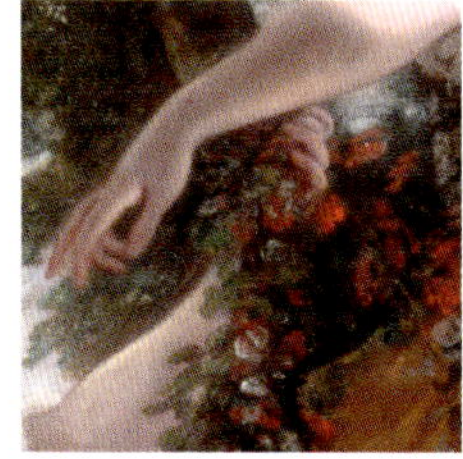

The sisters' outstretched arms echo the serpentine shape of the garland as they lead the viewer's eye from lower left to upper right.

A garland links the sisters in one continuous movement, reinforced by the use of light to foreground the figures.

In the ancient world, rams were associated with sexual potency, fertility, and wealth. They were often sacrificed to the gods.

A carving of Pan, god of the wild, shepherds, and flocks, decorates the wine flagon.

The women's poses are reminiscent of the Three Graces—Mirth, Beauty, and Elegance—of Greek mythology, as seen in historical paintings.

The Tribuna of the Uffizi

Johan Joseph Zoffany 1772–1777, oil on canvas, 49 x 61 in (123.5 x 155 cm), Royal Collection Trust, Windsor Castle, UK

Zoffany's painting re-creates numerous masterpieces from the Grand Duke of Tuscany's art collection, while also lampooning the boorish behavior of the English aristocrats, intellectuals, and other tourists viewing them. Queen Charlotte, who commissioned the work, had asked Zoffany to paint "the Florence Gallery," and reportedly did not appreciate the artist's social commentary or inclusion of socially unimportant sitters.

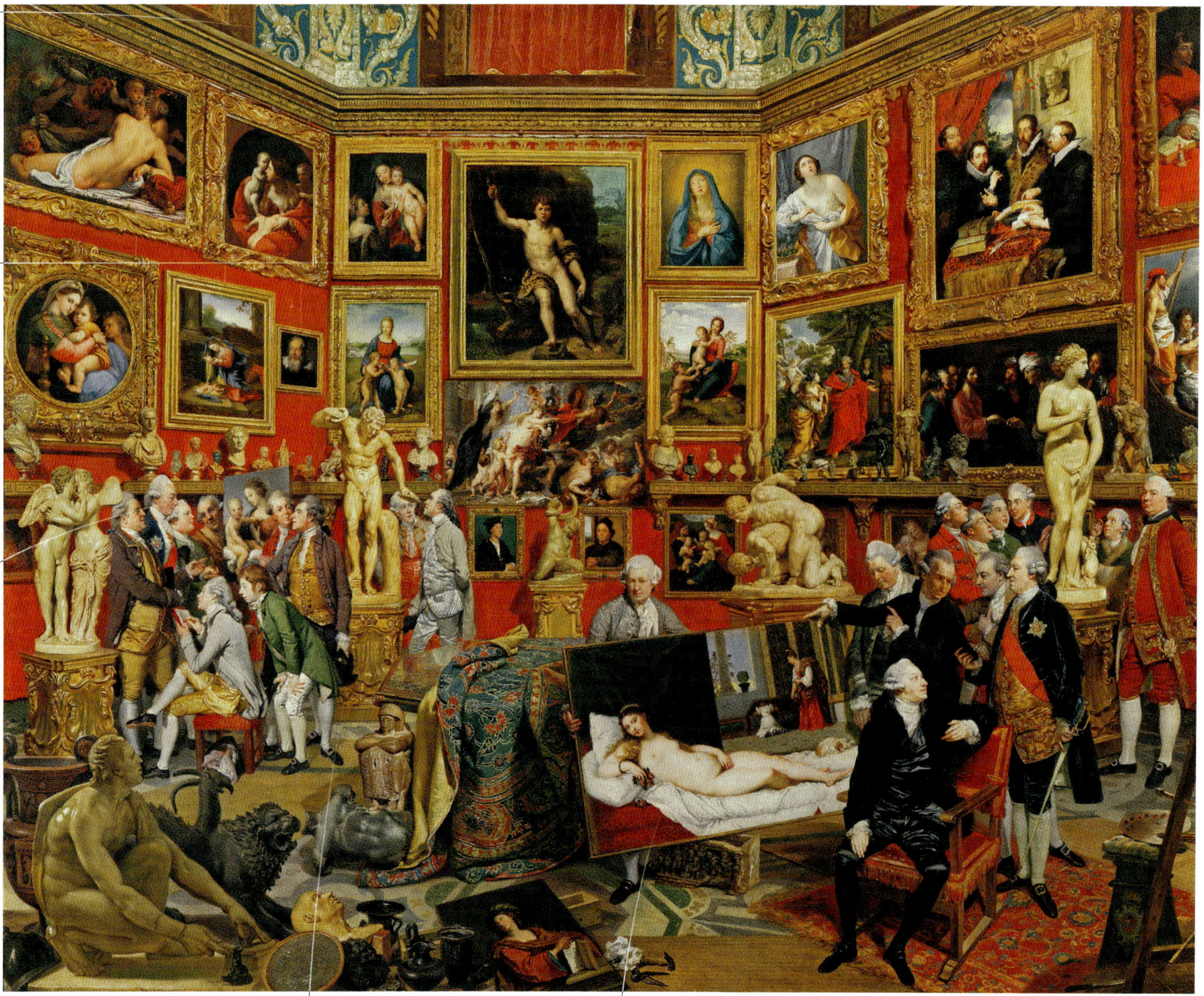

A small part of the domed roof of the Tribuna is visible. The space is octagonal, though Zoffany's painting includes only three of its walls.

Raphael's *Saint John the Baptist as a Boy* has a place of honor in the gallery.

A self-portrait is included. Zoffany holds Raphael's *Niccolini-Cowper Madonna*, a painting he had recently purchased.

Zoffany relocated several sculptures to fit them into this painting.

Titian's *Venus of Urbino* occupies a central position. Pietro Bastianelli, curator of the Uffizi collection, stands immediately behind it.

Several men, including George Finch, the Earl of Winchilsea, lasciviously ogle the rear end of the *Medici Venus*.

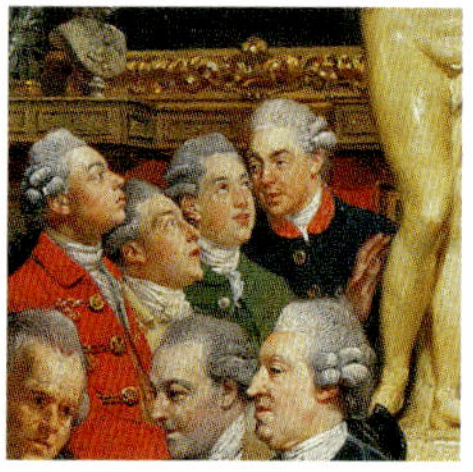

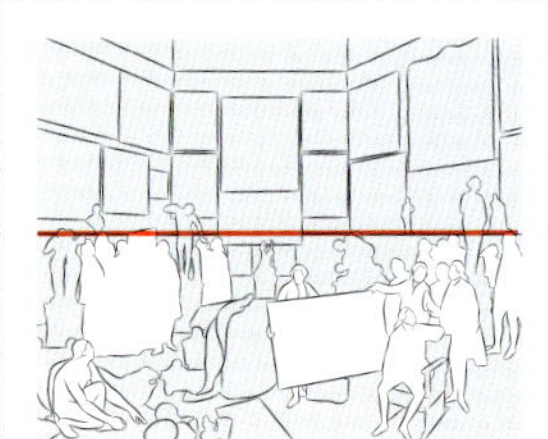

Packed with people
The perspective is skewed—the artwork and people in the foreground appear smaller than they should. Zoffany's priority was to squeeze in as much as possible.

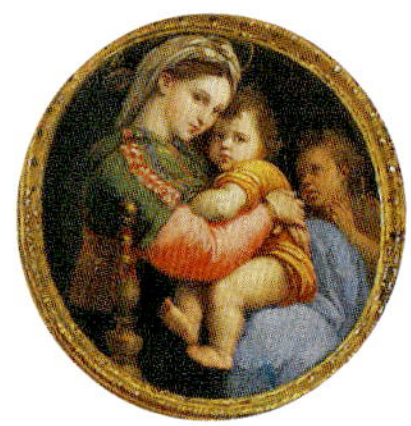

Intricate copies
Zoffany painted with such attention to detail—shown here in Raphael's *Madonna della Seggiola*—that viewers could appreciate the beauty of the paintings without going to Florence.

Watson and the Shark

John Singleton Copley 1778, oil on canvas, 72 × 90 in (182.1 × 229.7 cm), National Gallery of Art, Washington, D.C., US

Copley depicts a real-life moment in 1749 when a shark attacked 14-year-old cabin boy Brook Watson in Havana harbor. The gripping scene freezes time and invites contemplation of Watson's fate. Lauded upon its unveiling, Copley's adept play of light and shadow conveys a fierce struggle between man and nature. The work draws on Biblical themes of resurrection and salvation, with critics also observing references to the transatlantic slave trade and the American Revolution.

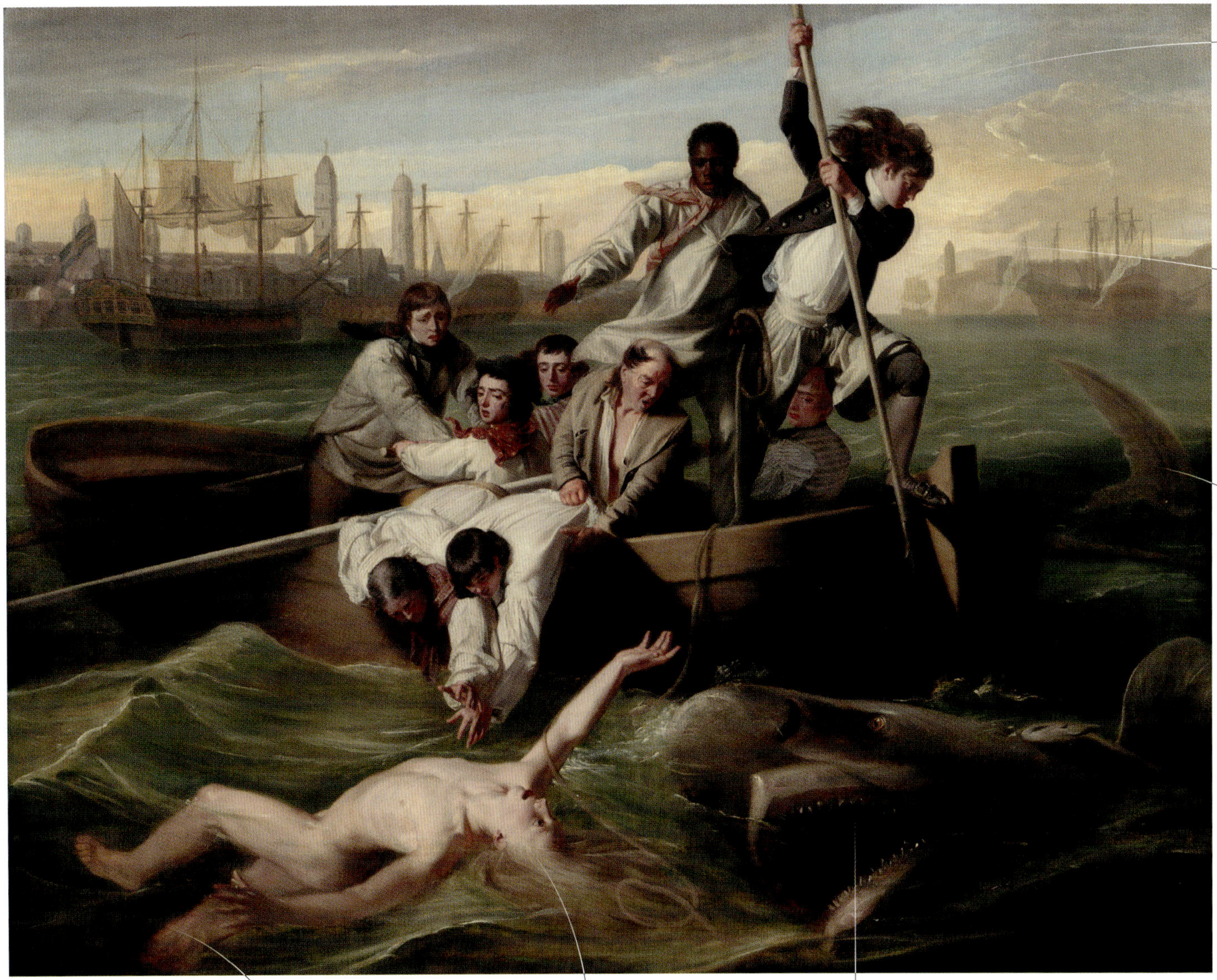

A Black sailor holds Watson's lifeline, contrasting sharply with the lack of mercy given to enslaved Africans during this period.

The harpooner's stance evokes Raphael's depiction of Archangel Michael vanquishing Satan out of heaven.

The shark's tail on the opposite side of the boat suggests that Copley has exaggerated the creature's length.

The bloody water hints at gore beneath the waves but leaves graphic details to the viewer's imagination.

Watson is naked and bathed in light, suggesting a figure of resurrection.

The shark's head, which has lips and forward-facing eyes, reveals Copley's lack of firsthand observation.

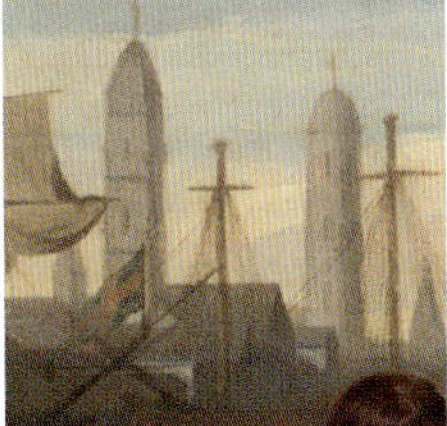

Copley used maps, prints, and engravings, to craft a credible cityscape despite never having visited Cuba.

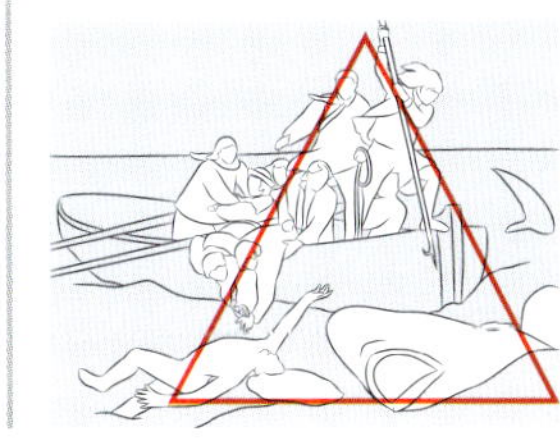

Center of action
Copley maintains equilibrium and symmetry through a pyramidal arrangement, guiding the viewer's focus toward the central point of the attack.

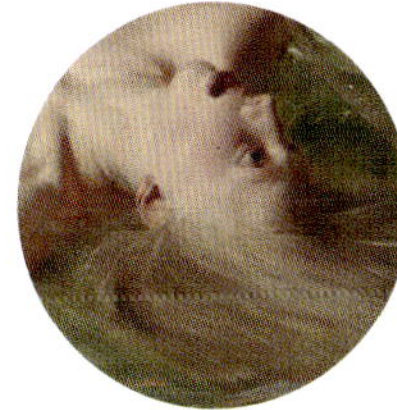

Low perspective
Copley applies a low vantage point, pulling the viewer into the water with Watson and placing them at eye level with the life-and-death struggle.

Pancratium Maritinum

Mary Delany 1778, colored paper, body color, and watercolor on black ink background, 14 × 9 in (35 × 22.2 cm), British Museum, London, UK

At first glance, this image looks like a traditional, painted botanical illustration. In fact, it is composed of tiny slivers of paper cut out and pasted onto a background. Delany, an experienced botanist and botanical artist, produced beautiful and scientifically accurate flower reproductions using a technique that she invented. She called her assemblages "paper mosaiks," a method that came to be known as collage.

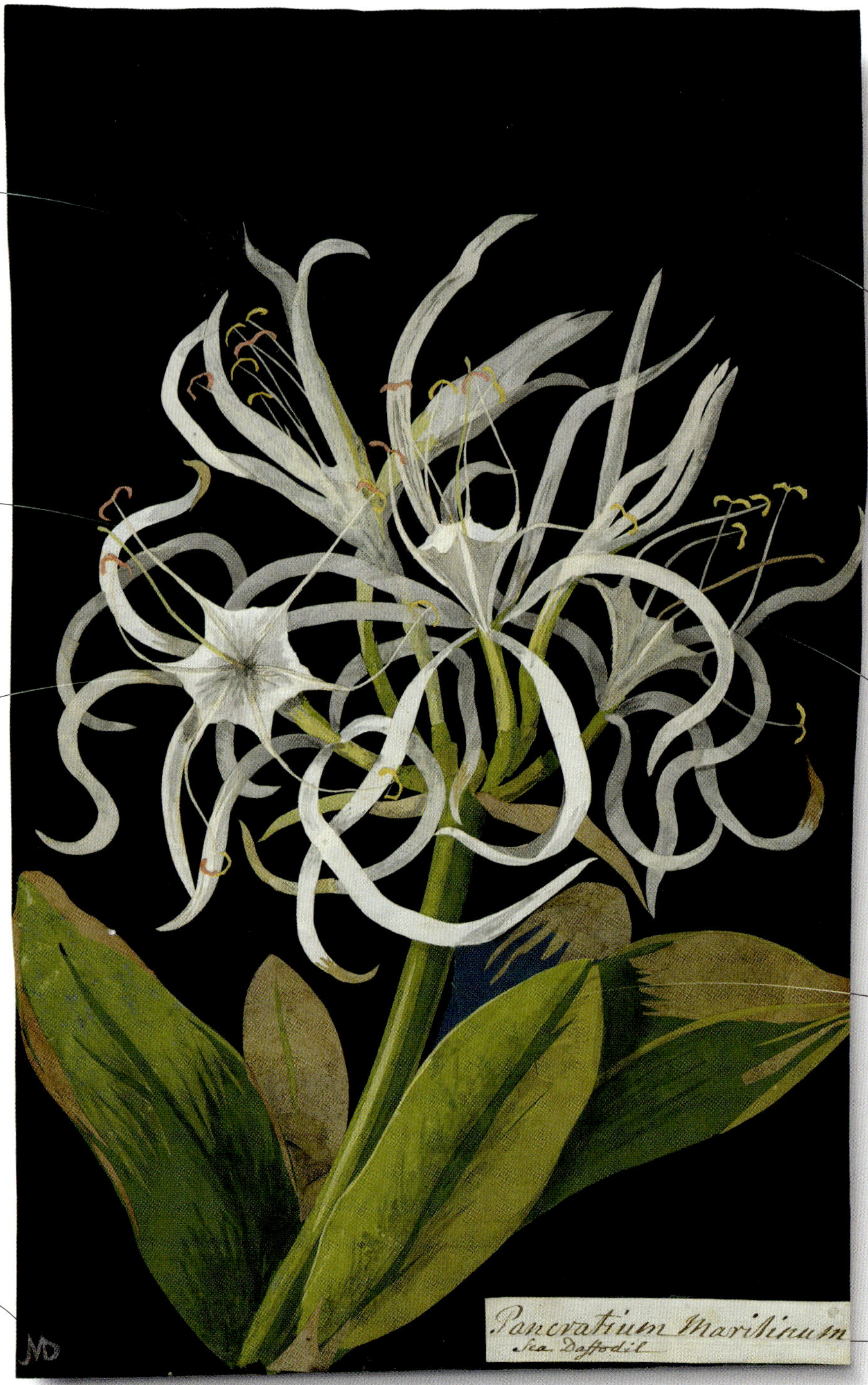

Unlike traditional botanical illustrations, which have a white background, the flower is assembled on a black background for dramatic effect.

Delany used a combination of hand-colored papers and tissue paper.

Nuances of shading were added using watercolor.

The artist has signed the work with a collaged monogram.

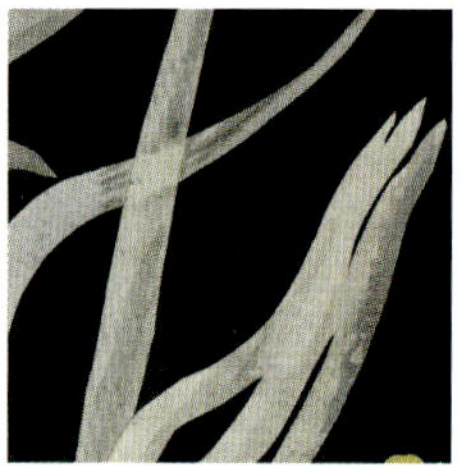

Tiny slivers of paper are cut out and superimposed on top of each other.

The black background was painted first and pieces of paper glued to it. The artist mixed honey into the black paint to enhance its finish.

A thin sliver of a lighter tone is overlaid on darker paper to form a highlight.

The central vein in the leaf is formed from a darker strip of paper.

The artwork is labeled with a variant spelling of the sea daffodil's scientific name—*Pancratium maritimum*.

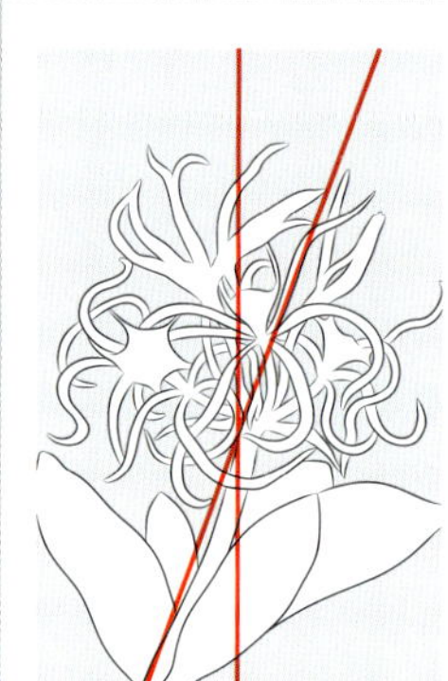

Ideal setting
The flower is centrally placed, with a slight diagonal bend to add a sense of movement. The leaves are arranged around the base so they balance the flower.

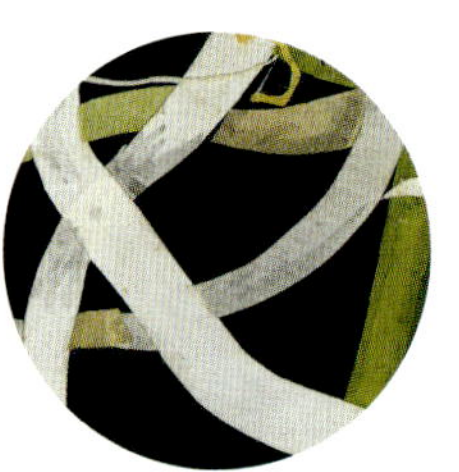

Trick of the light
Light tendrils have been superimposed over progressively darker ones for a three-dimensional feel.

> "I have invented a new way of imitating flowers."
>
> Mary Delany, 1772

Voltaire Seated

Jean-Antoine Houdon 1781, marble, 65 in (165 cm) high, Comédie Française, Paris, France

In this sculpture, Houdon conveys the intellectual authority yet also the physical frailty of the French Enlightenment philosopher Voltaire. The figure is draped in a voluminous cloak, with his hands grasping the arms of the chair. Houdon's expressive sculptures of intellectuals and politicians established him as a preeminent Neoclassical sculptor.

The wig and band tied around his head are typical of men's fashions in the 18th century.

Voltaire's piercing yet sunken eyes reflect his sharp intellect, tempered with the weariness of age.

His upper lip gently presses against his gum as he smiles, indicating a toothless mouth.

Voltaire's gaunt cheeks accentuate his wrinkles, alluding to his age and wisdom.

"One of the most beautiful attributes of the difficult art of statuary is that it preserves forms in all their truth and renders almost imperishable the images of men who have brought their nation glory or happiness."

Jean-Antoine Houdon

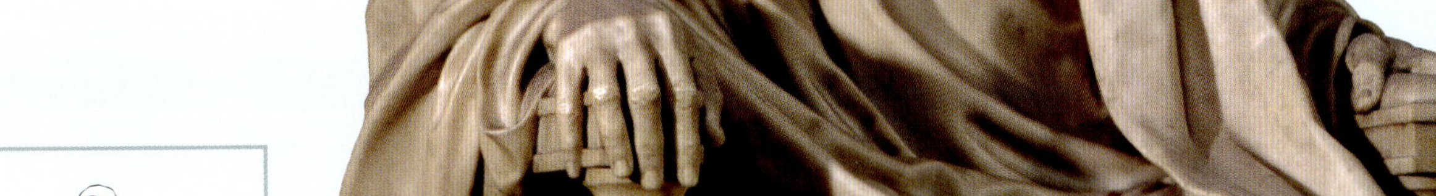

The feet are firmly grounded. One peeps out from his robe, as if he were about to rise from the chair.

Voltaire sits on a plinth with his name inscribed on the front, reminding the viewer of the philosopher's legacy.

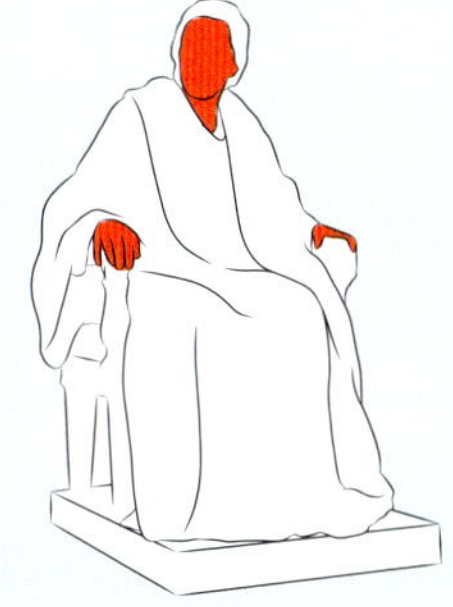

Visual contradiction
The bulkiness and weight of the drapery contrast with Voltaire's fragile and emaciated body, particularly his cheeks, throat, and bony fingers.

Careful positioning
Although Voltaire's shoulders and neck are centrally grounded, he turns to the side, as if lost in thought, adding a sense of movement to the static composition.

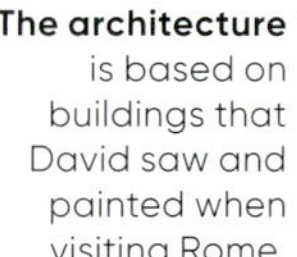

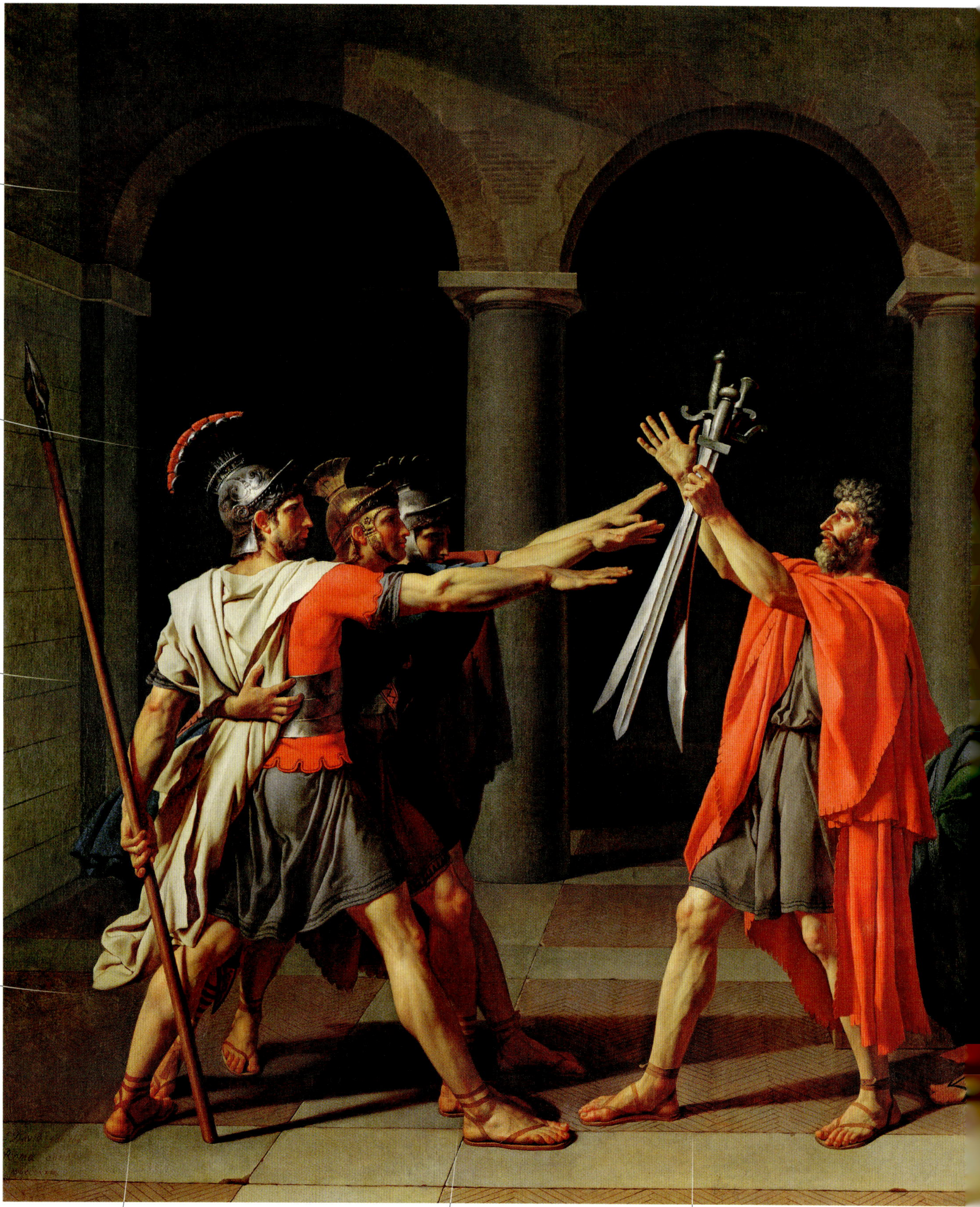

The architecture is based on buildings that David saw and painted when visiting Rome.

Chiaroscuro is used to draw attention to the foreground, emphasizing the figures' contours and expressions.

The men assume a rigid, upright posture that mirrors the columns behind them.

Muscular arms and legs form a triangular shape, emphasizing determination, stability, and unity.

The subject matter is arranged in threes—three fighters, swords, arches, and women—mirroring the triangular motifs.

David forges life-size figures on a canvas of monumental scale, depicting musculature with meticulous precision.

A single curved sword foreshadows one sole survivor among the brothers.

Oath of the Horatii

Jacques-Louis David 1784–1785, oil on canvas, 130 × 167 in (329.8 × 424.8 cm), Louvre, Paris, France

David's seminal work marks a milestone in French Neoclassicism. Rejecting Rococo ornamentation and drawing on classical elements and Enlightenment ideals, it depicts an episode in Roman legend—the solemn oath-taking before their father of the Horatii brothers, who vow to defend Rome against the Curiatii brothers of neighboring Alba Longa. David champions patriotism, honor, and civic duty over allegiance to family and the Church. The painting resonated deeply with a disenfranchised France, emerging as an icon for the looming Revolution and ultimately cementing David as a leading propagandist for the Napoleonic Empire.

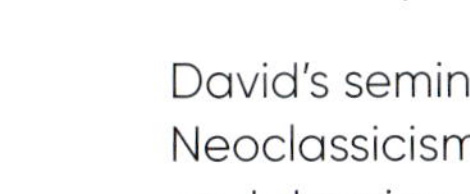

Crowning the columns are Doric capitals, considered the most masculine order in classical architecture.

Stoic gazes convey the gravity of the brothers' oath and the burden of their responsibility.

Connected through blood and marriage to both families, the women embody a scenario where no true winners prevail.

The curvilinear posture of the women contrasts with the men's verticality, echoing the arches upheld by the columns.

The children are being comforted: the young girl hides her face while the boy refuses to have his eyes shielded.

Vanishing point
The upright swords mark a central vanishing point in perspective composition. The arms, central arch, and converging lines of the walls and checkerboard floor all lead to this point.

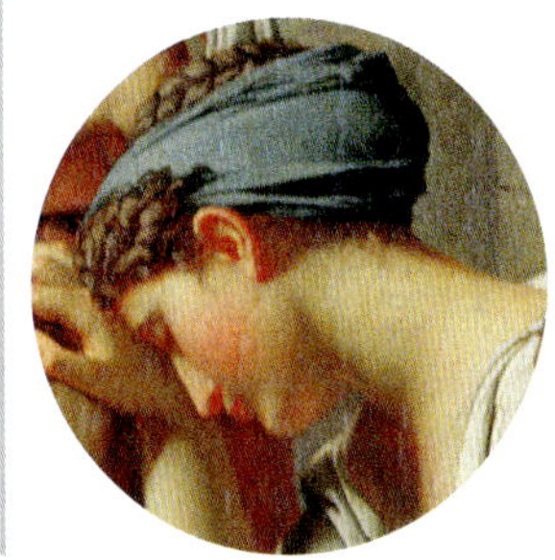

True to life
In a manner typical of Neoclassicism, David used very fine brushes to conceal brushstrokes and achieve a controlled, sculptural quality and photographic realism in his figures.

> "[This is] the moment which must have preceded the battle, when the elder Horatius, gathering his sons in their family home, makes them swear to conquer or die."
>
> Jacques-Louis David

Portrait of a Youth in an Embroidered Vest

Marie-Victoire Lemoine 1785, oil on canvas, 65.1 × 54.6 cm, Cummer Museum, Jacksonville, Florida, US

By portraying a young boy of African descent engaging confidently with the viewer, Lemoine challenges the convention of portraying Black figures waiting upon their white enslavers. Yet his opulent clothing would have been chosen to elevate the standing of the family to whom he is enslaved rather than his own status. He was probably a page or doorman to a wealthy household.

Warm brown tones in the background reflect and enhance the sitter's complexion.

Delicate curls on the boy's head stand out against the soft background.

The muted, hazy backdrop focuses the viewer's gaze on the subject.

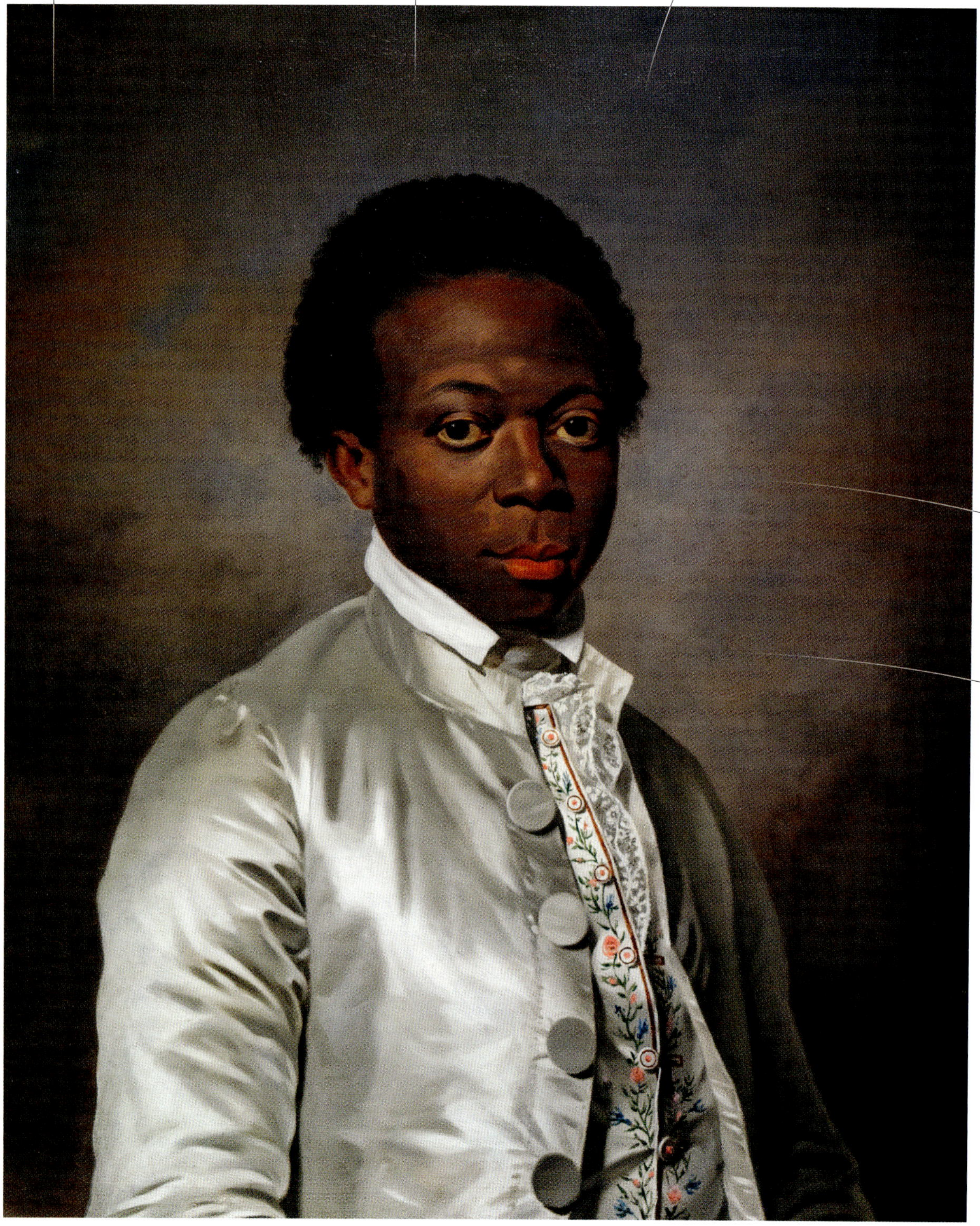

Light comes from the front left, casting a gentle shadow over the opposite side of the boy's face.

The crisp, white collar contrasts with the dark skin tone. This would have added to his "exoticism" in the European imagination.

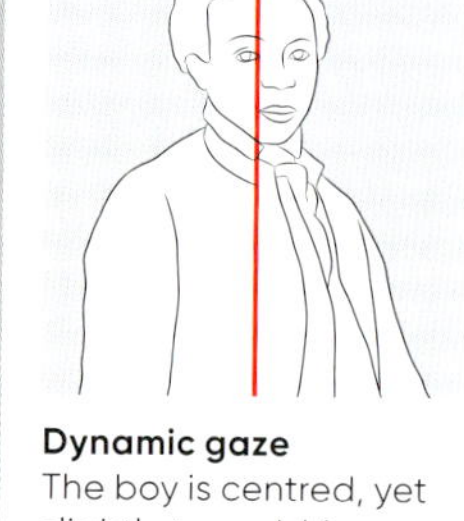

Dynamic gaze
The boy is centred, yet slightly turned, his gaze directed towards the viewer, adding a subtle dynamism to the otherwise static composition.

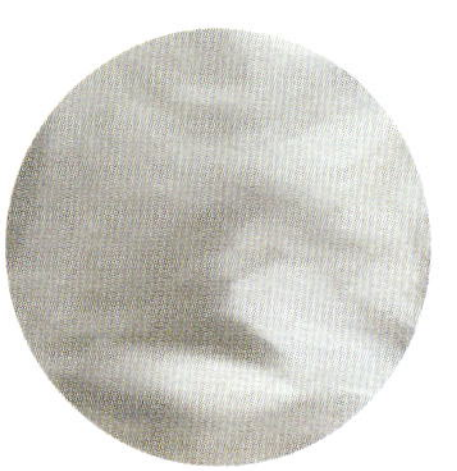

Creating texture
The paint is applied with broad brushstrokes, wet-on-wet and loosely blended, to create the smooth, silky texture of the figure's coat.

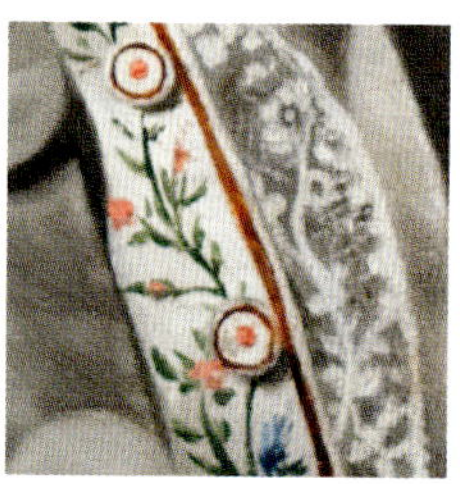

Ornate embroidery on clothing was popular among affluent Frenchmen, who dressed their servants in a similar fashion.

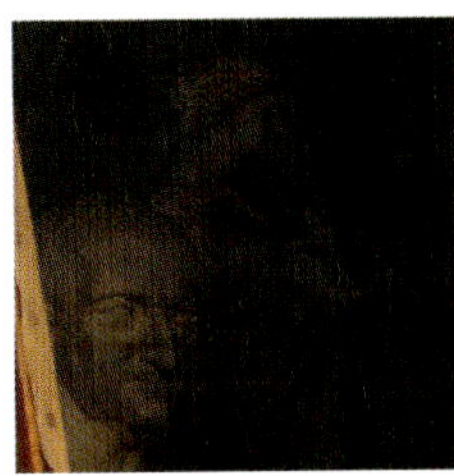

Statues at the back of the studio demonstrate the importance of classical sculpture in art education at the time.

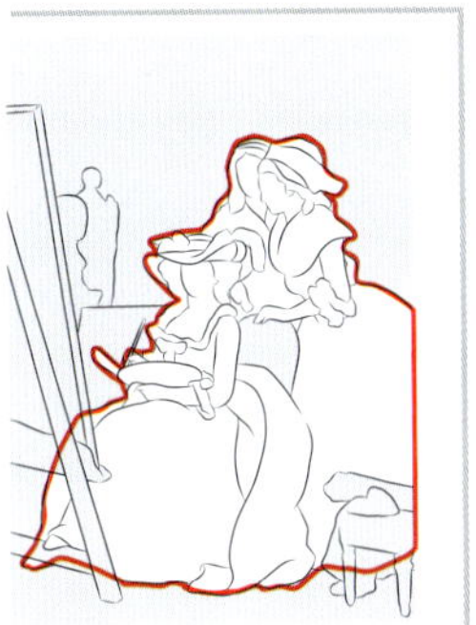

Inspiration
The grouping of the women is reminiscent of the *Three Graces*, the subject of many Renaissance paintings, but here, the women are creators rather than subjects.

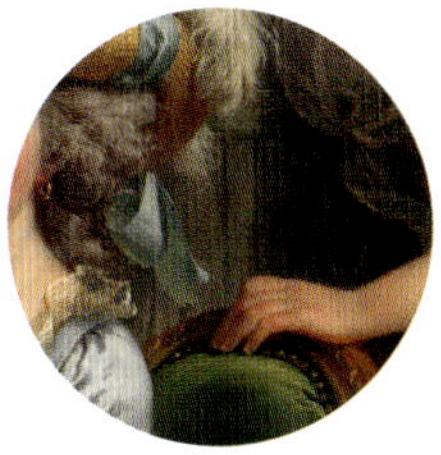

Intricate detail
Small touches of thick white paint on the lace; thin, translucent washes on the scarf; and delicate wisps of hair show the artist's ability to imitate textures.

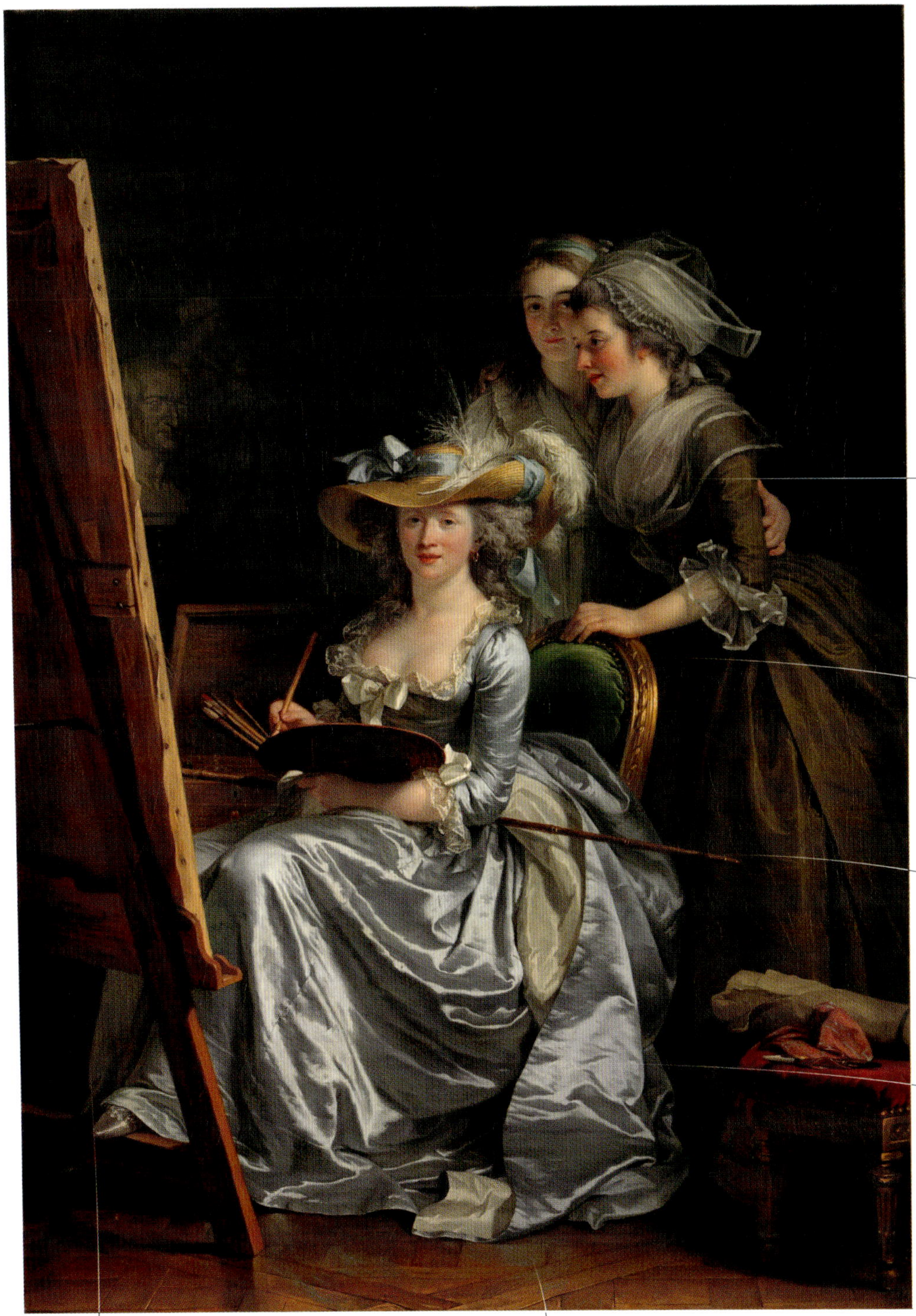

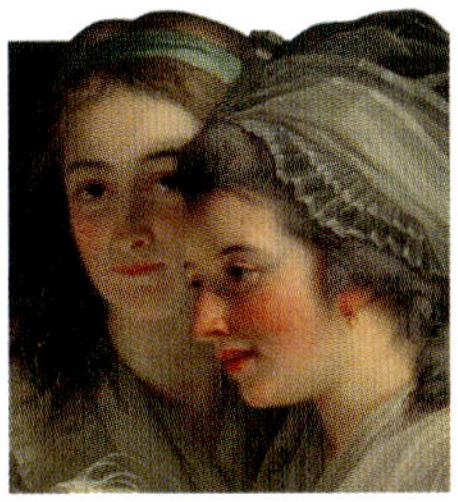

The two pupils are Marie Marguerite Carreaux de Rosemond (left) and Marie Gabrielle Capet (right).

The two students wear simpler styles of dress in muted colours typical of the Neoclassical style.

The artist sits at a large canvas, gazing out towards the viewer, as if she is painting them.

A mahlstick, a light stick with a soft leather or padded ball at one end, was used by painters to support and steady the working hand.

Labille-Guiard wears a sumptuous, Rococo-style dress and straw hat, in keeping with her status as an academician and society portrait painter.

Labille-Guiard's signature adorns the back of her easel, proof of her artistic activity.

The polished parquet floor reflects the shimmering blue dress, as does the underside of the palette.

Self-Portrait with Two Pupils

Adélaïde Labille-Guiard 1785, oil on canvas, 210.8 × 151.1 cm, Metropolitan Museum of Art, New York, US

An advocate for art training for women, Labille-Guiard, whose portraits were celebrated for their naturalism, portrays herself as a successful artist. She highlights her teaching role, too, at a time when the French Royal Academy, who admitted her in 1783, allowed only four female members and excluded them from its classes.

A client waits in another room, casting a shadow on the screen. A courtesan stands at the door, about to enter.

Boats float on a calm sea as clouds waft over the moon.

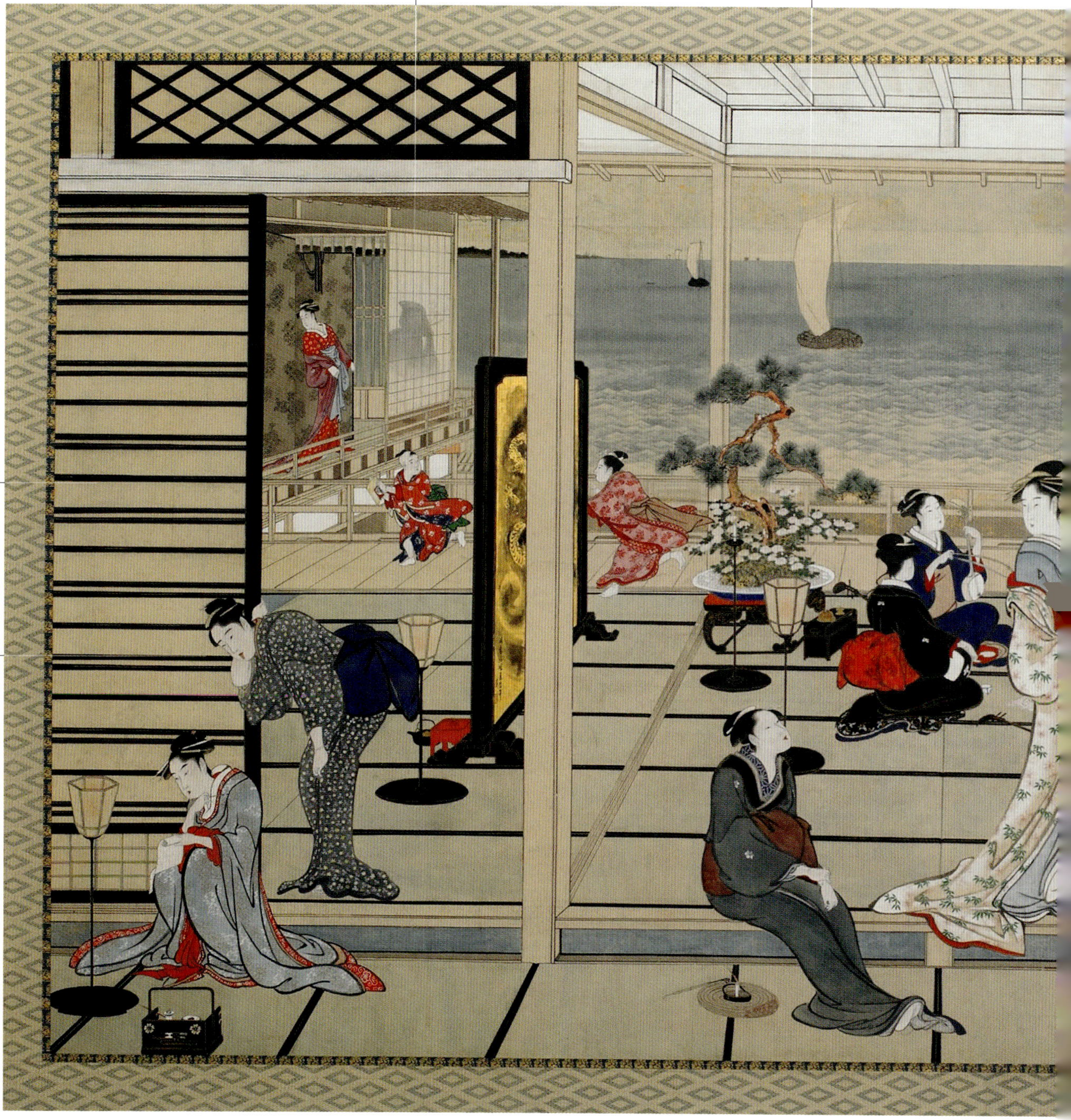

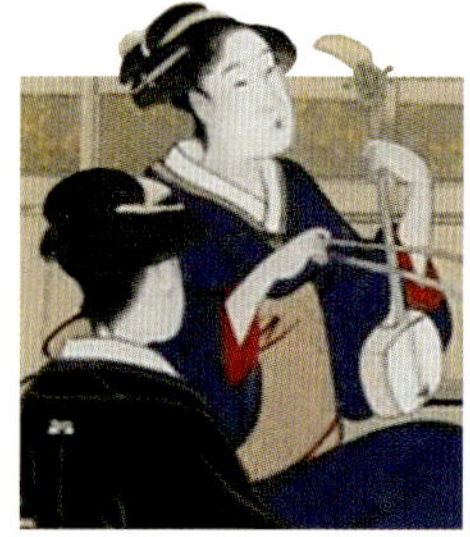

Geishas prepare to entertain guests with traditional musical instruments—a *shamisen*, played like a banjo; a *kokyu* (a small *shamisen* played with a bow); and a *koto*, played on a flat surface.

Sliding doors separate the veranda from the interior of the building.

A maid stands behind her mistress, who is reading a letter.

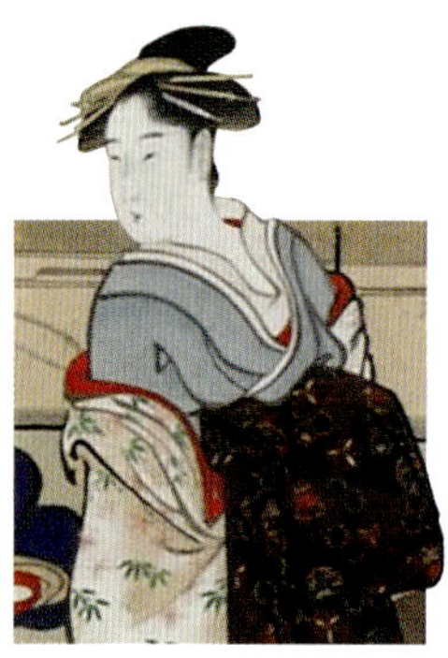

Courtesans wore obi sashes, which tied at the front, and often had many hair ornaments.

Moon at Shinagawa

Kitagawa Utamaro Late 1780s–early 1800s, hanging scroll, ink and mineral colors on paper, 58 × 126 in (148 × 321 cm), Freer Gallery of Art, Washington, D.C., US

This painting was originally part of a triptych celebrating Edo's three famous pleasure districts, Shinagawa, Yoshiwara, and Fukagawa, using the traditional theme of Snow, Moon, and Flowers. In this work, the scene is the elegant Sagamiya pleasure house in Shinagawa, near Edo (the old Japanese name for Tokyo). As the moon rises, five courtesans, several geisha, and a number of maids prepare to entertain the evening's clients. The women are all intent on their own activities, such as reading, playing instruments, chatting, carrying a tea tray, and lighting an oil lamp. Meanwhile, at the back of the room, a maid chases a mischievous boy while a courtesan looks out over the bay beyond.

The moon is associated with an appreciation of beauty.

This framed poem by Ōta Nampo (1749–1823) uses nature metaphors to ponder the passage of time.

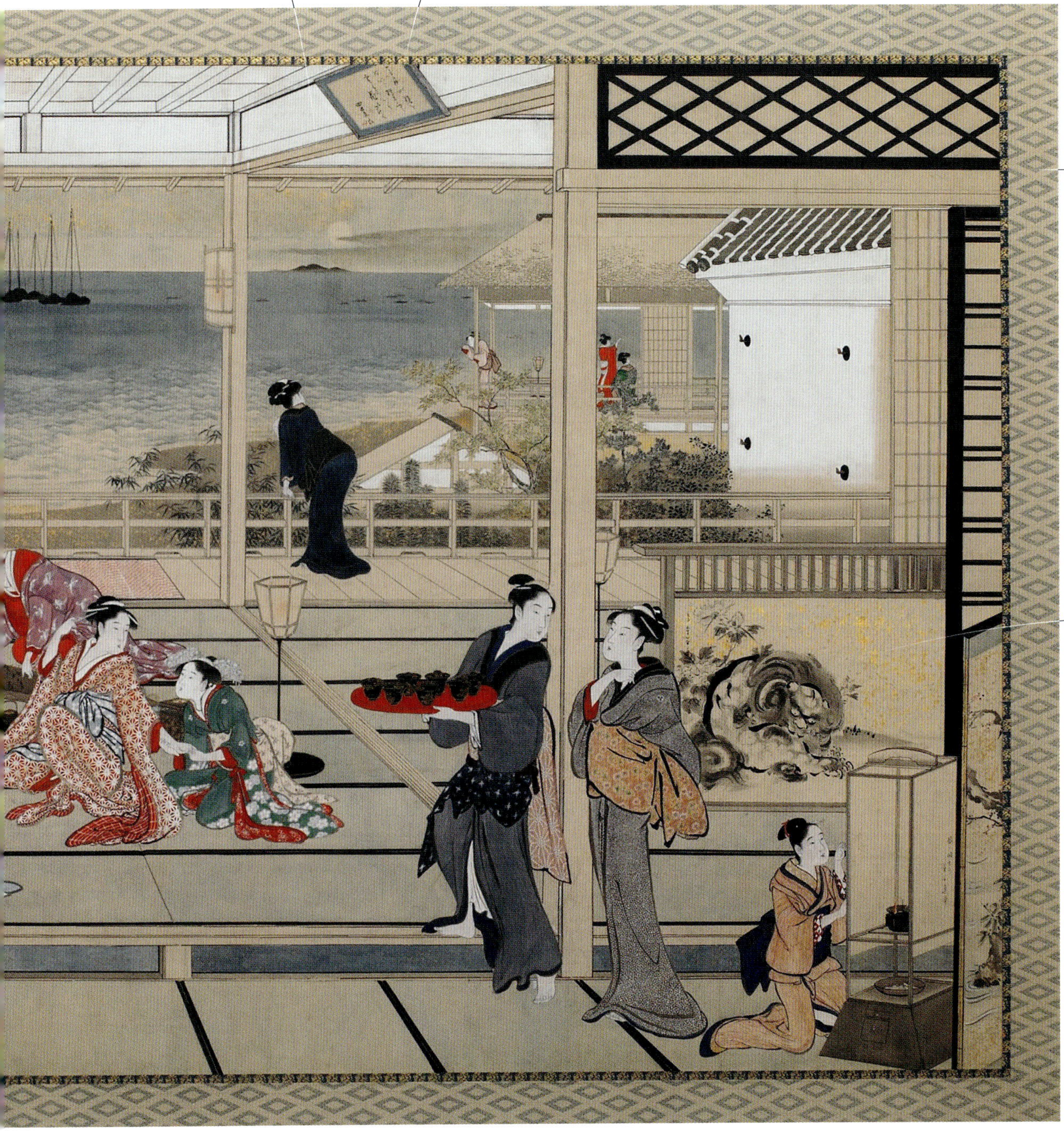

The painting was originally mounted as a hanging scroll, a traditional mounting that can be rolled up and stored. In Europe in the 1880s, it was remounted with a Western frame.

An ink painting (*sumi-e*) decorates the single panel standing screen (*tsuitate*) that divides the space.

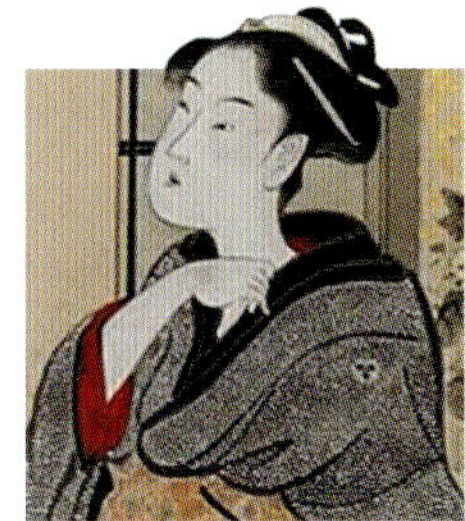

One woman, probably a servant, wears the family crest of Zenno Ihē, the merchant who commissioned Utamaro.

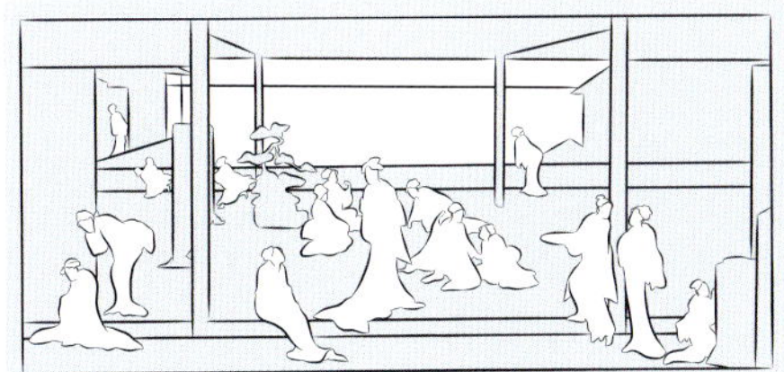

Composition
The building's architecture draws the eye through the room to the view of the bay, while strong vertical figures highlight areas of interest along the way.

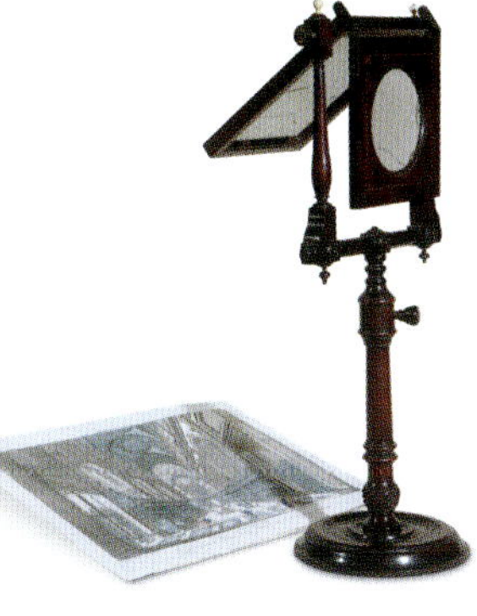

Perspective
This is a *uki-e* (perspective picture). In the 18th century, the Dutch introduced European science to Japan. Optical devices, such as this zograscope (used to give flat prints an illusion of depth) were imported, and artists experimented with European ways of depicting space.

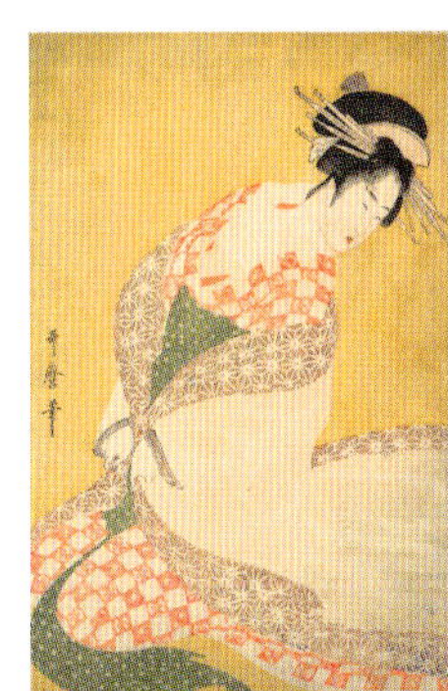

Images of beauty
Flourishing from the 17th to 19th centuries, *ukiyo-e* (pictures of the floating world) featured many images of beauty. Utamaro, among its most famous artists, is best known for woodblock prints of courtesans.

Tomb of Pope Clement XIV

Antonio Canova 1783–1787, marble, 291 in (740 cm) high, Santi Apostoli, Rome, Italy

Rejecting the twisting figures and complex compositions of Baroque sculpture, Canova based his figures on classical Greek statues, preferring their balance and simplicity. This shift to a Neoclassical style was not his only innovation. Previous funerary monuments celebrated the qualities of the deceased. Here, Canova concentrates attention on the grief of the two female figures in the foreground.

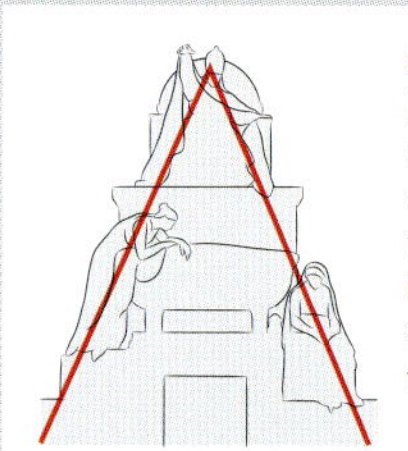

Composition
Pope Clement sits at the apex of a cone. The two female figures balance each other while leading the eye upward.

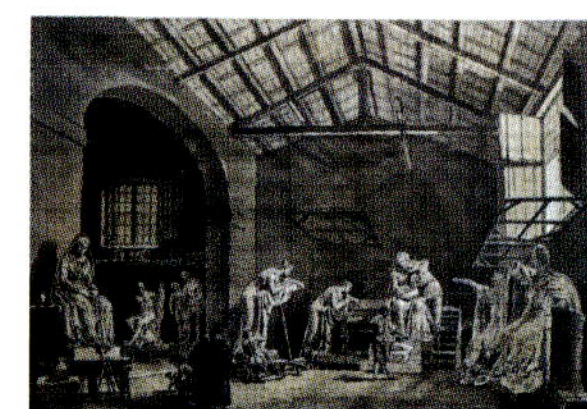

Studio support
Canova began with a detailed clay model, which he scaled up to full size and then cast in plaster to use as a guide. Assistants produced the initial carving, and Canova did the detailed carving and finishing.

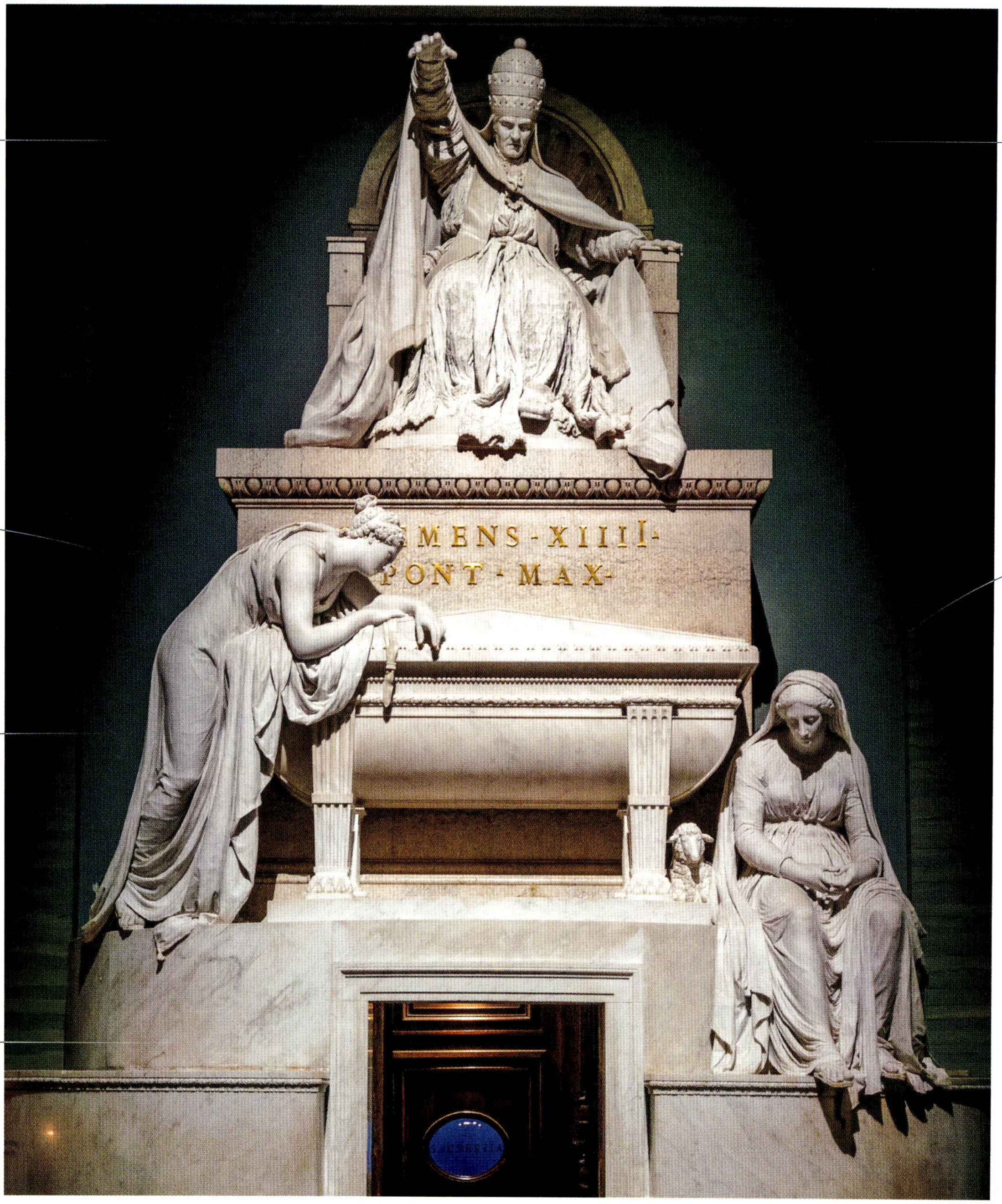

Clement XIV sits atop the monument, his arm outstretched in blessing.

Canova used white Carrara marble for the three figures and the base in a bid to create simple, elegant figures to be gazed on with reverence.

A female figure personifying Temperance caresses the sarcophagus, unwilling to accept the pontiff's death.

The sacristy door was a preexisting element that the artist incorporated into the monument.

The Pope's chair is carved in lumachella, or "fire marble," a pink-tinged rock composed of fossilized snails and clamshells.

Humility is represented by the right-hand figure. She faces forward, her hands clasped and her eyes looking down in quiet contemplation.

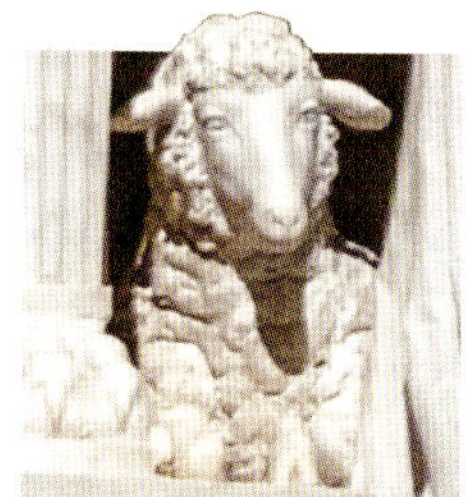

A lamb, the symbol of Christ, sits beside the statue of Humility.

Invention of the Art of Drawing

Joseph-Benoît Suvée 1791, oil on canvas, 105 × 52 in (267 × 131.5 cm), Groeningemuseum, Bruges, Belgium

According to classical myth, Dibutades, the daughter of the Greek potter Butades, created the first drawing when she traced the outline of her lover's shadow on a wall. Suvée illustrates this story in a pure Neoclassical style of simple lines and muted colors. He was an astute draftsman, and the painting pays homage to drawing as an art form.

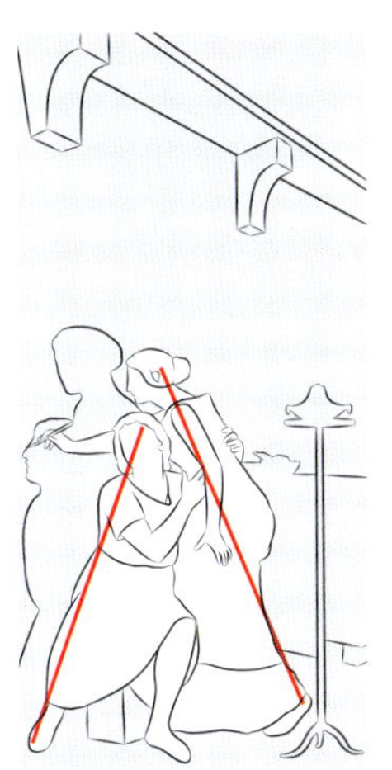

Dynamic effect
Strong diagonal lines following the contours of the two figures create a sense of energy and movement.

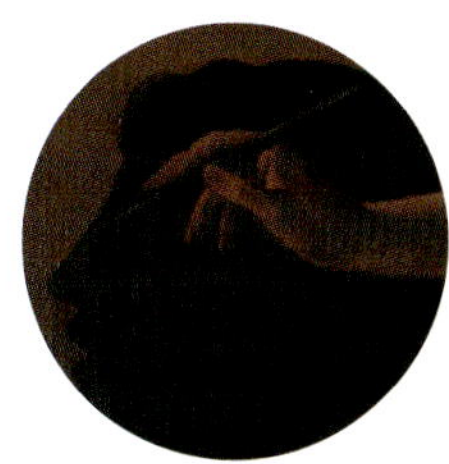

Emphasis on line
The woman draws around the outline of the shadow, indicating the importance of line in Neoclassical painting

A stone wall and wooden beams create a perspectival grid onto which the woman draws the shadow.

Dibutades traces her lover's shadow in order to remember him clearly while he is away.

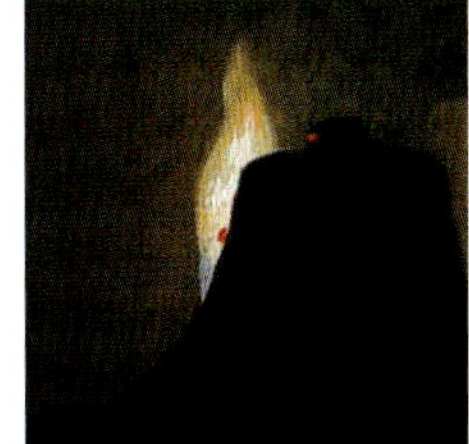

A single flame, almost hidden from the viewer, casts an intense light over the couple.

A strong contrast between light and dark adds a sense of drama to the illicit meeting.

The woman's white robe stands out against the muted colors of the interior, focusing the viewer's attention on her.

Folds in the drapery have a sculptural quality. Drawing from classical sculptures was a key part of an artist's training.

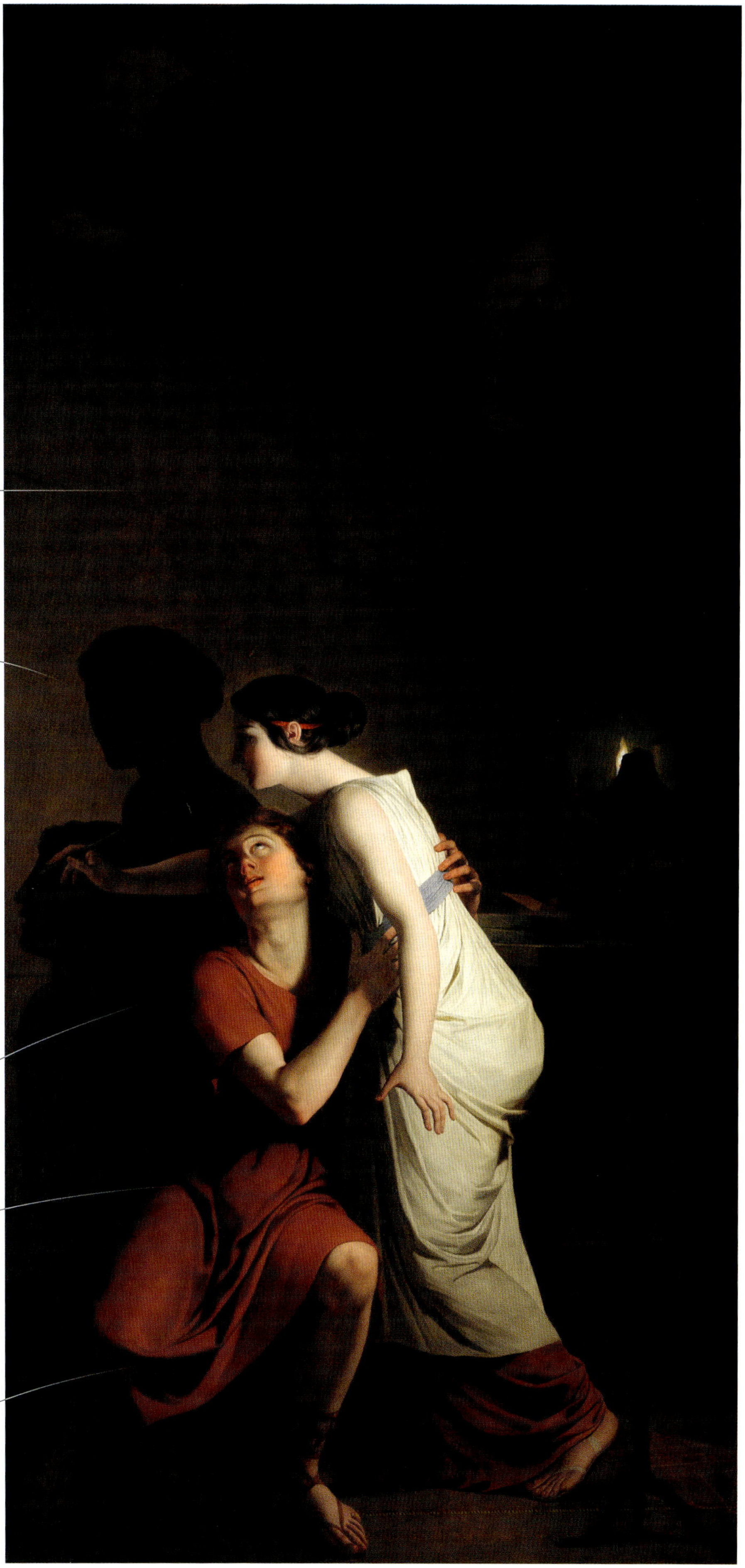

The Nightmare

Henry Fuseli 1790–1791, oil on canvas, 30 × 25 in (77 × 64 cm), Goethe Museum, Frankfurt, Germany

In this dramatic and haunting painting, Fuseli gives shape to the dreams tormenting a sleeping woman. His use of tenebrism (juxtaposition of dark and light) enhances the mysterious, ghostly ambience. The scene had an immediate, powerful impact on its viewers, reflecting an emerging fascination with Gothic horror.

The nocturnal palette gives the work a darkly lyrical quality, characteristic of the Gothic horror subgenre of Romanticism.

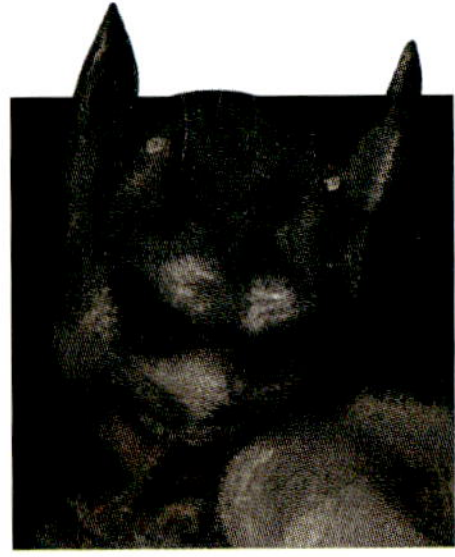

Perched on her chest, the apelike incubus (a demon said to seek sex with sleeping women), adds a sinister, sexual element to the painting.

The woman's swooning pose may reflect theories about "hysteria," a medical diagnosis that was later associated with female sexual frustration.

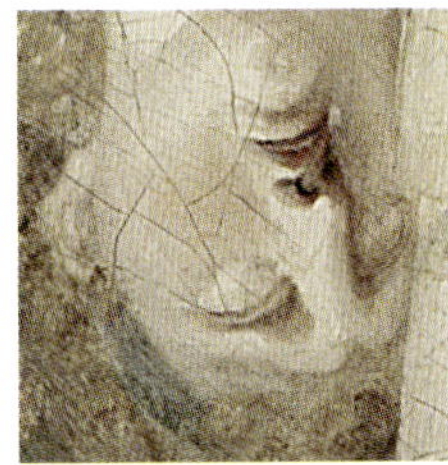

Fuseli offers a voyeuristic glimpse into the mental state of the woman as she sleeps—an insight into the fears that haunt her dreams.

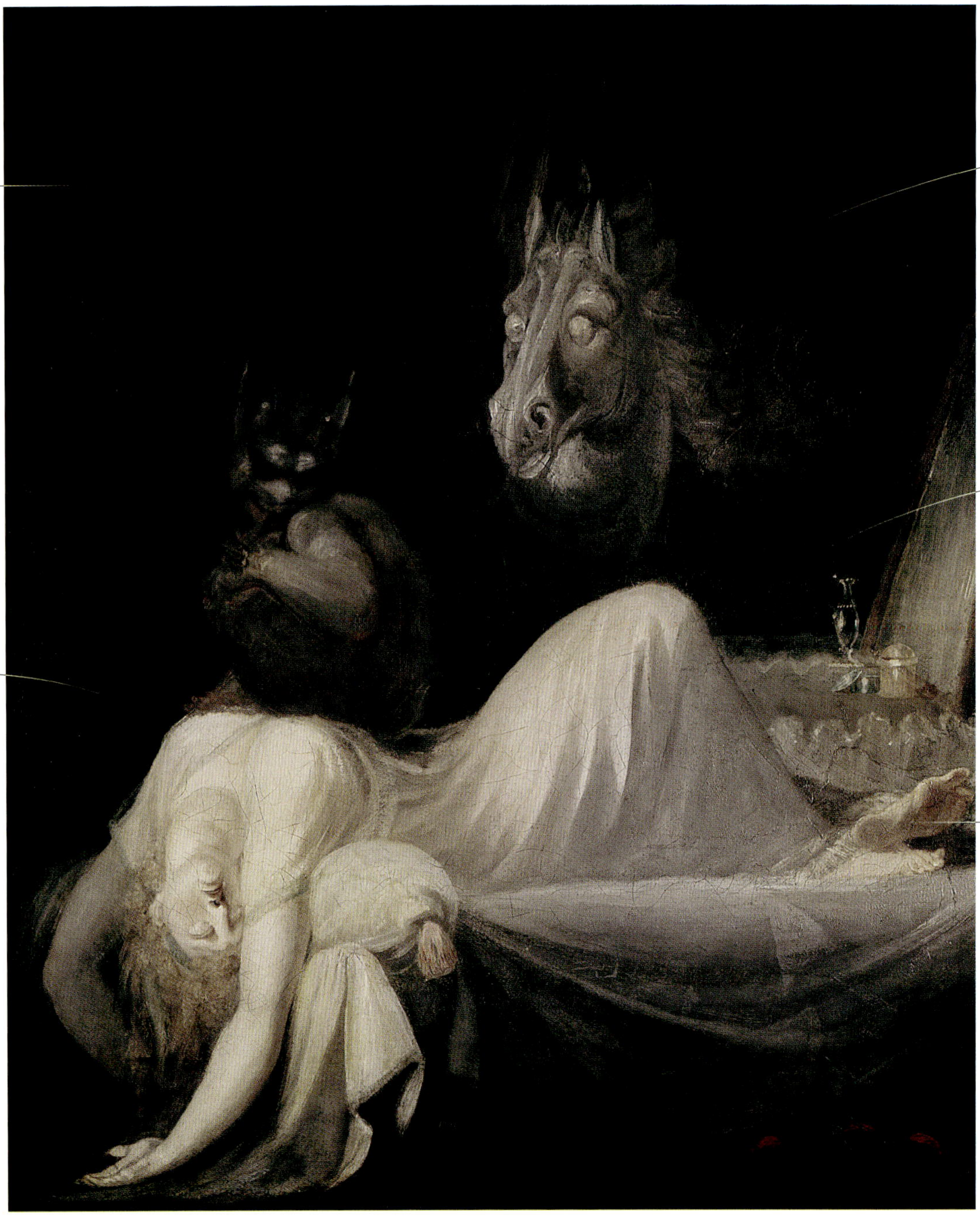

A ghostly horse, interpreted as male sexual power or an evil "mare" spirit, adds to the melodramatic atmosphere.

The white dress suggests purity and vulnerability. It also reflects the spiritual nature of dreams and imagination.

The woman's curved and contorted body suggests discomfort and restlessness, indicating the disturbing emotions and twisted reality that bad dreams can conjure.

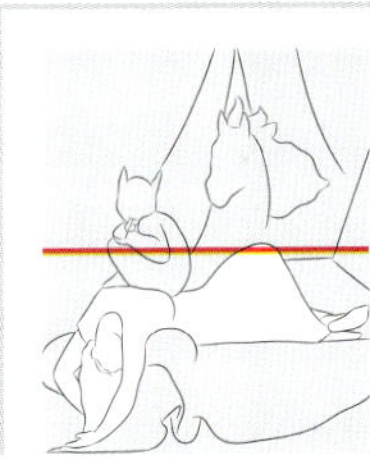

Symbolic contrast
The top half of the painting—the realm of the woman's nightmare—is shrouded in darkness, while her figure is bathed in light, symbolizing the transitional space between sleep and wakefulness.

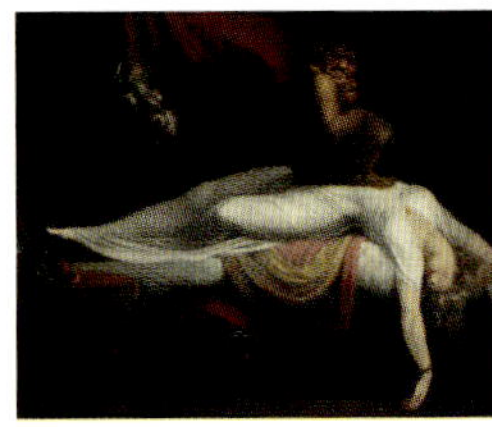

First version, 1781
Fuseli created many versions of *The Nightmare*. The first, deemed shocking by critics when it was exhibited at London's Royal Academy in 1782, attracted thousands of viewers. Prints were produced that the public could afford to buy.

> "One of the most unexplored regions of art are dreams."
>
> Henry Fuseli

Rice Threshing

Kim Hong-do 18th century, ink on paper, 11 × 9 in (28 × 23.9 cm), National Museum of Korea, Seoul, South Korea

With animated faces, peasants collect and transport sheaves of rice before threshing it on stones. They are overseen by their master, in the top right corner, who is relaxing and smoking his long pipe. This is a page from an album of 25 genre scenes in which the artist depicted the everyday life of his time.

One figure seems more downcast, perhaps tired from his work.

The blank background, with no landscape detail, focuses attention on the action.

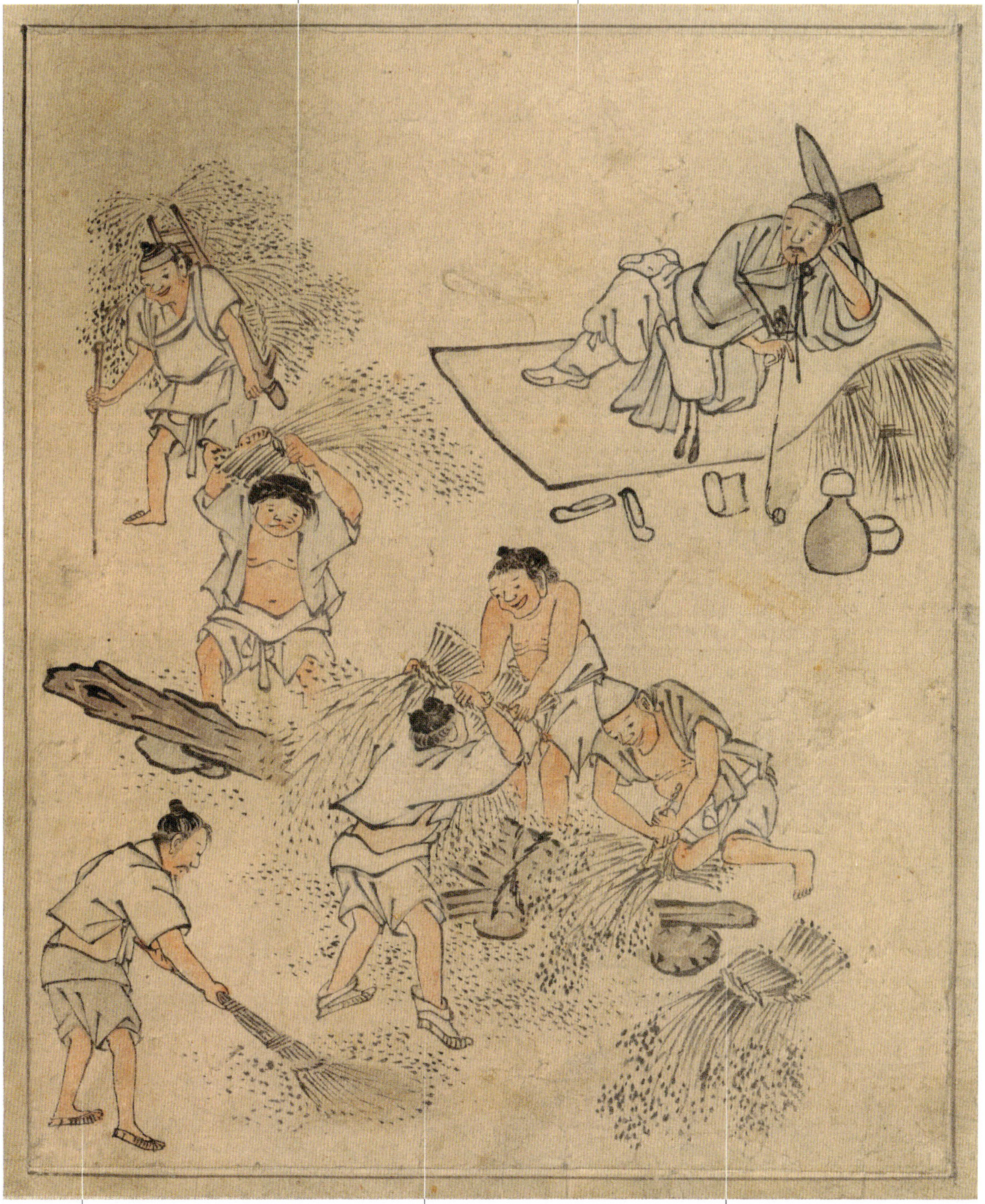

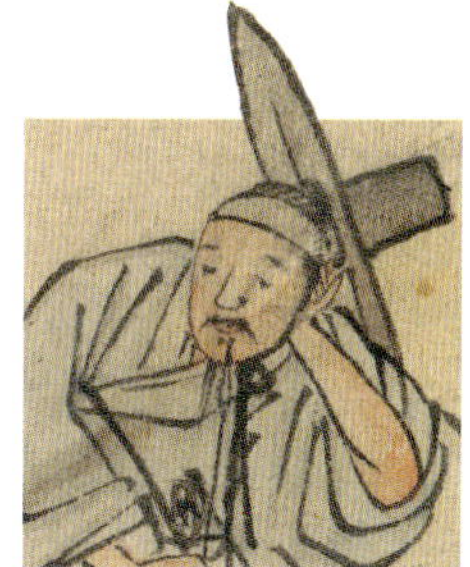

Lounging on a mat, the landowner remains apart from the workers. He wears a *gat*, a traditional Korean hat, and smokes a *gombangdae*, a long bamboo pipe.

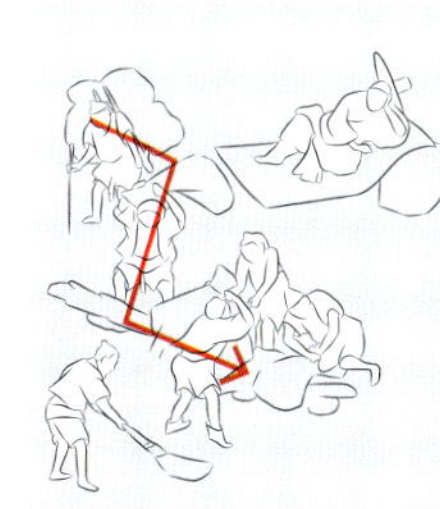

Composition
The zigzag positioning of the workers injects movement into the image, and guides the narrative from the delivery of the sheaves (top left) to threshing (bottom right).

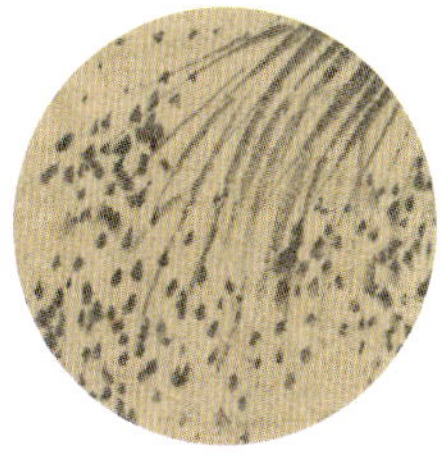

Brushstrokes
The artist created rich texture with minimal detail by varying the brushstrokes, from stippling (dotting) for rice grains to straight lines for stems, and flowing lines to outline the figures.

The limited palette of muted blues and flesh tones adds to the simplicity of the scene.

Figures are outlined with thin black lines, a necessity due to the restricted use of color.

Most of the workers look cheerful, suggesting they enjoy the communal activity.

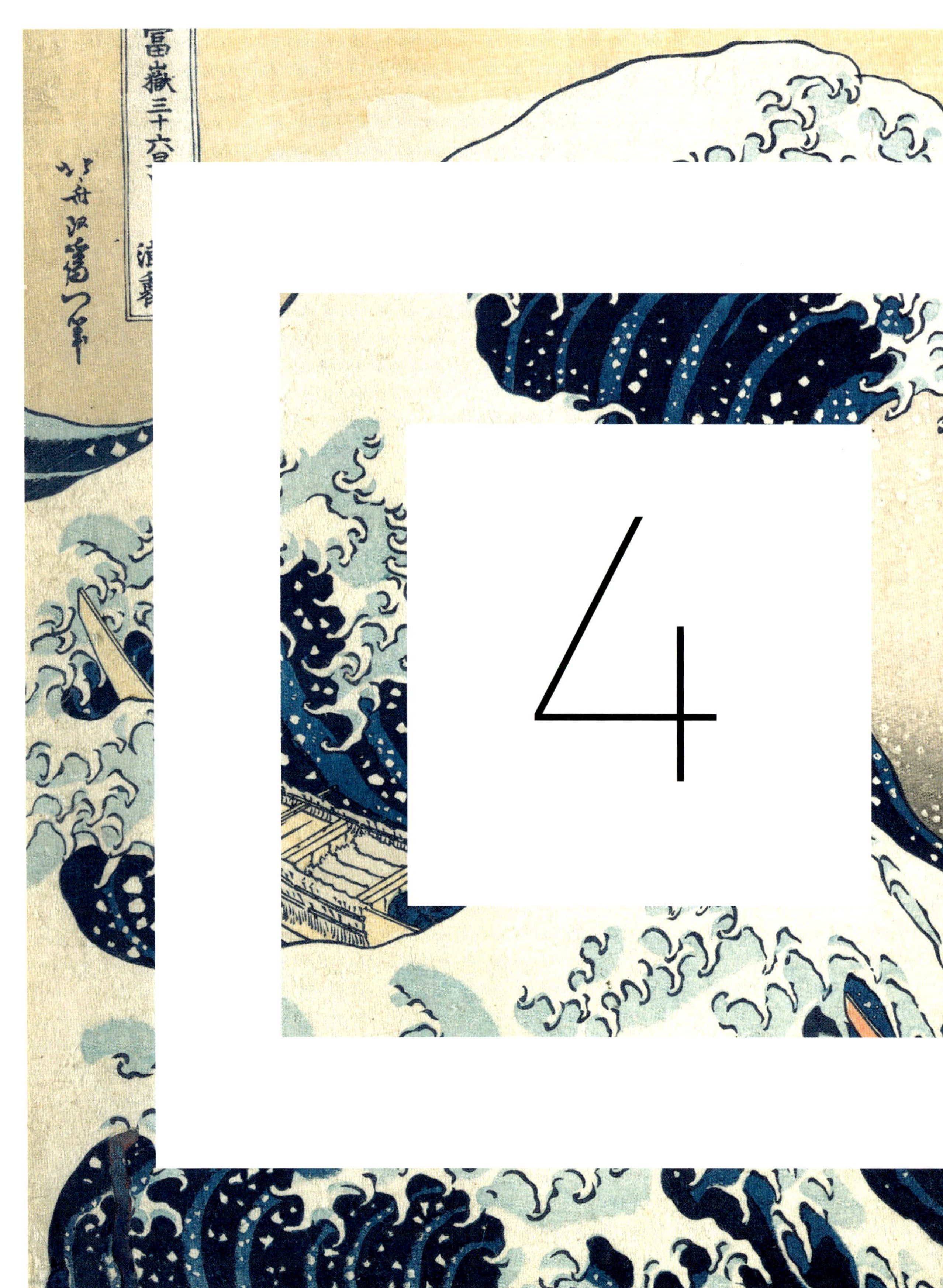

4

Colour and innovation

1800 - 1900

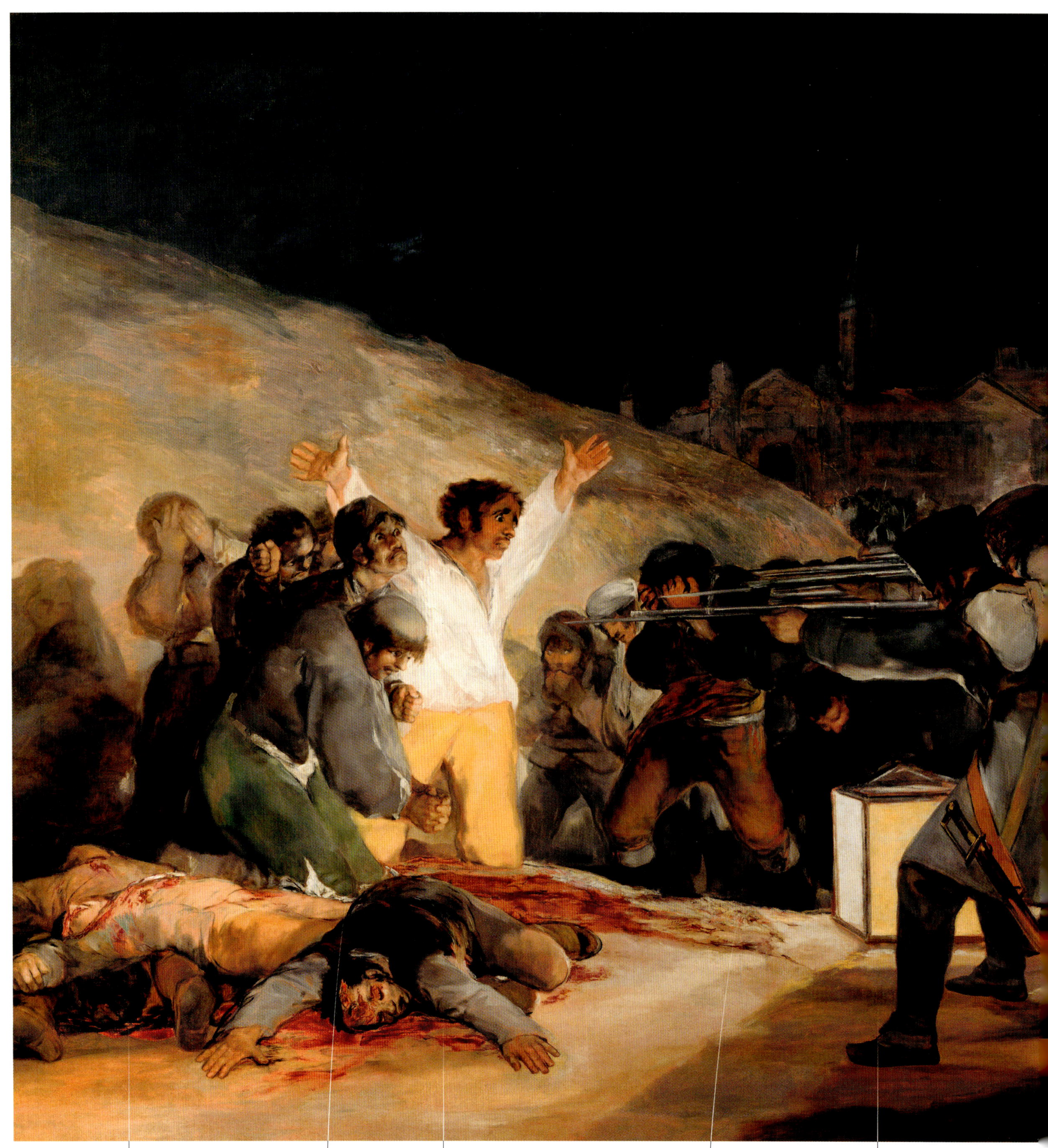

Those rebels who have already been executed are piled in a pool of blood.

The rebels are all portrayed as individuals. Their faces show expressions of fear, anguish, and despair.

With arms outstretched, the central figure takes up a surrendering position. His pose echoes that of Christ on the cross.

The turbulent arrangement of the victims is set against the horizontal lines of the soldiers' rifles.

A lantern is the only source of light. It reflects off the white shirt worn by the man in the center of the group.

The Third of May 1808

Francisco de Goya 1814, oil on canvas, 106 × 137 in (268 × 347 cm), Museo del Prado, Madrid, Spain

On May 2, 1808, the people of Madrid rose up against a French army of occupation. The following day, French troops rounded up hundreds of rebels and bystanders and executed them in retaliation. Six years later, after the expulsion of the French, Goya produced this atypical history painting of the event. It features anonymous members of the public rather than national heroes, and is painted in a realistic and expressive style. Unlike many of his fellow artists, who glorified war, Goya condemns human cruelty and the pointlessness of political violence.

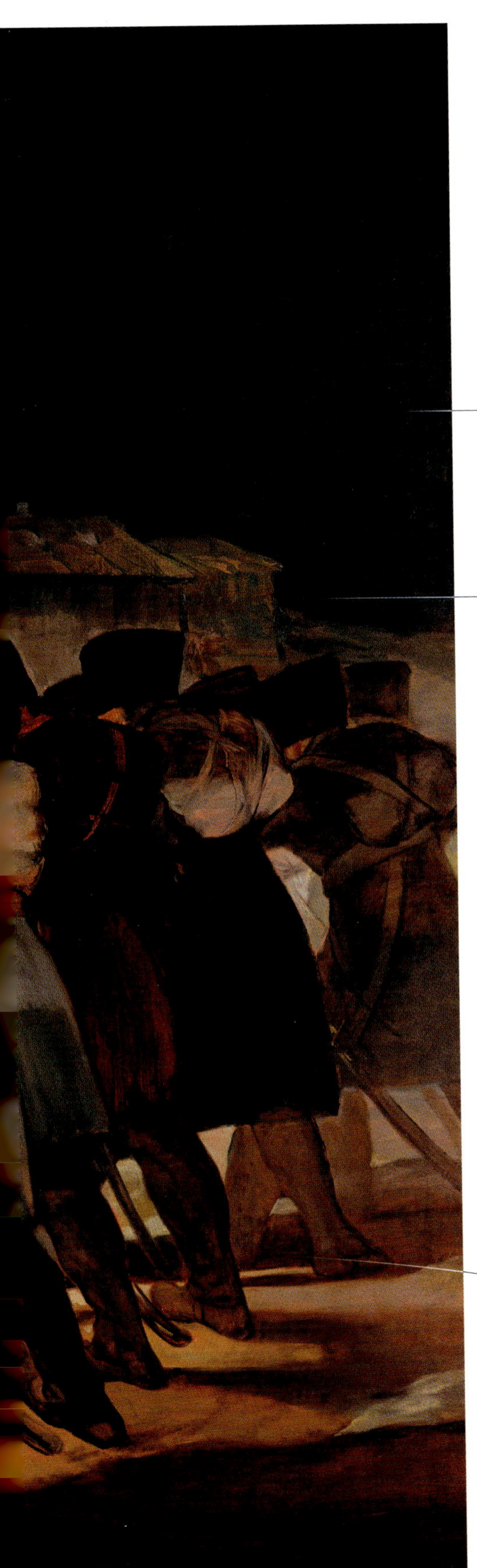

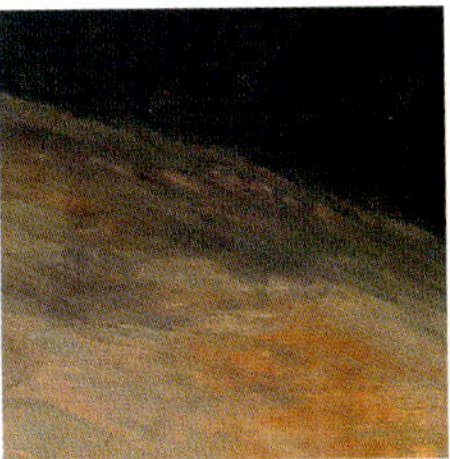

The hillside is sketched in with rough strokes of paint so there are no details to distract from the focal point.

Darkness fills a large part of the painting, making the central figure stand out.

A church dominates the town in the background. The building symbolizes the Church's inability to prevent the executions from taking place.

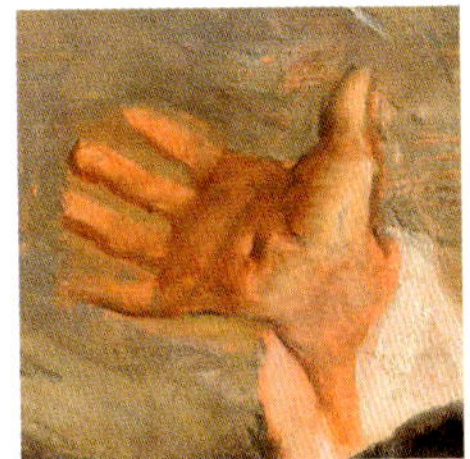

A mark on the man's hand suggests the stigmata of Christ.

The repetition of the soldiers' stance and their averted faces suggest the mechanical, inhuman nature of the firing squad.

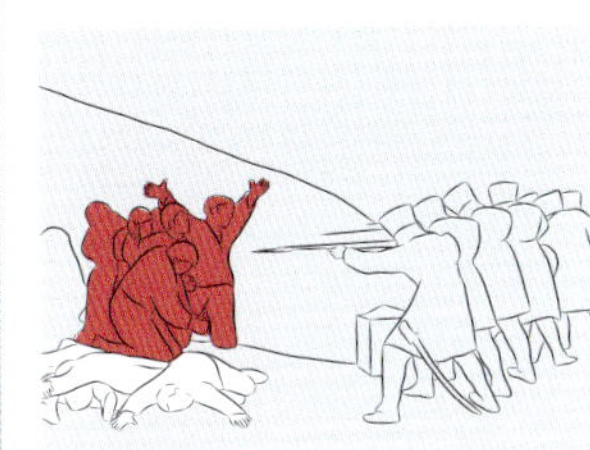

Creating a focus
Light concentrates attention on the group of rebels, revealing their fear, which contrasts with the detachment of the soldiers.

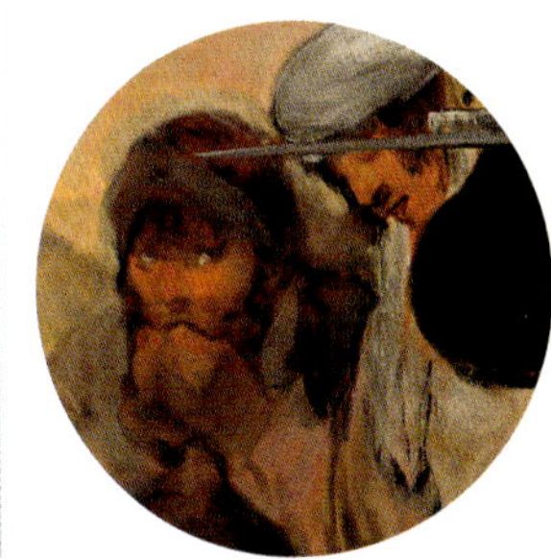

Expressive style
The brushwork across most of the canvas is loose and expressive and details have been sketched in quickly. The effect is very different from the precise and polished style that was common at the time.

> "With Goya, we do not think of the studio or even of the artist at work. We think only of the event."
>
> Kenneth Clark, 1960

Wanderer Above the Sea of Fog

Caspar David Friedrich c.1818, oil on canvas, 37 x 29 in (94.8 x 74.8 cm), Kunsthalle, Hamburg, Germany

A masterpiece of the Romantic movement, *Wanderer Above the Sea of Fog* depicts a man before a sublime landscape, his back to the viewer. One interpretation sees the man as an explorer, who has conquered the mountain and now casually surveys the land. Other readings of the painting propose the opposite: alone in an unknowable landscape, the wanderer watches the fog encroaching upon his feet.

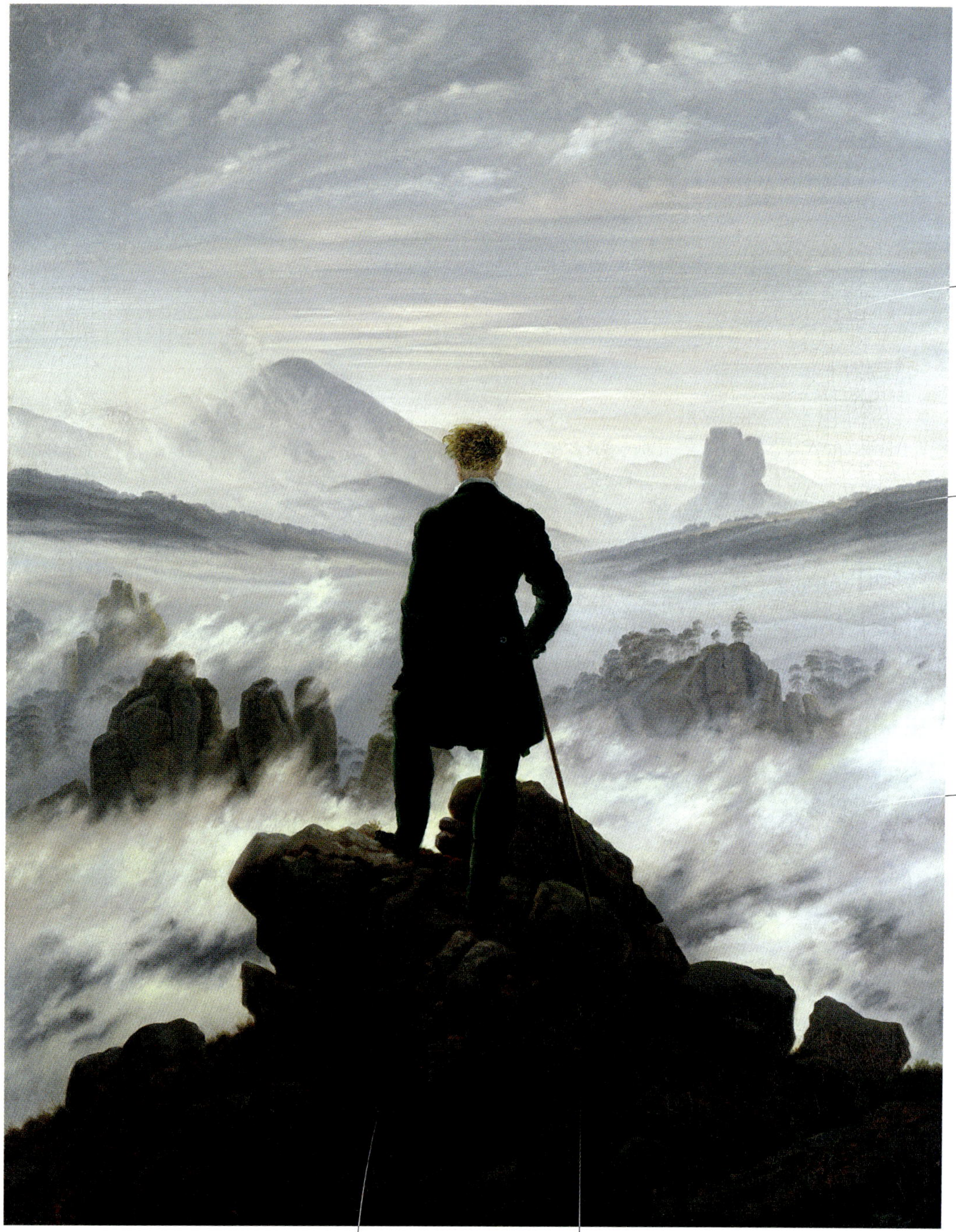

Unlike most landscape paintings, this work is taller than it is wide, emphasizing the figure of the man.

The focal point is the man's core, the seat of emotion—the response to nature demanded by Romantic artists and poets.

The figure is counterpoised—with one leg supporting the body's weight and the other with knee bent. This adds a sense of dynamism.

The figure is seen from behind, allowing the viewer to share his experience of the boundless immensity of nature without the distraction of portraiture.

The dark foreground creates a hard edge against the lighter scenery, causing it to fade into the distance as though receding.

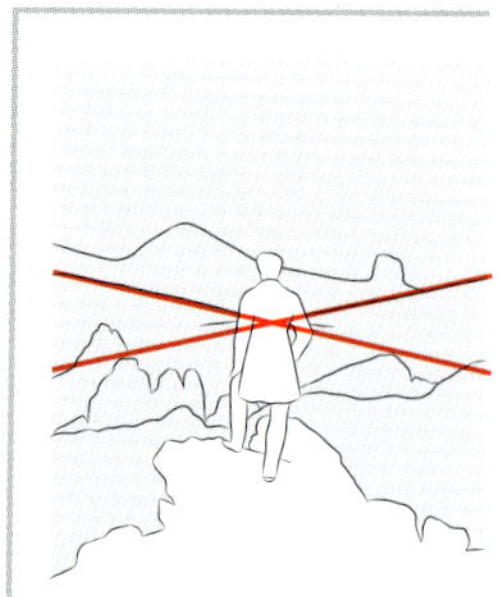

Commanding figure
Two diagonal lines cross to form an x, dividing the figure's torso and highlighting the monumental structure on which he stands.

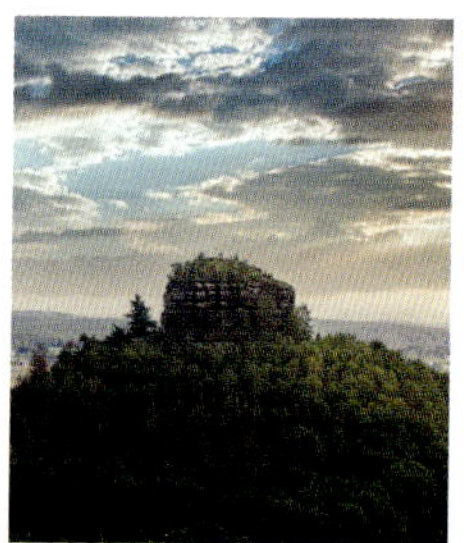

Romantic inspiration
Friedrich sketched several mountain ranges then combined specific elements in his studio. The man is probably looking at the Zirkelstein in Switzerland.

"Friedrich's landscapes rarely depict daylight or sunlight; rather, the paintings portray dawn, dusk, fog, or mist—phenomena that invite mystery."

Metropolitan Museum of Art, 2001

The Raft of the Medusa

Théodore Géricault 1818–1819, oil on canvas, 193 × 282 in (490 × 716 cm), Louvre, Paris, France

Cast adrift in tumultuous waters, a makeshift raft becomes a scene of desperation. This history painting refers to a naval tragedy in 1816, when the *Medusa* ran aground off the coast of West Africa. The shortage of lifeboats condemned 150 passengers to a perilous raft, on which survival depended on cannibalism. Géricault's painting captures the moment when a ship appears in the distance.

A wave threatens the raft and creates a stark contrast to the brightness and hope on the horizon.

This torso is based on the *Belvedere Torso*, a classical sculpture. Géricault accentuates its muscularity through chiaroscuro—the manipulation of light and dark.

Hints of deep red and the brighter yellows on the horizon symbolize hope.

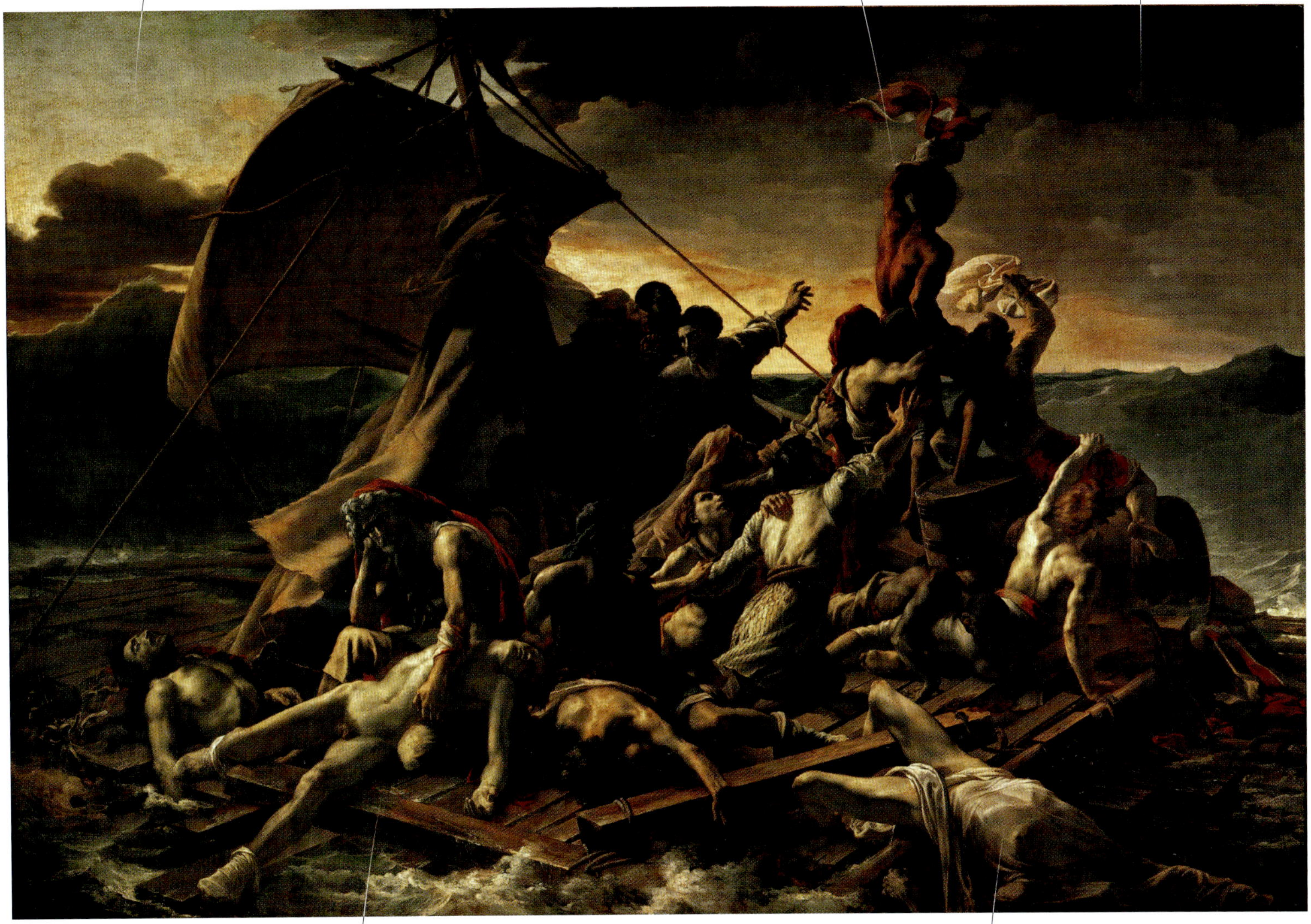

An elderly man loses hope as he clutches the body of his son.

A limp body droops overboard, beyond the confines of the image and its frame.

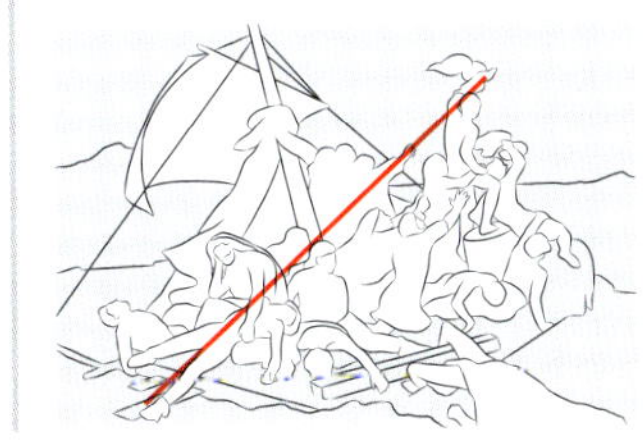

Composition
Dynamic diagonal lines guide the viewer from the lifeless bodies in the lower left toward the upper right, where hopeful survivors seek help by waving pieces of cloth at a rescue vessel.

> "With the brush we merely tint, while the imagination alone produces color."
>
> Théodore Géricault

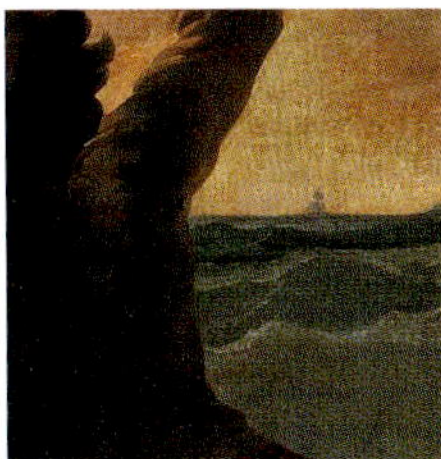

The *Argus*, the boat that rescued the survivors, emerges as a tiny speck on the distant horizon.

The Hay Wain

John Constable 1821, oil on canvas, 51 × 73 in (130.2 × 185.4 cm), National Gallery, London, UK

Constable depicts his family's millpond and meadows in Suffolk, England, during high summer. The built environment—house, wagon, and boat—gives way to the grandeur of nature in the rolling fields and clouds above and beyond. The naturalistic depiction marked a shift in landscape painting toward showing contemporary rather than historic, imagined landscapes.

Rigid shapes delineate the cottage, wagon (wain), and mill—features imposed by humans on the landscape.

Amorphous shapes depict natural subjects, such as the trees and clouds.

The use of bright green was frowned upon by English critics, who preferred the muted tones of historical paintings.

Constable is particularly famous for his realistic depictions of clouds.

Vivid green trees and fields are balanced by highlights of red and the expansive blue sky.

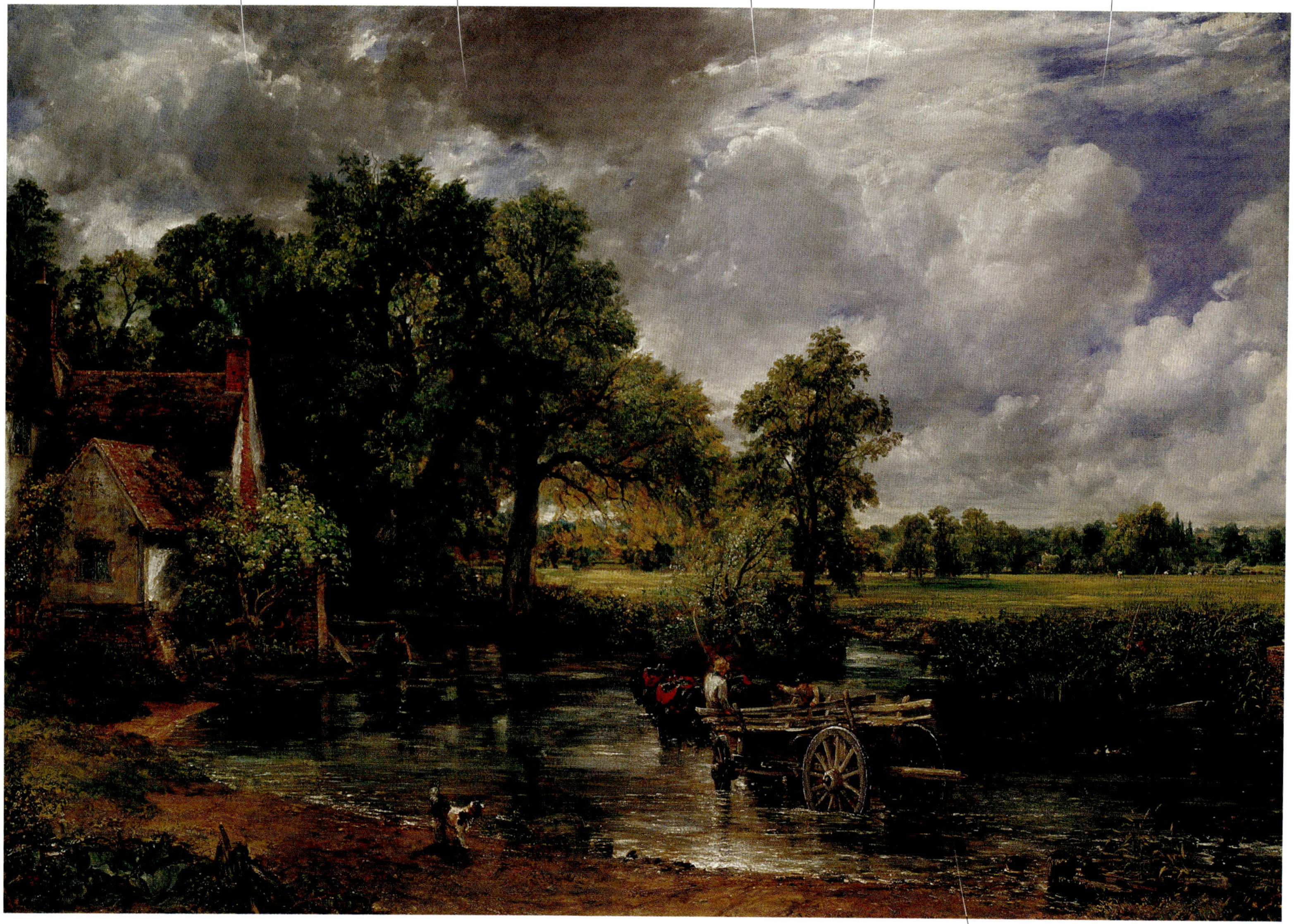

The monumental scale of *The Hay Wain* defied the traditional hierarchy of art subjects, which ranked landscapes at the bottom.

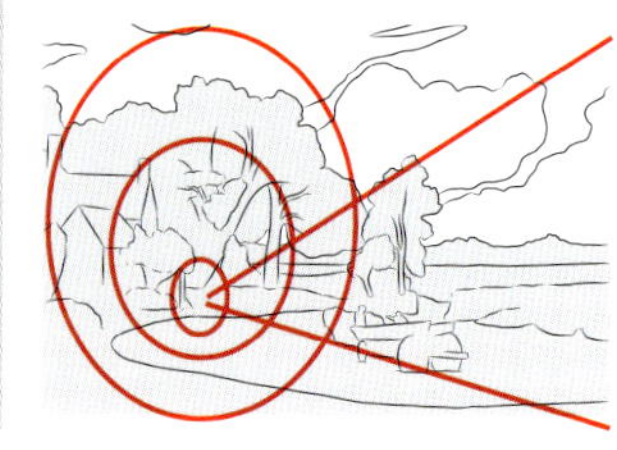

In the moment
Deeper colors on the left give way to lighter colors on the right, providing a sense of cool shade versus bright heat.

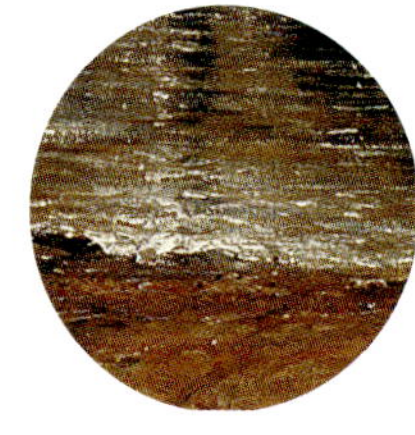

Capturing nature
Constable used loose brushwork and white highlights to express the restless changes in nature. Some of his critics disparaged his work for its lack of polish.

Carolina Parakeet

John James Audubon c.1825, watercolor on paper, 30 × 21in (75.6 × 54cm), New York Historical Society, US

In this painting filled with color and movement, seven gorgeously feathered Carolina parakeets have alighted on a cocklebur bush. The artist, ornithologist John James Audubon, risked everything to pursue his goal of depicting all the bird species in North America, even spending time in debtor's prison to finance his passion. This preparatory watercolor was made for Audubon's book *Birds of America.*

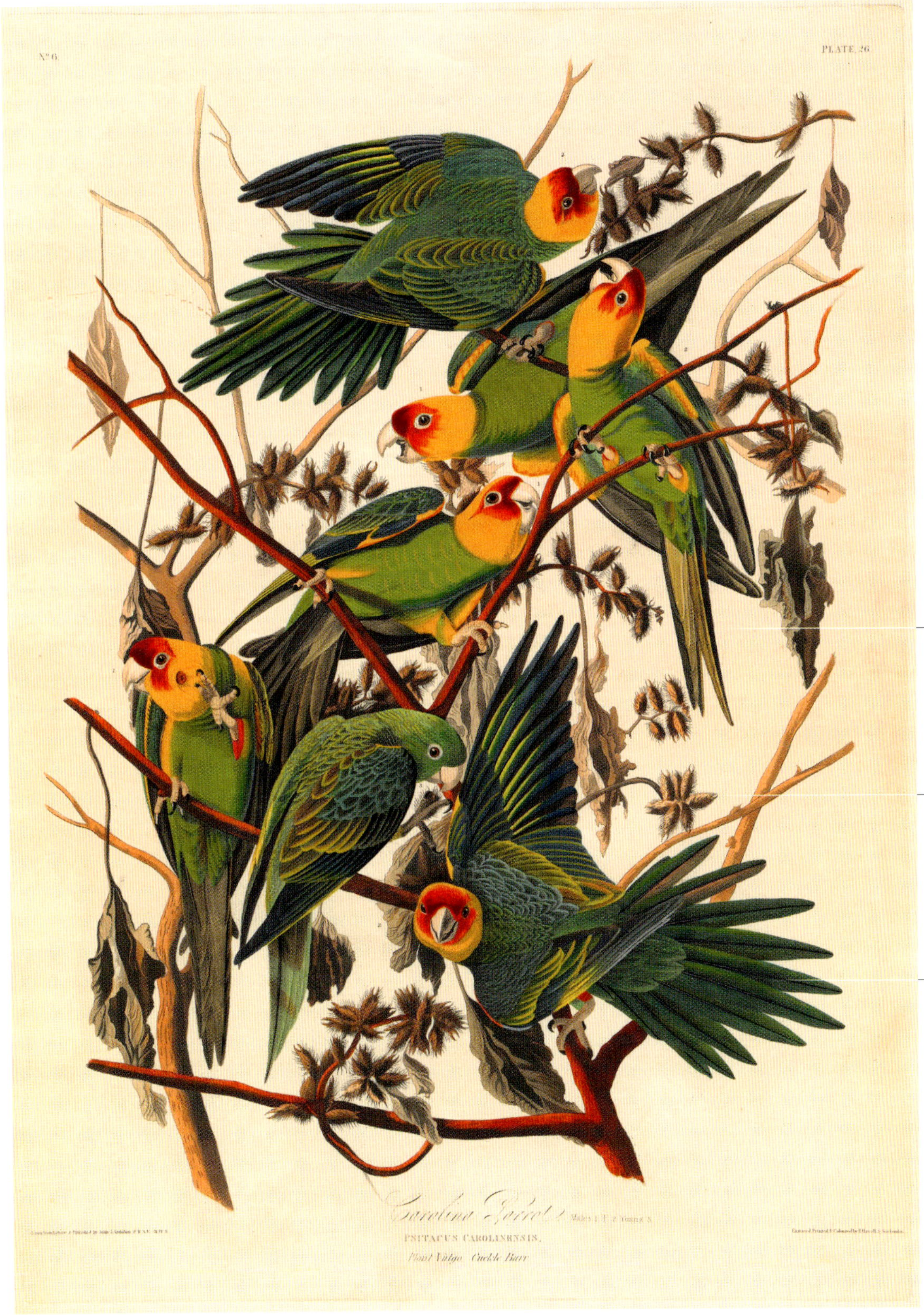

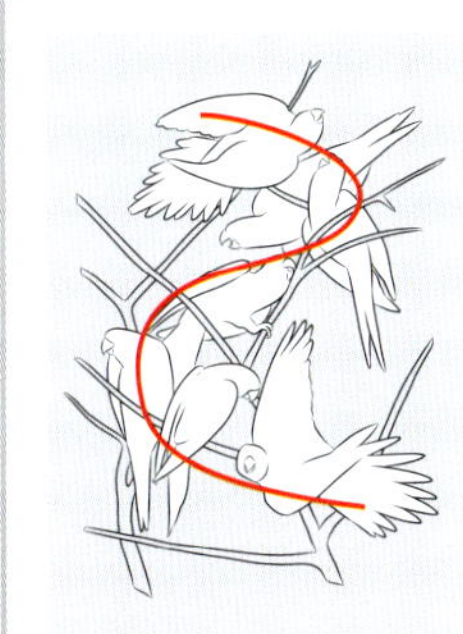

All angles
The birds are displayed in an S shape, allowing them to be seen from different angles.

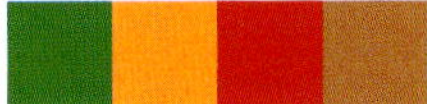

Brilliant plumage
Green, yellow, and red emphasize the sight of the birds against the brown foliage.

The only native parrot species in the US, the last Carolina parakeet (*Conuropsis carolinensis*) died in 1904.

The parakeets are devouring the common cocklebur, a native plant species that produces 2,000 burrs on a single plant.

Audubon combined watercolor, graphite, pastel, gouache, and black ink to achieve the effect he wanted.

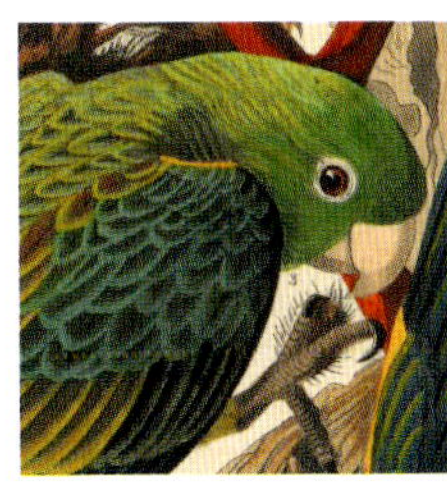

A single female, distinguished by her blue-green head, contrasts with the more flamboyant male birds.

History

History paintings and sculptures portray stories about people and events. They are narrative in character, usually sizable, and often involve large groups of figures and complex compositions. In commemorating events, some artists idealize their subjects to encourage the viewer to see them from a particular point of view. Some works depict legendary or historical tales in contemporary settings to draw parallels between a glorious past and the present.

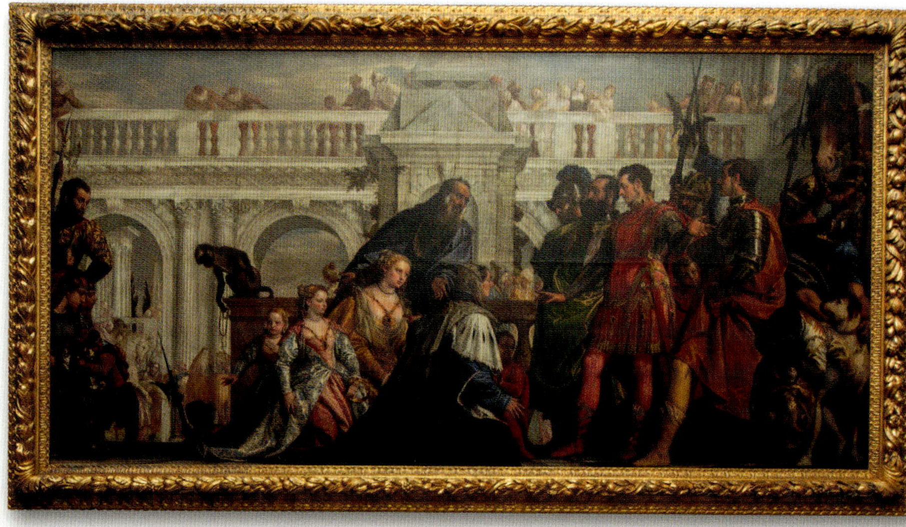

2

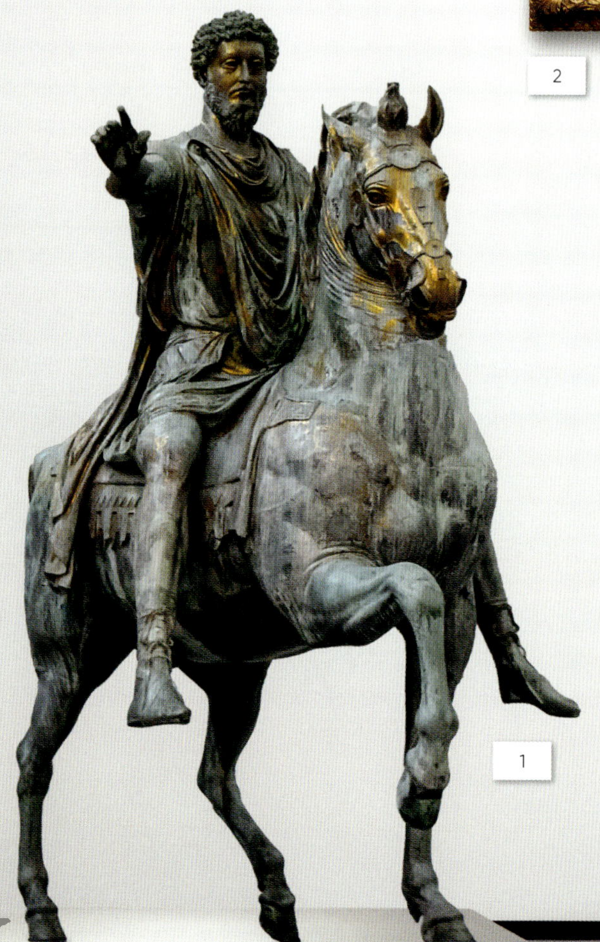

1

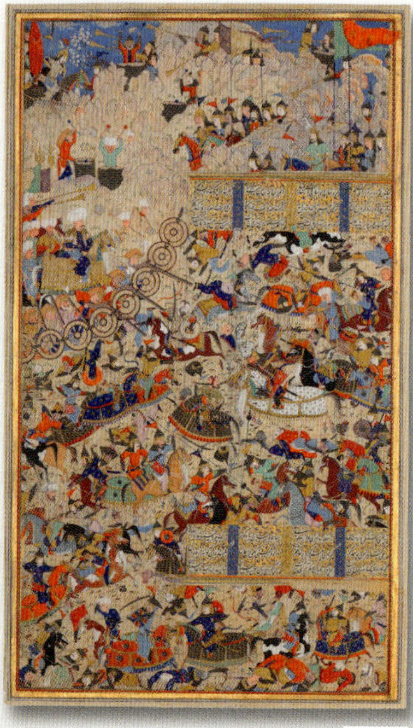

3

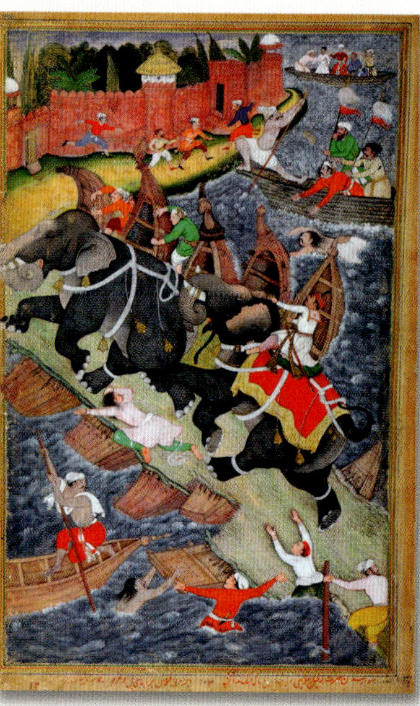

4

1. ***Marcus Aurelius*, 161–180 CE.** It was common for statues of Roman emperors to portray them as martial and all-conquering. In this example, Marcus Aurelius is wearing civic dress, without weapons or armor, indicating that he wanted to present himself as the bringer of peace.

2. ***The Family of Darius Before Alexander*, Veronese, 1545.** Veronese illustrates the magnanimity of Alexander the Great in sparing the family of Darius III, the defeated Persian leader. His figures are dressed in the style of Renaissance Venice to add grandeur to the scene.

3. ***Battle Between Iranians and Turanians*, Muhammad ibn Taj al-Din Haidar Muzahhib Shirazi, 1562–1583.** In a scene from the *Shahnama* (Book of Kings), the legendary Iranian hero Rustam is shown defeating his opponents, celebrating his strength in battle.

4. ***Akbar's Adventures with the Elephant Hawa'i*, Basawan and Chetar Munti, 1590.** This illustration from the *Akbarnama* (Book of Akbar) shows Mughal emperor Akbar mounted on Hawa'i, chasing rogue elephant Ran Bagha. The scene illustrates Akbar's bravery.

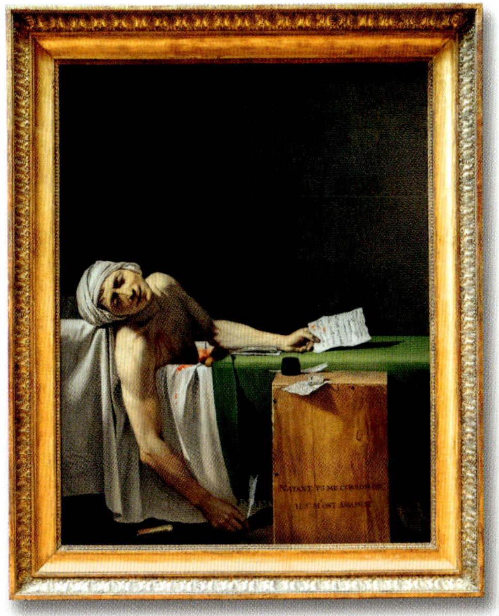

5

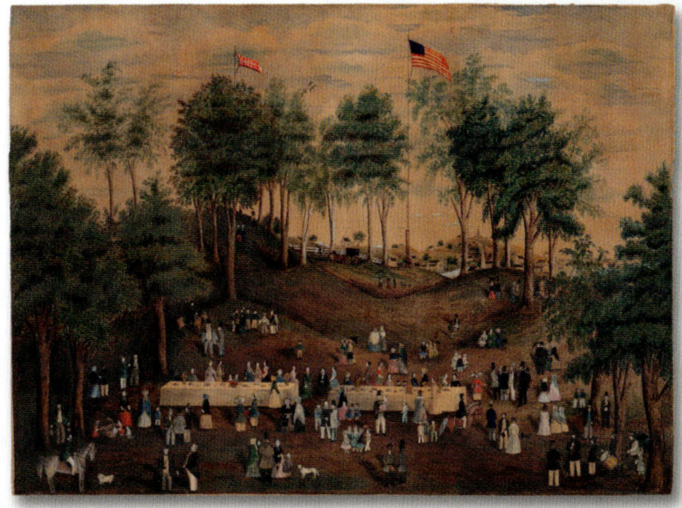

7

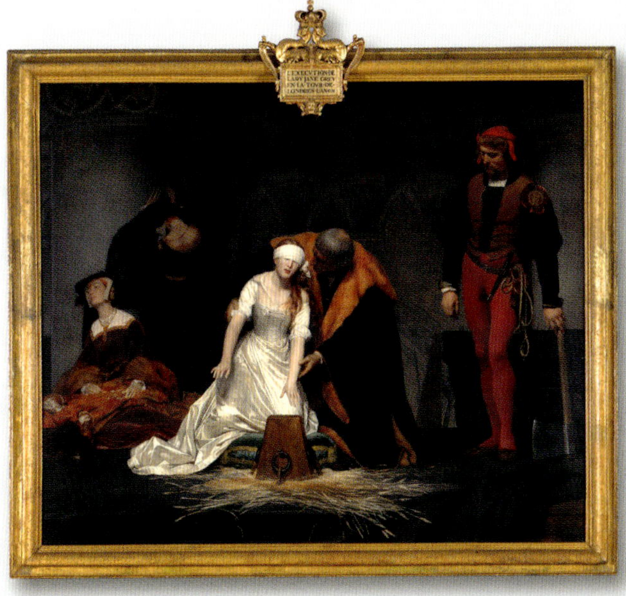

6

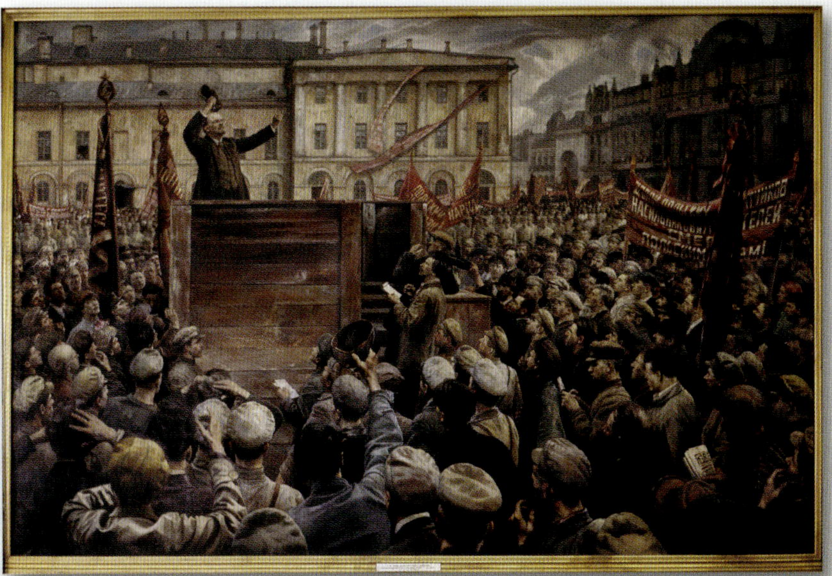

8

5. ***The Death of Marat*, Jacques-Louis David, 1793.** Jean-Paul Marat, a leader of the French Revolution, was murdered in his bathtub. David, a sympathizer, presents Marat as a Christlike figure in this propagandist image. When Marat later fell out of favor, David hid the picture.

6. ***The Execution of Lady Jane Grey*, Paul Delaroche, 1833.** The French painter Delaroche took inspiration from an event in British history. The beheading of a titular monarch and Jane's martyr-like figure were designed to elicit the sympathy of post-Revolutionary France.

7. ***Fourth of July Picnic at Weymouth Landing*, Susan Torrey Merritt, 1840–1850.** The Abolitionist flag on the left and the US flag on the right, together with people of all ethnic backgrounds, indicate that this is an antislavery picnic. Weymouth proudly supported the abolitionist cause.

8. ***Lenin and Soldiers of the Red Army on the Way to Poland*, Isaak Brodsky, 1920.** Brodsky, founder of the Socialist Realist style, shows Lenin as a commanding presence surrounded by a large crowd. It is an accurate rendition of the event, intended to rally Lenin's supporters.

Liberty Leading the People

Eugène Delacroix 1830, oil on canvas, 102 × 128 in (260 × 325 cm), Louvre, Paris, France

Delacroix captures the act of resistance when the French people, guided by the embodiment of Liberty, who triumphantly holds the French national flag, rise against the oppressive Bourbon monarchy. This stirring painting not only immortalized a moment in history but transcended its context to become a symbol of revolution and the struggle for freedom for people all over the world.

A man with a tailored jacket and top hat stands next to a factory worker, indicating the unity of social classes in this revolt.

The tricolor waved by Liberty extends beyond the confines of the canvas, creating a continuity with the space outside the pictorial frame.

The statuesque figure of Liberty strides toward the viewer, encouraging a surge of revolutionary zeal.

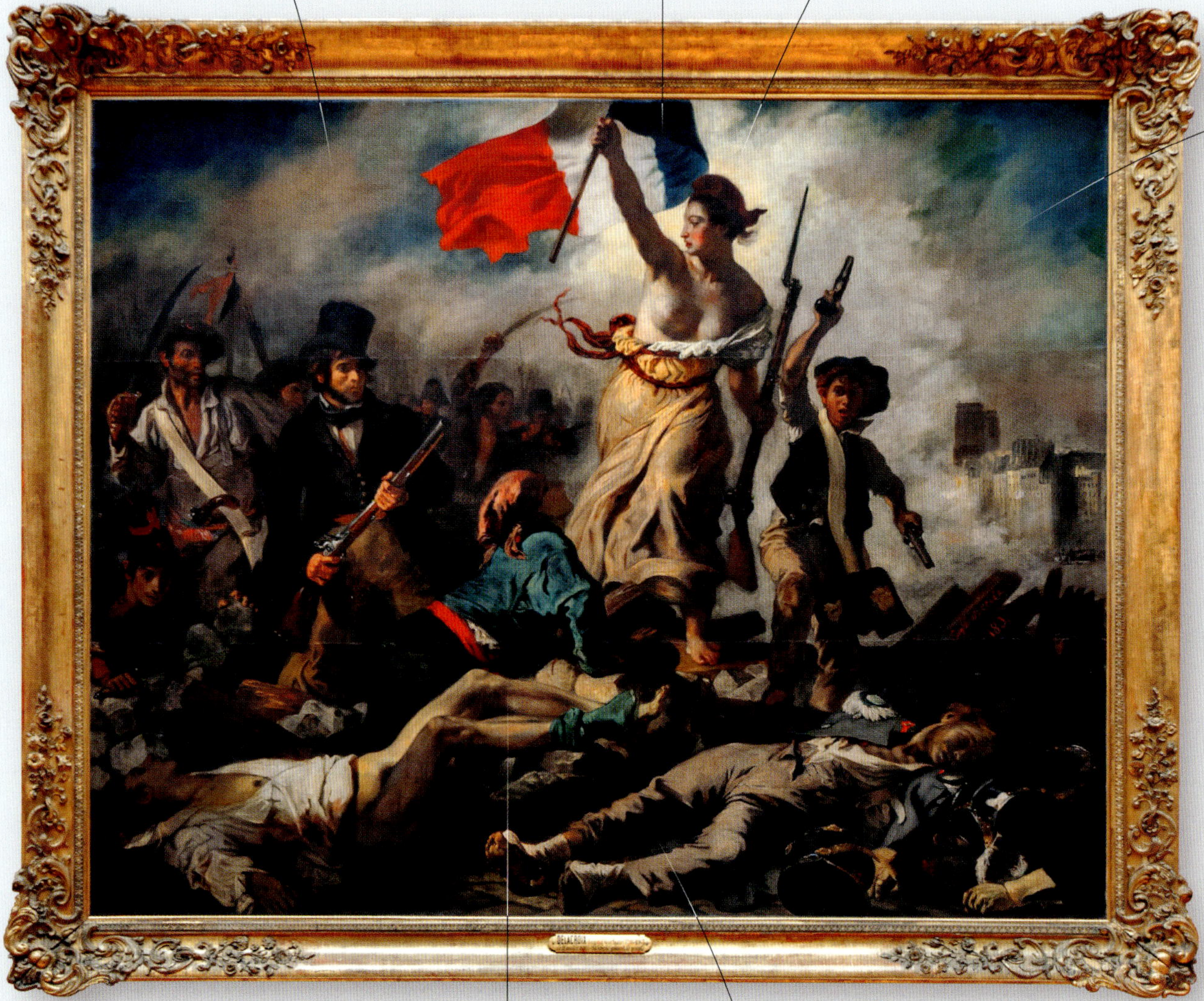

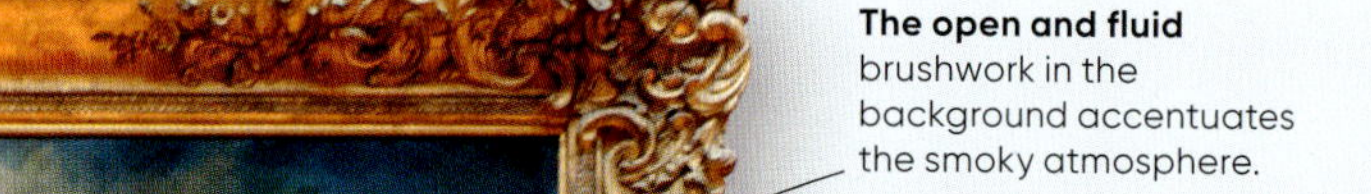

The open and fluid brushwork in the background accentuates the smoky atmosphere.

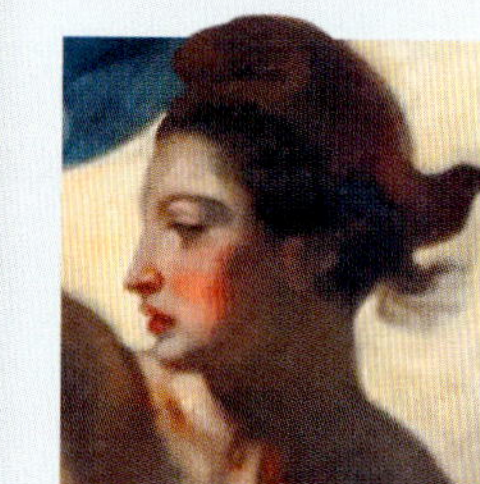

Liberty wears a Phrygian cap, which denotes freedom. In ancient Rome, freed slaves wore them to show their status.

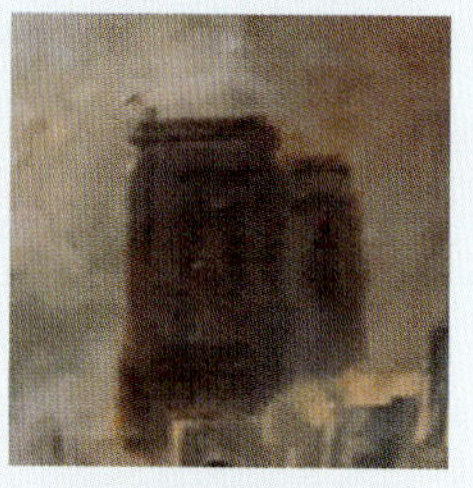

A tiny tricolor flag flying from the towers of Notre Dame Cathedral is a reminder that Paris is the backdrop for this revolutionary moment.

The figure on all fours looks longingly toward Liberty, and wears red, white, and blue, the colors of the tricolor.

The lifeless figures in the foreground are foreshortened to enhance the illusion of depth and draw the viewer into the pictorial frame.

> "I do not care for reasonable painting at all. My turbulent mind needs agitation, needs to liberate itself."
>
> Eugène Delacroix

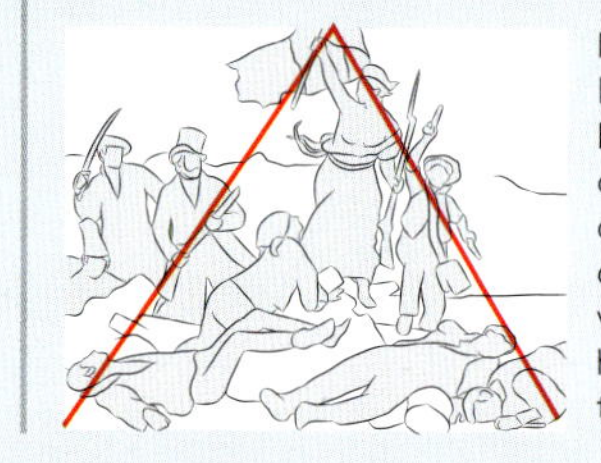

Liberty rises
Despite the chaos of bodies, Delacroix created a strong pyramidal composition. The limbs and muskets direct the viewer toward Liberty holding the tricolor at the apex.

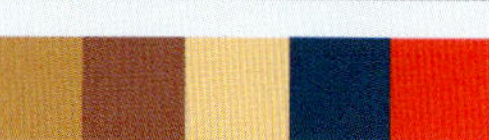

Color contrasts
Delacroix contrasts the muted palette of earthy yellows and browns in the foreground with pale yellows, deep blues, and brilliant reds in the top half of the painting.

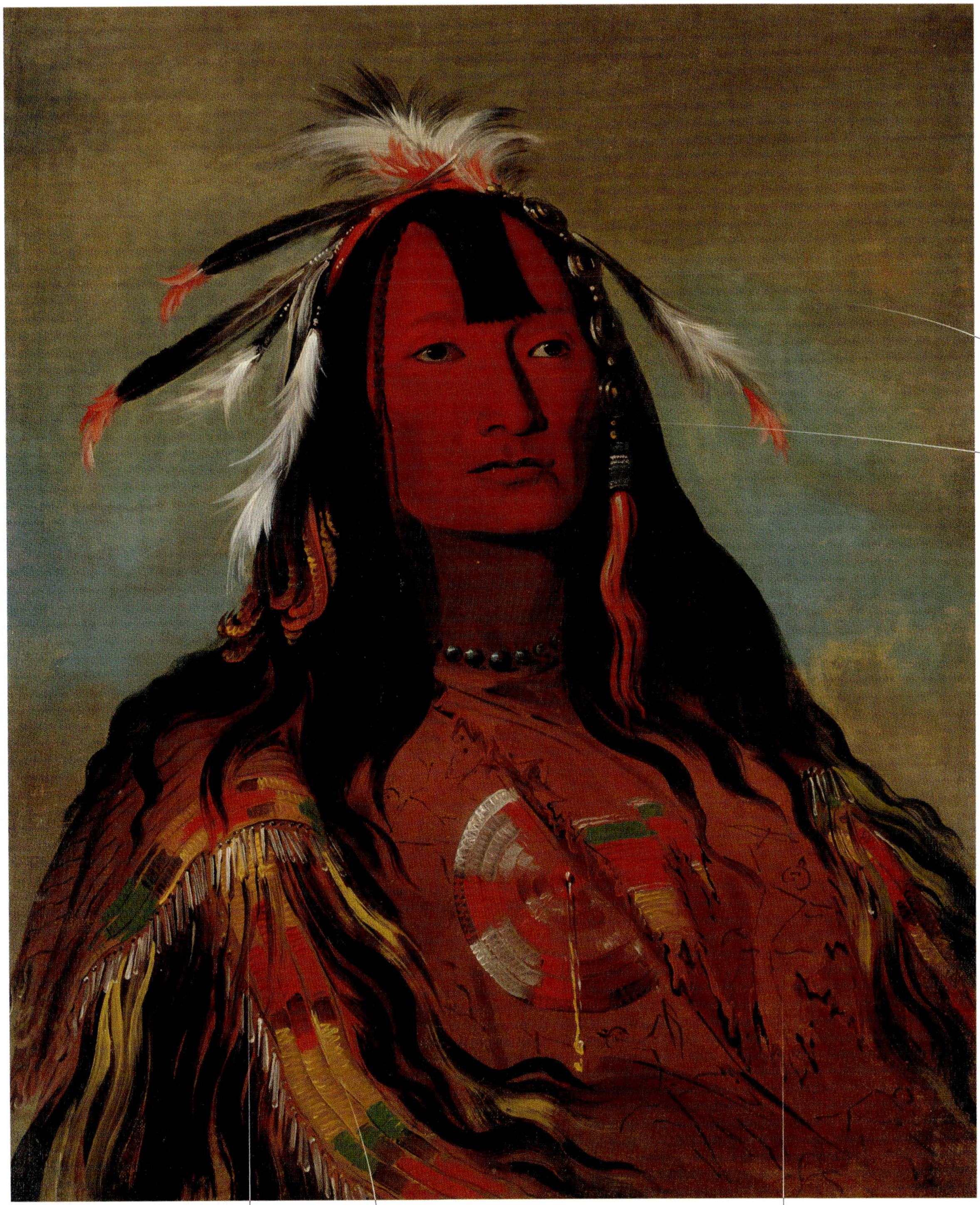

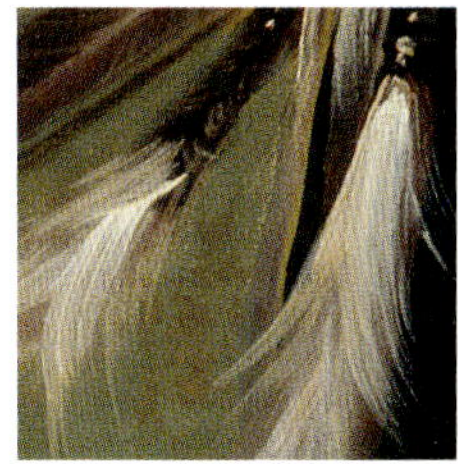

Ornaments such as feathers, fringes, and beads, are painted in naturalistic detail.

The simple background of sky focuses the viewer's attention on the subject.

Hee-oh'ks-te-kin's features, which convey dignity and solemnity, are recorded in a simple, precise style.

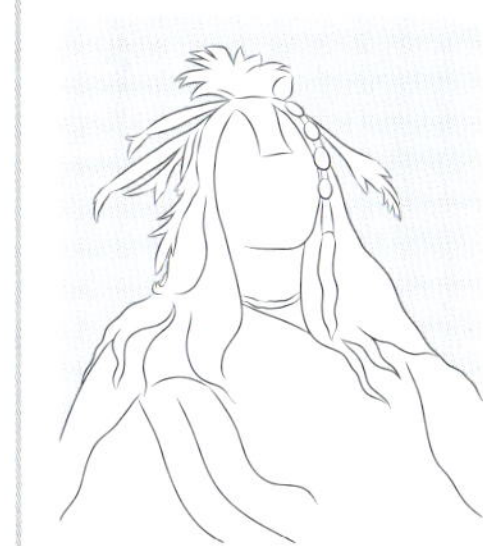

Classic pose
Drawing on the European tradition, Catlin placed Hee-oh'ks-te-kin centrally, at half-length, and turned toward the viewer, at a slight angle to the picture plane.

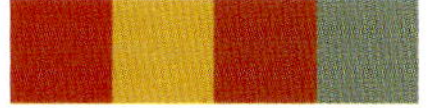

Color
Warm oranges, yellows, and browns are amplified by the cooler, less saturated colors in the sky.

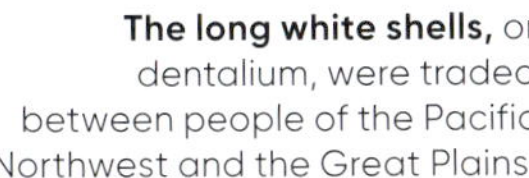

The long white shells, or dentalium, were traded between people of the Pacific Northwest and the Great Plains.

The embroidery on the tunic is depicted with small, descriptive brushstrokes.

Catlin loosely sketched the images on Hee-oh'ks-te-kin's embroidered buckskin tunic.

Hee-oh'ks-te-kin (Rabbit's Skin Leggings)

George Catlin 1832, oil on canvas, 29 × 24 in (73.7 × 60.9 cm), Smithsonian American Art Museum, Washington, D.C., US

Hee-oh'ks-te-kin, a Nimíipuu warrior of the Pacific Northwest, is depicted in full regalia. Wishing to document a disappearing way of life, Catlin specialized in portraits of Indigenous Americans at a time when they were being driven from their lands. He looked for willing participants and made portraits that convey strength and personality, but has faced accusations of exploiting his subjects.

Women of Algiers in Their Apartment

Eugène Delacroix 1834, oil on canvas, 71 × 90 in (180 × 229 cm), Louvre, Paris, France

Delacroix combines observations from his own travels with European fantasies of North Africa in this portrayal of a harem. Drawing from the Orientalist tradition at a time of French colonial expansion in North Africa, the painting inspired tributes from Picasso and Renoir and cemented his reputation as an experimental colorist.

Intricately patterned tiles, textiles, and carpets immerse the viewer in a faraway land.

The inclusion of the Black maidservant enabled Delacroix to further heighten the exoticism of the scene

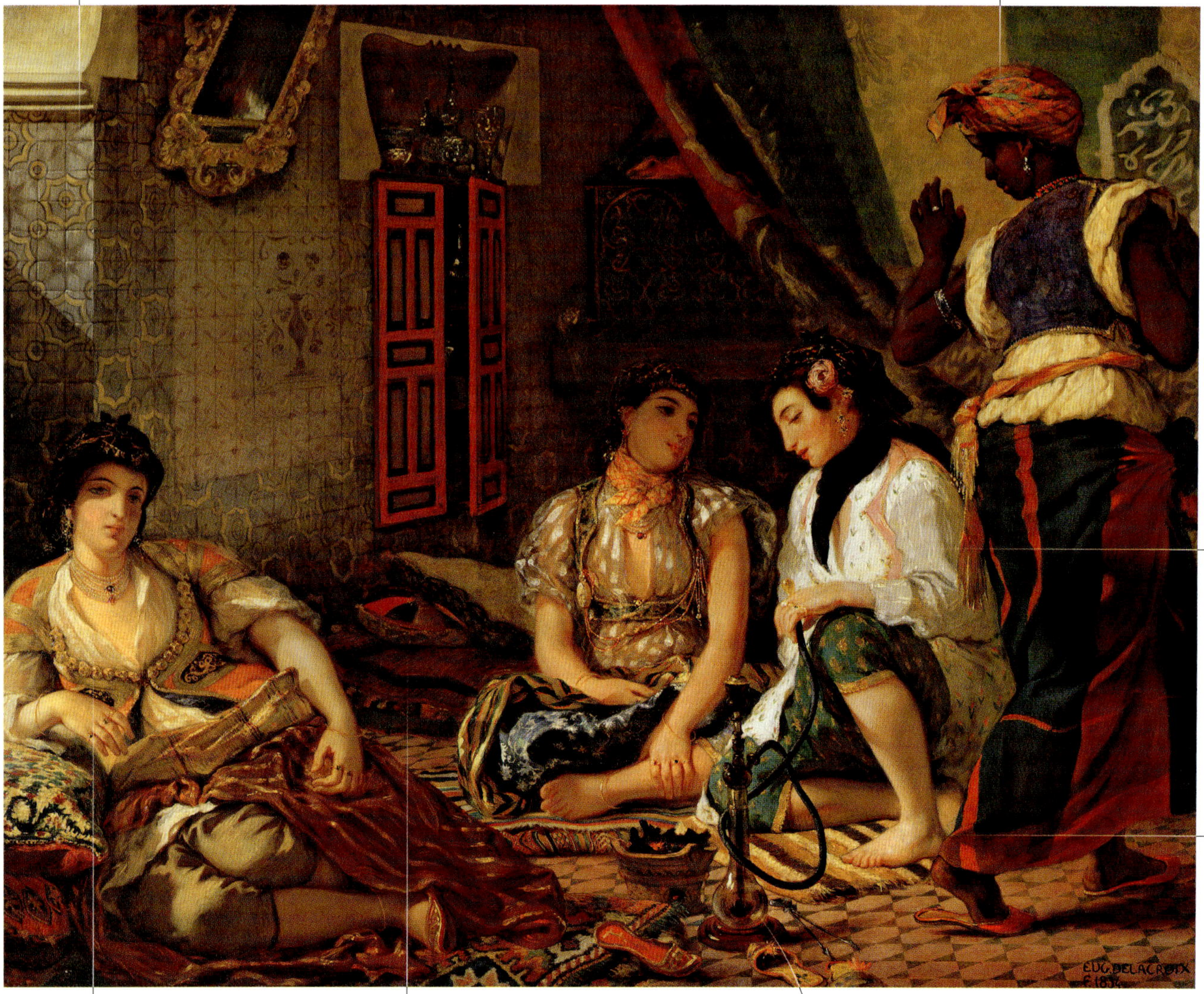

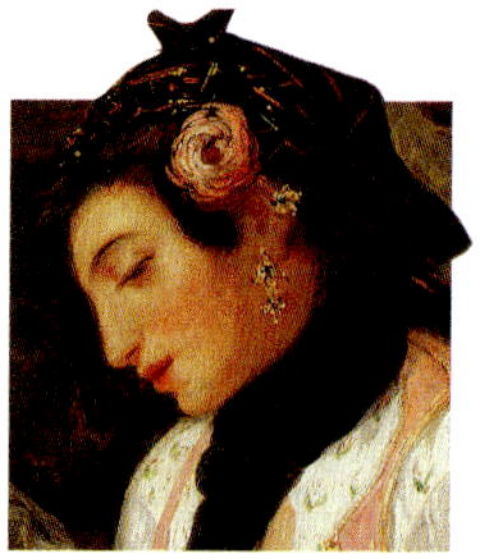

Generalized facial features depict the women as a European fantasy of harem beauty, rather than showing them as distinct individuals.

The women are bathed in a bright glow, enhancing their glamour.

Bare feet and loose slippers hint at feminine sensuality in an otherwise demure portrait.

A steely gaze keeps viewers at bay, suggesting that they are intruding into a private space.

Jewels, cushions, and billowing garments convey a sense of material richness and luxury.

A water pipe is an invitation to decipher new and exotic cultural codes and narratives.

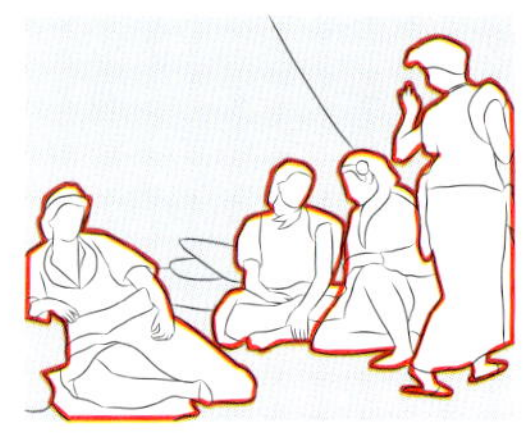

Mood over narrative
The women are disengaged from one another, across a tableau with no obvious focal point. Their lack of dynamism accentuates decorative mood rather than narrative drive.

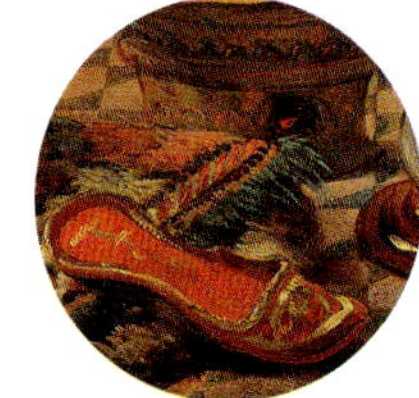

New technique
Flochetage, Delacroix's own innovation, involves placing small flecks of complementary colors together to make them vibrate with energy. The red slippers set against green carpet tassels intensifies the vibrancy of the red.

The Slave Ship

Joseph Mallord William Turner 1840, oil on canvas, 36 × 48 in (90.8 × 122.6 cm), Museum of Fine Arts, Boston, US

This painting is based on an incident in 1781 when the captain of the Jamaican-bound ship *Zong* ordered 132 enslaved people to be thrown overboard in order to claim insurance money. The iniquity of enslavement is highlighted by showing this horrendous scene of cruelty and death, emphasized by the dramatic use of color.

Strong colors in the sky—red, orange, yellow, purple, and blue—intensify each other and heighten the turbulent atmosphere.

Sea and sky become one at the horizon, creating a continuous world of powerful elements.

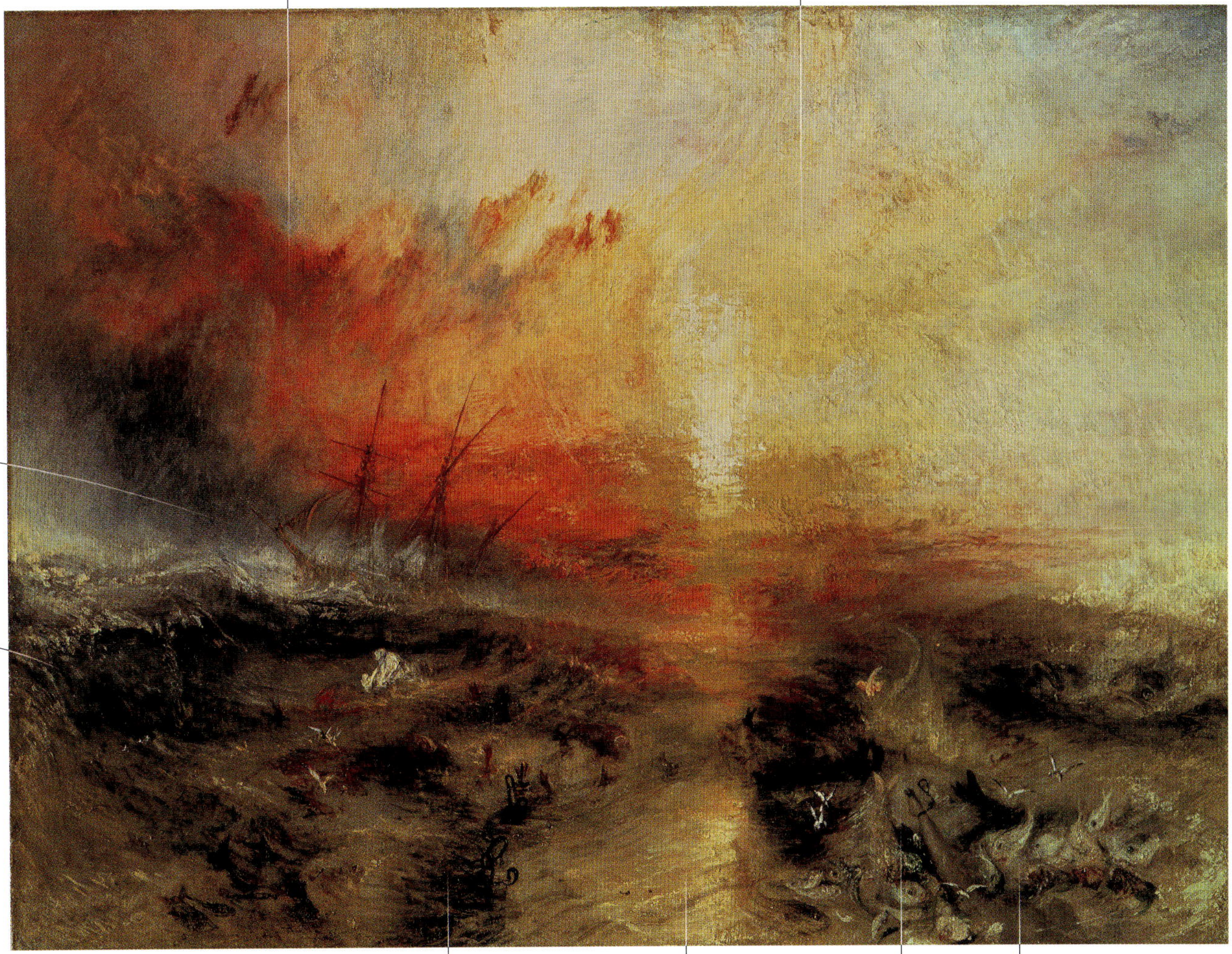

The ship flounders in the storm. Some commentators interpret the typhoon as retribution for the murder of the enslaved people.

The waves have been modeled to look like a solid wall of water.

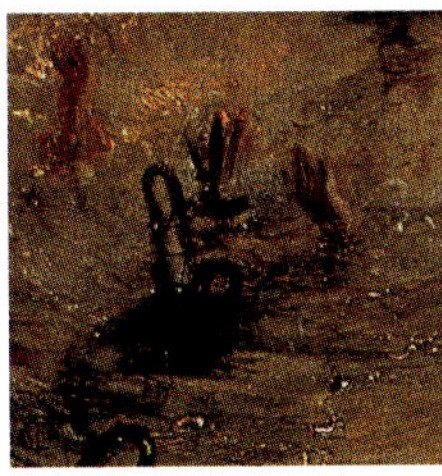

Turner used single strokes of the brush to paint the hands reaching out of the water.

Drowned bodies, still wearing shackles, are visible in the foreground.

A shaft of sunlight on the water acts as a spotlight on the scene.

The foot of this drowning body points to the ship.

The surface of the sea churns with fish, bodies, and swelling waves.

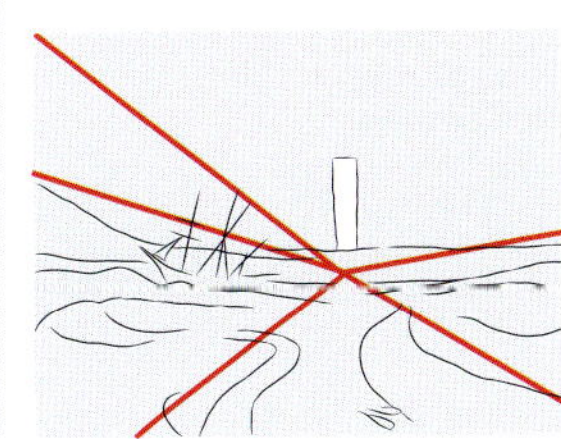

Distant focal point
A series of diagonal lines in the sea and sky lead to a distant point where the beam of sunlight meets the reflection on the water.

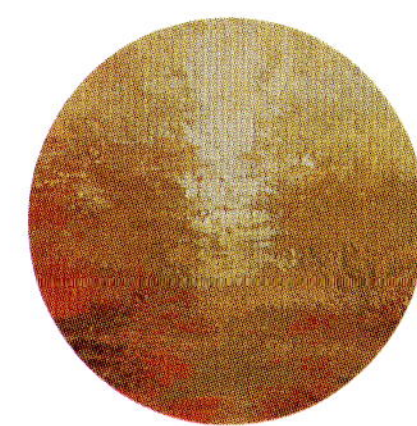

Paint effects
For the column of light, Turner scraped on thick white paint over the underlying layers. In the deepest red areas, he repeatedly scraped through the top layer to create a striated effect.

> "If I were reduced to test Turner's immortality upon any single work, I should choose this."
>
> John Ruskin, 1858

The Romans in Their Decadence

Thomas Couture 1847, oil on canvas, 186 × 304 in (472 × 772 cm), Musée d'Orsay, Paris, France

An orgy unfolds against a backdrop of classical architecture, its participants reveling in their excess. Drawing a parallel between the decadence of ancient Rome and the moral corruption of French society in the mid-19th century, the painting was exhibited in the Paris Salon the year before the 1848 revolution, which toppled the French monarchy. Reminiscent of Raphael's work, it is also representative of the French classic style.

Detached from the revelries, a young man symbolizes disillusion with the French bourgeoisie.

The classical sculptures look down on the orgy with contempt, their dignity contrasting with the frivolity of the revelers.

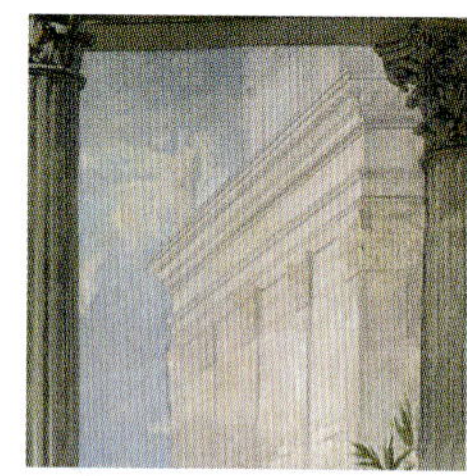

The hazy background glimpsed through the columns symbolizes the retreating values of the past.

A reveler offers a drink to a statue, representing the foolish behavior that accompanies moral downfall.

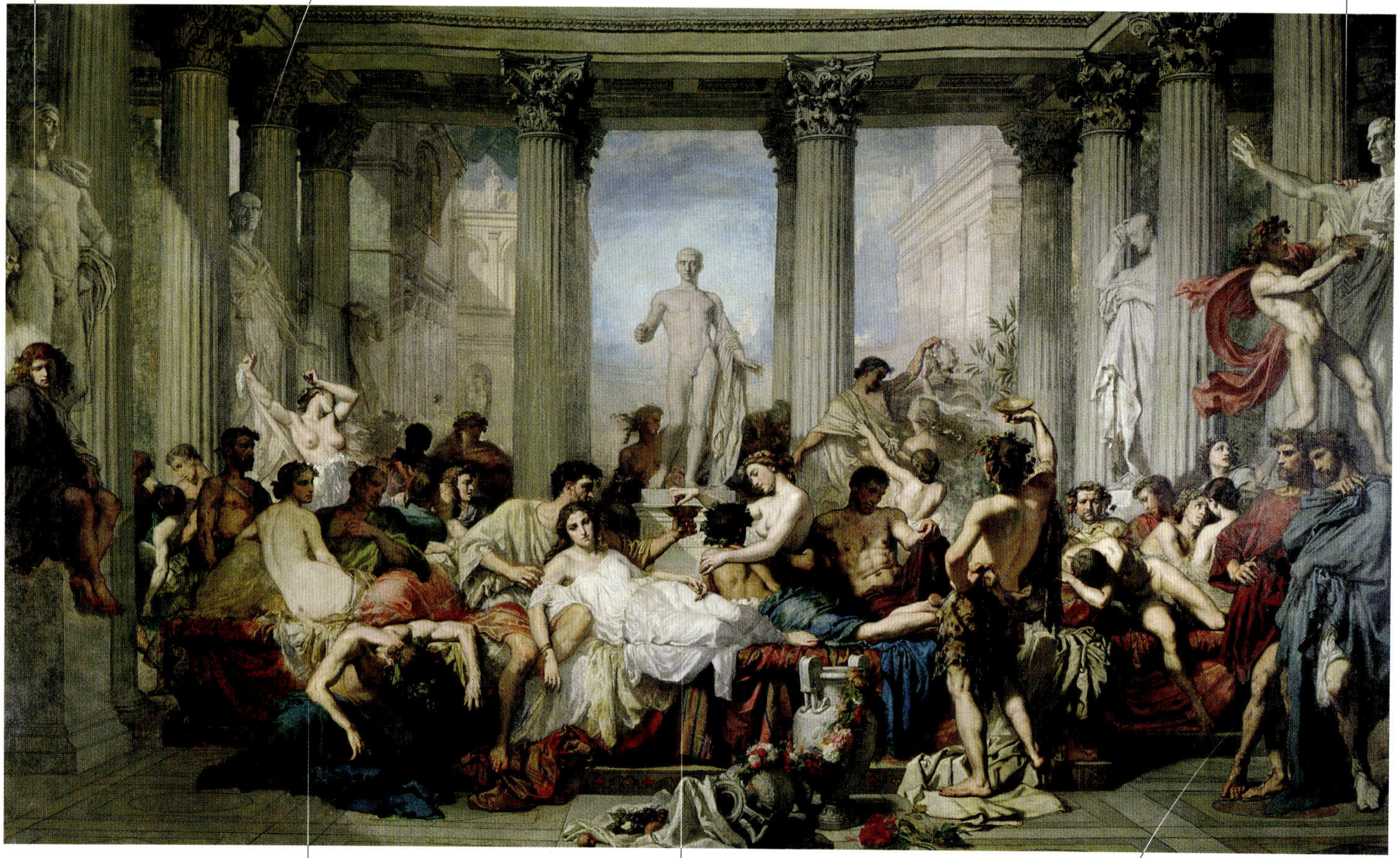

A nude woman poses as an odalisque (member of a Turkish harem). The odalisque was a common motif in French Romanticism, which eroticized the East.

A man offers grapes to a woman who embraces another man, emphasizing the sexual and political corruption at the core of French aristocratic society.

Two foreign visitors, not taking part in the drunken revels, cast disapproving glances over the unfolding scene.

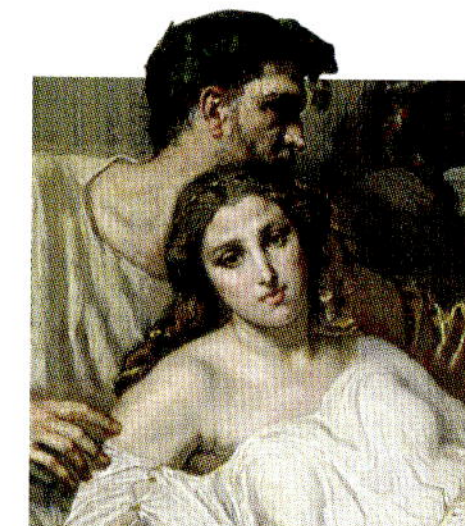

This reclining woman in the center of the painting gazes toward the viewer as if warning about the consequences of excess.

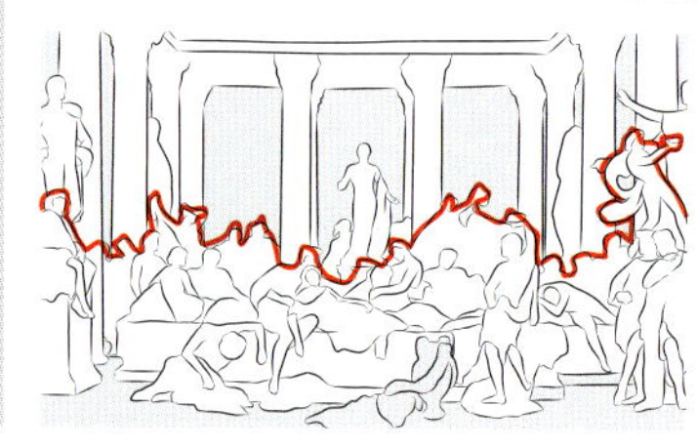

Contrasting angles
Architectural regularity and geometry in the background are disrupted by the curves of the revelers in the foreground.

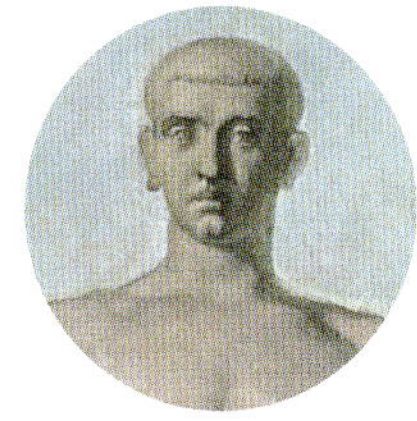

Cautionary symbol
The central statue, based on a work in the Louvre, depicts the Roman general Germanicus. While Germanicus was popular and principled, his son was Caligula, an emperor famously cruel and debauched.

Raftsmen Playing Cards

George Caleb Bingham 1847, oil on canvas, 28 × 38 in (71.3 × 96.7 cm), Saint Louis Art Museum, St. Louis, Missouri, US

George Caleb Bingham forged his artistic career in Missouri. He produced two types of painting: one portraying the cut and thrust of frontier politics, and the other depicting life on the Mississippi and Missouri rivers. *Raftsmen Playing Cards* romanticizes the lives of the boatmen—here they enjoy a card game in the early morning. Bingham uses light and invisible brushstrokes to create an ethereal sense of calm.

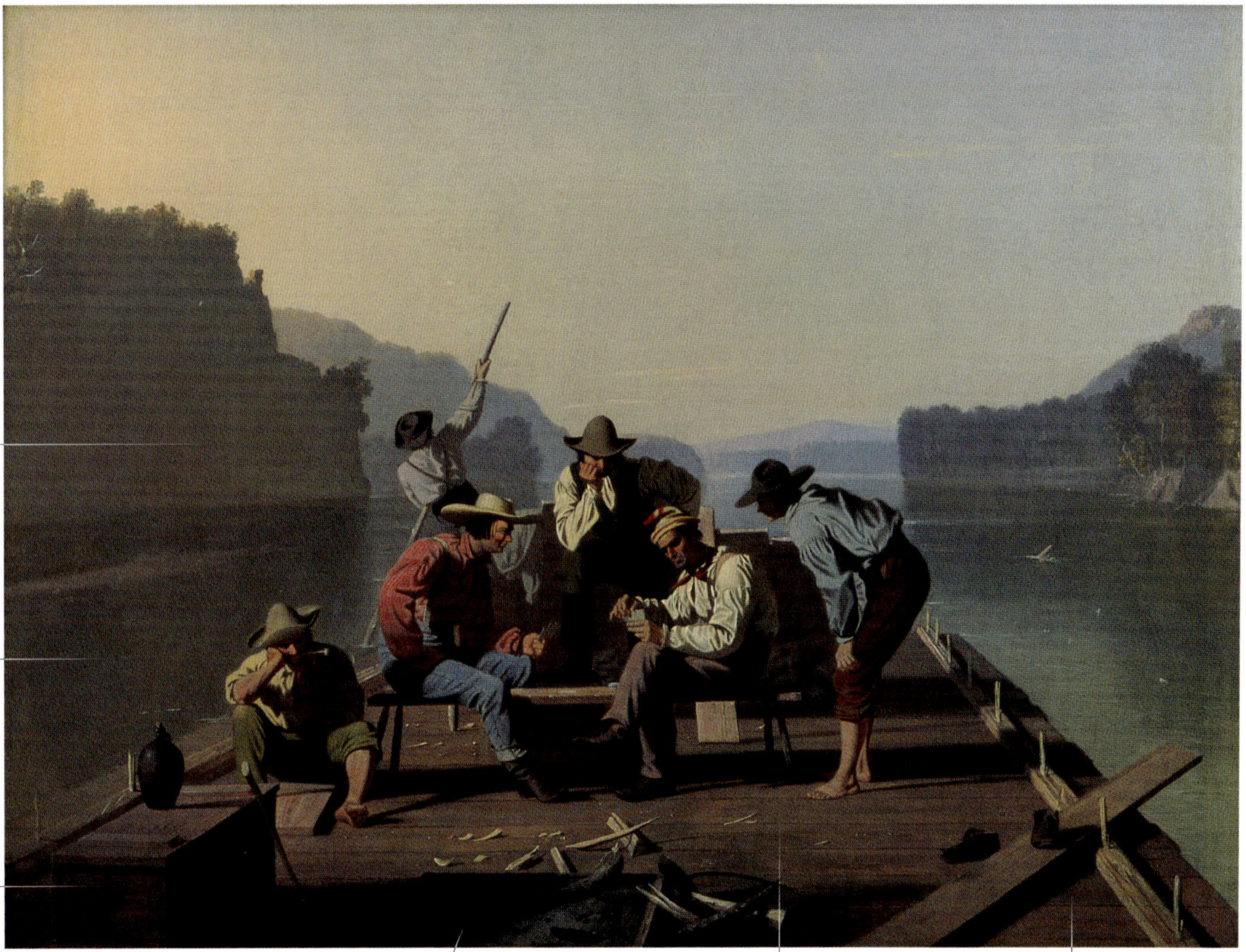

A pole man directs the raft down the river, correcting the course and avoiding sandbars that could beach the vessel.

The river is still and calm, reinforcing the air of relaxation.

Hard outlines in the foreground define the space, but the details soften as the scene recedes.

The friendly cast play cards with an intense and quiet focus. There is no sense of the raucousness found in Dutch genre scenes.

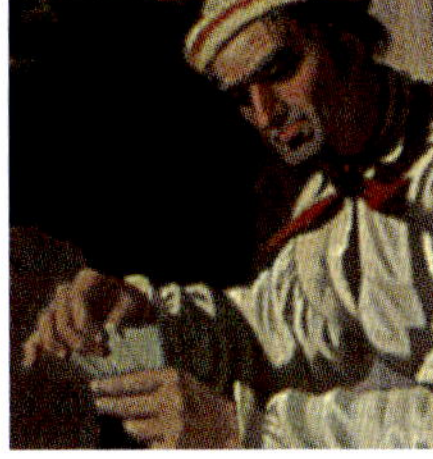

The remains of a campfire suggest that this is a long voyage taking several days.

This grouping appears in other works by Bingham, including *Mississippi Raftsmen at Cards*. Bingham drew on his huge collection of sketches when composing his paintings.

This type of boat was common on the Mississippi at the time. Unlike the steamers, they could navigate shallow water.

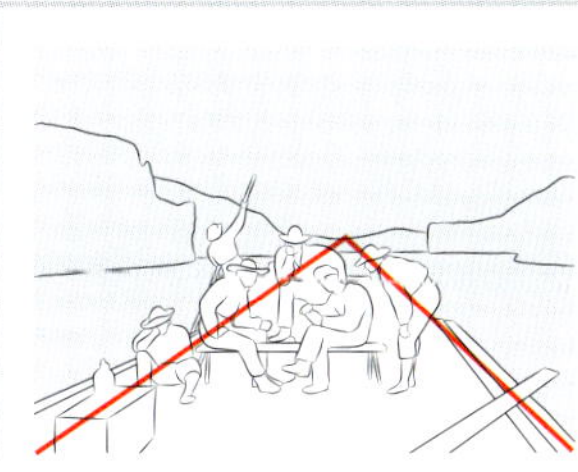

Pyramidal formation
As in many of Bingham's paintings, the composition forms a pyramid. The boat projects into the painting, inviting the viewer to join the men. A strong light source appears to the left, casting deep shadows.

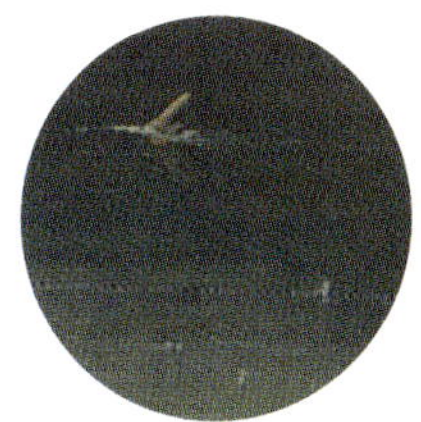

Fine surface
Bingham achieved the smooth surface of the paint by brushing out ridges with a sable brush, then applying flaxseed oil.

Mandu Yenu Throne

nji Nkome c. 1870, wood and beads, 69 in (175 cm) high, Ethnologisches Museum, Berlin, Germany

Mandu Yenu, meaning rich in beads, is a throne from the Kingdom of Bamum in the Cameroon grasslands, known for its opulent, courtly art. The impressive throne is carved of solid wood and covered in cloth, onto which beads have been stitched. The materials and symbolism communicate the economic, military, and spiritual power associated with kingship among the Bamum. On the side of the footstool, a trapdoor spider motif symbolizes the king's access to the ancestral realm, just as the spider burrows into the underworld.

Royal gift
The throne was made for King Nsangu (who reigned c. 1860–1886). His son, King Ibrahim Njoya, gave it to Kaiser Wilhelm II in 1908, during German colonial rule. Here, he sits on a copy of the original.

> "The court in all its splendor was the focal point of Bamum society."
>
> Christraud M. Geary

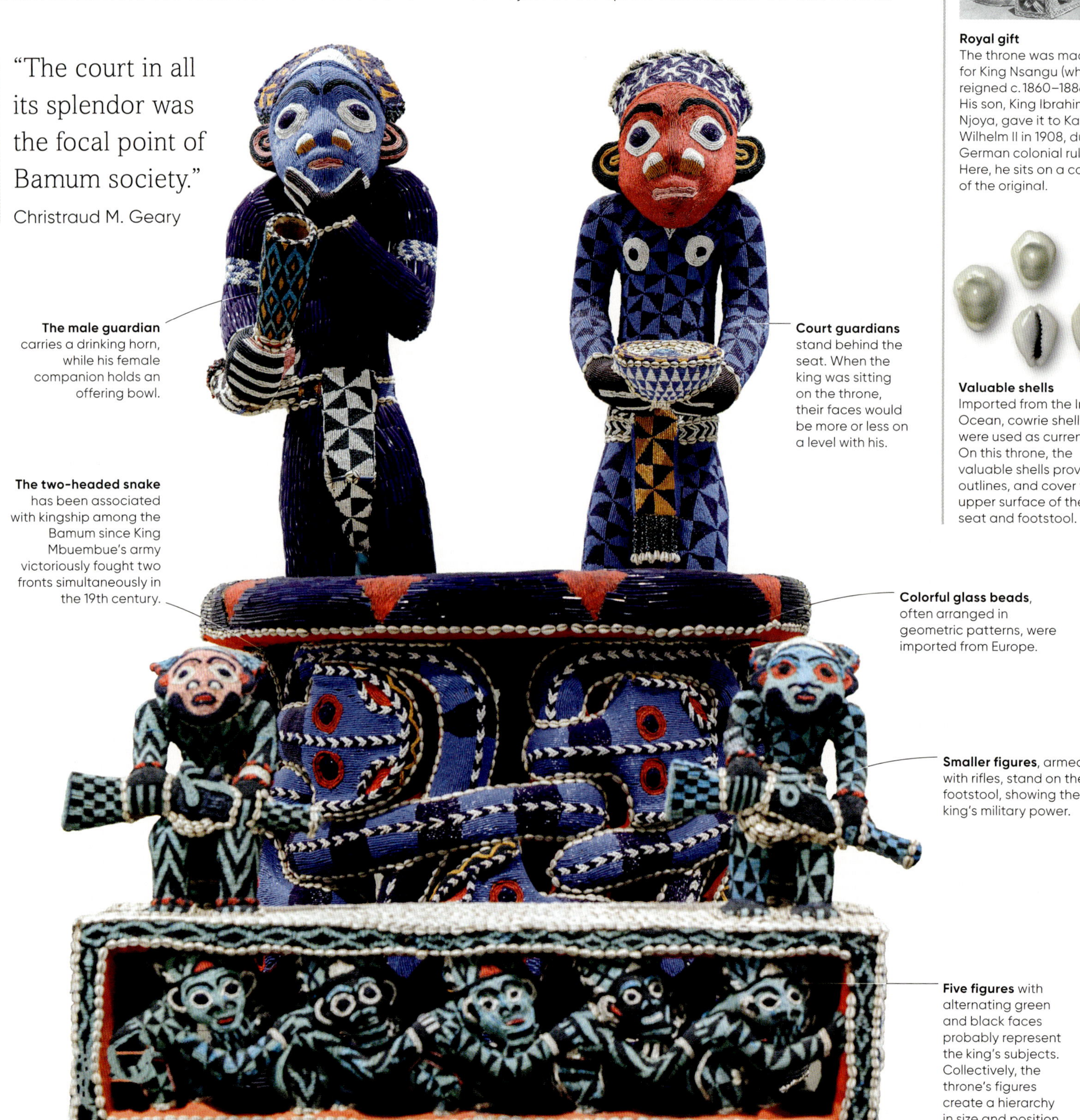

The male guardian carries a drinking horn, while his female companion holds an offering bowl.

Court guardians stand behind the seat. When the king was sitting on the throne, their faces would be more or less on a level with his.

Valuable shells
Imported from the Indian Ocean, cowrie shells were used as currency. On this throne, the valuable shells provide outlines, and cover the upper surface of the seat and footstool.

The two-headed snake has been associated with kingship among the Bamum since King Mbuembue's army victoriously fought two fronts simultaneously in the 19th century.

Colorful glass beads, often arranged in geometric patterns, were imported from Europe.

Smaller figures, armed with rifles, stand on the footstool, showing the king's military power.

Five figures with alternating green and black faces probably represent the king's subjects. Collectively, the throne's figures create a hierarchy in size and position.

The Great Day of His Wrath

John Martin 1851–1853, oil on canvas, 77 × 119 in (196.5 × 303.2 cm), Tate Britain, London, UK

A city is torn up and thrown into the abyss in Martin's portrayal of the apocalyptic events foretold in the Book of Revelation (6:12-17), the last book of the New Testament, describing the end of the world.

Full of drama and spectacle, this cataclysmic vision of destruction is the third part of Martin's Judgment Series triptych, along with *The Plains of Heaven* (1851–1853) and *The Last Judgment* (1853).

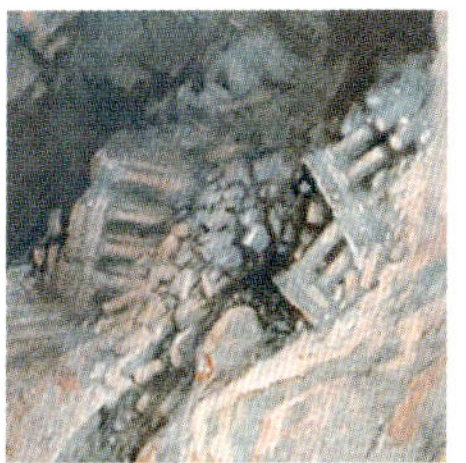

The buildings are historic classical structures. This painting was conceived as entertainment rather than as a warning urging its 19th-century viewers to repent.

Lightning from the heavens seems to break the mountains apart; Martin is emphasizing that this is God's will.

A tower is tumbling into the abyss. It appears to take a direct strike from the lightning.

The red glowing orb represents the moon, which the text says "became as blood."

Martin's earthquake is a crashing wave of earth; Revelation says "every mountain and island were moved out of their places."

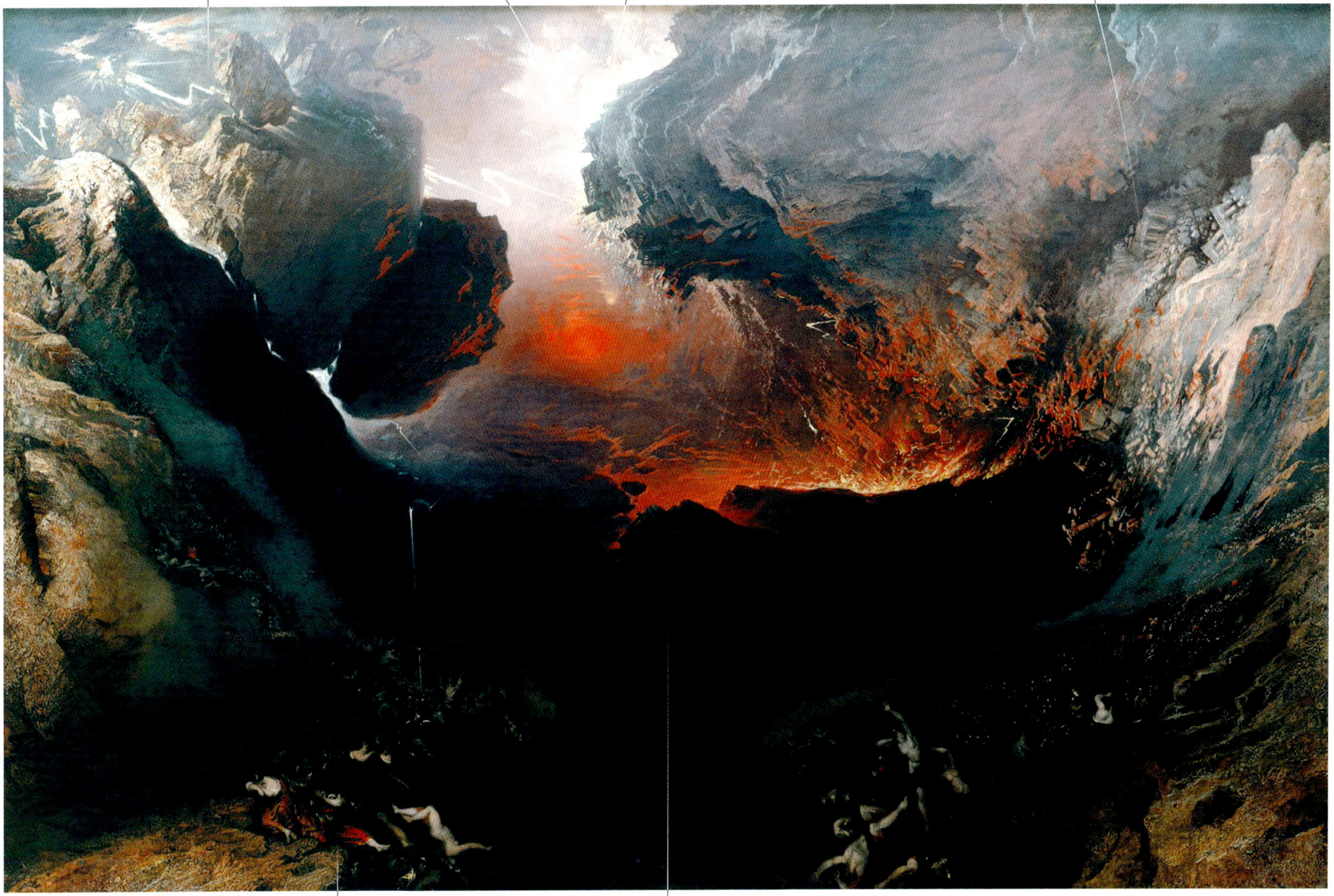

People fall into the abyss; those who are clothed seem to wear classical garb, not 19th-century attire.

The red glow was reportedly inspired by the glow of iron foundries at night.

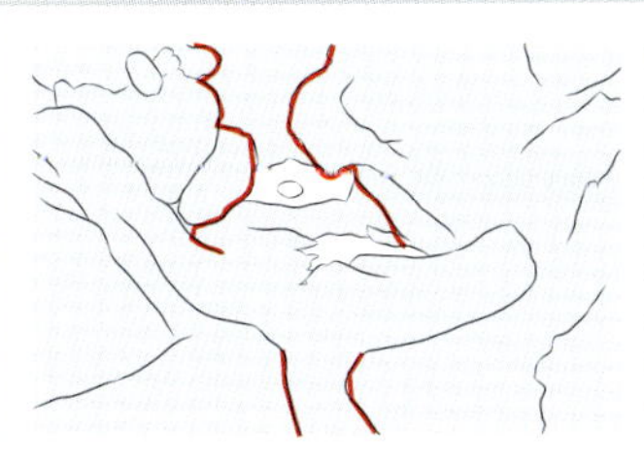

Perspective
Converging lines created by the cliffs collapsing inward and the abyss in the foreground draw the viewer's eye toward the center of the painting, with its extreme contrast of bright fire against deep black.

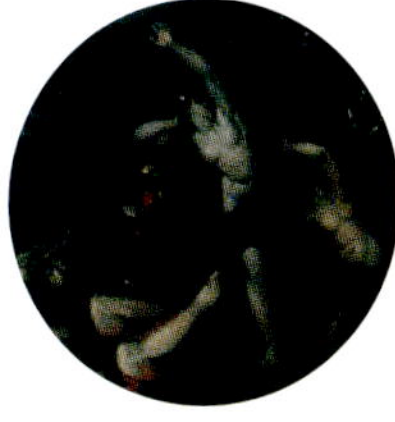

Tiny figures
The people falling into the abyss are tiny, emphasizing the scale of the events unfolding and the terrifying power of God's wrath. They also add interest to the foreground—an effect known as staffage.

"... there was a great earthquake; and the sun became black as sackcloth of hair, and the moon became as blood ..."

Book of Revelation, The Bible

A Burial at Ornans

Gustave Courbet 1849–1850, oil on canvas, 124 × 260 in (315 × 660 cm), Musée d'Orsay, Paris, France

Courbet's painting commemorates the burial of a common man as if he were royalty. It set aside artistic tradition in favor of creating a glorious depiction of ordinary people, and in doing so caused a scandal. The work is on the massive scale traditionally reserved for images on religious, mythological, or historical themes. The deceased is thought to be Courbet's great uncle Oudot, but *A Burial at Ornans* does not celebrate him—he is not even identified in the painting's title—so much as his community. Around 50 local residents, from the mayor to Courbet's own family, proceed in a serpentine path toward the open grave.

The sky is not used to add drama to the scene, unlike many paintings about death which use symbols such as a ray of sunlight breaking through clouds to illuminate the coffin.

A crucifix extends above the distant horizon into the heavens.

The village gravedigger Antoine Joseph Cassard (kneeling), is more prominent in the painting than the priest.

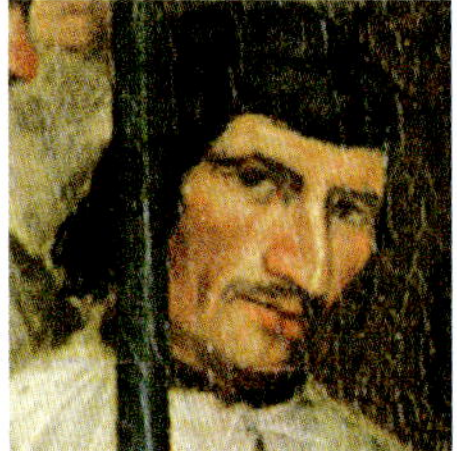

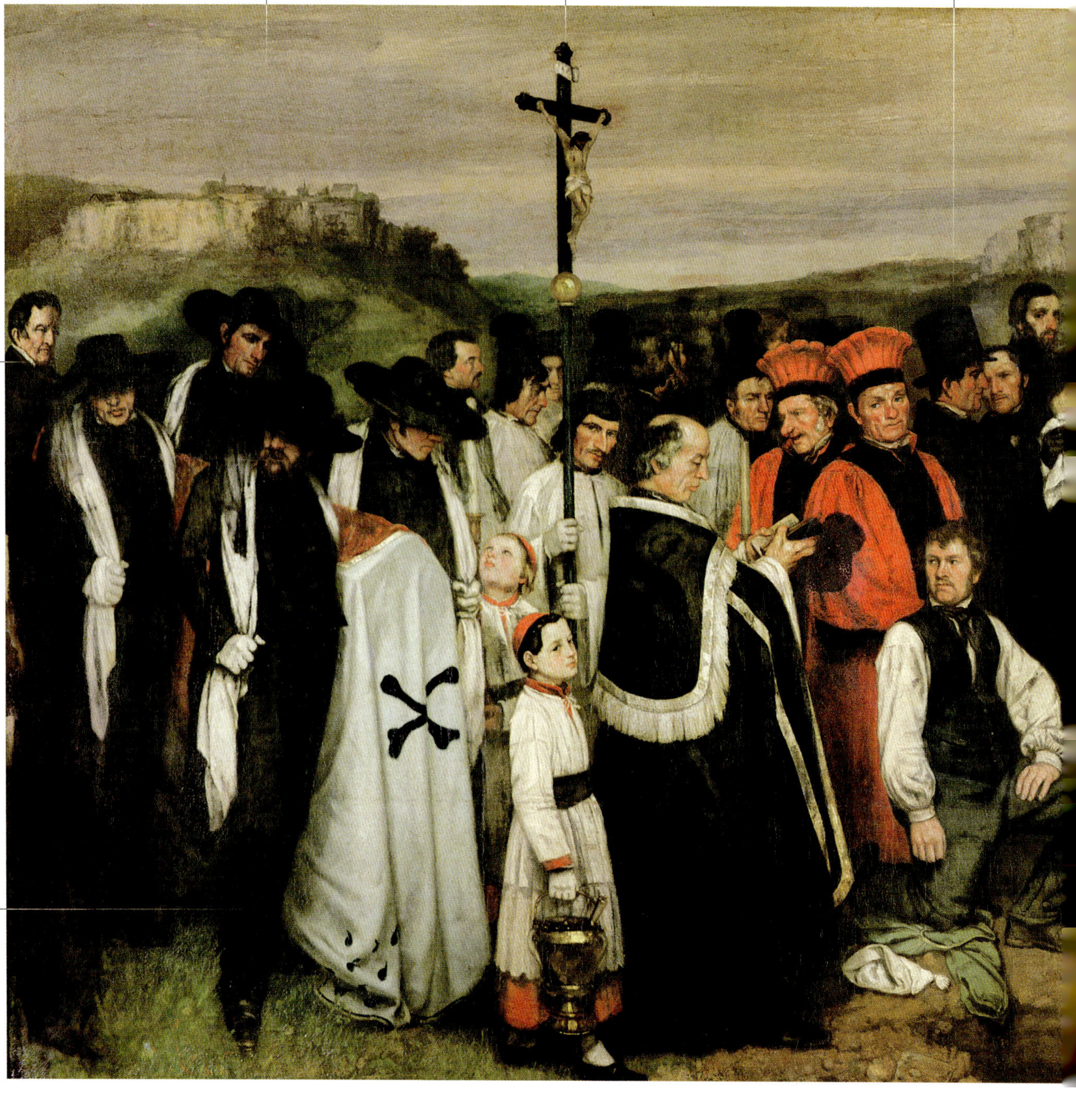

The man holding the crucifix (believed to be a local vigneron) stares directly at the viewer.

This man is believed to be Oudot, the deceased, attending his own funeral.

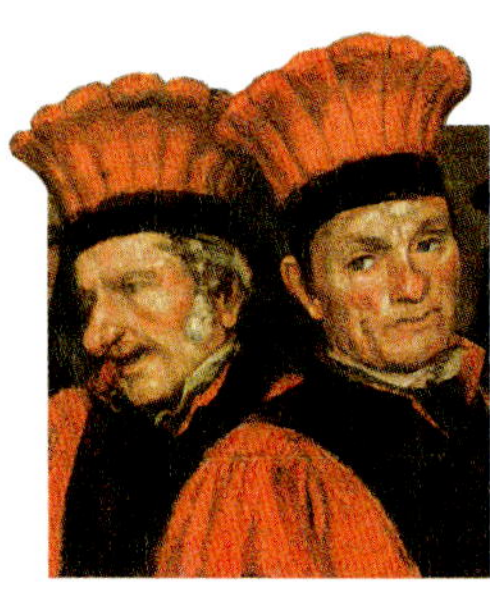

Church officials in red are painted in a less-than-flattering fashion, reflecting Courbet's skeptical view of religion.

Oudot's cloth-draped coffin is barely visible. Courbet's focus is on the community and the cycle of life, not eulogizing the dead.

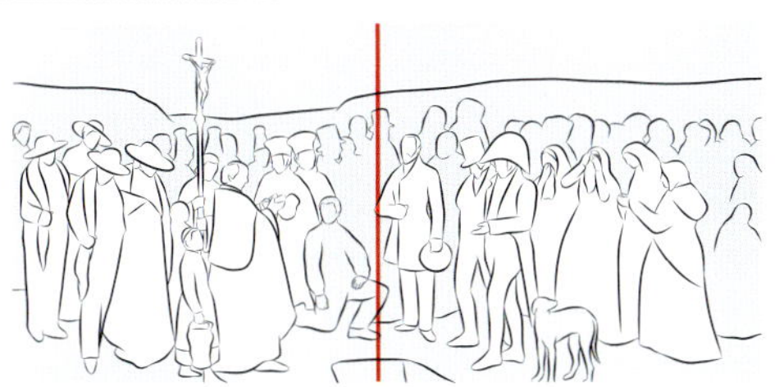

Composition
The grave divides the painting in two—clergy, pallbearers, and the deceased on the left, secular figures on the right. Repeated poses and gestures create visual harmony. The figures are grouped in a shallow foreground, almost as if in a classical frieze.

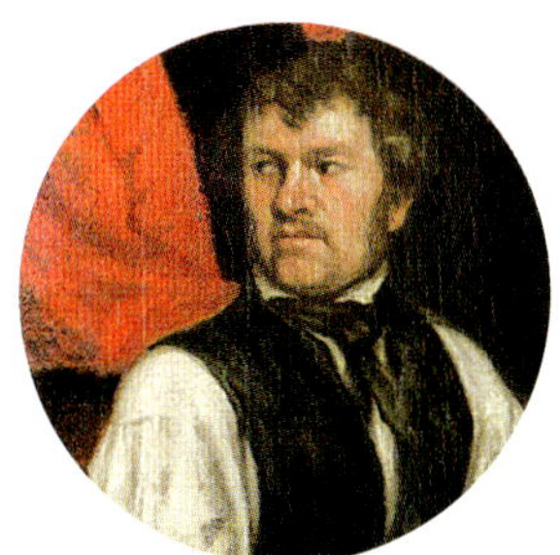

Brushwork
Courbet's brushstrokes are loose and full of feeling, not the smooth, imperceptible strokes found in academic works at the time. The texture varies—rougher for the earth, smoother for clothing—adding depth, interest, and realism.

> "*Burial at Ornans* ... is the portrait of a community, Courbet's own community, gathered around the grave of one of its members."
>
> Linda Nochlin

Two men are incongruously dressed in the fashion of French revolutionaries from 1793. Courbet's uncle Oudot had been a revolutionary.

Ornans is in a mountainous region near the Swiss border. These cliffs appear to contain and protect the community.

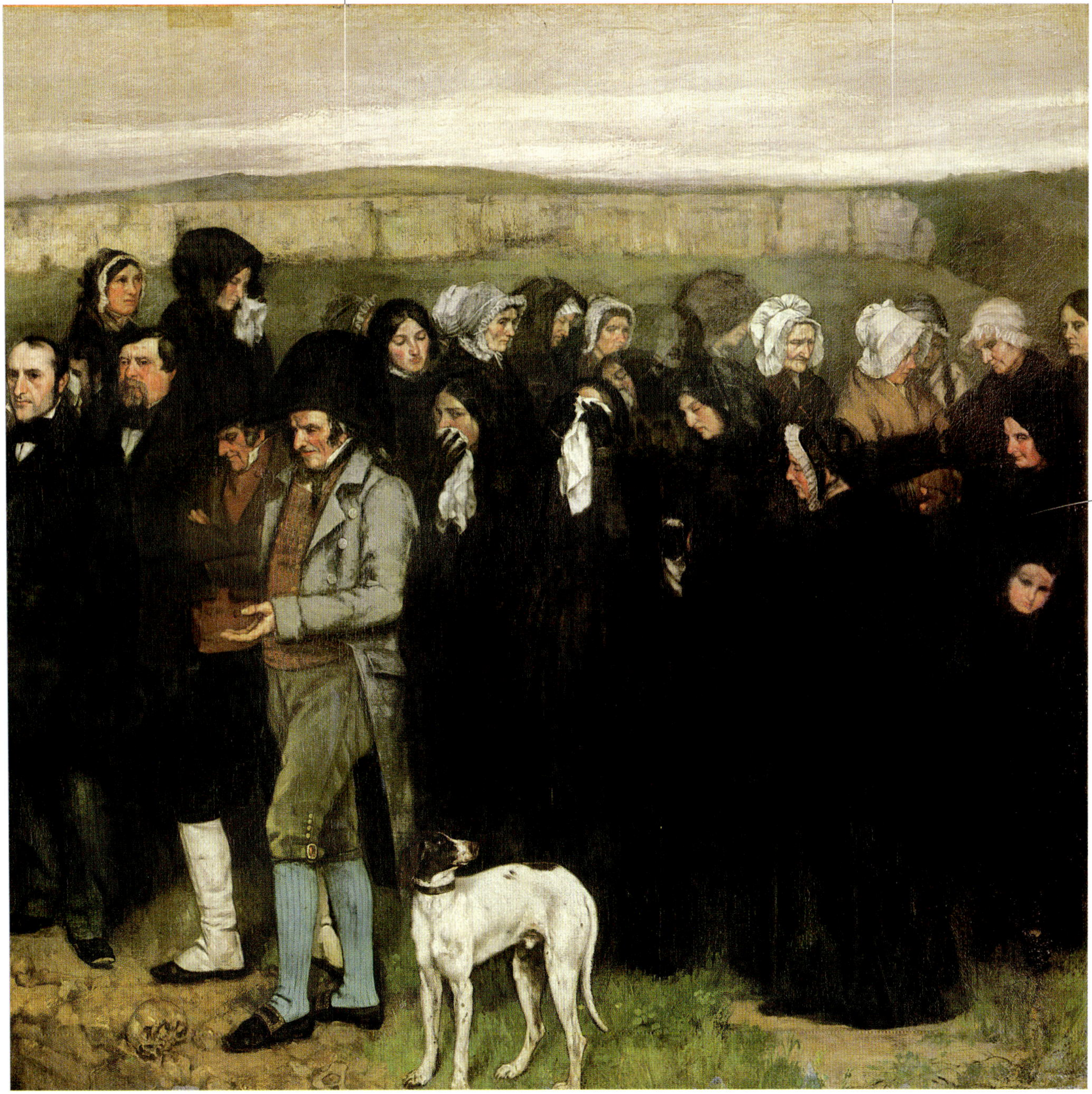

The black clothes of the women—Courbet's mother and sisters among them—meld into a mass, suggesting the unity of the community.

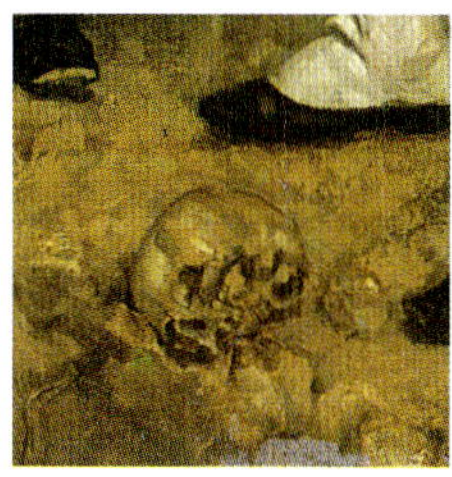

A skull, a traditional reminder of death, rests at the feet of the revolutionaries.

Madame Moitessier

Jean-Auguste-Dominique Ingres 1844–1856, oil on canvas, 48 × 36 in (121.3 × 90.9 cm), National Gallery, London, UK

By 1844, Ingres was well known for his history painting and reluctant to accept portraiture commissions, which were considered "low art." He made an exception upon meeting Madame Moitessier, the wife of a wealthy banker. Impressed by her commanding manner, he portrayed her in the grandiose style of Roman sculpture.

> "Never has a beauty … of a type more like Juno delivered its proud lines to the trembling crayons of an artist."
>
> Théophile Gautier

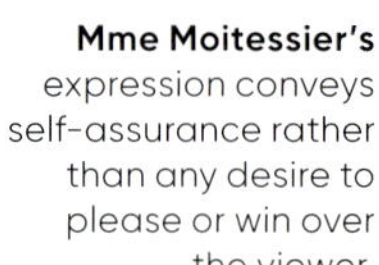

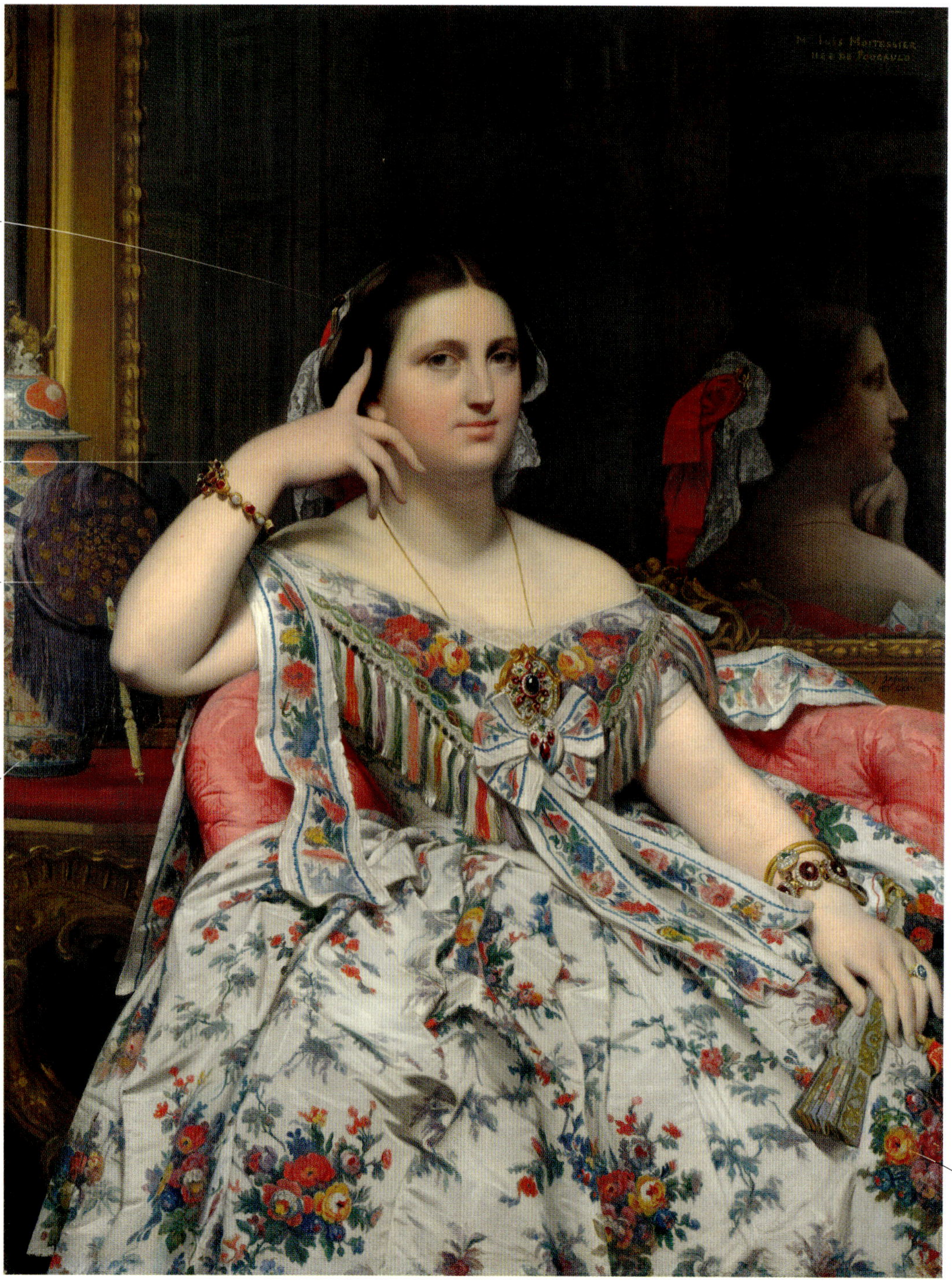

Mme Moitessier's expression conveys self-assurance rather than any desire to please or win over the viewer.

This floppy-fingered hand is unlifelike when considered closely, but in the context of the painting it sets off the severity of the subject's face.

Mme. Moitessier would have held up this silk hand-screen to shield her face from the reddening effect of a fire.

Gilded walls and luxury imports, such as this Japanese Imari vase, emphasize the family's wealth and status.

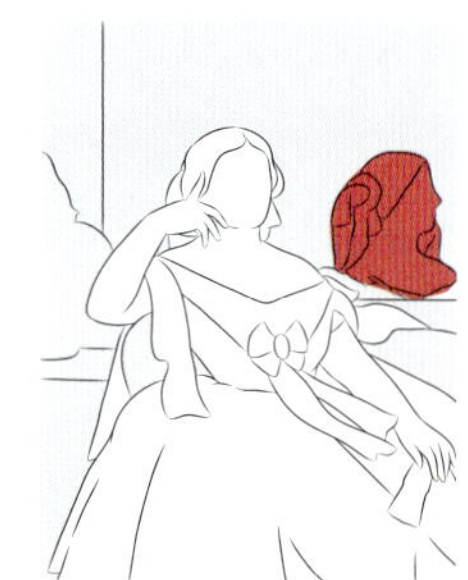

Multiple perspectives The reflection in the mirror behind Mme Moitessier is not scientifically accurate. By offering an additional perspective, the artist anticipates the later experimentation of the Cubists.

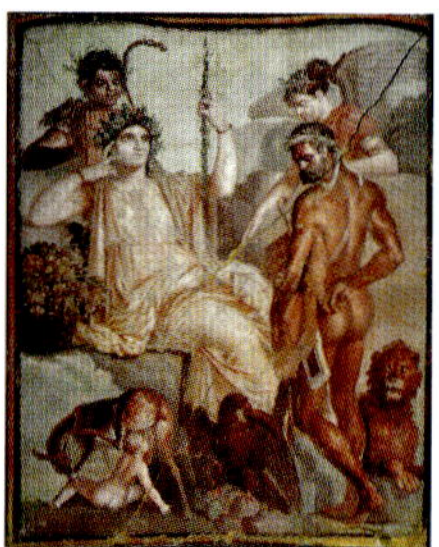

Classical influences Ingres portrayed Mme. Moitessier with the regal air of Juno, queen of the Roman goddesses. Her pose—including the languid hand—is explicitly modeled on that of the goddess of Arcadia in a famous fresco found in the ruins of Herculaneum, near Pompeii.

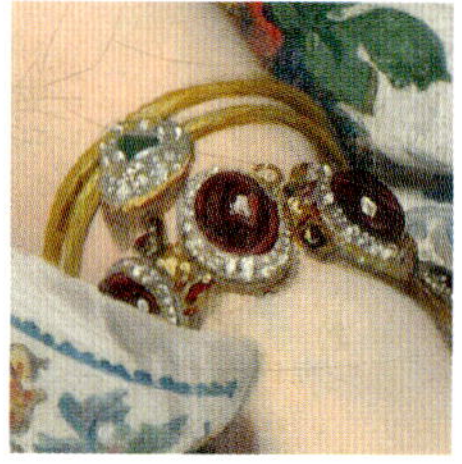

Ingres himself picked out the jewelery that Mme. Moitessier wears. Its bright, hard gemstones draw a contrast with the soft plumpness of her arm.

The bright colors and elaborate ornamentation of the dress highlight the smooth simplicity of the woman's skin.

Sudden showers were a favorite subject of Edo-period painters and poets.

The distant shore depicts Atake, an area of Edo (present-day Tokyo).

A boatman rushes along on a log raft, seemingly impervious to the evening rain.

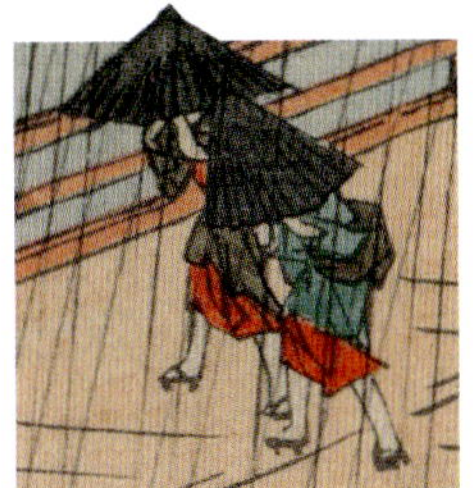

Seven figures cross the bridge, sheltering from the rain under hats, umbrellas, and capes.

The bridge is the Shin-Ōhashi Bridge over the Sumida River.

Although the signature reads *Hiroshige ga* (painted by Hiroshige), a woodblock image was a collaborative effort, involving an engraver, a printer, and a publisher.

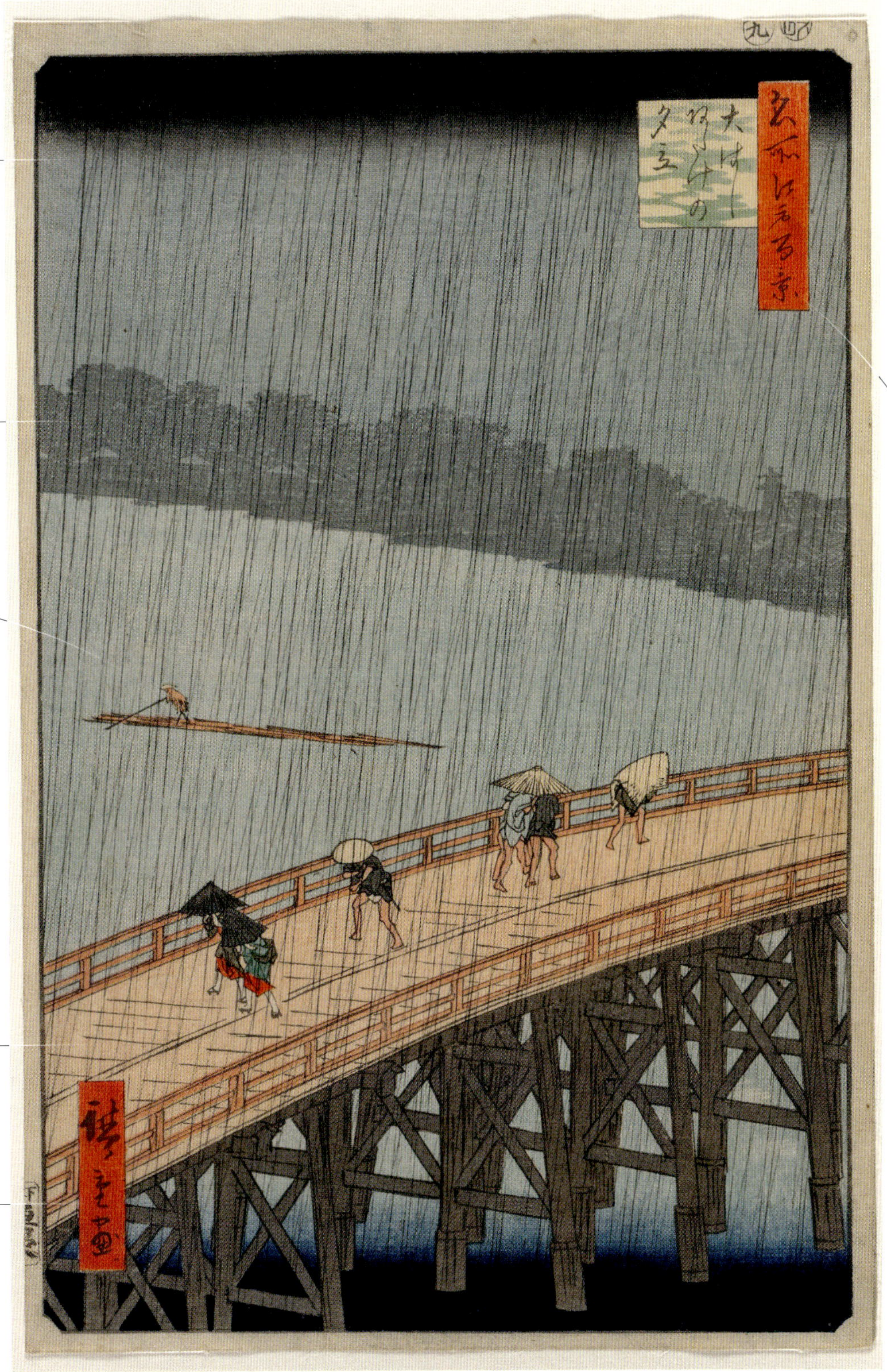

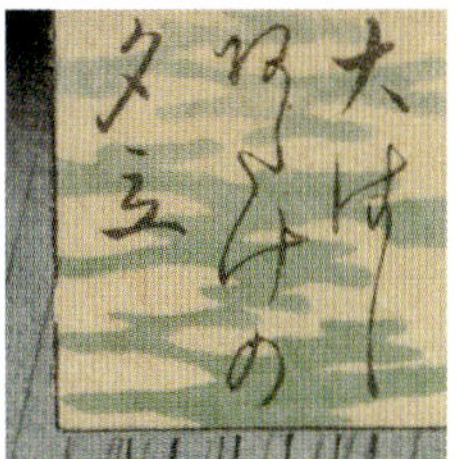

The series title, *Meisho Edo hyakkei* (One Hundred Famous Views of Edo), is inscribed in the top right corner, since Japanese is read from right to left.

A second inscription gives the artwork's title, *Ōhashi Atake no yūdachi.*

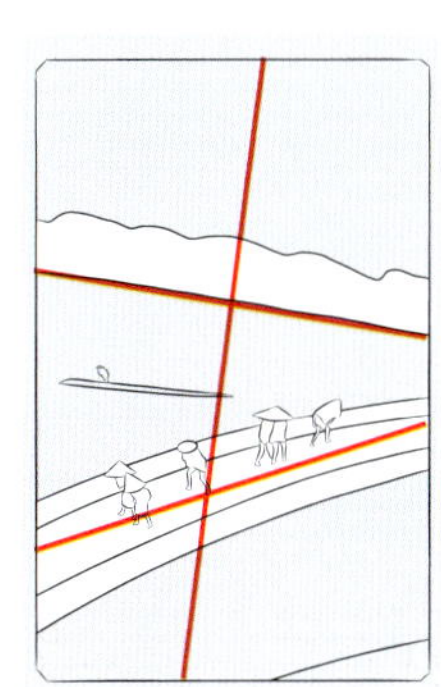

Composition
The strong diagonals of the bridge, shoreline, and oblique rain help create a dynamic composition.

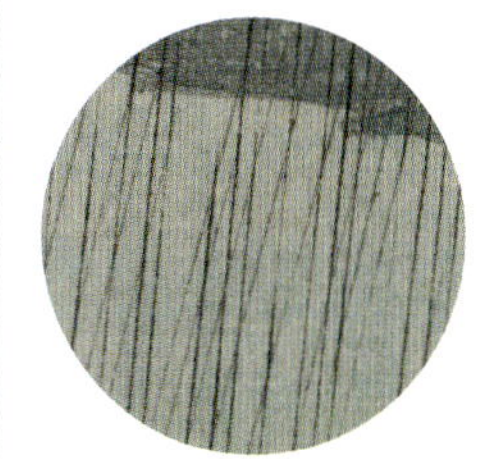

A hidden jigsaw puzzle
Ukiyo-e prints used a different woodblock for each color. The intricate crisscrossing pattern of the rain in this image would have presented a significant technical challenge, as consistency of thickness and orientation needed to be maintained across all of the carved and inked blocks.

Sudden Shower over Shin-Ōhashi and Atake

Utagawa Hiroshige 1857, woodblock print on paper, 13 × 9 in (34 × 24.1 cm), Cleveland Museum of Art, US

This depiction of people caught in a heavy shower on a summer evening epitomizes the *ukiyo-e* (floating world) artist Hiroshige's mastery of woodblock printing. One in a series of views of Edo, it perfectly demonstrates the Edo-period penchant for capturing momentary natural phenomena, representing cross-sections of urban life and referencing traditional landmarks.

The Horse Fair

Rosa Bonheur 1853, oil on canvas, 96 × 199 in (244.5 × 506.7 cm), Metropolitan Museum of Art, New York, US

Bonheur's horses circle in a roiling mass, their energy barely contained within the frame of the painting as their handlers struggle to show them off to best advantage. They are placed in the foreground, close to the viewer, introducing a sense of danger. Bonheur, an expert animal painter, spent 18 months making studies at a Paris horse fair, and visited abattoirs to examine horse anatomy, before making the painting. Its realism is almost photographic, and it became one of the most famous animal paintings of the 19th century.

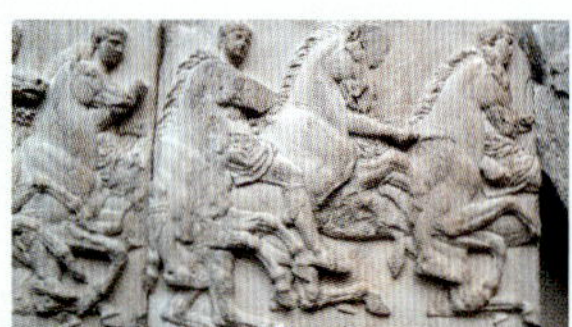

Classical inspiration
The horses are ranged across the lower half of the canvas. Bonheur was influenced by a line of horsemen on the frieze of the Parthenon.

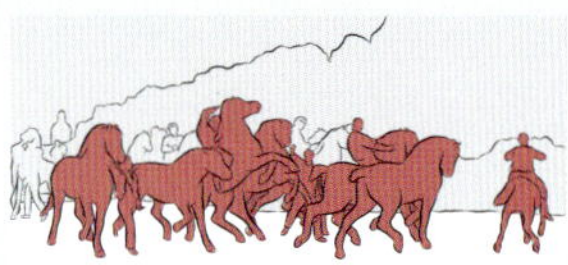

Creating depth
The artist has used aerial perspective. Strong colors and sharp outlines occur in the foreground. Forms become less distinct and colors softer in the distance.

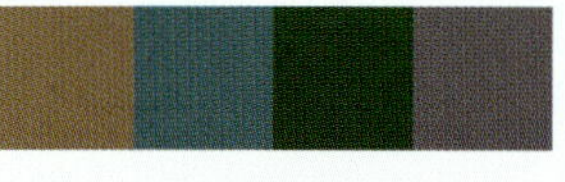

Conveying mood
Strong light/dark contrasts dominate, with accents of blue sandwiched between warm earth tones in the foreground and muted greens and blue-grays in the distance.

"It is my dream to show horses snorting fire and dust welling up around their hooves. I want this infernal waltz, this wild tornado to make people's heads spin."
Rosa Bonheur

A calmer horse is shown head on. The horses are portrayed from different angles and with different temperaments, demonstrating Bonheur's skill.

The receding row of trees limits the activity of the horses to the lower half of the painting.

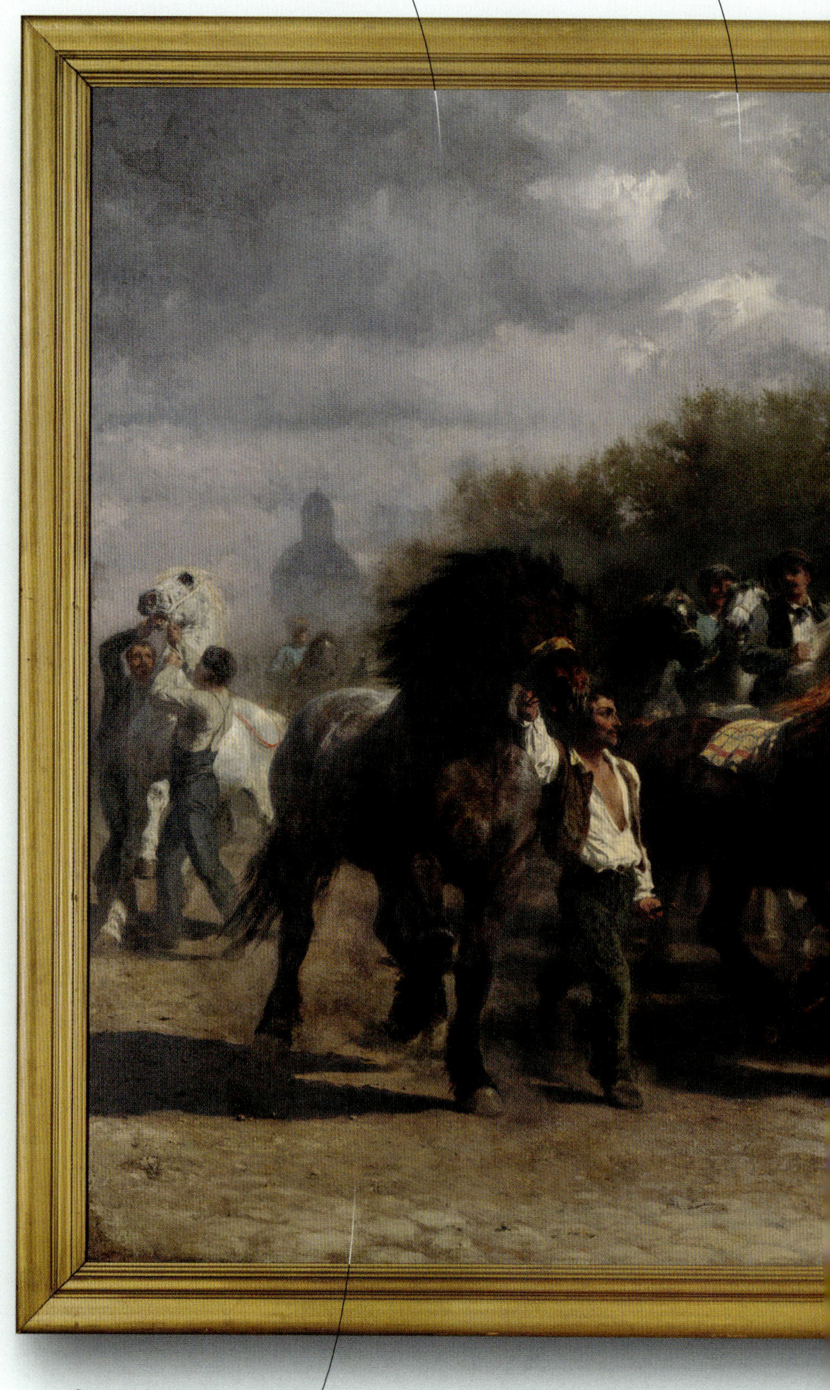

Strong shadows are cast on the ground. The contrasts of light and shadow across the scene create fully three-dimensional forms.

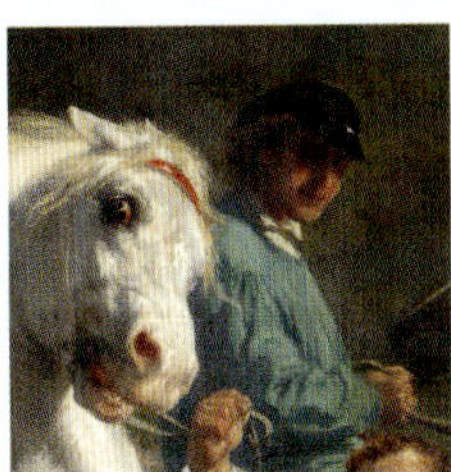

Bonheur has included herself in the picture. The artist dressed in men's clothing to avoid attracting attention while she sketched the market.

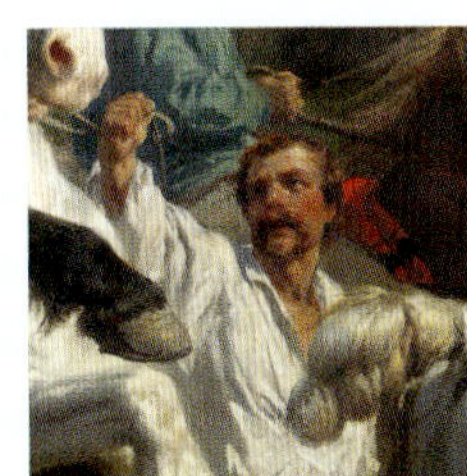

In the center of the painting, a handler struggling to control his horse adds extra drama to the scene.

A crowd has been drawn to the spectacle beside Paris's tree-lined Boulevard de l'Hôpital.

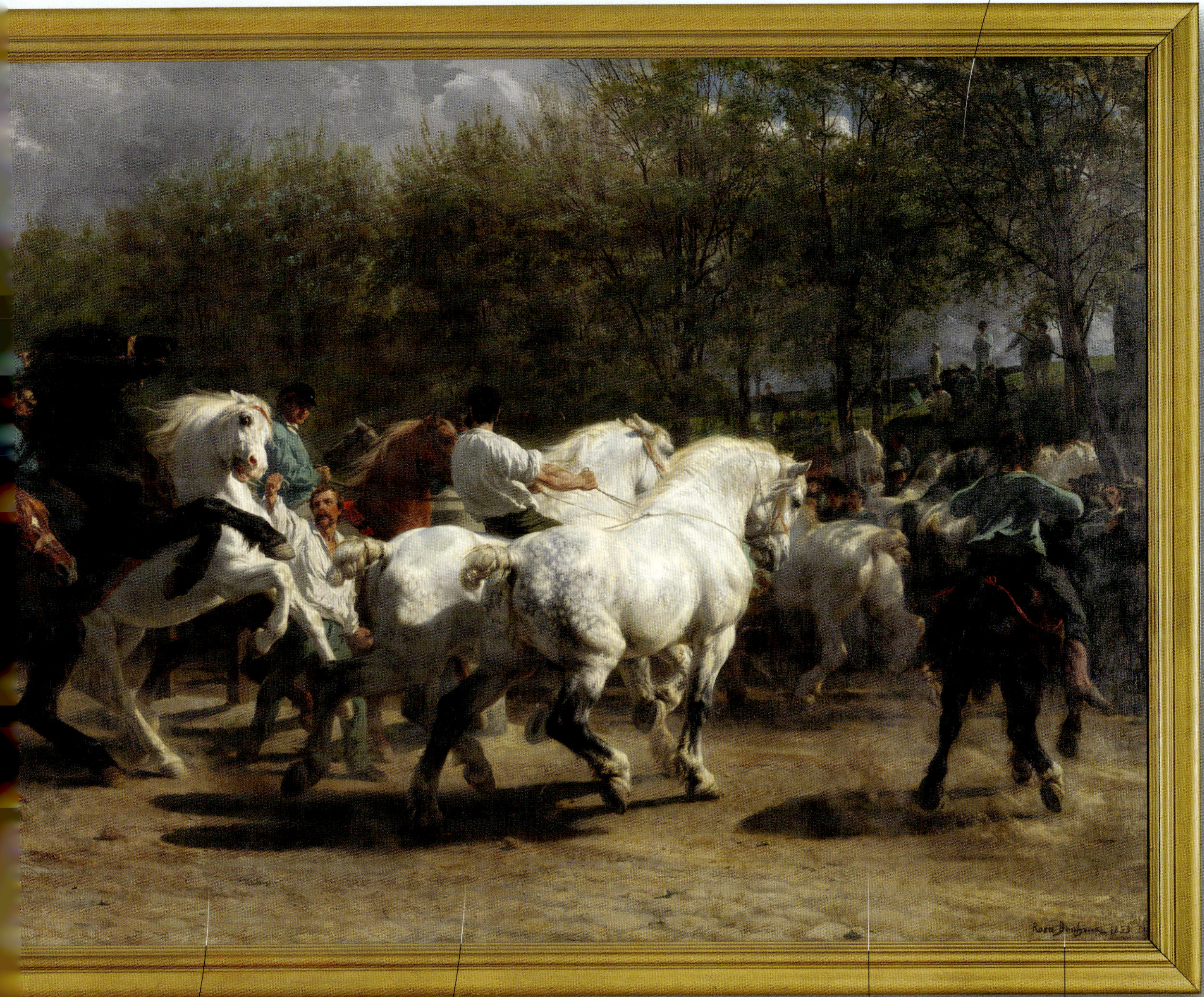

A strong white light falls like a spotlight through the center of the painting.

The white horses are Percherons, a breed of large, powerful draft horses. Their musculature is modeled in detail.

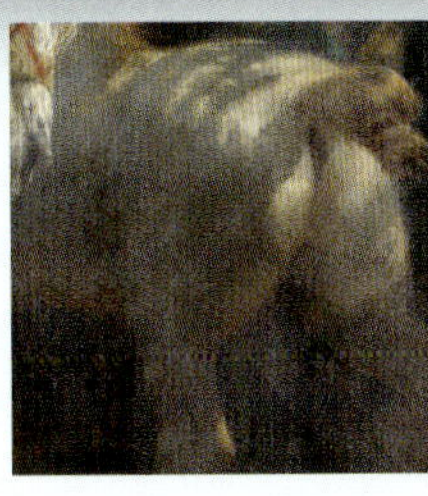

Bright light falling from the right-hand side catches the horses' rumps, which seem to glisten.

Clouds of dust kicked up by the boisterous activity add to the realism.

Bonheur retouched the painting and added a second date, 1855.

The Gleaners

Jean-François Millet 1857, oil on canvas, 33 × 43 in (83.5 × 110 cm), Musée d'Orsay, Paris, France

French peasant women gather the grain that remains in a field following harvest in an image that captures the struggles of rural poverty. Gleaners were not farm employees but poor people, often women, who scavenged harvested fields for overlooked grain, as had been their legal right since Biblical times.

The field's furrow lines do not meet at a single vanishing point, perhaps symbolizing the differences between the gleaners and farmers.

Seen in the distance, the actual harvest is far removed from the women gleaning in the foreground.

The colors, light, and tone of the painting are soft and warm; some critics argue Millet is sanctifying these women.

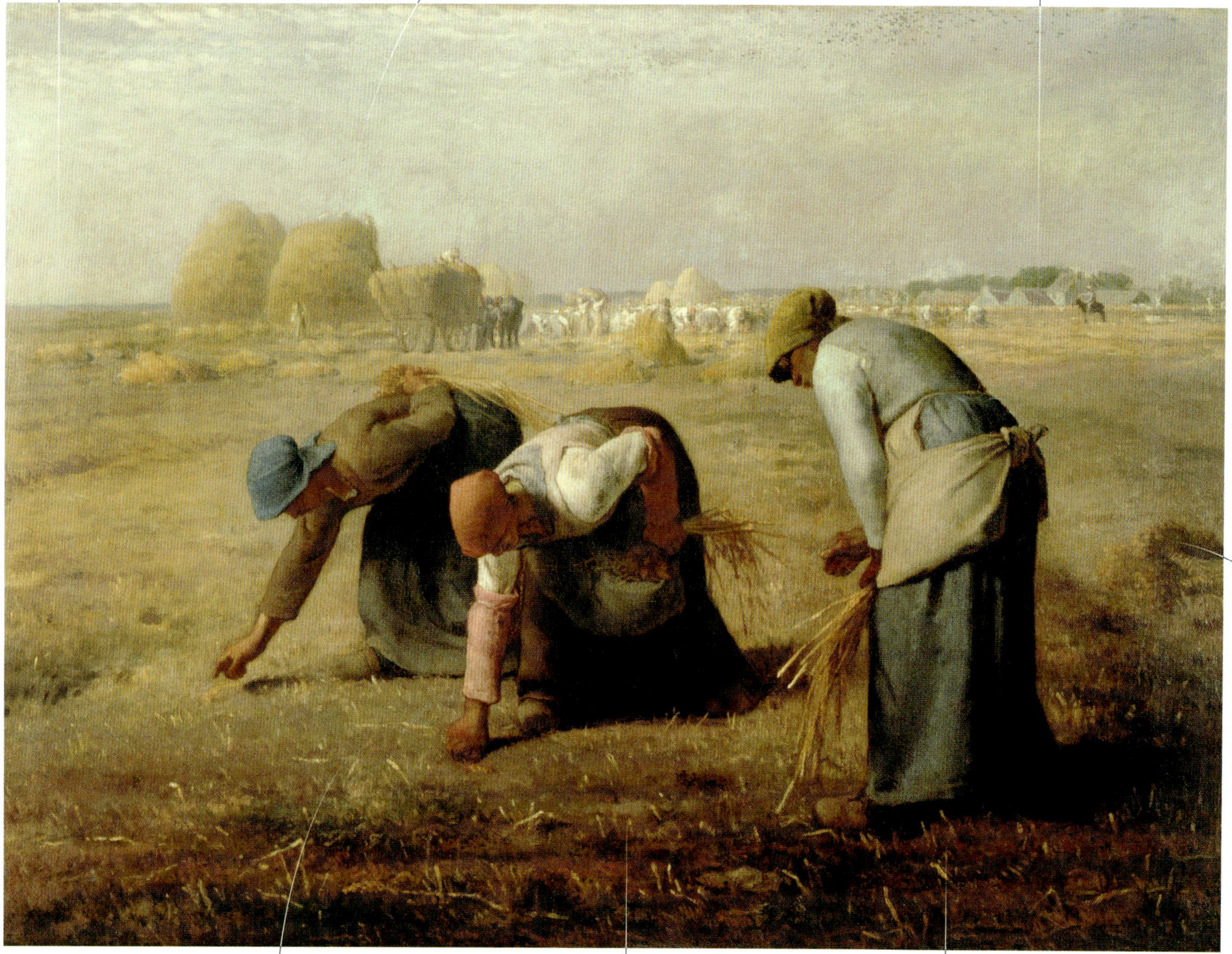

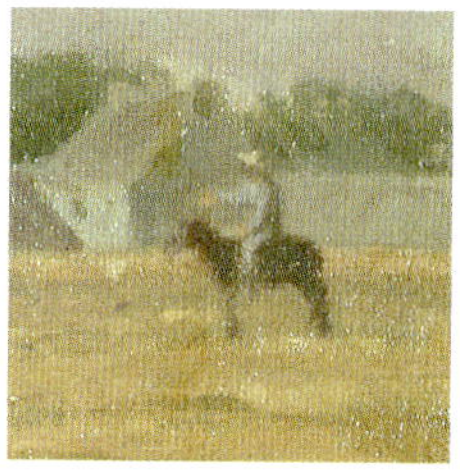

As an overseer, the rider would ensure the gleaners took only the fallen grain allowed by law.

The small pile of grain the women have collected contrasts with the heavily loaded wagon in the background.

The women wear humble clothing, but not rags. These women are dignified peasants, not beggars; gleaning was their legal right.

Varied ages are shown—with the youngest on the left and oldest on the right—suggesting the inescapable nature of rural poverty.

Straightening up for a moment, this woman highlights the arduous nature of the work.

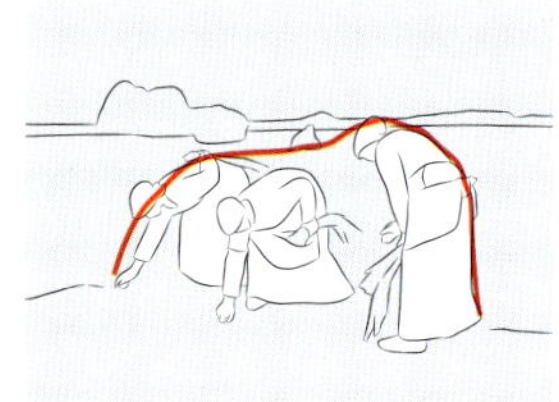

Haystack symbolism
Viewed as a group, the three women suggest the shape of a haystack, emphasizing the gleaners' connection to the fields.

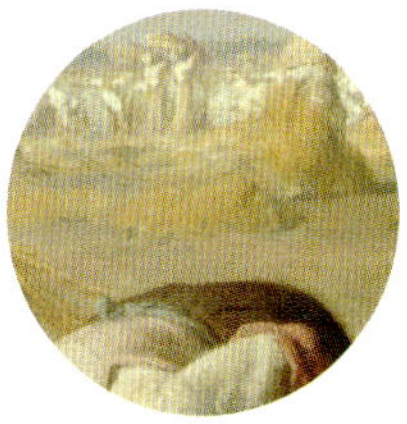

Aerial perspective
Millet's lack of detail and use of light colors in the background create a sense of distance from the more detailed, darker figures and landscape in the foreground.

"Millet's painting is in many ways a celebration of the tenuous balance between beauty and despair, labor and reward in the precarious cycle of country life."

Alexandra R. Murphy, 1984

The Bellelli Family

Edgar Degas c. 1858–1867, oil on canvas, 79 × 98 in (201 × 249.5 cm), Musée d'Orsay, Paris, France

The artist's aunt, Laure de Gas, her husband Baron Gennaro Bellelli, and their two daughters are the subjects of this unsettling portrait. Degas, who stayed with them in Italy when in his twenties, depicts each family member looking in a different direction, isolated in their own world. It is a study of marital discord.

Giulia, the eldest daughter, is the only person who looks toward the viewer, her prim expression and folded hands demonstrating compliance.

Laure is in mourning following the death of her father, Hilaire de Gas, whose framed portrait hangs next to her.

Giovanna, the youngest daughter, sits restlessly with one leg tucked up—a childlike pose in a scene full of adult conventions.

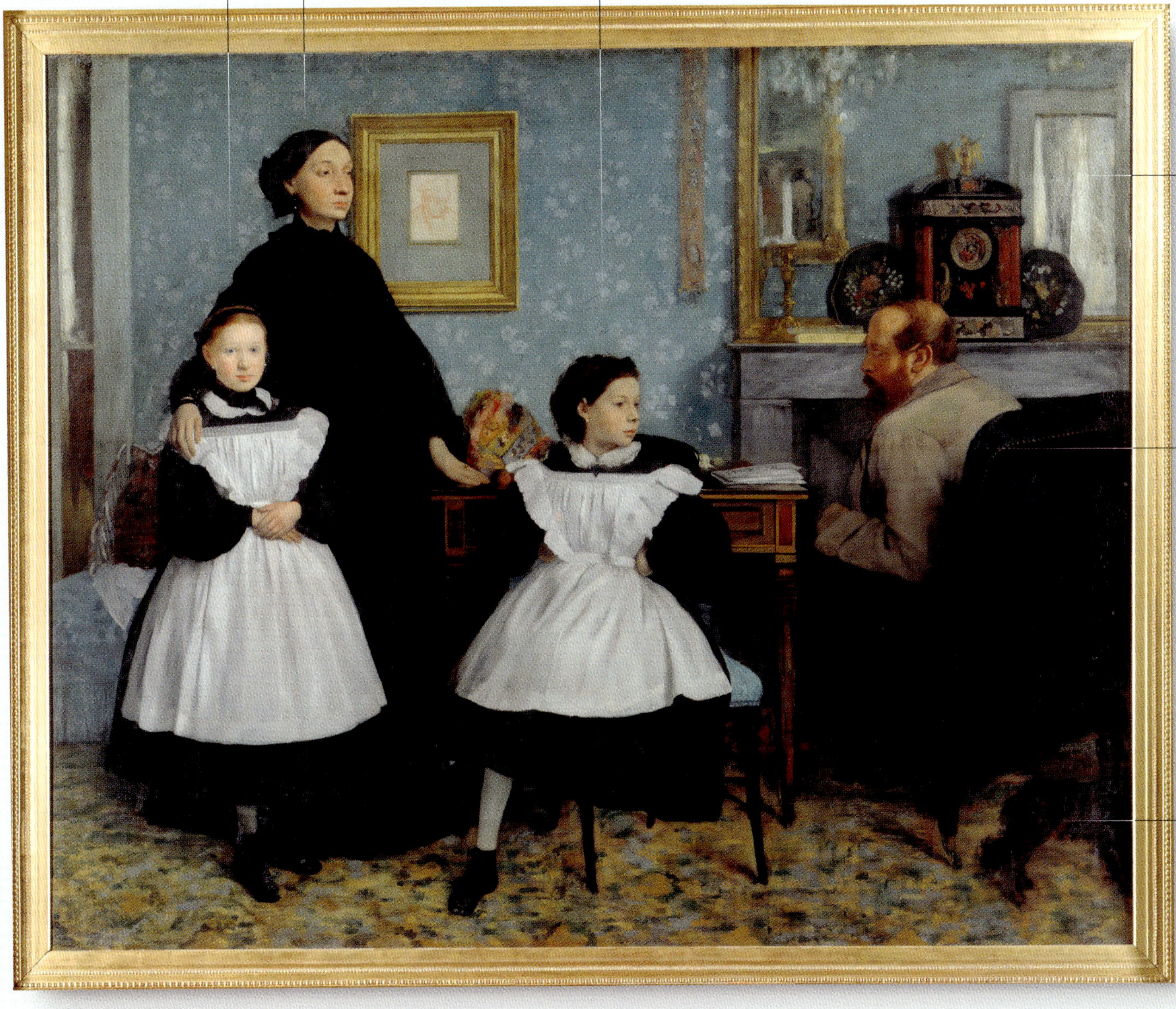

The claustrophobic mood of the room is increased by this mirror, reflecting what appears to be another mirror.

With his back toward the viewer, Baron Bellelli appears aloof, half-heartedly twisting around in his upholstered chair.

A small dog disappearing out of the frame emphasizes the "freeze-frame" approach evident in much of Degas's work.

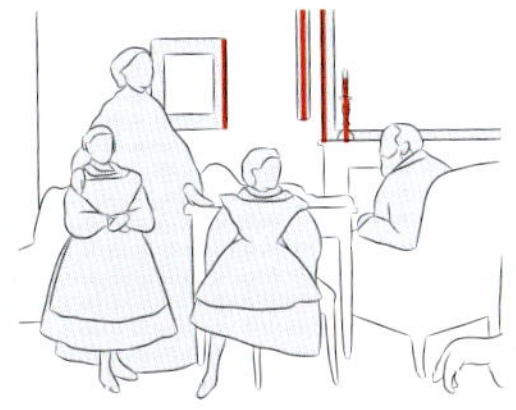

Family divisions
A series of vertical forms, including the frames, pull-cord, and candlestick, dominate the top of the picture and further isolate the Baron from his family.

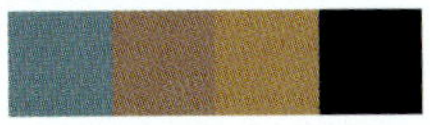

Dark truths
Degas used a restricted palette, concentrating on somber colors to create an oppressive atmosphere.

> "I assure you no art was ever less spontaneous than mine."
>
> Edgar Degas

Zenobia in Chains

Harriet Hosmer 1859, marble, 82 × 27 × 33 in (208.3 × 68.6 × 83.8 cm), The Huntington, San Marino, CA, US

Hosmer's marble sculpture of a 3rd-century queen recalls classical Greek sculpture but conveyed a provocative message of female strength and leadership to 19th-century viewers. Zenobia ruled Palmyra (now Syria) until she was defeated by Roman forces. Hosmer presents her as their captive, but the attitude is unyielding, with just the chain and the downward tilt of her head betraying her prisoner status.

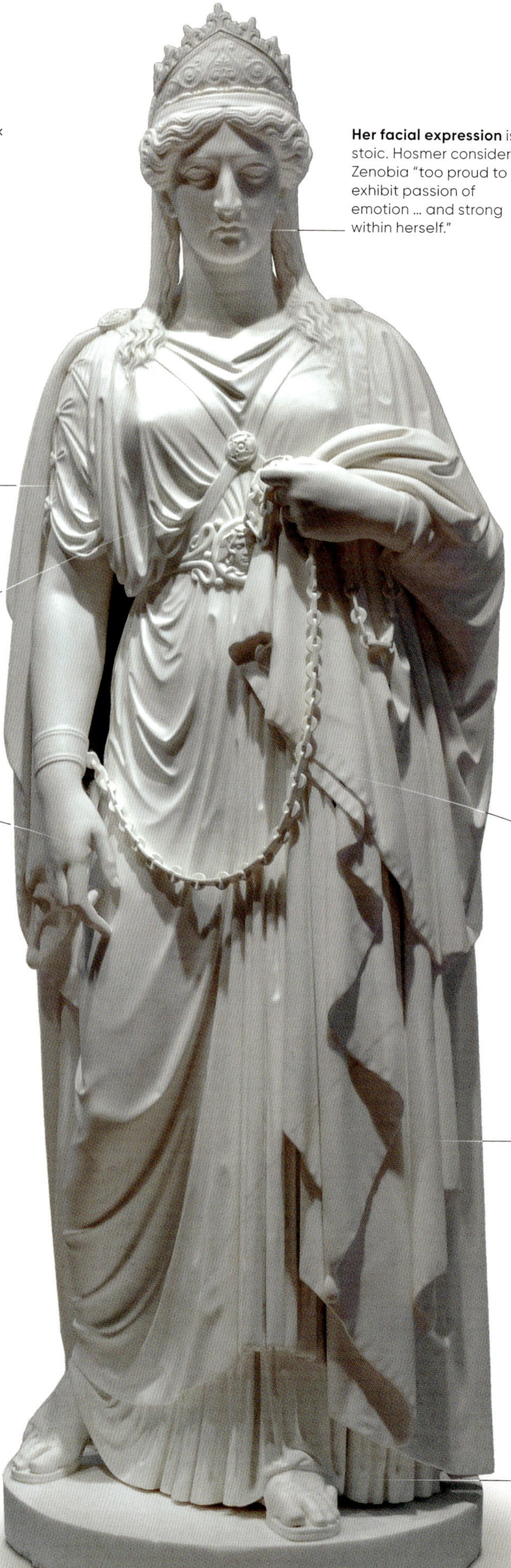

Her facial expression is stoic. Hosmer considered Zenobia "too proud to exhibit passion of emotion ... and strong within herself."

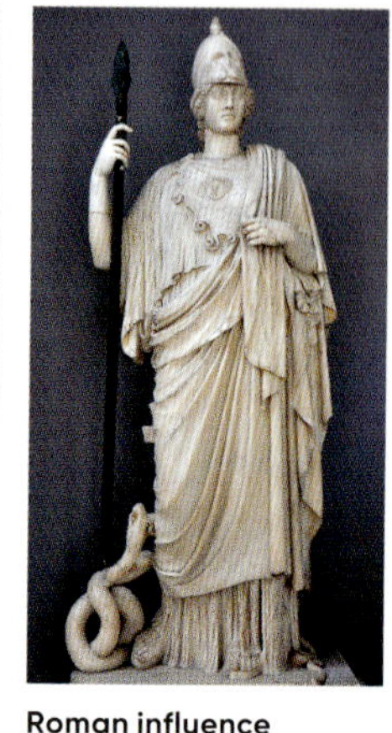

Roman influence
Zenobia's posture and robes are believed to be based on the ancient Roman statue *Athena Giustiniani*, who is also depicted exuding majestic strength.

Shaped from earth
Hosmer originally sculpted *Zenobia in Chains* from clay. She turned to marble to evoke the statuary of classical Greece.

Zenobia appears regal. Her elaborate court dress and crown emphasize her power and dignity.

The queen's hand grips the chain, exerting control over it.

Hosmer excelled at sculpting the human body. She attended anatomy classes at a St. Louis medical college to improve her skills.

The chain used to shackle the queen is understated—she is not defined by her current status as a prisoner.

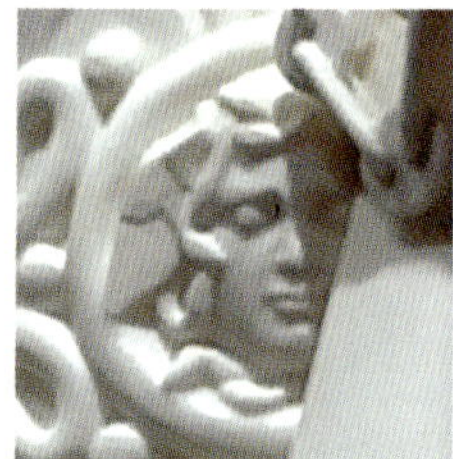

Medusa is depicted on the medallion. This associates Zenobia with Athena, Greek goddess of wisdom and war, who is often depicted wearing an image of the gorgon.

Even in captivity, Zenobia exhibits poise and grace. The folds of her robe fall with an almost perfect symmetry.

> "A very noble and remarkable statue indeed, full of dignity and beauty."
>
> Nathaniel Hawthorne, 1871

Zenobia steps forward, again suggesting that chains and captivity cannot fully restrain her.

Twilight in the Wilderness

Frederic Edwin Church 1860, oil on canvas, 40 × 64 in (101.6 × 162.6 cm), Cleveland Museum of Art, US

A spectacular sunset over Maine's Mount Katahdin celebrates the majesty of the American wilderness but also foretells the tumult of the looming Civil War. In Church's painting, the dramatic clouds, colors, and lighting suggest an approaching conflagration—or even the potential twilight of a nation.

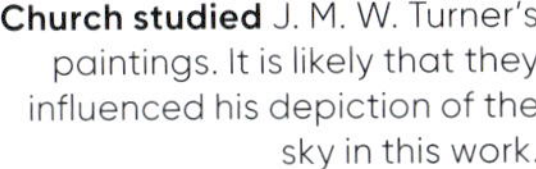

Church studied J. M. W. Turner's paintings. It is likely that they influenced his depiction of the sky in this work.

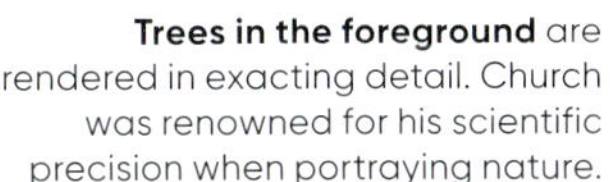

Trees in the foreground are rendered in exacting detail. Church was renowned for his scientific precision when portraying nature.

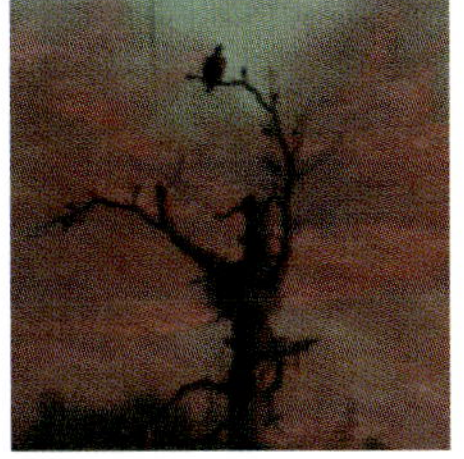

A bald eagle (a symbol of the US) surveys the scene from a dead or dying tree.

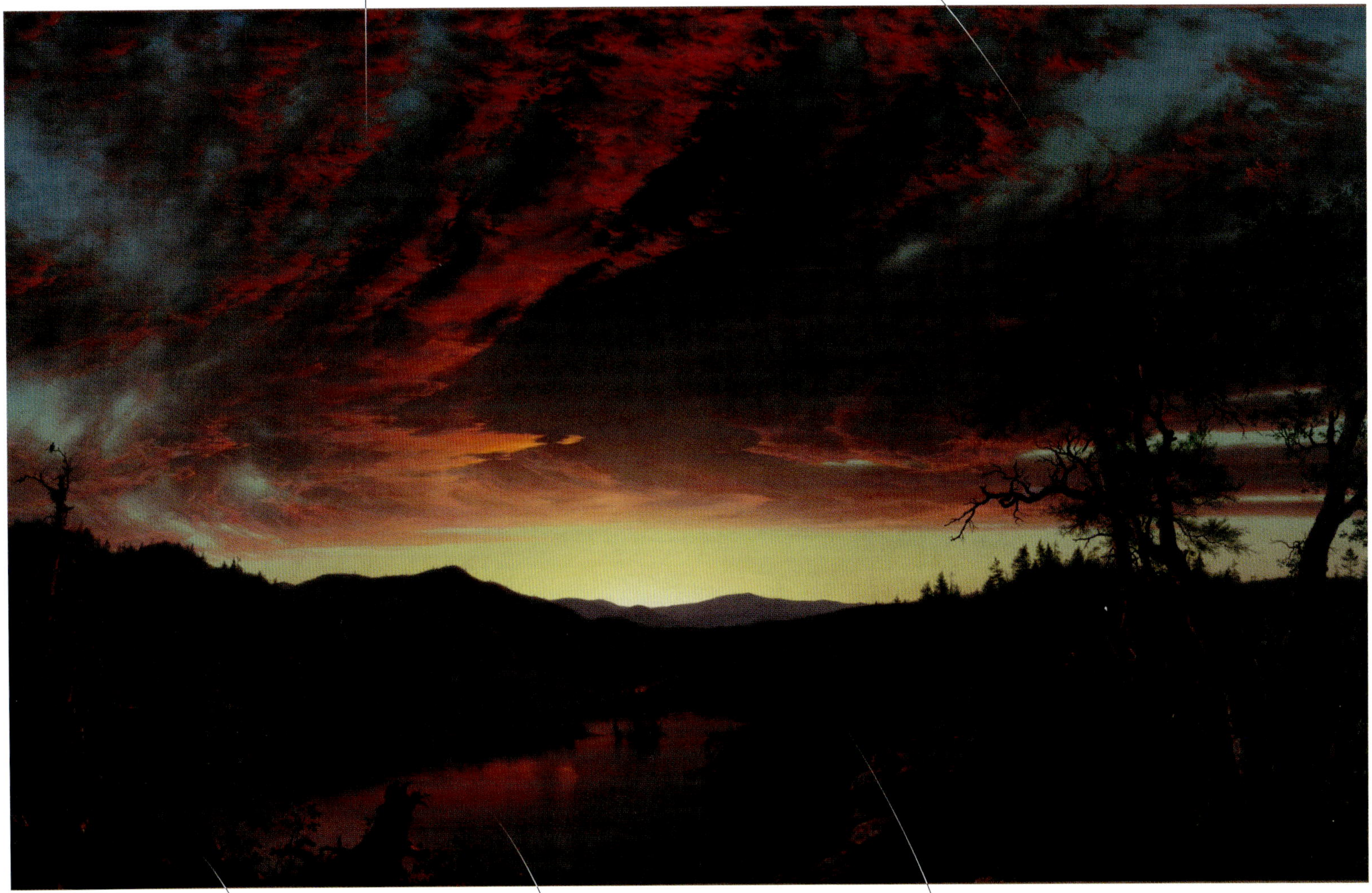

Dead and dying trees may symbolize deaths on the battlefield, or concern about the nation's potential demise.

The water in the lake looks deep red. Some see it as a symbolic lake of blood, others as "pillars of fire gleaming below the ... water."

In the background, the majestic purple mountains feel distant, perhaps unreachable in the coming night.

Barely visible on the top of a tree stump, a small cross suggests divine judgment, or it may be a grave marker.

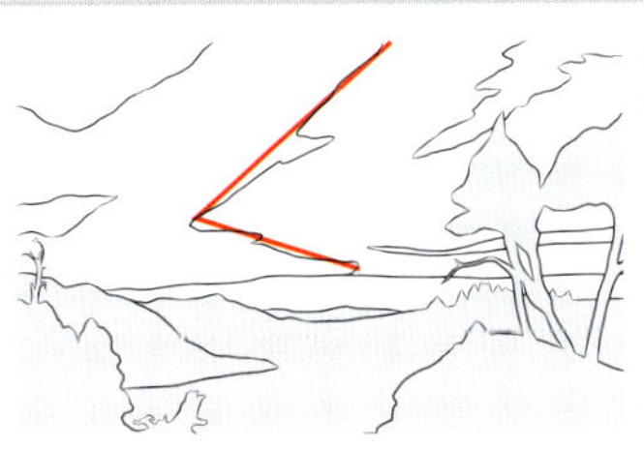

Depiction of movement
Church gives his clouds substance and suggests the direction in which they are moving by creating glowing red stripes.

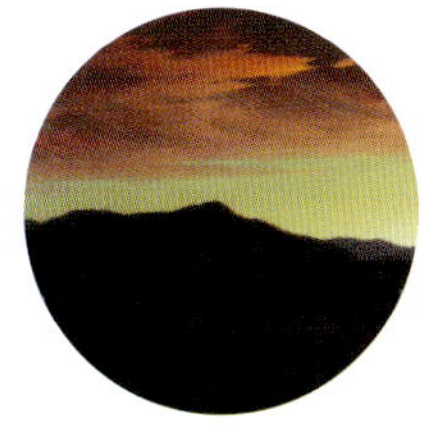

Creating a mood
The sky fills most of the canvas, but this is not a bright, open sky—only a narrow sliver of clear sky and sunlight remains between the imposing clouds and the distant horizon.

Landscape with Rainbow

Robert Duncanson 1859, oil on canvas, 30 × 52 in (76.3 × 132.7 cm), Smithsonian American Art Museum, Washington, D.C., US

A young couple walk down a road toward a cabin at the end of a rainbow in this pastoral, optimistic landscape. Bucolic scenes of Americans carving civilization from the wilderness were prevalent in 19th-century US art, but the timing and location of this optimistic image is notable—Duncanson painted it in 1859, when the American Civil War was looming. US landscapes painted in these antebellum years often featured threatening skies or thunderstorms, symbolizing trouble ahead, but Duncanson—among the era's most prominent Black American artists—has here painted largely blue skies and a rainbow, suggesting hope and God's blessing.

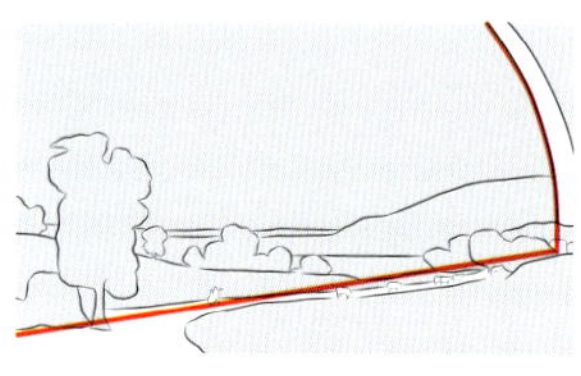

Focal point
The diagonal path, the man's pointing gesture, and the direction of the cattle lead the viewer's eye to the right and up toward the cabin; the rainbow directs the eye down toward the cabin as well.

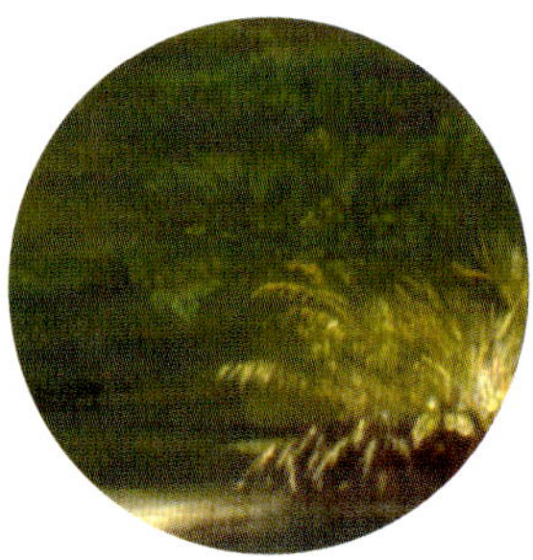

Idyllic lighting
Diffuse lighting contributes to the painting's peaceful, bucolic atmosphere. An obvious stripe of illumination in the foreground runs parallel to the path in the middle ground, pointing toward the cabin at the rainbow's base.

> "[T]he landscape is not a menacing, sublime force, but a fertile field receptive to man's use for farming, fishing, and raising a family."
>
> Joseph D. Ketner, 1993

An elm tree may symbolize liberty. In the American Revolution, a Boston elm was dubbed "The Liberty Tree."

The clouds directly above the couple are not rain clouds; the few dark clouds in the sky are passing by.

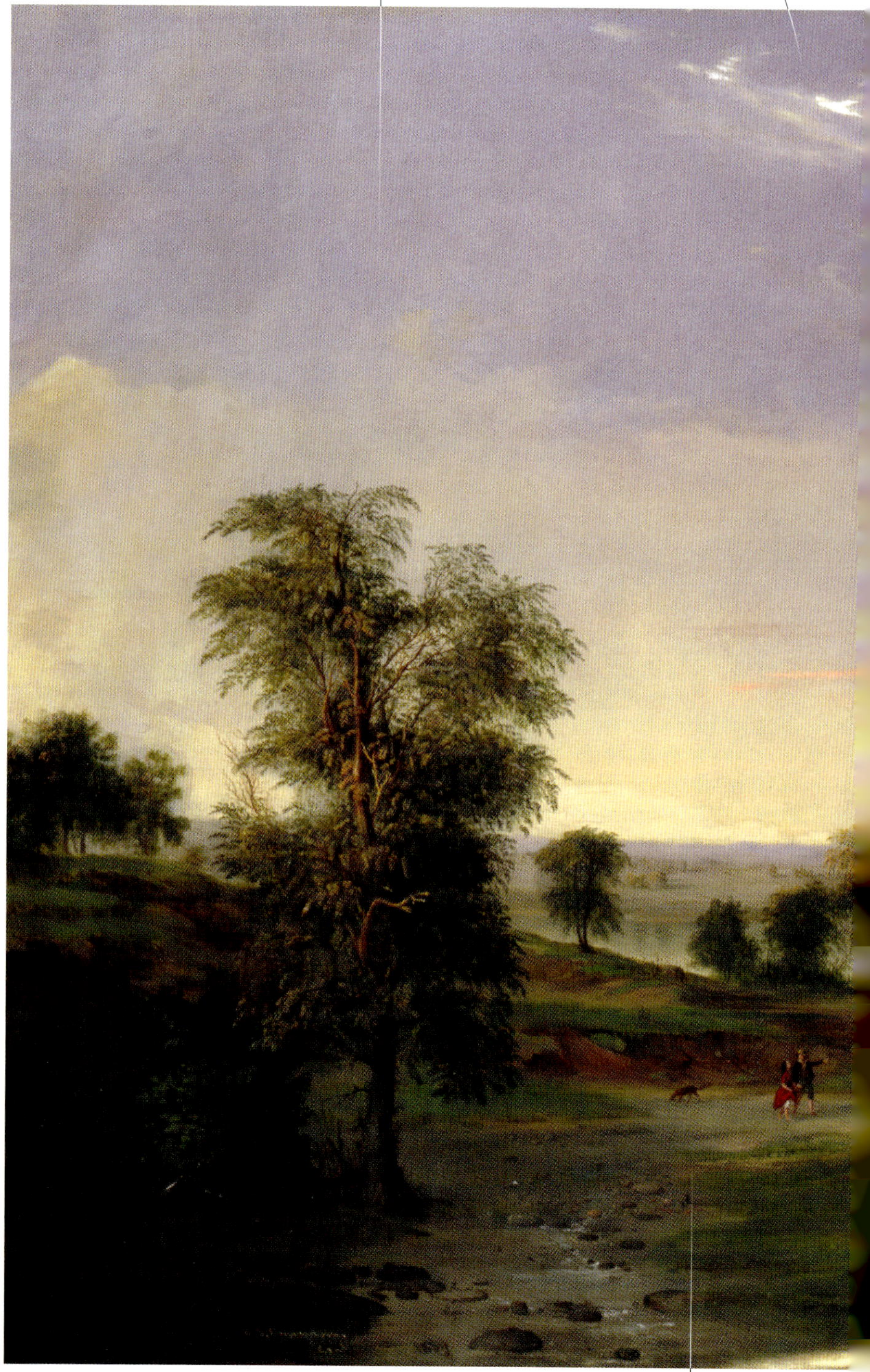

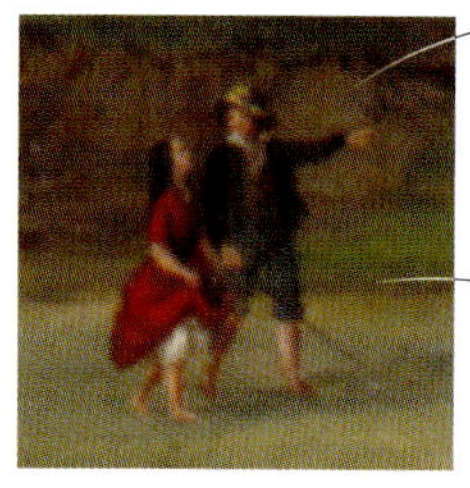

Pointing toward the rainbow, the man directs the couple toward their warm home and auspicious future.

The woman holds up the hem of her dress; like her country, she will endure some mud to reach her destination.

Sniffing the road, the couple's dog is the only figure in the painting not facing toward the rainbow.

The rainbow expresses that God looks favorably upon the US. He will see the nation through its looming crisis.

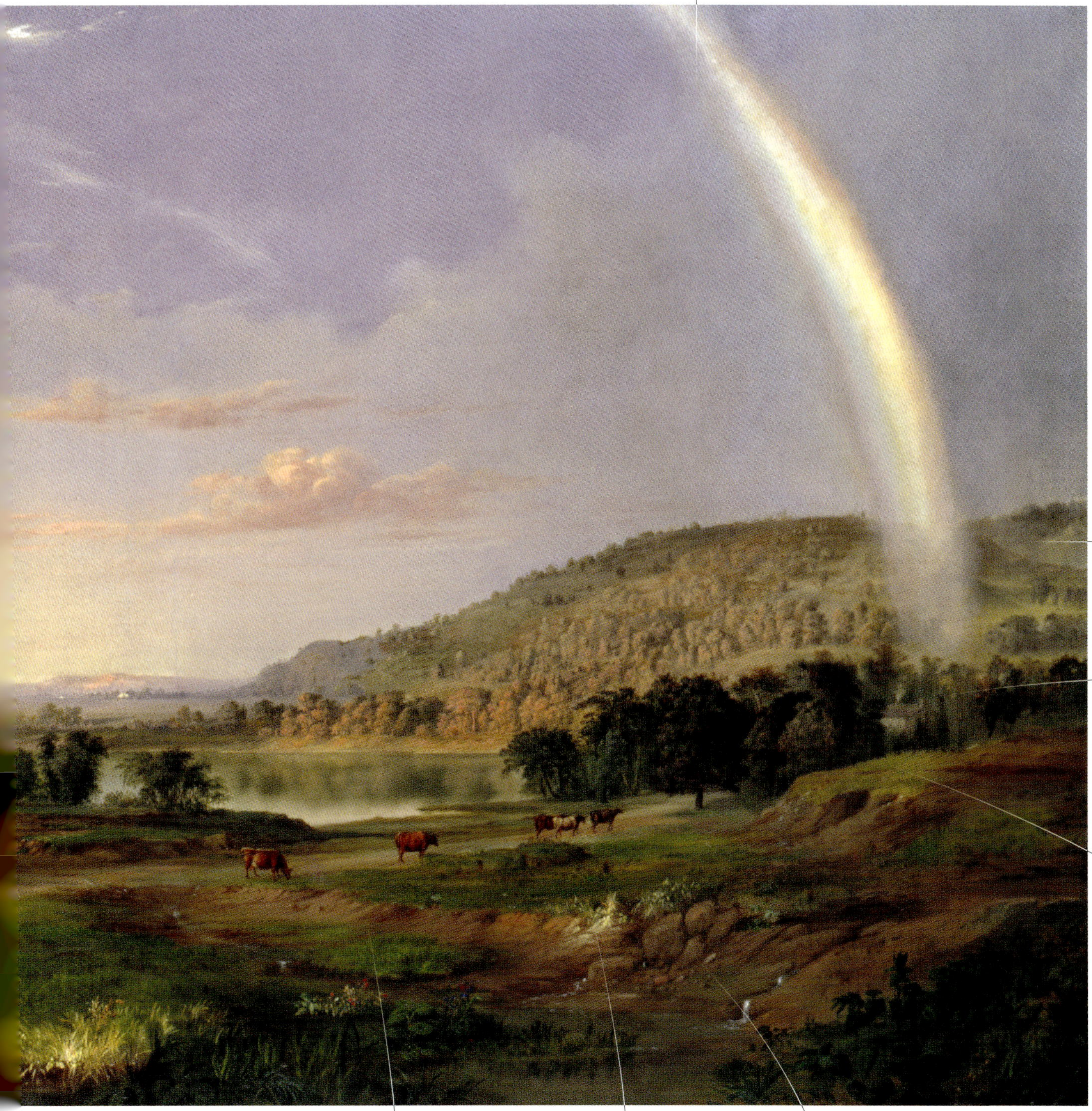

Beyond the cabin, the hills are illuminated by sunshine; better times will arrive.

The couple's cabin is near the base of the rainbow; smoke rises from its chimney signaling warmth and welcome within.

The cabin is nestled in a copse of trees; this couple is living in harmony with nature, not replacing it.

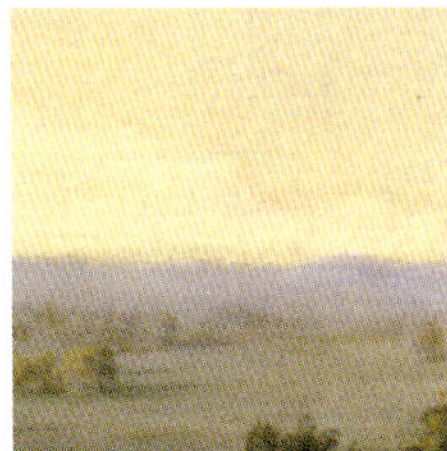

The horizon is relatively low in the painting. The expansive sky emphasizes the vastness of America's lands and future.

The water is probably the Ohio River separating Ohio, a northern state, from Kentucky, where slavery was legal in 1859.

Five head of cattle graze contentedly along the path, suggesting that this couple is not at risk of going hungry.

An uneven, rocky landscape may hint that life here will not be without challenges.

The Third-Class Carriage

Honoré Daumier 1862–1864, oil on canvas, 26 × 36 in (65.4 × 90.2 cm), Metropolitan Museum of Art, New York, US

Weary, working-class people ride in a crowded, dimly lit train car. In the foreground, an older woman with a calm expression is flanked by a napping boy and a young woman who holds a baby, probably her own. Unlike many works by Daumier, who also worked as a caricaturist, the image is sympathetic, not satirical. This is an unfinished version of this painting—a finished oil painting and a similar watercolor also exist.

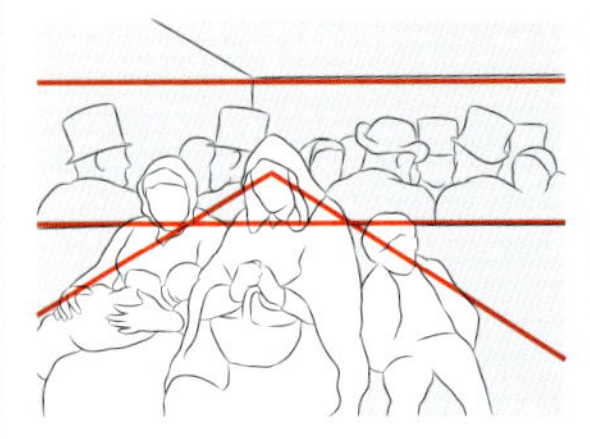

Narrative sweep
Diagonals created by the outer arms of the boy and young woman draw the eye up to the older woman's face. Horizontals created by the top of the bench and the roofline then draw the eye along the faces in the rows behind.

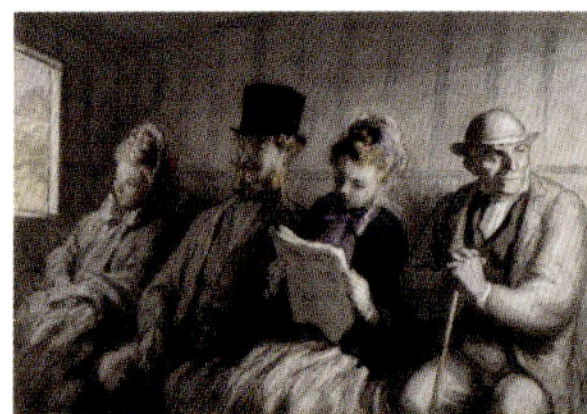

The First-Class Carriage
Daumier created multiple versions of *The Third-Class Carriage*, as well as images of first- and second-class carriages. He portrayed the passengers in those more expensive carriages as less cramped, but not necessarily more content.

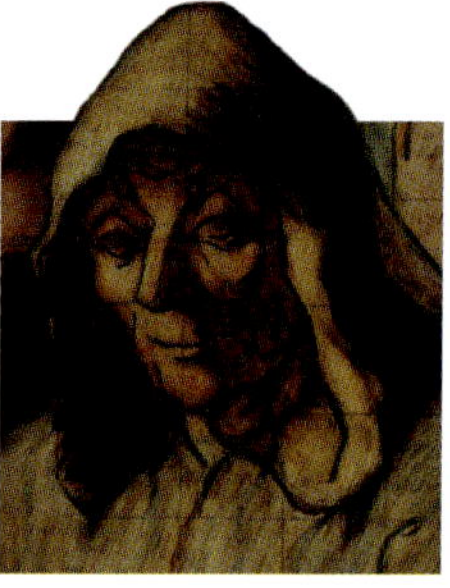

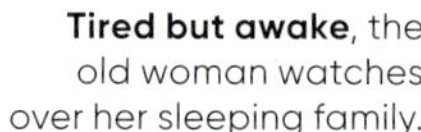

Tired but awake, the old woman watches over her sleeping family.

This top hat does not signify wealth—the hat is well-worn, its corners rounded.

The countryside is visible through the windows. This is a long-distance journey, not a cross-town hop.

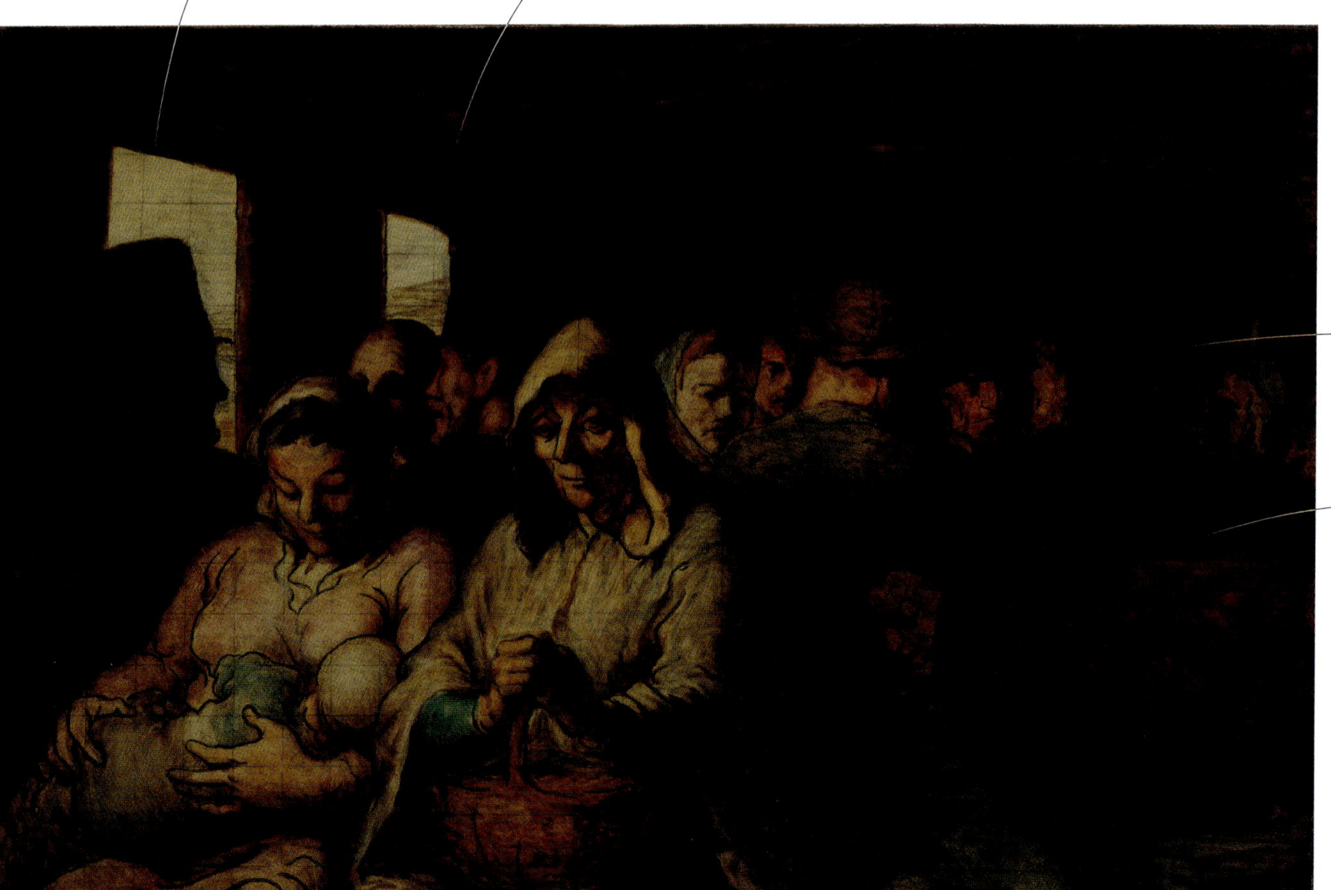

Passengers who were once strangers interact, conveying the communal, social atmosphere in the carriage.

There is no center aisle; the benches span the carriage and passengers board the train via doors at the end of each row.

An open space on the bench in the foreground contrasts with the crowded carriage behind, perhaps reflecting this family's isolation.

Three generations sitting together—baby to elderly woman—symbolize the inescapability of poverty in 19th-century France.

The boy sleeps, and the mother and baby rest as well. Their journey has perhaps been a long one.

Le Déjeuner sur l'herbe

Édouard Manet 1863, oil on canvas, 81 × 104 in (207 × 265 cm), Musée d'Orsay, Paris, France

Two fully dressed men picnic with a nude woman as a second woman bathes in the background. This painting was scandalous in 1863—its lack of depth and sense of unreality unusual, its nudity far less acceptable than in mythological scenes. Marking a new freedom from traditional subjects and modes of representation, *Le Déjeuner sur l'herbe* is often cited as one of modern art's starting points.

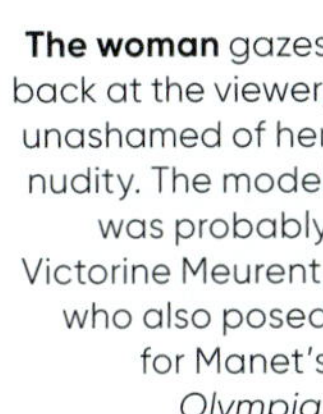

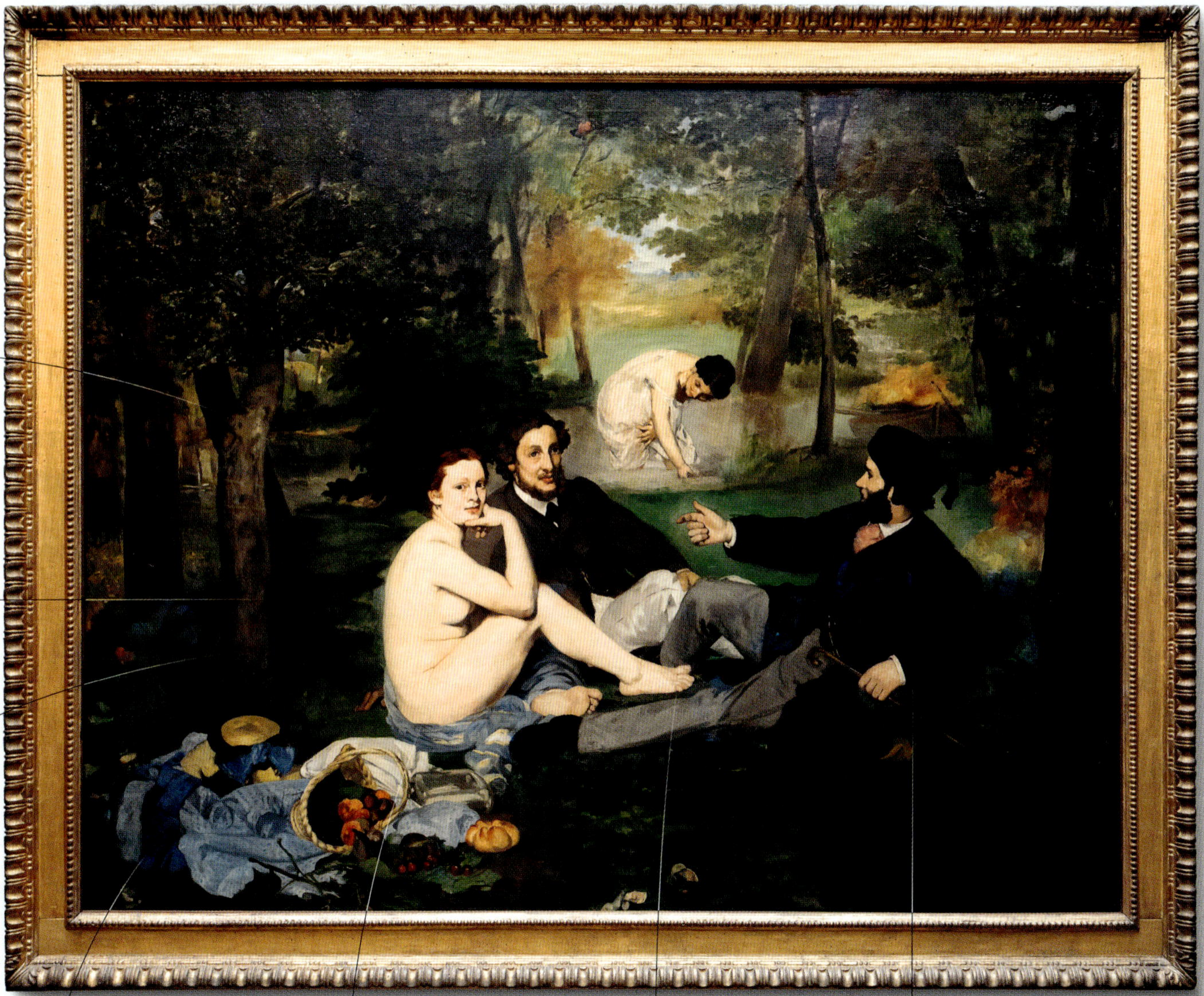

The woman gazes back at the viewer, unashamed of her nudity. The model was probably Victorine Meurent, who also posed for Manet's *Olympia*.

Portions of the background have been quickly and loosely painted, which was unusual in fine art prior to Impressionism.

The woman is more brightly lit than the men, contributing to the overall sense of unreality. Manet painted the sitters separately.

A pile of clothes indicates that this nude is not a mythological nymph; she is a woman sunning herself after bathing.

Sitting behind the naked woman is sculptor Ferdinand Leenhoff, Manet's brother-in-law.

The hand of the bearded man almost touches that of the woman bending down, even though she is far away.

This man is probably an amalgamation of Manet's brothers Eugène and Gustave.

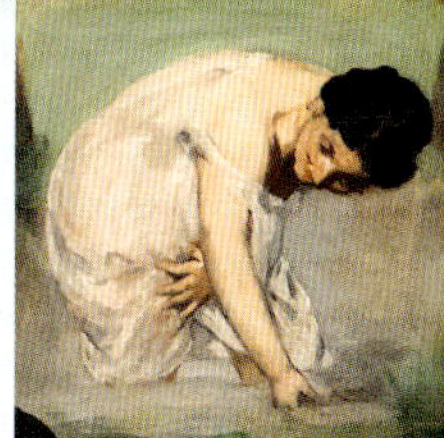

The bathing woman is much too large, considering that she is far away. She dwarfs a nearby rowing boat.

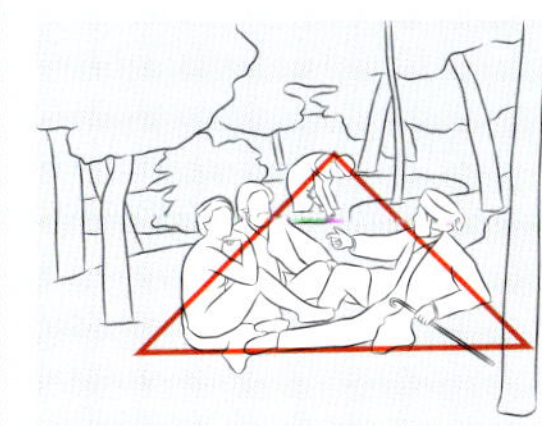

Balance
The figures form a triangle, with the woman in the river at its apex. Triangular compositions can make paintings feel balanced and stable.

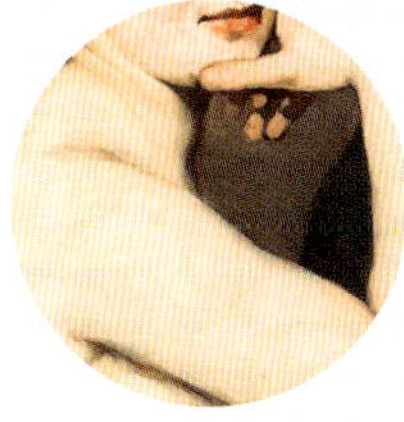

Lack of shadows
Manet painted the nude woman virtually without chiaroscuro—there is very little dark shadowing to contrast her light skin and create a sense of volume. This contributes to the painting's overall sense of flatness.

Ville-d'Avray

Jean-Baptiste-Camille Corot c. 1865, oil on canvas, 19 × 26 in (49.3 × 65.5 cm), National Gallery of Art, Washington, D.C., US

The pond and grounds in this painting belonged to a house bought by the artist's parents in 1817. They were a continual source of inspiration for Corot, who liked to paint *en plein air* (outdoors). The soft light, silvery trees, and still water evoke a moment of tranquility, an effect that anticipated Impressionism.

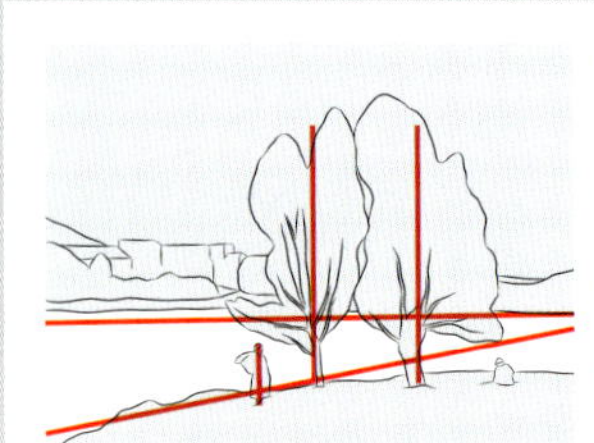

Contrasting lines
The water and bank form a gentle diagonal that tapers toward the skyline. This contrasts with the strong verticals of the trees and the figure on the left.

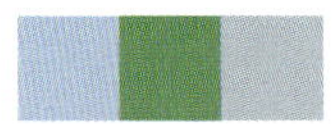

Sky and water
Bright colors typically dominate Corot's early sketches and paintings, but later works such as this are filled with blue-greens and grays.

> "There is only one master here—Corot. We are nothing compared to him, nothing."
> Claude Monet, 1897

Almost half of the canvas is devoted to a serene expanse of pale blue sky and puffy clouds.

Corot was a collector of early landscape photographs. The blurry nature of such images may have influenced his painting style.

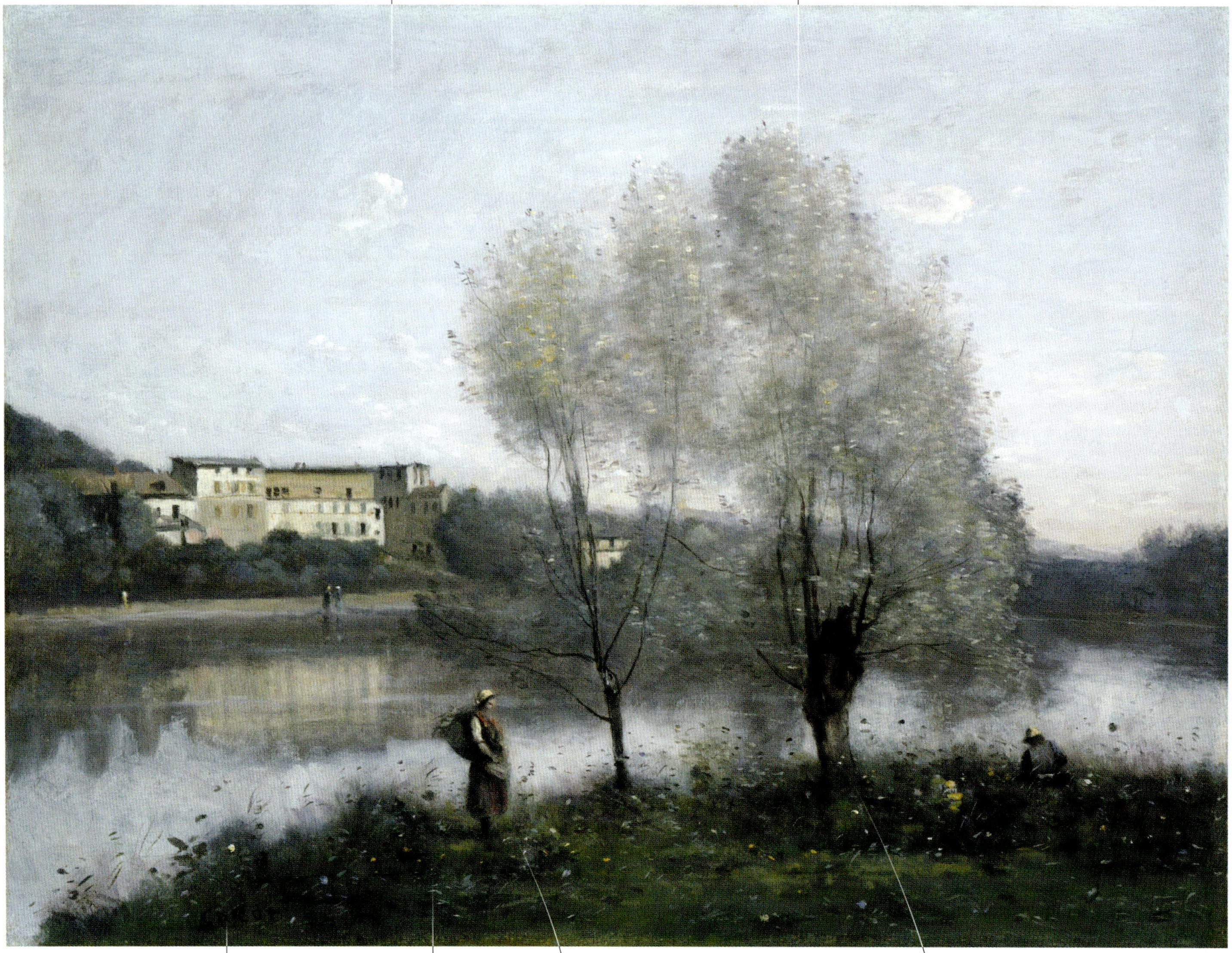

Corot has signed this painting. He did not always do this, and there are many Corot forgeries, some with fake signatures.

Dots of blue, yellow, and white suggest flowers.

Corot frequently featured two figures in the foreground, often drawing attention to them with a spot of bright color.

Sizable trees backed by water are often a feature in Corot's landscapes.

The bridge resembles the Ponte Vecchio over the Arno in Dante's Florence.

Beatrice is undergoing a spiritual transformation, sitting with her eyes closed, lips parted, and hands cupped as if receiving the Eucharist, the Christian sacrament commemorating the Last Supper.

After Rossetti's death, Ford Madox Brown completed this version of the painting's background.

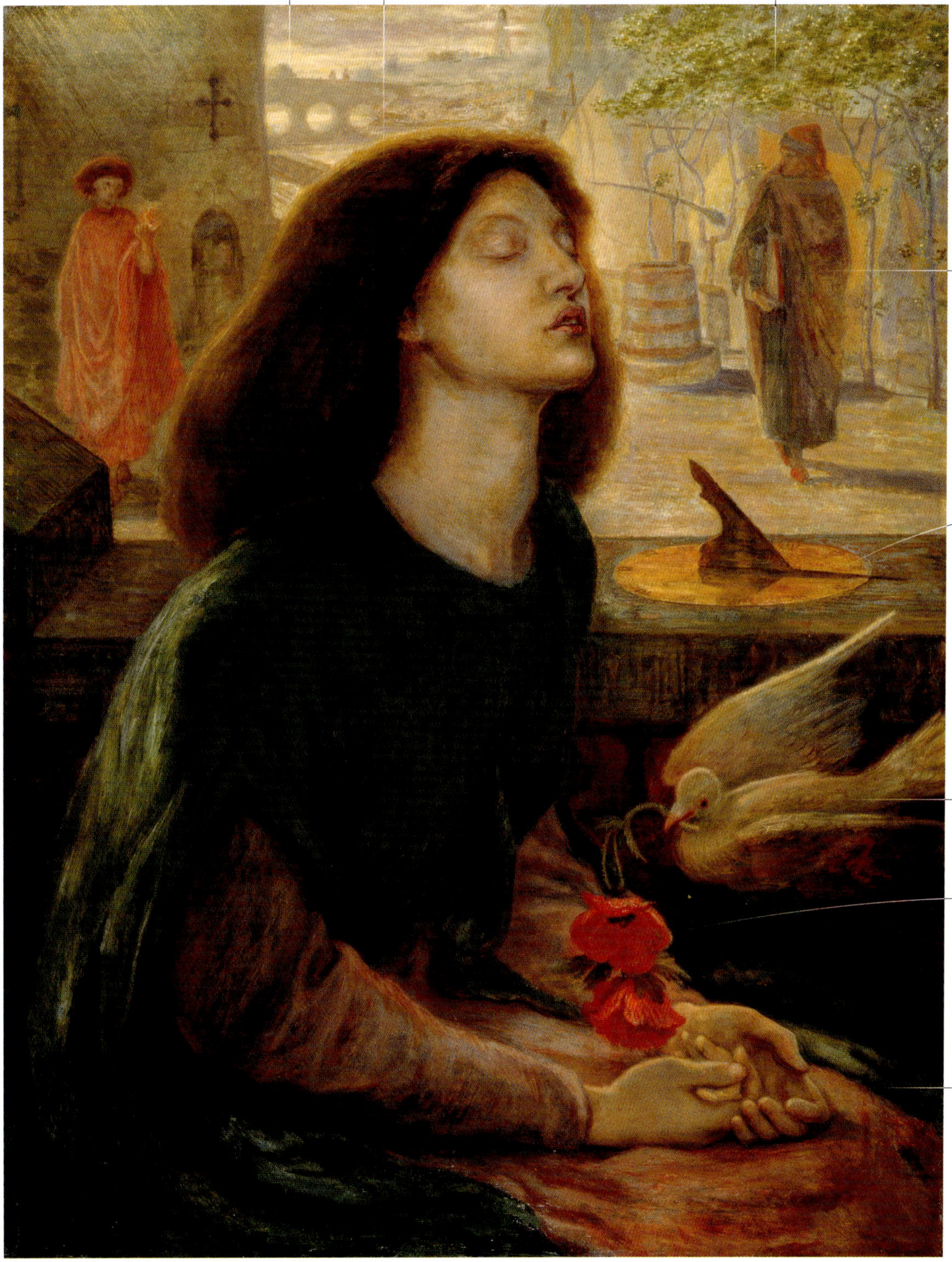

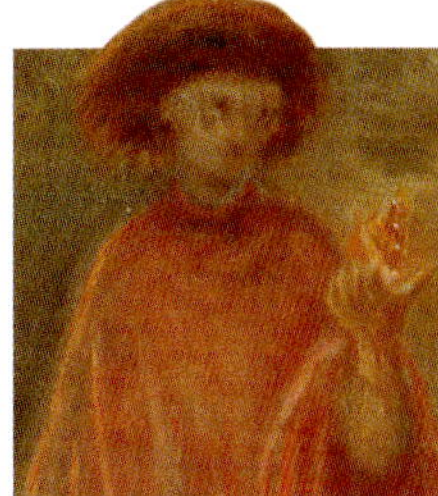

The figure of Love holds a flaming heart, in front of an arbor vitae plant, which is also known as the tree of life.

Symbolist composition
The woman sits surrounded by symbols, with the emblematic figures of Love and Dante placed at the same level on either side.

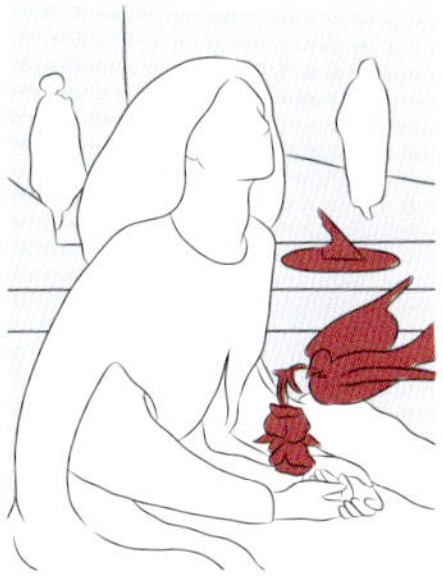

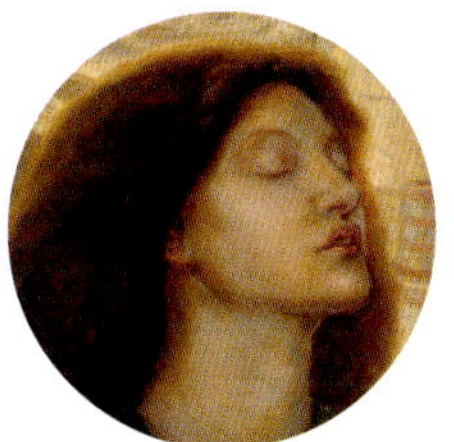

Aureole
The lighting is not treated realistically. Particular elements, such as the sundial and figure of Love, are illuminated, and Beatrice's head is surrounded by a circle of light, or aureole.

Dante stands in the background. The book under his arm may be Dante's *La Vita Nuova* (*The New Life*), which Rossetti had translated into English in 1848.

The shadow from the sundial rests on the figure nine, as Beatrice died at nine o'clock on June 9, 1290.

The dove, often used to symbolize love, is tinged with red. It appears here as a messenger of death.

The red poppy, a symbol of both death and peace, may refer to the laudanum Siddal overdosed on.

Siddal posed for many Pre-Raphaelite paintings, including Walter Howell Deverell's *Twelfth Night* and Sir John Everett Millais' *Ophelia*.

Beata Beatrix

Dante Gabriel Rossetti c. 1864–1870 (1877 version), oil on canvas, 34 × 26 in (86.4 × 66 cm), Birmingham Art Gallery, UK

Rich with symbolism, this painting depicts Beatrice Portinari, the muse of Italian poet Dante Alighieri, with whom Rossetti identified. However, Beata Beatrix is also intended as a memorial for Rossetti's wife, Elizabeth Siddal, who was the model for the artist's initial studies of Beatrice, and who had died in 1862.

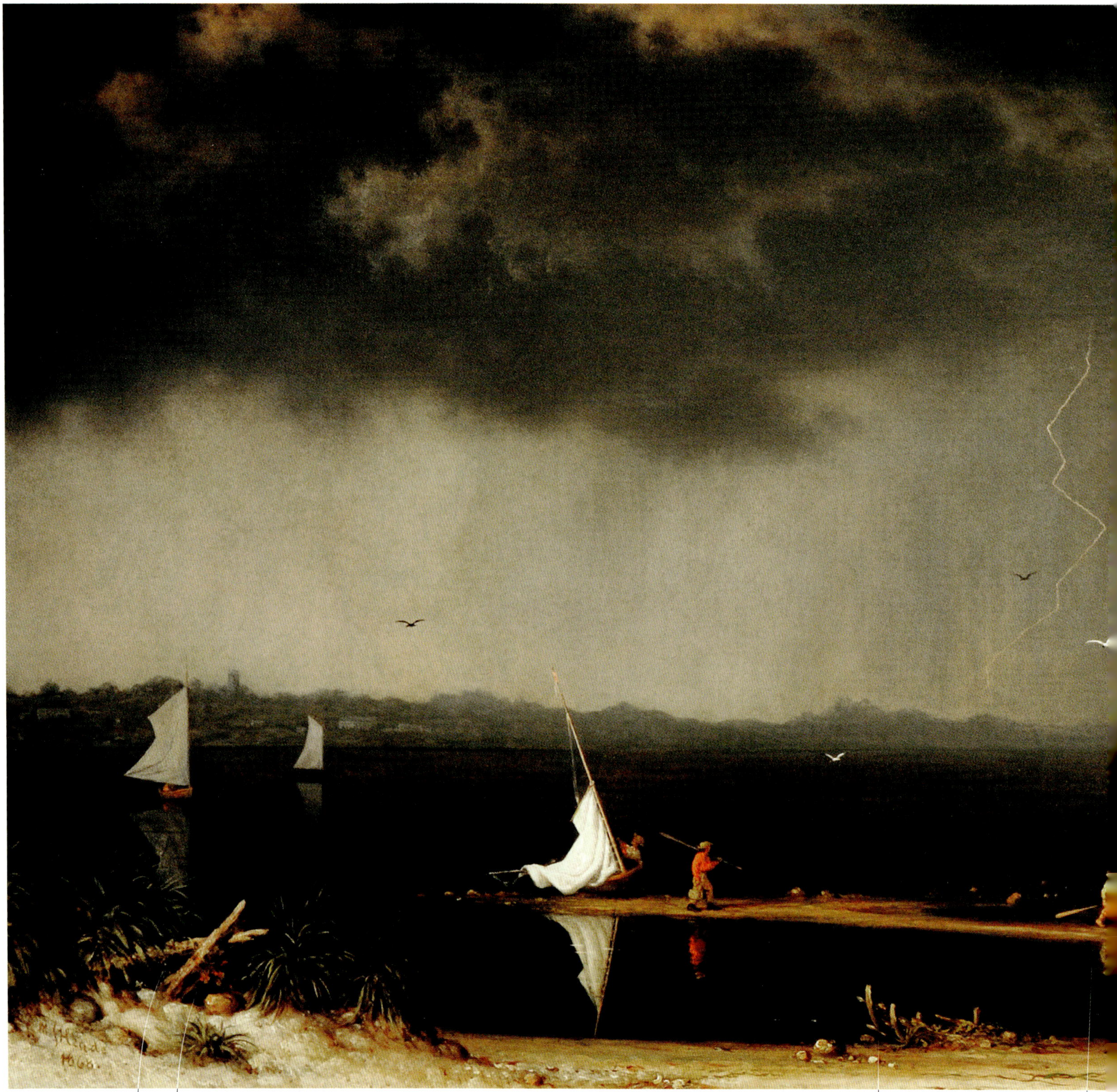

Fallen fence posts forming a cross are perhaps intended to suggest a grave marker.

A vine climbing the fence post may be a Biblical reference to God and salvation: "I am the true vine" (John 15:1).

The structure on the far shore, directly above the wooden cross, may be a church tower.

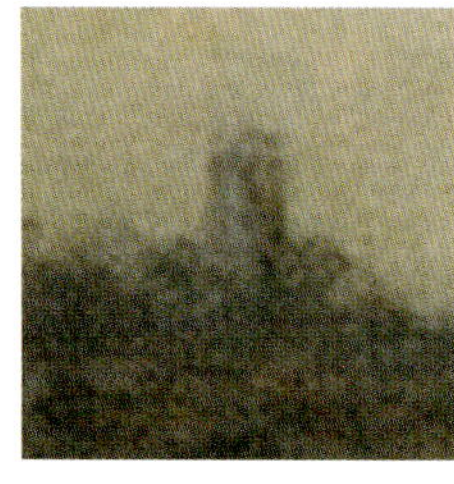

Some critics consider the bones of the old boat a vanitas symbol—a reminder of death's inevitability.

The three figures appear to be different ages. Like the boats at varying distances from the shore, they may represent the stages of life.

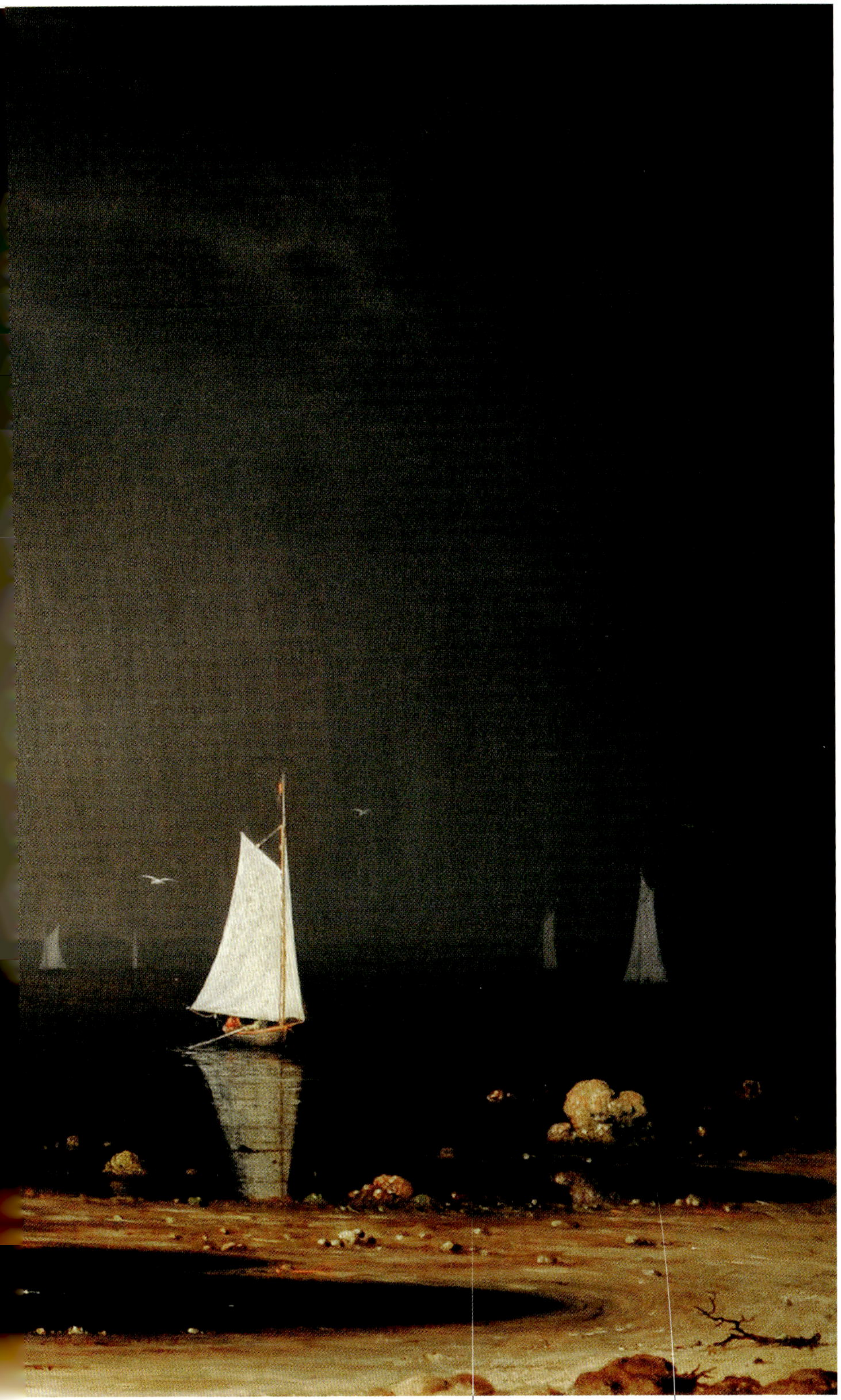

Thunderstorm Over Narragansett Bay

Martin Johnson Heade 1868, oil on canvas, 32 × 54 in (82 × 138 cm), Amon Carter Museum of American Art, Fort Worth, TX, US

Heade's seascape depicts the ominous quiet just before a storm arrives. Lightning flashes in the distance and menacing clouds approach, yet the sailors and seabirds appear oddly unconcerned about the impending tempest. Numerous Heade paintings feature thunderstorms, which in the 1860s often symbolized God's power or sometimes the tumult of the American Civil War. Some art historians have suggested that Heade is alluding to the stages of life and the inevitability of death. The painting received little attention until it was rediscovered in an antique shop in New York State in 1943, its provenance unclear.

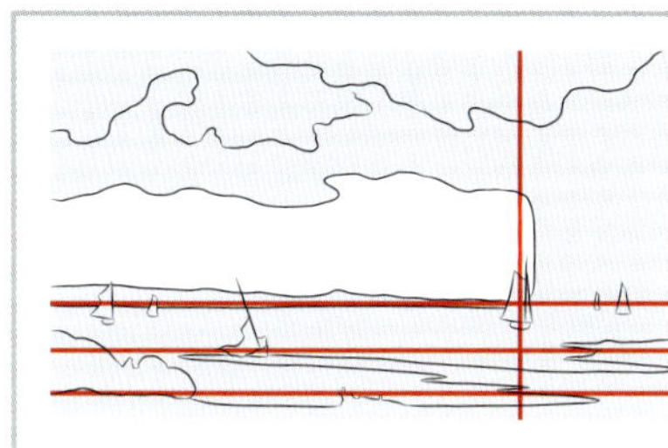

Colliding lines
The horizon, shoreline, and sandbar meet the vertical lines of a downpour until even the horizon line is swallowed by the blackness of the storm.

Mirror effect
Heade's carefully blended brushwork creates a mirrorlike surface—most brushstrokes are barely visible, while long strokes are used to convey sheets of powerful rain.

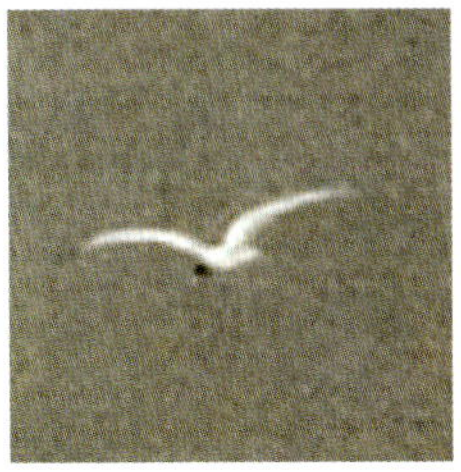

Seabirds, which are sometimes associated with angels, fly calmly through the stormy sky.

The darkness is so oppressive that some boats seem all but lost in the storm.

The rocks near the shoreline suggest skulls, another reminder of death.

> "[Heade's] paintings ... speak less to the keenness of observation than to the richness of the painter's imagination."
>
> Theodore E. Stebbins Jr., 2000

A Studio at Les Batignolles

Henri Fantin-Latour 1870, oil on canvas, 108 × 80 in (273.5 × 204 cm), Musée d'Orsay, Paris, France

Providing a glimpse into the artistic scene in the Batignolles neighborhood of Paris in the late 19th century, this painting shows artists and writers watching Édouard Manet paint Zacharie Astruc's portrait. It depicts the moment of artistic creation while also celebrating the members of the group.

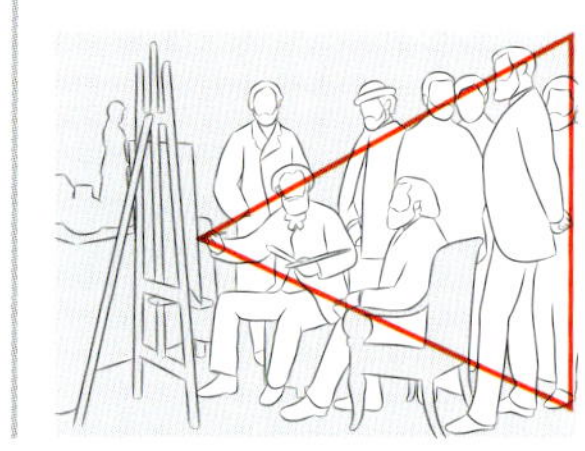

Establishing relationship The paintbrush forms the apex of a triangular arrangement that enfolds the men, arranged in friezelike composition on the right-hand side.

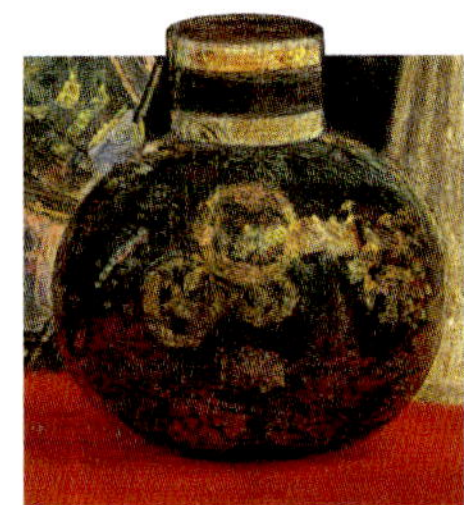

The Japanese-style vase was made by Laurent Bouvier and signifies the role of *Japonisme* in French Modernism.

Hands in pockets, German painter Otto Schölderer watches closely. He had come to Paris to get to know the followers of Gustave Courbet.

Renoir stands in front of a frame, creating a visual play on portraiture.

Claude Monet is almost hidden at the back of the group.

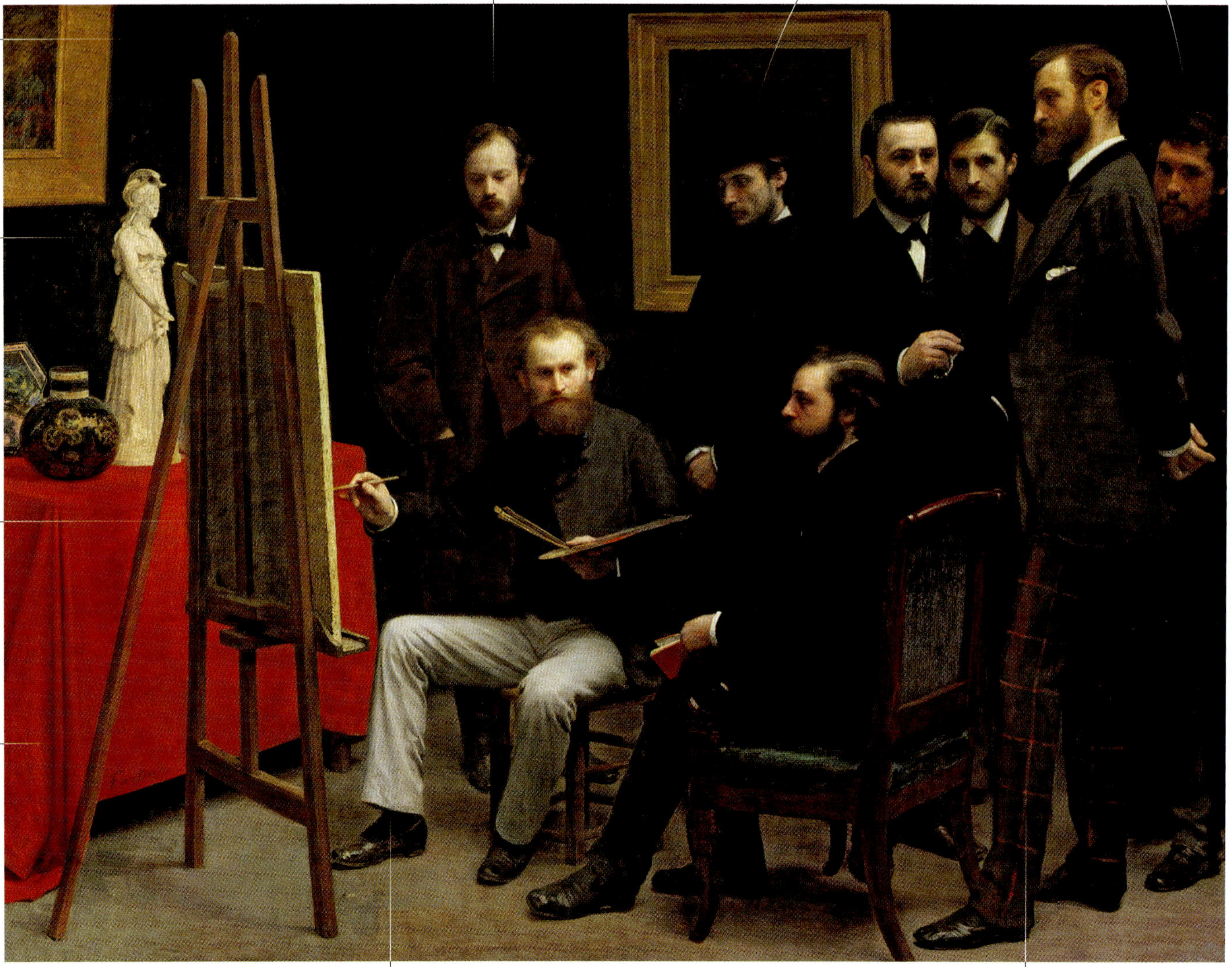

The dark and somber palette reflects the serious tone of the painting.

A small statue of Minerva, the Roman goddess of wisdom and patron of the arts, symbolizes the artists' respect for classical tradition.

The reverse of Manet's canvas faces the viewer, adding an element of mystery to the painting.

A red tablecloth adds a splash of color while highlighting the objects it holds.

Manet sits in the center of the composition, working on his portrait. This signifies his importance to the French avant-garde at the time.

By depicting the men in formal suits, the artist deliberately enhances their respectability.

Impression, Sunrise

Claude Monet 1872, oil on canvas, 19 × 25 in (48 × 63 cm), Musée Marmottan, Paris, France

The sun rises over Le Havre harbor on a hazy morning. Small boats scud across the water and the shapes of chimneys and the cranes being used to construct a new dock are visible in the distance. The subject—the light and color of the sunrise and its reflections in water—was revolutionary at the time, as was the way Monet painted them. The painting's title was used to define a whole movement—Impressionism.

> "What freedom, what ease of workmanship!"
>
> Louis Leroy, 1874

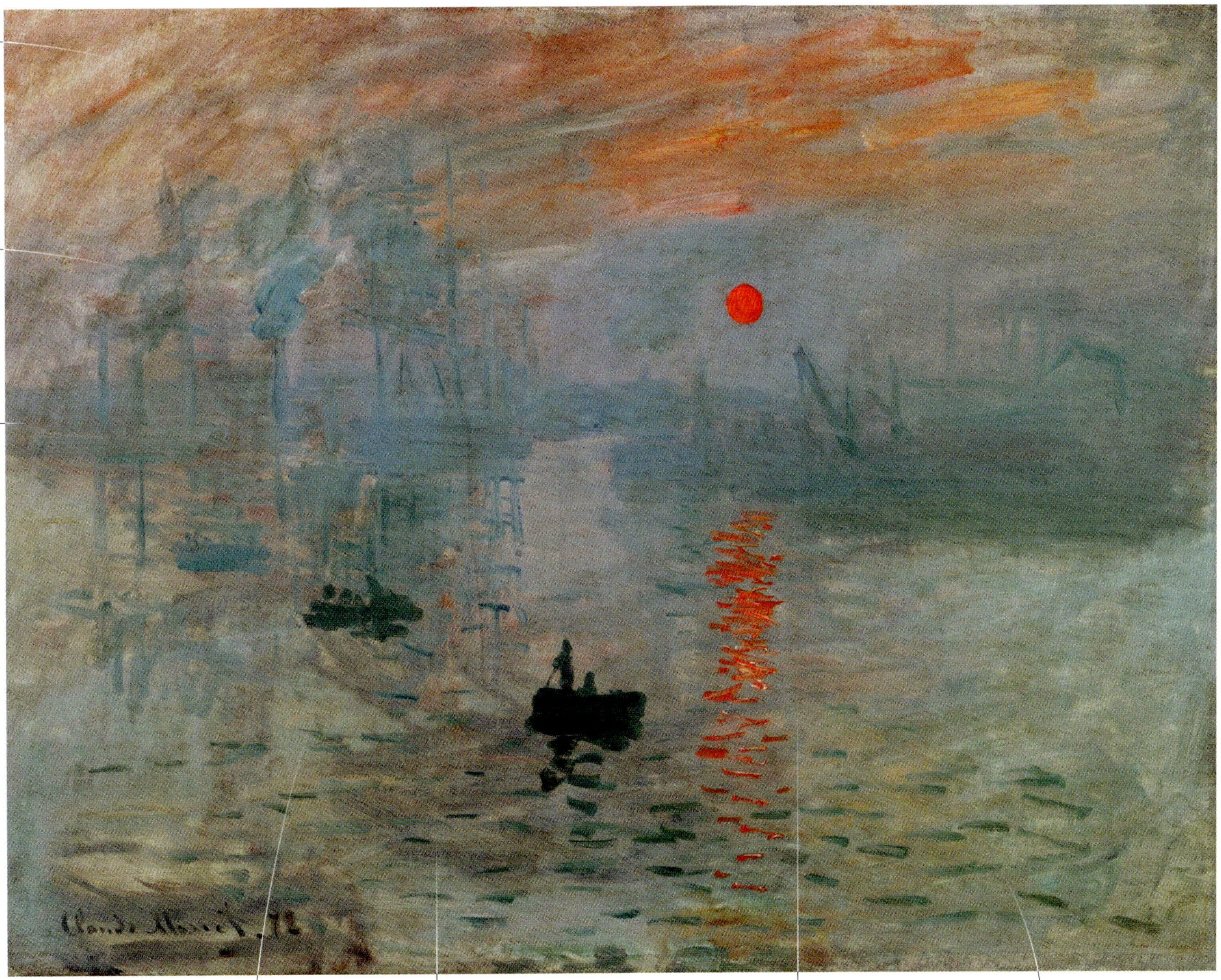

The sky is painted with brushstrokes that were made quickly. Patches of bare canvas can be seen in some places.

Smoke rises from chimneys in the distance, adding to the haziness of the early morning.

Continuing beyond the edges of the canvas on both sides, the scene creates the impression of a quick snapshot instead of a traditionally composed landscape.

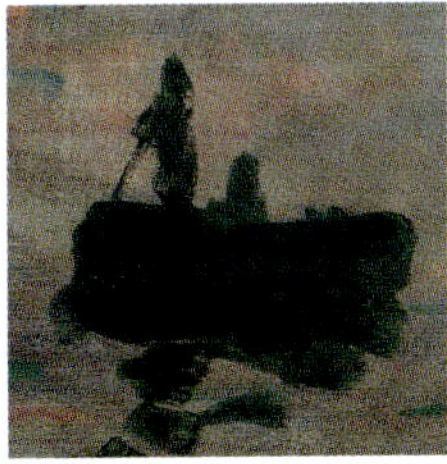

The boat and figures are just shapes. No details have been included.

The position of the three boats in a diagonal line creates a sense of recession.

Industrial buildings were not usually included in landscape paintings at the time.

Cranes indicate construction. At the time, the harbor was being enlarged.

Ripples on the water's surface are painted with unblended, broken brushstrokes.

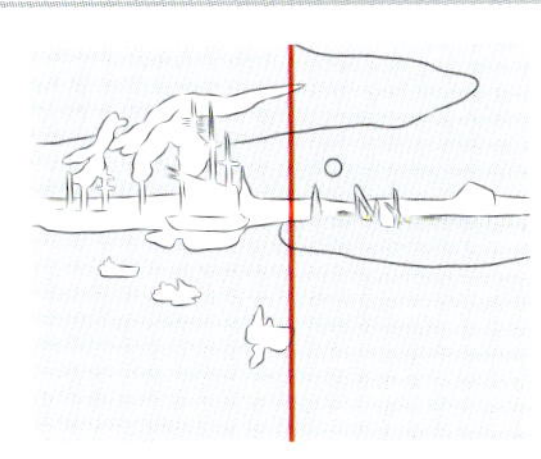

Balanced format
The more densely filled left-hand side, containing the boats and smoking chimneys, is balanced by the larger, more open right-hand side.

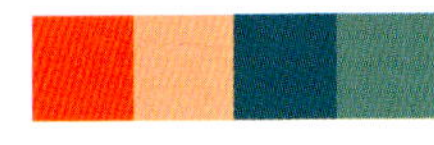

Color contrasts
The painting is built on contrasts of color—between orange and yellow and blue and green—rather than on a traditional contrast between light and dark.

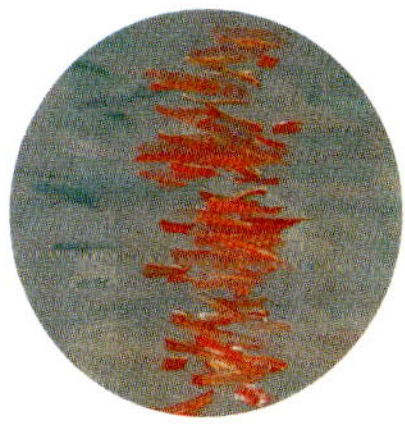

Different depths
Layers of thin washes in varying tones of blue and gray provide a base. The reflections were painted over the top with individual strokes of thick paint, or impasto.

Landscapes

At different times, artists have portrayed the natural world as ordered, or idealized, or wild and awe-inspiring. Some artists have used landscape painting to convey the power of God; others to express their own emotions. In China, where it was an independent genre from the 4th century CE, the natural world was portrayed as a retreat from city life. In Europe, landscapes did not develop into a separate genre until the 17th century, when Dutch artists began painting specific places.

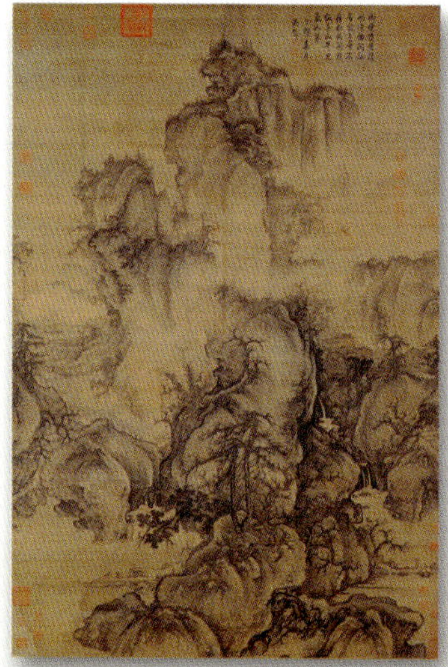

2

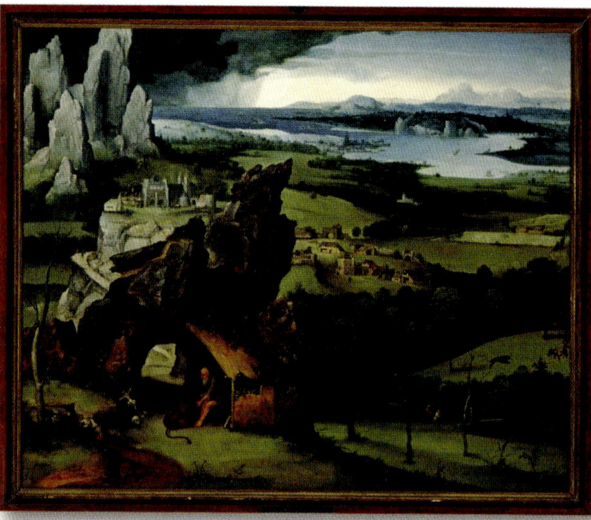

3

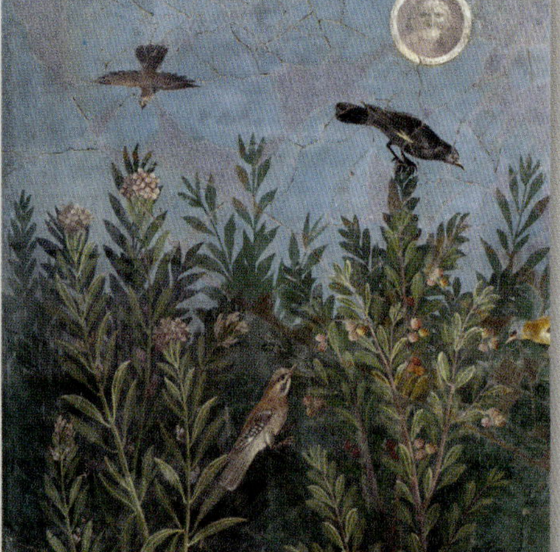

1

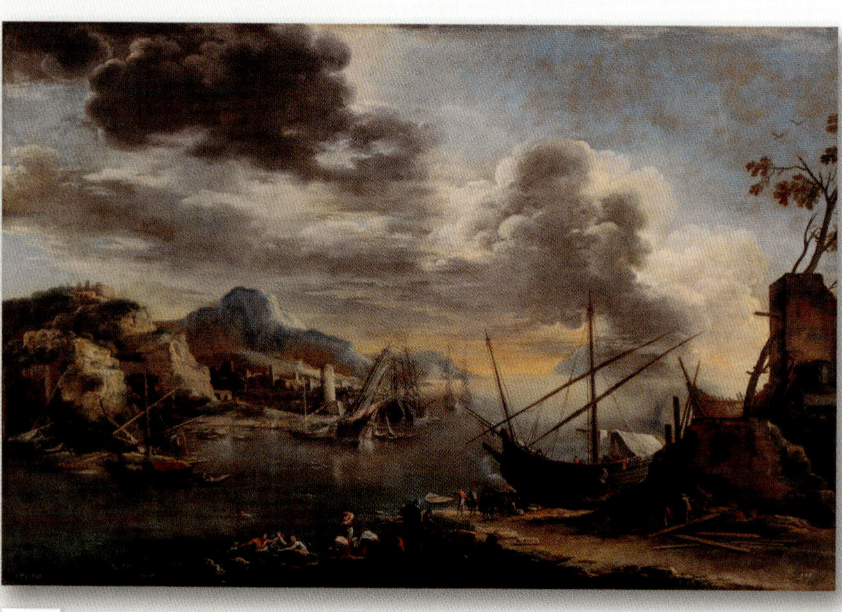

4

1. ***Garden Fresco*, artist unknown, 20–100.** Garden scenes celebrating nature were painted on the walls of the garden room in the House of the Golden Bracelet, Pompeii. These accurate renditions of plants and birds were intended to create the atmosphere of a country villa.

2. ***Early Spring*, Guo Xi, 1072.** In his most famous masterpiece, a type of painting called shan shui, or mountain-water, Guo Xi developed a multiple-perspective technique for showing "tall, deep, and flat distances." Strong brushstrokes build up the forms of mountains and trees.

3. ***Landscape with St. Jerome*, Joachim Patinir, 1516–1517.** A small religious scene is set in an extensive landscape. Patinir was one of the first European artists to give more weight to the landscape than to figures. His work influenced the development of European landscape painting.

4. ***View of the Gulf of Salerno*, Salvator Rosa, 1640–1645.** Rosa's rugged scenes under turbulent skies started a fashion for romanticized landscapes that lasted 200 years. This one is peopled with small figures, including two who are fighting, adding to the wild atmosphere.

En plein air

A French term meaning "in the open air," *en plein air* refers to paintings produced outdoors. British artist John Constable made studies of landscapes and weather this way, as did Jean-Baptiste-Camille Corot in France. This type of painting was made possible by the introduction of portable equipment and paint in tubes. Plein air painting was central to the Impressionists, who strove to capture changing light.

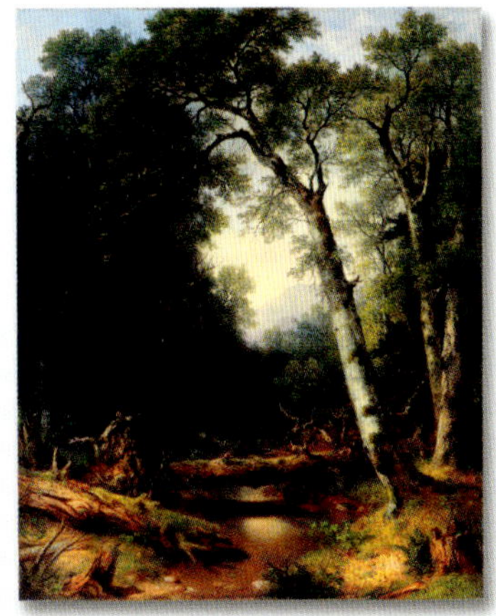

6

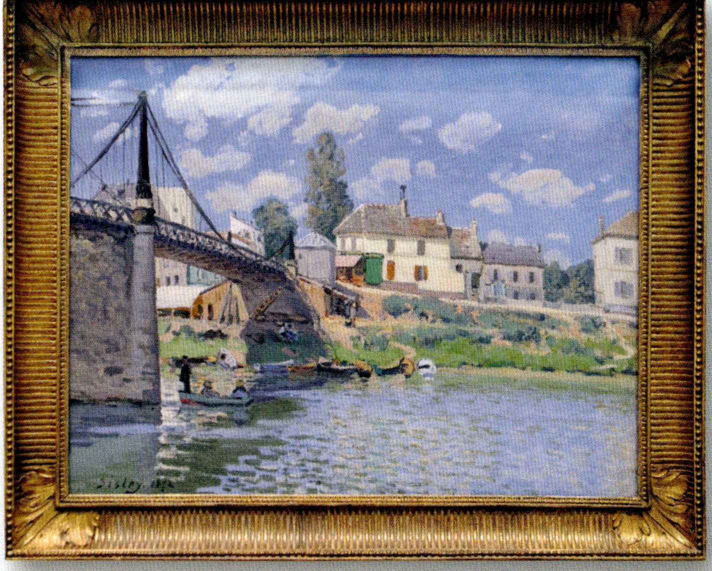

7

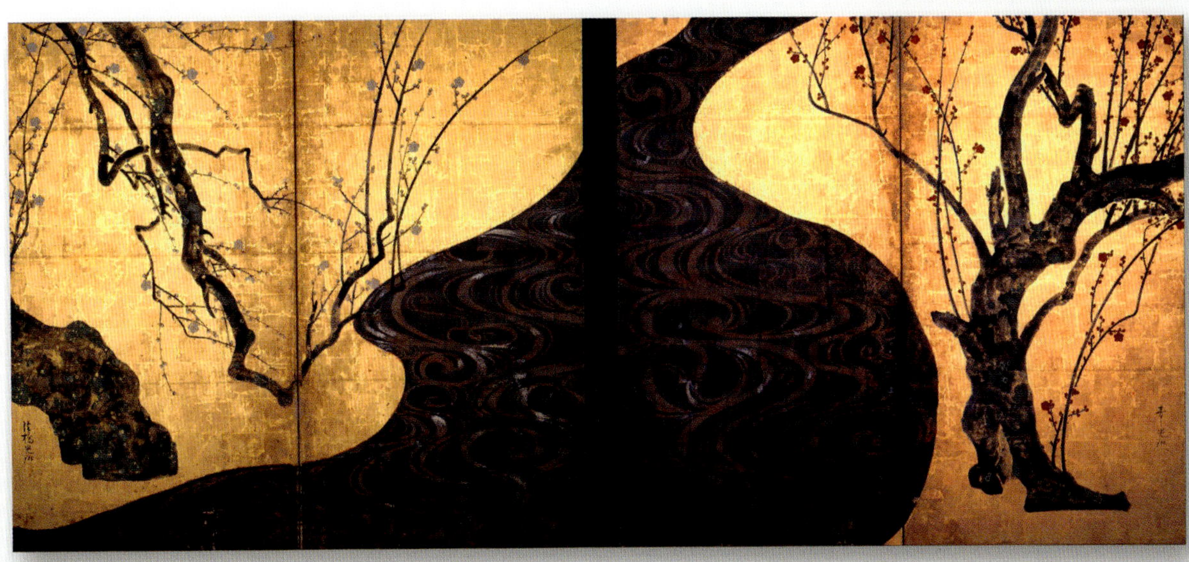

5

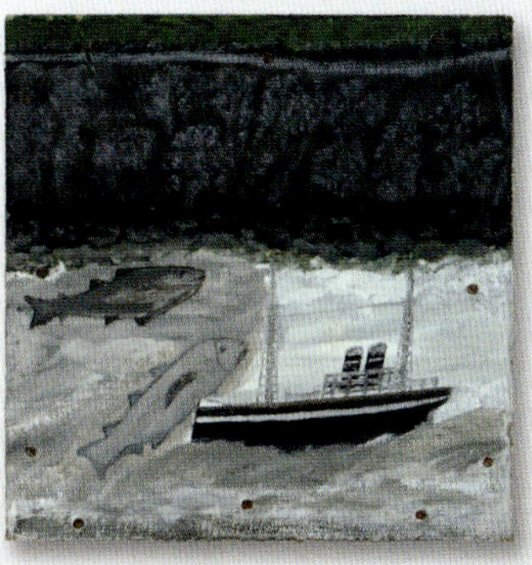

8

5. ***Red and White Plum Blossoms*, Ogata Kōrin, 18th century.** Kōrin was an early and influential member of the Japanese Rinpa School of painting. His simplified, abstract style and strong feeling for nature influenced later European painters such as Van Gogh and Gustave Klimt.

6. ***A Creek in the Wood*, Asher B. Durand, 1865.** A member of the Hudson River School of landscape painting, Durand produced luminous, detailed portrayals of the American wilderness as an unspoiled paradise. He presented nature as an expression of the majesty of God.

7. ***The Bridge at Villeneuve-la-Garenne*, Alfred Sisley, 1872.** As is typical of Impressionism, Sisley painted with quick brushstrokes of bright color to capture the ephemeral effects of light. Of all the Impressionists, he remained the most dedicated to painting outdoors.

8. ***Land, Fish and Motor Vessel*, Alfred Wallis, 1932–1937.** A Cornish fisherman, Wallis had no formal art training. He painted from memories of his early life at sea. The multiple perspectives, variations in scale, and lively paint surface produce a highly personal and expressive style.

Barge Haulers on the Volga

Ilya Repin 1870–1873, oil on canvas, 52 × 111 in (131.5 × 281 cm), State Russian Museum, St. Petersburg, Russia

Eleven weathered *burlaks* (barge haulers) strain to pull a barge upstream, their weary bodies and resigned expressions a testament to the enduring resilience of humanity. Repin's painting is both a portrayal of physical exertion and a comment on the sociopolitical realities of 19th-century Russia. Repin traveled extensively through the country, and meticulously captured the real-life faces of haulers he met along the way. This unfiltered representation of working men and their struggle against oppression is a departure from the romanticized, state-sponsored art being produced in Russia at the time.

In stark contrast to the barge being pulled by the men, a boat travels full-sail downstream, powered by the strong current.

Repin highlights the disparity between the fatigued laborers and the idyllic, bright riverscape behind them.

Most of the barge haulers look down, as if resigned to their fate.

A boy, brightly lit because he has not yet given in to his fate, tries to remove his harness in a gesture of youthful rebellion.

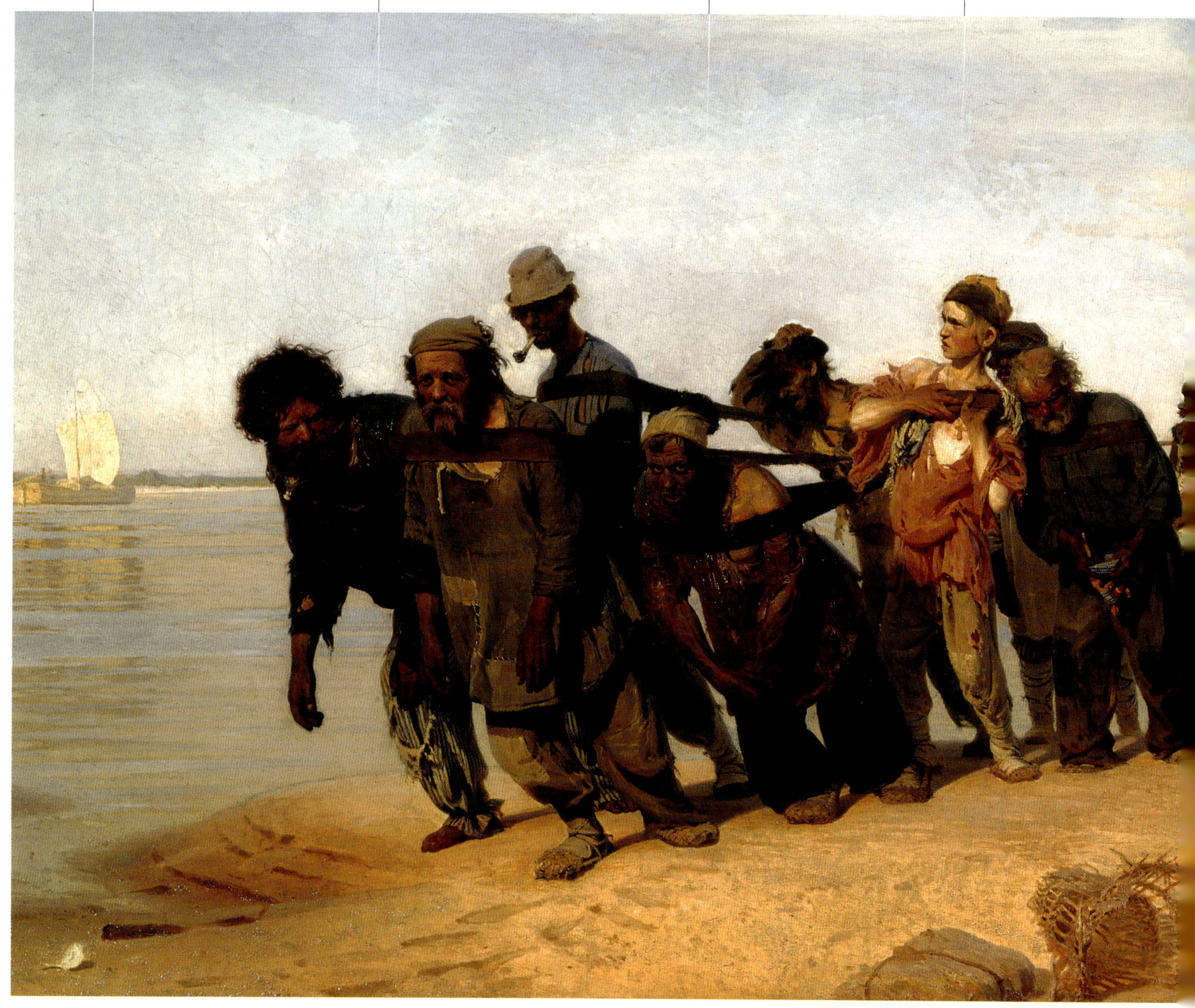

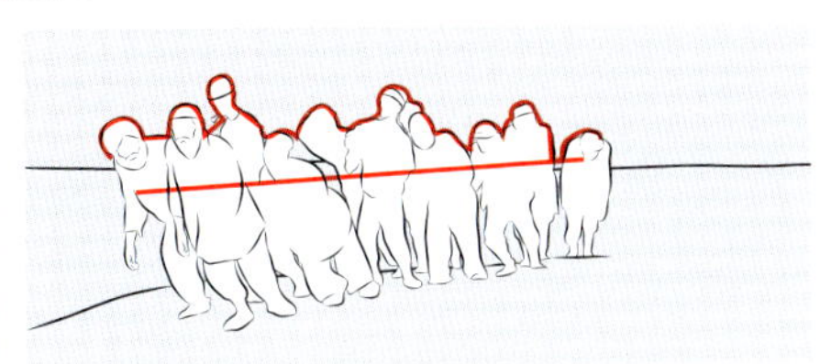

Physical effort
The contours of the heads create an undulating rhythm of movement; the diagonal arrangement of the torsos emphasizes intense exertion.

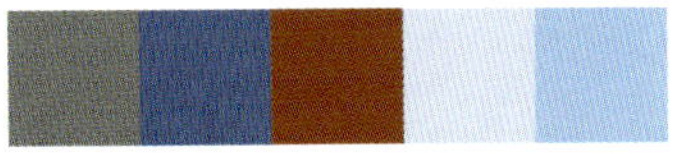

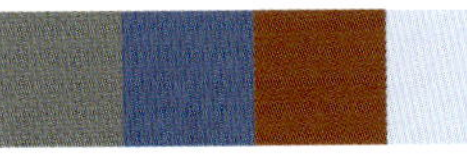

Stark contrast
Repin sets a foreboding palette of muted grays, blues, and browns for the laborers against the pale blues and lavenders of the sky on a beautiful, sunny day.

"[Repin] has … plunged headfirst into the very heart of the people's life … and the people's oppressive reality."
Vladimir Stasov

The man at the back appears to be on the verge of collapsing from exhaustion.

An upside-down national flag is Repin's call for social reform within the Russian state.

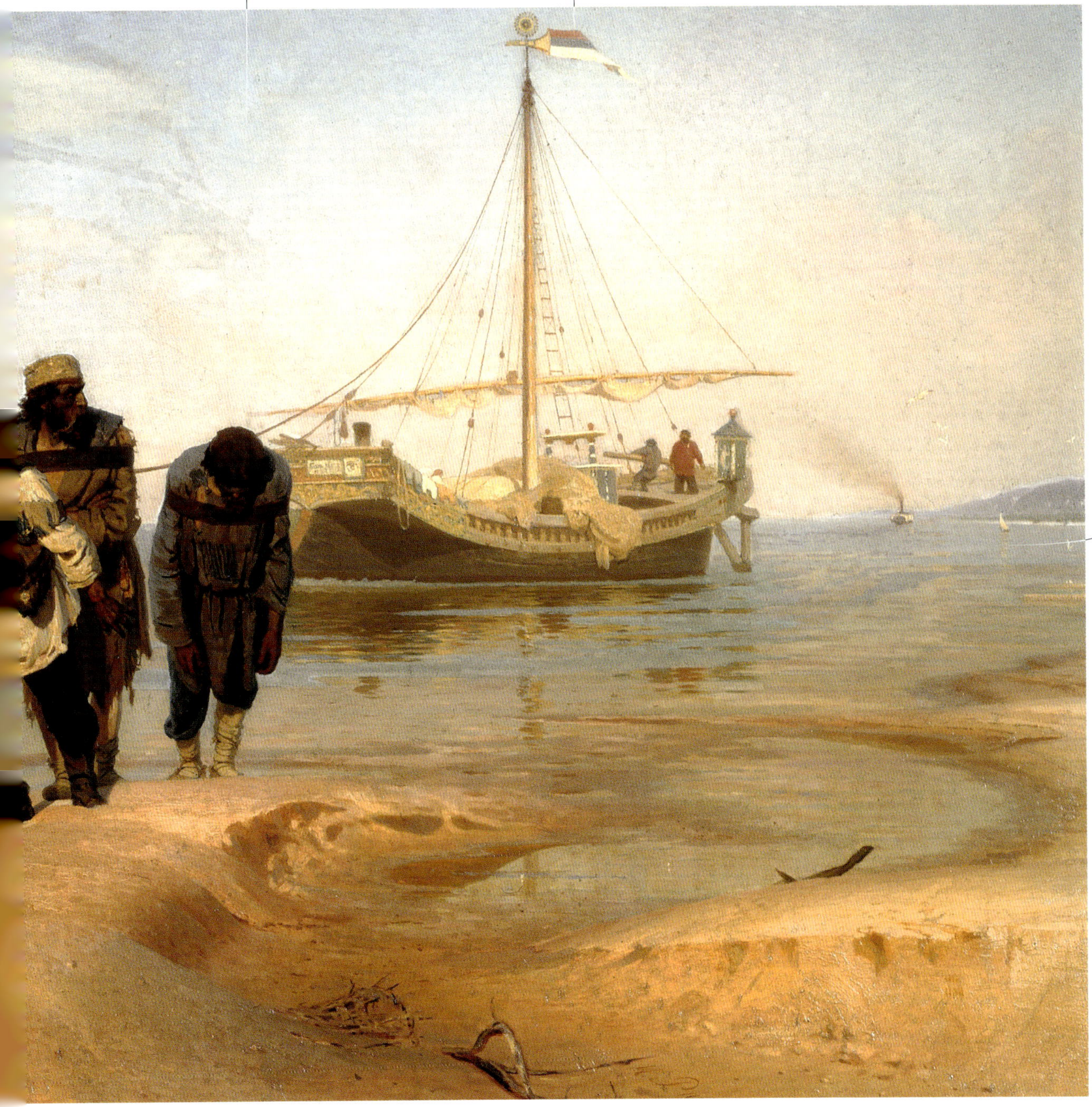

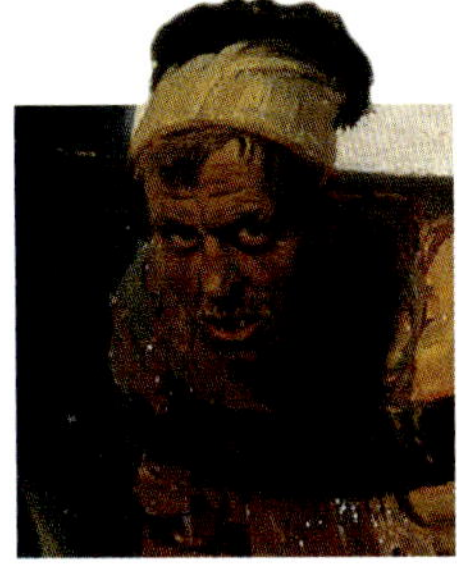

Each facial expression is distinct and detailed. In this way, Repin casts a spotlight on a tapestry of unique personal stories, dreams, and struggles.

The Volga River, with its historical trade routes and transportation links, represents the lifeblood of rural Russia.

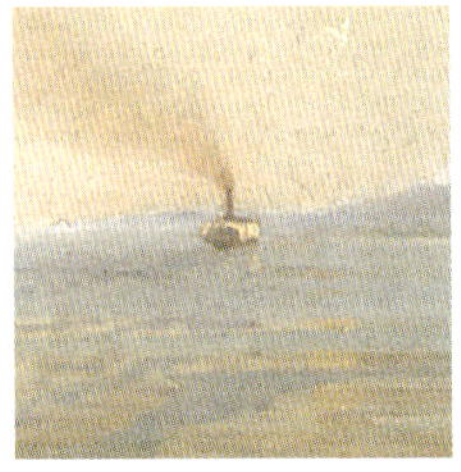

A steam-powered vessel in the distance hints at the dawn of Russian industrialization, and the possible end of this back-breaking labor.

The River Oise Near Pontoise

Camille Pissarro 1873, oil on canvas, 15 × 22 in (38 × 55.2 cm), Indianapolis Museum of Art, US

Considered by some to be the "father of Impressionism," Pissarro painted *en plein air* (outdoors) at a time when most artists worked in studios. He chose views that already had the makings of a picture, and would then paint the whole scene at once. This rural landscape encroached upon by modern industry shows Pissarro's fascination with how the changing light affected the impression of a scene.

Even on a gray day, Pissarro's vibrant sky dominates the scene.

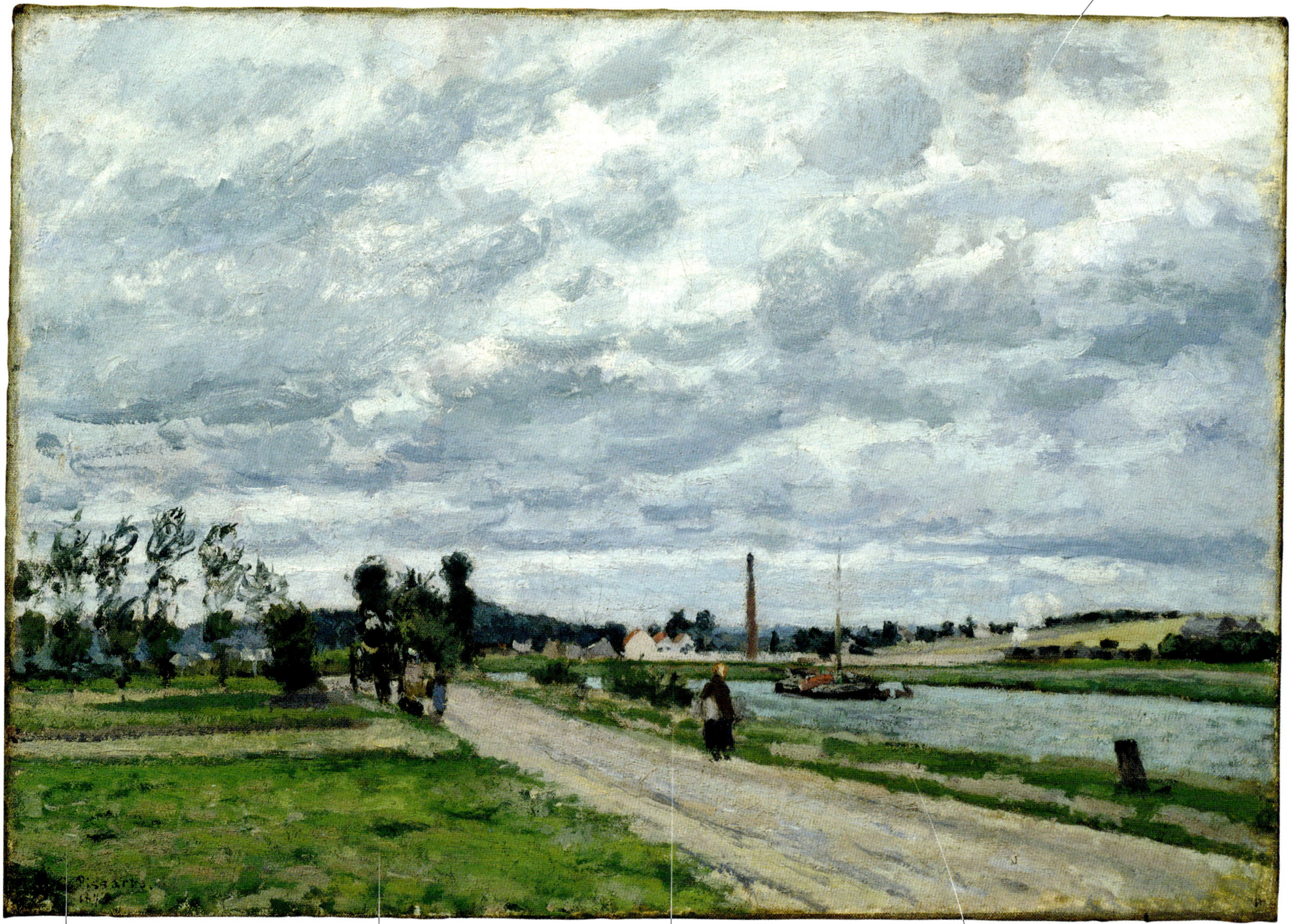

Patches of color on the ground conjure up a sense of shifting sunlight and a breeze ruffling the grass.

A horse and cart evoke ways of transportation before industrialization.

This blurred factory appears in several of Pissarro's paintings. He was interested in the loss of clarity created by distance.

A barge and train give the painting energy and a sense of life. They make it clear that this is no pastoral idyll but an industrial landscape.

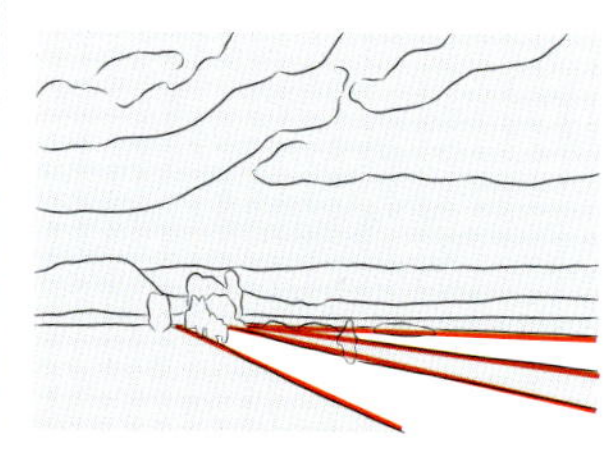

Composition
The river and road cut abruptly between the expanses of sky and landscape, establishing a unifying structure.

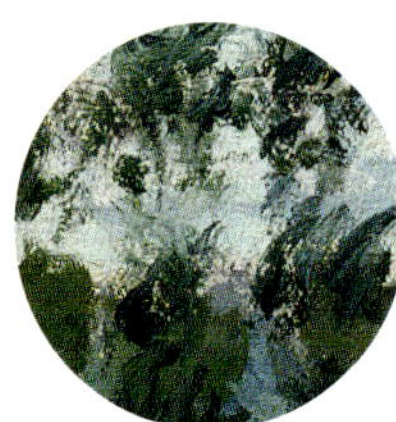

Brushwork
Loosely dabbed trees give an impression of airiness, light, and dynamism. "Drawing is dry," Pissarro told Louis Le Bail, a younger artist. He advised against defining the outlines of things.

Nocturne in Black and Gold, the Falling Rocket

James Abbott McNeill Whistler 1875, oil on panel, 24 × 18 in (60.3 × 46.7 cm), Detroit Institute of Arts, US

Fireworks light up the sky at the end of an evening's entertainment in Cremorne Gardens, a pleasure park on the Thames River in London. The work was thought to be unusually modern at the time because it depicted a fleeting moment rather than telling a story or being a portrait.

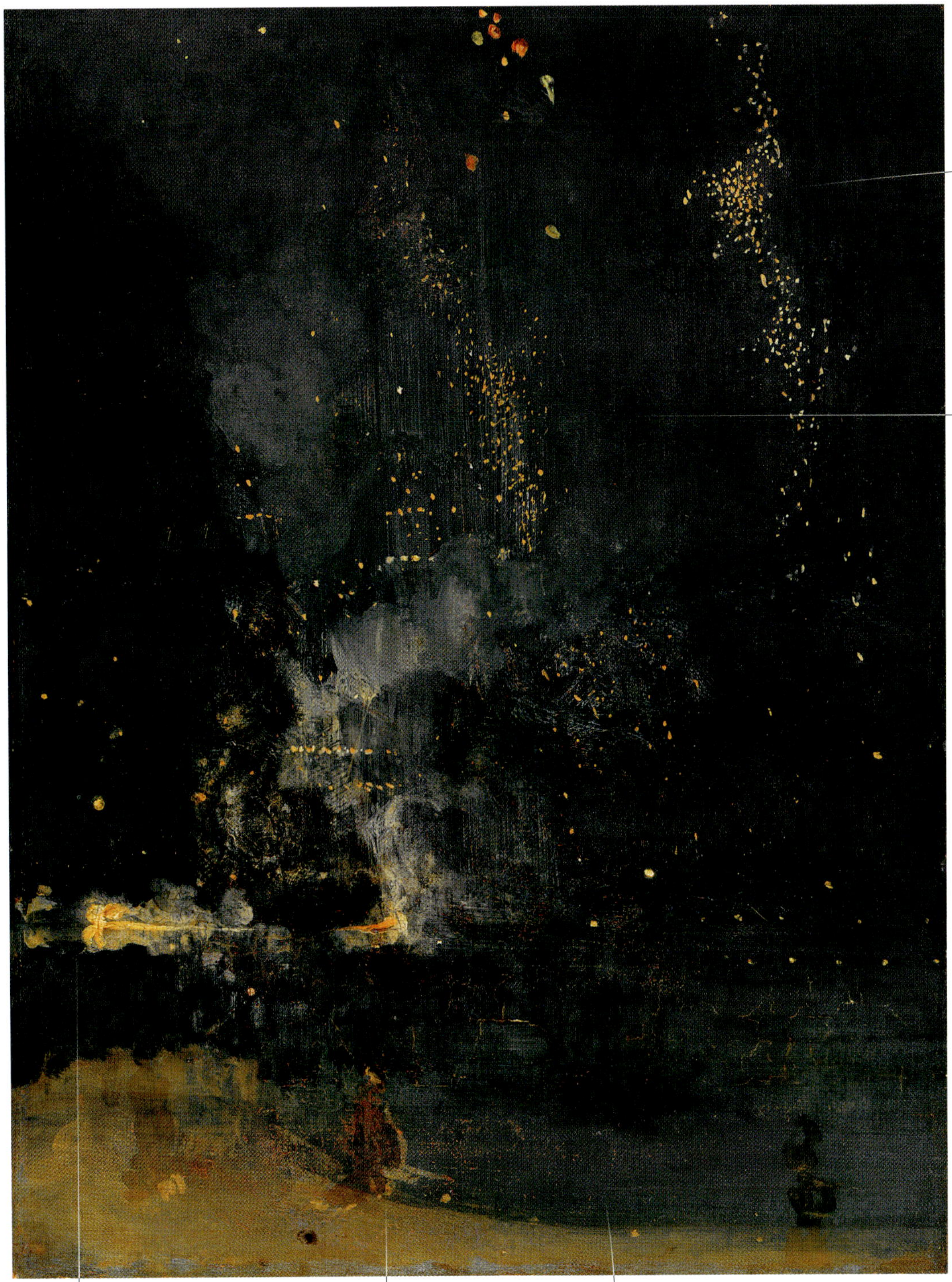

Golden sparks descend from an exploding firework; their snaking line suggests that they have been blown off course by the wind.

The river and sky form a contrast with the billowing smoke which disperses into the night air.

A large shape, perhaps a tree, fills one side of the canvas. It is another clue to the possible location.

Several people, including this indistinct genderless figure, watch the firework display.

A sweeping line of blue-green against old gold paint suggests the shoreline of the Thames River.

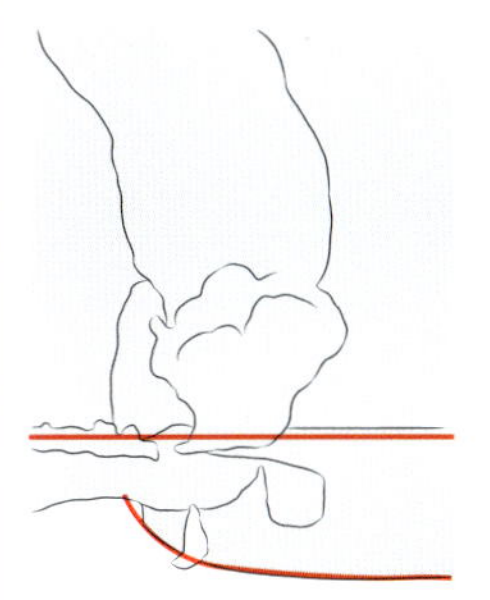

Detailed work
Despite the hurried feel of the work, there is a subtle shaping. A horizon line divides the sky from the water below, and a curve delineates the shoreline.

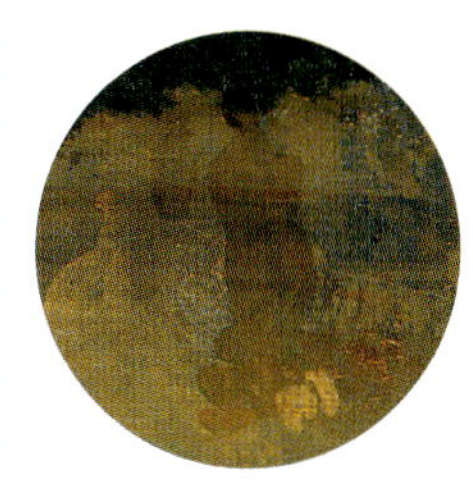

Thin layers
Whistler worked from memory in his studio rather than in the open air at night. He thinned the oil paints and then built up layers of color to create atmosphere.

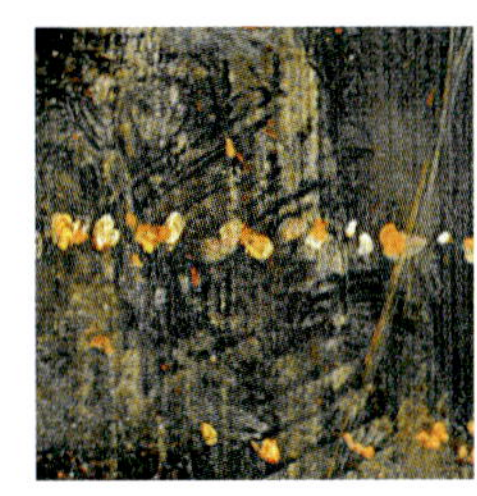

Sparks appear in a regular line, rather like the notes in a musical score. This echoes the title of the painting—a nocturne is a composition that is evocative of the night.

> "By using the word 'nocturne' I wished to indicate an artistic interest alone, divesting the picture of any outside anecdotal interest … A nocturne is an arrangement of line, form and color first."
>
> James Abbott McNeill Whistler, c. 1872

Le Moulin de la Galette

Pierre-Auguste Renoir 1876, oil on canvas, 52 × 69 in (131.5 × 176.5 cm), Musée d'Orsay, Paris, France

This joyful scene, one of Renoir's largest paintings, captures a summer afternoon at an outdoor dance hall. At the time, artists were only just beginning to depict contemporary leisure pursuits, and the painting's sense of energy combined with the sheer size of the canvas is a celebration of working-class life in Paris.

Le Moulin de la Galette was a popular dance hall in Montmartre, named after the 17th-century *moulin* (windmill) that once stood there.

Renoir once claimed that black was "not a color." He used mostly dark blue for the revelers' coats.

Dappled lighting falling through the trees softens the vibrant color.

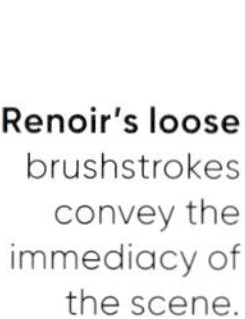

Renoir's loose brushstrokes convey the immediacy of the scene.

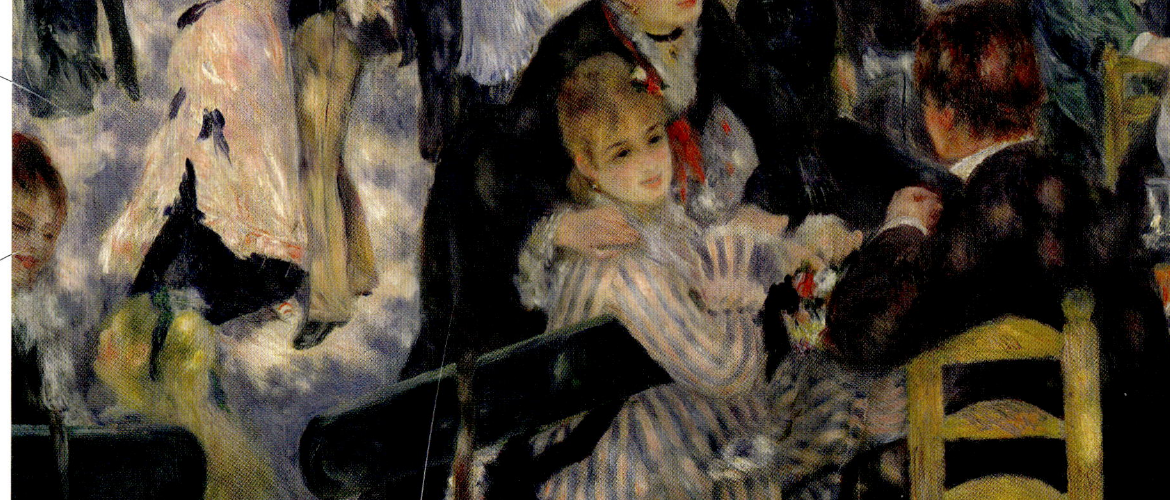

Figures are cut off at the edge of the painting, as though this lively scene continues outside the frame.

This figure may be Jeanne Samary, an actress who also modeled for Renoir's *Luncheon of the Boating Party.*

The joie de vivre of youth is celebrated by the attractive young men and women who populate the foreground.

Art critic Georges Rivière, who was a friend of Renoir, is depicted sitting at a table.

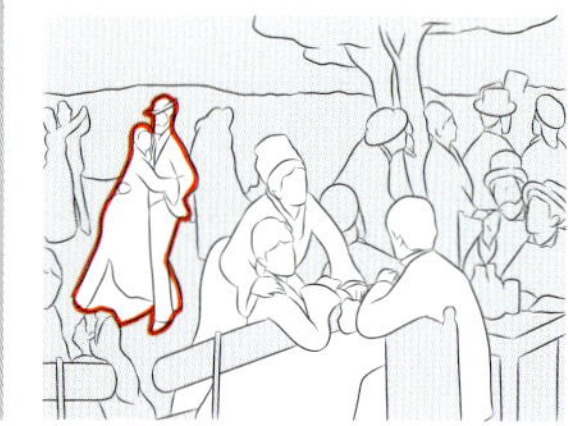

Asymmetry
The painting is full of people but most of the closer figures are on the right. On the left, one prominent couple is singled out by the space around them.

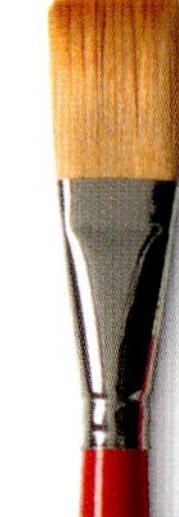

Flat-bristled brush
The emergence of the Impressionist movement coincided with the introduction of a flat-bristled brush, perfect for the application of short strokes of paint.

> "The joyful light fills every corner of the canvas, and even the shadows reflect it."
>
> Stéphane Mallarmé, 1876

Girl Awakening

Eva Gonzalès c. 1877–1878, oil on canvas, 32 × 39 in (81.1 × 100.1 cm), Kunsthalle Bremen, Bremen, Germany

This portrait shows a young woman caught in the moment between sleeping and waking. Gonzalès was Édouard Manet's only formal student, and the painting—also known as *Woman Awakening* and *Morning Awakening*—displays Impressionist traits, such as an emphasis on light and a photographic viewpoint. Like many women artists in the 19th century, Gonzalès focused on portraits and domestic scenes.

The woman looks out sleepily, perhaps at someone else in the room.

The inky blackness of the woman's hair draws attention. Gonzalès's paintings often contrasted light with dark for dramatic effect.

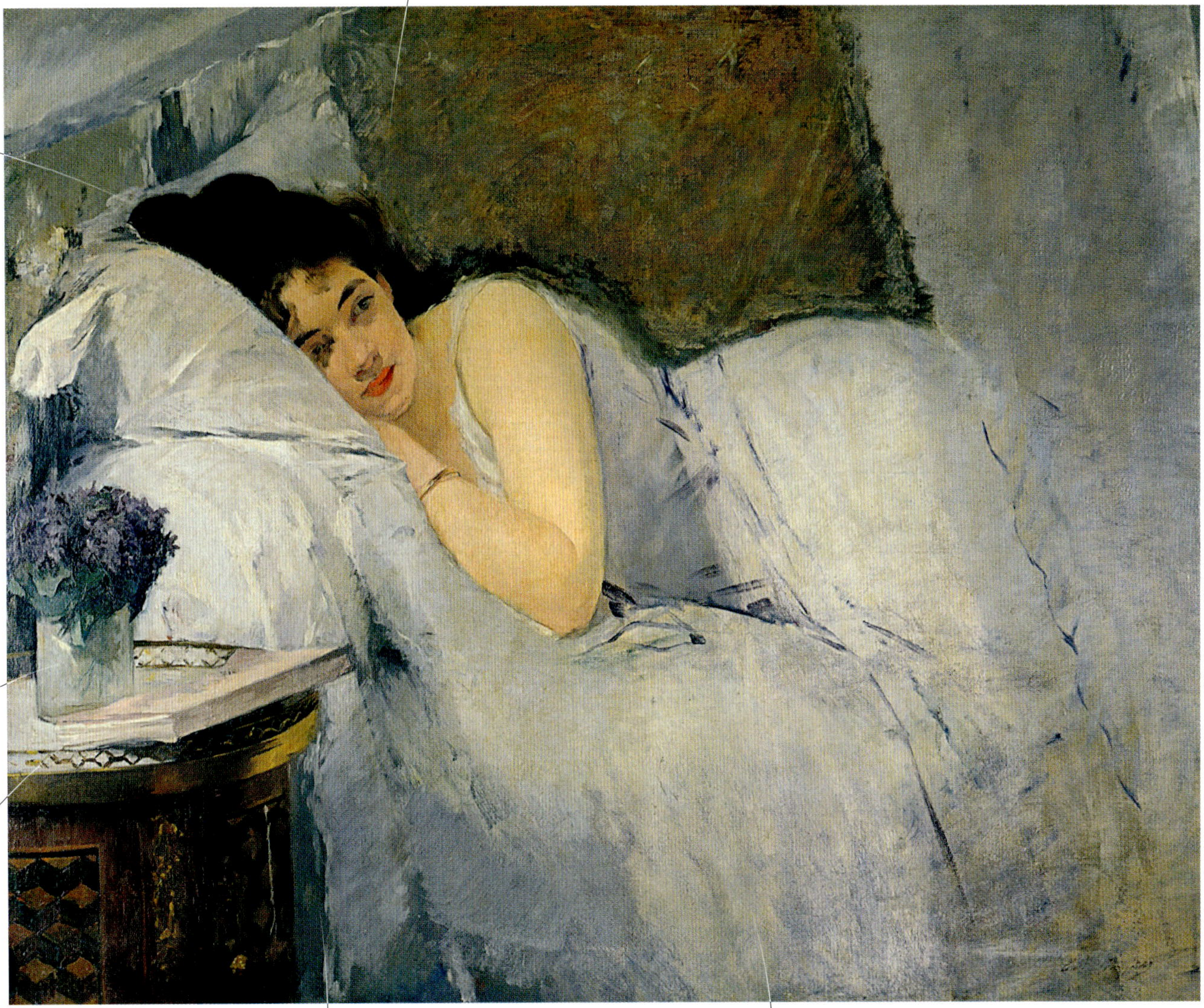

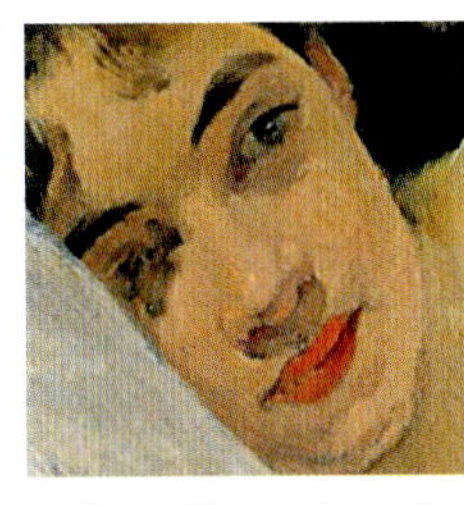

Gonzalès captures the intimate act of waking. One of the chief aims of Impressionism was to convey a specific moment in time.

The blue flowers on the bedside table may be violets.

A book blends with the subtle colors of the bedlinen and the woman's nightdress.

Shadows on the bedding are suffused with shades of blue, pink, and beige, possibly suggesting daybreak.

The model is Gonzalès's sister, Jeanne, who posed for many of her works and was said to closely resemble her.

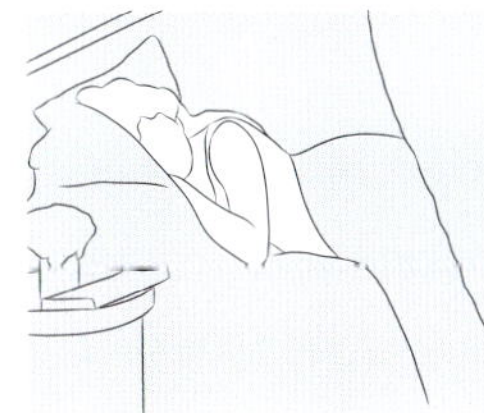

Sense of intimacy
The painting is closely cropped, and sections of the bed, curtain, and table are not visible. This heightens the sensation that the viewer is also present in the room.

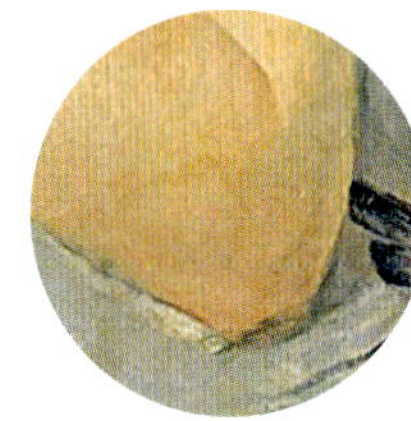

Dawn's rays
The waking woman is bathed in gentle morning light. Her pale skin glows, accentuated by the white bedding.

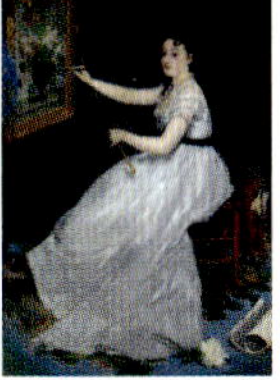

Manet's student
Before Gonzalès became his student at the age of 22, Manet painted this portrait of her painting at her easel.

Death of Cleopatra

Edmonia Lewis 1876, marble, 63 × 31 × 46 in (160 × 79.4 × 116.8 cm), Smithsonian American Art Museum, Washington, D.C., US

Lewis depicts Cleopatra, queen of Ptolemaic Egypt and enemy of Rome, enthroned at the moment of her dramatic death by suicide in 30 BCE. The sculpture was shown to great acclaim at the 1876 Centennial Exposition in Philadelphia, but then fell into obscurity and was lost to the public for more than 100 years.

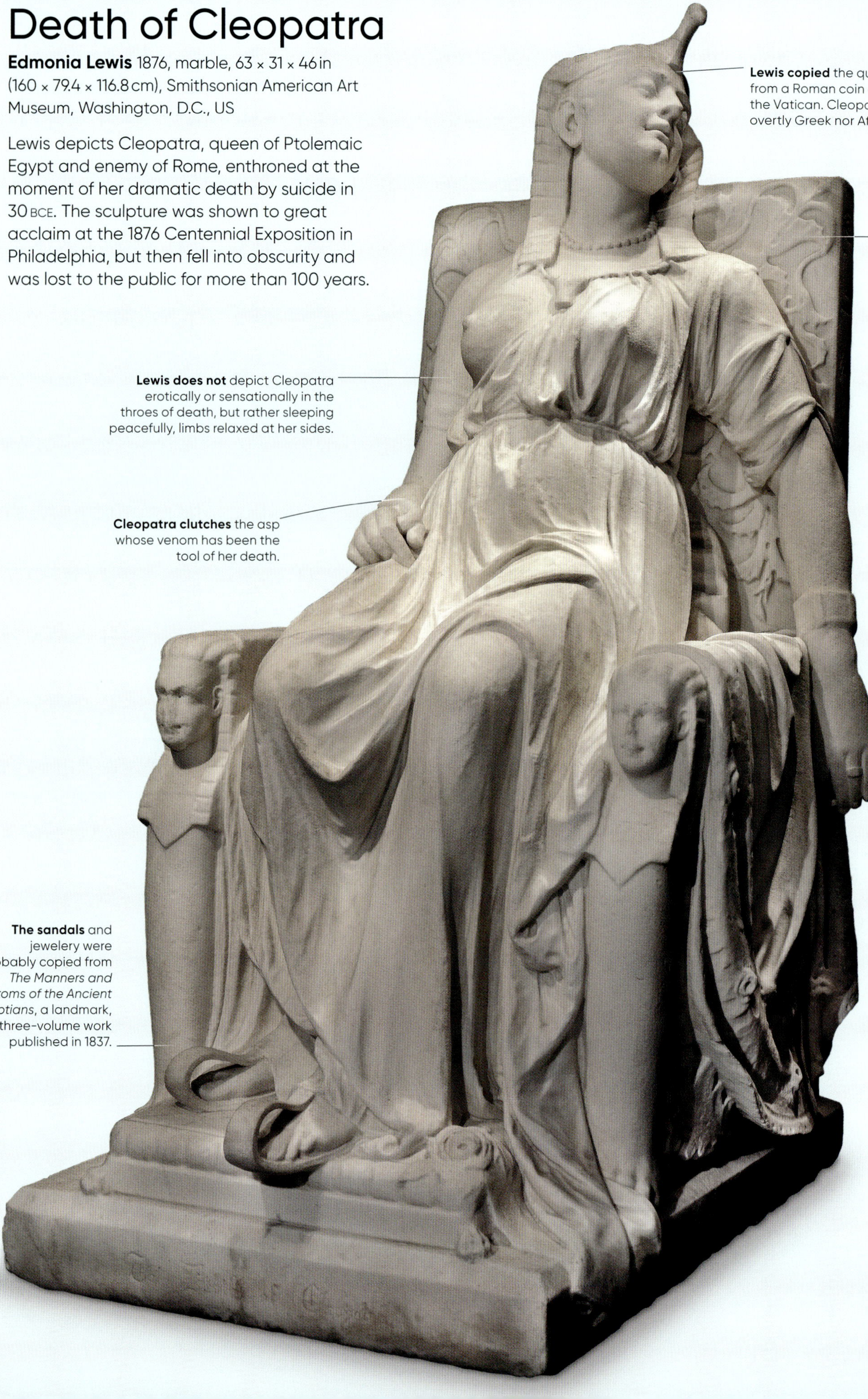

Lewis copied the queen's profile from a Roman coin on display at the Vatican. Cleopatra is neither overtly Greek nor African.

Stylized lotus flowers adorn the throne. The Egyptomania that gripped Europe in the 19th century popularized this ancient motif.

Lewis does not depict Cleopatra erotically or sensationally in the throes of death, but rather sleeping peacefully, limbs relaxed at her sides.

Cleopatra clutches the asp whose venom has been the tool of her death.

The sandals and jewelery were probably copied from *The Manners and Customs of the Ancient Egyptians*, a landmark, three-volume work published in 1837.

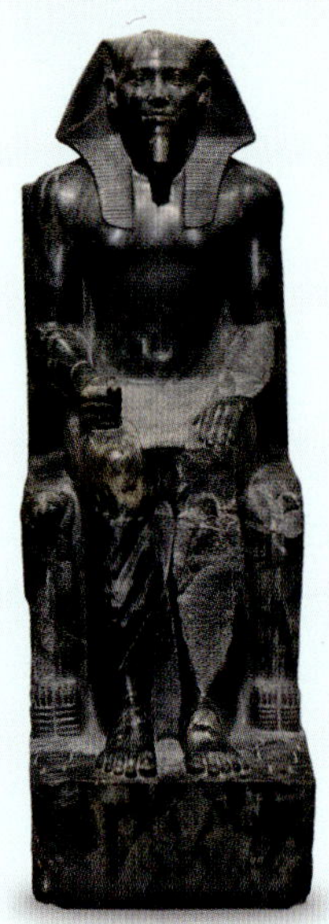

Inspiration
Lewis studied sculptures of Egyptian kings and queens, copying the shape and the position of the animals adorning their thrones.

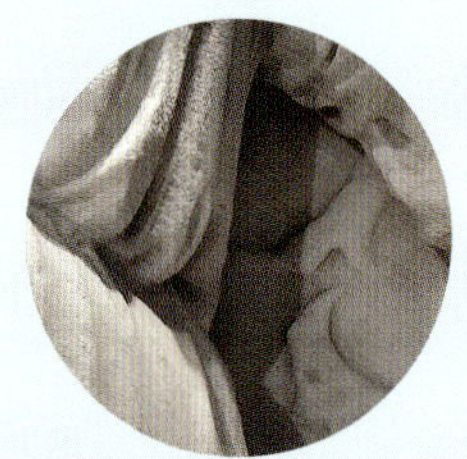

Damage
The 3-ton sculpture was used for many years to mark the grave of a horse. This time outdoors has left its once highly polished surface pitted.

Paris Street; Rainy Day

Gustave Caillebotte 1877, oil on canvas, 7 × 9 ft (2.12 × 2.76 m), Art Institute of Chicago, Illinois, US

On an anonymous street in Haussmann's newly redeveloped Paris, with its wide avenues, people walk alone in their own world. Caillebotte captures a vast, stark modernity and achieves a realistic, rain-soaked quality through the use of cool blues and grays, with shimmering touches of peach on the stones.

The sky, once hidden under a yellow varnish, was revealed as brighter and more varied after cleaning in 2013.

Beneath a sign reading *Pharmacie*, a shop stands at a crossroads. It is the only sign in the wide expanse.

The umbrella introduces a note of impending conflict; it will soon be caught between that of the couple and the wall to the far right.

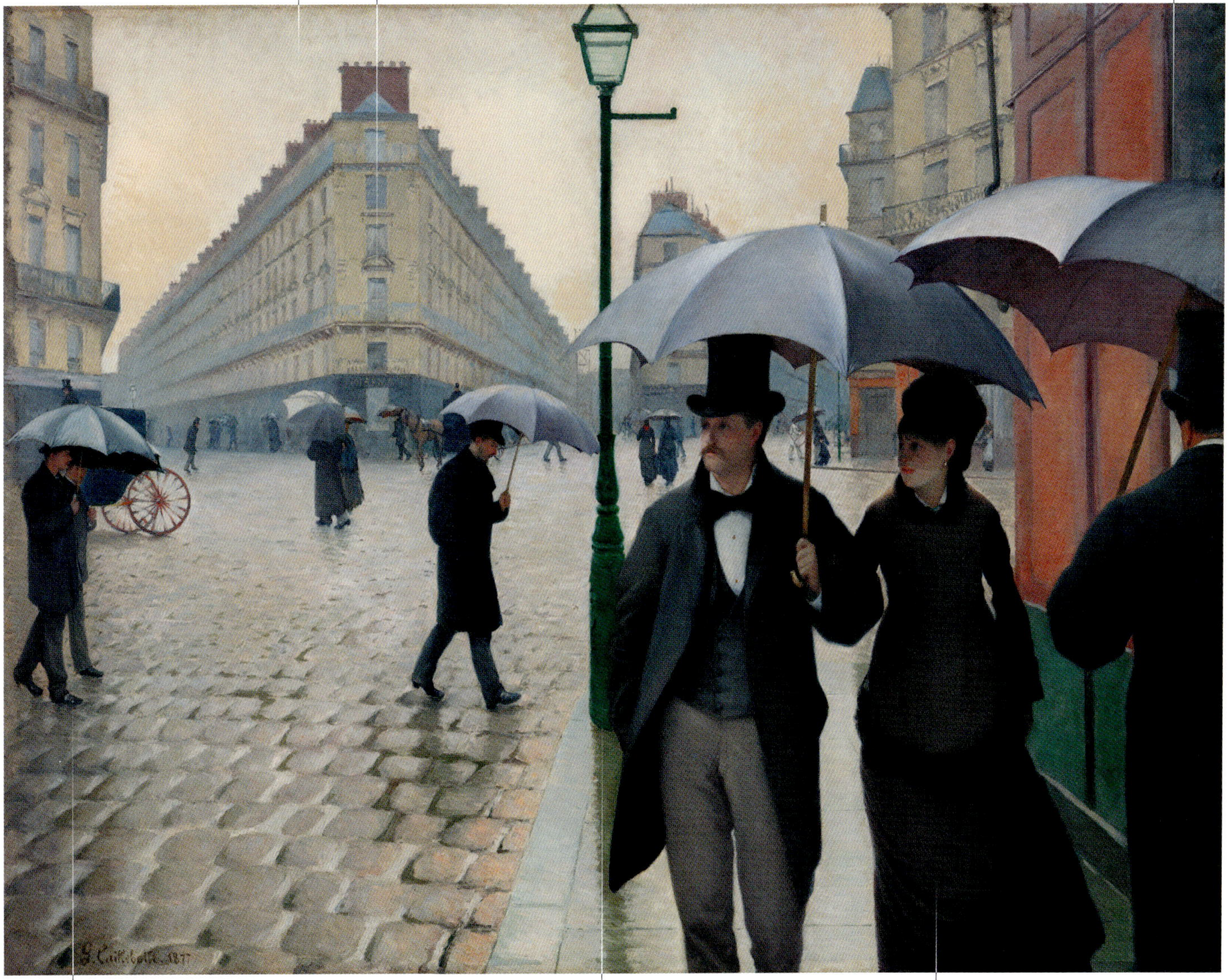

The retractable umbrella was a relatively new invention, and available in only two Parisian department stores.

Distinctive green lampposts became part of the city scape.

This elegant couple, painted at nearly life-size, wear the latest fashions.

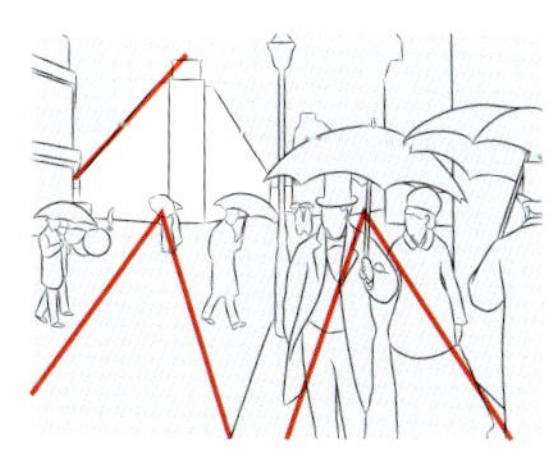

Linear perspective
Caillebotte uses at least two vanishing points: one left of the lamppost, the other on the right. The buildings taper toward the horizon, and the people grow smaller as they get farther away.

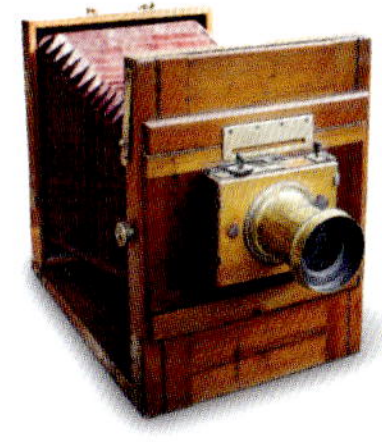

Photography
Caillebotte depicts the city as if through a camera lens; the man on the far right, for example, has been partially cut from the shot. At this time, when photography was still fairly new, the two art forms often influenced each other.

The behind-the-scenes approach is epitomized by an exhausted ballerina, resting her head on her left hand.

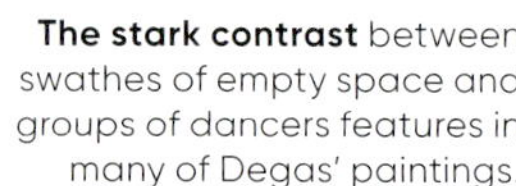

The stark contrast between swathes of empty space and groups of dancers features in many of Degas' paintings.

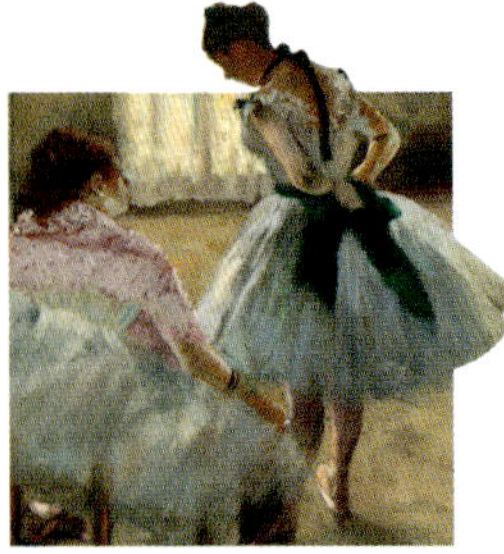

Most of the dancers have their backs to the artist. This creates tension, as Degas is present but simultaneously remote from the action.

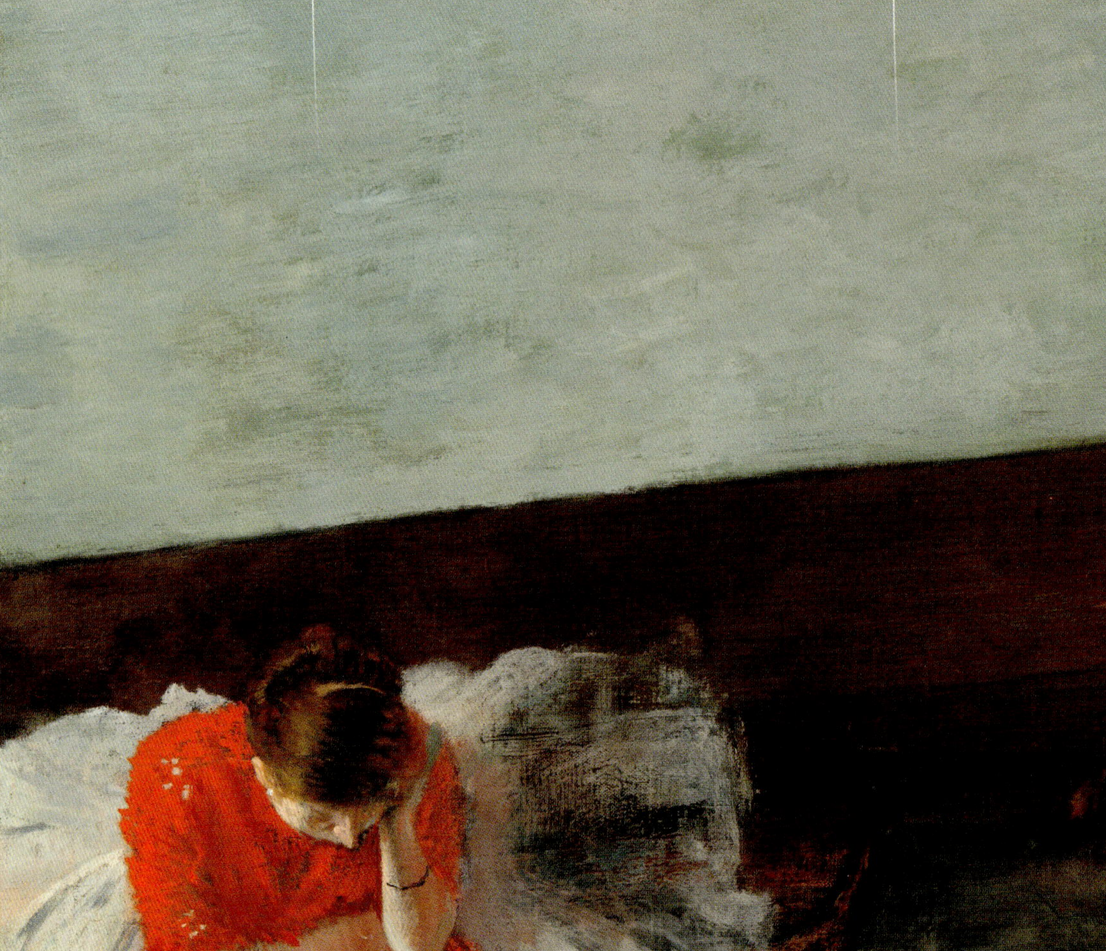

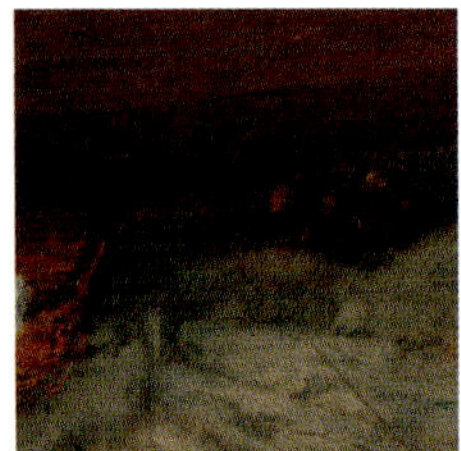

The artist's initial sketch contained several details, including the double bass, before most of the dancers were added.

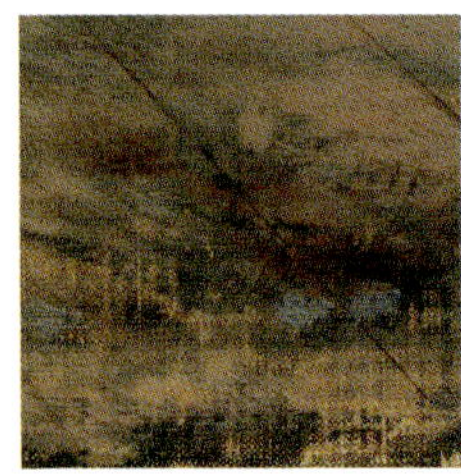

Degas often altered details. This open violin case has been painted over, but is still visible.

The Dance Lesson

Edgar Degas c.1879, oil on canvas, 15 × 35 in (38 × 88 cm), National Gallery of Art, Washington, D.C., US

The first in a series of about 40 works that Degas produced of ballet dancers, *The Dance Lesson* takes the viewer behind the scenes to a ballet class at the Paris Opera. At the time, ballet was not viewed as respectable, and Degas was criticized for depicting an improper theme in the style of classical works. *The Dance Lesson* has a spontaneous feel, but it was carefully composed. Degas made numerous sketches of ballerinas backstage at the Paris Opera before reproducing them in his studio.

Degas repeated figures in other works. A version of this ballerina adjusting her sash appears in several paintings and pastels.

Degas was influenced by the flattened forms of Japanese woodblock prints. This can be seen in the unusual rising floor.

The window provides a light source for the whole room, placing the focus on all of the dance students.

Photography was one of Degas' interests. This painting, with dancers half out of the frame, has the mood of a photograph.

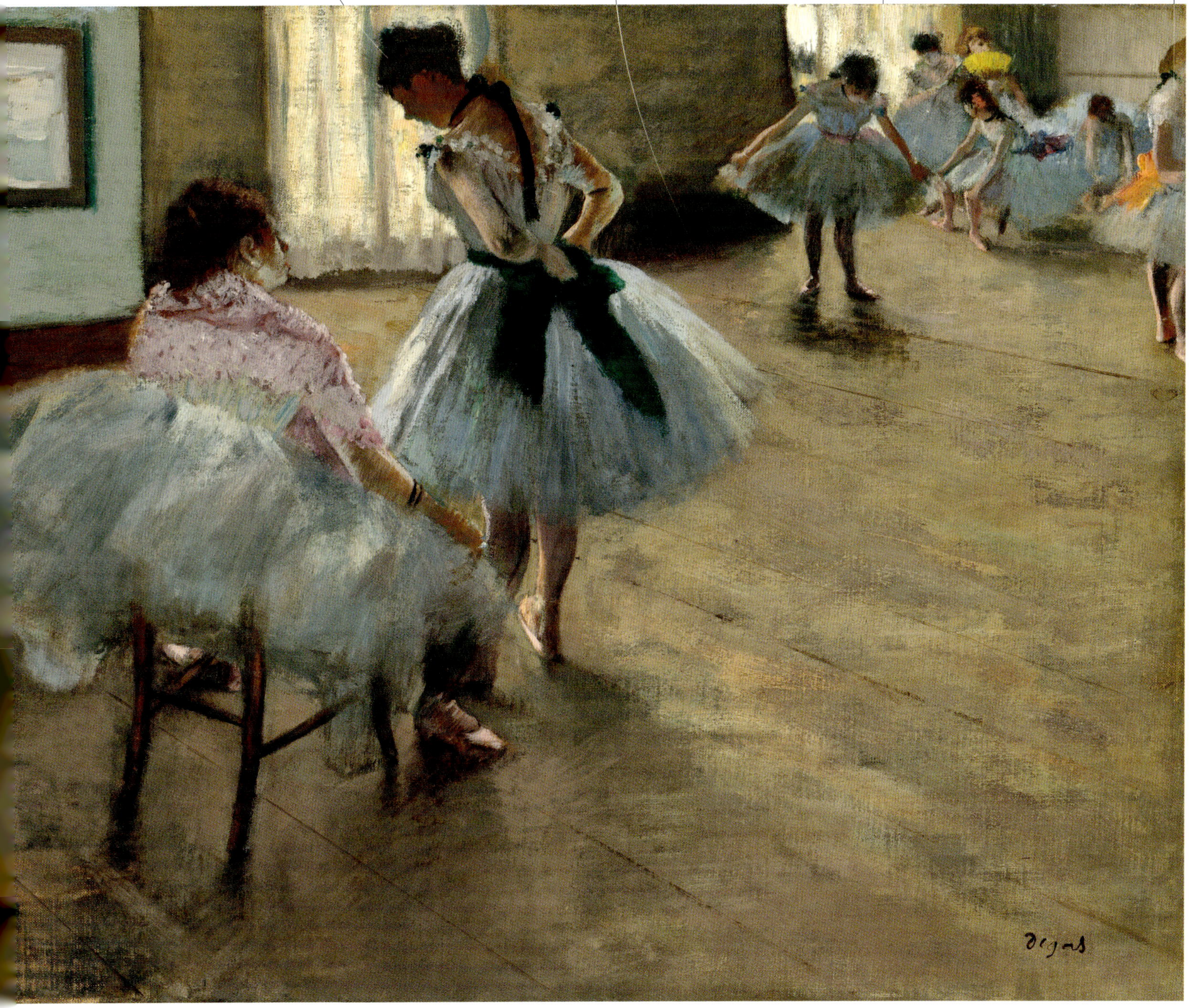

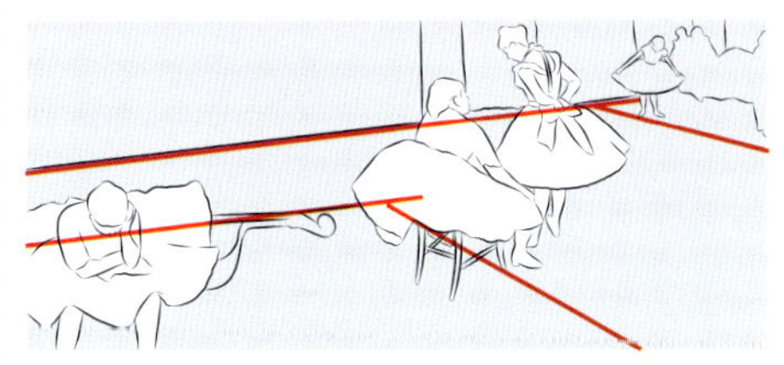

A class divided
The diagonals on the floorboards intersect with those along the walls, separating the dancers into three distinct groups.

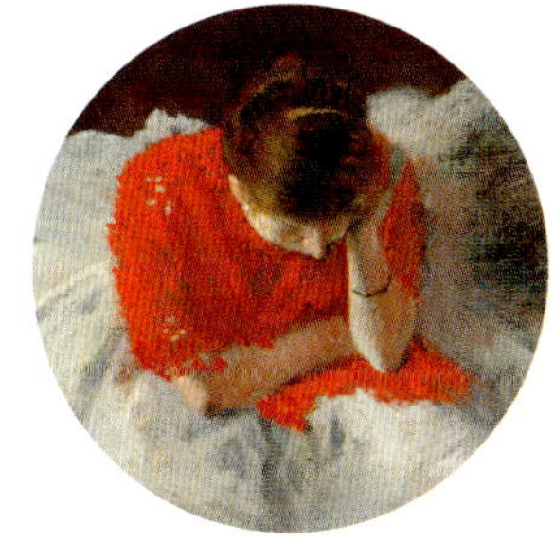

Splashes of color
The studio is depicted using earth tones but these are punctuated by the bright sashes and shawls.

"It has never occurred to them that my chief interest in dancers lies in rendering movement and painting pretty clothes."

Edgar Degas

Summer's Day

Berthe Morisot c. 1879, oil on canvas, 18 × 30 in (45.7 × 75.2 cm), National Gallery, London, UK

Morisot's quintessential Impressionist work depicts two fashionably dressed women in a boat in a Paris park. Characteristically for Impressionism, it is an image of ordinary people at leisure painted en plein air—not in a studio—using vigorous, visible brushstrokes and emphasizing sparkling natural light.

A horse-drawn carriage, barely visible on the shore, provides a reminder that this tranquil scene is set in an urban park.

One woman gazes directly at the viewer—or perhaps the painter—creating an emotional connection, though her expression is enigmatic.

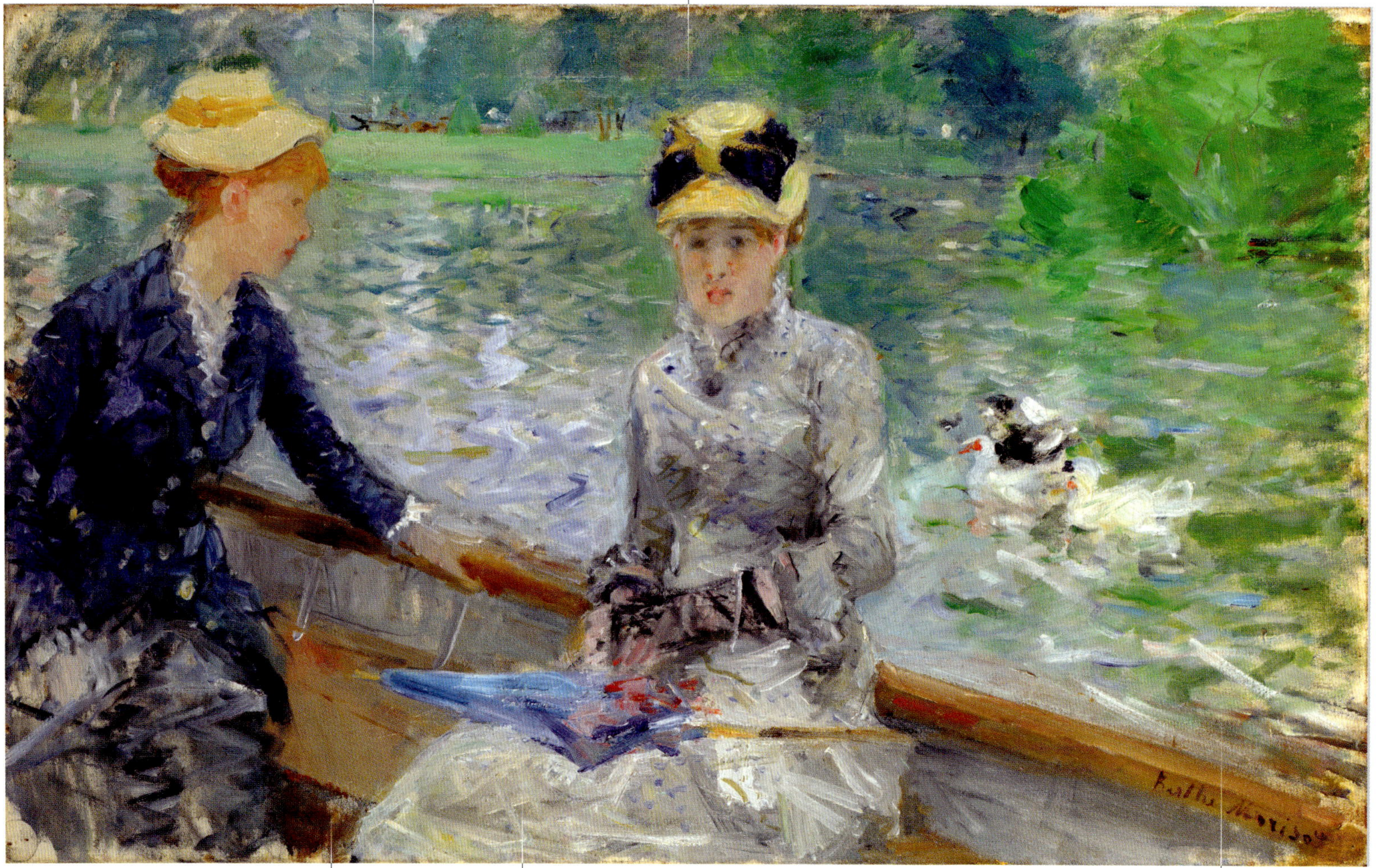

Morisot positions the viewer inside the boat with the women—unlike Renoir's otherwise comparable painting, *The Skiff*.

The same women probably modeled for Morisot's *In the Bois de Boulogne*; their clothes appear identical.

This lake is almost certainly in the Bois de Boulogne, a public park in western Paris, which was frequented by Morisot.

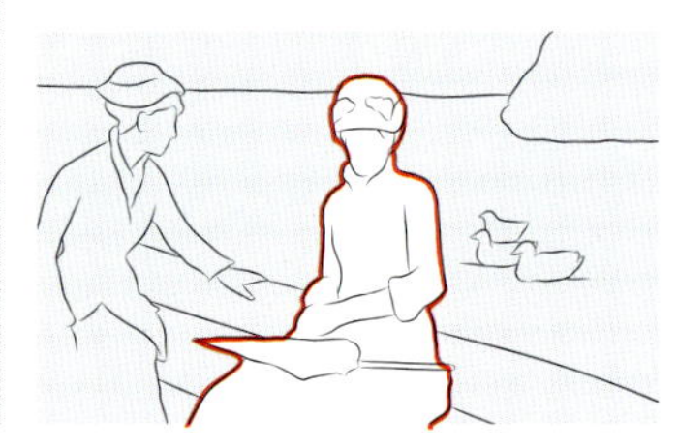

Leading lady
The woman in blue and the waterbirds all face inward, drawing the viewer's attention toward the central woman in white.

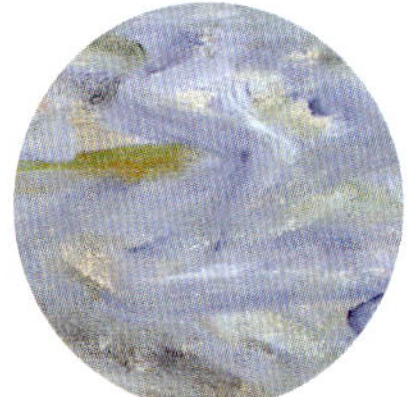

Brushstrokes
Morisot uses distinctive zigzag brushstrokes that bring a dynamic energy to *Summer's Day*.

> "The touch, sure and light [is] fixing something of the passing moment."
>
> Berthe Morisot, 1882

In the Studio

Marie Bashkirtseff 1881, oil on canvas, 74 × 61 in (188 × 154 cm), Dnipropetrovsk Art Museum, Dnipro, Ukraine

Bashkirtseff evokes a scene of female solidarity within the confines of an all-women studio at the Académie Julian in Paris, where she studied. This canvas stands as a rare firsthand account of women channeling their gaze and skills to create works during a transformative period in women's art education.

Fifteen women dominate a small space, contributing to a sense of congestion.

Figure studies stand sentinel over the students below, representing the realm toward which they aspire.

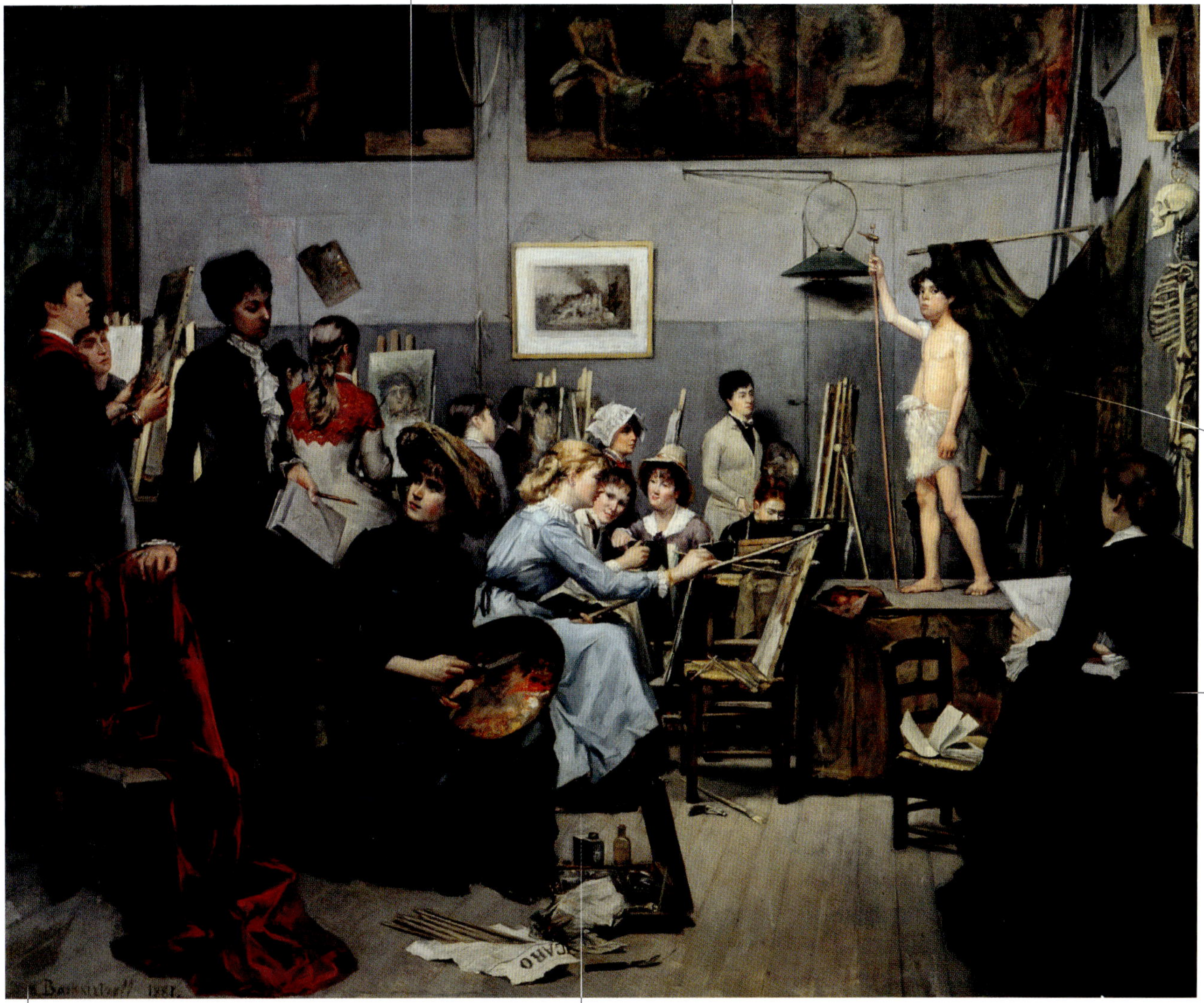

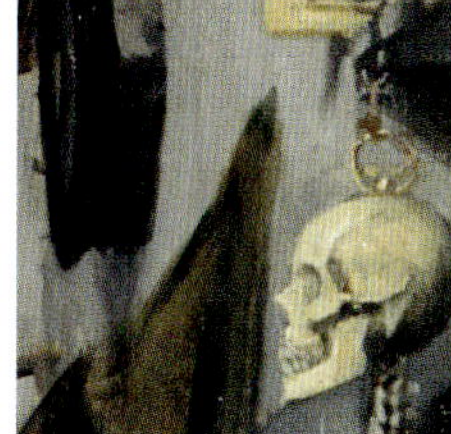

A skeleton and clock are the specter of Bashkirtseff's mortality looming over her head. She died of tuberculosis in 1884.

A young boy, perhaps posing as John the Baptist, serves as a minority figure in a female-controlled environment.

This woman with her back to the viewer may be Bashkirtseff herself. The woman isolates herself at the margins of the canvas and focuses on her art.

The initial M conceals Marie Bashkirtseff's gender: a common strategy used by women to gain acceptance in a male-dominated discipline.

Fellow student Marie Magdeleine Real del Sarte would go on to achieve success as a painter and art teacher.

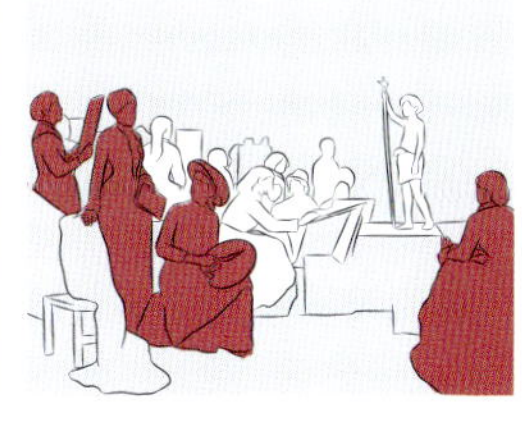

In the spotlight
Peripheral figures in low light and dark dresses frame brightly lit figures within, shaping an enclosed three-dimensional space that draws the gaze inward.

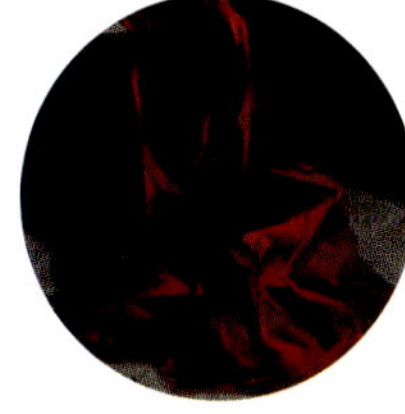

Bravura performance
Harmonized by red accents around it, the striking red shawl demonstrates a refined mastery of color gradation and a nuanced interplay between highlights and shadows.

> "In the studio all distinctions disappear. One has neither name nor family, one is no longer the daughter of one's mother, one is one's self."
>
> Marie Bashkirtseff, 1877

The white circles might be early electric lights; they produced a harsher light than gas lighting.

The chandelier—along with the champagne, fruit, and clientele's wardrobe—make it clear that this is an upscale establishment.

A Folies-Bergère barmaid called Suzon served as Manet's model for this painting.

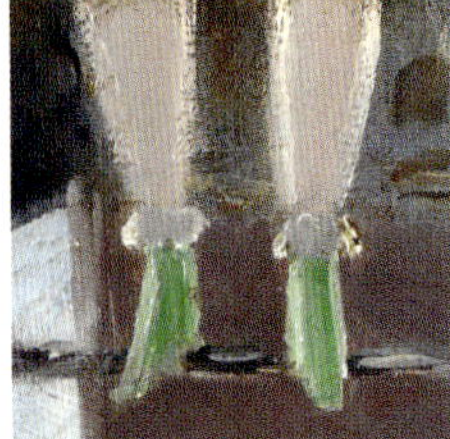

A trapeze artist's legs are visible in the corner, hinting at the excitement of the entertainment.

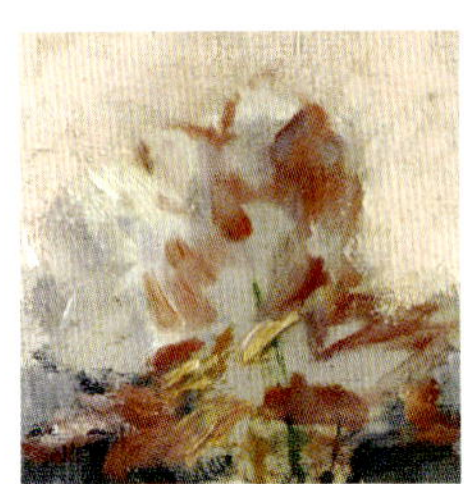

Flowers in the barmaid's décolletage echo the logo on the bottles of Bass beer.

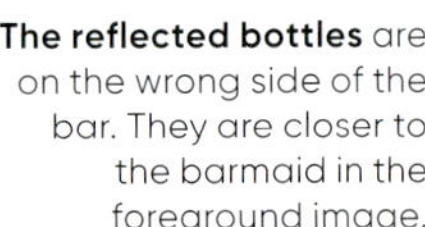

The reflected bottles are on the wrong side of the bar. They are closer to the barmaid in the foreground image.

The red triangular logo of Bass beer is visible on some bottles; other bottles contain champagne and liquor.

Manet's signature is on the label of this bottle.

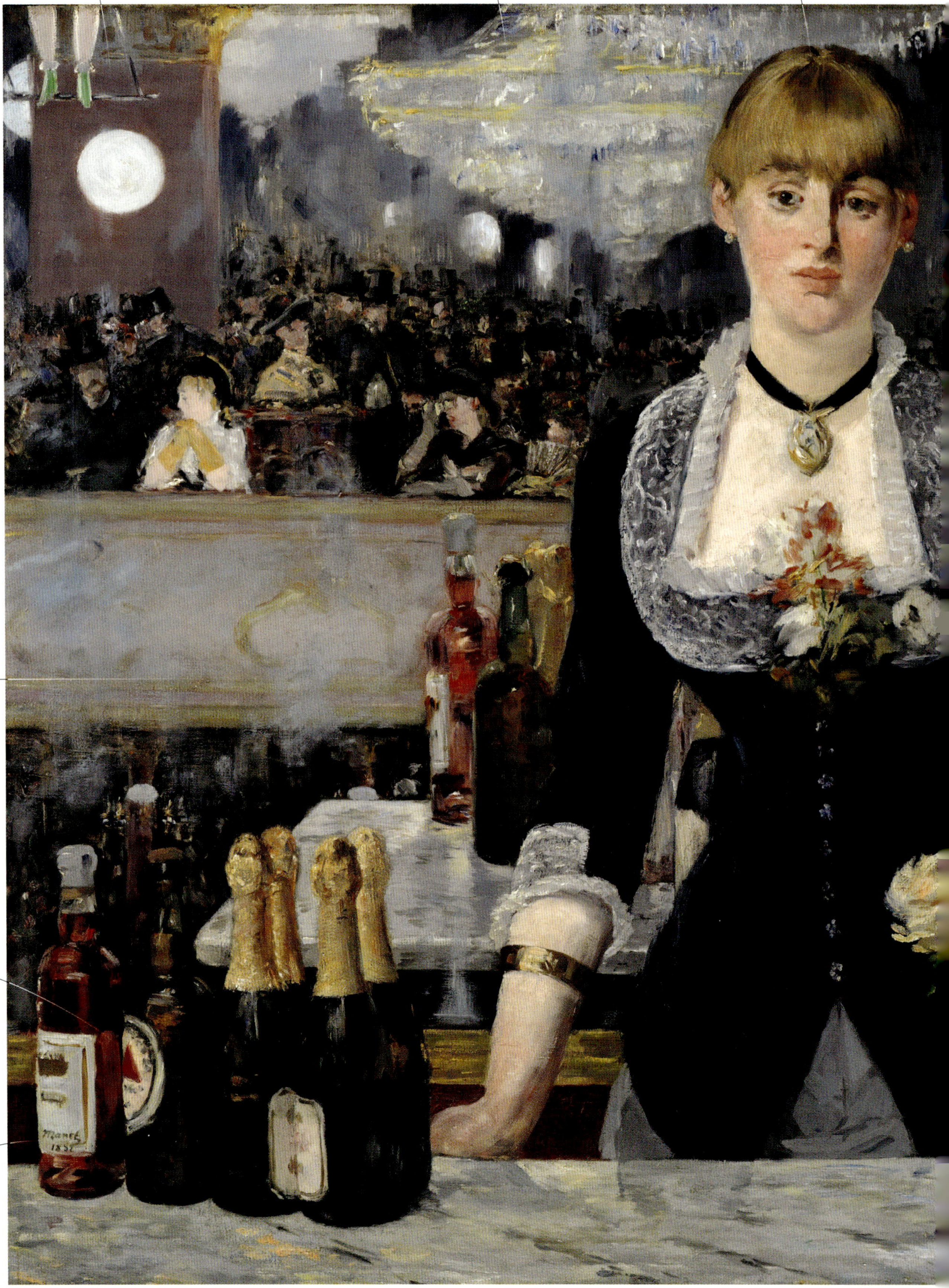

In the reflection, the barmaid is interacting with the male customer.

The reflection indicates that the man should be blocking the viewer, but he is not, suggesting he may be a dream, Manet himself, or represent the viewer.

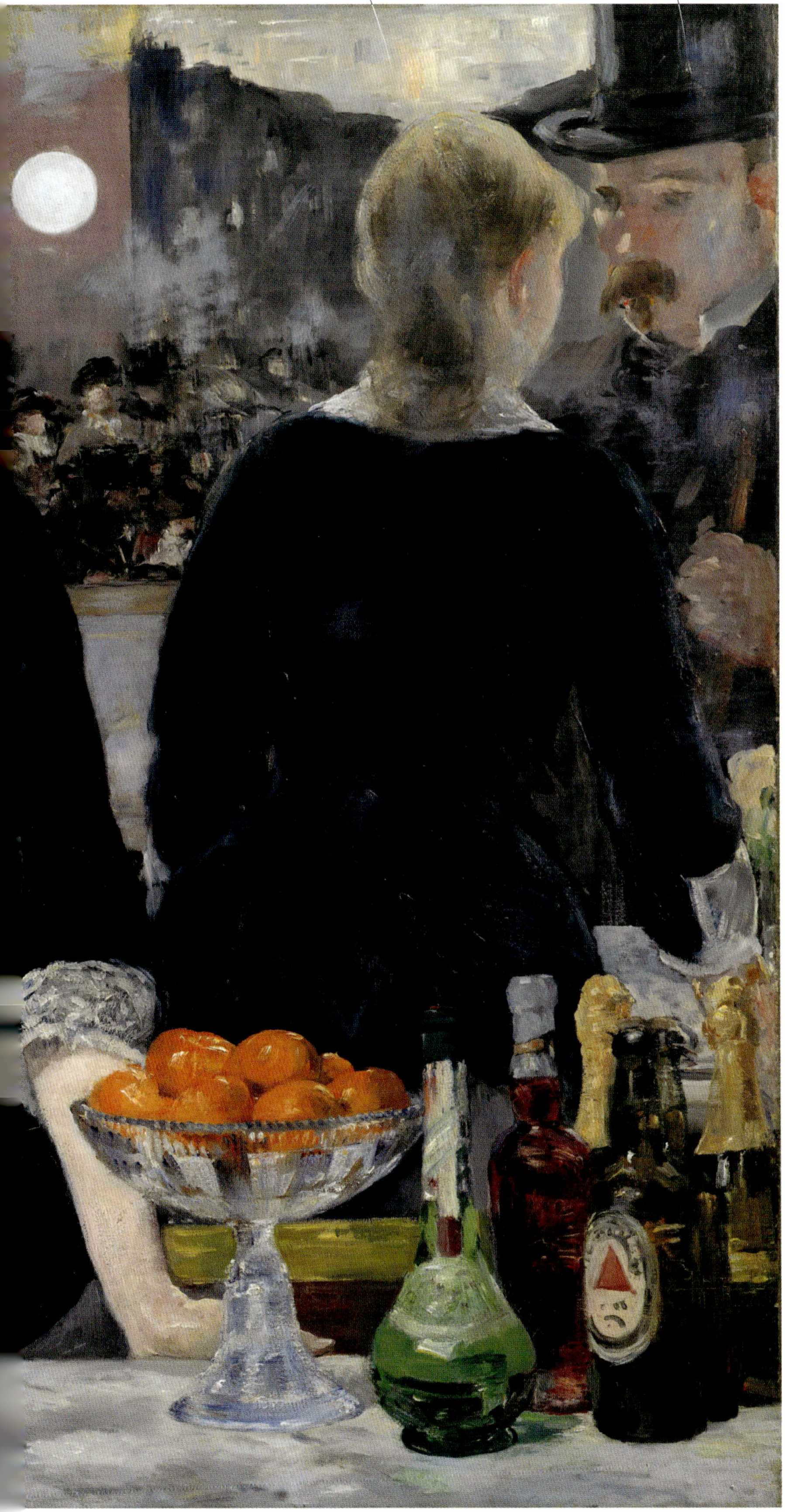

A Bar at the Folies-Bergère

Édouard Manet 1882, oil on canvas, 38 x 51 in (96 x 130 cm), Courtauld Institute, London, UK

In this large painting, a working-class woman stands behind a bar at a Parisian nightclub, bored or tired, despite the venue's excitement. The scene in front of the barmaid—a fashionable crowd enjoying an acrobatic performance—is visible in the mirror behind her. This mirror image also suggests that the barmaid is interacting with a male customer, but he is only seen in the reflection. Some art historians have interpreted the painting as a comment on the ills of Parisian nightlife. This was one of Manet's late masterpieces; he would soon succumb to the complications of syphilis.

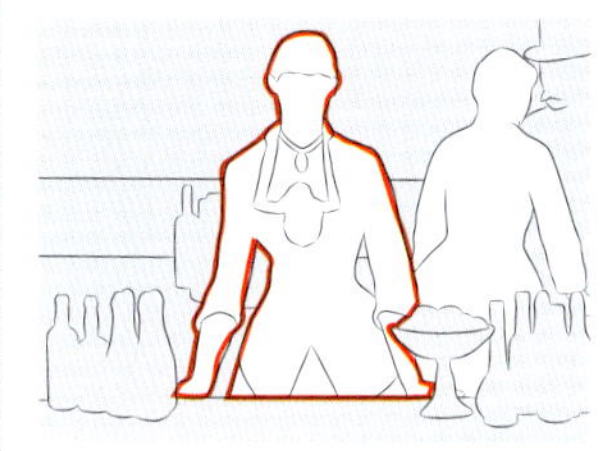

Mirror image
The mirror behind the barmaid disrupts traditional linear perspective. The reflective surface effectively acts as a picture within a picture, somewhat flattening the scene.

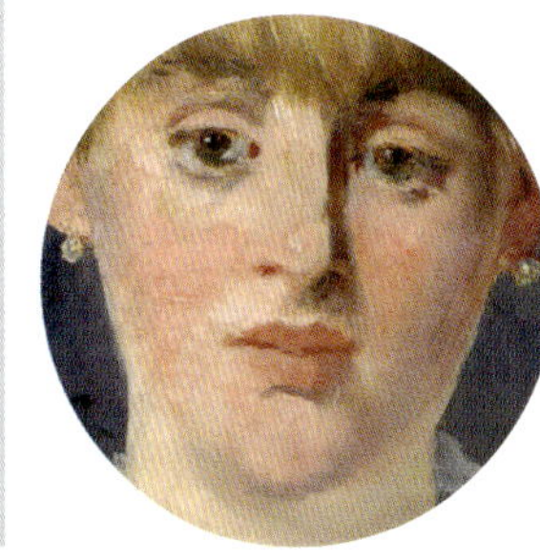

Focal point
Manet's brushwork is more precise on the barmaid's face and attire than on the figures in the reflection, increasing the sense that this barmaid is disengaged from the scene.

> "[Barmaids at the Folies-Bergère] might themselves become commodities, like the bottles on the bar. Manet's picture, with its willful distortion of perceived experience, seems designed to enshrine this uncertainty."
>
> John House

El Jaleo

John Singer Sargent 1882, oil on canvas, 91 × 137 in (232 × 348 cm), Isabella Stewart Gardner Museum, Boston, US

In a scene filled with a sense of drama and energy, a flamenco dancer plays the castanets and sways to the rhythm of the music, cheered on by members of the group. Using loose, gestural brushwork, Sargent brought all the passion and sensuousness of the dance to this large canvas. Best known for his society portraits, he painted *El Jaleo* after a visit to Spain. The work allowed him to explore capturing the effects of light, something he admired in Impressionism. It may also reflect an interest in Spanish culture in American society at the time.

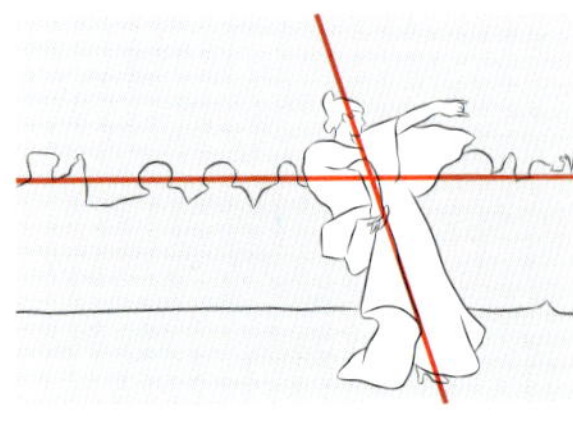

Composition
An off-center diagonal through the dancer captures her in an off-balance pose, creating a strong sense of movement. This contrasts with the horizontal arrangement of the band seated in a row along the canvas behind her.

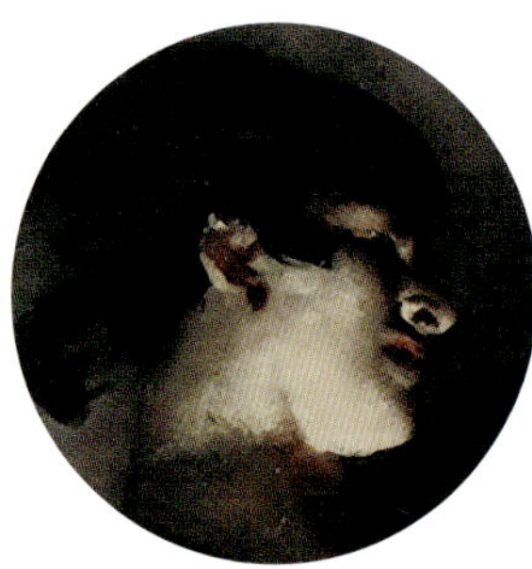

Light source
The light is coming from footlights across the front of the stage, creating a succession of highlights and deep shadows. The uplighting catches the dancer's face, hands, and skirt, and casts large shadows on the wall behind her.

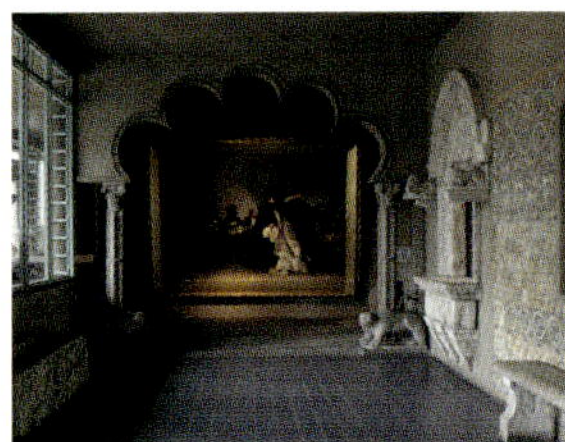

Evocative setting
Isabella Stewart Gardner acquired *El Jaleo* as a gift from T. Jefferson Coolidge in 1914. It became the focal point of the Spanish Cloister, a new gallery Gardner had created with Moorish-style features and walls covered in 17th-century Mexican tiles.

> "It is original. It is beautiful and approximately true to the effect intended in tone, in color, and in light."
>
> *The Critic*, 1882

One of the musicians claps out the rhythm.

Black and white intervals along the back wall create a staccato rhythm of their own.

A strong light reflecting off the guitar draws attention to the musician's hand as he plays.

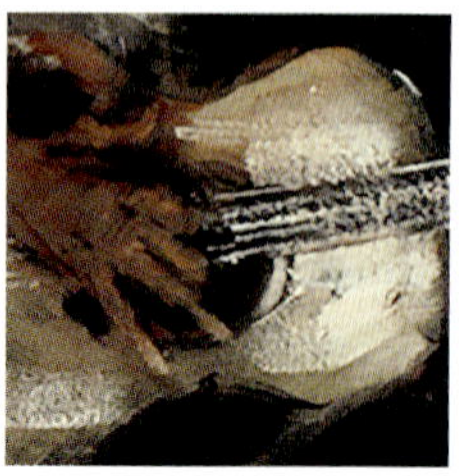

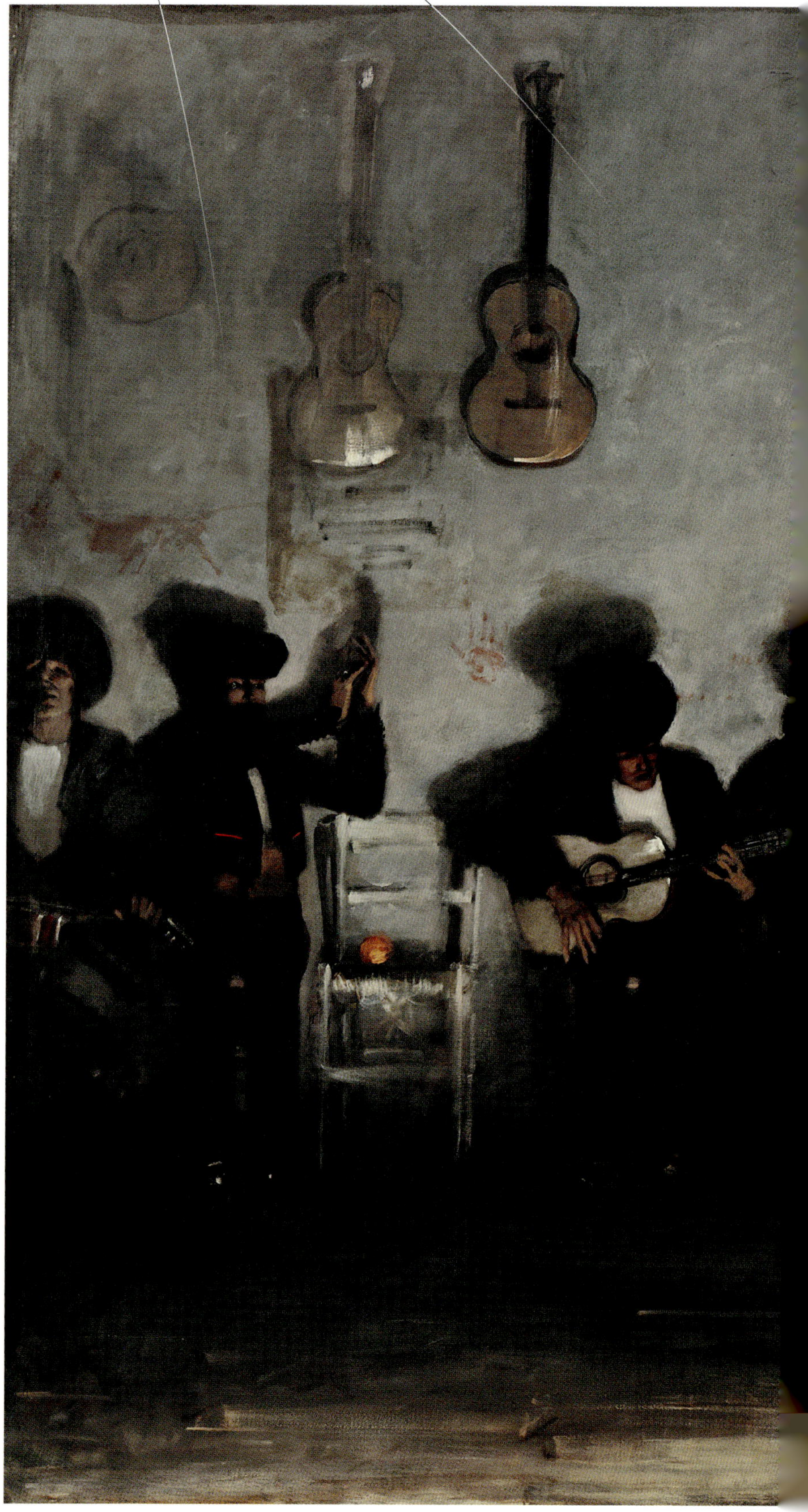

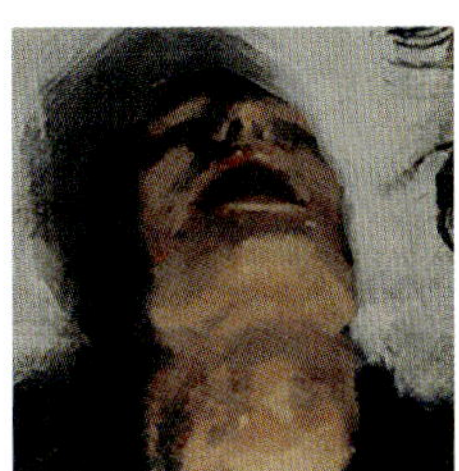

The singer's upturned face reflects the drama and passion of the performance.

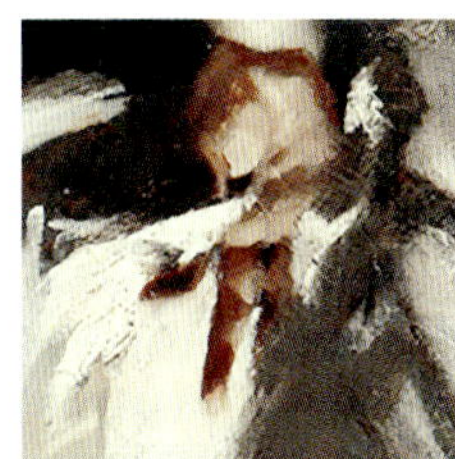

A flurry of broad brushstrokes convey the way the dancer uses her skirt for dramatic effect.

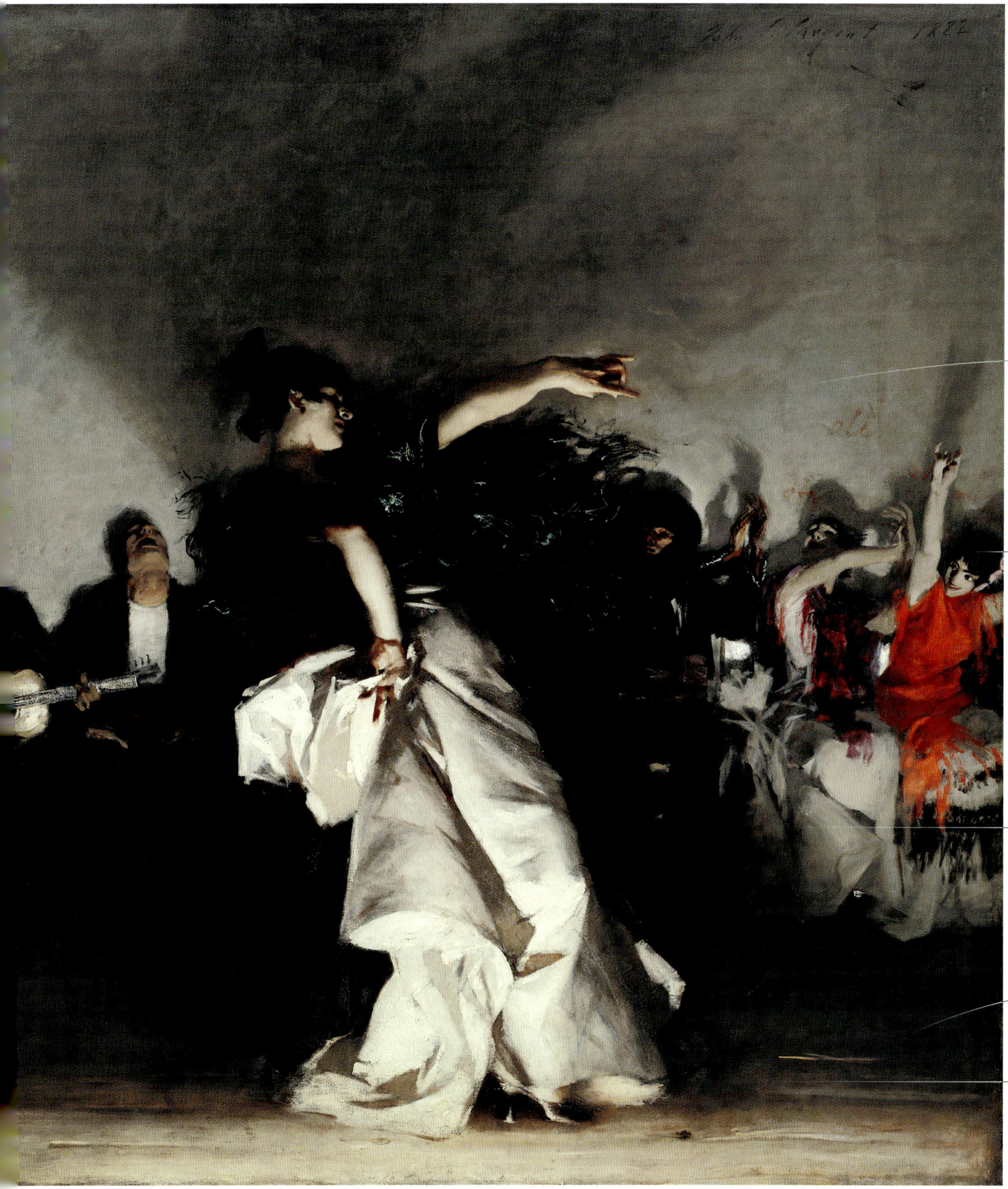

The lace mantilla is painted loosely. This creates the impression that it is flying through the air.

A woman in orange stops the eye at the right edge of the painting and sends the energy of the group back into the picture.

The dancer's skirt catches and reflects the light. The deep, diagonal folds in the fabric draw the audience's attention.

The lit area of the floor tapers as it recedes toward the back wall, creating a limited sense of depth.

By placing the dancer's foot low in the painting, Sargent brings the performance closer to viewers of the painting.

Free Period in the Amsterdam Orphanage

Max Liebermann 1881–1882, oil on canvas, 31 × 42 in (78.5 × 107.5 cm), Städel Museum, Frankfurt, Germany

Orphaned girls work, play, and chat in the courtyard of an orphanage. The challenges facing them are apparent—some toil during their recess—but there is also light, hope, and joy. The image is balanced between girls working on the right and playing on the left, reflecting the equilibrium between responsibility and childhood innocence. The style reflects Liebermann's transition from realism toward Impressionism.

This doorway leads to a courtyard for the younger girls.

The girl skipping in the background was not in Liebermann's preliminary studies—he opted to add this youthful energy.

Liebermann often combined solitude and sociability. Some girls seem lost in private thought.

The uniformity of the building's windows and architecture contrasts with Liebermann's irregular placement of the girls.

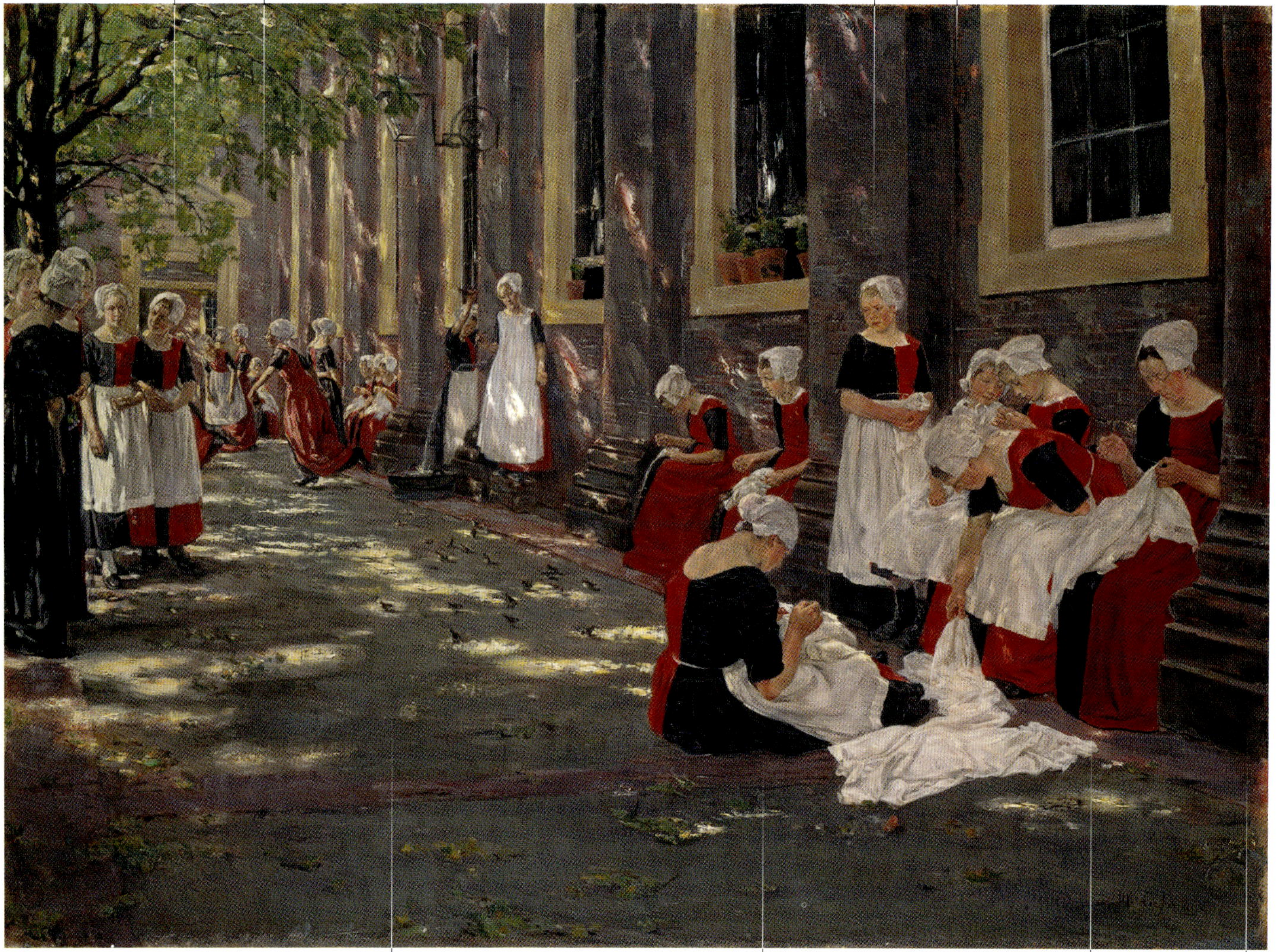

Simple gray birds contrast with the girls' bright uniforms. Birds can fly away, yet it is the confined orphans who seem more alive.

Some girls sew during recess. Although he was not overtly political, Liebermann often portrayed the dignity of working people.

The colorful uniforms were one of the factors that drew Liebermann to paint the orphanage.

This building is now the Amsterdam Museum.

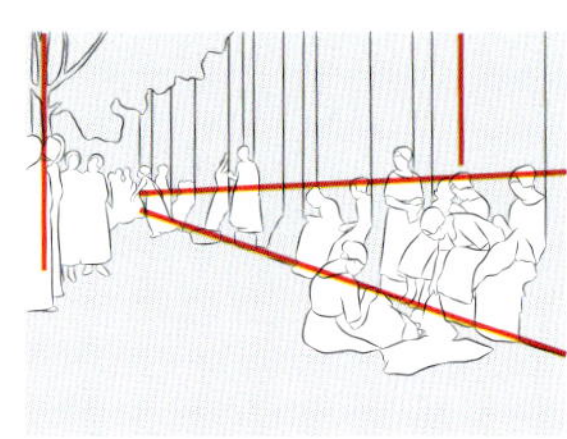

Diagonals and verticals
The strong diagonal lines of the building are echoed in the girls' heads, which are largely positioned along a diagonal. The verticals of the windows and trees are echoed by creases in their uniforms.

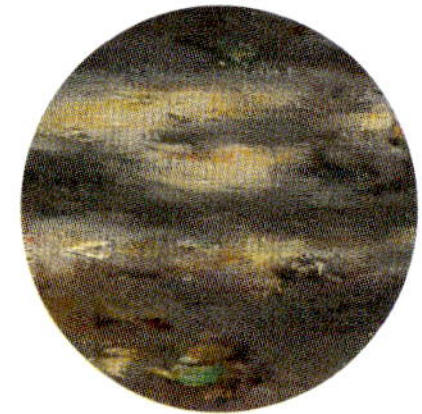

Light effects
Dappled sunlight creates the sense of being in nature, despite the imposing building behind the girls. Liebermann was known for his skill in capturing the effects of light.

The Writing Master

Thomas Eakins 1882, oil on canvas, 30 × 34 in (76.2 × 87 cm), Metropolitan Museum of Art, New York, US

Eakins's portrait of his father Benjamin, a writing master, focuses on the man's industriousness, skill, and wisdom. It conveys the artist's deep respect for his father's work—Benjamin's professional and investment successes subsidized Eakins's art career—and draws parallels between the father's calligraphy and the son's art. The delineation of his father's head and hands reveals the artist's own skills of observation.

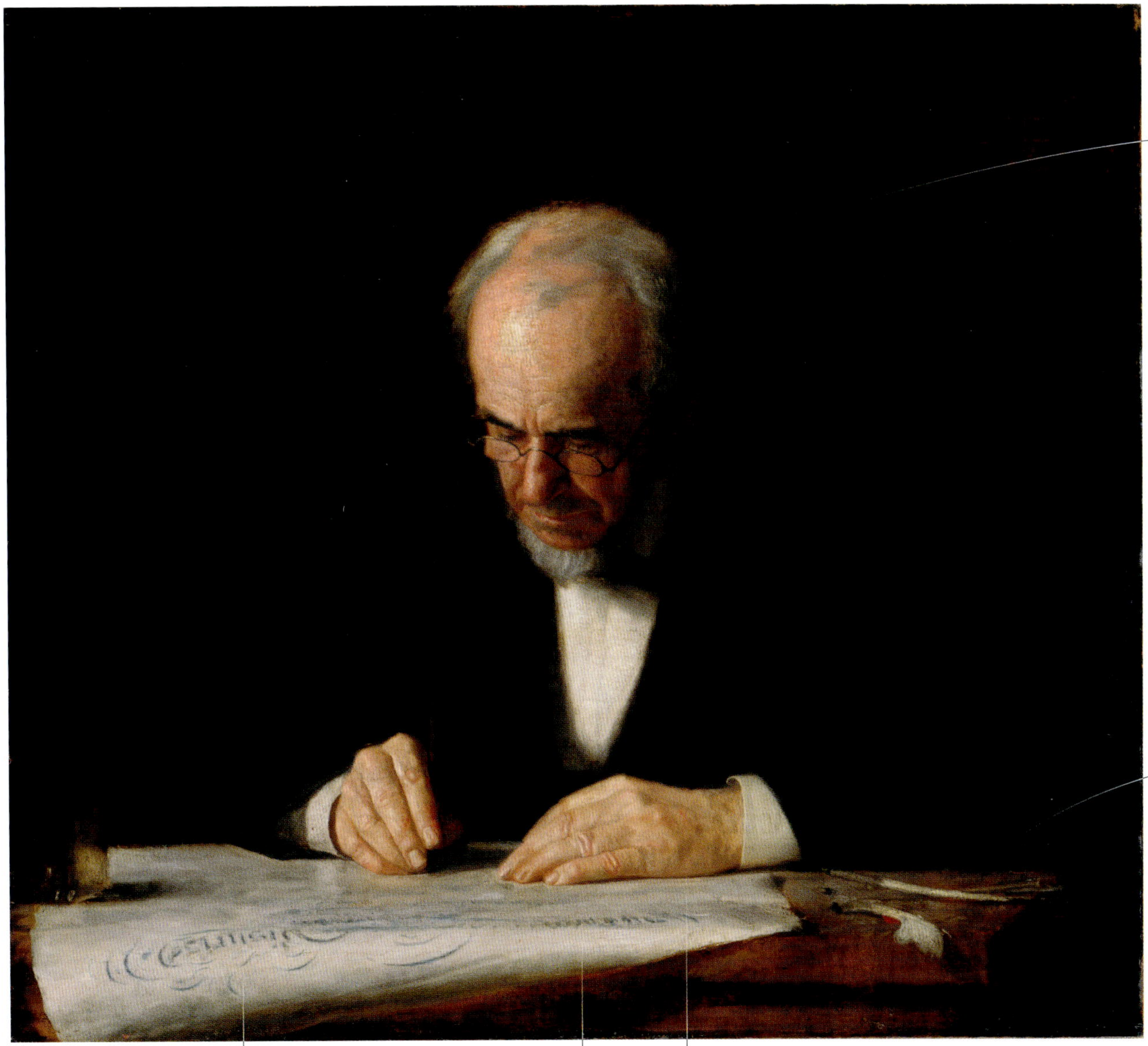

The focus on the balding pate of his father's head, not his face, symbolically emphasizes the older man's wisdom.

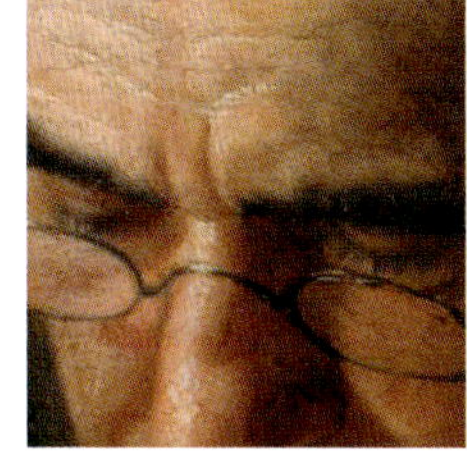

Benjamin's eyes remain focused on his task. Even without eye contact, the portrait conveys warmth and affection.

A quill appears to be positioned for the artist to take up, linking the father's calligraphy to the son's painting.

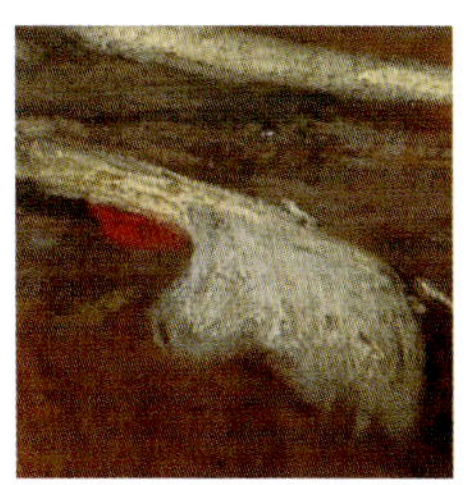

A red spot of wax appears under one of the quills; some see this as a reference to the blood in Eakins's *The Gross Clinic* (1875), a painting depicting a surgical procedure.

The calligraphy is a type known as "copperplate script." It would have been old-fashioned even when Eakins painted this work.

The brightly lit hands stand out against the dark background. Hands were central to both the father's calligraphy and the son's painting.

Eakins makes no attempt to minimize his father's advancing age. The hands are painted with great realism.

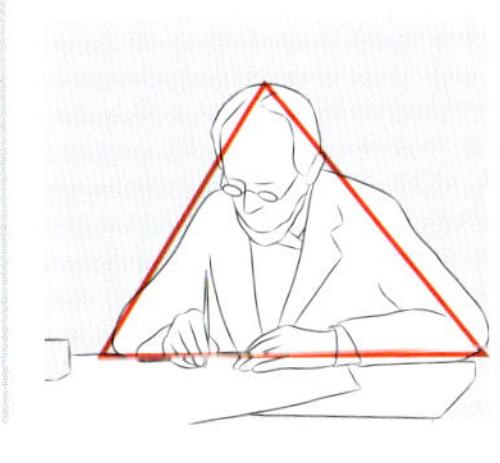

Triangular structure
The image creates a triangle, with Benjamin's head at its top, his arms forming its sides, and the desk at its base.

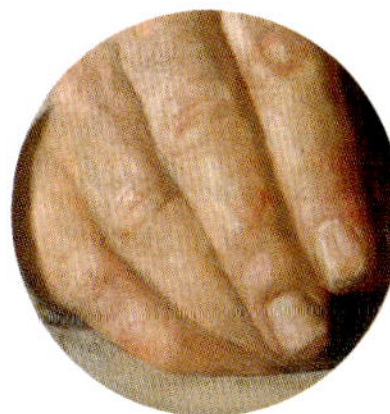

Sombre canvas
Precise lighting illuminates only the elements the artist wishes to highlight. This dark composition was different from the bright canvases of the era's Impressionist movement.

Gates of Yosemite

Albert Bierstadt 1882, oil on paper mounted on canvas, 14 × 20 in (35.6 × 50.8 cm), Smithsonian Art Museum, Washington, D.C., US

Bierstadt celebrates the Gates of the Valley in what would become Yosemite National Park. The huge scale of the valley is developed through the massive cliffs and rocks in the foreground, which contrast with the diminutive size of the distant trees. Bierstadt often painted Yosemite, contributing to the park's fame.

The vertical cliff face is likely to be El Capitan, the now-iconic 3,000-ft (914-m) wall of granite.

The sky is naturalistic. By 1882, Yosemite was well known, not a new wonder as in Bierstadt's earlier paintings of it.

The cliff faces seem daunting and impossible to climb, but even here, trees have taken root, suggesting that obstacles can be overcome.

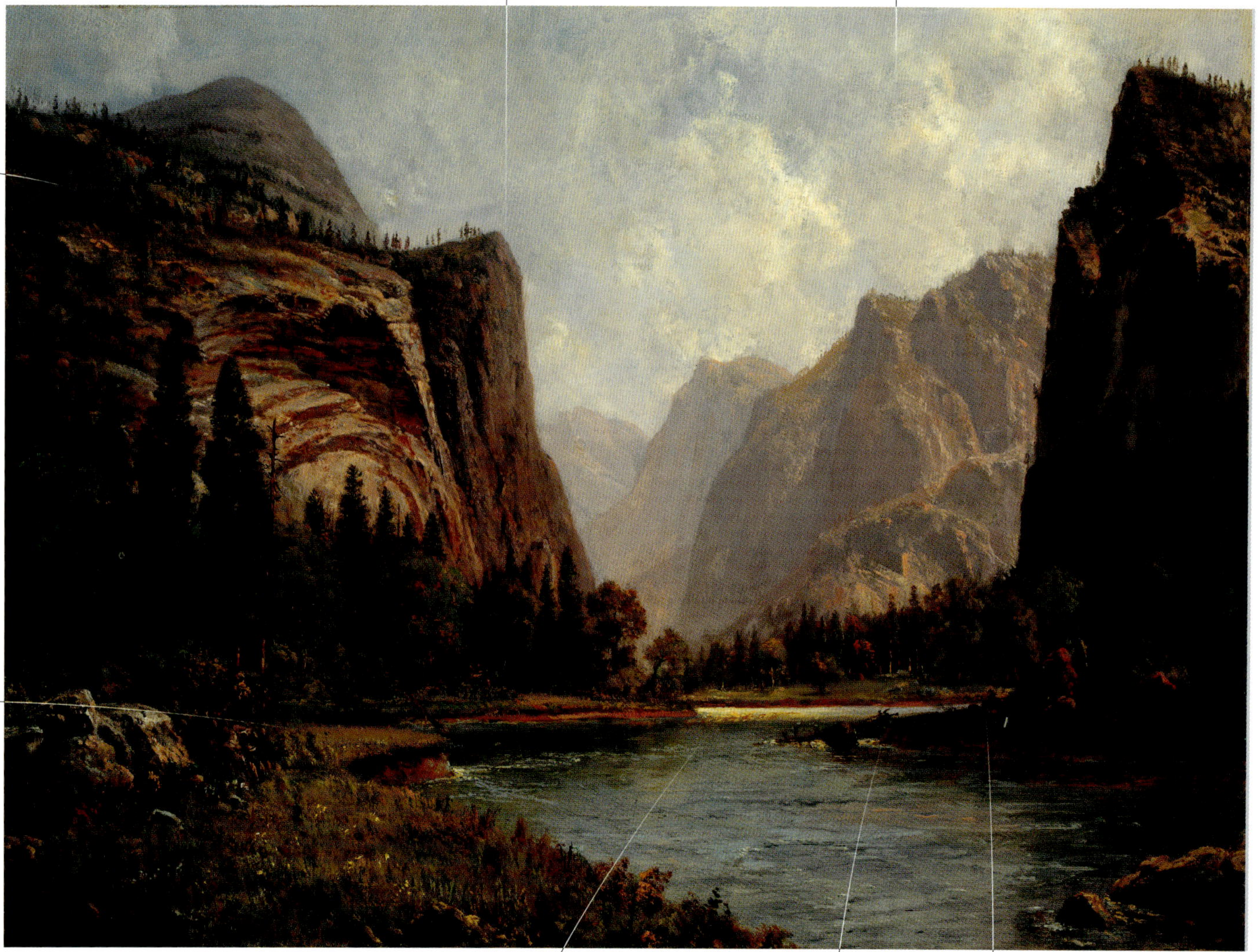

Bierstadt wrote that he had found the Garden of Eden after his 1863 visit to the then largely unknown Yosemite.

The sun breaks through the clouds and illuminates a distant shoreline, a spot that is seemingly out of reach.

A tree has been violently snapped in half, hinting at a past storm.

Boulders litter the shore, having fallen from the cliffs above. This meadow might not be as peaceful as it seems.

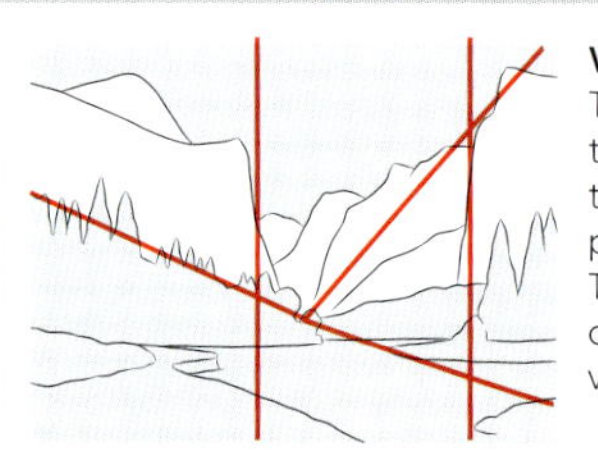

Vanishing point
The lines of the cliffs, trees, and river converge toward a vanishing point on the horizon. The towering verticals of the cliffs pull the viewer's eye inward.

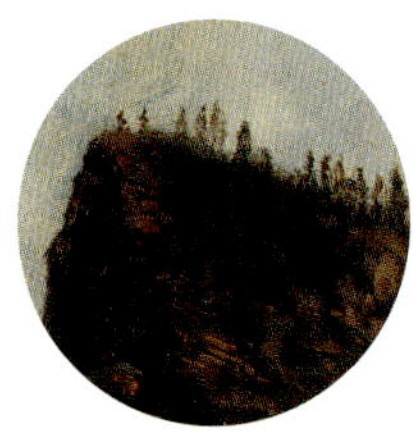

Emphasizing grandeur
The lighter, cooler tones and less distinct detail on the mountains and trees in the distance contribute to the sense of the valley's tremendous size and depth.

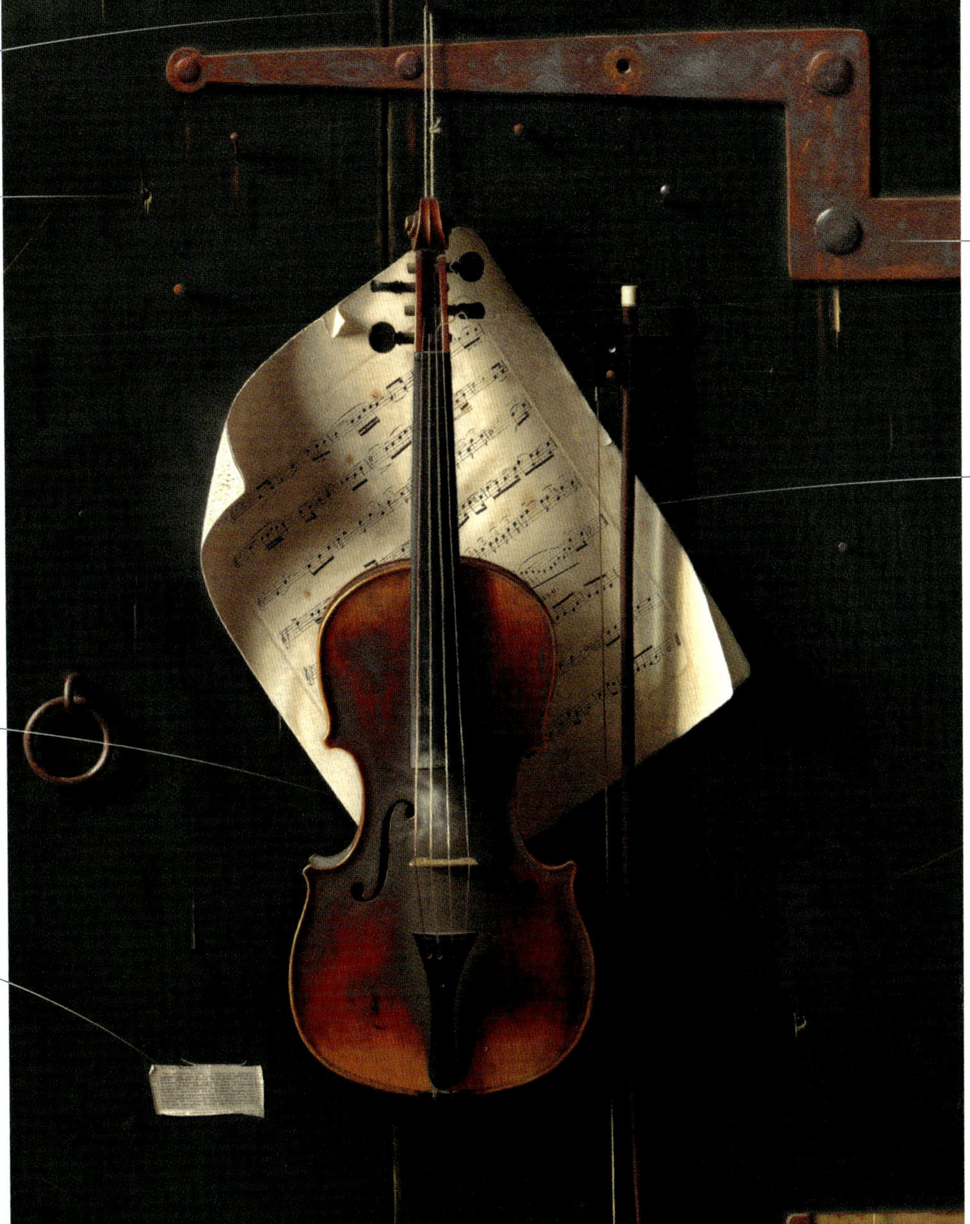

The violin and bow hang from nails, enhancing the illusion that they are real.

Nails and nail holes suggest that many other items, once important, now gone and forgotten, previously hung on this door.

Scuffed and rosin-dusted, the violin has been well loved and frequently played, embodying past pleasures.

A newspaper clipping is illegible. Deciphering the unsolvable mystery of how it relates to the other items pictured engages viewers.

The postmark reads PARIS, 3 27, AVRIL 86. Harnett painted this work shortly after returning to the US from Europe.

The envelope shows Harnett's actual studio address: W. M. Harnett, 28 East 14th St., New York.

The door's metal hardware is rusty and one hinge is broken, a sign of its age.

Sheet music contains melodies exploring a longing for the past, such as "*Vi ravviso, o luoghi ameni*" (O lovely scenes, again I see you).

Trompe l'oeil
When the painting was first exhibited, a guard was posted to prevent viewers from touching it to confirm it was only paint.

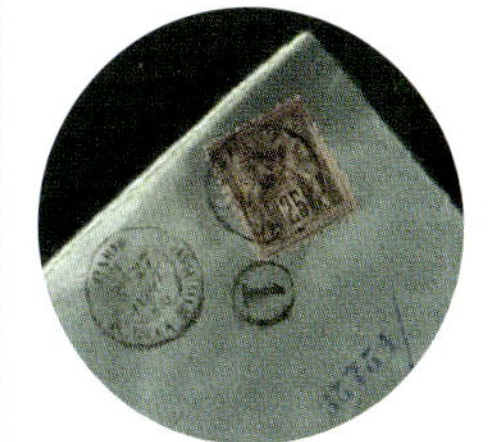

True to life
Harnett painted each object life size to increase the illusion of reality.

The Old Violin

William Michael Harnett 1886, oil on canvas, 38 × 24 in (96.5 × 60 cm), National Gallery of Art, Washington, D.C., US

A violin, a bow, sheets of music, a newspaper clipping, and a blue envelope are positioned against a green wooden door in Harnett's stunningly realistic still life, one of his most famous paintings. This simple composition is a work of multilayered meanings involving the relationships between illusion and reality, old and new, and the momentary and the enduring. The passage of time is central—the items appear aged and worn, conveying a sense of nostalgia for past pleasures.

The landscape is simplified, like a stage set on which to place the figures.

Seurat made many on-site sketches of the setting. He then separated the figures from the sketch and placed them in new configurations.

In the center, a woman and child are walking straight toward the viewer, yet they seem frozen in place.

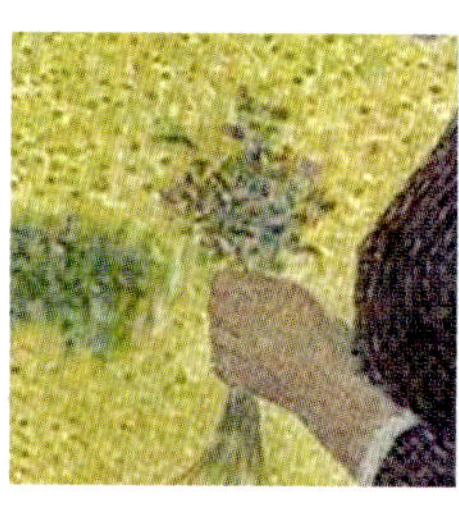

Seurat creates tonal shifts by using colors from the lighter end of the spectrum for sunlit areas and from the darker end for areas in shadow.

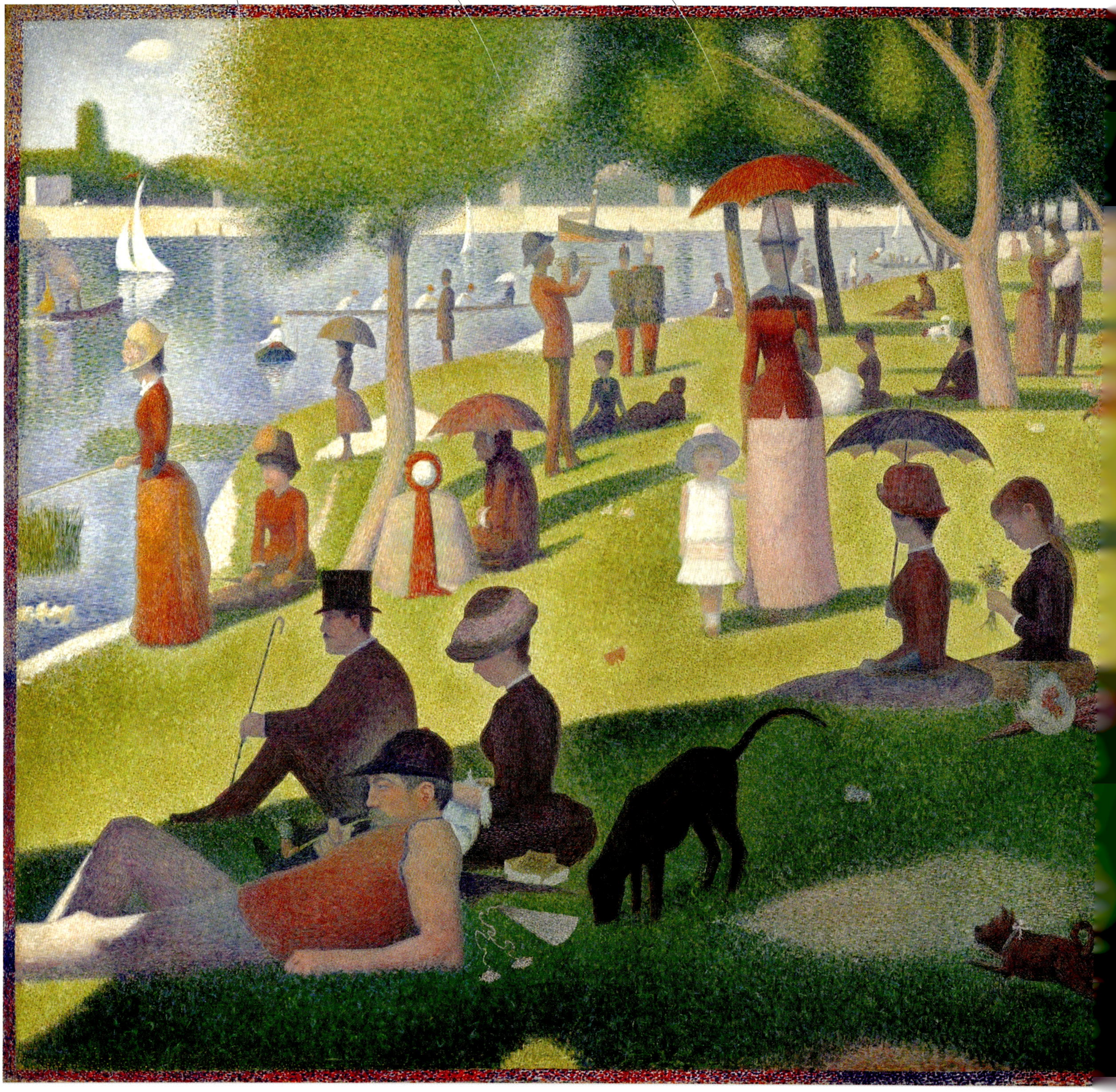

Sunday Afternoon on La Grande Jatte

Georges Seurat 1884–1886, oil on canvas, 82 × 121 in (207.5 × 308.1 cm), Art Institute of Chicago, US

In his best-known painting, Seurat depicted people from different social classes relaxing in a park on La Grande Jatte, an island in the Seine River. Although his subject was modern life, Seurat tried to evoke a sense of timelessness by creating a tension between stasis and movement. He planned his painting carefully, making around 60 studies before deciding on the final composition. The painting caused a sensation when it was shown at the last Impressionist Exhibition, held in Paris in 1886, and has since become an icon of Post-Impressionist art.

The sharp outlines of the figures isolate them from one another, creating an impersonal effect.

The tree trunks and the figures create a strong vertical emphasis, balanced by horizontal shadows and the distant shoreline.

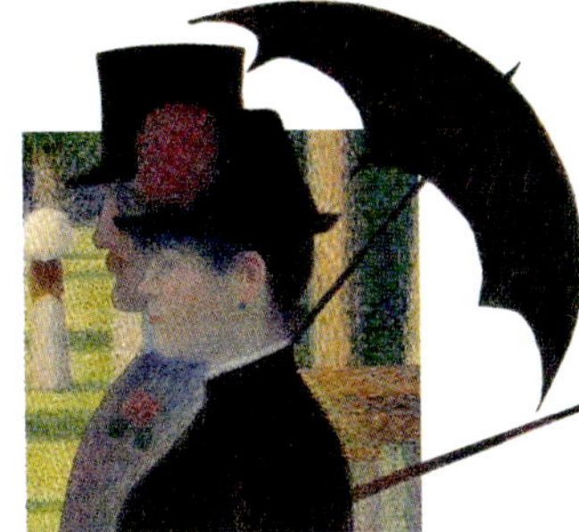

Parasols and hats are two motifs repeated in profile across the painting, creating a sense of rhythm.

Strong tonal contrasts and smaller dots are used to create sharp outlines.

Seurat added the painted border a few years later to soften the transition from painting to frame.

Most of the figures are in profile, silhouetted against the bright grass or river. This couple is disproportionately large.

Monkeys were popular pets at the time, but they also sometimes symbolized prostitution.

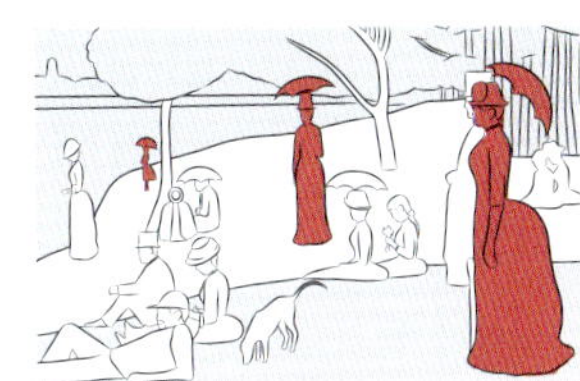

Unifying effect
The three standing figures holding umbrellas link the three zones of the painting: shadowed foreground, sunlit middle ground, and distance.

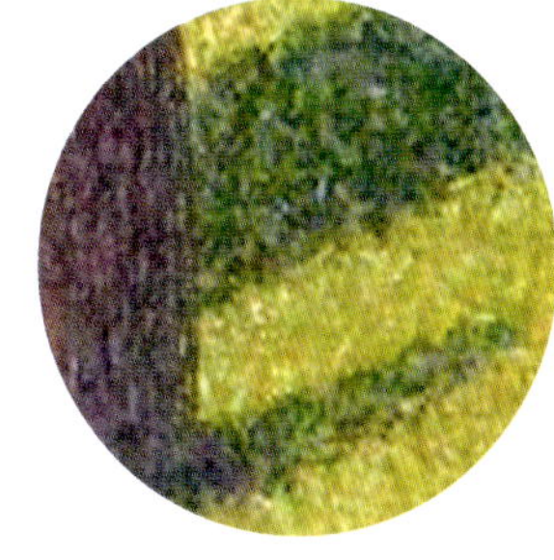

Pointillism
Small dots of pure color mix optically in the viewer's eye to create solid areas of light and shadow when the painting is viewed from several feet away.

> "Great things are done by a series of small things brought together. Some say they see poetry in my paintings. I see only science."
> Georges Seurat, 1897

Outdoors

Anders Zorn 1888, oil on canvas, 52 × 78 in (133 × 197.5 cm), Gothenburg Museum of Art, Gothenburg, Sweden

Being "at one with nature" was a widely held ideal in the post-Romantic period. Nakedness was one way to achieve it, but sea bathing was banned in the Stockholm archipelago at this time. With an Impressionist appreciation for light and the outdoors, Zorn captures these women's secret rebellion.

The darkened background creates a sense of depth.

An empty boat underlines the remoteness of the location, while also reminding us of the civilization the women are escaping.

The women huddle, fearing the water's chill, but also perhaps the unknown consequences of their transgression.

Tinged pink, perhaps by a setting sun, the water echoes the color of the bathers' flesh and of the granite rocks.

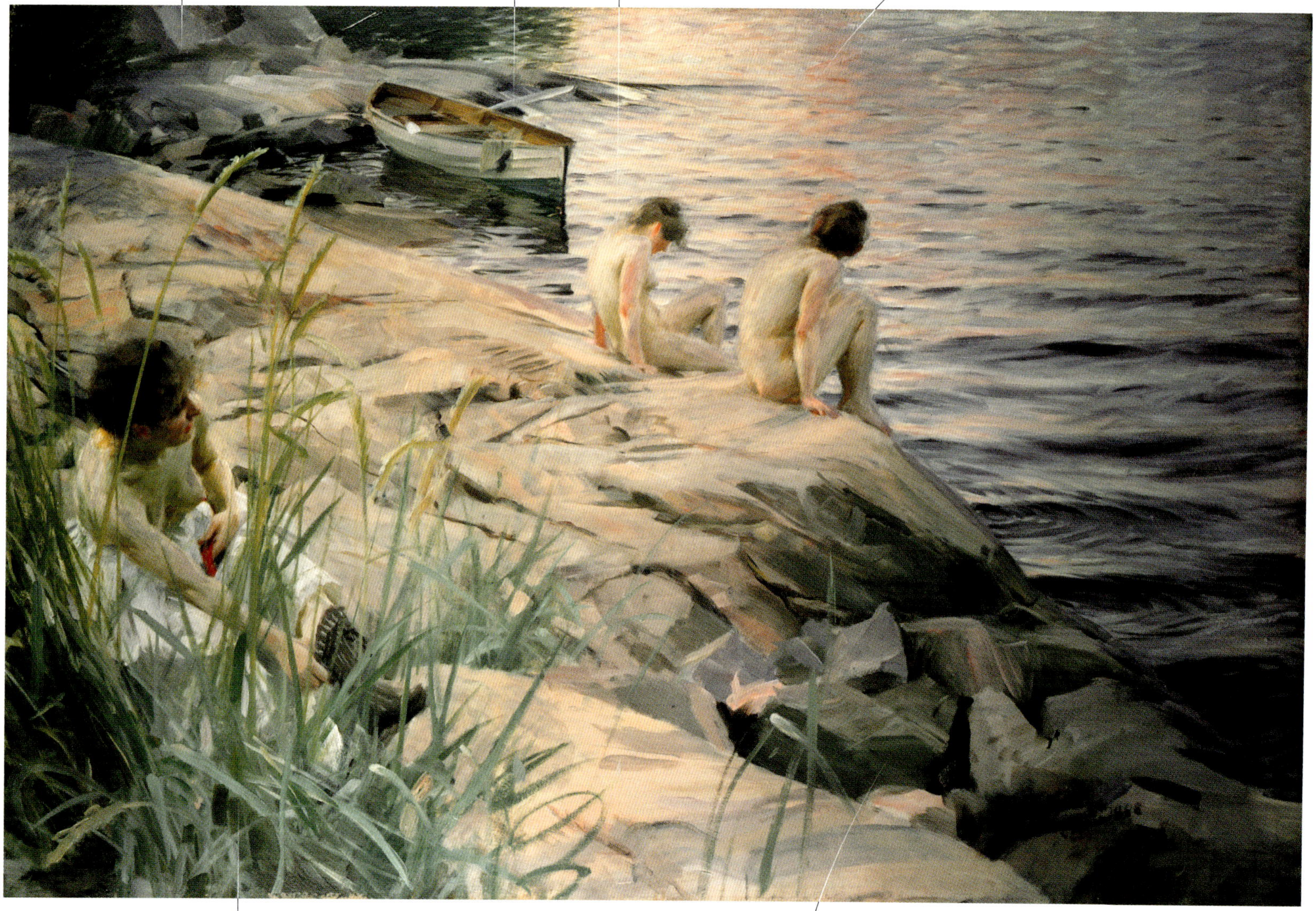

Wild reeds form an inadequate screen for a woman changing.

This untidy pile of rocks underlines the anarchic abandon the women's expedition represents.

> "Genius nothing. All a painter has to do is to know his trade perfectly—and then, of course, he has got to have a little taste."
>
> Anders Zorn

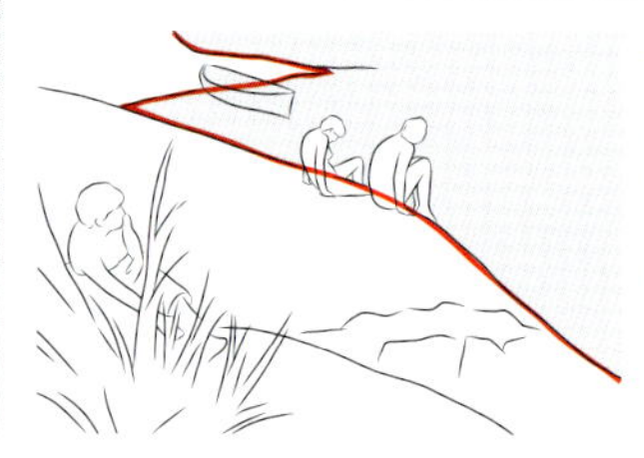

Zigzag line
The scene is held together by the meandering line formed by the rocks.

Color
Zorn was known for using a very limited color palette. In this painting, the rocks, water, and bathers all fall within a narrow range of hues and tones, creating a sense of harmony.

Nkisi

Artist unknown 19th to mid-20th centuries, wood, glass, iron, pigment, cloth, plant fiber, horn, nails, 17 × 10 × 8 in (42.7 × 26.6 × 19.3 cm), National Museum of African Art, Washington, D.C., US

Minkisi (plural of *nkisi*) are used by the Kongo (Bakongo) people in what is now the Democratic Republic of the Congo for healing, protection, divination, punishment, or ensuring success. Their power comes when the spiritually potent medicines added by a specialist called an *nganga* are activated.

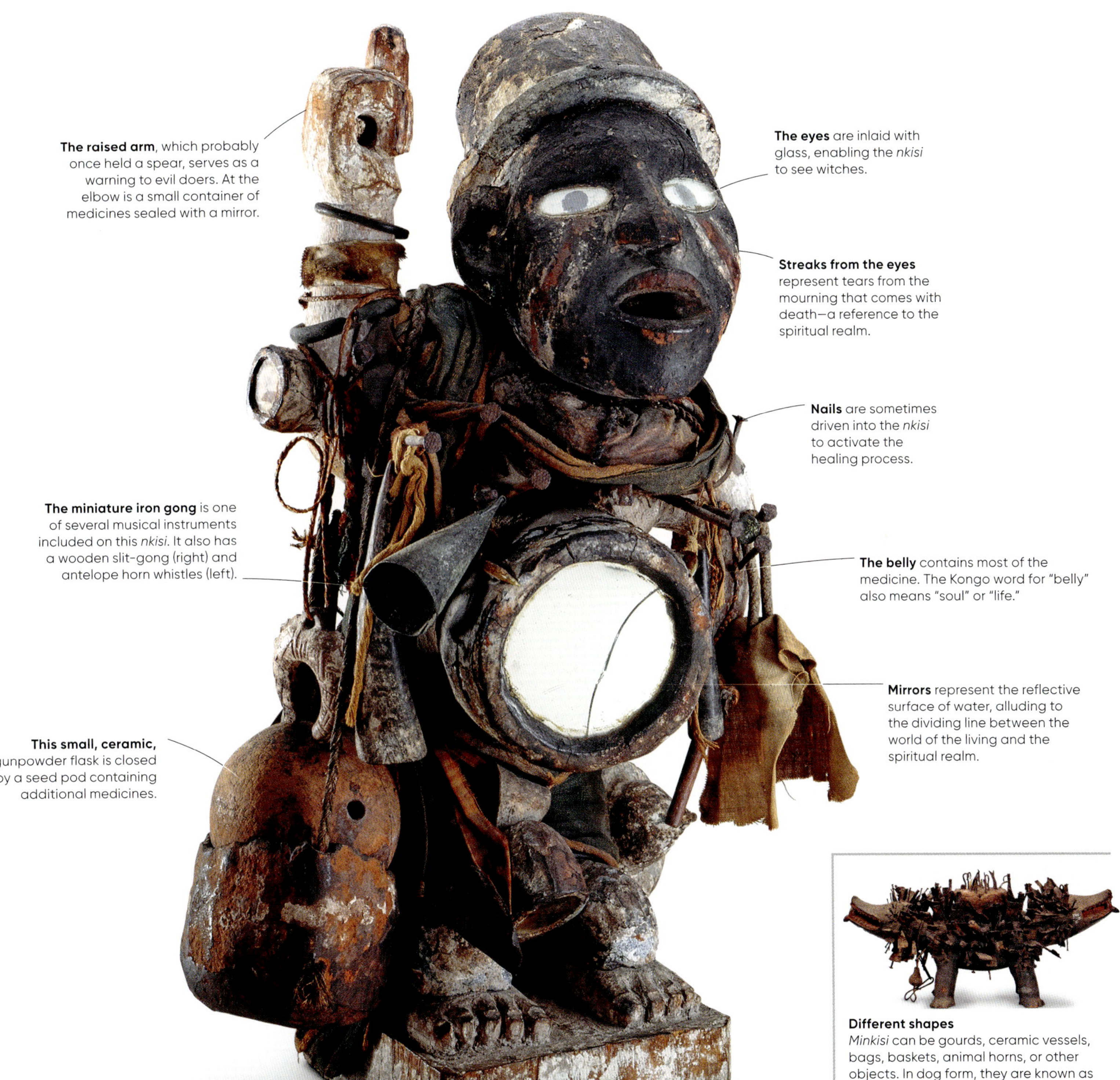

Different shapes
Minkisi can be gourds, ceramic vessels, bags, baskets, animal horns, or other objects. In dog form, they are known as *nkisi kozo*. Because dogs live both in the village and the bush, they are considered liminal creatures, as demonstrated here by this *nkisi kozo*'s two heads.

Vision After the Sermon (Jacob Wrestling with the Angel)

Paul Gauguin 1888, oil on canvas, 28 × 36 in (72.2 × 91 cm), Scottish National Gallery, Edinburgh, UK

After attending a religious sermon, a group of traditionally dressed Breton women experience a vision of the Biblical story of Jacob wrestling an angel (Genesis 32:22–32). Considered to be an important work of Post-Impressionism, the painting represented a departure from both Realism and Impressionism. Gauguin did not want the painting to look real; instead, he hoped to create something visionary and spiritual.

Traditional Breton clothing and customs were completely out of step with fashionable 19th-century France.

The cow is extremely small, as Gauguin himself noted in a letter. Gauguin did not explain its size.

The story of Jacob wrestling an angel is thought to symbolize the battle between man's earthly desires and God's will.

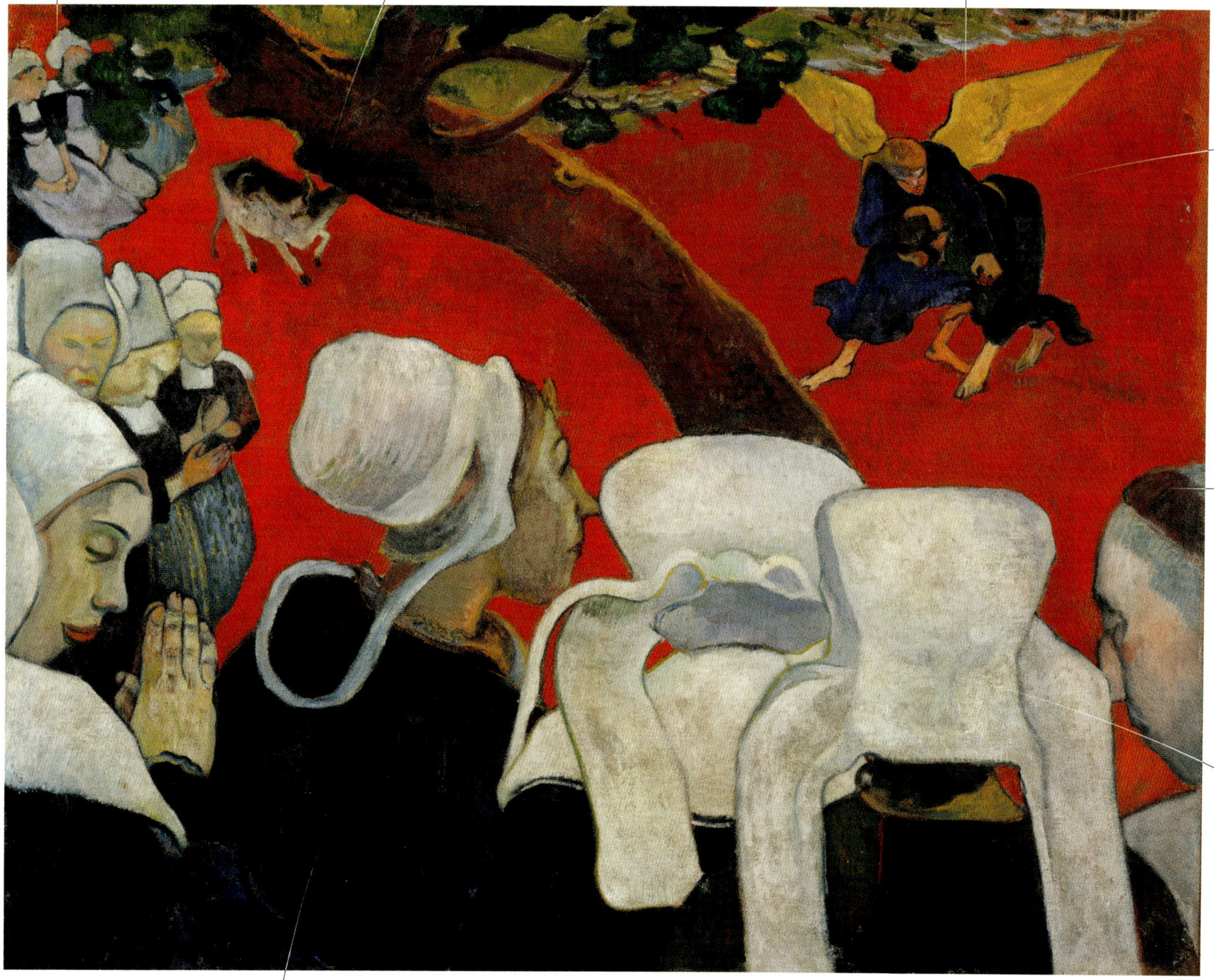

Wrestling has a long tradition in Brittany and probably helped inspire this work.

Gauguin added this man to the painting late in the process. He is probably a priest—perhaps Gauguin himself depicted as a priest.

In a letter to Vincent van Gogh, Gauguin called these bonnets "monstrous helmets."

This woman who is depicted watching the wrestling may be Madeleine Bernard, who Gauguin was attracted to.

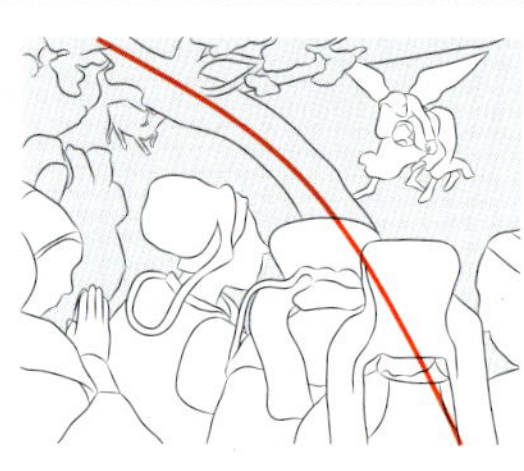

Tree of division
An apple tree separates the real world of Brittany below and the imaginary world of the Breton women's vision above. Two praying figures in profile, a woman on the left and a man on the right, frame the scene.

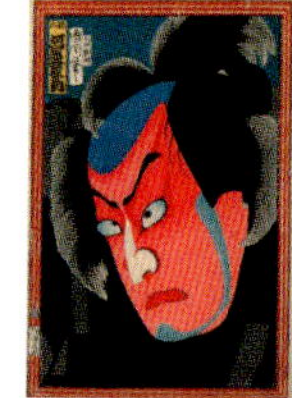

Japanese inspiration
The thick outlines, lack of shadow, and disdain for the rules of perspective create a flatness similar to that of Japanese woodblock prints, such as those by Toyohara Kunichika, whom Gauguin greatly admired.

The Kiss

Auguste Rodin 1888-1898, marble, 71 × 44 × 46 in (181.5 × 112.5 × 117 cm), Musée Rodin, Paris, France

Two lovers are about to exchange a kiss. At the time, sculpture was influenced by classical myths and allegory, but *The Kiss*, like many of Rodin's pieces, is a realistic representation of passion and the human body. It has become a universal symbol of love.

> "Sculpture is the art of the hole and the lump."
>
> Auguste Rodin

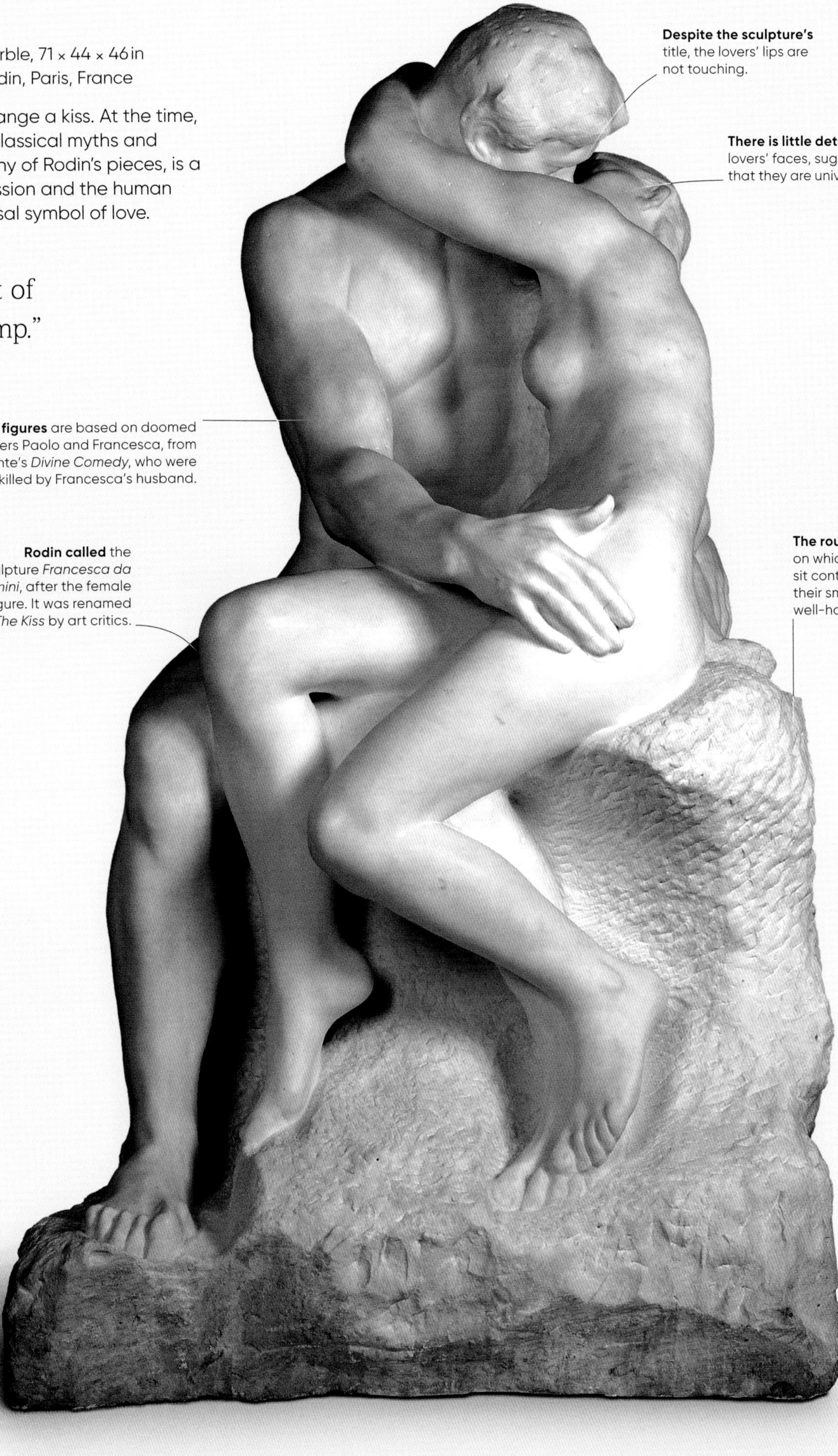

Despite the sculpture's title, the lovers' lips are not touching.

There is little detail in the lovers' faces, suggesting that they are universal.

The figures are based on doomed lovers Paolo and Francesca, from Dante's *Divine Comedy*, who were killed by Francesca's husband.

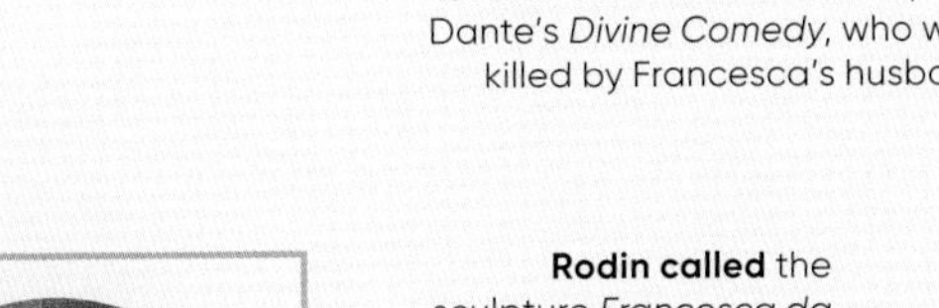

Rodin called the sculpture *Francesca da Rimini*, after the female figure. It was renamed *The Kiss* by art critics.

The rough rock on which the lovers sit contrasts with their smooth, well-honed bodies.

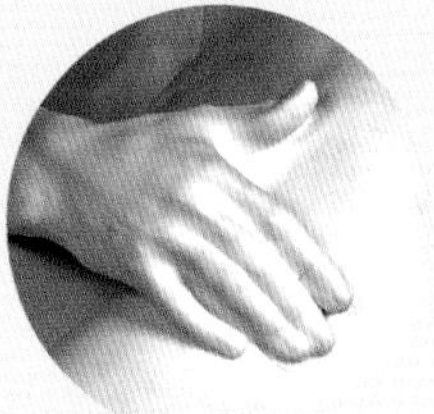

Strength in scale
The hands and feet are out of proportion with their bodies. Rodin often worked on hands and feet separately; the larger sizes symbolize strength.

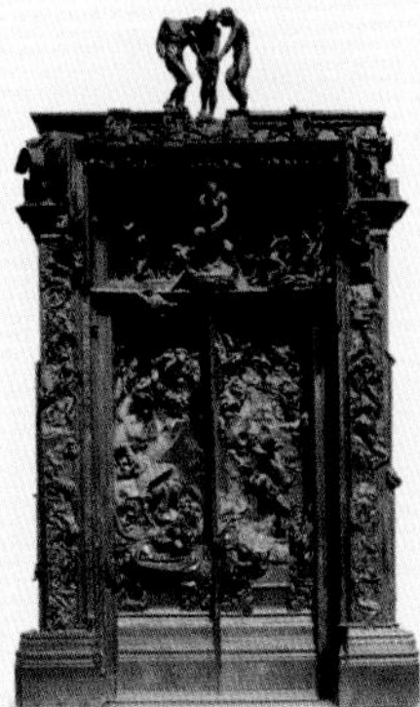

The Gates of Hell
The Kiss was originally conceived as an element for *The Gates of Hell*, a monumental bronze entrance for a museum of decorative arts that was never built. Now displayed in the Musée Rodin, the doors illustrate the Gates of Hell in Dante's *Inferno*, the first section of his *Divine Comedy*.

Ci Wara Kun

Artist unknown, late 19th–early 20th century, wood and metal, 32 × 14 × 3 in (80.6 × 34.3 × 7 cm), Brooklyn Museum, New York, US

According to the Bamana people in what is now Mali, the *ci wara* (pronounced chi wara) is a mythical creature who taught humans to farm. Performers wear these sculptures of the *ci wara* on their heads and dance to drums as young people compete in agricultural contests. This performance is an important way to honor the *ci wara*, who hid himself in the earth, offended by the wastefulness of humans.

The horns are tall, like those of antelope or millet stalks. However, in some regions of Mali, the head of the *ci wara* is lifted up and the horns lie horizontally, perhaps in reference to the harvest.

As well as being smaller and lacking a crest, the female *ci wara* can be identified by her straight horns.

The carver incised the horns, faces, ears, and added grooves on the bodies near the tails to add texture and visual interest.

The male is recognizable by his elaborate openwork mane, bent horns, long ears, and penis.

The female carries a baby on her back to emphasize fertility. The sculpture would, however, be worn and danced by a man.

The base of the sculpture would be attached to a basketry cap tied onto the head of the performer.

Composite creature
The *ci wara* is believed to be a conglomerate of different animals including the antelope, aardvark, and pangolin, animals associated with persistence, protection, digging, and connection to the earth.

Dance of the *ci wara*
Performers dance when crops are sown and harvested. They conceal themselves in costumes made of long raffia stalks that have been dyed black or brown, and may hold sticks to represent the *ci wara*'s front legs.

The Starry Night

Vincent van Gogh 1889, oil on canvas, 29 × 36 in (73.7 × 92.1 cm), MoMA, New York, US

Van Gogh painted this swirling masterpiece inspired by the sight of the night sky while he was a patient at an asylum in St-Rémy-en-Provence, southern France. Evoking feelings of the overwhelming power of the universe and the relative insignificance of humans, the painting is disturbing and uplifting in turn. The small village is a composite, combining different views around the asylum, earlier paintings, and memories.

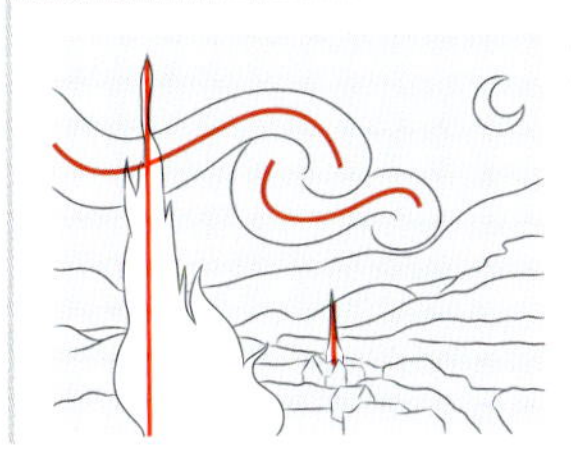

Composition The cypress tree and spire provide strong verticals, contrasting with the curving lines in the sky and stabilizing the composition.

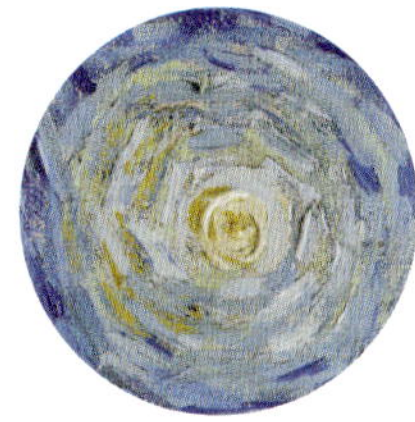

Solid swirls Van Gogh squeezed paint directly onto the canvas from the tube to create the painting's impasto surface. This is especially evident in the sky.

"It often seems to me that the night is even more richly colored than the day."

Vincent van Gogh, 1888

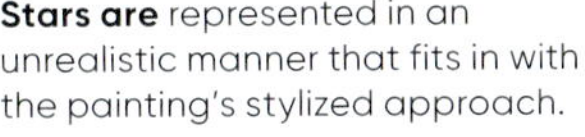

Stars are represented in an unrealistic manner that fits in with the painting's stylized approach.

The moon's vibrant luminosity, produced by the complementary contrast of blue and orange, is balanced by the dark tree in the opposite corner of the painting.

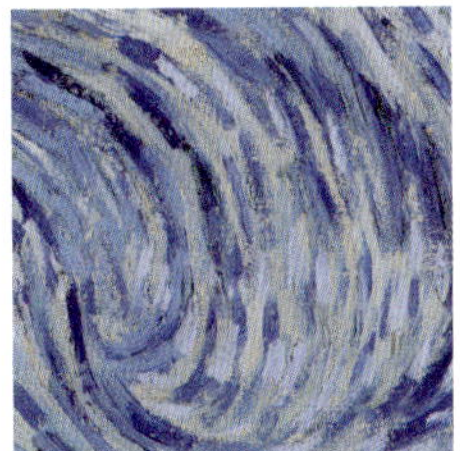

Undulating lines in the sky reflect the rise and fall of the mountaintops.

Van Gogh thought cypress trees had the same proportions and lines as Egyptian obelisks. He used them to represent the lasting splendor and monumentality of nature.

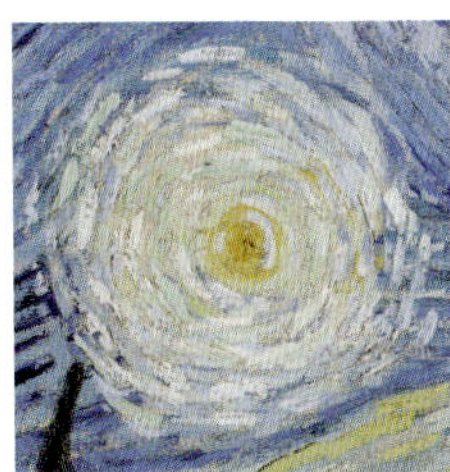

The brightest star may be Venus, also known as the morning star, which van Gogh described in letters to his brother Theo.

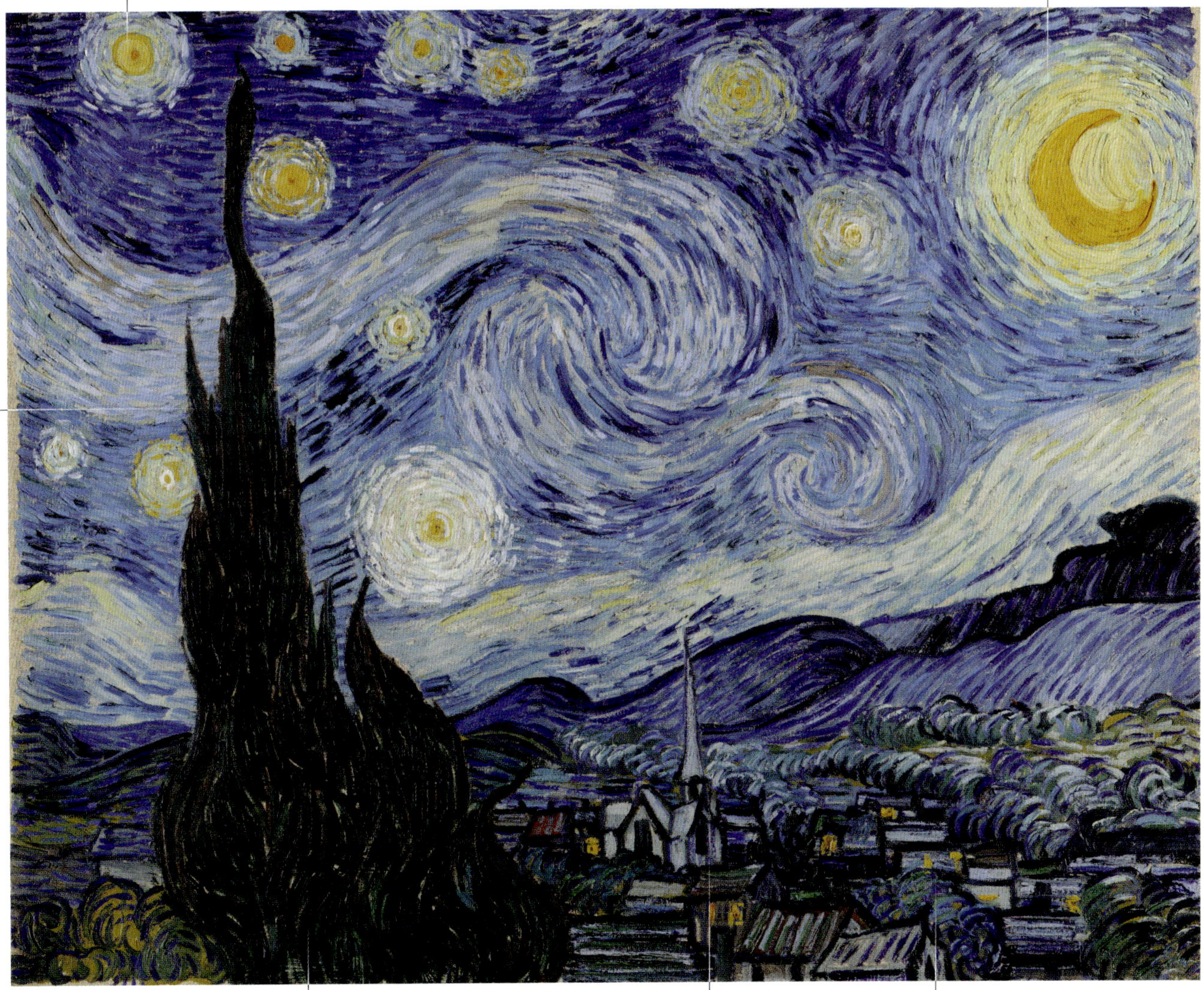

The tree has been placed at the very front of the picture, with the landscape receding behind it.

The steeple resembles those of Dutch churches and may be based on van Gogh's early memories.

Blocky buildings provide a sense of permanence beneath the dynamic sky.

The retreating soldiers wave pistols and look back over their shoulders as they take aim at their pursuers.

War bonnets are decorated with eagle feathers; the Lakota believed the eagle was an exceptionally powerful bird.

A Lakota fighter holds the reins of two horses that have been captured from the US Army.

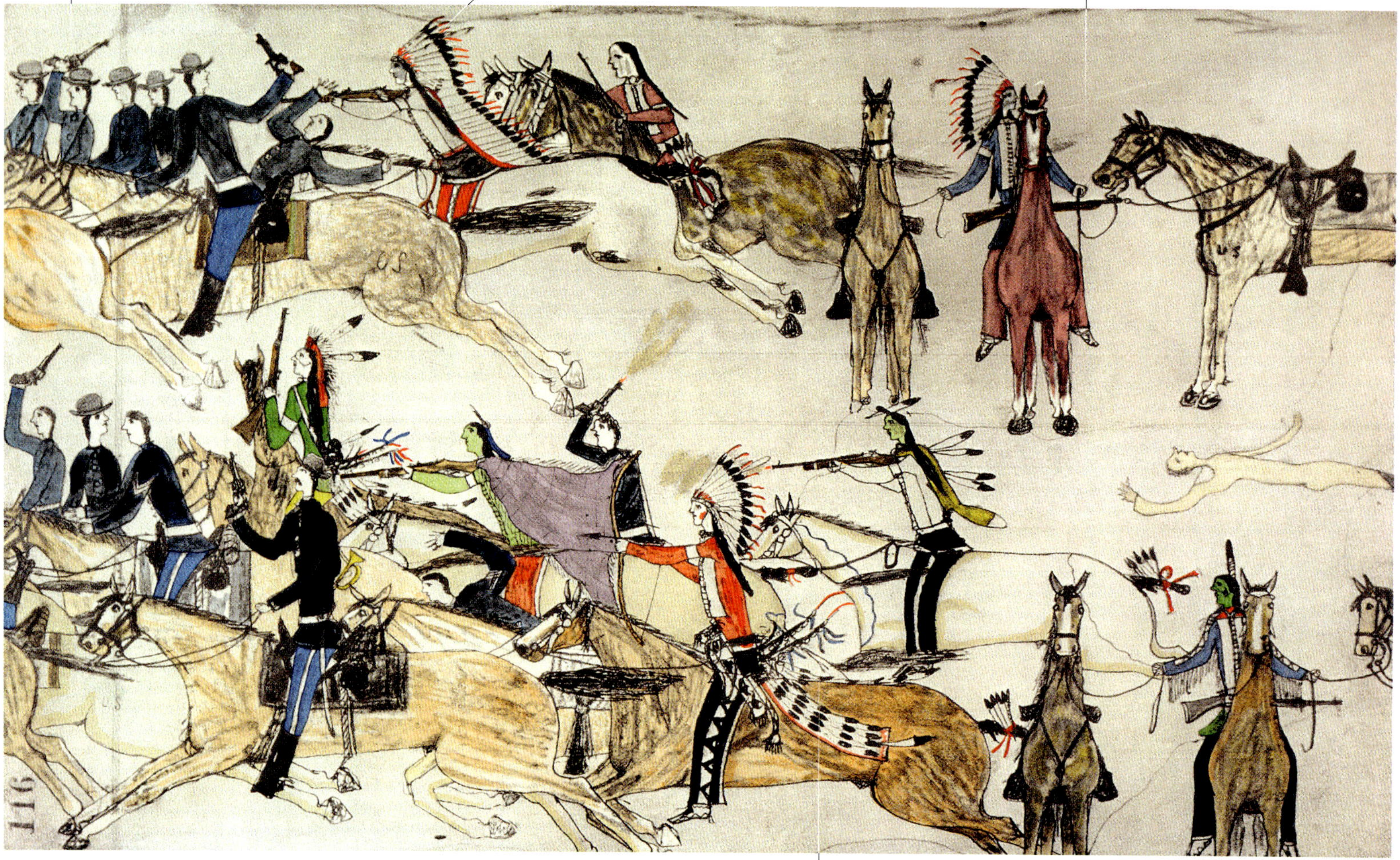

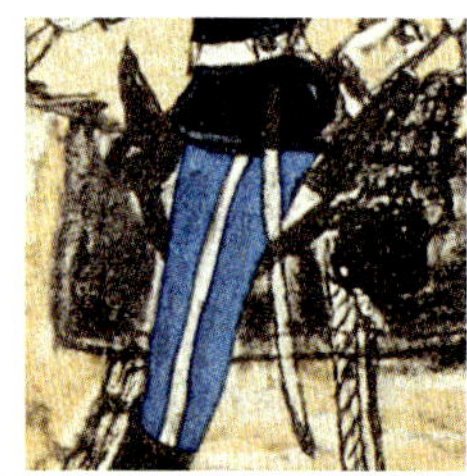

Swords were carried by some troops but may not have been used in the battle.

Winchester repeating rifles were used by both sides in this battle. Although not shown here, bows and arrows were still used by the Lakota, as well as tomahawks and medicine clubs.

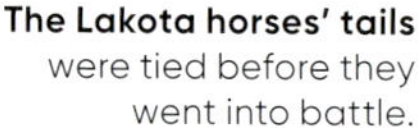

The Lakota horses' tails were tied before they went into battle.

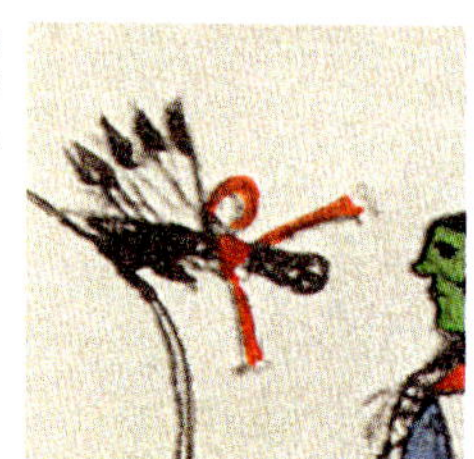

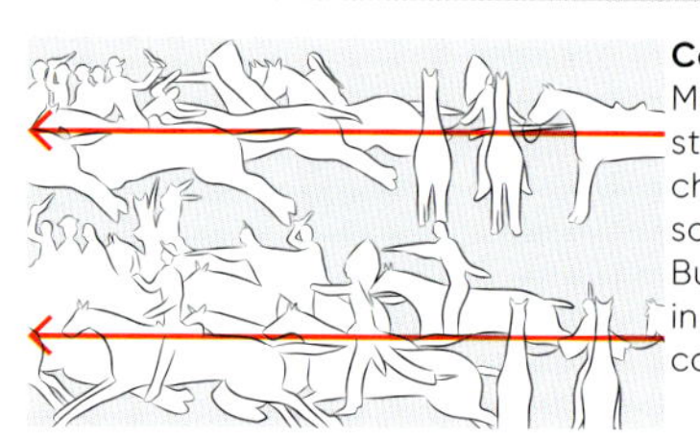

Composition
Moving in two parallel streams, the Lakota chase the fleeing US soldiers. Bad Heart Bull outlined the figures in black and then colored them in.

Ledger book art
For many years, Indigenous peoples had drawn battles on buffalo hides. In the 1890s, they began to use ledger books to record them, using ink, crayon, and watercolors.

Retreat of Major Marcus Reno's Command

Amos Bad Heart Bull 1890–1913, ink on paper, National Anthropological Archives, Washington, D.C., US

This detailed scene shows the US Army cavalry fleeing from superior Lakota warriors following a battle for the control of the gold-rich Black Hills of Dakota in 1876. Although only a child when the incident took place, Bad Heart Bull drew on firsthand accounts for his work. He created this accurate record of a major victory for the Lakota in a ledger book, and made 415 drawings of Lakota life between 1890 and 1913.

View of Moret

Alfred Sisley 1889, oil on canvas, 24 × 29 in (60.5 × 73.5 cm), private collection

In the cold light of a winter sunrise, a small town southeast of Paris comes to life. Impressionist painter Alfred Sisley worked in landscape all his life, using spontaneous brushstrokes and vibrant color to convey the fleeting effects of light. This is one of many views of Moret-sur-Loing that he painted.

Bare trees are loosely drawn in over the sky.

The sky is painted with long, loose brushstrokes in pink and a cold, green-blue.

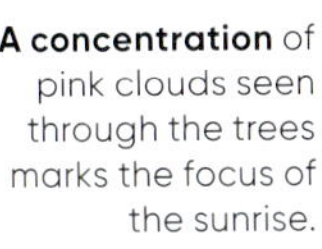

A concentration of pink clouds seen through the trees marks the focus of the sunrise.

Buildings seen between the trees become indistinct in the distance, increasing the sense of recession.

Two human figures help draw the eye into the scene. They are small in relation to their surroundings.

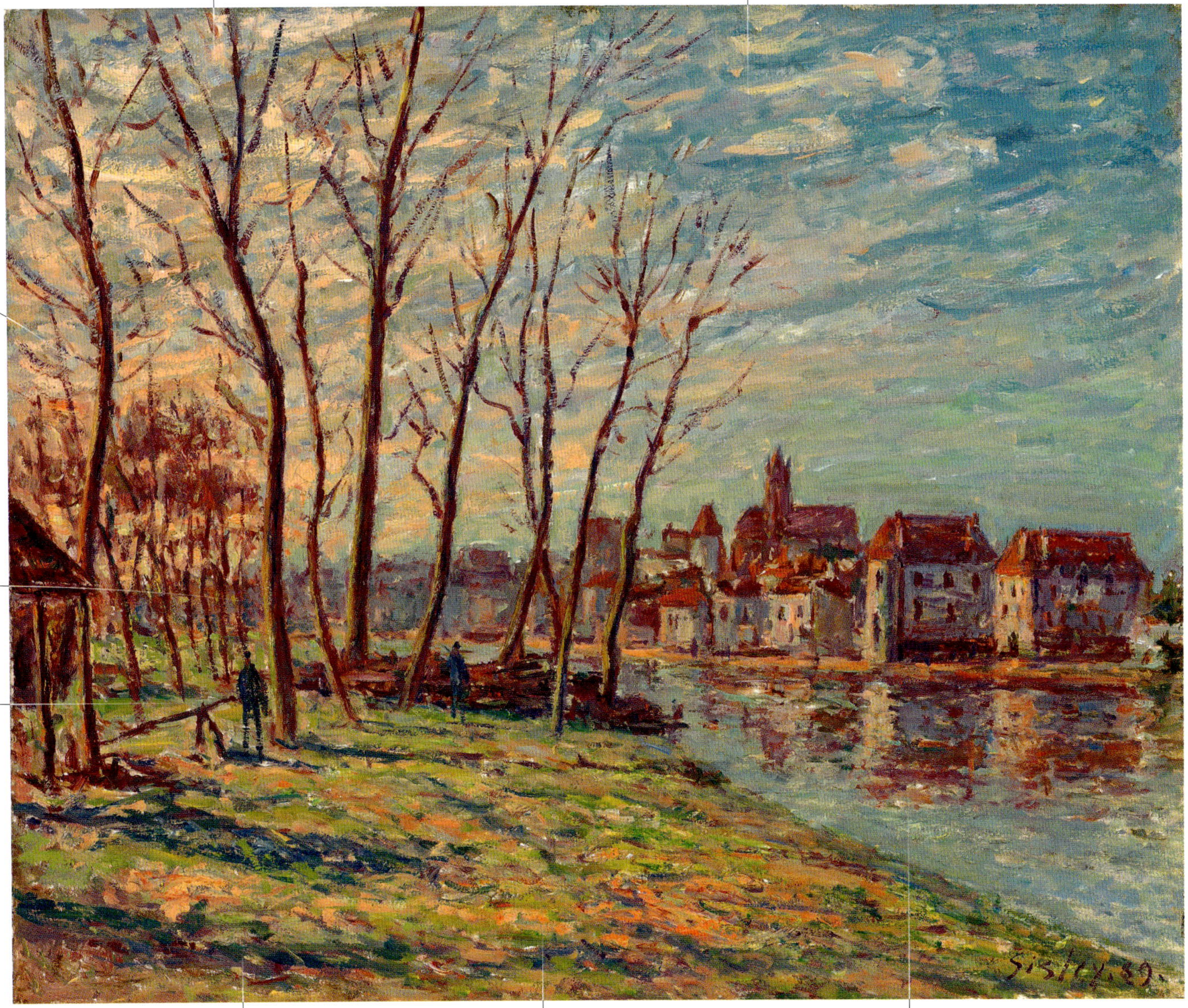

Horizontal shadows in the foreground balance the verticals of the trees.

Warm pink from the sunrise is dispersed throughout the scene—in the clouds, along the far bank, and in the foreground.

Loose, spontaneous brushstrokes create the impression of reflections on rippling water.

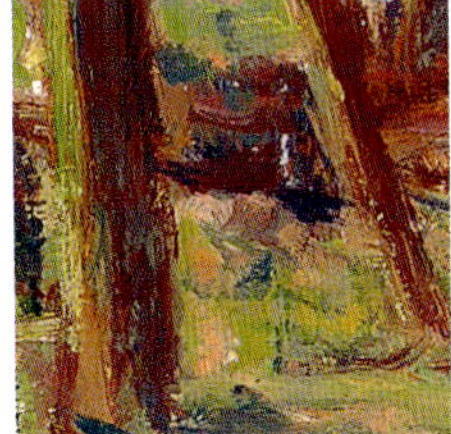

Sisley uses pale green to show sunlight on one side of a tree trunk, and deep red for the side in shadow.

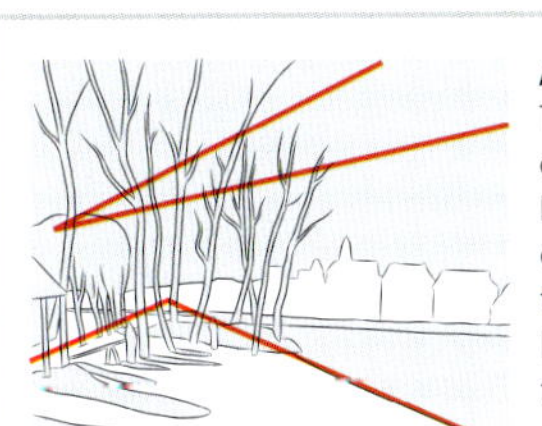

Arrangement
The composition is carefully structured. Diagonal lines radiate out from the focus of the sunrise, while others lead through the trees to the distant buildings.

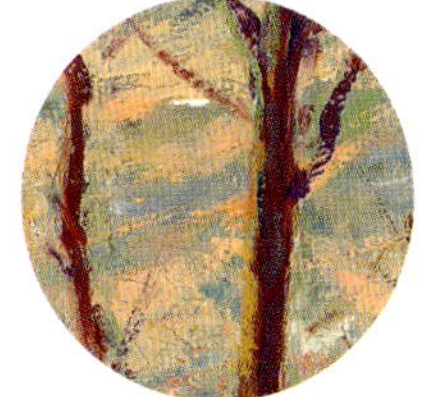

Technique
Alternating patches of light pink and greenish blue in similar tones create a shimmering light in the sky between the dark tree trunks.

At the Moulin Rouge, the Dance

Henri de Toulouse-Lautrec 1889–1890, oil on canvas, 46 × 59 in (115.6 × 149.9 cm), Philadelphia Museum of Art, US

This lively scene captures the clientele and performers of the Moulin Rouge, a popular nightclub in the Montmartre district of Paris frequented by artist Toulouse-Lautrec. Two dancers practice a routine, which may be the can-can, surrounded by an eclectic mix of onlookers and revelers.

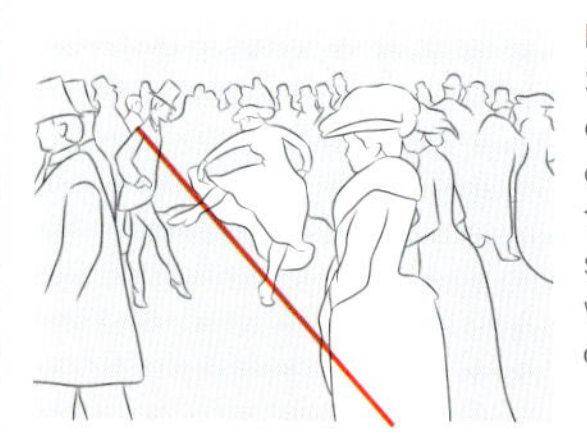

Pinks and reds
Starting with the pink dress in the foreground, a diagonal line through the dancer's red stockings and the waiter's hair and jacket draws in the viewer.

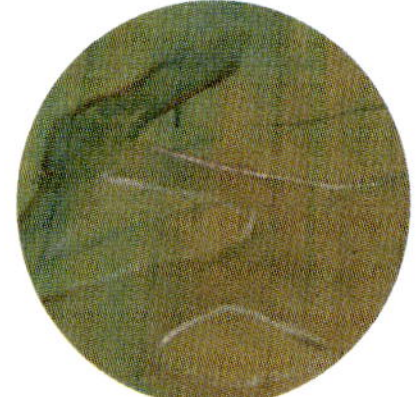

Shadow play
Like almost all of Toulouse-Lautrec's paintings, this nighttime scene is lit by harsh artificial light, with shadows in the foreground mirroring the dancers' bodies.

> "I paint things as they are. I don't comment. I record."
>
> Henri de Toulouse-Lautrec

This figure, whose face slightly resembles a skull, is believed to be the artist's father, Alphonse.

Drinks are served at the bar, where this painting was eventually hung—after the Moulin Rouge's owner bought it.

Wearing fashionable top hats, a line of men at the bar give the painting a voyeuristic element.

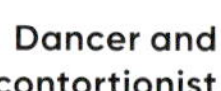

Dancer and contortionist Valentin le Désossé, (Valentin the Boneless), is shown teaching a new step.

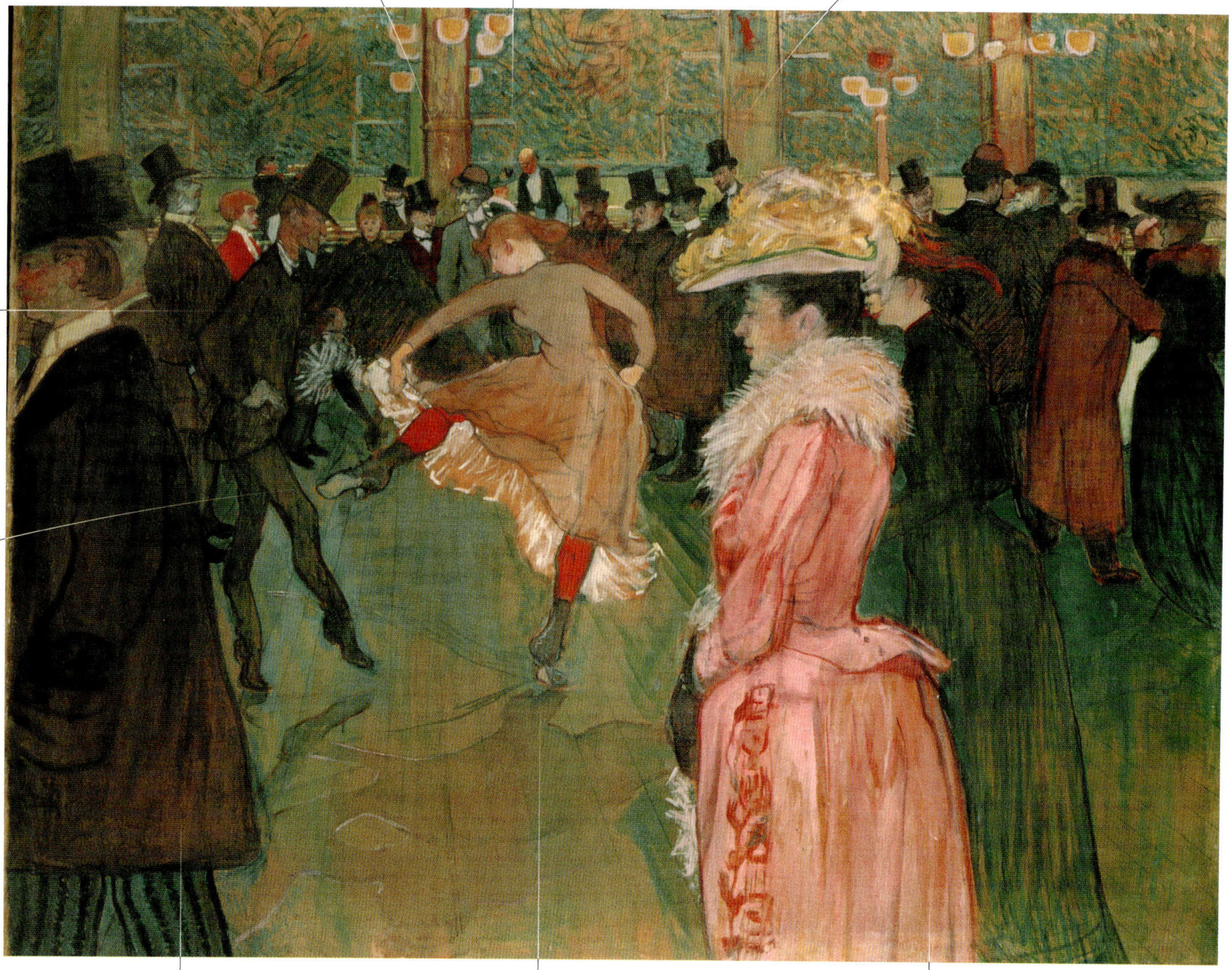

Valentin's pupil is probably dancer Louise Weber, who was known for being able to stand on one leg while raising the other above her head.

The customers cut off on either side of the painting contribute to the work's "snapshot" feel.

The dancer reveals her ankles and stockings—audacious behavior for the time.

The well-dressed visitor in pink appears out of place, but her slight smirk hints at her enjoyment of her surroundings.

Shearing the Rams

Tom Roberts 1890, oil on canvas on composition board, 48 × 72 in (122.4 × 183.3 cm), National Gallery of Victoria, Melbourne, Australia

Roberts presents a dynamic tableau of teamwork, harmony, and comradeship in this tribute to pastoral life and the honest working bushman. In an era when the Australian colonies dominated global wool production—and the sense of Australian nationalism was on the rise—the painting celebrates sheep as a symbol of national prosperity and their shearers as enduring folk heroes.

Shearers were paid by the fleece. Their progress and payment were tracked on wooden boards.

A bell signals the start and end of the working day, symbolizing order and the cyclical nature of shearing.

Candid moments of pause play out as one shearer sips from his billycan.

A tobacco pipe and hanging hat add still-life touches to this animated scene.

Oil, used to sharpen blades, is painted in golden hues, mirroring the glow of sunlight.

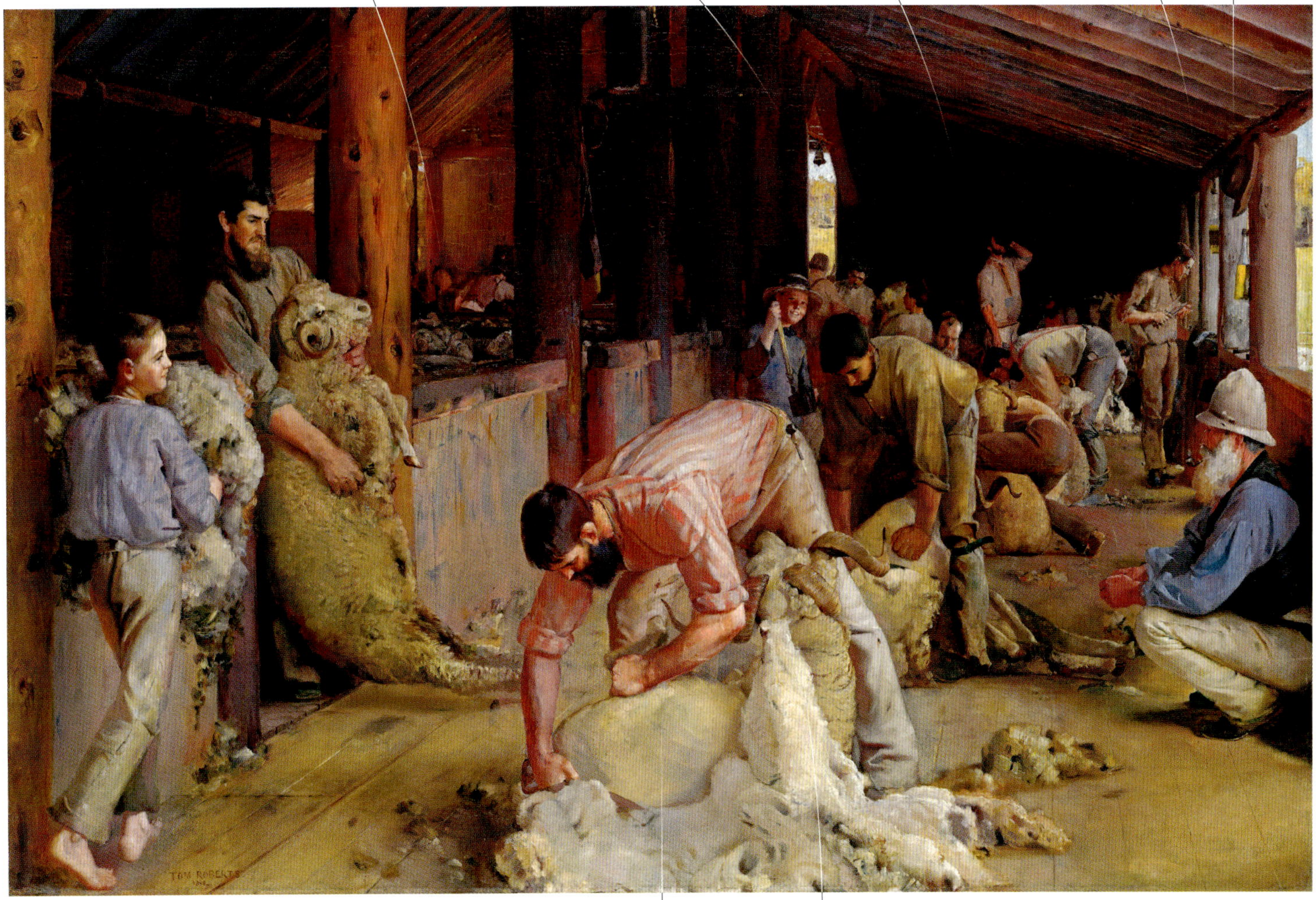

Prominent muscles and veins evoke "the Australian man" for whom skill, grit, and strength are prized.

A pink and white striped shirt spotlights the lead shearer.

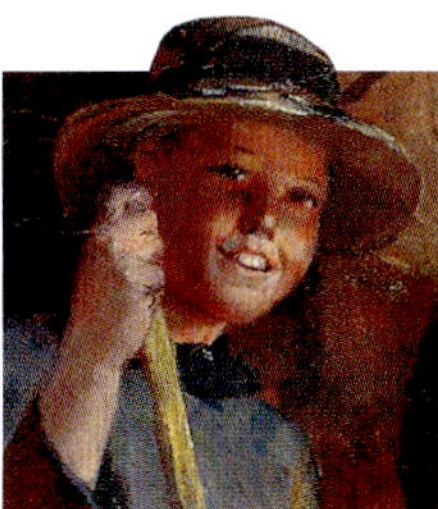

The tarboy was based on a local girl, who created atmosphere by sweeping dust around the shed while Roberts painted.

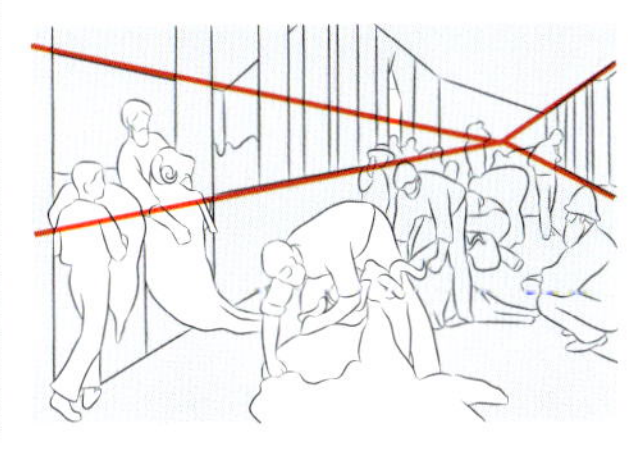

Composition
Roberts creates an illusion of space with architectural features converging toward a vanishing point. Quiet spaces below the ceiling and outdoors give the eye a break from the busy scene, creating harmony and balance.

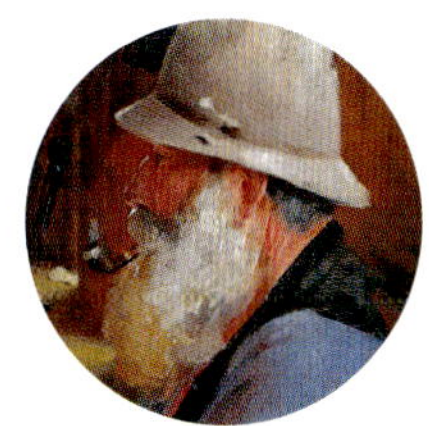

Three generations
Prominently positioned from left to right, three generations of shearers unfold: a spirited youth, a middle-aged shearer in his prime, and a reflective older figure, perhaps now a foreman.

The Card Players

Paul Cézanne 1892–1895, oil on canvas, 24 × 29 in (60 × 73 cm), Musée d'Orsay, Paris, France

Two men sit across a table playing cards in one of Cézanne's five paintings on this theme. They seem silent and immobile, engrossed in their game and as permanent as the Provence landscape. The men, farmworkers on Cézanne's late father's estate, contrast with each other, yet form a balanced composition.

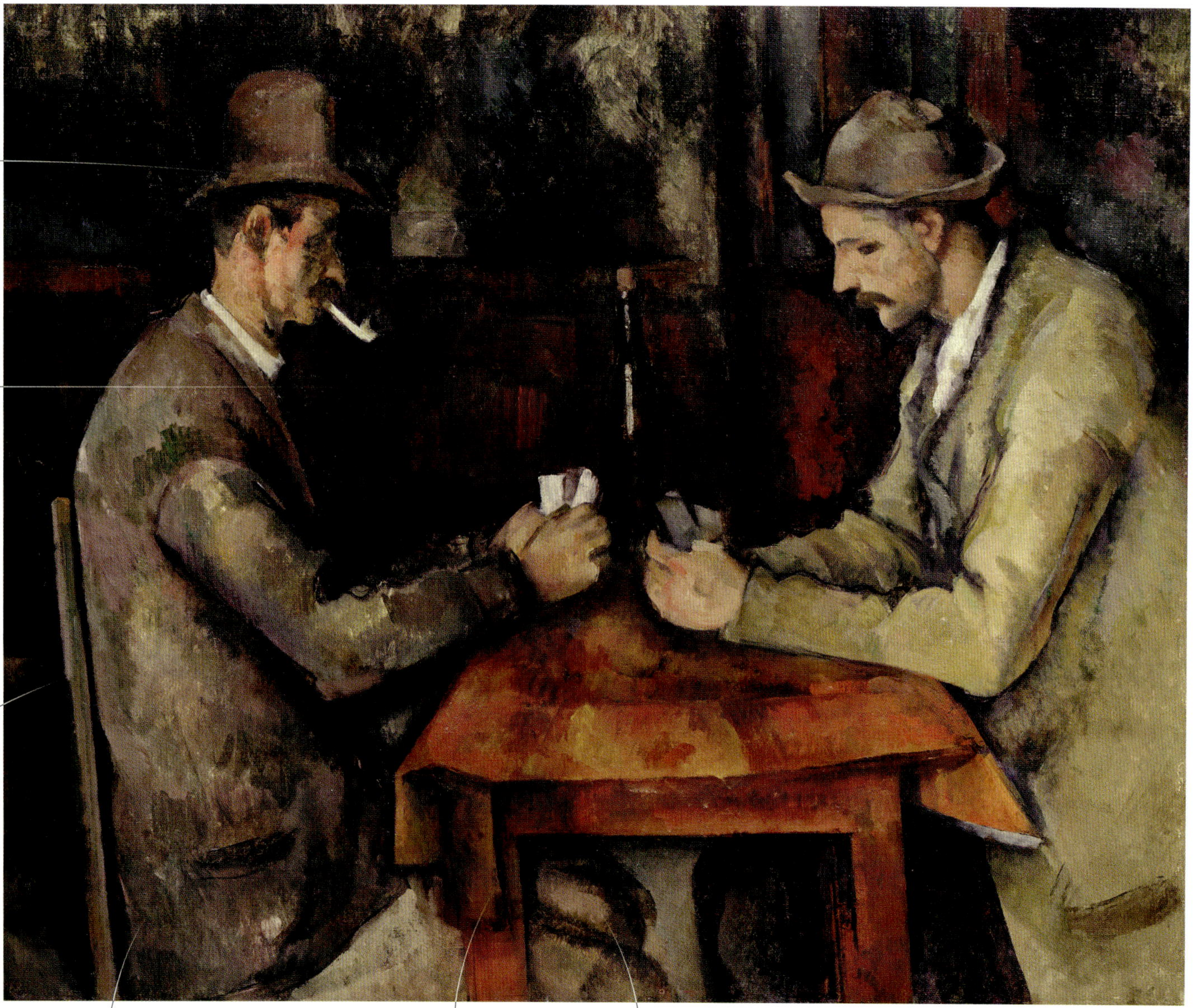

The brim of the pipe smoker's hat bends down; the other man's flicks up.

There is a wine bottle but no glasses, and no money is on the table; these are not drunken, boorish gamblers.

This straight-back chair echoes its occupant's upright posture—even his hat has straight sides. This contrasts with the other man's sloping posture and rounded hat.

Cézanne portrays card playing in a positive light. At the time, the French government was thinking of introducing a tax on playing cards to combat the ills of gambling.

The colors in the painting are warm, suggesting a welcoming haven.

The knees of the pipe smoker extend unnaturally far, balancing his opponent's long arms.

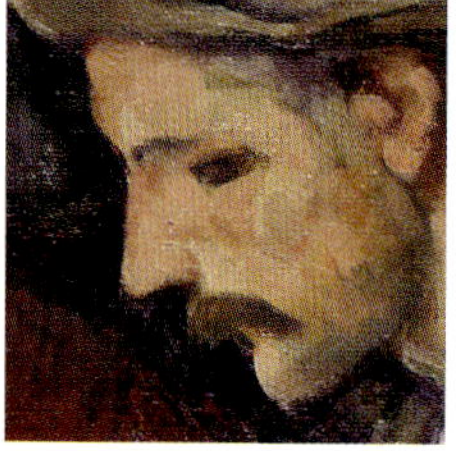

The men are focused on their cards; they interact through their game, not conversation.

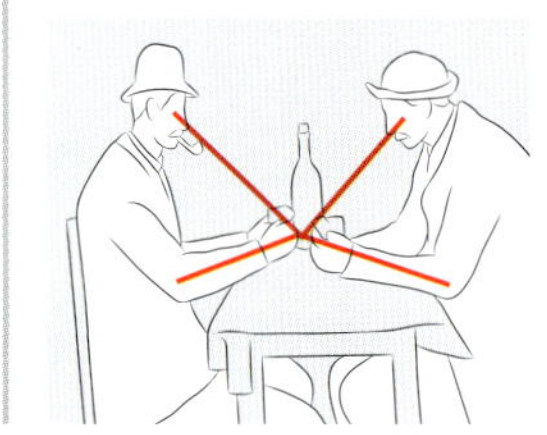

Diagonals
The downward gazes and upward slant of the forearms create diagonals that converge near the wine bottle, equal distance between the two men.

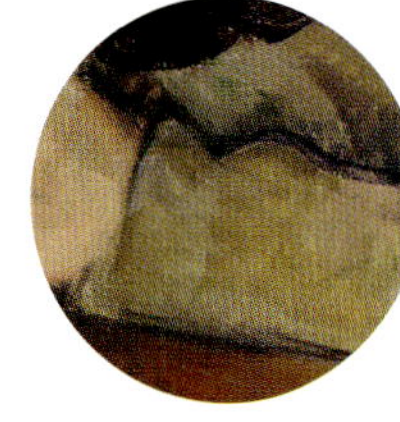

Focus
Thick black outlines around the men help convey a sense of solidity and permanence, the essence of the painting. In contrast, the loosely painted background is indistinct.

The Flowered Dress

Édouard Vuillard 1891, oil on canvas, 15 × 18 in (38 × 46 cm), Museu de Arte de São Paulo, São Paulo, Brazil

An intimate, almost autobiographical look inside a family home that also served as a workplace, this painting depicts Vuillard's mother, Marie, sewing. The image is informed by blocks of color and fabric patterns, heavily inspired by the works of Paul Gauguin. Vuillard's beloved mother, whom he lived with until he was 60, made women's clothes to pay the bills following her husband's death. His sister (also named Marie) and grandmother are probably the other women in the painting.

The mirror's reflection is inaccurate. It does not match the angle of the woman in the foreground.

Floral wallpaper echoes the flowers on the woman's dress. The home is a reflection of these hard-working women.

With its bold floral pattern, this dress is eye-catching. Vuillard's paintings often featured patterned fabrics; he was surrounded by these from a young age.

Vuillard's grandmother does not seem to be working as quickly as the other women.

None of the women make eye contact with each other or the viewer; they are concentrating solely on their work.

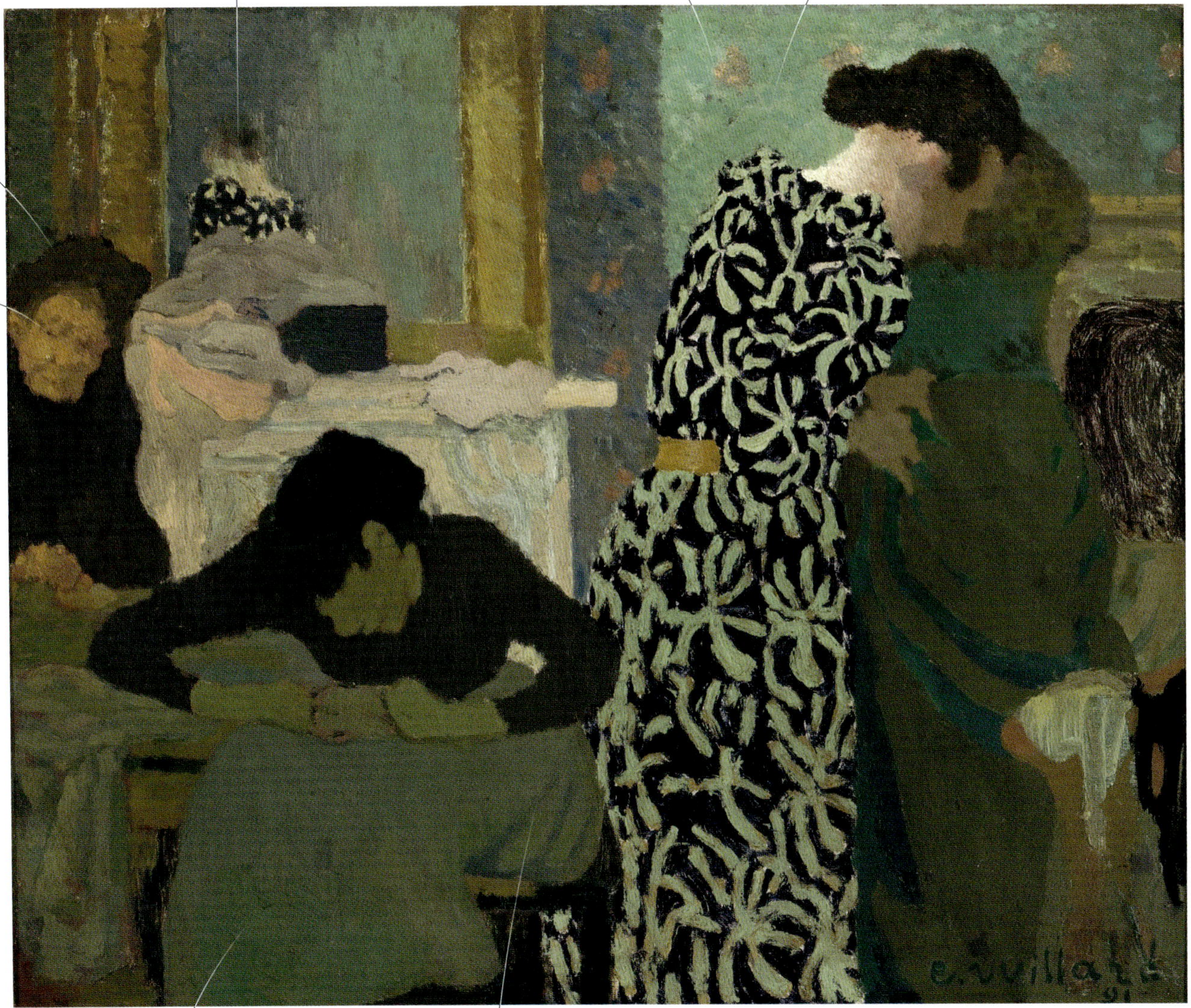

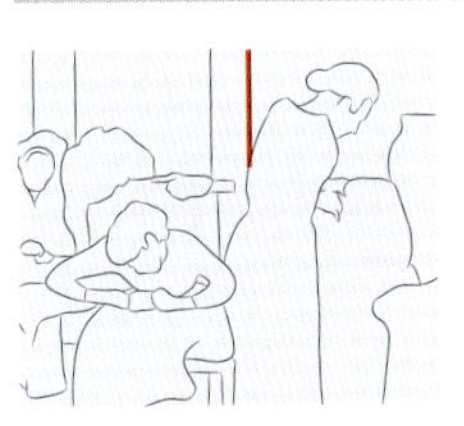

Two-dimensionality
Vuillard has flattened the space. The vertical line separating the light-green wallpaper from the darker-looking wallpaper is the room's corner, yet these walls seem parallel rather than perpendicular.

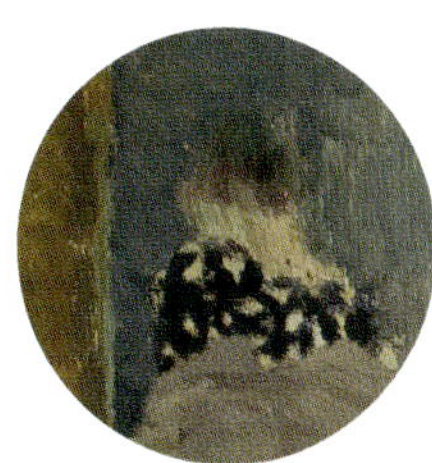

Focus on work
The image is tightly framed, with relatively little of the room visible beyond the women's work area. Even the mirror fails to show the viewer anything beyond the women's activities.

The mother's pose displays determination and force.

The mother's elbows and chair extend over the other women, exerting symbolic dominance over the scene, even though the title of the painting highlights the woman in the flowered dress.

"Family life, confined within these ever-present walls, aroused Vuillard's most powerful emotions, so that his interiors also function as theaters."

Elizabeth Wynne Easton

Hesiod and the Muse

Gustave Moreau 1891, oil on panel, 23 × 14 in (59 × 34.5 cm), Musée d'Orsay, Paris, France

Symbolist painters sought to express deep truths by drawing on the imaginative resonance of emblematic images and myths. In this symbolic representation of artistic creativity, Moreau invokes the ancient Greek poet Hesiod, author of *Theogony*, and one of the Muses, maiden-goddesses said to inspire the creativity of mortals. She tenderly guides his hands as he attempts to play a lyre—the symbol of poetry.

A star blazes above the figures, symbolizing the truth and hope that humanity will derive from this scene, the birth of poetry.

Mount Helicon, traditionally held to be the seat of poetic inspiration, is topped by a classical temple

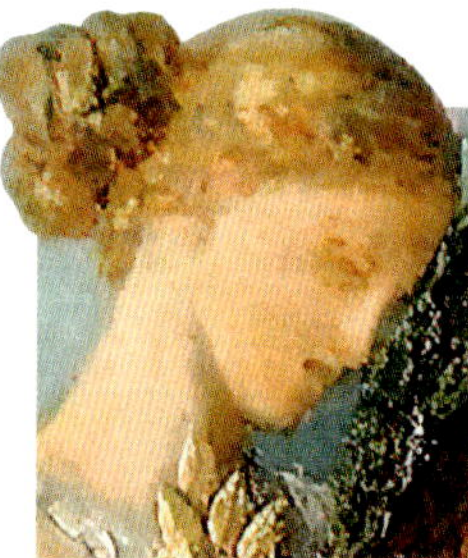

Eyes closed, the muse concentrates on conjuring inspiration from within.

The Muse has her own lyre, but focuses on nurturing the creativity of humankind.

The Muse guides Hesiod's hand to his lyre as she whispers into his ear.

The mythic Valley of the Muses was green and fertile, but poetry can be produced even in rocky terrain.

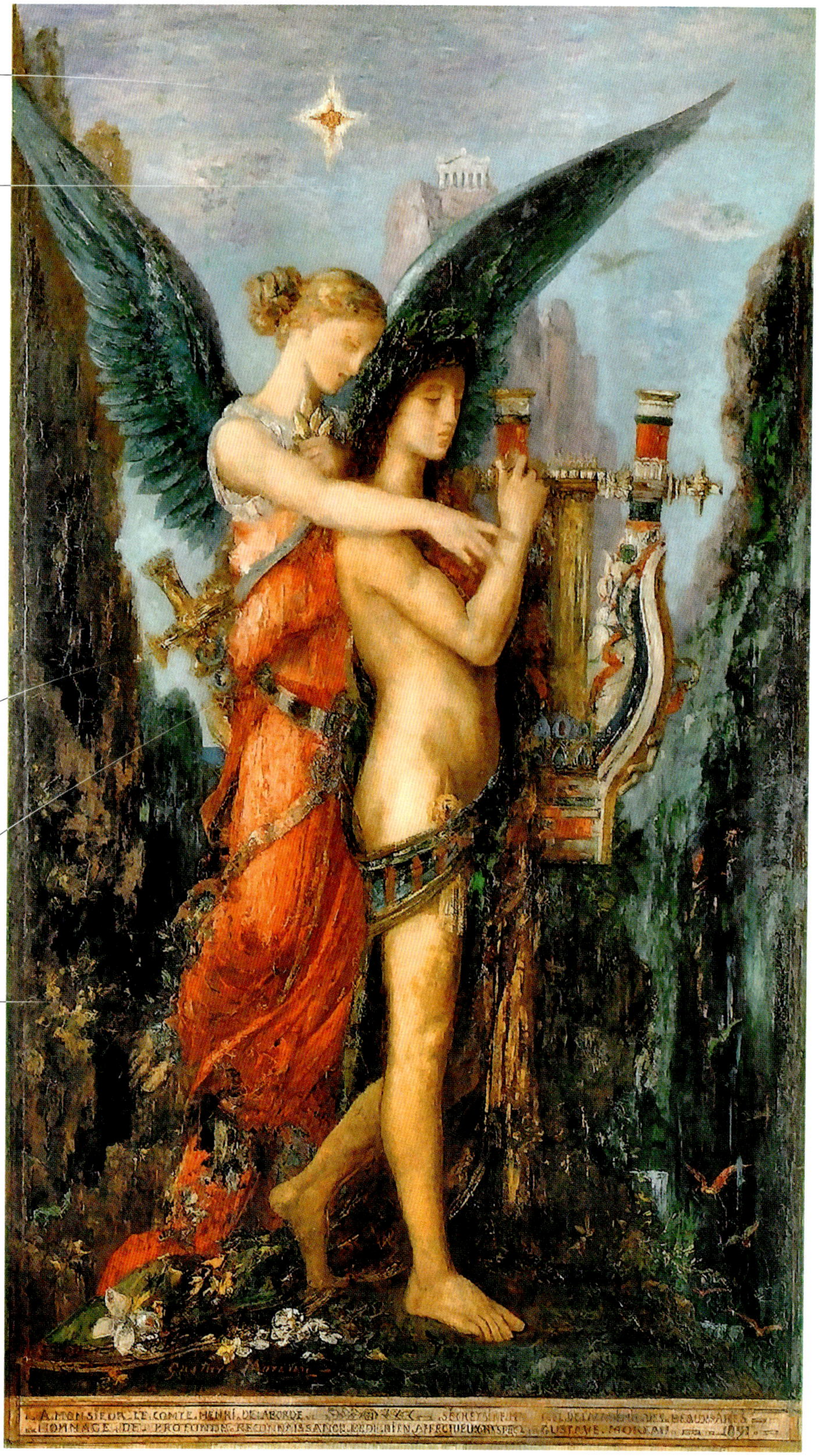

> "Divination, the intuition of things, belongs to the artist and the poet alone."
>
> Gustave Moreau

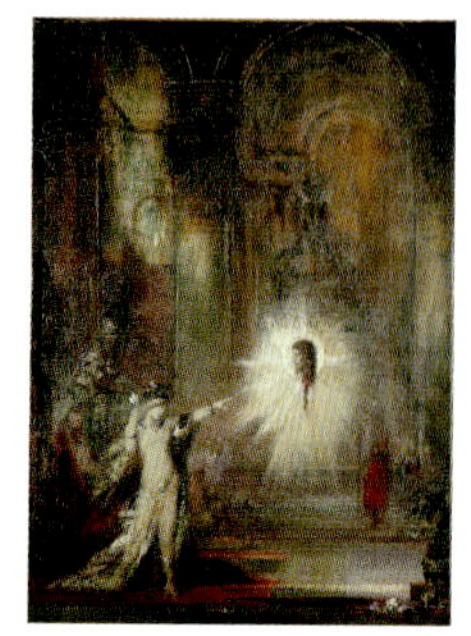

Symbolist themes
Moreau also painted Biblical themes. *The Apparition* (c. 1876) imagines John the Baptist appearing to Salome, his killer.

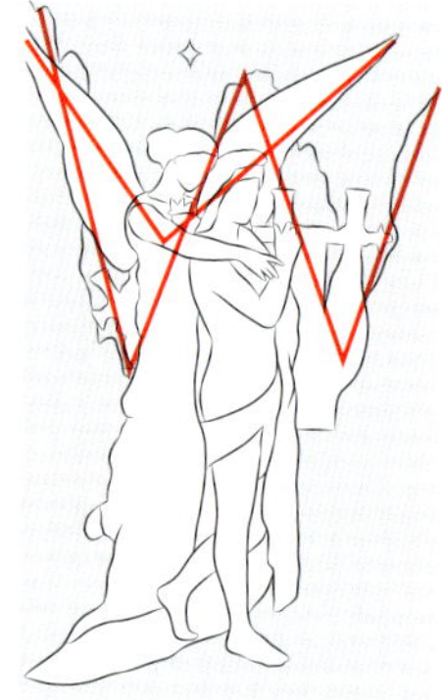

Composition
The "V" of the Muse's wings cuts across the "W" formed by the ravines that frame the scene, emphasizing the height of the central figures.

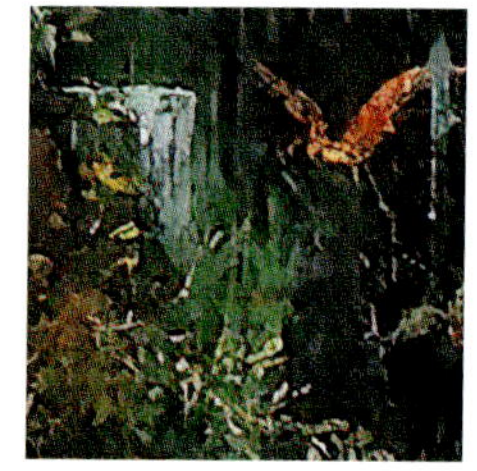

The Hippocrene spring was a source of inspiration in Greek legend. Here it reinforces the dominant theme of Moreau's painting.

The Waltz

Camille Claudel 1891, bronze, 17 × 9 × 14 in (43.2 × 23 × 34.3 cm), Musée Camille Claudel, Paris, France

Claudel's heavy statue seems about to float away, borne up by the gravity-defying force of the dancers' passion. Yet some interpretations suggest the work is about the destructive capacity of love rather than its joyful sensuality. Did Claudel wonder if her passionate affair with her mentor, sculptor Auguste Rodin, was costing her too much?

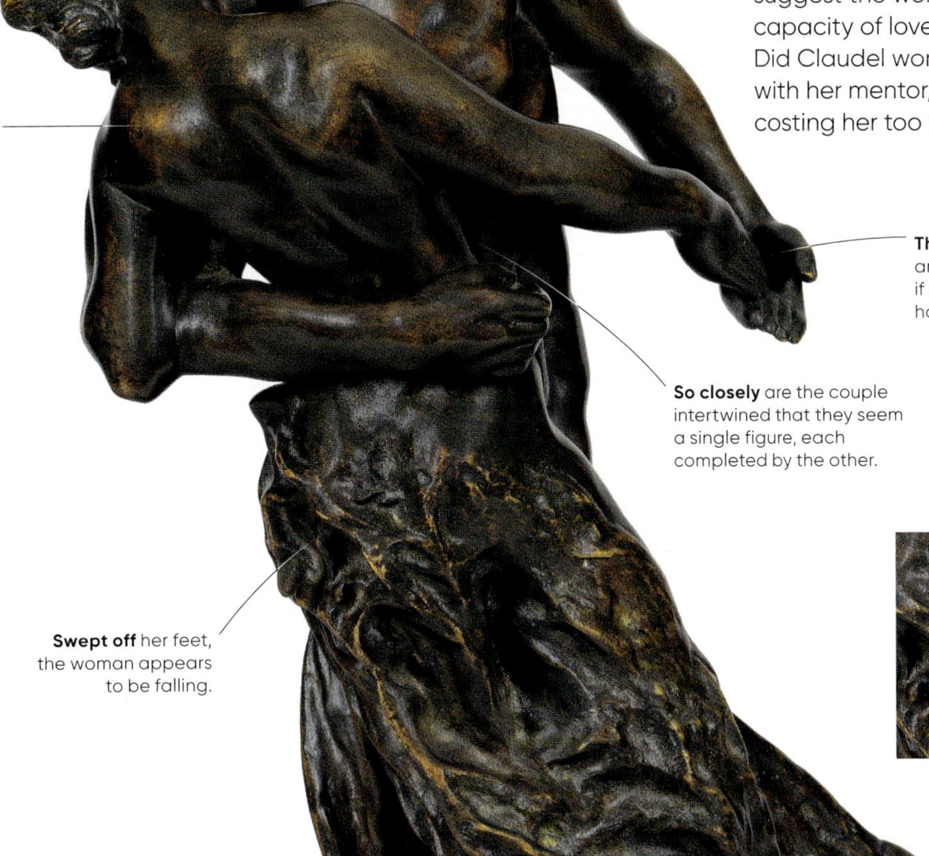

The man leans in to nuzzle the woman's neck, but also appears to be consuming her.

Near-nudity makes the dancers appear timeless and universal, symbols rather than individuals.

The hands may indicate ambivalence. It is unclear if she is withdrawing her hand or about to grasp his.

So closely are the couple intertwined that they seem a single figure, each completed by the other.

Swept off her feet, the woman appears to be falling.

The female dancer dissolves into drapery. She may be engulfed by passion or a woman robbed of her autonomy by love.

In the round
The statue was designed to be viewed from all sides. While disapproval led Claudel to clothe the woman in the hope she would receive a state commission to produce the work in marble, the man is naked. He lifts his left leg to begin a new step of the dance.

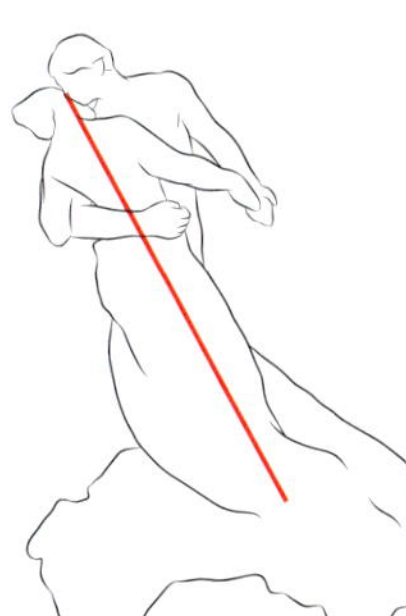

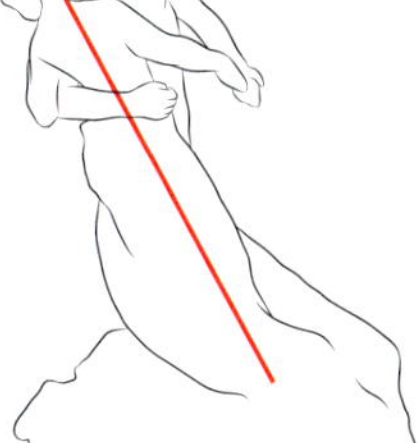

Sense of movement
The dancers' off-kilter stance and the woman's swirling skirt suggest both the madness of their passion and the movement of the dance. It seems they could fall to the ground at any moment.

At the Seaside

William Merritt Chase c. 1892, oil on canvas, 20 × 34 in (50.8 × 86.4 cm), Metropolitan Museum of Art, New York, US

Chase's painting of women and children relaxing along a seashore shows the growing influence of European Impressionism on US art in the 1890s. Chase did not think of himself as an Impressionist—he painted in varied styles and considered the Impressionists overly formulaic—but he saw value in the way Impressionists sacrificed detail to convey an impression of a scene's light and air. Unlike many 19th-century seascapes, *At the Seaside* does not depict a breathtaking view or foreboding storm, but simply ordinary people enjoying a pleasant summer's day. "Paint the commonplace," Chase advised, "so that it will be distinguished."

The sky, which fills the upper half of the canvas, seems to have depth. "Try to paint the sky as if we could see through it," advised Chase. It adds to the sense of bright airiness.

Scudding clouds artfully echo the white forms of the central parasol and children's dresses.

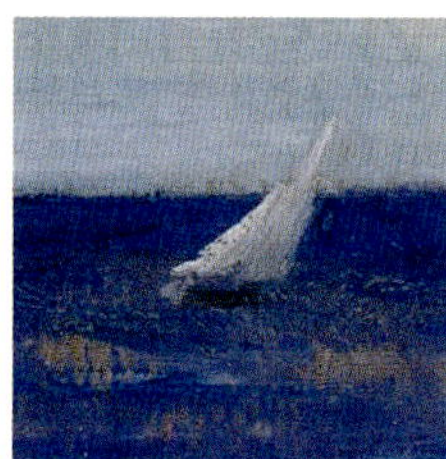

A sailboat keels to one side, suggesting a breeze in the sea air and giving the painting a sense of motion.

Cool blue water, bright blue sky, and even blue tones in the sand are accentuated by the red and yellow parasols and beach gear.

The beach is believed to be Southampton, New York, where Chase ran a summer art school between 1891 and 1902.

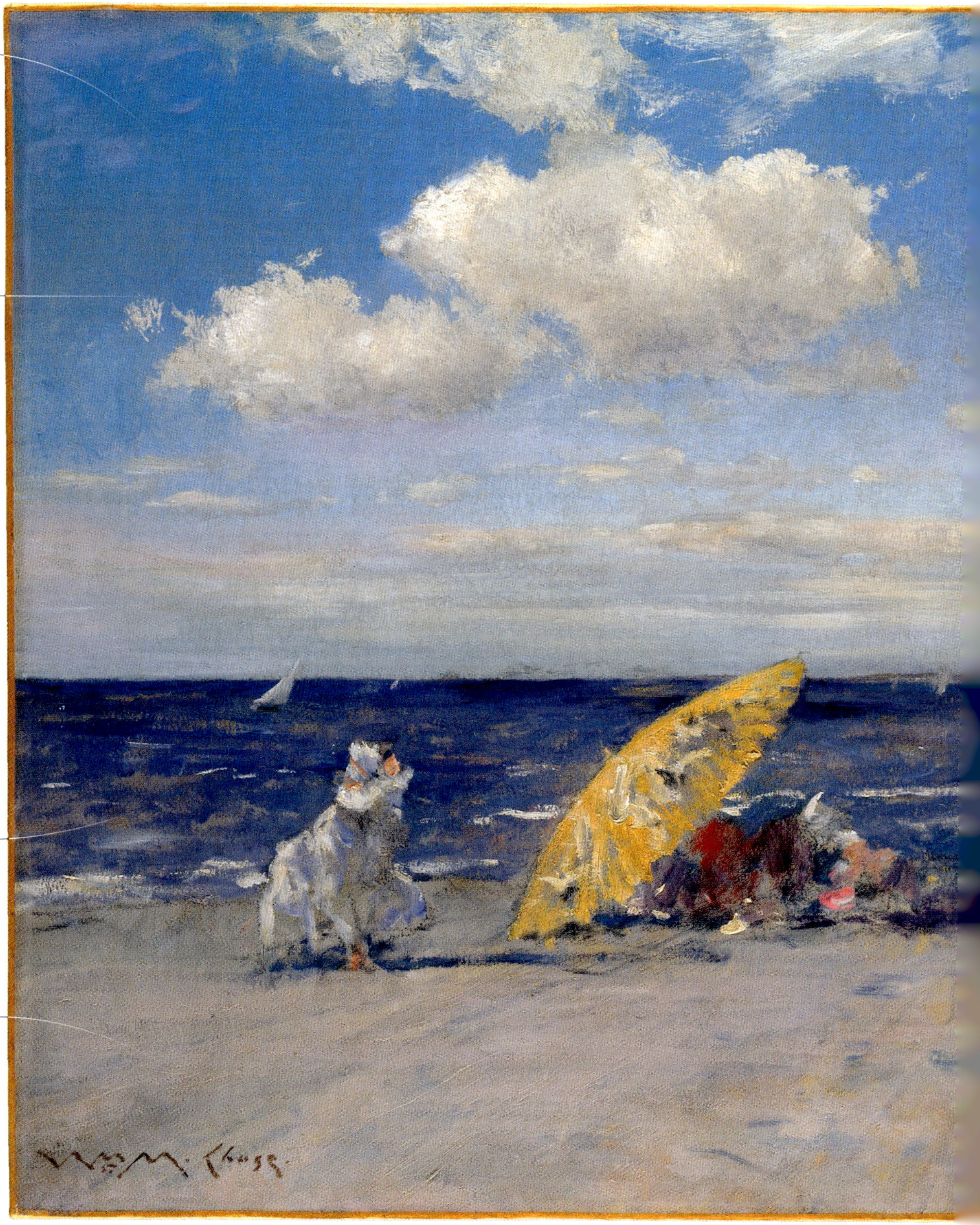

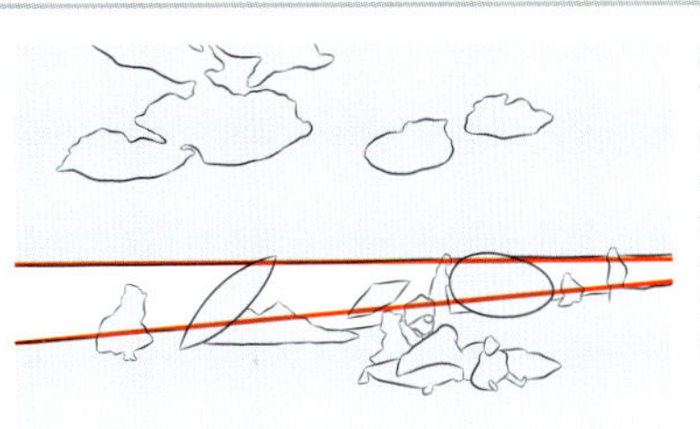

Broad view
The horizon line and diagonal shoreline converge outside the painting to the right. A wide, open foreground draws the viewer into the scene.

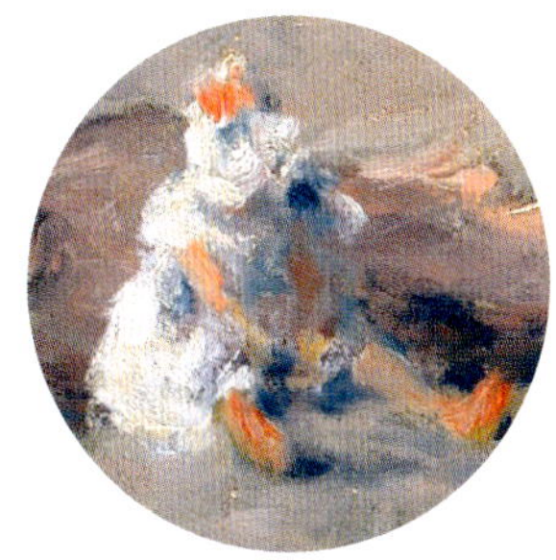

Creating an impression
Chase paints with loose, spirited brushwork; just one or two brushstrokes create a limb or face.

> "These things by Mr. Chase of sea and sky and sandy shore are like a breath of salt-sea air itself."
>
> Orson Lowell

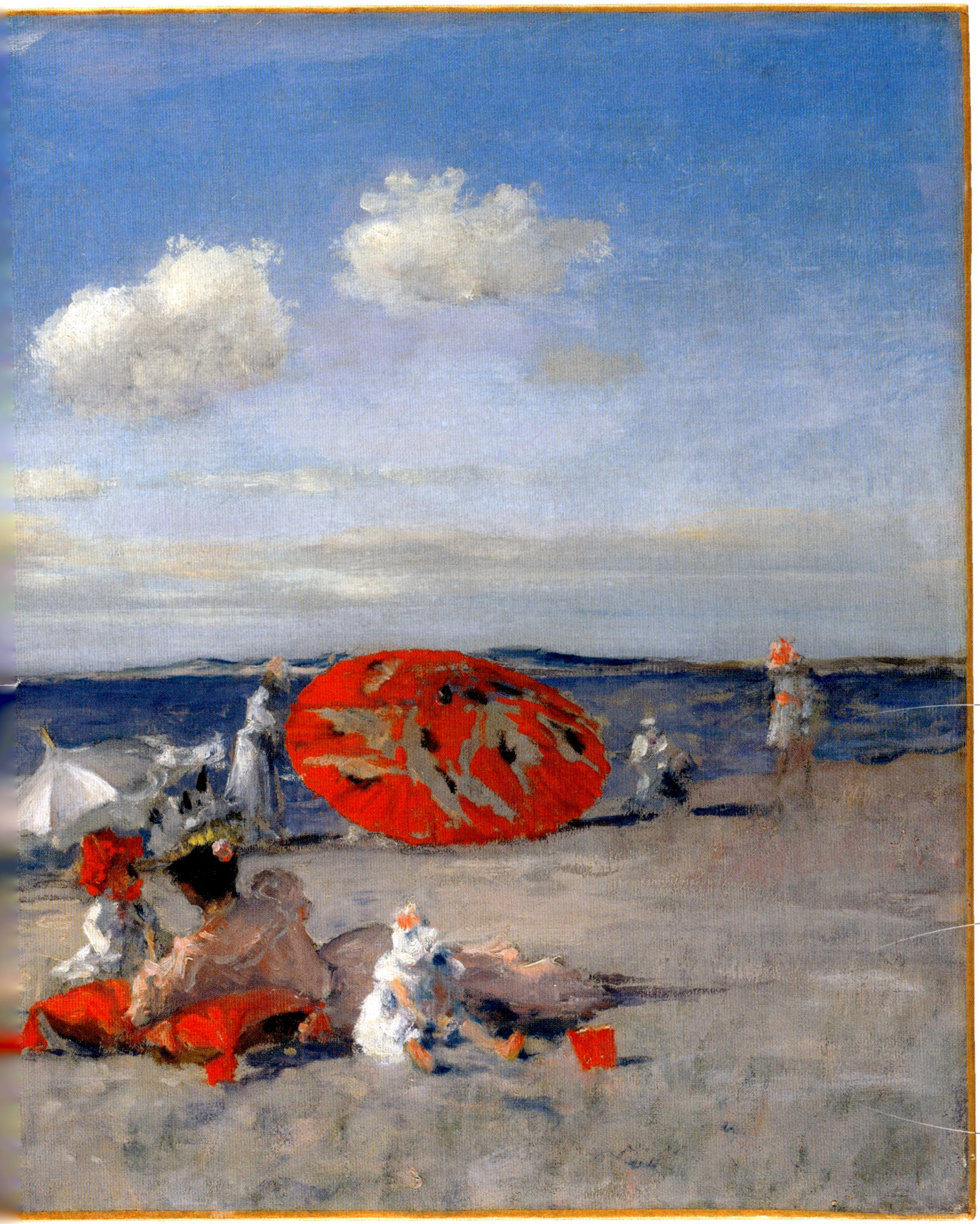

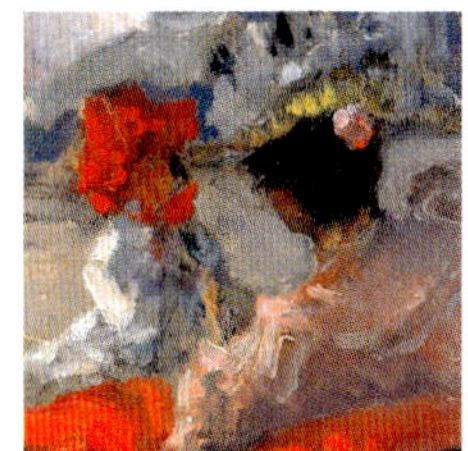

Chase's wife and child are probably among the beachgoers; Chase painted them often.

Japanese parasols, incongruous on a New York beach, reflect Chase's interest in Japanese art and design.

Uneven sand suggests footprints. "In painting a sandy beach," Chase suggested, "try to imagine that you are walking upon it."

Facial expressions are not visible. This painting offers a sense of being on a beach, not the thoughts of the beachgoers.

Surprised!

Henri Rousseau 1891, oil on canvas, 51 × 64 in (129.8 × 161.9 cm), National Gallery, London, UK

A tiger crouches in a colorful, dreamlike jungle during a thunderstorm, about to surprise its prey. The painting's two-dimensional, naïve style, despite the layering of jungle plants, has been compared to that of Japanese woodblock prints. It was not an artistic choice—Rousseau had limited technical skill. His abandonment of naturalism influenced many modern artists who admired him.

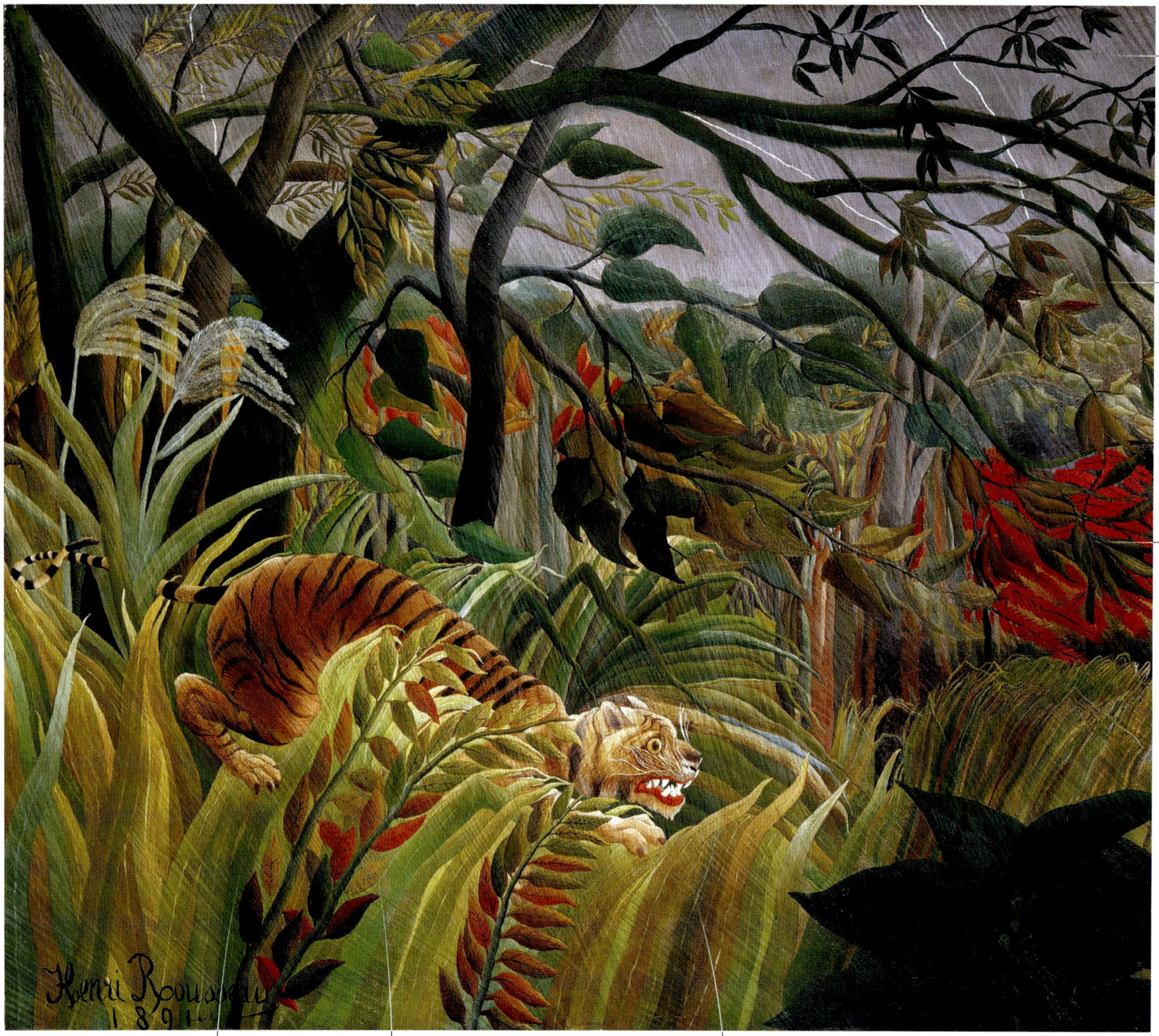

Falling rain, jungle grasses, and tiger stripes create myriad slanting lines, providing visual interest.

The jungle plants provide attractively layered color.

These red leaves might foreshadow the blood from the tiger's coming strike.

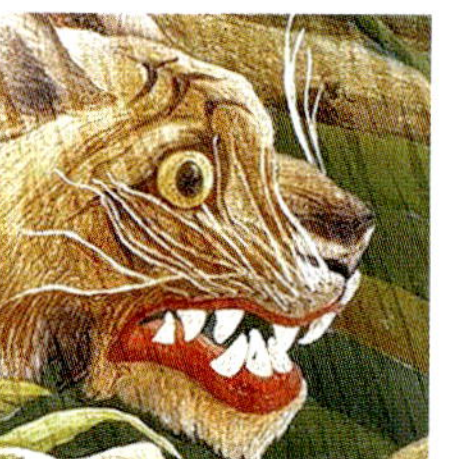

The tiger's upward-pointing whiskers reflect the angle of the rain and lightning flashes.

A paw seems to float above the ground. Rousseau struggled to paint realistic feet throughout his career.

Rousseau's tiger could have been drawn by a child. Some in the Parisian avant-garde saw his primitive style as a virtue.

The tiger's expression is one of surprise, throwing doubt on who or what is the subject of the title. Rousseau claimed the tiger was about to surprise people unseen to the right.

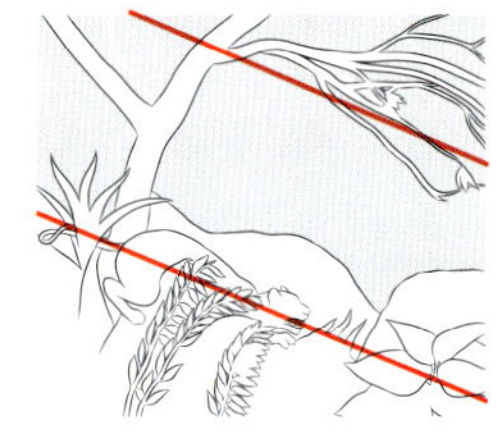

Windswept effect
The momentum of the painting is diagonal, from top left to bottom right. The wind pushes a prominent tree branch and the rain in this direction. The lightning strikes and tiger pounce are at a similar angle.

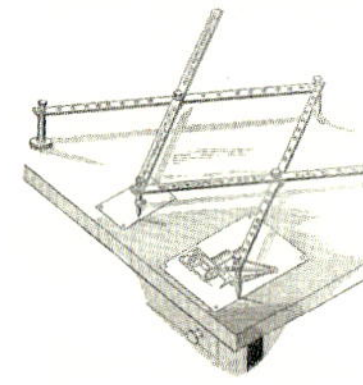

Artist's pantograph
Rousseau used a mechanical tool called a pantograph to trace and enlarge shapes and illustrations he found in other sources.

"His tiger surprising its prey ought not be missed; it's the alpha and omega of painting."

Félix Vallotton, 1891

The Scream

Edvard Munch 1893, oil, tempera, and pastel on cardboard, 36 × 29 in (91 × 73.5 cm), National Museum, Oslo, Norway

The Scream is part of Munch's The Frieze of Life, a series of autobiographical paintings on the themes of love, life, loss, loneliness, and death. He painted it after experiencing a panic attack while out for a walk, and sought to express the extreme anxiety and fear he was feeling at the time.

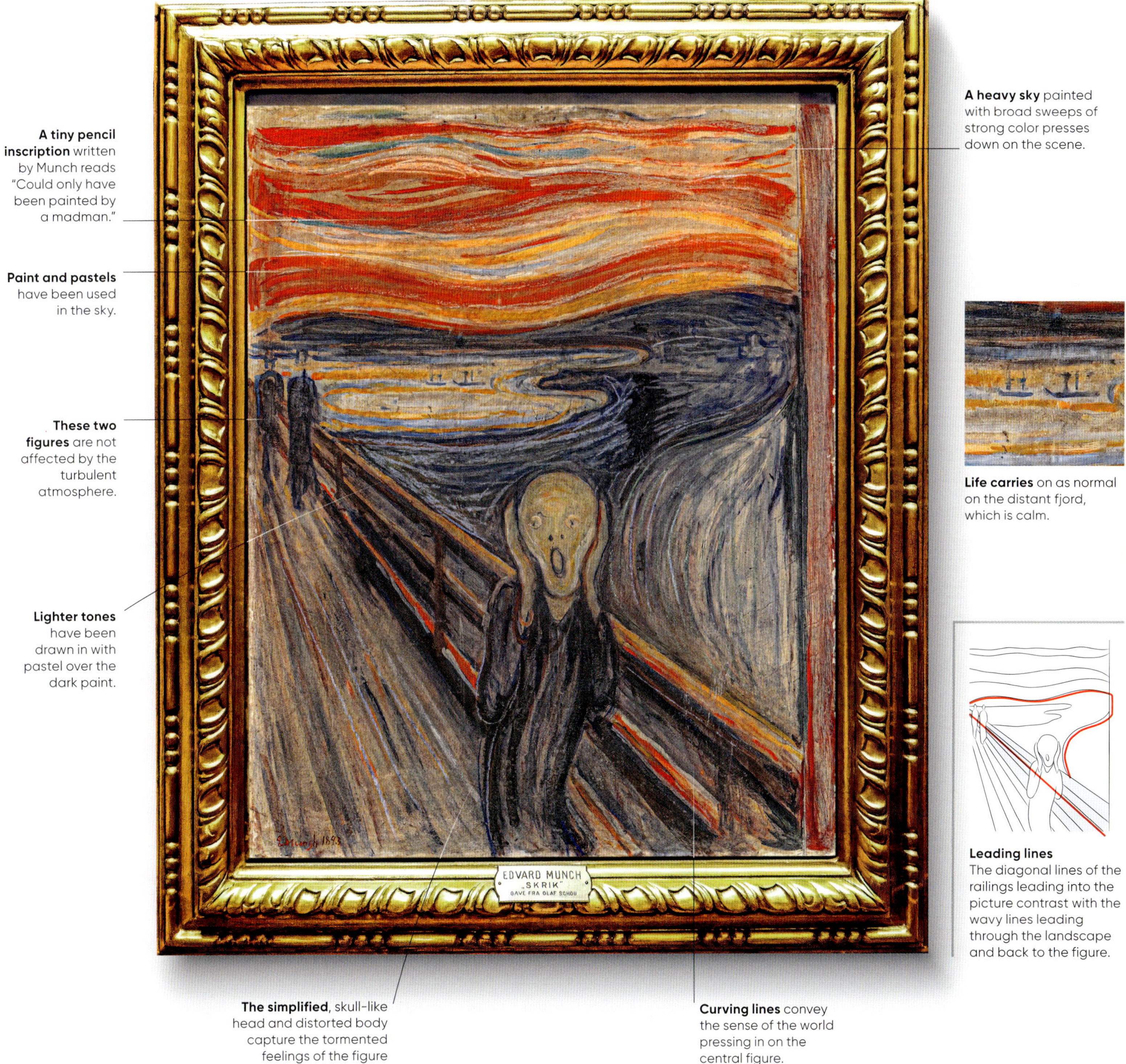

A tiny pencil inscription written by Munch reads "Could only have been painted by a madman."

Paint and pastels have been used in the sky.

These two figures are not affected by the turbulent atmosphere.

Lighter tones have been drawn in with pastel over the dark paint.

The simplified, skull-like head and distorted body capture the tormented feelings of the figure

Curving lines convey the sense of the world pressing in on the central figure.

A heavy sky painted with broad sweeps of strong color presses down on the scene.

Life carries on as normal on the distant fjord, which is calm.

Leading lines
The diagonal lines of the railings leading into the picture contrast with the wavy lines leading through the landscape and back to the figure.

Femme à l'ombrelle

Paul Signac 1893, oil on canvas, 32 × 26 in (81 × 65 cm), Musée d'Orsay, Paris, France

Berthe Roblès, the artist's wife, holds an orange parasol in a painting in the Pointillist or "divisionist" style founded by Signac and Georges Seurat. The power of the work lies in Signac's use of contrasting colors—green is next to orange; yellow is next to purple. The tasseled handle of the parasol, the arabesques in the sleeves, and the stylized flower also exaggerate the decorative look.

Berthe's orange parasol appears yellow close to her face, a choice made to maximize color contrast.

Berthe has a stoic, solemn expression. This painting is a study in color and light, not a lover's romantic portrait.

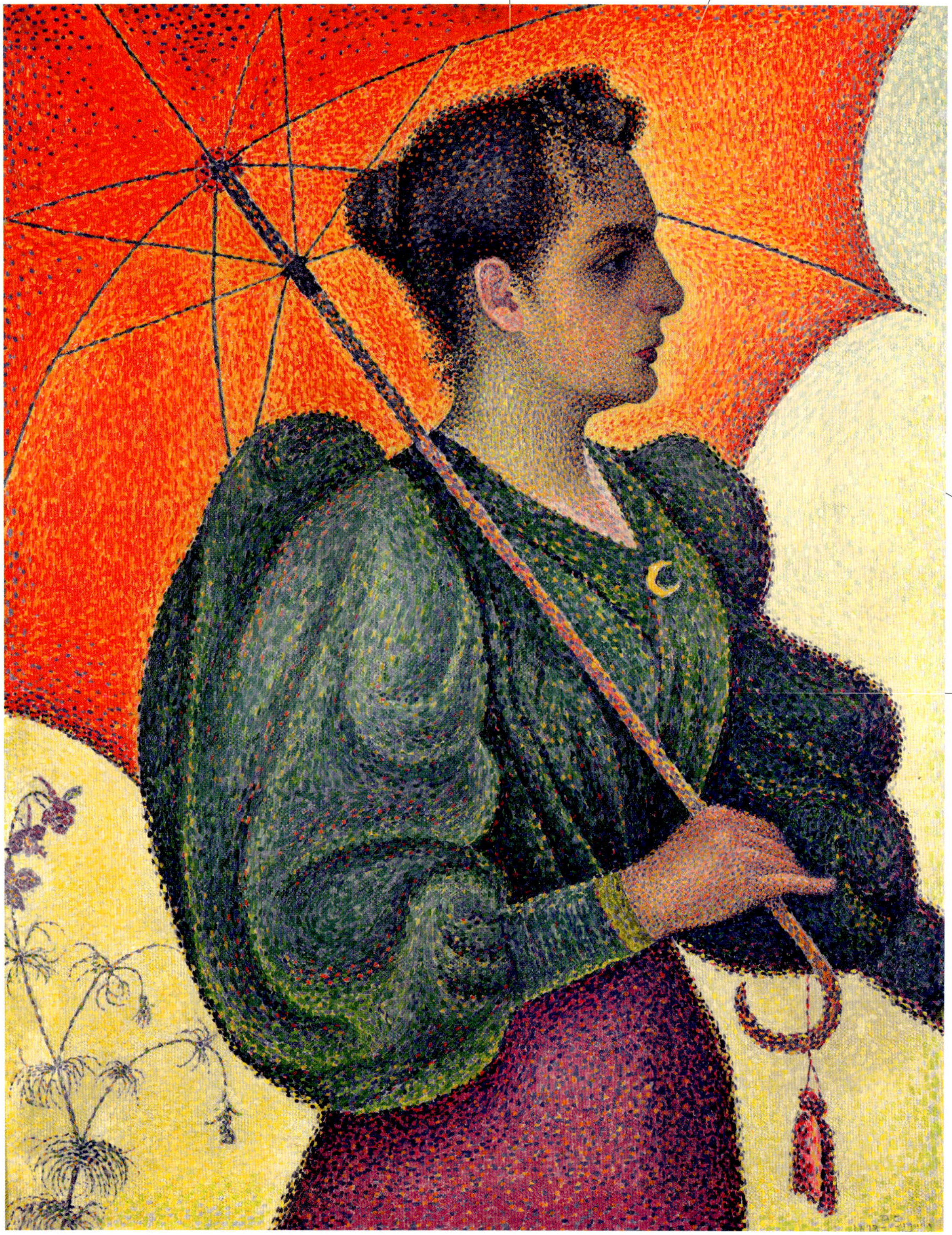

The parasol might allude to the woman holding a similar parasol in Seurat's *A Sunday on La Grande Jatte*.

The handle changes color to contrast with adjacent tones. Strong contrasts makes both colors seem more vibrant.

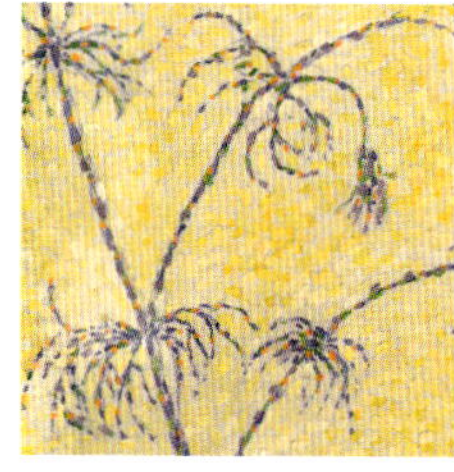

A lone plant appears against the uncluttered yellow background, perhaps reflecting Signac's interest in Art Nouveau and Japanese woodblock prints.

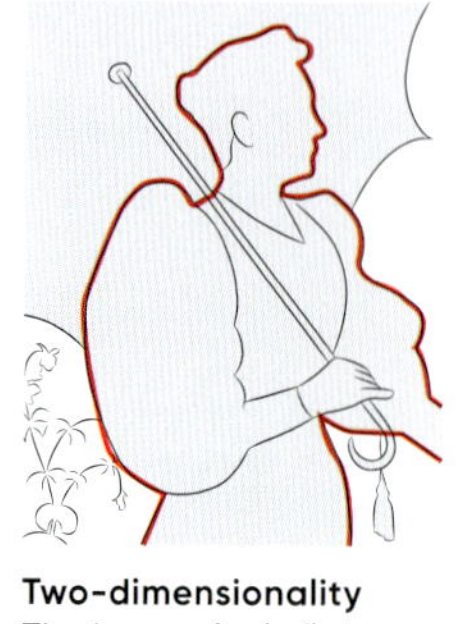

Two-dimensionality
The image feels flat, with very little to suggest depth beyond the modest shadowing in Berthe's blouse and face.

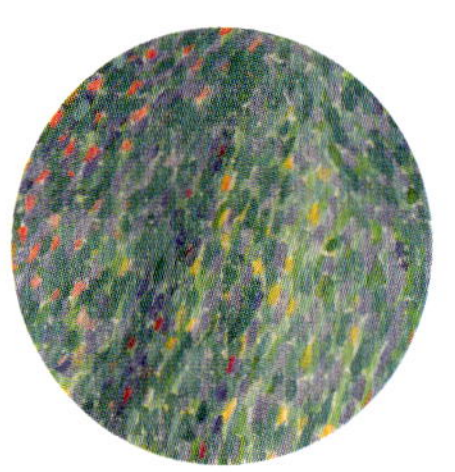

Dabs of color
Pointillist paintings are not made with brushstrokes but with tiny dabs of unblended pigment. The colors blend in the viewer's eye and mind.

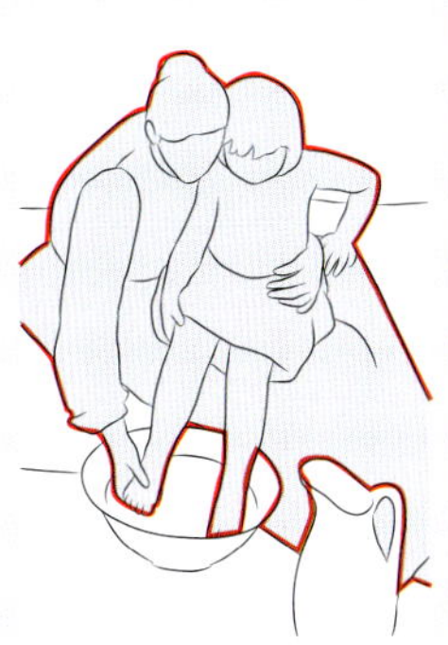

Two form one
The two figures lean together to form a single unit, their contours filling the picture frame.

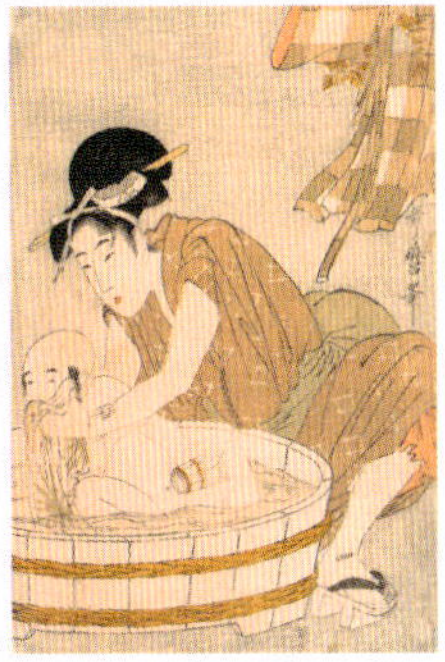

Japanese inspiration
Cassatt was inspired by the simplicity of Japanese woodcut prints, such as *Bathtime* by Kitagawa Utamaro.

A high viewpoint creates an unusual perspective, widely used in Japanese art. The viewer looks down at the mother and child, which creates a flat picture plane.

The figures are surrounded by pattern, such as the geometric and floral motifs of the oriental carpet and furnishings.

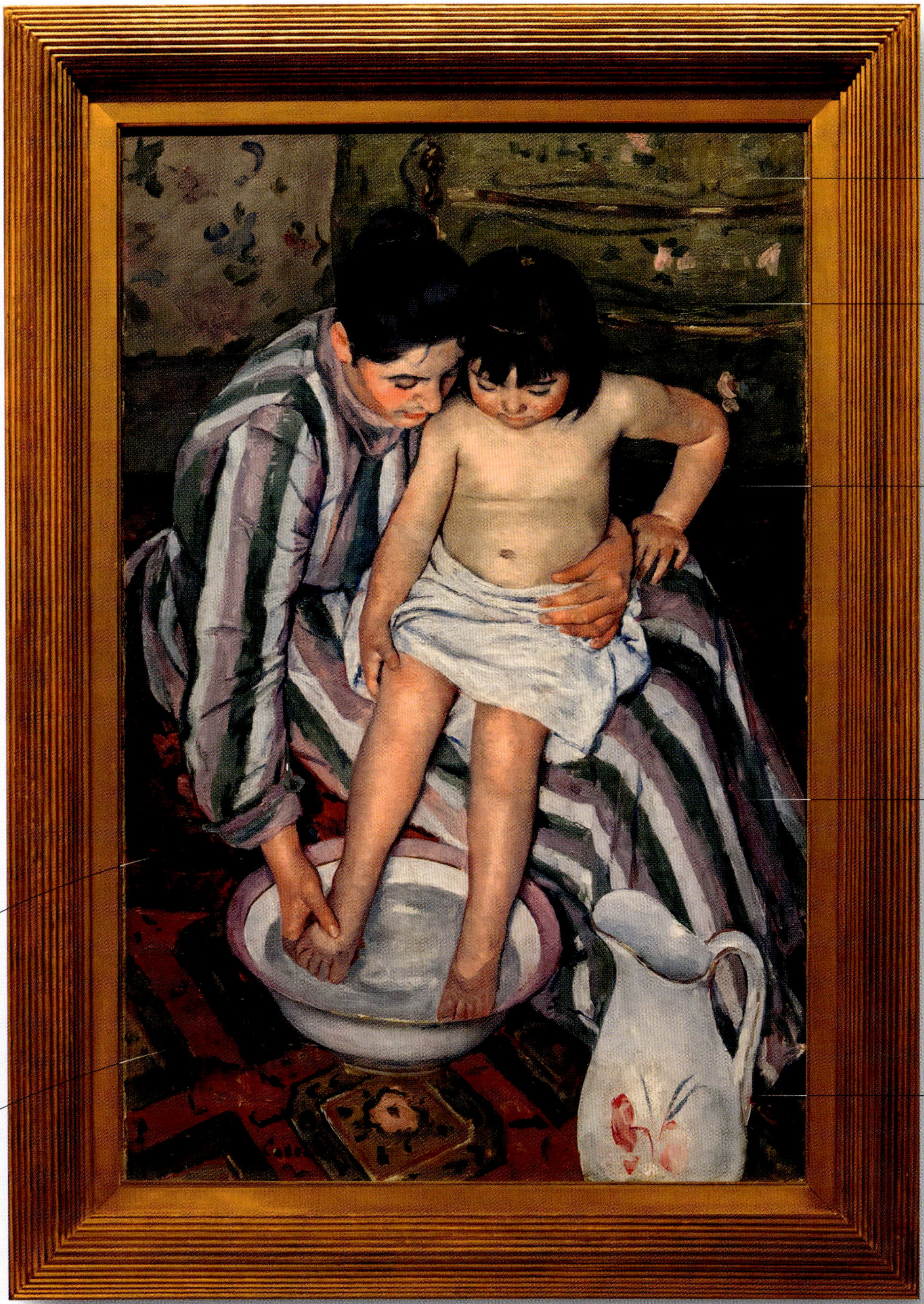

The barest of interior detail is shown behind the two figures.

Leaning together, the two heads form the focal point of the painting.

Bonds of affection between mother and child are shown by the encircling arms and gentle touch.

A simple striped dress indicates that the mother is a country woman or servant.

The details of the figures, the jug, and the bowl are boldly outlined to make them stand out against the background.

The Child's Bath

Mary Cassatt 1893, oil on canvas, 39 × 26 in (100.3 × 66.1 cm), Art Institute of Chicago, US

American Impressionist Mary Cassatt devoted much of her career to modern interpretations of the ancient theme of motherhood. *The Child's Bath* is a vibrant example of this, while also experimenting with compositional elements of Japanese art. This quiet scene of everyday life recalls images of the Virgin and Child, but above all it is a naturalistic and secular portrayal of the maternal bond.

The Butcher Shop

Lovis Corinth 1897, oil on canvas, 27 × 34 in (69 × 87 cm), Kunsthalle Bremen, Bremen, Germany

A smiling employee in a butcher shop stands in front of a row of hanging carcasses, holding a tray of meat. Because his father was a tanner, Corinth grew up surrounded by animal skins. He painted numerous genre paintings of slaughterhouses and butcher shops, subjects that were rarely depicted by artists.

The meat's fat glistens with a glossy sheen and greasy texture. It is far brighter than the man's face.

Smiling, even though he is surrounded by blood and death, the employee is proud of his work and of the products he sells.

This carcass is the most complete. The background carcasses become less animal-like and more meat-like as the eye moves left.

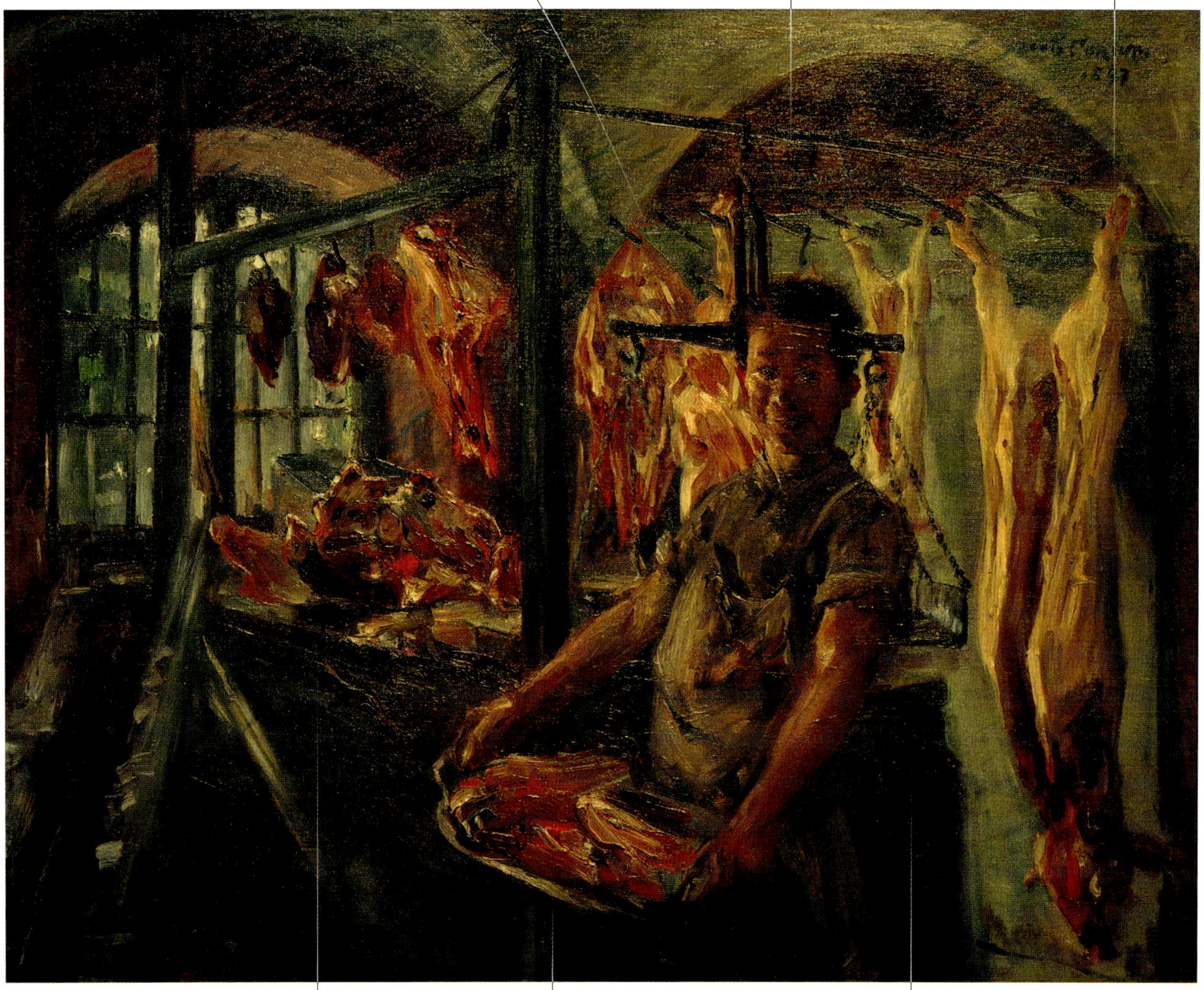

Animal heads—the cuts that clearly evoke the living animal—are not as brightly illuminated as the hanging carcasses.

The young man holds a tray containing cuts of meat for sale; the animals are now fully reduced to meat for eating.

The scales directly behind the man may refer to the scales the Archangel Michael uses to weigh souls on the Day of Judgment.

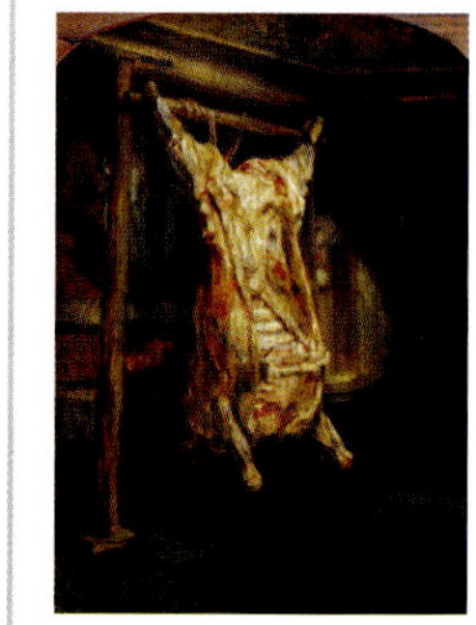

> "It was different when big animals were killed ... I would hide. But later, when I could no longer recognize the animal I had known before, I feasted my eyes on it."
>
> Lovis Corinth

Past inspiration
Animal carcasses might seem an unlikely subject matter, but it had a precedent—most notably, Rembrandt's *The Slaughtered Ox* (1655), a still-life study of a side of beef, which Corinth may have seen at the Louvre.

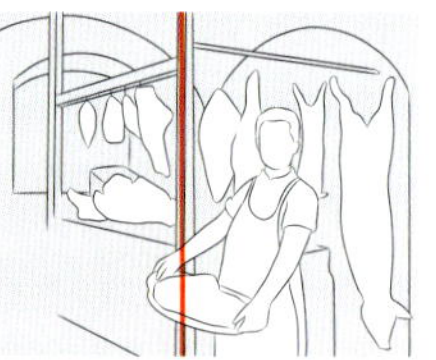

Physical separation
A pair of arches and a vertical post divide the painting into two parts: a red-toned area containing meat to the left and a green-toned area of recognizable creatures—including the young man—on the right-hand side.

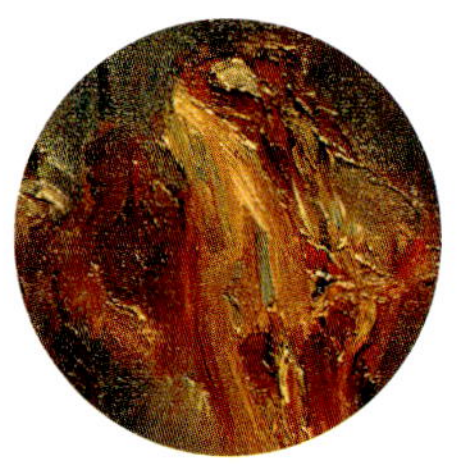

Play of light
The natural light from the shop's windows illuminates the meat in the background rather than the young man in the foreground, drawing the viewer's eye to the carcasses.

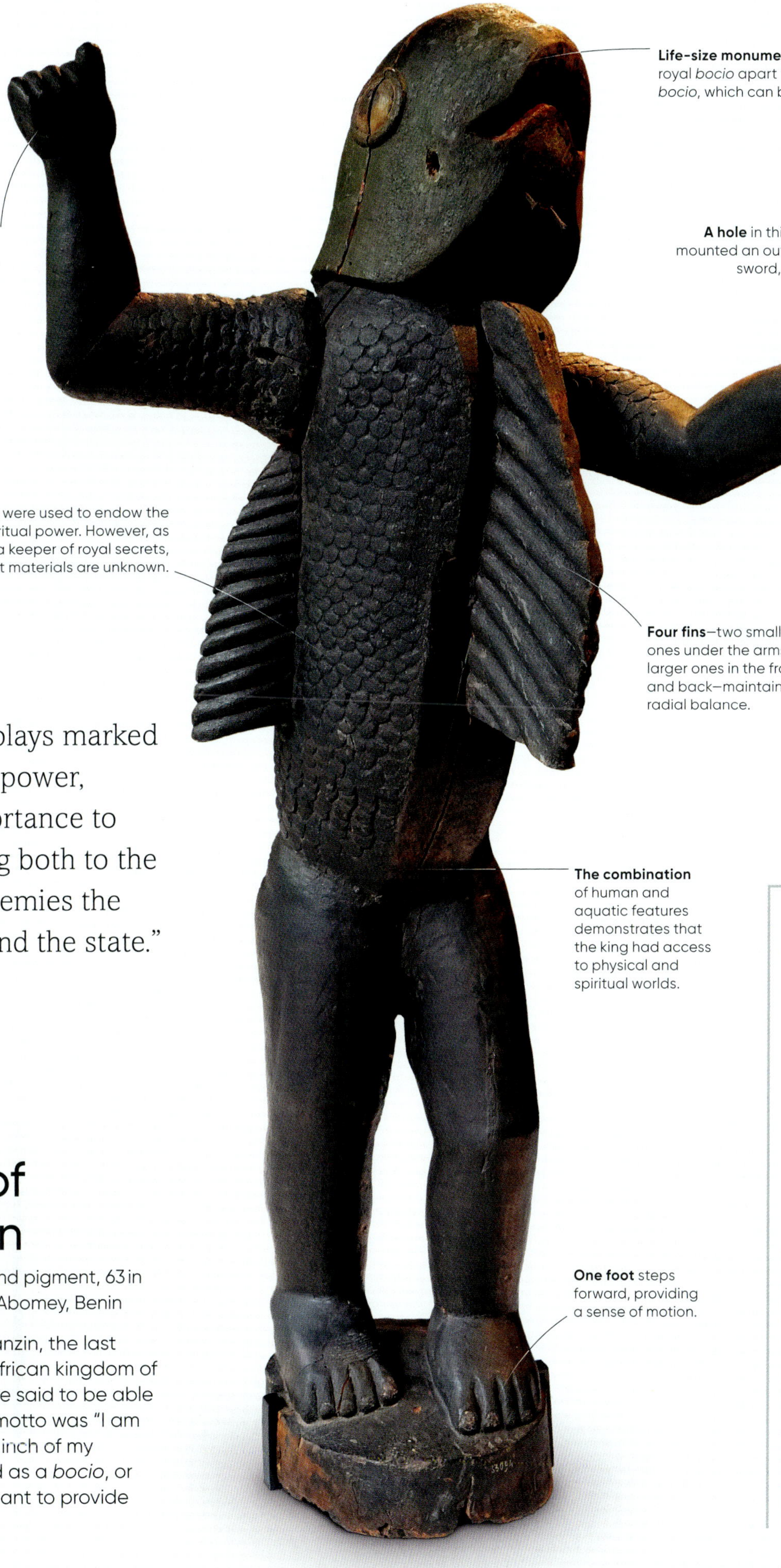

Life-size monumentality set this royal *bocio* apart from common *bocio*, which can be very small.

Aggressively clenched fists and raised arms suggest that this *bocio* may have been made for the purpose of display during warfare.

A hole in this fist once mounted an outstretched sword, since lost.

Special materials were used to endow the sculpture with spiritual power. However, as Sosa Adede was a keeper of royal secrets, the exact materials are unknown.

Four fins—two small ones under the arms and larger ones in the front and back—maintain a radial balance.

"The shark figure displays marked attributes of physical power, qualities of vital importance to the kings in conveying both to the public and to their enemies the strength of the king and the state."

Suzanne Preston Blier, 1995

The combination of human and aquatic features demonstrates that the king had access to physical and spiritual worlds.

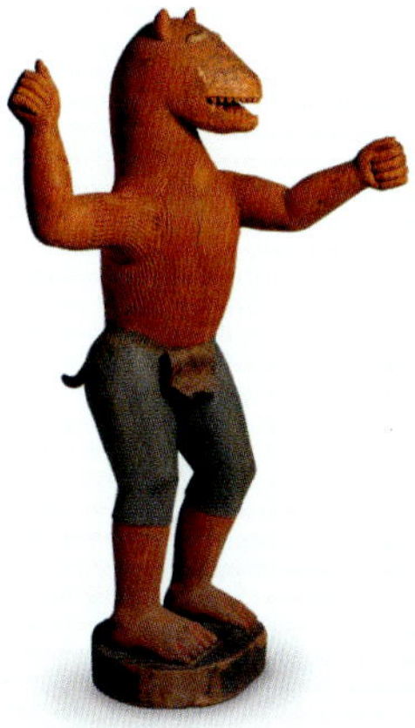

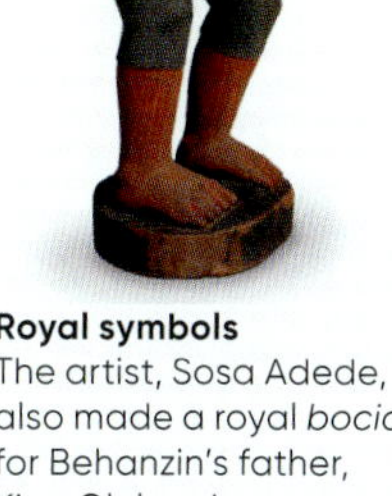

Royal symbols
The artist, Sosa Adede, also made a royal *bocio* for Behanzin's father, King Glele, whose symbol was the lion.

Repatriation
Benin's royal *bocio* were looted from the city during the French conquest of Dahomey in 1894. They were repatriated to the Republic of Benin in 2021.

Royal Bocio of King Behanzin

Sosa Adede 1890–1892, wood and pigment, 63 in (160 cm) high, Historic Museum of Abomey, Benin

This shark-man represents Behanzin, the last independent king of the West African kingdom of Dahomey. Dahomean kings were said to be able to shape-shift, and Behanzin's motto was "I am the shark: I will not relinquish an inch of my kingdom." This figure functioned as a *bocio*, or empowered figure, who was meant to provide spiritual protection.

One foot steps forward, providing a sense of motion.

The Gulf Stream

Winslow Homer 1899, oil on canvas, 28 × 49 in (71.4 × 124.8 cm), Metropolitan Museum of Art, New York, US

A man is beset by danger in Homer's depiction of a lone sailor on a badly damaged boat at sea. Sharks circle below, waves rise up behind, and a waterspout looms in the distance. It is not coincidental that this sailor is Black—the painting is thought to be a metaphorical representation of the perils that continued to face Black Americans after the abolition of slavery, a common theme of Homer's. The meaning of the ship on the horizon is unclear—is it offered to provide hope that this sailor will be rescued or is it sailing past, either unaware of the man's fate or unwilling to help?

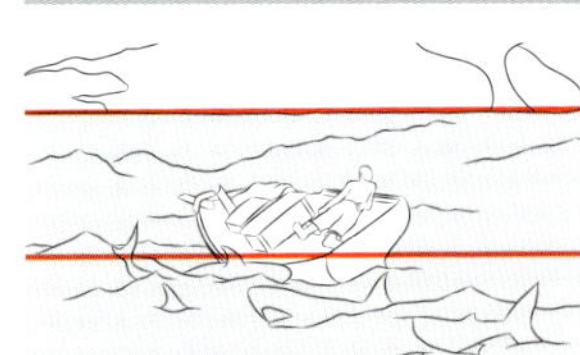

Triple threat
The painting is divided into three roughly horizontal sections: a stormy sky, the face of a wave, and a darker, shark-infested sea in the foreground.

All-encompassing sea
Blues and grays dominate the image, making the browns and whites of the small boat stand out.

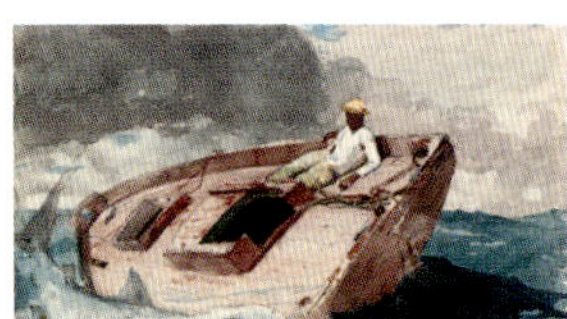

Preparatory work
This oil painting was based on a watercolor Homer had previously completed. The watercolor was inspired by sketches of a distressed boat that Homer had made in 1885.

> "If there is a God of the Gulf it is a God of water, not waves but water, all the globe turned water pocked rising and falling tireless, forever."
>
> Joyce Carol Oates, 1987

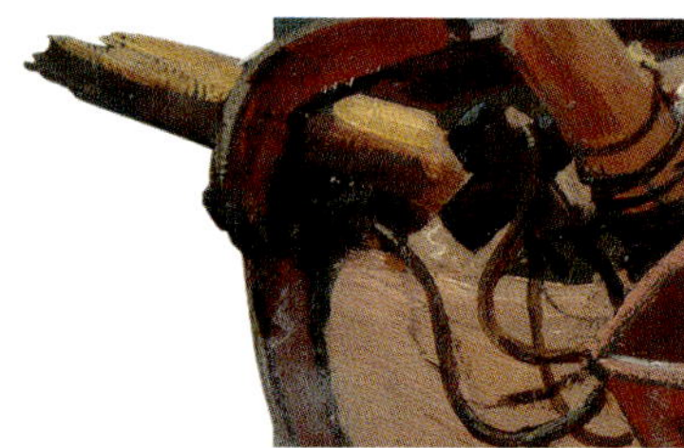

A cross is visible near the boat's broken mast, perhaps hinting that this boat will become the sailor's grave.

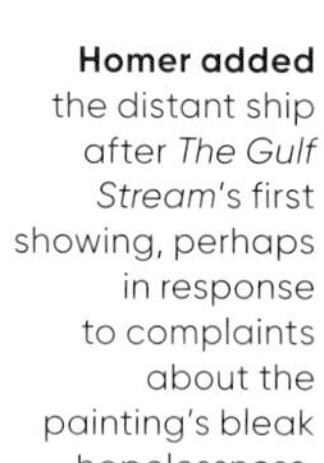

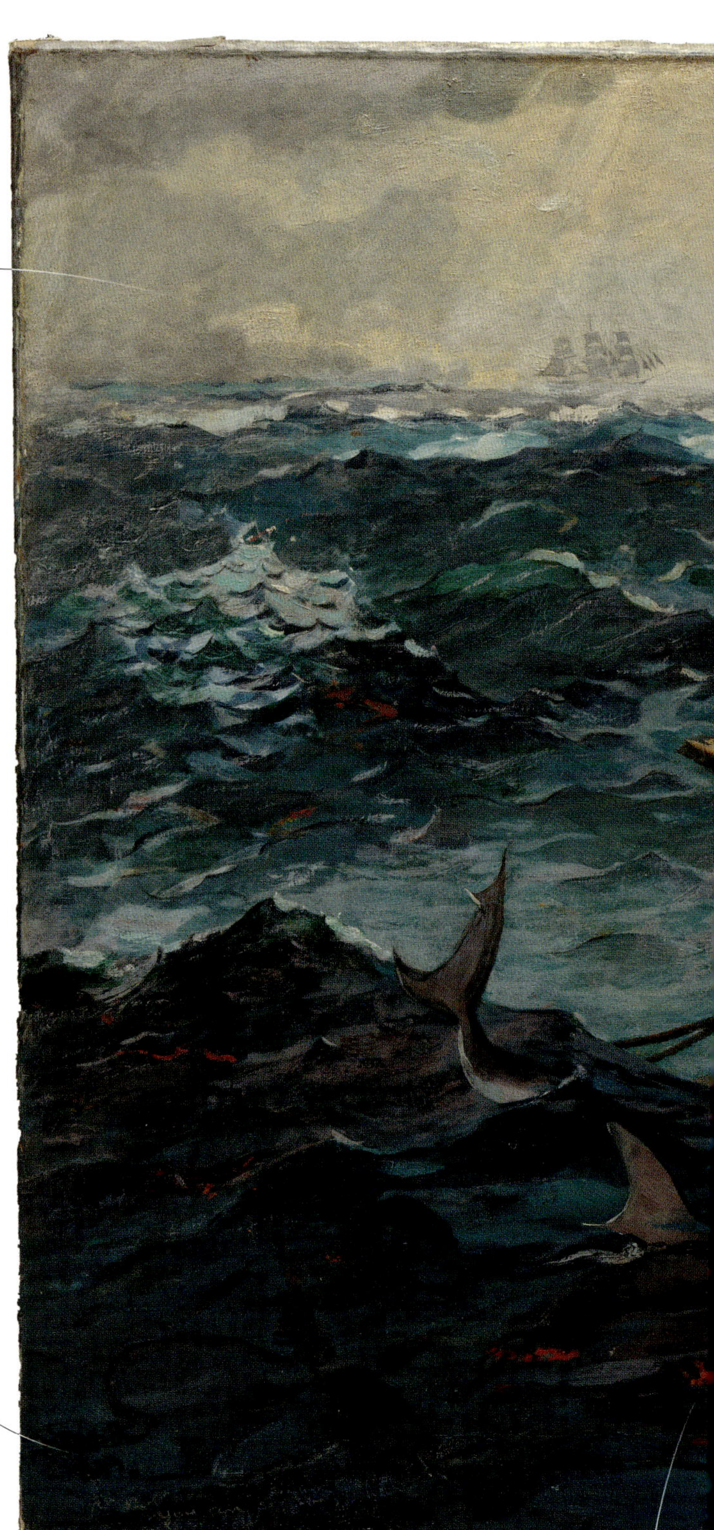

Homer added the distant ship after *The Gulf Stream*'s first showing, perhaps in response to complaints about the painting's bleak hopelessness.

Homer wrote in tiny script below his signature, "At 12 feet from the picture you can see it." He wanted the painting to be viewed from a specific distance.

Red splatters in the water suggest the sharks have already claimed a sailor or perhaps foreshadow what will soon occur.

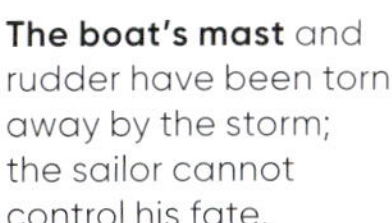

The boat's mast and rudder have been torn away by the storm; the sailor cannot control his fate.

Powerful waves might toss the sailor overboard. Homer associated this work with *Slave Ship*, J. M. W. Turner's painting of enslaved people who had been thrown overboard.

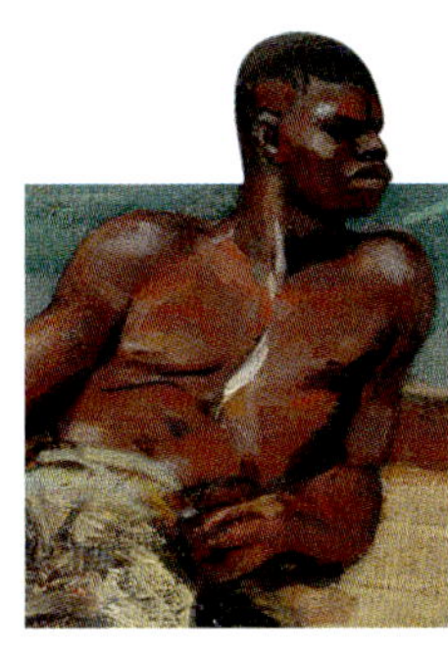

The sailor appears strangely stoic, worn down by his struggles or perhaps resigned to a fate that he has long anticipated.

Homer increased the size of the waterspout after *The Gulf Stream* was first shown, likely to emphasize the sailor's peril.

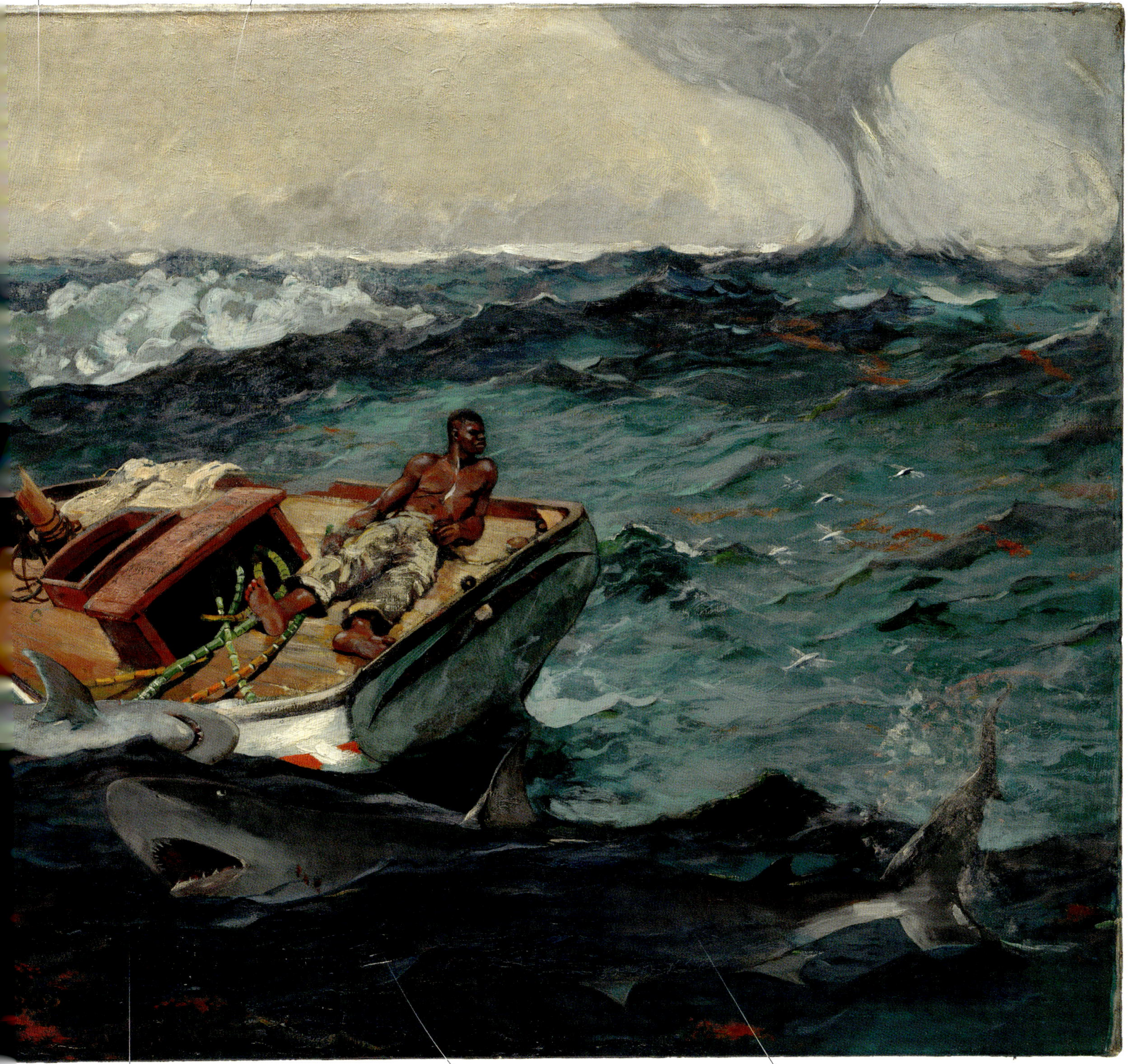

Homer added the fallen sail after *The Gulf Stream* was originally shown, perhaps to represent the sailor's funeral shroud.

Stalks of sugar cane on the deck act as a reminder of the hard life of Black people working on plantations.

The boat is labeled "Anna" and "Key West"—indicating that this is an American man.

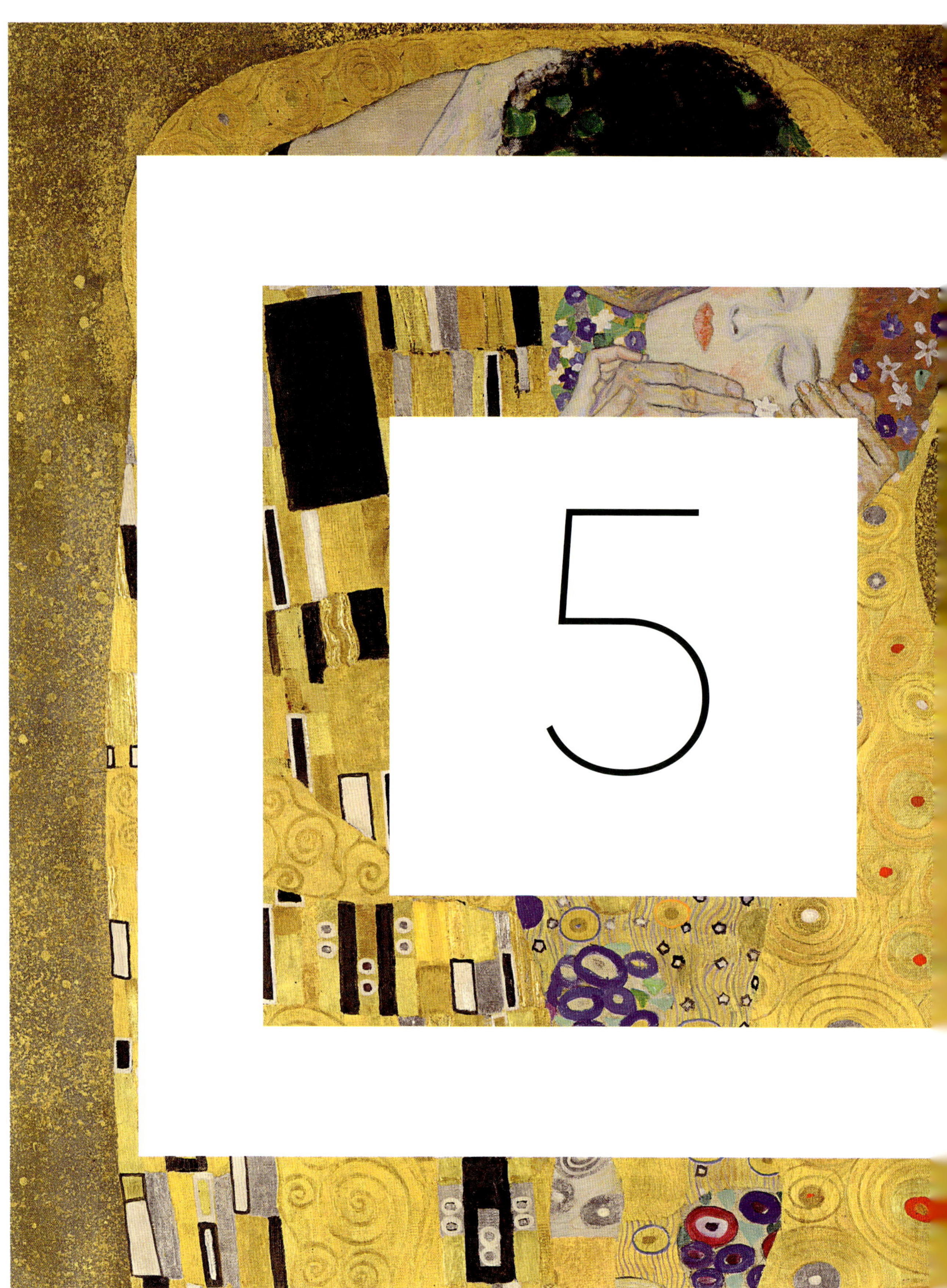

5

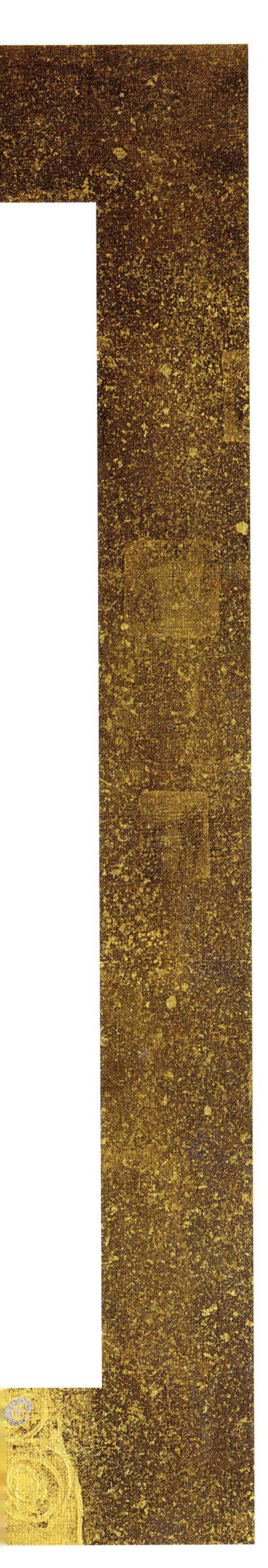

Towards abstraction

1900 - 1945

Interior with Woman at Piano, Strandgade 30

Vilhelm Hammershøi 1901, oil on canvas, 22 × 18 in (55.9 × 44.8 cm), private collection, New York, US

Hammershøi's wife Ida sits at a piano with her back to the viewer, her face unseen, in a somber painting that portrays loneliness and the unknowability of other people, even in marriage. The room is portrayed with measured distance and uniform structure. Hammershøi often painted the interior of his Copenhagen apartment, creating peaceful but unsettling works of solitude and stillness.

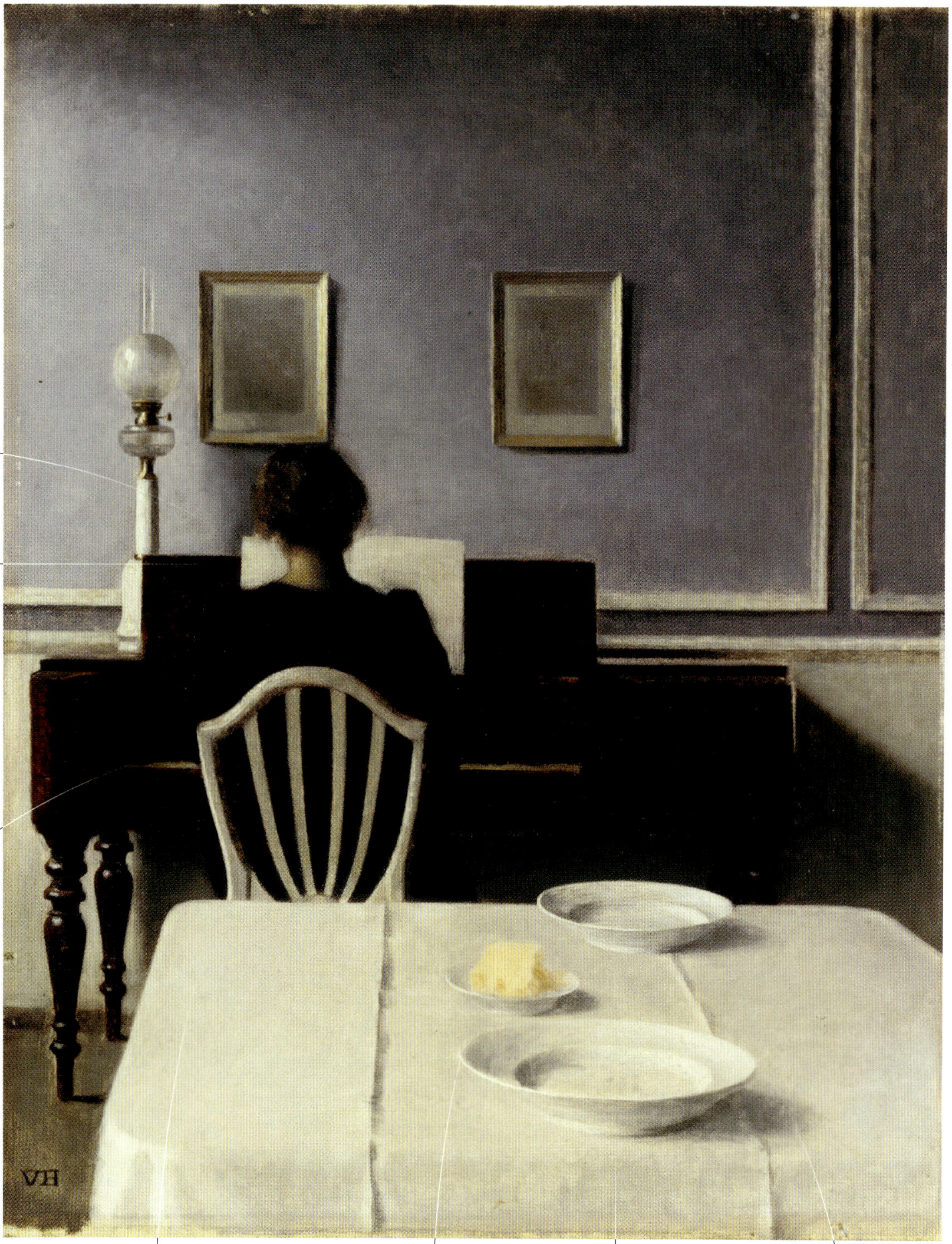

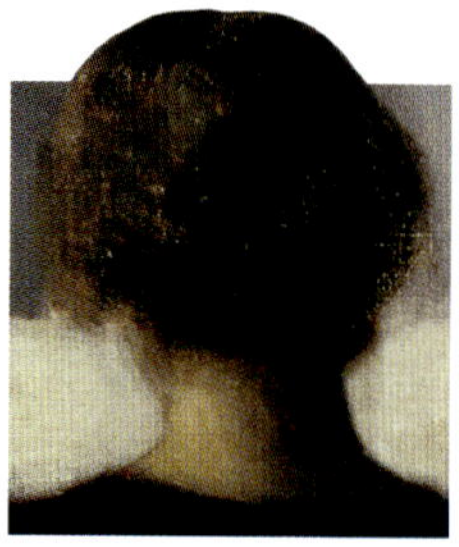

Ida's head fits perfectly between the bottom of the picture frame and the top of the piano, visually enclosing her.

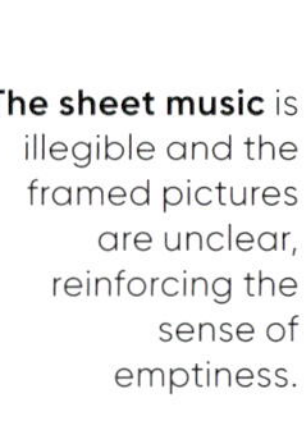

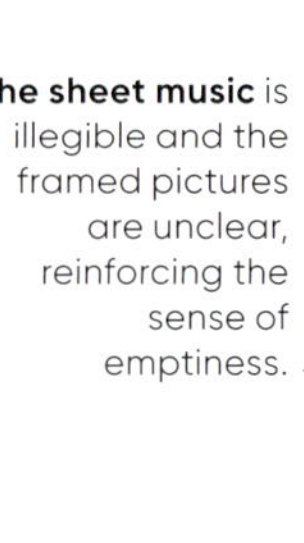

The sheet music is illegible and the framed pictures are unclear, reinforcing the sense of emptiness.

The nape of Ida's neck was "Hammershøi's favorite erotic allusion," according to one art historian.

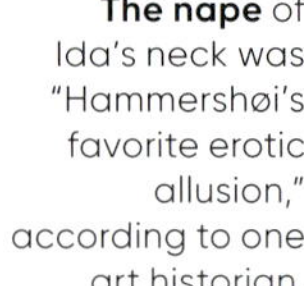

A black dress hides Ida's figure, while her face is unseen. She is absorbed in playing the piano.

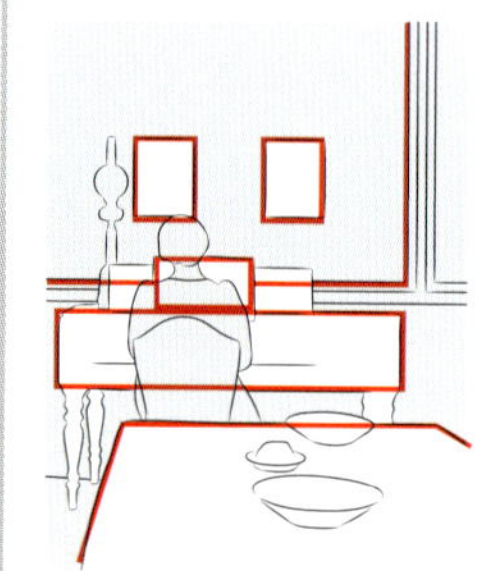

Confinement
The painting seems to enclose Ida within an array of confining squares and rectangles: the pictures above her, the table behind her, the sheet music, the piano, and details of the wall in front of her.

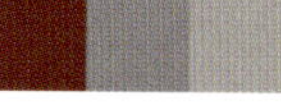

Muted color
The melancholic character of the painting is reflected in the limited color palette. The blue-gray walls convey a somber mood. Even the sunlight illuminating the space adds no warmth.

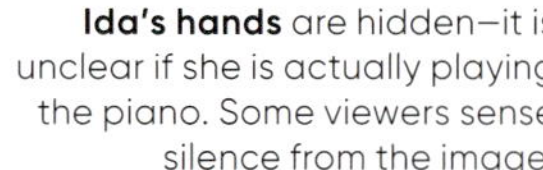

Ida's hands are hidden—it is unclear if she is actually playing the piano. Some viewers sense silence from the image.

The warm yellow of the butter makes the rest of the space seem cold in comparison.

Two plates sit on the table, suggesting that a couple shares this home.

The plates are out of alignment in this otherwise highly structured image, creating a sense of unease.

Open Window, Collioure

Henri Matisse 1905, oil on canvas, 22 × 18 in (55.3 × 46 cm), National Gallery of Art, Washington, D.C., US

This view from an open window in the coastal town of Collioure in the south of France depicts a group of sail boats on a sunny day. The striking choice of non-naturalistic colors, such as the pink ripples on the water, was a hallmark of the short-lived Fauvist movement, which Matisse helped develop.

Matisse chose colors in complementary pairs, such as turquoise and fuchsia (top left- and right-hand corners of the canvas).

The window is positioned off-center to the left, which gives the scene an informal feel.

The balcony and window create a series of frames within frames.

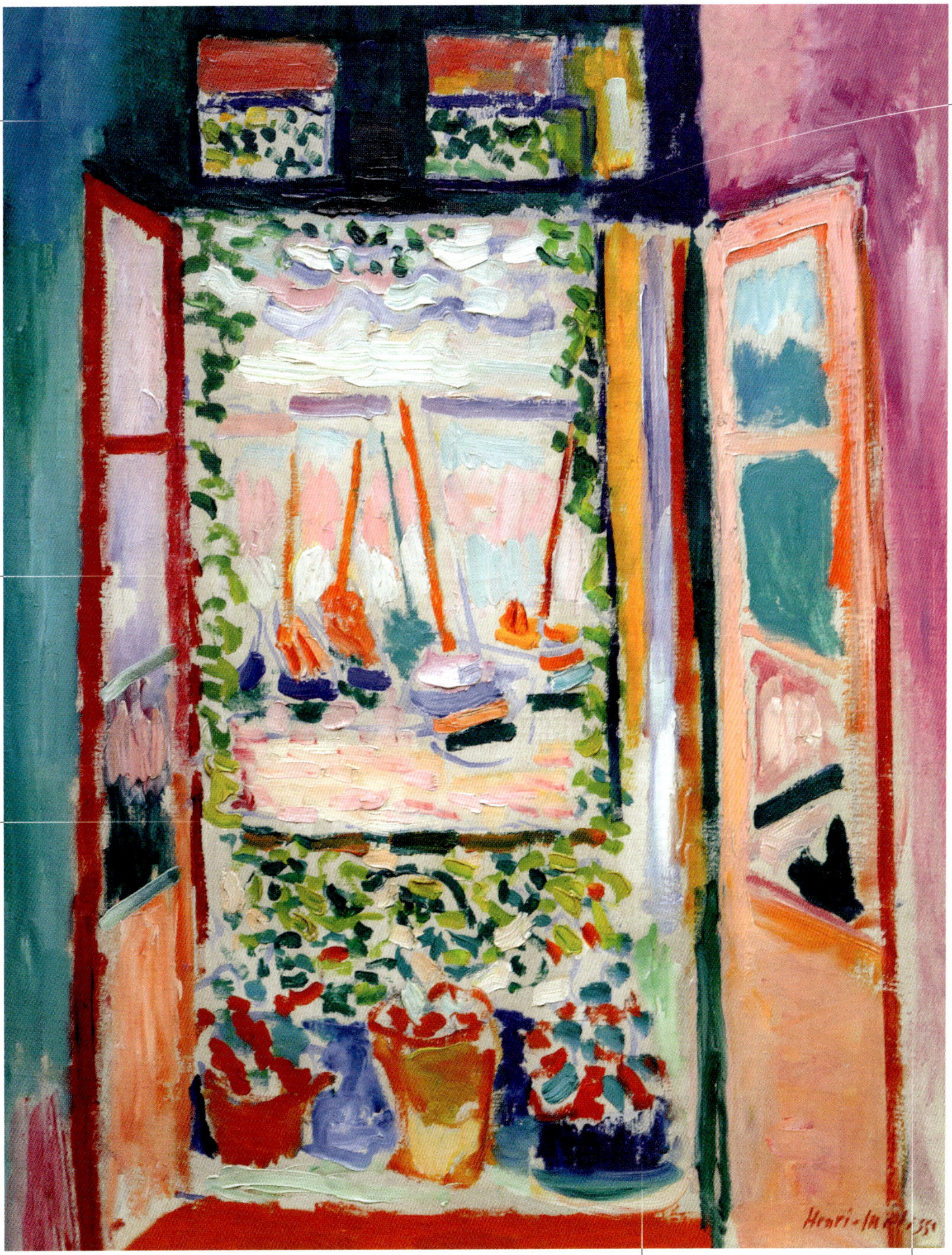

Matisse often used open windows as frames, adapting a visual strategy used since the Renaissance.

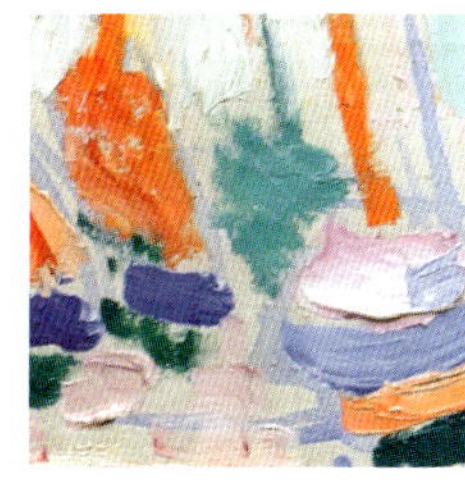

The light, vibrant colors of the outside world appear inviting. They contrast with the darker tones inside the room.

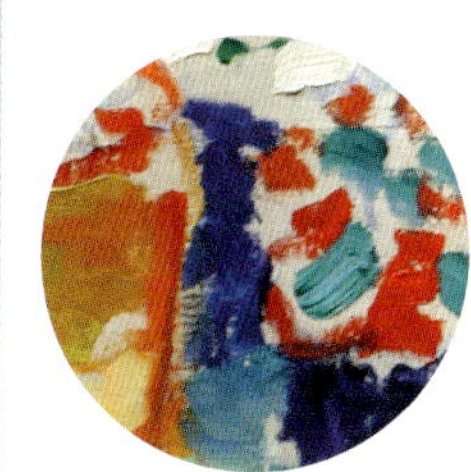

Trademarks
Matisse used a variety of brush marks, including blended strokes, wavy lines, and thick, staccato-like dabs.

Fauvism and color
Emerging in France in 1904–1905, Fauvism was led by Matisse, Derain, de Vlaminck, and Braque. The Fauves and Matisse used intense colors to portray emotions. In his 1914 work *French Window at Collioure*, Matisse painted the view as a black rectangle, reflecting a world overshadowed by the start of World War I.

> "When I put a green, it is not grass. When I put a blue, it is not the sky."
>
> Henri Matisse

The contrasting colors of the flowerpots at the bottom of the painting pick up the color combinations at the top.

Some patches of the canvas are left bare, emphasizing that this is an artwork rather than an actual window.

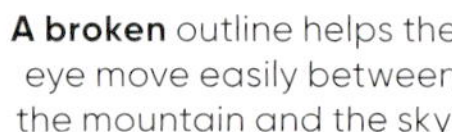

A broken outline helps the eye move easily between the mountain and the sky.

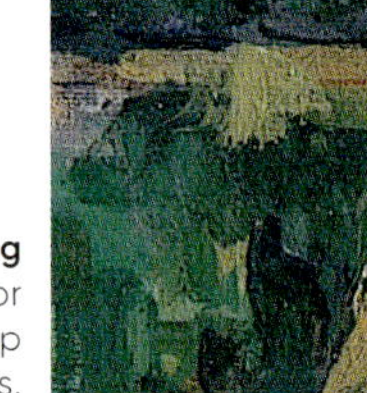

Contrasting patches of color represent a rooftop against the trees.

The solid face of the mountain is built up with carefully controlled contrasts in color and tone combined with directional brushstrokes.

The double outline produces a "vibration" along the edge of the mountain, as if it is being seen in very bright light.

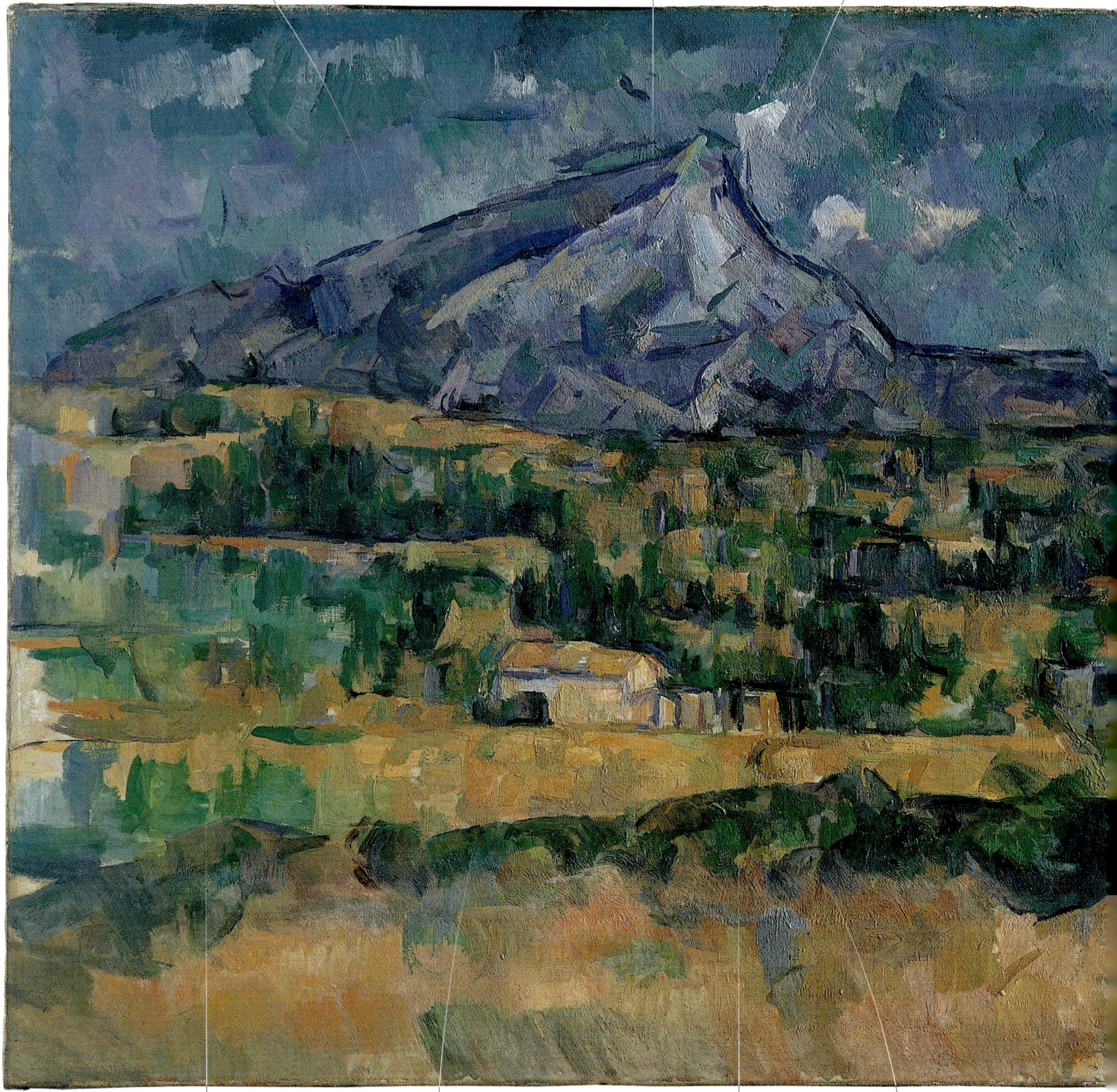

Blocks of color are used in an architectural way to build the structure of the landscape.

A farmhouse is recognizable, but no details are included. It is just part of the overall pattern.

Rows of emphatic brushstrokes emphasize the flatness of the canvas, yet the land also appears to recede toward the mountain.

Small patches of different colors are used to convey the curved form of the rock.

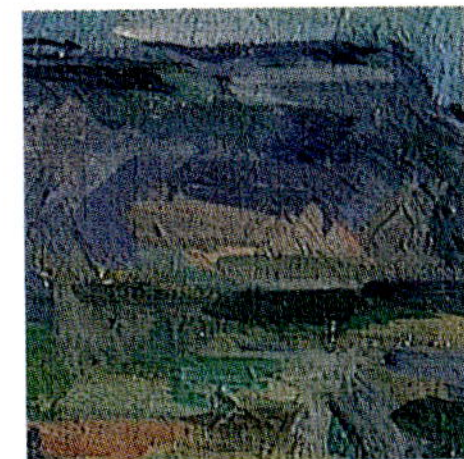

Brushstrokes become smaller as the landscape recedes into the distance.

Saturated sky colors echo those in the landscape, removing any sense of depth.

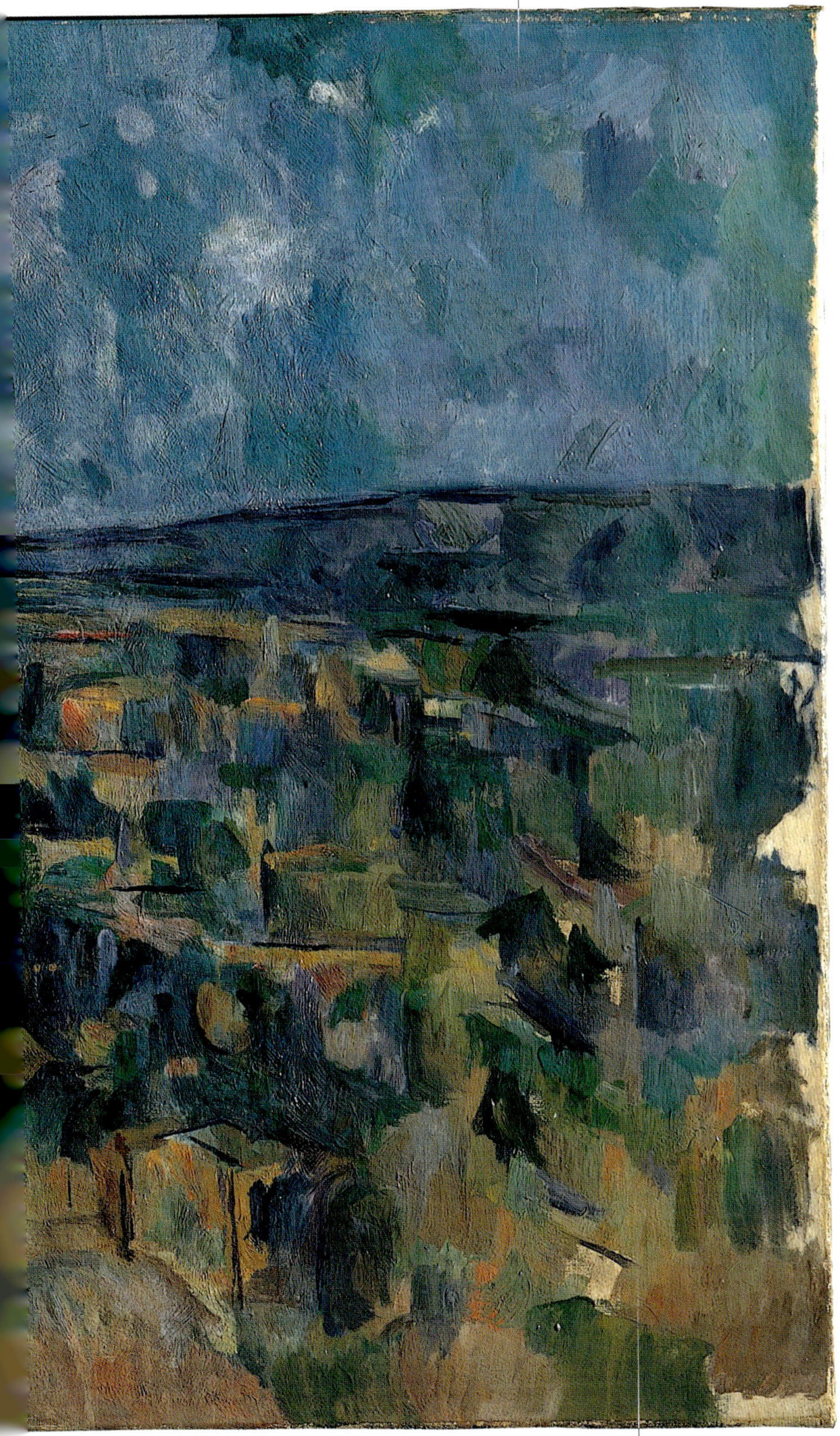

Cézanne added an extra strip of canvas on the right-hand side to broaden the composition.

Mont Sainte-Victoire

Paul Cézanne c. 1902–1906, oil on canvas, 23 × 38 in (57.2 × 97.2 cm), Metropolitan Museum of Art, New York, US

In his later years, Cézanne returned to this view of Mont Sainte-Victoire rising above the Provençal landscape many times. He was determined to record both his painstakingly accurate observations of the subject and his emotional response to it in a way that produces a pleasing and harmonious painting. He used rows of small, overlaid brushstrokes to structure the painting, building up an overall pattern that captures the solidity and permanence of the landscape. Regarded by many as the father of modern art, Cézanne had a profound influence on younger artists, such as the Cubists.

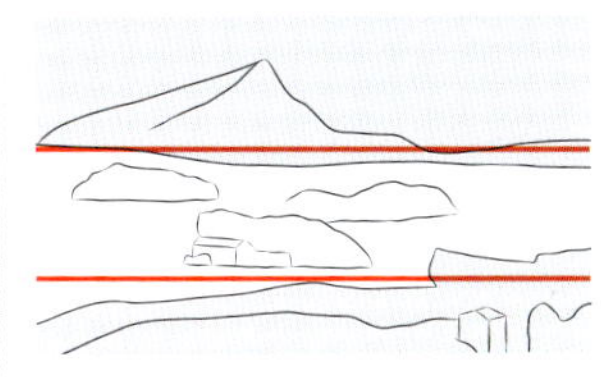

Composition
The canvas is divided into three horizontal bands that move progressively into the distance. The lowest features warm colors; the middle one alternating warm and cool colors; and the top band uses cool colors.

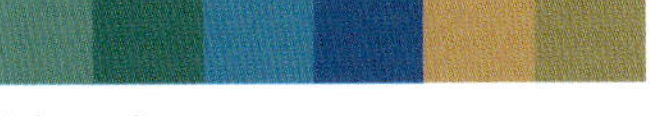

Color palette
Predominantly strong greens—viridian and emerald—alternate with vibrant blues and subdued earth colors. They play against each other to produce a harmonious whole.

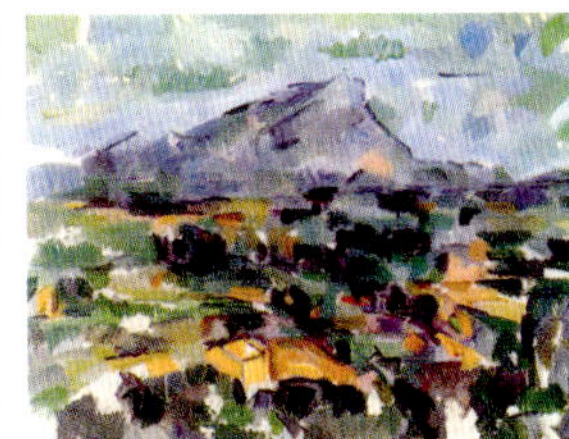

Evolving view
Cézanne painted the view of Mont Sainte-Victoire more than 60 times, at different times of the year, in oils and watercolors. The paintings reveal how the artist's style developed. This example, from 1904–1906, shows his movement toward even more abstract forms.

> "One must see one's model clearly and feel it exactly right and then express oneself with distinction and force."
>
> Paul Cézanne, 1904

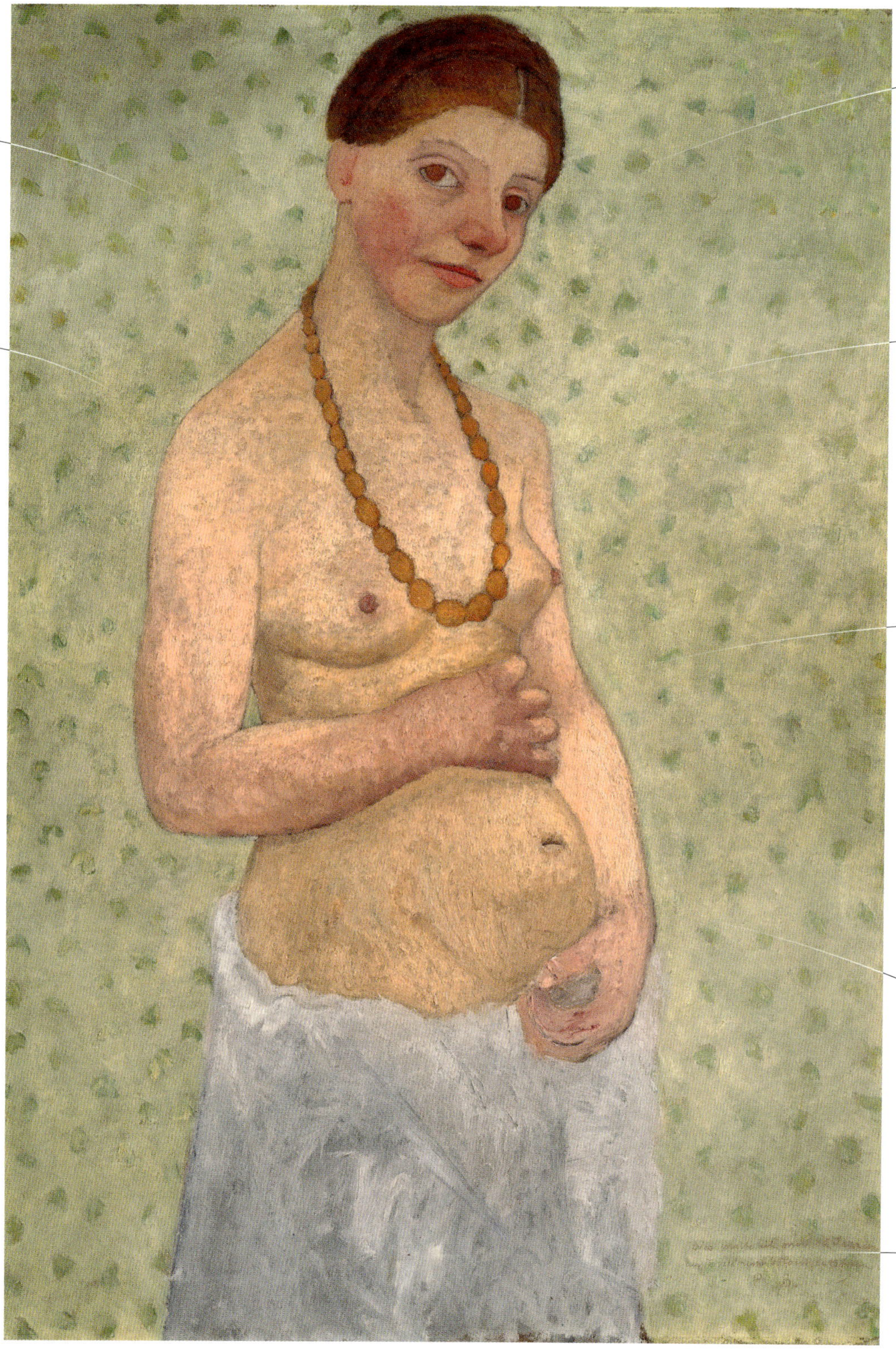

Modersohn-Becker is not shown in a conventionally feminine pose. The result is not the type of erotic nude favored by male painters.

Simplicity of form is a hallmark of Modersohn-Becker's work. It allowed her to show the true character of the subject.

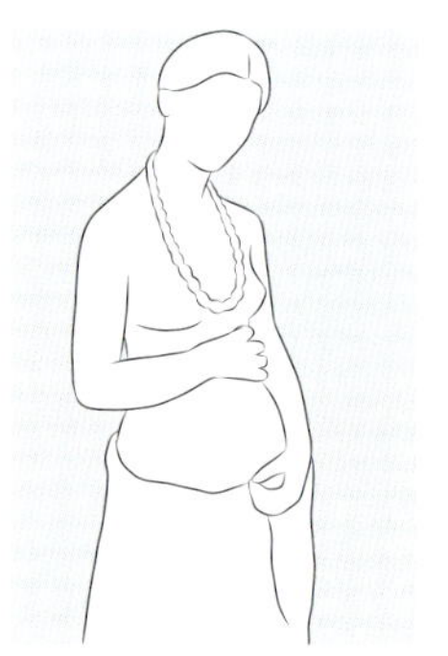

Artistic heritage The three-quarter-length nude is common in art. Here, Modersohn-Becker recalls the depictions of Venus, with drapery around her hips.

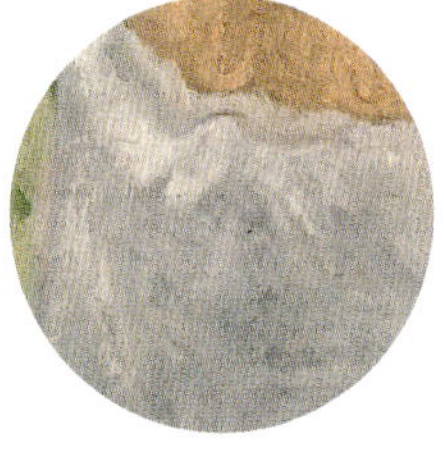

Surface texture Modersohn-Becker built up areas on the canvas with paint, then scratched into it with the other end of the brush to create a sculptural quality. This emphasizes the shape of the belly.

The gaze is direct, but not aggressive. She acknowledges the viewer while still seeming introspective.

Glowing colors were inspired by those of other avant-garde artists working in Paris such as Paul Cézanne, Paul Gauguin, and Vincent van Gogh.

Her reddened hands and face proclaim her to be a working woman, an artist, whose face and hands have encountered work and weather.

Modersohn-Becker depicts herself as being pregnant (she was not at the time) to express her potential as an artist.

An inscription says: "I painted this at age 30 / on my 6th wedding day / P.B." By omitting the letter M from her signature, she wished to signal her freedom from her husband, Otto Modersohn.

Self-Portrait on Her 6th Wedding Anniversary

Paula Modersohn-Becker 1906, oil on canvas, 40 × 28 in (101.8 × 70.2 cm), Paula Modersohn-Becker Museum, Bremen, Germany

This life-size painting is said to be the first nude self-portrait by a woman. Although its title commemorates the artist's wedding anniversary, she had in fact just left her husband and moved to Paris.

The Ten Largest, Group IV no. 3, Youth

Hilma af Klint 1907, tempera on paper, mounted on canvas, 124 × 92 in (315 × 234 cm), Hilma af Klint Foundation, Stockholm, Sweden

In a vibrant composition filled with spirals and circular motifs, af Klint depicts youth. It is part of a series, *The Ten Largest*, in which she explored life's stages, from childhood to old age. Guided by transcendental spiritualism, af Klint claimed that she was commissioned to paint the series by a spirit guide.

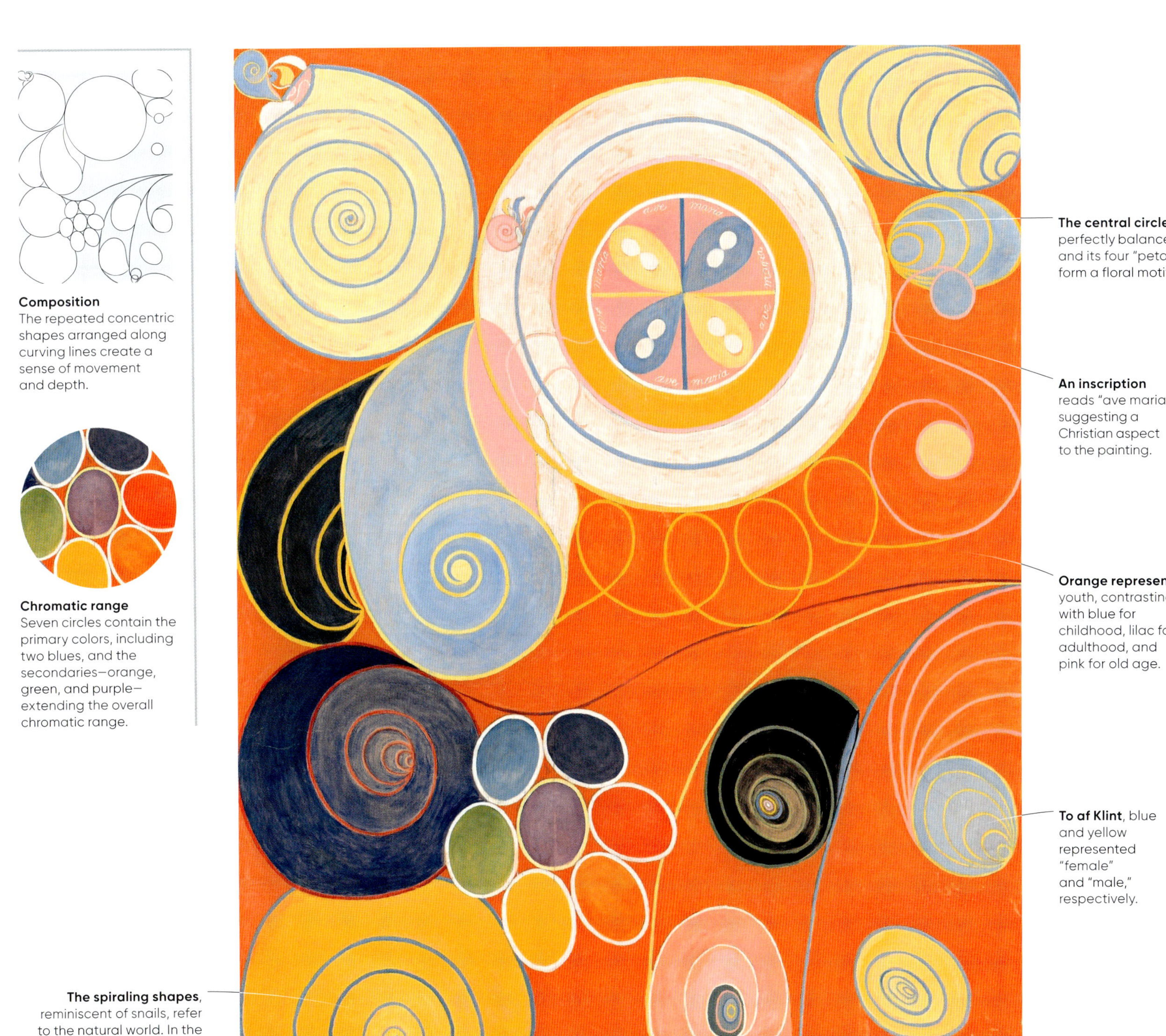

Composition
The repeated concentric shapes arranged along curving lines create a sense of movement and depth.

Chromatic range
Seven circles contain the primary colors, including two blues, and the secondaries—orange, green, and purple—extending the overall chromatic range.

The central circle is perfectly balanced, and its four "petals" form a floral motif.

An inscription reads "ave maria," suggesting a Christian aspect to the painting.

Orange represents youth, contrasting with blue for childhood, lilac for adulthood, and pink for old age.

To af Klint, blue and yellow represented "female" and "male," respectively.

The spiraling shapes, reminiscent of snails, refer to the natural world. In the artist's visual language, they evoke growth and evolution.

The Kiss

Gustav Klimt 1907–1908, oil and gold leaf on canvas, 71 × 71 in (180 × 180 cm), Belvedere Museum, Vienna, Austria

A man kisses a kneeling woman on a hill of wildflowers below a starry sky, both figures clad in gold. Some see in *The Kiss* the transportive power of romantic love—perhaps even representing that between Klimt himself and fashion designer Emilie Flöge—but others consider the woman's response ambivalent.

The man kisses the woman—but she does not kiss him back.

The gold around the couple's heads has been compared to a halo, as in Byzantine icons.

The woman's eyes are closed, her expression passive. It is not clear if she is lost in bliss or powerless, even lifeless.

The man's thick neck suggests strength and virility; the viewer sees little else of his body or face.

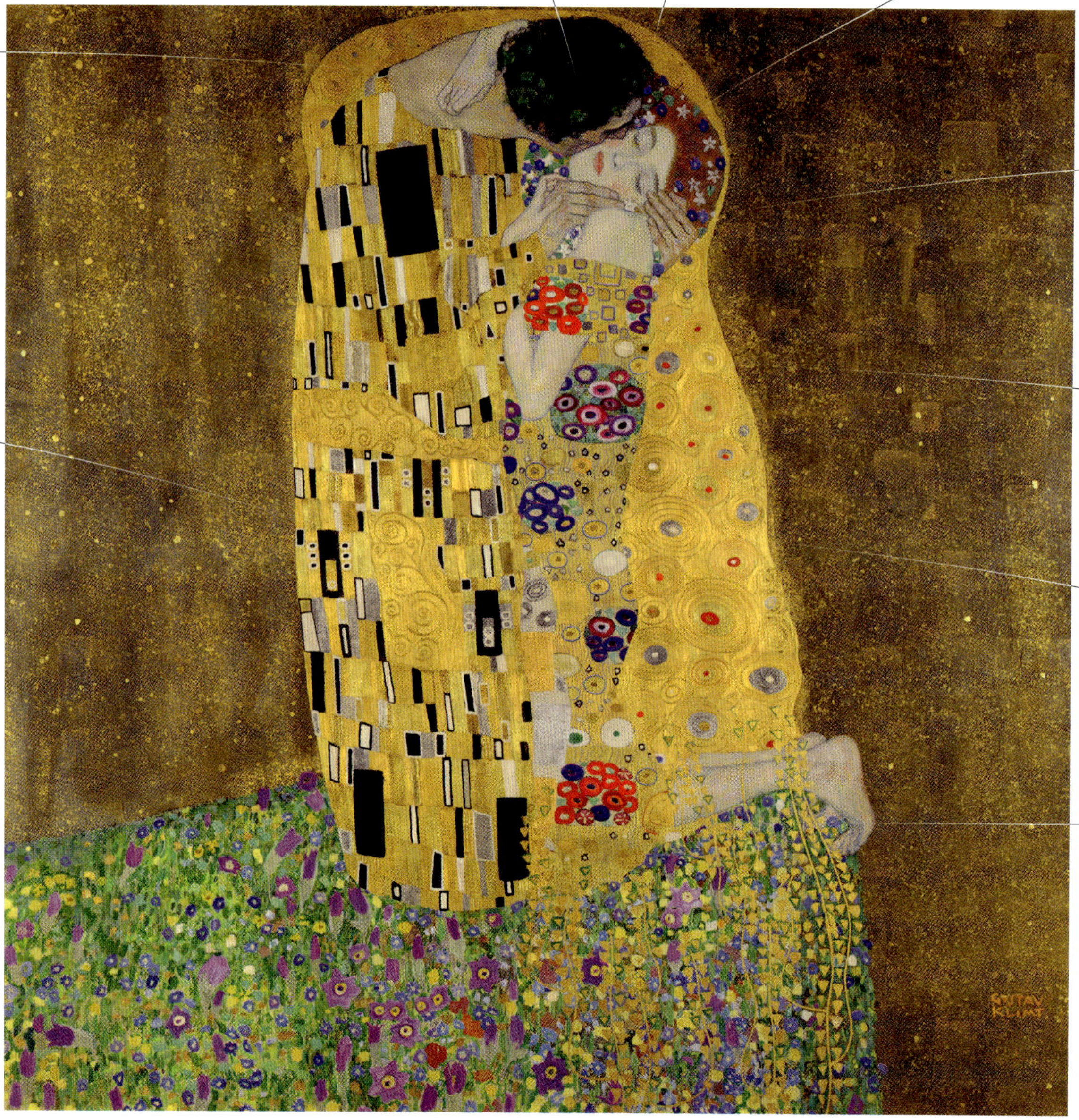

The woman's face and the lovers' hands are realistically drawn, contrasting with the abstract bodies and background.

Curved, feminine shapes embellish the woman's dress.

Vertical rectangles, considered to be a masculine or even phallic shape, decorate the man's robe.

The couple's golden clothing melds, suggesting the union of lovers.

According to some theories, the gold "vines" allude to Daphne, the nymph in Greek mythology who turns into a tree.

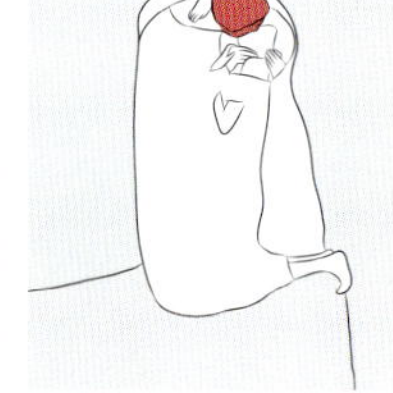

Composition
The man's head sits extremely high in the composition by the standards of European art. This might reflect the influence of Japanese woodblock prints on Klimt's art.

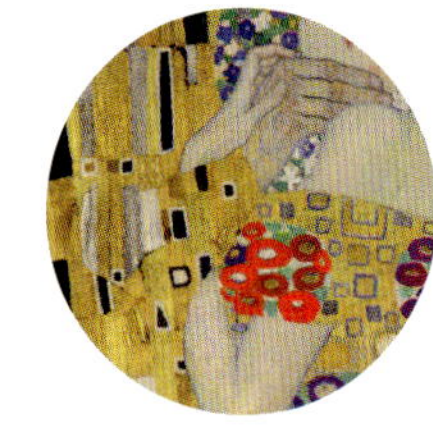

2D and 3D
Klimt deliberately painted his figures flat, but created physical depth by building up the surface before applying gold leaf.

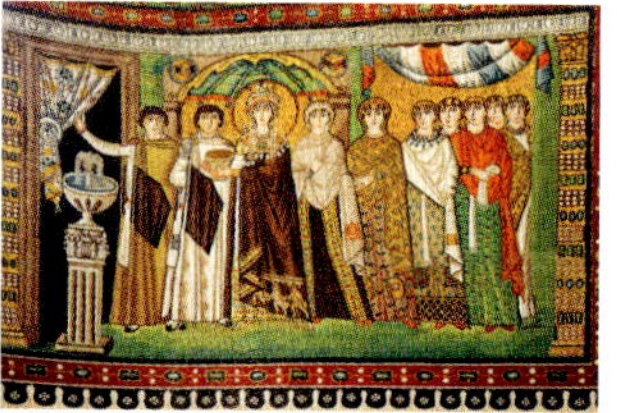

Golden inspiration
Klimt is known for his lavish use of gold leaf. He was probably inspired by the Byzantine mosaics in the church of San Vitale, Ravenna, Italy, which he visited twice in 1903.

My Wife and Daughters in the Garden

Joaquín Sorolla 1910, oil on canvas, 65 × 81 in (166 × 206 cm), private collection

At the center of Sorolla's composition, his wife, Clotilde, holds the hand of their youngest daughter. At the same time, Clotilde looks toward their eldest daughter, who looks out at the viewer. Sorolla's characteristic manipulation of light enhances the tenderness of this intimate family portrait, completed by the family dog.

Sorolla conveys his daughters' youth through their rosy cheeks, the roses in their hair, and the dappled light reflected from their faces.

Clotilde, the artist's wife, is depicted in profile, concealing her facial expression and thus placing more emphasis on the beauty of their daughters.

The curve of the bench forms a delicate cradle around the women, giving them a harmonious unity.

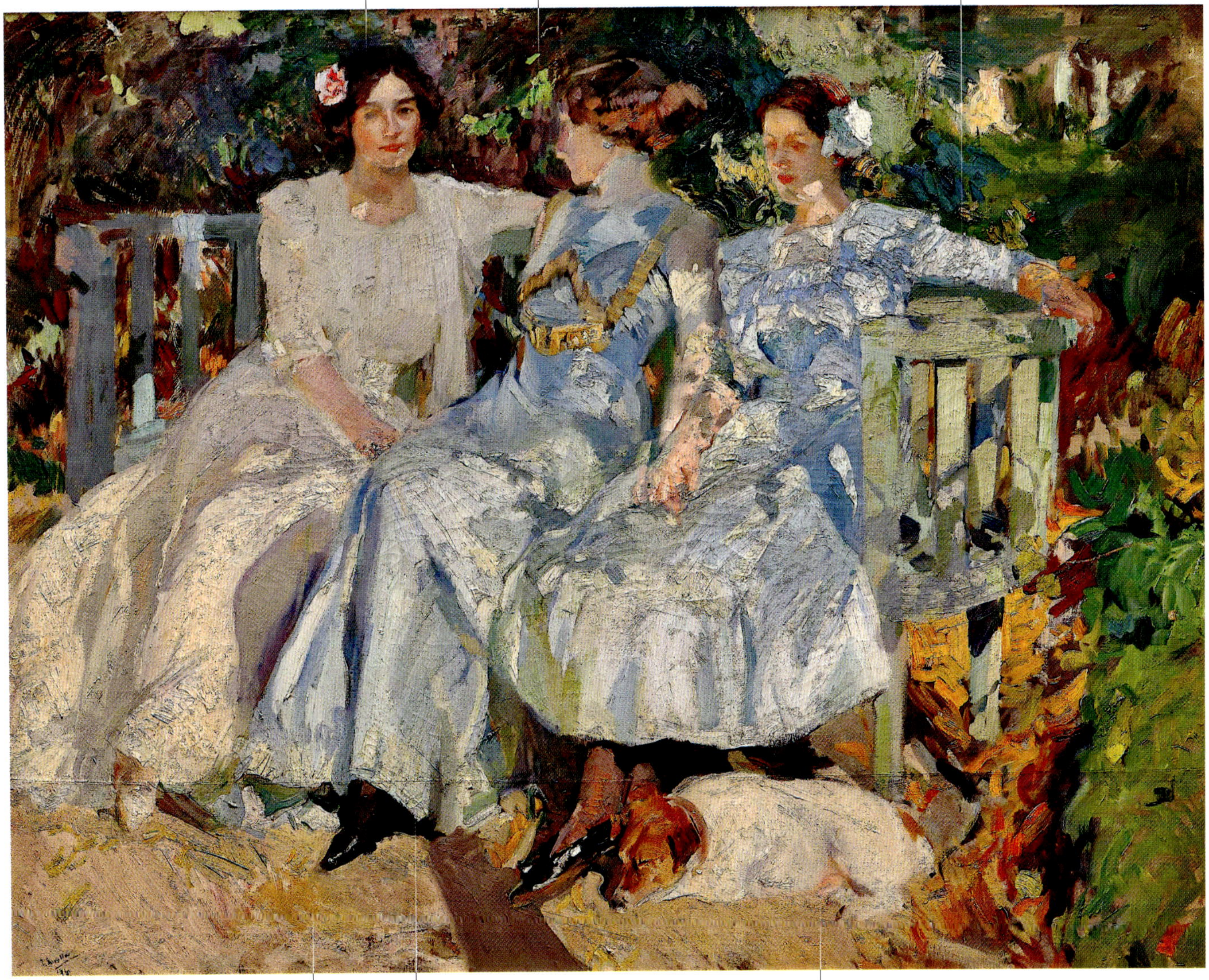

Sorolla's composition subtly refers to the Three Graces in Greek mythology, intertwining personal sentiment with art-historical allusion.

The vibrant colors of the women's dresses and the luscious greenery contribute to the composition's overall sense of joy.

A dog lies sleeping at the feet of the artist's youngest daughter, evoking a sense of tranquility as well as symbolizing family loyalty.

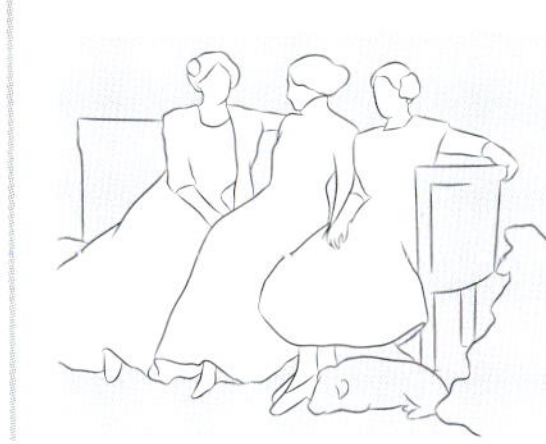

Close cropping
The tight, almost photographic, framing contributes to the painting's profound sense of close relationships.

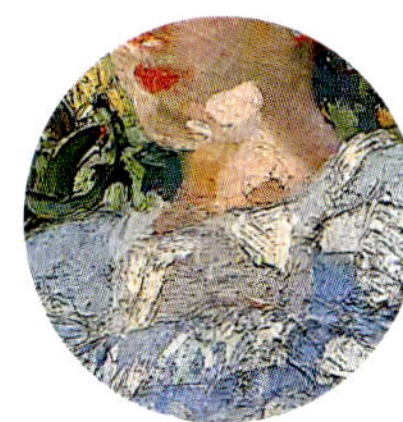

Dappled light
The fluid brushstrokes and manipulation of light through color capture the dappled sunlight as it shines through the trees and onto the women.

> "I do not know any brush that contains as much sun."
>
> Henri Rochefort, 1909

Portraits

Classical artists took an idealized approach to portraiture, though later Roman art displayed more naturalism. In Renaissance Italy, artists tended to idealize their subject, while Northern European painters took a more realistic approach. Artists became increasingly interested in conveying the character of their sitters, and even status-symbol portraits conveyed psychological insight. In the 18th and 19th centuries, artists tended to romanticize their subjects. From the late 19th century, portraits showed an increasing degree of psychological insight.

1

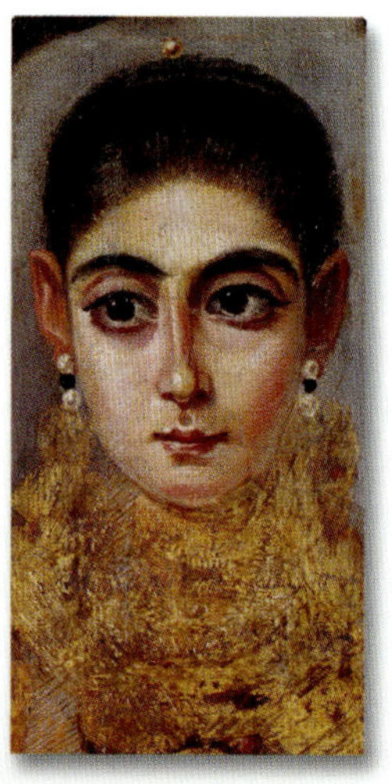

2

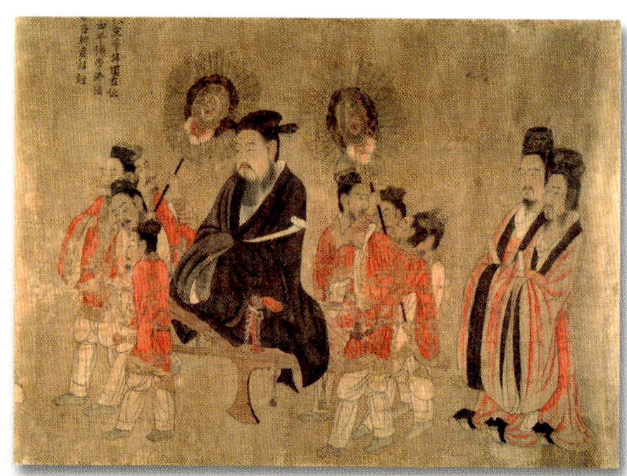

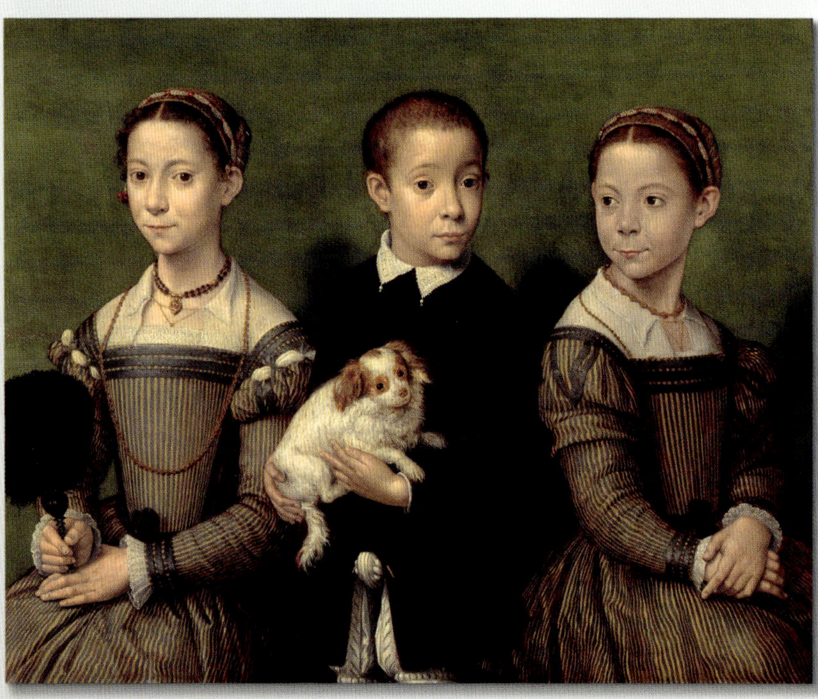

3

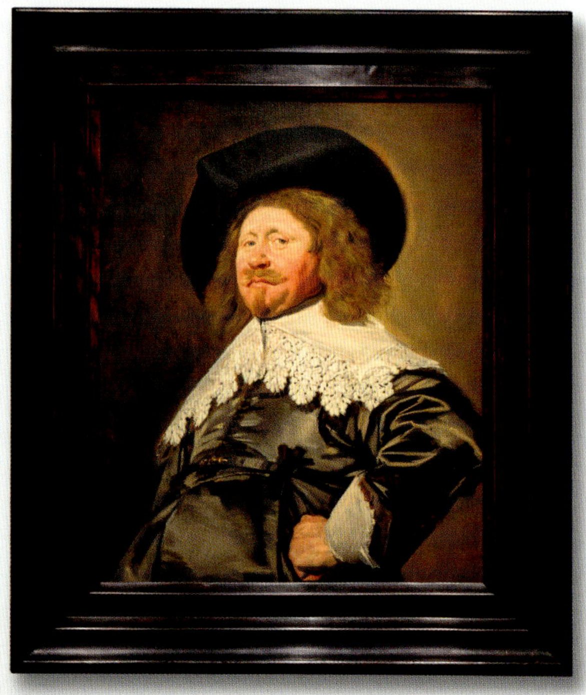

4

1. **Portrait of a young woman, artist unknown, 2nd century CE.** In the Fayum district of Egypt, highly realistic portraits were painted on the mummy of the deceased prior to burial. Some were painted while the subject was still alive, but most portraits were made just after death.

2. **Thirteen Emperors Scroll, attributed to Yan Liben, 650–700.** The 6th-century Chinese Emperor Xuan is one of several emperors included in this scroll painting. The artist portrayed the character of the figures with a restrained use of line and color.

3. ***Two Sisters and a Brother of the Artist*, Sofonisba Anguissola, c. 1555.** As a female artist in the 16th century, Anguissola was limited mainly to portraiture. In this painting of three of her siblings, the children are formally posed, but she has captured the personality of each.

4. ***Portrait of a Man, Possibly Nicolaes Pietersz Duyst van Voorhout*, Franz Hals, 1636-1638.** The three-quarter view, which first became popular in the 15th century, invites a connection between subject and viewer. This man is thought to have been a Haarlem brewer.

5

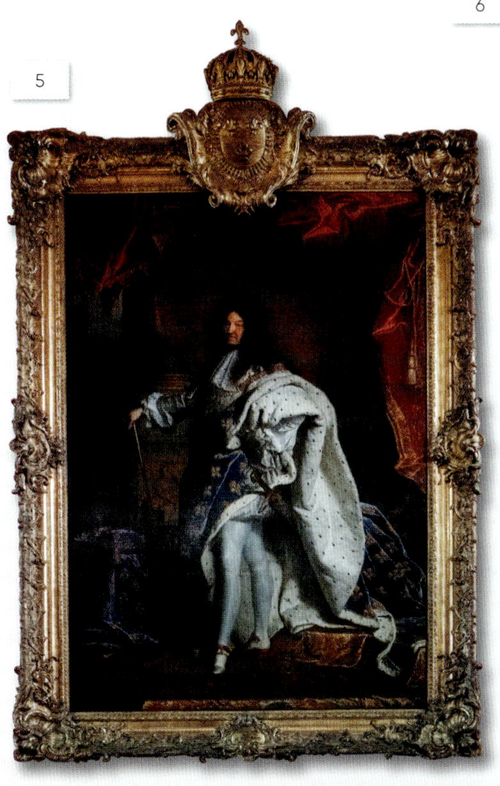

6

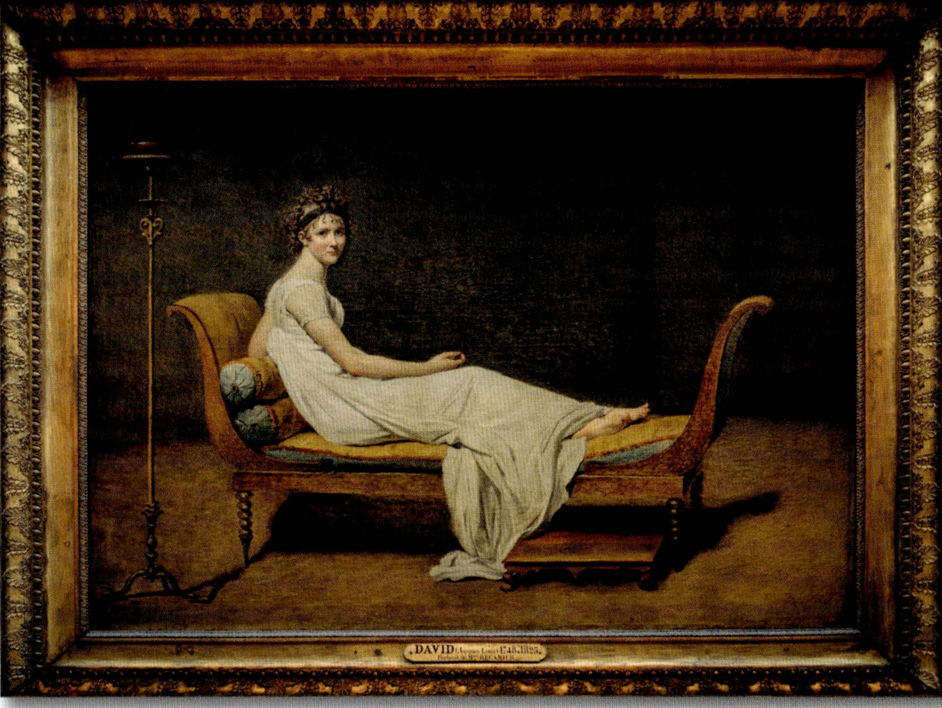

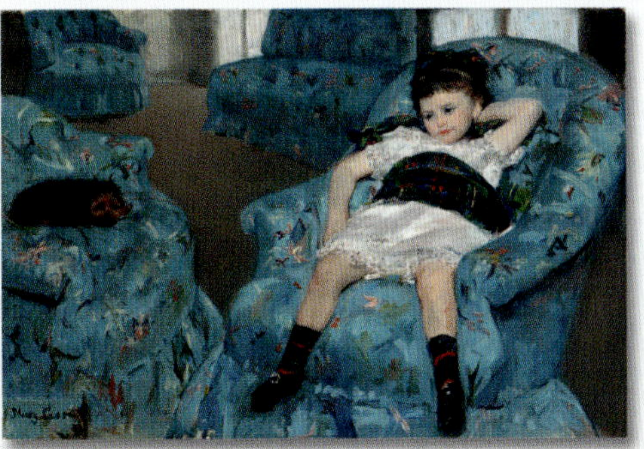

7

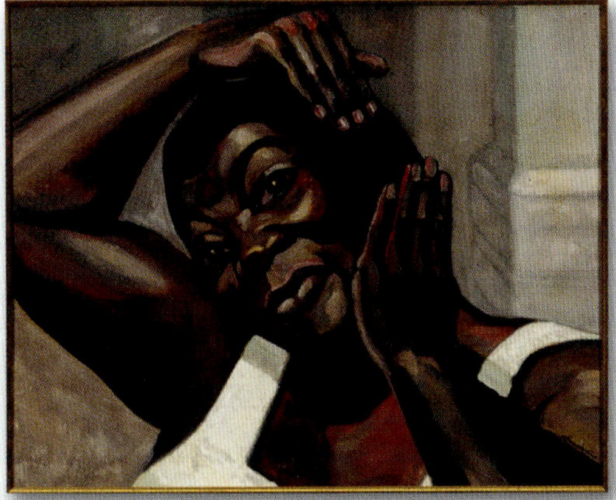

8

The royal portrait

All portraits have to strike a balance between an identifiable image and one that presents the subject as they would like to be seen. To this end, royal portraits are usually large-scale and full length. Physical flaws are modified and subjects are presented with inexpressive faces, wearing luxurious robes, and surrounded by symbols of divine and political power.

5. ***Portrait of Louis XIV in Coronation Robes*, Hyacinthe Rigaud, 1701.** Ceremonial portraits proclaim the grandeur of their subjects, and Rigaud's portrait of the French king represents the pinnacle of the style. Louis is presented as physically strong, surrounded by royal regalia.

6. ***Portrait of Madame Récamier*, Jacques-Louis David, 1800.** David's portrayal of a socialite in post-Revolutionary Paris recalls the refinement of classical art. The subject's simple dress and bare arms, and the sparse surroundings, were unusual at the time.

7. ***Little Girl in a Blue Armchair*, Mary Cassatt, 1878.** Cassatt concentrated on painting domestic scenes from the lives of women and children. In this informal portrait, she has captured a brief private moment in the life of a child, who sits slumped in a chair, her attention elsewhere.

8. ***Ruby Elzy in "Porgy and Bess,"* Sergei Yurevich Sudeikin, 1935.** Sudeikin has painted American opera singer Ruby Elzy as the character Serena adjusting her hair. Elzy challenged stereotypes, and this intimate image portrays both strength and vulnerability.

Door Panels

Olowe of Ise 1910–1914, Wood, 91 × 62 × 18 in (230 × 156.5 × 46 cm), British Museum, London, UK

Originally carved for the palace in Ikere, these doors illustrate the power dynamics in Nigeria under British colonial rule. The left door portrays the *ogoga*, or king of Ikere, and his court, while the right door shows the arrival of the colonial administrators between 1899 and 1901. Carved in high relief, the scenes are divided into registers (rows) with dynamically patterned painted backgrounds.

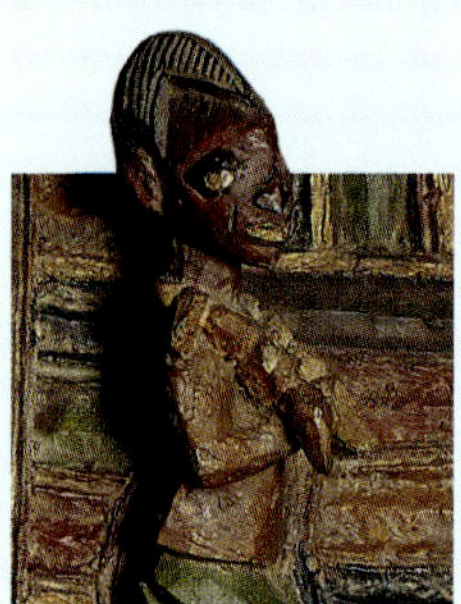

Olowe of Ise follows the conventions of Yoruba art: the eyes are rimmed and the lips do not meet at the corners.

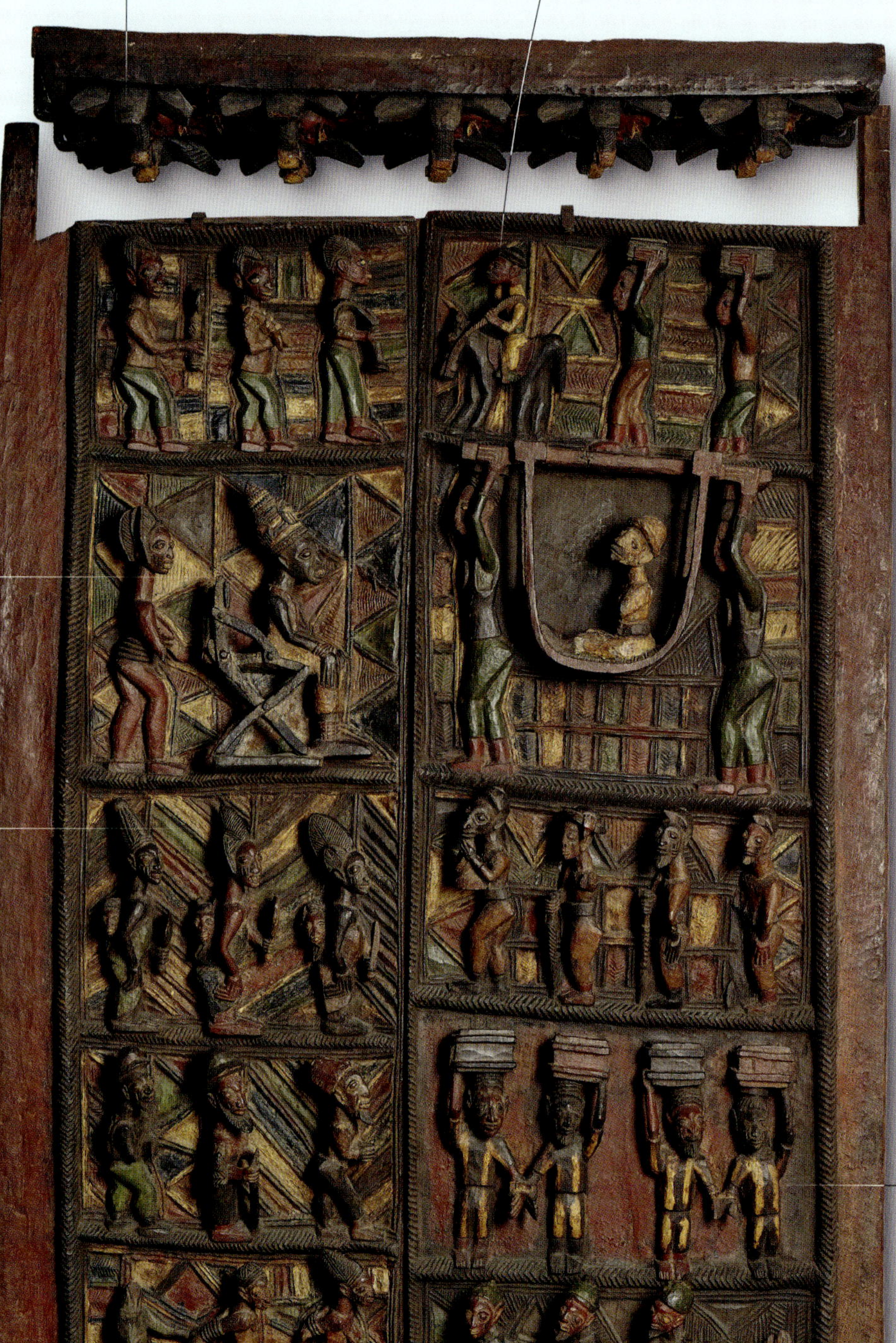

The five human faces whose eyes are being pecked by vultures may be a covert reference to human sacrifice—a practice that the British outlawed.

Major Reeve-Tucker, the traveling commissioner, is shown on horseback followed by his porters.

The *ogoga* of Ikere, Onijagbo Obasoro Alowolodu, is recognizable by his conical, beaded crown and throne. He is accompanied by his principal wife.

The beautifully coiffured wives of the *ogoga*, with scarification on their cheeks, carry children on their backs.

Four shackled porters illustrate the injustices of colonization. They are probably carrying boxes of cowrie shells, which were collected as taxes.

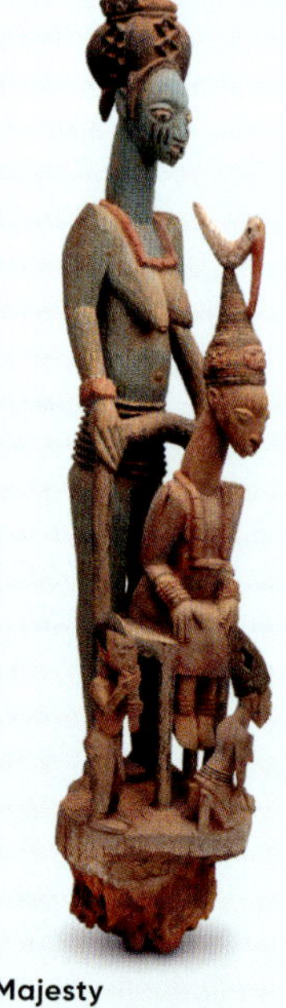

Majesty
Olowe of Ise carved several figurative posts, also for the Ikere palace. Like the doors, this one portrays the *ogoga* enthroned and wearing his crown. Behind him, originally holding up the palace roof, is either his principal wife or mother.

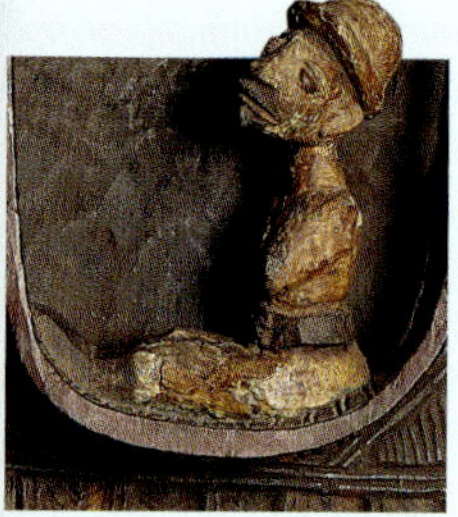

Wearing a pith helmet, Captain W. G. Ambrose is carried in a hammock. His chin tilts up in anticipation of meeting the *ogoga*.

> "Olowe was not only a prolific sculptor but also arguably the most celebrated Yoruba artist of the twentieth century."
>
> Rowland Abiodun, 2014

States of Mind II: Those Who Go

Umberto Boccioni 1911, oil on canvas, 28 × 38 in (70.8 × 95.9 cm), MoMA, New York, US

Melancholic passengers sit in a train as it hurtles along the track. Boccioni was a Futurist, who rejected the values of the past. Like other Futurists, he sought to convey the speed and dynamism of modern life, and especially modern machines, using a fragmented, multi-viewpoint approach. This is the central panel in a triptych bookended by two contrasting scenes, *The Farewells* and *Those Who Stay*.

Overlapping circular and angular shapes suggest the front of the engine.

Clouds of steam billow from the engine's chimney.

The yellow building provides a burst of color as the train flashes past.

Diagonal brushstrokes cut across the passengers, highlighting their unsettled thoughts.

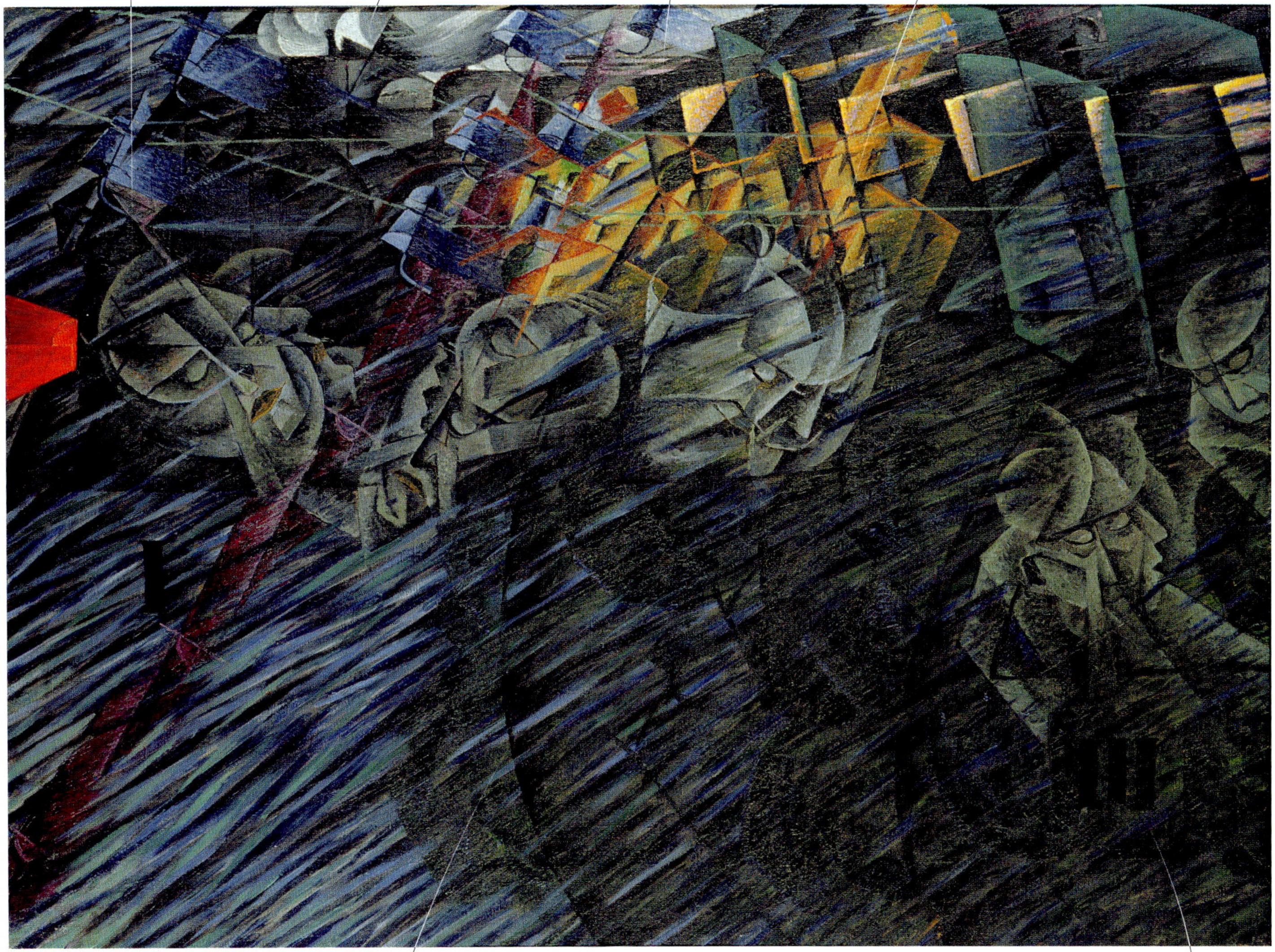

Forceful blue brushstrokes extend across the canvas, conveying a sense of speed.

The passengers' expressions suggest a somber, silent atmosphere. Boccioni said he was trying to convey "loneliness, anguish, and dazed confusion."

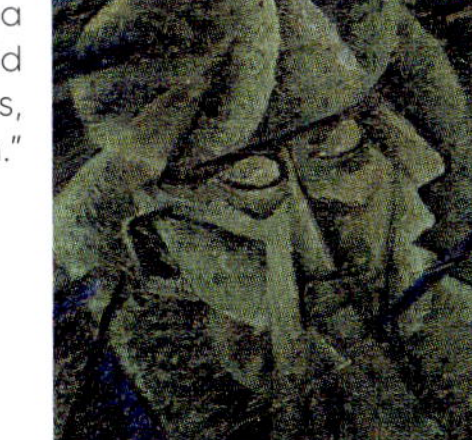

Roman numerals reminiscent of the style used on clock faces suggest the passage of time.

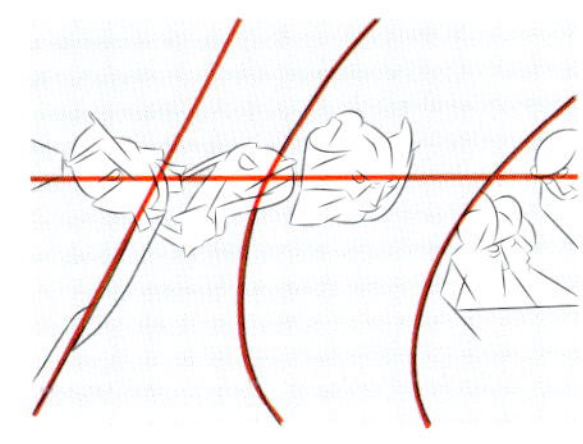

Composition
The heads of the passengers fall along a horizontal band, providing an element of stability among the many tilting diagonal and curving lines.

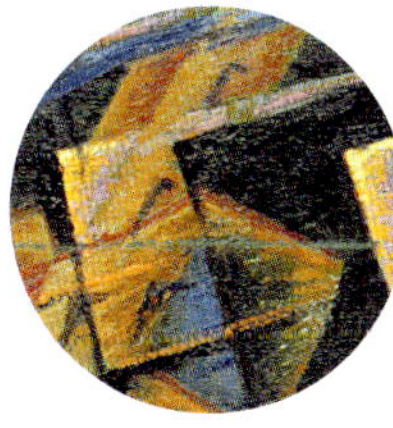

Abstract approach
Boccioni's style altered after he discovered Cubism. Intimations of this are apparent in the fractured but recognizable yellow building and passengers' faces.

Homme à la guitare

Georges Braque 1911, oil on canvas, 46 × 32 in (116.2 × 80.9 cm), MoMA, New York, US

In this visionary work, Braque breaks down his subject into geometric shapes and intersecting planes. Between 1907 and 1914, he and Pablo Picasso subverted spatial perspective to create a style known as Analytical Cubism. In its pursuit, Braque likened himself and Picasso to mountain-climbers roped together.

Rigid angles sketch a left-facing profile. The point suggests a nose, while semicircles give the impression of eyes.

A rope and nail motif recurs in Braque's Cubist works, perhaps invoking the curtain tie-back of a café scene.

Hard lines and cylinders resemble pistons and axles.

Hints of a fretboard and sound hole remind the viewer that this is a guitar. Braque avoided purely abstract painting.

A sharp angle implies the crook of the guitarist's elbow below a rounded plane, possibly a chair back.

A scroll could be architectural or decorative and also suggests the lower curl of a treble clef.

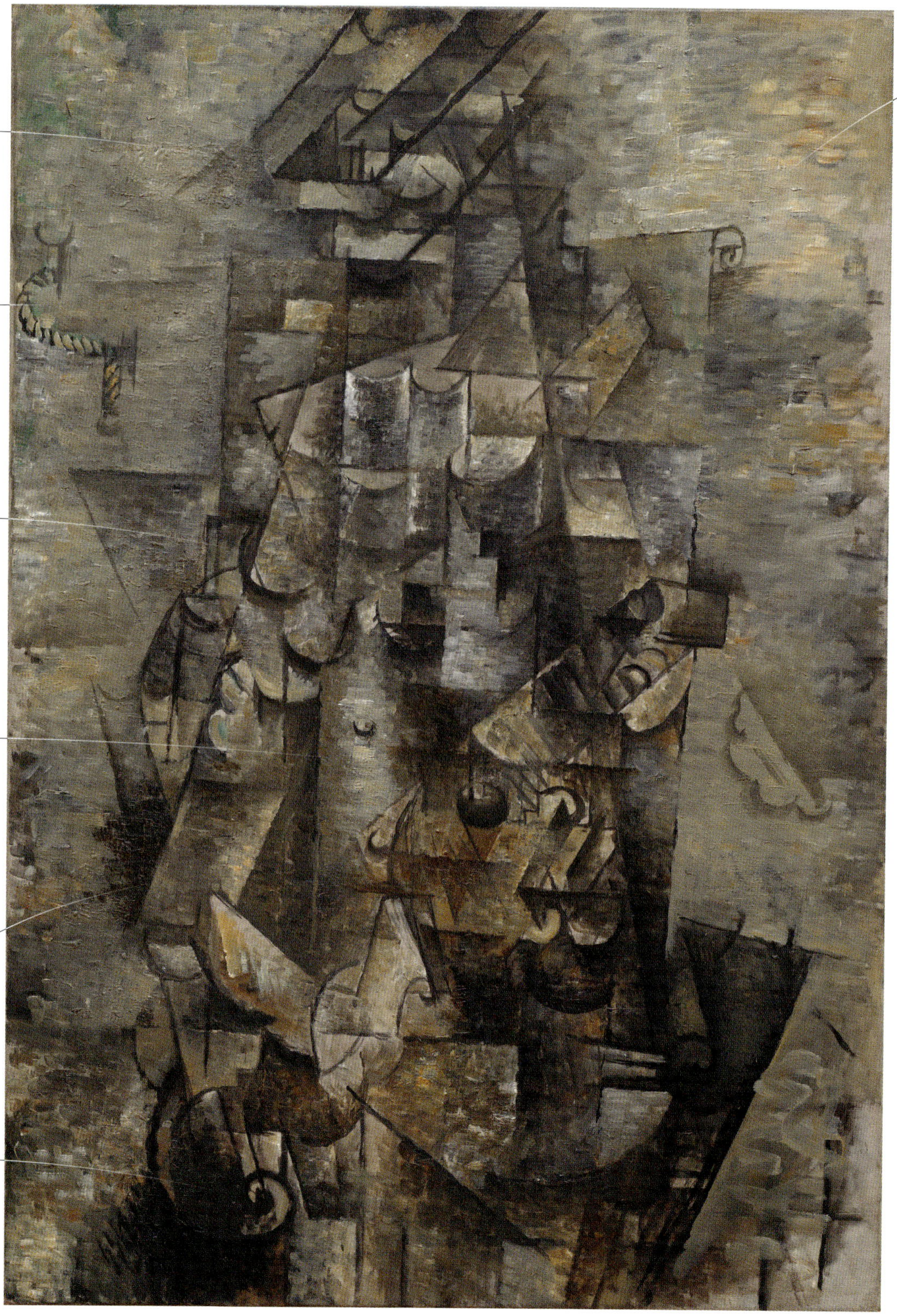

Another scroll, evoking sheet music, punctuates the composition in a quieter zone of the canvas.

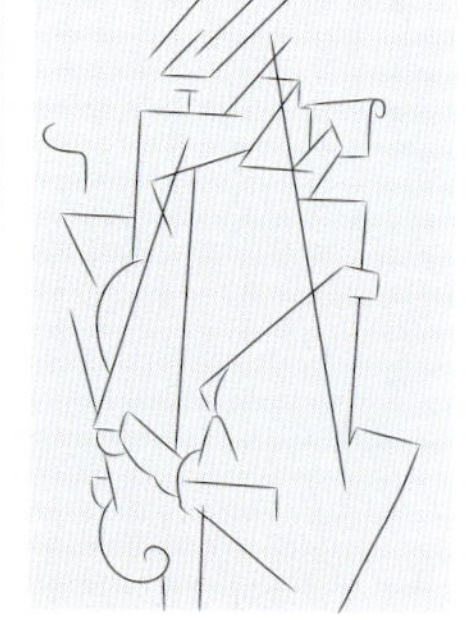

Perspective
Braque reduces and fractures reality into myriad coexisting viewpoints within the same space. By rejecting the illusion of depth in conventional perspective, the real, actual flatness of the canvas is emphasized.

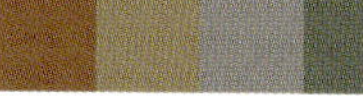

Focus on form
A subdued palette of browns, grays, and greens is typical of Braque's Cubist works. He believed that color would detract attention from structure and form.

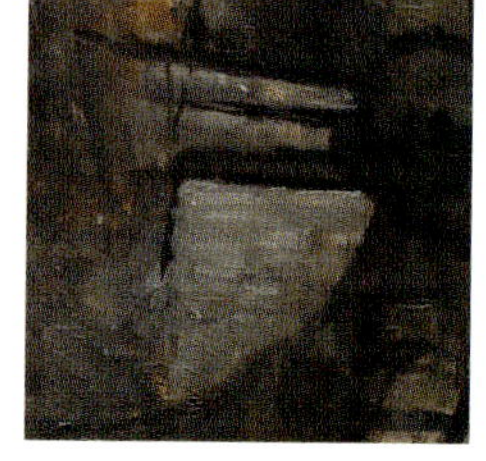

By fragmenting the body of the guitar, Braque invites the viewer to see it more realistically from multiple angles.

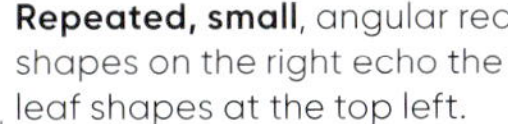

A man and woman in historical dress evoke the frolicking couples who populate Rococo paintings.

Repeated, small, angular red shapes on the right echo the leaf shapes at the top left.

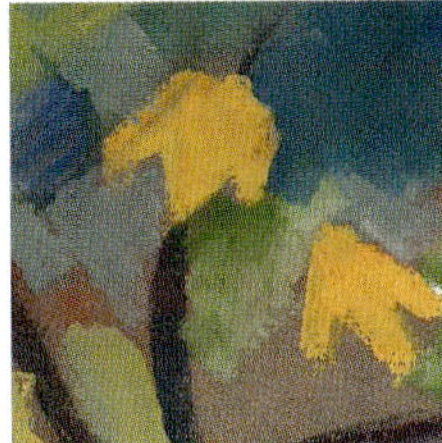

Three, short brushstrokes, repeated across the top left of the composition, effectively portray the leaves of the tree.

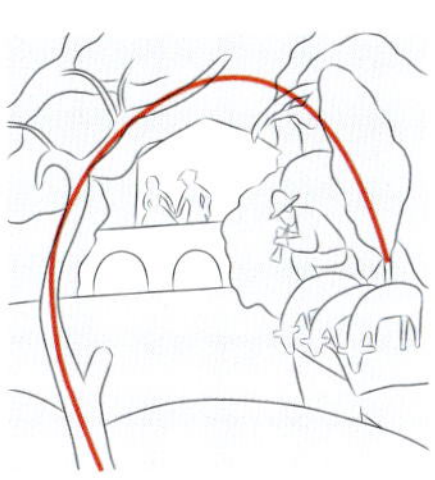

Composition
The two trees create an arch around the building and figures in the center.

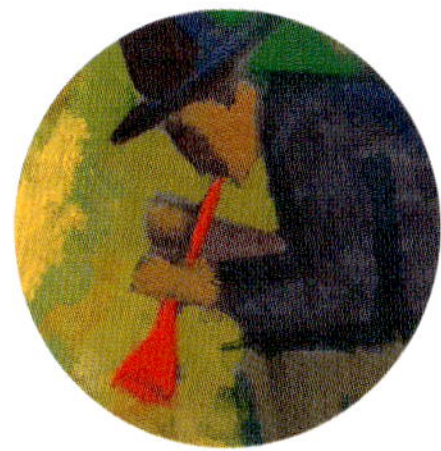

Brushstrokes
A dynamic interplay of brushstrokes, ranging from thin washes to thick dabs of paint and bold outlines, gives the painting an expressive depth.

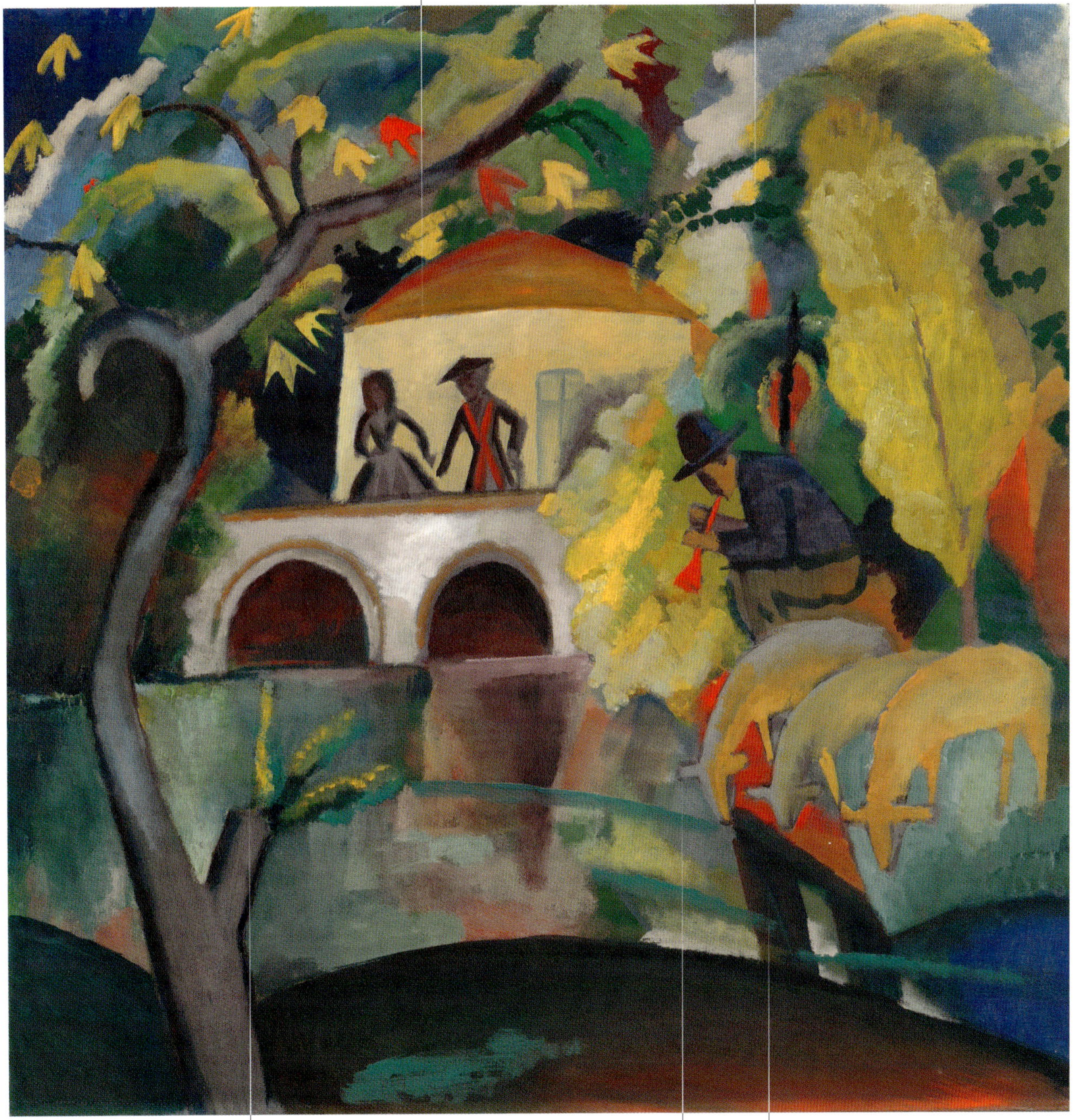

The two arches are an allusion to classical architectural motifs that feature in many Rococo paintings.

The vivid red trumpet complements the deep blue of the shepherd's outfit, enhancing the brightness of the composition.

The gently curving forms of three sheep and other horizontal curves in the foreground produce a tranquil effect.

Rokoko

August Macke 1912, oil on canvas, 35 × 35 in (89 × 89 cm), Sparebankstiftelsen DNB, National Museum, Oslo, Norway

Macke depicts a shepherd, his flock, and a traditionally dressed couple set against a lush, rural landscape and an imposing building—subject matter that recalls 18th-century Rococo pastoral scenes. While evoking a nostalgic yearning for a simpler life, the painting signals modernity as it is infused with Expressionist brushwork and a saturated Fauvist palette. Two years after its completion, Macke was killed in action in World War I.

Simultaneous Windows on the City

Robert Delaunay 1912, oil on canvas with painted wood frame, 16 × 18 in (40 × 46 cm), Hamburger Kunsthalle, Hamburg, Germany

Delaunay melds a view from a window overlooking the Eiffel Tower with the reflection of a person looking out at that view, erasing the boundaries between interior and exterior spaces. The two views are seen simultaneously and Delaunay coined the term "Simultanism" to describe this new style.

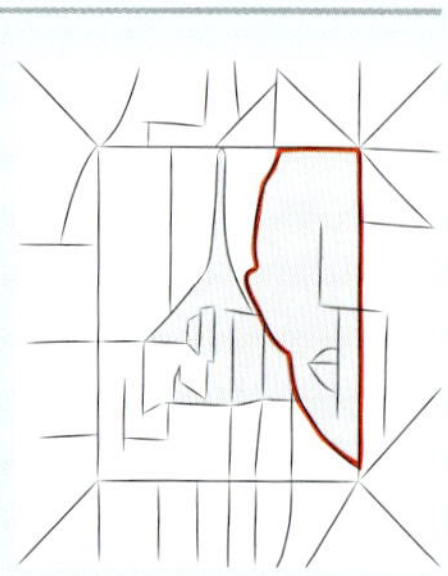

Vivid yellows and oranges evoke warm sunlight while vibrating in contrast with cool sky blues.

The green silhouette of the Eiffel Tower is an instantly recognizable landmark—a beacon of progress and modernity.

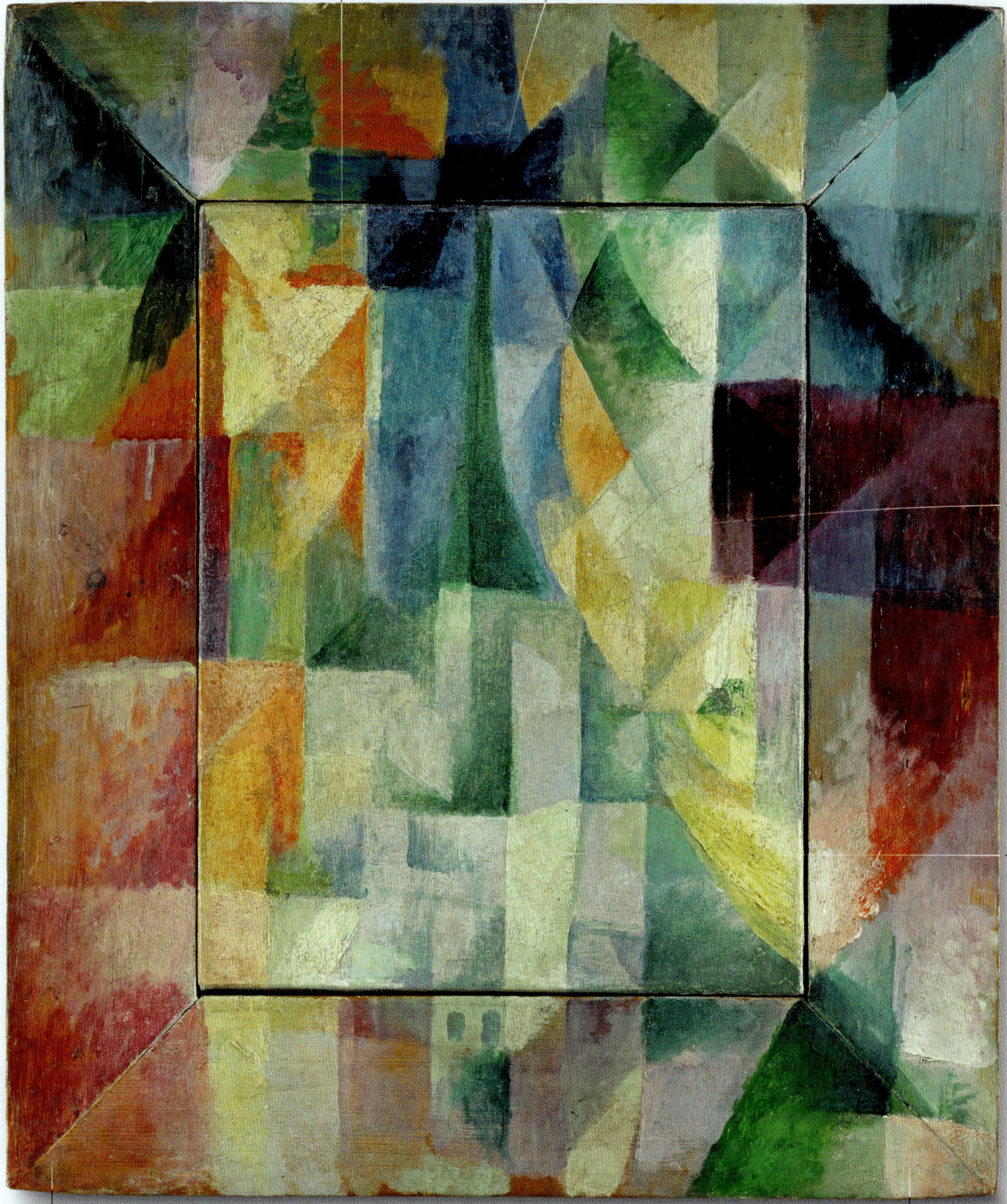

A face gradually unfolds, with a pale orange ear, and a green smear and yellow quarter-circle hinting at lips and a chin.

A curving yellow shape represents a curtain being pulled back.

The frame's miters (joints) work in tandem with Delaunay's manipulation of diagonal color planes, helping to guide the viewer's gaze to the focal point.

The painting continues onto the frame, paradoxically giving it vitality and meaning while negating its very existence.

Hidden forms
On the right, a concealed face comes into focus. In the center, shifting hues trace a diagonal rectangle, conjuring an aerial view of the Champ de Mars which runs southeast from the Eiffel Tower.

The Windows Series
Delaunay painted 22 variations on this painting in 1912. Gone were the muted colors of Cubism—these window views vibrated with bright contrasting colors and set the stage for his move into abstract art.

> "The Windows truly began my life as an artist."
> Robert Delaunay

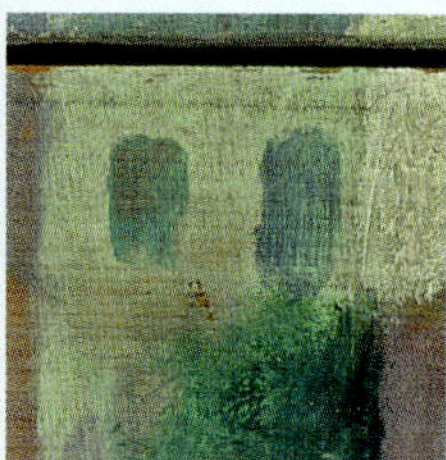

Twin blue rectangles might be windows or eyes peering back at the viewer.

The ocean spreads almost to the top of the painting, suggesting that Appledore Island is an escape from the world. At the time, World War I was looming.

Surf crashes against a rocky shore, suggesting a rugged, untamed island. In fact, Appledore had an upmarket hotel.

A single boat is just visible on the distant horizon, emphasizing that Appledore Island is separate from the larger world.

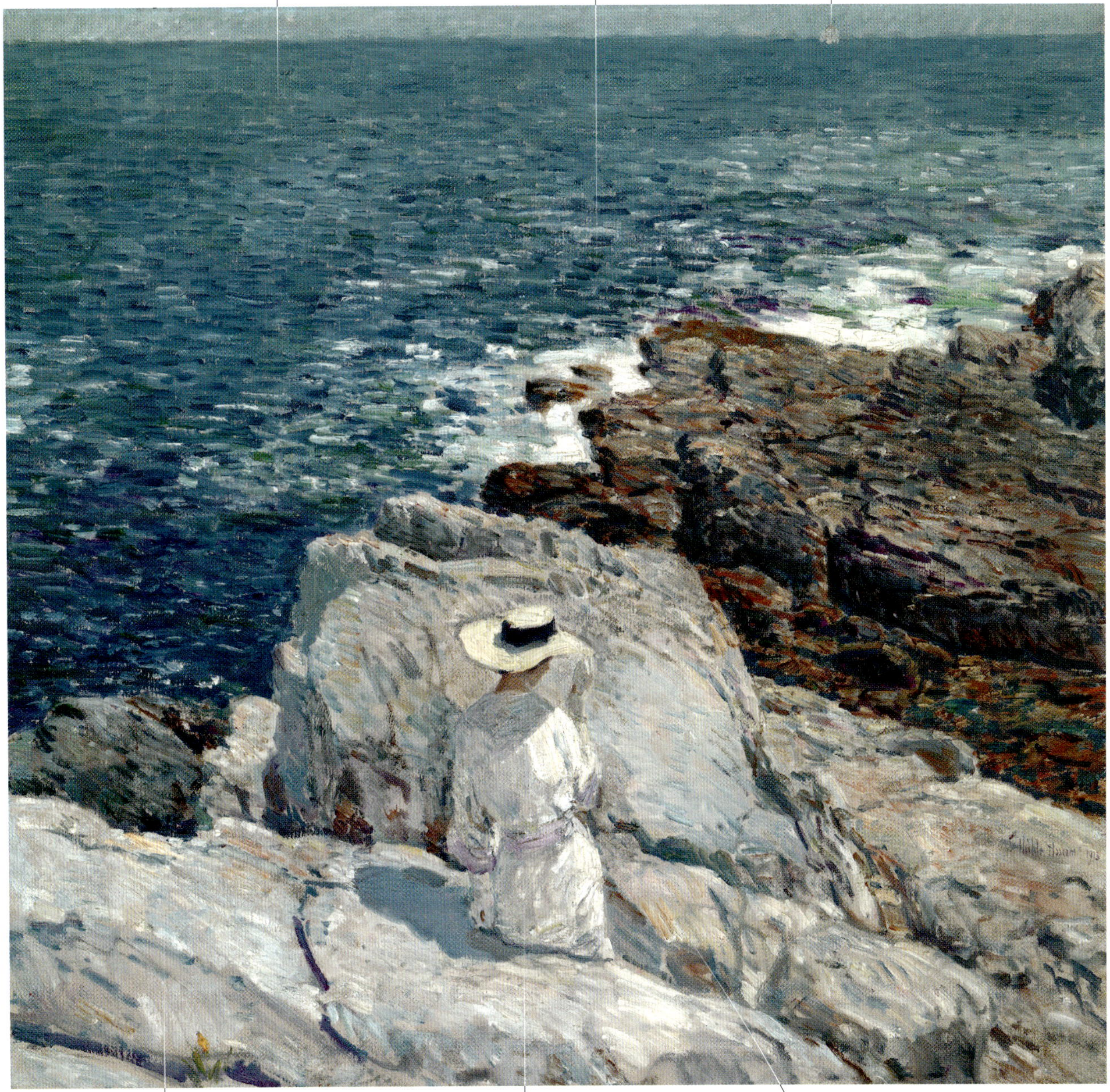

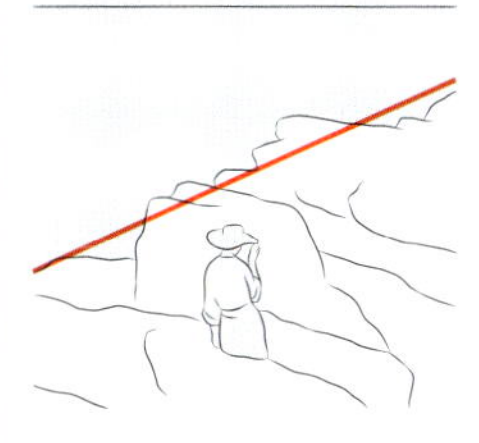

Two parts
A strong diagonal line divides the nearly square canvas in two, separating water from land. The viewer is positioned above and behind the woman.

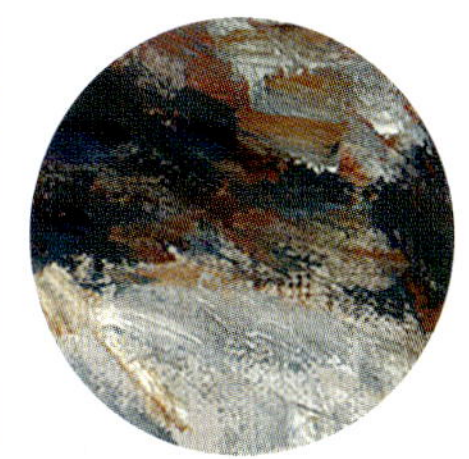

Method
Hassam often applied paint directly from tubes without first mixing colors on a palette, resulting in thickly applied and contrasting pigment.

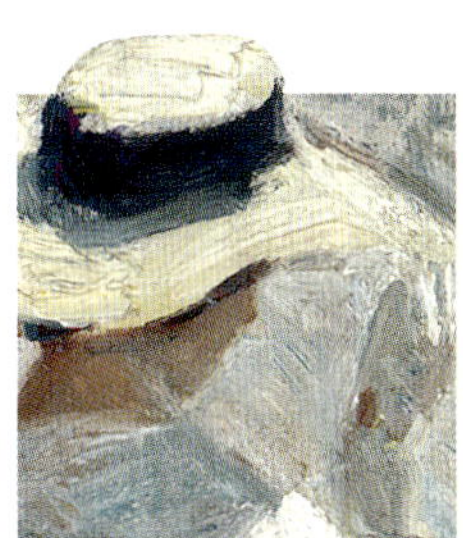

The woman holds the brim of her hat, perhaps to shade her eyes from the sun's rays.

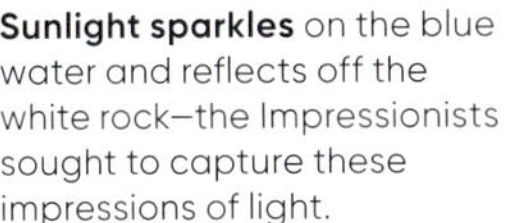

Sunlight sparkles on the blue water and reflects off the white rock—the Impressionists sought to capture these impressions of light.

The woman's clothes are fashionable—Appledore Island in Maine was an escape for the wealthy.

Looking down and away, the woman is seemingly lost in thought, interested in neither viewer nor sea.

The South Ledges, Appledore

Childe Hassam 1913, oil on canvas, 34 × 36 in (87 × 91.6 cm), Smithsonian American Art Museum, Washington, D.C., US

On a warm summer day, a woman sits by the sea, her white dress blending into the surrounding rocks. The scene is calm but there is a sense of unease and isolation. Hassam's loose, visible brushstrokes, characteristic of Impressionism, led to him being known as "The American Monet."

Composition VII

Wassily Kandinsky 1913, oil on canvas, 119 × 79 in (302.3 × 200.7 cm), The State Tretyakov Gallery, Moscow, Russia

In this piece, Kandinsky explores the expressive potential of color, form, and abstraction in search of a pure form of painting. He saw relationships between art and music, color and sound, and line and rhythm, and embraced the concept of synesthesia—the perception of one sense through another. He developed a deeply personal iconography. In *Composition VII*, an overwhelming sense of drama unfolds, involving apocalyptic and Biblical themes of catastrophe and salvation.

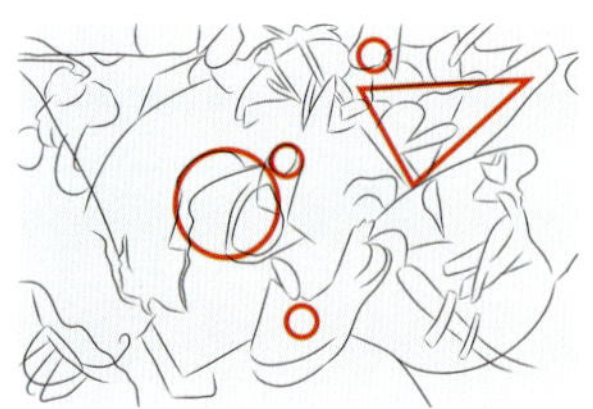

Shape combinations
Tension is created by the interaction of a triangular element, emphasizing diagonal movement, and circular forms, within which the turbulence unfolds.

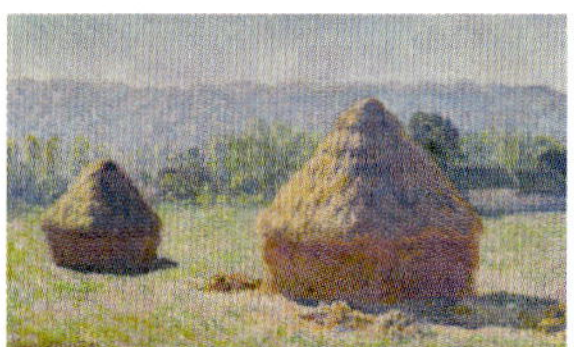

Influence
Kandinsky claimed to have embraced abstraction after seeing Monet's *Haystacks* hung upside down at an exhibition in 1896. He realized that color and form could be independent of subject.

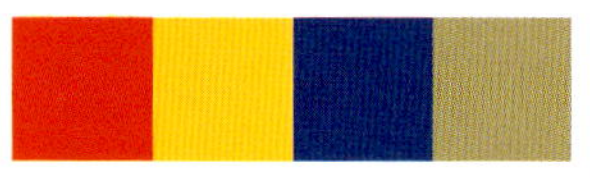

Hearing color
Colors represent how Kandinsky heard the instruments of the orchestra. Yellow represents trumpets, red symbolizes violins, and blues denote cellos and organs.

"Color is the keyboard, the eyes are the hammers, the soul is the piano with many strings. The artist is the hand which plays, touching one key or another, to cause vibrations in the soul."

Wassily Kandinsky, 1911

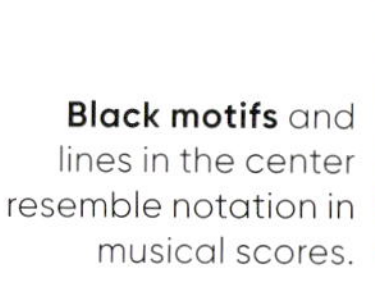

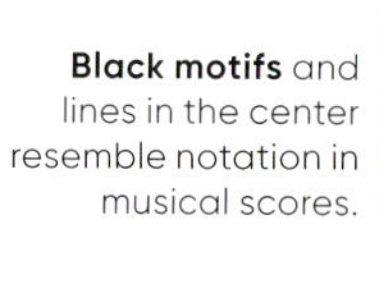

Black motifs and lines in the center resemble notation in musical scores.

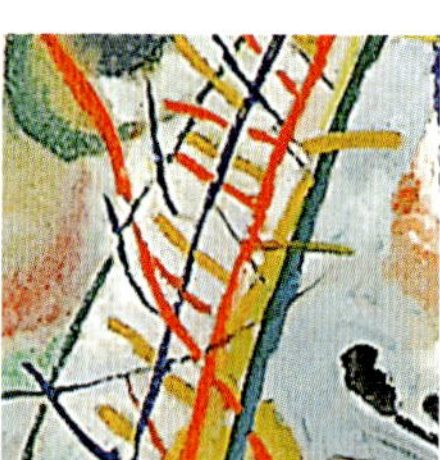

Crosshatched lines resemble barbed wire, perhaps representing the build up to World War I. Barbed wire had been widely used in the Russo-Japanese War of 1904–1905.

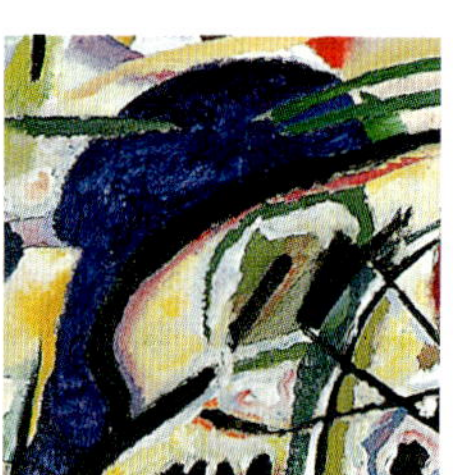

Circular forms in the center of the painting create the sense of a violent vortex.

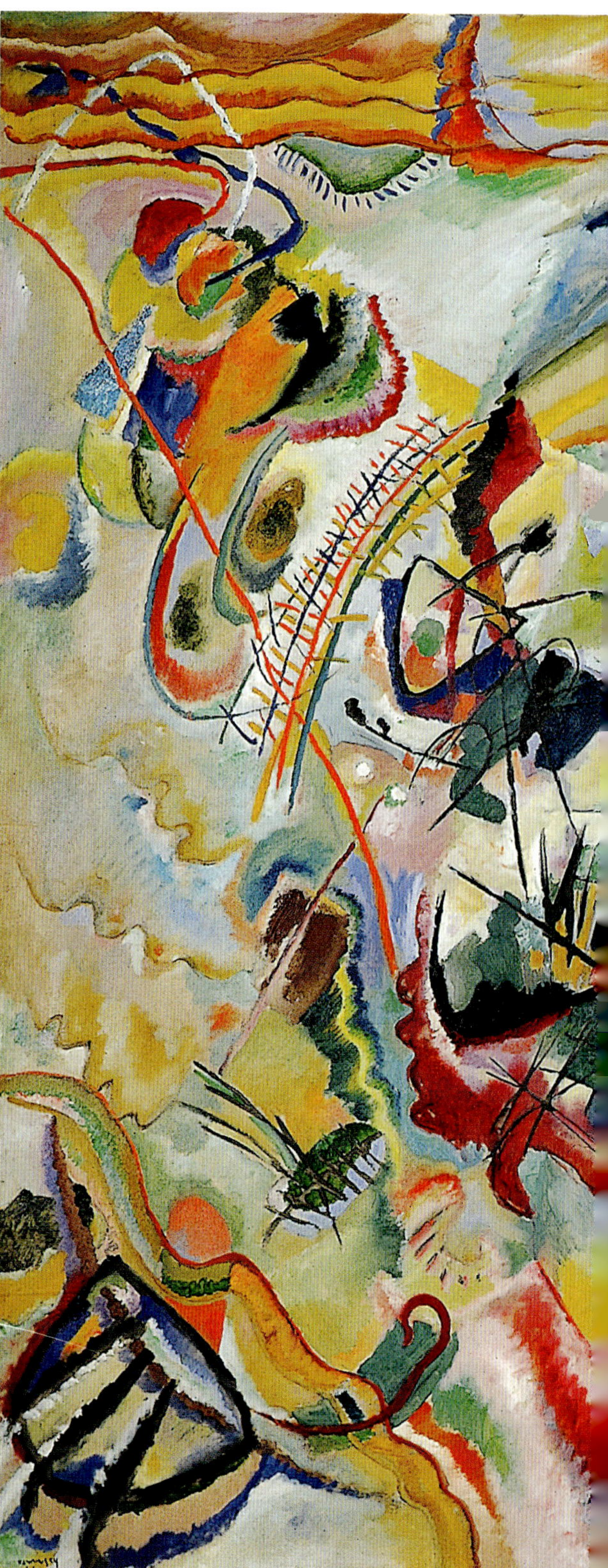

Boats with curved bows and straight oars represent Noah's ark in the Bible's Book of Genesis. They symbolize themes of destruction and renewal.

A blue angel blows on a yellow trumpet, a motif of the Last Judgment.

A patch of red depicts the prophet Elijah's chariot of fire, with which he ascended to heaven. The development of this abstracted form can be traced in the artist's earlier work.

Quieter areas in the corners balance the crescendo of chaos in the center.

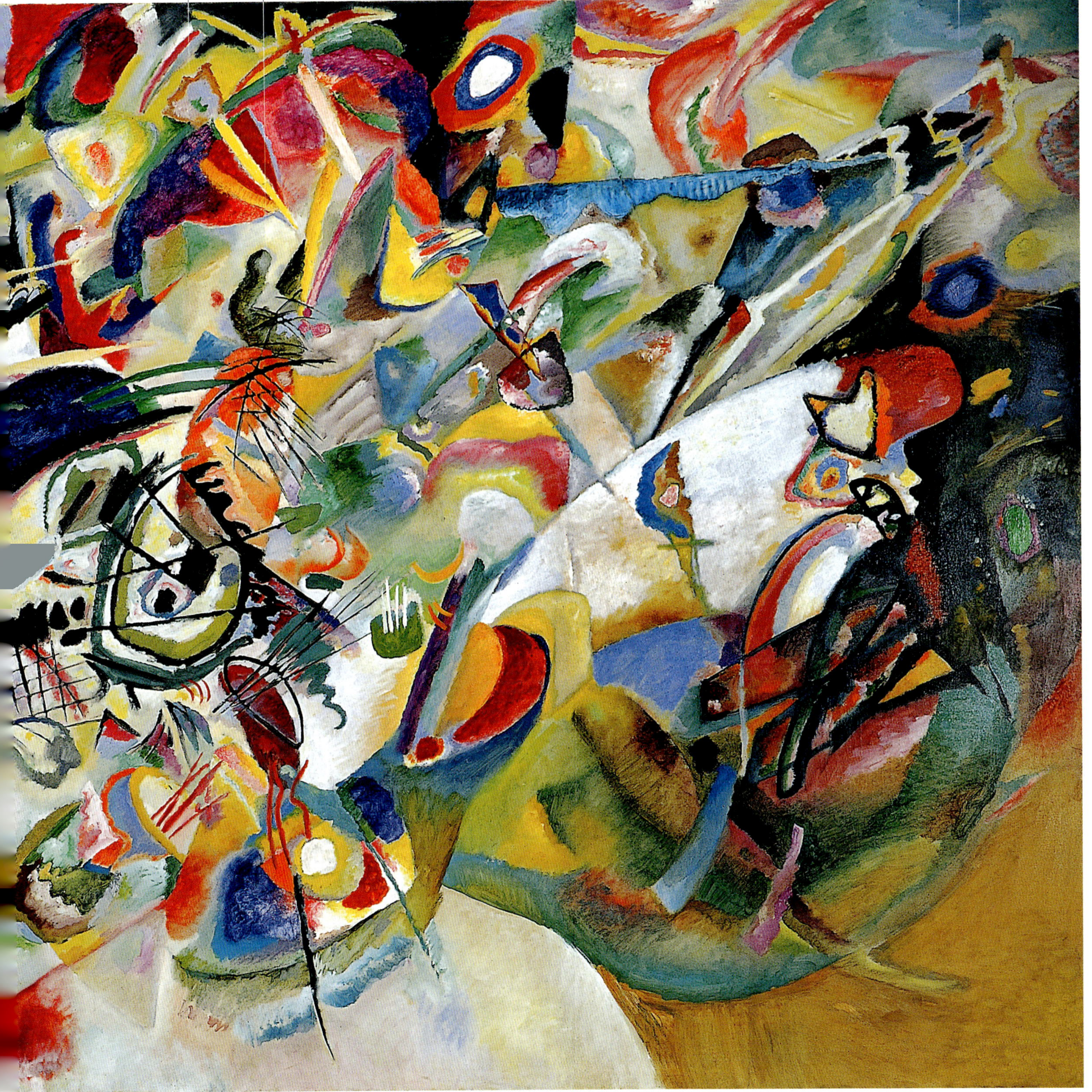

The use of red in the dress and feathers identifies the two women as the protagonists.

Two horses pulling a carriage contribute to the dynamic energy of the scene.

The elongated, angular figures give the painting a rhythmic energy, evoking the vibrant nighttime streets of Berlin.

Kirchner regarded sex workers as examples of independent, modern women.

In contrast to the extravagantly dressed women, the men wear sober blue coats and hats.

Orange appears in the foreground and in the distance, flattening the space and adding to a sense of claustrophobia.

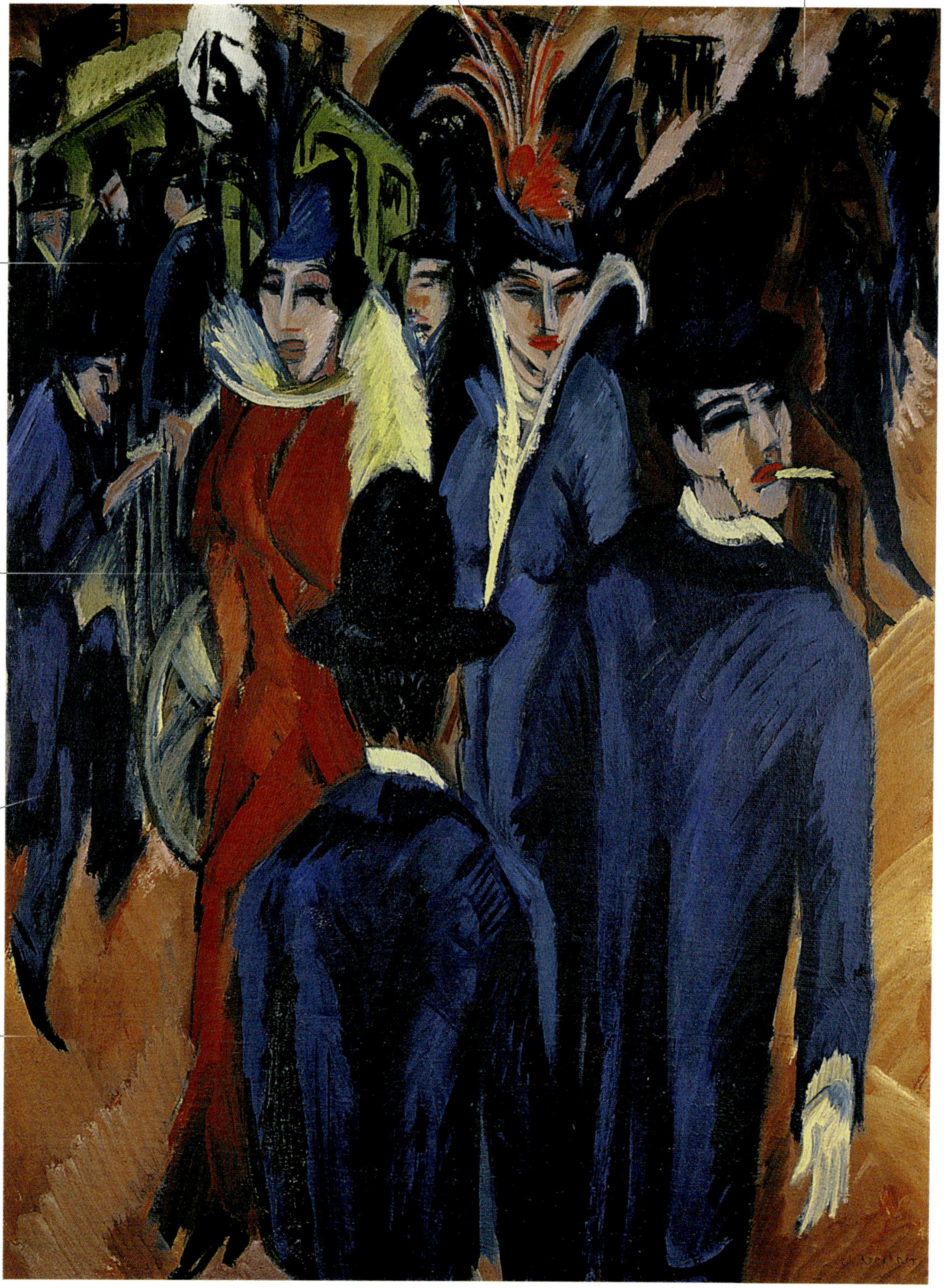

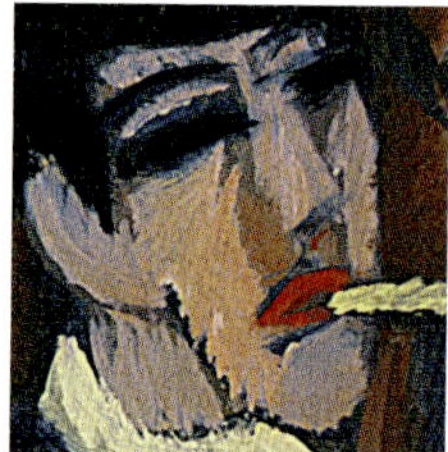

One man turns away from the women, a cigarette hanging from his mouth. His expression suggests contemplation or perhaps disgust.

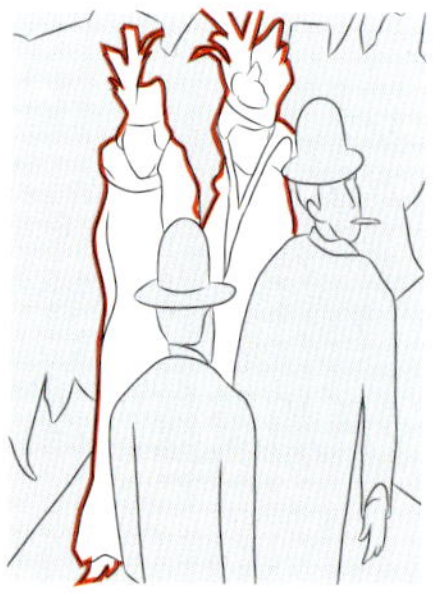

Composition
The close cropping and elevated perspective accentuate the subtly slanting vertical lines that guide the focus to the central figures.

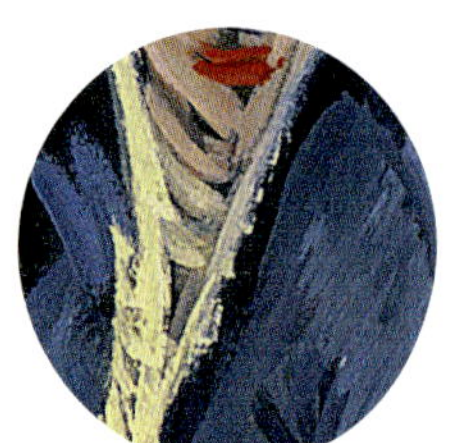

Striking brushstrokes
Bold, dynamic hatched brushstrokes heighten the figures' angular lines, contributing to the work's vibrant atmosphere and emotional intensity.

Berlin Street Scene

Ernst Ludwig Kirchner 1913, oil on canvas, 48 × 37 in (121 × 95 cm), private collection and Neue Galerie, New York, US

Men jostle around two fashionably dressed sex workers striding down a bustling Berlin street. In this scene from a series on the same subject, Kirchner, a leading German Expressionist, used a crowded composition, dynamic brushstrokes, and vivid color to convey the essence of modern decadence and social upheaval on the eve of World War I. The cropped portrayal of the two men in the foreground suggests a snatched moment in time.

After the Meeting

Cecilia Beaux 1914, oil on canvas, 41 × 28 in (104 × 71.4 cm), Toledo Museum of Art, Ohio, US

The elegant sitter may be "as pretty as a picture," but she is not interested in being viewed that way, engrossed as she is in earnest conversation. The woman is the artist's friend and possible romantic partner Dorothea Gilder; no clues are provided as to what the "meeting" may have been.

Women enjoy each other's company in the background of the gathering. Beaux made her name as a painter of American high society.

The elegant gloves draw attention to Gilder's enthusiastic gestures, perhaps suggesting that being "fashionable" is not the same as "frivolous."

Gilder's knees point left toward the mystery person with whom she is speaking.

The arm of the chair cold-shoulders the viewer, closing off Beaux's subject from view.

Rose-covered fabric evokes a feminine world.

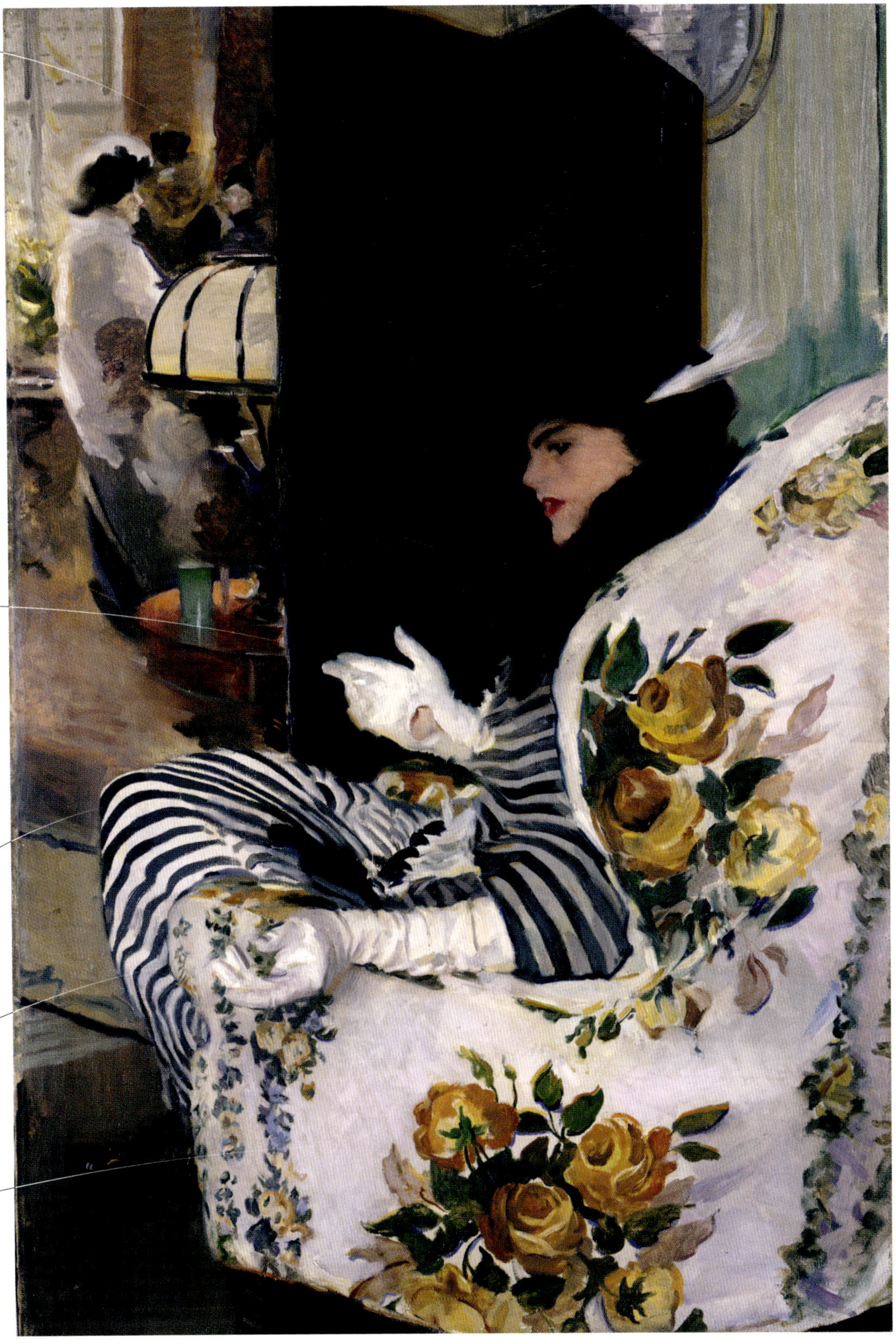

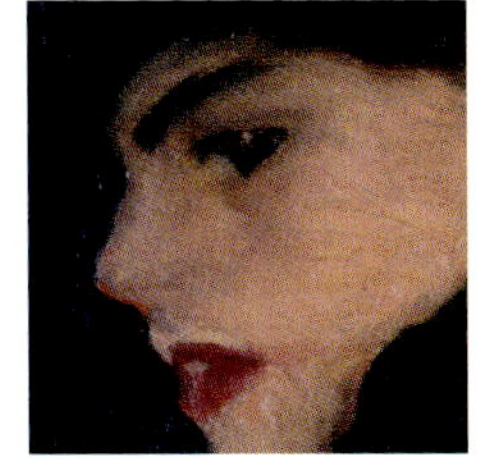

Gilder does not meet the viewer's gaze or seek their admiration; she is fully engaged in conversation.

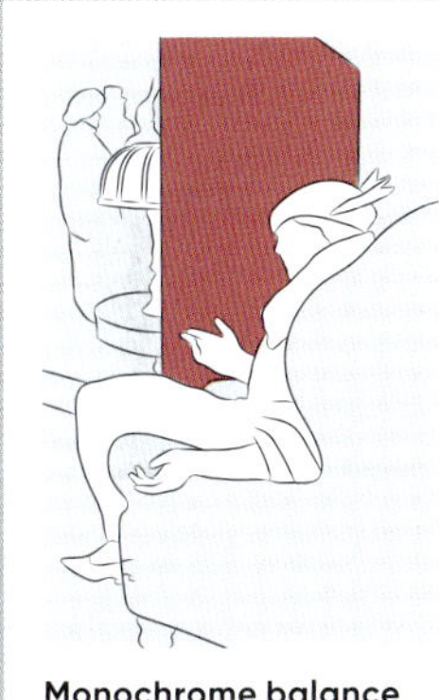

Monochrome balance
A dark screen provides a backdrop for the subject's face while also creating a sense of intimacy. The black-and-white lampshade counterbalances the playful monochromatic patterns of the sitter's dress.

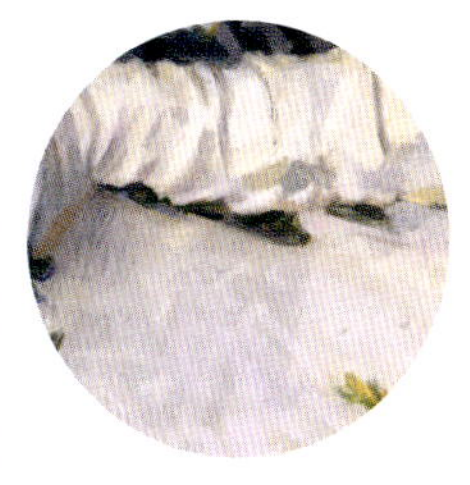

The use of white
White fabric unifies the armchair, the sitter's gloves, and the distant woman's dress.

Portrait of a German Officer

Marsden Hartley 1914, oil on canvas, 68 × 41 in (173.4 × 105.1 cm), Metropolitan Museum of Art, New York, US

Hartley's painting is a homage to his close, possibly intimate, friend Lieutenant Karl von Freyburg. It is partly Cubist in style, as its subject is depicted with a collage-like assemblage of fragments, but it is also Expressionist in its use of color and dynamic shapes. By depicting Freyburg through the symbols of his identity as a German officer rather than by painting a physical likeness, Hartley redefined portraiture.

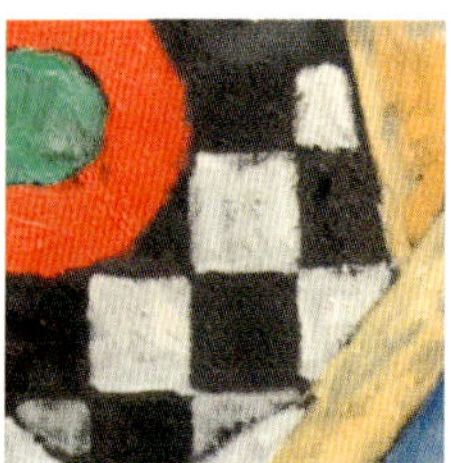

Black and white checks celebrate Freyburg's love of chess—a game the men played together.

The Iron Cross, the highest German military decoration for bravery, was awarded posthumously to Freyburg, who was killed at the start of World War I.

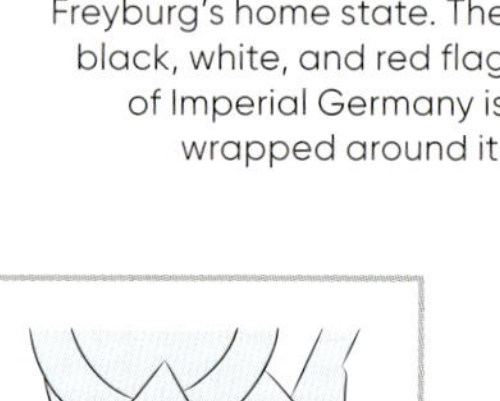

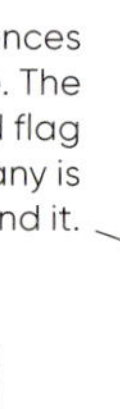

The Bavarian flag references Freyburg's home state. The black, white, and red flag of Imperial Germany is wrapped around it.

"4" refers to von Freyburg's regiment.

Composition
The Iron Cross is the portrait's "heart," from which a series of intricately clustered symbols radiate.

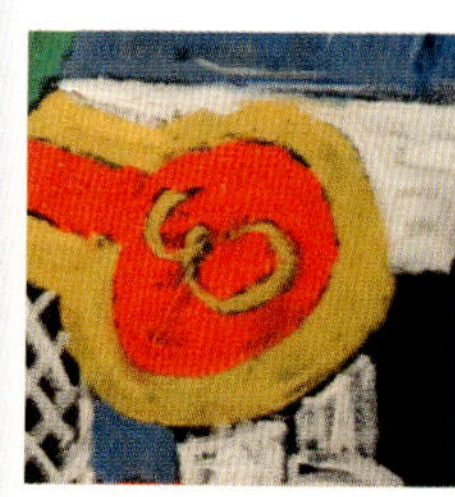

The gold, cursive "E" on the epaulet may stand for Edmund, Hartley's birth name. The central, red, cursive "E" beneath the Iron Cross signifies Freyburg's regiment.

"24" denotes the lieutenant's age when he died, deepening the poignancy of this tribute.

The silver star, reminiscent of a boot spur, indicates that Von Freyburg was a cavalry officer.

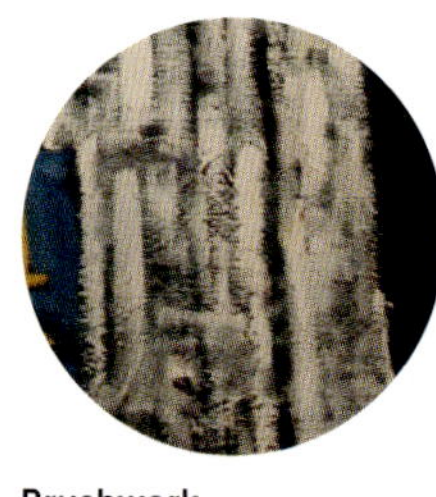

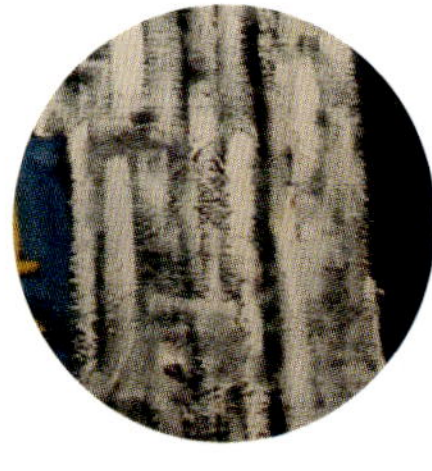

Brushwork
Hartley's expressive brushwork, which varies in direction and thickness, has echoes of German Expressionism.

Von Freyburg appears symbolically through his initials "K.v.F.".

The flags of Germany's enemies, England and Belgium, sit at the portrait's base, like doormats beside the lieutenant's boots.

A classical arcade links modern Europe to antiquity. It also creates space and blurs time.

A wall of darkness seems to trap the viewer in the piazza; a village in the distance feels unreachable.

Two people are visible, but their distance from the foreground contributes to a sense of loneliness in this public space.

The factory chimneys lack a factory. They also do not have shadows. De Chirico's chimneys are often thought to be phallic symbols.

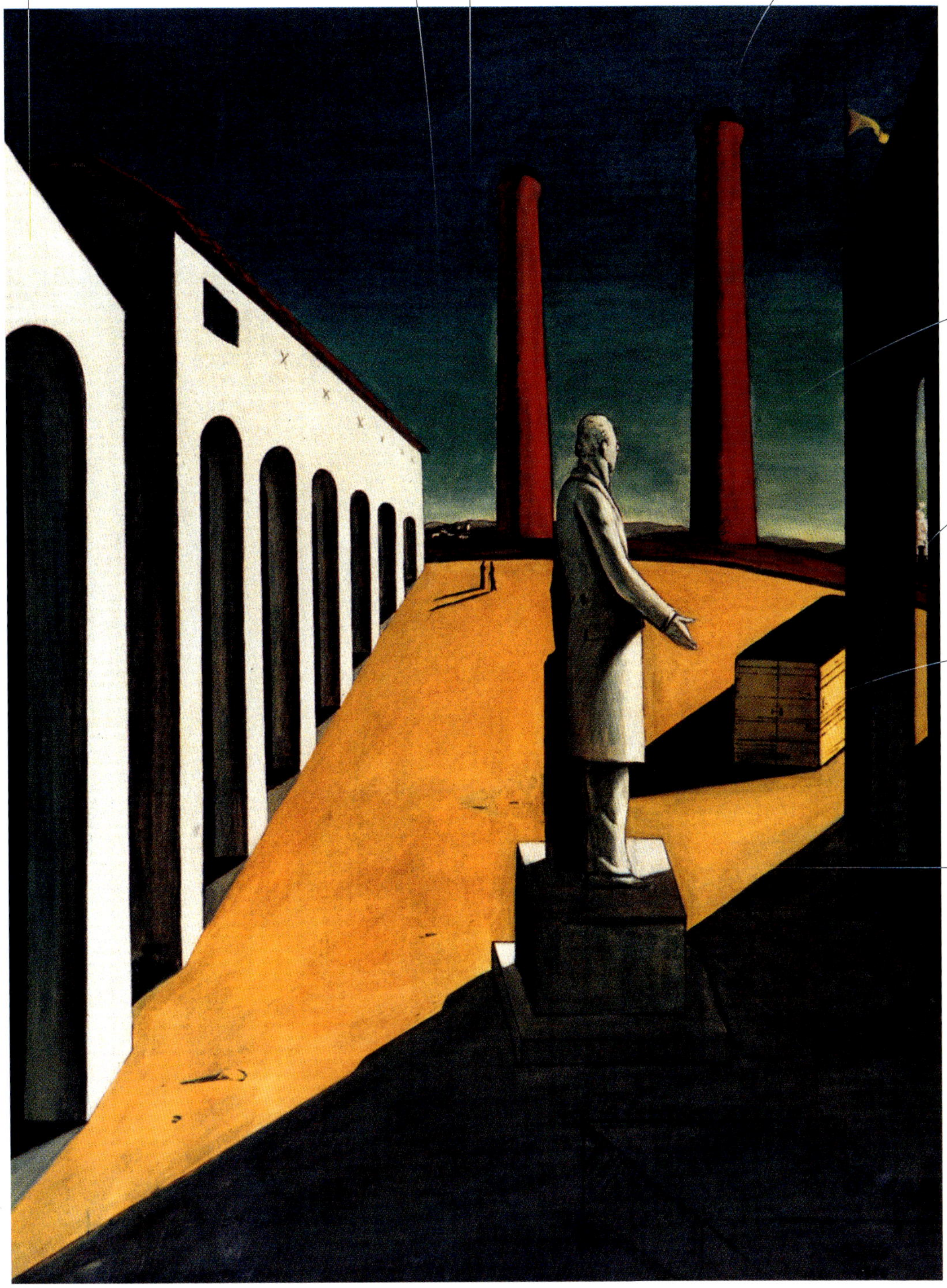

A statue of Count Camillo Benso di Cavour, the father of Italian unification, might also represent the Greek god Apollo or even de Chirico's father.

A train is just visible. De Chirico's trains probably symbolize the journey into the unconscious.

The "shed" is actually a train car without wheels.

The yellow ground evokes a desert landscape rather than any actual European piazza.

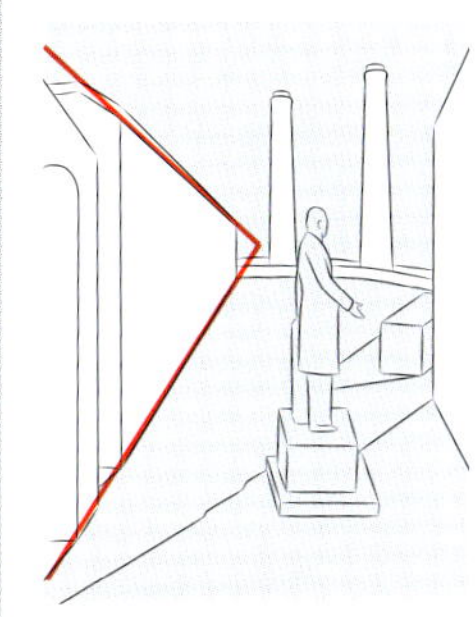

Spatial inconsistencies
The painting has many vanishing points. That of the arcade is well above the horizon. This leaves the viewer feeling insecure and ungrounded.

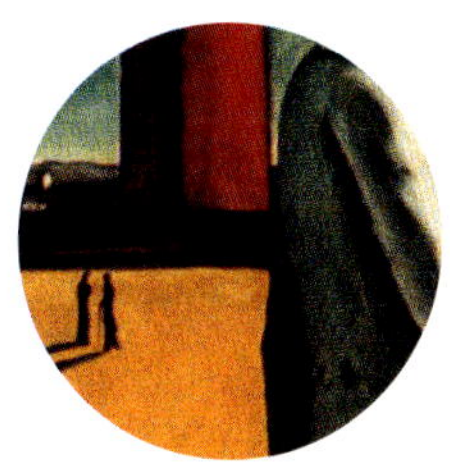

Unconventional viewpoints
The angle of view is unsettling. The observer is looking at a statue but from the side, gazing at a wide, sunlit piazza from the dark shadows. The two people are too far away to add context or meaning to the scene.

> "The painting of de Chirico is not painting, in the sense that we use that word today. It could be defined as a writing down of dreams."
>
> Ardengo Soffici, 1914

The Enigma of a Day

Giorgio de Chirico 1914, 73 × 55 in (185.5 × 139.7 cm), oil on canvas, MoMA, New York, US

Two shadowy, faraway figures stand in an otherwise deserted European piazza in this disquieting scene. De Chirico marries classical architectural elements with Cubism to create the lonely landscape, using bold, simple shapes, compressed space, and muted tones. He wanted to paint the hidden meaning of familiar objects, and his images later influenced the Surrealists. French Surrealist poet André Breton owned this work.

Painterly Architectonic

Lyubov Popova 1916, oil on canvas, 63 × 49 in (159 × 125 cm), State Tretyakov Gallery, Moscow, Russia

Dynamic, overlapping planes of color push a large red rectangle forward, toward the viewer, creating a sense of space suggestive of Cubism but purely abstract. Popova titled many of her paintings "architectonic," referring to their clear structure; she treated planes almost as solid entities.

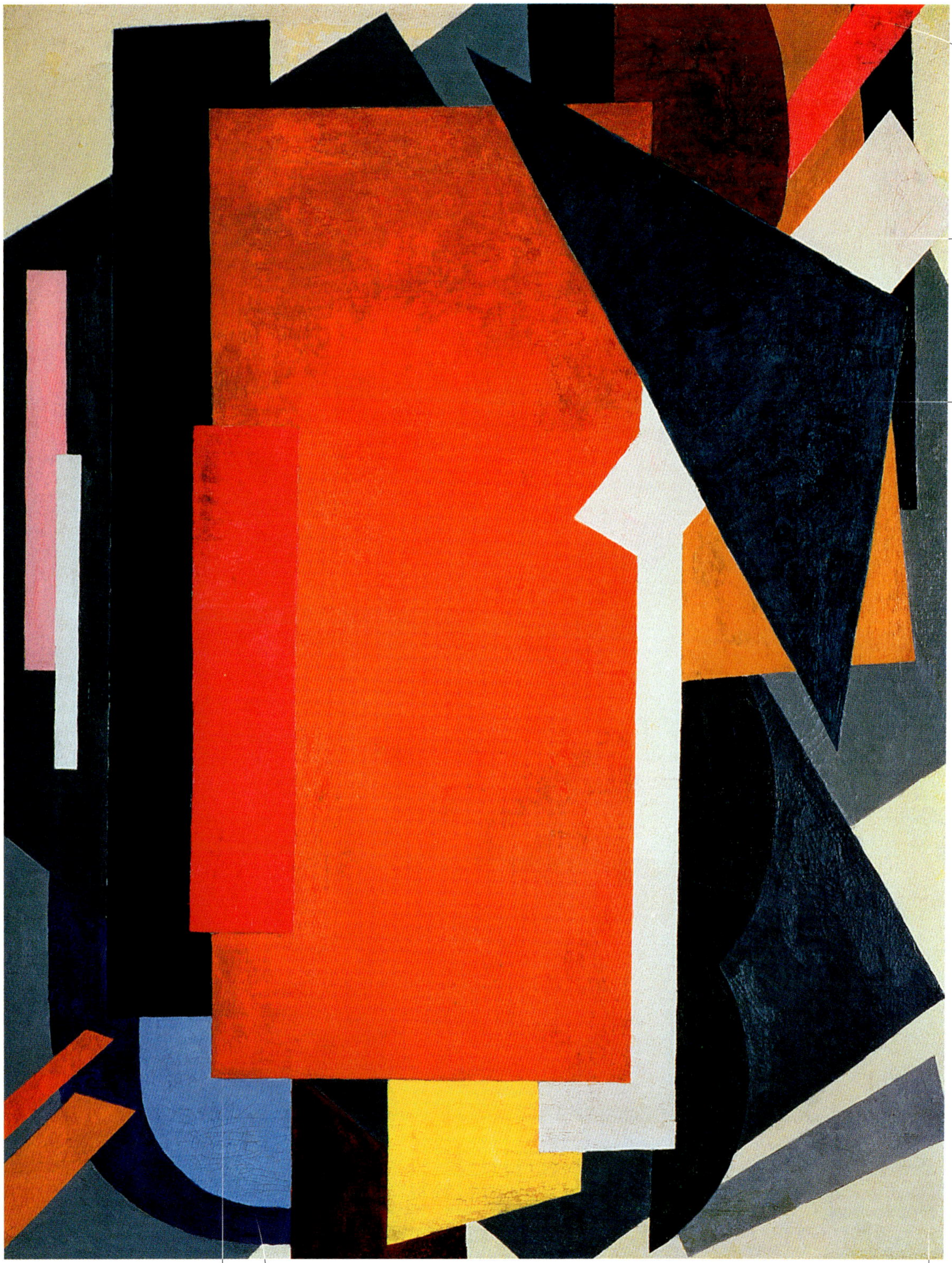

Shapes are cut off at the edges of the painting, suggesting space beyond it.

A simple palette of yellow, red, and blue, black and white, with hints of pink and orange, produces chromatic harmony.

Two dark blue triangles—one of which overlays the central red block—add a dynamic depth to the composition.

A monolithic red rectangle grounds the composition and acts as an entry into the work.

Curvilinear shapes along the bottom edge disrupt the otherwise angular work and give it a sense of movement.

Off-white areas in the bottom-right and top left-hand corners provide a backdrop against which other planes advance.

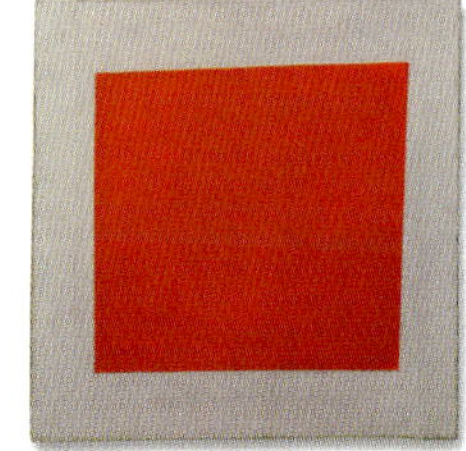

Influence
Kazimir Malevich's *Red Square* (above) inspired Popova's dominant red rectangle. However, Popova transformed the simplicity of Malevich's work into a varied and unified composition.

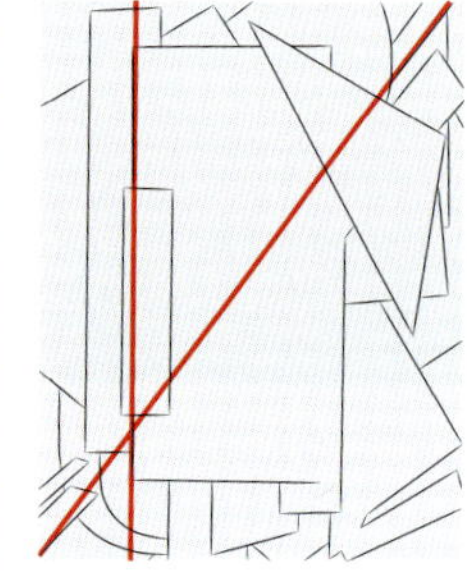

Composition
The dominant vertical movement, driven by the rectilinear forms, is interrupted by the subtle diagonal axis formed by smaller shapes at the corners and edges.

Jeanne Hébuterne

Amedeo Modigliani 1919, oil on canvas, 51 × 32 in (129.5 × 81.5 cm), private collection

Art student Jeanne Hébuterne was 19 when she met Modigliani, and soon began a passionate affair with the Italian artist. During their time together, he painted more than 20 portraits of her. Pregnant here with their second child, she is portrayed with great tenderness. The long oval face, elongated body, and bold contours characterize Modigliani's style.

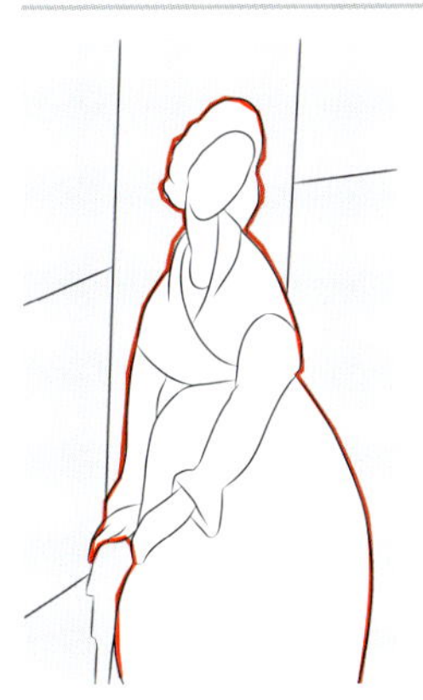

Asymmetry
The asymmetrical, three-quarter-length portrait references 16th-century Italian Mannerist portraits.

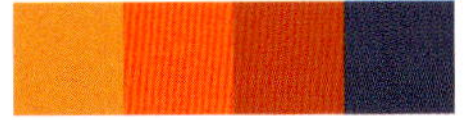

Warm colors
Vibrant ochers and strong reds dominate. They are set against the cool blues of the skirt.

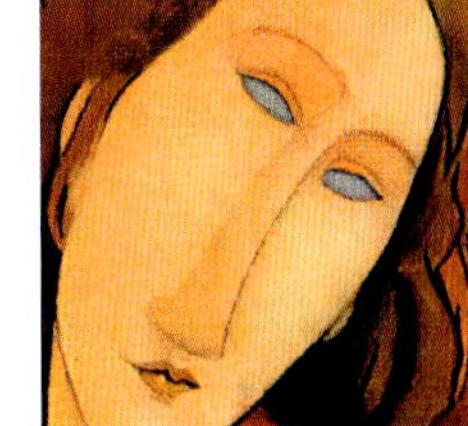

The masklike, oval face with its blank eyes is similar in style to the sculptures that Modigliani created.

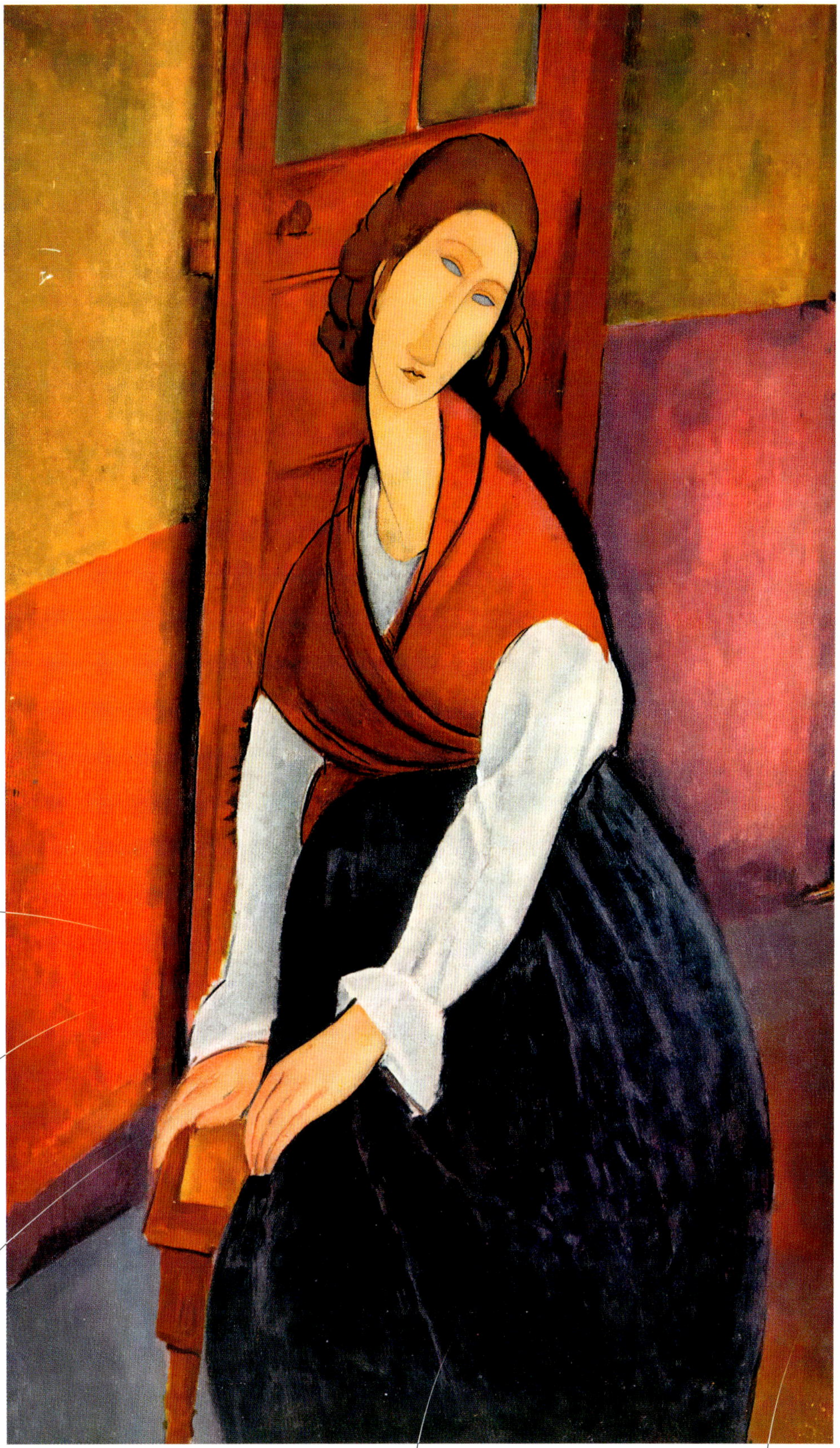

Strong verticals and horizontals form a simplified background. The painted door frames Hébuterne's figure.

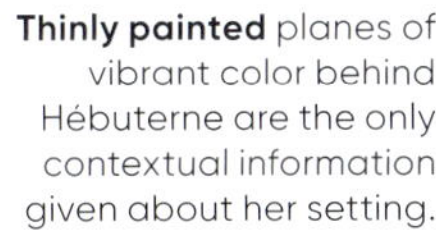

Thinly painted planes of vibrant color behind Hébuterne are the only contextual information given about her setting.

The long, slender hands are stylized rather than realistic. The fingers—all identical—are delineated by a thin brown line.

The simple clothing is sculptural in form. The voluminous skirt suggests the swelling stomach beneath.

Variations in tone between the right and left sides of the painting create a flattened background rather than one in perspective.

> "What I am seeking is not the real and not the unreal but rather the unconscious, the mystery of the instinctive in the human race."
>
> Amedeo Modigliani

Water Lilies

Claude Monet 1919, oil on canvas, 40 × 79 in (101 × 200 cm), Metropolitan Museum of Art, New York, US

For nearly 30 years, from 1897 until his death in 1926, Claude Monet devoted much of his time to painting the water garden in his Giverny estate in Normandy, France. The *Water Lilies*, or *Nymphéas*, cycle contains about 250 paintings, all exploring Monet's fascination with the changing effects of light on water. Unlike much of the artist's later work, this 1919 composition, painted in the wake of World War I, was signed by Monet and released to his dealers to be sold, along with three other paintings of the same scene. It is the left-hand panel of a pair—its sister painting presents a murkier, more foreboding version of the same scene.

Lacking a visible horizon, the painting has a sense of flatness, and the pond appears to go on forever.

Monet claimed that the flowers were just the "accompaniment" to the mirror of the water, with its constantly changing appearance.

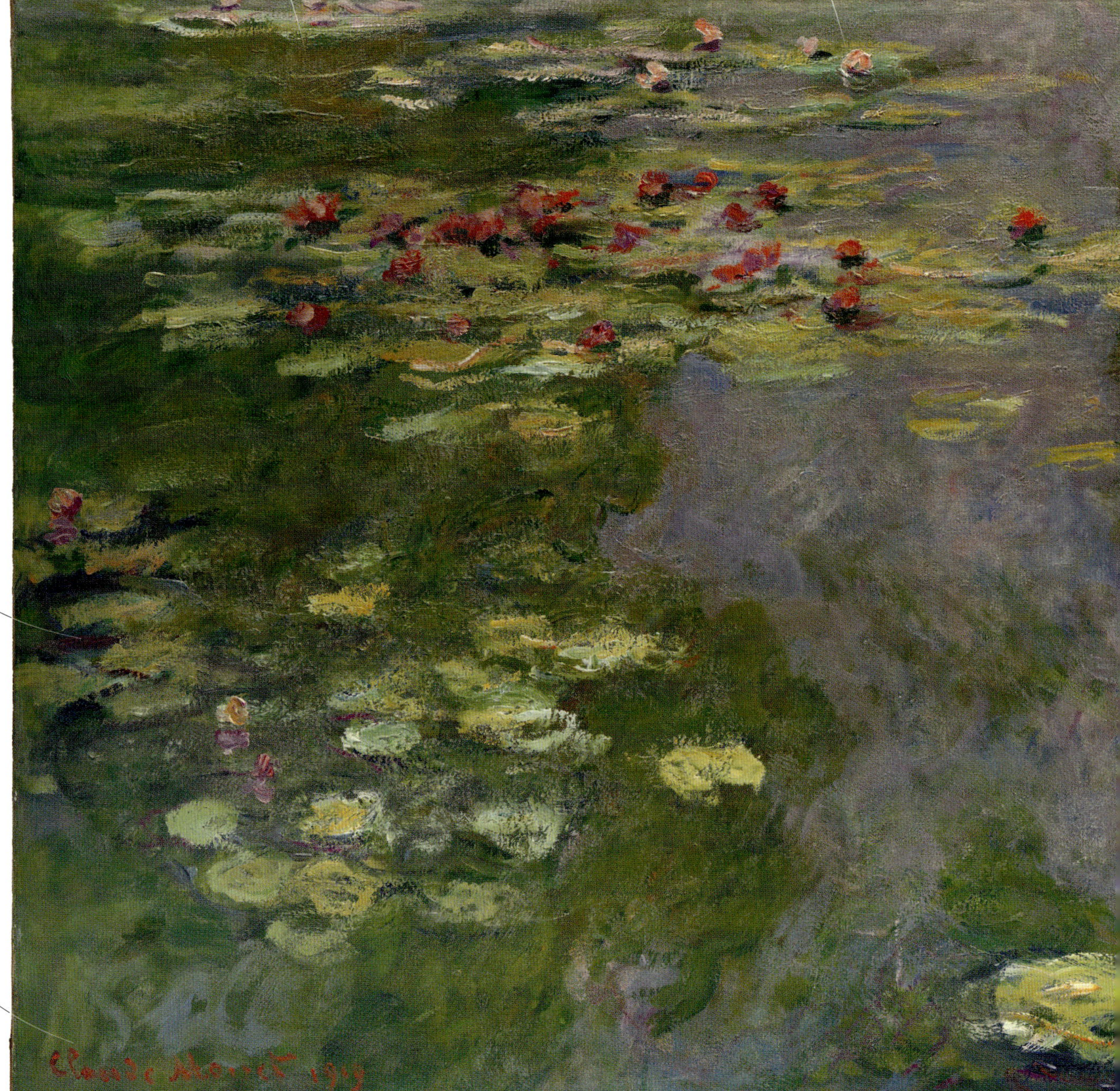

Instead of blending paints, Monet placed strokes of different colors next to one another, so they blend together in the viewer's gaze.

The painting is signed and dated in red, a complementary color to the predominant green tones.

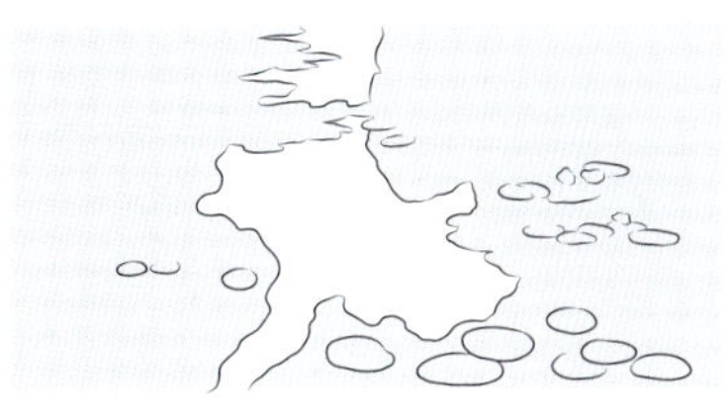

Light effects
The sun's rays reflecting off the water provide a central focus, emphasizing the interplay of light, water, and air.

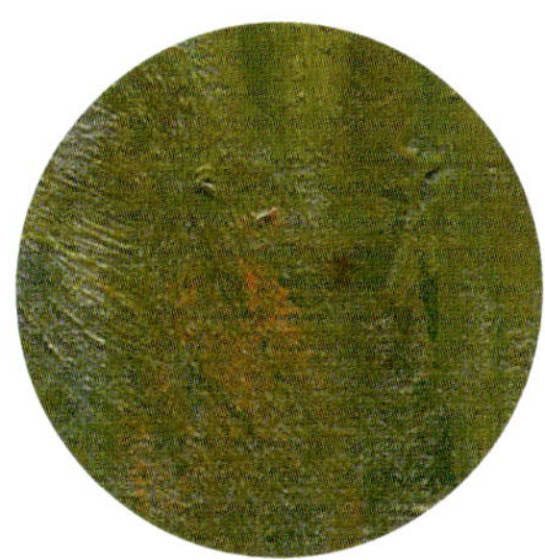

Color adjustment
From 1908, cataracts distorted Monet's vision, and some of the later Water Lilies paintings, such as this one, have a reddish-yellow tinge, or blue where he tried to neutralize the shift.

"The richness I achieve comes from nature, the source of my inspiration."
Claude Monet

The weeping willows around the pond are seen only as reflections, created by swirling, energetic brushstrokes.

Nymphaea, a scientific name for a water lily, is derived from a Greek myth about a goddess of the waters.

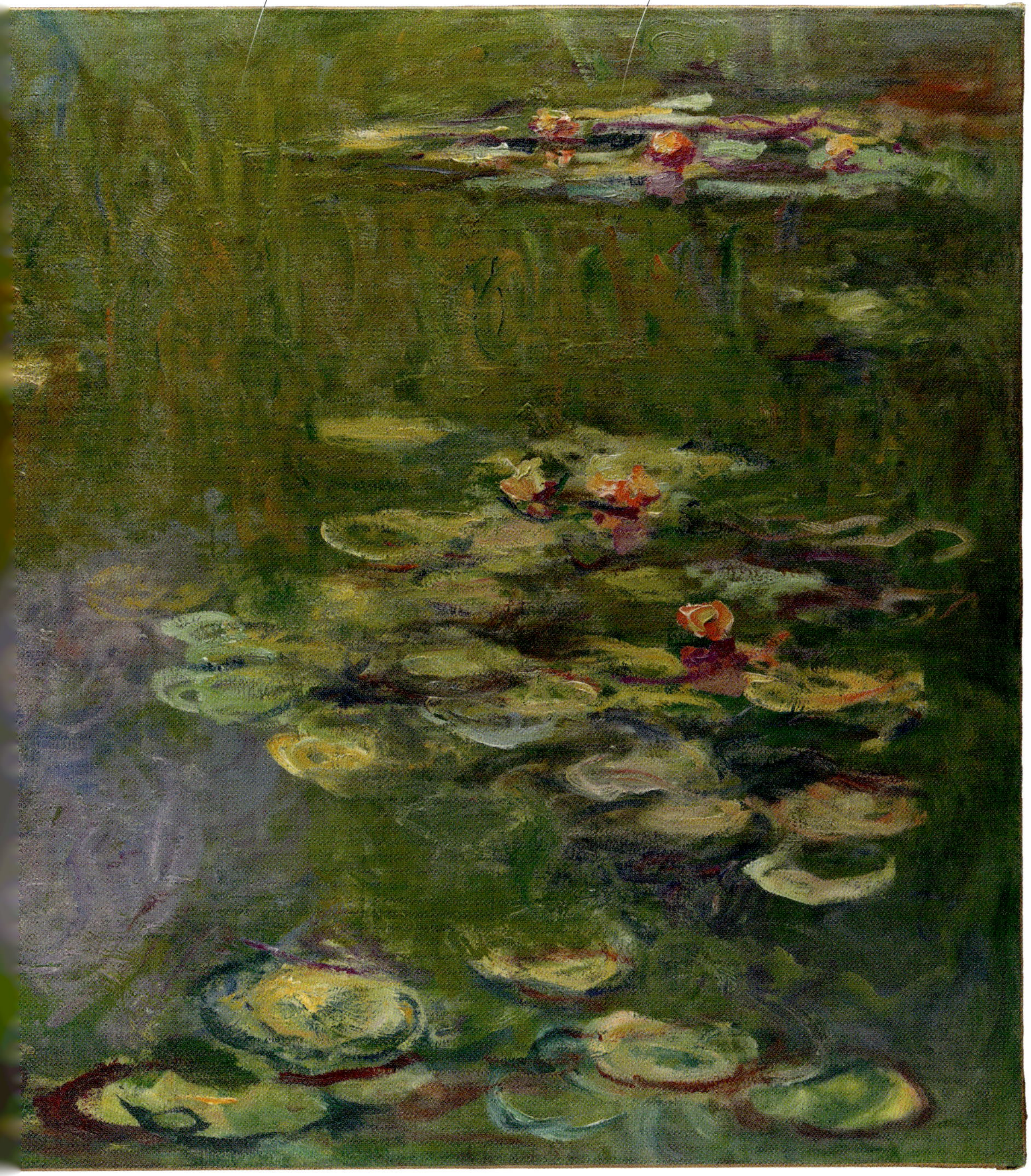

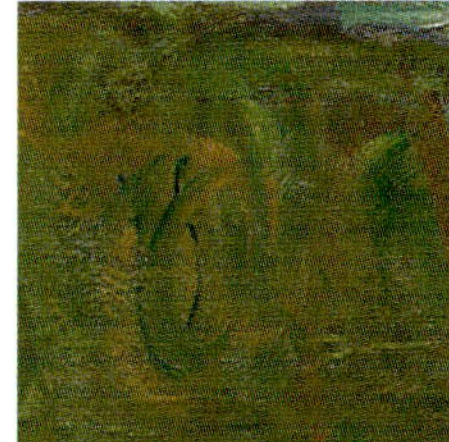

Thickly applied paint gives the brushwork a textured, almost 3D appearance.

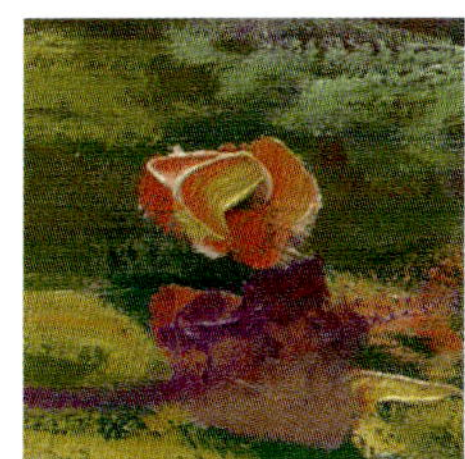

Red, pink, and yellow lilies provide small, but punchy, accents.

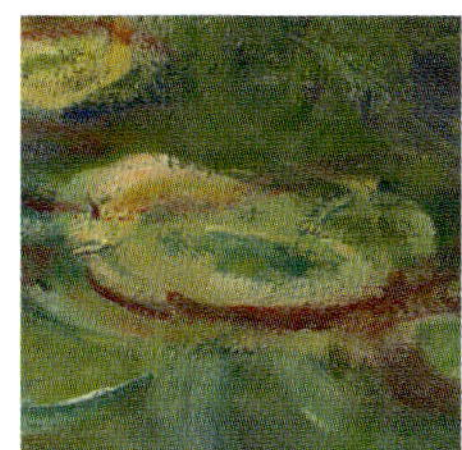

Monet's focus on color and simplified composition in later works like this relate to Post-Impressionism and Abstract art.

The Menin Road

Paul Nash 1919, oil on canvas, 72 × 125 in (182.8 × 317.5 cm), Imperial War Museum, London, UK

An apocalyptic scene of shell-holes and water-filled bomb craters, dead trees, and an endless sea of mud, *The Menin Road* depicts an area in Belgium that saw some of the fiercest fighting of World War I. Nash, who was an official war artist, drew on sketches he made while serving in the trenches to portray the devastated landscape and the mechanized nature of the war. The painting's harsh light, hard edges, and overall angular treatment add to the unreality of the scene and help convey the terrible ravaging of nature.

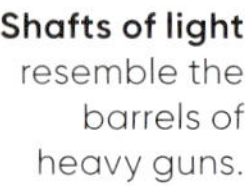

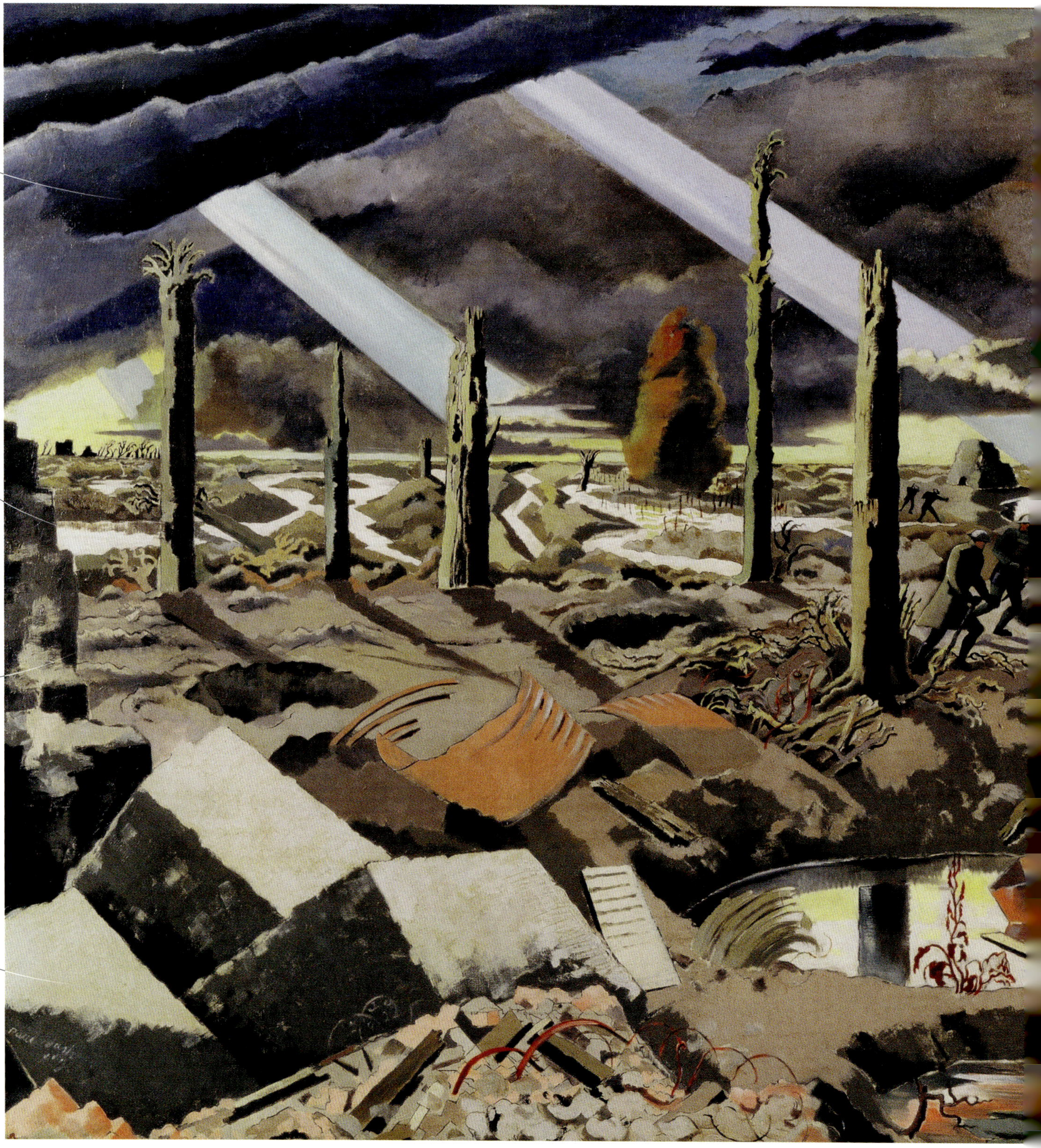

Shafts of light resemble the barrels of heavy guns.

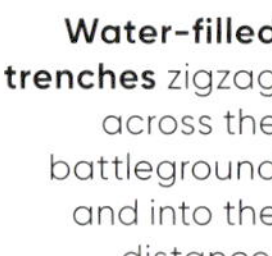

Water-filled trenches zigzag across the battleground and into the distance.

Elements reduce in size quickly as they recede into the distance, creating a vast space and an unreachable horizon.

Three concrete blocks create an obstacle at the front of the painting.

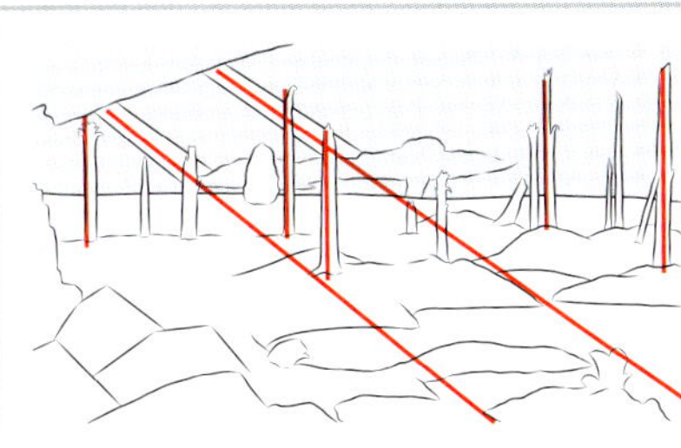

Verticals and diagonals
The eye is drawn across the painting from upper left to lower right by the shadows of the vertical trees and the shafts of light. The edge-to-edge composition suggests that the world of the painting extends beyond the confines of the canvas.

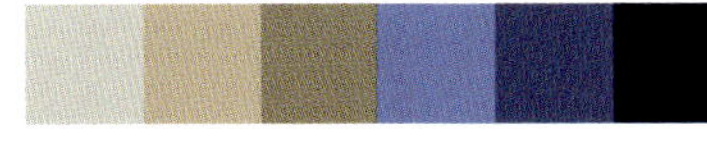

Inspired by Flemish craftsmen
The palette of earthy browns, blues, and black is said to be based on the color schemes of Flemish tapestries.

> "I am a messenger ... to those who want the war to go on for ever ... may it burn their lousy souls."
>
> Paul Nash, 1917

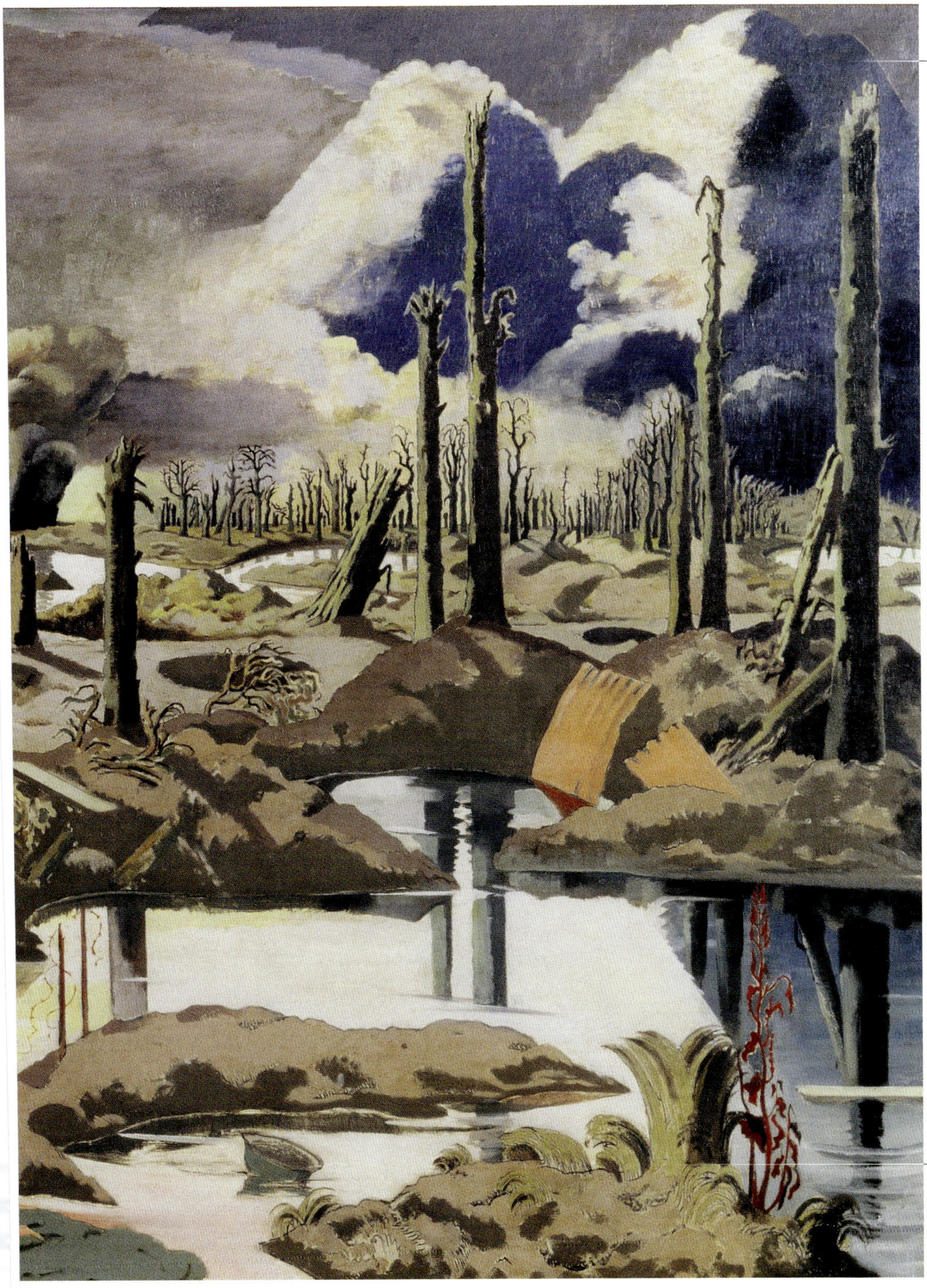

Dark clouds—which could be due to the weather or plumes of smoke—echo the concrete blocks in the opposite corner.

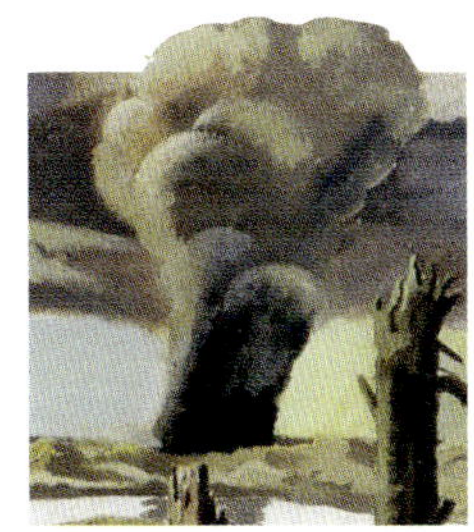

An exploding artillery shell sends up a column of mud, evidence that the battle continues to be fought elsewhere.

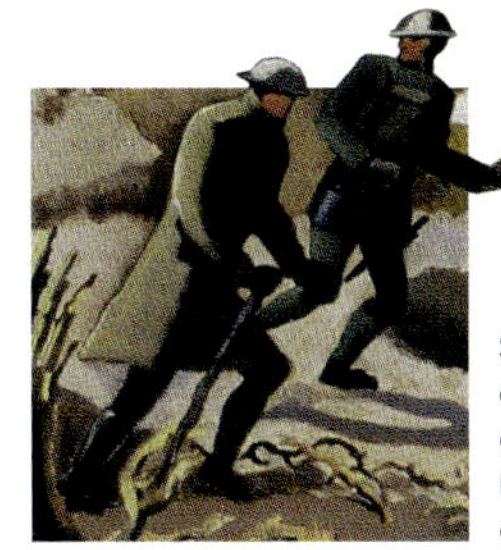

Soldiers are depicted as small figures who are overwhelmed by the huge scale of the landscape.

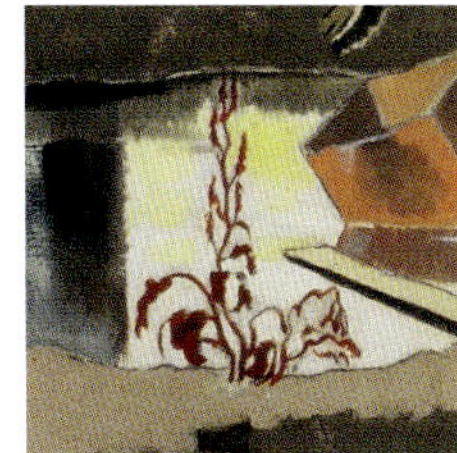

Small plants have survived the onslaught and act as a symbol of hope or endurance.

A soldier's helmet floats in the water.

The Convalescent

Gwen John 1923–1924, oil on canvas, 16 × 13 in (41.2 × 33 cm), Fitzwilliam Museum, Cambridge, UK

In this quiet but affecting painting, a young woman sits in an armchair and looks at a letter in her hands. John approached this introspective subject again and again—there are at least 10 versions of this painting, while the unknown girl appears in at least 50 of her later works. This example is characteristic of her style.

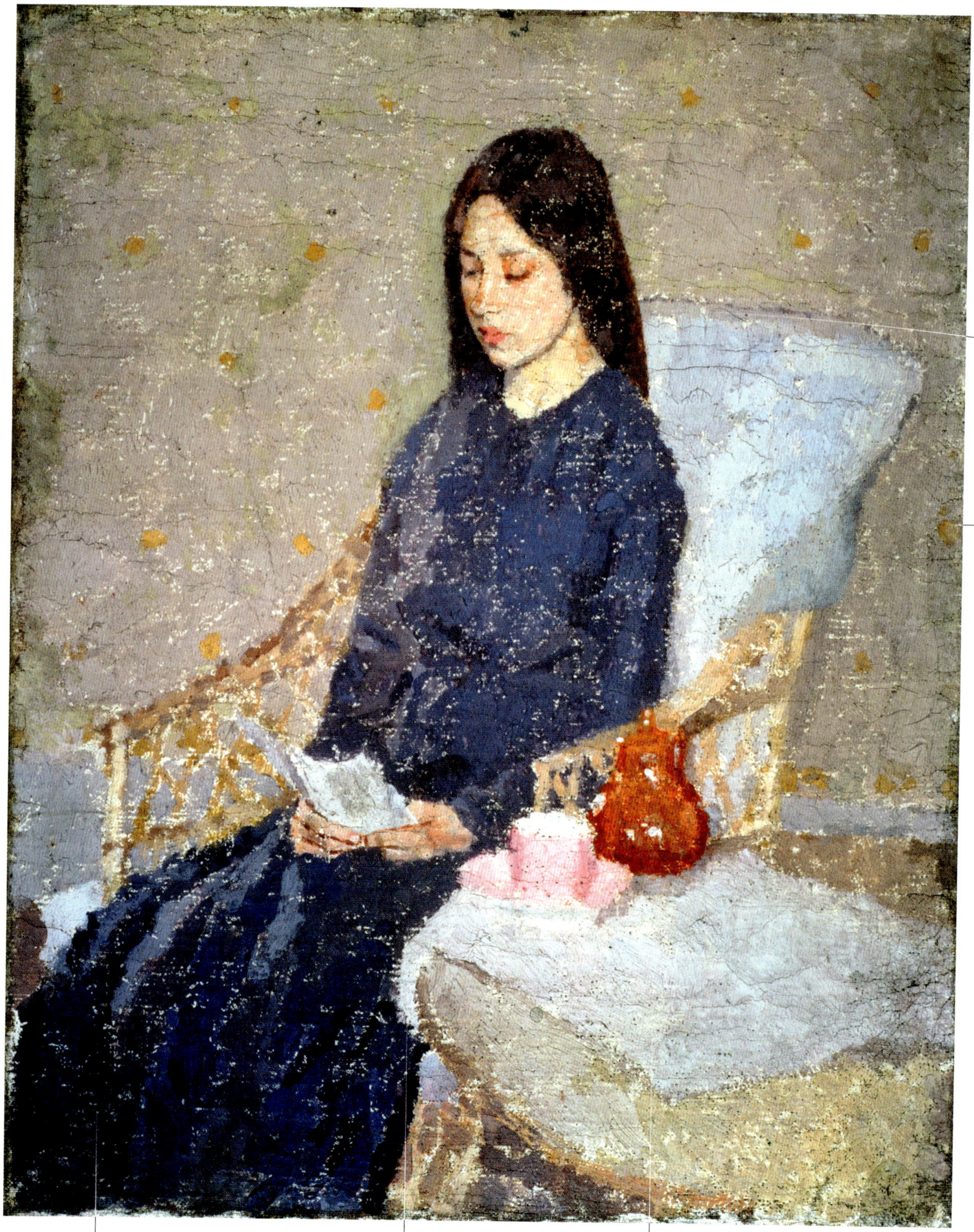

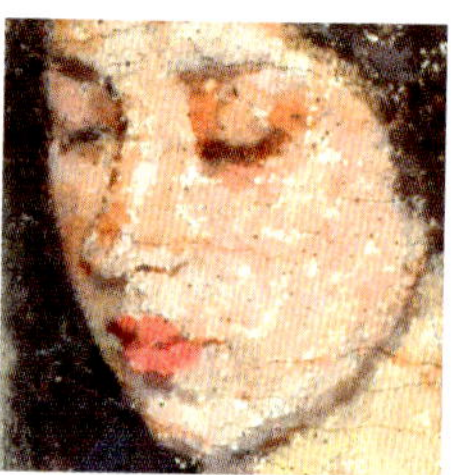

Her face is modeled using careful splodges of color, which combine to form a pleasing whole.

The sitter reads the letter, but the absence of expression on her face suggests she may be rereading it or perhaps is lost in thought.

Gold circles probably represent yellow flowers on the wallpaper.

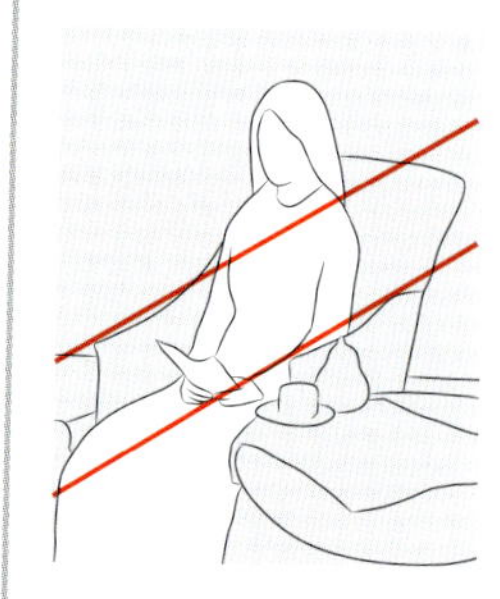

Center stage
The diagonals in the lines of the chair and table drive attention toward the face and torso of the figure.

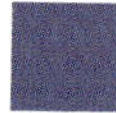
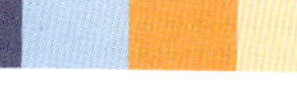

Complementary colors
The painting is a study in the contrast between the cool prominent blue of the dress, emphasized in the blue shading of the blanket over the back of the chair, versus the warm gold of the jug, the bamboo chair, and the girl's skin.

The folds of the dress are implied with broad strokes of differing shades of blue, gray, and purple.

The pose echoes the frailty suggested by the title.

A pink teacup and terra-cotta jug add balance to the composition by highlighting those colors in the rest of the work.

The Blue Room

Suzanne Valadon 1923, oil on canvas, 35 × 46 in (90 × 116 cm), Musée National d'Art Moderne, Paris, France

Valadon's self-portrait pokes fun at the famous nudes painted by male artists. Like the models in Ingres's *Grande Odalisque* or Manet's *Olympia*, Valadon lies on a bed, but she is fully dressed, wearing the clothes in which she feels most comfortable rather than an outfit to please the "male gaze."

Books piled up on the bed establish that Valadon is no man's plaything, but an intelligent woman with ideas of her own.

This hanging drape is a more colorful version of the one seen above the bed in Manet's *Olympia* (1863).

The cigarette recalls the hookah pipe in Ingres's *Grande Odalisque* (1814), while challenging 1920s taboos on women smoking.

With her hair tied up—she has work to do—Valadon looks off to one side, without meeting the viewer's gaze.

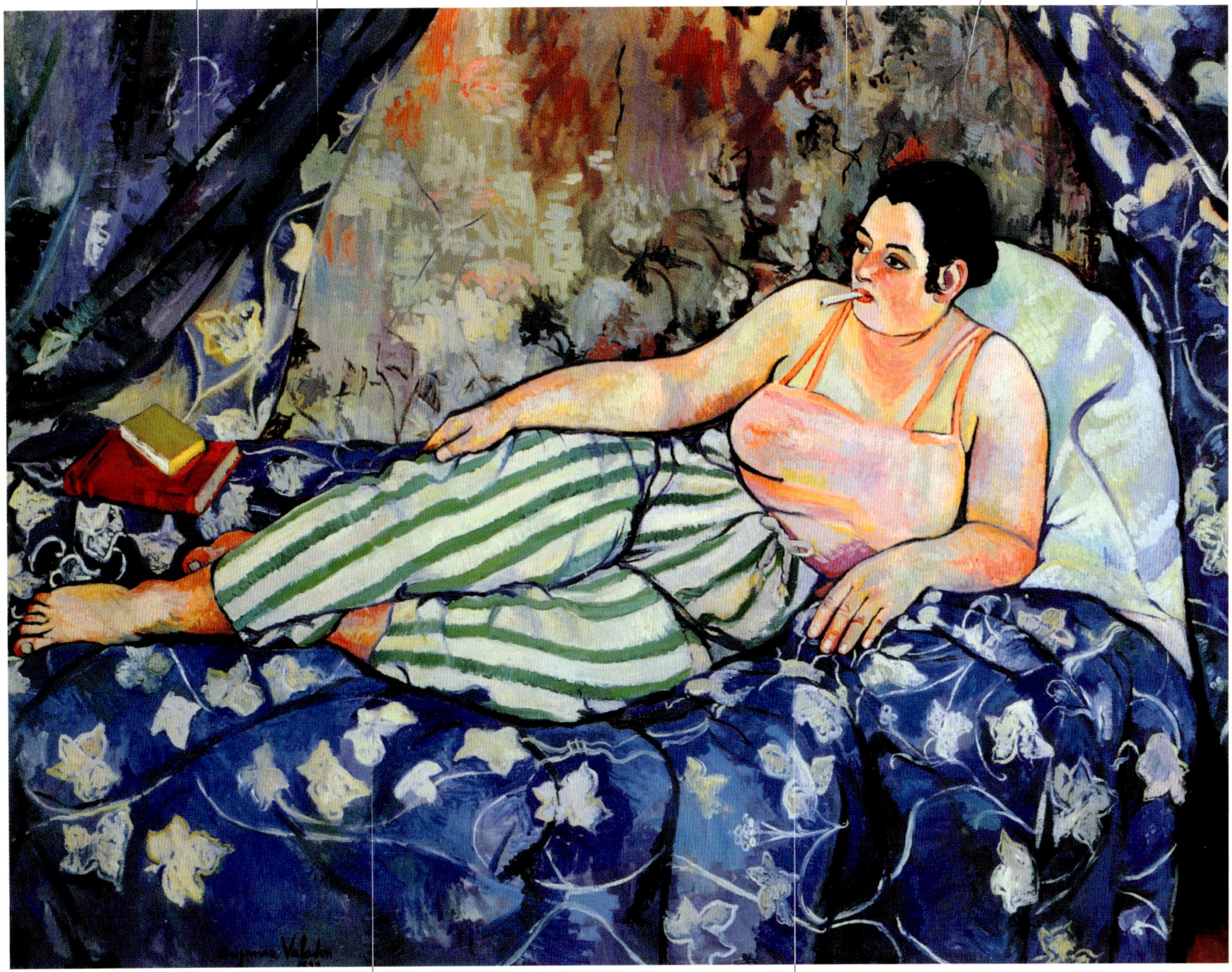

Harem pants, fashionable at the time, mock Ingres's *Odalisque*, as Valadon rejects the role of sultan's concubine.

Valadon's bodice, almost matches the color of her flesh, ridiculing the viewer's momentary expectation of nudity.

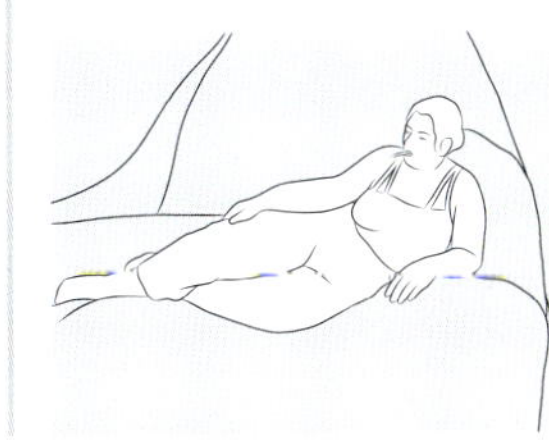

The model
Valadon had modeled for male painters, so she made the perfect model for herself. Her pose is that of the classic 19th-century nude—except for her expression of indifference, and her clothes.

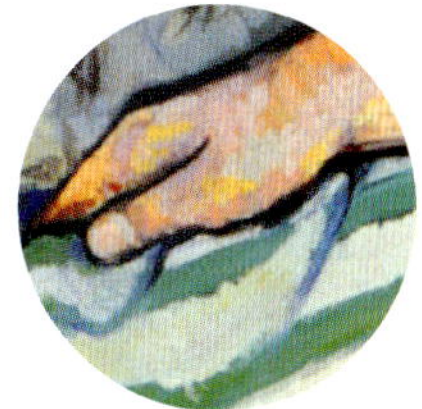

Bold approach
The self-confident outline of the subject and the use of bold brushstrokes echo much Post-Impressionist art.

> "At the center of a maelstrom of color, on display but in command, she's perfectly at ease."
>
> Will Heinrich, 2021

Two Calla Lilies on Pink

Georgia O'Keeffe 1928, oil on canvas, 40 × 30 in (101.6 × 76.2 cm), Philadelphia Museum of Art, Pennsylvania, US

Distilled down to their contours, curves, and colors, O'Keeffe's calla lilies are neither fully realistic nor indecipherably abstract. The flowers are dramatically larger than their actual size, with their petals painted as sweeping broad waves, encouraging viewers to see them anew and appreciate nature's beauty.

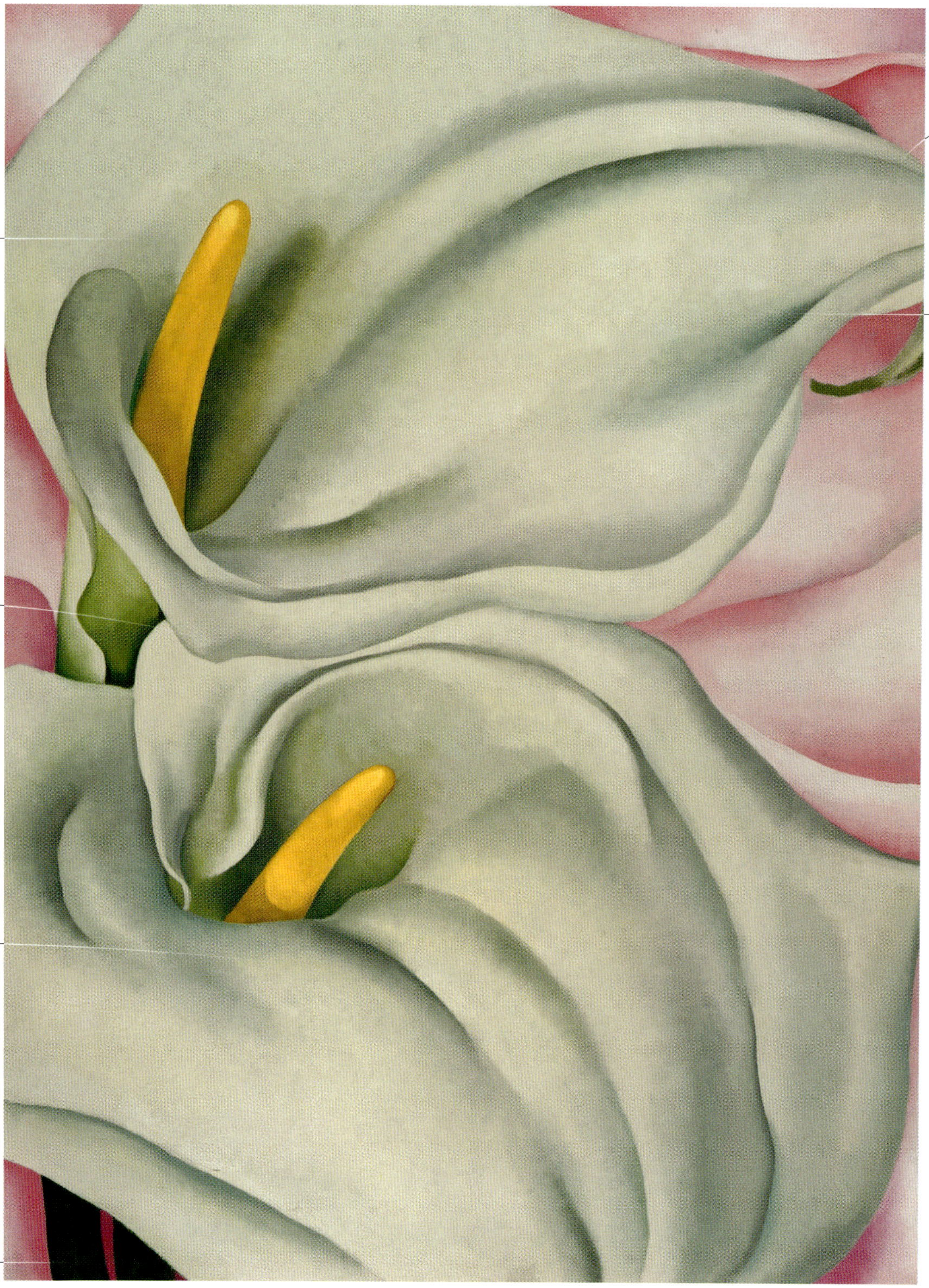

Many see sexual imagery in the erect spadices extending into the soft concavity of spathes. O'Keeffe denied any sexual meaning.

Here the two lilies seem to almost melt together, contributing to the sense of softness and fluidity.

White calla lilies have more than one symbolic meaning—they are associated with both death and innocence.

Stems are barely visible and there is no vase; O'Keeffe painted calla lilies, not a still-life containing them.

The tips of calla lily spathes taper to points; O'Keeffe frames out these points, leaving only soft, curving shapes.

Calla lilies preoccupied O'Keeffe more than any other flower. In 1928 alone, she painted them six times.

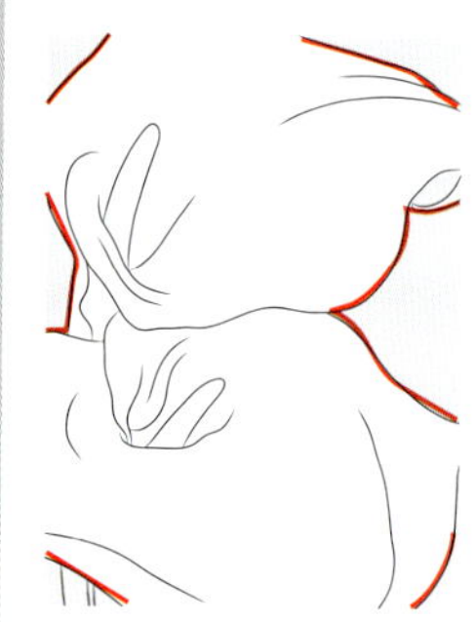

Close up
The flowers' impressive size—the two lilies essentially fill a yard-high canvas—contributes greatly to their impact. Using a single color behind the blooms ensures the focus remains on them.

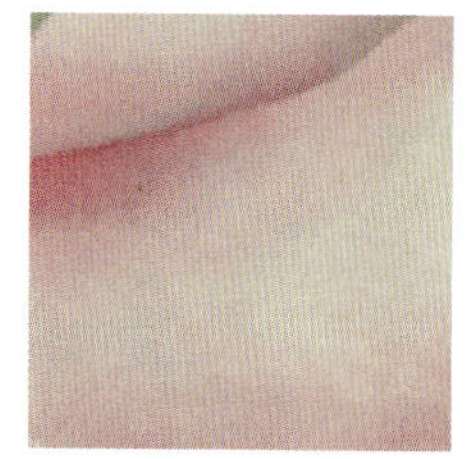

Artistic perfection
The abstraction of O'Keeffe's calla lilies hides her attention to detail; she often mixed paint for hours to achieve a precise color.

American Gothic

Grant Wood 1930, oil on beaver board, 31 × 26 in (78 × 65.3 cm), Art Institute of Chicago, Illinois, US

Wood's iconic image of a man and woman standing before a house both extols and gently satirizes rural Midwestern Americans. Wood, a rural Midwesterner himself, saw the absurdity of these people but also their fundamental goodness and unshakable work ethic. Just as this man, woman, and house were out of step with the modern world in 1930, Wood's painting was at odds with the art movements of the day.

The pattern of the curtain fabric echoes that featured on the woman's apron.

A steeple visible on the horizon echoes the lightning rod at the top of the farmhouse and notes Midwestern Christian values.

Nan Wood Graham, Wood's sister, modeled for the woman—he elongated her face and she changed her hair.

It is believed that the brooch belonged to Wood's mother—she wore it in his painting *Woman with Plant*.

Their clothing already looked dated when Wood painted *American Gothic*. Like the architecture, it suggests the late 19th century.

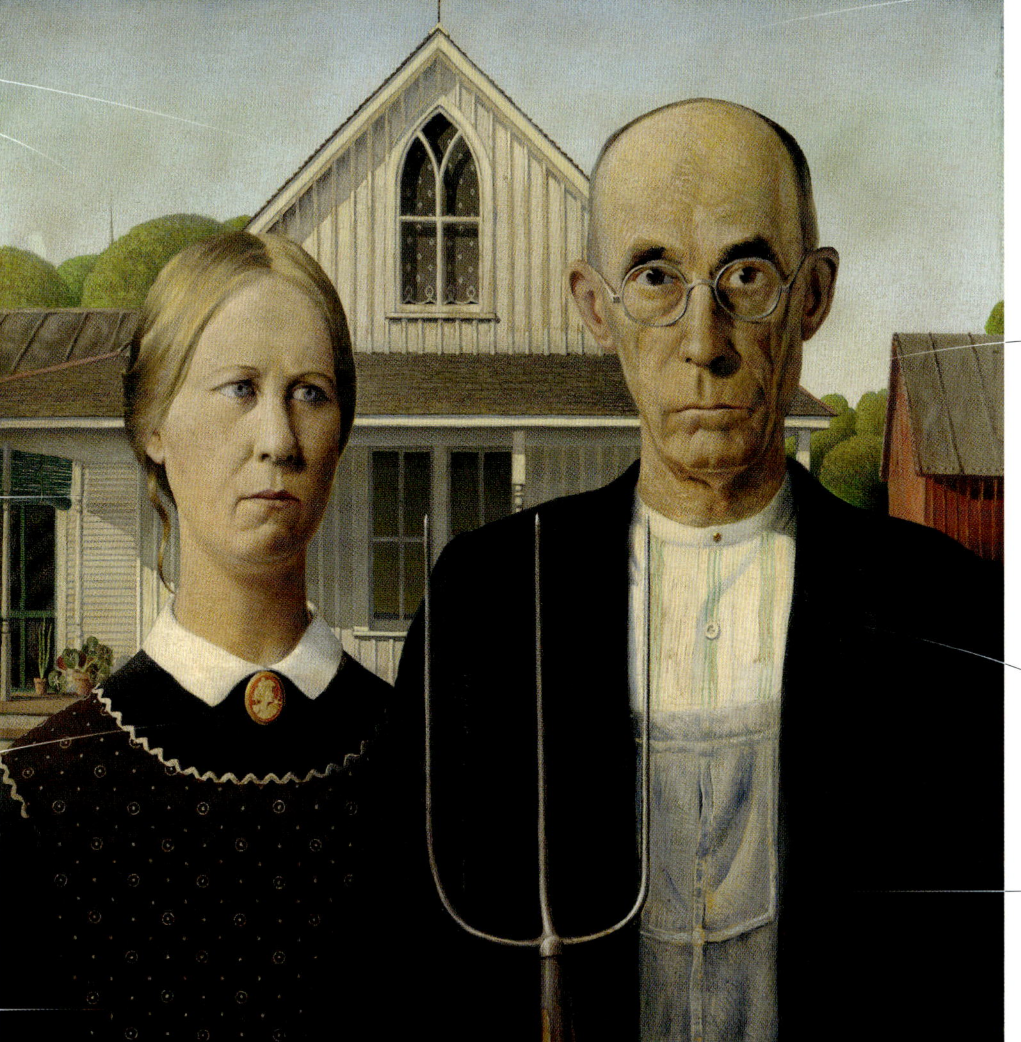

An incongruous "Carpenter Gothic" farmhouse—a humble abode with a pretentious Gothic window—in Eldon, Iowa, inspired *American Gothic*.

Wood's dentist, Dr. Byron McKeeby, reluctantly modeled for the man; Wood liked the long, straight lines of his face.

Wood initially said the couple were man and wife, but later claimed they were father and daughter.

Stitching in the bib of the man's overalls echoes the shape of the pitchfork.

There is a suggestion of confrontation in the dominant pitchfork. In the initial sketch for the painting, the man holds a rake, not a pitchfork.

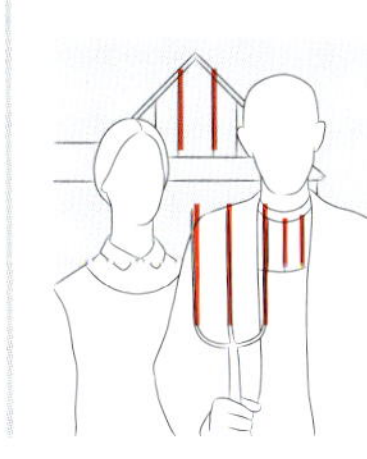

Keeping things straight
Repeating vertical lines—pitchfork tines, details in the house and barn, and stripes on the man's shirt—reinforce the couple's elongated faces and help convey their upright values.

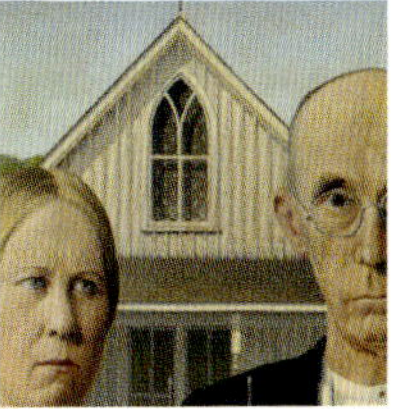

Joined as a pair
The angled roof line of the farmhouse in the background ties together the portraits of the man and woman in the foreground.

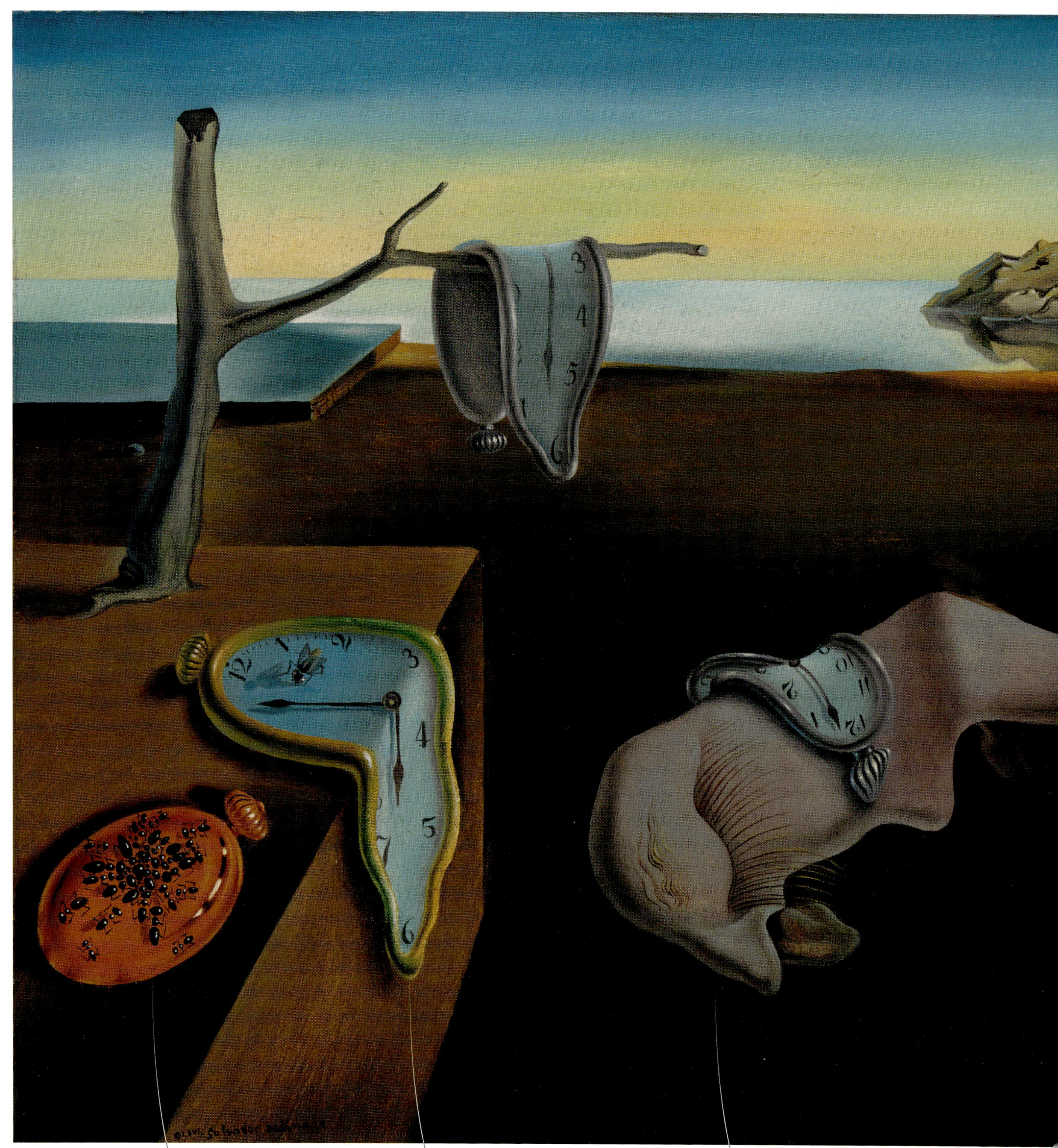

Ants consume a gold pocket watch as if it were rotting fruit. Ants and flies symbolize decay and often appear in Dalí's work.

The watches are a symbol of time, but their malleable shapes emphasize the distorting nature of time.

The amorphous face shape in the center is a self-portrait of the artist dreaming the scene around him.

The Persistence of Memory

Salvador Dalí 1931, oil on canvas, 9 x 13 in (24.1 x 33 cm), MoMA, New York, US

Dalí depicts a dreamscape, possibly based on Port Lligat, the village in Spain where he grew up. The work is an example of the artist's paranoiac-critical method, in which he sought to discredit reality by distorting and subverting everyday objects and concepts, such as clocks and time, and placing them in imagined contexts. Its title and content allude to the idea of memories and dreams as unconscious time that cannot be measured by clocks. Characteristic of Dalí, and Surrealism, the painting is disturbing yet elusive, its symbols and juxtapositions compelling and repelling in turn.

Hard and jagged, the coastline contrasts with the soft organic shapes in the foreground.

A barren and empty landscape reinforces a feeling of uneasiness.

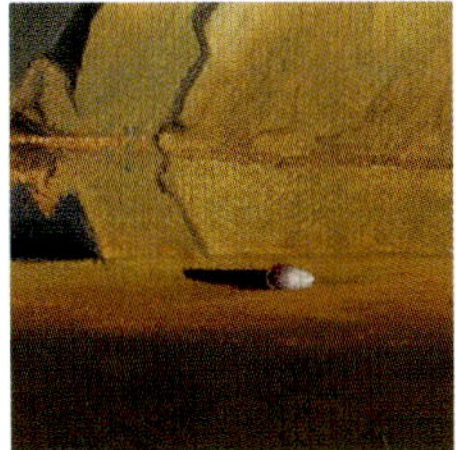

A tiny egg in the background symbolizes birth and represents Dalí's interest in the contrast between "soft" (the egg's contents) and "hard" (the shell).

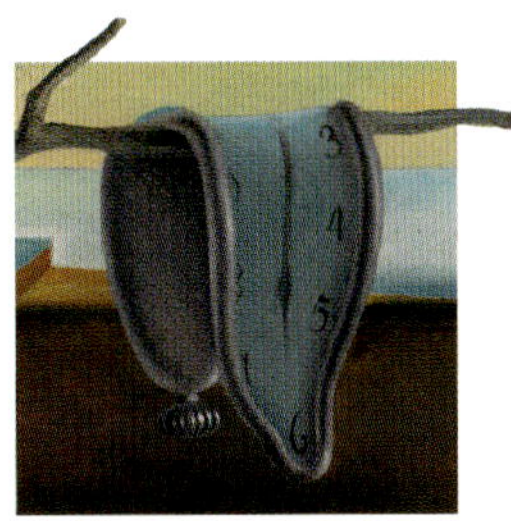

Dalí likened the soft, limp clocks, one of which hangs on a dead branch, to overripe Camembert.

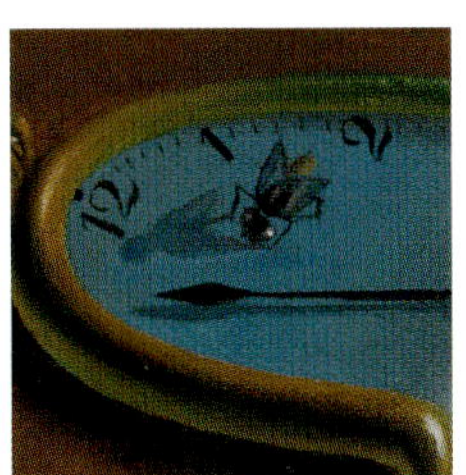

The fly and its reflection in the watch glass allude to the tradition of still-life painting and memento mori—reminders of death.

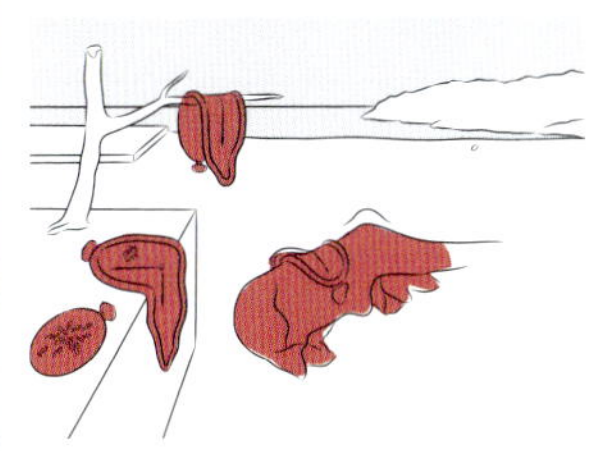

High horizon
The surreal objects on the left are balanced by a more traditional landscape in the distance on the right, creating a high-horizon composition that directs attention to the foreground.

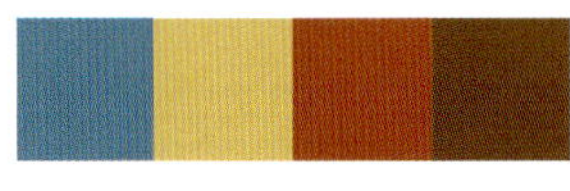

Creating a mood
The cool blues and yellows of the distant skyline contrast with the warmer oranges and browns of the foreground, creating a dreamlike atmosphere.

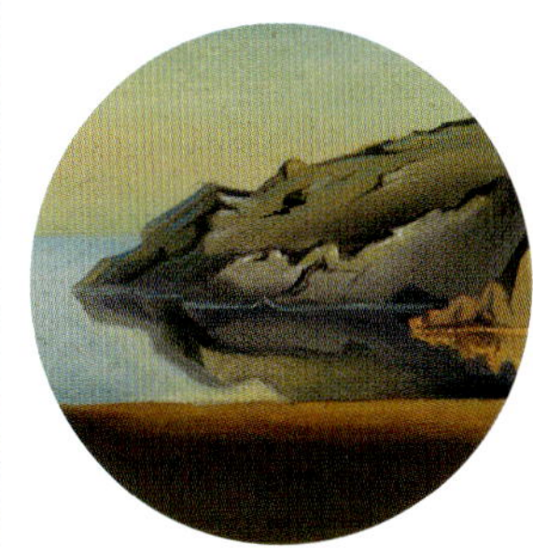

Hyperrealism
Dalí described his technique as "hand-painted color photography," in which fine brushstrokes emphasize a sense of reality juxtaposed with the irrationality of the subject matter.

> "[The] flabby watches are nothing else than the tender, extravagant and solitary paranoiac-critical Camembert of time and space."
>
> Salvador Dalí

Animals

In European art, animals were originally included in paintings because they were associated with certain saints or as symbols of virtues. In all cultures, an interest in natural history increasingly led to animals being the subjects of paintings in their own right and being portrayed in naturalistic styles, alongside their continuing symbolic roles. Above all, animal art celebrates the beauty and power of animals and the pleasure they provide for humans.

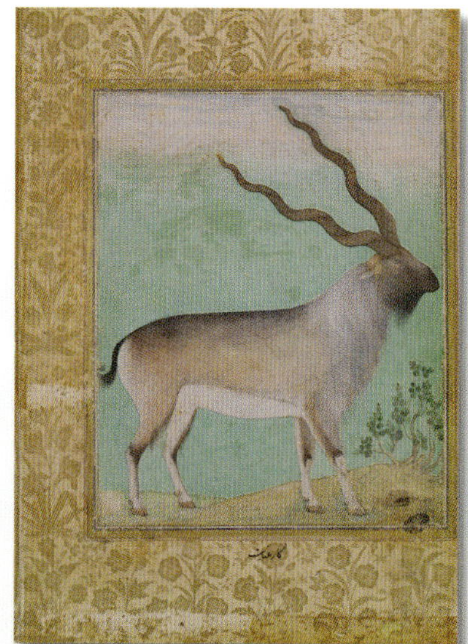

2

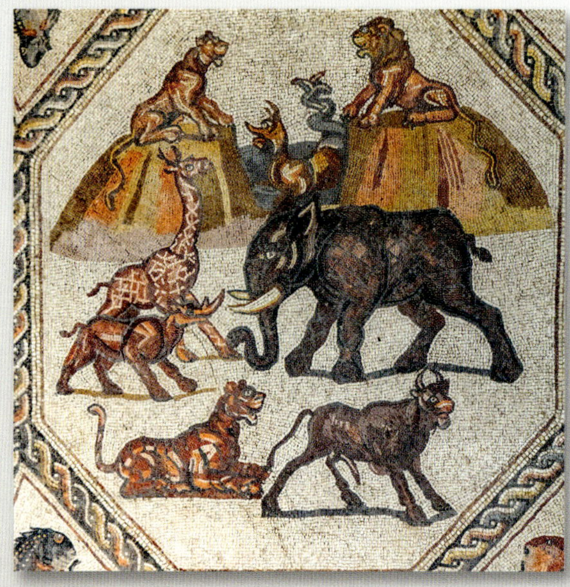

1

3

4

1. ***The Lod Mosaic*, c. 300 CE.** This Roman floor mosaic, uncovered in the Israeli town of Lod, depicts a selection of wild animals, including a giraffe and a rhinoceros, species that rarely appeared in ancient art. The mosaic may refer to animals that appeared in Roman amphitheaters.

2. ***Ibex*, Mughal School, 1612.** An ibex, a symbol of agility and resilience in many cultures, is depicted standing against a plain background. The artist, working during the artistically rich Jahangir period (1605–1627), has picked out the animal's fur and horns in exquisite detail.

3. ***Goldfinch*, Carel Fabritius, 1654.** It was unusual for a bird to be the main subject of a painting in the 17th century. This goldfinch is chained to the feeder by its foot, but it looks as though it is about to fly away. The bird may symbolize the crucified Christ, or perhaps captive love.

4. ***Walking Tiger*, unknown artist, 16th century.** In Japanese mythology, the tiger represented the earth and its roar created the wind. This expressive style of ink painting and the subject—tigers did not exist in Japan—were based on examples of Chinese ink painting.

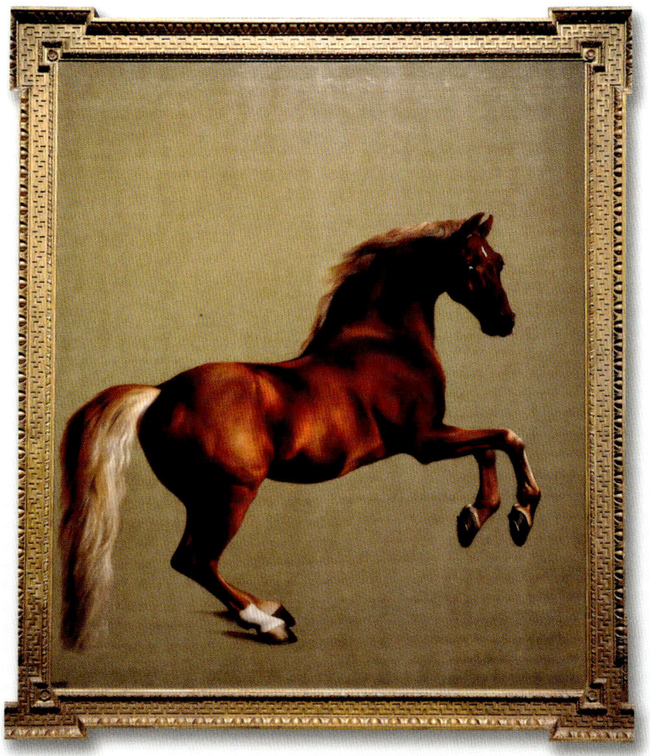

5

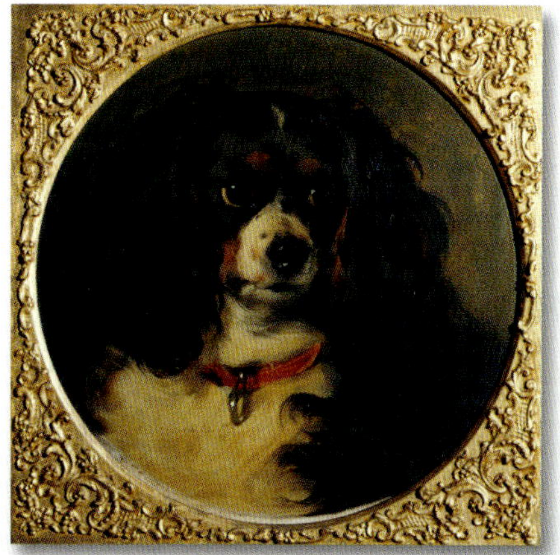

7

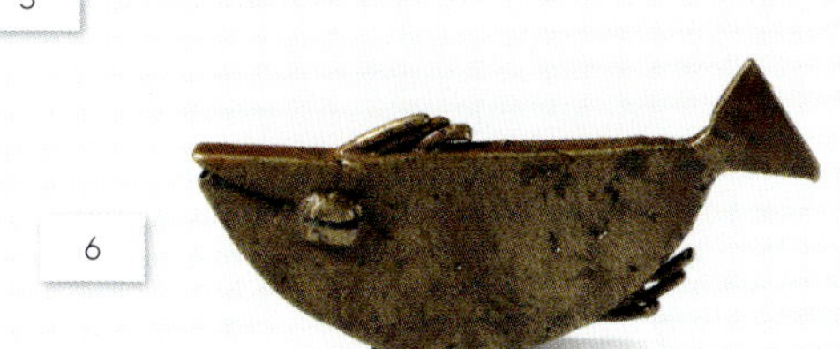

6

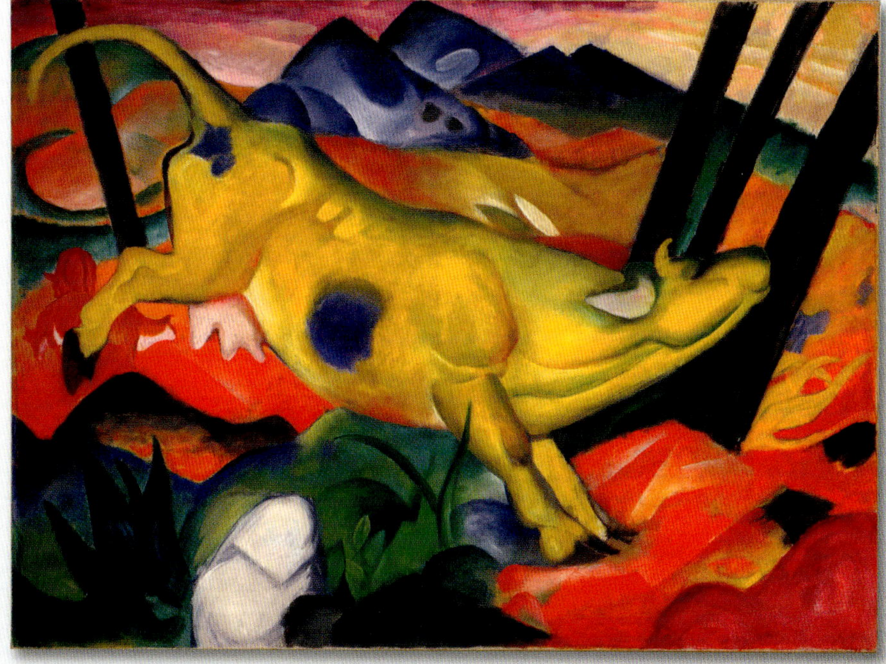

8

5. ***Whistlejacket*, George Stubbs, 1762.** This detailed portrait captures the energy, power, and tension of a successful racehorse, as well as its temperamental character. Stubbs was famous for his studies of horses; his understanding of their anatomy was based on careful observation.

6. **Asante *Gold Weight Fish*, 1800.** Weights cast in brass were used for balancing gold dust, the currency in the Akan region of West Africa. The weights, which could be figurative or geometric, also allude to proverbs and myths, illustrating the character of the person who made them.

7. ***Dash*, Sir Edwin Landseer, 1836.** This characterful portrait is of a King Charles spaniel owned by Britain's Queen Victoria. Landseer specialized in animal paintings, especially of dogs, that tended toward the anthropomorphic and sentimental.

8. ***The Yellow Cow*, Franz Marc, 1911.** Marc used color symbolically: yellow for the feminine principle, blue for the masculine, and red for the earth. Here, the repetition of the three colors links the cow to the background. The work may celebrate Marc's marriage to Maria Franck.

Let My People Go

Aaron Douglas c. 1935–1939, oil on Masonite, 48 x 36 in (121.9 x 91.4 cm), Metropolitan Museum of Art, New York, US

Douglas depicts Moses leading the Israelites out of Egyptian enslavement, as described in the Bible's Book of Exodus. This is the seventh of eight panels in a series of illustrations originally accompanying James Weldon Johnson's book of poems, *God's Trombones: Seven Negro Sermons in Verse*. Douglas, a Black American, used the Biblical story to reflect the end of enslavement in the US.

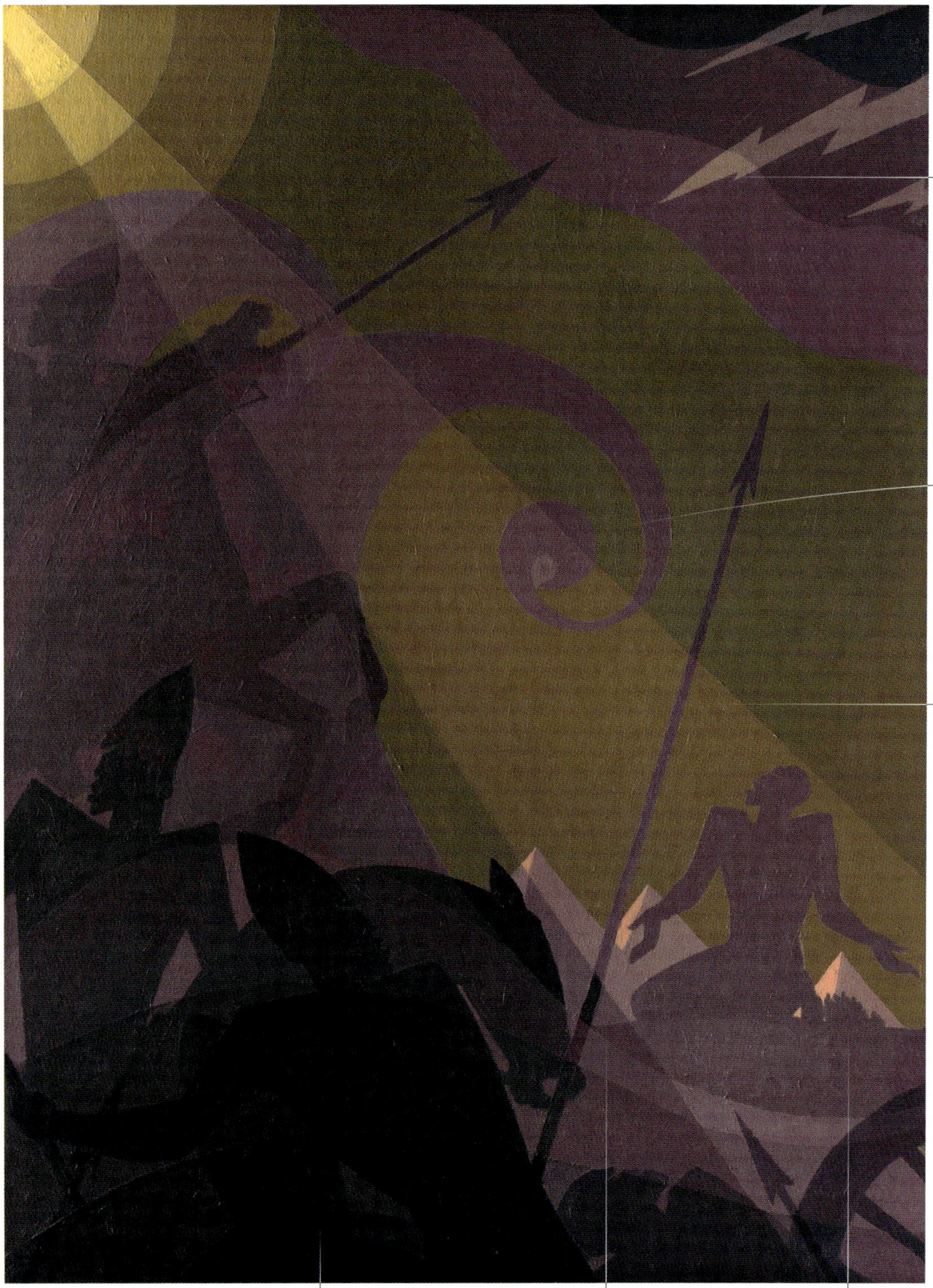

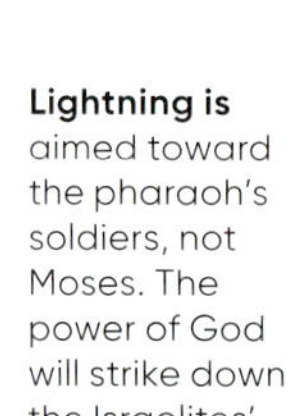

Lightning is aimed toward the pharaoh's soldiers, not Moses. The power of God will strike down the Israelites' pursuers.

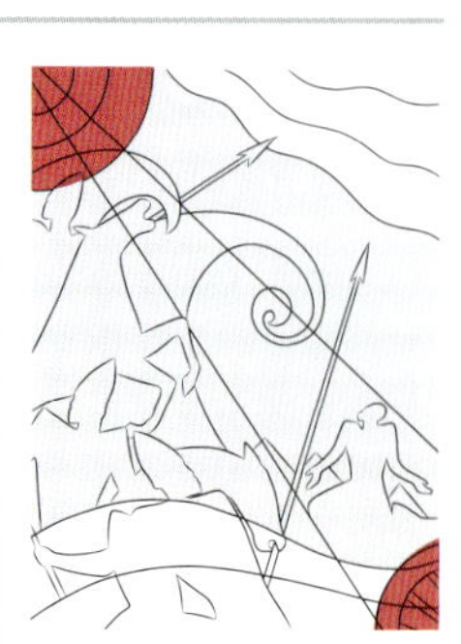

Complementary shapes Repetition of geometric forms creates symmetry and harmony. Circles representing God in the upper left are echoed by a wagon wheel in the lower right. The waviness of the clouds in the upper right is subtly echoed by wavy lines low on the painting.

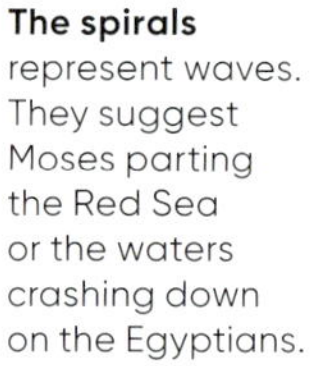

The spirals represent waves. They suggest Moses parting the Red Sea or the waters crashing down on the Egyptians.

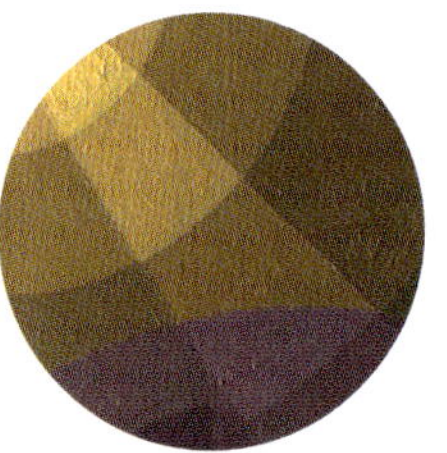

Diagonal spotlight Divine light provides directional lighting, leading the viewer's eye toward Moses, the painting's key figure, while also creating contrast.

A beam of light shines on Moses, representing God's guidance or Moses's enlightenment.

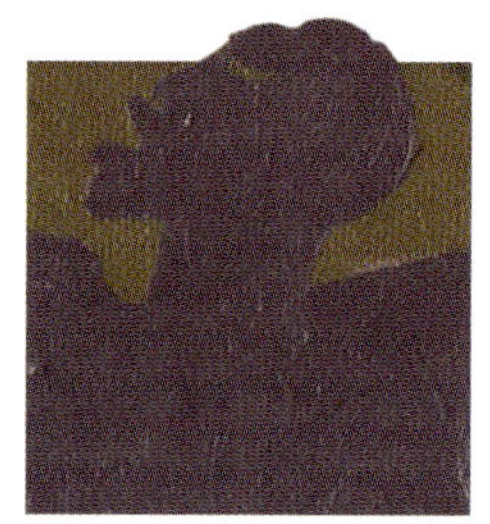

Moses kneels in deference to God. Douglas's silhouetted Moses appears to be ethnically from south of the Sahara.

Pharaoh's soldiers have the darkest value (amount of black or white in the hue). The pyramids have the lightest value, which makes them appear distant.

Behind Moses, the triangles represent Egyptian pyramids—perhaps the three pyramids of Giza.

This dark mass of lines may represent Israelites in the distance, following Moses out of Egypt.

> "[Douglas] was looking at Biblical history, but he was also looking at the social plight—that African Americans were under the rule of the Pharaoh, so to speak."
>
> David Driskell, 2015

Medallion

Gluck 1936, oil on canvas, 12 × 14 in (30.5 × 35.6 cm), private collection

This small double portrait of the artist Gluck and Nesta Obermer, wife of wealthy American Seymour Obermer, is an unapologetic announcement of a lesbian love affair at a time when such relationships were socially unacceptable. The painting was inspired by an evening at the opera, during which the two women felt fused into one person through the intensity of the music.

The simple background emphasizes the profiles of the two women.

Nesta is presented as a classical beauty with blonde hair, rose-colored lips, and blue eyes. She gazes up, her face bathed in light.

The outline of Nesta's hair behind Gluck suggests that the two women are fused together.

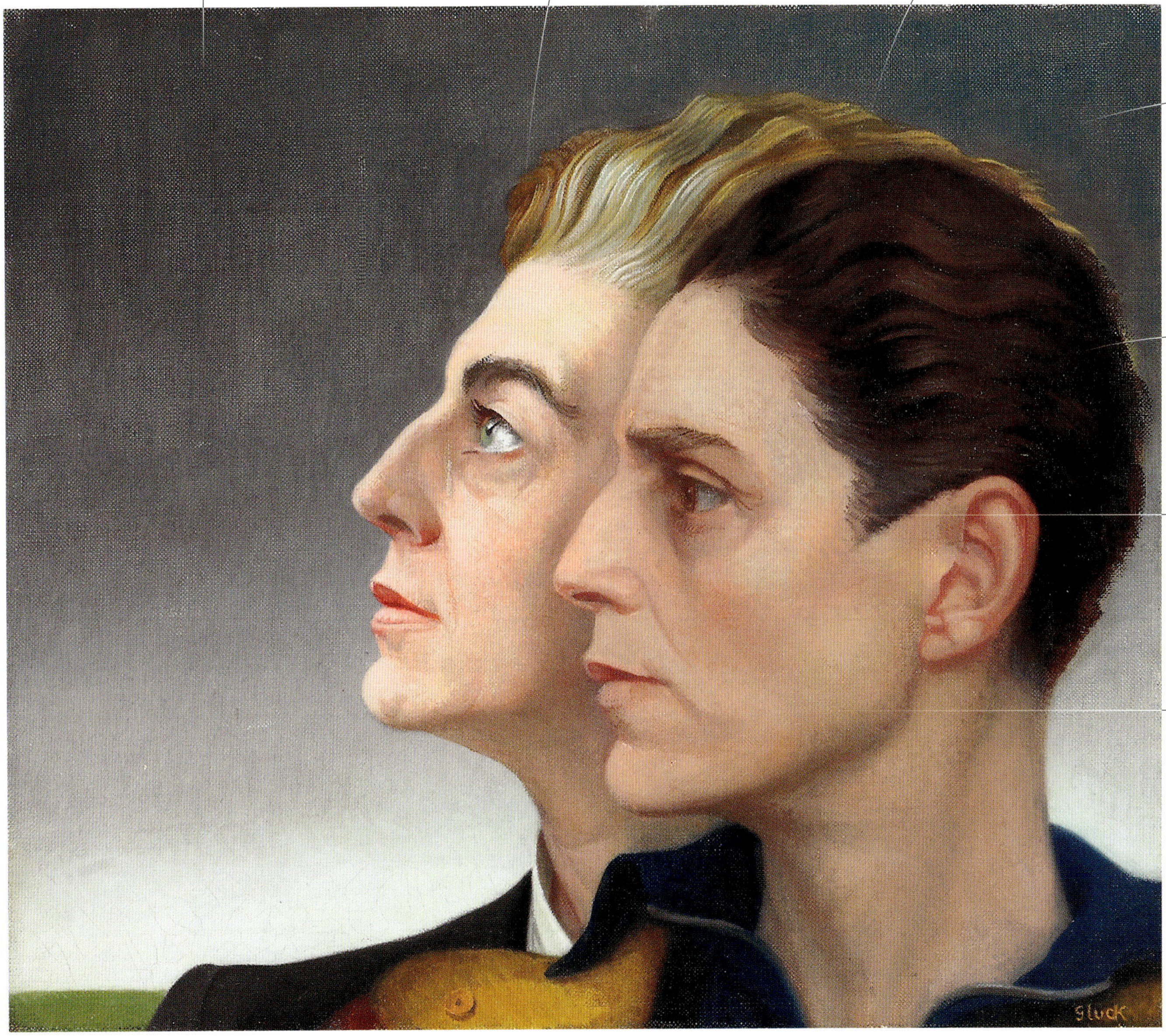

The subdued colors against a neutral background convey a mood of seriousness and intensity.

Gluck gazes straight ahead, her face in shadow.

The viewer is allowed to look at Gluck closely. Nesta is partly shielded.

Gluck's strong jawline is emphasized.

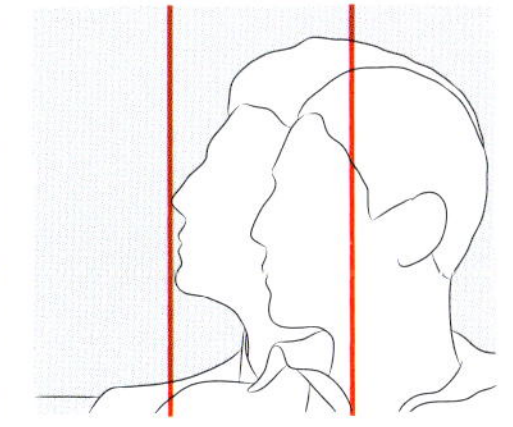

Central focus The women's faces are packed close together in the central third of the canvas.

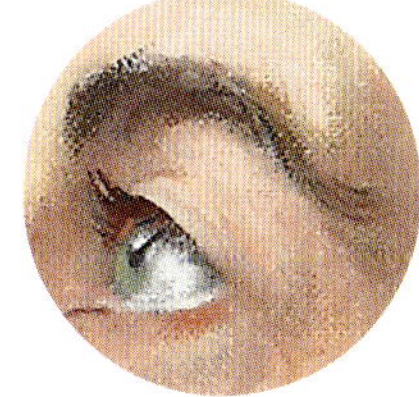

Tiny details The features are modeled with layers of fine brushstrokes and thin paint. Small details such as hair and eyelashes are drawn in individually.

> "Now it is out and to the rest of the Universe I call Beware! Beware! We are not to be trifled with."
>
> Gluck, 1936

Guernica

Pablo Picasso 1937, oil on canvas, 138 × 306 in (349.3 × 776.6 cm), Museo Reina Sofía, Madrid, Spain

Guernica records an event during the Spanish Civil War. In April 1937, German planes bombed this Basque town in northern Spain in support of General Franco's fascist forces, who were attacking Spain's Republican government. Picasso immediately began work on the painting, spending several weeks making sketches and repeatedly changing the composition before arriving at the final version. It has many elements of a traditional history painting, but the event is presented in a violently fragmented image. The succession of contrasts between light and dark across the canvas prevents the eye from settling anywhere.

A bird, which may represent peace, is just visible in the darkness.

The light bulb, surrounded by a spiked flash of light, resembles an exploding bomb.

The dying horse, its body pierced through by a spear, represents the suffering of the innocent.

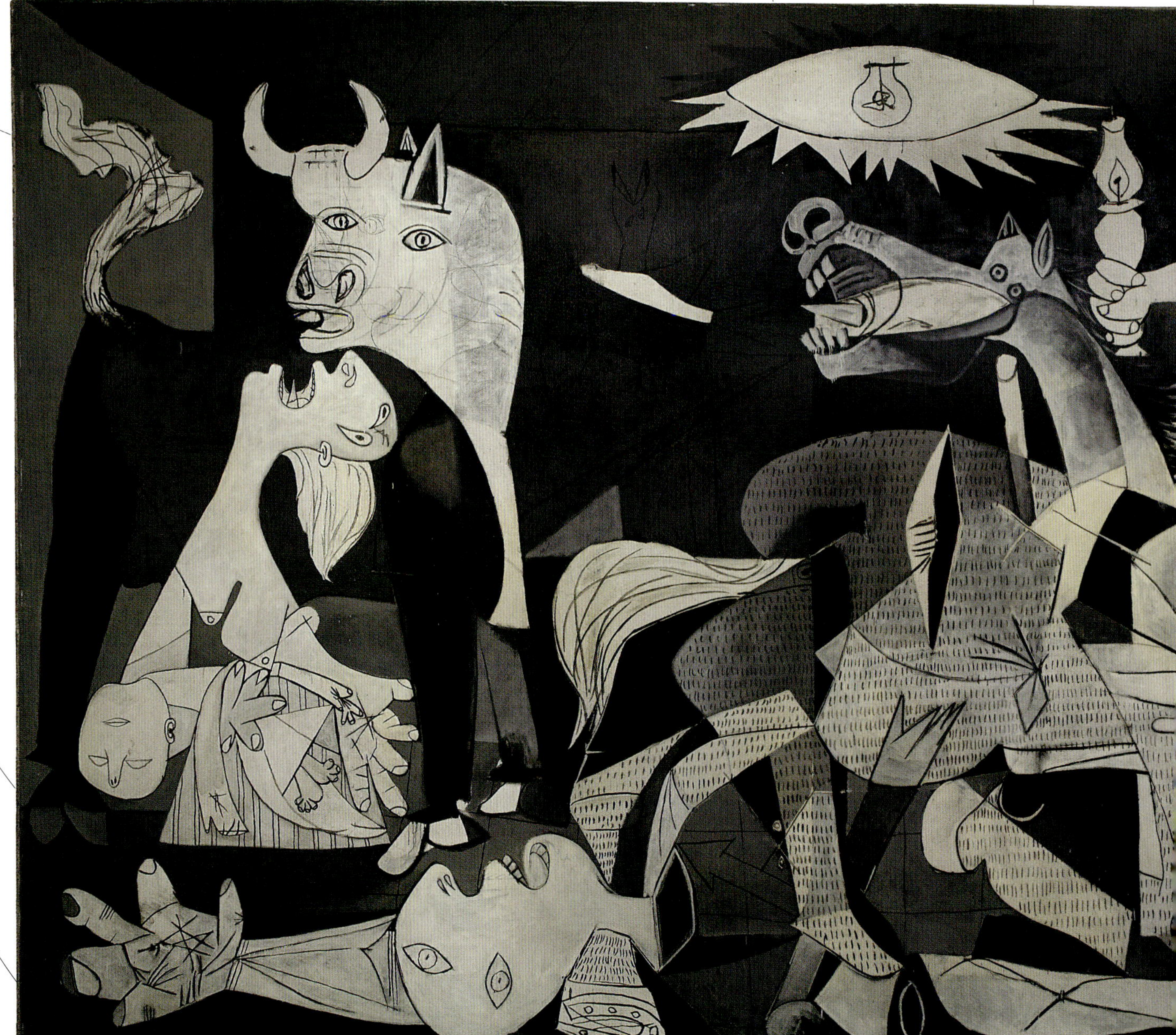

The bull could represent fascism or brutality in general.

A fallen warrior, emblematic of the fight against tyranny, lies across the front of the painting.

A lack of perspective in the tiled flooring contributes to the sense of a shallow, condensed picture space.

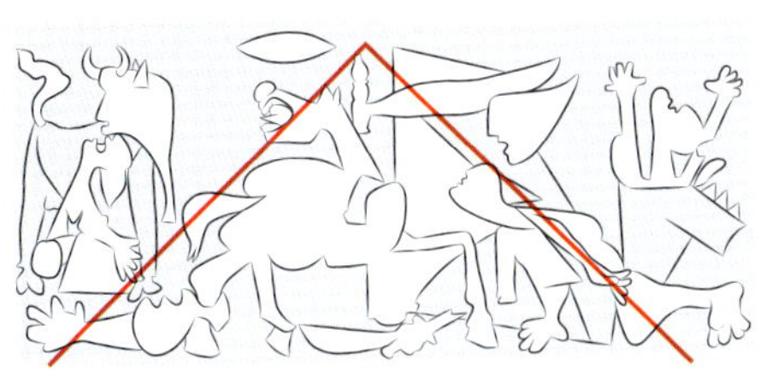

Human pyramid
A melee of body parts and abstract shapes is contained in a central triangle, flanked by Individual incidents at the sides.

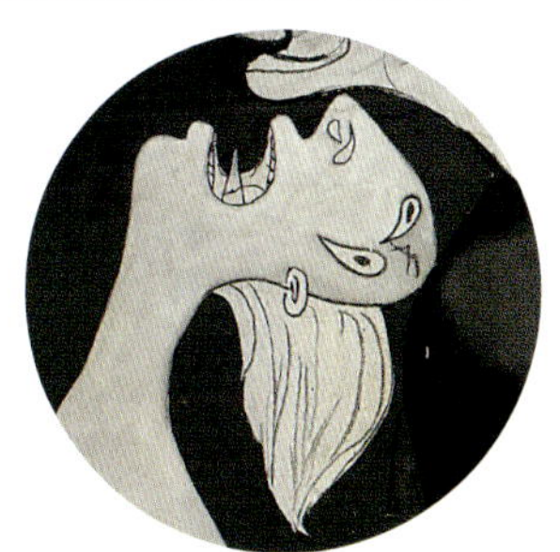

Distortion
The mother's elongated neck, head thrown back, wide scream, and eyes out of position convey extreme distress.

> "Even when he painted the agonizing women of Guernica he did so as a detached observer."
>
> Roland Penrose, 2006

A woman personifying the spirit of the Spanish Republic holds a lamp, casting light on the atrocity that has been committed.

Flames engulf a building, trapping a woman.

The pose of the woman in the burning building recalls that of the central figure in *The Third of May 1808* by Francisco de Goya.

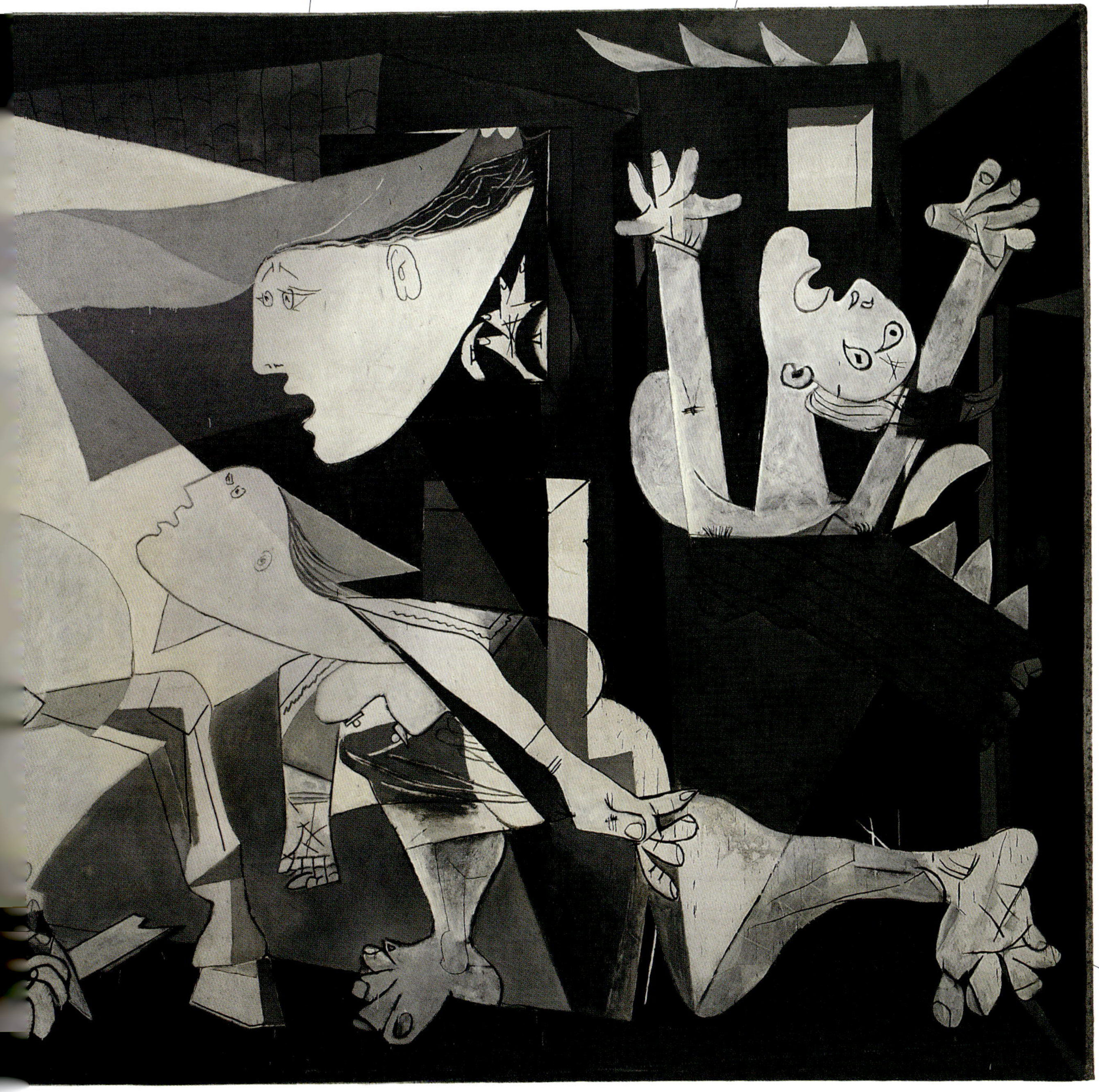

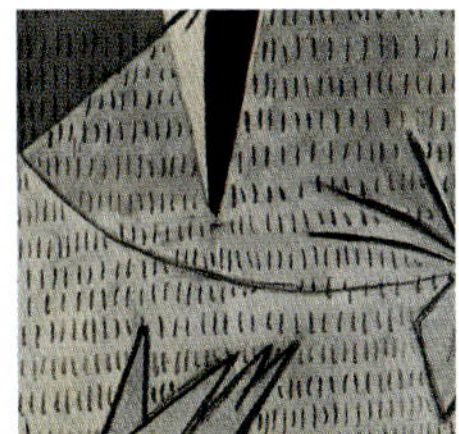

Combined with the monochromatic color scheme, rows of small marks give the impression of newsprint.

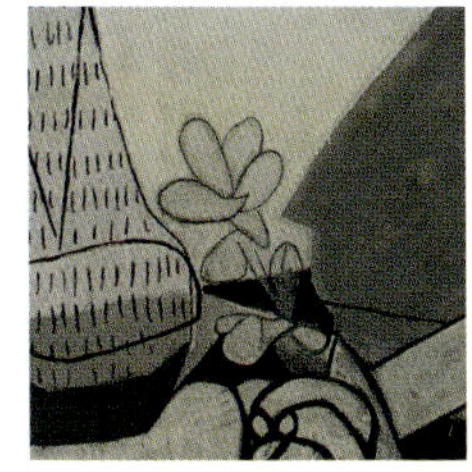

A small flower clasped in the man's hand represents hope.

A naked woman runs from her house, her twisted limbs dragging behind her.

Composition with Yellow, Blue, and Red

Piet Mondrian 1937–1942, oil on canvas, 29 × 27 in (72.7 × 69.2 cm), Tate Modern, London, UK

Mondrian's grid paintings consist of asymmetric arrangements of primary color held in place with straight black horizontal and vertical lines on a white background. The artist regarded these elements as the purest means of expression and referred to his style as Neoplasticism. He viewed his paintings as meditations on harmony, which would make the world a better place.

Groups of vertical lines create a syncopated rhythm across the canvas.

Black paint is not painted over the white; instead white paint is applied just to the edge of the black.

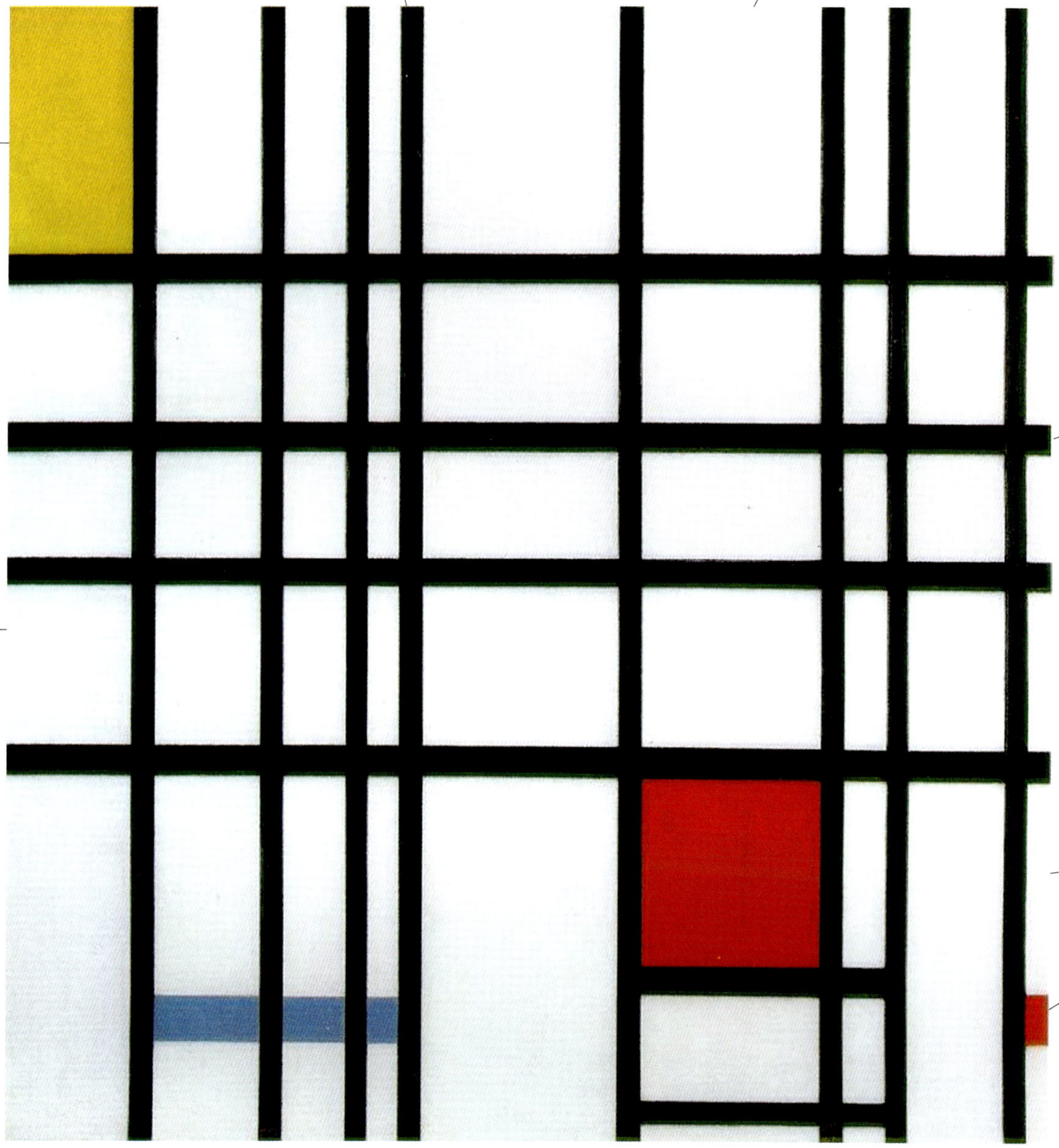

Brushmarks are visible in the dense, carefully worked paint surface. They were laid down in different directions—depending on the color area.

The edge between the black and white areas has been adjusted. Mondrian made numerous changes in pursuit of his desired effect.

To position the lines, Mondrian probably attached adhesive tape to the canvas.

Different colored areas appear nearer or farther away, creating movement in depth.

This small red area appears lighter than the larger one because it is surrounded by white.

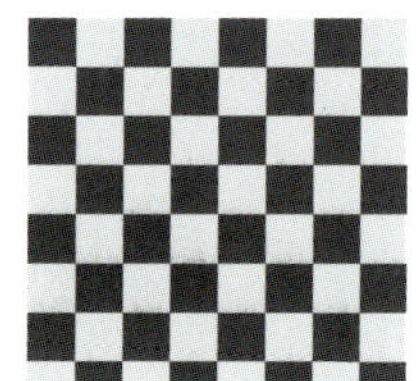

Straight lines
The vertical and horizontal lines play a variation on a regular checkerboard grid.

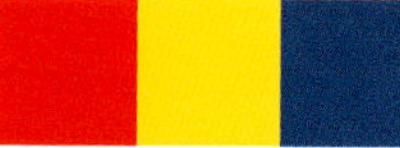

Primary colors
The colors work purely in relation to each other within the painting. They do not carry any naturalistic, cultural, or other associations.

Recumbent Figure

Henry Moore 1938, green Hornton stone, 35 × 52 × 29 in (88.9 × 132.7 × 73.7 cm), Tate Britain, London, UK

Commissioned to produce a figure for an outdoor rural setting, Moore decided on a reclining female freestanding figure, which echoed the undulating forms of the landscape of the nearby South Downs. The body is made up of a series of abstracted, simplified shapes that appear to shift and change as the viewer moves around the figure. It is carved from green Hornton stone, which cannot be quarried in large blocks, so three pieces were bonded together at the quarry—one for the head and two for the body.

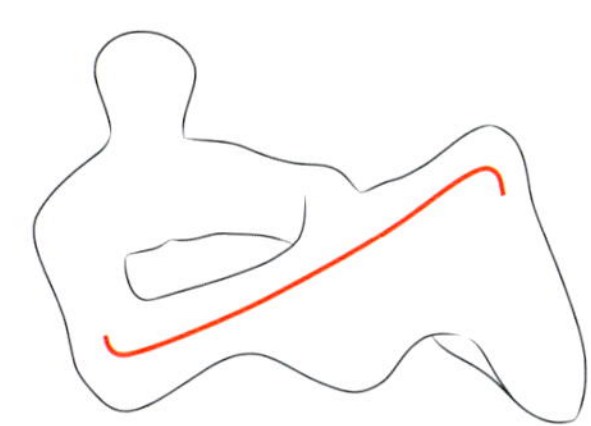

Organic form
From the front, a diagonal axis runs from the elbow up to the knee. Other lines in the body echo the undulating lines of rolling landscape.

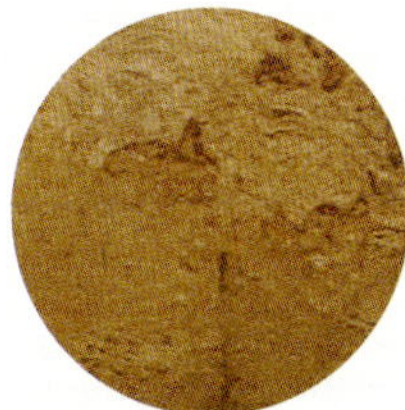

Hornton stone
Moore used Hornton stone again and again in his work. He chose this Jurassic limestone for its matte appearance and color, which varies from green to gray and brown.

"Rounded forms convey an idea of fruitfulness, maturity."

Henry Moore, 1937

The facial features are suggested by shallow indentations for the eyes and chin.

The upper body appears unsupported in space, but is counterbalanced by the weight of the lower body and legs.

Surface imperfections in the stone are part of its appeal.

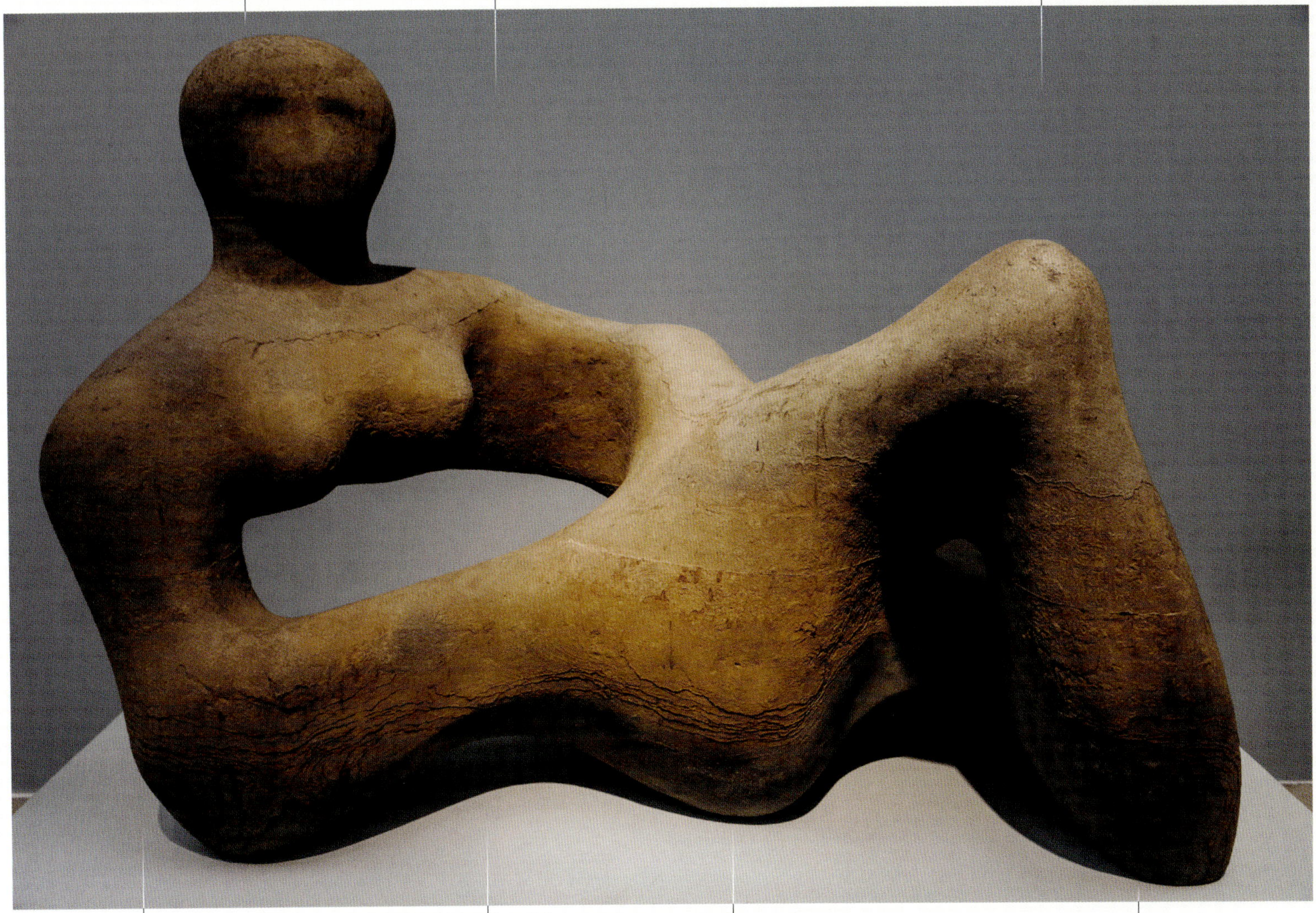

A seam joining two pieces of stone is just visible.

Holes in the figure connect one side with another and make the sculpture appear more three-dimensional.

The figure balances on three points: the elbow, hip, and feet.

The physical shape of the body is conveyed without realism.

The Two Fridas

Frida Kahlo 1939, oil on canvas, 68 × 68 in (173.5 × 173 cm), Museo de Arte Moderno, Mexico City, Mexico

Two identical women sit side by side holding hands, their hearts exposed, in front of a cloud-filled sky. In this double self-portrait, painted soon after her divorce from the Mexican artist Diego Rivera, Kahlo addresses her suffering through the juxtaposition of two identities: one European and the other Mexican.

Still inside her chest, the heart is torn open and exposed, suggesting the pain and loneliness Kahlo felt following her separation from Rivera.

A blood vessel connects the two Fridas and echoes their clasped hands.

The heart, which is resting on top of her dress, is revealed but is whole, suggesting strength and endurance.

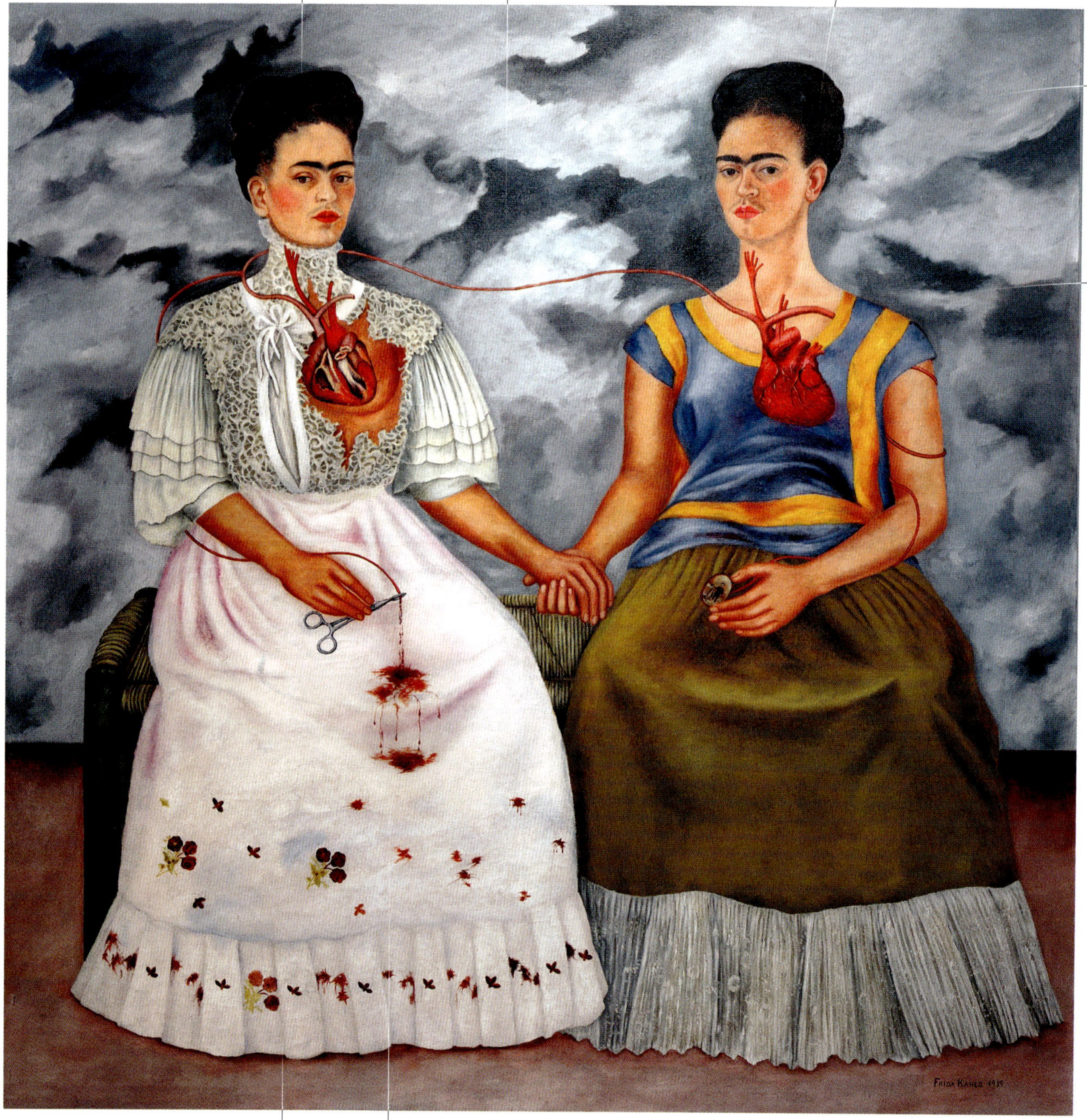

The sky is dark and stormy, filled with foreboding.

The right-hand Frida wears a traditional Tehuana outfit, reflecting her mother's Spanish and Indigenous heritage.

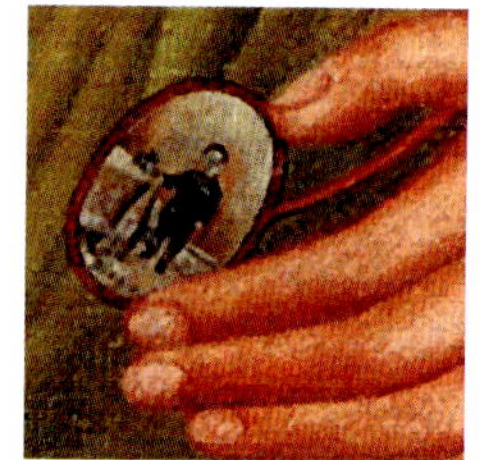

Mexican Frida holds a miniature painting of her former husband Rivera as a child.

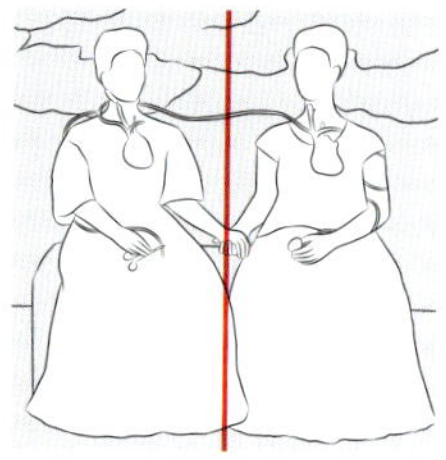

Composition
The two halves are perfectly balanced. The figures' poses mirror each other, except for the positions of their hearts. The different costumes provide the only other variation. The figures occupy a shallow space, achieved by the use of flat, somber colors and a sky that acts more as a backdrop than as sky.

The left-hand Frida wears a German-style dress, reflecting her European heritage on her father's side. It shows how she dressed before she met her husband.

European Frida holds a clamp on the blood vessel in her lap, but it is failing to stem the flow of blood, signifying her struggle to contain her feelings.

> "I never painted dreams. I painted my own reality."
>
> Frida Kahlo, 1953

Portrait Head of John Henry

Augusta Savage c. 1940, patinated plaster, 7 × 4 × 5 in (16.8 × 8.9 × 12.1 cm), Museum of Fine Arts, Boston, US

Exuding confidence, Savage's bust of a young Black man was a realistic and positive image in an era when unflattering racial caricatures of Black Americans remained common. The name John Henry may allude to the Black American legend celebrated in song: "John Henry was a Steel-Drivin' Man."

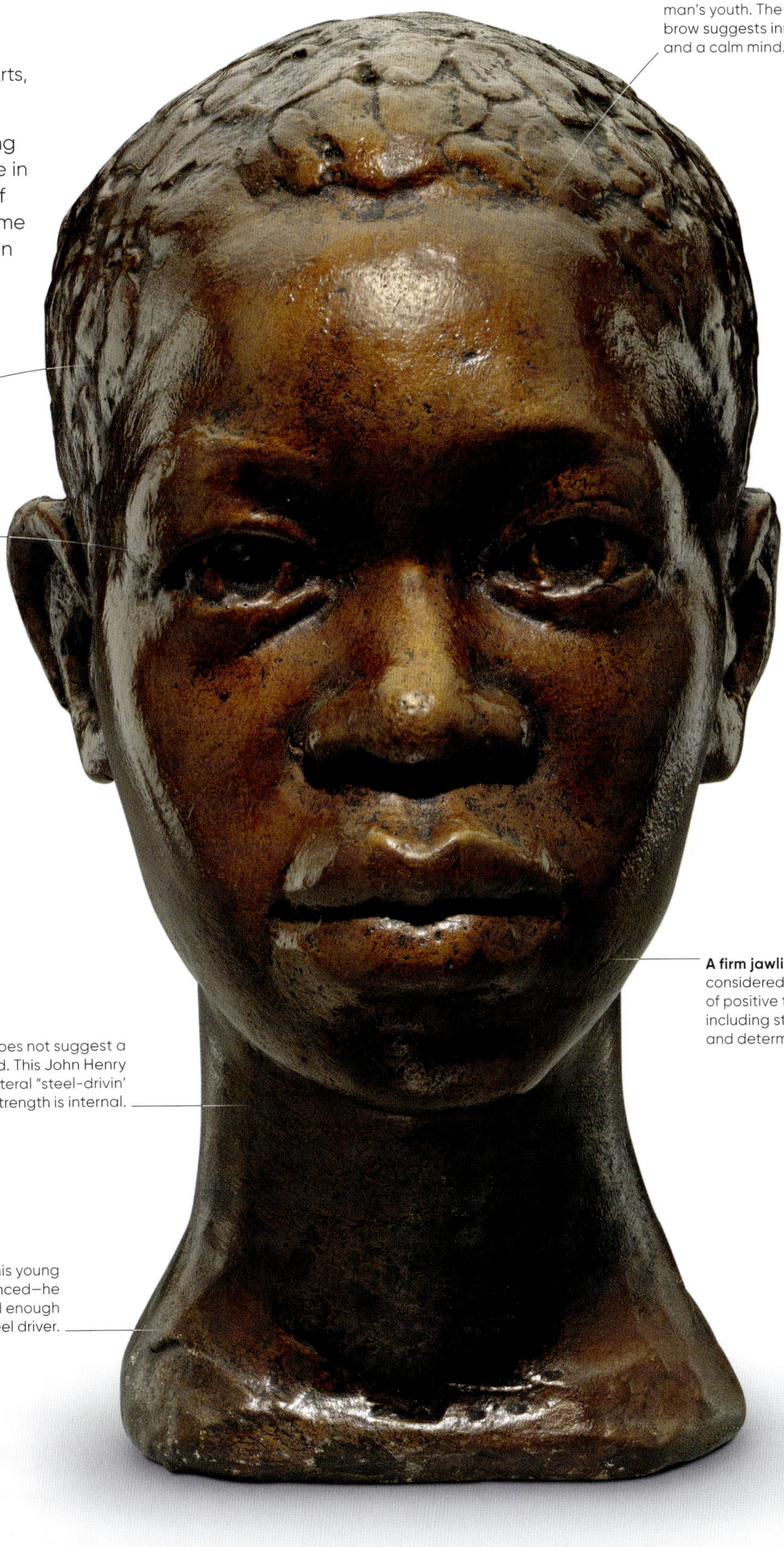

Smooth skin reflects the man's youth. The unfurrowed brow suggests inner peace and a calm mind.

The understated depiction of a short hairstyle echoes that of some statues of 3rd-century Roman military leaders.

The level eye line creates a firm, unwavering gaze, suggesting a sense of purpose and resolve.

A firm jawline is often considered symbolic of positive traits, including strength and determination.

The neck does not suggest a muscular build. This John Henry is not a literal "steel-drivin' man"—his strength is internal.

The youth of this young man is pronounced—he does not look old enough to work with a steel driver.

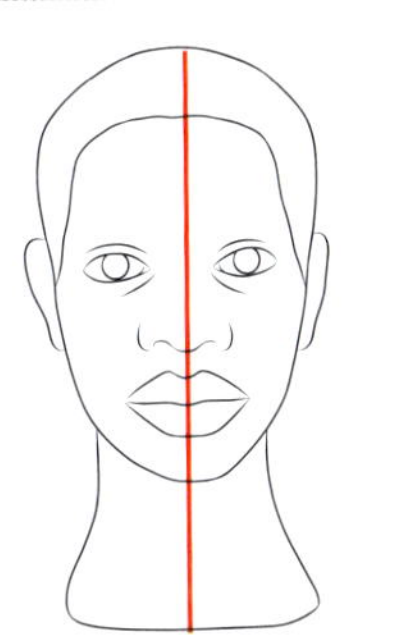

Facial symmetry
The symmetry of the young man's face—the left and right side are virtually identical—contributes greatly to his physical attractiveness.

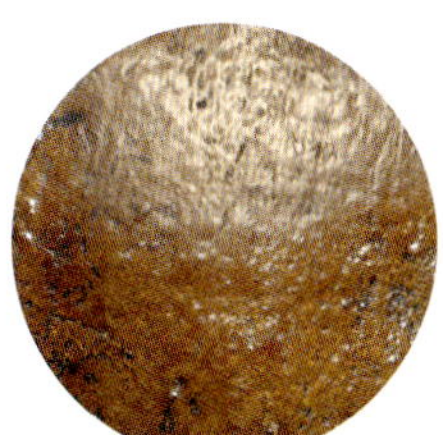

Patinated plaster
This form of plaster mimics the appearance of bronze but is less expensive. Plaster dries quickly, however, forcing the artist to work fast and with precision.

Nude in the Bath and Small Dog

Pierre Bonnard c. 1940–1946, oil on canvas, 48 × 60 in (122.4 × 151.5 cm), Carnegie Museum of Art, Pittsburgh, US

The walls pulse with intense color in this painting of the artist's wife, Marthe de Méligny, bathing. From writings at the time, Marthe was described as "difficult," even "neurotic," and the bath was her sanctuary. From their first meeting in 1893 to her death in 1942, Bonnard painted Marthe—often nude and in the bath—almost 400 times. This work was completed after her death.

The curtain glows bright yellow where the sunlight shines through the window.

The bath seems to wrap itself around the woman within.

Marthe appears ageless. She was in her early seventies when Bonnard started this painting.

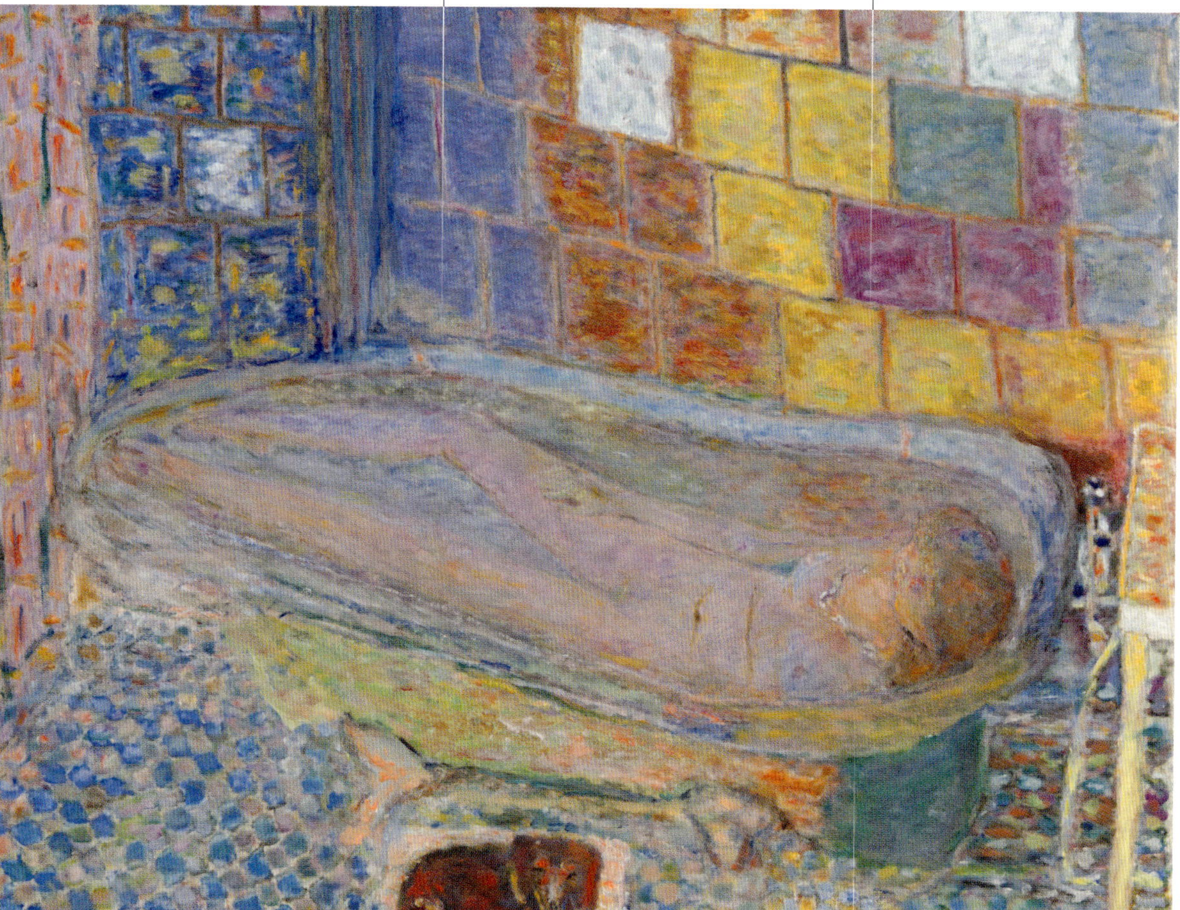

A dog sitting on a mat stares out at the viewer.

At first sight, the waterline looks like a jeweled necklace.

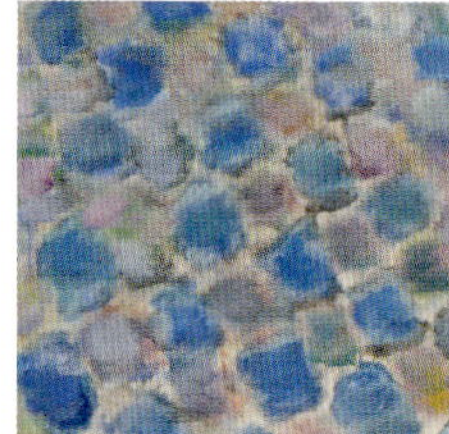

Checkered patterns were a common motif in Bonnard's paintings. He cited Japanese prints as his inspiration.

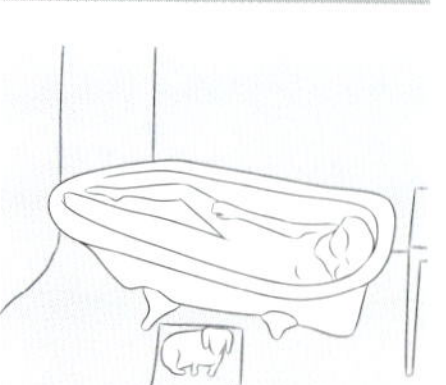

Unique perspective Bonnard looks down on the scene from high above but sees the walls straight on. The result is similar to a panoramic photo taken from a high viewpoint in a confined space.

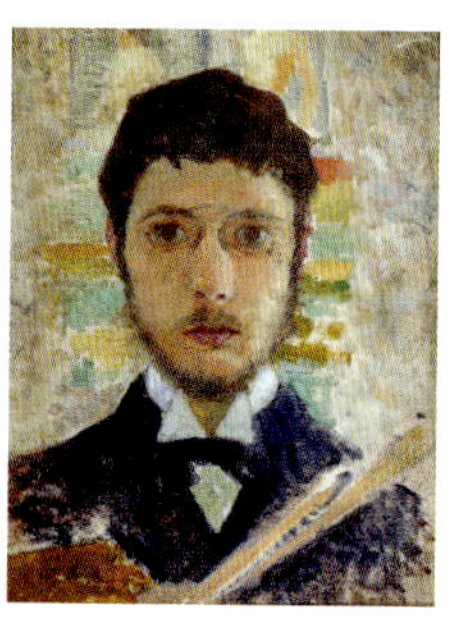

Impressionist beginnings Bonnard (seen here in a 1889 self-portrait) began his career in the heyday of Impressionism. His late paintings retain Impressionism's sense of light and spontaneity, but their flatness and bright colors show the influence of Modernism.

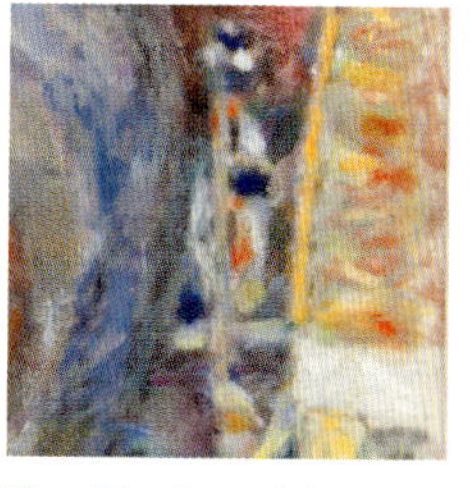

The side view of the faucet shows that Bonnard could render perspective "correctly," emphasizing that all other angles in the work are a deliberate choice.

> "There is a formula, which fits painting perfectly: Lots of little lies for the sake of one big truth."
>
> Pierre Bonnard, 1945

Anschluss—Alice in Wonderland

Oskar Kokoschka 1942, oil on canvas, 25 × 29 in (63.5 × 73.6 cm), Vienna Insurance Group, on permanent loan in the Leopold Museum, Vienna, Austria

As Vienna burns, a nude woman stands behind a barbed-wire fence surrounded by scenes of violence. Kokoschka was in exile in Britain when he painted this condemnation of Hitler's annexation of Austria in 1938 and the Allies' appeasement of Nazi Germany on the eve of World War II.

Figures in the background wring their hands in anguish at the unfolding terror.

Flames engulf a neoclassical building with "WIEN" (Vienna) inscribed on its facade.

The three men in military helmets epitomize the proverb "see no evil, hear no evil, speak no evil."

A headless mother and child echo the mother and child in the foreground.

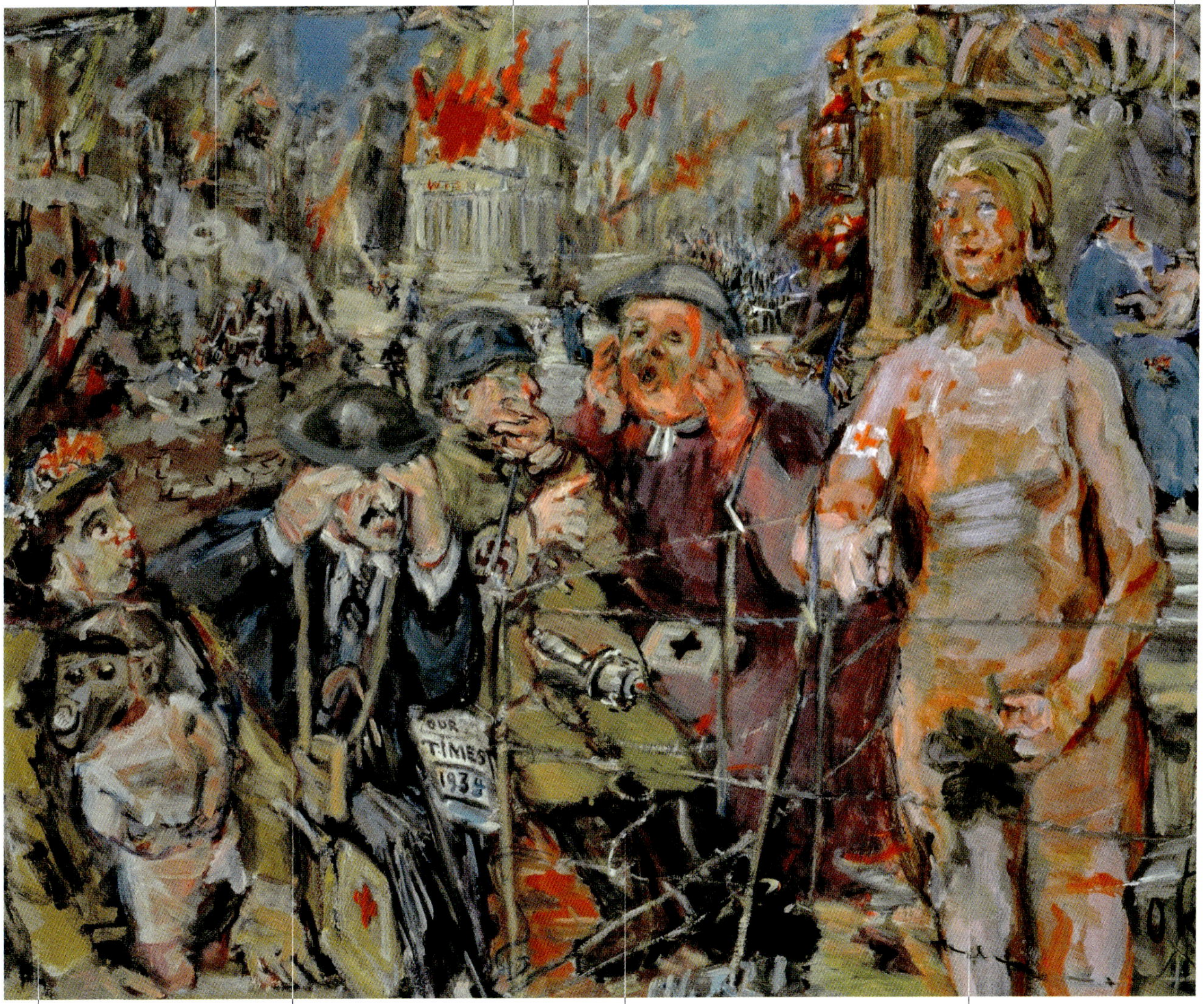

A mother holds a baby wearing a gas mask and looks woefully toward Alice.

This figure represents Neville Chamberlain, the British prime minister who advocated appeasement of Nazi Germany.

A man in military uniform and a cleric personify Germany and France respectively.

Naked Alice embodies the resilience of the Austrian people as they watched their country being invaded.

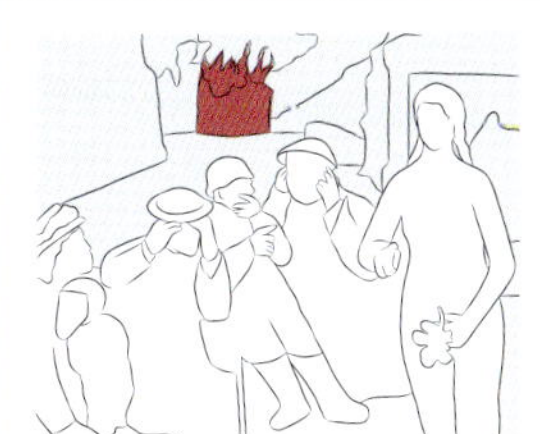

Hectic background
The foreground figures form a gently sloping frieze. Beyond, a scene of panic and distress unfolds, centered on the blazing building.

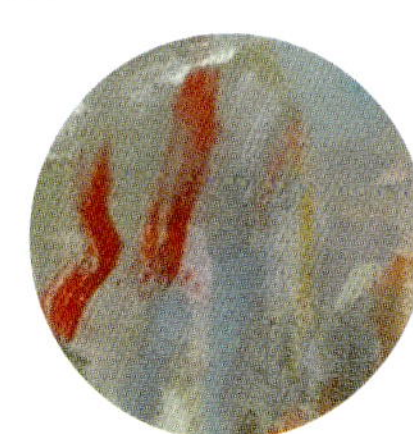

Building atmosphere
The loose, expressive brushstrokes in the background create a chaotic and tumultuous atmosphere, amplifying the emotional intensity of the artwork.

> "I see creative art as a source, a spring, like Nature itself."
>
> Oscar Kokoschka, 1974

Nighthawks

Edward Hopper 1942, oil on canvas, 33 × 60 in (84.1 × 152.4 cm), Art Institute of Chicago, Illinois, US

Hopper captures the loneliness of urban life and the unknowability of other people in an iconic image of customers sitting silently at the counter of a late-night New York diner. The city streets outside are strangely dark and empty, drawing the viewer's eye to the diner, which is well lit but bleak and unwelcoming. The lack of clear narrative encourages the viewer to speculate about the diners' thoughts and stories, though the date of the work—*Nighthawks* was painted in the weeks following the bombing of Pearl Harbor—hints that these diners might have been experiencing the anxiety of a nation plunged into war.

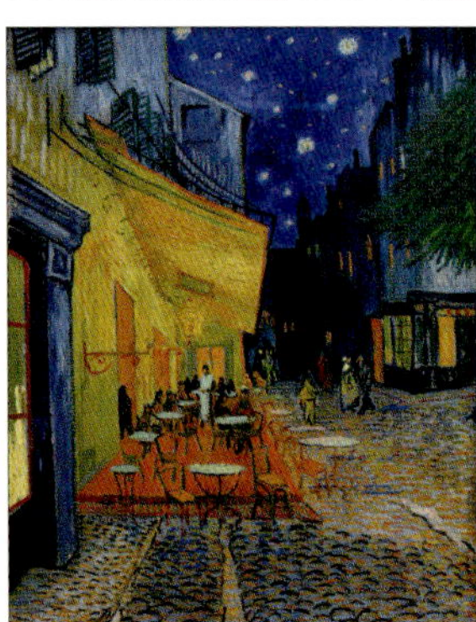

Precedent
Hopper might have been inspired by Van Gogh's *Café Terrace at Night* (1888), a comparable scene of a cafe at night.

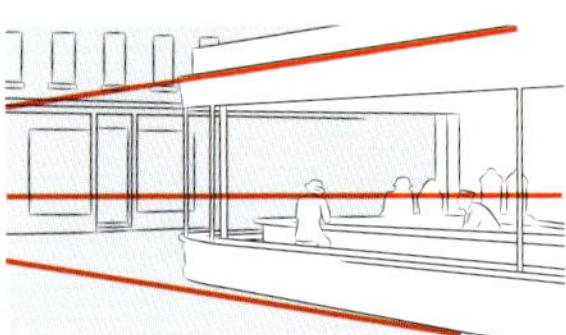

Outside presence
Strong diagonal lines converge outside the painting to the left. The customers' heads are placed along the painting's horizontal midpoint.

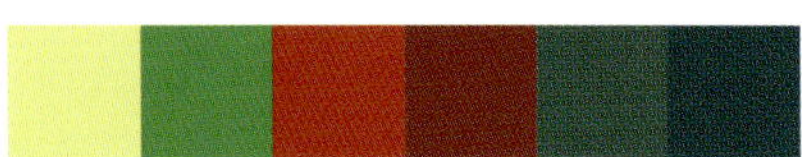

Colorful yet somber
The bright yellows, jade greens, and cherry-colored wood counter inside the diner draw the eye, while muted brownish-reds, dark greens, and grays dominate the outside world.

> "It is a timeless image that exposes an inescapable fear … we are all ultimately alone and vulnerable."
>
> Will Gompertz, 2012

It is disquietingly empty outside the diner. There is no evidence of life in the nearby building.

An ad for cigars is the only visible signage. The diner itself is unnamed, adding to a sense of universality.

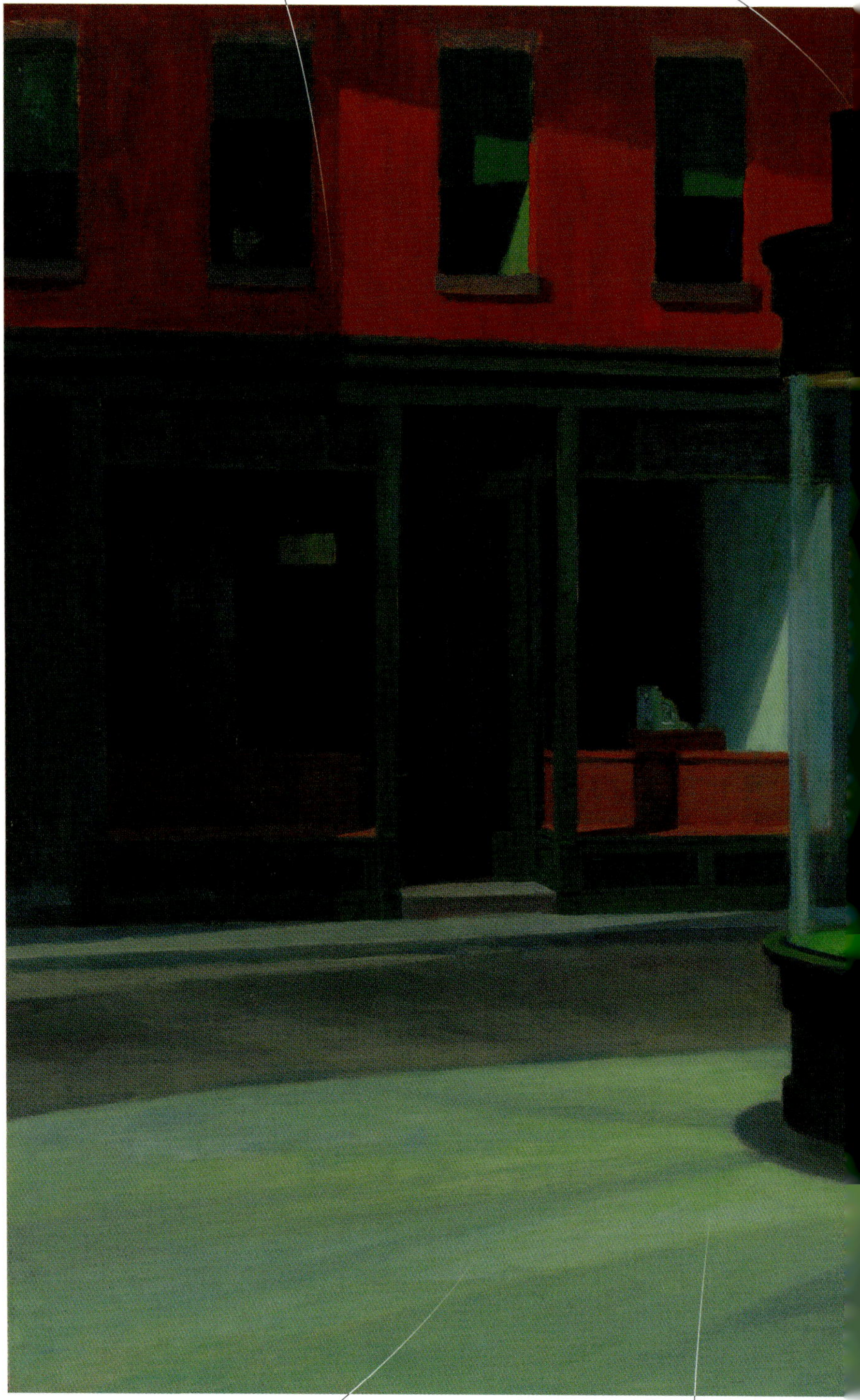

The diner's harsh fluorescent lighting is the main source of illumination for the street.

There is no door to the diner. Viewers have no way to enter the establishment, and the customers have no way out.

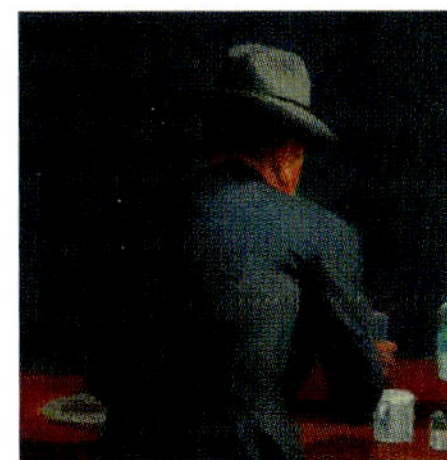

A customer in the foreground faces away from the viewer, completely unknowable. Hopper's wife, Jo, who was the model for the woman, described him as "sinister."

The apparent lack of conversation among the diner's customers and the emptiness of the street create a sense of silence.

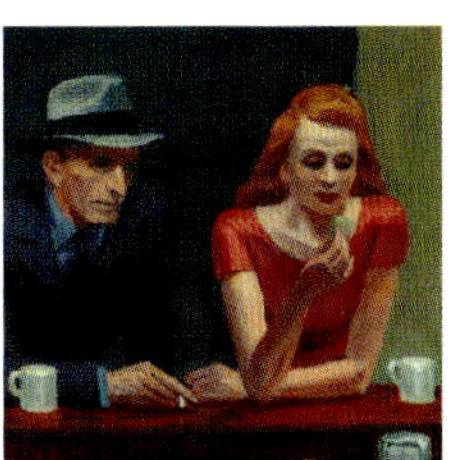

The couple seems disengaged—their expressions blank, their hands not quite touching. Her coffee is steaming while his appears cold.

More detailed than the exterior, the diner's interior contains items such as coffee urns, napkin dispensers, and salt shakers, but it still feels stark.

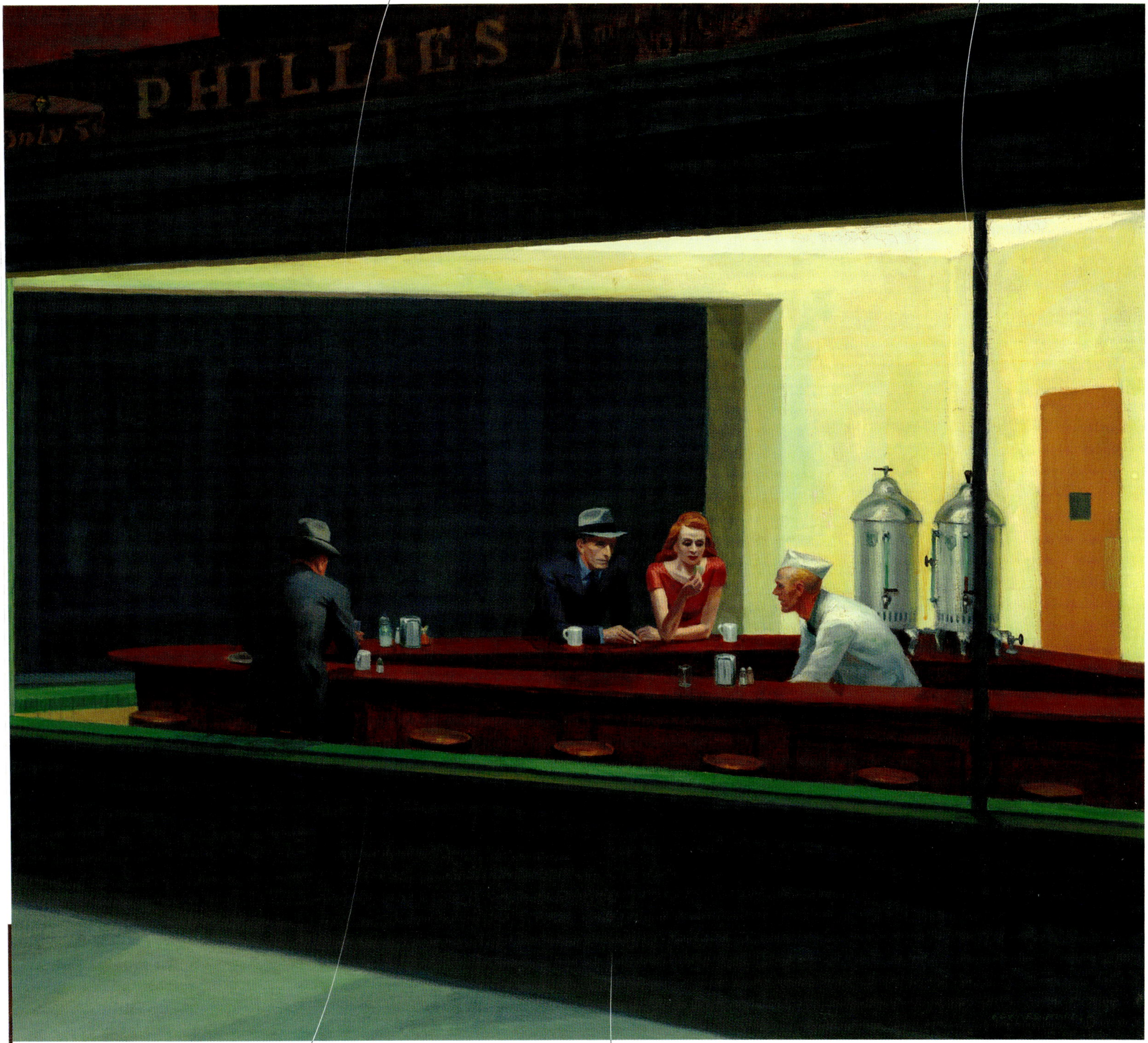

The large window provides a voyeuristic view, but it also serves as a barrier.

The diner was reportedly inspired by a restaurant Hopper had seen on New York's Greenwich Avenue.

The Agony

Arshile Gorky 1947, oil on canvas, 40 × 51 in (101.6 × 128.3 cm), MoMA, New York, US

Gorky painted *The Agony* a year before he died by suicide following a series of setbacks, including cancer and a car accident. An Armenian émigré in the US, he was the link between European organic Surrealism and Abstract Expressionism, using shapes based on natural forms to produce abstract works that seem to contain actual figures. In *The Agony*, the anguished quality of the forms is matched by intense colors.

Thin veils of color produce a luminous effect.

Biomorphic shapes come together to suggest a suspended, tormented figure.

An armature of fine lines, painted with a signwriter's brush, link and create shapes.

The red areas may refer to a studio fire that destroyed a large number of his paintings.

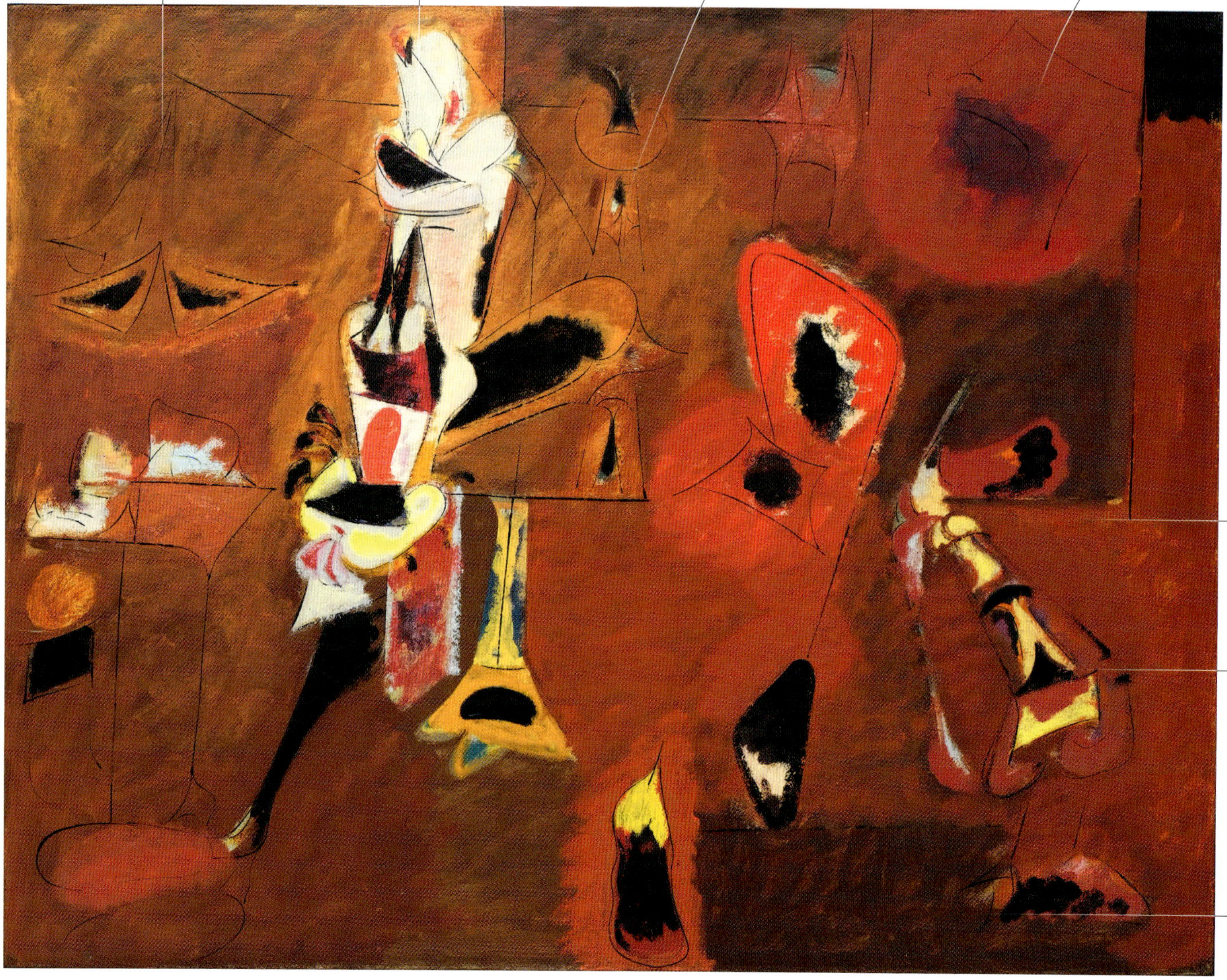

The horizontal line helps identify the background as an interior.

A second, small figure is hinted at.

The darker background colors insert a sense of melancholy.

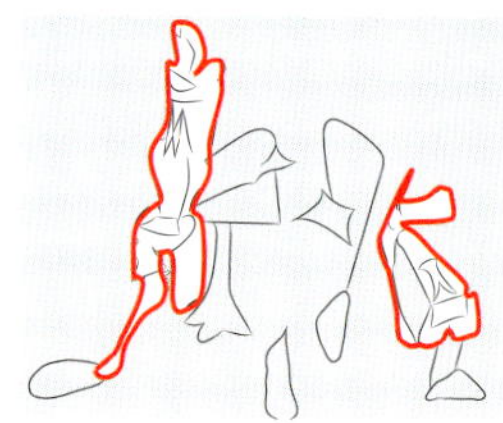

Composition
The large main figure on the left is balanced by smaller shapes on the right.

Scumbling
Gorky used scumbling, the application of a thin layer of paint with a dry brush, to soften the transition from one area to another.

Eidos

Barbara Hepworth 1947, stone, synthetic polymer paint, 13 × 20 × 11 in (32.2 × 50.7 × 28.2 cm), National Gallery of Victoria, Melbourne, Australia

A leading figure in British Modernist art, Hepworth was inspired by the landscape and the human figure. She made very pure, abstract sculptures that expressed the relationship between the two. In *Eidos*, meaning "form" in Greek, Hepworth evokes the beauty of the landscape through the beauty of a simple form.

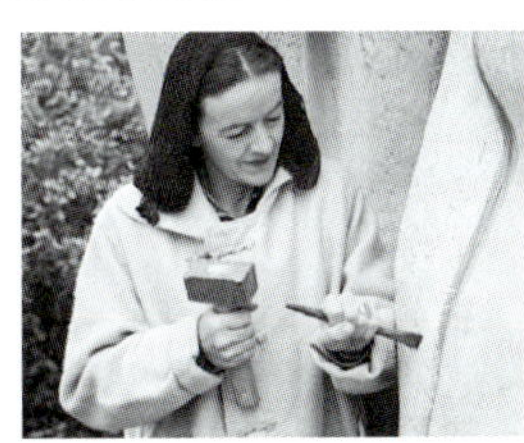

Direct carving
Hepworth regarded her tools as an extension of herself: her right hand, working with the hammer, provided the motor for sculpting while her left hand felt the way.

"All my early memories are of forms and shapes and textures."
Barbara Hepworth

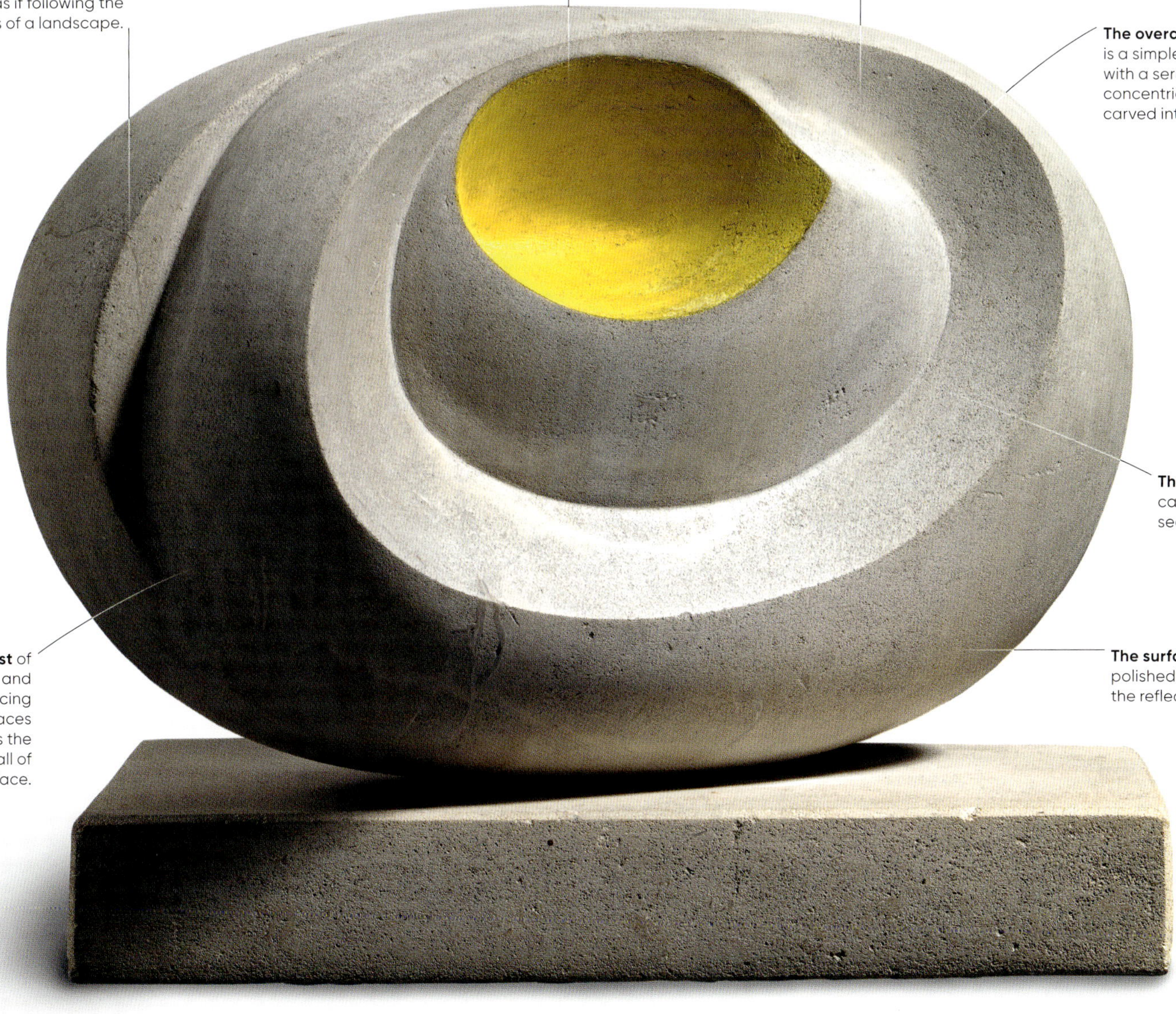

Yellow hints at sunlight, but seen from a different angle, the color creates a deep shadow in the hollow.

One form appears to be nestling inside another, hinting at the theme of motherhood.

The viewer's eye follows the continuous curves and hollows as if following the contours of a landscape.

The overall form is a simple ovoid, with a series of concentric circles carved into it.

The inner form can also be seen as an eye.

The contrast of inward- and outward-facing surfaces emphasizes the rise and fall of the surface.

The surface is highly polished to maximize the reflection of light.

Christina's World

Andrew Wyeth 1948, egg tempera on board, 32 × 48 in (82 × 121 cm), MoMA, New York, US

Set in the stark landscape of coastal Maine, Wyeth's haunting painting of a woman lying in a field, gazing back at a weathered farmhouse, conveys a yearning for America's pastoral past. The viewer is drawn to try to understand this woman's story, but the image offers few clues to the overriding sense of mystery.

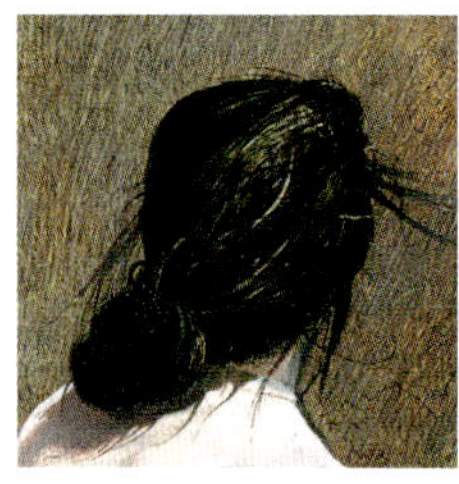

Christina's face is hidden, allowing the viewer to imagine what she might be feeling.

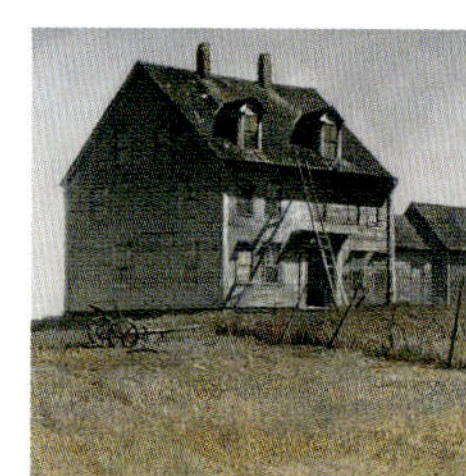

The gentle curves of the driveway and the grassy hill separate Christina from the farmhouse.

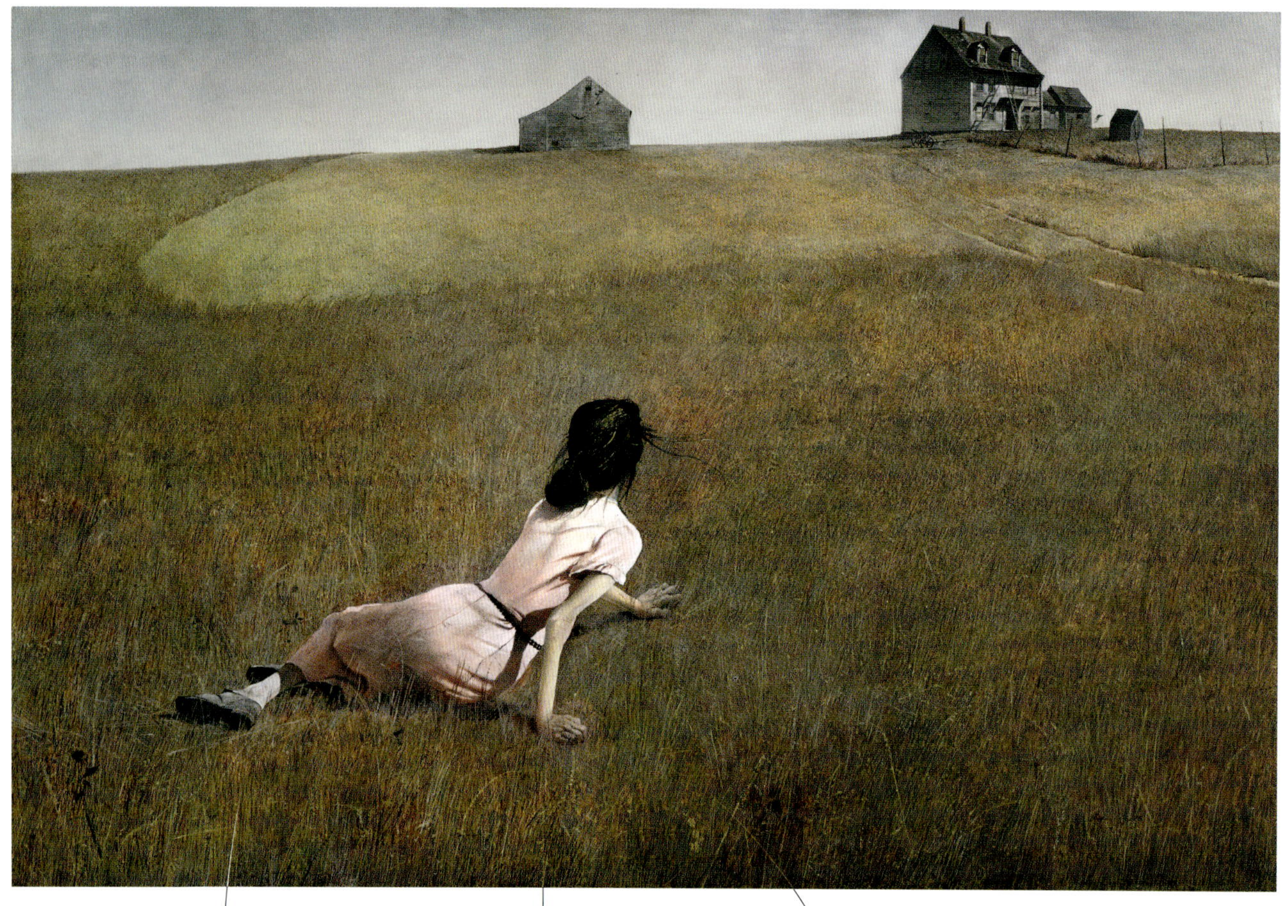

Christina pulls herself up the hill. The figure was inspired by Anna Christina Olson, a friend of Wyeth with a disease that left her unable to walk.

The woman's thin, contorted arms and gnarled hands hint that this is not merely a young woman in a pastoral idyll.

Physically, the woman is both middle-aged (arms) and young (torso). Youthful Christina was modeled on Wyeth's 26-year-old wife.

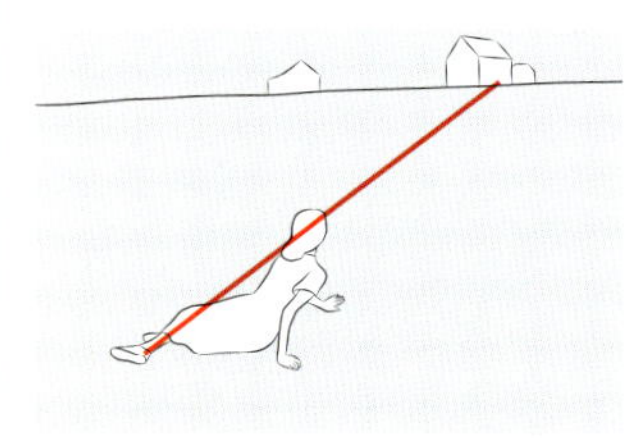

Looking up
The angle of Christina's body and direction of her gaze draw the viewer's eye from the lower left up to the house at the top right.

Meticulous detail
Wyeth painted in tempera applied with tiny brushes to slow himself down and capture fine detail, such as individual blades of grass.

"… her world may be limited physically but by no means spiritually …"
Andrew Wyeth

> "A painting is not about an experience. It is an experience."
> Mark Rothko

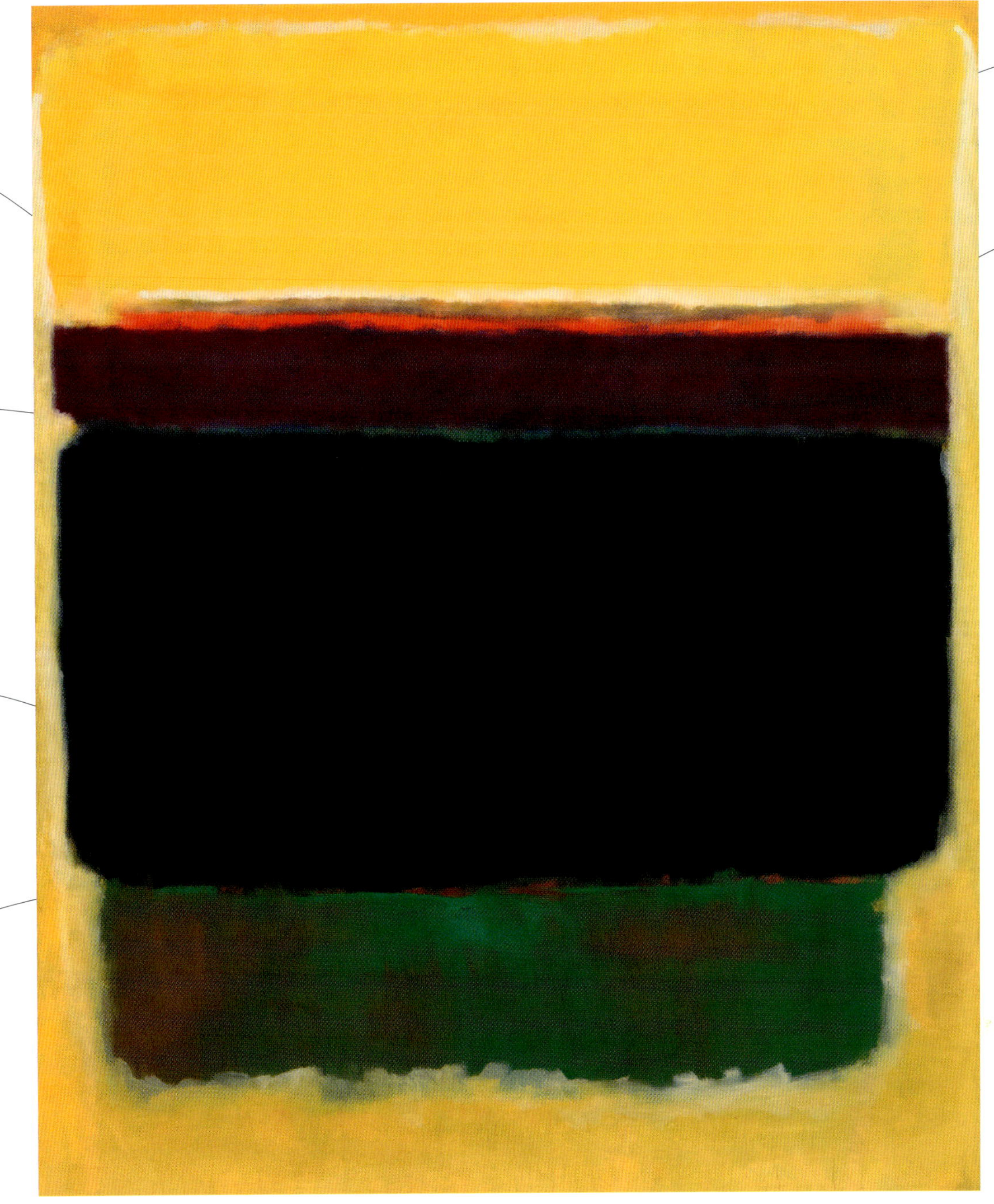

The orange-red strip glows due to its proximity to the darker bluish magenta.

A thin green strip enhances the contrast between purple and black and releases the top edge of the black area to move forward.

The opacity of the dark central block contrasts with the thinner areas of color.

A small area of thicker green paint with a sharp upper edge forms a focal point against areas of color that merge into each other.

Yellow pigment mixed into animal hide glue went on first. Thinned oil paint was applied over the top in overlapping layers of color.

All color areas are free of the picture edge, allowing them to hover in space.

Spiritual plane
A stack of horizontal rectangles and bands of color are centrally placed. The horizontal shapes create a sense of calm.

Broad brushmarks soften the edge and allow the eye to move from the yellow ground into the green and orange area.

Untitled

Mark Rothko 1949, pigmented hide glue and oil on canvas, 80 × 66 in (204.2 × 168.6 cm), National Gallery of Art, Washington, D.C., US

Rothko was the leading Color Field painter—an approach characterized by large areas of flat color and the rejection of three-dimensionality. In his abstract paintings of stacked rectangles and bands of saturated colors, he used tone, transparency, and brushmarks to express intense emotions and create an immersive, transcendental experience for the viewer.

Abstract art

Around the end of the 19th century, artists working in the Western tradition began to depict experiences in nonrepresentational ways. Rather than telling stories or describing the world in an illusionistic or naturalistic way, they used shape, color, line, and texture, and the relationships between them, to express their ideas. Some strands of abstract art are purely geometric while others are more obviously connected to the material world.

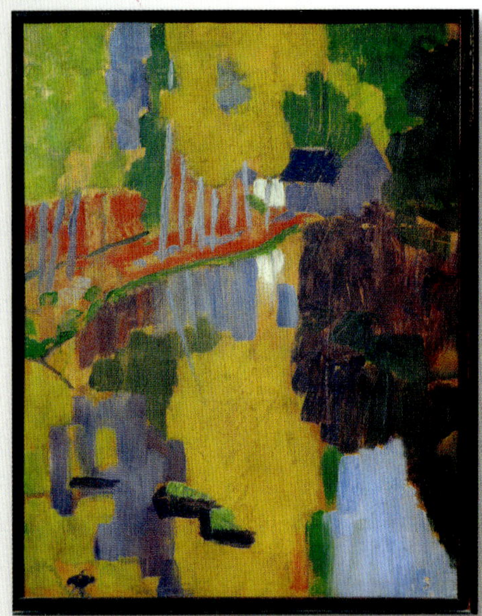

1

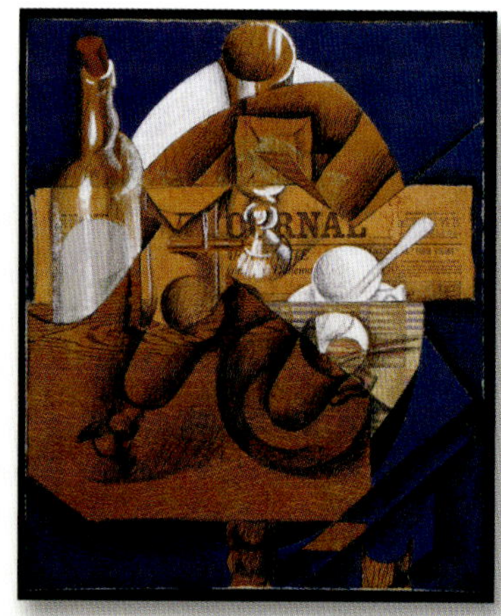

4

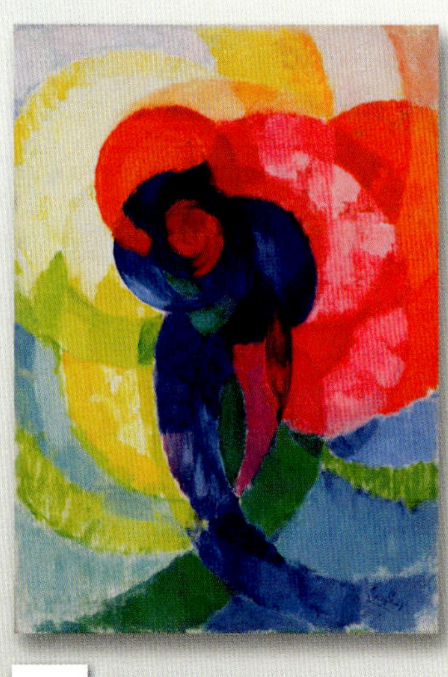

2

3

1. ***The Talisman*, Paul Sérusier, 1888.** An actual scene in a wood is rendered in simplified, flat areas of contrasting colors that are used for their expressive potential. Influenced by Paul Gauguin, Sérusier painted this early example of abstraction based on landscape.

2. ***Red and Blue Disks*, František Kupka, 1911–1912.** Some claim Kupka was one of the first purely abstract artists. He sought visual analogies for the rhythms of music and turning of the cosmos, and found them by using a limited number of colors in arrangements of circular forms.

3. ***Composition IV*, Wassily Kandinsky, 1911.** In moving toward abstraction, Kandinsky wanted to reach an inner truth beyond outward appearances. Through the arrangement of colors and shapes, he hoped to achieve an emotional effect similar to that of music.

4. ***Cup, Glasses, and Bottle*, Juan Gris, 1914.** This richly layered, mixed-media composition by Gris, a leading Cubist, has multiple viewpoints. The combination of collaged newspaper and trompe l'oeil effects raises questions about what is real and what is illusory.

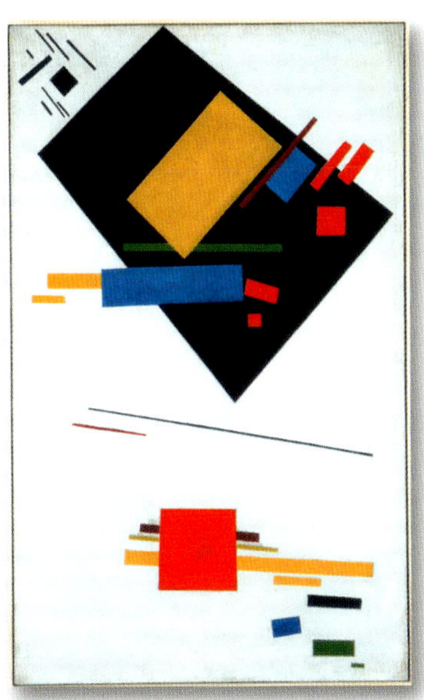

5

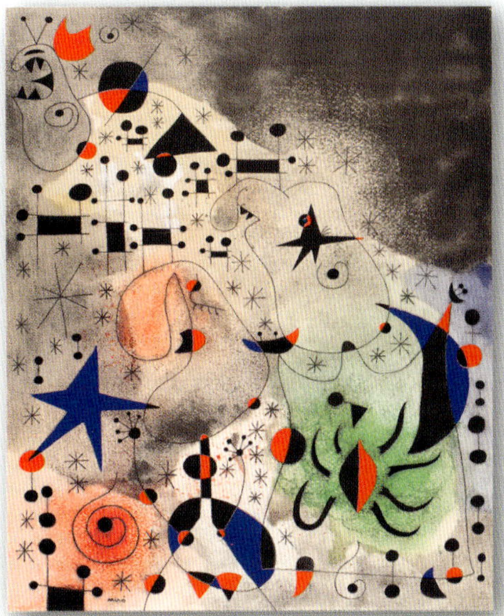

7

Color Field painting

This relies on the expressive power of color. The term covers Abstract Expressionists such as Mark Rothko and Helen Frankenthaler. Producing an immersive experience, they avoided a figure-ground (object and background) approach in favor of compositions in which the space, or "field," extends beyond the painting's edges.

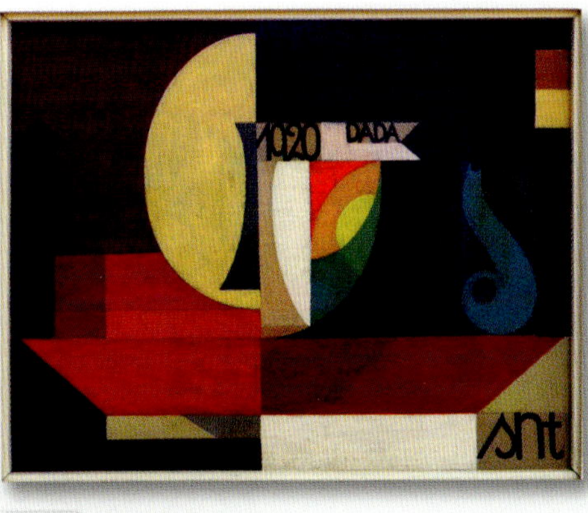

6

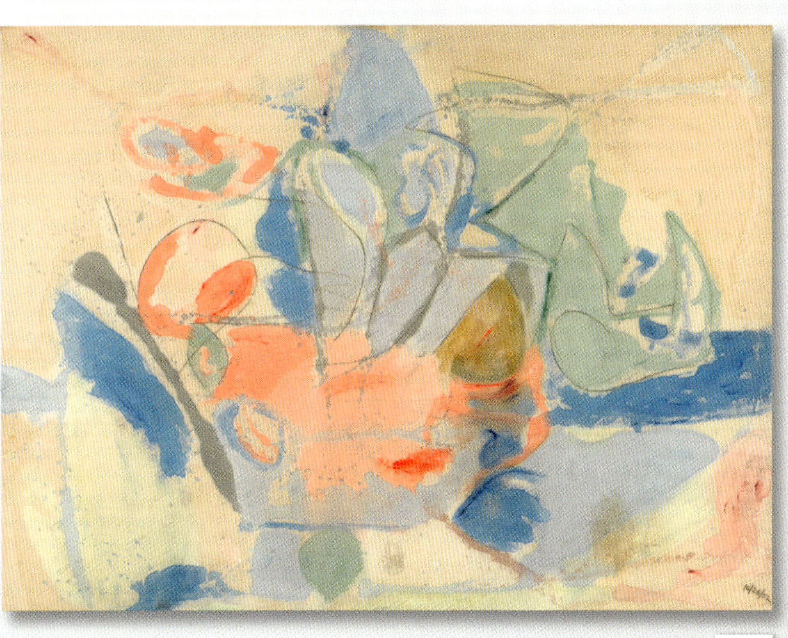

8

5. ***Suprematist Painting (with Black Trapezium and Red Square)*, Kazimir Malevich, 1915.** Malevich used geometric shapes, which he has overlapped and tilted, to create a sense of dynamism and space. He believed that pure feeling could best be accessed through abstraction.

6. ***Composition Dada*, Sophie Taeuber-Arp, 1920.** Dada artists such as Taeuber-Arp believed that the middle-class attitudes associated with representational art had led to World War I. Resembling a collage, this work is made up of circular and rectangular forms and clear colors.

7. ***The Migratory Bird*, Joan Miró, 1941.** This image was produced at a time when Miró returned to Spain from Nazi-occupied Paris. It includes his personal language of motifs, such as birds and constellations, but also two large forms resembling heads, their mouths open in a fixed scream.

8. ***Mountains and Sea*, Helen Frankenthaler, 1952.** An Abstract Expressionist, Frankenthaler inspired a new approach to painting. She poured paint washes onto unprimed canvas and let them sink in. She eliminated brush marks so color could carry expressive power.

Four Women on a Base

Alberto Giacometti 1950, bronze, 29 × 16 × 6 in (74.5 × 41.5 × 16 cm), MAM, Rio de Janeiro, Brazil

In this piece, four elongated female figures balance on a tall base. The sculpture was inspired by four sex workers seen on the far side of a room in a Paris nightclub, distant and unreachable. Giacometti's thin figures of the 1950s exemplified a general sense of alienation and loneliness in the wake of the horrors of World War II.

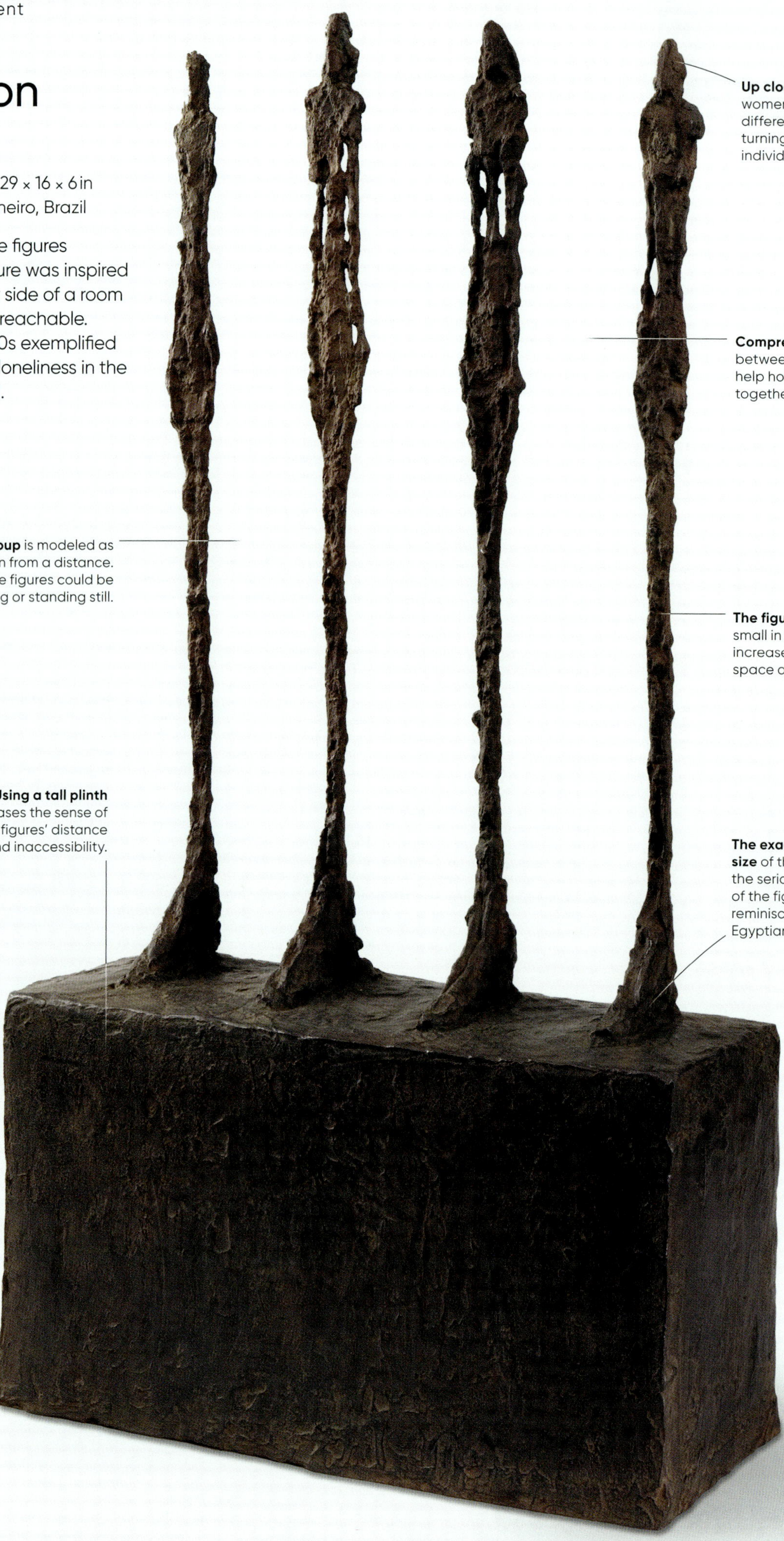

Up close, the four women have slightly different features, turning them into individuals.

Compressed spaces between the figures help hold the four together as a group.

The group is modeled as if seen from a distance. The figures could be moving or standing still.

The figures are small in size, which increases the sense of space around them.

Using a tall plinth increases the sense of the figures' distance and inaccessibility.

The exaggerated size of the feet and the serial nature of the figures is reminiscent of ancient Egyptian statues.

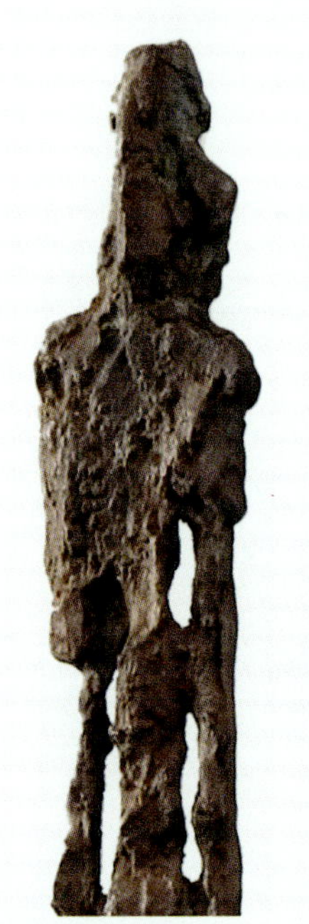

Forming figures
The figures were modeled in clay and cast in bronze. Giacometti repeatedly built up the clay and cut it away again to achieve the desired effect.

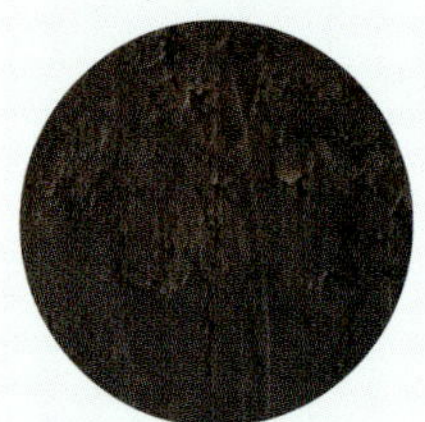

Working with bronze
Bronze expands in the mold as it solidifies, picking up fine details. It then shrinks as it cools, making it easier to remove the sculpture from the mold.

No. 1, 1950 (Lavender Mist)

Jackson Pollock 1950, oil, enamel, & aluminum on canvas, 87 × 118 in (221 × 299.7 cm), National Gallery of Art, Washington, D.C., US

This piece embodies Pollock's drip painting style, in which he worked instinctively by pouring and trailing industrial paint onto a large canvas to produce a densely structured image. The process is one of self-exploration. When seen from a distance, the black, white, russet, orange, silver, and stone blue colors merge to create the appearance of mauve, giving rise to the painting's title.

Thin lines of paint have been trailed over the top of dry areas.

The large canvas size creates an immersive experience for the viewer.

The marks are a record of Pollock's actions as he moved around the canvas.

Pollock's handprint appears in each top corner in lieu of a signature.

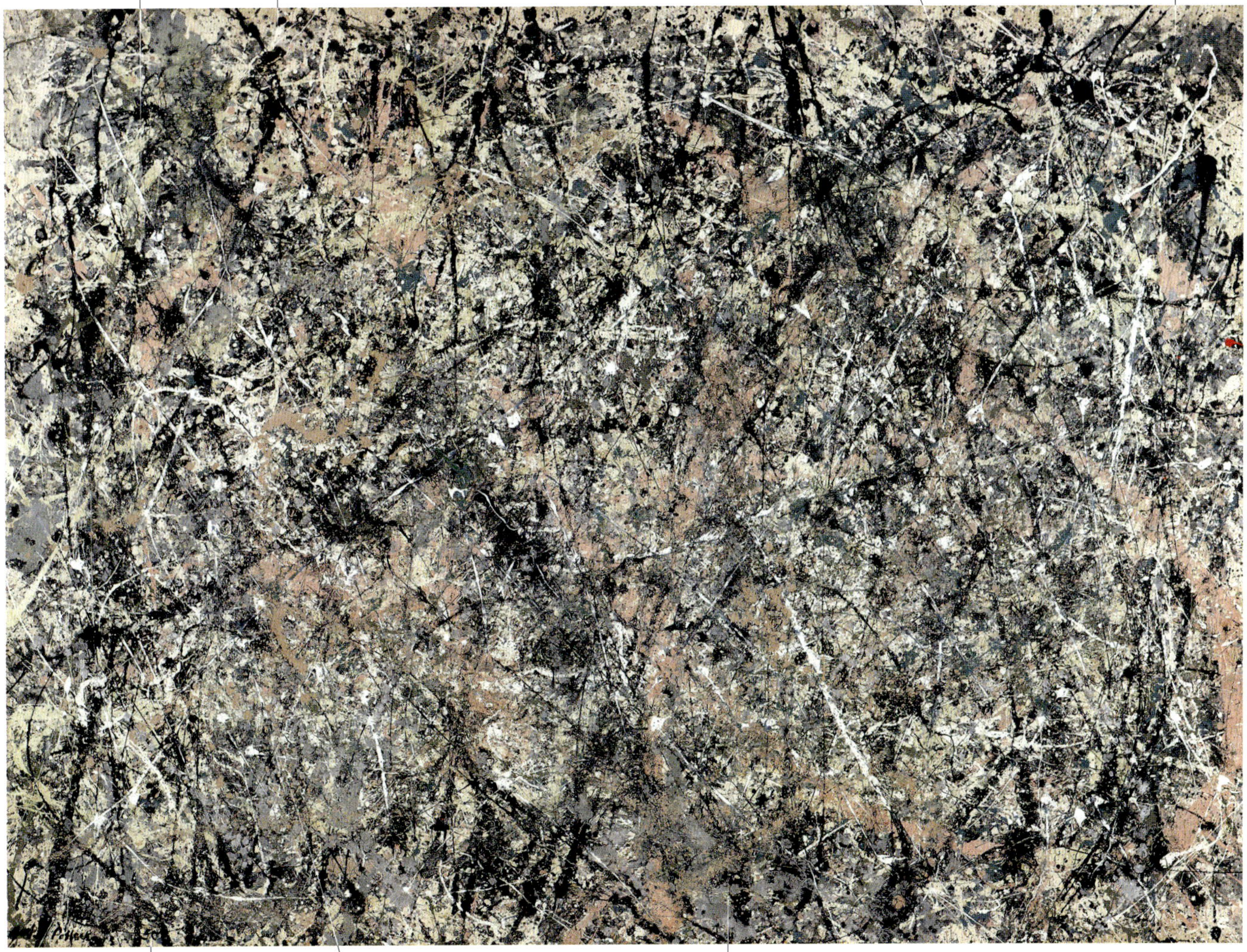

Marks continue off the canvas, suggesting that the world of the painting continues beyond its edges.

A dense web created by the lines and marks is reminiscent of nature.

Pools of wet paint have merged into each other.

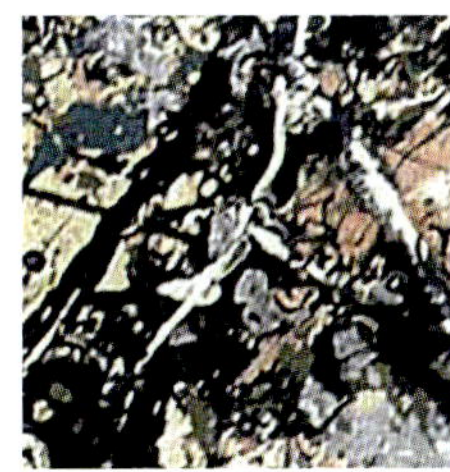

Layered marks in different sizes and textures, from thin paint to impasto, create a limited sense of depth.

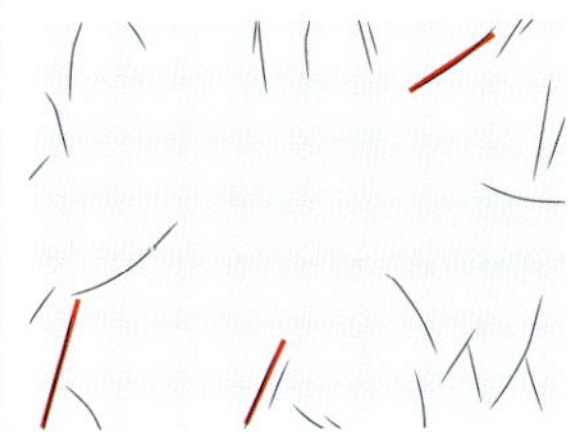

Lack of focus
The edge-to-edge composition has no central subject or focus. Diagonal black lines around the edges direct the viewer across the canvas.

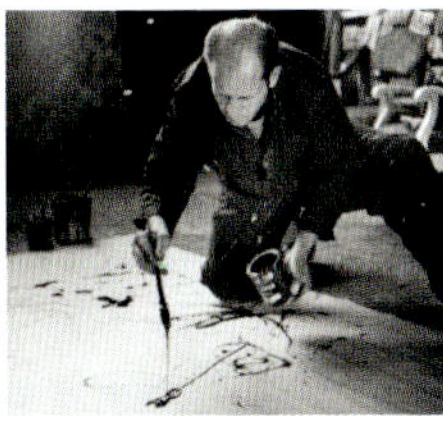

Drip technique
Pollock moved around a canvas placed on the floor, applying paint from all sides using implements such as brushes, sticks, and trowels, and different pouring and dripping actions.

Study After Velázquez's Portrait of Pope Innocent X

Francis Bacon 1953, oil on canvas, 60 × 46 in (152.1 × 117.8 cm), Des Moines Art Center, Des Moines, Iowa, US

A screaming figure appears to be trapped on a golden throne. This is one of nearly 50 paintings by Bacon based on a portrait of Pope Innocent X by 17th-century Spanish artist Diego Velázquez, a painter he admired. He replaced the formal portrait with an image of human suffering, using it to depict a distorted perspective of religion. He never saw the original painting, so worked from black-and-white reproductions.

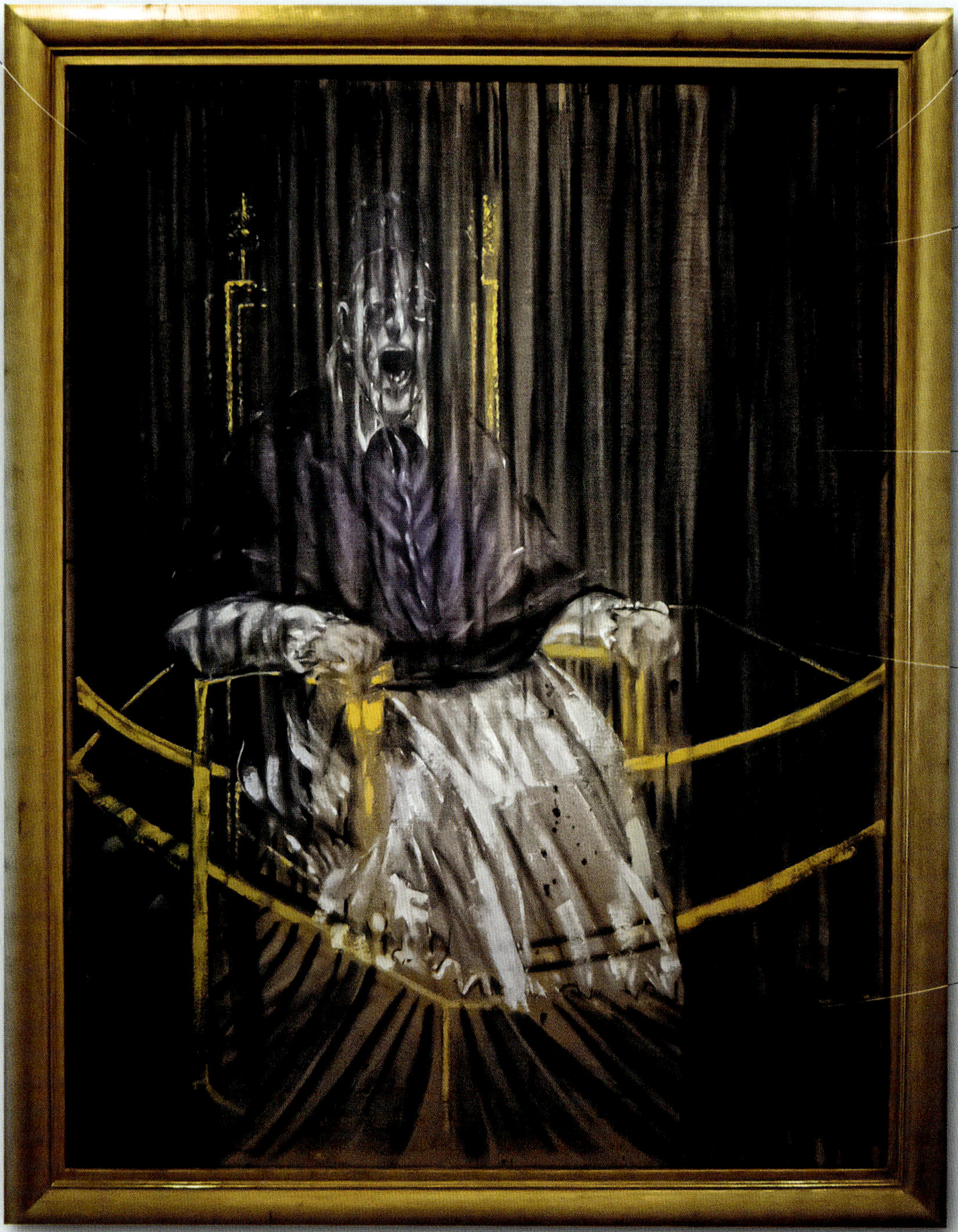

As in Velázquez's painting, the figure is centrally placed and takes up most of the canvas.

The dark, curtain-like background creates a shallow space.

At first sight, the vertical brushstrokes seem more prominent than the figure, but then the figure slowly comes to the fore.

Thin paint has been used to sketch the pope's cape, suggesting that the pope's authority is without substance.

Clenched hands and a screaming face create a sense of tension.

Thick, diagonal brushstrokes make the figure appear both three-dimensional and hollow at the same time.

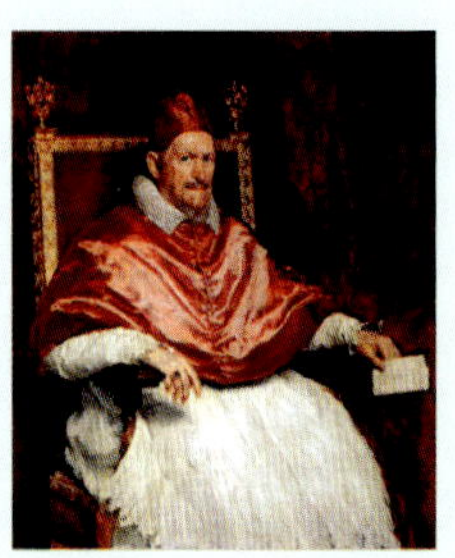

Inspiration
Diego Velázquez painted *Portrait of Pope Innocent X* in around 1650. The pope was said to be delighted with it.

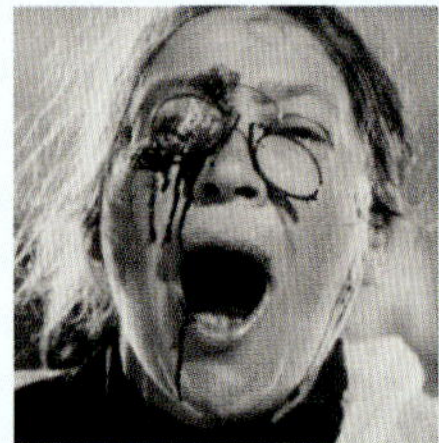

Haunting image
The pope's scream is based on the silent scream of the nurse in Sergei Eisenstein's 1925 film *Battleship Potemkin*.

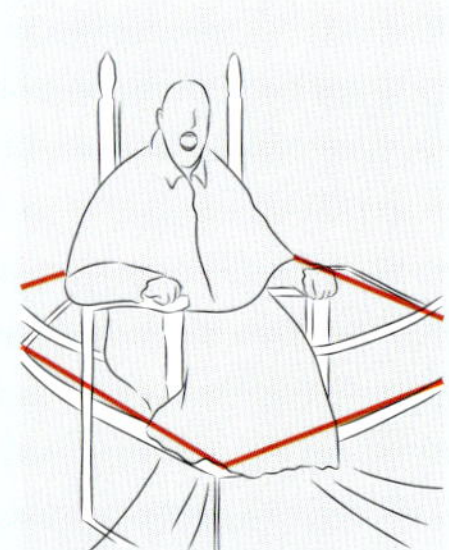

Subject in a frame
Bacon placed a cage-like space frame around the pope, suggesting psychological entrapment.

"I've always thought that this was one of the greatest paintings in the world, and I've used it through obsession."

Francis Bacon, on Velázquez's *Pope Innocent X*

> "This evocation of night and day seems to me to have the power to surprise and delight us. I call this power: poetry."
>
> René Magritte

A bright but sunless sky provides one source of light in the painting, but it does not illuminate the street below.

As is typical in Surrealism, the style is precise and naturalistic.

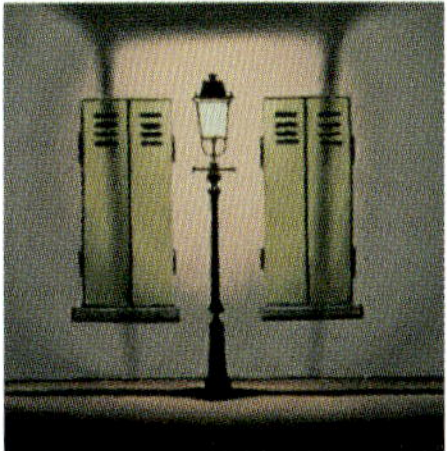

Another source of light is provided by a streetlight, which is the focal point of the scene.

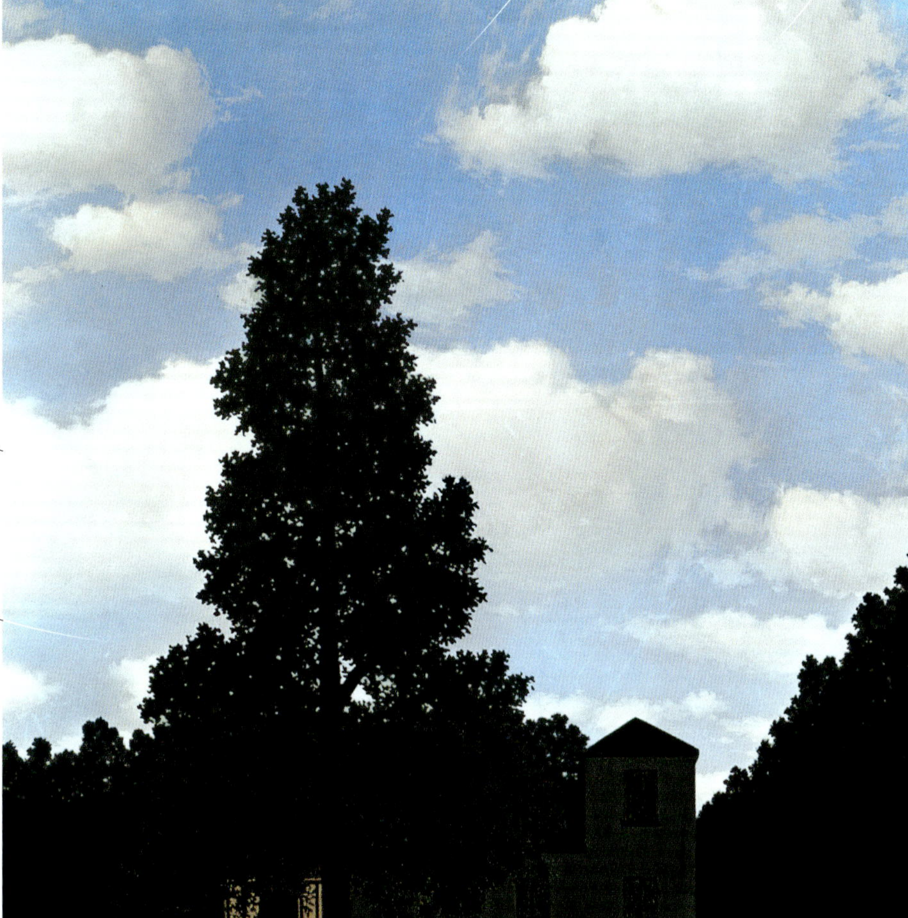

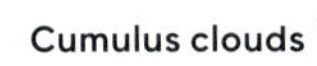

Cumulus clouds are portrayed in a naturalistic way.

The tree has been painted as if in darkness, but glimpses of sky between the branches link the two worlds of the painting.

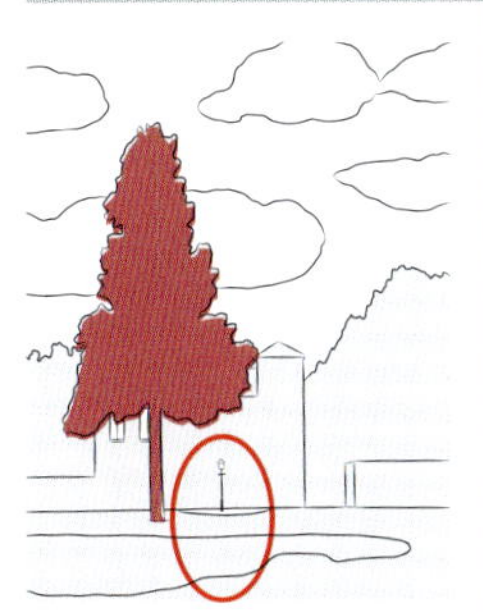

Achieving equilibrium
The pool of light in the street is balanced by the dark silhouetted tree that extends high into the sky.

Small details, such as the shuttered windows, draw the viewer into the scene.

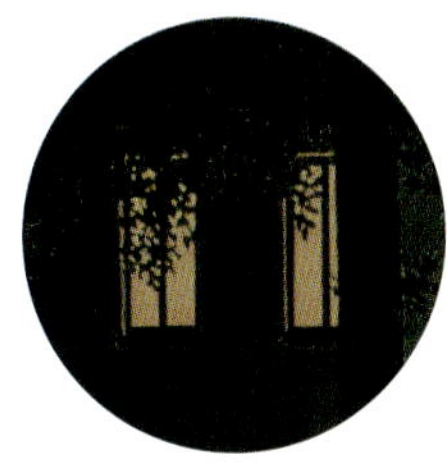

Creating contrast
The light in the windows is the only touch of warm color against the cold glow of the streetlight and the sky.

Water in the foreground reflects the lamp and buildings but not the sky.

Empire of Light

René Magritte 1954, oil on canvas, 57 × 45 in (146 × 114 cm), Royal Museums of Fine Arts, Brussels, Belgium

The juxtaposition of a nocturnal scene with a blue sky poses a simple but disturbing paradox: can day and night, or light and dark, coexist? Magritte, who was a Surrealist, liked to surprise people with unexpected associations and upturned assumptions. *Empire of Light* appears both real and unreal.

Composition with Bottle and Three Boxes

Giorgio Morandi 1954, oil on canvas, 12 × 14 in (31.2 × 36.3 cm), Fondazione Roberto Longhi, Florence, Italy

Morandi spent his life painting deceptively simple still lifes that vibrate with light. He used household objects that consist of basic rectangular or curved forms to create works that combine naturalism and abstraction. Careful placement and sensuous brushwork give each item a sense of individuality.

The large and empty upper half of the canvas is balanced by the tightly packed forms in the smaller, lower half.

The form of the vase is suggested by its contours, not by tonal modeling.

Loosely brushed, thin paint gives the painting texture.

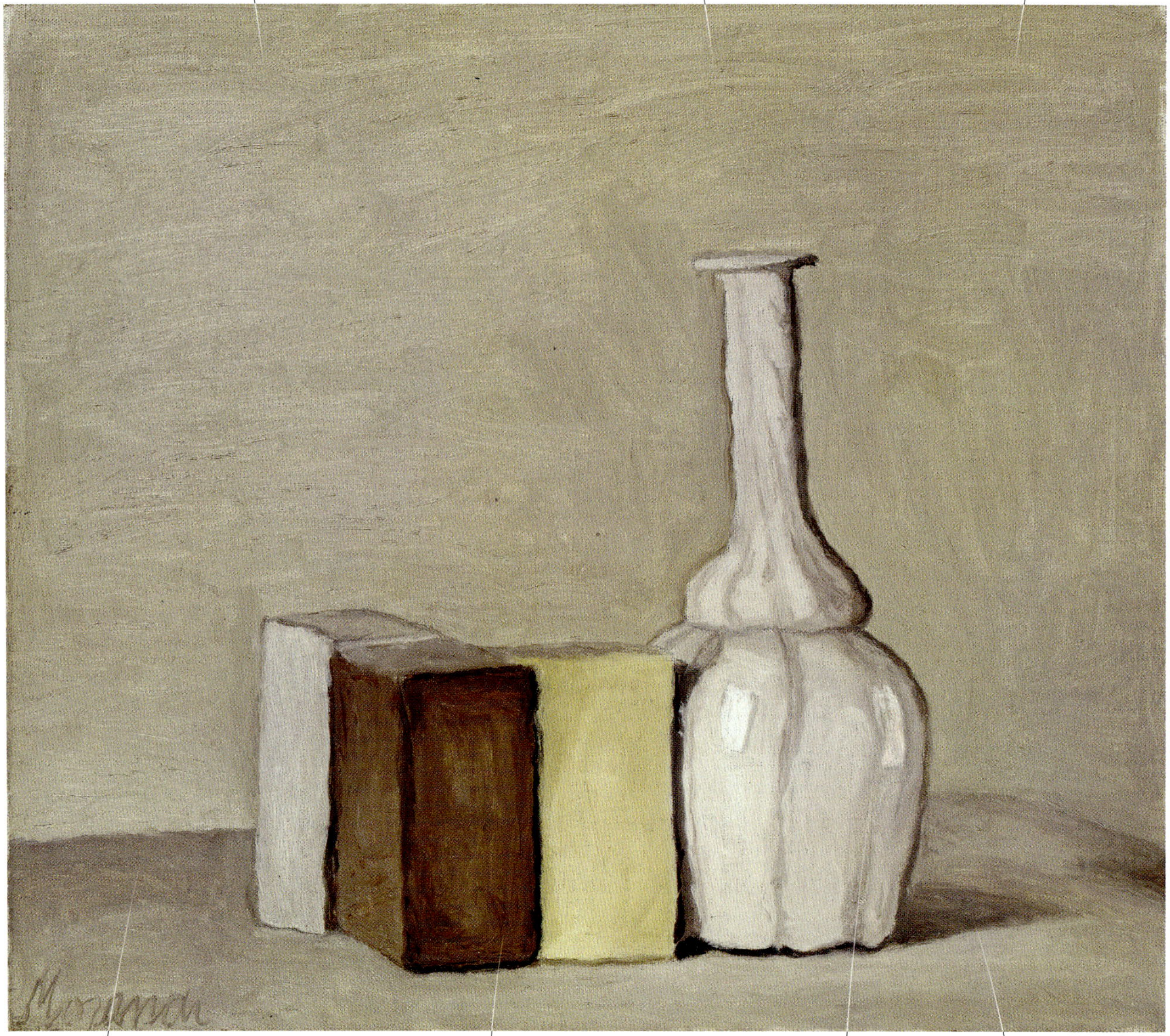

The low eye level gives the objects a sense of monumentality.

Setting the boxes at a slight angle to the picture plane helps give them a sense of volume.

This highlight is not consistent with the direction of the light source. Morandi often did this in his paintings.

Shadow indicates the direction of the light source to the left of the picture.

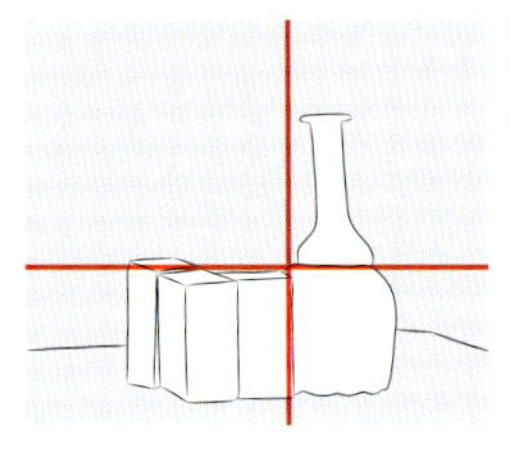

Golden section
The intersection of the top line of the boxes and the left-hand side of the vase fall on the golden section. This gives the composition a harmonious and pleasing balance.

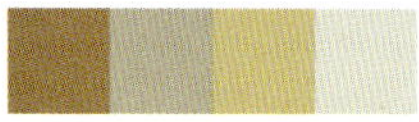

Tones
The quality of light is created with carefully juxtaposed tones. White paint combined with yellows and browns produces muted shades, creating a quiet but luminous effect.

Three Flags

Jasper Johns 1958, encaustic on canvas, 31 × 46 × 5 in (77.8 × 115.6 cm × 11.7 cm), Whitney Museum of American Art, New York, US

In the 1950s, Johns began a long series of works based on the American flag. Choosing a familiar subject, he used artistic means to shift attention from the flag's symbolic meaning to its aesthetic qualities in order to question the difference between the composition as a flag and as a painting.

Only 48 states are represented; Alaska and Hawaii had not yet become part of the US.

The red varies between lighter and darker, and brighter and duller, adding to the painterly quality of the surface.

A layered structure draws attention to the fact that the work is a picture, not a flag. The effect is reminiscent of a mirror reflected in a mirror.

The flag's stars and stripes are transformed into a pattern of repeating shapes and colors.

Conventional perspective is reversed by displaying the smallest canvas uppermost.

Superimposed canvases cast shadows that reinforce the work's three-dimensional nature and its existence as a physical object.

Encaustic paint has a sculptural quality that draws attention to the sensual surface texture.

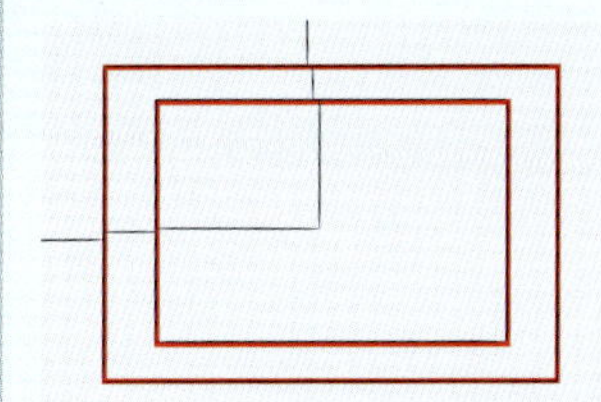

Size differences
The three canvases are positioned centrally; each one is about 25 percent smaller than the one beneath it.

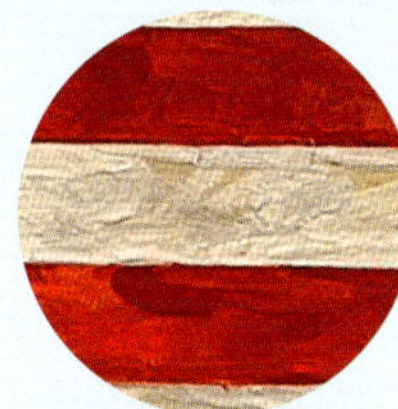

Encaustic painting
This ancient technique involves mixing a colored pigment with warm beeswax. The paint solidifies as each brush stroke is applied, building up a highly textured surface.

"While I was painting a flag, I was aware that it was not a flag that I was painting."
Jasper Johns

Warhol cropped in on Marilyn's face, bringing her closer to the viewer.

Bold colors and graphic lines reflect Warhol's background as an artist in advertising.

Outlines of the image were traced onto the canvas, and the silkscreen image was then placed on top.

The silkscreen process produces hard edges and flat areas of color.

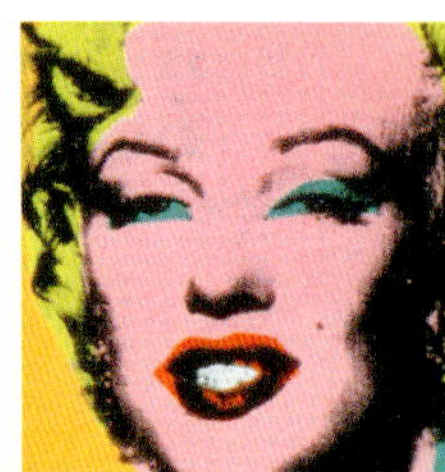

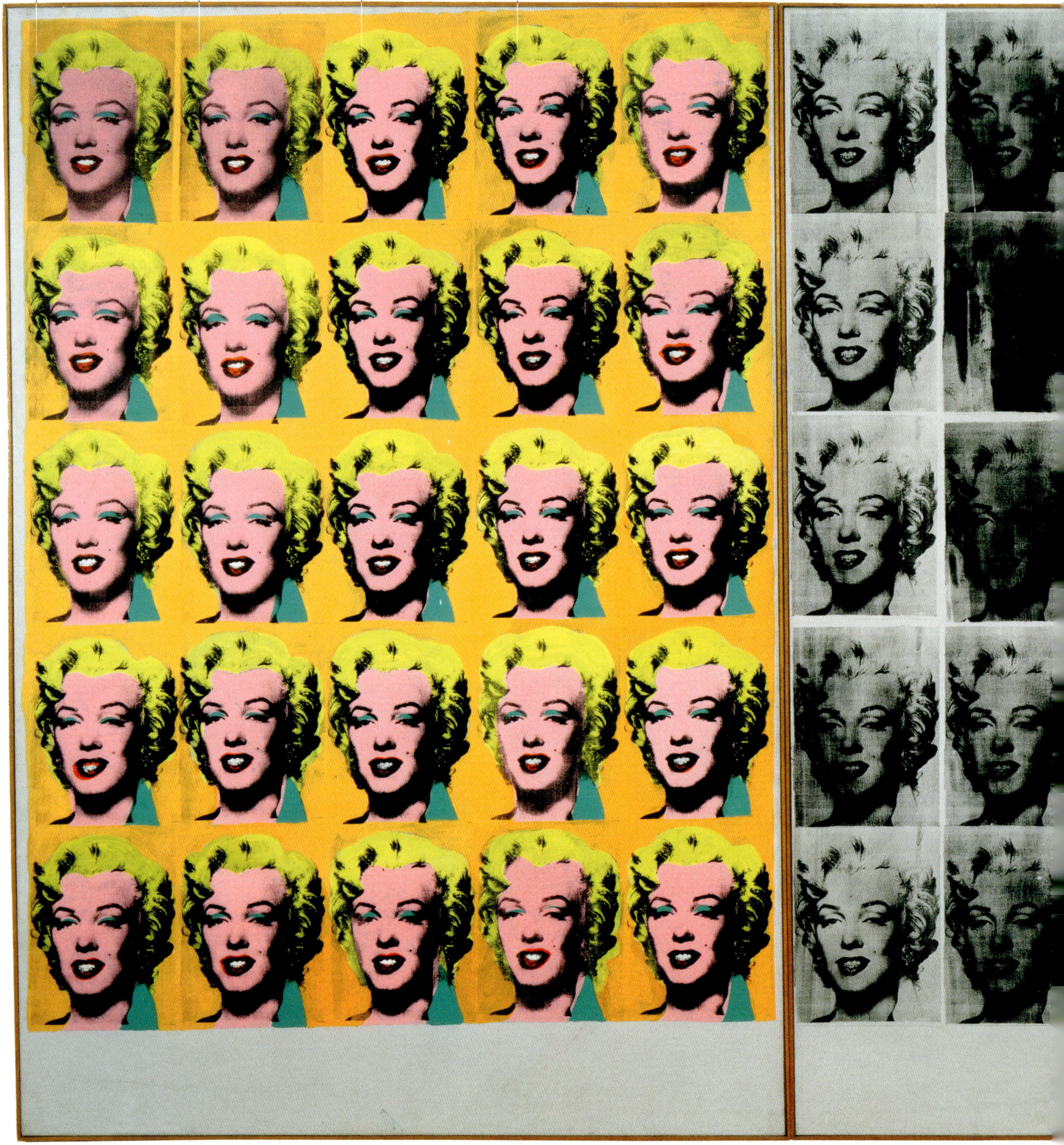

Patches of hand-painted color do not always match the printed image, creating slight variations between the images.

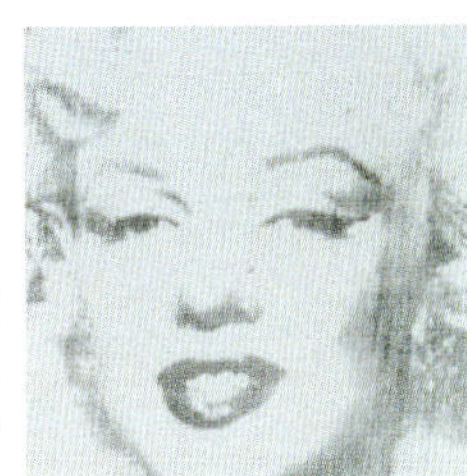

As the images fade toward the right-hand side, Marilyn seems to disappear in front of the viewer's eyes.

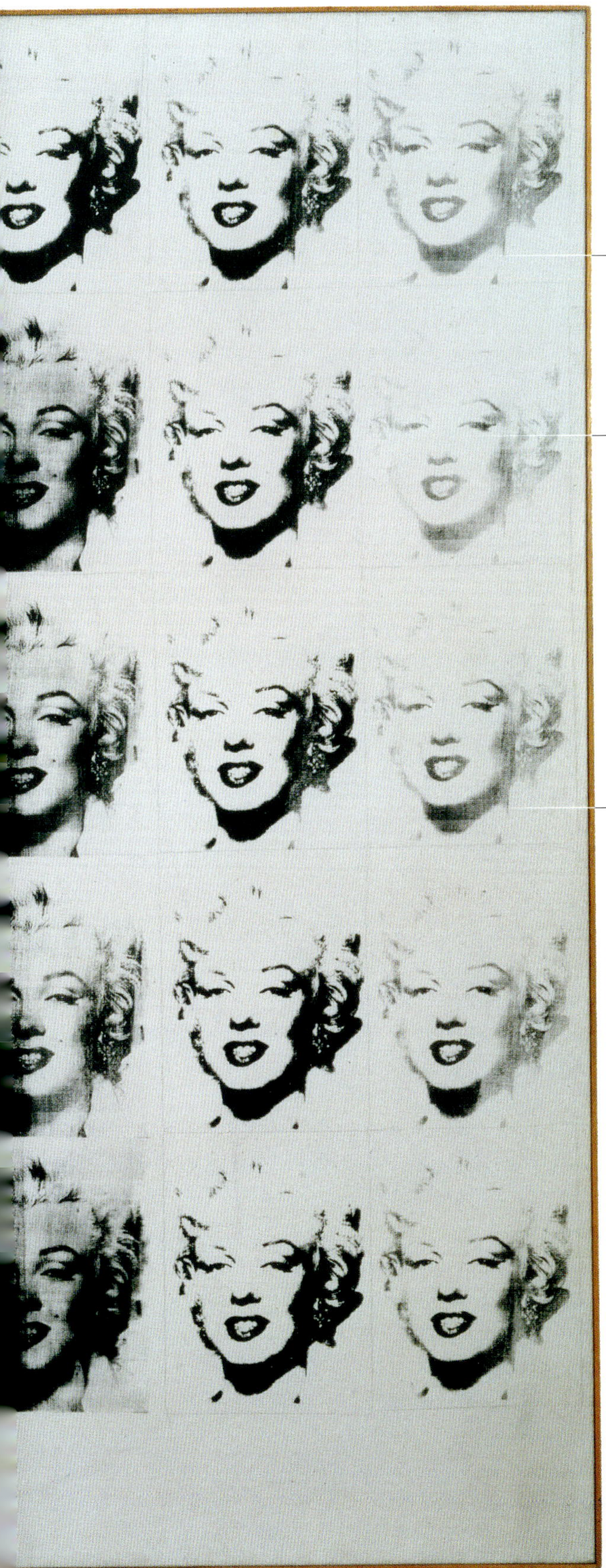

The silver background echoes the "silver screen" of Hollywood.

The repetition reflects Marilyn's constant presence in the media and also suggests mass-production.

Irregularities of the screen printing process create a flickering effect.

Marilyn Diptych

Andy Warhol 1962, silkscreen ink and acrylic paint on canvas, 81 × 114 in (205.4 × 289.8 cm), Tate Modern, London, UK

After Marilyn Monroe died in August 1962, Warhol began making silkscreen prints of her face using a publicity photo from her 1953 film *Niagara* as his source material. He then combined these images with hand-painted backgrounds on canvas, a technique he used to produce many works of art. In the *Marilyn Diptych*, Monroe's face is repeated 50 times. On the left, it is presented in full technicolor as a product of Hollywood; on the right, the actress is shown in monochrome as a private person. The use of screen printing creates an impersonal, mass-produced aesthetic typical of Warhol's art.

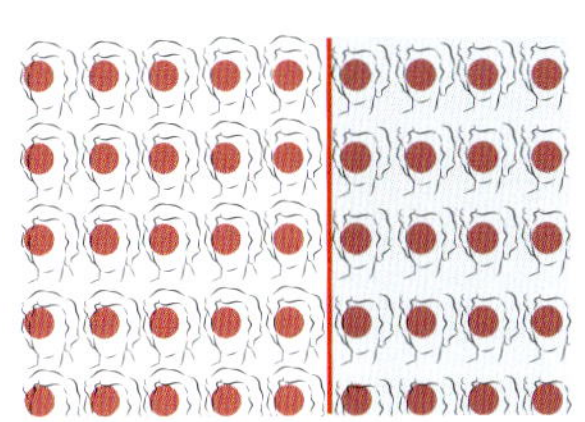

Repeat pattern
Each panel is laid out on a strict grid. The viewer's eye wanders from face to face without focusing on a particular spot.

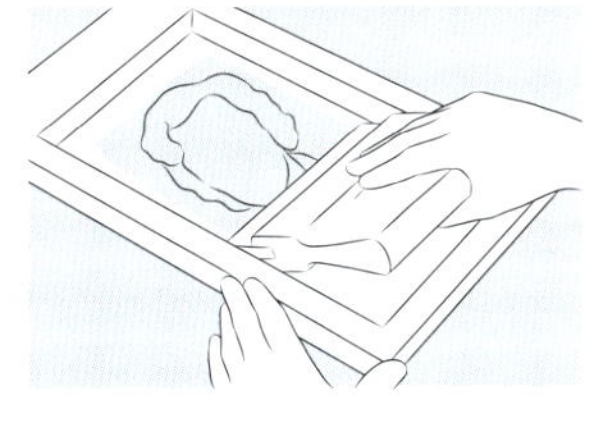

Silkscreen printing
Prints are produced by transferring the image onto fine mesh screens. Ink is then spread across the screen and pushed through the mesh onto the surface to be printed.

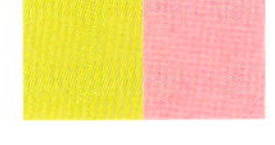

Color effects
Five colors—yellow, pink, white, aqua, and orange—are used for the underpainting on the left. On the right, black ink is printed over a silver underpainting.

> "When Marilyn happened to die that month, I got the idea to make screens of her beautiful face—the first Marilyns."
>
> Andy Warhol

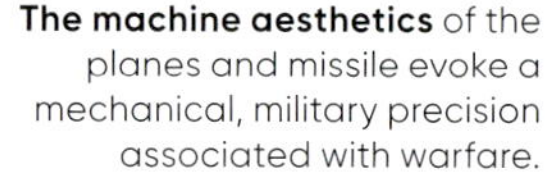

The machine aesthetics of the planes and missile evoke a mechanical, military precision associated with warfare.

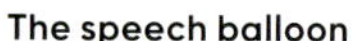

The speech balloon provides narrative context and underlines the work's comic-book inspiration.

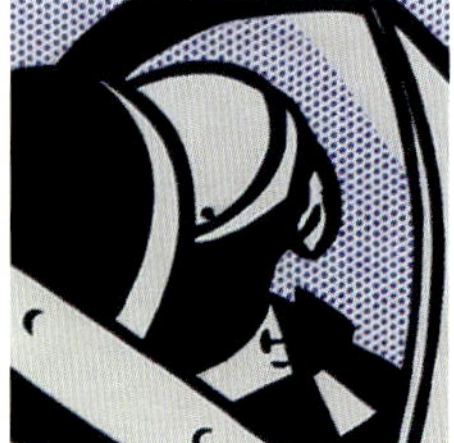

A purposefully concealed pilot's face underscores the reality of war, where soldiers are stripped of all human value and identity.

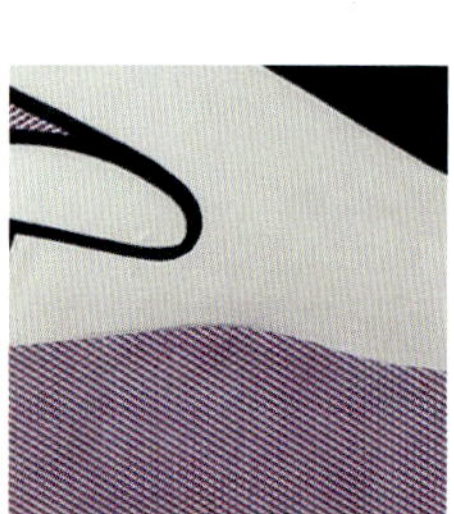

Lichtenstein emulated the Ben-Day dots of the comic strip, named after American illustrator Benjamin Henry Day Jr., inventor of the technique. Color, tone, and shade are created by overlapping different colored dots or changing their density.

The smoke from the fired missile links the two planes, suggesting a mutually destructive relationship.

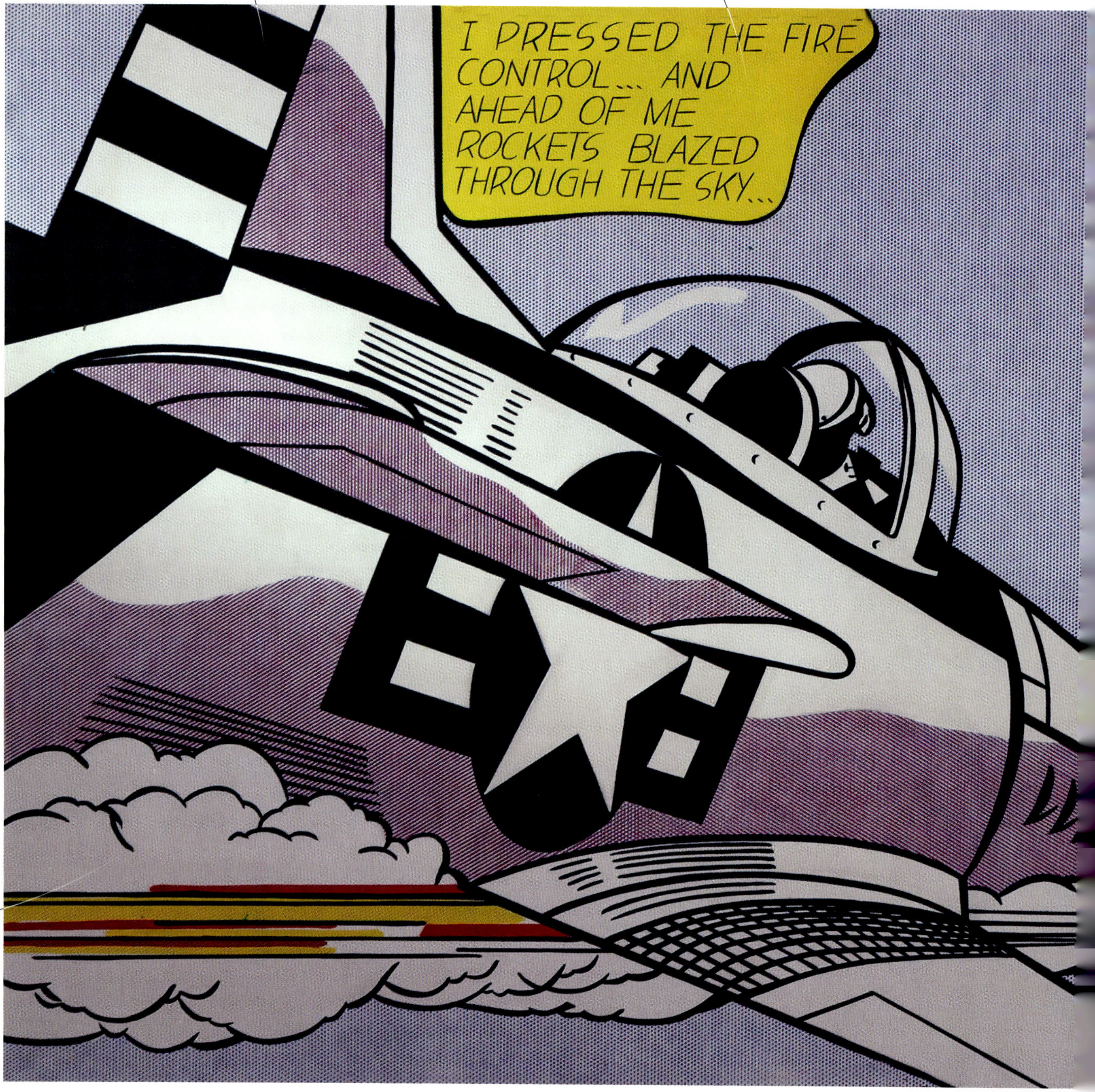

Whaam!

Roy Lichtenstein 1963, acrylic and oil paint on canvas, 680 × 1,600 in (1,727 × 4,064 cm), Tate Modern, London, UK

In this two-panel painting, Lichtenstein captures the intense moment in aerial combat when an American fighter jet launches a missile into an approaching enemy plane, resulting in a resounding onomatopoeic *Whaam!* Painted in response to the East–West tensions of the Cold War and to the particular involvement of the US in the Vietnam War, it reimagines a DC Comics panel drawn by Irv Novick for the 1962 edition of *All-American Men of War*, a long-running series of comics glorifying the adventure of battle. *Whaam!* celebrates the undeniable thrill of aerial combat while also dismantling the idealized notions of warfare promoted by American pop culture during the Cold War.

A calm and featureless expanse of sky contrasts with the chaos of warfare.

WHAAM! emblazoned across the sky produces an instant visual response to the pilot's actions and injects comic-book humor.

Thick black lines encase lettering, speech bubbles, and primary colors, painting a dramatic scene in a graphic manner.

Jagged bursts of color create an eye-catching focal point and emphasize the intensity of the explosion.

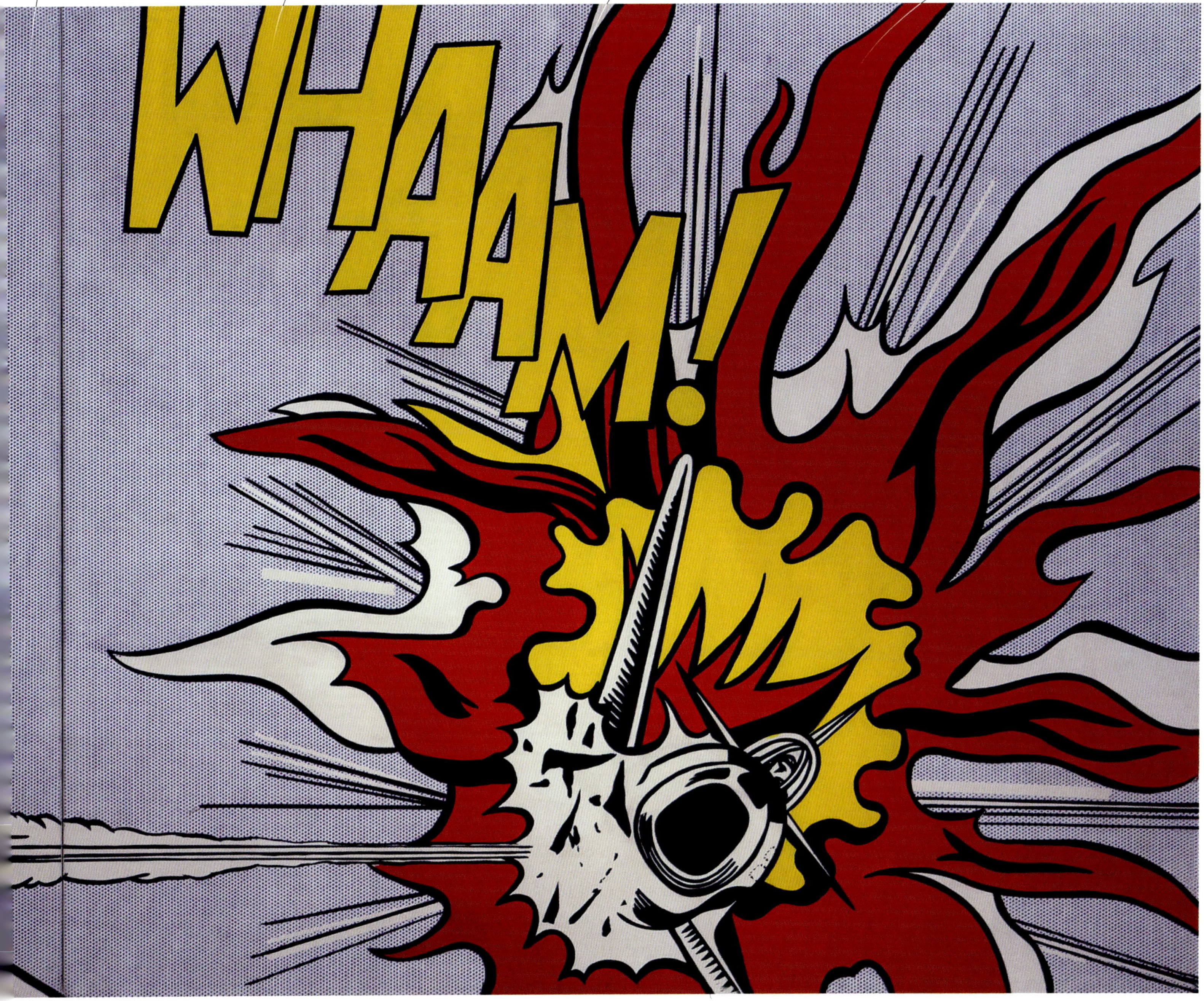

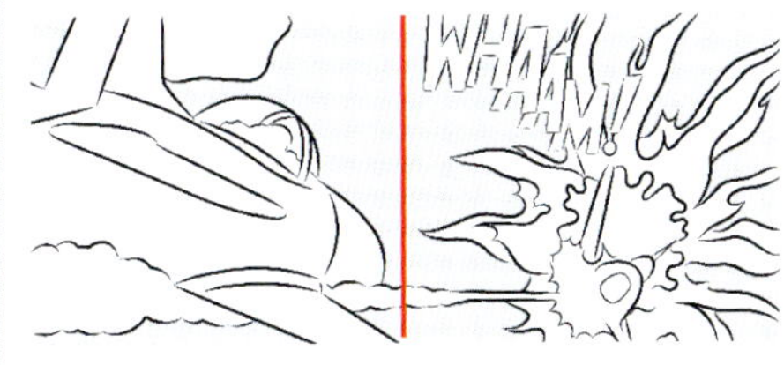

Composition
The mirrored position of the planes creates balance, while splitting the scene across two panels highlights the relationship between action and consequences in war.

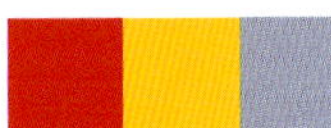

Heat of battle
Dominating the point of impact, red and yellow primary colors stand out against a cool and muted gray-blue sky.

"I am nominally copying, but I am really restating the copied thing in other terms … The original acquires a totally different texture."

Roy Lichtenstein

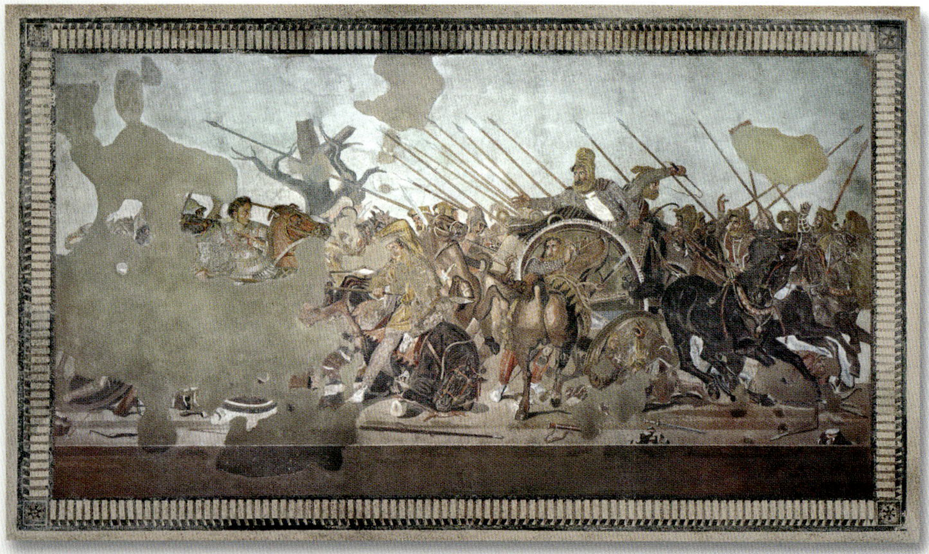

1

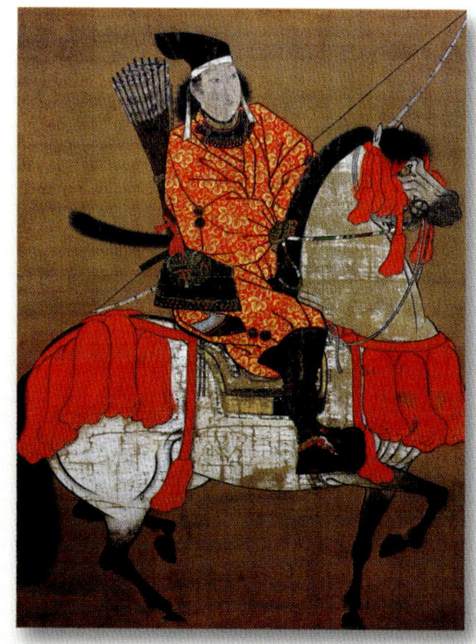

3

War

A form of history painting and sculpture, war art provides a visual impression of the realities and effects of conflict. It may commemorate leaders or combatants, glorify heroism, document events, or provide personal expressions of suffering. Some scenes are inventions based on historical or journalistic accounts. Others, especially since the early 20th century, are based on the firsthand experiences of combatants and official war artists.

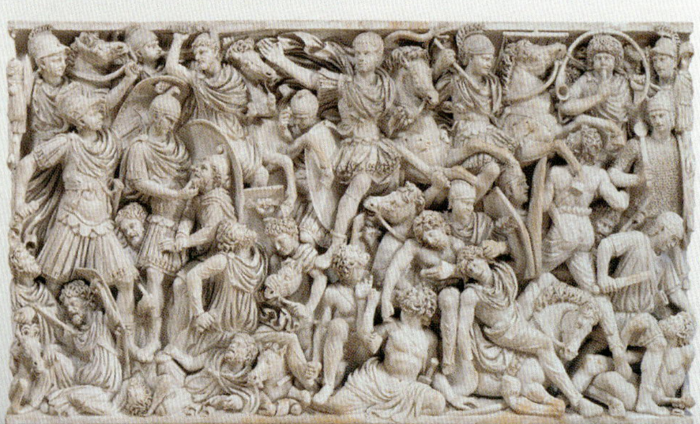

2

4

1. ***The Alexander Mosaic*, artist unknown, c. 120–100 BCE.** Found at Pompeii, this mosaic illustrates a key moment in the Battle of Issus (333 BCE), between the Greek and Persian armies. The Persian leader Darius III, in a chariot, looks back at Alexander the Great, the eventual winner.

2. ***Ludovisi Battle Sarcophagus*, artist unknown, 250 CE.** A battle scene between Roman soldiers and Barbarians is in full flow. Celebrating heroism and the preservation of Roman civilization, this sarcophagus was probably made for the soldier on horseback in the center.

3. ***Portrait of Ashikaga Yoshihisa*, artist unknown, 1489.** Yoshihisa was the ninth Japanese Ashikaga shogun. He succeeded to the title following a civil war over succession and dealt with a series of rebellions. This portrait was painted in the year of his death at the age of 24.

4. ***The Death of General Wolfe*, Benjamin West, 1770.** West has presented the British general, who died at the Battle of Quebec in 1759, as a Christlike figure. He is shown surrounded by others, many of whom were not there at the time. The work helped make Wolfe a national hero.

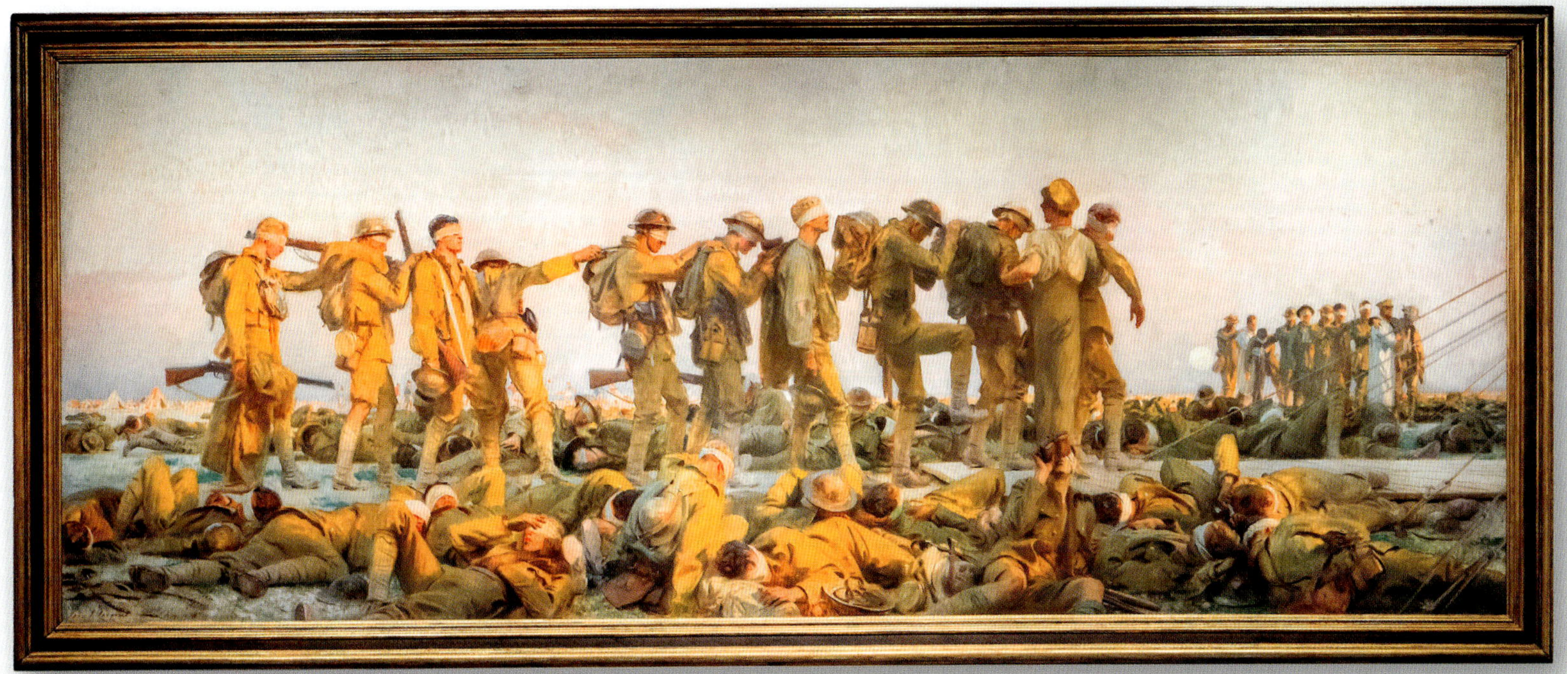

6

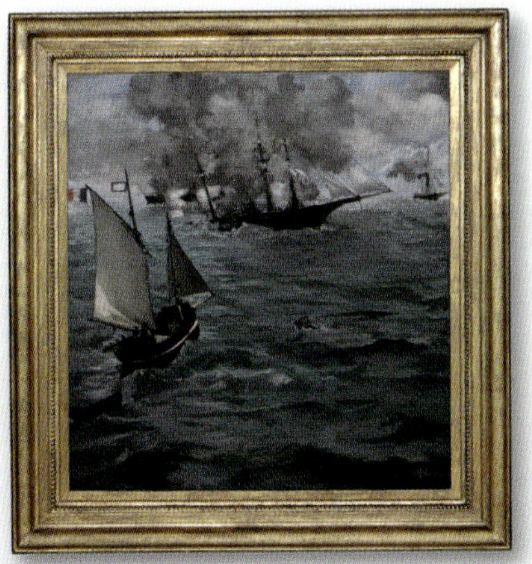

5

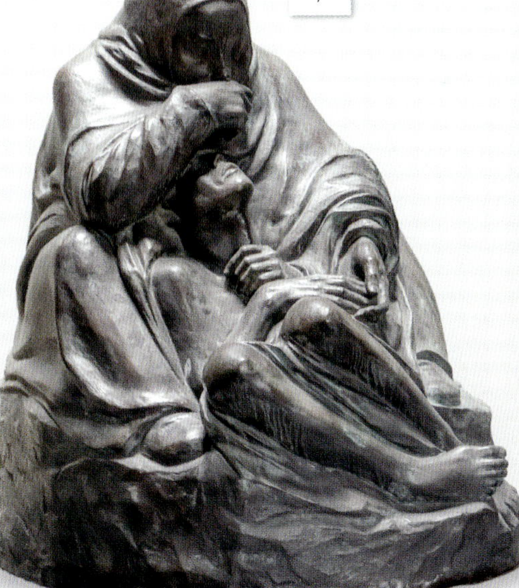

7

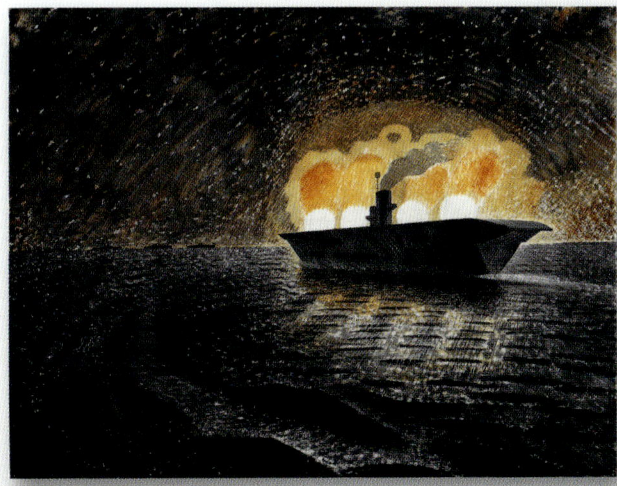

8

5. ***The Battle of the* Kearsarge *and the* Alabama, Édouard Manet, 1864.** The battle between these two US ships during the American Civil War took place so close to the French coast that people could watch it. Manet did not see the battle, so he based his painting on press reports.

6. ***Gassed*, John Singer Sargent, 1918.** Sargent, who spent time with British troops in World War I, has depicted a line of soldiers affected by a mustard-gas attack being led to a field hospital. The image captures both the suffering and the routine nature of such an event.

7. ***Mother with her Dead Son*, Käthe Kollwitz, 1937.** Kollwitz's pietà—based on statues of the Virgin cradling the dead Christ—expresses the suffering caused by war. Her younger son was killed during World War I, and the theme of the grieving mother recurred throughout her work.

8. ***HMS* Ark Royal *in Action*, Eric Ravilious, 1940.** Ravilious, an official British war artist, painted the *Ark Royal* firing its guns while on board a ship that was escorting it. The deceptive simplicity of his style captures the power of the weaponry and the danger of the situation.

A Bigger Splash

David Hockney 1967, acrylic on canvas, 95 × 96 in (242.5 × 243.9 cm), Tate Britain, London, UK

Inspired by the strong California light, Hockney made several paintings of swimming pools, looking for ways to represent the appearance of water. In this image, which portrays the absolute stillness of a hot day broken by a momentary burst of activity, the splash was copied from a photograph, while the 1960s modernist building was based on a sketch. The diver who caused the splash is presumably still under the water.

The raw canvas surround suggests the border of a Polaroid photograph.

Surrounding buildings are indicated by reflections in the windows.

A human presence is implied by the splash and the empty chair.

Large blocks of color—the sky, building, and pool—were applied with a roller in two or three layers to give a smooth, opaque surface.

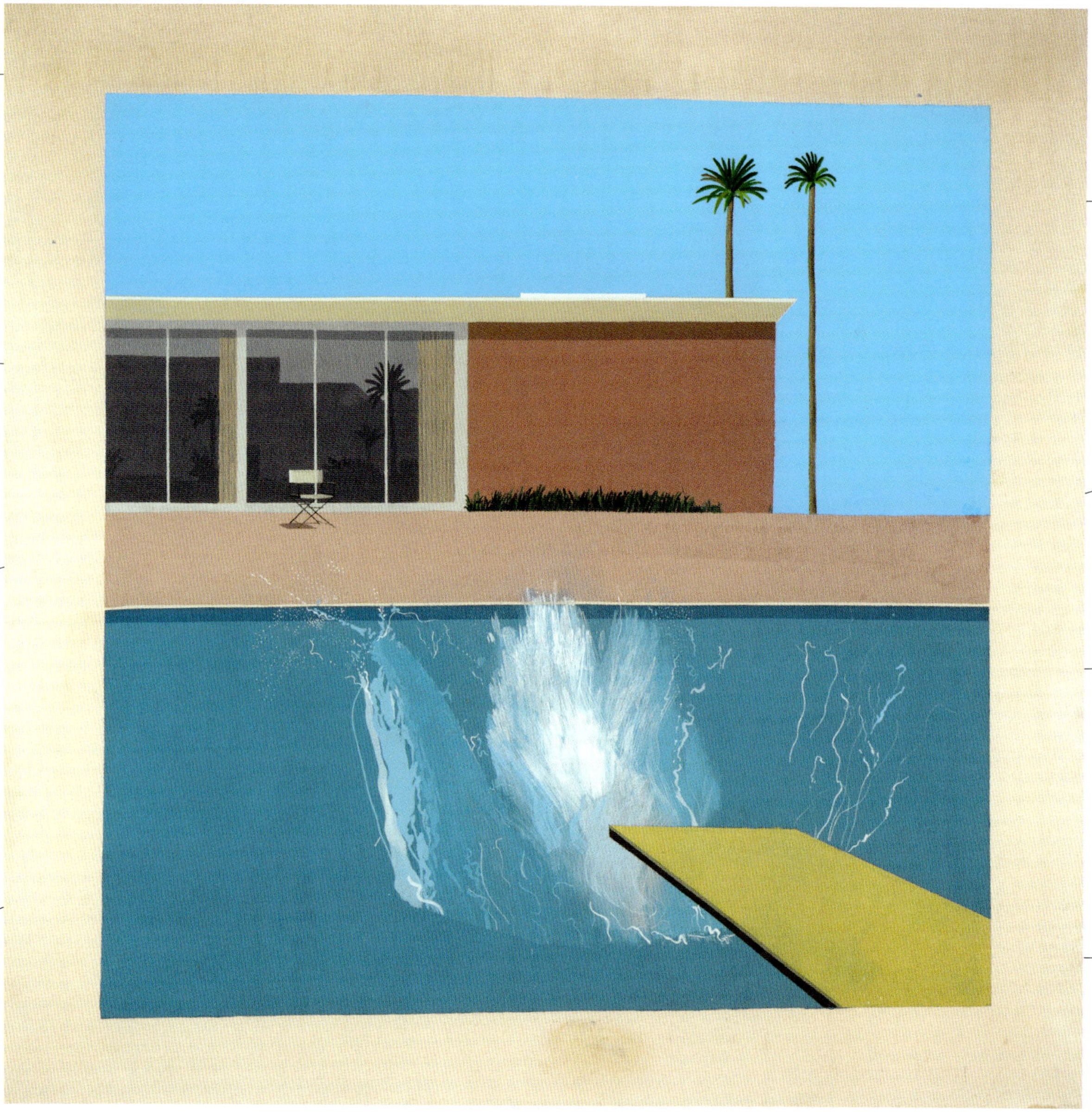

Small brushes were used for painting details, such as the vegetation and palm trees, as well as the splash.

An absence of shadows indicates that the sun is directly overhead.

The splash, which is frozen in a moment of time, took two weeks to paint. Hockney copied a photograph meticulously.

The large diving board compared to the small size of the chair creates a sense of perspective despite the flat blocks of color.

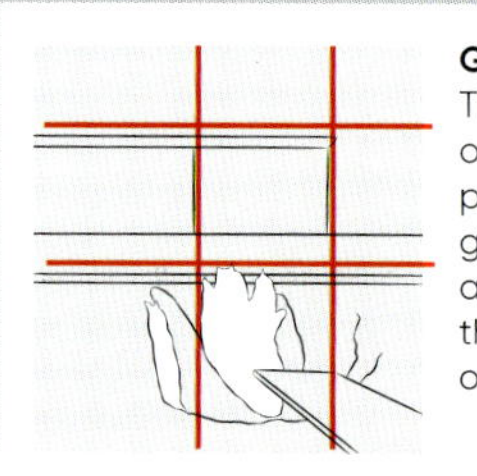

Grid structure
The straight lines of the building and pool edge form a grid, which accentuates the explosive energy of the splash.

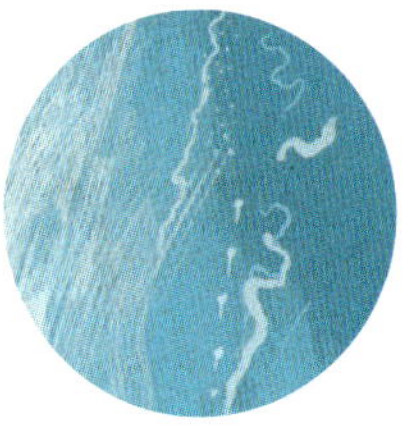

Brushstrokes
Hockney used small brushes and a wide variety of marks, together with contrasts between thick and thin paint, to apply white paint over the blue of the pool.

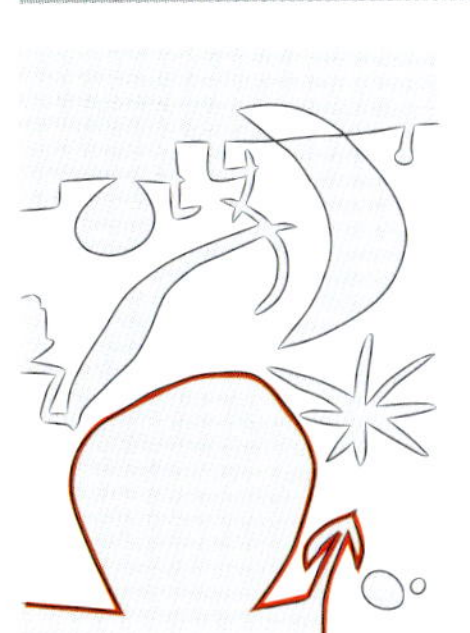

Sense of movement The large, dark shape fills most of the lower half of the canvas, creating a sense of weight and immobility, against which curving, diagonally placed shapes seem to move.

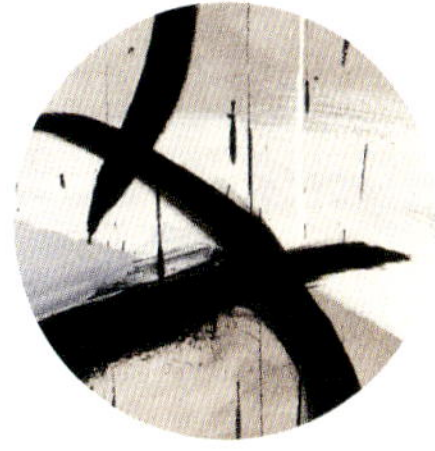

Paint handling Very diluted paint contrasts with more thickly applied areas. The thinly washed-on gray underpainting resembles the infinity of the sky compared to the thicker areas.

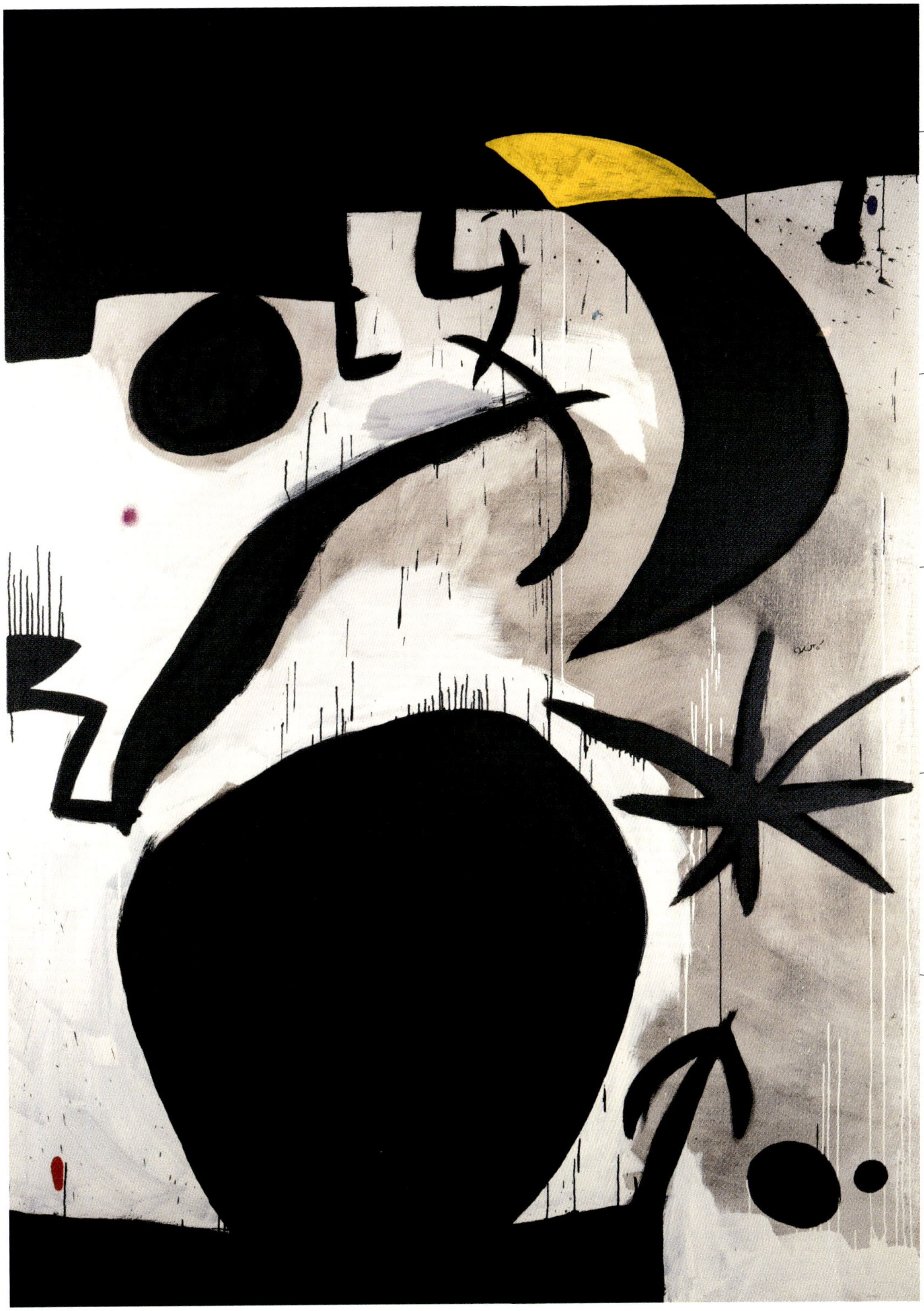

The yellow shape mediates between two black areas and draws the eye.

A curving shape resembling a bird in flight streaks across the sky, introducing an impression of movement.

The soft edges and small drips of paint draw the eye into the distance. Miró must have painted at least part of this work upside-down.

Shapes resembling a star and a sliver of moon suggest night time, yet they are dark forms against a light background.

A large, dark, static form consisting of a large circle resting on a rectangular band sits on the bottom edge of the canvas.

Woman and Birds in the Night

Joan Miró 1969, acrylic on canvas, 96 × 69 in (244 × 174 cm), Joan Miró Foundation, Barcelona, Spain

Simplified, familiar shapes are placed on a ground of opaque white and thin gray paint, while a band of black at the top of the painting holds everything in place. Mirò, who was associated with the Surrealists, developed a personal language of visual forms that appear recognizable yet also abstract. He used these to explore ideas such as flight, infinity, and a harmonious relationship between humans and nature. Here, the viewer has the sense of standing on the ground and looking up into the heavens.

Margarethe

Anselm Kiefer 1981, oil, acrylic, emulsion, and straw on canvas, 110 × 157 in (280 × 400 cm), San Francisco Museum of Modern Art, US

Margarethe is the last in a series of paintings Kiefer based on the poem "Death Fugue" by Paul Celan, a Holocaust survivor. Set in a concentration camp, the poem features Margarethe, a German woman, and Shulamite, a prisoner. Kiefer used the poem to explore the themes of national identity in Germany. His dense layering of materials suggests the accretion of layers of history, while the burned straw and ashes are symbolic of the transformative power of fire to bring about cleansing and renewal.

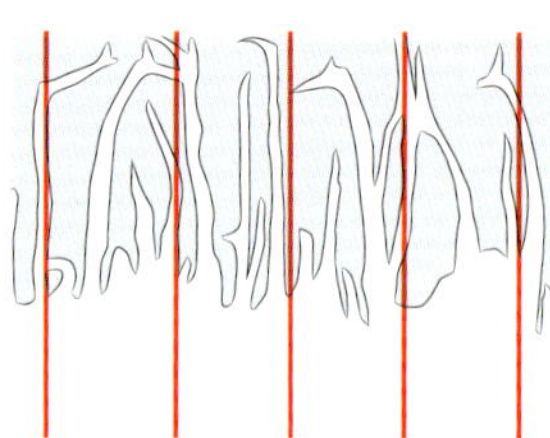

Imprisoned Vertical strands of straw are arranged across the canvas like prison bars, suggesting that both women were prisoners of history.

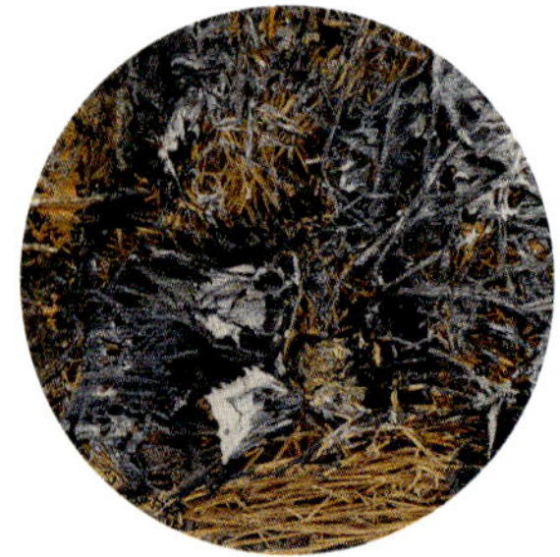

The identities of the women are woven together, reflecting Kiefer's hopes for eventual reconciliation.

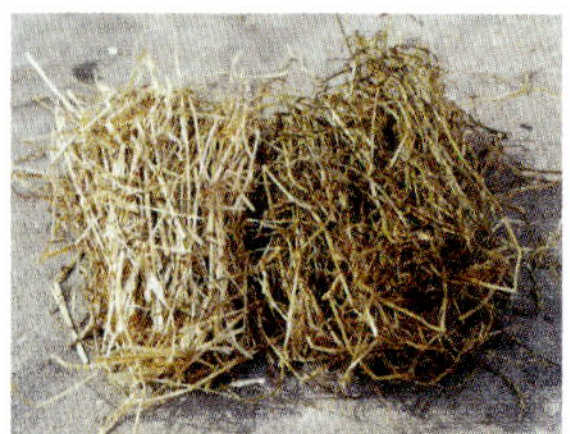

Symbolic meaning Kiefer often incorporates natural materials such as soil and plants into his paintings. Straw may be emblematic of the German people's love of the land.

> "History speaks to artists. It changes the artist's thinking and is constantly reshaping it into different and unexpected images."
>
> Anselm Kiefer, 2012

The combination of paint and straw creates a heavily textured surface, giving the painting a strong material presence.

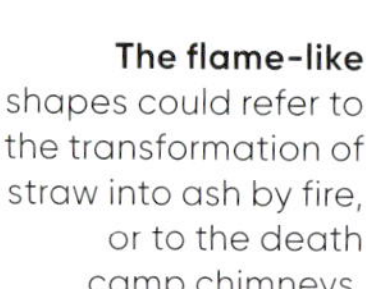

The flame-like shapes could refer to the transformation of straw into ash by fire, or to the death camp chimneys.

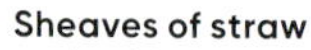

Sheaves of straw embedded in the paint represent Margarethe's golden hair, a personification of Aryan identity.

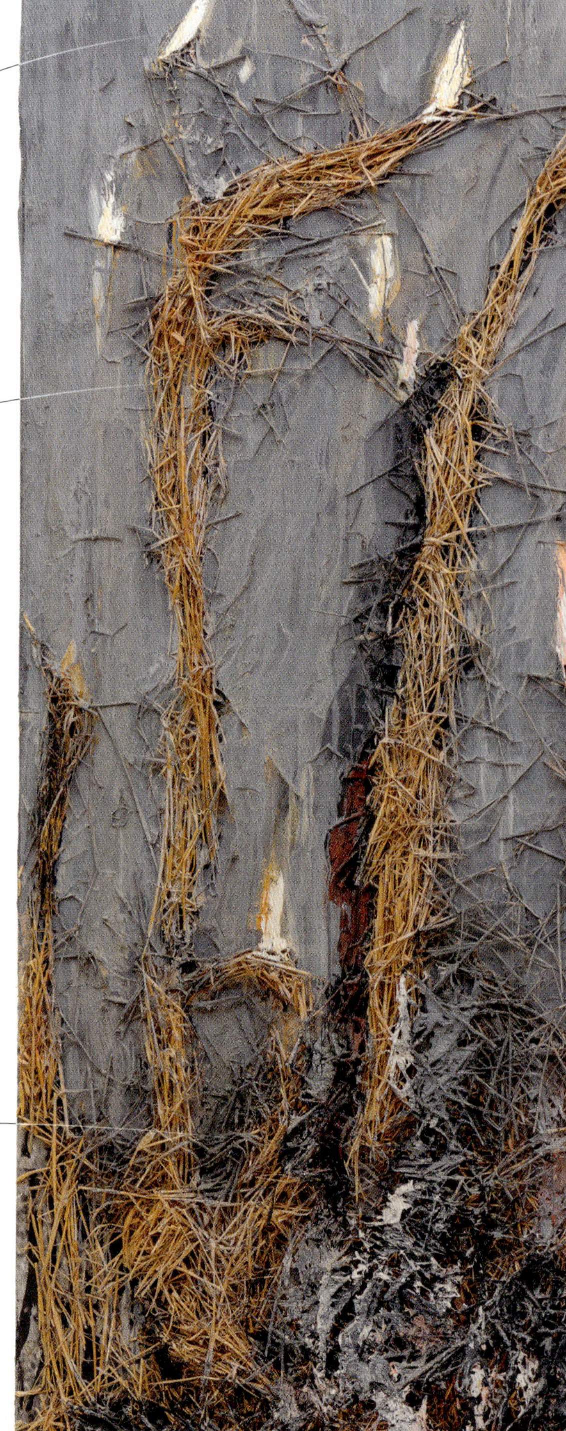

Black areas represent the ashen hair of Shulamite, who personifies Jewish identity. They could also refer to the piles of human hair found at Auschwitz.

The charred soil symbolizes a land that is scarred by history.

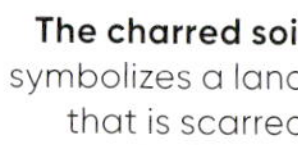

Margarethe's name is inscribed across the painting like graffiti.

The neutral gray of the background unifies light and dark elements.

Thick paint creates a solid, wall-like background, against which the sheaves of straw stand out.

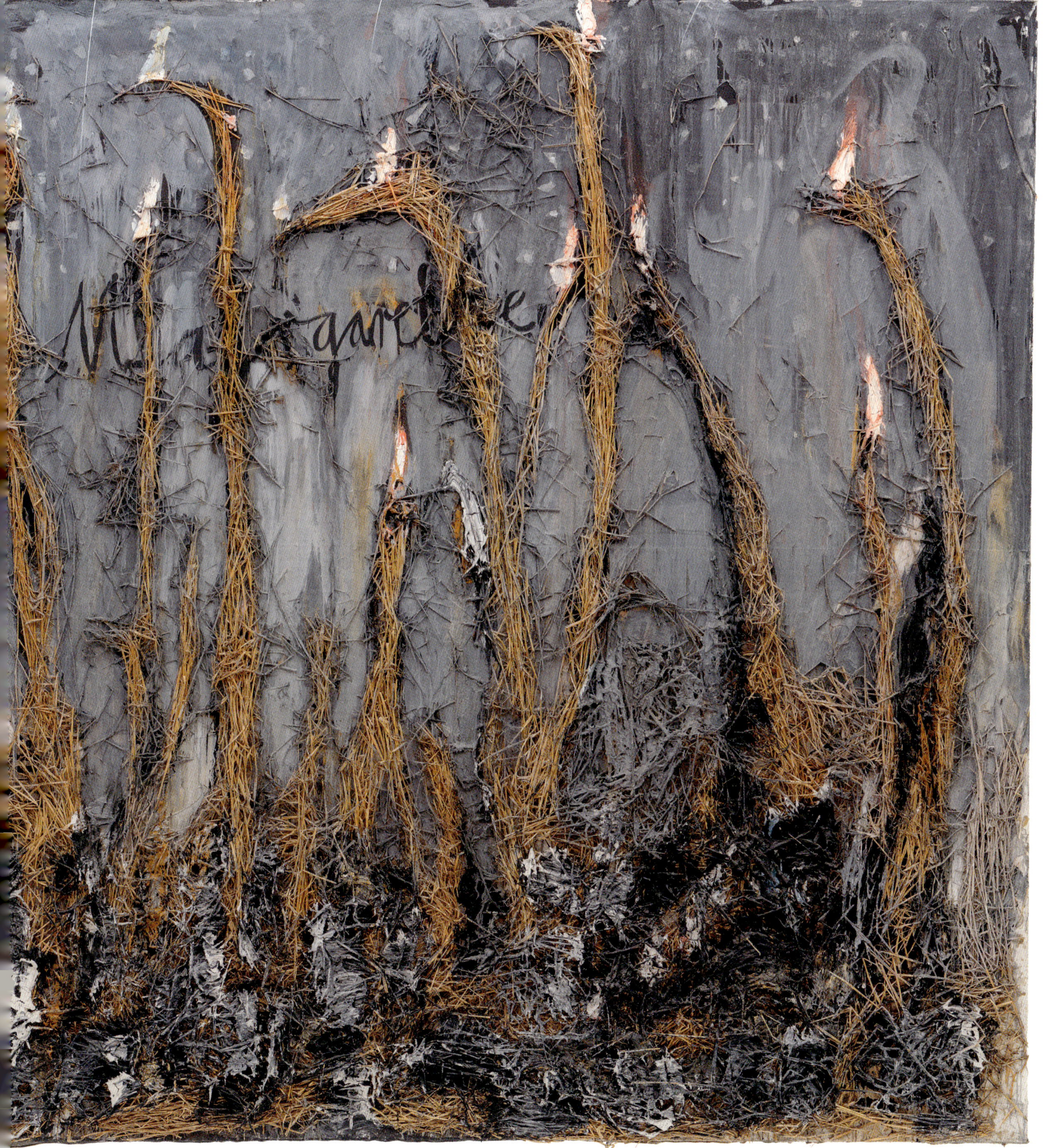

The Dance

Paula Rego 1988, acrylic on paper on canvas, 84 × 108 in (212.6 × 274 cm), Tate Modern, London, UK

In this dreamlike painting, a group of eight figures dance on a beach in the moonlight. Their rhythmic movements contrast with the stillness of the setting and with the imposing fortresslike building in the background. Rego is known for her narrative paintings and works inspired by her childhood. This appears to be a dance of life, with the single figure, couples, and group representing the stages in a woman's life.

The passing of time is represented by this group, comprising a grandmother, mother, and child.

Rego's husband and son inspired the two men in the painting.

A young woman stands alone, inviting the viewer into the scene. She is proportionately larger than the other figures.

Elongated shadows on the ground link the figures in each group, rather than being naturalistic.

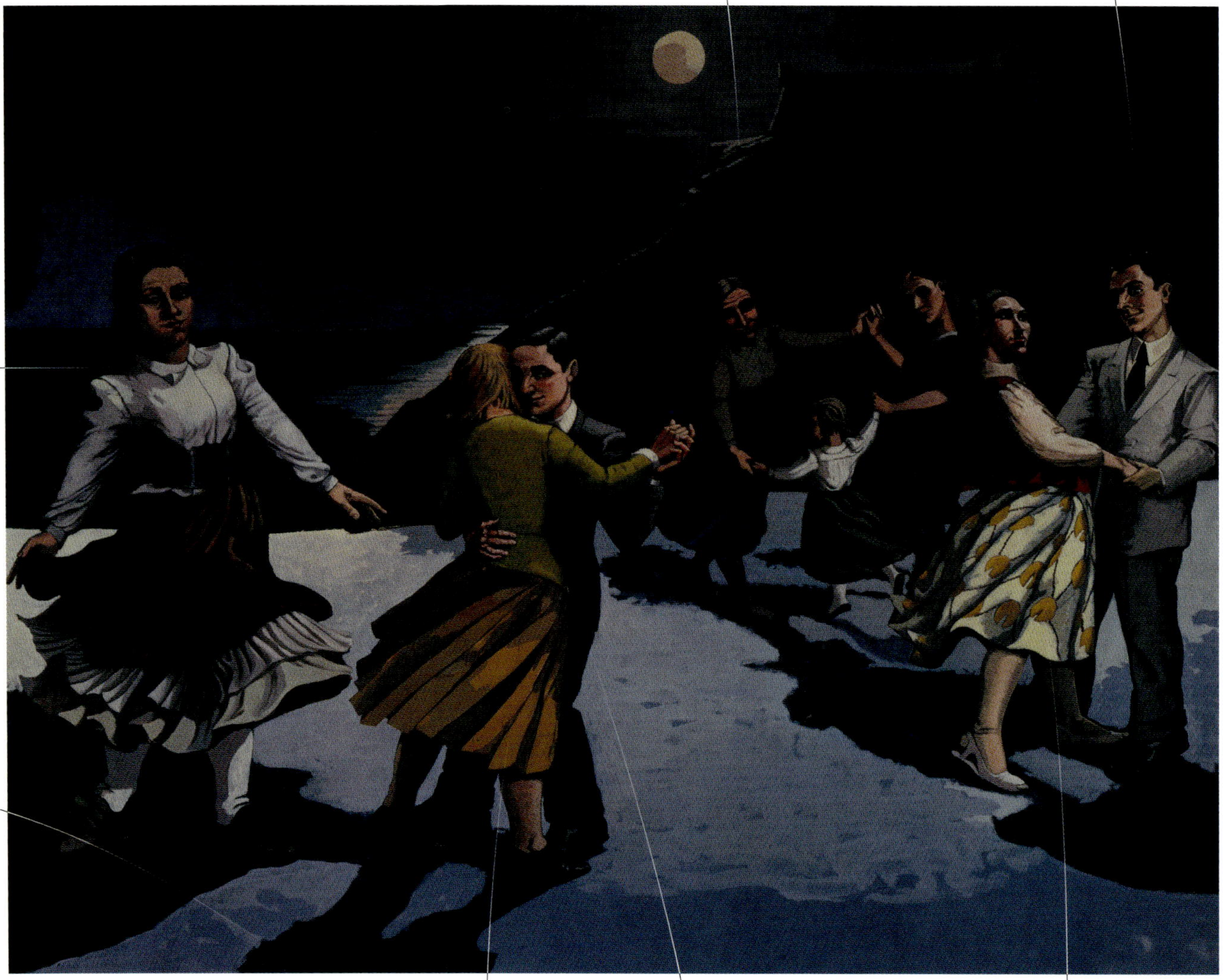

Thin black paint outlines the figures and forms, giving them a statuesque quality, but the swirling skirts suggest movement.

A courting couple takes center stage.

The pregnant woman suggests this is a married couple.

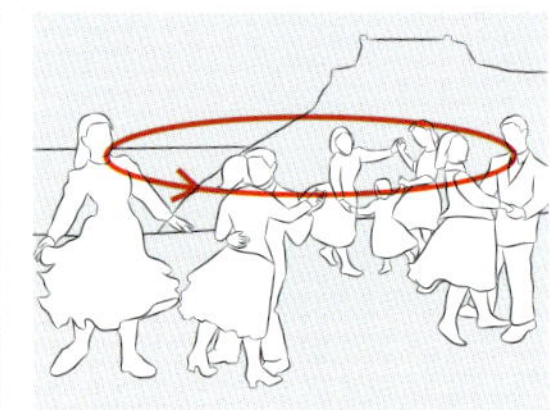

Sweeping composition
The figures are arranged in a circle, and the eye follows them counterclockwise. Implied diagonals between the opposite corners add to the painting's sense of depth.

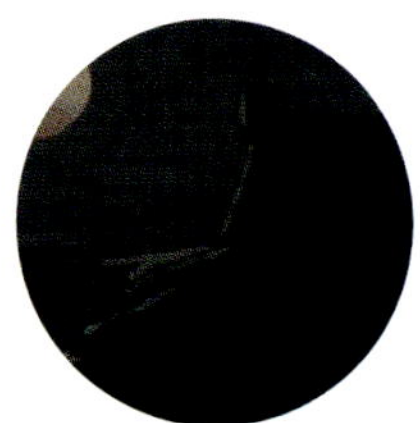

Bleak history
The building may be a military fort that was used as a prison during the *Estado Novo*, Portugal's period of dictatorship in the mid-20th century.

Goanna Dreaming

Clifford Possum Tjapaltjarri 1988, acrylic on canvas, 76 × 48 in (193 × 122 cm), Corbally Stourton Contemporary Art, Sydney, Australia

Drawing on the "dot art" tradition of the Papunya communities in Australia's Western Desert, Tjapaltjarri's paintings evoke the Dreaming—the creation period in Aboriginal culture when ancestor spirits, who emerged from the earth and sky, shaped the land, law, and society. *Goanna Dreaming* honors the goanna (large lizard) as a totemic spirit for the Anmatyerre people, sustaining their profound connection to the land.

Two goannas are the focus. The rest of the painting has a symbolism outsiders are unable to understand.

Golden stars enhance the timelessness of this Dreaming narrative.

Wormlike figures suggest serpents or land formations.

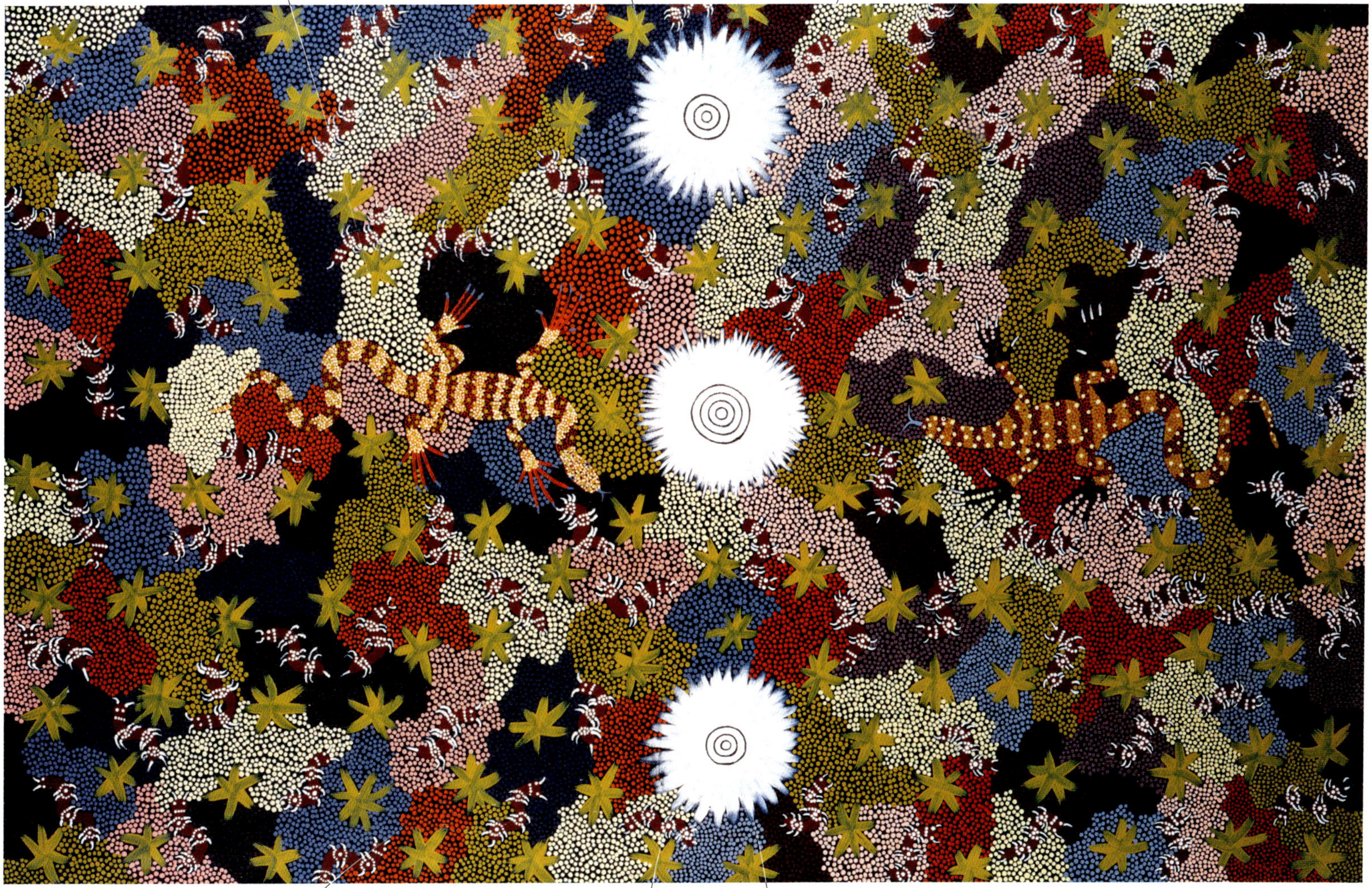

Ocher dots evoke the dabs of paint traditionally applied to peoples' bodies during Aboriginal rituals.

Glowing white bursts depict fires, a reference to Tjapaltjarri's bushfire Dreaming in *Dreaming Story at Warlugulong* (1976).

Concentric circles form roundels and convey many meanings in Aboriginal art, including hills, waterholes, campsites, and ceremonial places.

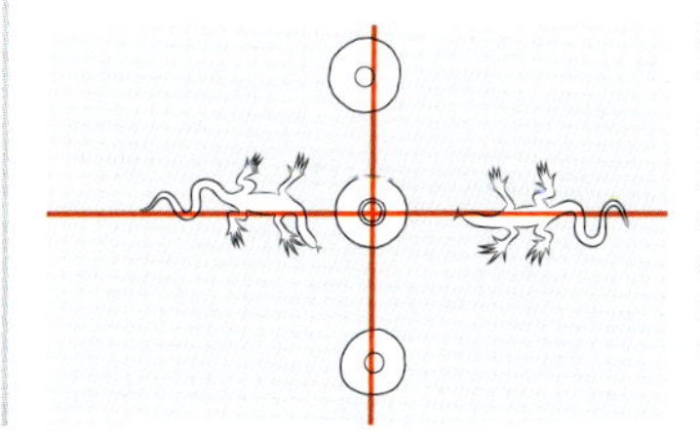

Structure
The symmetrical painting has a vertical line, and the mirrored goannas converge at the focal point. The central roundel's extra ring makes it more significant than the others.

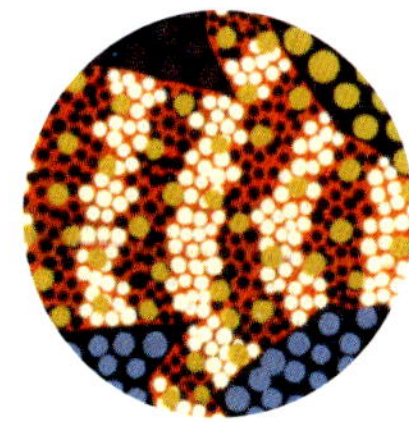

Keeping it neat
Tjapaltjarri's meticulous precision is evident in the consistent spacing of the dots, a hallmark of Papunya art. The rhythm of the dots remains consistent across a seamless patchwork of colors.

By shifting from foreground focus to background blurring, the image imitates a shallow depth-of-field in a photograph.

The focus is on the back of the head and the left shoulder and arm, which are closest to the viewer.

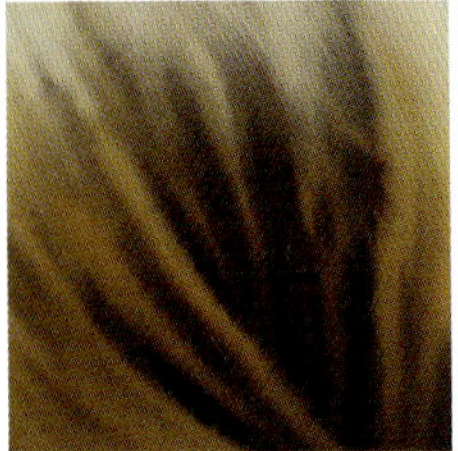

Very fine brushstrokes are just evident in the strands of hair.

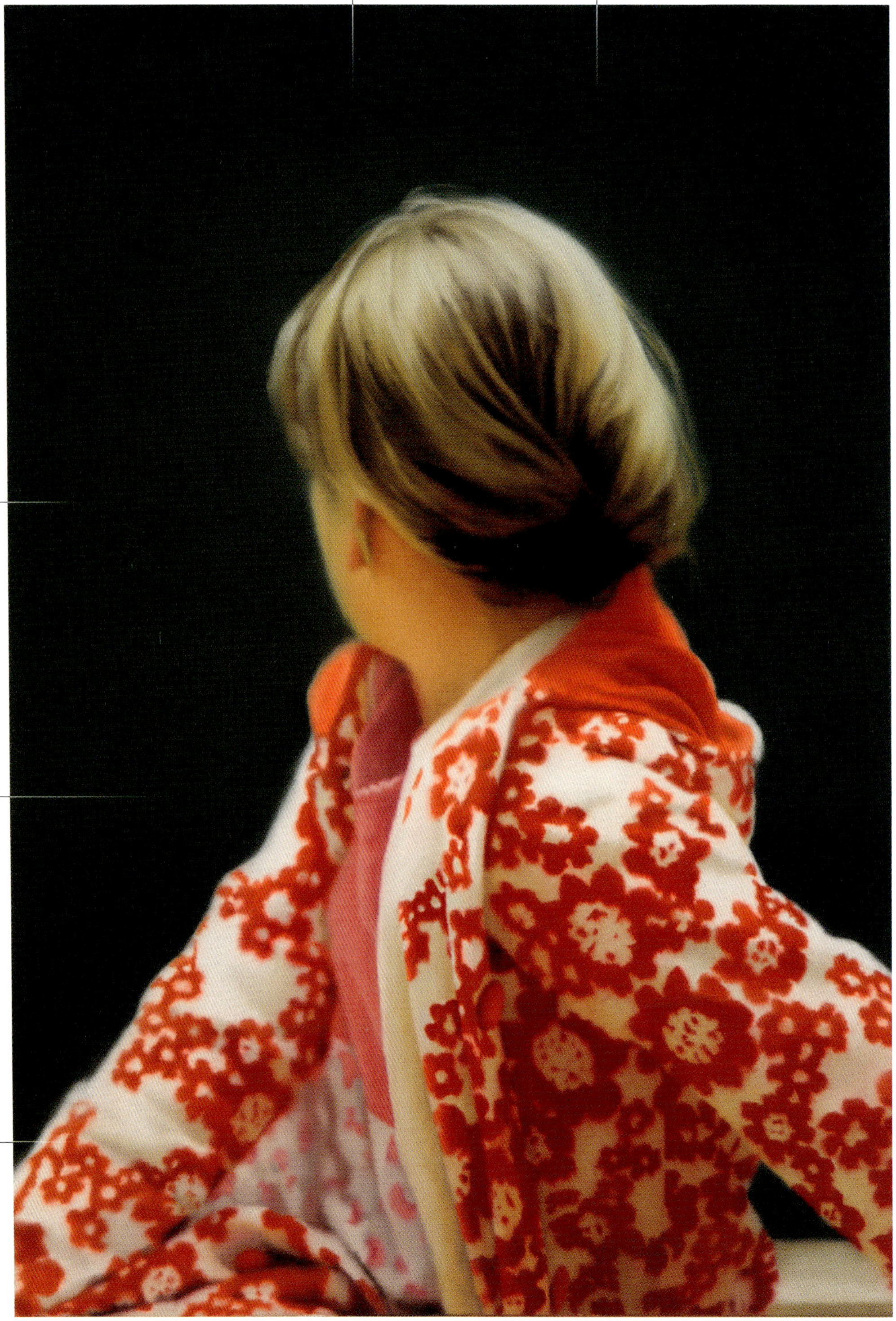

The figure is set against a plain dark background. Some commentators suggest that Betty is looking at one of Richter's Gray paintings behind her.

Textures are very accurately rendered, as in this hooded top.

The portrait is painted in a traditional way to produce a smooth paint surface.

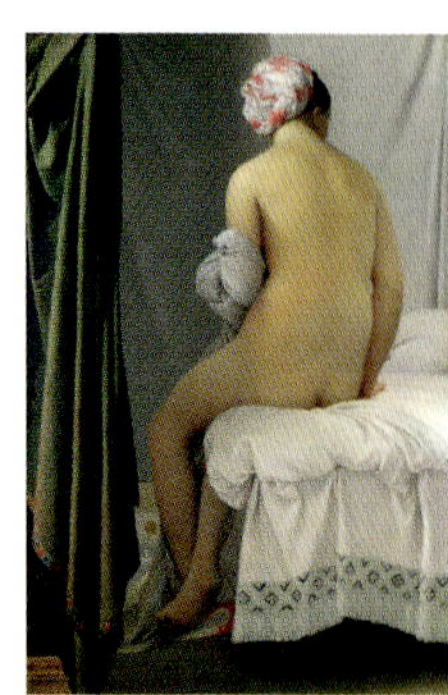

Classic pose
Women are often depicted with their head turned away, as in *The Bather of Valpinçon* by 19th-century French painter Jean-Auguste-Dominique Ingres.

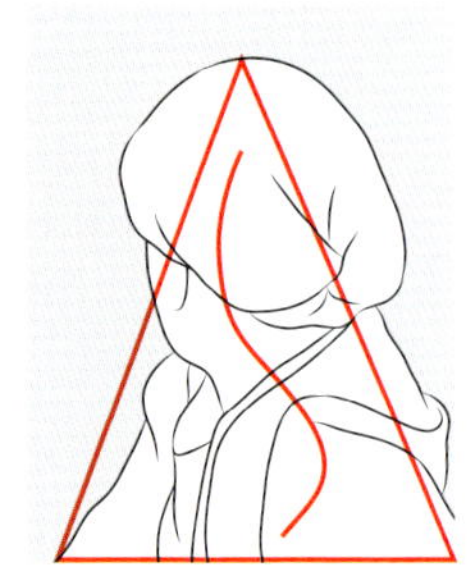

Pleasing shape
The composition is based on a triangle, which gives it stability. The turning body forms an S within the triangle.

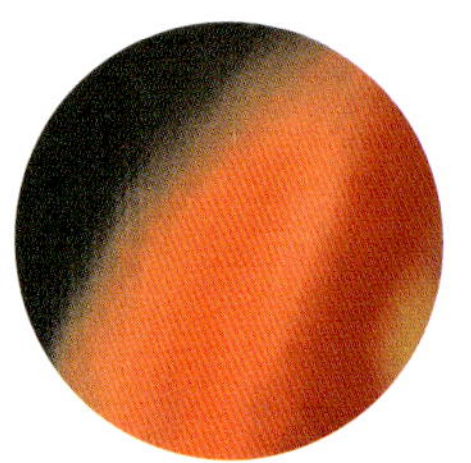

Soft effect
Richter paints a sharp edge between areas, then drags a dry brush through the wet paint to achieve slightly blurred outlines.

Betty

Gerhard Richter 1988, oil on canvas, 40 × 29 in (102.2 × 72.4 cm), Saint Louis Art Museum, US

At first sight this portrait appears to be a photograph, but look closely and fine brush marks are just visible. The work is, in fact, a painting of a photograph. Richter is more interested in the process of painting than in personal expression. He uses traditional oil-painting techniques to re-create photographic effects, producing works of great beauty that juxtapose the classical with the modern.

Double Portrait

Lucian Freud 1988-1990, oil on canvas, 46 × 38 in (117.3 × 95.5 cm), private collection

In this double portrait, Freud depicts a woman with his family's pet whippet, Pluto, in a poignant exploration of intimacy and companionship. Freud's emotional examination of the two subjects imbues them with a psychological depth, creating a sense of equality between his friend and his dog.

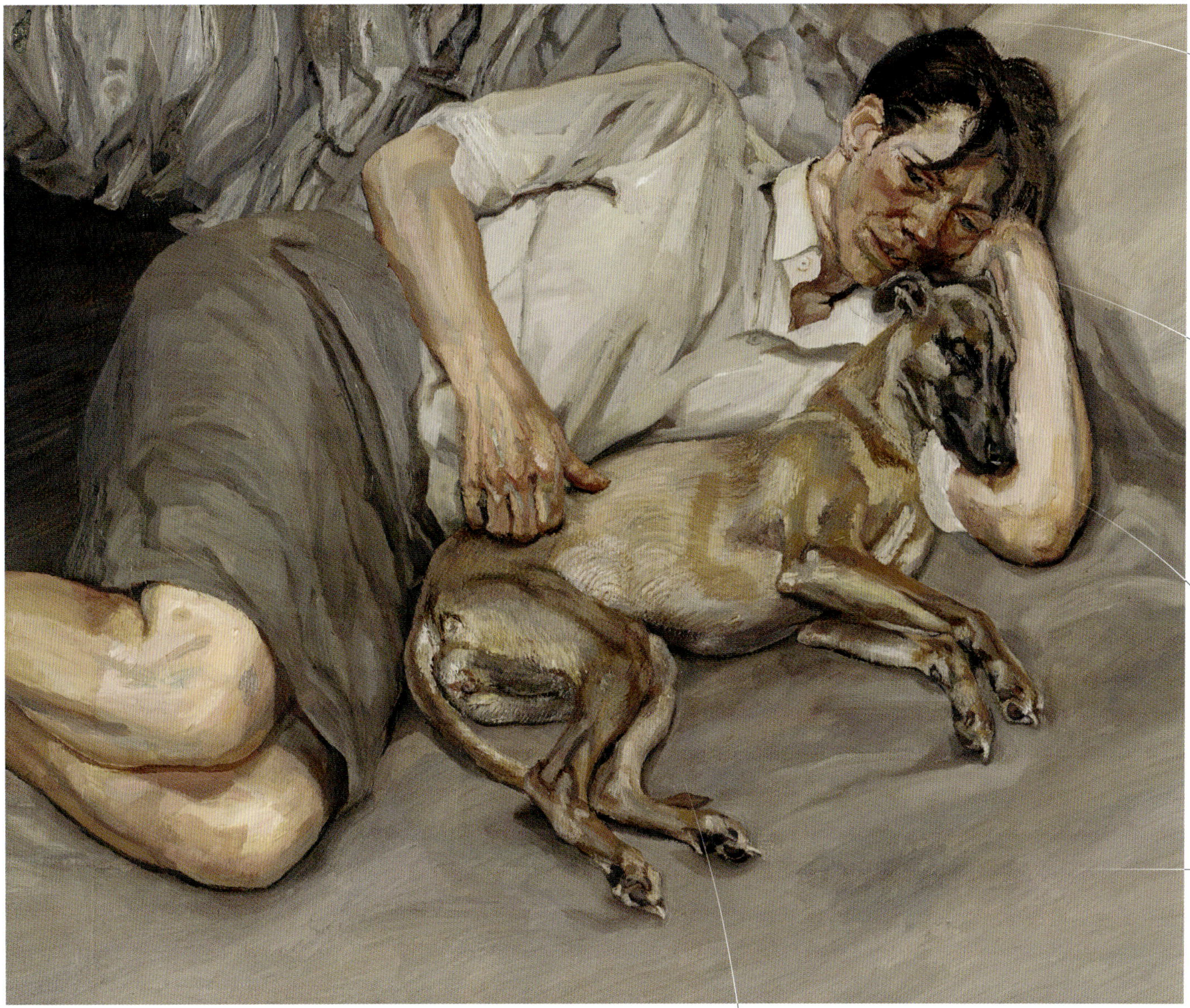

The composition's tight crop and downward-looking framing directs focus on the sitters. A glimpse of furniture in the background hints at the domestic setting.

The woman is lost in thought, as if unaware the artist is painting her.

Pluto's eyes are half closed, his snout nestling into the crook of the woman's elbow, a testament to his trust in her.

A muted color palette of earthy tones reflects the emotional tone of the painting.

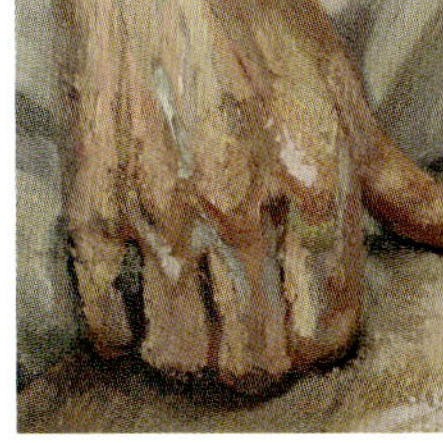

The interplay of subtle chromatic variation and expressive brushstrokes capture the nuanced texture of human skin, particularly on the woman's face and hand.

The woman gently strokes Pluto with her right hand, a tender and affectionate gesture encapsulating the unspoken language between the two sitters.

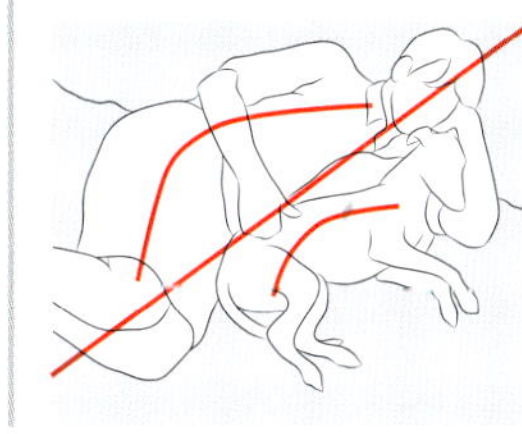

Strong diagonal
The woman's curled body forms a sinuous curve that echoes the dog she caresses, creating an attractive diagonal line.

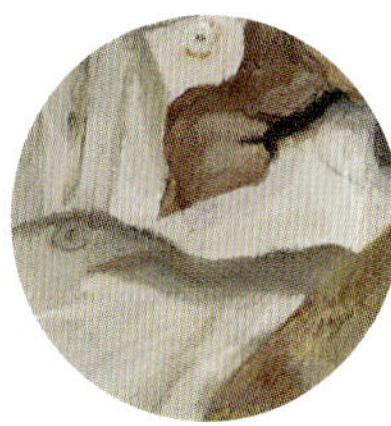

Thickly applied
Freud employed impasto, thick and textured paint using broad brushstrokes, with liberal amounts of Cremnitz white, a particularly heavy pigment. He used this technique in many of his works.

Shadow Rhythm

Bridget Riley 1989, oil on canvas, 65 × 90 in (165.7 × 228 cm), private collection

Shadow Rhythm is one of a series of paintings in which Riley uses a vertical and diagonal structure of simple repeating shapes to evoke visual sensations experienced in the natural world. The interplay of varying degrees of color contrasts creates shimmering, ever-changing effects that draw the viewer's attention in and out of space and across the canvas.

The blocks of strong red next to the dark blue and black sit on the same plane in space.

Individual colors weave in and out of the vertical structure, drawing the viewer's eye across the canvas.

The diagonal patches of color are known as "zigs" in Riley's studio. They work like individual brushstrokes.

Stacks of strong colors appear to advance toward the viewer next to the more muted colors.

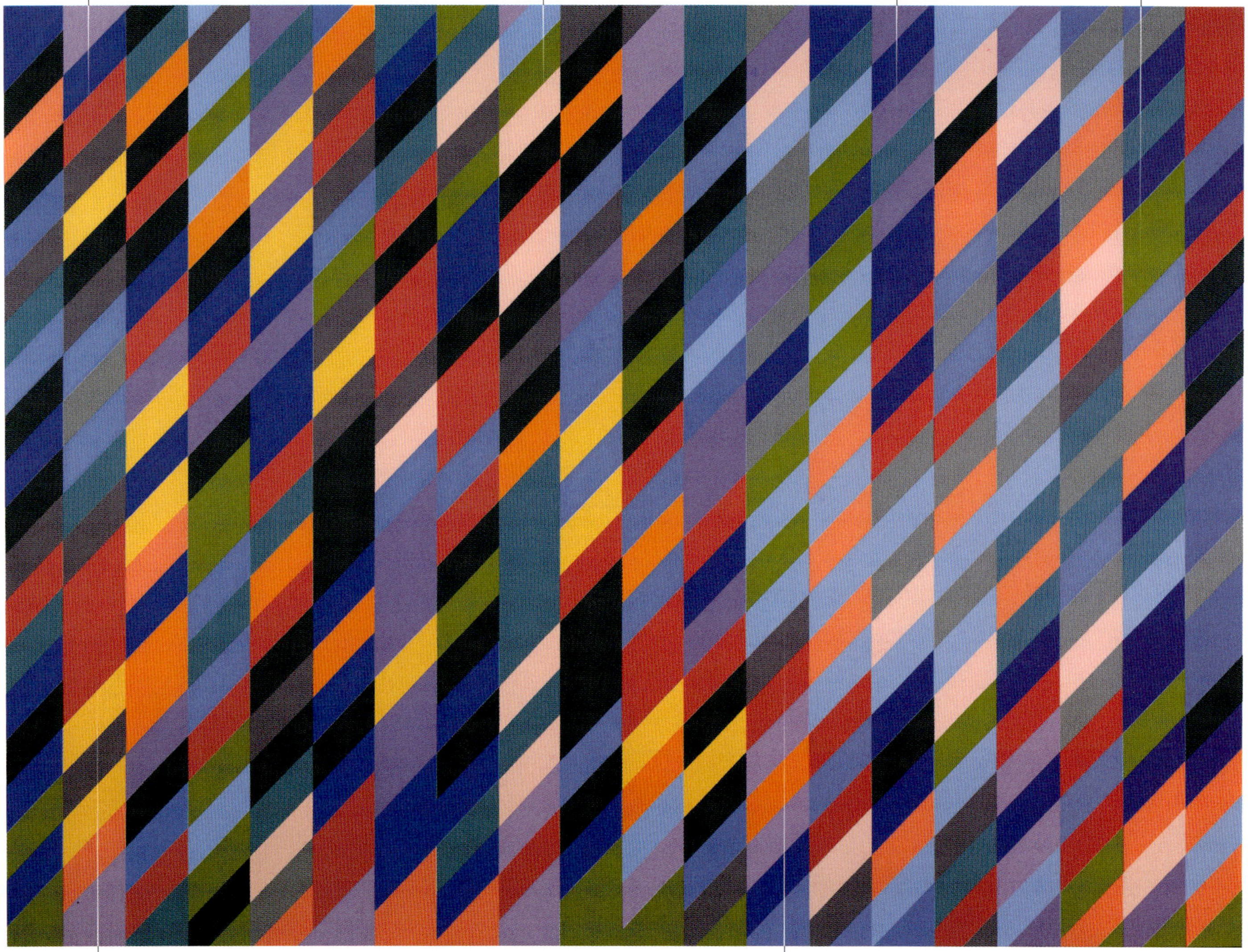

Stacks of patches of the same color emphasize the vertical axis.

The cooler, more muted light blue and green patches recede away from the viewer against the strong blue and red.

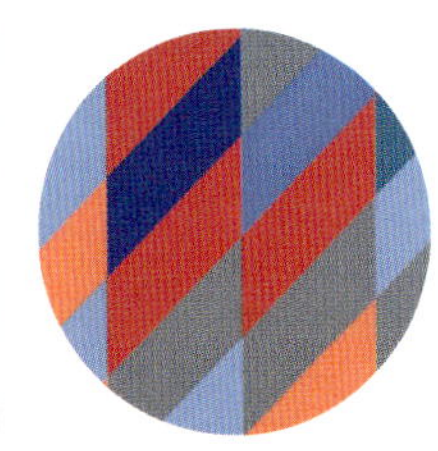

Color effect
On the right side of the canvas, a strong red dispersed through more muted colors creates a flickering effect.

Op art
Riley's style is known as Op art (short for optical art). First explored by Hungarian-French artist Victor Vasarely in the 1950s, it combines repetitive shapes, patterns, and colors to create optical illusions, especially of movement.

> "No painter, alive or dead, has ever made us more conscious of our eyes than Bridget Riley."
>
> Robert Melville, 1971

The Holy Virgin Mary

Chris Ofili 1996, acrylic, oil, polyester resin, paper collage, glitter, map pins, elephant dung on canvas, 96 × 72 in (243.8 × 182.8 cm), MoMA, New York, US

This is a contemporary, sensual, and tradition-defying representation of a traditional subject in European art. Using unconventional materials, Ofili challenges the usual portrayal of the Virgin Mary as European and white. In a work that reflects on Western art history, racial identity, and the teachings of the Catholic faith, he poses the question: could the Virgin Mary have been Black?

The use of gold recalls Byzantine icons and medieval paintings, in which it was used to represent divine light.

Lines appear to radiate from the Virgin's head, suggesting a halo.

The forms floating cherublike around the Virgin are from illustrations in pornographic magazines. They provide a shocking contrast to the iconic presentation of the Virgin.

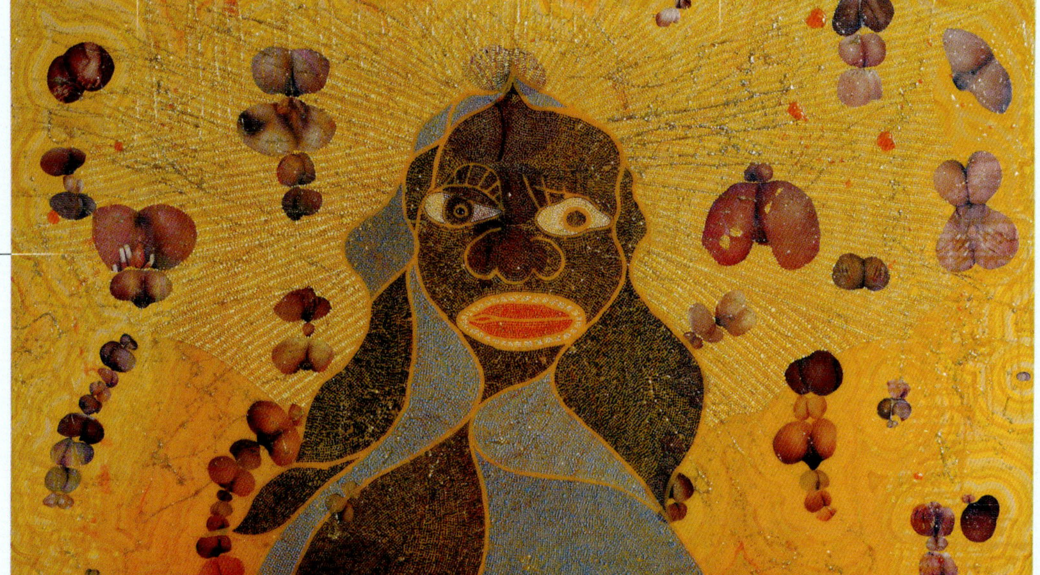

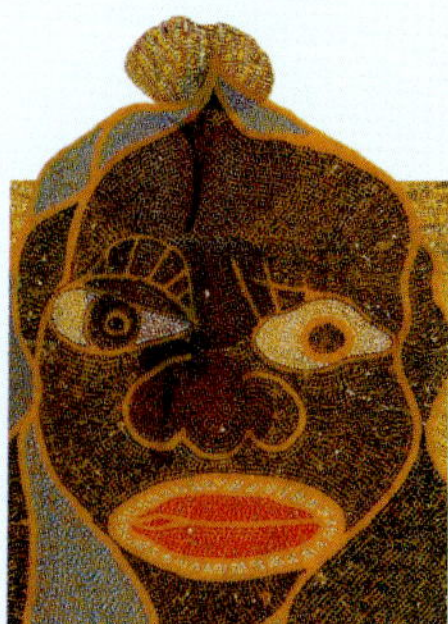

The Virgin looks straight out at the viewer. The image challenges racial stereotypes and the tradition of representing Biblical figures as white.

The Virgin's dress is drawn back to reveal a piece of varnished elephant dung where her breast should be.

The glowing background consists of layers of transparent paint and resin impressed with a batik-like pattern. Glitter creates extra sparkle.

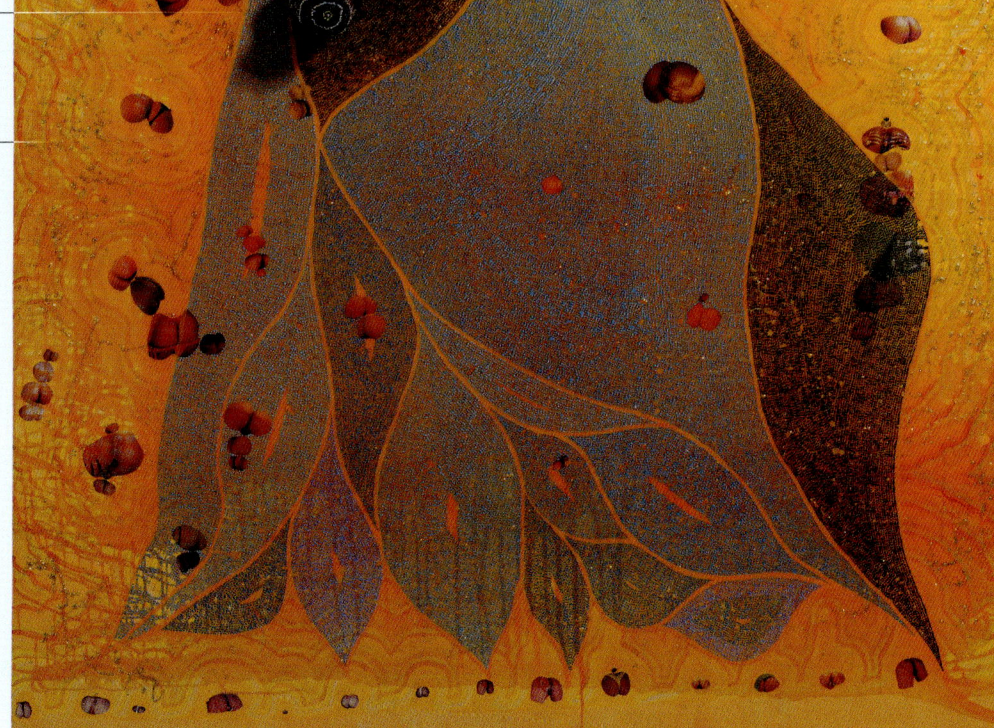

Pieces of elephant dung connect the painting to the African landscape. The Virgin's name is spelled out with map pins.

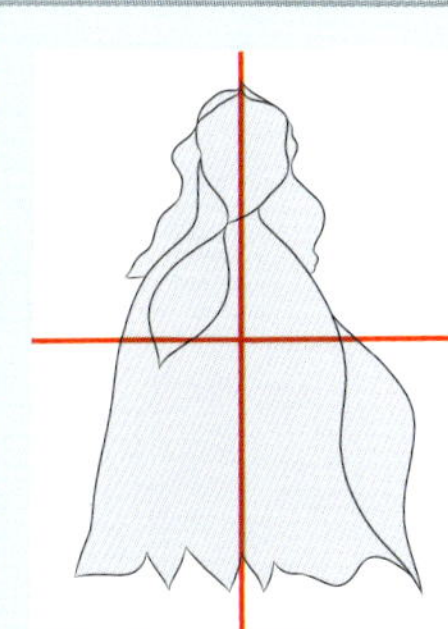

Composition
The figure is centrally placed and shown in a three-quarter view, as in a traditional European portrait of the Virgin.

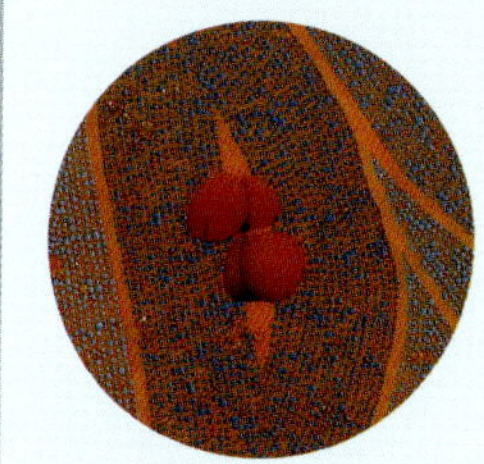

Technique
The Virgin's robe is painted with small spots of blue paint over a background built up with layers of paint and orange-colored resin.

The Sunflower Quilting Bee at Arles

Faith Ringgold 1996, color lithograph, 22 × 30 in (55.9 × 76.2 cm), Philadelphia Museum of Art, Pennsylvania, US

In a field of sunflowers, a group of distinguished Black American women from past and present hold up a quilt decorated with the blooms while Vincent van Gogh stands in the background. This is inspired by a series of 12 story quilts that Ringgold made to celebrate the contribution of Black American women in public life. It also highlights their absence in the established art world, here represented by Vincent van Gogh.

The women are campaigners in the fields of freedom, justice, education, and civil rights.

The flowers in the field represent the work of van Gogh, the solitary male painter.

Van Gogh, the most famous painter of sunflowers, offers the women a pot of the flowers in recognition of their work.

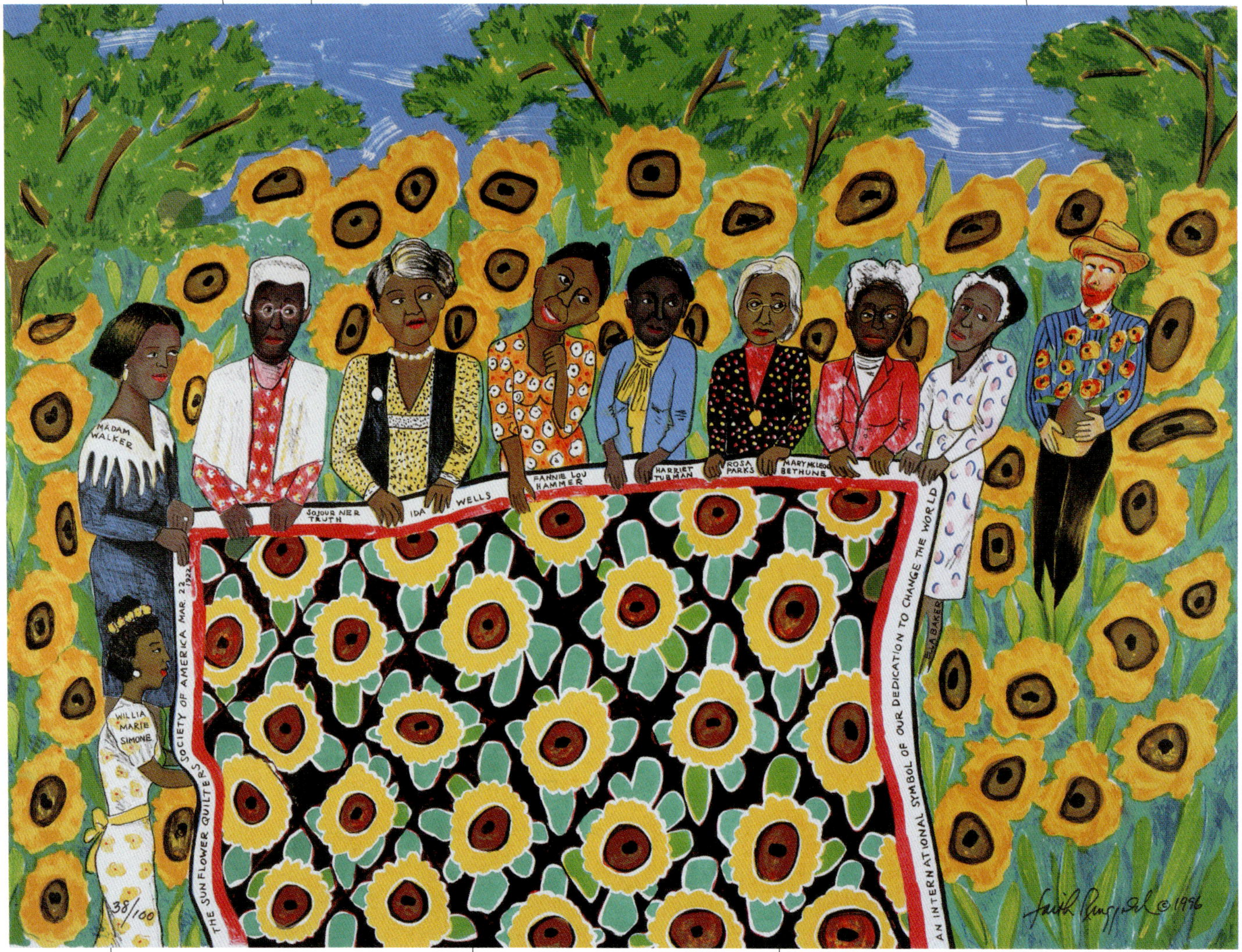

Willia Marie Simone is a fictional character in Ringgold's Sunflower Quilters series who goes to study art in 1920s Paris.

The quilt is the product of Black American women's artistry and skill. It represents communal endeavor and achievement.

The sunflowers on the quilt symbolize the solidarity and collective creative work of the quilters.

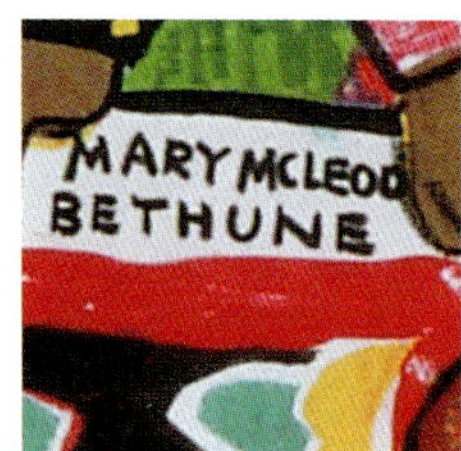

Text around the edge states that the quilt is an international symbol of the women's dedication to changing the world.

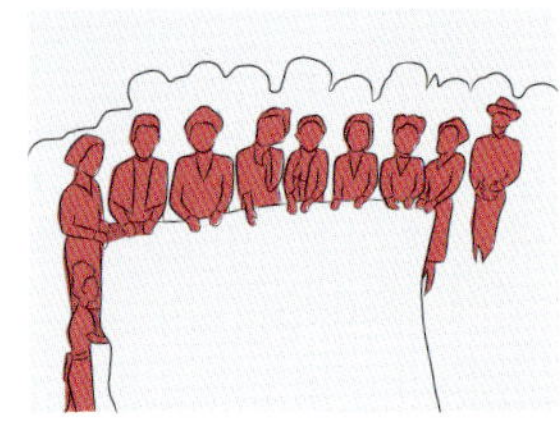

Composition
The figures are placed in a row—as equals, an arrangement that deliberately defies traditional perspective.

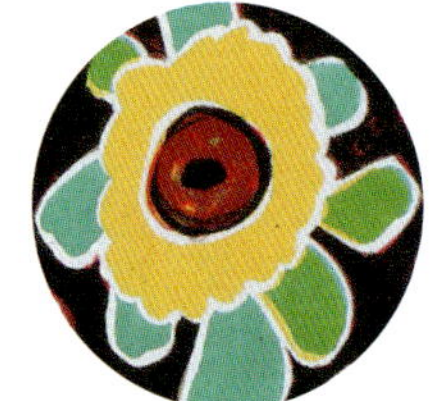

Technique
By employing flatness and bright colors, which are usually associated with a "craft" style, the image calls into question the distinction between "high" and "low" art.

Maman

Louise Bourgeois 1999, cast 2001, bronze, marble, and stainless steel, 365 × 351 × 403 in (927 × 891 × 1,023 cm), Guggenheim Museum, Bilbao, Spain

A monumental bronze spider several times the height of a person balances on tensed limbs, as if ready to strike its prey. Bourgeois, who made many sculptures of spiders, associated the creature with strength and resilience and with the maternal qualities of nurture and protection. To her, their constant round of weaving and repairing webs was also symbolic of the creative identity of the artist.

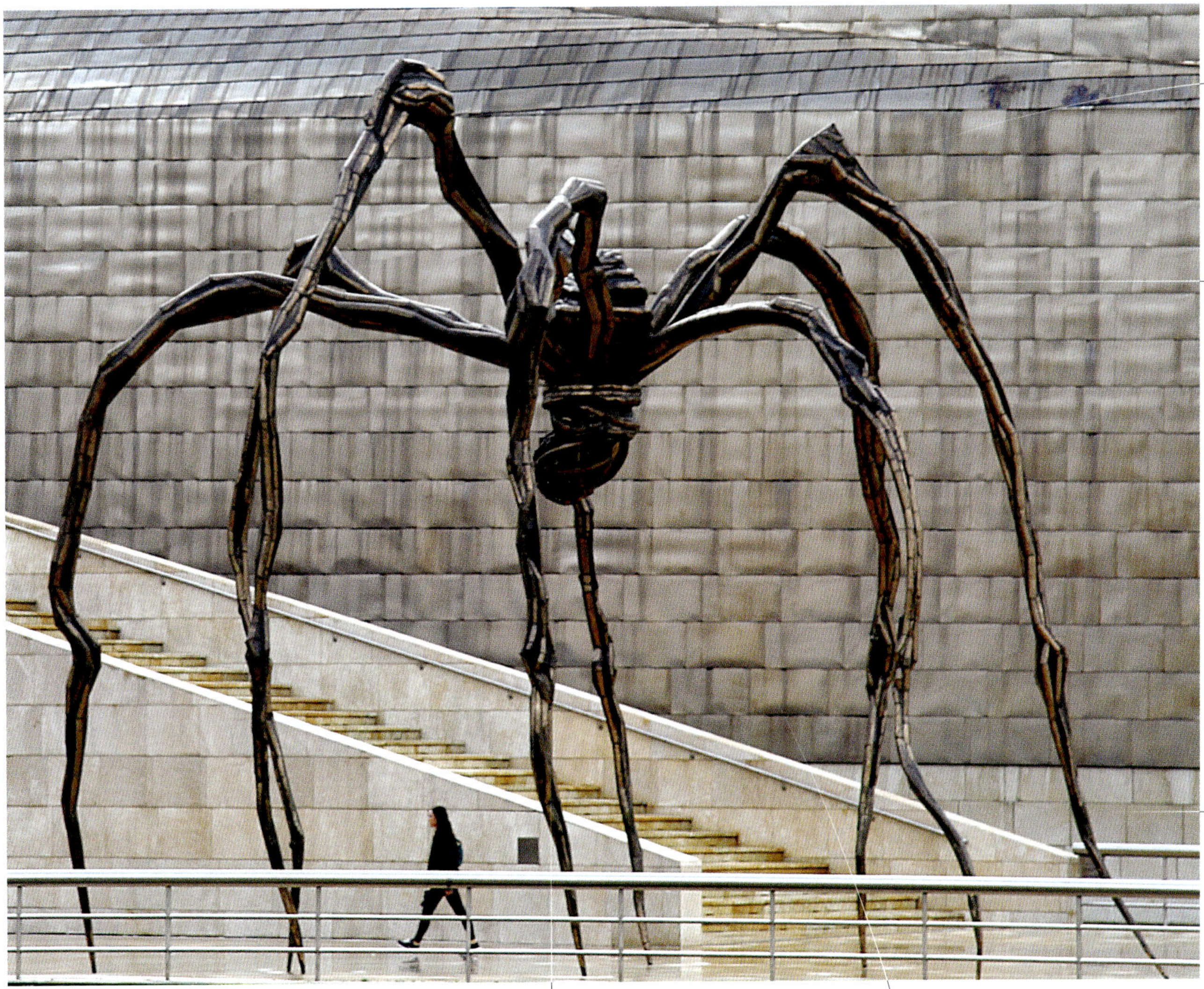

The representation of the spider is expressive rather than anatomical.

The body is formed from thick strands of bronze spiraling around a central oval form.

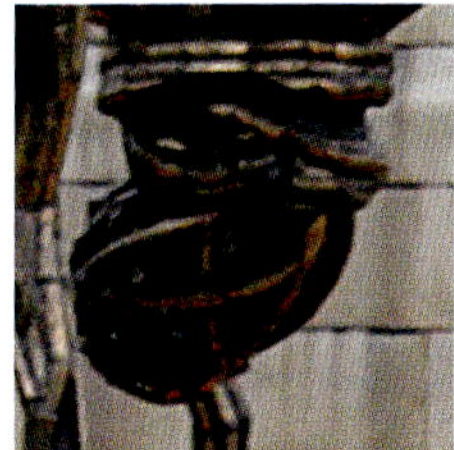

Thirty-two carved marble eggs are carried in a cage-like sac under the spider's body. The sac is formed from steel.

Bundles of tube-shaped segments welded together. form the legs.

The spider stands on long, slender, segmented legs, evoking a feeling of vulnerability.

The huge space under the body makes the spider seem protective and threatening at the same time.

"The spider is a repairer. If you bash into the web of a spider, she doesn't get mad. She weaves and repairs it."

Louise Bourgeois, 1998

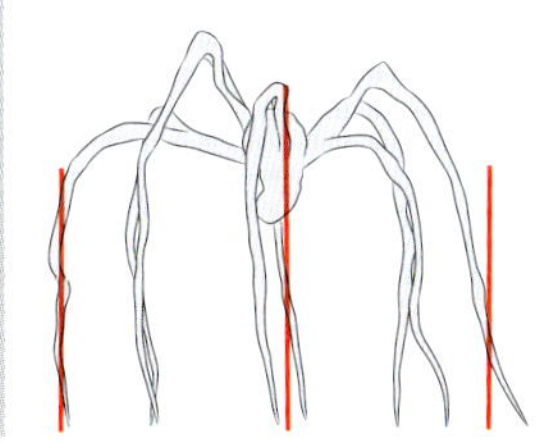

Balance
The body is suspended at the center. The legs radiate out in all directions to provide eight widely spaced points of balance.

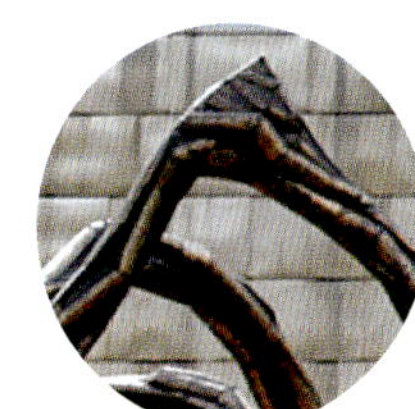

Sense of movement
A rhythm of upward and downward thrusts through the body and legs creates the impression that the spider is moving.

State Names

Jaune Quick-to-See Smith 2000, oil, collage, and mixed media on canvas, 48 × 72 in (121.9 × 182.9 cm), Smithsonian American Art Museum, Washington, D.C., US

On first look, this resembles a familiar map showing the states of the US, but several state names are missing and others are obscured by long runs of paint. The names that are included are those that have their origins in the Indigenous languages of the original communities who lived there. For Smith, maps tell stories, and this is a story of lands that were colonized by European settlers.

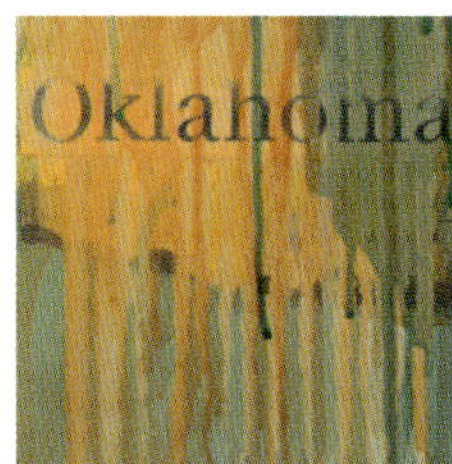

Layers of different colors make explicit that land long occupied by Indigenous communities has been divided up without regard for preexisting territories.

The runs of paint are evocative of blood and sweat.

Minnesota comes from the Sioux word for "cloudy water" or "sky-tinted water," referring to the Minnesota River.

Empty areas represent states whose names have European origins.

Massachusetts comes from the Algonquin word "Massadchu-es-et," meaning "great hill small place."

Borders with Mexico and Canada appear as arbitrary as those between the states.

State borders are heavily outlined in places, which reinforces their imposed and arbitrary nature.

State names are collaged onto the map.

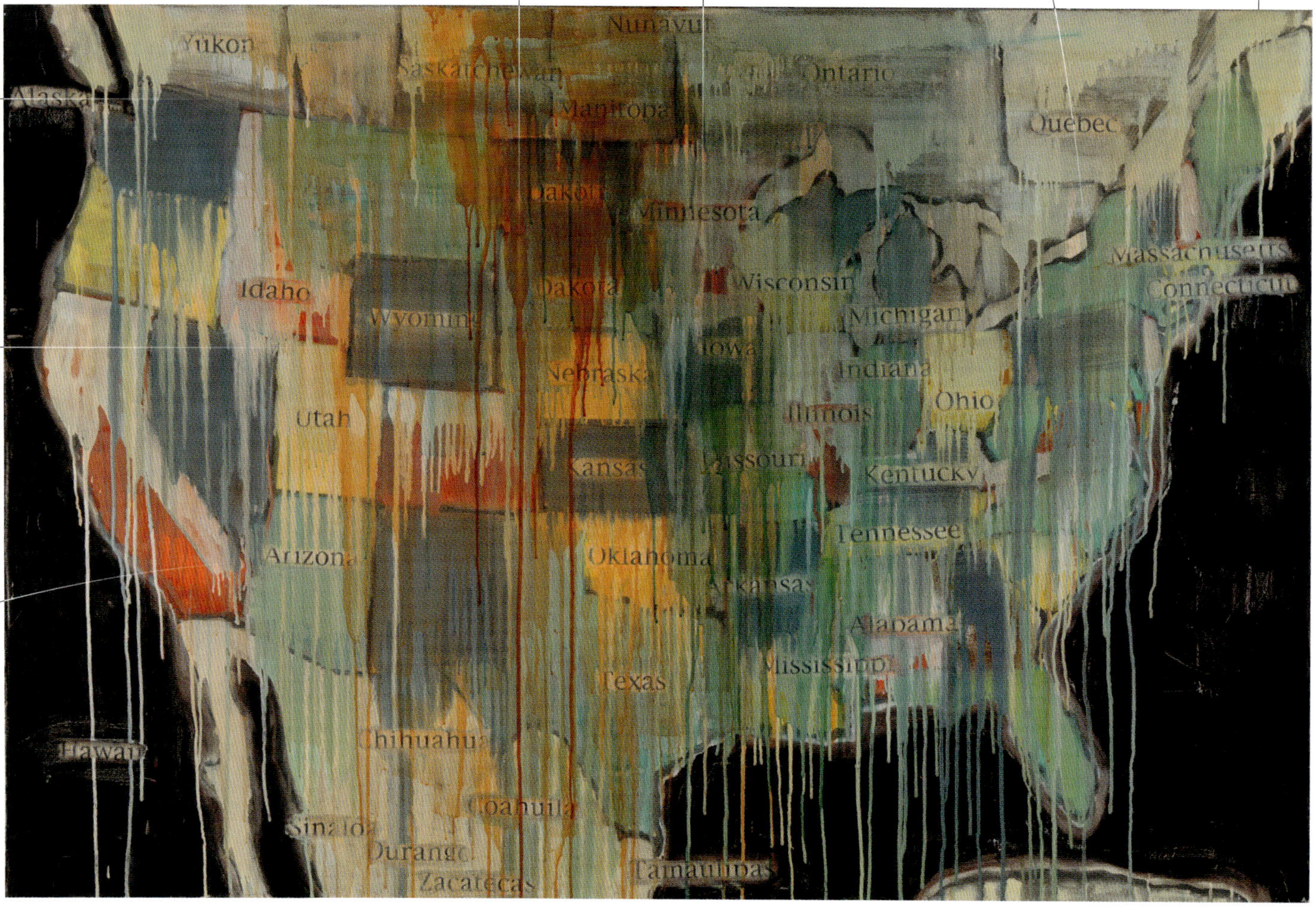

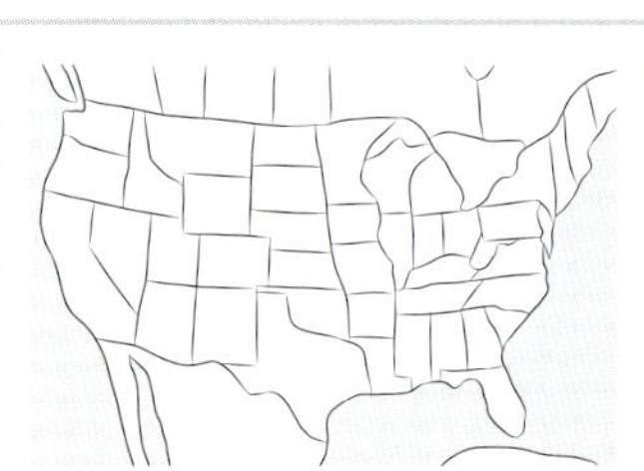

Composition
Smith has cropped in on a standard map. The close-cropping and areas of black ocean create a sense of isolation and abstraction.

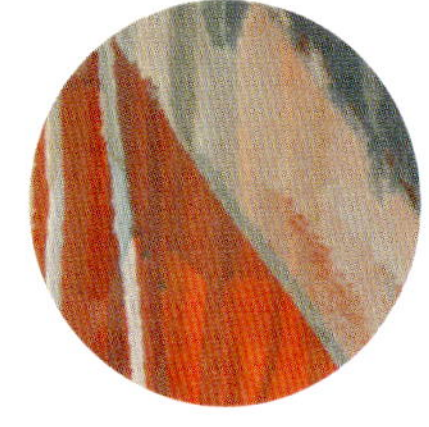

Layering
Several layers of transparent color and runs of paint create a spatial depth that suggests the layering of time and history.

Smith repurposed Abstract Expressionist techniques such as dripping paint and collage to make a statement about her own identity and heritage.

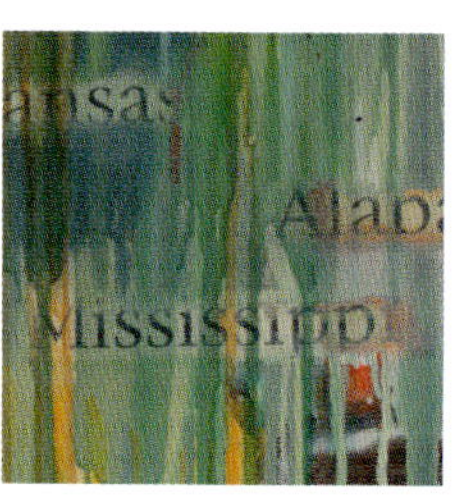

Girl With Balloon

Banksy 2002, spray paint and stencil, Waterloo Bridge, London, UK

A small girl reaches out toward a balloon—has she let go accidentally or is she releasing it? Is this mural an image of loss, freedom, nostalgia, or hope? The original work appeared in various London locations. Although these images are now lost, many versions of *Girl With Balloon* exist as screen prints and on canvas. "There is always hope," written on the wall at the Waterloo Bridge site, was the original title.

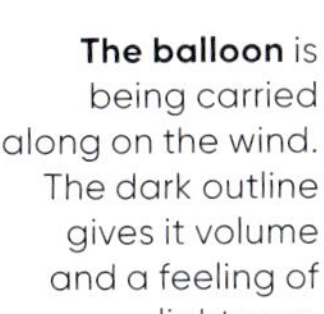

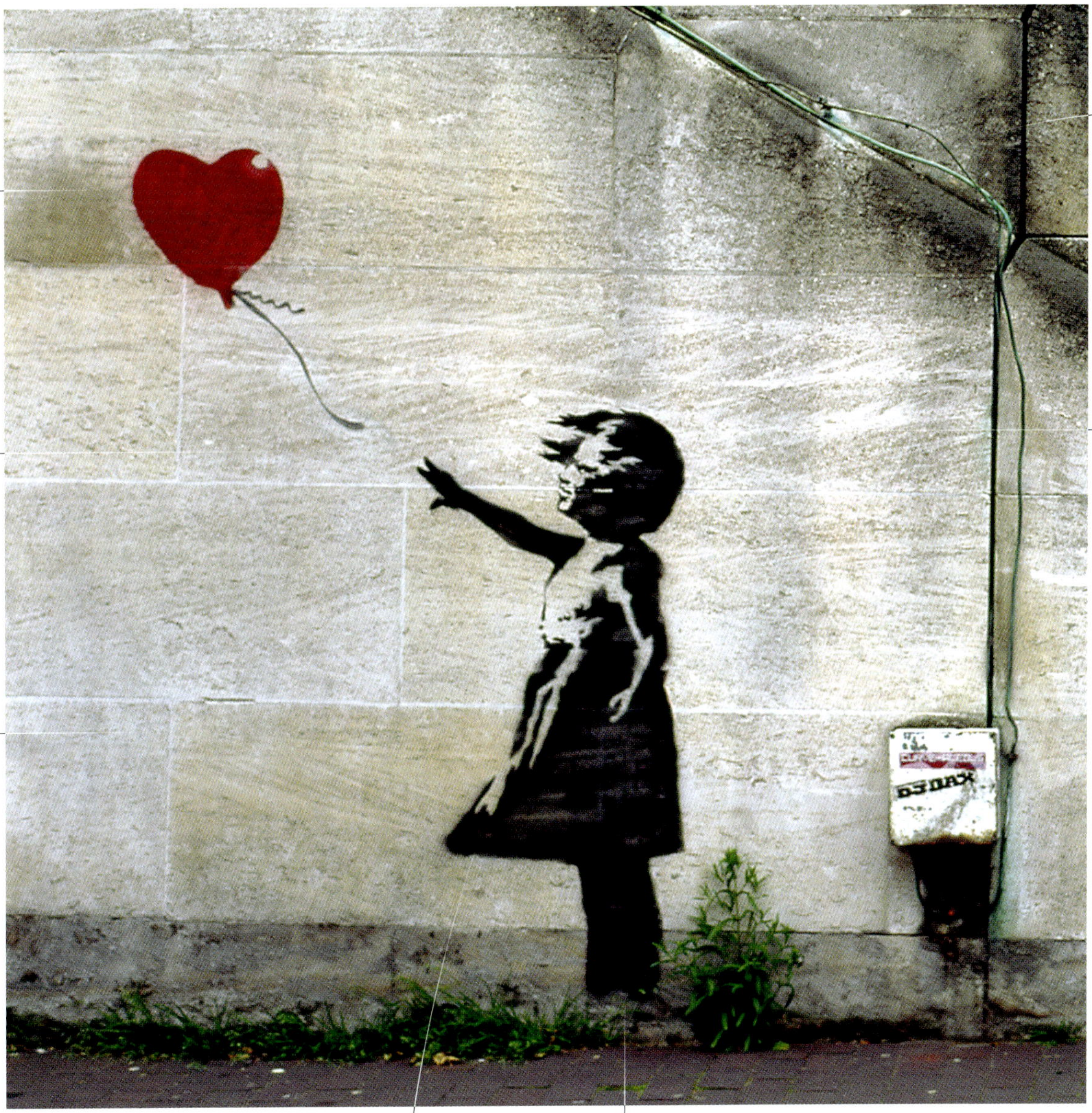

The balloon is being carried along on the wind. The dark outline gives it volume and a feeling of lightness.

The size of the gap between the girl's outstretched hand and the end of the string puts the balloon just out of her reach.

Areas of bare wall form the highlights on the figure.

The artwork is framed by cables and weeds. Urban decay is a feature of many of the locations chosen by Banksy.

The direction of the girl's windswept hair and skirt suggest that the balloon is being swept away from her grasp.

Light and dark shapes are used to create a three-dimensional figure. The graphic approach produces a powerful image.

Dark areas have been stenciled with black and gray paint.

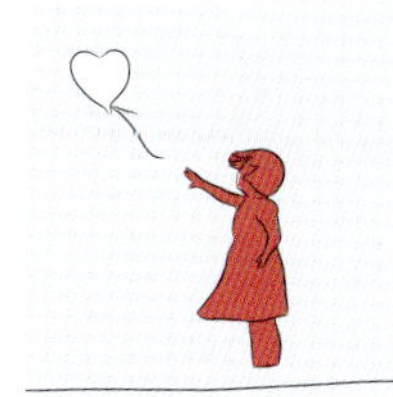

Up, up, and away
The solidly based, static figure emphasizes the lightness of the floating balloon.

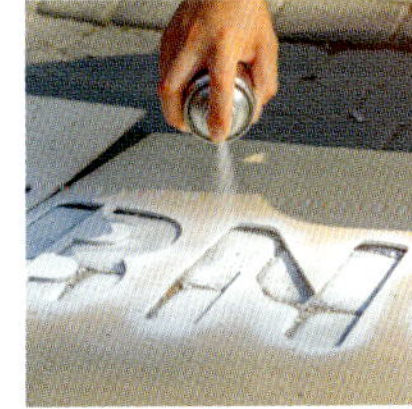

Stenciling
The stencil technique (applying paint or ink through a cut-out design) is common to street art, for its speed, and to screen printing.

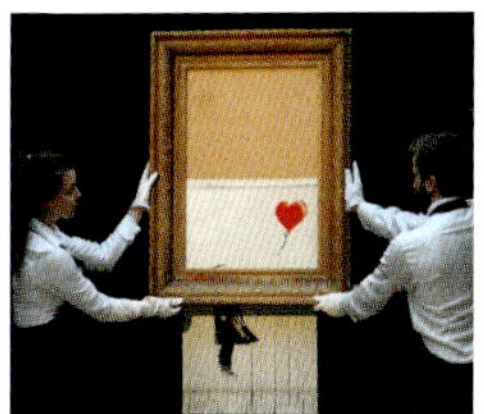

Shredding
In 2018, a reproduction on canvas was auctioned at Sotheby's London. Afterward, the canvas was partially passed through a shredder Banksy had hidden in the frame. This increased the value of the work, which he retitled *Love Is In the Bin*.

Focus

El Anatsui 2015, aluminum and copper, 112 × 120 in (284 × 304 cm), private collection

Jewellike areas of color glow against a shimmering background in what looks like a swathe of fabric draped across the wall. It is, in fact, comprised of thousands of small, tesserae-like pieces of metal. The work, which references traditional African textiles, reuses the detritus of consumerism, in the form of bottle tops and labels, to create a beautiful object that also alludes to the exploitative nature of colonialism in Africa.

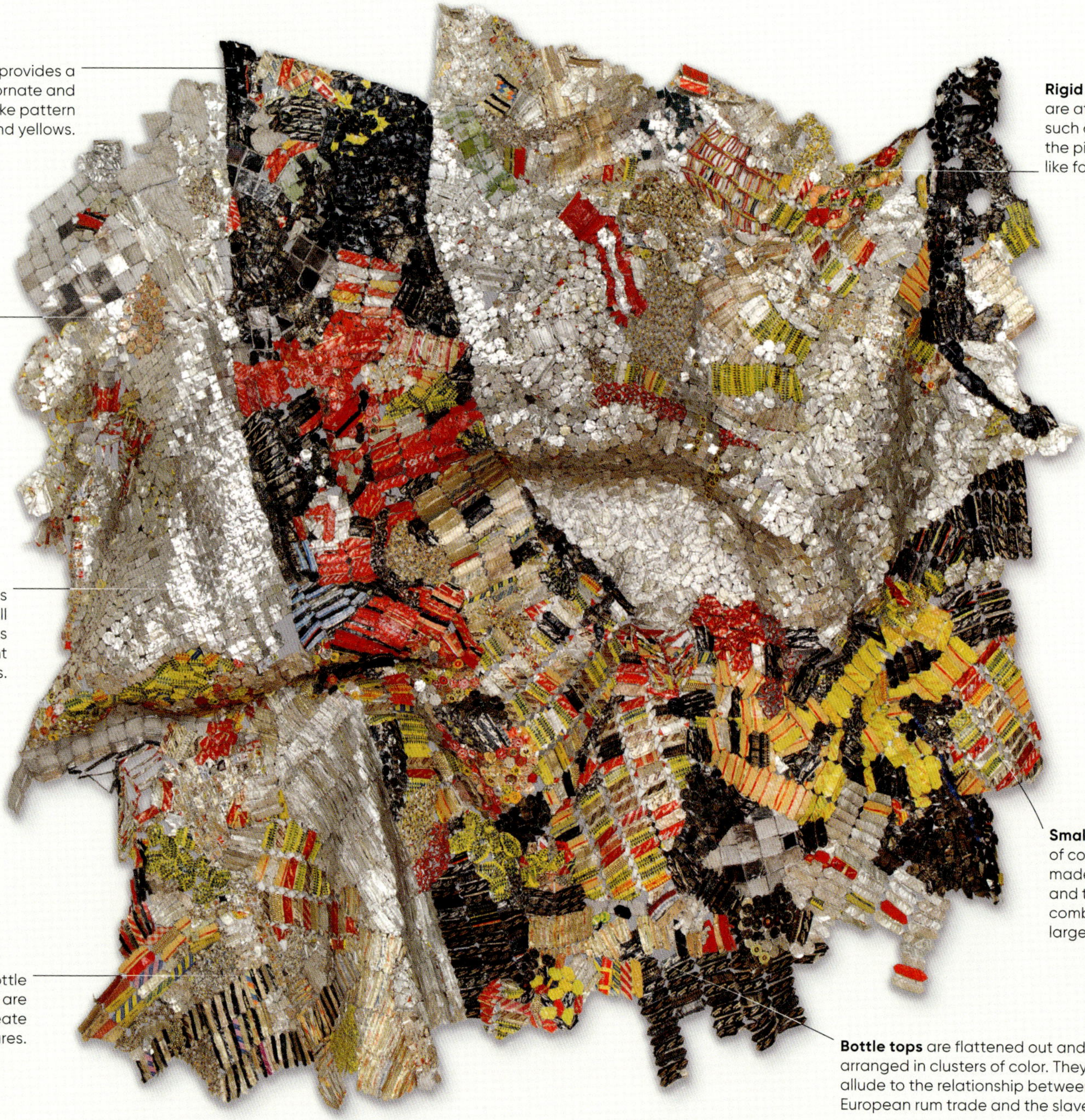

The dark area provides a background for an ornate and complex, tapestry-like pattern of reds and yellows.

Rigid materials are attached in such a way that the piece hangs like fabric.

The use of discarded materials references the way wealthy nations treat Africa as a dumping ground.

The hanging is arranged on the wall so that it catches and reflects light from all directions.

Smaller areas of color are made first, and then combined into larger blocks.

Blocks of bottle tops and labels are juxtaposed to create contrasting textures.

Bottle tops are flattened out and arranged in clusters of color. They allude to the relationship between the European rum trade and the slave trade.

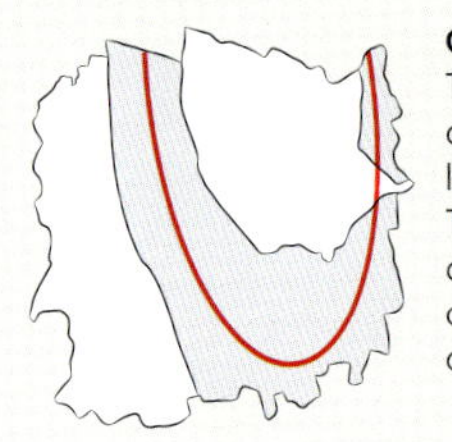

Composition
The materials are organized into large light and dark areas. The asymmetrical, dipping U-shape creates an impression of movement.

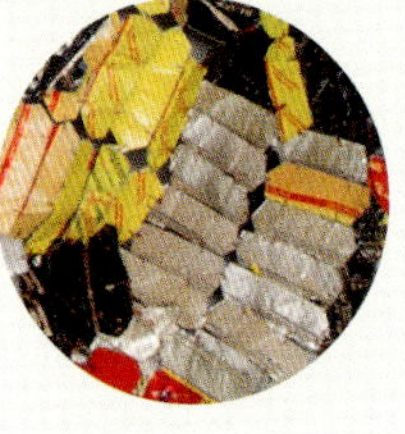

Technique
The bottle caps and labels are joined together with copper wire so the finished piece is flexible and can hang in folds and drapes.

Iona Miriam's Christmas Visit To & from Brighton

Frank Bowling 2017, acrylic and mixed media on collaged canvas, 74 × 48 in (189 × 122.5 cm), private collection

Drifts and pools of vibrant color appear to melt into each other in some areas and float apart in others. In an image of pure abstraction filled with color, light, texture, and drama, and in the making of which chance and improvisation played a part, Bowling records a specific family event.

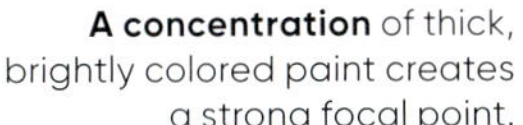

A concentration of thick, brightly colored paint creates a strong focal point.

The varied application of the paint draws attention to its physicality and sensuousness.

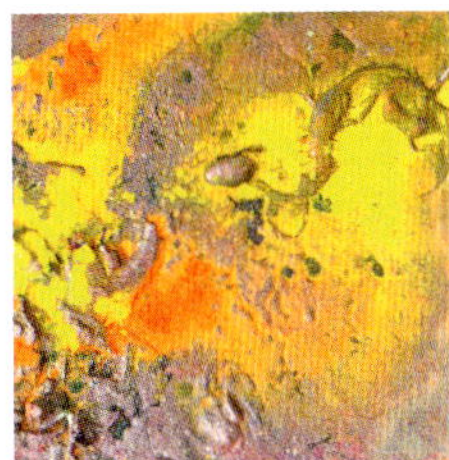

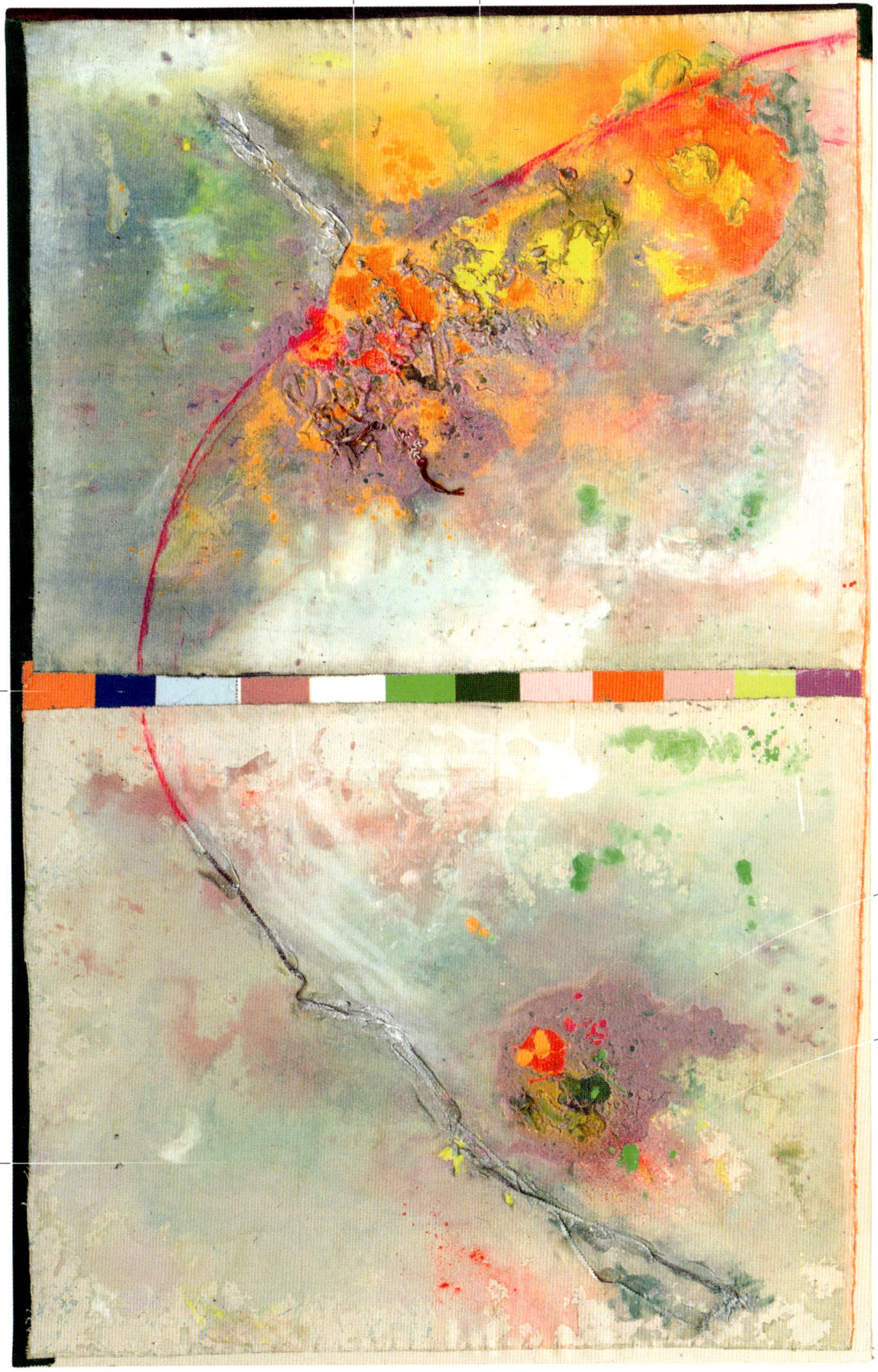

Pieces of plastic toys and other objects are embedded in the paint to add texture. They may be souvenirs or gifts.

In an act of collaboration, Bowling has incorporated a printed strip cut from a work by a friend, the artist Arlington Weithers, across the center of the painting.

Stains of very dilute color merge and drift across the lower part of the canvas.

A smaller area of bright color balances the larger area in the upper half.

Drips and larger areas of thick paint lie over thin paint. The contrast gives the thin areas great depth.

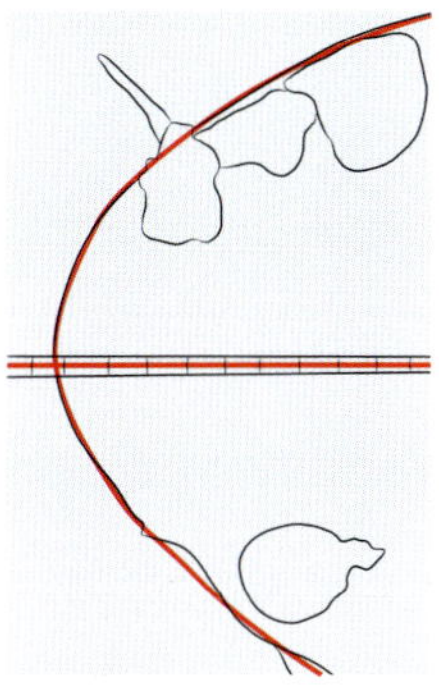

Composition
The two halves of the painting are linked by the background colors, the curving red line, the repetition of vibrant reds and violet, and multiple circular shapes.

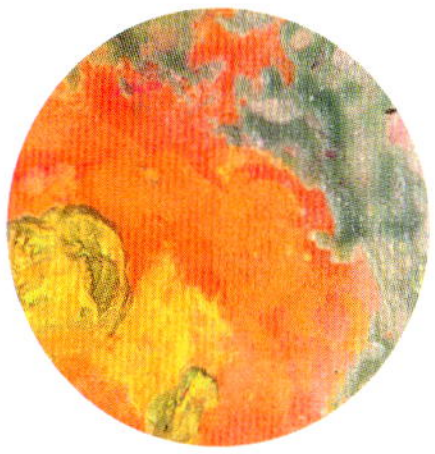

Texture
Bowling added acrylic gel, which hardens as it dries, to the paint to give it body and create texture. When dry, it is strong enough to "glue" objects to the canvas.

"I want the materials to speak to people, as intensely as possible."

Frank Bowling

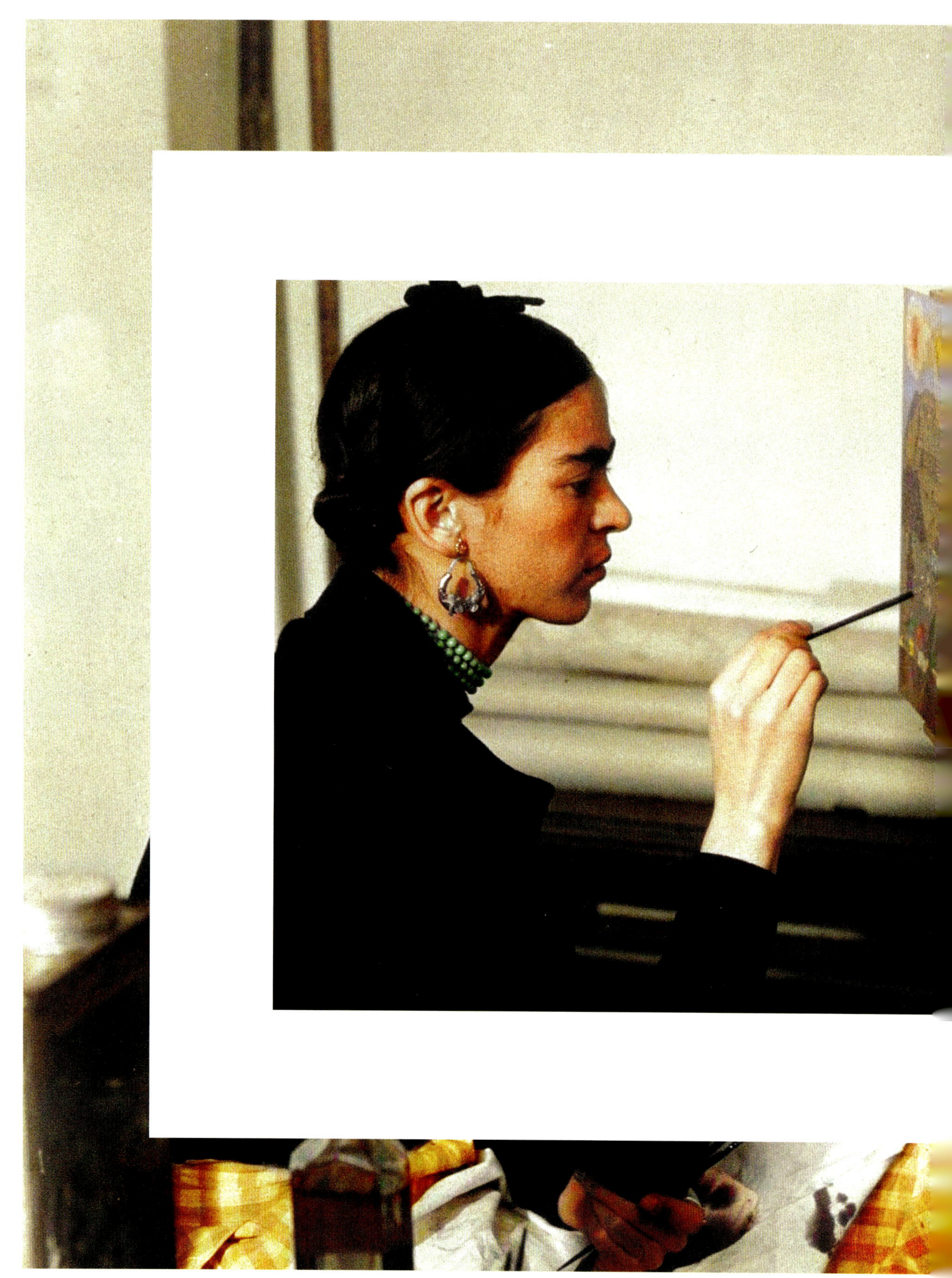

Directory of artists

NICCOLA PISANO P. FEDI

▲ **Portrait statue of Nicola Pisano**, Pio Fedi, 1849, marble, Piazzale des Uffizi, Florence, Italy

Polykleitos

Active c. 450–420 BCE

Ancient Greek sculptor Polykleitos produced the statue *Doryphoros*, based on the mathematical proportions of the human body and celebrated as the standard of male beauty. None of Polykleitos's works are believed to survive, but later copies of some do exist. His ivory-and-gold statue of the goddess Hera was especially acclaimed, but is now known only through descriptions and images on coins.

Heraclitus

Active 2nd century CE

A Roman mosaic maker, Heraclitus is known for a mosaic, *The Unswept Floor*. It creates the impression that trash remains on a dining room floor following a banquet. Had he not signed this work, it is likely that Heraclitus's name would be lost to history.

Yan Liben

c. 600–673

A leading Chinese figure painter, Yan Liben was highly regarded in his day for his images of emperors and scholars, among other works. Yan was the son of a prominent government official and architect; he achieved success in those fields in addition to his painting.

Ende

c. 10th century

Ende was one of the illuminators who illustrated the *Gerona Beatus*, a Spanish manuscript completed in 975. Little is known about her life beyond the inscription linking her to that work: *Ende pintrix et di aiutrix* (Ende painter and helper of God). She was probably a nun and is considered to be the first female manuscript illuminator whose work can be established through an inscription.

Guo Xi

c. 1020–1090

An 11th-century Chinese landscape painter, Guo produced hand scrolls and large paintings that decorated the walls of prominent buildings. An innovative and influential artist whose paintings were prized by Emperor Shenzong, Guo created a system known as "the angle of totality" or "the floating perspective," which presented multiple viewpoints in a single image.

Zhang Zeduan

1085–1145

A prominent court artist whose work influenced the Chinese landscape artists who followed him, Zhang is believed to have created the highly detailed hand scroll *Along the River During the Qingming Festival*, portraying life in a city during the spring festival.

Nicola Pisano

c. 1220–1284

Together with his son and collaborator, Giovanni, Pisano is generally regarded as the preeminent sculptor of his era and even as the founder of western sculpture. He carved religious images in the Gothic style, and his work conveyed a naturalism that helped set the stage for the sculptors of the Renaissance. His greatest works were completed in Pisa, although he may have trained as a sculptor in southern Italy.

Margarito of Arezzo

Active c. 1260–1290

An Italian painter believed to have been based in Tuscany, Margarito of Arezzo painted Christian images in a vivid, linear, Romanesque style. He is among the few Italian artists of the era to sign his work, but little is known about his life. One source mentions that he was an architect as well as a painter.

Cimabue

c. 1240–1302

Cimabue is generally regarded as the greatest European artist prior to the emergence of Giotto—a reputation cemented by Dante, who described him as such in *The Divine Comedy*. Based in Florence, he created frescoes of Christian images in a Byzantine style, but he is credited with beginning the transition from the "flat" Byzantine style to the more modern and naturalistic style that followed.

Zhao Mengfu

1254–1322

Generally regarded as the leading painter and calligrapher of China's Yuan dynasty, Zhao produced images of horses, landscapes, and other subjects influenced by Chinese artists of earlier dynasties. Zhao descended from the Song imperial family, but he served the Mongols who ruled during the Yuan dynasty. His wife, Guan Daosheng, was also a notable artist.

Duccio di Buoninsegna

c. 1255–c. 1319

Generally considered the first great Sienese painter, Duccio imbued his Christian images with a naturalism that was new for Byzantine art. He is best remembered for his masterwork, the double-sided Maestà altarpiece created for the cathedral in Siena.

Guan Daosheng

1262–1319

An acclaimed painter, calligrapher, and poet, Guan specialized in paintings of natural subjects, such as bamboo, flowers, or birds. Born into a prominent family, she married the artist and government official Zhao Mengfu (their son, Zhao Yong, achieved fame as a painter as well). Guan is regarded as the most accomplished female artist of her era.

Giotto

c. 1266–1337

A Florentine artist sometimes called the founder of modern Western painting, Giotto produced frescoes on Christian themes that featured a naturalism, depth, expression, and emotion not typically found in earlier Byzantine art. Famously cited by Dante in *The Divine Comedy* as the painter who eclipsed Cimabue as the greatest artist of all, he remained relevant and influential for centuries.

Simone Martini

c. 1284–1344

A painter and manuscript illuminator of Christian images, the Siena-based Martini was probably a student of Duccio. Religious works such as altarpieces figure prominently among his works, but unusually for the time he is also credited with secular works, such as *Guidoriccio da Fogliano at the Siege of Montemassi*, a fresco of a Sienese military commander on horseback. Later in life, he lived and worked at the papal court in Avignon, France, where he befriended Petrarch.

Ambrogio Lorenzetti

c. 1285–c. 1348

A Sienese painter who was probably a student of Duccio, Lorenzetti embraced a naturalism that was unusual at the time. His most notable works are frescoes in Siena's town hall known as *Good and Bad Government*, considered the first Italian paintings to use landscape as a background. Little is known about Lorenzetti's life, except that both he and his brother Pietro, also an artist, probably died of the plague.

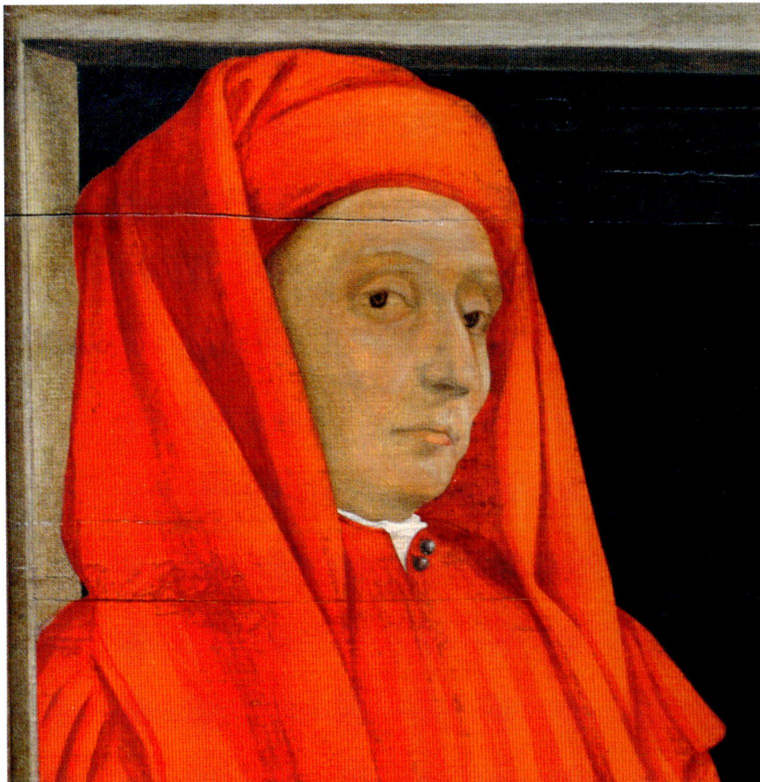

▲ **Giotto**, detail from *Five Famous Men*, artist unknown, c. 1490s, tempera on wood, Louvre, Paris, France

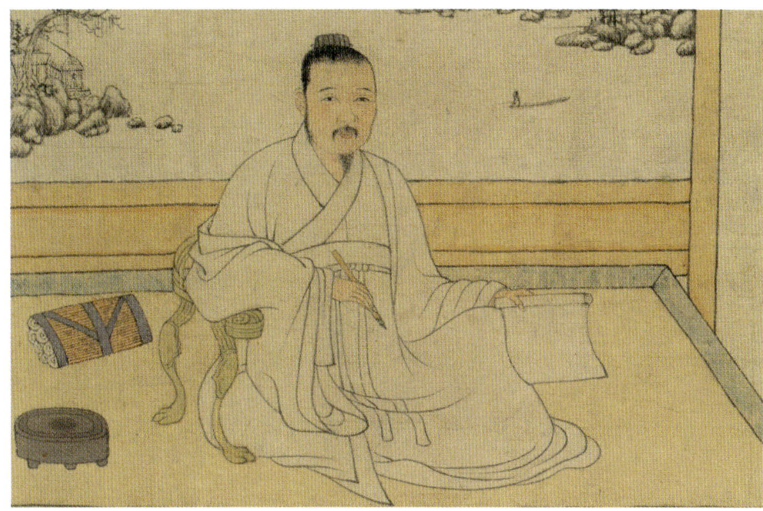

▲ ***Inscribing a Portrait of Ni Zan***, Zhang Yu, 14th century, ink and color on paper, National Palace Museum, Taipei

Jean Pucelle

c. 1300–1350

A manuscript illuminator and miniaturist, Pucelle operated a large workshop in Paris. He is thought to have traveled to Italy, and some credit him with bringing the artistic innovations of Giotto and Duccio to Northern Europe. His religious images were in the Gothic style, but with a degree of depth and naturalism. He was highly regarded at the French court and his art sold for significant sums.

Ni Zan

1301–1374

A highly influential Chinese painter of landscapes and other scenes, Ni was one of the artists later referred to as the "Four Masters of the Yuan dynasty." His work is characterized by open space and monochrome ink. Born into a wealthy family in Jiangsu province, Ni chose to pursue painting, calligraphy, and poetry rather than serve the Mongols, who then ruled China.

Theophanes the Greek

c. 1330–c. 1410

A painter of Byzantine-style frescoes and icons, Theophanes is considered one of the greatest Russian artists of the Middle Ages. He worked mainly in Novgorod and, later in his life, in Moscow, although he probably came from Constantinople. At least one source reports that he was also a manuscript illuminator.

Claus Sluter

c. 1340–c. 1405

An influential Netherlandish sculptor and founder of the Burgundian School, Sluter is generally regarded at the greatest Northern European sculptor of the late 14th century. Born in Haarlem, he moved to Brussels and then to Dijon, France, were he served as chief sculptor for Philip the Bold, Duke of Burgundy. His work is noted for its naturalism and the skillful portrayal of drapery.

Andrei Rublev

c. 1360–1430

This Russian monk was the leading painter of religious icons in Russia in the early 15th century. His works are often described as more graceful and delicate than those being made in the traditional Byzantine style by the other Russian icon painters of his day. He is known to have worked with Theophanes the Greek on the Cathedral of the Annunciation in the Kremlin.

Gentile da Fabriano

1370–1427

One of Italy's foremost painters in the International Gothic style, Gentile is known to have created elaborate frescoes and other works in numerous Italian cities, although many of his pieces are now lost. The *Adoration of the Magi*, painted for a church in Florence, is generally regarded as his greatest surviving work. His use of light and space was innovative for the time, as was the careful attention he paid to natural detail.

Limbourg brothers

Active 1390s–c.1416

Brothers Paul, Herman, and Jean Limbourg were born in Holland. They worked as manuscript illuminators for Philip the Bold, Duke of Burgundy. Following his death in 1404, they worked for his brother, Jean, Duc de Berri, a prominent art collector. The Limbourgs' creative, intricate work in *Les Très Riches Heures* is regarded as one of the greatest surviving works of manuscript illumination. The spellings of the brothers' given names vary.

Lorenzo Ghiberti

c.1378–1455

An Italian sculptor, Ghiberti was the leading caster of bronze in Florence during the first half of the 15th century. The elaborate bronze doors of the Baptistry in Florence are his most famous work. Ghiberti was also a goldsmith, a stained-glass artist, and wrote extensively on art, most notably his three-volume *Commentarii*, a discussion of art theory and history from antiquity to his time.

Donatello

c.1386–1466

The leading sculptor of the early Renaissance, Donatello created expressive and inventive works that combined naturalism and emotion. His sculpture greatly influenced many other artists, including Michelangelo. Sometimes called "the father of the Renaissance," Donatello (real name Donate di Niccolò di Betto Bardi) was tremendously versatile, creating everything from relief sculpture to nudes, and working in numerous mediums, including bronze, stone, terra-cotta, and wood.

Jan van Eyck

1390–1441

One of the first European painters to create portraits of the merchant class and bourgeoisie, van Eyck is considered the leading artist of the early Netherlands school. His work is known for its naturalism, the exacting attention he paid to the details of his subjects' facial features, and his use of luminous color. He is renowned for having perfected the technique of painting with oils. In addition to his artistic career, van Eyck served in a diplomatic capacity for Philip the Good, Duke of Burgundy.

Hubert van Eyck

Unknown–1426

The brother of Jan van Eyck, Hubert is believed to have worked on the Ghent Altarpiece—an inscription on that work states that it was begun by Hubert van Eyck and completed by Jan. Little else is known about Hubert, however, and art historians have never conclusively separated one brother's work from the other on the altarpiece.

Fra Angelico

c.1395–1355

A Dominican friar, Angelico bridged the divide between earlier Gothic Christian art and more modern Renaissance styles—his use of perspective was decidedly modern, for example. The figures in Angelico's paintings are typically described as happy and innocent, conveying a message of the goodness of God's creation, and bright pinks and blues abound. Born Guido di Pietro in Tuscany, he created frescoes for popes Eugenius IV and Nicholas V.

Pisanello

c.1395–1455

A painter popular in the courts of Italy, Pisanello was noted not only for his paintings but also for his drawings and portrait medals, which were inspired by Roman coins. He is considered to be the leading medalist of his era, and his drawings of animals reveal detail and character. Pisanello is a nickname that translates as "The Little Pisan"; it is probable that he was from Pisa but his actual name was Antonio Pisano.

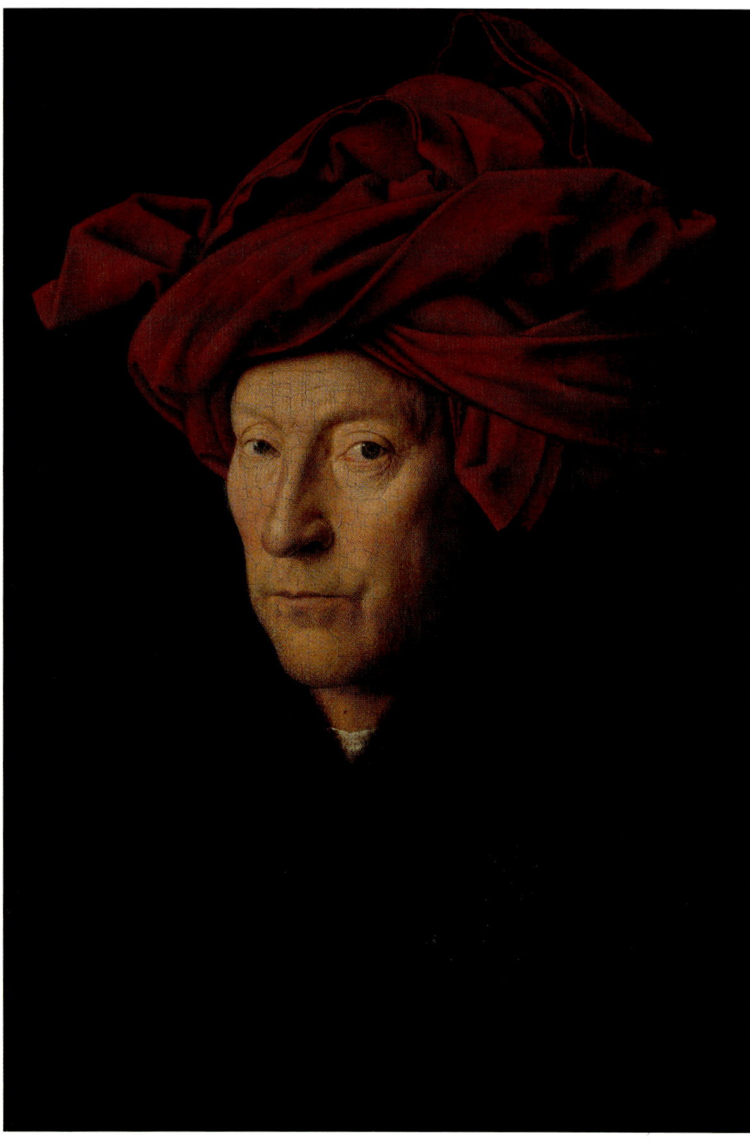

▲ **Jan van Eyck**, *Portrait of a Man* (possibly a self-portrait), 1433, oil on oak, National Gallery, London, UK

Paolo Uccello

1397–1475

Florentine painter Uccello is known for his extreme use of perspective and foreshortening. In fact, he often seemed more interested in solving the problems associated with rendering three-dimensional space on a two-dimensional surface than any other aspect of painting. Uccello was reportedly known as "the bird" due to his love of birds and animals; his real name was Paolo di Dono.

Rogier van der Weyden

1399–1464

Following the death of Jan van Eyck, the Brussels-based van der Weyden was the leading northern European painter of the mid-15th century. He painted figures with great detail and deep, meaningful emotion, although his figures were often positioned in stiff, unrealistic poses, and his use of gold was somewhat dated by this time. His paintings were typically religious in nature.

Masaccio

1401–1428

Regarded as the leading painter of the Florentine early Renaissance, Masaccio's simple compositions feature realistic human figures who convey deep, meaningful emotions. He is often cited as the first painter to use scientific perspective and foreshortening. He died before reaching the age of 30, and left few surviving works. The name Masaccio tends to be translated as "Clumsy Tom" or "Big Ugly Tom"; his real name was Tommaso di Ser Giovanni de Simone.

Stefan Lochner

c.1410–1451

The greatest painter working in mid-15th-century Cologne, Lochner painted Christian images featuring figures with soft, rounded, luminous faces. His oeuvre reflects the transition from a late Gothic style to the early Renaissance. His later paintings in particular show increasing naturalism. Little is known about his personal life.

Konrad Witz

c.1400–1445

Generally regarded as the greatest Swiss painter of the 15th century, Witz was born in Germany and settled in Basel in the 1430s. An innovative artist, he is best known

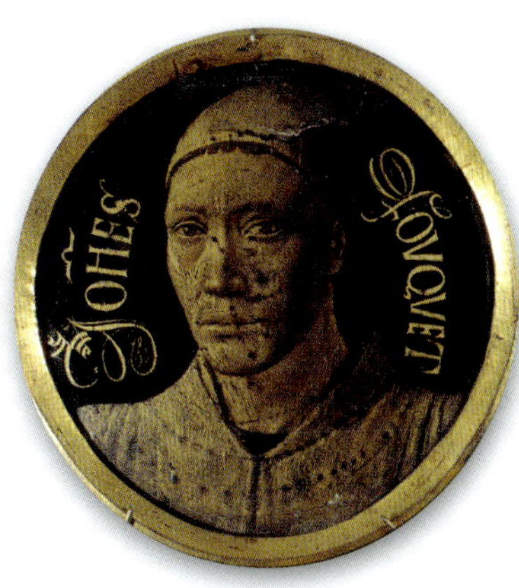

▲ **Jean Fouquet**, *Self-Portrait*, 1452-1455, enamel-painted copper, Louvre, Paris, France

for *The Miraculous Draft of Fishes*, featuring a highly detailed and topographically accurate view of Lake Geneva and skillful study of the reflection of sunlight on water.

Jean Fouquet

c.1420–1481

The leading French painter and manuscript illuminator of the 15th century, Fouquet brought the artistic innovations of the Renaissance to France after traveling to Italy in the late 1440s. He was born in Tours and operated a large workshop there for several decades following his Italian trip. Heavily influenced by the early Italian Renaissance, his work was popular with the French royal court.

Piero della Francesca

c.1416–1492

An Italian painter now regarded as among the greatest of the early Renaissance, Piero was not tremendously well known in his day and was largely forgotten until the 20th century. The Christian images he created are notable for their attention to perspective and proportion, both rooted in his interest in mathematics. He also served as town councilor in the town of Sansepolcro, east of Florence.

Sesshū Tōyō

1420–1506

A major figure in the history of Japanese monochrome ink painting, or *sumi-e*, Sesshū spent two years in China. This interlude influenced his style, and he incorporated Chinese techniques into Japanese art. Born into a samurai family, Sesshū became a Zen Buddhist monk as a child. His most famous works are landscapes, but he also painted other subjects, including Buddhist scenes.

Benozzo Gozzoli

c.1421–1497

A Florentine painter of early Renaissance frescoes and altarpieces, Gozzoli originally trained as a goldsmith. A student of Fra Angelico, he worked with Ghiberti on the east doors of the Baptistry in Florence. Gozzoli's best-known works are probably the *Procession of the Magi* frescoes in Florence's Medici Riccardi Palace. Some of his greatest frescoes were badly damaged by bombing during World War II.

Petrus Christus

Active c.1444–1475

The greatest painter in Bruges following the death of Jan van Eyck, Christus produced Christian images and portraits that were often extremely similar to the work of van Eyck. Indeed, his paintings have been misattributed to van Eyck. Christus is sometimes cited as the first Northern European painter to employ single-point perspective.

Hans Memling

c.1430–1494

The leading artist in Bruges during the late 15th century, German-born Memling is regarded as the successor to Rogier van der Weyden. He may have worked under van der Weyden and certainly borrowed ideas from him. However, Memling's work, mainly consisting of altarpieces and portraits, is softer, quieter, and more decorative than that of van der Weyden. Memling is sometimes spelled Memlinc.

Giovanni Bellini

c.1430–1516

A key early Renaissance figure generally regarded as the father of Venetian painting, Bellini is known for his depictions of natural light and cloudy skies, which were revolutionary for their time. The most accomplished member of a prominent family of artists, his paintings usually reflected religious themes. He was hugely influential on the generation of Venetian artists who followed him, including his students Titian and Giorgione.

Carlo Crivelli

c.1430–1495

A Venetian painter of religious works, Crivelli employed a Gothic-influenced ornamental style that was already somewhat out of date in his own time. However, he combined this with great attention to detail and modern linear perspective and foreshortening to produce a distinctive result. He was knighted by Prince Ferdinand of Capua in 1490, suggesting he had achieved fame and respect.

Andrea Mantegna

1431–1506

A northern Italian painter and engraver, Mantegna brought a distinctive viewpoint, attention to detail, and a mastery of scientific perspective and foreshortening to Renaissance Christian scenes and portraits. He had a passionate interest in Roman Antiquity. His style is sometimes criticized as dry and scholarly. He was court painter to the dukes of Gonzaga.

Pollaiuolo brothers

c.1432–1498 and c.1441–1496

Antonio and Piero Pollaiuolo were versatile artists who operated a successful workshop in Florence. Painters, engravers, and sculptors, they took a great interest in anatomy—reports suggest they even dissected corpses to further their understanding of the human body. They also created detailed and innovative landscapes.

Andrea della Robbia

1435–1525

A major Florentine sculptor during the Renaissance, della Robbia was from a family of acclaimed artists—his uncle Luca della Robbia pioneered a successful technique for glazed terra-cotta. Andrea inherited that technique—along with his uncle's artistic style and successful workshop—and passed them on to his sons.

Hugo van der Goes

c.1440–1482

Van der Goes was a talented and distinctive Dutch painter, but only one surviving work is definitively attributed to him—the *Portinari Altarpiece*, commissioned for a Florentine chapel. Probably born in Ghent, van der Goes became dean of that city's artist's guild. Toward the end of his life, he moved to a monastery and became a lay monk but he suffered from declining mental health.

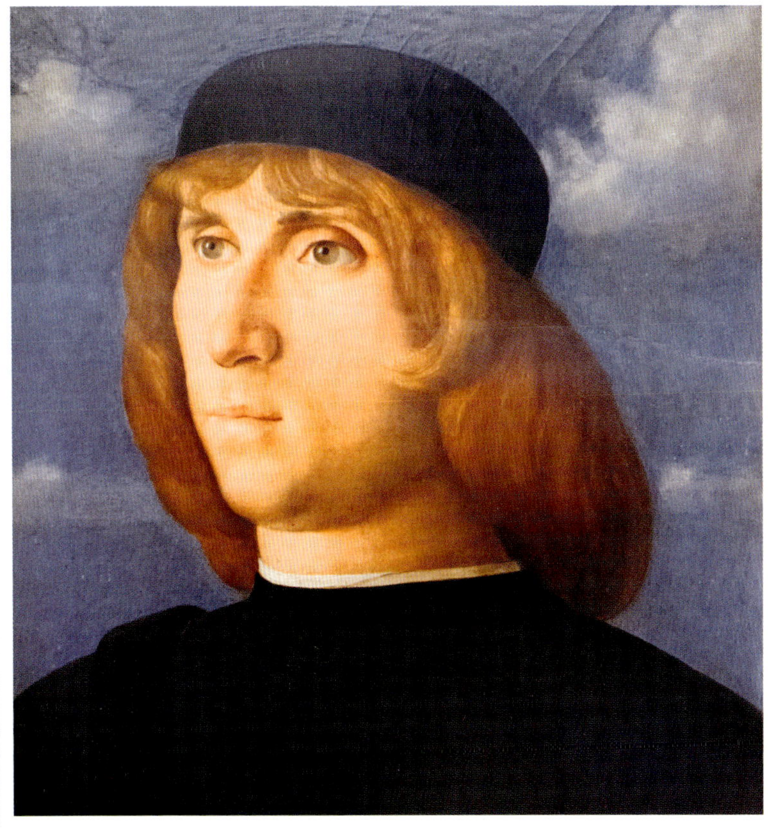

▲ **Giovanni Bellini**, *Self-Portrait*, c.1500, oil on panel, Capitoline Museums, Rome, Italy

Bartolomé Bermejo

c.1440–1498

Perhaps the greatest Spanish painter prior to the 16th century, Bermejo may have trained in Holland, because his work shows influences from the region. The *Pietà* in Barcelona Cathedral is generally considered his greatest surviving work. Believed to be from Córdoba, he worked in Aragon and later in Barcelona. His actual name was Bartolomé de Cardenas; "Bermejo" means red, perhaps suggesting that he had red hair.

Martin Schongauer

c.1445–1491

Perhaps the most famous German artist of the 15th century, Schongauer was renowned for his engravings. He was the leading German engraver prior to Albrecht Dürer, who was greatly influenced by Schongauer's work. The son of a goldsmith, he worked in Colmar, Alsace, producing both engravings and paintings, usually on Christian themes but sometimes depicting scenes of everyday life.

Sandro Botticelli

c.1445–1510

A key figure of the Florentine Renaissance, Botticelli painted religious and mythological subjects with tremendous beauty, although without the attention to scientific perspective that was becoming common among artists at the time. He was perhaps the first major artist since antiquity to paint mythological subjects on a large scale, and was regarded as an excellent draftsman. His work was starting to fall out of fashion by the end of his life.

▲ **Self-portrait of Sandro Botticelli**, detail of *Adoration of the Magi*, 1470-1475, tempera grassa on wood, Uffizi, Florence, Italy

Perugino

c.1450–1523

A painter of Christian art and portraits during the Renaissance, Perugino trained in Florence, but was born and worked around Perugia. That town is the source of his nickname; his actual name was Pietro Vannucci. Perugino's style has been described as soft and sentimental, but his status during his day was lofty enough for him to receive commissions from Pope Sixtus IV. The frescoes Perugino painted in the Vatican's Sistine Chapel were lost when Michelangelo painted his *Last Judgment* on the altar wall.

Hieronymus Bosch

c.1450–1516

The last of the great Northern European medieval painters, Bosch is primarily known for his highly distinctive, detailed, and disquieting pieces focusing on the wickedness of humanity and the eternal damnation that awaits sinners. Otherworldly creatures and torture abound. Although Bosch was active during the Renaissance, his imaginative works stand apart from the art of his contemporaries, although he painted conventional religious themes, too.

Leonardo da Vinci

1452–1519

Born the illegitimate son of a notary near Florence, Leonardo became the Renaissance man who gave meaning to the phrase "Renaissance man." He was not just a painter, draftsman, and sculptor but also a scientist, inventor, writer, architect, engineer, and more—his extraordinarily versatile genius making him one of the most famous people in history. However, his active mind and wide-ranging interests resulted in him leaving behind relatively few paintings for an artist of his stature—perhaps only 17. Still, these show a masterful ability to express emotion, and his study of anatomy represented a leap forward in naturalism. Leonardo's works significantly influenced the Renaissance artists who followed him.

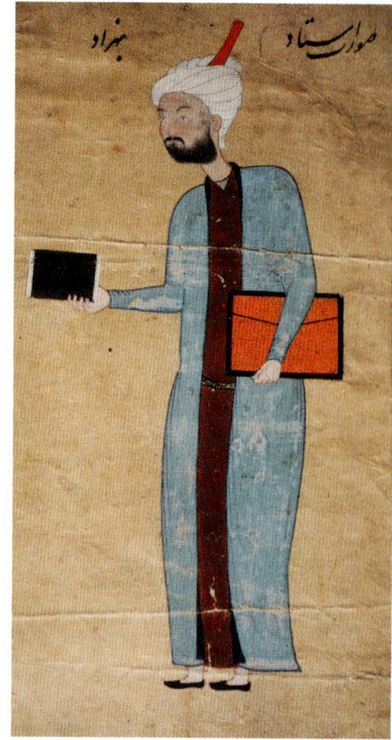

▲ ***Portrait of the Painter Bihzad*** from the album of Shah Tahmasp I, artist unknown, 15th century, gouache on paper, Istanbul University Library, Türkiye

Bihzad

c.1455–c.1536

An influential and skilled painter of Persian miniatures and a manuscript illuminator, Bihzad brought dynamism and realism to Persian art. An orphan, he studied under the artist Mirak Naqqash in Herat (modern-day Afghanistan). Bihzad led the Herat academy from 1486 until 1506, and was later director of the royal library at Tabriz (in modern-day Iran), helping to establish the city's artistic reputation.

Vittore Carpaccio

c.1460–c.1525

The leading Venetian narrative painter of the early Renaissance, Carpaccio painted religious and mythological scenes, although they were often set in the Venice of his own time. The naturalism of his paintings and his modern use of space were notable. Carpaccio is often ranked with Bellini as the most important Venetian artist of his day.

Wen Zhengming

1470–1559

A Chinese painter, calligrapher, and poet during the Ming dynasty, Wen Zhengming is regarded as one of the leaders of the Wu School of

Chinese art, and was one of the acclaimed "Four Masters of the Ming dynasty." A diligent scholar from a distinguished family, he studied calligraphy and art styles from earlier periods of Chinese art. He usually painted landscapes, but his style was varied, reflecting wide-ranging influences.

Albrecht Dürer

1471–1528

The leading artist of the Northern European Renaissance, Dürer is best remembered for his woodcuts and engravings, although he was also a talented painter. After completing an apprenticeship, he traveled to Italy and incorporated the artistic advances of the Italian Renaissance into Northern European traditions. The son of a Hungarian-born goldsmith, Dürer opened a successful workshop in Nuremberg and, from 1512, worked extensively for the Holy Roman Emperor Maximilian I.

Lucas Cranach the Elder

1472–1553

A leading painter and engraver during the German Renaissance, Cranach produced mainly religious works and portraits, although he was also known for his mythological scenes featuring female nudes. Very popular and financially successful in his day, he was an acquaintance of Protestant theologian Martin Luther and painted many portraits of him.

Michelangelo

1475–1564

One of the towering figures of the Italian Renaissance, sculptor and painter Michelangelo was regarded as the greatest artist of his era by contemporaries, and he exerted great influence over Western art in the centuries that followed. His work glorified the human form, reflecting his study of anatomy (including participation in dissections) in order to better understand the body. Michelangelo also drafted detailed anatomical drawings. His sculpture—often statues of mythological or Biblical heroes—combined idealism with emotional insight.

Giorgione

c.1476–1510

An important Venetian painter during the Renaissance, Giorgione is now mainly known for small pieces, sometimes described as mysterious and dreamlike, that he painted for private collectors. His provocative scenes are not always easily linked to religious, historical, or mythological stories, though he also painted more conventional Christian images. Little is known about his life. Only a small number of works can be confidently attributed to him.

Lü Ji

1477–unknown

A Chinese painter during the Hongzhi reign in the early Ming Dynasty, Lü Ji specialized in painting birds and flowers, images generally interpreted as symbolic of political authority. Lü worked in the "ink wash" style, in which varied concentrations of black ink are applied using a brush, a style that had been in vogue centuries earlier. Appointed a court painter, he was given an honorary title as an officer of the imperial guard.

Jan Gossaert

c.1478–c.1532

An early 16th-century painter, influenced by Jan van Eyck and Albrecht Dürer, Gossaert introduced the artistic ideas of the Italian Renaissance to the Low Countries (modern-day Belgium, Luxembourg, and the Netherlands) following a 1508 visit to Rome. A skilled draftsman, he was highly regarded in his day and served as master of Antwerp painter's guild. Gossaert was also known as Mabuse and probably came from Maubeuge in modern-day northern France.

Matthias Grünewald

c.1480–1528

A German painter of powerful Christian images, Grünewald is known for his unexpected colors and distorted figures. He paid minimal attention to naturalism in many of his works, which had more in common with medieval German art than with the more modern, Renaissance painting of his day. The spiritual intensity of Grünewald's work made it very popular during his lifetime—he served as court painter for the archbishop of Mainz—but his fame faded quickly following his death from the plague. However, centuries later, Grünewald's paintings influenced the work of the German Expressionists.

Albrecht Altdorfer

c.1480–1538

A German painter and printmaker, Altdorfer created mainly Christian-themed images and is considered to be one of the first European artists to treat landscapes as a genre of their own. The human figures in Altdorfer's distinctive and imaginative works are often seemingly of less importance than their surroundings. Altdorfer held positions in local government in Regensburg, Germany.

Raphael

1483–1520

One of the most famous Western artists of all time, Raphael excelled at draftsmanship, composition, and conveying emotion. The son of Giovanni Santi, a successful painter in Urbino, Italy, Raphael was a prodigy whose greatness had already been recognized by the time he reached his early twenties. At the age of 21, he moved to Florence, where he was influenced by Leonardo and Michelangelo, and later settled in Rome. He spent much of his career working on commissions from popes Julius II and Leo X, including serving as an architect in charge of the rebuilding of St. Peter's Basilica from 1514. He also worked for Agostino Chigi, Europe's leading banker. Raphael died of fever on or around his 37th birthday.

Joachim Patinir

c. 1485–1524

Flemish painter Patinir is often cited as one of the first European artists to specialize in landscape painting. These scenes generally feature stories from the Bible or the lives of the saints, and are not pure landscapes because they included figures. Highly regarded in his day, Patinir also painted background landscapes for other artists, including his friend Quentin Massys. Massys served as the guardian of Patinir's two daughters after his death.

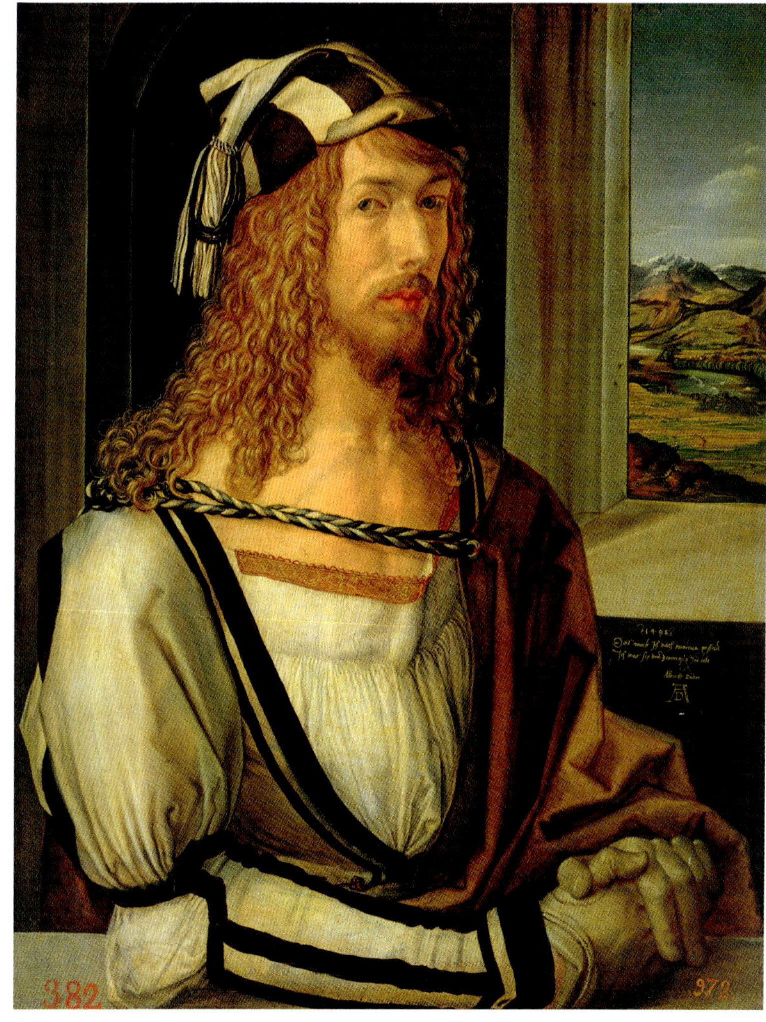

▲ **Albrecht Dürer**, *Self-Portrait*, 1498, oil on panel, Prado, Madrid, Spain

Titian

c.1490–1576

The leading painter of 16th-century Venice, Titian is widely regarded as one of the greatest painters in the history of European art. During a long career, Titian, whose real name was Tiziano Vecelli, produced remarkably expressive, moving paintings on religious, mythological, and historical subjects, as well as portraits. He counted emperors, kings, and popes among his patrons, including Holy Roman Emperor Charles V, King Philip II of Spain, and Pope Paul III.

Correggio

c.1494–1534

A northern Italian artist known for the gentle, misty delicacy of his Christian and mythological images, Correggio was not hugely famous in his day, but his paintings became popular in the centuries following his death. His innovative use of lighting to focus attention on religious themes, such as light radiating from an image of the Christ Child, was much copied. His work was influential among the Baroque painters who followed.

Qiu Ying

c.1494–c.1552

A Chinese painter in Suzhou, Qiu was known for his meticulous, detailed and realistic *gongbi* technique. Born a peasant, he showed early talent as an artist and attracted wealthy patrons, eventually being acclaimed as one of the "Four Masters of the Ming dynasty." His works were varied in subject, including images of flowers, landscapes, humans, and buildings. Most of his paintings feature vibrant colors, although he also created some monochromatic works.

Jacopo Pontormo

1494–1557

Among the leading painters of early 16th-century Florence, Pontormo is considered a key figure in what became known as Italian Mannerism—the Late Renaissance style that led to the Baroque. His works are emotionally intense and marked by an experimental, energetic style. Most of his paintings were on Christian themes, although he also produced portraits.

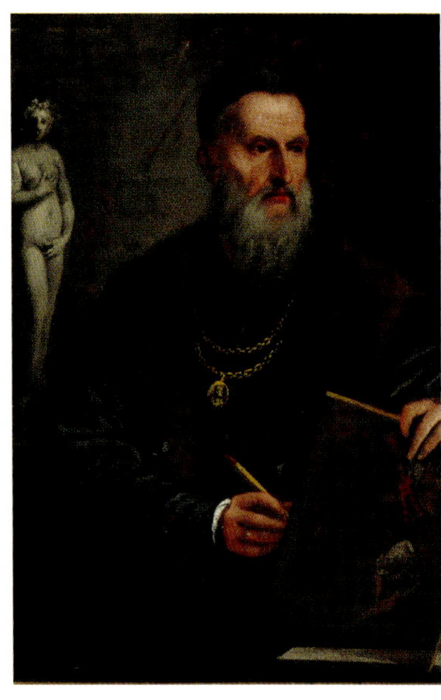

▲ ***Imaginary Self-Portrait of Titian***, Pietro della Vecchia, c.1650s, oil on canvas, private collection

Hans Holbein the Younger

c.1497–1543

Holbein is remembered as one of the greatest portrait painters of the 16th century, a claim based on his portraits of Henry VIII and other powerful people. A versatile artist, Holbein also produced altarpieces, murals, woodcuts for books, jewelery, and other works. Born in Augsburg, Germany, to an artist father, his career took him to England where he became the court painter.

Martin van Heemskerk

1498–1574

A prominent painter from Holland, van Heemskerk created portraits, religious works, and mythological scenes. Born the son of a farmer, he worked largely in Haarlem, but spent several years in Rome, and his work shows Italian influences. He was also a skilled draftsman, and many of his images were turned into engravings.

Benvenuto Cellini

1500–1571

A 16th-century Florentine sculptor, engraver, and goldsmith, Cellini is remembered for his colorful and sometimes violent life story as much as for his art. He created large statues and small, precisely executed pieces, and his patrons included Cosimo I de' Medici in Florence and Frances I of France. Cellini was exiled from Florence for dueling in 1523 and was imprisoned on multiple occasions.

Parmigianino

1503–1540

An early 16th-century Italian Mannerist painter and engraver, Parmigianino created religious works and portraits that were elegant, refined, distinctive, and notable for their strangely elongated figures. Born in Parma, hence his nickname (his real name was Girolamo Francesco Maria Mazzola), he was also active in Rome and Bologna. Parmigianino's widely distributed etchings helped his fame and influence spread through Italy despite his early death. He was one of the first Italian engravers to create etchings of his own artwork.

Agnolo Bronzino

1503–1572

An Italian painter, Bronzino is best known for his stylish portraits. His works are well composed and often feature bold colors, but his sitters stare arrogantly out at viewers, creating little emotional connection—the purpose of these paintings being to convey the sitters' wealth and power, not their personalities. He spent much of his career in Florence working for Duke Cosimo I de' Medici. Bronzino was a nickname meaning "bronze colored," perhaps a reference to the artist's skin tone; his real name was Agnolo di Cosimo.

Mir Sayyid Ali

c.1510–1572

The son of artist Mir Musawwir, Persian painter Mir Sayyid Ali was known for his brightly colored, finely detailed miniatures. He emigrated to India at the invitation of the Mughal emperor, and, together with Abd-us-Samad, played a key role in establishing the Mughal school of painting. He died in Mecca.

Giorgio Vasari

1511–1574

A 16th-century Italian painter, architect, and writer, Vasari is primarily remembered as the author of the biographies that came to be known as *The Lives of the Artists*, an important and influential work detailing the history of Renaissance art. His most important work as an architect was the Uffizi Gallery in Florence. Vasari's paintings were created in a decorative Mannerist style.

Kanō Yukinobu

c.1513–1575

A Japanese painter, Kanō Yukinobu was a member of the family that founded the Kanō school of painting (known for its bold brushwork), which attracted important patrons and dominated Japan's art scene for centuries. Kanō Yukinobu was the younger brother of the more famous Kanō Motonobu, who led the family's artistic dynasty during its second generation.

Tintoretto

1518–1594

Among the most prominent Venetian painters of the 16th century, following Titian, the prolific Tintoretto was perhaps best known for his large, passionate, religious and mythological works featuring thick brushwork and dramatic lighting. He reportedly boasted that his work combined the drawing skill of Michelangelo and the color of Titian. He also produced numerous portraits.

Pieter Bruegel the Elder

c.1525–1569

Bruegel was the leading Flemish artist of the mid-16th century. His paintings and prints of landscapes and scenes of peasant life were distinct from the overtly religious and mythological works that dominated the era. An extended visit to Italy in the early 1550s influenced his style, and his work would influence Dutch artists in the 17th century.

Giovanni Moroni

c.1525–1578

Among the greatest portrait painters of mid-16th-century Italy, Moroni produced dignified, detailed, realistic, and expressive likenesses, often of ordinary middle-class people. He also painted religious works, but those are not as highly regarded as his portraits.

Giuseppe Arcimboldo

c.1527–1593

The court painter to several Hapsburg emperors, including Maximilian II, the Milan-born Arcimboldo is remembered for painting "composite heads"—portraits cleverly created by combining numerous small objects on a theme, such as books to form a librarian or birds to form a personification of the element of air. Centuries later, these works would influence the Surrealists.

Catharina van Hemessen

c.1528–after 1566

A Flemish portrait painter during the Renaissance, van Hemessen is generally credited with having created, in 1548, the first self-portrait to capture an artist at work on a self-portrait. She was the daughter of Jan Sanders van Hemessen, a leading painter of religious images; her patrons included Mary of Hungary, regent of the Netherlands.

Veronese

c.1528–1588

Among the greatest Venetian painters of the generation that followed Titian, the prolific Veronese was at his best creating large, colorful scenes, both religious and secular. He also painted portraits, but those were less notable than his large frescoes. Veronese is a nickname reflecting his birthplace of Verona; his actual name was Paolo Caliari.

Alonso Sánchez Coello

c.1531–1588

Born to Portuguese parents and trained in Flanders, Coello was a court portrait painter to Phillip II of Spain. He is an influential early figure in the history of formal Spanish portraiture. His figures tended to be dignified, if somewhat stiff, with careful attention paid to their wardrobe. He also painted religious pieces.

Sofonisba Anguissola

c.1532–1625

An Italian portrait painter during the Renaissance, Anguissola is generally considered the best-known female artist of her time and, arguably, the first female artist to achieve international acclaim. Born into an aristocratic family in Cremona, she was one of six sisters, all of whom painted. She became a portrait painter to the court of Philip II of Spain, although her self-portraits and portraits of her own family are considered her best work. She was a courtier rather than a professional artist.

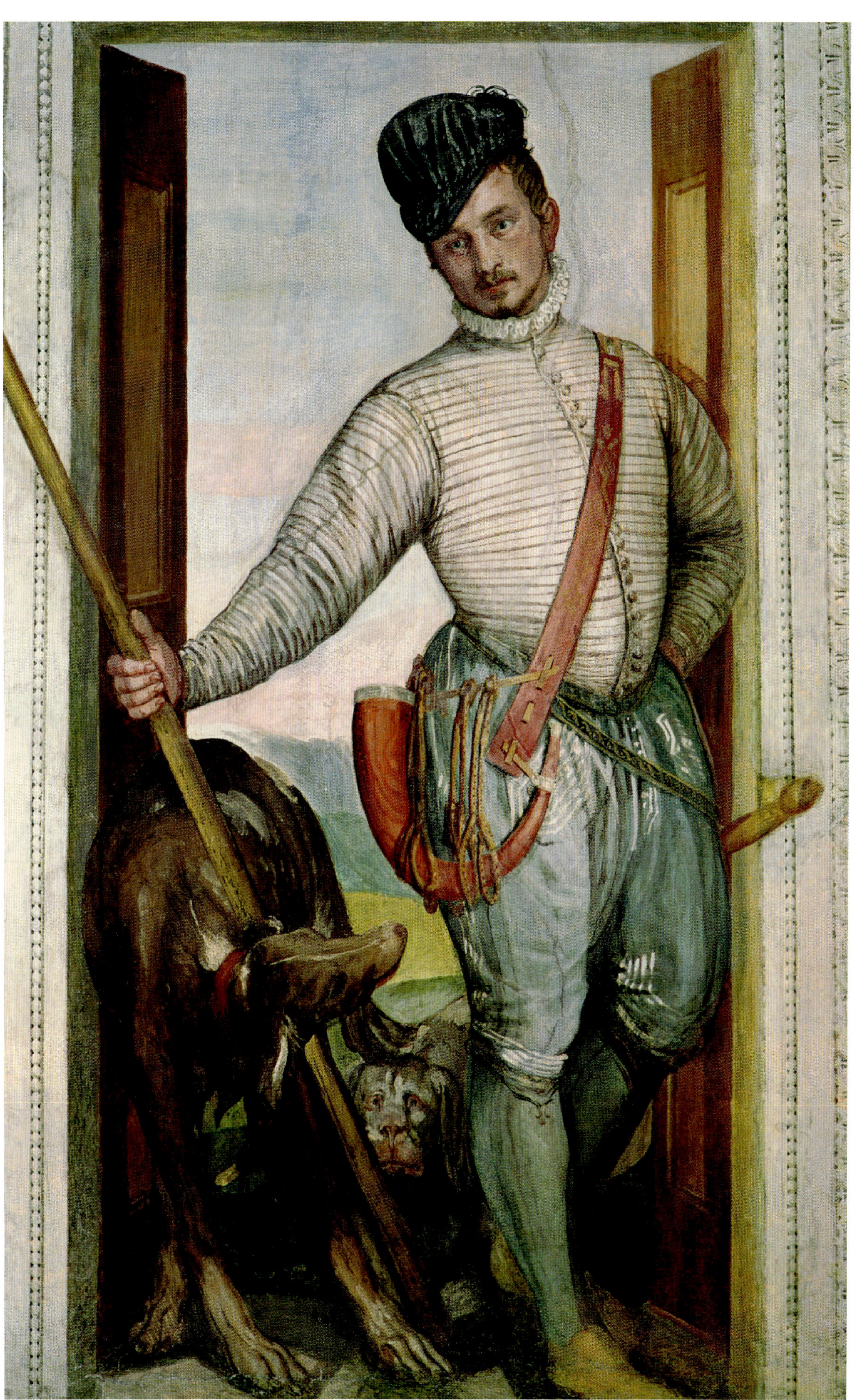

▶ **Veronese**, *Self-Portrait in Hunting Costume*, 1562, fresco, Villa Barbaro, Maser, Italy

Muhammad ibn Taj al-Din

Active 1583

Persian artist Muhammad ibn Taj al-Din is known for the illustrations he added, in 1583, to a manuscript of the *Shahnama* that had been created two decades earlier. This lengthy poem celebrates the real and mythical achievements of Iranian kings; it is sometimes called the *Book of Kings* or the Persian national epic.

Basawan

Active 1556–1600

A court painter to the Mughal emperor Akbar, Basawan created manuscript illustrations and other miniatures in the Mughal style. He is noted for his strong use of color and ability to create scenes and figures that speak to aspects of human nature. His son, Manohar, was also a prominent painter.

El Greco

1541–1614

Born in Crete and trained in Italy, El Greco painted religious works and portraits. He began his artistic career creating Byzantine-style icons but, by 1577, he had relocated to Spain—first to Madrid and later Toledo—where he produced unique art that showed wide-ranging influences. The nickname El Greco simply meant "The Greek"; his real name was Domenikos Theotokopoulos. He would come to be seen as perhaps the greatest Spanish painter of his era.

Kanō Eitoku

1543–1590

A member of the fifth generation of the hugely influential and well-connected Kanō family of Japanese artists, Kanō Eitoku is credited with several important innovations that added a sense of energy to the family's artistic style, including thicker outlines and the use of a dramatic gold background to their works. Most of his paintings were of natural subjects, such as trees, flowers, birds, and animals.

Nicholas Hilliard

1547–1619

Queen Elizabeth I made English painter and goldsmith Nicholas Hilliard her official miniature painter, a role he retained under her successor, James I. Hilliard created images not only of the queen, but many of the prominent figures of the era. He completed some larger portraits as well. The Exeter-born son of a goldsmith, Hilliard is known to have experienced financial struggles during his career.

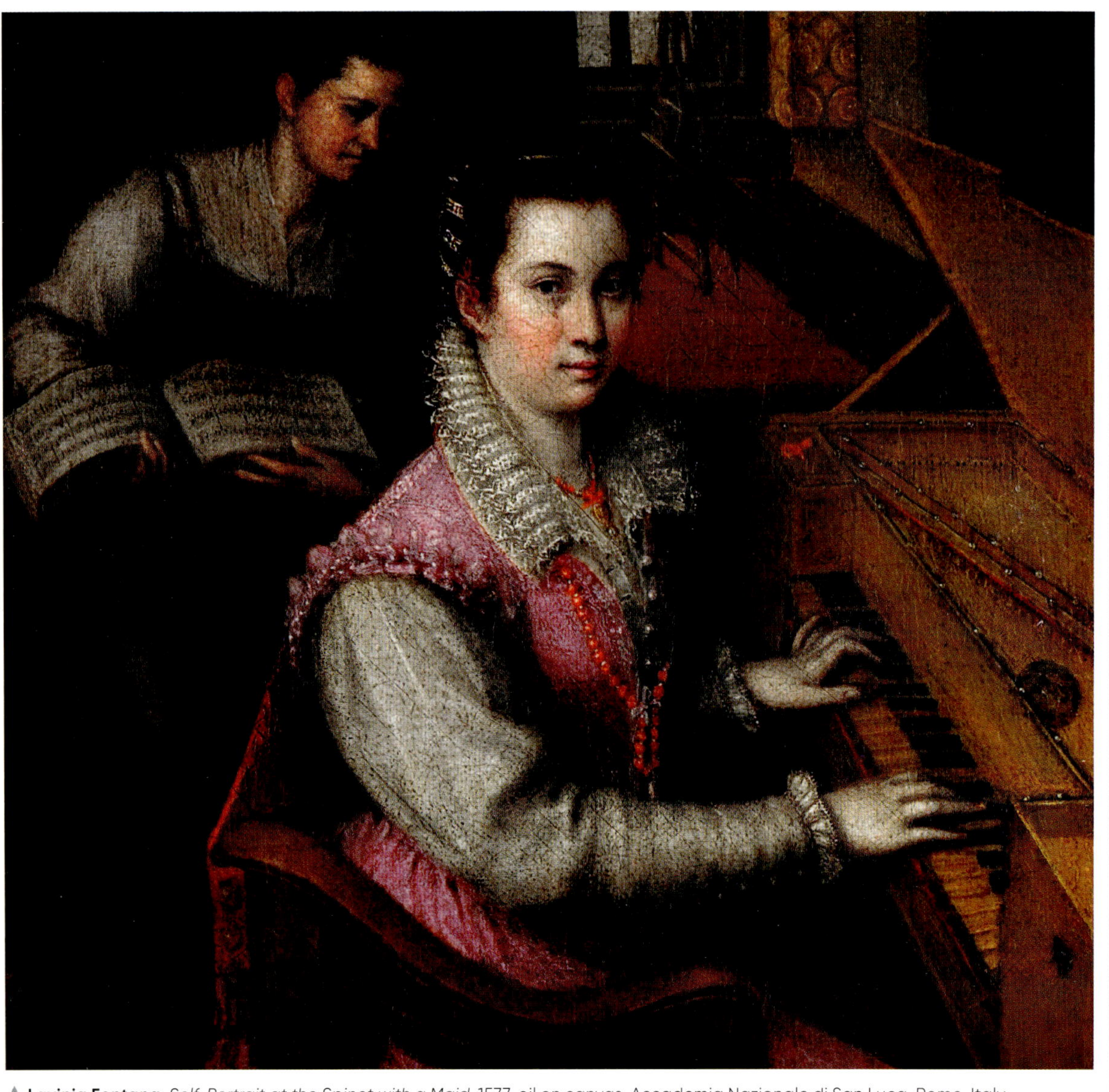

▲ **Lavinia Fontana**, *Self-Portrait at the Spinet with a Maid*, 1577, oil on canvas, Accademia Nazionale di San Luca, Rome, Italy

Lavinia Fontana

1552–1614

A highly regarded Italian portrait painter and the first professional woman painter in Renaissance Europe. Fontana was the daughter and student of the successful Bolognese Mannerist painter Prospero Fontana. She remained in demand as a portrait painter in Bologna and, later, in Rome, while raising a large family. Fontana also painted religious works, which have been compared to those of Correggio.

Annibale Carracci

1560–1609

The most talented member of a Bologna-based family of artists, Carracci—together with his brother Agostino and cousin Ludovico—founded an academy that established Bologna as an important center of art in the late 16th century. Carracci was an eclectic artist and his works included religious and genre works, landscapes, and portraits. Together with his brother and cousin, he is sometimes credited with the invention of caricature.

Juan Sanchez Cotán

1561–1627

An early and influential Spanish painter of still lifes, Sanchez Cotán's images of food—often fruits and vegetables—against a simple, dark background were executed with impressive naturalism and depth. The deeply religious artist also painted Christian images, plus some portraits and other works, but he is remembered for his still lifes.

Jan Brueghel the Elder

1568–1625

A Flemish painter specializing in landscapes and flowers, Brueghel was known for his skill with delicate textures, earning him the nickname "Velvet" Brueghel. The son of Pieter Bruegel the Elder, he was a friend and sometime collaborator of Peter Paul Rubens. He worked in Italy in the 1590s before moving to Antwerp, where he spent the remainder of his career.

Caravaggio

1571–1610

Caravaggio's bold naturalism and dramatic content and lighting proved revolutionary in the late 16th and early 17th centuries.

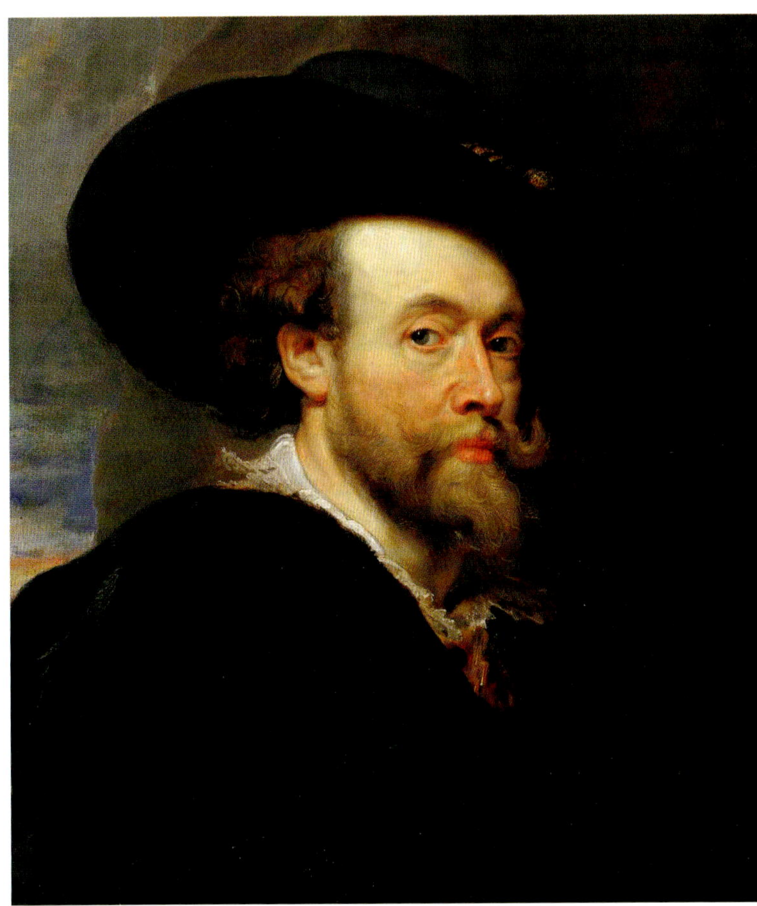

▲ **Peter Paul Rubens**, *Self-Portrait*, 1623, oil on panel, Royal Collection Trust, London, UK

A hugely influential and innovative Italian painter, Caravaggio was also a temperamental man, who became embroiled in multiple legal problems and had to flee Rome after killing a man in a fight. He died of malarial fever.

Ambrosius Bosschaert the Elder

1573–1621

An early and influential Dutch painter of still lifes, Bosschaert created bright and attractive images of floral arrangements or, occasionally, fruit. Most of his still lifes have simple backgrounds, but some feature windows that offer views of distant landscapes. He was also an art dealer and teacher, and three of Bosschaert's sons followed him into the flower-painting profession.

Guido Reni

1575–1642

Perhaps Bologna's leading artist in the early to mid-17th century, Reni combined classicism and naturalism in beautiful, if melodramatic, works on religious and mythological themes. His large and successful studio created paintings that were in demand across Europe, and he was held in high regard by art collectors for centuries after his death. However, it is reported that Reni was often in debt despite his professional success, and that his financial problems were rooted in gambling.

Sir Peter Paul Rubens

1577–1640

Northern Europe's most influential Baroque artist, the Flemish painter Rubens is renowned for his bold, energetic, expressive, and colorful images of religious, mythological, and historical scenes. He also painted portraits and landscapes, and his drawings are held in great esteem. From the 1620s, Rubens served as a diplomat, and was knighted by both Charles I of England and Philip IV of Spain.

Adam Elsheimer

1578–1610

An influential painter of small, precisely rendered landscapes and religious works, Elsheimer usually painted on copper plate. His exacting attention to detail helped make his work distinctive—his use of multiple sources of lighting in landscapes was innovative—but it also forced him to work very slowly, contributing to financial problems. Although he was born in Germany, Elsheimer trained and worked in Italy.

Domenichino

1581–1641

Among Rome's leading painters during the early 17th century, the Bologna-born Domenichino created religious and mythological works in a style that was rooted in antiquity but that tended toward the early Baroque as his career progressed. He was also a pioneer of landscape painting, a skilled draftsman, and a notable portrait painter. Domenichino means "Little Dominic." His real name was Domenico Zampieri.

Frans Hals

c. 1581–1666

An influential Dutch portrait painter, Hals was known for his bold, spontaneous brushstrokes and the sense of vitality and expression that he brought to his subjects. Based in Haarlem throughout his entire career, he achieved professional acclaim but not financial success—he was often in debt, in part because of the expenses related to his large family. He is known for his paintings of individuals and groups such as families and the civic guard.

Fede Galizia

c. 1587–c. 1630

An early Italian painter of still lifes, Galizia created striking and naturalistic pictures of fruit before that subject matter was common in European art. She also painted portraits and religious works, although these are less acclaimed than her still lifes. She was the daughter of Nunzio Galizia, a noted miniaturist.

Jusepe de Ribera

1591–1652

The leading painter in the Italian city of Naples during the first half of the 17th century, the Spanish-born Ribera is best known for his realistic and memorable images of unpleasant scenes, such as the martyrdom of saints. He is also celebrated for his skill with lighting, which has been compared to that of Velázquez. In addition to religious images, he painted mythological scenes and portraits, among his other works.

Gerard van Honthorst

1592–1656

A follower of Caravaggio, Dutch painter Gerard van Honthorst was acclaimed for his nocturnal scenes, a specialty that earned him the nickname "Gerardo della Notte" (Gerard of the Night). His historical, mythological, and genre images were popular with collectors and royal patrons in Italy and across Europe. He served as the painter at the Dutch court for 15 years.

Georges de la Tour

1593–1652

A 17th-century French artist largely forgotten until the 20th century, Georges de la Tour is now held in high regard, in particular for his candlelit, nocturnal scenes. He often painted images of peasants, rogues, and other colorful characters in a realistic style, as well as some religious works. De la Tour seems to have been relatively successful in his own day—the Duke of Lorraine was a patron, and Louis XIII owned one of his paintings—but he fell into obscurity toward the end of his life.

Nicolas Poussin

1594–1665

Poussin was the most influential painter in 17th-century France. His classical paintings on historical, mythological, and religious themes became the standard against which future generations of French classical artists would be judged. Poussin became court painter to Louis XIII in the early 1640s. Despite his central position in the history of French art, he spent much of his career in Rome.

Clara Peeters

1594–after 1657

A Flemish painter of still lifes, Peeters is best known for her "breakfast pieces"—images depicting the components of a meal laid out on a table. Her work is characterized by close attention to detail and her use of a low viewpoint. Almost nothing is known about her life, and Peeters had disappeared from both the art world and public records by 1657.

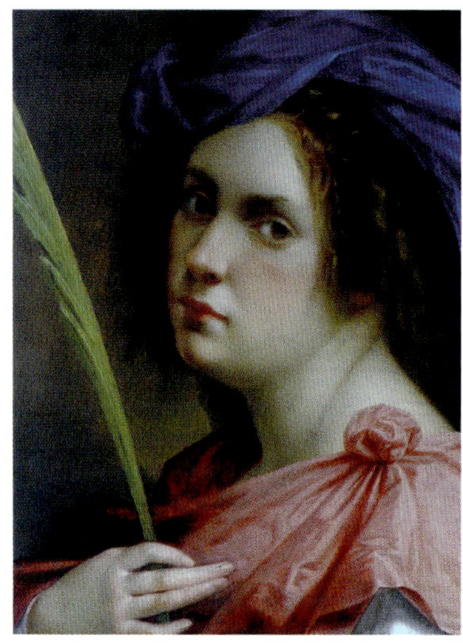

▲ **Artemisia Gentileschi**, *Self-Portrait as a Martyr*, c.1615, oil on panel, private collection

Bichitr
Active 1615–1640

A 17th-century Indian painter to the Mughal court, Bichitr was known for his portraits, as well as paintings commemorating important events. Based on his attire in a self-portrait that he included in one of his works, he seems to have been Hindu. He is known to have studied European art—he included European-style cherubs in some of his work—but otherwise very little is known about his life.

Artemisia Gentileschi
c.1593–c.1654

A 17th-century Italian painter often compared to Caravaggio, Gentileschi created dramatic works sometimes depicting violence. The daughter of painter Orazio Gentileschi, and the first female member of the Florentine Academy, she tended to paint images of women being victimized by men—or exacting revenge on men who had victimized them. Raped as a teenager, Gentileschi was tortured during the subsequent trial to test the honesty of her testimony. She has become renowned for her technical skill, particularly her use of chiaroscuro.

Pieter Saenredam
1597–1665

A 17th-century Dutch painter, Saenredam specialized in "architectural portraits"—essentially accurate images of real buildings, often churches. He painted interiors and exteriors, showing a strong understanding of linear perspective. He was the son of engraver Jan Saenredam, who died when Peter was still a boy.

Francisco de Zurbarán
1598–1664

A 17th-century Spanish painter of mainly religious works and portraits, de Zurbarán received numerous important commissions from Spanish religious orders in the 1630s, before his work fell out of fashion in the 1640s. A friend of Velázquez, de Zurbarán is best known for his naturalistic and idealistic portraits of saints or monks in prayer against simple backgrounds.

Gianlorenzo Bernini
1598–1680

The leading sculptor of the 17th century Baroque style, Bernini was said to have an unparalleled ability to create a realistic sense of movement and expression from stone. The son of sculptor Pietro Bernini, he showed talent from an early age and attracted many important patrons within the Catholic church, most notably Pope Urban VIII. Bernini worked as an architect as well as a sculptor.

Sir Anthony van Dyck
1599–1641

A Flemish painter, van Dyck is famous for his elegant portraits of Charles I and other members of the English aristocracy, which convey a strong sense of dignity and privilege. Van Dyck painted religious and mythological images, too. The son of a successful silk merchant, he served as an assistant to Peter Paul Rubens before becoming successful in his own right.

Diego Velázquez
1599–1660

The greatest Spanish painter of the 17th century, Velázquez is considered one of history's most accomplished portrait painters, lauded for his ability to convey character and realistic expression. Born the son of a lawyer in Seville, Velázquez spent much of his adult life as a close acquaintance and court painter to Philip IV of Spain. He painted the portraits of court dwarves as movingly as he did royalty. He also painted religious, mythological, and genre scenes.

Claude Lorrain
c.1600–1682

One of the most influential and popular landscape and seascape painters of the 17th century, the Lorraine-born, Rome-based artist created well-composed works that were poetic and harmonious, often with mythological or religious themes. Also known as Claude Gellée, Le Lorrain, or simply Claude, he was revered for his ability to capture light falling on landscapes.

Giovanna Garzoni
1600–1670

A 17th-century Italian painter of still lifes, Garzoni was known for her naturalistic images of plants, fruits, vegetables, and animals, usually painted in tempera on vellum. The Medici family were important patrons of her work for many years. Early in her career, she painted other subject matter, including religious and mythological works.

Philippe de Champaigne
1602–1674

A 17th-century painter of portraits and religious images, Philippe de Champaigne brought a measure of restraint and austerity to the Baroque style. Born in Brussels, he moved to Paris in 1621 and found considerable success, counting Louis XIII and Cardinal Richelieu among his patrons.

Michaelina Wautier
1604–1689

A 17th-century Flemish painter, Wautier was virtually unknown until the late 20th century, her work often misattributed to other artists such as her brother, Charles. She painted a wide range of subjects, including portraits; still lifes of flowers; and genre, mythological, religious, and historical scenes. She was born into a well-connected family, and Archduke Leopold Wilhelm of Austria was her patron.

Rembrandt van Rijn

1606–1669

The leading figure of Dutch art in the 17th century, Rembrandt painted perceptive, expressive, naturalistic portraits, often of himself—he left more than 70 self-portraits. Both a painter and printmaker, Rembrandt was a versatile, prolific artist and painted and etched Biblical, historical, and mythological scenes as well as landscapes. Born the son of a successful Leiden miller, Rembrandt settled in Amsterdam, where he endured financial struggles despite his fame.

Juan de Pareja

c.1608–1670

A Spanish-born painter of at least partially African ancestry, de Pareja was enslaved in the studio of artist Diego Velázquez before gaining freedom and achieving his own artistic success. One story, probably apocryphal, holds that Philip IV insisted that de Pareja be freed after seeing his skill as an artist. De Pareja painted mainly religious and genre scenes. He was the subject of a famous portrait by Velázquez.

Judith Leyster

1609–1660

A 17th-century Dutch painter of genre scenes as well as portraits and still lifes, Leyster may have studied under Frans Hals, and her work is often compared to his. Like those of Hals, her paintings are noted for their bold, spontaneous brushstrokes. Born the daughter of a brewer, she married artist Jan Miense Molenaer.

Salvator Rosa

1615–1673

A 17th-century Italian Baroque painter, engraver, poet, actor, satirist, and musician, the versatile Rosa created a wide range of unconventional works. Born in Naples, he is remembered for his highly dramatic landscapes, battle scenes, and images portraying witchcraft. A flamboyant figure, his satirical efforts sometimes earned him enemies.

Carel Fabritius

1622–1654

Often called Rembrandt's most talented student, Fabritius was an innovative 17th-century Dutch painter whose works are noted for their distinctive use of lighting. His paintings include historical images, portraits, still lifes, and cityscapes—a variety that's all the more impressive considering that only around a dozen of Fabritius's works survive. He died at the age of just 32, a victim of a gunpowder warehouse explosion that destroyed much of Delft.

Jan Steen

c.1625–1679

A 17th-century Dutch painter, Steen is particularly known for his witty genre scenes, often set in taverns—he was a tavern owner himself and the son of a brewer. His paintings often conveyed a moral message about drunkenness or other vices. The prolific Steen also painted portraits and historical and mythological scenes, but he experienced financial struggles throughout his career.

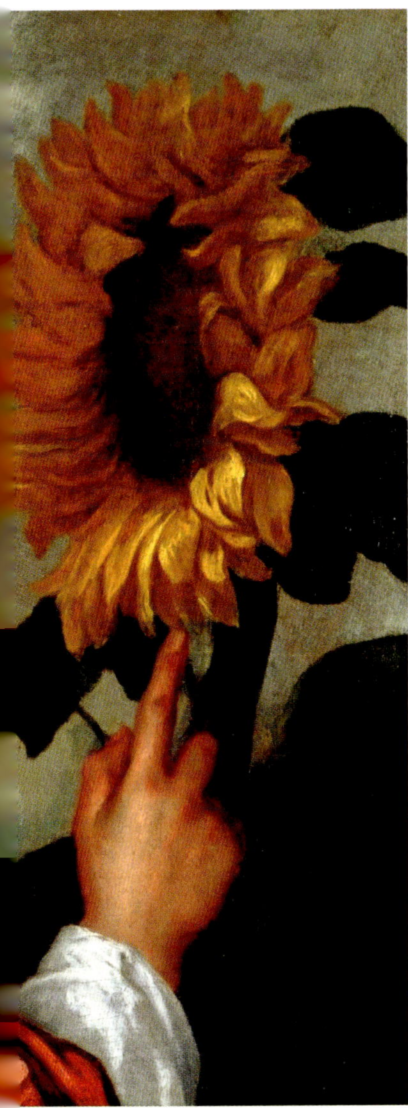

◀ **Sir Anthony van Dyck**, *Self-Portrait with a Sunflower*, c.1632-1633, oil on canvas, private collection

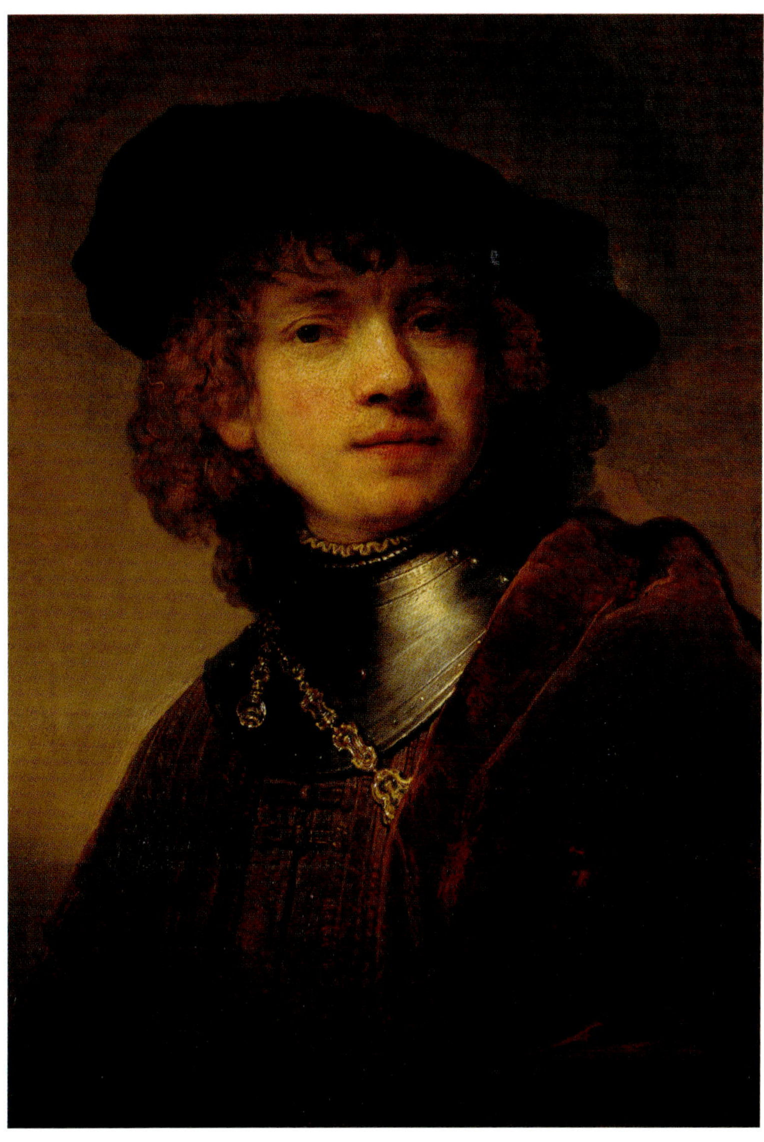

▲ **Rembrandt van Rijn**, *Self-Portrait as a Young Man*, c.1623, oil on panel, Uffizi, Florence, Italy

Jacob van Ruisdael

1628–1682

An important 17th-century Dutch landscape painter, the prolific van Ruisdael's images are naturalistic in style, but they often display a melancholic or even tragic tone. The nephew of landscape painter Salomon van Ruysdael—the men differed in how they spelled the family name—Jacob van Ruisdael was a surgeon as well as a prolific painter.

Josefa de Óbidos

1630–1684

The most prominent female artist in 17th-century Portugal, Spanish-born Óbidos is best remembered for her Baroque still lifes, many of them featuring food, flowers, or fruit. She also painted religious works and portraits, including altarpieces for numerous Portuguese churches. The daughter of a painter, Óbidos never married and she achieved financial independence through her art.

Maria van Oosterwijck

1630–1693

A 17th-century Dutch painter of still lifes—usually flowers—van Oosterwijck was highly regarded in her day, and her impressive list of patrons included Louis XIV of France and Holy Roman Emperor Leopold I. Many of her still lifes feature elements that have a symbolic meaning, often religious in nature.

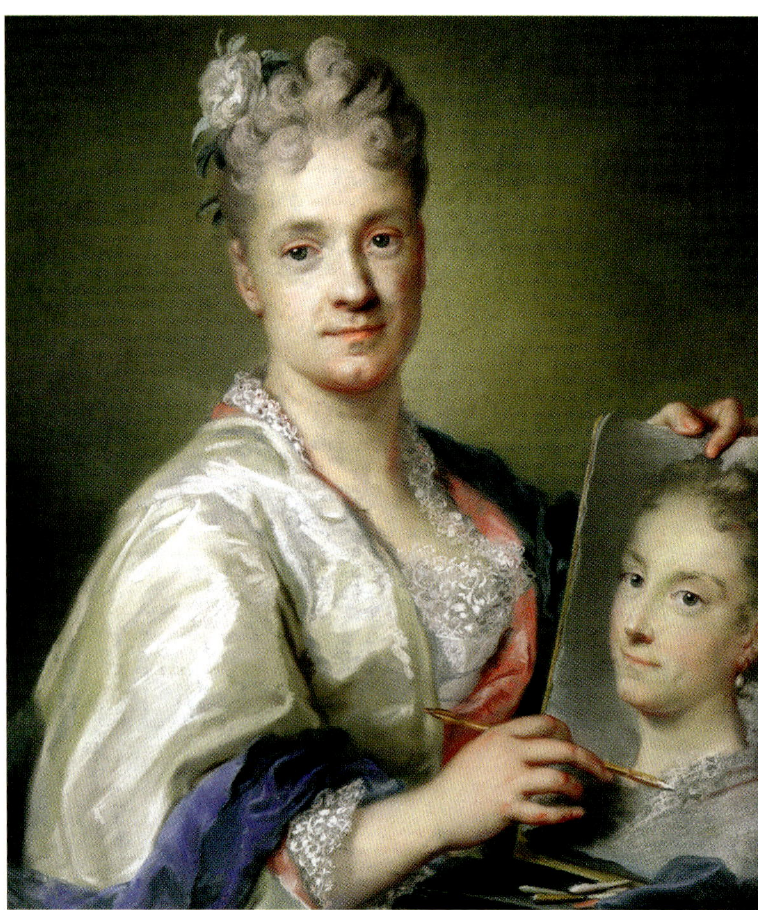

▲ **Rosalba Carriera**, *Self-Portrait Holding a Portrait of Her Sister*, 1715, pastel on paper, Uffizi, Florence, Italy

Wang Hui

1632–1717

The leading painter of late-17th century China, Wang came from a well-established lineage of painters, and his landscapes looked back to earlier traditions of Chinese art. Scholarly opinion is divided on the degree to which Wang brought new ideas to the traditional artistic styles he adopted, but he is today the best known of the Chinese painters collectively referred to as the "Four Wangs."

Johannes Vermeer

1632–1675

Now ranked among history's greatest Dutch artists for his luminous interior scenes of ordinary 17th-century life, Vermeer was little known outside Delft and Amsterdam until the late 19th century. The son of a successful weaver and art dealer, Vermeer sold his work to local collectors, but left fewer than 40 paintings in total and died in debt. He also painted religious and mythological scenes early in his career.

Elisabetta Sirani

1638–1665

A 17th-century Bolognese painter, Sirani mainly produced religious, mythological, and allegorical pieces. The daughter of painter Giovanni Sirani, she took over the family workshop after her father was incapacitated (two of her sisters were also artists). Reported to be an extremely fast painter, Sirani produced well over 100 paintings despite the fact that she died at the age of just 27.

Ogata Kōrin

1658–1716

A leading artist during Japan's Tokugawa period (1603–1867), Ogata painted vibrant images of natural subjects on folding screens. He also produced lacquerwork and textile designs, and created designs for ceramics crafted by his brother, Ogata Kenzan, a highly regarded potter. Born into a successful family, Ogata Kōrin pursued professional art in earnest relatively late in his life, after squandering a sizable inheritance.

Hyacinthe Rigaud

1659–1743

Ranked alongside Nicolas de Largillière as the leading French portrait painter of the Baroque era, Rigaud's formal paintings of French aristocracy—most notably Louis XIV—are notable for the exacting attention he paid to his sitters' expensive garments and surroundings, in order to emphasize their wealth and position. His sitters' posture and facial expressions also tend to convey their power rather than their personality.

Rachel Ruysch

1664–1750

A Dutch painter of flowers and other still lifes, Ruysch had a long and successful artistic career, including an eight-year stint as court painter to the Elector Palatine of Bavaria. The daughter of an esteemed botanist—which might help explain her choice of subject matter—she managed to achieve artistic success while also raising a large family.

Rosalba Carriera

1675–1757

A Venetian pastel artist best known for her portraits, Carriera helped elevate pastels as a medium. She was probably self-taught and created portraits of foreign visitors to Venice, including King Louis XV of France and Frederick-Augustus II, the Elector of Saxony. She went on to fill a room of the latter's palace in Dresden with more than 100 of her works. Her career ended when she lost her sight in the late 1740s.

Jeong Seon

1676–1759

A Korean landscape painter, Jeong created realistic "true view" landscapes based on actual mountains and other settings in Korea, rather than painting imaginary or idealized locations as was common at the time. He is known for his bold brushstrokes. Born into a poor family, he held a series of civil service positions while pursuing his interests as an artist.

Jean-Antoine Watteau

1684–1721

One of the most important French artists of the early 18th century, Watteau is credited with helping create the ornamental, sensuous Rococo style. Many of his paintings depict aristocratic people wearing extravagant clothing in lush outdoor settings, but despite the apparent frivolity of his images there is sometimes an undercurrent of melancholy—perhaps due to Watteau's own struggle with tuberculosis, from which he died at the age of just 36.

Giulia Lama

c.1685–c.1747

Lama was a Venetian painter of religious and historical scenes and portraits, but very little is known about her life and career. She is known to have painted highly regarded altarpieces for three Venetian churches, and she is thought to be among the first female artists to paint and draw female and male nudes. Many of Lama's paintings were misattributed to other artists. She also wrote poetry.

Jin Nong

1687–c.1764

An acclaimed Chinese painter, Jin depicted traditional subjects, such as bamboo, plum blossom, and other flowers, although he also painted self-portraits, horses, and Buddhist images. Also a successful poet and calligrapher (he created the "lacquer calligraphy" style), he pursued painting seriously relatively late in life. He is the best remembered of a group of artists known as the "eight eccentrics of Yangzhou."

Miguel Cabrera

1695–1768

A highly acclaimed artist in 18th-century Mexico, Cabrera was in great demand as a painter of Christian images, and completed many commissions for churches and religious leaders. He also painted portraits and "casta paintings"—images that aimed to trace the complex racial mixing of the population. Cabrera himself reportedly was of mixed Spanish and Indigenous heritage.

Giambattista Tiepolo

1696–1770

A Venetian painter, Tiepolo is known for grand, airy, exquisitely executed frescoes and other works featuring religious, historical, or mythological scenes. By the mid-18th century, he was in great demand across Europe. Also a skilled draftsman and etcher, he was strongly influenced by the Later Renaissance style—which had ended two centuries earlier.

William Hogarth
1697–1764
The most important English artist of his time, Hogarth was an engraver as well as a painter. He produced portraits and other images, but achieved fame and financial success by selling prints of his satirical, moralizing images that made fun of human follies and vanities. "The Harlot's Progress" and "The Rake's Progress"—two extremely popular series of images that told a story—are often cited as forerunners of the modern comic strip. Hogarth also played an important role in the passage of England's 1735 Engraving Copyright Act.

Canaletto
1697–1768
A popular Venetian "view painter," Canaletto created images of Venice's canals, buildings, and other attractions, mainly for tourists. He was also skilled at drawing and etching. Extremely popular with aristocratic English travelers, Canaletto spent a decade of his career painting in England. His real name was Giovanni Canal; he was born the son of Bernardo Canal, a painter of theatrical scenery.

Jean-Siméon Chardin
1699–1779
A leading French painter of small still lifes and genre scenes, Chardin is known for the naturalism and intimacy of his work and the simplicity of his compositions.

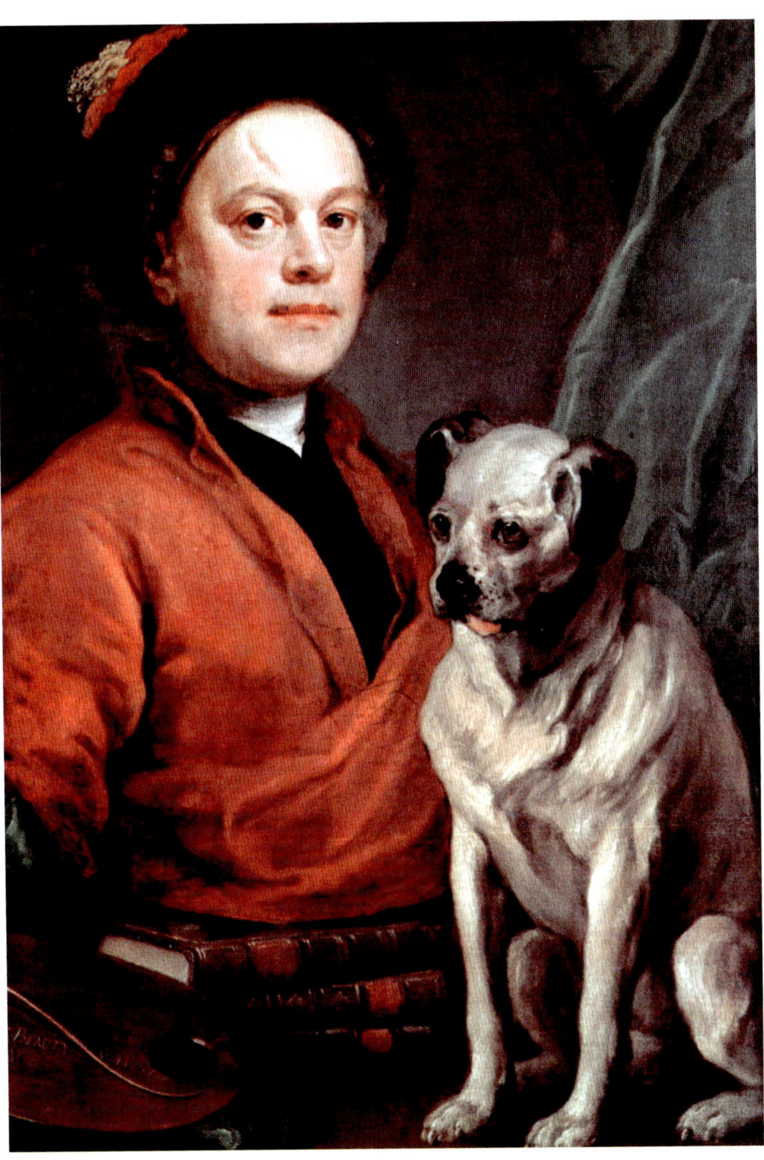
▲ **William Hogarth**, self-portrait entitled *The Painter and His Pug*, 1745, oil on canvas, Tate Britain, London, UK

Popular and successful for most of his career—Louis XV was an important patron—his style fell out of favor late in his life, when he also suffered from eye problems. In his later years, he mainly made pastel portraits.

Mary Delany
1700–1788
An 18th-century British artist, Delany is known for the botanically accurate images of plants that she created through decoupage, cutting and attaching pieces of colored paper to a background. Her artistic career did not begin until she was in her seventies and twice widowed, but the engaging and well-connected Delany produced nearly 1,000 "paper mosaiks," as she called them, before failing eyesight ended her artistic career.

Manaku
c.1700–1760
An Indian painter, Manaku played a pivotal role in the creation of the Pahari School of miniature painting and manuscript illustration that thrived for centuries in the foothills of the Himalayan Mountains. Manaku belonged to a family of artists—he shared an artistic style with his father, Pandit Seu, and his brother and sons were also notable artists.

Pietro Longhi
1702–1785
A Venetian painter, Longhi is known primarily for his small interior scenes of upper- and middle-class life in the republic. His work shows careful observation, subtle wit, and a modest dose of social commentary. The son of a silversmith, Longhi painted at least one large-scale historical scene early in his career, but it was not well received.

François Boucher
1703–1770
The quintessential Rococo artist, Boucher painted lush, lavish, but largely frivolous images that would help define 18th-century French art. Best known for his extravagant mythological scenes, the prolific and popular Boucher also painted portraits, landscapes, and other works, and designed tapestries and porcelain. Louis XV and his mistress Madame de Pompadour were patrons.

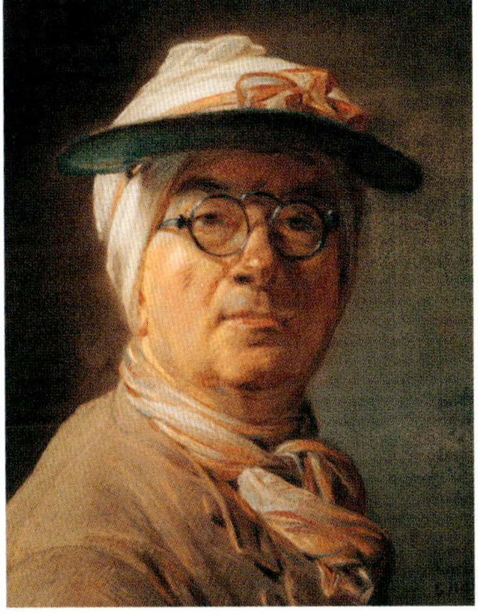
▲ **Jean-Siméon Chardin**, *Self-Portrait with a Visor*, c.1776, pastel on blue laid paper, mounted on canvas, Art Institute of Chicago, US

Sir Joshua Reynolds
1723–1792
A leading English portrait artist, Reynolds was extremely well regarded in his day and elected the first president of the Royal Academy when it was founded in 1768. The son of a headmaster, Reynolds was intellectual by nature—Samuel Johnson and Edmund Burke were among his friends—and often included references to classical mythology and sculpture in his portraits. He promoted the grand manner style of history painting.

George Stubbs
1724–1806
This English artist is best known for his paintings of horses—often images of racehorses painted as a commission from their aristocratic owners. The works were wonderfully accurate as they were rooted in Stubbs' extensive study of horse anatomy. He also painted images of other animals, scenes of peasant life, portraits, and historical works.

Thomas Gainsborough
1727–1788
An important and imaginative English painter, Gainsborough was one of the most popular and talented portrait painters of his era, rivaled only by Reynolds. He disliked working with aristocratic sitters, however, and greatly preferred painting landscapes, at which he also excelled. Gainsborough was a founding member of the Royal Academy.

Jean-Honoré Fragonard

1732–1806

A French painter in the lavish Rococo style, Fragonard is best known for the lighthearted, titillating, and sometimes outright erotic images he painted for private clients. He first found artistic success as a painter of large works on traditional historical themes, before abandoning that mainstream artistic path. Madame du Barry, mistress of Louis XV, was an important patron. Fragonard's art fell out of fashion following the French Revolution.

Joseph Wright

1734–1797

An 18th-century English painter, Wright was known for his innovative and dramatic use of artificial lighting—many of his scenes were set at night, lit by candles or the glow of a furnace. Wright often painted portraits, but his works also include landscapes and images related to industry, such as numerous paintings of forges and blacksmith's shops.

Johan Zoffany

1733–1810

A German-born painter with an adventurous streak, Zoffany found success in England painting portraits, theatrical scenes, and informal group portraits known as "conversation pieces." He agreed to join Captain Cook's second expedition as the onboard artist, but when that failed, he accepted a commission from Britain's Queen Charlotte to travel to Florence and paint the *Tribuna of the Uffizi*. Zoffany made the commission last for most of the 1770s and eventually delivered a controversial painting, damaging his relationship with the English royal family, his most important patrons. Zoffany later lived and worked in India.

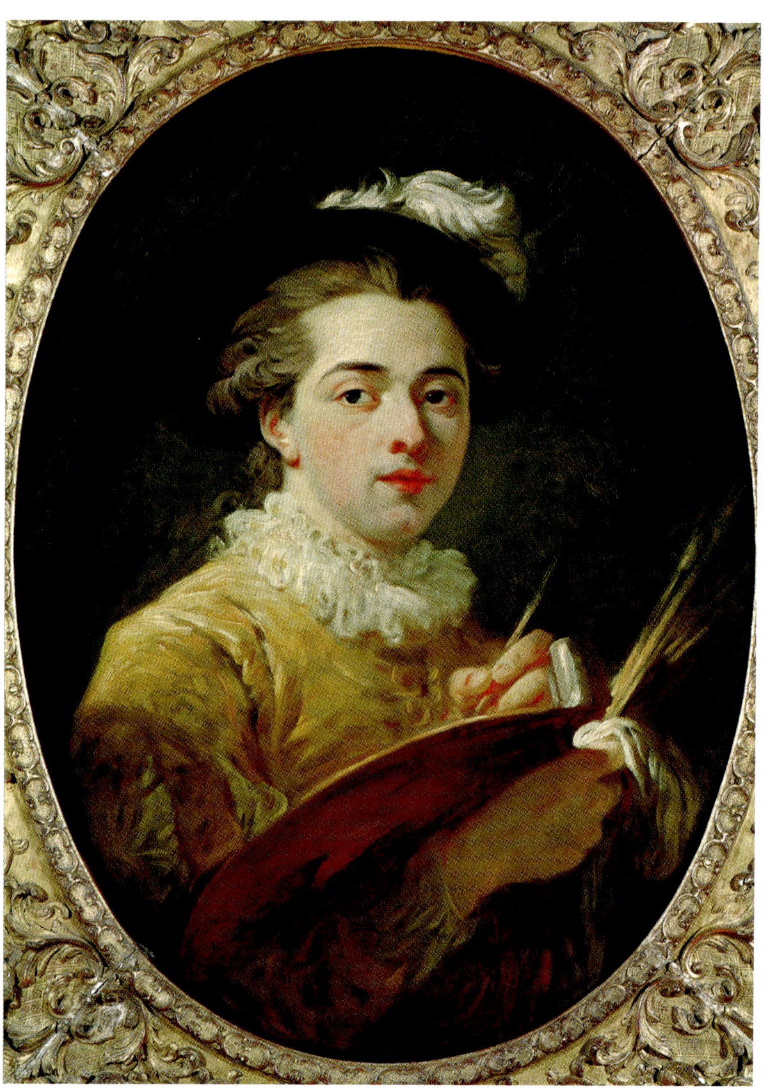

▲ **Jean-Honoré Fragonard**, *Self-Portrait with Palette* (or *Self-Portrait in a Renaissance Costume*), c. 1760-1770, oil on canvas, Musée Fragonard, Grasse, France

John Singleton Copley

1738–1815

The leading artist of colonial America, the Boston-based Copley was a popular, successful, and largely self-taught portrait painter. He left America in 1774, concerned about the coming war, never to return. After a brief stay in Italy, he settled with his family in London, where he was well received as a painter of large historical images.

Benjamin West

1738–1820

An American-born painter who worked mainly in London, West is remembered for his historical paintings—most notably, *The Death of General Wolfe*. One of the first American-born artists to achieve international acclaim, West was a founder of the Royal Academy and for many years the official history painter to King George III. He managed to remain on good terms with the king despite expressing loyalty to the American revolutionaries.

Angelica Kauffman

1741–1807

A Swiss-born artist who worked mainly in London and Italy, Kauffman was a highly regarded and successful painter of portraits and historical images. She painted some of the most powerful people of her time, while many of her history paintings focused on female subjects from classical history and mythology. Kauffman was one of only two women to be founding members of the Royal Academy in London.

Henry Fuseli

1741–1825

A Swiss-born artist who worked mainly in England, Fuseli is known for painting intense, imaginative, emotional scenes rich in drama and, sometimes, eroticism and fantasy. He painted many scenes based on the works of William Shakespeare. Born the son of Johann Caspar Fuseli, a portrait and landscape painter, he was ordained as a minister before following his father in an artistic career. He spent much of his later life as a professor of painting at London's Royal Academy.

Jean-Antoine Houdon

1741–1828

An important French sculptor, Houdon is best remembered for his portrait busts, including well-received images of famous subjects, such as philosophers Denis Diderot and Voltaire, and American statesman Benjamin Franklin. His works suggest the classical style of ancient Greek and Roman statuary. Houdon survived the French Revolution, but his career went into decline after 1800.

Joseph-Benoît Suvée

1743–1807

A Bruges-born painter known for his historical, mythological, and religious scenes as well as portraits, Suvée worked in the restrained French Neoclassical style. He was imprisoned during the French Revolution but survived and, in 1801, became director of the French Academy in Rome, where he served until his death.

Kim Hong-do

c. 1745–c. 1806

One of the most famous Korean artists, Kim painted images of ordinary life during the Joseon era. He worked in a simple style consisting largely of ink drawing with minimal colors and backgrounds, yet his scenes reveal character, wit, and social commentary, offering insight into the time and place. Kim painted landscapes, portraits, and natural and religious subjects as well.

Francisco de Goya

1746–1828

The leading Spanish artist of his era, Goya was initially known for his portraits—he was named painter to the king by Charles III in 1786, then court painter by Charles IV in 1789. Goya's subjects diversified following a 1793 illness that left him deaf. He ventured into social commentary, and painted modern historical scenes related to the violence of Napoleon's occupation of Spain, as well as some dark and disturbing images.

Jacques-Louis David

1748–1825

David was the leading painter of the French Neoclassical style, which rejected the decorative Rococo style in favor of a return

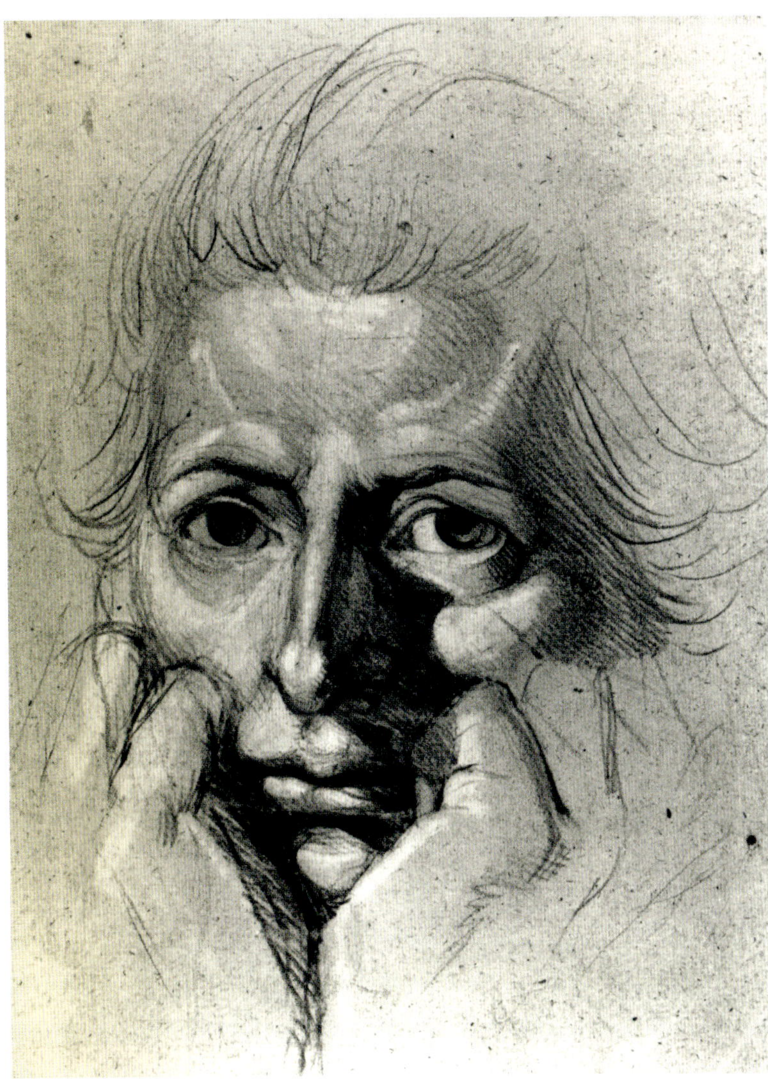

▲ **Henry Fuseli**, *Self-Portrait*, 1780s, black and white chalk on paper, V&A, London, UK

to the artistic ideals of ancient Greece and Rome. David wielded great influence over French art following the French Revolution, thanks to his political appointments and connections. His austere historical, mythological, and allegorical paintings embodied the period.

Adélaïde Labille-Guiard

1749–1803

A French artist known for her informal portraits, Labille-Guiard became a noted art teacher of female students. She specialized in pastel miniatures early in her career, but later shifted toward larger paintings, often in oil paint. In 1787, Labille-Guiard was named official painter to the maiden aunts of Louis XVI. Some of her works were destroyed during the French Revolution, even though she reportedly had republican sentiments herself.

Kitagawa Utamaro

1753–1806

A Japanese printmaker and painter during the Edo period, Utamaro is considered the leading artist of *ukiyo-e*, an affordable style of woodblock print. He was best known for his woodblock prints of attractive women, including some that now would be classified as erotica. In 1804, he was arrested for violating strict new censorship laws, an event that seems to have damaged his health and effectively ended his career.

Marie-Victoire Lemoine

1754–1820

A French painter of genre scenes, miniatures, and portraits, Lemoine excelled above all at portraits of women, including aristocrats such as Princess de Lamballe and Mademoiselle de Chartres. Born into a middle-class family, two of her sisters painted in a similar style. In 1796, post-Revolutionary reforms allowed her to exhibit her work at the prestigious Paris Salon for the first time.

Elisabeth Vigée Le Brun

1755–1842

A prominent and prolific French portrait artist best known for her many images of Queen Marie Antoinette, Vigée Le Brun was one of the most celebrated and successful female artists in Europe during the late 18th and early 19th centuries. The daughter of artist Louis Vigée, she was a prodigy, and was painting professionally by the age of 15. Forced to flee revolutionary France in 1789, fearing that her association with the queen put her in danger, Vigée Le Brun returned to Paris permanently in 1805.

Jean-Baptiste Frédéric Desmarais

1756–1813

A French Neoclassical painter who worked mainly in Italy, Desmarais is known for his historical works that often featured gory content, as well as for his male nudes. He probably settled in Italy to avoid the tumult of the French Revolution, and found success there as a painter and art teacher.

Sir Henry Raeburn

1756–1823

The leading Scottish portrait painter of his era, Raeburn captured not only the naturalistic appearance of his usually prominent and wealthy sitters but also something of their character. Apprenticed to a goldsmith in his youth, Raeburn was a confident and largely self-taught painter, working directly on canvas with no preliminary sketches or underdrawing. He was the first Scottish painter to be knighted.

Antonio Canova

1757–1822

The leading Neoclassical sculptor, the Italian Canova was lionized in his day, credited with reviving the fading art of sculpting, and celebrated for his ability to make marble appear lifelike. His wide-ranging work included mythological and religious subjects as well as portraits, and his prominent commissions included funerary monuments for popes Clement XIII and Clement XIV and a famed bust of Napoleon. Pope Pius VII appointed Canova Inspector General of Antiquities and Fine Arts of the Papal States.

Hokusai

1760–1849

An influential Japanese artist during the Edo period, Hokusai created some tremendously famous *ukiyo-e* woodblock prints during his long and prolific career. His prints and paintings covered a wide range of subjects, but images from his series of landscape and seascape prints collectively known as "Thirty-Six Views of Mount Fuji" have become icons of Japanese art.

Caspar David Friedrich

1774–1840

The preeminent German Romantic landscape and seascape painter of his era, Friedrich specialized in moody, atmospheric nature scenes set in fog or at night, dawn, or dusk. When Friedrich included figures in his works, they often faced away from the viewer. While his work is generally not overtly religious, it often contains symbolic content related to the artist's Christian faith.

Tōshūsai Sharaku

Active 1794–1795

A Japanese *ukiyo-e* woodblock printmaker, Tōshūsai Sharaku was known for his intense, probably satirical prints of kabuki actors. The artist's actual identity is uncertain—some suspect he may have been an actor himself. All of his known works were produced within a two-year period (1794–1795); they were not highly regarded in Japan at the time.

Joseph Mallord William Turner

1775–1851

An important British painter of landscapes and seascapes, Turner is famous for his expressive and atmospheric—if not always completely naturalistic—use of color and light. His willingness to set aside naturalism helped set the stage for the abstract artists who followed. The son of a barber, Turner's artistic career was financially successful although not well received by all critics; his status as one of England's greatest artists only evolved after his death.

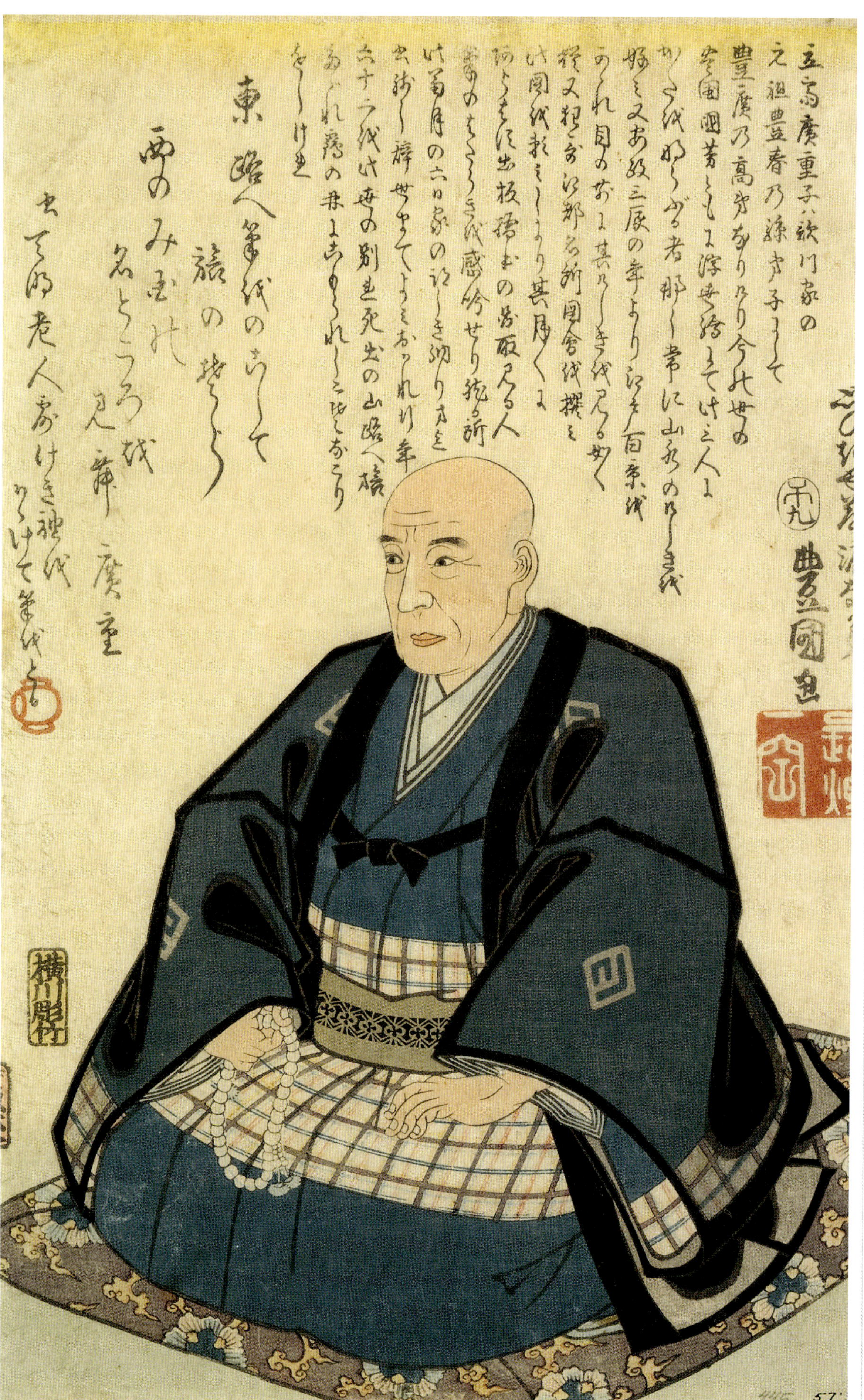

John Constable

1776–1837

A leading British landscape painter, Constable created naturalistic images of the countryside northeast of London—he painted the same rural region so often that it eventually became known as "Constable country." The son of a successful miller and corn merchant, he only achieved modest acclaim during his life, but is now often ranked alongside Turner as one of the most important English landscape artists of his time.

Jean-Auguste Dominique Ingres

1780–1867

A leading 19th-century French Neoclassical painter, he painted portraits, nudes, and historical, mythological, and religious images with a precise, unromantic style. However, Ingres's work was controversial as he often distorted the human form in unnatural ways, such as extending the spine of female nudes. He was director of the French Academy in Rome.

John James Audubon

1785–1851

A largely self-taught artist, Audubon is remembered for *The Birds of America*, an 1838 multi-volume work that contained 435 engravings of 490 species of birds. The visually stunning images were detailed, engaging, and largely accurate, although ornithologists have noted some scientific errors. Born the illegitimate son of a French sea captain in what is now Haiti, Audubon was raised in France but went to America in 1803, and worked in varied fields, including taxidermy.

Utagawa Kunisada

1786–1865

A popular and astoundingly prolific maker of *ukiyo-e* woodblock prints, Kunisada is best known for his portraits of actors and attractive women, although he created prints on a wide range of other subjects, as well as paintings. A Japanese artist in the late Edo period, his prints influenced several European Post-Impressionist artists, including van Gogh and Gauguin.

◀ ***Memorial Portrait of Utagawa Hiroshige***, Utagawa Hiroshige, 1858, ink and color on paper (woodblock print), San Diego Museum of Arts, US

John Martin
1789–1854
A British painter, Martin painted bombastic, apocalyptic scenes, many of them taken straight from the Bible. Martin's works were very popular in their day and exhibited on successful tours—they have been compared to modern Hollywood disaster blockbusters. Late in life, Martin pursued an ultimately unsuccessful plan to improve London's water and sewer system.

Théodore Géricault
1791–1824
A leading French Romantic painter, and a skilled lithographer and sculptor, Géricault is best remembered for *The Raft of the Medusa*, a masterpiece of early 19th-century social commentary, but he painted a wide range of images, including portraits. One of his favorite subjects was horses, which he loved to ride. Born into a wealthy family, he did not need to worry about earning a living from his art. Géricault died young, the result of illness and several serious riding accidents.

George Catlin
1796–1872
An 18th-century American artist, writer, and explorer, Catlin traveled the American West in the 1830s, painting and drawing portraits and scenes of Indigenous peoples, images that served as illustrations in his various books about them. Catlin's efforts were not financially successful at the time, but later came to be seen as an important record of Indigenous American society. He was a portrait painter in Philadelphia before venturing West.

Jean-Baptiste-Camille Corot
1796–1875
A French landscape and portrait painter, Corot initially produced paintings in the classical landscape tradition that were rich in color. Those painted later in his career were more lyrical, softer, hazier, and often dominated by silvery green tones. Corot's landscapes were so popular that he is said to be one of the 19th-century artists most often faked by forgers. His portraits were often of women and tend to receive fewer plaudits than his landscapes.

Asher Brown Durand
1796–1886
A 19th-century American artist, Durand, together with his friend Thomas Cole, was a leading figure in the loosely affiliated group of US romantic landscape painters who would come to be known as the Hudson River School. Durand was a successful engraver and portrait painter before turning to landscapes, and his writings about art—the "Letters on Landscape Painting"—were influential.

Paul Delaroche
1797–1856
An early 19th-century French painter who was tremendously popular in his day, Delaroche is known for creating large, highly detailed, and often highly dramatic historical scenes. He also painted portraits and religious images. A well-regarded teacher, his students included Jean-François Millet and Jean-Léon Gérôme.

Utagawa Hiroshige
1797–1858
A Japanese *ukiyo-e* woodblock print artist during the late Edo period, and often cited as a source of inspiration for the Impressionists, Hiroshige is best known for his landscapes. He was a prolific artist who also produced prints of birds, flowers, and, early in his career, figures including girls and samurai. He died during a cholera epidemic.

Eugène Delacroix
1798–1863
A leading French Romantic painter, Delacroix employed a bold style and rich colors, and often chose dramatic subject matter. He influenced generations of subsequent artists; his use of color, for example, can be seen in the work of the Impressionists. A prolific artist, Delacroix painted works on historical, mythological, literary, and contemporary themes. He was born the son of a diplomat, though rumors held that he was the illegitimate son of the French statesman Charles de Talleyrand.

Thomas Cole
1801–1848
An important 19th-century American landscape painter, the British-born Cole is considered the founder of the Hudson River School, a loose collection of landscape artists who painted images that gloried in the grandeur of the American wilderness. Some Cole landscapes not only captured the United States' natural beauty but also reflected on the growth of the American nation. Cole also painted religious images, but those are not regarded as favorably.

Sir Edwin Landseer
1802–1873
A British artist, Landseer is remembered for his paintings and sculptures of animals. He also painted the occasional portrait of a person—notably Queen Victoria, who was a great fan of his work. Tremendously popular in his day, Landseer's animal works display a knowledge of anatomy, although many were later criticized as overly sentimental. He was primarily a painter, but he also created the bronze lions that guard the base of Nelson's Column in London's Trafalgar Square.

Honoré Daumier
1808–1879
An important French caricaturist and social satirist, Daumier produced prints and paintings that lampooned politicians, the bourgeoisie, and other classes of French society. His lithographs have been the source of his greatest fame, but he also created notable naturalistic paintings, as well as sculptures. He endured failing eyesight and financial challenges late in his life.

George Caleb Bingham
1811–1879
An American painter based in Missouri, Bingham was noted for his images of the American frontier and, especially, life on and around the Missouri River. A largely self-taught artist, Bingham also painted portraits of prominent local residents. He held political posts in Missouri, and late in life taught art at the University of Missouri.

Jean-François Millet
1814–1875
A 19th-century French painter associated with the Barbizon School, Millet painted portraits, landscapes, and, most notably, dignified images of French peasants—he was born into a farming family. His sympathetic images of peasants were viewed as politically subversive in some quarters, and while respected in the art community, he was not financially successful until relatively late in his career.

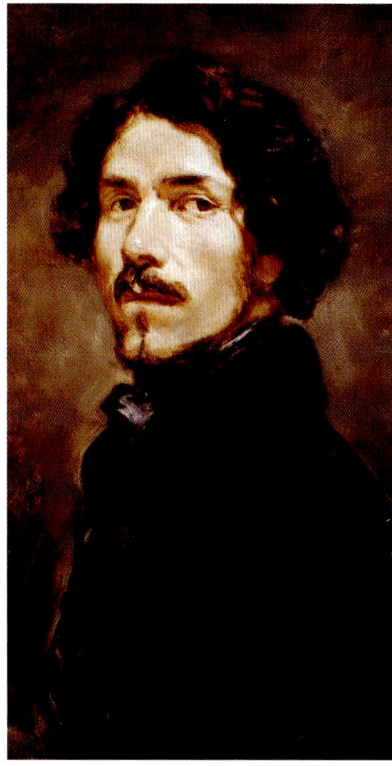

▲ **Eugène Delacroix**, *Self-Portrait*, 1860, oil on canvas, Uffizi, Florence, Italy

Thomas Couture
1815–1879
A 19th-century French painter of portraits and historical and genre scenes, Couture is best remembered for *The Romans of the Decadence*, an orgy scene that was the hit of the Paris Salon of 1847. He was a highly regarded art teacher, and his bold use of tonal contrast probably influenced his most successful student, Édouard Manet.

Gustave Courbet
1819–1877
An important French painter, Courbet rejected Romanticism and instead created bold images, many offering an unromantic look at ordinary French people. He also painted landscapes, seascapes, and female nudes. Courbet developed the term Realism to reflect the need to paint lived and witnessed experiences. Anti-authoritarian and occasionally radical, Courbet was forced out of France for his role in the destruction of the Vendôme Column, a Napoleonic symbol. He died in exile in Switzerland.

Sosa Adede

19th century

A sculptor for the court of Dahomey in West Africa, Sosa Adede (sometimes spelled Sossa Dede) was descended from King Agoli-Agbo (r. 1789–1797). He worked for the kings Guezo, Glele, and Behanzin in the 19th century. His best known works are the monumental power figures, or *bocio*, representing Glele and Behanzin, and his sculpted palace doors. Adede is also remembered as a singer.

Martin Johnson Heade

1819–1904

A 19th-century American painter of landscapes and seascapes, Heade is among the leading artists of the Luminist art style. This emphasized dramatic natural lighting, and he was especially noted for his ability to capture the sense of foreboding in the sky immediately before the onset of a storm. Heade also painted well-regarded images of hummingbirds and orchids. He did not achieve substantial fame during his career and was largely forgotten until his work was rediscovered in the 1940s.

Robert Duncanson

1821–1872

A prominent 19th-century American landscape painter, Duncanson was the first Black artist to achieve international fame. A painter of both straightforward landscapes and landscapes linked to historical or literary themes, he was well received in Canada, Britain, and continental Europe—the king of Sweden bought one of his most important pieces. Duncanson developed dementia and died in 1872, just as his particular style of landscape painting was fading from popularity.

Rosa Bonheur

1822–1899

The most successful French female artist of the 19th century, Bonheur is best known for her detailed and naturalistic paintings and sculptures of animals, which she observed at animal markets. She trained with her painter father and began exhibiting at the Paris Salon at the age of 19. She was the first woman artist to be awarded the Legion of Honor.

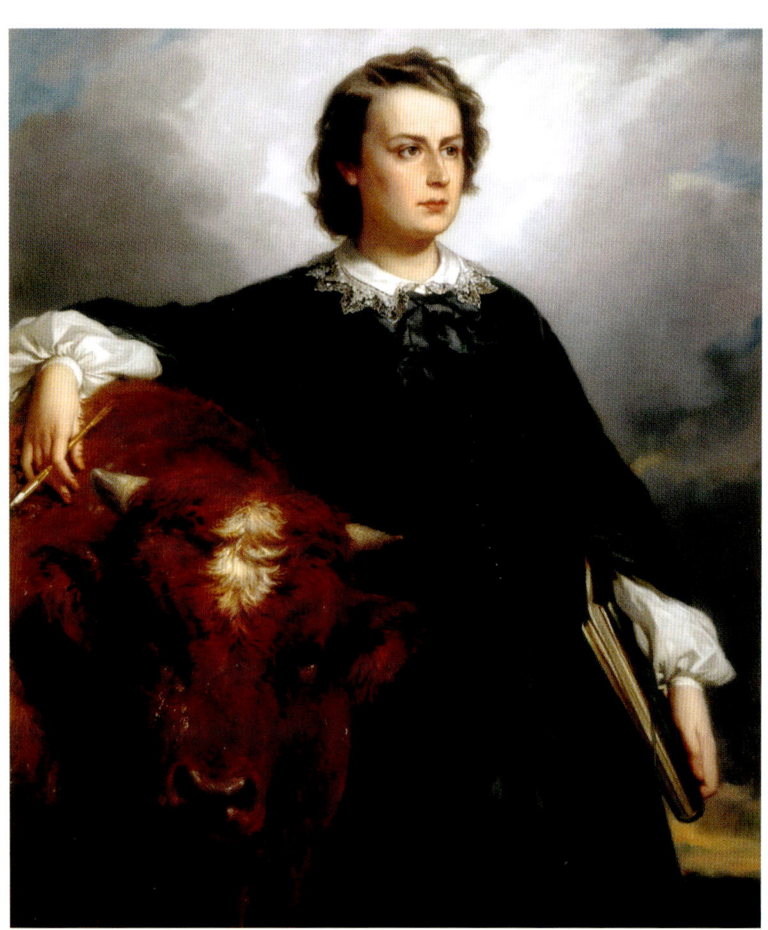

▲ ***Portrait of Rosa Bonheur***, Édouard Louis Dubufe, 1857, oil on canvas, Musée de l'histoire de France, Versailles, France

Lilly Martin Spencer

1822–1902

American artist Lilly Martin Spencer is best known for her upbeat, sentimental paintings of domestic life. She also produced portraits, still lifes, and other works. Born in England, she moved to the US with her family while she was a child. Spencer's husband was supportive of her career and took charge of raising their family, leaving her to paint.

Susan Torrey Merritt

1826–1879

A 19th-century American amateur folk artist, Merritt is remembered for the image she created of an 1845 picnic held in support of the abolitionist cause in Weymouth Landing, Massachusetts. This innovative work is technically a collage—she painted the figures individually, then pasted them onto the watercolor background.

Gustave Moreau

1826–1898

A 19th-century French painter, Moreau was a central figure in the Symbolist movement, which used symbolism to suggest emotions or ideas and rejected the naturalistic depiction of scenes. The prolific Moreau's mythological and religious paintings were influenced by his interest in Byzantine and Italian Renaissance art, yet they are also sensuous, and sometimes described as erotic or decadent. Later in his career, Moreau taught at the École des Beaux-Arts in Paris, where his students included Henri Matisse.

Frederic Edwin Church

1826–1900

A leading American landscape painter, Church created grand, stunning, dramatic images that extolled the glory of God's creation. He is associated with the Hudson River School, although he painted images of South American landscapes as well as the US wilderness. Church was popular in the 1850s and 1860s, but by the final decades of his life, the Hudson River School style had declined in popularity and arthritis limited his ability to paint.

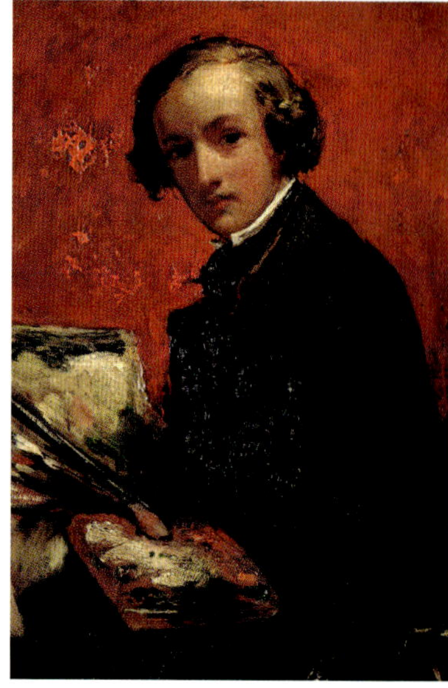

▲ **Sir John Everett Millais**, *Self-Portrait*, 1847, oil on board, Walker Art Gallery, Liverpool, UK

Dante Gabriel Rossetti

1828–1882

A 19th-century poet and painter, Rossetti was one of the founders of the Pre-Raphaelite Brotherhood, a group of artists who hoped to revive the nonacademic art styles that prevailed before the 16th century and the time of Raphael. He worked in watercolors and oils, and is best known for his paintings of beautiful women, although he also painted romantic medieval subjects. Rossetti struggled with drug addiction following the death of his wife, Elizabeth Siddal, in 1862.

Sir John Everett Millais

1829–1896

A 19th-century British painter, Millais was one of the founders of the Pre-Raphaelite Brotherhood, which sought to revive the simple, sincere, nonacademic art that had prevailed before the Later Renaissance. A popular and financially successful artist, Millais painted religious, historical, and genre scenes as well as portraits. He became a baronet in 1885 and was made president of the Royal Academy shortly before his death.

Albert Bierstadt

1830–1902

A German-born, American-raised landscape painter, Bierstadt achieved considerable fame in the 1860s and '70s for his romantic images of awe-inspiring vistas in the American West, including

Yosemite, the Rocky Mountains, and the Sierra Nevada Mountains. His work helped popularize the wonders of the West, but it had fallen out of fashion by the 1880s and he died largely forgotten.

Camille Pissarro

1830–1903

A central figure of French Impressionism, Pissarro was the only artist to show his work at all eight of the now-famous Impressionist exhibitions. Known for his landscapes and cityscapes, he also briefly worked in the Pointillist style before returning to Impressionism. Born on the Caribbean island of St. Thomas, Pissarro struggled financially for much of his artistic career, but was a valued mentor to a number of his contemporaries, including Cézanne and Gauguin.

Harriet Hosmer

1830–1908

One of the most prominent 19th-century American female sculptors, Hosmer is said to have made sculpture a suitable career for women. She studied anatomy, a subject usually not open to women, in the US. Hosmer then moved to Rome where she found success creating Neoclassical sculptures of mythological and historical figures and achieved financial independence.

Édouard Manet

1832–1883

An influential late 19th-century French artist, Manet painted in a bold, modern style and selected contemporary, often controversial, subjects. His paintings *Dejeuner Sur L'Herbe* (1862) and *Olympia* (1863) shocked the establishment with their depiction of female nudity. With Monet, he helped found the Impressionist movement. Unlike his predecessors, who waited for one layer of paint to dry before adding another, Manet used layers of wet oil paint to create his works. The composition of his paintings shows the influence of photography.

James Abbott McNeill Whistler

1834–1903

An American-born artist who worked in Europe, Whistler was a leading figure in the aesthetic movement, which stressed the idea "art for art's sake," and considered it more important that a work have a pleasing color and form than meaningful subject matter or symbolism. A noted dandy and wit, Whistler was greatly influenced by the Japanese art that reached Europe in the late 19th century.

Edgar Degas

1834–1917

An influential late 19th-century French painter, sculptor, and printmaker, Degas created modern images of contemporary Parisian life across varied social classes, often with a particular interest in women and ballet dancers. Although frequently grouped with the Impressionists, with whom Degas sometimes exhibited his work—and with whom he shared an unwillingness to work within the confines of academic painting—Degas never embraced the philosophies of the Impressionists, preferring to work in a studio rather than *en plein air*. Failing eyesight reduced his output later in his life.

Henri Fantin-Latour

1836–1904

A late 19th-century French painter, Fantin-Latour is known for his popular, detailed still lifes of flowers as well as for portraits and group portraits of important French painters and writers of his era. Although he painted in an academic style, he was friendly with many Impressionist and Post-Impressionist artists. He produced works on other subjects as well, including, late in his career, imaginative lithographs and paintings related to the music of Wagner and Berlioz.

Winslow Homer

1836–1910

A leading 19th-century American painter, Homer is best known for his naturalistic, energetic images, often related to the power of the sea and people's relationship with it. Originally an illustrator—his well-regarded drawings of the American Civil War appeared in popular magazines—he later worked effectively in watercolors as well as oil paint.

Alfred Sisley

1839–1899

A 19th-century Impressionist landscape painter, Sisley's work was shown at the first Impressionist exhibition in 1874, as well as several of the Impressionist exhibitions that followed. Born in France to wealthy English parents, his family's finances were ruined by the Franco-Prussian War of 1870–1871, after which Sisley lived in poverty. His art attracted little attention until after his death. He worked mainly in France but held British citizenship.

Paul Cézanne

1839–1906

Cézanne was an important French Post-Impressionist painter, whose explorations of color and form were a crucial step toward the Cubism and abstraction that emerged in the early 20th century. Influenced both by the classic French art style epitomized by Poussin and new Impressionist ideas, he painted distinctive still lifes, portraits, many landscapes of Provence, and other works, often returning to the same subject time and again. Cézanne was virtually unknown until 1895, when an exhibition of his work helped shape the artistic direction of many young Paris-based artists including Picasso and Matisse.

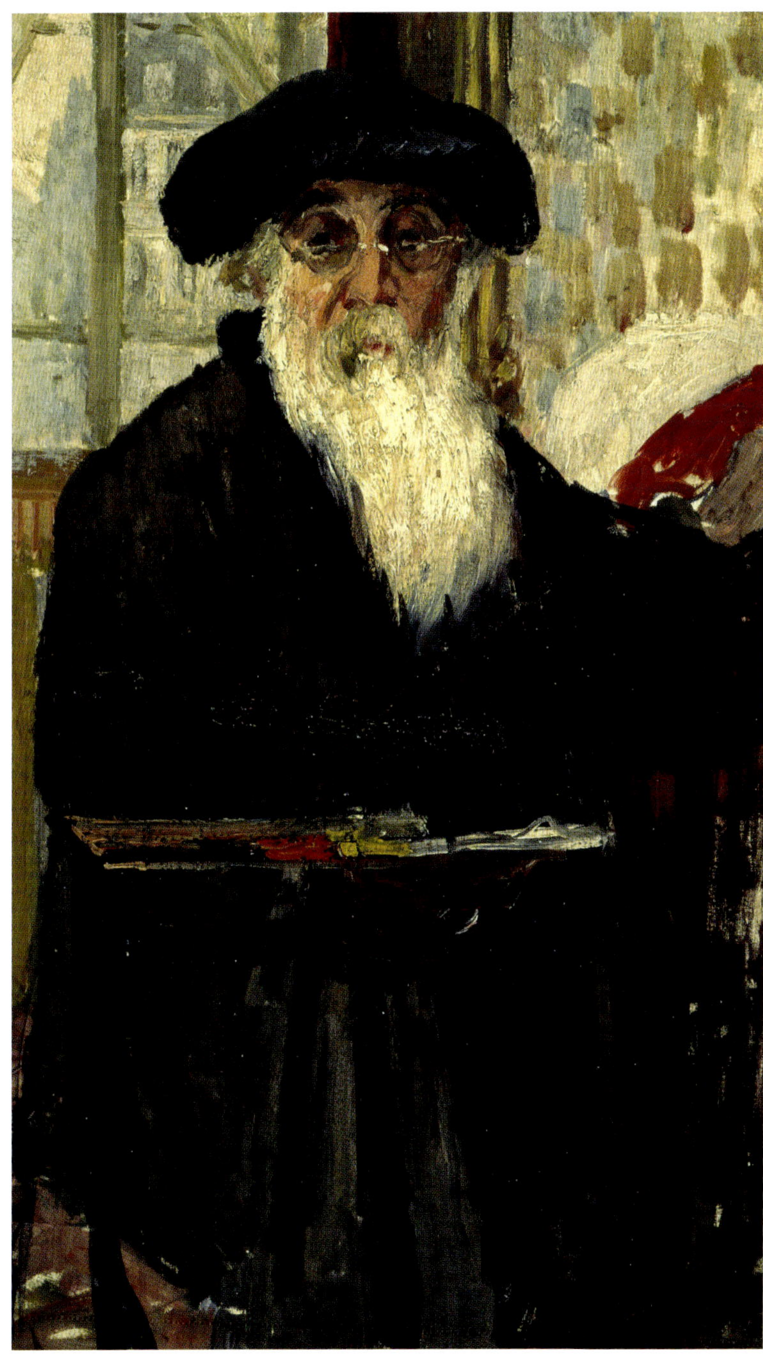

▲ **Camille Pissarro**, *Self-Portrait*, c.1898, oil on canvas, Dallas Museum of Art, US

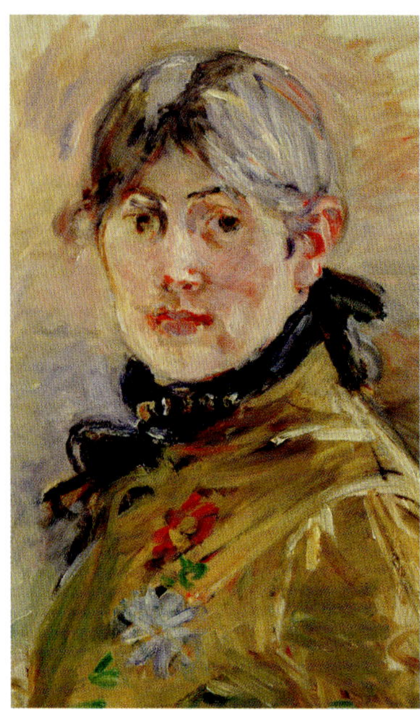

▲ **Berthe Morisot**, *Self-Portrait*, 1885, oil on canvas, Musée Marmottan Monet, Paris, France

Odilon Redon
1840–1916
An important French Symbolist artist, Redon began his career creating lithographs and charcoal drawings that often feature dark, dreamlike, macabre, or even monstrous imagery. Some of his early pieces were inspired by the work of Edgar Allan Poe and Charles Baudelaire. Later, he shifted to painting and drawing in color, often using pastels, and created floral still lifes, religious works, portraits, scenes from mythology, and other images.

Auguste Rodin
1840–1917
The leading sculptor of his day, Rodin created some of the most iconic artwork of modern times, such as *The Thinker* and *The Kiss*. He was born into a poor family in Paris, and success did not come quickly—Rodin was 40 before he was taken seriously as an artist—yet by the time he died he was hailed as the modern equivalent of Michelangelo. He worked in a range of materials.

Claude Monet
1840–1926
The leading Impressionist painter, Monet painted outdoor scenes of Paris and the Normandy coast with bold brushstrokes, working quickly to convey a sense of the light and color of the moment, not to re-create a view. Now regarded as one of the most important painters in modern art, he did not achieve financial success until well into the 1880s. Monet suffered from failing eyesight late in life yet continued to paint, completing numerous paintings of the waterlilies in his garden at Giverny, Normandy.

Berthe Morisot
1841–1895
A 19th-century French painter, Morisot was a central figure in the Impressionist movement, showing works at seven of the eight Impressionist exhibitions. She is best known for her portraits of women and interior scenes of women and children, although she also painted light-and-airy outdoor scenes more typical of Impressionism. Morisot was a friend, model, and the sister-in-law of Édouard Manet.

Pierre-Auguste Renoir
1841–1919
A founding member of the Impressionist movement, leading French painter Renoir produced landscapes and group scenes noted for their bright colors, dappled light, and soft, sensuous quality. He broke away from Impressionism in the early 1880s, and his later works have a more classical style. He was born the son of a French tailor, and his son Jean became an important film director.

Wang Zhensheng
1842–1922
A well-regarded painter during the final decades of the Qing dynasty, China's last imperial dynasty, Wang is best known for his paintings of flowers and birds, in addition to his calligraphy. In 1874, he earned the degree of *jinshi*, the highest rank on the imperial civil service exam.

Edmonia Lewis
1844–1907
A noted late 19th-century American Neoclassical sculptor, Lewis was the first Black and first Indigenous American artist (her father was Black, her mother Chippewa) to win international success in sculpture. Lewis was also one of the few women of her era to do so. Orphaned and raised by her mother's nation, she spent a few tumultuous years at Oberlin College in Ohio, but eventually moved to Rome where her marble statues on Biblical, mythological, and racial themes were well received.

Henri Rousseau
1844–1910
An eccentric, self-taught French artist, Rousseau's work has a decidedly primitive style . Nicknamed "Le Douanier" (the Customs Officer) Rousseau held a menial government job before leaving in middle age to pursue an art career. His colorful works influenced early 20th-century art. Rousseau is best known for his jungle fantasy pictures

Mary Cassatt
1844–1926
An American artist who worked in Paris and became a member of the Impressionist movement, Cassatt often painted and made prints of mothers with their children, as well as other themes related to the private lives of women. Degas was a friend and mentor. Born into a prosperous family in Pennsylvania, Cassatt was well connected and encouraged her wealthy acquaintances to purchase Impressionist art, helping it gain popularity in the US. Failing eyesight reduced her artistic output in the final years of her life.

Thomas Eakins
1844–1916
An important American Realist painter, Eakins produced honest, unflinching portraits and genre scenes, which ranged from bloody images of surgeons at work to sunny images of boating and swimming. His work was not well received during his lifetime—his father provided him with much-needed financial support—but after his death he came to be seen as one of the greatest American artists of the 19th century. Eakins was also a pioneering photographer.

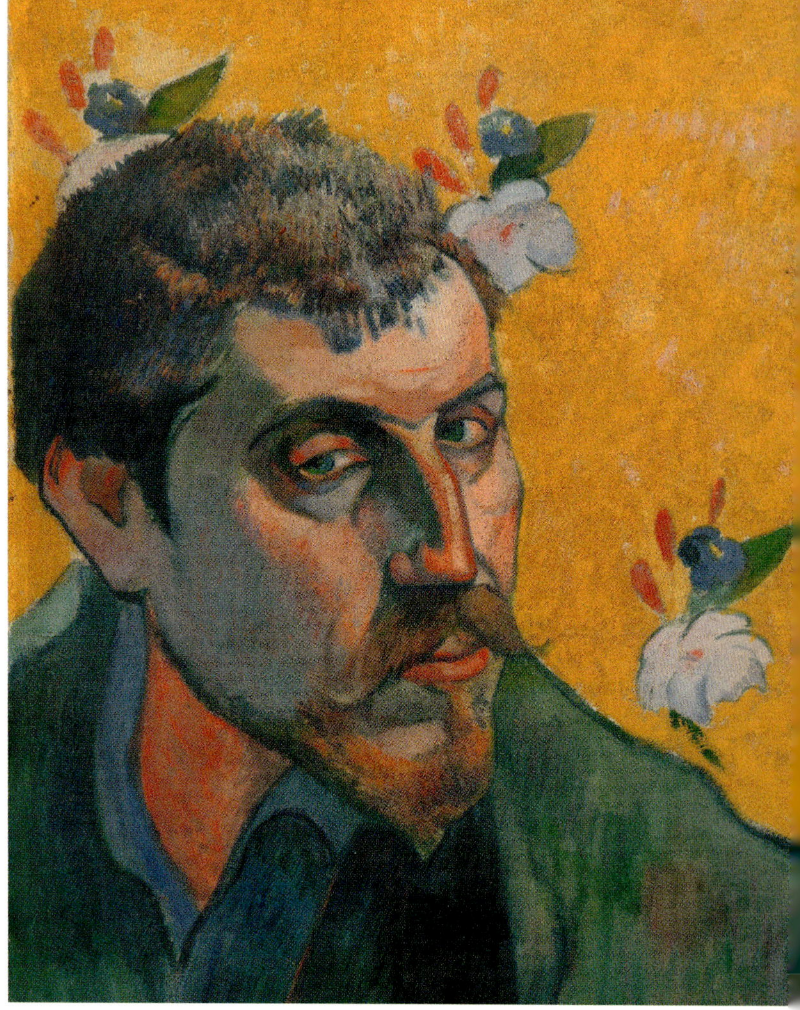

Ilya Repin

1844–1930

A Russian painter known for his powerful historical and genre images, Repin is sometimes credited with setting the stage for the Soviet Socialist Realist painters who followed. He frequently focused on political content, such as the struggles of Russian peasants, but he painted portraits, landscapes, religious images, and other works as well. His style was influenced by the Impressionists. In 1894, he became a professor of art in St. Petersburg.

Max Liebermann

1847–1935

Liebermann is best known for his paintings of contemporary urban life, especially of the poor, although he also painted landscapes. A leading figure in early 20th-century German art, and in particular of the Berliner Sezession that broke from German academic painting endorsed by the state, he became president of the Berlin Academy, until forced by the Nazis to resign due to his Jewish heritage.

William Harnett

1848–1892

An Irish-born, American-raised painter of still lifes, Harnett was famous in his day for his astoundingly realistic trompe l'oeil images, which often featured musical instruments, game, guns, or letter racks. Although popular with the public, his paintings were not embraced by 19th-century art critics. Illness reduced his artistic output late in his life, and he died at the age of 44.

Gustave Caillebotte

1848–1894

French painter Gustave Caillebotte is closely associated with the Impressionists and his best-known works include urban street scenes and interiors. The son of a successful businessman, he could afford to purchase works from struggling fellow artists and is perhaps most notable as an early collector of Impressionist art. His patronage was much welcomed in the years before this modern style attracted widespread acclaim.

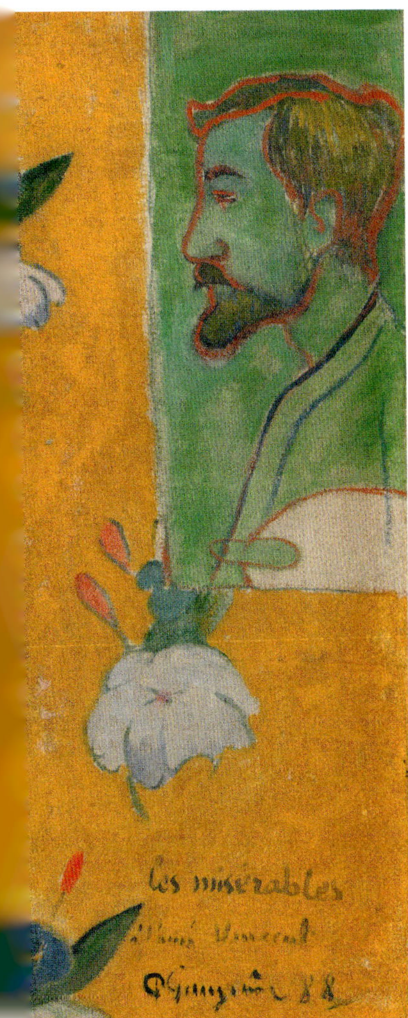

◀ **Paul Gauguin**, detail from *Self-Portrait with Portrait of Émile Bernard (Les Misérables)*, 1888, oil on canvas, Van Gogh Museum, Amsterdam, the Netherlands

Paul Gauguin

1848–1903

A French painter who developed a primitive style that featured bold colors, simplified forms, and rich symbolism, Gauguin was greatly influenced by Japanese and ancient Greek art. His life story is as famous as his paintings—he lost his job as a stockbroker and then left his family to become an artist. In 1888, he spent nine weeks living and working with van Gogh in the south of France; in 1891, he moved to Tahiti but failed to realize his dream of living in an unspoiled earthly paradise because the traditional culture was being overtaken by Western values. However, he produced many paintings. His work became popular after his death.

Eva Gonzalès

1849–1883

A 19th-century French painter associated with the Impressionists, Gonzales was a student of Édouard Manet. Her work was similar to that of Manet early in her career, but her style became more distinct later in her short life. The daughter of writer Emmanuel Gonzales, she died in childbirth at the age of 34.

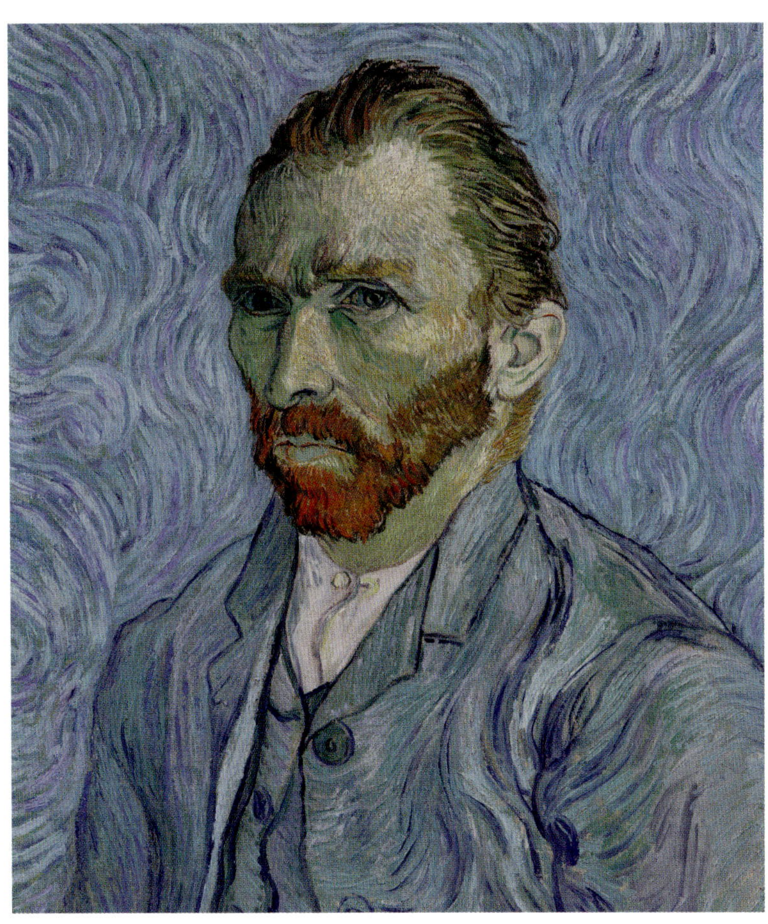

▲ **Vincent van Gogh**, *Self-Portrait*, 1889, oil on canvas, Musée d'Orsay, Paris, France

William Merritt Chase

1849–1916

A prolific and versatile American painter, Chase created a wide variety of works, including somber, elegant portraits; bright outdoor scenes in the style of the French Impressionists, many painted along the coast of New York's Long Island; and still lifes, often featuring fish. He was talented with pastels as well as oil paint, and was a popular art teacher. Georgia O'Keeffe and Edward Hopper were among his pupils.

John William Waterhouse

1849–1917

An English painter, Waterhouse was popular in his day and created large works on classical, historical, and literary themes. His best-known paintings tend to be richly colored, romantic, and frequently feature attractive women. Waterhouse was born in Rome but had English parents and spent most of his life in London.

nji Nkome

Active late 19th century

Nji Nkome worked for the Fon, or king, of the Bamum Kingdom in the grasslands of Cameroon during the 19th century. His sculptures show knowledge of the iconography and style of the Bamum culture.

Vincent van Gogh

1853–1890

Dutch artist Vincent van Gogh developed a distinctive, expressive style characterized by thickly applied paint, unexpected colors, and emotional intensity. Suffering from a psychiatric disorder and financially unsuccessful—almost none of his art sold during his lifetime—he died by suicide in Auvers-sur-Oise, France, at the age of. 37 He had taken up painting only 10 years before his death, yet the work he left behind includes some of the best known, and most valuable artwork, ever created.

Cecilia Beaux
1855–1942
A leading American portrait artist, Beaux painted pictures of New York and Philadelphia's rich and powerful people in the late 19th and early 20th centuries. Her work was often compared to that of John Singer Sargent, the other major American portrait artist of the time. She was the first woman to serve as instructor at the Pennsylvania Academy of Fine Arts.

Alfred Wallis
1855–1942
A British fisherman who took up painting at the age of 70 following his wife's death, Wallis created images of ships, ports, and St. Ives, Cornwall, in a naïve style. He painted on cardboard or wood rather than canvas to save money. His work was embraced by the artistic community—Ben Nicholson and Christopher Wood were key supporters—but Wallis died in poverty.

John Singer Sargent
1856–1925
A Florence-born American portrait painter who worked mainly in London, Sargent produced flattering but aloof images featuring bold brushwork that were popular with the English upper classes during the late 19th century. Not satisfied with painting portraits, Sargent turned to other subjects later in his career, perhaps most notably watercolors of Venice and the Swiss Alps.

Tom Roberts
1856–1931
A leading Australian Impressionist painter, Roberts is known for his landscapes, portraits, and genre paintings of rural Australian life. Born in England, his family moved to Australia in 1869 following the death of his father. Roberts was the central figure of the Heidelberg School, a group of artists known for their Impressionist paintings of Australian subjects.

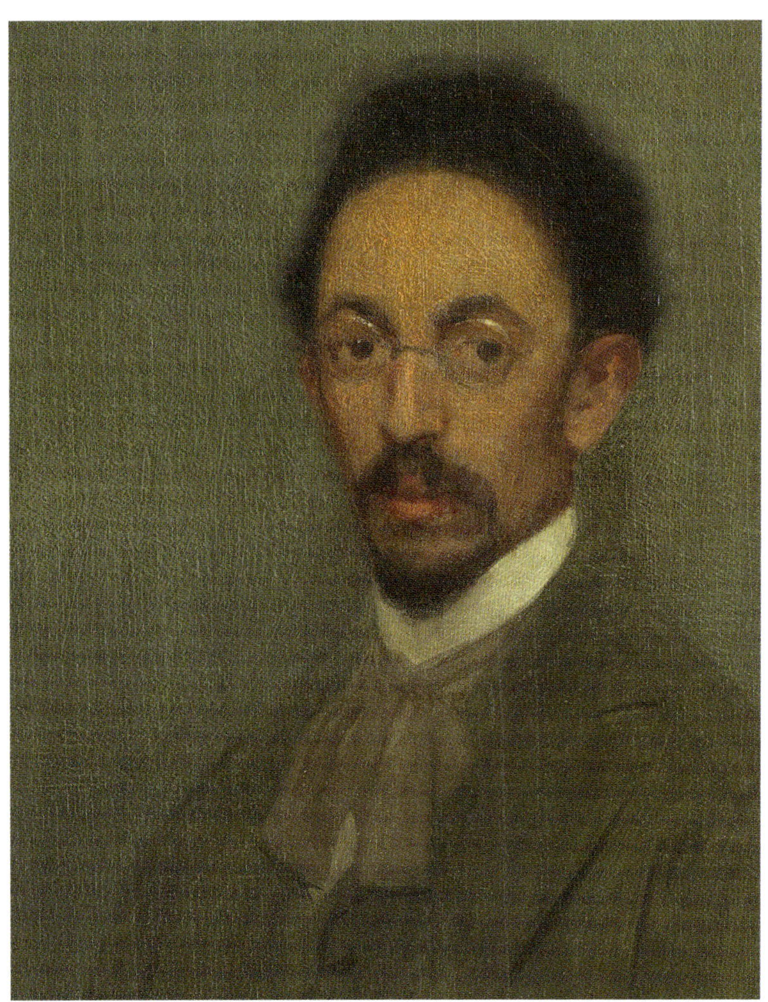

▲ ***Portrait of Henry Ossawa Tanner***, Hermann Dudley Murphy, c.1891-1896, oil on canvas, Art Institute of Chicago, US

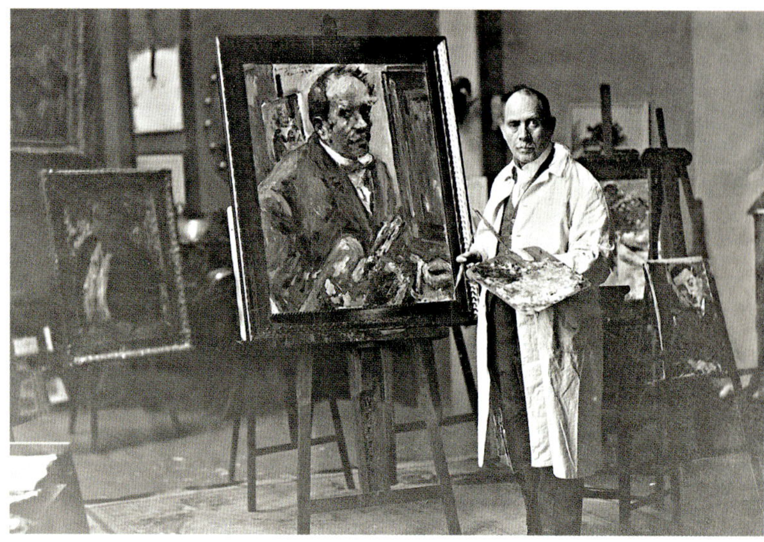

▲ **Lovis Corinth** working on a self-portrait in his studio, 1925

Marie Bashkirtseff
1858–1884
A Russian writer and painter who worked in France, Bashkirtseff created well-received oil paintings, pastels, statues, and drawings. These were often portraits or genre scenes, but she is best remembered for her diary, which was published after her death. Born into a noble family, she planned to pursue a singing career before tuberculosis claimed her voice, her health, and eventually, her life. She died at the age of just 25.

Lovis Corinth
1858–1925
A prominent German painter and printmaker, whose style evolved over the course of his career, Corinth produced largely naturalistic works early in his career but was later at the forefront of German Expressionism. His work following a 1911 stroke exhibits the intense emotion, bold brushwork, and vibrant colors typical of the style, although Corinth himself expressed reservations about Expressionist art. He painted landscapes, nudes, portraits, and Biblical and genre scenes, among other subjects.

Childe Hassam
1859–1935
A leading American Impressionist artist, Hassam is known for his coastal, garden, and urban images. Originally an illustrator, he studied art in Paris in the late 1880s, soaking up the French Impressionist style, which was then becoming popular in the US, before returning to New York in 1889. During World War I, Hassam painted numerous patriotic images featuring the US flag, and sometimes also the flags of its wartime allies.

Henry Ossawa Tanner
1859–1937
Among the first Black painters to achieve international fame, Tanner mainly painted religious images and landscapes. *The Banjo Lesson*, a scene of Black life, is probably his best-known work, but it is something of an outlier in his oeuvre. A student of Thomas Eakins, Tanner spent most of his career in France, where he faced less racism than he did in the US at the time.

Georges Seurat
1859–1891
A French Post-Impressionist artist, Seurat is remembered as the inventor of the art style known as Divisionism as well as its close cousin Pointillism—painting not with brushstrokes, but by painstakingly applying tiny dabs of unmixed pigment to produce a luminous image. An innovative, influential, and intellectually curious artist, Seurat died at the age of just 31.

Anders Zorn
1860–1920
A Swedish painter best known for his female nudes, many of them set outdoors, Zorn also painted portraits, landscapes, and genre scenes, which were often related to

Scandinavian life. A versatile artist, he began his career working largely with watercolors, and later switched to oils. He was also skilled at etching.

Walter Sickert

1860–1942

A major figure in late 19th- and early 20th-century British avant-garde art, Sickert is best known for his paintings of music halls and often dimly lit interiors in a style that was heavily influenced by Impressionism—Degas was a close acquaintance. Sickert was also noted for his skill as an etcher, teacher, and writer. He was a founding member of the Camden Town Group who painted suburban landscapes and modest interiors in bold colors inspired by the Post-Impressionists.

Frederic Remington

1861–1909

A sculptor, painter, and illustrator, Remington's popular depictions of cowboys, Indigenous Americans, cavalrymen, horses, and vast landscapes helped shape the heroic image of the American West. Initially known for his illustrations, which often appeared in popular magazines, he took up sculpting with great success in the mid-1890s. Although he liked to portray himself as an authentic cowboy, Remington was actually a Yale-educated easterner who lived only briefly in the West, although he traveled there often.

Gustav Klimt

1862–1918

Austrian painter Klimt's best-known works are the highly ornamental and sensual images of women that he painted in the final 20 years of his life. Many of these feature extensive use of gold leaf (Klimt's father had been a gold engraver). In the closing years of the 19th century, Klimt was a leader of the Vienna Secession movement, which rejected academic art. His earlier works included traditional murals for public buildings.

Hilma af Klint

1862–1944

A pioneering Swedish painter Hilma af Klint is known for her abstract, colorful, séance-inspired images, which she painted years before the early abstract works of Kandinsky and Mondrian. Af Klint did not display her abstract works publicly, however, and left instructions that they not be shown until 20 years after her death, removing them from art history until recent decades. Af Klint also painted conventional landscapes as well as portraits and works featuring flowers.

Helene Schjerfbeck

1862–1946

A leading Finnish Modernist painter, Schjerfbeck is best remembered for her many self-portraits, which often have a haunted quality. She also painted other portraits, still lifes, and landscapes. Her work is highly celebrated in Finland, although it is less well known elsewhere. Her sequence of self-portraits demonstrates her fascination with the process of aging.

Joaquín Sorolla y Bastida

1863–1923

A popular and prolific Spanish painter—he was considered Spain's greatest artist in the late 19th century—Sorolla is known for bright Valencian beach scenes influenced by Impressionism. He also painted landscapes, genre paintings, portraits, and historical works. Tremendously famous in his home country, he found success in the US late in his career and was commissioned to paint a series of canvases for the Hispanic Society of America's New York library.

Paul Signac

1863–1935

A French Neo-Impressionist painter, Signac was the most important painter working in the Divisionism and Pointillism styles following the early death of Seurat. Divisionism involves applying small areas of unmixed colors to a canvas so they seem to mix together in the eyes of viewers; Pointillism refers to doing this using tiny dots of paint. He liked to sail, and many of his paintings are of harbors.

Edvard Munch

1863–1944

A prolific Norwegian painter and printmaker who is best known for a single image—*The Scream*—Munch trained in Germany. He set the stage for German Expressionism, a movement in which naturalism is distorted to convey emotion. Munch's family was plagued by illness and death during his childhood and early adulthood, probably contributing to the dark, troubled themes that dominated much of his art. Following a nervous breakdown in 1908, his work rarely recaptured its earlier emotional intensity.

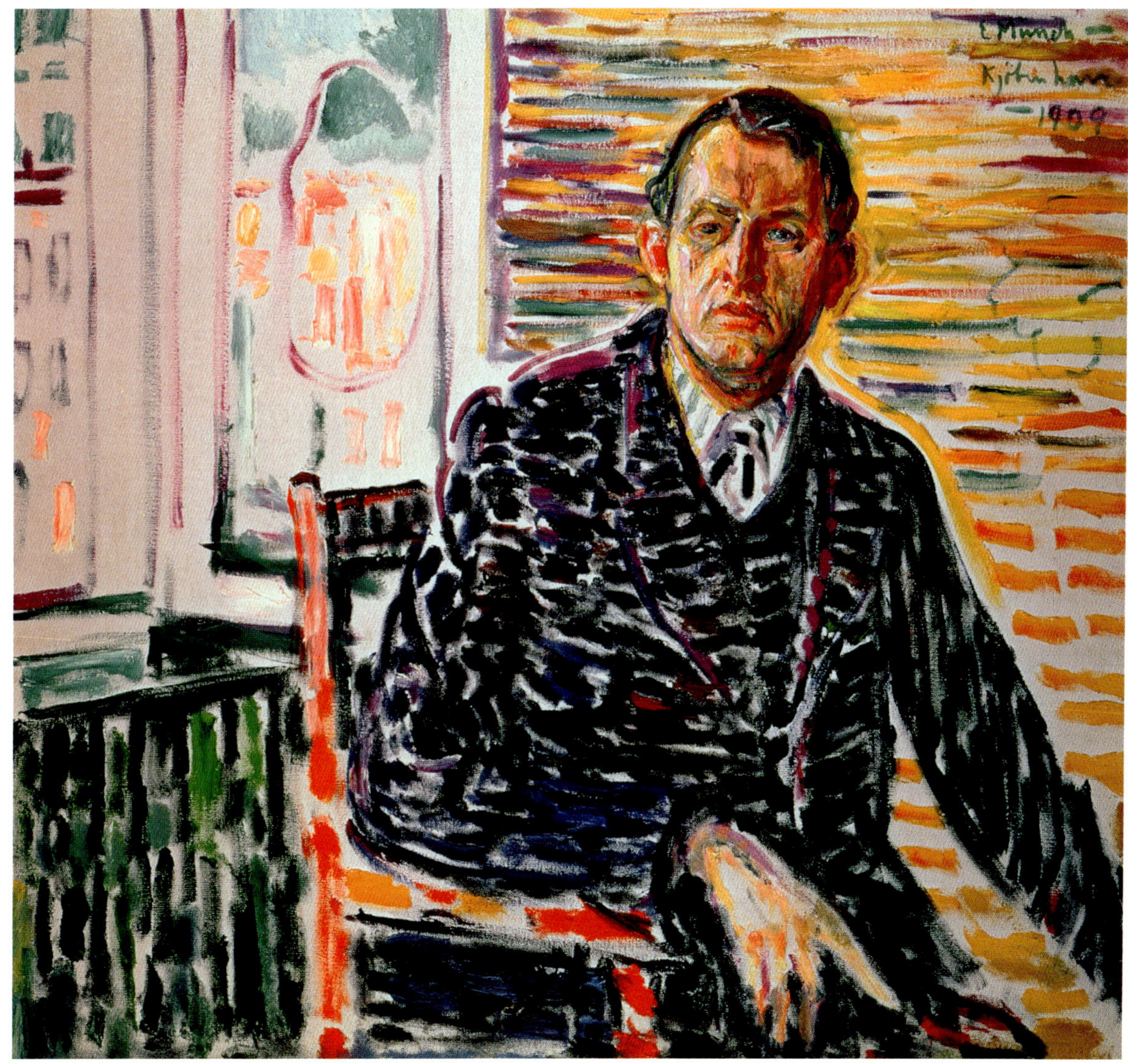

▲ **Edvard Munch**, *Self-Portrait in the Clinic*, 1909, oil on canvas, KODE Art Museums, Bergen, Norway

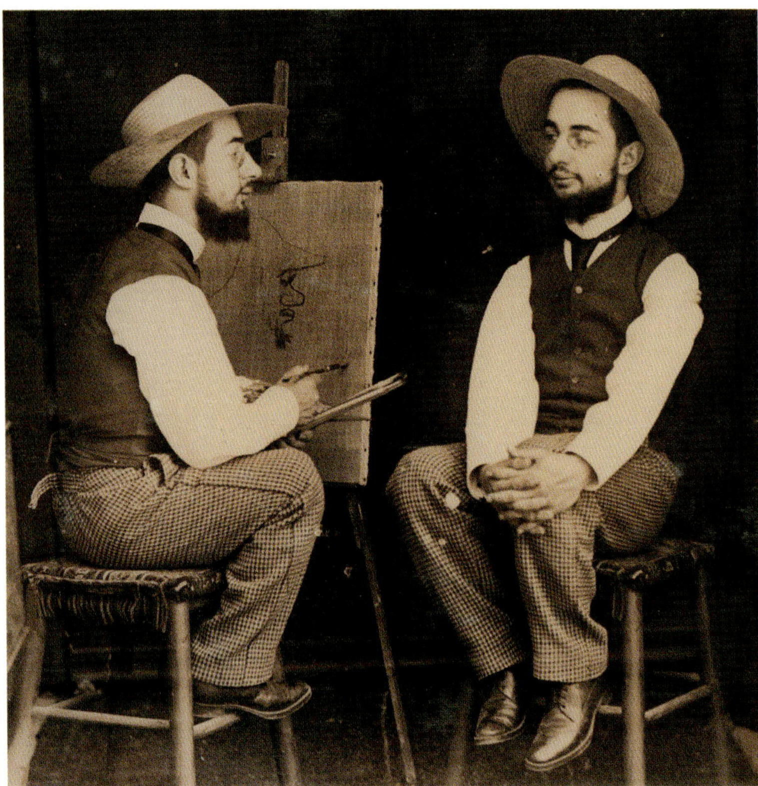

▲ ***Lautrec Paints Lautrec***, Musée Toulouse-Lautrec, Albi, France

Henri de Toulouse-Lautrec
1864–1901
French artist Toulouse-Lautrec's paintings, posters, and drawings often focus on themes related to Parisian nightlife, including clubs and brothels. His work was influenced by Japanese *ukiyo-e* prints. Born into an aristocratic family, he broke his legs in separate accidents as a teenager, after which they failed to grow properly. This left him short in stature, with mobility problems. He died at just 36, his death linked to complications from alcoholism and syphilis.

Vilhelm Hammershøi
1864–1916
The leading Danish painter of the late 19th and early 20th centuries, Hammershøi used muted tones to create enigmatic images on the theme of loneliness. Among his most powerful works are quietly haunting images of empty rooms or rooms containing a lone woman who faces away from the viewer. The woman in these paintings is his wife, Ida, and the rooms were in their Copenhagen home. He also painted disturbingly unpopulated urban scenes, as well as portraits and landscapes.

Paul Sérusier
1864–1927
An important French Post-Impressionist painter, Sérusier was one of the founders of Les Nabis ("prophets" in Hebrew), a group of artists inspired by Gauguin's use of color and flattened perspective; he met Gauguin in Pont-Aven in 1888. His early works often depicted the people and landscapes of Brittany, while his later paintings tended to have religious themes. Sérusier's 1921 book *ABC of Painting* was influential.

Camille Claudel
1864–1943
A French sculptor, Claudel was a notable artist, creating powerful, expressive, often sensual works in bronze and marble. However, she is primarily remembered as the student, model, and mistress of Rodin. She contributed to his work in the 1880s and early 1890s, possibly modeling hands and feet for his *Burghers of Calais*. She struggled financially and psychologically after her romantic and professional relationship with him ended, and she spent the final three decades of her life in an asylum although her doctors told her family she was well.

Akseli Galen-Kallela
1865–1931
Among the most important figures in the history of Finnish art, Galen-Kallela is best known for his images of Finland's folklore, people, and landscapes, including his illustrations of Finland's national epic, the *Kalevala*. Although he occasionally lived and painted in locations as distant as the southwestern US and what is now Kenya, Galen-Kallela was a proud Finn who changed his name to sound more Finnish and fought in the country's 1918 Civil War.

Suzanne Valadon
1865–1938
A French artist in the first half of the 20th century, Valadon painted and drew nudes, still lifes, and portraits. Previously a circus acrobat, she became a model for numerous important Paris artists of the era, including Toulouse-Lautrec and Degas, who encouraged her artistic efforts. Her work achieved critical and popular success by the 1920s, as did that of her son, Maurice Utrillo.

Wassily Kandinsky
1866–1944
An innovative Russian-born painter, Kandinsky created increasingly abstract art in the years leading up to World War I. He is often credited with painting the first fully abstract images, in or around 1911, though the long unknown works of Hilda af Klint can also lay claim to this. Trained as a lawyer, Kandinsky left that profession at the age of 30 in order to pursue art. He was an influential art writer and teacher, including at the Bauhaus school of art.

Käthe Kollwitz
1867–1945
A German printmaker and sculptor whose work is associated with the Expressionist movement, Kollwitz typically confronted social issues, such as poverty, worker's rights, war, and the suffering of women and children. Her son was killed fighting in World War I, and her home and many of her works were destroyed by bombing in World War II. She was the first woman in more than 80 years to be elected to the Prussian Academy, although she was forced to resign by the Nazis in 1933.

Pierre Bonnard
1867–1947
A French painter and illustrator, Bonnard is best remembered for his brightly colored, intimate, interior scenes, often featuring his wife, Marthe, whom he sometimes depicted bathing. In the 1890s, Bonnard was associated with Les Nabis, a group of artists inspired by Gauguin and Japanese prints. Some of his work is influenced by Impressionism.

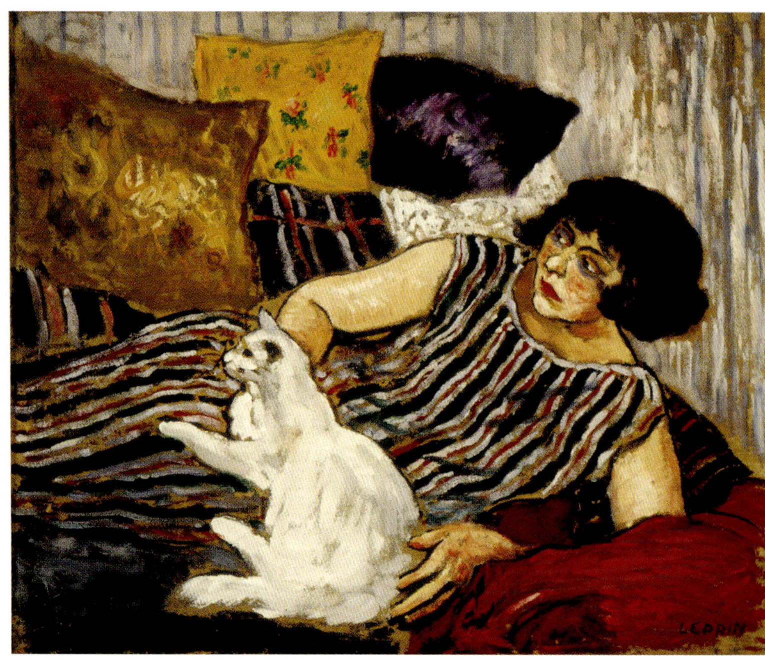

▲ ***Suzanne Valadon and Her Cat***, Marcel Leprin, undated, oil on canvas, Musée Regards de Provence, Marseille, France

Édouard Vuillard

1868–1940

A French painter and printmaker, Vuillard is best known for his interior scenes of middle-class French life, which often featured bold patterns and usually included women, often his widowed mother. Vuillard also painted portraits and landscapes. He is associated with Les Nabis, a group of painters in 1890s Paris who were influenced by Gauguin's use of color, pattern, and flattened sense of space.

Amos Bad Heart Bull

c. 1869–1913

An Oglala Lakota artist, Bad Heart Bull illustrated events from the history of his people. Included among his images was a drawing of his cousin, the famed Lakota war leader Crazy Horse. In 1967, more than 400 of Bad Heart Bull's drawings were published in *A Pictographic History of the Oglala Sioux*, bringing them to the world's attention more than half a century after his death.

Henri Matisse

1869–1954

Alongside Picasso, Matisse was one of the most influential figures in early 20th century modern art. He is best remembered for his expressive, nondescriptive use of intense color. Born into a family of weavers in northern France, he trained as a lawyer before pursuing art. In addition to painting, Matisse was a skilled sculptor and printmaker. Late in life, he worked extensively in paper collage.

František Kupka

1871–1957

An influential Czech painter and illustrator who worked mainly in France, Kupka was among the first artists to produce fully abstract works. Kupka believed painters could use color and form to evoke emotions and ideas much as musicians did with musical notes. Kupka later served as a Paris-based professor for the Prague Academy.

Pauline Powell Burns

1872–1912

A Black painter and pianist, Powell Burns's artwork included still lifes and landscapes. In her day, she was better known as a pianist and piano teacher, and left relatively few paintings when she died of tuberculosis. She was the first African American artist to exhibit her work in California.

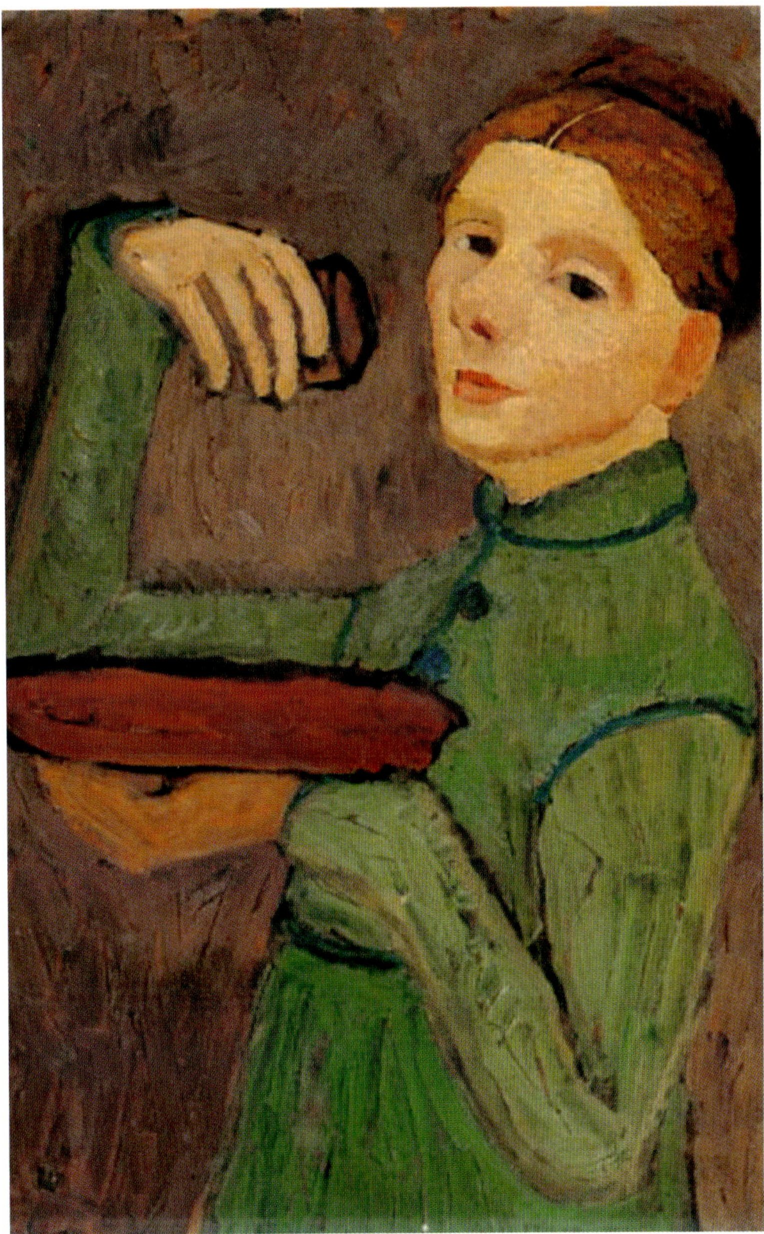

▲ **Paula Modersohn-Becker**, *Self-Portrait with a Bowl and a Glass*, c. 1904, oil on cardboard, Louisiana Museum of Modern Art, Humlebaek, Denmark

Piet Mondrian

1872–1944

Among the first artists to create fully abstract works, Mondrian is best known for his "grid" paintings of the 1920s and 1930s, which included only straight black lines and rectangles of primary colors, white, or, initially, gray. Born in the Netherlands, Mondrian worked mainly in Paris, but after its fall to the Nazis in 1940 he spent the final years of his life in New York. The bustling city brought a new vitality to his work.

Paula Modersohn-Becker

1876–1907

An early 20th-century German modernist painter, Modersohn-Becker is known for her portraits of women and girls—including many self-portraits—that rejected traditional norms of female beauty. She also painted landscapes, still lifes, and genre scenes. Financially unsuccessful during her career, she died shortly after giving birth to her only child.

Gwen John

1876–1939

A Welsh painter in the early 20th century, John specialized in solemn, understated portraits of women, often pictured seated with their hands in their laps. During her life, John was best known for the people she knew—she was the model and mistress of Rodin, and her brother was artist Augustus John—but her artwork has received increased attention in recent decades.

Constantin Brancuşi

1876–1957

A hugely influential Romanian sculptor who worked in France, Brancuşi typically carved his highly abstract works directly from stone or wood, rather than make models to be cast, as was common. Born into a peasant family, Brancuşi studied under Rodin, and by the 1910s his work was internationally popular. He became a French citizen in 1952.

Marsden Hartley

1877–1943

An experimental American artist in the first half of the 20th century, Hartley was influenced by several modern art styles—some of his early works are Impressionistic, while later works suggest German Expressionism and abstraction. The final decade of Hartley's life was spent in his home state of Maine, where he mostly painted landscapes and coastal scenes.

Raoul Dufy

1877–1953

A French artist whose style evolved over the course of his career, Dufy is best known for his colorful, decorative paintings depicting leisure scenes, such as boating, beaches, and riding horses. He experimented with Cubism, but is most closely associated with Fauvism, a style featuring intense, nondescriptive colors. Dufy was also a skilled book illustrator and designed tapestries and furniture.

Olowe of Ise

c. 1878–1938

An important and innovative early 20th-century Yoruba wood sculptor, Olowe carved palace doors, figures, veranda posts, and other objects, mainly for Yoruba kings. Born in Efon-Alaaye, but working mainly in Ise—a town in modern-day Nigeria—he developed a distinctive style featuring deeply carved figures and abstract forms.

Kazimir Malevich
1879–1935
An influential early 20th-century Russian avant-garde painter, Malevich worked in a wide range of styles during his career. But he is best remembered for his fully abstract images of geometric shapes, such as *Black Square*, a painting that delivered precisely what its title promised. He labeled this art style Suprematism. Although generally identified as Russian, Malevich was actually born to ethnically Polish parents in what is now Ukraine.

Paul Klee
1879–1940
A Swiss/German artist associated with *Der Blaue Reiter*, the Munich-based Expressionist group, Klee created colorful, largely abstract works. The son of a father who taught music and a mother who sang professionally, Klee was also a talented violinist. He taught art in the 1920s and early 1930s, including at the Bauhaus school of art, but left Germany for Switzerland when Hitler rose to power.

Franz Marc
1880–1916
An early 20th-century German artist, Marc is best known for his vibrantly colored paintings of horses and other animals. His work explored the emotive and symbolic value of colors, and he was among the founders of the Expressionist art group Der Blaue Reiter. He died at the age of just 36, killed while fighting in the Battle of Verdun during World War I.

▲ **Ernst Ludwig Kirchner**, *Self-Portrait*, 1931, oil on canvas, Bündner Kunstmuseum, Chur, Switzerland

Ernst Ludwig Kirchner
1880–1938
A German painter and printmaker, Kirchner is known for his use of intense color in paintings that include portraits, street scenes, and, especially, nudes. He was among the founders of the art movement Die Brücke (The Bridge), which helped pave the way for German Expressionism, a style that elevated emotional content over naturalism. Kirchner was discharged from the military after suffering a mental breakdown during World War I. He died by suicide in 1938, not long after his art was classified as degenerate by the Nazis.

Natalia Goncharova
1881–1962
A leading Russian avant-garde artist, Goncharova created modern, Primitivist works inspired by Russian folk art and religious icons. Although known for her paintings, she was a versatile artist who also sculpted, illustrated books, made prints, and became involved with theater design, fashion design, and more. She left Russia in 1915, settled in Paris after World War I, and lived there for the rest of her life.

Pablo Picasso
1881–1973
Among the most famous and important artists of the 20th century, Picasso cocreated, along with Georges Braque, the innovative art style known as Cubism, where multiple views of a subject are combined into a single image. Cubism was, however, only one aspect of Picasso's long career. He worked in an astonishing range of styles and pursued many artistic endeavors. In addition to producing iconic paintings, he was an influential sculptor, printmaker, designer, and ceramic artist.

Alexandra Exter
1882–1949
A prominent Russian avant-garde artist, Exter created fully abstract works. She was also a key figure in the Russian abstract art movement known as Suprematism, and is credited with playing an important role in Russia's Constructivist art movement. Successful as a stage designer as well as a painter, she was based in Paris after 1924.

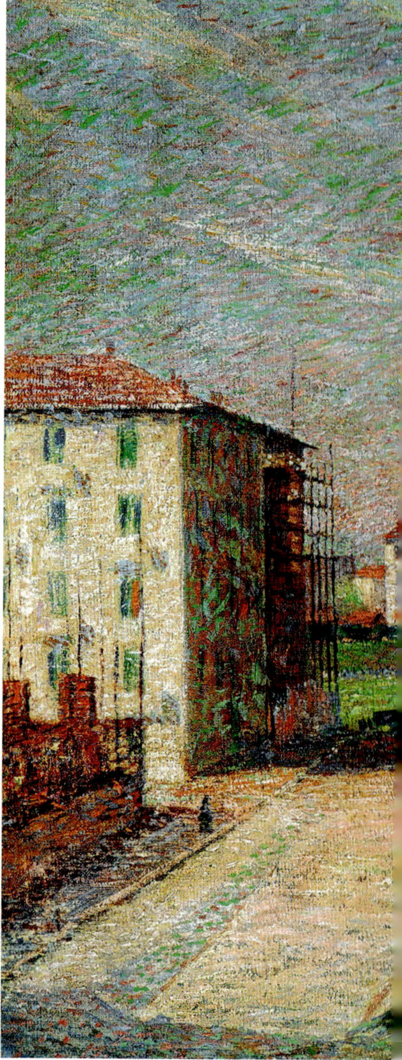

Umberto Boccioni
1882–1916
Boccioni was a leading Italian painter and sculptor associated with Futurism, a pre–World War I Italian art movement that sought a break with art's past and celebrated the power, speed, dynamism, and machinery of the modern world. He created Cubist-influenced art of great energy and excitement. Neither the Futurist movement nor Boccioni survived the war; he was thrown from his horse during a cavalry training exercise and died at the age of 33.

Sergei Sudeikin
1882–1946
A prominent Russian theatrical set and costume designer in the first half of the 20th century, Sudeikin was also a notable painter whose works includes theatrical scenes, portraits—sometimes of actresses and dancers—landscapes, and still lifes. Based in St. Petersburg in the 1910s, Sudeikin moved to Paris in

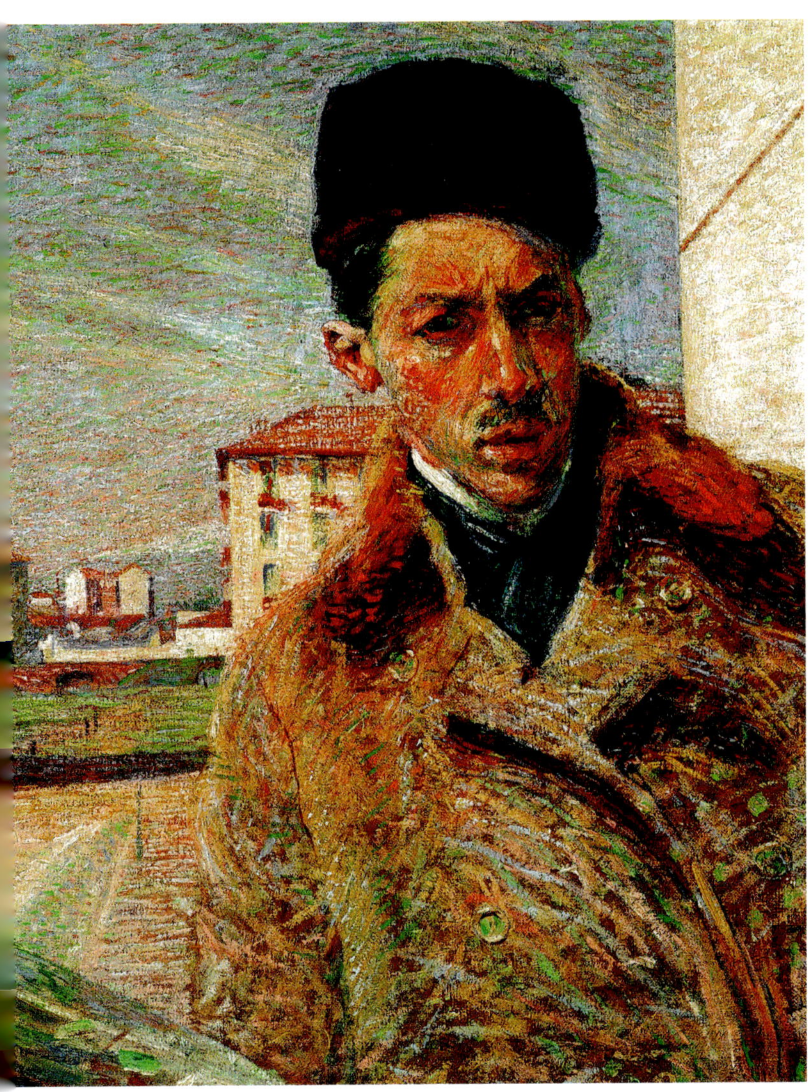

1920, then to the US in 1923, where he designed the sets for the original production of George Gershwin's *Porgy and Bess*.

Georges Braque

1882–1963

During the early decades of the 20th century, Braque worked closely with Picasso producing Cubism, an art style in which multiple views of an image are combined to create fragmented, increasingly abstract work. An innovative avant-garde painter and maker of mixed-media pieces, he was born the son of a French house painter. After World War I his work became freer, but it became more grounded in reality by the end of the 1920s.

Edward Hopper

1882–1967

An important 20th-century American Realist painter, Hopper is known for creating spare but evocative images that capture the loneliness of modern life, urban environments in particular. His city streets are often devoid of people and strangely silent; the figures who do populate his images tend to be lost in their own troubled worlds and are disconnected from other figures in the work. Originally an illustrator, watercolorist, and etcher, Hopper achieved artistic recognition and financial success after the age of 40.

Isaak Brodsky

1884–1939

Soviet artist Isaak Brodsky played a major role in the development of Social Realist art, which glorified communism and the Soviet state. His oeuvre includes portraits of prominent statesmen—most notably Lenin and Stalin—and scenes celebrating significant moments in Soviet history, but he also painted landscapes and other works. Brodsky was named the director of the Russian Academy of Arts in 1934.

◀ **Umberto Boccioni**, *Self-Portrait*, 1908, oil on canvas, Pinacoteca di Brera, Milan, Italy

Amedeo Modigliani

1884–1920

An Italian painter and sculptor who worked largely in France, Modigliani is known for creating distinctive, elongated, and often asymmetrical nudes and portraits. The elongated shape was inspired at least in part by African masks and sculpture. He died of tuberculosis at age 35, his work largely ignored until after his death.

Robert Delaunay

1885–1941

An innovative French painter, Delaunay, with his wife Sonia and others, created the style known as Orphism, which combined the fragmented shapes of Cubism with bright colors. Many paintings from later in Delaunay's career are abstract—he began to experiment with nearly or fully abstract images as early as 1912.

Oskar Kokoschka

1886–1980

An Austrian Expressionist painter, Kokoschka is best known for his intense, modern, psychologically probing portraits and self-portraits. He also painted landscapes, townscapes, and views of the Thames River, often from a high viewpoint. He was wounded during World War I, and left Austria in the 1930s due to the rise of the Nazis, obtaining Czech citizenship in the 1930s, and British citizenship in 1947. Later, he taught in Switzerland.

Diego Rivera

1886–1957

Leading Mexican painter Diego Rivera is best known for his large-scale murals, which reflect Mexican history and Marxist political themes. While he was working in Paris in the 1910s, his style was strongly influenced by Cubism. On returning to Mexico in 1921, he developed a style that combined Mexican and European influences. He married the artist Frida Kahlo twice.

Auguste Macke

1887–1914

An important German artist in the early years of the 20th century, Macke's work after 1909 was noted for its bold, nondescriptive use of color, influenced by the Fauves. Generally labeled as an Expressionist artist, he was among the founders of the Munich-based art group Der Blaue Reiter (The Blue Rider), which included Marc and Kandinsky. Macke was killed in battle during the first months of World War I, at the age of 27.

Juan Gris

1887–1927

A Spanish artist working in the early 20th century, Gris is best known for his still lifes painted in the Cubist style (he is generally regarded as the third most important Cubist after Picasso and Braque). Originally an illustrator specializing in humorous drawings, he only took up painting seriously after 1910. He died of kidney failure at the age of 40.

Kurt Schwitters

1887–1948

Working in the first half of the 20th century, Schwitters was an innovative avant-garde painter and maker of mixed-media pieces. He experimented with a wide range of styles and art forms, but is best known for the assemblage sculptures he called "Merz," made from discarded items that he scavenged. He fled Germany for Norway and eventually England after the Nazis declared his art degenerate. His masterwork, the original installation *Merzbau*, was destroyed during World War II.

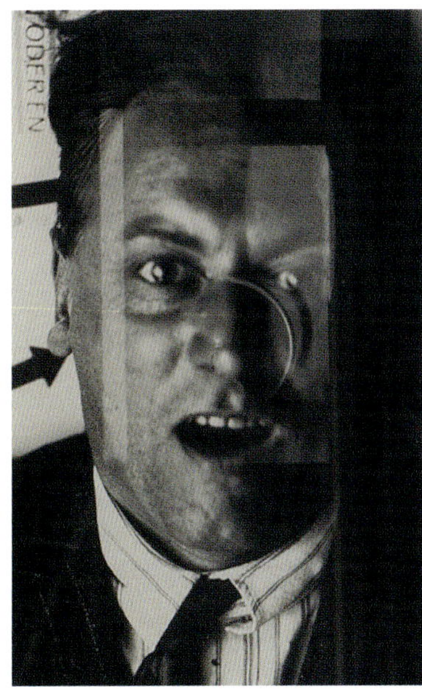

▲ **Portrait of Kurt Schwitters**, c. 1924, photograph by El Lissitzky

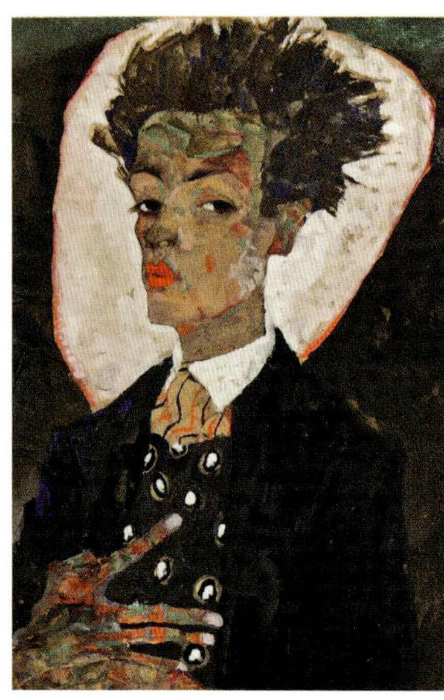

▲ **Egon Schiele**, *Self-Portrait with Peacock Waistcoat*, 1911, gouache, watercolor, and black crayon on paper, Albertina Museum, Vienna, Austria

Marc Chagall

1887–1985

A prolific Jewish artist born in what is now Belarus, Chagall created colorful, dreamlike images that combine 20th-century European art trends with Russian and Jewish folk art. Many of his paintings are about love—wedding scenes or romantic partners who seem to float on air—but Chagall produced many works on other subjects, including religion; the circus; and Vitebsk, the peasant village of his youth.

Georgia O'Keeffe

1887–1986

One of the most prominent female artists of the 20th century, O'Keeffe painted simplified forms mainly of natural subjects such as animal skulls, landscapes, and—most famously—flowers. Born in Wisconsin, she moved to New York in 1918 and married photographer Alfred Stieglitz, an early and important advocate of her work. She often visited and eventually settled in New Mexico, where desert plants and rugged landscapes provided inspiration.

Giorgio de Chirico

1888–1978

A Greek-born Italian painter, de Chirico is known for the mysterious, dreamlike scenes of largely deserted piazzas, distorted perspectives, enigmatic objects, and mannequins that he created between 1910 and 1919. He referred to these often perplexing, sometimes disturbing paintings as "metaphysical" works, and they had a great influence on the Surrealist artists who followed. De Chirico turned to a classical style later in his career; these works are not regarded as highly.

Lyubov Popova

1889–1924

A Russian avant-garde painter, textile designer, and theatrical set designer, Popova was an important figure in Constructivist art, a Russian abstract art movement that sought to connect the work of artists with the needs of the people. Her earlier, semiabstract work shows the influence of Cubism and Futurism. Born into a successful family in the Moscow area, she died at just 35.

Paul Nash

1889–1946

A leading British landscape painter in the first half of the 20th century, Nash combined the traditions of pastoral landscape painting with the modern styles of his era, most notably Surrealism and abstraction. Appointed an official war artist during each of the world wars, he produced powerful, deceptively simple images of both conflicts. He was also a successful book illustrator.

Egon Schiele

1890–1918

Austrian painter and draftsman Egon Schiele created intense, Expressionist images, often of male or female nudes that tend to be disturbing rather than sensual. In 1912, he was briefly imprisoned for public immorality charges related to his art. Schiele also drew and painted landscapes and portraits. He died of influenza during the epidemic of 1918.

Giorgio Morandi

1890–1964

A 20th-century Italian painter and etcher, Morandi painted delicate still lifes of simple objects such as bottles, bowls, and vases, invariably in subdued tones. He also produced landscapes. Early in his career Morandi experimented with a number of avant-garde art styles, most notably the Metaphysical style that helped inspire Surrealism.

Grant Wood

1892–1942

Specializing in scenes of the rural Midwest, American painter Grant Wood is known for one of the country's most iconic paintings, *American Gothic*. An important figure in the American art movement known as "Regionalism," which favored old-fashioned folk aesthetics and local subject matter over the European modern art ideas of the era, Wood also created stylized landscapes of his native Iowa.

Augusta Savage

1892–1962

American sculptor Augusta Savage's best-known works are on Black themes. She overcame substantial challenges to become a leading figure in the Harlem Renaissance of the 1920s and 1930s. The naturalistic way in which Savage depicted her subjects questioned the stereotypical ways that Black people were shown in art at the time. Her sculptures of young boys in particular helped humanize working-class Black American children in a way that challenged their popular image as mischief-makers. Savage was the first Black member of the organization now known as the National Association of Women Artists, but she was not financially successful.

Dora Carrington

1893–1932

A British painter of landscapes, portraits, and other works, Carrington is best remembered as a member of the Bloomsbury Group. Her work was influenced by Impressionism, Primitivism, and Surrealism. Carrington died by suicide at the age of 38. Her artwork was rarely exhibited and was largely unknown until decades after her death.

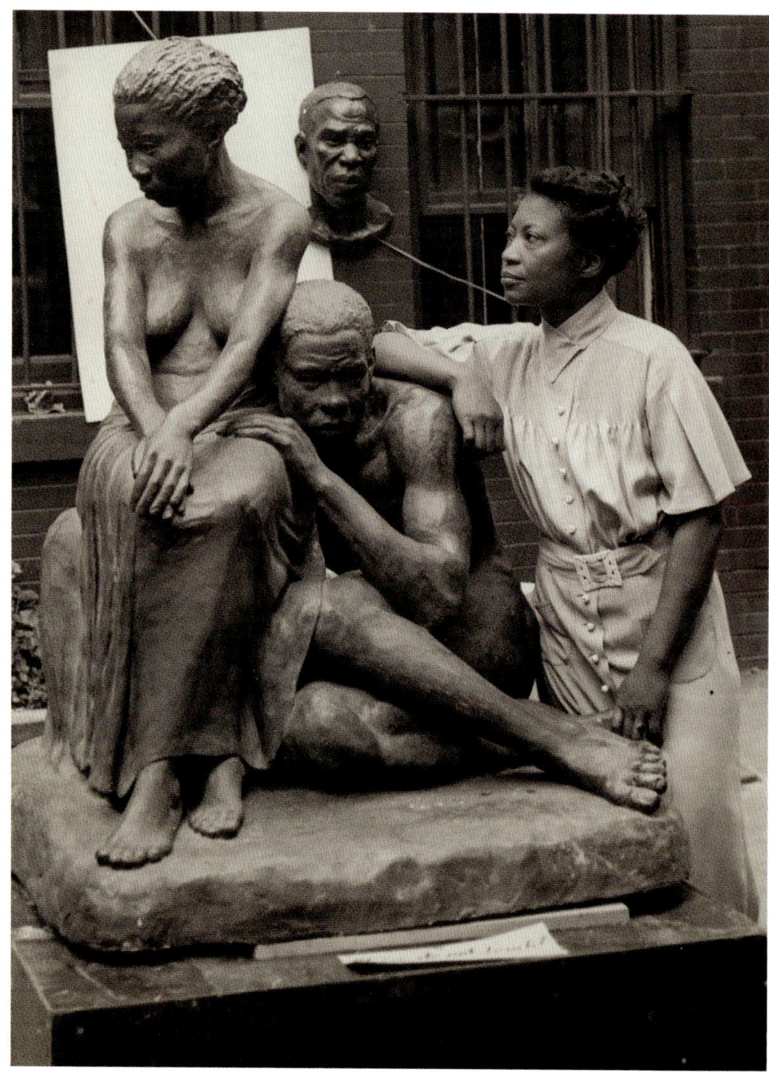

▲ **Augusta Savage** with her sculpture *Realization*, 1938, photograph by Andrew Herman

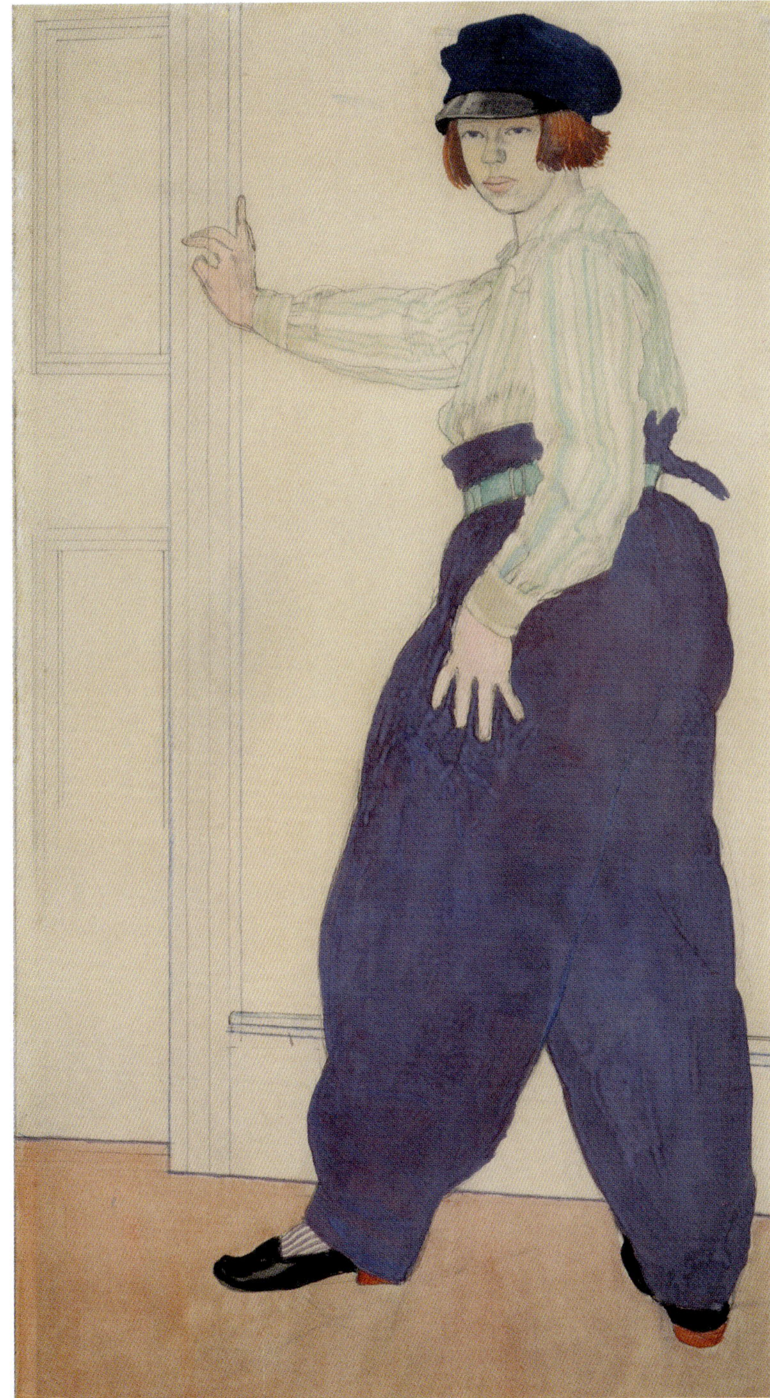

▲ **Dora Carrington**, *Self-Portrait*, 1913, pencil, watercolor, gouache, and chalk on paper, Jerwood Collection of Modern and Contemporary Art, Ludlow, UK

Joan Miró

1893–1983

One of the first artists to work in the Surrealist style, Miró is best known for his highly abstract, experimental paintings, which often featured simple forms floating above colored or white backgrounds. Miró was also a prominent abstract sculptor. Born the son of a Barcelona goldsmith and watchmaker, he had a successful career as an artist but preferred privacy to self-promotion.

Gluck

1895–1978

A 20th-century British painter best known for portraits and floral images, Gluck selected the genderless name in 1918. Born into a wealthy Jewish family, Gluck achieved significant artistic acclaim in the 1920s and 1930s, and caused controversy by wearing men's clothes and painting a double portrait featuring the artist with a female romantic partner. Gluck's artistic output declined in later decades. They refused to conform to any particular artistic school or style.

René Magritte

1898–1967

Belgium-born Surrealist painter Magritte painted mysterious images in which ordinary things are presented in unusual or even incomprehensible ways, encouraging viewers to search for explanations that probably do not exist. These included erotic objects that were juxtaposed in dreamlike settings. He became a leading figure in Surrealism after moving to Paris in 1927.

Henry Moore

1898–1986

A leading 20th-century British sculptor, Moore is known for his abstracted, often monumental statues, including reclining female nudes. Most of his figures and abstract forms feature smooth, flowing shapes inspired by landscapes or other aspects of nature—they are designed to be displayed outdoors—although other works were influenced by the carvings of ancient cultures. Early in his career, he worked in stone or wood, but later mainly used bronze.

Aaron Douglas

1899–1979

During the Harlem Renaissance of the 1920s, painter and illustrator Aaron Douglas developed a distinctive style that featured vibrant colors and silhouettes. His work shows the influence of both traditional African art and European modernism, and it often has African or Black themes. Douglas taught art at Fisk University in Nashville, Tennessee, for more than two decades.

Alberto Giacometti

1901–1966

The elongated human figures that Swiss-born sculptor Alberto Giacometti created from the late 1940s are among the most iconic works of modern sculpture. They are often interpreted as expressing the anxiety, desolation, and tragedy of postwar Europe. The sculptures he created before World War II were often Surrealist in style. Giacometti was a skilled painter and draftsman as well as a sculptor; his father was the noted painter Giovanni Giacometti.

Eric Ravilious

1903–1942

A 20th-century British watercolor painter and printmaker, Ravilious is perhaps best known for the distinctive works he created while serving as an official war artist during World War II, and for his prewar landscapes. A versatile artist, he also created highly regarded prints, which often served as book illustrations, and designs for ceramics, textiles, furniture, and glass. He married artist Tirzah Garwood.

Mark Rothko

1903–1970

Russian-born American painter Rothko is best known for his abstract Color Field paintings, which he started to create in the late 1940s. These featured large blocks of just a few colors that filled most or all of a very large canvas; the goal of these works was to express emotion. Rothko's work began to receive favorable attention in the 1950s and 1960s; he died by suicide in 1970.

Dame Barbara Hepworth

1903–1975

Sculptor Barbara Hepworth was a pivotal figure in the development of British abstract art. In 1931, she unveiled the first of her sculptures that was pierced by a hole, a use of negative space that proved influential. In 1938, she married painter Ben Nicholson and a year later they moved to Cornwall. Her work became more individual in style, exploring the interiors of round or pointed oval shapes using strings and colored paint and wood rather than stone.

Salvador Dalí

1904–1989

An influential Spanish painter, Dalí is remembered largely for the enigmatic Surrealist images that he painted between 1929 and the late 1930s—most notably 1931's *The Persistence of Memory*. During the final half century of Dalí's life, he was known as much for his endless self-promotion and extravagant mustache as for his art.

Arshile Gorky

c.1904–1948

A pioneering figure in the Abstract Expressionist movement, Gorky is best known for abstract images

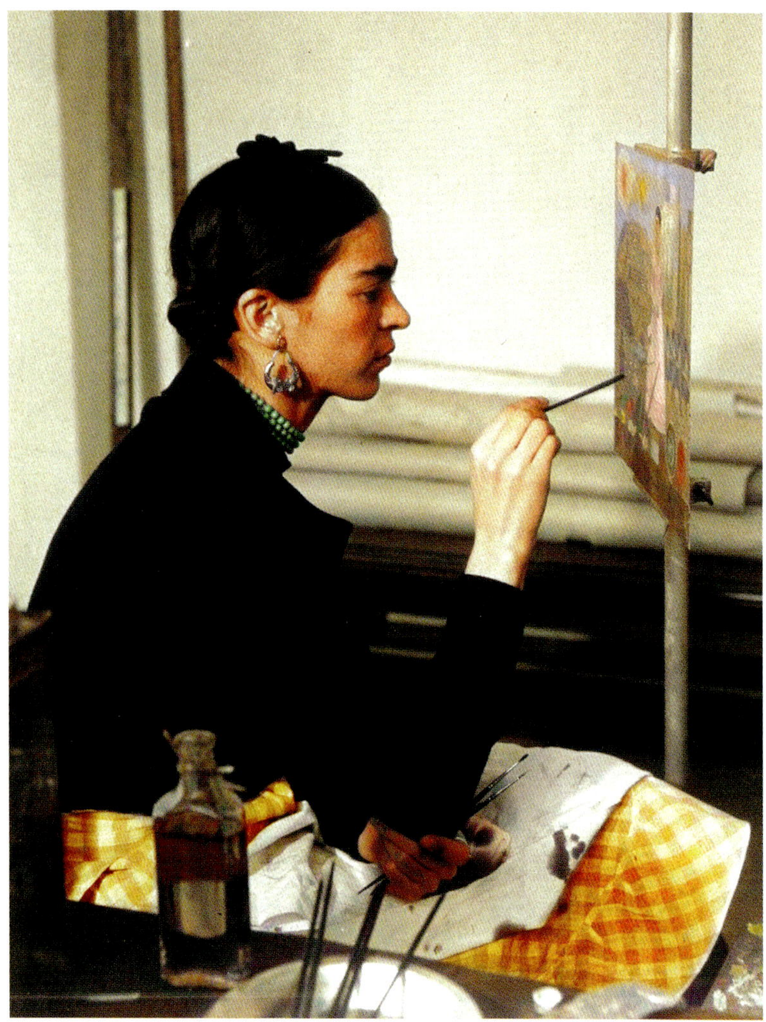

▲ **Frida Kahlo** painting, 1932

featuring organic forms. His early work was clearly influenced by Picasso and Cézanne. An Armenian born in modern-day Türkiye, he moved to the US as a teenager. Gorky died by suicide in 1948 following a series of setbacks that included cancer, a serious car accident, and the loss of numerous works in a studio fire.

Frida Kahlo

1907–1954

One of Mexico's most famous artists, Kahlo is best known for her richly colored self-portraits, inspired by Mexican artistic traditions. These often feature inventive dreamlike imagery, which led her to be associated with the Surrealists, an association she did not accept. Gravely injured in a bus accident as a teenager, Kahlo endured severe pain throughout her life, something reflected in many of her self-portraits. She married the artist Diego Rivera twice.

Francis Bacon

1909–1992

Among the most distinctive—and disturbing—painters of the mid-20th century, this Irish-born British artist created powerful, unsettling images of isolation and anguish, as well as deeply distorted and disturbing portraits. Many of Bacon's most important works are triptychs. A largely self-taught artist, he worked as an interior decorator before finding success as an artist in the mid-1940s.

Louise Bourgeois

1911–2010

A major figure in the history of modern and contemporary art, Bourgeois is known for installations and sculptures—some of them abstract, others figurative—that explored her own memories and life experiences, including of childhood family drama. Born and raised in France, she moved to New York in 1938. She also painted, drew, and created prints.

Jackson Pollock

1912–1956

A leading figure in the American Abstract Expressionist movement, Pollock is best known for his "drip paintings," which he created by pouring or splashing paint onto horizontal canvases, leading to works characterized by frenetic energy and a sense of spontaneity. Pollock created the first of these drip paintings in 1947. He was an alcoholic and died in a drunk driving accident at the age of 44.

Sir Sidney Nolan

1917–1992

An acclaimed 20th-century Australian painter, Nolan is best known for his landscapes, which capture the vastness of the Australian bush. He is also notable for paintings related to the country's folklore and historical figures, such as the outlaw Ned Kelly. An experimental artist, Nolan produced a great variety of work over the course of his career. His early works were largely abstract. He was knighted in 1981.

Andrew Wyeth

1917–2009

A 20th-century American Realist painter, Wyeth mainly created watercolor and tempera images of the people and landscapes of two rural locations that he knew well—his hometown of Chadds Ford, Pennsylvania, and Cushing, Maine, where he had a summer home. His works are sometimes labeled nostalgic, but they have proved enduringly popular. Wyeth's 1948 painting *Christina's World* is among the most famous American artworks of the 20th century. His father was the acclaimed illustrator N. C. Wyeth.

Lucian Freud

1922–2011

A German-born British artist, Freud created expressive, psychologically probing portraits and unidealized nudes, typically of sitters he knew well—and often of himself. The grandson of Sigmund Freud, Lucian Freud was among the most important and acclaimed figurative painters of his era. His early works were influenced by Surrealism, while those from the 1950s tend to be highly detailed and realist. Freud's later paintings feature bolder, looser brushwork.

Roy Lichtenstein

1923–1997

An important figure in the American Pop Art movement, Lichtenstein produced large paintings based very closely on panels from comic strips and comic books—perhaps the ultimate example of elevating low art to the status of fine art. Lichtenstein discovered this subject matter in the early 1960s when he was nearly 40 years old; until then, he had supported himself largely through teaching, including at Rutgers University. Lichtenstein was also a sculptor and printmaker.

Andy Warhol

1928–1987

Warhol was a leading figure of the 1960s Pop Art movement. His paintings and silkscreen prints of popular consumer products and celebrities are among the most recognizable artworks of the second half of the 20th century. Born in Pittsburgh, Warhol was a successful commercial illustrator in New York before finding artistic fame. His art both satirized and exalted consumer and celebrity culture; it catapulted Warhol himself to celebrity status.

Helen Frankenthaler

1928–2011

An important American painter in what is considered to be the second generation of Abstract Expressionism, Frankenthaler created her most notable works by pouring thin paints onto canvases that she had laid on the floor. The strategy was inspired by Jackson Pollock's drip paintings, but produced very different results that contributed to the development of Color Field painting. She was also a skilled printmaker. For a time, she was married to artist Robert Motherwell.

Jasper Johns

1930–

A key figure in American Pop Art, which used ordinary objects and popular culture as the basis for fine art, Johns is best known for his paintings of two-dimensional items, including targets, maps, numbers, letters, and US flags, which he started painting in the mid-1950s, shortly after serving in the US Army. He was also a sculptor, producing re-creations of everyday objects, such as beer cans and light bulbs.

Faith Ringgold

1930–

An important Black American artist, Ringgold's work often focuses on the themes of US race relations and women's rights. In addition to oil paintings and prints, she is known for creating quilts, soft sculptures, and other artwork involving fabric. Ringgold's mother, who worked as a fashion designer, collaborated with her on some of these projects. Ringgold is also an illustrator and author of children's books.

Bridget Riley

1931–

Featuring colors, lines, patterns, and curves, the work of British abstract painter Bridget Riley creates optical illusions, such as the illusion of movement or depth, a branch of Abstract art known as Op Art. A more conventional painter early on in her career, Riley was inspired to explore the use of optical effects from 1959, after studying the Pointillist paintings of Georges Seurat.

Gerhard Richter

1932–

German Contemporary artist Gerhard Richter has explored a range of abstract styles. He is best known for paintings he created in the 1960s that were based on photographs from magazines and newspapers. From the 1970s, his work tended toward Abstraction and Minimalism, though he continued to experiment, including with glass sculpture, photography, and stained glass. From 2011 Richter began to use digital technology, too. In 1961, he defected from communist East Germany to live in West Germany.

Clifford Possum Tjapaltjarri

1932–2002

A leading figure in 20th-century Australian Aboriginal art, Possum Tjapaltjarri is known for his paintings of the Dreaming, the creation period in Aboriginal culture. His abstracted "map paintings" are rooted in traditional Aboriginal sand drawing, but introduced new ideas and iconography, which influenced future Aboriginal artists. Wood carving was his main artistic outlet before the 1970s. He was one of the first artists to become involved with the Aboriginal Art Movement.

Sir Frank Bowling

1934–

A British Guiana-born painter, Bowling is known for the large, colorful abstract works that he created after moving to New York in 1966. Among the most notable are his "map paintings," which feature maps, often of continents, stenciled onto large fields of color. An experimental artist whose work has continued to evolve throughout his long career, Bowling was knighted in 2020.

Dame Paula Rego

1935–2022

An influential and imaginative artist, Rego was born in Portugal but lived and worked largely in the UK. She created challenging, sometimes unsettling works about the plight of women—one series confronted the aftermath of illegal abortions, another portrayed women behaving like dogs. Rego also painted images inspired by children's stories. She was made a Dame Commander of the British Empire in 2010.

David Hockney

1937–

The leading British artist of his generation, Hockney was a major figure in the Pop Art movement of the 1960s. He is best known for his bright, sunny paintings of swimming pools, created after he moved to Los Angeles in 1964; portraits and double portraits, usually of people he knows well; and vibrantly colored abstract landscapes, especially of his native Yorkshire, which he returned to in 2004. A versatile artist, Hockney has also achieved considerable success in drawing, printmaking, stage design, and photography often exploiting the possibilities presented by new technology.

Jaune Quick-to-See Smith

1940–

The art of this leading Indigenous American artist often focuses on contemporary Indigenous themes and issues, such as the misrepresentation of Indigenous culture in white society. She incorporates traditional Indigenous American influences and modern styles associated with artists of European heritage, such as Robert Rauschenberg.

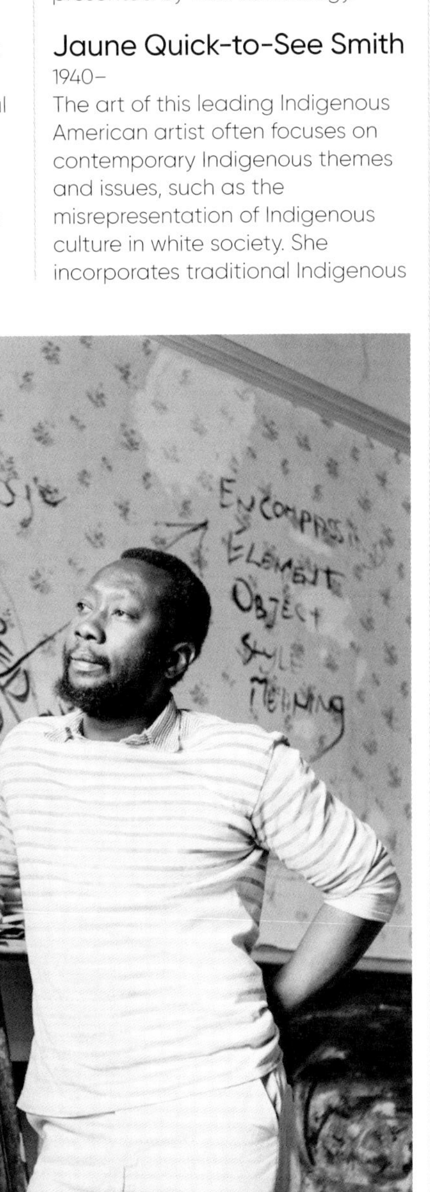

▲ **Frank Bowling** in his studio, 1962, photograph by Tony Evans

El Anatsui

1944–

A Ghanaian sculptor based in Nigeria, Anatsui is best known for his large-scale curtains made from thousands of bottle caps connected by wires. These works have been described as metallic tapestries; his father was a weaver and fisherman. Anatsui's early works included innovative wood and ceramic sculptures. He tends to give his works new forms every time they are installed.

Anselm Kiefer

1945–

Leading German Neo-Expressionist artist Anselm Kiefer has confronted difficult topics related to German history and culture—most notably the Nazi era. His paintings, sculptures, mixed-media works, and installations are poignant, grim, and typically muted in color. He often applies thick layers of paint and sometimes incorporates objects such as dried plants or broken glass.

Chris Ofili

1968–

A British artist of Nigerian descent, Ofili is known for his provocative works on topics such as race and religion. Most famously, he has incorporated elephant dung into his paintings, including those that are Christian images. In 1998, Ofili was the first Black artist to win Britain's prestigious Turner Prize. He now lives and works in Trinidad and Tobago.

Banksy

Active since the early 1990s, Graffiti artist Banksy works mainly in the UK, but he is internationally famous for creating witty anti-authoritarian murals, often in public places at night when nobody is around and usually with the help of stencils. He has also created performance art pieces. Despite his tremendous fame, Banksy is celebrated for his anonymity—the name Banksy is a pseudonym. As of early 2024, Banksy has still not revealed his true identity, ostensibly because of the illegal nature of graffiti, though many theories abound.

INDEX

A

B

C

M

N

O

P

PICTURE CREDITS

The publisher would like to thank the following for their kind permission to reproduce their photographs:

(Key: a-above; b-below/bottom; c-center; f-far; l-left; r-right; t-top)

2 akg-images: © Sotheby›s. **4-5 Bridgeman Images. 6-7 Bridgeman Images:** Photograph © 2024 Museum of Fine Arts, Boston. All rights reserved. / Gift of Quincy A. Shaw, Jr. (detail). **9 Courtesy National Gallery of Art, Washington:** Chester Dale Fund (detail). **10-11 Getty Images:** Universal History Archive / Contributor. **12 Bridgeman Images:** © Iberfoto (r); Photo © Heini Schneebeli (cla). **13 Alamy Stock Photo:** Nick Hill (b, cr). **13 Kremer Pigmente GmbH & Co. KG** (tl). **14-15 Alamy Stock Photo:** CPA Media Pte Ltd. **16-17 © The Trustees of the British Museum. All rights reserved. 18 Bridgeman Images:** Photo © Andrea Jemolo. **19 Alamy Stock Photo:** CPA Media Pte Ltd (cl). **Bridgeman Images** (c, cra). **Getty Images / iStock:** Sergey Strelkov / Getty Images Plus (bl). **20-21 Photo Scala, Florence:** Marie Mauzy. **22 © The Trustees of the British Museum. All rights reserved** (br). **Getty Images:** Photo12 (c, tr, bl). **23 Kremer Pigmente GmbH & Co. KG.** (br). **SuperStock:** Leonardo Diaz Romero / age fotostock (l, c, bc). **24 Getty Images:** Werner Forman / Contributor / Universal Images Group Editorial (c, cl). **The Metropolitan Museum of Art:** The Michael C. Rockefeller Memorial Collection, Bequest of Nelson A. Rockefeller, 1979 (br). **Jill Mollenhauer** (cr). **25 Getty Images:** Universal History Archive / Contributor (c). **SuperStock:** A. Burkatovski / Fine Art Images (bc). **26 Photo Scala, Florence. 27 Bridgeman Images:** Granger (bl). **Dreamstime.com:** Sulozone (c); Aleksandar Todorovic (bc). **28 Bridgeman Images:** G. Dagli Orti / © NPL—DeA Picture Library. **29 Bridgeman Images:** Photo © Andrea Jemolo (cl); Photo © Stefano Baldini (c, cr). **30 Dreamstime.com:** Steve Allen (cr, c, clb). **Getty Images:** MediaProduction (bc). **Kremer Pigmente GmbH & Co. KG.** (br). **31 Bridgeman Images** (l, c); © Frank Buffetrille. All rights reserved 2024 (cr). **© The Trustees of the British Museum. All rights reserved:** (crb). **32 Bridgeman Images** (bl); Photo © Stefano Baldini (c, tr); © Look and Learn (bc). **33 Bridgeman Images** (tr); Photo © Raffaello Bencini (c); Luisa Ricciarini (tc). **34 Alamy Stock Photo:** Album (tr); Rosa Irene Betancourt (c). **Getty Images:** Fine Art Images / Heritage Images (crb). **Minneapolis Institute of Art:** The John R. Van Derlip Fund and Gift of funds from Bruce B. Dayton, an anonymous donor, Mr. and Mrs. Kenneth Dayton, Mr. and Mrs. W. John Driscoll, Mr. and Mrs. Alfred Harrison, Mr. and Mrs. John Andrus, Mr. and Mrs. Judson Dayton, Mr. and Mrs. Stephen Keating, Mr. and Mrs. Pierce McNally, Mr. and Mrs. Donald Dayton, Mr. and Mrs. Wayne MacFarlane, and many other generous friends of the Institute (bl). **35 Alamy Stock Photo:** Classic Image (tc); Heritage Image Partnership Ltd (tr); Franck Legros (cl). **SuperStock:** Photo DeAgostini / © Succession H. Matisse/ DACS 2024 (cr). **36 Bridgeman Images:** (c, bl). **37 Bridgeman Images:** Kimbell Art Museum, Fort Worth, Texas. **38 Bridgeman Images:** Dinodia (c, tr). **Getty Images:** Christophe Boisvieux / Corbis (bc). **39 The Metropolitan Museum of Art:** The Michael C. Rockefeller Memorial Collection, Bequest of Nelson A. Rockefeller, 1979. **40 Getty Images:** Pictures from History / Contributor / Universal Images Group Editorial. **41 akg-images:** Jean-Louis Nou (c, cla, br). **Depositphotos Inc:** saiko3p (clb). **42-43 Dreamstime.com:** Tinamou. **44 Alamy Stock Photo:** ephotocorp (br). **Shutterstock.com:** sharptoyou (c, tr). **45 123RF.com:** brankobjovanovic (cr). **National Museum of Korea:** (c, cl, tr, cra). **46 Bridgeman Images:** Photograph © 2024 Museum of Fine Arts, Boston. All rights reserved. / Denman Waldo Ross Collection (c). **Kremer Pigmente GmbH & Co. KG.** (cl). **47 Dreamstime.com:** Nagoruni (c, cla, cl, br); Penchan Pumila (cr). **The Metropolitan Museum of Art:** The Michael C. Rockefeller Memorial Collection, Bequest of Nelson A. Rockefeller, 1979 (tr). **48 Bridgeman Images:** © British Library Board. All Rights Reserved. **49 Bridgeman Images:** Pictures from History. **50 © The Trustees of the British Museum. All rights reserved:** (c, tl, cl). **Dreamstime.com:** Bobhilscher (bl). **51 123RF.com:** swisshippo (br). **Alamy Stock Photo:** Lindra Hismanto (c, bl). **52 Bridgeman Images** (cra); **Tarker** (c, cla, clb, br, bl). **53 akg-images:** Joseph Martin. **54 The Metropolitan Museum of Art:** Bequest of Cora Timken Burnett, 1956. **55 Alamy Stock Photo:** Photo 12. **56 Bridgeman Images:** Museum of Fine Arts, Houston / Gift of Mr & Mrs Harris Masterson III. **Getty Images:** Universal History Archive / Contributor (cl). **The Metropolitan Museum of Art:** Louis V. Bell Fund, 1967 (tr). **SuperStock:** Tolo Balaguer / age fotostock (tc). **57 Alamy Stock Photo:** Stephen Chung / Alamy Live News (cl). **Bridgeman Images** (c); Photo: Turku Art Museum /Kari Lehtinen (tr). **Shutterstock.com:** Eileen Tweedy (tl). **58 © The Trustees of the British Museum. All rights reserved. 59 The Metropolitan Museum of Art:** Gift of R. H. Ellsworth Ltd., in honor of Susan Dillon, 1987. **60 Bridgeman Images:** © Kimbell Art Museum. **61 The Metropolitan Museum of Art:** Samuel Eilenberg Collection, Bequest of Samuel Eilenberg, 1998 (c, cla, c, bl). **Photograph by Emma Natalya Stein:** (tr). **62-63 Getty Images:** Pictures from History / Contributor / Universal Images Group. **63 Dreamstime.com:** Pattanawit Chancharastong (bc). **64 Bridgeman Images:** © Iberfoto (c, bl, cra); Luisa Ricciarini (crb). **65 Bridgeman Images:** Universal History Archive / UIG. **66 © The Trustees of the British Museum. All rights reserved. 67 Bridgeman Images:** © Peter Willi (cl, c, cla, bl). **Dreamstime.com:** Fuzja44 (br). **68 Alamy Stock Photo:** Azoor Photo (br). **Getty Images:** G. Nimatallah / De Agostini / Contributor (c). **69 Bridgeman Images:** Photograph © 2024 Museum of Fine Arts, Boston. All rights reserved. / Fenollosa-Weld Collection. **70-71 Bridgeman Images** (b). **71 Kremer Pigmente GmbH & Co. KG.** (cla). **72 Bridgeman Images:** Luisa Ricciarini (c). **Courtesy National Gallery of Art, Washington:** Gift of Mrs. Otto H. Kahn (br). **73 The Metropolitan Museum of Art:** Gift of John M. Crawford Jr., 1988. **74 SLUB Dresden/Digital Collections:** Mscr.Dresd.R.310. **75 Bridgeman Images:** Photo © Luca Tettoni (bl). **© The Trustees of the British Museum. All rights reserved** (c, tl, cra). **76 Bridgeman Images:** Photo © Raffaello Bencini (c, clb); Cameraphoto Arte Venezia (bc). **77 National Palace Museum, Taipei, Taiwan. 78-79 Photo Scala, Florence:** Photo Opera Metropolitana Siena. **79 Alamy Stock Photo:** LightField Studios Inc. (tc). **80 Bridgeman Images:** Luisa Ricciarini. **81 Bridgeman Images. 82-83 Photo Scala, Florence. 83 SuperStock:** Universal Images (tc). **84 © The Trustees of the British Museum. All rights reserved. 85 The Metropolitan Museum of Art:** Bequest of John M. Crawford Jr., 1988. **86, 87 Bridgeman Images. 88-89 Alamy Stock Photo:** GL Archive. **90 Getty Images:** DEA / A. Dagli Orti / Contributor. **91 Bridgeman Images** (br). **Getty Images:** Andia / Contributor / Universal Images Group (c, bl, bc). **92 Bridgeman Images:** Photo © Andrea Jemolo. **93 Bridgeman Images:** (cl); © Musée Condé, Chantilly (c). **94-95 Bridgeman Images:** Photo © Raffaello Bencini. **95 Dreamstime.com:** Anna Pakutina (tc). **96-97 Bridgeman Images:** © Art in Flanders. **98 Bridgeman Images:** Mondadori Portfolio / Archivio Antonio Quattrone. **99 Bridgeman Images. 100 Bridgeman Images:** Photo © Photo Josse. **101 Alamy Stock Photo:** photosublime. **102 Alamy Stock Photo:** World History Archive (cr, tc, tr). **Bridgeman Images** (clb). **103 Alamy Stock Photo:** Adam Eastland (c); Neil Setchfield (bc). **104-105 Bridgeman Images. 106 Alamy Stock Photo:** Prisma Archivo. **107 Bridgeman Images:** Luisa Ricciarini (r, bc). **Photo Scala, Florence:** courtesy of the Ministero Beni e Att. Culturali e del Turismo (clb). **108 Bridgeman Images. 109 Getty Images:** Heritage Images / Contributor / Hulton Fine Art Collection. **110 Bridgeman Images** (cr); © Art in Flanders (c); © NPL—DeA Picture Library (br). **111 Bridgeman Images. 112 Photo Scala, Florence:** courtesy of the Ministero Beni e Att. Culturali e del Turismo. **113 Bridgeman Images:** © Museo Nacional Thyssen-Bornemisza, Madrid. **114 Alamy Stock Photo:** Heritage Image Partnership Ltd (tr); The Picture Art Collection (c). **Bridgeman Images:** © NPL—DeA Picture Library (crb). **The Cleveland Museum Of Art:** Leonard C. Hanna, Jr. Fund (clb). **Dreamstime.com:** Marcus0711 (bl). **115 Alamy Stock Photo:** dpa picture alliance (cl); Lanmas (c). **Bridgeman Images:** © Francesco Turio Bohm. All rights reserved 2023 (tr); Luisa Ricciarini (tl). **116 Bridgeman Images:** © National Museum in Gdansk. **117, 118 Bridgeman Images. 119 Alamy Stock Photo:** B. O'Kane. **120 Bridgeman Images** (c, l, cb). **Kremer Pigmente GmbH & Co. KG:** (br). **121 Getty Images:** Fine Art / Contributor / Corbis Historical. **122, 123, 124-125 Bridgeman Images. 126 Bridgeman Images** (c, cla, clb). **Dreamstime.com:** Montree Nanta (br). **127 Bridgeman Images. 128-129 Alamy Stock Photo:** Album. **129 Bridgeman Images** (crb). **130 Bridgeman Images:** Pictures from History. **131 Bridgeman Images:** Tarker. **132-133 Dreamstime.com:** Giorgio Morara. **133 Bridgeman Images** (tc). **134 Bridgeman Images. 135 Alamy Stock Photo:** The Picture Art Collection. **136 Getty Images:** Leemage / Contributor / Corbis Historical. **137 Bridgeman Images** (c, tl). **The Metropolitan Museum of Art:** The Friedsam Collection, Bequest of Michael Friedsam, 1931 (cr). **138 The Metropolitan Museum of Art:** Ex coll.: C. C. Wang Family, Gift of Oscar L. Tang Family, 2005. **139 Bridgeman Images. 140 Dreamstime.com:** Jakub Zajic. **141 Bridgeman Images. 142 The Art Institute of Chicago:** Major Acquisitions Fund. **143 Dreamstime.com:** Vlad Ghiea. **144-145 Dreamstime.com:** Ilfede. **145 Dreamstime.com:** Tatiana Sidorenko (bc). **146-147 Alamy Stock Photo:** World History Archive. **147 Bridgeman Images:** © Veneranda Biblioteca Ambrosiana / Mauro Ranzani / Mondadori Portfolio (cr). **148 Bridgeman Images:** Stefano Bianchetti (l, br). **Dreamstime.com:** Lukelake (cra). **Kremer Pigmente GmbH & Co. KG.** (crb). **149 Dreamstime.com:** Giorgio Morara (r, tl). **The Metropolitan Museum of Art:** Fletcher Fund, 1919 (detail) (b). **150 Alamy Stock Photo:** Peter Barritt (c, cr). **151 Bridgeman Images. 152 Courtesy National Gallery of Art, Washington:** Widener Collection. **153 Bridgeman Images. 154 Getty Images:** Heritage Images / Contributor / Hulton Fine Art Collection (c, br). **Kremer Pigmente GmbH & Co. KG.** (cr). **155 Alamy Stock Photo:** GL Archive. **156 Bridgeman Images:** Pictures from History. **157 Bridgeman Images:** © NPL—DeA Picture Library. **158 Bridgeman Images. 159 © The Trustees of the British Museum. All rights reserved** (clb). **Photo Scala, Florence:** Image copyright The Metropolitan Museum of Art / Art Resource / Scala, Florence (c, tl, tr). **160 Photo Scala, Florence:** bpk, Bildagentur fuer Kunst, Kultur und Geschichte, Berlin. **161 The J. Paul Getty Museum, Los Angeles:** (cra). **The Metropolitan Museum of Art:** H. O. Havemeyer Collection, Bequest of Mrs. H. O. Havemeyer, 1929 (c, br). **162 The Metropolitan Museum of Art:** Mary and Cheney Cowles Collection, Gift of Mary and Cheney Cowles, 2018. **163 Bridgeman Images** (c, cla). **Alamy Stock Photo:** Album (bl). **164 Dreamstime.com:** Scaliger (c). **164-165 Alamy Stock Photo:** Azoor Collection. **166 Bridgeman Images. 167 The Metropolitan Museum of Art:** Gift of Paul and Ruth W. Tishman, 1991 (c, bl, br). **168 Dreamstime.com:** Vladimirs Koskins (c). **Getty Images:** DEA / Biblioteca Ambrosiana / Contributor / DeAgostini Editorial (cl). **169 National Palace Museum, Taipei, Taiwan. 170 Alamy Stock Photo:** Stephen Chung / Alamy Live News (cr). **Bridgeman Images:** Photo © Stefano Baldini (tc); Royal Collection Trust / © His Majesty King Charles III, 2024 (tr). **Getty Images:** DEA Picture Library / Contributor (cl). **171 Alamy Stock Photo:** John Bracegirdle (tr); Michael Sawyer / Associated Press (cl); Heritage Image Partnership Ltd (c). **Bridgeman Images** (tl). **172 Alamy Stock Photo:** Penta Springs Limited (c, cl). **Dreamstime.com:** Vladimirs Prusakovs (bc). **173 Los Angeles County Museum of Art:** Bequest of Edwin Binney, 3rd (M.90.141.1). **174 The Metropolitan Museum of Art:** Gift of Mr. and Mrs. Earl Morse, 1972. **175 Bridgeman Images. 176-177 Alamy Stock Photo:** GL Archive. **178 Bridgeman Images. 179 SuperStock:** A. Burkatovski / Fine Art Images. **180 © The Trustees of the British Museum. All rights reserved** (br). **The Metropolitan Museum of Art:** Gift of Mr. and Mrs. Klaus G. Perls, 1990 (c, tl, clb). **181 Alamy Stock Photo:** Art Heritage. **182 National Portrait Gallery, London. 183 Bridgeman Images. 184 Bridgeman Images:** Photograph © 2024 Museum of Fine Arts, Boston. All rights reserved. / Gift of Quincy A. Shaw, Jr. **185 Bridgeman Images:** © CSG CIC Glasgow Museums Collection. **186-187 Bridgeman Images:** Pictures from History. **187 Freer Gallery of Art, Smithsonian Institution, Washington DC:** Gift of Charles Lang Freer / Freer Gallery of Art Collection (bl). **188 Alamy Stock Photo:** ARTGEN. **189 Dreamstime.com:** Alvaro German Vilela. **190-191 Alamy Stock Photo:** Album. **192, 193 Bridgeman Images. 194 Bridgeman Images:** © San Diego Museum of Art / Gift of Anne R. and Amy Putnam. **195 Bridgeman Images:** © NPL—DeA Picture Library (b, ca, cra). **Dorling Kindersley:** Dave King / Science Museum, London (tr). **196 Bridgeman Images. 197 Bridgeman Images:** Photo © Christie's Images. **198 Bridgeman Images. 199 Bridgeman Images** (c, br). **Depositphotos Inc:** Prokrida (bc). **200 akg-images:** MPortfolio / Electa (cl). **Alamy Stock Photo:** world masterpiece (tr). **Getty Images:** De Agostini / Contributor (tl). **The Metropolitan Museum of Art:** Bequest of Joan Whitney Payson, 1975 (cr). **201 Alamy Stock Photo:** Guy Bell / Alamy Live News (cl). **Collection of the Smithsonian National Museum of African American History and Culture:** (tl). **Getty Images:** Sepia Times / Contributor / Universal Images Group (cr). **Photo Scala, Florence:** Museo Nacional Thyssen-Bornemisza (tr). **202 Bridgeman Images. 203 Bridgeman Images:** The Stapleton Collection. **204 Bridgeman Images** (c); Luisa Ricciarini (cl). . **205 Photo Scala, Florence:** Copyright The National Gallery, London. **206 Getty Images:** Grafissimo / DigitalVision Vectors (cl); Mondadori Portfolio / Contributor / Hulton Fine Art Collection (c, br). **207 Alamy Stock Photo:** Heritage Image Partnership Ltd. **208 Bridgeman Images:** © National Galleries of Scotland. **209, 210 Bridgeman Images. 211 Courtesy National Gallery of Art, Washington:** Gift of the 50th Anniversary Gift Committee. **212-213 Bridgeman Images. 214 Photo Scala, Florence:** RMN-Grand Palais / Angle Dequier / Dist. **215 The Metropolitan Museum of Art:** Gift of Mr. and Mrs. Charles Wrightsman, 1978. **216 Dreamstime.com:** Nicoleta Raluca Tudor. **217 Bridgeman Images:** Photo © Fine Art Images. **218-219 Rijksmuseum, Amsterdam:** On loan from the City of Amsterdam. **220 Bridgeman Images:** Photo © Stefano Baldini (c, br). **Getty Images:** Heritage Images / Contributor / Hulton Archive (cra). **221 The Metropolitan Museum of Art:** Purchase, Fletcher and Rogers Funds, and Bequest of Miss Adelaide Milton de Groot (1876-1967), by exchange, supplemented by gifts from friends of the Museum, 1971. **222 Bridgeman Images:** Alinari Archives, Florence—Reproduced with the permission of Ministero per i Beni e le Attività Culturali. **223 Bridgeman Images:** Stefano Bianchetti. **224 Bridgeman Images:** Photo © Sotheby's (c); Photo © Christie's Images (cr). **225 SuperStock:** Iberfoto Archivo. **226-227 Bridgeman Images. 228-229 SuperStock:** Artist—Jan Steen / Peter Barritt. **230, 231 Bridgeman Images. 232 Alamy Stock Photo:** Stefano Politi Markovina (tl). **Bridgeman Images:** © Kimbell Art Museum (cl); © National Galleries of Scotland (tr). **Dreamstime.com:** Inna Felker (cr). **233 Alamy Stock Photo:** Mihai Barbat (cl); De Agostini Picture Library (cr). **Bridgeman Images:** The Phillips Collection, Washington, D.C., USA / Acquired 1923 (tr). **National Museum of Korea** (tl). **234 SuperStock:** De Agostini. **235 Bridgeman Images:** © Ashmolean Museum. **236 The Metropolitan Museum of Art:** Purchase, The Dillon Fund Gift, 1979. **237 The Metropolitan Museum of Art:** Purchase, Barbara and William Karatz Gift and funds from various donors, 2004. **238 Getty Images:** Werner Forman / Contributor / Universal Images Group (bl). **The Metropolitan Museum of Art:** Gift of Lester Wunderman, 1977 (r, cl, c). **239 Bridgeman Images. 240-241 Alamy Stock Photo:** GL Archive. **241 Bridgeman Images** (cr). **242 Museo Nacional de Arte, La Paz, Bolivia. 243 Getty Images:** Heritage Images / Contributor / Hulton Fine Art Collection. **244 The Metropolitan Museum of Art:** Rogers Fund, 1919. **245 The Art Institute of Chicago:** The Regenstein Collection (c, bl). **Dreamstime.com:** Jianghongyan (cl). **246-247 Alamy Stock Photo:** © Fine Art Images / Heritage Images. **247 Dreamstime.com:** Erick Nguyen / Erickn (crb). **248 Bridgeman Images:** © Sir John Soane›s Museum. **249 Alamy Stock Photo:** Album. **250 The Metropolitan Museum of Art:** Bequest of Walter C. Baker, 1971 (bc). **Photo Scala, Florence:** RMN-Grand Palais / Mathieu Rabeau / Dist. (c, br). **251 Getty Images:** Universal History Archive / Contributor / Universal Images Group. **252-253 Alamy Stock Photo:** GL Archive. **254 Alamy Stock Photo:** PAINTING (br). **Photo Scala, Florence:** Copyright The National Gallery, London (c, tr). **255 Bridgeman Images:** © Brooklyn Museum / Museum Collection Fund and Dick S. Ramsay Fund. **256 Photo Scala, Florence:** Image copyright The Metropolitan Museum of Art / Art Resource. **257 Bridgeman Images. 258 Bridgeman Images:** © Wallace Collection, London, UK. **259 Alamy Stock Photo:** The Archives. **260-261 Alamy Stock Photo:** Album. **262 Bridgeman Images:** Royal Collection Trust / © His Majesty King Charles III, 2024. **263 Image Courtesy National Gallery Of Art, Washington:** Ferdinand Lammot Belin Fund. **264 © The Trustees of the British Museum. All rights reserved. 265 Bridgeman Images:** © Peter Willi. **266-267 Bridgeman Images. 268 SuperStock:** ACME Imagery. **269 The Metropolitan Museum of Art:** Gift of Julia A. Berwind, 1953. **270-271 Alamy Stock Photo:** © Fine Art Images / Heritage Images. **271 Bridgeman Images:** © London Metropolitan Archives (bc). **The Metropolitan Museum of Art:** The Howard Mansfield Collection, Purchase, Rogers Fund, 1936 (br). **272 Alamy Stock Photo:** Agenzia Sintesi (tc). **Dreamstime.com:** Stefano Valeri (c, br). **273 Bridgeman Images:** © Art in Flanders. **274 The Metropolitan Museum of Art:** Andrew W. Mellon Collection. **275 Bridgeman Images:** © Brooklyn Museum (c, clb). **The Metropolitan Museum of Art:** Rogers Fund, 1922 (br). **276 Bridgeman Images:** © Detroit Institute of Arts (bc); © Peter Willi (c, cla, clb). **277 National Museum of Korea. 278-279 The Metropolitan Museum of Art:** H. O. Havemeyer Collection, Bequest of Mrs. H. O. Havemeyer, 1929. **280-281 Alamy Stock Photo:** Niday Picture Library. **282 Bridgeman Images** (c). **Shutterstock.com:** Kay Wiegand (cr). **283, 284 Bridgeman Images. 285 Alamy Stock Photo:** ARTGEN. **286 Alamy Stock Photo:** Malcolm Park (tr). **Bridgeman Images** (cr). **Dreamstime.com:** Legacy1995 (cl);

Chumphon Whangchom (bl). **The Metropolitan Museum of Art:** Purchase, Joseph Pulitzer Bequest, 1952 (c). **287 Alamy Stock Photo:** Hayk Shalunts (tl). **The Art Institute of Chicago:** Gift of Elizabeth R.Vaughan (tr). **Photo Scala, Florence:** bpk, Bildagentur fuer Kunst, Kultur und Geschichte, Berlin (cr); Copyright The National Gallery, London (cl). **288 Alamy Stock Photo:** Ayhan Altun. **289 Smithsonian American Art Museum:** Gift of Mrs. Joseph Harrison Jnr., 1985.66.145_1. **290–291 The Metropolitan Museum of Art:** H. O. Havemeyer Collection, Bequest of Mrs. H. O. Havemeyer, 1929. **291 The Metropolitan Museum of Art:** Henry L. Phillips Collection, Bequest of Henry L. Phillips, 1939 (br). **292 Bridgeman Images**. **293 Bridgeman Images:** Photograph © 2024 Museum of Fine Arts, Boston. All rights reserved. / Henry Lillie Pierce Fund. **294–295 The Metropolitan Museum of Art:** Gift of Mrs. Russell Sage, 1908. **296 Bridgeman Images**. **297 Bridgeman Images:** © Saint Louis Art Museum / Bequest of Ezra H. Linley by exchange. **298 Getty Images:** Jens Schlueter / Contributor / AFP (c). **Marie Pauline Thorbecke, Rautenstrauch-Joest Museum:** Inv.no. T 123 (tr). **299 Alamy Stock Photo:** GL Archive. **300–301 Bridgeman Images**. **302 Alamy Stock Photo:** Charlie J Ercilla (c, br). **Bridgeman Images** (bc). **303 The Metropolitan Museum of Art:** Gift of Max N. Berry, 2015. **304 Bridgeman Images** (c, br); Luisa Ricciarini (cr). **305 The Cleveland Museum Of Art:** Gift from J. H. Wade. **306–307 The Metropolitan Museum of Art:** Gift of Cornelius Vanderbilt, 1887. **306 Dreamstime.com:** Rixie (cl). **308, 309 Bridgeman Images:** Photo © Photo Josse. **310 Dreamstime.com:** Nicoleta Raluca Tudor (tr). **Shutterstock.com:** Roka (c, clb). **311 The Cleveland Museum Of Art:** Mr. and Mrs. William H. Marlatt Fund. **312–313 Smithsonian American Art Museum:** Gift of Leonard and Paula Granoff. **314 The Metropolitan Museum of Art:** H. O. Havemeyer Collection, Bequest of Mrs. H. O. Havemeyer, 1929 (b, cra). **The Walters Art Museum, Baltimore:** Commissioned by William T. Walters, 1864 (tc). **315 Alamy Stock Photo:** Franck Legros. **316 Courtesy National Gallery of Art, Washington:** Gift of Count Cecil Pecci-Blunt. **317 Bridgeman Images**. **318–319 Alamy Stock Photo:** FineArt. **320, 321 Bridgeman Images**. **322 akg-images:** Erich Lessing (tr). **Bridgeman Images:** © NPL–DeA Picture Library (tc). **Photo Scala, Florence:** courtesy of the Ministero Beni e Att. Culturali e del Turismo (cl). **SuperStock:** Album Archivo / Album (cr). **323 Alamy Stock Photo:** Album (c); IanDagnall Computing (tc). **Bridgeman Images:** © Kettle›s Yard (cr). **SuperStock:** © Tomas Abad / age fotostock (tr). **324–325 Getty Images:** Sovfoto / Contributor / Universal Images Group. **326 Courtesy of Indianapolis Museum of Art at Newfields.:** James E. Roberts Fund. **327 Bridgeman Images:** © Detroit Institute of Arts / Gift of Dexter M. Ferry Jr. **328 Bridgeman Images** (c). **329 Bridgeman Images:** Photo © Fine Art Images (br). **SuperStock:** Artepics / age fotostock (c, cl, bl). **330 Bridgeman Images:** Photo © Stefano Baldini (cr). **Smithsonian American Art Museum:** Gift of the Historical Society of Forest Park, Illinois (c, br). **331 The Art Institute of Chicago:** Charles H. and Mary F. S. Worcester Collection (c). **Getty Images / iStock:** stocksnapper (bc). **332–333 Courtesy National Gallery of Art, Washington:** Collection of Mr. and Mrs. Paul Mellon. **334 Bridgeman Images**. **335 Bridgeman Images:** Photo © Fine Art Images. **336–337 Bridgeman Images:** Photo © The Courtauld. **338–339 Bridgeman Images:** © Isabella Stewart Gardner Museum. **338 Bridgeman Images:** © Isabella Stewart Gardner Museum / Photo © Sean Dungan (bl). **340 Bridgeman Images**. **341 The Metropolitan Museum of Art:** John Stewart Kennedy Fund, 1917. **342 Smithsonian American Art Museum:** Bequest of Marvin J. and Shirley F. Sonosky in memory of Harryette Cohn. **343 Image Courtesy National Gallery Of Art, Washington:** Gift of Mr. and Mrs. Richard Mellon Scaife in honor of Paul Mellon. **344–345 Dreamstime.com:** Giorgio Morara. **346 akg-images**. **347 © The Trustees of the British Museum. All rights reserved** (br). **National Museum of African Art, Smithsonian Institution:** Gift of Dr. and Mrs. Robert Kuhn (c). **348 Alamy Stock Photo:** Skimage (br). **Getty Images:** National Galleries of Scotland / Contributor / Hulton Fine Art Collection (c). **349 Bridgeman Images:** © Philippe Galard (c, cl). **Dreamstime.com:** Wrangel (bl). **350 Bridgeman Images:** © Brooklyn Museum / Gift of Rosemary and George Lois (c). **Getty Images:** Michel Huet / Contributor / Gamma-Rapho (cra). **351 Bridgeman Images**. **352 Bridgeman Images:** The Stapleton Collection. **353 Bridgeman Images:** Photo © Christie's Images. **354 Bridgeman Images:** Philadelphia Museum of Art, Pennsylvania, PA, USA / The Henry P. McIlhenny Collection. **355 Alamy Stock Photo:** Archivart. **356 Bridgeman Images**. **357 Bridgeman Images:** Photo: © Granger. **358 Alamy Stock Photo:** Artepics (c, cl, br). **Bridgeman Images:** Photo © Photo Josse (tr). **359 Camille CLAUDEL (1864–1943), La Valse, 1889–1905, bronze, cast Eugne Blot N 5, 1905, H.45.9 L.31.9 P.22.9 cm, Musée Camille Claudel Nogent-sur-Seine, inv.2010.1.10, purchased from Reine-Marie Paris in 2008, Photograph Marco Illuminati**. **360–361 The Metropolitan Museum of Art:** Bequest of Miss Adelaide Milton de Groot (1876–1967), 1967. **362 Alamy Stock Photo:** M&N (bc). **Getty Images:** Fine Art / Contributor / Corbis Historical (c, crb). **363 Depositphotos Inc:** YUNUSI. **364 Bridgeman Images**. **365 Alamy Stock Photo:** Bosiljka Zutich (c). **The Metropolitan Museum of Art:** H. O. Havemeyer Collection, Bequest of Mrs. H. O. Havemeyer, 1929 (cl). **366 Collection of the Hampton University Museum, Hampton, VA**. **367 The Metropolitan Museum of Art:** Bequest of Helen R. Bleibtreu, 1985 (c); Rogers Fund, 1928 (crb). **368 Alamy Stock Photo:** Artefact (c, crb). **Bridgeman Images** (tr). **369 Alamy Stock Photo:** Michel Euler / Associated Press (c). **Photo Scala, Florence:** RMN-Grand Palais / Patrick Gries / Dist. (br). **370–371 The Metropolitan Museum of Art:** Catharine Lorillard Wolfe Collection, Wolfe Fund, 1906. **370 The Art Institute of Chicago:** Mr. and Mrs. Martin A. Ryerson Collection (clb). **372–373 Bridgeman Images**. **374 akg-images:** © Sotheby›s. **375 SuperStock:** Photo Peter Barritt/ © Succession H. Matisse/ DACS 2024. **376–377 The Metropolitan Museum of Art:** The Walter H. and Leonore Annenberg Collection, Gift of Walter H. and Leonore Annenberg, 1994, Bequest of Walter H. Annenberg, 2002. **377 Alamy Stock Photo:** incamerastock (br). **378 Bridgeman Images:** Photo © Fine Art Images. **379 Alamy Stock Photo:** Hà Frankhauser. **380 Bridgeman Images** (c, bc). **Dreamstime.com:** Tinamou (br). **381 Bridgeman Images:** Photo © Fine Art Images. **382 Alamy Stock Photo:** Malcolm Park (cr). **Bridgeman Images** (cl); Photo © Photo Josse (tc); Photograph © 2024 Museum of Fine Arts, Boston. All rights reserved. / Denman Waldo Ross Collection (tr). **383 Alamy Stock Photo:** Lana Rastro (tr). **Bridgeman Images:** Photo © Fine Art Images (c). **Dreamstime.com:** Albertophotography (tl). **Courtesy National Gallery of Art, Washington:** The Collection of Mr. and Mrs. Paul Mellon (cl). **384 The Art Institute of Chicago:** Major Acquisitions Centennial Fund (tr). **© The Trustees of the British Museum. All rights reserved** (c, cr, cla). **385 Bridgeman Images:** Photo © Boltin Picture Library. **386 Bridgeman Images:** UPRAVIS 2024/ © Natalia Goncharova. **387 Bridgeman Images** (br); Photo © Fine Art Images (c, cr). **388 Photo Scala, Florence:** Digital image, The Museum of Modern Art, New York /© ADAGP, Paris and DACS, London 2024. **389 Bridgeman Images**. **390 akg-images**. **391 Collection of the Smithsonian American Art Museum:** Gift of John Gellatly. **392–393 Photo Scala, Florence:** Album. **392 Bridgeman Images** (cl). **394 Bridgeman Images**. **395** Cecilia Beaux (American, 1855–1942), After the Meeting, 1914, oil on canvas, 40 15 / 16 x 28 1 / 8 in. (104 x 71.5 cm), **Toledo Museum of Art (Toledo, Ohio), Gift of Florence Scott Libbey, 1915.163**. **396 Alamy Stock Photo:** Tracey Whitefoot. **397 Bridgeman Images:** Luisa Ricciarini / © DACS 2024. **398 Courtesy National Gallery of Art, Washington:** Chester Dale Fund. **399 Bridgeman Images**. **400 Bridgeman Images** (c); Photo © Fine Art Images (cr). **401 Alamy Stock Photo:** Artefact. **402–403 Getty Images:** Sepia Times / Contributor / Universal Images Group. **404–405 Bridgeman Images:** © Imperial War Museums. **406 Alamy Stock Photo:** Richard Manning (br). **Photo Scala, Florence:** Buffalo AKG Art Museum / Art Resource, NY / © Succession Brancusi–All rights reserved. ADAGP, Paris and DACS, London 2024 (c, crb). **407, 408 Bridgeman Images**. **409 Bridgeman Images:** Photo © Heini Schneebeli (tr). **Photo Scala, Florence:** Image copyright The Metropolitan Museum of Art (c, crb). **410 Bridgeman Images:** © Fitzwilliam Museum. **411 Alamy Stock Photo:** ARTGEN. **412 Bridgeman Images:** Photo: Philadelphia Museum of Art, Pennsylvania, PA, USA / Bequest of Georgia O'Keeffe for Alfred Steiglitz Coll, 1987. **413 Bridgeman Images:** © Art Institute of Chicago / Friends of American Art Collection. **414–415 Photo Scala, Florence:** Digital image, The Museum of Modern Art, New York/ © Salvador Dali, Fundació Gala-Salvador Dali, DACS 2024. **416 Alamy Stock Photo:** Richard Dyson (c). **Bridgeman Images:** The Stapleton Collection (tc). **Minneapolis Institute of Art:** Gift of Harriet and Ed Spencer (r). **Shutterstock.com:** Kateryna Mashkevych (cl). **417 Alamy Stock Photo:** Album (br). **Bridgeman Images:** Royal Collection Trust / © His Majesty King Charles III, 2024 (tc). **The Cleveland Museum Of Art:** Gift of William Ellery Greene (clb). **Dreamstime.com:** Yujie Chen (tl); Olga Kurbatova (bl). **418 Bridgeman Images:** Photo © Photo Josse (c, bc); Photo © Christie's Images (br). **419 Bridgeman Images:** © Detroit Institute of Arts / © Banco de México Diego Rivera Frida Kahlo Museums Trust, Mexico, D.F. / DACS 2024; © Detroit Institute of Arts (cr). **420 Photo Scala, Florence:** Image copyright The Metropolitan Museum of Art / Art Resource / © Heirs of Aaron Douglas/VAGA at ARS, NY and DACS, London 2024. **421 Bridgeman Images:** Photo © Christie's Images / © The Gluck Estate. All rights reserved, DACS 2024. **422–423 Photo Scala, Florence**: Photo Art Resource / John Bigelow Taylor/ © Succession Picasso/DACS, London 2024. **424 Bridgeman Images:** © Mondrian / Holtzman Trust. **425 SuperStock:** Steve Vidler / © The Henry Moore Foundation. All Rights Reserved, DACS / www.henry-moore.org 2024. **426 Bridgeman Images:** Luisa Ricciarini / © Banco de México Diego Rivera Frida Kahlo Museums Trust, Mexico, D.F. / DACS 2024. **427 Photograph © 2024 Museum of Fine Arts, Boston:** The John Axelrod Collection Frank B. Bemis Fund, Charles H. Bayley Fund, and The Heritage Fund. **428 Art Resource, NY:** Carnegie Museum of Art, Pittsburgh, PA (c, br, bl). **Bridgeman Images** (cra). **429 akg-images**/ © Fondation Oskar Kokoschka/ DACS 2024. **430–431 SuperStock:** A. Burkatovski / Fine Art Images. **430 Dreamstime.com:** Giorgio Morara (cl). **432–433 Bridgeman Images:** Luisa Ricciarini. **434 Alamy Stock Photo:** Peter Barritt / © ADAGP, Paris and DACS, London 2024 (c, br). **Bridgeman Images:** Photo © Andrusier (bc). **435** ***Sidney Nolan, Ned Kelly 1946 enamel paint on hardboard 90.8 (h) x 121.5 (w) cm framed (overall) 91.3 (h) x 122.2 (w) x 3 (d) cm.*** **National Gallery of Australia, Canberra. Gift of Sunday Reed 1976** /© The Sidney Nolan Trust. All rights reserved, DACS. 2024 (c). **Getty Images:** Hulton Archive / Stringer (bl). **436 Photo Scala, Florence:** Digital image, The Museum of Modern Art, New York. **437 Bridgeman Images:** Barbara Hepworth © Bowness (c). **Getty Images:** Haywood Magee / Stringer / Picture Post (tl). **438 Photo Scala, Florence:** Digital image, The Museum of Modern Art, New York/© Wyeth Foundation for American Art / ARS, NY and DACS, London 2024. **439 Alamy Stock Photo:** Peter Barritt / © 1998 Kate Rothko Prizel & Christopher Rothko ARS, NY and DACS, London 2024. **440 Bridgeman Images:** Luisa Ricciarini (br). **Getty Images:** Christophel Fine Art / Contributor / Universal Images Group (tl). **Photo Scala, Florence:** Christie's Images, London (tr). **SuperStock:** A. Burkatovski / Fine Art Images / © ADAGP, Paris and DACS, London 2024 (bl). **441 Alamy Stock Photo:** Heritage Image Partnership Ltd (tl); steeve-x-art (cl). **Helen Frankenthaler Foundation, Inc., on loan to the National Gallery of Art, Washington, National Gallery of Art, Washington X.16**/ **© Helen Frankenthaler Foundation, Inc.** / **ARS, NY and DACS, London 2024** (br). **The Menil Collection, Houston.** Photo: Caroline Philippone/ © Successió Miró / ADAGP, Paris and DACS London 2024 (tc). **442 Bridgeman Images:** © Succession Alberto Giacometti / DACS 2024. **443 Bridgeman Images:** © The Pollock-Krasner Foundation ARS, NY and DACS, London 2024 (c, br). **Shutterstock.com:** Martha Holmes / The LIFE Picture Collection (bc). **444 Alamy Stock Photo:** Archivart (cla); Pictorial Press Ltd (clb). **SuperStock:** Album Archivo / Album / © The Estate of Francis Bacon. All rights reserved. DACS 2024 (c). **445 Bridgeman Images**/ © ADAGP, Paris and DACS, London 2024. **446 Bridgeman Images:** Mondadori Portfolio / Electa / Vincenzo Silvestri / © DACS 2024. **447 Alamy Stock Photo:** David Grossman / © Jasper Johns/VAGA at ARS, NY and DACS, London 2024. **448–449 © DACS 2024:** © The Andy Warhol Foundation for the Visual Arts, Inc. / Licensed by DACS / Artimage, London. **448 © DACS 2024:** Derivative Andy Warhol Artwork created by DK in 2024 and used with permission from The Andy Warhol Foundation for the Visual Arts, Inc. / Licensed by DACS / Artimage, London (t). **449 © DACS 2024:** Derivative Andy Warhol Artwork created by DK in 2024 and used with permission from The Andy Warhol Foundation for the Visual Arts, Inc. / Licensed by DACS / Artimage, London (tc). **450–451 SuperStock:** Peter Barritt /© Estate of Roy Lichtenstein/DACS 2024. **452 Alamy Stock Photo:** World History Archive (cr); **Bridgeman Images** (tl, bl); Pictures From History (tr). **453 Alamy Stock Photo:** Guy Bell / Alamy Live News (t). **Bridgeman Images:** © Imperial War Museums (cr); Philadelphia Museum of Art, Pennsylvania, PA, USA / John G. Johnson Collection, 1917 (cl). **Dreamstime.com:** Chumphon Whangchom (bc). **Shutterstock.com:** Kiev.Victor (c). **454 © Tate, London 2024:** © David Hockney. **455 Bridgeman Images:** Mondadori Portfolio / © Successió Miró / ADAGP, Paris and DACS London 2024. **456–457 Copyright Anselm Kiefer.** Anselm Kiefer, Margarethe, 1981 oil, straw, emulsion, and gelatin silver print on linen; 114 ¼ x 157 ¾ in. (290.2 x 400.69 cm). **San Francisco Museum of Modern Art, The Doris and Donald Fisher Collection at the San Francisco Museum of Modern Art. Photograph: Katherine Du Tiel** (c). **458 Bridgeman Images:** Paula Rego. All rights reserved 2024. **459 Bridgeman Images:** © The Estate of Clifford Possum Tjapaltjarri/Copyright Agency. Licensed by DACS 2024. **460 Bridgeman Images** (tr). **© Gerhard Richter.** Gerhard Richter, German, born 1932; Betty, 1988; oil on canvas; 40 ¼ x 28 ½ inches; Saint Louis Art Museum, Funds given by Mr. and Mrs. R. Cosby Kemper Jnr. through the Cosby Kemper Foundation, The Arthur and Helen Baer Charitable Foundation, Mr and Mrs. Van Lear Black III, Anabeth Calkins, John Weil, Mr. and Mrs. Gary Wolff and the Honorable and Mrs. Thomas F. Eagleton; Museum Purchase, Dr. and Mrs. Harold J. Joseph, and Mrs. Edward Mallinckrodt, by exchange 23:1992, © Gerhard Richter 2019. **461 Bridgeman Images:** © The Lucian Freud Archive. All Rights Reserved 2024. **462 © Bridget Riley 2024. All rights reserved**. **463** Chris Ofili. The Holy Virgin Mary, 1996. Acrylic, oil, polyester resin, paper collage, glitter, map pins and elephant dung on linen 243.8 x 182.8 cm, 96 x 72 in. **© Chris Ofili. Courtesy the artist and Victoria Miro**. **464 Bridgeman Images:** Philadelphia Museum of Art, Pennsylvania, PA, USA / Gift of Anne d'Harnoncourt, 1996 / © Faith Ringgold / ARS, NY and DACS, London, Courtesy ACA Galleries, New York 2024. **465 SuperStock:** Felix Gonzlez / age fotostock / © The Easton Foundation/VAGA at ARS, NY and DACS, London 2024. **466 Smithsonian American Art Museum:** Gift of Elizabeth Ann Dugan and museum purchase, 2004.28 / Courtesy of the artist and Garth Greenan Gallery, New York. **467 Bridgeman Images:** Girl with red heart balloon mural 2002 by Banksy, Waterloo Bridge, South London, 2004 (photo), Banksy (b.1975) / Private Collection (c). **Dreamstime.com:** Twinsen123 (bc). **Getty Images:** Tristan Fewings / Stringer (br). **468** El Anatsui. Focus, 2015. Aluminum and copper wire, 284 x 304 cm. **© El Anatsui. Private Collection. Courtesy the Artist and October Gallery, London. Photo: © Jonathan Greet**. **469 © Frank Bowling**. All Rights Reserved, DACS 2024/Artimage. Courtesy Hales Gallery. Photo: Charlie Littlewood. **470–471 akg-images. 472 Alamy Stock Photo:** Peter Horree. **473 Bridgeman Images** (b). **National Palace Museum, Taipei, Taiwan** (t). **474 Bridgeman Images. 475 Bridgeman Images:** Photo © Stefano Baldini (b); Photo © Photo Josse (t). **476 akg-images:** Roland and Sabrina Michaud (t). **Bridgeman Images:** Photo © Fine Art Images (b). **477 Bridgeman Images. 478 Bridgeman Images:** Photo © Christie's Images. **479 Bridgeman Images. 480 Bridgeman Images:** Photo © Fine Art Images. **481 Getty Images:** Heritage Images / Contributor / Hulton Fine Art Collection. **482 Bridgeman Images** (tl). **482–483 Alamy Stock Photo:** Heritage Image Partnership Ltd (b). **483 Getty Images:** Thekla Clark / Contributor / Corbis Historical (tr). **484 Bridgeman Images:** Photo © Raffaello Bencini. **485 Alamy Stock Photo:** World History Archive (b). **Bridgeman Images** (t). **486 Bridgeman Images. 487 Bridgeman Images:** © NPL–DeA Picture Library. **488 Bridgeman Images:** © San Diego Museum of Art / Bequest of Mrs. Cora Timken Burnett. **489 Bridgeman Images:** Luisa Ricciarini. **490 Alamy Stock Photo:** Heritage Image Partnership Ltd (b). **Bridgeman Images:** © National Museums Liverpool (t). **491 Bridgeman Images:** The Wendy and Emery Reves Collection. **492 Bridgeman Images** (tl). **492–493 Bridgeman Images** (b). **493 Bridgeman Images** (tr). **494 Bridgeman Images:** © Art Institute of Chicago / Friends of American Art Collection (b); © SZ Photo / Scherl (t). **495 Bridgeman Images. 496 Bridgeman Images:** © Jean Bernard. All rights reserved 2024 / Collection fondation regards de Provence, Marseille (b). **Getty Images:** Heritage Images / Contributor / Hulton Archive (t). **497 Alamy Stock Photo:** The Picture Art Collection. **498 akg-images** (bl). **498–499 Bridgeman Images:** Luisa Ricciarini (t). **499 Getty Images:** Heritage Images / Contributor / Hulton Archive (br). **500 Bridgeman Images:** Photo © Fine Art Images (t). **The New York Public Library:** (b). **501 Bridgeman Images:** © Jerwood Collection. **502 akg-images. 503 Getty Images:** Tony Evans / Timelapse Library Ltd. / Contributor / Hulton Archive.

Front cover image: Bridgeman Images: Luisa Ricciarini.

Back cover image: Alamy Stock Photo: GL Archive.

All other images © Dorling Kindersley

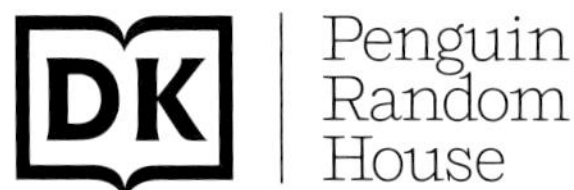

DK LONDON
Senior Editor Angela Wilkes
Senior Art Editor Mark Cavanagh
Senior US Editor Megan Douglass
Managing Editor Gareth Jones
Senior Managing Art Editor Lee Griffiths
Production Editor Rob Dunn
Senior Production Controller Rachel Ng
Jacket Designer Surabhi Wadhwa
Jacket Design Development Manager Sophia M.T.T.
Illustrator Emma Fraser Reid
Associate Publishing Director Liz Wheeler
Art Directors Karen Self, Maxine Pedliham
Publishing Director Jonathan Metcalf

CREATED FOR DK BY TOUCAN BOOKS LTD.
Editorial Director Ellen Dupont
Senior Art Editor Thomas Keenes
Senior Editor Dorothy Stannard
Picture Research Sharon Southren
Designers Tessa Bindloss, Leah Germann, Dave Jones, Lee Riches
Editors Julie Brooke, Helen Douglas-Cooper, Beth Dymond, Jen Moore
Assistant Cora Green
Proofreader Danielle Carter
Indexer Marie Lorimer

First American Edition, 2024
Published in the United States by DK Publishing,
a division of Penguin Random House LLC
1745 Broadway, 20th Floor, New York, NY 10019

26 27 28 10 9 8 7 6 5
009–341458–Sep/2024

Published in Great Britain by Dorling Kindersley Limited

A catalog record for this book
is available from the Library of Congress.
ISBN 978-0-5938-4409-0

Printed and bound in China

www.dk.com

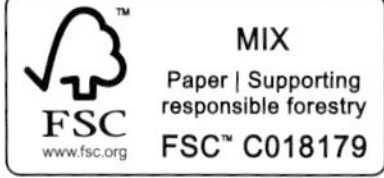